Econometric Theory

This book is for my family, with love.

Econometric Theory

James Davidson

Blackwell
Publishing

BLACKWELL PUBLISHING
350 Main Street, Malden, MA 02148-5020, USA
108 Cowley Road, Oxford OX4 1JF, UK
550 Swanston Street, Carlton, Victoria 3053, Australia

First published 2000
Reprinted 2001, 2004

Library of Congress Cataloging-in-Publication Data

Davidson, James
Econometric theory / James Davidson.
p. cm.
Includes bibliographical references and index.
ISBN 0-631-17837-6 (hb.: alk. paper) — ISBN 0-631-21584-0 (pb.: alk. paper)
1. Econometrics. 2. Regression analysis. I. Title.

HB139.D366 1999
330'.01'5195 21—dc21 99-045659

A catalogue record for this title is available from the British Library.

Set in 10 pt Computer Modern by the author

The publisher's policy is to use permanent paper from mills that operate a sustainable forestry policy, and which has been manufactured from pulp processed using acid-free and elementary chlorine-free practices. Furthermore, the publisher ensures that the text paper and cover board used have met acceptable environmental accreditation standards.

For further information on
Blackwell Publishing, visit our website:
http://www.blackwellpublishing.com

Contents

Figures

Symbols and Abbreviations

§ denotes a section or subsection in the text. The symbol □ is used to terminate assumptions, definitions, and theorems whose proofs do not follow immediately. The symbol ■ is used to terminate proofs. Lists of conditions or assumptions are labelled (a), (b),... The parts of a multipart theorem are labelled (i), (ii),...

Vectors and matrices are always shown in boldface, usually in lower case and upper case respectively, although this convention is not rigid. Other standard but not rigid usages in mathematical notation include calligraphic symbols (e.g. $\mathcal{I}$) for sigma fields and blackboard bold (e.g. $\mathbb{R}$) for spaces.

$\Longrightarrow$	converges weakly to
$[x]$	the largest integer not exceeding x
$\lVert \boldsymbol{x} \rVert$	norm (length) of a vector
$\{x_t\}$	sequence with coordinates x_t, $t = \ldots, -1, 0, 1, \ldots$
$\lVert X \rVert_p$	L_p-norm of a random variable
$[a, b]$	the closed interval bounded by a and b
(a, b)	the open interval bounded by a and b
$\forall$	for all
$(\boldsymbol{A})_{ij}$	the i,jth element of matrix $\boldsymbol{A}$
ACov	asymptotic covariance
AE	adaptive expectations
ADF	augmented Dickey–Fuller
AIC	Akaike information criterion
ALR	analogue likelihood ratio
AR	autoregressive process
ARI	integrated autoregressive process
ARCH	autoregressive conditional heteroscedasticity
ARDL	autoregressive distributed lag
arg min	the argument that minimizes
ARMA	autoregressive moving average
ARMADL	autoregressive moving average distributed lag
ARIMA	autoregressive integrated moving average
a.s.	almost surely
a.s.lim	almost sure limit
$\underset{\text{asy}}{\sim}$	has same asymptotic distribution

AVar	asymptotic variance
BAN	best asymptotically normal
BFGS	Broyden–Fletcher–Goldfarb–Shanno
BHHH	Berndt–Hall–Hall–Hausman
BLUE	best linear unbiased estimator
BM	Brownian motion
$\subseteq$	is a subset of
$C(\cdot)$	criterion function
$C[0,1]$	the space of continuous functions on $[0,1]$
CAN	consistent and asymptotically normal
CLT	central limit theorem
CM test	conditional moment test
CO	Cochrane–Orcutt
CR	Cramér–Rao
CRDW	cointegrating regression Durbin–Watson
$D[0,1]$	the space of cadlag functions on $[0,1]$
$\xrightarrow{\text{D}}$	converges in distribution to
d.f.	degrees of freedom
DF	Dickey–Fuller
DFP	Davidon–Fletcher–Powell
DWH	Durbin–Wu–Hausman
DW	Durbin–Watson
Δ^d	dth difference
Δ_d	d-period difference
c.d.f.	cumulative distribution function
$\boldsymbol{\nabla}$	gradient
$\exists$	there exists
$\in$	set inclusion; *also*
$\cdot \in \mathcal{A}$	($\mathcal{A}$ a σ-field) measurable with respect to $\mathcal{A}$
$E(\cdot)$	expected value
$E(\cdot\|\mathcal{G})$	expected value conditional on σ-field $\mathcal{G}$
ECM	error correction model
EWMA	exponentially weighted moving average
FCLT	functional central limit theorem
$\sim F(n_1, n_2)$	distributed as F with n_1 and n_2 degrees of freedom
GARCH	generalized autoregressive conditional heteroscedasticity
FIML	full information maximum likelihood
FMLS	fully modified least squares
GLS	generalized least squares
GMM	generalized method of moments
GTP	general to particular
H_0	the null hypothesis
H_A	the alternative hypothesis
H_M	the maintained hypothesis
HQC	Hannan–Quinn criterion

$\sim \mathrm{I}(d)$	is integrated of order d
$\mathcal{I}_t$	σ-field generated by conditioning variables
$\mathfrak{I}$	information matrix
$\boldsymbol{I}_n$	identity matrix of order n
$\boldsymbol{\iota}$	unit vector (column of 1s)
i.i.d.	independent and identically distributed
IMA	integrated moving average process
inf	infimum
$\mathrm{int}(\Theta)$	interior of the set Θ
IV	instrumental variables
JB	Jarque–Bera
KLIC	Kullback–Leibler information criterion
KPSS	Kwiatkowski–Phillips–Schmidt–Shin
$\mathcal{L}(\cdot)$	likelihood function
$L(\cdot)$	log-likelihood function
LGV	least generalized variance
LGVR	least generalized variance ratio
LVR	least variance ratio
LIE	law of iterated expectations
LIML	limited information maximum likelihood
LM	Lagrange multiplier
ln	natural logarithm
LR	likelihood ratio
M test	moment test
MA	moving average process
MLE	maximum likelihood estimator
m.d.	martingale difference
MDE	minimum distance estimator
MP	Moore–Penrose
MSE	mean squared error
$\cap$	intersection of sets
$\sim \mathrm{N}(\mu, \sigma^2)$	is Gaussian with mean μ, variance σ^2
$\sim \mathrm{NI}(0, \sigma^2)$	is Gaussian and serially independent (of sequence)
NED	near-epoch dependent
NLFIML	nonlinear full information maximum likelihood
NLIV	nonlinear instrumental variables
NLLS	nonlinear least squares
$\emptyset$	the empty set
$\otimes$	Kronecker product
$O_p(\cdot)$	stochastic order of magnitude
$o_p(\cdot)$	stochastic order of magnitude, 'little-oh' form
OE	optimization estimator
OLS	ordinary least squares
OPG	outer product of the gradient
PA	partial adjustment
PDL	polynomial distributed lags

p.d.f.	probability density function
plim	probability limit
$\xrightarrow{\text{pr}}$	converges in probability to
PTG	particular to general
QML	quasi-maximum likelihood
QN	quasi-Newton
RE	rational expectations
R^2	coefficient of determination
RESET	Ramsey's test of functional form
r.v.	random variable
SBC	Schwarz Bayesian criterion
$\sigma(X)$	the sigma field generated by X
σ^2	variance
SLLN	strong law of large numbers
2SLS	two stage least squares
3SLS	three stage least squares
sup	supremum
$\sim t_p$	distributed as Student's t with p degrees of freedom
$\cup$	union of sets
UDE	unrestricted dynamic equation test
$\vee$	union of σ-fields
Var	variance
VARMA	vector autoregressive moving average
Vec	vectorized matrix
VECM	vector error correction model
v.m.d.	vector martingale difference
W test	Wald test
WLLN	weak law of large numbers
w.p.1	with probability 1
$\sim \chi^2(p)$	distributed as chi-squared with p degrees of freedom
$\mathcal{X}_t$	σ-field generated by $\{\boldsymbol{x}_s,\ s \leq t\}$
$p \times q$	dimensions of a matrix
$A \times B$	(of sets) Cartesian product

Preface

This book has its origin in a set of lecture notes prepared for a mixed group of graduates and advanced undergraduates at the London School of Economics. The graduate students come from a range of academic backgrounds, but most had taken mainstream econometrics courses using a text at the level of Johnston's (1972) *Econometric Methods* or Maddala's (1977) *Econometrics*. The undergraduates had also attended such a course, and most had taken a second-year course in probability and distribution theory.

The lectures evolved to try to meet the differing needs of these students. It was not possible to assume that all of them were rigorously drilled in the ramifications of the general linear model, though all should have been exposed to it, and some revision was deemed necessary. The degree of probabilistic intuition of the group also tended to vary widely. These topics needed to be reviewed with some care, but at the risk of boring the upper echelon of the class with repetition of familiar material. The compromise sought was to spend some time looking at old material in a new way. Rather than attempting to survey a wide range of advanced topics, the core of the course was an in-depth examination of the regression model. The written notes distributed to the class form the basis for several of the present chapters, although the opportunity has been taken to update the material, to treat some topics in more depth, and to add extra ones. Some of the additional material has been developed from lectures given for the M.Sc. Econometrics and Mathematical Economics at LSE, including the sections on nonlinear estimation, unit roots and cointegration. However, while the format of a book affords both author and reader more leisure to pursue the details than was possible in the lectures, the treatment remains self-contained and technically unified.

Something the lectures attempted, with what success the reader may judge, is to take the probabilistic foundations of the subject seriously. Given that economics is a non-experimental discipline, with nearly all observed variables being stochastically generated and not chosen by the investigator, the 'stochastic regressor' framework seems the appropriate one, and was adopted from the outset. Regression analysis is motivated by direct appeal to the notion of conditional expectation. One advantage of focusing on the conditioning approach to regression is that it neatly resolves an issue that often lands teachers and students in a tangle, that of correct and incorrect model specification. Students are traditionally told, for example, that regressors and disturbances should be uncorrelated for consistent estimation. This sounds sensible enough at first, but as one delves further into the analysis, puzzles creep in. The regressors are part of the data set, whereas the disturbances are not merely unobserved but are really fictional, having no existence outside the context of the model postulated. It is more satisfactory to focus on the properties of the conditional mean of a variable, deviations from which are orthogonal to the conditioning variables by construction. This leads naturally to the idea that every regression involves two sets of variables: the valid conditioning variables (those that may explain the regressand) and the explanatory variables (those that do explain it). The crucial step in model specification (defining the problem) is to specify the conditioning set. Model evaluation techniques can then be understood as guiding the choice of regressors from this set. Virtually the whole arsenal of regression diagnostics and modelling procedures can be accommodated in this basic framework. The disturbances would not even need to be mentioned to put the basic ideas across.

An attempt has also been made to unify the treatment of estimation theory through the notion of optimization estimators. A few simple results allow least squares, maximum likelihood, instrumental variables, GMM and other procedures to be viewed as different implementations of the same underlying principle. This approach saves a lot of duplication of effort in understanding the properties of the estimators, and yields results in many cases that are otherwise intractable. It also provides valuable insight, helping us to understand why, for example, an estimator described as 'maximum likelihood' can have good properties even when the data are not really distributed in a way that justifies the claim.

Thus, another aim has been to face up to the reality of partial specification and potential misspecification, which besets econometric practice. Students are often shown tightly specified models, involving features such as linearity, normality and independence of the disturbances, and stationarity of the time series composing the data set. While we all know that these are at best approximations to reality, there has been a pedagogic tendency to pile in all these conditions at the outset, and only subsequently (and probably sketchily) consider how to relax them. The inability of the classical statistical theory to handle data features such as dependence and heterogeneity is perhaps the chief reason why this approach is traditionally pursued. So far as is compatible with a reasonably straightforward treatment, the aim here has been to derive the theory of estimation and inference in the context of the minimum assumptions needed to justify it. For example, normality of the disturbances is not needed for most of the desirable asymptotic properties of the popular estimators (large sample efficiency being the chief exception). We also know that our models can sometimes throw up outliers in the residuals of a magnitude that sits unhappily with the normality assumption. Accordingly, this property is not emphasized: and the least squares estimator is not billed as maximum likelihood unless this assertion is specifically justified.

Likewise, the assumption of independence of disturbances really has no place in time series regression analysis. Almost all the economic time series we ever observe are serially dependent in some respect, and except in the context of joint (never mind conditional) normality, conditioning models do not induce independence of the disturbances. It must be imposed as an extra, arbitrary feature of the model, a *deus ex machina* that in any case has no essential role in the asymptotic analysis.

After the introductory chapters, independence is hardly used at all in the book except sometimes for illustration. Instead, appeal is made to the simple and very powerful concept of a martingale difference process, which has nearly all the desirable properties of an independent process, but a much better chance of being either generated in nature, or at worst, as the residuals from our modelling efforts.

This approach is made feasible by introducing some results from modern limit theory and, for this purpose, extensive reference is made at certain points to my book *Stochastic Limit Theory* (Davidson 1994a). There is a sense in which the two works can be viewed as companions, representing theory and application respectively. However, a knowledge of the mathematics used in *Stochastic Limit Theory* is not assumed here. Readers need to consult that book only to follow up the various proofs that are cited, and this is strictly optional.

There are always two sorts of question that an econometrics text must try to answer: the hows and the whys. The how questions (how to construct a model, and estimate it) are generally well covered by a range of existing texts. The why questions (why a particular technique is used in empirical work, or in other words, how its use can be justified) often receive less attention, because to answer them coherently requires the ground to be carefully prepared. This book does not try to answer all the how questions, and the coverage of models and methods is selective, although hopefully representative of current time series techniques. It does attempt to address some of the why questions seriously, which is the main excuse for the word 'theory' appearing in the title.

An Overview of the Chapters

The book has been structured with a view to serving as the basis of a two-semester graduate course, and contains as much material as such a course could reasonably cover. The subject matter falls fairly naturally into four parts, and the chapters are grouped accordingly. Each part is reasonably self-contained, although making use of the preceding material. A one-semester course on regression analysis for time series might be based on Parts I and II (Chapters 1 to 8). These chapters deal with the classical linear regression model and its extension into time series analysis. No nonlinear analysis is attempted here, and the estimators are of the simplest kind, just ordinary least squares and two-stage least squares.

The first three chapters deal with the classical regression model specifically in the sense that the observations are treated as independently sampled. All the variables in the analysis are nonetheless treated as stochastic from the outset, so that notions of conditioning can be introduced. Chapter 1 introduces the main ideas and summarizes the matrix algebra, Chapter 2 explores the exact inference theory based on conditionally Gaussian disturbances (mostly identical to the fixed regressor theory) and Chapter 3 does the asymptotic version of the analysis, without the Gaussianity.

Part II (Chapters 4 to 8) is explicitly about time series analysis. The main idea developed here is that samples are not generally independent, but that sequential conditioning arguments yield a close analogue of the classical asymptotic analysis under independence. Chapters 4 and 5 survey the concepts of model building in time series, and the latter part of Chapter 5 is a digression into schemes for modelling phenomena such as lagged adjustment and rational expectations. Apart from their intrinsic interest, an important object of these sections is to motivate the later discussion of nonlinear modelling in time series. Chapter 6 develops the time series extensions of the asymptotic analysis, focusing for clarity on the estimation of the first-order autoregressive model. The key role of sequential conditioning is emphasized in the derivation of the properties of the estimators. Then, Chapter 7 looks at the asymptotic analysis of the multiple regression model, and goes on to deal with the issues of specification testing and model choice. Chapter 8 extends the analysis to simultaneous equations and thoroughly studies two-stage least squares. Although much of this material has a general application, the assumptions are once again relevant to the time series case.

Part III is an introduction to the general theory of optimization estimators (OEs, or M estimators) although, as in Part II, concepts of sequential conditioning are used throughout. Chapter 9 covers the main ideas, and Chapter 10 applies them to well-known problems, including nonlinear models, joint estimation of mean and variance, and misspecified models. Maximum likelihood estimation is deliberately covered, in Chapter 11, following the treatment of the general class of OEs in Chapters 9 and 10, so that readers can put this method into context and appreciate its special properties. This means that certain concepts are given a slightly unusual treatment. Something looking much like the Gaussian log-likelihood function for the linear model is analysed using OE theory, with no mention of Gaussian disturbances. The information matrix equality and likelihood ratio tests (which we generally refer to as 'analogue LR' tests) are among other topics treated in a novel manner, although hopefully one that clarifies the issues. Chapter 12 deals with the general theory of hypothesis testing, again in an OE framework. Emphasis is placed here on the role of the information matrix equality in simplifying test procedures, but also on the importance of robust procedures that do not depend on it. Chapter 13 covers classical system estimation, including the nonlinear case.

Finally, Part IV deals with unit roots and cointegration theory. This subject area has now become so large that a specialized text would be required to cover it comprehensively. A number of interesting topics have had to be given a cursory treatment. Rather, the aim has been to cover the basics thoroughly, and convey the flavour of the methods of analysis used in this field, especially the Brownian calculus. Chapter 14 discusses the probability essentials, and details the standard tests for unit roots. Chapter 15 looks at the estimation of cointegration models in a single-equation context. Chapter 16 deals with what is commonly known as Johansen's approach, and concludes the work with some considerations of structural cointegration modelling.

Although there is, unavoidably, a good deal of notation, the book aims as far as possible at a narrative and informal style. Proofs are set out formally in the text only if they are brief and essential to the development. Some longer and more technical proofs are segregated in chapter appendices, where they can be studied or ignored according to taste. The main appendices summarize the most important of the technical prerequisites, including matrix algebra and the elements of probability and distribution theory. Some readers may be surprised to find elementary material juxtaposed with some quite sophisticated arguments. This is deliberate. The book is intended to be accessible, at least in part, to students with no more mathematical training than accompanies the typical degree in economics, and things such students might not know are often pointed out. However, there is no attempt to censor difficult stuff where it is important to the story. In some books, technically advanced sections are 'starred' to warn off the timid reader, and this option was considered, but in the end it seemed better to let readers and teachers decide for themselves what was important and worth giving the effort to.

Literature references of two sorts are provided for the student who wishes to pursue the topics in greater depth. A list for 'Further Reading' is appended to each chapter, but with a few exceptions, these references are to textbooks, surveys and monographs, where the student might find more specialized coverage, or an alternative view. Most references to the journal literature, by contrast, are given in context.

Acknowledgements

I must thank the people who, as they say, made this book possible. First and foremost, the remarkable people who taught me econometrics: Andy Chesher, Meghnad Desai, Jim Durbin, Terence Gorman, David Hendry, Grayham Mizon, the late Denis Sargan, and Ken Wallis. The econometrics group at LSE later provided a most congenial and stimulating working environment. Colleagues who at various times collaborated on the econometrics teaching, and participated in lively discussions at the Tuesday Econometrics workshops, have included Andrew Harvey, Javier Hidalgo, Jan Magnus, Stephen Pudney, Danny Quah, Peter Robinson, and Hugh Wills. Latterly my collaborator on various research projects, Robert de Jong, has been a source of indispensable insights on asymptotics. I am conscious of the debt I owe all the above-named and many others in developing the themes of this book, though needless to say, none are to blame for its undoubted shortcomings. The excellent students who attended the lectures contributed more than they could imagine. I don't just mean the ones who argued the case, pointed out errors and suggested improvements. Equally important were the majority whose enthusiasm and hard work made the enterprise worthwhile and enjoyable.

Blackwells commissioned the book longer ago than I now dare to admit, and the gestation process has proved tougher than I foresaw. Other projects have intervened, and for a while it seemed as though it might never be finished. The one consolation is that this one is a much better book than it would have been if delivered to the original schedule. Al Bruckner and Katie Byrne deserve credit for finally taking the thing by the scruff of the neck and driving it through to completion. It badly needed their encouragement, and I am grateful. Bruce Hansen, Len Gill, Brendan McCabe, and two anonymous referees have perused the manuscript at various stages, and I thank them for their helpful and encouraging comments.

For the typesetting design, created with the benefit of LaTeX, the author must take any additional credit that may be going for himself. The original lecture notes and the first draft of the book were created in Chiwriter, but this word-processing package has since fallen by the wayside, and I must thank Jenny Firth for carefully retyping the manuscript in TeX using Scientific Word. The final version of the text has been developed from her files.

James Davidson

Cwmystwyth, Wales
September 1999

Part I

Basic Regression Theory

Chapter 1

The Linear Regression Model

1.1 The Model

Let us begin by defining some symbols and writing down some notation, without any preconceptions, initially, as to what the context of these relationships might be. Let $x_{1t}, \ldots, x_{kt}, y_t$ for $t = 1, \ldots, n$ denote a sample of n observations on $k+1$ variables, and consider the linear equation

$$y_t = \beta_1 x_{1t} + \beta_2 x_{2t} + \cdots + \beta_k x_{kt} + u_t \tag{1.1.1}$$

where $\beta_1, \ldots, \beta_k$ are fixed but unknown parameters. The variable u_t is defined by the equation, being that function of the observables that balances the equation for observation t. If the parameters are unknown, then u_t is likewise unknown. The variable y_t is called the *regressand*, and the x_{it} variables for $i = 1, \ldots, k$ are the *regressors*. Usually one of the regressors is fixed at unity, say $x_{kt} = 1$, all t, and its coefficient β_k is called the *intercept* of the equation.

The observations are typically either a *time series*, relating to successive time periods in the study of economic aggregates, or a *cross-section* of individual economic units – households, firms, industries, countries and so forth, observed at a point of time.[1] The intercept apart, the variables in the equation, the y_t and usually the x_{it} too (subject to the considerations discussed in §1.3) are assumed to be *random variables*. This means that the observations are supposed to be generated by a random experiment, in advance of which their values are unknown. The notion of 'experiment' here is rather loose, and might refer merely to the act of collecting the sample. The relevant probability theory is summarized in Appendix B, but for present purposes it will do no harm to treat the concept of randomness in a purely intuitive fashion. It aims to capture the idea that the experiment

[1] The case of *panel data* in which the observations have both dimensions, e.g. the same sample of households observed in successive years, is treated only briefly in this book; see §2.3.1.

might in principle be performed repeatedly, in each case throwing up a new sample whose particular values are not predictable in advance. All we need to assume is that the notion of an *expected value* is well-defined, and there exist constants $E(y_t)$, $E(x_{it})$ and $E(u_t)$ representing central tendencies of the distributions of the indicated variables.

To provide a convenient shorthand form of the equation, define the vectors

$$\boldsymbol{\beta} = \begin{bmatrix} \beta_1 \\ \vdots \\ \beta_k \end{bmatrix} \quad (k \times 1) \qquad \boldsymbol{x}_t = \begin{bmatrix} x_{1t} \\ \vdots \\ x_{kt} \end{bmatrix} \quad (k \times 1)$$

and then write $y_t = \boldsymbol{\beta}'\boldsymbol{x}_t + u_t$, or equivalently $y_t = \boldsymbol{x}_t'\boldsymbol{\beta} + u_t$. The usual practice is to write down all the observations in one vector equation. Letting

$$\boldsymbol{y} = \begin{bmatrix} y_1 \\ \vdots \\ y_n \end{bmatrix} \quad (n \times 1) \quad \boldsymbol{X} = \begin{bmatrix} \boldsymbol{x}_1' \\ \vdots \\ \boldsymbol{x}_n' \end{bmatrix} \quad (n \times k) \quad \boldsymbol{u} = \begin{bmatrix} u_1 \\ \vdots \\ u_n \end{bmatrix} \quad (n \times 1)$$

the complete sample of equations is represented by

$$\boldsymbol{y} = \boldsymbol{X}\boldsymbol{\beta} + \boldsymbol{u}. \tag{1.1.2}$$

In the context of econometrics, equation (1.1.1) is usually thought of as a model of economic behaviour. The variable y_t typically represents the response of economic agents to a collection of 'stimulus' variables $\boldsymbol{x}_t$. The equation 'explains' y_t as a function of $\boldsymbol{x}_t$. Such a model is typically suggested by economic theory when agents are assumed to formulate a plan for y_t based on $\boldsymbol{x}_t$, for example, a plan for consumption expenditure given income received and prices observed. The notion of a systematic rule of behaviour is embodied in the assumption that the coefficients $\beta_1, \ldots, \beta_k$ are constants. u_t is called the *disturbance* term, or the *error* term and, in the context of the behavioural model, represents the deviations from the plan. We assume $E(u_t) = 0$, although note that unless the intercept β_k is constrained in some way, this assumption is trivially valid. By estimating $\boldsymbol{\beta}$ and setting $u_t = 0$ the model can be used to predict y_t, given predictions or observations of $\boldsymbol{x}_t$.

1.2 The Least Squares Estimator

1.2.1 Derivation of the Estimator

An *estimator* is a rule (for example, a formula) for computing an *estimate* (a number) from sample data. The method of least squares is the standard technique for extracting an estimate of $\boldsymbol{\beta}$ from a sample of observations. Consider

$$\boldsymbol{e}(\boldsymbol{b}) = \boldsymbol{y} - \boldsymbol{X}\boldsymbol{b} \quad (n \times 1) \tag{1.2.1}$$

a vector of functions with k-dimensional vector argument $\boldsymbol{b}$. Choosing a vector $\boldsymbol{b}$ to represent the unknown $\boldsymbol{\beta}$, $\boldsymbol{X}\boldsymbol{b}$ may be thought of as a predictor of $\boldsymbol{y}$, and then

$\boldsymbol{e}$ is the corresponding prediction error. The sum of the squared prediction errors is

$$S(\boldsymbol{b}) = \boldsymbol{e}(\boldsymbol{b})'\boldsymbol{e}(\boldsymbol{b}). \tag{1.2.2}$$

If the criterion of a good estimator is one that yields a good predictor of $\boldsymbol{y}$ given $\boldsymbol{X}$, a natural choice is $\hat{\boldsymbol{\beta}}$ such that $S(\hat{\boldsymbol{\beta}}) \leq S(\boldsymbol{b})$ for all k-vectors $\boldsymbol{b}$, denoted more formally by

$$\hat{\boldsymbol{\beta}} = \arg\min_{\boldsymbol{b}} S(\boldsymbol{b}) \tag{1.2.3}$$

where 'arg min' is shorthand for 'the argument that minimizes' the function in question. This is called the *ordinary least squares* (OLS) estimator. The corresponding estimator of $\boldsymbol{u}$ is denoted by $\hat{\boldsymbol{u}} = \boldsymbol{y} - \boldsymbol{X}\hat{\boldsymbol{\beta}}$, the *least squares residuals*, such that $S(\hat{\boldsymbol{\beta}}) = \hat{\boldsymbol{u}}'\hat{\boldsymbol{u}}$.

As is well known, $\hat{\boldsymbol{\beta}}$ is obtained from the data by a simple mathematical formula. One way to derive this formula is from the following result:

Theorem 1.2.1 Necessary and sufficient conditions for a vector $\hat{\boldsymbol{\beta}}$ to be the unique minimizer of S are

(a) $\text{rank}(\boldsymbol{X}) = k$

(b) $\boldsymbol{X}'\hat{\boldsymbol{u}} = \boldsymbol{0}$.

Proof Substitute $\hat{\boldsymbol{u}} + \boldsymbol{X}\hat{\boldsymbol{\beta}}$ for $\boldsymbol{y}$, so as to write

$$\begin{aligned} S(\boldsymbol{b}) &= (\boldsymbol{y} - \boldsymbol{X}\boldsymbol{b})'(\boldsymbol{y} - \boldsymbol{X}\boldsymbol{b}) \\ &= (\hat{\boldsymbol{u}} + \boldsymbol{X}(\hat{\boldsymbol{\beta}} - \boldsymbol{b}))'(\hat{\boldsymbol{u}} + \boldsymbol{X}(\hat{\boldsymbol{\beta}} - \boldsymbol{b})) \\ &= S(\hat{\boldsymbol{\beta}}) + 2(\hat{\boldsymbol{\beta}} - \boldsymbol{b})'\boldsymbol{X}'\hat{\boldsymbol{u}} + (\hat{\boldsymbol{\beta}} - \boldsymbol{b})'\boldsymbol{X}'\boldsymbol{X}(\hat{\boldsymbol{\beta}} - \boldsymbol{b}). \end{aligned} \tag{1.2.4}$$

$\boldsymbol{X}'\boldsymbol{X}$ is positive definite if and only if condition (a) holds, by Lemma A.7.1, and hence $S(\boldsymbol{b})$ is minimized uniquely at the point $\hat{\boldsymbol{\beta}} = \boldsymbol{b}$ if and only if both the conditions hold, by Lemma A.7.3. ∎

Let us see what this result implies. According to the orthogonality condition (b), the sample covariances of the residuals and each regressor are identically zero, noting that since one column of $\boldsymbol{X}$ is the column of ones, the residuals also sum to 0 by construction. If this were not so, some linear function of $\boldsymbol{X}$ could be used to predict $\hat{\boldsymbol{u}}$. The least squares predictor of $\boldsymbol{y}$,

$$\hat{\boldsymbol{y}} = \boldsymbol{X}\hat{\boldsymbol{\beta}} = \boldsymbol{y} - \hat{\boldsymbol{u}} \tag{1.2.5}$$

could be improved by adding this predictor to it. $\hat{\boldsymbol{\beta}}$ is the linear estimator which cannot be so improved, for all such corrections have been made. It can easily be verified that

$$\hat{\boldsymbol{u}}'\hat{\boldsymbol{y}} = 0. \tag{1.2.6}$$

It is straightforward to obtain the formula for $\hat{\boldsymbol{\beta}}$ from condition (b) of Theorem 1.2.1, which may be written as

$$\boldsymbol{X}'\boldsymbol{y} = \boldsymbol{X}'\boldsymbol{X}\hat{\boldsymbol{\beta}}. \tag{1.2.7}$$

These are the so-called *normal equations* of least squares. Noting that $\boldsymbol{X}'\boldsymbol{X}$ is nonsingular by Lemma A.7.1, they have the unique solution

$$\hat{\boldsymbol{\beta}} = (\boldsymbol{X}'\boldsymbol{X})^{-1}\boldsymbol{X}'\boldsymbol{y}. \tag{1.2.8}$$

This completes the derivation of the OLS estimator. Notice that calculus has not been used. Solving the first-order conditions for the minimization of S is an alternative and more common way to obtain the formula, and is an easy exercise using the results of §A.9.

1.2.2 Goodness of Fit

Condition (1.2.6) implies the well-known *sum of squares decomposition*,

$$\boldsymbol{y}'\boldsymbol{y} = \hat{\boldsymbol{y}}'\hat{\boldsymbol{y}} + \hat{\boldsymbol{u}}'\hat{\boldsymbol{u}}. \tag{1.2.9}$$

The square of the sample correlation coefficient between $\boldsymbol{y}$ and $\hat{\boldsymbol{y}}$ has the formula

$$r^2_{y\hat{y}} = \frac{(\boldsymbol{y}'\hat{\boldsymbol{y}} - n\bar{y}^2)^2}{(\boldsymbol{y}'\boldsymbol{y} - n\bar{y}^2)(\hat{\boldsymbol{y}}'\hat{\boldsymbol{y}} - n\bar{y}^2)} \tag{1.2.10}$$

where $\bar{y}$ is the sample mean of $\boldsymbol{y}$ and also, note, the mean of $\hat{\boldsymbol{y}}$ by construction. This statistic, known as the *coefficient of determination* and more popularly denoted by R^2, is conventionally used to measure the goodness of fit of the regression, since it must lie between 0 and 1. It also has the more commonly quoted formulae

$$R^2 = \frac{\hat{\boldsymbol{y}}'\hat{\boldsymbol{y}} - n\bar{y}^2}{\boldsymbol{y}'\boldsymbol{y} - n\bar{y}^2} \tag{1.2.11}$$

and, in view of (1.2.9),

$$R^2 = 1 - \frac{\hat{\boldsymbol{u}}'\hat{\boldsymbol{u}}}{\boldsymbol{y}'\boldsymbol{y} - n\bar{y}^2}. \tag{1.2.12}$$

It can be verified that provided the regression includes an intercept, all three definitions are identical.

1.2.3 The Projection Matrices

The residual decomposition

$$\hat{\boldsymbol{u}} = \boldsymbol{y} - \boldsymbol{X}\hat{\boldsymbol{\beta}} = \boldsymbol{y} - \boldsymbol{X}(\boldsymbol{X}'\boldsymbol{X})^{-1}\boldsymbol{X}'\boldsymbol{y} \tag{1.2.13}$$

leads to the definition of two fundamental $n \times n$ matrices,

$$\boldsymbol{Q} = \boldsymbol{X}(\boldsymbol{X}'\boldsymbol{X})^{-1}\boldsymbol{X}' \tag{1.2.14}$$

and

$$\boldsymbol{M} = \boldsymbol{I}_n - \boldsymbol{X}(\boldsymbol{X}'\boldsymbol{X})^{-1}\boldsymbol{X}' \tag{1.2.15}$$

such that $\hat{\boldsymbol{y}} = \boldsymbol{Q}\boldsymbol{y}$ and $\hat{\boldsymbol{u}} = \boldsymbol{M}\boldsymbol{y}$. Note that $\boldsymbol{Q}\boldsymbol{X} = \boldsymbol{X}$, and hence $\boldsymbol{M}\boldsymbol{X} = \boldsymbol{0}$. $\boldsymbol{Q}$ is called a *projection matrix.* In geometrical terms, think of it as projecting any n-vector into the space spanned by $\boldsymbol{X}$. $\boldsymbol{M}$ is the *orthogonal projection matrix*, projecting into the space orthogonal to $\boldsymbol{X}$. These matrices have the important properties of *symmetry:*

$$\boldsymbol{Q}' = \boldsymbol{Q}, \qquad \boldsymbol{M}' = \boldsymbol{M} \tag{1.2.16}$$

idempotency:

$$\boldsymbol{Q}\boldsymbol{Q} = \boldsymbol{X}(\boldsymbol{X}'\boldsymbol{X})^{-1}\boldsymbol{X}'\boldsymbol{X}(\boldsymbol{X}'\boldsymbol{X})^{-1}\boldsymbol{X}' = \boldsymbol{Q} \tag{1.2.17}$$

$$\boldsymbol{M}\boldsymbol{M} = (\boldsymbol{I} - \boldsymbol{Q})(\boldsymbol{I} - \boldsymbol{Q}) = \boldsymbol{I} - \boldsymbol{Q} - \boldsymbol{Q} + \boldsymbol{Q}\boldsymbol{Q} = \boldsymbol{I} - \boldsymbol{Q} = \boldsymbol{M} \tag{1.2.18}$$

and *mutual orthogonality:*

$$\boldsymbol{Q}\boldsymbol{M} = \boldsymbol{M}\boldsymbol{Q} = \boldsymbol{Q} - \boldsymbol{Q}\boldsymbol{Q} = \boldsymbol{0}. \tag{1.2.19}$$

Since the rank of an idempotent matrix is equal to its trace (see §A.6) it is easily shown that $\boldsymbol{Q}$ has rank k and $\boldsymbol{M}$ has rank $n - k$. Also note the relation

$$\hat{\boldsymbol{u}} = \boldsymbol{M}\boldsymbol{y} = \boldsymbol{M}\boldsymbol{X}\boldsymbol{\beta} + \boldsymbol{M}\boldsymbol{u} = \boldsymbol{M}\boldsymbol{u}. \tag{1.2.20}$$

One cannot of course use this to recover $\boldsymbol{u}$ from $\hat{\boldsymbol{u}}$ since $\boldsymbol{M}$ is singular, but it does yield the formula

$$S(\hat{\boldsymbol{\beta}}) = \hat{\boldsymbol{u}}'\hat{\boldsymbol{u}} = \boldsymbol{u}'\boldsymbol{M}'\boldsymbol{M}\boldsymbol{u} = \boldsymbol{u}'\boldsymbol{M}\boldsymbol{u}. \tag{1.2.21}$$

1.2.4 Linear Transformations

Let $\boldsymbol{A}$ be a $k \times k$ nonsingular matrix, and define $\boldsymbol{Z} = \boldsymbol{X}\boldsymbol{A}$. Each column of $\boldsymbol{Z}$ is a linear combination of columns of $\boldsymbol{X}$. The model can be written in terms of the new variables as

$$\boldsymbol{y} = \boldsymbol{Z}\boldsymbol{\delta} + \boldsymbol{u} \tag{1.2.22}$$

where $\boldsymbol{\delta} = \boldsymbol{A}^{-1}\boldsymbol{\beta}$. Note that the same transformation applies to the regression coefficients, since

$$\hat{\boldsymbol{\delta}} = (\boldsymbol{Z}'\boldsymbol{Z})^{-1}\boldsymbol{Z}'\boldsymbol{y} = (\boldsymbol{A}'\boldsymbol{X}'\boldsymbol{X}\boldsymbol{A})^{-1}\boldsymbol{A}'\boldsymbol{X}'\boldsymbol{y} = \boldsymbol{A}^{-1}\hat{\boldsymbol{\beta}} \tag{1.2.23}$$

where the final equality is obtained using (A.2.3). It follows directly that

$$\boldsymbol{y} - \boldsymbol{Z}\hat{\boldsymbol{\delta}} = \boldsymbol{y} - \boldsymbol{X}\hat{\boldsymbol{\beta}} = \hat{\boldsymbol{u}} \tag{1.2.24}$$

so that an invertible linear transformation of the regressors leaves the residuals unchanged. The transformed model is statistically identical to the original, with only the interpretation of the coefficients changed.

1.2.5 The Partitioned Linear Model

Partition the regressors by columns as $\boldsymbol{X} = [\boldsymbol{X}_1\ \boldsymbol{X}_2]$, where $\boldsymbol{X}_1$ is $n \times k_1$ and $\boldsymbol{X}_2$ is $n \times k_2$, where $k_1 + k_2 = k$, and let $\boldsymbol{\beta} = \begin{bmatrix}\boldsymbol{\beta}_1\\ \boldsymbol{\beta}_2\end{bmatrix}\begin{matrix}k_1\\ k_2\end{matrix}$ conformably. The regression model $\boldsymbol{y} = \boldsymbol{X\beta} + \boldsymbol{u}$ can then be written as

$$\boldsymbol{y} = \boldsymbol{X}_1\boldsymbol{\beta}_1 + \boldsymbol{X}_2\boldsymbol{\beta}_2 + \boldsymbol{u}. \tag{1.2.25}$$

It is frequently useful to have a formula for the k_1-dimensional sub-vector $\hat{\boldsymbol{\beta}}_1$, and this can be obtained by partitioning the normal equations $\boldsymbol{X}'\boldsymbol{X}\hat{\boldsymbol{\beta}} = \boldsymbol{X}'\boldsymbol{y}$ as

$$\begin{bmatrix}\boldsymbol{X}_1'\boldsymbol{X}_1 & \boldsymbol{X}_1'\boldsymbol{X}_2\\ \boldsymbol{X}_2'\boldsymbol{X}_1 & \boldsymbol{X}_2'\boldsymbol{X}_2\end{bmatrix}\begin{bmatrix}\hat{\boldsymbol{\beta}}_1\\ \hat{\boldsymbol{\beta}}_2\end{bmatrix} = \begin{bmatrix}\boldsymbol{X}_1'\boldsymbol{y}\\ \boldsymbol{X}_2'\boldsymbol{y}\end{bmatrix} \tag{1.2.26}$$

or

$$\boldsymbol{X}_1'\boldsymbol{X}_1\hat{\boldsymbol{\beta}}_1 + \boldsymbol{X}_1'\boldsymbol{X}_2\hat{\boldsymbol{\beta}}_2 = \boldsymbol{X}_1'\boldsymbol{y} \tag{1.2.27a}$$

$$\boldsymbol{X}_2'\boldsymbol{X}_1\hat{\boldsymbol{\beta}}_1 + \boldsymbol{X}_2'\boldsymbol{X}_2\hat{\boldsymbol{\beta}}_2 = \boldsymbol{X}_2'\boldsymbol{y}. \tag{1.2.27b}$$

To solve these equations, first obtain $\hat{\boldsymbol{\beta}}_2$ from (1.2.27b), as

$$\hat{\boldsymbol{\beta}}_2 = (\boldsymbol{X}_2'\boldsymbol{X}_2)^{-1}(\boldsymbol{X}_2'\boldsymbol{y} - \boldsymbol{X}_2'\boldsymbol{X}_1\hat{\boldsymbol{\beta}}_1). \tag{1.2.28}$$

Substitution in (1.2.27a) and rearrangement yields

$$\begin{aligned}\hat{\boldsymbol{\beta}}_1 &= [\boldsymbol{X}_1'\boldsymbol{X}_1 - \boldsymbol{X}_1'\boldsymbol{X}_2(\boldsymbol{X}_2'\boldsymbol{X}_2)^{-1}\boldsymbol{X}_2'\boldsymbol{X}_1]^{-1}[\boldsymbol{X}_1'\boldsymbol{y} - \boldsymbol{X}_1'\boldsymbol{X}_2(\boldsymbol{X}_2'\boldsymbol{X}_2)^{-1}\boldsymbol{X}_2'\boldsymbol{y}]\\ &= (\boldsymbol{X}_1'\boldsymbol{M}_2\boldsymbol{X}_1)^{-1}\boldsymbol{X}_1'\boldsymbol{M}_2\boldsymbol{y}\end{aligned} \tag{1.2.29}$$

where $\boldsymbol{M}_2 = \boldsymbol{I} - (\boldsymbol{X}_2'\boldsymbol{X}_2)^{-1}\boldsymbol{X}_2'$. It may be verified that applying the partitioned inverse formula in (A.2.13) to the solution of (1.2.26) yields the same result.

Because of the idempotency and symmetry of $\boldsymbol{M}_2$ one can also write

$$\hat{\boldsymbol{\beta}}_1 = (\boldsymbol{X}_1'\boldsymbol{M}_2'\boldsymbol{M}_2\boldsymbol{X}_1)^{-1}\boldsymbol{X}_1'\boldsymbol{M}_2'\boldsymbol{y} \tag{1.2.30}$$

so that $\hat{\boldsymbol{\beta}}_1$ can be seen as the result of regressing $\boldsymbol{y}$ on $\boldsymbol{M}_2\boldsymbol{X}_1$. The latter is, in turn, the matrix of residuals from the regression of $\boldsymbol{X}_1$ on $\boldsymbol{X}_2$. The result that multiple regression coefficients can be computed by this two-stage procedure is the *Frisch–Waugh theorem.* It was very useful in the days when regressions were computed by hand, see Frisch and Waugh (1933), and also Lovell (1963). Also note that replacing $\boldsymbol{y}$ by $\boldsymbol{M}_2\boldsymbol{y}$ in the formula leads to exactly the same result.

Another approach to the partitioned algebra is to apply an orthogonalizing transformation to the regressors. Define

$$\boldsymbol{A} = \begin{bmatrix}\boldsymbol{I}_{k_1} & \boldsymbol{0}\\ -(\boldsymbol{X}_2'\boldsymbol{X}_2)^{-1}\boldsymbol{X}_2'\boldsymbol{X}_1 & \boldsymbol{I}_{k_2}\end{bmatrix} \tag{1.2.31}$$

and so represent the model in the style of (1.2.22) as

$$\boldsymbol{y} = \boldsymbol{M}_2\boldsymbol{X}_1\boldsymbol{\delta}_1 + \boldsymbol{X}_2\boldsymbol{\delta}_2 + \boldsymbol{u} \tag{1.2.32}$$

where it is easily verified that $\boldsymbol{\delta}_1 = \boldsymbol{\beta}_1$ and $\boldsymbol{\delta}_2 = (\boldsymbol{X}_2'\boldsymbol{X}_2)^{-1}\boldsymbol{X}_2'\boldsymbol{X}_1\boldsymbol{\beta}_1 + \boldsymbol{\beta}_2$. Since $\boldsymbol{X}_2'\boldsymbol{M}_2\boldsymbol{X}_1 = \boldsymbol{0}$, the partitioned inverse formula yields simply

$$\begin{bmatrix} \hat{\boldsymbol{\delta}}_1 \\ \hat{\boldsymbol{\delta}}_2 \end{bmatrix} = \begin{bmatrix} (\boldsymbol{X}_1'\boldsymbol{M}_2\boldsymbol{X}_1)^{-1}\boldsymbol{X}_1'\boldsymbol{M}_2\boldsymbol{y} \\ (\boldsymbol{X}_2'\boldsymbol{X}_2)^{-1}\boldsymbol{X}_2'\boldsymbol{y} \end{bmatrix} \tag{1.2.33}$$

according to (1.2.23), where $\hat{\boldsymbol{\delta}}_1 = \hat{\boldsymbol{\beta}}_1$.

Finally, consider the residuals of the partitioned model. These are

$$\begin{aligned} \hat{\boldsymbol{u}} &= \boldsymbol{y} - \boldsymbol{X}_1\hat{\boldsymbol{\beta}}_1 - \boldsymbol{X}_2\hat{\boldsymbol{\beta}}_2 \\ &= \boldsymbol{y} - \boldsymbol{X}_1\hat{\boldsymbol{\beta}}_1 - \boldsymbol{X}_2(\boldsymbol{X}_2'\boldsymbol{X}_2)^{-1}(\boldsymbol{X}_2'\boldsymbol{y} - \boldsymbol{X}_1\hat{\boldsymbol{\beta}}_1) \\ &= \boldsymbol{M}_2\boldsymbol{y} - \boldsymbol{M}_2\boldsymbol{X}_1\hat{\boldsymbol{\beta}}_1 \\ &= \left[\boldsymbol{M}_2 - \boldsymbol{M}_2\boldsymbol{X}_1(\boldsymbol{X}_1'\boldsymbol{M}_2\boldsymbol{X}_1)^{-1}\boldsymbol{X}_1'\boldsymbol{M}_2\right]\boldsymbol{y} \end{aligned} \tag{1.2.34}$$

where the second equality substitutes from (1.2.28). However, since $\hat{\boldsymbol{u}} = \boldsymbol{M}\boldsymbol{y}$, and these equalities hold for arbitrary $\boldsymbol{y}$, it follows that

$$\boldsymbol{M} = \boldsymbol{M}_2 - \boldsymbol{M}_2\boldsymbol{X}_1(\boldsymbol{X}_1'\boldsymbol{M}_2\boldsymbol{X}_1)^{-1}\boldsymbol{X}_1'\boldsymbol{M}_2. \tag{1.2.35}$$

1.3 The Statistical Model

So much for computation. The next fundamental question concerns interpretation. Minimizing the sum of the squared prediction errors is not the only criterion for choosing an estimator of $\boldsymbol{\beta}$, so we would like to know how good an estimator $\hat{\boldsymbol{\beta}}$ is, and how it might compare with alternatives. To deal with these issues, some additional details about the observational setup, and the goals of the investigation, need to be filled in.

In the context of the linear model, an obvious question is the following: why in (1.1.1) is y_t placed on the left-hand side, with coefficient fixed at unity, and all the other variables on the right-hand side with unspecified coefficients? What is special about y_t? Two kinds of answer to this question have been offered above. The first relates to the purpose of the investigation. If this is prediction, in a situation where we observe (or have previously predicted) $\boldsymbol{x}_t$ and wish to predict y_t, an equation to predict y_t is what is needed. The second relates to the interpretation of the data generation mechanism. If y_t is the response of economic agents to the effects of $\boldsymbol{x}_t$, it is the natural choice for normalization because of the way the β_i are interpreted, as response coefficients.

This type of argument explains why the model is set up as it is, but it does not explain why least squares is the most suitable estimator. To do this requires a more formal approach. The set of assumptions about the way the sample data are generated go under the name of the *statistical model*. Broadly, three distinct statistical models of the data generation mechanism can be distinguished.

Model A: Fixed regressors

Elementary treatments of the regression model make the assumption that the regressors are *fixed in repeated samples*. This is basically a simplifying assumption to make the statistical analysis tractable, but it is as well to see just what it implies. This is the model most applicable to experimental situations. An experimenter chooses the experimental design, the cases $\boldsymbol{X} = [\boldsymbol{x}_1, \ldots, \boldsymbol{x}_n]'$, and then $\boldsymbol{y} = (y_1, \ldots, y_n)'$ represents the experimental outcomes. In the regression model $\boldsymbol{y} = \boldsymbol{X\beta} + \boldsymbol{u}$, the $\boldsymbol{u}$ stands for errors in measuring $\boldsymbol{y}$, and other factors outside the experimenter's control. For example, consider an investigation of crop yields by agrobiologists. Let $\boldsymbol{y}$ represent the yields of a crop grown on n experimental plots, and let the rows of $\boldsymbol{X}$ represent the seed varieties, irrigation, fertilizer and other experimental variables for each plot. $\boldsymbol{u}$ represents the effects of uncontrolled differences from plot to plot, soil and sunlight variations for example, or errors in measuring the yield.

In this situation, the experiment can, in principle, be repeated as often as desired, with the same design matrix $\boldsymbol{X}$ but different, randomly drawn $\boldsymbol{u}$, and it is sensible to think of $\boldsymbol{X}$ as being fixed in repeated samples. The regression model is a natural basis for the analysis because only one of the variables, $\boldsymbol{y}$, is random.

Model B: Random regressors with independent sampling

Imagine a survey of household budgets, conducted by economists or government statisticians. A sample of families is drawn at random, and their incomes and expenditures on various commodities are recorded. An econometrician regresses (say) food expenditure on income and other relevant variables pertaining to consumption habits, things such as family size, number of children, etc. In this model the data are non-experimental, and the regressors cannot be described as fixed in repeated samples. If we draw a new sample of families, a new $\boldsymbol{y}$ *and* a new $\boldsymbol{X}$ are randomly selected each time.

However, the regression is still a valid device for predicting what a family with a given income etc. will spend on food, because it estimates the *conditional expectation* of y_t given $\boldsymbol{x}_t$. Thanks to the fact that the families are randomly sampled, it turns out that this model 'mimics' the fixed regressor model, and as we shall see in Chapter 2, many of the statistical properties of least squares in the fixed regressor model continue to hold. There are nonetheless some important differences from model A.

Model C: Time series regression (dependent sampling)

Suppose the data consist of annual or quarterly observations on national income and expenditures, drawn from the national accounts. In this model, the random sampling assumption does not apply. Successive periods in the history of the national economy are obviously highly dependent on one another, reflecting the business cycle, technological trends, and other factors carrying over from one year or quarter to the next. The same is true of nearly all economic data taking the form of a time series. When the sample points are dependent, the statistical model has *completely* different properties from cases such as randomly sampled households. It is fundamentally unlike the fixed regressor model. Special statistical treatment is called for here, although there are still important situations in which the least squares estimator is the correct tool of analysis.

This book will have little to say about model A, for the simple reason that economics (a basically non-experimental discipline) throws up little data of this type. In the present chapter, and Chapters 2 and 3, we are going to study model B in detail. Most of the remainder of the book will deal, implicitly or explicitly, with model C. In either model, the crucial concept in the analysis is going to be the conditional expectation. The formalities of conditioning theory are dealt with in Appendix B, but for present purposes, we will focus on intuition.

$E(y_t)$, the ordinary expected value of the random variable y_t, is usually to be thought of as the best predictor of y_t based on its behaviour in repeated sampling *and nothing else.* All the random influences that make one sample different from another are averaged out. On the other hand, in a sampling experiment generating the random vector $(y_t, \boldsymbol{x}_t)$, such as our sample survey, the conditional expectation $E(y_t|\boldsymbol{x}_t)$ can be thought of as the best predictor of y_t based on knowledge of $\boldsymbol{x}_t$. In essence, this is like a thought experiment. Compare the two questions: 'what does the average family spend on food?' and 'what does a family of two adults and two children living on £15,000 per annum expect to spend on food?'. The answers to both these questions can be expressed as mathematical expectations, but in the latter case it is a conditional expectation, corresponding to a thought experiment in which variables that actually vary randomly are given fixed chosen values.

Since $E(y_t|\boldsymbol{x}_t)$ is a function of $\boldsymbol{x}_t$, from the viewpoint of an observer to whom $\boldsymbol{x}_t$ is unknown it is itself a random variable. A fundamental property of conditional distributions is the *law of iterated expectations* (LIE), which states that the expectation of $E(y_t|\boldsymbol{x}_t)$ under the marginal distribution of $\boldsymbol{x}_t$ is identical with the expectation of y_t. That is,

$$E_x[E(y_t|\boldsymbol{x}_t)] = E(y_t) \tag{1.3.1}$$

where $E_x[\cdot]$ denotes the expectation under the marginal distribution.[2] (See Theorem B.6.1.)

In this context, constants can be thought of as a special variety of random variable, called *degenerate* (having zero variance). The intercept dummy and other 'non-random' elements of $\boldsymbol{x}_t$ are subsumed under this distribution. The linear regression model can now be understood as embodying the basic assumption,

$$\boldsymbol{x}_t'\boldsymbol{\beta} = E(y_t|\boldsymbol{x}_t) \tag{1.3.2}$$

or equivalently, $E(u_t|\boldsymbol{x}_t) = 0$.[3]

To show the implication of this assumption is very easy. Premultiply the expression by the vector $\boldsymbol{x}_t$ and take expectations through to give

$$E(\boldsymbol{x}_t\boldsymbol{x}_t')\boldsymbol{\beta} = E[\boldsymbol{x}_t E(y_t|\boldsymbol{x}_t)] = E[E(\boldsymbol{x}_t y_t|\boldsymbol{x}_t)] = E(\boldsymbol{x}_t y_t) \tag{1.3.3}$$

[2] Henceforth this subscript will usually be omitted, since the context should always make clear which variables are being 'averaged'.

[3] This statement of the model is technically imprecise, although the amendment required is generally of no practical importance. See §2.1 for an explanation, and also §B.6 and §B.10 for details.

where the second equality uses the fact that $\boldsymbol{x}_t$ can be treated 'like a constant' with respect to the distribution conditioned on it, and the last one is an application of the LIE. Assume that the matrix $E(\boldsymbol{x}_t\boldsymbol{x}_t')$ is positive definite, and hence nonsingular. This is equivalent to assuming that $E(\boldsymbol{x}_t'\boldsymbol{a})^2 > 0$ for an arbitrary vector of constants $\boldsymbol{a}$ (compare inequality (B.8.6)) and so does not do more than rule out any redundancy in the set of regressors. Then

$$\boldsymbol{\beta} = E(\boldsymbol{x}_t\boldsymbol{x}_t')^{-1}E(\boldsymbol{x}_t y_t) \tag{1.3.4}$$

is the expression that uniquely defines the coefficients of the linear conditional expectation of $y_t|\boldsymbol{x}_t$. There is an obvious resemblance to the formula for the OLS estimator. Indeed, replacing expectations by sample averages leads immediately to the formula

$$\hat{\boldsymbol{\beta}} = (\boldsymbol{X}'\boldsymbol{X})^{-1}\boldsymbol{X}'\boldsymbol{y} \tag{1.3.5}$$

noting that $\boldsymbol{X}'\boldsymbol{X} = \sum_{t=1}^n \boldsymbol{x}_t\boldsymbol{x}_t'$ and $\boldsymbol{X}'\boldsymbol{y} = \sum_{t=1}^n \boldsymbol{x}_t y_t$. Sums are equivalent to averages in this expression since factors of n^{-1} cancel.

1.4 Model Specification

1.4.1 Linearity

Formula (1.3.4) suggests the link between the least squares principle and a model of conditional expectations. However, the *linearity* in model (1.3.2) is no more than an assumption. For full generality, one should write

$$E(y_t|\boldsymbol{x}_t) = f_t(\boldsymbol{x}_t) \tag{1.4.1}$$

where $f_t(\cdot)$ is an arbitrary function, possibly depending on t. It may then be necessary to justify the linear function as an *approximation* to $f_t(\boldsymbol{x}_t)$. To see how linear regression should be interpreted in this case, consider the mean squared error function $E[E(y_t|\boldsymbol{x}_t) - \boldsymbol{x}_t'\boldsymbol{b}]^2$. One could think of the value of $\boldsymbol{b}$ that minimizes this expression as providing the 'best' linear approximation to $E(y_t|\boldsymbol{x}_t)$.

Theorem 1.4.1 If $E(\boldsymbol{x}_t\boldsymbol{x}_t')$ is positive definite, the mean squared approximation error is minimized by setting $\boldsymbol{b} = \boldsymbol{\beta}_t$ where

$$\boldsymbol{\beta}_t = \left[E(\boldsymbol{x}_t\boldsymbol{x}_t')\right]^{-1} E(\boldsymbol{x}_t y_t). \tag{1.4.2}$$

Proof Substituting and rearranging yields

$$\begin{aligned} E(E(y_t|\boldsymbol{x}_t) - \boldsymbol{x}_t'\boldsymbol{b})^2 &= E[E(y_t|\boldsymbol{x}_t) - \boldsymbol{x}_t'\boldsymbol{\beta}_t + \boldsymbol{x}_t'(\boldsymbol{\beta}_t - \boldsymbol{b})]^2 \\ &= E[E(y_t|\boldsymbol{x}_t) - \boldsymbol{x}_t'\boldsymbol{\beta}_t]^2 + (\boldsymbol{\beta}_t - \boldsymbol{b})'E(\boldsymbol{x}_t\boldsymbol{x}_t')(\boldsymbol{\beta}_t - \boldsymbol{b}) \\ &\quad + 2(\boldsymbol{\beta}_t - \boldsymbol{b})'E[\boldsymbol{x}_t(E(y_t|\boldsymbol{x}_t) - \boldsymbol{x}_t'\boldsymbol{\beta}_t)]. \end{aligned} \tag{1.4.3}$$

However, since $E[\boldsymbol{x}_t E(y_t|\boldsymbol{x}_t)] = E(\boldsymbol{x}_t y_t)$ by the LIE,

$$E[\boldsymbol{x}_t(E(y_t|\boldsymbol{x}_t) - \boldsymbol{\beta}_t'\boldsymbol{x}_t)] = E(\boldsymbol{x}_t y_t) - \boldsymbol{\beta}_t'E(\boldsymbol{x}_t\boldsymbol{x}_t') = \boldsymbol{0}. \tag{1.4.4}$$

Hence, (1.4.3) is minimized by setting $\boldsymbol{b} = \boldsymbol{\beta}_t$, by Lemma A.7.3. ∎

It further follows that for any given $\boldsymbol{x}_t$, $\boldsymbol{\beta}_t'\boldsymbol{x}_t$ is the linear predictor that minimizes the mean squared error in predicting y_t from $\boldsymbol{x}_t$.

Theorem 1.4.2 The function $E(y_t - \boldsymbol{b}'\boldsymbol{x}_t)^2$ is minimized by setting $\boldsymbol{b} = \boldsymbol{\beta}_t$.

Proof

$$\begin{aligned} E(y_t - \boldsymbol{b}'\boldsymbol{x}_t)^2 &= E[(y_t - E(y_t|\boldsymbol{x}_t) + E(y_t|\boldsymbol{x}_t) - \boldsymbol{b}'\boldsymbol{x}_t]^2 \\ &= E[y_t - E(y_t|\boldsymbol{x}_t)]^2 + E[E(y_t|\boldsymbol{x}_t) - \boldsymbol{b}'\boldsymbol{x}_t]^2 \\ &\quad + 2E[(y_t - E(y_t|\boldsymbol{x}_t))(E(y_t|\boldsymbol{x}_t) - \boldsymbol{b}'\boldsymbol{x}_t)]. \end{aligned} \tag{1.4.5}$$

The cross-product term vanishes, since by the LIE

$$\begin{aligned} E[(y_t - E(y_t|\boldsymbol{x}_t))(E(y_t|\boldsymbol{x}_t) - \boldsymbol{b}'\boldsymbol{x}_t)] &= E[(E(y_t|\boldsymbol{x}_t) - E(y_t|\boldsymbol{x}_t))(E(y_t|\boldsymbol{x}_t) - \boldsymbol{b}'\boldsymbol{x}_t)] \\ &= E(0) = 0. \end{aligned} \tag{1.4.6}$$

The result therefore follows by Theorem 1.4.1. ∎

Equation (1.4.2) differs from (1.3.4) since it is not necessarily the case that $\boldsymbol{\beta}_t = \boldsymbol{\beta}$, independent of t. This would be true if, for example, the data were identically distributed, implying in particular that $E(\boldsymbol{x}_t\boldsymbol{x}_t')$ and $E(\boldsymbol{x}_t y_t)$ are constants which do not depend on t. Later on, we show that $\hat{\boldsymbol{\beta}}$, more generally, estimates a weighted average of the $\boldsymbol{\beta}_t$,

$$\boldsymbol{\beta}_n = \left(\sum_{t=1}^{n} E(\boldsymbol{x}_t\boldsymbol{x}_t')\right)^{-1} \sum_{t=1}^{n} E(\boldsymbol{x}_t y_t) = \sum_{t=1}^{n} \boldsymbol{A}_{nt}\boldsymbol{\beta}_t \tag{1.4.7}$$

where

$$\boldsymbol{A}_{nt} = \left(\sum_{t=1}^{n} E(\boldsymbol{x}_s\boldsymbol{x}_s')\right)^{-1} E(\boldsymbol{x}_t\boldsymbol{x}_t') \tag{1.4.8}$$

having the property $\sum_{t=1}^{n} \boldsymbol{A}_{nt} = \boldsymbol{I}_k$. The term 'estimate' is used here in the rather special sense that $\boldsymbol{\beta}_n$ and the least squares estimator are converging to the same limit (appropriately defined, and assuming such limits exist) as n tends to infinity. The technical details are covered in §10.5.

Unless stated specifically to the contrary, in what follows we will always appeal to the so-called *axiom of correct specification*, or in other words assume (1.3.2) is true. The properties of the OLS estimator to be derived in Chapter 2 and subsequently do not generally hold without (1.3.2), but these remarks may serve to reassure us that the assumption need not be too critical.

1.4.2 Included Variables

Even if linearity is assumed, our model may be *incomplete* in the following sense. Suppose there are some other variables $\boldsymbol{z}_t$ ($l \times 1$) relevant to the explanation of y_t, such that

$$E(y_t|\boldsymbol{x}_t, \boldsymbol{z}_t) = \boldsymbol{x}_t'\boldsymbol{\beta} + \boldsymbol{z}_t'\boldsymbol{\delta}. \tag{1.4.9}$$

Then, evidently,

$$E(y_t|\boldsymbol{x}_t) = \boldsymbol{x}_t'\boldsymbol{\beta} + E(\boldsymbol{z}_t'|\boldsymbol{x}_t)\boldsymbol{\delta}. \tag{1.4.10}$$

In general, the second term is an arbitrary function of $\boldsymbol{x}_t$. However, if the linearity assumption is extended by assuming that $E(\boldsymbol{z}_t|\boldsymbol{x}_t) = \boldsymbol{D}\boldsymbol{x}_t$ where

$$\boldsymbol{D} = E(\boldsymbol{z}_t\boldsymbol{x}_t')E(\boldsymbol{x}_t\boldsymbol{x}_t')^{-1} \quad (l \times k) \tag{1.4.11}$$

is independent of t, then

$$E(y_t|\boldsymbol{x}_t) = \boldsymbol{x}_t'\boldsymbol{\gamma} \tag{1.4.12}$$

where $\boldsymbol{\gamma} = \boldsymbol{\beta} + \boldsymbol{D}'\boldsymbol{\delta}$. The vectors $\boldsymbol{\gamma}$ and $\boldsymbol{\beta}$ are called respectively the *simple* and *partial* regression coefficients of $\boldsymbol{x}_t$. The least squares coefficients have a corresponding decomposition. Note that the formula (1.2.28) applied to the regression

$$\boldsymbol{y} = \boldsymbol{X}\boldsymbol{\beta} + \boldsymbol{Z}\boldsymbol{\delta} + \boldsymbol{u} \tag{1.4.13}$$

yields $\hat{\boldsymbol{\gamma}} = \hat{\boldsymbol{\beta}} + \hat{\boldsymbol{D}}'\hat{\boldsymbol{\delta}}$ where $\hat{\boldsymbol{\beta}}$ and $\hat{\boldsymbol{\delta}}$ are the multiple regression coefficients, $\hat{\boldsymbol{\gamma}} = (\boldsymbol{X}'\boldsymbol{X})^{-1}\boldsymbol{X}'\boldsymbol{y}$, and $\hat{\boldsymbol{D}} = \boldsymbol{Z}'\boldsymbol{X}(\boldsymbol{X}'\boldsymbol{X})^{-1}$. These formulae reveal how the computational and the interpretive relationships between the simple and partial coefficients are closely linked.

It is possible that $\boldsymbol{\gamma}$ represents the parameters of interest in the investigation. For example, $\boldsymbol{x}_t'\boldsymbol{\gamma}$ is the best (minimum mean squared error) predictor of y_t given $\boldsymbol{x}_t$, and if $\boldsymbol{z}_t$ were unobserved, prediction by $\boldsymbol{x}_t$ might be the object of the exercise so $\boldsymbol{\gamma}$ is what we wish to know. However, $\boldsymbol{\beta}$ is more commonly regarded as containing the parameters of interest, because they show how y_t and $\boldsymbol{x}_t$ are directly related, after controlling for the effects of $\boldsymbol{z}_t$. They are commonly identified with theoretical economic magnitudes (e.g. elasticities of demand or supply, technological coefficients) whereas no such interpretation is available for composite parameters such as $\boldsymbol{\gamma}$. Moreover, the assumption $E(\boldsymbol{z}_t|\boldsymbol{x}_t) = \boldsymbol{D}\boldsymbol{x}_t$ is entirely *ad hoc*. If in reality $E(\boldsymbol{z}_t\boldsymbol{x}_t')E(\boldsymbol{x}_t\boldsymbol{x}_t')^{-1} = \boldsymbol{D}_t$, depending on t, the composite coefficients are $\boldsymbol{\gamma}_t = \boldsymbol{\beta} + \boldsymbol{D}_t'\boldsymbol{\delta}$ and linearity fails for the incomplete model even if it holds for the complete one. Therefore, unless $\boldsymbol{z}_t$ is included in the regression, the model is misspecified.

However, in econometrics, the number of relevant variables may be very large, often exceeding the number of observations available, and choices of a practical nature are forced on the investigator. If the elements of $\boldsymbol{\delta}$ are of no interest, so-called *nuisance* parameters, and also $\boldsymbol{\beta} = \boldsymbol{\gamma}$, a case can often be made for excluding $\boldsymbol{z}_t$. Note that the latter condition holds if $\boldsymbol{D} = \boldsymbol{0}$, or more generally if $E(\boldsymbol{z}_t|\boldsymbol{x}_t) = \boldsymbol{0}$,[4] and need not imply $\boldsymbol{\delta} = \boldsymbol{0}$. In principle, it would be preferable to include the variables in every case where $\boldsymbol{\delta} \neq \boldsymbol{0}$, because otherwise $\boldsymbol{z}_t'\boldsymbol{\delta}$ becomes

[4] This is a mild abuse of notation since strictly, when $\boldsymbol{z}_t$ is not predictable from $\boldsymbol{x}_t$ the conditional mean is a constant, not necessarily zero. Similarly, if $x_{kt} = 1$, the kth column of $\boldsymbol{D}$ should not vanish. However, this term can be subsumed by adding it to the intercept of the regression, and it can be conveniently neglected by assuming the variables are expressed in deviations from the mean.

a component of the error term. Even if $\boldsymbol{\beta} = \boldsymbol{\gamma}$, $\hat{\boldsymbol{\gamma}}$ is an inferior estimator of $\boldsymbol{\beta}$ relative to $\hat{\boldsymbol{\beta}}$, other things equal, because the error term has a larger variance in that case. However, if $\boldsymbol{\delta} = \mathbf{0}$ while $\boldsymbol{D} \neq \mathbf{0}$, it is also known that $\hat{\boldsymbol{\beta}}$ is typically inferior to $\hat{\boldsymbol{\gamma}}$.[5] The case where $\boldsymbol{\delta}$ is nonzero but 'small', in some suitable sense, may therefore represent a balance of advantage between inclusion and exclusion. Given that prior knowledge of all these relations is inevitably lacking in practice, there can be no simple rule underlying the choice of regressors. A good deal of our subsequent analysis will focus on this problem.

1.4.3 Relevant Variables

We neglected an important and difficult question in the previous section by speaking of the *relevant* variables in the model. A distinction needs to be made is between *explanatory variables*, and what may be called the *valid conditioning variables*. To be relevant, a variable must fall into both of these categories. Suppose the object of the exercise is to forecast y_t in a situation where $\boldsymbol{x}_t$ is observed, but y_t and also $\boldsymbol{z}_t$ are unobserved. Then, no matter how 'good' an equation (1.4.9) may be in terms of least squares fit, it is of no interest. Trivially, putting $\boldsymbol{z}_t = y_t$ one could write $E(y_t|\boldsymbol{x}_t, y_t) = y_t$ and obtain a model that forecasts perfectly, but is useless. For this problem, y_t is not a valid conditioning variable.

Similarly, a behavioural model must make economic sense. It is possible to 'explain' a families' total income in terms of its food expenditure, in the sense that these tend to move together in a predictable fashion, and either can be used to predict the other. However, we aren't usually interested in the regression of income on expenditure. This is because a model of economic behaviour based on the conditional expectation $E(y_t|\boldsymbol{x}_t)$ embodies an assumption about the order of causation. $\boldsymbol{x}_t$ must be given (i.e., observed by agents) at the moment when y_t is determined, such that no feedback from y_t to $\boldsymbol{x}_t$ is possible. If, in a model of economic behaviour, the disturbance term represents the deviation between plans and outcomes due to unforeseen events, it is appropriate for it to be unpredictable by the conditioning variables, in the sense $E(u_t|\boldsymbol{x}_t) = 0$.

In the context of the food demand example, a valid conditioning variable is any variable that the household has observed when the spending decision is made. It is also an explanatory variable if it actually influences their decision. The expenditure model would not be valid if households were to plan *jointly* what to earn and what to spend on food, so that the two decisions are interdependent rather than sequential. Over a longer time-scale (say, lifetimes rather than months or years), we would typically recognize the existence of such an interdependence. In general, the simple regression model is appropriate to cases where a single variable is chosen conditional on others. The alternative possibility, with two or more variables being jointly determined, is a model involving several simultaneous equations. This type of model is studied in Chapters 8 and 13.

---

[5] The statistical arguments underlying these claims are explored in Chapter 2 and subsequently.

Further Reading: Alternative accounts of the linear regression algebra can be found in many popular textbooks. Theil (1971) is recommended. Rao (1973), Madansky (1976), Seber (1980) offer good advanced treatments. For a geometric interpretation of the algebra, see Davidson and MacKinnon (1993). Goldberger (1991) and Spanos (1986) emphasize the 'conditional expectation' interpretation. On nonlinear regression, see Gallant (1987), Davidson and MacKinnon (1993), Malinvaud (1970).

Chapter 2

Statistical Analysis of the Regression Model

2.1 Statistical Assumptions

In this chapter we investigate the properties of the OLS estimator

$$\hat{\boldsymbol{\beta}} = (\boldsymbol{X}'\boldsymbol{X})^{-1}\boldsymbol{X}'\boldsymbol{y} \tag{2.1.1}$$

under a set of assumptions corresponding to sampling model B, as defined in §1.3. The primary assumption is

$$E(y_t|\boldsymbol{x}_t) = \boldsymbol{x}_t'\boldsymbol{\beta} \quad t = 1, \dots, n. \tag{2.1.2}$$

However, this must be augmented by a range of other assumptions, some merely simplifying, but others substantive from the point of view of the statistical properties of the model. The most critical of these is *random sampling*, which is to say that the $(k+1)$-dimensional sample points $(y_t, \boldsymbol{x}_t')$ are independently drawn. In this case, knowing $\boldsymbol{x}_s$ for any $s \neq t$ cannot help in predicting y_t, and (2.1.2) can be extended to

$$E(y_t|\boldsymbol{x}_1, \dots, \boldsymbol{x}_t, \dots, \boldsymbol{x}_n) = \boldsymbol{x}_t'\boldsymbol{\beta} \quad t = 1, \dots, n. \tag{2.1.3}$$

As a matter of fact, random sampling would equally imply that

$$E(y_t|\boldsymbol{x}_1, \dots, \boldsymbol{x}_t, \dots, \boldsymbol{x}_n, y_1, \dots, y_{t-1}, y_{t+1}, \dots y_n) = \boldsymbol{x}_t'\boldsymbol{\beta} \tag{2.1.4}$$

but (2.1.3) is just what we need.

Consider initially the following assumptions on the model represented by (1.1.2). The first, given the definition of the disturbance u_t, is just a restatement of (2.1.3).

Assumption 2.1.1 $E(\boldsymbol{u}|\boldsymbol{X}) = \boldsymbol{0}$ a.s. □

Assumption 2.1.2 $E(\boldsymbol{u}\boldsymbol{u}'|\boldsymbol{X}) = \sigma^2\boldsymbol{I}_n$ a.s. □

Assumption 2.1.3 $\text{rank}(\boldsymbol{X}) = k$ a.s. □

The tag 'a.s.', standing for almost surely, is attached here since the quantities in question are random variables, and it is formally correct to include it in (2.1.2)–(2.1.4) similarly. It means the same as 'with probability 1'; see §B.4 for further details. In this chapter, statements involving $\boldsymbol{X}$, especially expectations conditional on $\boldsymbol{X}$, should strictly speaking be qualified in the same way. However, to avoid clutter this will often be taken as implicit.

Assumptions 2.1.1 and 2.1.2 virtually rule out time-series data. Time series, by their nature, almost always exhibit interdependence of the data points. Elements of $\boldsymbol{y}$ feed back through dynamic interactions to influence post-dated elements of $\boldsymbol{X}$ and, hence, are predictable by these, invalidating (2.1.3).

In Assumption 2.1.2, σ^2 is a constant not depending on $\boldsymbol{X}$. Given Assumption 2.1.1, $\sigma^2\boldsymbol{I}_n$ is the conditional covariance matrix of $\boldsymbol{u}$ and, since it does not depend on $\boldsymbol{X}$, it is also the *un*conditional covariance matrix. Thus, Assumptions 2.1.1 and 2.1.2 imply that

$$\begin{aligned} E(u_t) = 0, \text{Var}(u_t) = \sigma^2 \quad t = 1, \dots, n \\ \text{Cov}(u_t, u_s) = E(u_t u_s) = 0 \quad t \neq s \end{aligned}$$

(unconditionally, note). The uncorrelatedness part of this assumption follows from independent sampling, but the uniformity of the variances is essentially a simplifying requirement since, otherwise, it is necessary to know what the variances are. See §2.3.1 on the ways this assumption could fail.

Assumption 2.1.3 ensures that the model is well-specified for estimation, and has already been seen to be a condition for the existence of the OLS estimator in any given sample. The 'near' failure of this assumption, manifested in the matrix $\boldsymbol{X}'\boldsymbol{X}$ being poorly conditioned for inversion, is known as *multicollinearity*. We refer to the actual failure of Assumption 2.1.3 as exact (or perfect) multicollinearity.

2.2 The Properties of OLS

2.2.1 Mean and Variance

Assumptions 2.1.1–2.1.3 imply the following results. First, the estimator *exists*. Assumption 2.1.3 implies that $|\boldsymbol{X}'\boldsymbol{X}| \neq 0$ with probability 1, by Lemma A.7.1. Second, there is the well-known result that $\hat{\boldsymbol{\beta}}$ is unbiased. The estimator is conveniently decomposed into the true value and the error-of-estimate,

$$\hat{\boldsymbol{\beta}} = (\boldsymbol{X}'\boldsymbol{X})^{-1}\boldsymbol{X}'(\boldsymbol{X}\boldsymbol{\beta} + \boldsymbol{u}) = \boldsymbol{\beta} + (\boldsymbol{X}'\boldsymbol{X})^{-1}\boldsymbol{X}'\boldsymbol{u}. \tag{2.2.1}$$

Hence

$$E(\hat{\boldsymbol{\beta}}|\boldsymbol{X}) = \boldsymbol{\beta} + (\boldsymbol{X}'\boldsymbol{X})^{-1}\boldsymbol{X}'E(\boldsymbol{u}|\boldsymbol{X}) = \boldsymbol{\beta} \tag{2.2.2}$$

by Assumption 2.1.1. This result holds for any $\boldsymbol{X}$, so that applying the LIE to (2.2.2) yields $E(\hat{\boldsymbol{\beta}}) = \boldsymbol{\beta}$, unconditionally. In repeated samples, the distribution of the estimates has the true value as its central tendency, which is reassuring, although by no means a sufficient condition for the estimator to be useful. The third result is the formula for the covariance matrix of the estimator. In view of (2.2.2), this is

$$\begin{aligned}\operatorname{Var}(\hat{\boldsymbol{\beta}}|\boldsymbol{X}) &= E[(\hat{\boldsymbol{\beta}}-\boldsymbol{\beta})(\hat{\boldsymbol{\beta}}-\boldsymbol{\beta})'|\boldsymbol{X}] \\ &= (\boldsymbol{X}'\boldsymbol{X})^{-1}\boldsymbol{X}'E(\boldsymbol{uu}'|\boldsymbol{X})\boldsymbol{X}(\boldsymbol{X}'\boldsymbol{X})^{-1} \\ &= (\boldsymbol{X}'\boldsymbol{X})^{-1}\boldsymbol{X}'(\sigma^2\boldsymbol{I})\boldsymbol{X}(\boldsymbol{X}'\boldsymbol{X})^{-1} \\ &= \sigma^2(\boldsymbol{X}'\boldsymbol{X})^{-1} \end{aligned} \tag{2.2.3}$$

where the penultimate equality is by Assumption 2.1.2.

The covariance matrix measures how informative the sample is about the parameters. A perspective on this question in multiple regression is provided by considering the extreme case of multicollinearity, where $\boldsymbol{X}'\boldsymbol{X}$ is near singular. If its determinant is close to zero the elements of the inverse are liable to be large, with the consequence that the regression coefficients are poorly determined, having large conditional variances. This phenomenon has nothing to do with goodness of fit, and multicollinearity can coexist with a high R^2. While the problem cannot be eliminated except possibly by obtaining more data, a judicious transformation of the model as in §1.2.4 may relieve it. In other words, it may be possible to choose $\boldsymbol{A}$ so that particular elements of $\hat{\boldsymbol{\delta}} = \boldsymbol{A}^{-1}\hat{\boldsymbol{\beta}}$ have smaller conditional variances than those of $\hat{\boldsymbol{\beta}}$ itself.

Since, unlike the conditional mean, the formula in (2.2.3) depends on $\boldsymbol{X}$, it is not the unconditional variance. However, applying the LIE, we obtain

$$\operatorname{Var}(\hat{\boldsymbol{\beta}}) = E[\operatorname{Var}(\hat{\boldsymbol{\beta}}|\boldsymbol{X})] = \sigma^2 E[(\boldsymbol{X}'\boldsymbol{X})^{-1}] \tag{2.2.4}$$

Be careful to note that $E[(\boldsymbol{X}'\boldsymbol{X})^{-1}] \neq [E(\boldsymbol{X}'\boldsymbol{X})]^{-1}$. It must be assumed that the former expectation exists, since otherwise the variance, conditional or unconditional, is not well-defined.[1]

In repetitions of the random experiment with randomly drawn $\boldsymbol{X}$, the distribution of $\hat{\boldsymbol{\beta}}$ is described by (2.2.4). However, it may be that the conditional variance is the relevant measure of dispersion for practical purposes. Since $\boldsymbol{X}$ is observed, in the thought experiment of repeated sampling a case can be made for confining attention to the distribution of those samples having this $\boldsymbol{X}$ (the conditional distribution) for which (2.2.3) is the relevant formula. Thus, if there is a large amount of variation in the rows of $\boldsymbol{X}$ so that $\boldsymbol{X}'\boldsymbol{X}$ is big, the conditional variance is small, and better estimates are also to be expected than in the case of small variations in $\boldsymbol{X}$, other things equal. From this point of view, the performance of the estimator in repeated sampling of the $\boldsymbol{X}$ is irrelevant. On the other hand, the variance is also the basis for comparing the efficiency of alternative estimators and, for this purpose, it is natural to consider the average case, a point discussed further in §2.2.3. There is no 'correct' answer to the question of which formula is the relevant one. Fortunately, in the important matter of interval estimation (see §2.4) the distinction proves to be immaterial.

---

[1] For any random variables y and x, $E(y|x)$ is well defined only if $E|y| < \infty$. See §B.6 for details.

2.2.2 The Residuals

Although they estimate uncorrelated variables by assumption, the least squares residuals are correlated, for

$$E(\hat{\boldsymbol{u}}\hat{\boldsymbol{u}}'|\boldsymbol{X}) = E(\boldsymbol{M}\boldsymbol{u}\boldsymbol{u}'\boldsymbol{M}|\boldsymbol{X}) = \sigma^2\boldsymbol{M}. \tag{2.2.5}$$

It can be seen that their conditional distribution is singular, the covariance matrix having rank of $n-k$, the rank of $\boldsymbol{M}$. This is the consequence of their orthogonality with $\boldsymbol{X}$ since the null space of $\boldsymbol{M}$ is the space spanned by $\boldsymbol{X}$. An unbiased estimator of σ^2 is provided by the formula

$$s^2 = \frac{\hat{\boldsymbol{u}}'\hat{\boldsymbol{u}}}{n-k}. \tag{2.2.6}$$

To see this, use (1.2.21) and (A.1.12) (and the fact that a scalar is its own trace), to obtain

$$\boldsymbol{u}'\boldsymbol{M}\boldsymbol{u} = \mathrm{tr}\boldsymbol{u}'\boldsymbol{M}\boldsymbol{u} = \mathrm{tr}\boldsymbol{M}\boldsymbol{u}\boldsymbol{u}'. \tag{2.2.7}$$

Hence,

$$E(\hat{\boldsymbol{u}}'\hat{\boldsymbol{u}}|\boldsymbol{X}) = E(\mathrm{tr}\,\boldsymbol{M}\boldsymbol{u}\boldsymbol{u}'|\boldsymbol{X}) = \mathrm{tr}\,\boldsymbol{M}E(\boldsymbol{u}\boldsymbol{u}'|\boldsymbol{X}) = \sigma^2\,\mathrm{tr}\,\boldsymbol{M}. \tag{2.2.8}$$

Using (A.1.11) and (A.1.12),

$$\mathrm{tr}\,\boldsymbol{M} = \mathrm{tr}\,\boldsymbol{I}_n - \mathrm{tr}\,\boldsymbol{X}'\boldsymbol{X}(\boldsymbol{X}'\boldsymbol{X})^{-1} = n-k \tag{2.2.9}$$

so that $E(\hat{\boldsymbol{u}}'\hat{\boldsymbol{u}}) = \sigma^2(n-k)$, unconditionally.

2.2.3 The Gauss–Markov Theorem

We would like to show that OLS is the optimal estimator, in some sense. In particular, given that it is unbiased, we would like it to have the smallest possible variance amongst estimators sharing that property. This is the property called *efficiency*, in the sense of making the most efficient use of the information in a given sample. In the following analysis, the standard approach is somewhat modified because of the random $\boldsymbol{X}$ assumption.

Consider the class of linear estimators,

$$\boldsymbol{\beta}_L = \boldsymbol{L}\boldsymbol{y} \tag{2.2.10}$$

defined on the set of $k \times n$ stochastic matrices $\boldsymbol{L}$ that satisfy the following assumptions, which must hold in addition to Assumptions 2.1.1–2.1.3.

Assumption 2.2.1 $E(\boldsymbol{u}|\boldsymbol{X},\boldsymbol{L}) = \boldsymbol{0}$ a.s. □

Assumption 2.2.2 $E(\boldsymbol{u}\boldsymbol{u}'|\boldsymbol{X},\boldsymbol{L}) = \sigma^2\boldsymbol{I}_n$ a.s. □

Assumption 2.2.3 $\boldsymbol{L}\boldsymbol{X} = \boldsymbol{I}_k$ a.s. □

Then, note that under Assumptions 2.2.1 and 2.2.3

$$E(\boldsymbol{\beta}_L) = E(\boldsymbol{LX})\boldsymbol{\beta} + E[\boldsymbol{L}E(\boldsymbol{u}|\boldsymbol{X}, \boldsymbol{L})] = \boldsymbol{\beta} \tag{2.2.11}$$

using the LIE, so that $\boldsymbol{\beta}_L$ is unbiased. OLS belongs to this class of linear unbiased estimators, representing the case $\boldsymbol{L} = (\boldsymbol{X}'\boldsymbol{X})^{-1}\boldsymbol{X}'$. Further, under Assumption 2.2.2, we obtain

$$\text{Var}(\boldsymbol{\beta}_L|\boldsymbol{X}, \boldsymbol{L}) = E(\boldsymbol{Luu'L'}|\boldsymbol{X}, \boldsymbol{L}) = \sigma^2\boldsymbol{LL'} \tag{2.2.12}$$

and hence,

$$\text{Var}(\boldsymbol{\beta}_L) = \sigma^2 E(\boldsymbol{LL'}). \tag{2.2.13}$$

The following result generalizes the well-known Gauss–Markov (GM) theorem to the stochastic regressor case.

Theorem 2.2.1 Let Assumptions 2.1.1–2.1.3 hold. Then the difference between $\text{Var}(\boldsymbol{\beta}_L)$ and $\text{Var}(\hat{\boldsymbol{\beta}})$ is a positive semi-definite matrix for every $\boldsymbol{L}$ satisfying Assumptions 2.2.1–2.2.3.

Proof Define $\boldsymbol{D} = \boldsymbol{L} - (\boldsymbol{X}'\boldsymbol{X})^{-1}\boldsymbol{X}'$, so that $\boldsymbol{DX} = \boldsymbol{0}$ a.s. by assumption. Then note that

$$\begin{aligned}\boldsymbol{LL'} &= (\boldsymbol{X}'\boldsymbol{X})^{-1}\boldsymbol{X}'\boldsymbol{X}(\boldsymbol{X}'\boldsymbol{X})^{-1} + (\boldsymbol{X}'\boldsymbol{X})^{-1}\boldsymbol{X}'\boldsymbol{D}' + \boldsymbol{DX}(\boldsymbol{X}'\boldsymbol{X})^{-1} + \boldsymbol{DD}'\\ &= (\boldsymbol{X}'\boldsymbol{X})^{-1} + \boldsymbol{DD}'. \end{aligned}\tag{2.2.14}$$

It follows that

$$\text{Var}(\boldsymbol{\beta}_L|\boldsymbol{X}, \boldsymbol{L}) = \text{Var}(\hat{\boldsymbol{\beta}}|\boldsymbol{X}, \boldsymbol{L}) + \sigma^2\boldsymbol{DD}' \tag{2.2.15}$$

where $\boldsymbol{DD}'$ is positive semi-definite by Lemma A.7.1. The theorem follows on taking unconditional expectations to obtain

$$\text{Var}(\boldsymbol{\beta}_L) = \text{Var}(\hat{\boldsymbol{\beta}}) + \sigma^2 E(\boldsymbol{DD}') \tag{2.2.16}$$

and noting that for arbitrary fixed k-vector $\boldsymbol{a}$,

$$\boldsymbol{a}'E(\boldsymbol{DD}')\boldsymbol{a} = E(\boldsymbol{a}'\boldsymbol{DD}'\boldsymbol{a}) \geq 0 \tag{2.2.17}$$

since $\boldsymbol{a}'\boldsymbol{DD}'\boldsymbol{a}$ is non-negative (a sum of squares) for any $\boldsymbol{D}$. ∎

To show what this result implies, consider the (scalar) variance of an arbitrary linear combination of the coefficients. Since $\text{Var}(\boldsymbol{a}'\boldsymbol{x}) = \boldsymbol{a}'\,\text{Var}(\boldsymbol{x})\boldsymbol{a}$ from (B.8.6), the theorem shows that for any k-vector $\boldsymbol{a}$,

$$\text{Var}(\boldsymbol{a}'\boldsymbol{\beta}_L) - \text{Var}(\boldsymbol{a}'\hat{\boldsymbol{\beta}}) = \boldsymbol{a}'[\text{Var}(\boldsymbol{\beta}_L) - \text{Var}(\hat{\boldsymbol{\beta}})]\boldsymbol{a} \geq 0. \tag{2.2.18}$$

As a simple example, let $\boldsymbol{a}' = (0, \dots, 0, 1, 0, \dots, 0)$, the 1 lying in position i. Then,

$$\text{Var}(\boldsymbol{\beta}_{Li}) \geq \text{Var}(\hat{\boldsymbol{\beta}}_i) \tag{2.2.19}$$

which holds for $i = 1, \ldots, k$. For any such linear combination of coefficients, the variance of OLS is no greater than that of any estimator in the class $\boldsymbol{\beta}_L$ and, in this sense, it is the efficient member of the class.

A simple example of a less-than-efficient linear unbiased estimator is OLS applied to a model containing redundant regressors. In other words, suppose $\boldsymbol{\beta}_2 = \mathbf{0}$ in (1.2.25). The model

$$\boldsymbol{y} = \boldsymbol{X}_1\boldsymbol{\beta}_1 + \boldsymbol{u} \tag{2.2.20}$$

satisfies Assumptions 2.1.1–2.1.3 and the OLS estimator is $\hat{\boldsymbol{\beta}}_1 = (\boldsymbol{X}_1'\boldsymbol{X}_1)^{-1}\boldsymbol{X}_1'\boldsymbol{y}$ with conditional covariance matrix $\sigma^2(\boldsymbol{X}_1'\boldsymbol{X}_1)^{-1}$. Including the redundant regressors, on the other hand, the estimator of $\boldsymbol{\beta}_1$ takes the form of (2.2.10) where

$$\boldsymbol{L} = (\boldsymbol{X}_1'\boldsymbol{M}_2\boldsymbol{X}_1)^{-1}\boldsymbol{X}_1'\boldsymbol{M}_2 \tag{2.2.21}$$

from (1.2.29). Call this estimator $\hat{\boldsymbol{\beta}}_{1(2)}$. Assumptions 2.2.1–2.2.3 are satisfied for this choice, and the conditional covariance matrix is the top-left $k_1 \times k_1$ submatrix of $\boldsymbol{\sigma}^2(\boldsymbol{X}'\boldsymbol{X})^{-1}$, given by the partitioned-inverse formula as

$$\mathrm{Var}(\hat{\boldsymbol{\beta}}_{1(2)}|\boldsymbol{X}_1, \boldsymbol{X}_2) = \sigma^2(\boldsymbol{X}_1'\boldsymbol{M}_2\boldsymbol{X}_1)^{-1}. \tag{2.2.22}$$

To show the conditional Gauss-Markov inequality is now a matter of noting that

$$\boldsymbol{X}_1'\boldsymbol{X}_1 - \boldsymbol{X}_1'\boldsymbol{M}_2\boldsymbol{X}_1 = \boldsymbol{X}_1'\boldsymbol{X}_2(\boldsymbol{X}_2'\boldsymbol{X}_2)^{-1}\boldsymbol{X}_2'\boldsymbol{X}_1 \tag{2.2.23}$$

is a positive definite matrix, and applying Lemma A.7.6. The difference between the unconditional covariance matrices is

$$\mathrm{Var}(\hat{\boldsymbol{\beta}}_{1(2)}) - \mathrm{Var}(\hat{\boldsymbol{\beta}}_1) = \sigma^2 E[(\boldsymbol{X}_1'\boldsymbol{M}_2\boldsymbol{X}_1)^{-1}] - \sigma^2 E[(\boldsymbol{X}_1'\boldsymbol{X}_1)^{-1}] \tag{2.2.24}$$

for which no closed formula exists, but it is positive definite by an argument similar to (2.2.17).

The Gauss–Markov theorem is often thought of as the principal justification for the use of OLS. In the classical version of the result that applies under model A of §1.3, $\boldsymbol{X}$ and $\boldsymbol{L}$ are non-stochastic, and the difference between the conditional and unconditional distributions disappears. In this case, equation (2.2.11) becomes simply

$$E(\boldsymbol{\beta}_L) = \boldsymbol{LX\beta} + \boldsymbol{L}E(\boldsymbol{u}) = \boldsymbol{\beta}. \tag{2.2.25}$$

For an unbiased estimator, such that this formula is valid for every value of $\boldsymbol{\beta}$, it is necessary that $\boldsymbol{LX} = \boldsymbol{I}_k$. Specialized to the non-stochastic case, Assumption 2.2.3 necessarily holds for every unbiased member of the class $\boldsymbol{\beta}_L$ and $\hat{\boldsymbol{\beta}}$ is said to be BLUE, meaning best (minimum variance) in the class of linear unbiased estimators.

However, we must be careful to see just how the theorem extends to model B. The main difference in this case is that (2.2.25) is replaced by

$$E(\boldsymbol{\beta}_L) = E(\boldsymbol{LX})\boldsymbol{\beta} + E(\boldsymbol{Lu}). \tag{2.2.26}$$

Thus, given Assumption 2.2.1, it is sufficient for unbiasedness if

$$E(\boldsymbol{LX}) = \boldsymbol{I}_k \tag{2.2.27}$$

which is weaker than Assumption 2.2.3. If $\boldsymbol{LX} \neq \boldsymbol{I}_k$ with positive probability, the estimator is conditionally biased, but under (2.2.27) the bias terms average out over the distribution of $\boldsymbol{X}$ and hence the estimator is unbiased in repeated sampling under model B. However, it is not possible to conclude just on the strength of (2.2.27) that $E[\boldsymbol{DX}(\boldsymbol{X}'\boldsymbol{X})^{-1}] = \boldsymbol{0}$ so, if such cases are admitted the proof of Theorem 2.2.1 fails. Therefore, in model B, it is not correct to claim that OLS is BLUE, except in the context of the conditional distribution.

What this means in practice is that, in a repeated sampling experiment in which $\boldsymbol{X}$ is held fixed but a new $\boldsymbol{u}$ is sampled at each replication of the experiment, OLS has variance of $\sigma^2(\boldsymbol{X}'\boldsymbol{X})^{-1}$ which is the best possible in the sense of (2.2.18). However, in repeated trials in which both $\boldsymbol{u}$ and $\boldsymbol{X}$ are sampled afresh each time, OLS has variance $\sigma^2 E[(\boldsymbol{X}'\boldsymbol{X})^{-1}]$ and, strictly speaking, the claim that it is best in the linear unbiased class cannot be made. However, there is no obvious candidate for a better estimator, and this fact is of more theoretical than practical significance.

2.3 Generalized Least Squares

2.3.1 Failure of the Assumptions

Suppose Assumption 2.1.2 fails and

$$E(\boldsymbol{uu}'|\boldsymbol{X}) = \sigma^2\boldsymbol{\Omega} \text{ a.s.} \tag{2.3.1}$$

where $\boldsymbol{\Omega}$ is $n \times n$ symmetric and positive definite, depending on $\boldsymbol{X}$ in general, but possibly just a constant matrix different from $\boldsymbol{I}_n$.

There are several ways that this phenomenon might arise. The simplest is where the different observations are randomly drawn from different conditional distributions having different variances, although independently sampled. This is the case of *heteroscedasticity*,[2] in which $\boldsymbol{\Omega}$ is a diagonal matrix, with $\omega_{tt} \neq 1$ although $\omega_{ts} = 0$ for $t \neq s$. If ω_{tt} is a random variable it is called *conditional* heteroscedasticity. Just one of the many ways this kind of thing could arise is where the data are drawn randomly from a distribution of heterogeneous models, with different linear regression coefficients. Suppose (introducing some simplifying assumptions for the sake of clarity) that the coefficients vary randomly according to $\boldsymbol{\beta}_t = \boldsymbol{\beta} + \boldsymbol{v}_t$ where $E(\boldsymbol{v}_t|\boldsymbol{x}_t) = \boldsymbol{0}$ and $E(\boldsymbol{v}_t\boldsymbol{v}_t'|\boldsymbol{x}_t) = \boldsymbol{\Sigma}_v$ (a constant matrix). The model might then take the form

$$y_t = \boldsymbol{\beta}_t'\boldsymbol{x}_t + e_t = \boldsymbol{\beta}'\boldsymbol{x}_t + u_t \tag{2.3.2}$$

[2]This word, from the Greek verb 'skedanime' meaning to disperse or scatter, is also to be found as heteroskedasticity in the literature. Either spelling appears acceptable.

where $u_t = e_t + \boldsymbol{v}_t'\boldsymbol{x}_t$. If e_t conforms to the usual assumptions, with conditional variance σ^2 and $E(e_t\boldsymbol{v}_t|\boldsymbol{x}_t) = \boldsymbol{0}$, note that

$$E(u_t|\boldsymbol{x}_t) = 0 \tag{2.3.3}$$

but

$$E(u_t^2|\boldsymbol{x}_t) = \sigma^2 + \boldsymbol{x}_t'\boldsymbol{\Sigma}_v\boldsymbol{x}_t = \sigma^2\omega_{tt}. \tag{2.3.4}$$

where $\omega_{tt} = 1 + \sigma^{-2}\boldsymbol{x}_t'\boldsymbol{\Sigma}_v\boldsymbol{x}_t$. If the random coefficients are independent of each other, ω_{tt} is just a linear function of the squared explanatory variables. Methods of estimating such models are discussed in §10.4.2.

A more complex case is that of panel data (see §1.1). If observations are grouped by virtue of relating to the same economic unit in T successive years, the corresponding disturbances are liable to be correlated, even if the units themselves form a random sample. In this case $\boldsymbol{\Omega}$ would have a 'block-diagonal' structure, with $\omega_{ts} \neq 0$ when t and s refer to the same unit at different times.

However, the independent sampling assumption maintained in this chapter (model B) is violated in the panel data set-up. The only way to maintain the present statistical approach would be to assume that the regressors are non-stochastic (model A) so that conditioning every observation on $\boldsymbol{X}$ becomes trivial. This is implausible in general. The statistical treatment of such models raises special problems, see for example Hsiao (1986) for a detailed account.

2.3.2 Aitken's Theorem

To show how all these cases might be dealt with, in principle, suppose that $\boldsymbol{\Omega}$ is known. This case was first analysed by Aitken (1935). According to Lemmas A.7.2 and A.7.4, there exists the factorization $\boldsymbol{\Omega}^{-1} = \boldsymbol{K}'\boldsymbol{K}$. Premultiplying both sides of (1.1.2) by $\boldsymbol{K}$ yields a linear relation between transformed data, with the same coefficients but a transformed disturbance vector:

$$\boldsymbol{Ky} = \boldsymbol{KX\beta} + \boldsymbol{Ku}. \tag{2.3.5}$$

Note the properties

$$E(\boldsymbol{Ku}|\boldsymbol{X}) = \boldsymbol{K}E(\boldsymbol{u}|\boldsymbol{X}) = \boldsymbol{0} \tag{2.3.6}$$

and, applying Lemma A.7.4,

$$E(\boldsymbol{Kuu}'\boldsymbol{K}'|\boldsymbol{X}) = \boldsymbol{K}E(\boldsymbol{uu}'|\boldsymbol{X})\boldsymbol{K}' = \sigma^2\boldsymbol{K\Omega K}' = \sigma^2\boldsymbol{I}_n. \tag{2.3.7}$$

Hence, the transformed regression satisfies Assumptions 2.1.1 and 2.1.2. The OLS coefficients from the regression of $\boldsymbol{Ky}$ on $\boldsymbol{KX}$ are

$$\tilde{\boldsymbol{\beta}} = (\boldsymbol{X}'\boldsymbol{K}'\boldsymbol{KX})^{-1}\boldsymbol{X}'\boldsymbol{K}'\boldsymbol{Ky} = (\boldsymbol{X}'\boldsymbol{\Omega}^{-1}\boldsymbol{X})^{-1}\boldsymbol{X}'\boldsymbol{\Omega}^{-1}\boldsymbol{y}. \tag{2.3.8}$$

It is easy to verify that $\tilde{\boldsymbol{\beta}}$ is unbiased. The conditional variance matrix is found by application of the OLS formulae to be

$$\text{Var}(\tilde{\boldsymbol{\beta}}|\boldsymbol{X}) = \sigma^2(\boldsymbol{X}'\boldsymbol{\Omega}^{-1}\boldsymbol{X})^{-1}. \tag{2.3.9}$$

This method is called generalized least squares (GLS). By construction, since the conditions of the Gauss-Markov theorem have been induced to hold by the transformation, it is BLUE for this model, under the conditional distribution. This is Aitken's theorem. Most important, the same arguments show that OLS is not BLUE in this case. GLS is not a feasible estimator, since it requires knowledge of $\boldsymbol{\Omega}$ that in practice is not available, but the formulae provide the basis for various feasible procedures involving estimates of $\boldsymbol{\Omega}$. For additional examples, see §10.2.3 and §10.2.5.[3]

If OLS is used when Assumption 2.1.1 and (2.3.1) hold, $\hat{\boldsymbol{\beta}}$ is unbiased but

$$\begin{aligned}\operatorname{Var}(\hat{\boldsymbol{\beta}}|\boldsymbol{X}) &= E\big((\boldsymbol{X}'\boldsymbol{X})^{-1}\boldsymbol{X}'\boldsymbol{u}\boldsymbol{u}'\boldsymbol{X}(\boldsymbol{X}'\boldsymbol{X})^{-1}|\boldsymbol{X}\big)\\ &= \sigma^2(\boldsymbol{X}'\boldsymbol{X})^{-1}\boldsymbol{X}'\boldsymbol{\Omega}\boldsymbol{X}(\boldsymbol{X}'\boldsymbol{X})^{-1}. \qquad (2.3.10)\end{aligned}$$

Thus, there is a double problem with the failure of Assumption 2.1.2. Not only is OLS is no longer BLUE, but possibly more important is the fact that the conditional OLS variance formula in (2.2.3) is incorrect. This means that the inferential procedures to which the remaining sections of this chapter are devoted would not be valid.

2.3.3 Interpreting Residual Autocorrelation

Although the distinction may sometimes appear tenuous, it is important not to confuse failures of Assumption 2.1.2 proper with failures of Assumption 2.1.1. If the latter fails, then we might write $\boldsymbol{u} = \boldsymbol{e} + \boldsymbol{g}(\boldsymbol{X})$, where $\boldsymbol{e}$ may satisfy Assumption 2.1.2 but the elements g_t for $t = 1, \ldots, n$ are nonlinear functions of $\boldsymbol{x}_t$. However, regardless of the form of $\boldsymbol{g}$ the regression residuals $\hat{\boldsymbol{u}}$ have a *sample* mean of zero by construction, so that they may appear to an investigator to satisfy Assumption 2.1.1. To the unwary, a problem in which the mean of u_t depends on t may then appear as a problem of correlation of the disturbances.

A good example of this phenomenon is analysed of one of the best-known of all applied econometric papers, Nerlove's (1963) study of cost functions for the US electricity supply industry, where the sample is a cross-section of 145 generating companies. In the linear (in logarithms) cost equation first fitted, the residuals turned out to show a pattern of correlation when the firms were placed in order of size, by output. The largest and smallest firms tended to have positive residuals, while most of those of intermediate size had negative residuals. This meant that the estimated ω_{ts} appeared positive for small values of $|t-s|$, and the Durbin–Watson test (see §7.6.2) revealed an apparent pattern of first-order autocorrelation.

However, this conclusion would be fallacious. Such a thing can occur only in the context of sampling model C, as detailed in Part II of this book. If a sample is independently drawn, any such correlation is necessarily spurious. The actual source of the observed pattern, as Nerlove's study demonstrates, was the omission of a quadratic term in log-output, in other words, a failure of Assumption 2.1.1.

[3]The cited examples are based on time series assumptions (model C) and hence their justification is different from the present case, but the same formulae apply.

Forcing them to have a mean of zero necessarily produced the sign-pattern observed in the *residuals*, but this was not due to what is commonly called autocorrelation of the disturbances. If Assumption 2.1.1 holds, there can be no tendency for the sign of u_t to depend on t, and only in this case can a failure of Assumption 2.1.2 be recognised. The case $\omega_{ts} > 0$, for example, represents a tendency of adjacent disturbances (under some ordering of the data) to take the same sign, but *which* sign should not depend on t. This distinction is important in practice, for the correct remedy in the former case is to amend the specification of the regression, and only in the latter case to undertake GLS estimation.

2.4 The Gaussian Linear Model

2.4.1 Interval Estimation

We now introduce a further assumption that (be careful to note) was not required for the foregoing results. Let the conditional distribution of $\boldsymbol{y}$ given $\boldsymbol{X}$ be the independent multivariate Gaussian distribution, otherwise known as the normal distribution; see Appendix C for details. This may be expressed as

Assumption 2.4.1 $\boldsymbol{y}|\boldsymbol{X} \sim \mathrm{N}(\boldsymbol{X\beta}, \sigma^2 \boldsymbol{I}_n)$ □

An equivalent form of the assumption is $\boldsymbol{u}|\boldsymbol{X} \sim \mathrm{N}(\boldsymbol{0}, \sigma^2\boldsymbol{I}_n)$. This implies that $\boldsymbol{u} \sim \mathrm{N}(\boldsymbol{0}, \sigma^2\boldsymbol{I}_n)$ unconditionally. Nonetheless, the conditional distribution must be stated explicitly, since the reverse implication does not hold.

Since $\hat{\boldsymbol{\beta}}$ is a linear function of $\boldsymbol{u}$,

$$\hat{\boldsymbol{\beta}}|\boldsymbol{X} \sim \mathrm{N}(\boldsymbol{\beta}, \sigma^2(\boldsymbol{X}'\boldsymbol{X})^{-1}). \tag{2.4.1}$$

In this case, the conditional distribution depends on $\boldsymbol{X}$, so no conclusions can be drawn about the unconditional distribution of $\hat{\boldsymbol{\beta}}$. In spite of this, Assumption 2.4.1 provides the basis for setting up confidence regions and performing hypothesis tests about $\boldsymbol{\beta}$. Consider first

$$\begin{aligned}\frac{(\hat{\boldsymbol{\beta}}-\boldsymbol{\beta})'\boldsymbol{X}'\boldsymbol{X}(\hat{\boldsymbol{\beta}}-\boldsymbol{\beta})}{\sigma^2} &= \frac{\boldsymbol{u}'\boldsymbol{X}(\boldsymbol{X}'\boldsymbol{X})^{-1}\boldsymbol{X}'\boldsymbol{X}(\boldsymbol{X}'\boldsymbol{X})^{-1}\boldsymbol{X}'\boldsymbol{u}}{\sigma^2} \\ &= \frac{\boldsymbol{u}'\boldsymbol{Q}\boldsymbol{u}}{\sigma^2}. \end{aligned} \tag{2.4.2}$$

Now,

$$\left.\frac{\boldsymbol{u}'\boldsymbol{Q}\boldsymbol{u}}{\sigma^2}\right|\boldsymbol{X} \sim \chi^2(k) \tag{2.4.3}$$

by Theorem C.3.3, since $\boldsymbol{Q}$ is an idempotent matrix having rank k, fixed under the conditional distribution and, by Assumption 2.4.1, $\sigma^{-1}\boldsymbol{u}|\boldsymbol{X} \sim \mathrm{N}(\boldsymbol{0}, \boldsymbol{I}_n)$. Moreover, since it does not depend on $\boldsymbol{X}$, this distribution is also the unconditional distribution! This is true, remarkably enough, regardless of what the distribution of $\boldsymbol{X}$ actually is, as long as this distribution is well-defined.

This result is not directly applicable, since σ^2 is unknown. However, it is also the case that

$$\frac{S(\hat{\boldsymbol{\beta}})}{\sigma^2} = \frac{\boldsymbol{u}'\boldsymbol{M}\boldsymbol{u}}{\sigma^2} \sim \chi^2(n-k) \tag{2.4.4}$$

by the same argument. These two quadratic forms are independent by Theorem C.4.1, since $\boldsymbol{MQ} = \boldsymbol{0}$ as we know from (1.2.19). Also, both are proportional to the unknown parameter $1/\sigma^2$, and it follows from Theorem C.4.2 that the distribution of the ratio of (2.4.3) to (2.4.4), after weighting for degrees of freedom, is $F(k, n-k)$. Using formula (2.2.6), the result is

$$\frac{(\hat{\boldsymbol{\beta}}-\boldsymbol{\beta})'\boldsymbol{X}'\boldsymbol{X}(\hat{\boldsymbol{\beta}}-\boldsymbol{\beta})}{ks^2} = \frac{\boldsymbol{u}'\boldsymbol{Q}\boldsymbol{u}/k\sigma^2}{\boldsymbol{u}'\boldsymbol{M}\boldsymbol{u}/(n-k)\sigma^2} \sim F(k, n-k). \tag{2.4.5}$$

One way to make use of this result is to let $F^*_\alpha(k, n-k)$ denote the critical value obtained from the tabulation of the $F(k, n-k)$ distribution, such that

$$P[F(k, n-k) > F^*_\alpha(k, n-k)] = \alpha \tag{2.4.6}$$

for $0 \leq \alpha \leq 1$. For various values of α, we may make statements of the form

$$P\big[(\hat{\boldsymbol{\beta}}-\boldsymbol{\beta})'\boldsymbol{X}'\boldsymbol{X}(\hat{\boldsymbol{\beta}}-\boldsymbol{\beta}) \leq ks^2 F^*_\alpha(k, n-k)\big] = 1-\alpha. \tag{2.4.7}$$

The sets of $\boldsymbol{\beta}$-values that satisfy this inequality for given values of α define so-called *confidence ellipsoids* in k-dimensional space, centred on $\hat{\boldsymbol{\beta}}$. Figure 2.1 illustrates two of these, for $k = 2$.

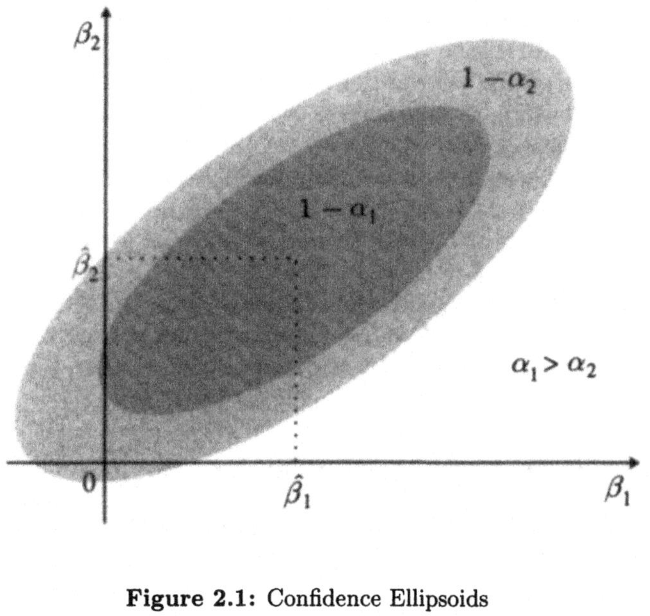

Figure 2.1: Confidence Ellipsoids

The proportions and alignment of the ellipsoids depend on the elements of $\boldsymbol{X}'\boldsymbol{X}$. For example, in the 2×2 case shown in the figure the quadratic form in

(2.4.7) reduces to

$$(\hat{\beta}_1 - \beta_1)^2 \sum_{t=1}^{n} x_{1t}^2 + 2(\hat{\beta}_1 - \beta_1)(\hat{\beta}_2 - \beta_2) \sum_{t=1}^{n} x_{1t}x_{2t} + (\hat{\beta}_2 - \beta_2)^2 \sum_{t=1}^{n} x_{2t}^2.$$

The contours of the implicit function $ax^2 + bxy + cy^2 = K$ are ellipses with centre $(x = 0,\ y = 0)$, inclined positively as illustrated in Figure 2.1 when $b < 0$. This corresponds to the well-known fact that $\hat{\beta}_1$ and $\hat{\beta}_2$ are (conditionally) positively correlated when $\sum_t x_{1t}x_{2t} < 0$, and negatively correlated when $\sum_t x_{1t}x_{2t} > 0$. In repeated independent samples, the probability that the $(1 - \alpha)$-ellipsoids so generated contain $\boldsymbol{\beta}$ is $1 - \alpha$, and one could say that $\boldsymbol{\beta}$ has a probability $1 - \alpha$ of lying inside an α-ellipsoid. However, be careful not to fall into the error of thinking this means $\boldsymbol{\beta}$ is a random variable. The parameters are fixed and given by nature, even though unknown. It is the ellipsoids whose positions and proportions are randomly determined by the data.

2.4.2 Testing Hypotheses

The confidence ellipsoid is a form of interval estimate for the vector $\boldsymbol{\beta}$. Hypothesis testing is closely related to interval estimation, but entails making a decision, on the basis of sample data, whether to accept that certain restrictions are satisfied by the basic assumed model.[4] In this context, Assumptions 2.1.1–2.1.3 and 2.4.1 are known as the *maintained hypothesis* H_M. According to the accepted terminology, the restricted form of the model is the *null hypothesis*, denoted H_0, and the *alternative hypothesis* is $H_A = H_M - H_0$. A statistical test is usually performed by computing a statistic from the data whose distribution under H_0 is known. By basing the decision on the value of this statistic, it is possible to fix the probability of rejecting H_0 when H_0 is true, what is called a Type 1 error, at a level α. This is called the *significance level* of the test.

The significance level is conventionally set at 5% (i.e., $\alpha = 0.05$) although 1% and 10% are also used. Note the judgement implicit in this choice: that 1-in-20 is a low enough probability to ignore. There is a deliberate asymmetry of the roles of H_0 and H_A in this testing framework. The probability of a Type 2 error (that of failing to reject a false null hypothesis) is unknown but, by setting the significance level low, we implicitly treat it as less important than a Type 1 error. Failure to reject H_0 does not mean it should be accepted as true. Rather, there is insufficient evidence from the data to reject it.

2.4.3 The F Test of Linear Restrictions

An α-level test of the hypothesis $H_0 : \boldsymbol{\beta} = \boldsymbol{\beta}_0$, based on the F statistic, is given if H_0 is accepted when $\boldsymbol{\beta}_0$ lies inside the $(1-\alpha)$-confidence ellipsoid. This particular

---

[4]This chapter assumes some familiarity with the elementary facts of hypothesis testing, and uses these concepts in an informal manner. The theory of statistical inference is treated more formally in §12.1.1.

form of test is not very useful because hypotheses are rarely so restrictive as to specify values for all elements of $\boldsymbol{\beta}$. More often one wants to test some set of r restrictions on $\boldsymbol{\beta}$, where $0 < r \leq k$. Restricting attention to the class of linear restrictions, these have the general form

$$H_0 : \boldsymbol{R\beta} = \boldsymbol{c} \tag{2.4.8}$$

where $\boldsymbol{R}$ $(r \times k)$ is a constant matrix with rank r and $\boldsymbol{c}$ $(r \times 1)$ is a constant vector. Specific examples are considered in §2.4.5.

If $\hat{\boldsymbol{\beta}}|\boldsymbol{X} \sim \mathrm{N}(\boldsymbol{\beta}, \sigma^2(\boldsymbol{X}'\boldsymbol{X})^{-1})$, then according to Theorem C.1.1

$$\boldsymbol{R}\hat{\boldsymbol{\beta}} - \boldsymbol{c}|\boldsymbol{X} \sim \mathrm{N}(\boldsymbol{R\beta} - \boldsymbol{c},\ \sigma^2\boldsymbol{R}(\boldsymbol{X}'\boldsymbol{X})^{-1}\boldsymbol{R}'). \tag{2.4.9}$$

To obtain the test, we derive the distribution under H_0, assuming that $\boldsymbol{R\beta}-\boldsymbol{c} = \boldsymbol{0}$. Note that

$$\boldsymbol{R}\hat{\boldsymbol{\beta}} - \boldsymbol{c} = \boldsymbol{R\beta} + \boldsymbol{R}(\boldsymbol{X}'\boldsymbol{X})^{-1}\boldsymbol{X}'\boldsymbol{u} - \boldsymbol{c} \tag{2.4.10}$$

and hence, under H_0,

$$\begin{aligned}(\boldsymbol{R}\hat{\boldsymbol{\beta}}-\boldsymbol{c})'&(\boldsymbol{R}(\boldsymbol{X}'\boldsymbol{X})^{-1}\boldsymbol{R}')^{-1}(\boldsymbol{R}\hat{\boldsymbol{\beta}} - \boldsymbol{c}) \\ &= \boldsymbol{u}'\boldsymbol{X}(\boldsymbol{X}'\boldsymbol{X})^{-1}\boldsymbol{R}'[\boldsymbol{R}(\boldsymbol{X}'\boldsymbol{X})^{-1}\boldsymbol{R}']^{-1}\boldsymbol{R}(\boldsymbol{X}'\boldsymbol{X})^{-1}\boldsymbol{X}'\boldsymbol{u} \\ &= \boldsymbol{u}'\boldsymbol{P}\boldsymbol{u}.\end{aligned} \tag{2.4.11}$$

The last equality defines $\boldsymbol{P}$, which, as can be verified, is a symmetric idempotent matrix of rank r satisfying $\boldsymbol{PM} = \boldsymbol{0}$. Hence, the earlier result has an immediate extension. On $H_0 : \boldsymbol{R\beta} = \boldsymbol{c}$,

$$\frac{(\boldsymbol{R}\hat{\boldsymbol{\beta}} - \boldsymbol{c})'[\boldsymbol{R}(\boldsymbol{X}'\boldsymbol{X})^{-1}\boldsymbol{R}']^{-1}(\boldsymbol{R}\hat{\boldsymbol{\beta}} - \boldsymbol{c})}{rs^2} \sim F(r, n-k). \tag{2.4.12}$$

The test procedure is to compute this statistic, and reject H_0 if its value lies in the *critical region* above F^*_α, such that it has a probability less than α of being a drawing from the $F(r, n-k)$ distribution.

2.4.4 The Constrained Estimation Approach

Another approach to generating test statistics is to obtain the least squares estimates subject to the constraints in H_0. This corresponds to finding a stationary point of the Lagrangian function[5] $\frac{1}{2}S(\boldsymbol{\beta}) + \boldsymbol{\lambda}'(\boldsymbol{R\beta} - \boldsymbol{c})$. The solutions to the problem, $\dot{\boldsymbol{\beta}}$ and $\dot{\boldsymbol{\lambda}}$, are solved from the first-order conditions

$$\boldsymbol{X}'(\boldsymbol{y} - \boldsymbol{X}\dot{\boldsymbol{\beta}}) + \boldsymbol{R}'\dot{\boldsymbol{\lambda}} = \boldsymbol{0} \tag{2.4.13a}$$

$$\boldsymbol{R}\dot{\boldsymbol{\beta}} - \boldsymbol{c} = \boldsymbol{0} \tag{2.4.13b}$$

and $\dot{\boldsymbol{\beta}}$ represents the constrained least squares estimator. The solutions are obtained by premultiplying (2.4.13a) by $(\boldsymbol{X}'\boldsymbol{X})^{-1}$ and rearranging using (1.2.8), as

$$\dot{\boldsymbol{\beta}} = \hat{\boldsymbol{\beta}} + (\boldsymbol{X}'\boldsymbol{X})^{-1}\boldsymbol{R}'\dot{\boldsymbol{\lambda}}. \tag{2.4.14}$$

[5] See for example Intriligator (1971).

Premultiplying (2.4.14) by $\boldsymbol{R}$ and solving yields the Lagrangian multipliers,

$$\begin{aligned}\dot{\boldsymbol{\lambda}} &= -[\boldsymbol{R}(\boldsymbol{X}'\boldsymbol{X})^{-1}\boldsymbol{R}']^{-1}\boldsymbol{R}(\hat{\boldsymbol{\beta}} - \dot{\boldsymbol{\beta}}) \\ &= -[\boldsymbol{R}(\boldsymbol{X}'\boldsymbol{X})^{-1}\boldsymbol{R}']^{-1}(\boldsymbol{R}\hat{\boldsymbol{\beta}} - \boldsymbol{c}) \end{aligned} \tag{2.4.15}$$

on substituting (2.4.13b). Finally, from (2.4.14),

$$\dot{\boldsymbol{\beta}} = \hat{\boldsymbol{\beta}} - (\boldsymbol{X}'\boldsymbol{X})^{-1}\boldsymbol{R}'[\boldsymbol{R}(\boldsymbol{X}'\boldsymbol{X})^{-1}\boldsymbol{R}']^{-1}(\boldsymbol{R}\hat{\boldsymbol{\beta}} - \boldsymbol{c}). \tag{2.4.16}$$

Note that

$$(\dot{\boldsymbol{\beta}} - \hat{\boldsymbol{\beta}})'\boldsymbol{X}'\boldsymbol{X}(\dot{\boldsymbol{\beta}} - \hat{\boldsymbol{\beta}}) = (\boldsymbol{R}\hat{\boldsymbol{\beta}} - \boldsymbol{c})'[\boldsymbol{R}(\boldsymbol{X}'\boldsymbol{X})^{-1}\boldsymbol{R}']^{-1}(\boldsymbol{R}\hat{\boldsymbol{\beta}} - \boldsymbol{c}) \tag{2.4.17}$$

so that the numerator in (2.4.12) has a representation in terms of the difference between the constrained and unconstrained estimates. Also, from (2.4.16),

$$\dot{\boldsymbol{u}} = \boldsymbol{y} - \boldsymbol{X}\dot{\boldsymbol{\beta}} = \hat{\boldsymbol{u}} + \boldsymbol{X}(\boldsymbol{X}'\boldsymbol{X})^{-1}\boldsymbol{R}'[\boldsymbol{R}(\boldsymbol{X}'\boldsymbol{X})^{-1}\boldsymbol{R}']^{-1}(\boldsymbol{R}\hat{\boldsymbol{\beta}} - \boldsymbol{c}). \tag{2.4.18}$$

It follows from (2.4.18), noting how the cross-products cancel since $\boldsymbol{X}'\hat{\boldsymbol{u}} = \boldsymbol{0}$, that

$$\dot{\boldsymbol{u}}'\dot{\boldsymbol{u}} - \hat{\boldsymbol{u}}'\hat{\boldsymbol{u}} = (\boldsymbol{R}\hat{\boldsymbol{\beta}} - \boldsymbol{c})'[\boldsymbol{R}(\boldsymbol{X}'\boldsymbol{X})^{-1}\boldsymbol{R}']^{-1}(\boldsymbol{R}\hat{\boldsymbol{\beta}} - \boldsymbol{c}). \tag{2.4.19}$$

Thus, the numerator in (2.4.12) also has a representation as the difference of the constrained and unconstrained sums of squares. The derivation establishes that this difference is always non-negative. The form

$$\frac{\dot{\boldsymbol{u}}'\dot{\boldsymbol{u}} - \hat{\boldsymbol{u}}'\hat{\boldsymbol{u}}}{\hat{\boldsymbol{u}}'\hat{\boldsymbol{u}}} \cdot \frac{n-k}{r} \sim F(r, n-k) \text{ on } H_0 : \boldsymbol{R\beta} = \boldsymbol{c} \tag{2.4.20}$$

is equivalent to (2.4.12).

2.4.5 Significance Tests

The problem of choosing the specification of the regression model discussed in §1.4.2 is often solved in practice by testing the hypothesis that the 'doubtful' variables have coefficients of zero. This test can be performed for single variables, or as a joint restriction on several coefficients. In (2.4.8), set $\boldsymbol{c} = \boldsymbol{0}$, $\boldsymbol{R} = [\boldsymbol{I}_r \; \boldsymbol{0}]$, and accordingly partition $\boldsymbol{\beta}$ as $(\boldsymbol{\beta}_1', \boldsymbol{\beta}_2')'$. Then, $\boldsymbol{R\beta} = \boldsymbol{c}$ corresponds to the hypothesis $\boldsymbol{\beta}_1 = \boldsymbol{0}$ in the partitioned model,

$$\boldsymbol{y} = \boldsymbol{X}_1\boldsymbol{\beta}_1 + \boldsymbol{X}_2\boldsymbol{\beta}_2 + \boldsymbol{u} \tag{2.4.21}$$

where the partition is into blocks of dimension r and $k-r$. This hypothesis asserts that $\boldsymbol{X}_1$ has no power to explain $\boldsymbol{y}$ once $\boldsymbol{X}_2$ has been taken into account. A more explicit way to state it is

$$H_0 : \boldsymbol{y} = \boldsymbol{X}_2\boldsymbol{\beta}_2 + \boldsymbol{u},\; \boldsymbol{u}|\boldsymbol{X}_1, \boldsymbol{X}_2 \sim \mathrm{N}(\boldsymbol{0}, \sigma^2\boldsymbol{I}). \tag{2.4.22}$$

The matrix $\boldsymbol{R}(\boldsymbol{X}'\boldsymbol{X})^{-1}\boldsymbol{R}'$ $(r \times r)$ in this case is the top-left submatrix of $(\boldsymbol{X}'\boldsymbol{X})^{-1}$, which is equal to $(\boldsymbol{X}_1'\boldsymbol{M}_2\boldsymbol{X}_1)^{-1}$ according to the partitioned inverse formula (A.2.13). Hence the F statistic in (2.4.12) takes the form

$$\frac{\hat{\boldsymbol{\beta}}_1'\boldsymbol{X}_1'\boldsymbol{M}_2\boldsymbol{X}_1\hat{\boldsymbol{\beta}}_1}{rs^2} = \frac{\boldsymbol{y}'\boldsymbol{M}_2\boldsymbol{X}_1(\boldsymbol{X}_1'\boldsymbol{M}_2\boldsymbol{X}_1)^{-1}\boldsymbol{X}_1'\boldsymbol{M}_2\boldsymbol{y}}{\boldsymbol{y}'\boldsymbol{M}\boldsymbol{y}} \cdot \frac{n-k}{r} \tag{2.4.23}$$

The equivalence between this form and (2.4.20) follows from the equality (1.2.35) so that an alternative representation of the numerator quadratic form is $\boldsymbol{y}'\boldsymbol{M}_2\boldsymbol{y} - \boldsymbol{y}'\boldsymbol{M}\boldsymbol{y}$, the difference between the restricted and unrestricted sums of squares in the present case. Hence, significance tests are easy to perform. Run the regressions including and excluding the test regressors, retrieve the sums of squared residuals for each case and compute the formula in (2.4.20).

Now consider the case $r = 1$, so that β_1 is a scalar. By reordering the variables, this can represent any element of $\boldsymbol{\beta}$. The model will be written as $\boldsymbol{y} = \boldsymbol{x}_1\beta_1 + \boldsymbol{X}_2\boldsymbol{\beta}_2 + \boldsymbol{u}$ where $\boldsymbol{x}_1$ is just a n-vector. For this case, the formula for the F-statistic specializes to

$$\frac{\hat{\beta}_1^2}{s^2(\boldsymbol{x}_1'\boldsymbol{M}_2\boldsymbol{x}_1)^{-1}} \sim F(1, n-k) \text{ on } H_0 : \beta_1 = 0 \tag{2.4.24}$$

where $(\boldsymbol{x}_1'\boldsymbol{M}_2\boldsymbol{x}_1)^{-1}$ is the $(1,1)$ element of $(\boldsymbol{X}'\boldsymbol{X})^{-1}$. Alternatively, applying (C.3.26) directly yields a null distribution of the form

$$\frac{\hat{\beta}_1}{s(\boldsymbol{x}_1'\boldsymbol{M}_2\boldsymbol{x}_1)^{-1/2}} \sim t_{n-k} \tag{2.4.25}$$

where t_{n-k} is Student's t distribution with $n-k$ degrees of freedom. This is the t-statistic in its familiar form as the ratio of the estimator to its standard error. Recall that $F(1, n-k) = t_{n-k}^2$, so that these two distributions are equivalent. The t form of the test is preferred since it allows us to perform tests against one-sided alternatives.

A *confidence interval* is defined by a statement of the form

$$P\left[\hat{\beta}_1 - t_\alpha^* s(\boldsymbol{x}_1'\boldsymbol{M}_2\boldsymbol{x}_1)^{-1/2} \leq \beta_1 \leq \hat{\beta}_1 + t_\alpha^* s(\boldsymbol{x}_1'\boldsymbol{M}_2\boldsymbol{x}_1)^{-1/2}\right] = 1 - \alpha \tag{2.4.26}$$

where t_α^* is the α-critical value from the tabulation of the t_{n-k} distribution. It is interesting to compare the information conveyed by the confidence interval for β_1 with the confidence ellipsoid defined earlier. Since now $1-\alpha$ is the probability of β_1 lying in the specified interval unconditionally, the interval defines a cylindrical region in $\boldsymbol{\beta}$-space, illustrated for $k = 2$ in Figure 2.2.

Significance tests are easy to perform because they just require two conventional regressions: one including the regressors under test, the other excluding them. Fortunately, tests of general linear restrictions can also be done in this way, if the data are first transformed suitably. The trick is to order the regressors so that the equations $\boldsymbol{R}\boldsymbol{\beta} = \boldsymbol{c}$ can be partitioned as

$$\boldsymbol{R}_1\boldsymbol{\beta}_1 + \boldsymbol{R}_2\boldsymbol{\beta}_2 = \boldsymbol{c} \tag{2.4.27}$$

where $\boldsymbol{R}_1$ is $r \times r$ nonsingular. If $\boldsymbol{R}$ has rank r, such an arrangement always exists. An equivalent form of the restrictions is then

$$\boldsymbol{\beta}_1 - \boldsymbol{R}_1^{-1}(\boldsymbol{c} - \boldsymbol{R}_2\boldsymbol{\beta}_2) = \boldsymbol{0}. \tag{2.4.28}$$

Substituting the expression $\boldsymbol{R}_1^{-1}(\boldsymbol{c} - \boldsymbol{R}_2\boldsymbol{\beta}_2) + \boldsymbol{\beta}_1 - \boldsymbol{R}_1^{-1}(\boldsymbol{c} - \boldsymbol{R}_2\boldsymbol{\beta}_2)$ for $\boldsymbol{\beta}_1$ in the partitioned regression

$$\boldsymbol{y} = \boldsymbol{X}_1\boldsymbol{\beta}_1 + \boldsymbol{X}_2\boldsymbol{\beta}_2 + \boldsymbol{u} \tag{2.4.29}$$

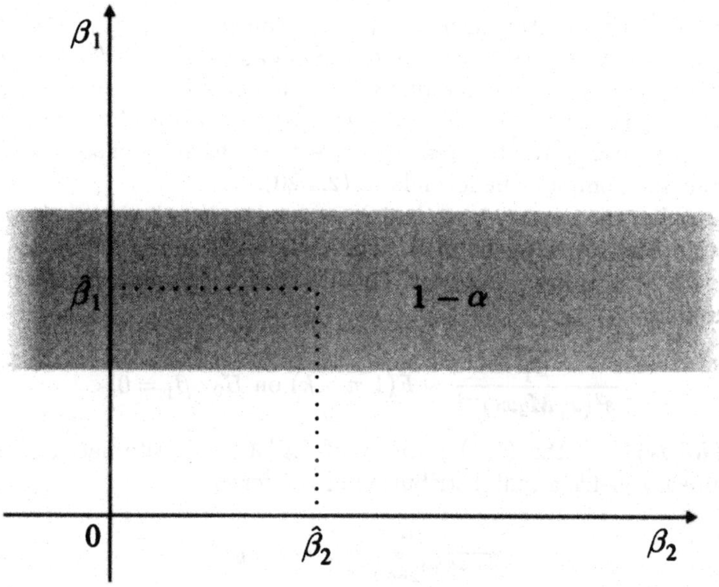

Figure 2.2: Confidence Interval

and rearranging the equation yields

$$y - X_1R_1^{-1}c = X_1[\beta_1 - R_1^{-1}(c - R_2\beta_2)] + (X_2 - X_1R_1^{-1}R_2)\beta_2 + u \quad (2.4.30)$$

Since R and c are known, creating the new variables to replace y and X_2 is straightforward, and could usually be done using the data transformation facilities of a regression package. The test of H_0 is accomplished by testing the significance of X_1 in this equation.

2.5 Stability Analysis

2.5.1 Structural Breaks

Let the data set be divided into two subsamples of sizes $n_1 \geq k$ and $n_2 = n - n_1 \geq k$, assumed to represent a grouping of the observations of known significance. After reordering the observations if required, the partitioning of the data set (by rows on this occasion) can be represented by

$$X = \begin{bmatrix} X_1 \\ X_2 \end{bmatrix} \qquad y = \begin{bmatrix} y_1 \\ y_2 \end{bmatrix}. \quad (2.5.1)$$

The hypothesis to be tested is whether the same regression model applies to both groups. Writing

$$y_1 = X_1\beta_1 + u_1 \quad (n_1 \times 1) \quad (2.5.2a)$$

$$y_2 = X_2\beta_2 + u_2 \quad (n_2 \times 1) \tag{2.5.2b}$$

the null hypothesis is $H_0 : \beta_1 = \beta_2$. To construct the test, it is assumed that the disturbances u_1 and u_2 are distributed independently with the same variance σ^2. Then, it reduces to a straightforward test of a linear restriction. The observations may be stacked up into a single equation with alternate forms

$$\begin{bmatrix} y_1 \\ y_2 \end{bmatrix} = \begin{bmatrix} X_1 & 0 \\ 0 & X_2 \end{bmatrix} \begin{bmatrix} \beta_1 \\ \beta_2 \end{bmatrix} + \begin{bmatrix} u_1 \\ u_2 \end{bmatrix} \tag{2.5.3}$$

and

$$\begin{bmatrix} y_1 \\ y_2 \end{bmatrix} = \begin{bmatrix} X_1 & 0 \\ X_2 & X_2 \end{bmatrix} \begin{bmatrix} \beta_1 \\ \delta \end{bmatrix} + \begin{bmatrix} u_1 \\ u_2 \end{bmatrix} \tag{2.5.4}$$

where $\delta = \beta_2 - \beta_1$ (see §1.2.4). Clearly, a significance test on δ in (2.5.4) will test the stability restriction. However, the regressors in (2.5.3) are orthogonal, and it is easily verified that the simple regressions of y_1 on X_1 and y_2 on X_2 in (2.5.2) yield the estimates from the combined regression in (2.5.3), $\hat{\beta}_1$ and $\hat{\beta}_2$ respectively. Applying (1.2.23), the residuals from these regressions, $\hat{u}_1$ and $\hat{u}_2$, are equivalent to those from regression (2.5.4) for the first n_1 and last n_2 observations respectively. It follows that the F statistic for this test takes the form

$$\frac{\hat{u}'\hat{u} - \hat{u}_1'\hat{u}_1 - \hat{u}_2'\hat{u}_2}{\hat{u}_1'\hat{u}_1 + \hat{u}_2'\hat{u}_2} . \frac{n_1 + n_2 - 2k}{k} \sim F(k, n_1 + n_2 - 2k) \text{ on } H_0 \tag{2.5.5}$$

where $\hat{u}$ are the residuals from fitting the same model to all observations. This is the Chow (1960) test of parameter stability, also called Chow's first test. It is not difficult to construct variants of this test in which only a subset of the coefficients are allowed to vary across the groups under the alternative. In this case, however, only form (2.5.4) of the model is available. 'Dummy' regressors, set equal to zero for the first group and duplicating the test variables in the second group, will have to be explicitly constructed and their significance tested in the usual way.

2.5.2 Prediction

Now, assume the data set is divided into subsets of size n_s and n_p, where $n_p \geq 1$, but is generally small relative to n_s. Write

$$y_s = X_s\beta + u_s \; (n_s \times 1) \tag{2.5.6a}$$

$$y_p = X_p\beta + u_p \; (n_p \times 1) \tag{2.5.6b}$$

where the data $\begin{bmatrix} y_s & X_s \end{bmatrix}$ are to be used for fitting the equation. The idea is to use the fitted model to generate out-of-sample predictions of y_p from X_p, and a test of model stability can be based on the comparison between predictions and out-turns. Note that β is the same vector in both (2.5.6a) and (2.5.6b), since the model stability hypothesis is formulated in this case as

$$H_0 : \; u|X_s, X_p \sim \mathrm{N}(0, \sigma^2 I_{n_s+n_p}) \tag{2.5.7}$$

where $\boldsymbol{u} = (\boldsymbol{u}_s', \boldsymbol{u}_p')'$. In this framework the maintained hypothesis is, in effect, that Assumptions 2.1.1–2.1.3 and 2.4.1 hold for the 'sample' observations only.

The predictor of $\boldsymbol{y}_p$ is $\hat{\boldsymbol{y}}_p = \boldsymbol{X}_p\hat{\boldsymbol{\beta}}$, and the prediction error, denoted $\boldsymbol{f}$, is

$$\begin{aligned}\boldsymbol{f} &= \boldsymbol{u}_p - \boldsymbol{X}_p(\hat{\boldsymbol{\beta}} - \boldsymbol{\beta}) \\ &= \boldsymbol{u}_p - \boldsymbol{X}_p(\boldsymbol{X}_s'\boldsymbol{X}_s)^{-1}\boldsymbol{X}_s'\boldsymbol{u}_s = \boldsymbol{B}\boldsymbol{u}\end{aligned} \tag{2.5.8}$$

where $\boldsymbol{B} = \left[-\boldsymbol{X}_p\left(\boldsymbol{X}_s'\boldsymbol{X}_s\right)^{-1}\boldsymbol{X}_s' \quad \boldsymbol{I}_{n_p}\right]$ $(n_p \times (n_s + n_p))$. Under H_0, Theorem C.1.1 implies that

$$\boldsymbol{f}|\boldsymbol{X}_s, \boldsymbol{X}_p \sim \mathrm{N}(\boldsymbol{0}, \sigma^2\boldsymbol{B}\boldsymbol{B}') \tag{2.5.9}$$

where $\boldsymbol{B}\boldsymbol{B}' = \boldsymbol{I}_{n_p} + \boldsymbol{X}_p\left(\boldsymbol{X}_s'\boldsymbol{X}_s\right)^{-1}\boldsymbol{X}_p'$. This result may be used to generate confidence intervals for the predictions, conditional on the explanatory variables. Alternatively it yields the key distributional result for the prediction test,

$$\boldsymbol{f}'\left[\mathrm{Var}\left(\boldsymbol{f}|\boldsymbol{X}\right)\right]^{-1}\boldsymbol{f} = \frac{\boldsymbol{u}'\boldsymbol{B}'\left(\boldsymbol{B}\boldsymbol{B}'\right)^{-1}\boldsymbol{B}\boldsymbol{u}}{\sigma^2} \sim \chi^2\left(n_p\right) \text{ on } H_0 \tag{2.5.10}$$

following from the fact that $\boldsymbol{B}'\left(\boldsymbol{B}\boldsymbol{B}'\right)^{-1}\boldsymbol{B}$ is symmetric and idempotent with rank n_p.

The sample-period residuals are $\hat{\boldsymbol{u}}_s = \boldsymbol{M}_s\boldsymbol{u}_s$ where

$$\boldsymbol{M}_s = \boldsymbol{I}_{n_s} - \boldsymbol{X}_s\left(\boldsymbol{X}_s'\boldsymbol{X}_s\right)^{-1}\boldsymbol{X}_s'. \tag{2.5.11}$$

Observe that $\hat{\boldsymbol{u}}_s'\hat{\boldsymbol{u}}_s = \boldsymbol{u}'\boldsymbol{M}^*\boldsymbol{u}$ where

$$\boldsymbol{M}^* = \begin{bmatrix}\boldsymbol{M}_s & \boldsymbol{0}\\ \boldsymbol{0} & \boldsymbol{0}\end{bmatrix}. \tag{2.5.12}$$

Since $\boldsymbol{M}_s\boldsymbol{X}_s = \boldsymbol{0}$,

$$\boldsymbol{M}^*\boldsymbol{B}' = \begin{bmatrix}\boldsymbol{M}_s & \boldsymbol{0}\\ \boldsymbol{0} & \boldsymbol{0}\end{bmatrix}\begin{bmatrix}-\boldsymbol{X}_s\left(\boldsymbol{X}_s'\boldsymbol{X}_s\right)^{-1}\boldsymbol{X}_p'\\ \boldsymbol{I}_{n_p}\end{bmatrix} = \boldsymbol{0}. \tag{2.5.13}$$

Theorem C.4.2 therefore establishes that

$$\frac{\boldsymbol{f}'(\boldsymbol{I}_{n_p} + \boldsymbol{X}_p\left(\boldsymbol{X}_s'\boldsymbol{X}_s\right)^{-1}\boldsymbol{X}_p')^{-1}\boldsymbol{f}}{n_p s^2} \sim F\left(n_p, n_s - k\right) \text{ on } H_0 \tag{2.5.14}$$

where $s^2 = \hat{\boldsymbol{u}}_s'\hat{\boldsymbol{u}}_s/\left(n_s - k\right)$. The test based on this statistic is known as the Chow (1960) prediction test, not to be confused with the parameter stability test of §2.5.1.

While the null hypothesis has been formulated as a distribution for $\boldsymbol{u}$ rather than as a parametric restriction, there is an implicit alternative hypothesis that may be expressed as

$$\begin{bmatrix}\boldsymbol{y}_s\\ \boldsymbol{y}_p\end{bmatrix} = \begin{bmatrix}\boldsymbol{X}_s\\ \boldsymbol{X}_p\end{bmatrix}\boldsymbol{\beta} + \begin{bmatrix}\boldsymbol{0}\\ \boldsymbol{I}_{n_p}\end{bmatrix}\boldsymbol{\delta} + \begin{bmatrix}\boldsymbol{u}_s\\ \boldsymbol{u}_p\end{bmatrix} \tag{2.5.15}$$

or

$$y = X\beta + Z\delta + u \tag{2.5.16}$$

where δ is a n_p-vector of parameters. In this context the null hypothesis can be stated as $H_0 : \delta = 0$. Note that

$$\begin{aligned} X'X &= X_s'X_s + X_p'X_p \\ X'y &= X_s'y_s + X_p'y_p \\ Z'X = X_p,\ Z'y &= y_p,\ Z'Z = I_{n_p} \end{aligned}$$

and, hence, the partitioned normal equations corresponding to (1.2.26) have the solutions

$$\hat{\beta} = (X_s'X_s)^{-1}X_s'y_s \tag{2.5.17a}$$

$$\hat{\delta} = y_p - X_p\hat{\beta}. \tag{2.5.17b}$$

Note, (2.5.17b) implies that the residuals in the prediction period are identically zero. To fit the unrestricted model, one simply fits the model to the sample observations only.

Therefore, consider the test based on the restricted and unrestricted sums of squares. Letting

$$\dot{\beta} = (X'X)^{-1}X'y \tag{2.5.18}$$

denote the regression under H_0, note that

$$\hat{\beta} = (X_s'X_s)^{-1}(X'y - X_p'y_p) = \dot{\beta} - (X_s'X_s)^{-1}X_p'\dot{u}_p \tag{2.5.19}$$

where $\dot{u}_p = y_p - X_p'\dot{\beta}$. The residuals from the restricted regression are

$$\dot{u} = \begin{bmatrix} \dot{u}_s \\ \dot{u}_p \end{bmatrix} = \begin{bmatrix} \hat{u}_s + X_s(X_s'X_s)^{-1}X_p\dot{u}_p \\ \dot{u}_p \end{bmatrix} \tag{2.5.20}$$

where the form of the third member follows from the relationship between $\dot{\beta}$ and $\hat{\beta}$ just given. Substituting from (2.5.20) into the sum of squares function yields

$$\begin{aligned} \dot{u}'\dot{u} &= \hat{u}_s'\hat{u}_s + \dot{u}_p'(I_{n_p} + X_p(X_s'X_s)^{-1}X_p')\dot{u}_p \\ &= \hat{u}_s'\hat{u}_s + \dot{u}_p'BB'\dot{u}_p. \end{aligned} \tag{2.5.21}$$

Note that the cross-product terms in the second member vanish since $X_s'\hat{u}_s = 0$. Moreover,

$$\dot{u}_p = f - X_p(X_s'X_s)^{-1}X_p'\dot{u}_p = (BB')^{-1}f \tag{2.5.22}$$

so

$$\dot{u}'\dot{u} - \hat{u}_s'\hat{u}_s = f'(BB')^{-1}f. \tag{2.5.23}$$

The right-hand side of this equation is the quadratic form appearing in the numerator of the Chow statistic, whereas the left-hand side is the difference between the residual sums of squares of the regression fitted to the whole data set, and of that fitted to the 'sample' observations only. We have therefore shown that an alternative form of the statistic in (2.5.14) is

$$\frac{\hat{u}'\hat{u} - \hat{u}_s'\hat{u}_s}{\hat{u}_s'\hat{u}_s} \cdot \frac{n_s - k}{n_p}. \tag{2.5.24}$$

The prediction test is therefore very straightforward to compute in practice.

Further Reading: Good accounts of this theory is to be found in many texts although not all emphasize the fact that the regressors can be random variables. Theil (1971) is excellent. For more advanced treatments, see in particular Silvey (1970), Rao (1973), Seber (1980), Gourieroux and Monfort (1995).

Chapter 3

Asymptotic Analysis of the Regression Model

3.1 Stochastic Convergence

3.1.1 Modes of Convergence

This chapter introduces the basic concepts of asymptotic theory, an approximate distribution theory for estimators based on the limiting case as the sample size goes to infinity. Outside the somewhat restrictive assumptions of §2.4, there is no exact distribution theory on which to base interval estimation and hypothesis testing, but approximate results exist based on variants of the two fundamental theorems of statistics: the law of large numbers and the central limit theorem. These results are found to yield an adequate approximation to the true, unknown or intractable distributions that actually prevail when the sample is reasonably large.

To begin at the very beginning, consider an infinite sequence of variables indexed on the natural numbers,

$$X_1, X_2, X_3, \dots, X_n, \dots = \{X_n\}. \tag{3.1.1}$$

The sequence as a whole is denoted by placing braces around the symbol for the typical element. If the sequence is non-stochastic, there is a simple definition of convergence of the sequence: $\{X_n\}$ converges to a variable X if for all real numbers $\varepsilon > 0$, there exists an integer $n_\varepsilon \geq 1$ such that $|X_n - X| < \varepsilon$ for all $n > n_\varepsilon$. This is denoted by writing $\lim_{n\to\infty} X_n = X$. A familiar example is given by $X_n = \sum_{t=1}^{n} \lambda^t$, for $|\lambda| < 1$. In this case, as is well known, $X = 1/(1-\lambda)$.

Now suppose that $\{X_n\}$ is a sequence of random variables, with a corresponding sequence of distribution functions $\{F_n\}$. Several different types of convergence are defined for X_n.

Definition 3.1.1 If the real sequences $\{F_n(x)\}$ converge to $F(x)$ whenever x is a continuity point of a function F, F_n is said to *converge weakly* to F, written

$F_n \Longrightarrow F$. In this case $\{X_n\}$ is said to *converge in distribution* to X, where X is a random variable with distribution function F, written $X_n \xrightarrow{\mathrm{D}} X$. □

Continuity points of F are points x such that $P\{X = x\} = 0$, so that weak convergence is the condition that

$$\lim_{n\to\infty} P(X_n \le x) = P(X \le x) \tag{3.1.2}$$

for all such x. Weak convergence is strictly a property of sequences of distribution functions, and the notation $X_n \xrightarrow{\mathrm{D}} X$ is slightly irregular. If Z is another random variable having distribution function F it is equally correct to write $X_n \xrightarrow{\mathrm{D}} Z$. In context, the meaning is usually clear.

Definition 3.1.2 If X is a random variable, and for all $\varepsilon > 0$

$$\lim_{n\to\infty} P(|X_n - X| < \varepsilon) = 1 \tag{3.1.3}$$

X_n is said to *converge in probability* to X, written $X_n \xrightarrow{\mathrm{pr}} X$. X is known as the *probability limit* of X_n, written $X = \operatorname{plim} X_n$. □

Definition 3.1.3 If for all $\varepsilon > 0$

$$P\Big(\lim_{n\to\infty} X_n = X\Big) = 1 \tag{3.1.4}$$

X_n is said to converge to X *almost surely* or with probability 1, written $X_n \xrightarrow{\mathrm{as}} X$, or a.s. $\lim X_n = X$. □

Definition 3.1.4 If

$$\lim_{n\to\infty} E(X_n - X)^2 = 0 \tag{3.1.5}$$

X_n is said to *converge in mean square* to X, written $X_n \xrightarrow{\mathrm{ms}} X$. □

These four modes of stochastic convergence (not an exhaustive list by any means) form a partial hierarchy. Almost sure convergence and mean square convergence both imply convergence in probability which in turn implies weak convergence, but the converse implications do not hold. The most important notions from our point of view are convergence in distribution and convergence in probability. Almost sure convergence is widely analysed in advanced treatments, but convergence in probability is easier to work with at an elementary level and is sufficient for most purposes. The chief role of mean square convergence is that of being easier to prove in certain contexts than convergence in probability directly, and sufficient for the latter.

While X is in principle a random variable in these definitions, in many applications it is a constant, or equivalently a degenerate random variable whose distribution is defined by $X = c$ with probability 1. In the case of convergence in distribution, the degenerate limiting distribution function F would then have the form

$$F(x) = \begin{cases} 0, & x < c \\ 1, & x \geq c. \end{cases} \tag{3.1.6}$$

In this case, convergence in distribution and in probability are equivalent. However, if $\operatorname{plim} X_n = c$ it does not necessarily follow that $\lim_{n\to\infty} E(X_n) = c$, as one might possibly expect. While this is true in 'well-behaved' cases, counter-examples can be devised, such as the one after Theorem 3.2.2.

3.1.2 Related Results

A number of useful results are available that allow us to infer the convergence of transformations of a sequence, of which the following are probably the most important.

Theorem 3.1.1 (Slutsky's Theorem) Let $\{X_n\}$ be a random sequence converging in probability to a constant a, and let $g(\cdot)$ be a function continuous at a. Then $\operatorname{plim} g(X_n) = g(a)$. □

Theorem 3.1.2 (Cramér's Theorem) Let $\{Y_n\}$ and $\{X_n\}$ be random sequences, with $Y_n \xrightarrow{\text{D}} Y$ and $X_n \xrightarrow{\text{pr}} a$ (a constant). Then

(i) $X_n + Y_n \xrightarrow{\text{D}} a + Y$

(ii) $X_n Y_n \xrightarrow{\text{D}} aY$

(iii) $\dfrac{Y_n}{X_n} \xrightarrow{\text{D}} \dfrac{Y}{a}$ when $a \neq 0$. □

Theorem 3.1.3 (Continuous Mapping Theorem) If $X_n \xrightarrow{\text{D}} X$ and $g(\cdot)$ is continuous, then $g(X_n) \xrightarrow{\text{D}} g(X)$. □

For the proofs of these results, see respectively Theorems 18.10, 22.14 and 22.11 of Davidson (1994a).

If a non-stochastic sequence $\{X_n\}$ has the property that the sequence $\{X_n/n^r\}$ remains bounded in the limit as $n \to \infty$, for some real r, it is customary to write $X_n = O(n^r)$, or in words, that X_n is 'of order of magnitude n^r'. The counterpart of this usage for stochastic sequences is the '$O_p(\cdot)$' and '$o_p(\cdot)$' notations due to Mann and Wald (1943a).

Definition 3.1.5 If for any $\varepsilon > 0$ there exists $B_\varepsilon < \infty$ such that

$$P\Big(\frac{|X_n|}{n^r} > B_\varepsilon\Big) < \varepsilon \tag{3.1.7}$$

for all $n \geq 1$, write $X_n = O_p(n^r)$. If $\operatorname{plim} X_n/n^r = 0$, write $X_n = o_p(n^r)$. □

A sufficient condition for $X_n = O_p(n^r)$ is that $\text{plim}\, X_n/n^r$ exists. If $Z_n = O_p(n^{r_1})$ and $W_n = O_p(n^{r_2})$ then

$$Z_n + W_n = O_p(n^{\max(r_1,r_2)}) \tag{3.1.8}$$

$$Z_n W_n = O_p(n^{r_1+r_2}). \tag{3.1.9}$$

The same rules for manipulation hold for $o_p(\cdot)$.

Finally, a word about *uniform* conditions. When stating conditions on the terms of a sequence, it may be necessary to make clear that they apply 'in the limit'. Thus, the statement '$X_n < \infty$ for every $n \geq 1$' is satisfied by (for example) the case $X_n = n$, but clearly this sequence is not bounded in the limit. To convey this condition one must say something like '$X_n \leq B$ for every $n \geq 1$' where B is a finite bound. The same meaning is conveyed by the phrase '$X_n < \infty$ uniformly in n'.

3.2 The Law of Large Numbers

In its simplest form, the *weak law of large numbers* (WLLN) is the result that, given a sample $x_1, \dots, x_n$ of random variables with mean $E(x_t) = \mu$, the sample mean

$$\bar{x}_n = \frac{1}{n}\sum_{t=1}^{n} x_t \tag{3.2.1}$$

converges in probability to μ as the sample size increases. The strong law of large numbers (SLLN) is the corresponding result with almost sure convergence. Although convergence results in econometrics are sometimes cast in the strong law format, convergence in probability is sufficient for all the distributional results in this book. The laws of large numbers formalize the intuitive concept of the result of averaging large numbers of random observations.

3.2.1 Independent Sequences

The best-known formulation of the weak law is Khinchine's Theorem:

Theorem 3.2.1 Let $\{x_t\}$ be independently and identically distributed, and integrable with $E(x_t) = \mu < \infty$. Then $\bar{x}_n \xrightarrow{\text{pr}} \mu$. □

See Davidson (1994a), Theorem 23.5 for the proof. 'Identically and independently distributed' (i.i.d.) means that the sequence is generated by successive random drawings from an infinite population[1] whose distribution has mean μ. Since the integrability condition is equivalent to the existence of a finite mean, the theorem asserts that, in the i.i.d. case, no supplementary conditions are needed.

[1] Drawing from a finite population *with replacement* is equivalent to drawing from an infinite population.

It is also possible to sample randomly from a heterogeneous sequence of distributions, such that y_t is drawn from F_t. A cross-sectional population (of firms say) might contain units of two or more distinct types, or a distribution might be evolving with time. In this case, the random sequence is said to be independent but not identically distributed. A particular possibility is non-identical means. However, given a sequence $\{y_t\}$ with $E(y_t) = \mu_t$ we can always consider the centred variables $x_t = y_t - \mu_t$ which have a common mean of zero. Showing that $\bar{x}_n \xrightarrow{\text{pr}} 0$ is sufficient for showing that $\bar{y}_n$ converges in probability to the limit of the sequence $\bar{\mu}_n = n^{-1}\sum_{t=1}^{n}\mu_t$. It is perfectly possible to have $\bar{\mu}_n$ diverge as n goes to ∞ and yet a weak law still holds in the sense that $|\bar{y}_n - \bar{\mu}_n| \xrightarrow{\text{pr}} 0$. In any case, there is no loss of generality in confining attention to the case $\mu = 0$, and this is assumed henceforth. However, the distributions of the centred variables may still be heterogeneous. The danger for the application of the weak law in this context is that without any restraints on the sequence $\{F_t\}$, the integrability condition for the centred variables could eventually fail as the sample size is increased. The following theorem, which is a corollary of Theorem 6.2.2 below, is obtained by imposing a condition sufficient to rule out this possibility.

Theorem 3.2.2 Let the sequence $\{x_t\}$ be independent, with $E(x_t) = 0$. If[2]

$$E|x_t|^{1+\delta} \leq B < \infty \quad \delta > 0,\ \forall\, t \tag{3.2.2}$$

then $\bar{x}_n \xrightarrow{\text{pr}} 0$. □

Khinchine's Theorem, by imposing identical distributions, permits $\delta = 0$ in (3.2.2). Otherwise, this condition is sufficient to impose on the sequence a technical property known as *uniform integrability*, forbidding extreme values tending to ∞ as t increases. This can frustrate convergence of the sample mean in spite of the population mean being apparently well-defined for every t. Interestingly enough, it is not sufficient for uniform integrability just to stipulate that $E|x_t| \leq B < \infty$ for all t. Something stronger is needed, which is hard to state in simple terms but for which (3.2.2) is sufficient.

We can illustrate the problem with a rather contrived example in which the distributions depend on t in a particular way. Let $y_t = 0$ with probability $1 - 1/t$, and $y_t = t$ with probability $1/t$. Note that $\mu_t = 1$ for every t, and hence $\bar{\mu}_n = 1$, but if $x_t = y_t - 1$ it is intuitively clear that $\bar{x}_n$ is close not to 0 but to -1, with high probability when n is large. In fact, it can be proved that $\operatorname{plim}\bar{x}_n = -1$, so that the WLLN fails in this case. Note that $E|x_t| \leq E|y_t| + 1 < \infty$, uniformly in t. Nonetheless, condition (3.2.2) rules this case out, because

$$E|x_t|^{1+\delta} = 1 - \frac{1}{t} + \frac{|t-1|^{1+\delta}}{t} = O(t^{\delta}) \tag{3.2.3}$$

For any choice of B, and $\delta > 0$, there is a t large enough that the inequality in (3.2.2) fails to hold.

[2] The symbol $\forall$ stands for 'for all'.

3.2.2 Chebyshev's Theorem

The two versions of the weak law just given have nothing to say about the existence of variances.[3] If it can be assumed that variances always exist, more extreme forms of heterogeneity are permitted. Assuming $E(x_t) = 0$ and letting $E(x_t^2) = \sigma_t^2$, note that, if the terms of the sequence are independent, they are also uncorrelated, and it is easy to show that the variance of the sample mean is

$$E(\bar{x}_n^2) = \frac{1}{n^2}\sum_{t=1}^{n}\sigma_t^2. \tag{3.2.4}$$

If $E(\bar{x}_n^2)$ converges to 0 as n increases, then according to Definition 3.1.4 one says that $\bar{x}_n$ converges in mean square to 0. The assertion made following Definition 3.1.4, that this is sufficient for convergence in probability, is now demonstrated by applying the Chebyshev inequality (B.4.14) for $p = 2$. This yields

$$P(|\bar{x}_n| > \varepsilon) \le \frac{E(\bar{x}_n^2)}{\varepsilon^2} \to 0 \tag{3.2.5}$$

for any $\varepsilon > 0$, which is convergence in probability according to Definition 3.1.2. This result, often known as Chebyshev's Theorem, is stated formally as follows:

Theorem 3.2.3 If $E(x_t) = 0\ \forall\ t$ and $\lim_{n\to\infty} E(\bar{x}_n^2) \to 0$, then $\operatorname{plim} \bar{x}_n = 0$. □

See Davidson (1994a), Theorem 19.1 for the proof. The assumption of uniformly finite variances, with $\sigma_t^2 \le B < \infty$ for every t, is clearly more than sufficient for convergence, since then $n^{-1}\sum_{t=1}^{n}\sigma_t^2 \le B$ for every n. In this case, note that $E(\bar{x}_n^2) \le B/n$ and thus the *rate* of convergence is quantified. We are able to say that

$$\bar{x}_n = o_p(n^{-\alpha}) \tag{3.2.6}$$

for all $\alpha < \frac{1}{2}$. This is the well-known 'square root' rule for the effect of increasing sample size. No such conclusion on the rate of convergence can be drawn from Theorem 3.2.2. Moreover, it is possible to have the variances increasing without limit. Suppose $\sigma_t^2 = O(t^{2\gamma})$ for some $\gamma > 0$. In this case, $E(\bar{x}_n^2) = O(n^{2\gamma-1})$, and the condition of Theorem 3.2.3 is satisfied provided $\gamma < \frac{1}{2}$. However, with $\gamma > 0$, $E|x_t|^{1+\delta}$ is an increasing function of t for $\delta = 1$, and the condition of Theorem 3.2.2 is violated. The square root rule does not hold in this case, since (3.2.6) can be asserted only for $\alpha < \frac{1}{2} - \gamma$.

---

[3] While the second moment is finite for most common distributions like the Gaussian, there are plenty of distributions for which $E(X^2) = \infty$. The Cauchy distribution is a well-known example, that also lacks a mean. By 'common' we mean, of course, commonly found in textbooks of statistics. What kind of distributions are to be found in nature could be another matter altogether.

3.3 The Central Limit Theorem

Like the laws of large numbers, the central limit theorem (CLT) concerns the convergence of scaled sums of random variables, but in this case the means of the variables must be zero, and the scale factor considered is $n^{-1/2}$ instead of n^{-1}. If $\mathrm{Var}(\bar{x}_n) = O(n^{-1})$, then $\mathrm{Var}(n^{1/2}\bar{x}_n) = O(1)$. The random sequence of normalized sample means $\{n^{1/2}\bar{x}_n\}$, having expected value 0, neither degenerates to 0 in the limit nor diverges to infinite values, except with probability 0. The interesting cases are those where it converges in distribution according to Definition 3.1.1, and the CLT states that, subject to various mild conditions on the sequence, this limit is the Gaussian (normal) distribution.

3.3.1 The i.i.d. Case

The simplest and best-known of these results is commonly known as the Lindeberg–Lévy Theorem:

Theorem 3.3.1 Let $\{x_t\}$ be i.i.d. with mean 0 and variance $\sigma^2 < \infty$. If $\omega_n = \sqrt{n}\bar{x}_n/\sigma$, then

$$\omega_n \xrightarrow{\mathrm{D}} \omega \sim \mathrm{N}(0,1). \quad \square \tag{3.3.1}$$

See for example Davidson (1994a) Theorem 23.3 for a proof. The notation

$$\sqrt{n}\frac{\bar{x}_n}{\sigma} \underset{\text{asy}}{\sim} \mathrm{N}(0,1) \tag{3.3.2}$$

can be used to express the result of this theorem more compactly. The conditions are comparable to those of Khinchine's Theorem, except that the variance must be finite. This is always a requirement for the CLT to hold.

It may not be immediately obvious how $X_n \xrightarrow{\mathrm{D}} X$ can mean something different from $X_n \xrightarrow{\mathrm{pr}} X$, when the limit is in each case a random variable. The difference is best appreciated by working through a counter-example. Consider

$$\omega_n = \frac{1}{\sqrt{n}}\sum_{t=1}^{n} x_t \tag{3.3.3}$$

where $x_1, \ldots, x_n$ are i.i.d. with mean 0 and variance σ^2. By the Lindeberg–Lévy CLT, $\omega_n \xrightarrow{\mathrm{D}} \omega \sim \mathrm{N}(0,\sigma^2)$. However, not only is it not the case that $\omega_n \xrightarrow{\mathrm{pr}} \omega$, but $\operatorname{plim}\omega_n$ does not even exist, so care is necessary when taking limits involving such variables.

The proof of this assertion is by contradiction. Assume $\omega_n \xrightarrow{\mathrm{pr}} \omega$. Then it must follow that $\omega_{2n} - \omega_n \xrightarrow{\mathrm{pr}} 0$, where

$$\omega_{2n} = \frac{1}{\sqrt{2n}}\sum_{t=1}^{2n} x_t. \tag{3.3.4}$$

However, $\omega_{2n} = 2^{-1/2}(\omega_n + \omega_n')$ where

$$\omega_n' = \frac{1}{\sqrt{n}} \sum_{t=n+1}^{2n} x_t \tag{3.3.5}$$

and hence,

$$\omega_{2n} - \omega_n = \left(\frac{1}{\sqrt{2}} - 1\right)\omega_n + \frac{1}{\sqrt{2}}\omega_n'. \tag{3.3.6}$$

Since ω_n and ω_n' are independent (they have no observations in common)

$$\mathrm{Var}(\omega_{2n} - \omega_n) = \sigma^2\left[\left(\frac{1}{\sqrt{2}} - 1\right)^2 + \left(\frac{1}{\sqrt{2}}\right)^2\right] = \sigma^2(2 - \sqrt{2}). \tag{3.3.7}$$

This is clearly true for any n. Since the assumptions of the Lindeberg–Lévy CLT are satisfied,

$$\omega_{2n} - \omega_n \underset{\text{asy}}{\sim} \mathrm{N}(0,\ \sigma^2(2 - \sqrt{2})) \tag{3.3.8}$$

which contradicts the assumption that $\omega_{2n} - \omega_n \xrightarrow{\text{pr}} 0$.

3.3.2 Heterogeneous Data

In the non-identically distributed case, when the variances of the variables in the sum may differ, the conditions for the CLT become more difficult to state. The fundamental sufficient condition on the distributions is Lindeberg's condition:

$$\lim_{n\to\infty} \frac{1}{s_n^2} \sum_{t=1}^{n} \int_{\varepsilon s_n^2}^{\infty} x_t^2 dP = 0 \text{ for all } \varepsilon > 0 \tag{3.3.9}$$

where $s_n^2 = E(\sum_{t=1}^n x_t)^2$, and $s_n^2 = \sum_{t=1}^n \sigma_t^2$ under independence. Basically, Lindeberg's condition ensures that no one term is so relatively large as to dominate the entire sample, in the limit. It is admittedly somewhat unintuitive and awkward to verify, and the following result, which is a variant of the so-called Liapunov Theorem, gives more transparent conditions that are sufficient for the Lindeberg condition to hold. The conditions of the following result are implied by those of Theorem 23.12 of Davidson (1994a), extended using Theorem 23.18 of the same source.

Theorem 3.3.2 Let x_t be distributed independently with mean 0 and variance σ_t^2, and let $\bar{\sigma}_n^2 = n^{-1}\sum_{t=1}^n \sigma_t^2$. If[4]

$$\frac{\max_{1\le t\le n} \|x_t\|_{2+\delta}}{\bar{\sigma}_n} \le B < \infty \quad \delta > 0,\ \forall\, n \ge 1 \tag{3.3.10}$$

then $\omega_n = \sqrt{n}\bar{x}_n/\bar{\sigma}_n \xrightarrow{\text{D}} \omega \sim \mathrm{N}(0,1)$. □

---

[4]See (B.4.15) for the definition of $\|\cdot\|_p$.

This result is presented in conventional style with ω_n represented as the sample mean of the data points normalized by dividing by its standard deviation. An equivalent representation is

$$\omega_n = \frac{\sum_{t=1}^n x_t}{\sqrt{E\left(\sum_{t=1}^n x_t\right)^2}} \tag{3.3.11}$$

which is simply the sum of n zero-mean independent terms, normalized to have unit variance for any n. Central limit theorems always concern this type of standardized sum, and the various applications to estimators and statistics of different kinds must imply the construction of something with the form of (3.3.11).

Condition (3.3.10) is really a two-part restriction. To ensure that a CLT operates, the fundamental requirement is that no finite collection of the terms be so influential as to dominate the entire sum, in the limit. This can happen either because of growth of the high-order moments implying an excessive probability of outliers in the limit, or because of eventual degeneracy of the distributions. If the $L_{2+\delta}$-norms are uniformly bounded in t, then to satisfy (3.3.10), it is enough for $\bar{\sigma}_n^2$ to be bounded uniformly away from 0. The individual variances σ_t^2 must nearly all be positive, such that their sum is $O(n)$ but not $o(n)$. Obviously, if all but a finite number of the x_t are equal to 0, there can be no central limit result. Similarly, if $\bar{\sigma}_n^2$ is uniformly bounded, then so must $\|x_t\|_{2+\delta}$ be.

To illustrate the role of the bounded norm condition, consider a counter-example. Let $x_t = y_t - E(y_t)$ where $y_t = 0$ with probability $1 - 1/t^2$, and $y_t = t$ with probability $1/t^2$. Then $E(y_t) = 1/t \to 0$, and

$$E(x_t^2) = \left(-\frac{1}{t}\right)^2\left(1 - \frac{1}{t^2}\right) + \left(t - \frac{1}{t}\right)^2\frac{1}{t^2} \to 1 \tag{3.3.12}$$

as $t \to \infty$. Hence, $\bar{\sigma}_n^2 \to 1$. Despite this, it is clear that x_t is converging to a degenerate random variable, taking the value 0 with probability 1. The CLT cannot apply in such a case. However, it is easily verified that $\|x_t\|_{2+\delta} = O(t^{\delta/(2+\delta)})$, so that with any $\delta > 0$, the condition in (3.3.10) must fail when n is large enough.

Condition (3.3.10) still permits a wide range of variation in the distributions of the sample points. It does not rule out both numerator and denominator diverging to ∞, provided the ratio remains bounded. Since $\|x_t\|_{2+\delta} \geq \sigma_t$ by the Liapunov inequality (B.4.16), one thing (3.3.10) says is that if the variances do grow with t, the largest variance must not grow faster than the average variance. It can be shown that $\sigma_t^2 = O(t^\alpha)$ is permissible for any $\alpha > 0$, although not $\sigma_t^2 = O(e^t)$.

Here is one further curious example, showing that although sufficient, the conditions of Theorem 3.3.2 are not necessary. Suppose $y_t = 0$ and 1 with probability $\frac{1}{2}(1 - 1/t^2)$ each, and t with probability $1/t^2$. In this case, y_t is tending to a simple Bernoulli random variable[5], and the CLT certainly applies in this case, yet (3.3.10) is not satisfied. Such cases are nonetheless exceptional.

[5] A Bernoulli r.v. takes the values 0 and 1 with fixed probabilities p and $1 - p$.

3.3.3 Vector Sequences

The foregoing results are for scalar random variables, whereas econometrics usually deals with vector quantities. The requisite multivariate generalizations are obtained using a result known as the *Cramér–Wold device*:

Theorem 3.3.3 If $\{\boldsymbol{X}_n\}$ is a sequence of random vectors, $\boldsymbol{X}_n \xrightarrow{\text{D}} \boldsymbol{X}$ if and only if for all conformable fixed vectors $\boldsymbol{\lambda}$, $\boldsymbol{\lambda}'\boldsymbol{X}_n \xrightarrow{\text{D}} \boldsymbol{\lambda}'\boldsymbol{X}$. □

For the proof see Davidson (1994a) Theorem 25.5. This approach yields the following vector form of the Lindeberg–Lévy CLT:

Theorem 3.3.4 If $\{\boldsymbol{x}_t\}$ is a sequence of m-vectors, $\boldsymbol{x}_t \sim$ i.i.d.$(\boldsymbol{0}, \boldsymbol{\Sigma})$ and $\bar{\boldsymbol{x}}_n = n^{-1}\sum_{t=1}^{n} \boldsymbol{x}_t$, then $\sqrt{n}\bar{\boldsymbol{x}}_n \xrightarrow{\text{D}} \text{N}(\boldsymbol{0}, \boldsymbol{\Sigma})$.

Proof $\boldsymbol{\lambda}'\boldsymbol{x}_t \sim$ i.i.d.$(0, \boldsymbol{\lambda}'\boldsymbol{\Sigma}\boldsymbol{\lambda})$ for any fixed $\boldsymbol{\lambda}$, so the result follows by Theorems 3.3.1 and 3.1.2. ■

Combining Theorems C.1.1 and 3.1.2 gives the following result, often referred to as Cramér's Theorem in the literature because it is a corollary of Theorem 3.1.2, the result given by Cramér (1946).

Theorem 3.3.5 Assume $\boldsymbol{X}_n \xrightarrow{\text{D}} \text{N}(\boldsymbol{\mu}, \boldsymbol{\Sigma})$, and $\boldsymbol{A}_n$ is a conformable matrix with $\text{plim}\, \boldsymbol{A}_n = \boldsymbol{A}$. Then $\boldsymbol{A}_n\boldsymbol{X}_n \xrightarrow{D} \text{N}(\boldsymbol{A}\boldsymbol{\mu}, \boldsymbol{A}\boldsymbol{\Sigma}\boldsymbol{A}')$. □

Slutsky's Theorem generalizes directly to random vectors and matrices. For example, if $\{\boldsymbol{A}_n\}$ is a sequence of square random matrices that are nonsingular with probability 1, and $\text{plim}\, \boldsymbol{A}_n = \boldsymbol{A}$, a nonsingular constant matrix, then $\text{plim}\, \boldsymbol{A}_n^{-1} = \boldsymbol{A}^{-1}$. These results are used repeatedly in the sequel.

3.4 Asymptotic Estimation Theory

Let $\hat{\boldsymbol{\theta}}_n$ $(p \times 1)$ be an estimator, applied to a sample of size n, of a vector of parameters $\boldsymbol{\theta}_0$. Both $\hat{\boldsymbol{\theta}}_n$ and $\boldsymbol{\theta}_0$ must be elements of the set Θ of all admissible values of the parameters, called the *parameter space.* In the case of the regression coefficients in the linear model, the parameter space can in principle be defined to be $\mathbb{R}^p$, or p-dimensional Euclidean space, where in this case $p = k$. In other words, there is no need to restrict it. All the cases to be considered in this chapter, and also in Part II of the book, are of this type. Subsequently, cases arise where the estimator does not have a closed formula, but is defined implicitly. In these cases, for technical reasons, Θ must in general be a *compact* subset of $\mathbb{R}^p$. Compactness is the property that the set is both bounded and *closed*, meaning that it contains its boundary points. It is further required in this case, for reasons discussed below, that $\boldsymbol{\theta}_0$ be an *interior* point of Θ. Technically, we say that $\boldsymbol{\theta}_0 \in \text{int}(\Theta)$ if there exists a real number $\delta > 0$ such that $\boldsymbol{\theta} \in \Theta$ whenever $\|\boldsymbol{\theta} - \boldsymbol{\theta}_0\| < \delta$. This excludes

$\boldsymbol{\theta}_0$ being on the boundary of the set. For further discussion of these issues, see §9.3.1.

The following terminology is standard.

Definition 3.4.1 $\hat{\boldsymbol{\theta}}_n$ is said to be consistent for $\boldsymbol{\theta}_0$ if $\text{plim}\,\hat{\boldsymbol{\theta}}_n = \boldsymbol{\theta}_0$. □

Consistency might be thought of as the minimum requirement for a useful estimator. If we cannot assume that eventually the error-of-estimate will be reduced by increasing the sample size, it is probably difficult to establish any interesting connection between the unknown parameter and the estimator.

Proofs of consistency play an important role in econometric theory, and it is worth noting the form these proofs often take. As shown in Theorem 3.2.3, if the sequence $E(\hat{\boldsymbol{\theta}}_n)$ has a limit and $\lim_{n\to\infty} \text{Var}(\hat{\boldsymbol{\theta}}_n) = \mathbf{0}$, then $\hat{\boldsymbol{\theta}}_n$ converges in probability to that limit. If $\lim_{n\to\infty} E(\hat{\boldsymbol{\theta}}_n) = \boldsymbol{\theta}_0$ then $\hat{\boldsymbol{\theta}}_n$ is said to be asymptotically unbiased. Asymptotic unbiasedness and zero limiting variance are jointly sufficient for consistency.

Suppose $\hat{\boldsymbol{\theta}}_n$ is consistent, and that $n^k(\hat{\boldsymbol{\theta}}_n - \boldsymbol{\theta}_0) = O_p(1)$ for some $k > 0$, and has a non-degenerate limiting distribution as $n \to \infty$. This distribution is called the asymptotic distribution of $\hat{\boldsymbol{\theta}}_n$, the centring and normalization by n^k being understood.

Definition 3.4.2 $\hat{\boldsymbol{\theta}}_n$ is said to be consistent and asymptotically normal (CAN) for $\boldsymbol{\theta}_0 \in \text{int}(\Theta)$ if there exists $k > 0$ such that $n^k(\hat{\boldsymbol{\theta}}_n - \boldsymbol{\theta}_0) \xrightarrow{\text{D}} \text{N}(\mathbf{0}, \boldsymbol{V})$, where $\boldsymbol{V}$ is a finite variance matrix. □

In most applications, $k = \frac{1}{2}$, although it can be larger than this in models containing deterministic trend terms; see §7.2.2. There are also the cases to be studied in Part IV, involving stochastic trends, in which $k > \frac{1}{2}$ but the limiting distribution is not Gaussian. Note the importance of the restriction $\boldsymbol{\theta}_0 \in \text{int}(\Theta)$ here. Since the Gaussian distribution has infinite support, the condition $\hat{\boldsymbol{\theta}}_n \in \Theta$ is incompatible with asymptotic normality when inadmissible values lie arbitrarily close to $\boldsymbol{\theta}_0$. Of course, no effective restriction is imposed in the case $\Theta = \mathbb{R}^k$.

Asymptotic normality is an important property to establish for an estimator, because it is often the only basis for constructing interval estimates and tests of hypotheses. $\boldsymbol{V}$ is usually referred to as the asymptotic variance matrix (AVM), although sometimes that term is applied to $\boldsymbol{V}/n$, which is the approximate variance matrix of $\hat{\boldsymbol{\theta}}_n$ itself, for large n when $k = \frac{1}{2}$. We use the generic notation $\text{AVar}(\hat{\boldsymbol{\theta}}_n)$ to denote the AVM, which is always understood to be defined like $\boldsymbol{V}$ (in general, a non-vanishing quantity) in this book.

Let $\boldsymbol{C}$ denote a class of CAN estimators of $\boldsymbol{\theta}_0$, and write $\hat{\boldsymbol{\theta}}_n \in \boldsymbol{C}$ to denote that the estimator belongs to this class.[6]

[6] This notion of inclusion is of course distinct from $\hat{\boldsymbol{\theta}}_n \in \Theta$, meaning that the estimates lie in the parameter space. Unfortunately the notation does not distinguish the estimator (rule for estimation) from the values generated by it from given samples, but the distinction is implicit.

Definition 3.4.3 $\hat{\theta}_n \in C$ is said to be best asymptotically normal for θ_0 (BAN) in the class C if $\text{AVar}(\tilde{\theta}_n) - \text{AVar}(\hat{\theta}_n)$ is positive semi-definite for every $\tilde{\theta}_n \in C$. □

This property is also called *asymptotic efficiency*, when the CAN property is understood. The linear estimators of the regression model analysed in §2.2.3 are shown in §3.6.1 to be a CAN class, under suitable assumptions. It is shown that least squares is the efficient case under the usual assumptions, so that BAN can be seen as an asymptotic counterpart of the BLUE property. When C is defined to be the class of all CAN estimators of a given parameter, the BAN estimator is known to correspond with the maximum likelihood estimator. This theory is discussed in §11.3.6.

3.5 Asymptotics of the Stochastic Regressor Model

3.5.1 Assumptions

Consider the statistical model B of §1.3 (independent sampling) whose exact distributional properties under the conditional Gaussianity assumption are analysed in Chapter 2. Without the Gaussianity assumption conventional statistical inference is not possible, and the asymptotic properties of the OLS estimator are interesting for this reason alone.

These are derived very simply using the limit theorems of §3.2 and §3.3, invoking some additional assumptions on the sampling model often referred to as regularity conditions. Writing the regression model as

$$y_t = \boldsymbol{x}_t'\boldsymbol{\beta} + u_t \quad t = 1, \dots, n \tag{3.5.1}$$

let Assumptions 2.1.1–2.1.3 hold for all $n \geq k$, and assume additionally that[7]

$$\operatorname*{plim}_{n\to\infty} \frac{1}{n}\sum_{t=1}^{n} \boldsymbol{x}_t\boldsymbol{x}_t' = \lim_{n\to\infty}\frac{1}{n}\sum_{t=1}^{n} E(\boldsymbol{x}_t\boldsymbol{x}_t') = \boldsymbol{M}_{XX} < \infty \text{ (positive definite)} \tag{3.5.2}$$

and that

$$E|\boldsymbol{\lambda}'\boldsymbol{x}_t u_t|^{2+\delta} \leq B < \infty \quad \delta > 0,\ \forall\, t,\ \forall \text{ fixed } \boldsymbol{\lambda} \text{ with } \boldsymbol{\lambda}'\boldsymbol{\lambda} = 1. \tag{3.5.3}$$

Condition (3.5.2), which can be written more compactly as $\operatorname{plim} n^{-1}\boldsymbol{X}'\boldsymbol{X} = \boldsymbol{M}_{XX}$, has two components. The weak law of large numbers must apply to the squares and cross-products of the elements of $\boldsymbol{x}_t$, and $\boldsymbol{M}_{XX}$ must have full rank. The latter condition can fail even though $\boldsymbol{X}$ has rank k for every finite n. To take a fairly trivial example, let $x_{1t} = 1/t$. Thus, the positive definiteness in (3.5.2) is an additional assumption, and does not follow from Assumption 2.1.3.

[7] The notation '$\boldsymbol{M} < \infty$', for a positive definite matrix $\boldsymbol{M}$, means $\boldsymbol{\lambda}'\boldsymbol{M}\boldsymbol{\lambda} < \infty$ for all vectors $\boldsymbol{\lambda}$ with $\boldsymbol{\lambda}'\boldsymbol{\lambda} = 1$.

3.5.2 Consistency

The least squares estimator can be written as

$$\hat{\boldsymbol{\beta}} = \left(\sum_{t=1}^{n} \boldsymbol{x}_t \boldsymbol{x}_t'\right)^{-1} \sum_{t=1}^{n} \boldsymbol{x}_t y_t = \boldsymbol{\beta} + \left(\sum_{t=1}^{n} \boldsymbol{x}_t \boldsymbol{x}_t'\right)^{-1} \sum_{t=1}^{n} \boldsymbol{x}_t u_t. \tag{3.5.4}$$

Consider the $k \times 1$ vector $\boldsymbol{x}_t u_t$. Since $E(u_t|\boldsymbol{x}_t) = 0$ by Assumption 2.1.1 and $E(u_t^2|\boldsymbol{x}_t) = \sigma^2$ by Assumption 2.1.2, the LIE gives

$$\operatorname{Var}(\boldsymbol{x}_t u_t) = E\left[E(u_t^2 \boldsymbol{x}_t \boldsymbol{x}_t'|\boldsymbol{x}_t)\right] = \sigma^2 E(\boldsymbol{x}_t \boldsymbol{x}_t') < \infty. \tag{3.5.5}$$

When the data points are independent, (3.5.5) is sufficient for the Chebyshev WLLN to hold for $\boldsymbol{x}_t u_t$ element by element, so that

$$\operatorname{plim} \frac{1}{n} \sum_{t=1}^{n} \boldsymbol{x}_t u_t = \mathbf{0} \tag{3.5.6}$$

which is written more compactly as $\operatorname{plim} n^{-1} \boldsymbol{X}'\boldsymbol{u} = \mathbf{0}$. Then, by (3.5.2) and the Slutsky Theorem,

$$\operatorname{plim} \hat{\boldsymbol{\beta}} - \boldsymbol{\beta} = \left(\operatorname{plim} \frac{1}{n} \boldsymbol{X}'\boldsymbol{X}\right)^{-1} \operatorname{plim} \frac{1}{n} \boldsymbol{X}'\boldsymbol{u} = \boldsymbol{M}_{XX}^{-1} \cdot \mathbf{0} = \mathbf{0} \tag{3.5.7}$$

which is the consistency result.

3.5.3 Asymptotic Normality

Consider condition (3.3.10) applied to the sequence $\{\boldsymbol{\lambda}'\boldsymbol{x}_t u_t\}$. Applying (3.5.5) and (3.5.2) gives

$$\lim_{n\to\infty} \frac{1}{n} \sum_{t=1}^{n} \operatorname{Var}(\boldsymbol{\lambda}'\boldsymbol{x}_t u_t) = \sigma^2 \boldsymbol{\lambda}' \boldsymbol{M}_{XX} \boldsymbol{\lambda}. \tag{3.5.8}$$

Since $\boldsymbol{M}_{XX}$ is positive definite, this condition bounds the denominator in (3.3.10) uniformly away from 0, but also ensures it is finite. Since (3.5.3) uniformly bounds the numerator in (3.3.10), these conditions suffice by Theorem 3.3.2 to yield

$$\frac{1}{\sqrt{n}} \sum_{t=1}^{n} \boldsymbol{\lambda}'\boldsymbol{x}_t u_t \xrightarrow{\mathrm{D}} \mathrm{N}(\mathbf{0}, \sigma^2 \boldsymbol{\lambda}' \boldsymbol{M}_{XX} \boldsymbol{\lambda}) \tag{3.5.9}$$

for each $\boldsymbol{\lambda}$ specified. By Theorem 3.3.3, this is equivalent to

$$\frac{1}{\sqrt{n}} \boldsymbol{X}'\boldsymbol{u} \xrightarrow{\mathrm{D}} \mathrm{N}(\mathbf{0}, \sigma^2 \boldsymbol{M}_{XX}). \tag{3.5.10}$$

Finally by Cramér's Theorem (Theorem 3.3.5), using $\boldsymbol{M}_{XX}^{-1} \boldsymbol{M}_{XX} \boldsymbol{M}_{XX}^{-1} = \boldsymbol{M}_{XX}^{-1}$,

$$\sqrt{n}(\hat{\boldsymbol{\beta}} - \boldsymbol{\beta}) = \left(\frac{1}{n} \boldsymbol{X}'\boldsymbol{X}\right)^{-1} \frac{1}{\sqrt{n}} \boldsymbol{X}'\boldsymbol{u} \xrightarrow{\mathrm{D}} \mathrm{N}(\mathbf{0}, \sigma^2 \boldsymbol{M}_{XX}^{-1}). \tag{3.5.11}$$

These conclusions may be summarized in the following theorem:

Theorem 3.5.1 If the sample is independently drawn, and Assumptions 2.1.1, 2.1.2 and 2.1.3 plus the regularity conditions in (3.5.2) and (3.5.3) hold, the OLS estimator of $\boldsymbol{\beta}$ in model (3.5.1) is CAN with the distribution given in (3.5.11). □

The practical implication of this result is that the confidence intervals and test procedures derived in §2.4–§2.5 can often be treated as holding approximately when n is 'large', even when Assumption 2.4.1 does not hold. The matrix $\boldsymbol{M}_{XX}$ is unknown, but is consistently estimated by $n^{-1}\boldsymbol{X}'\boldsymbol{X}$ which means that, in practice, the usual regression standard error estimates are utilized. How large is 'large' depends on the actual distribution of the disturbances. In 'well-behaved' cases exhibiting symmetry and bounded moments the convergence is very rapid. For example, simulation experiments show that if the data are drawn from the uniform (rectangular) distribution centred on 0, with 20 or so observations the limit is virtually attained. Extreme skewness on the other hand, or a high probability of large outliers, would call for a larger sample for a good approximation. Suffice it to say that it is customary in econometrics to quote asymptotic test results in research reports, and leave it to the reader to decide what confidence to place in them.

3.5.4 A Common Pitfall

The argument leading to (3.5.11) is one variant of the derivation of the asymptotic variance matrix of $\hat{\boldsymbol{\beta}}$,

$$\mathrm{AVar}(\hat{\boldsymbol{\beta}}) = \sigma^2 \boldsymbol{M}_{XX}^{-1}. \tag{3.5.12}$$

This derivation has often been done incorrectly. An early edition of one of the best known textbooks of econometrics contained the following argument, which is reproduced here to point out the pitfalls that can arise in reasoning about asymptotics:

$$\begin{aligned} \text{“}\,\mathrm{AVar}(\hat{\boldsymbol{\beta}}) &= \mathrm{plim}\big(\sqrt{n}(\hat{\boldsymbol{\beta}}-\boldsymbol{\beta})\sqrt{n}(\hat{\boldsymbol{\beta}}-\boldsymbol{\beta})'\big) \\ &= \mathrm{plim}\left(\frac{\boldsymbol{X}'\boldsymbol{X}}{n}\right)^{-1} \mathrm{plim}\left(\frac{\boldsymbol{X}'\boldsymbol{u}\boldsymbol{u}'\boldsymbol{X}}{n}\right) \mathrm{plim}\left(\frac{\boldsymbol{X}'\boldsymbol{X}}{n}\right)^{-1} \\ &= \boldsymbol{M}_{XX}^{-1}\sigma^2\boldsymbol{M}_{XX}\boldsymbol{M}_{XX}^{-1} = \sigma^2\boldsymbol{M}_{XX}^{-1}\text{”} \end{aligned}$$

To see the difficulty with this argument, note first that $\mathrm{plim}\, n^{-1}(\boldsymbol{X}'\boldsymbol{u}\boldsymbol{u}'\boldsymbol{X})$ (assuming it exists) cannot possibly be $\sigma^2\boldsymbol{M}_{XX}$. It would have to be a random matrix of rank 1, not a fixed matrix of rank k. Letting $\boldsymbol{p}_n = n^{-1/2}\boldsymbol{X}'\boldsymbol{u}$,

$$\boldsymbol{p}_n \xrightarrow{\mathrm{D}} \mathrm{N}(\boldsymbol{0}, \sigma^2\boldsymbol{M}_{XX}) \tag{3.5.13}$$

(as just shown) and hence $\boldsymbol{p}_n\boldsymbol{p}_n'$ must a random matrix of rank 1 for any value of n, and even as $n \to \infty$. Of course, $E(\boldsymbol{p}_n\boldsymbol{p}_n')$ is a fixed matrix of rank k. Beware of confusing the properties of probability limits and expectations!

In fact, even to write $\mathrm{plim}\,\boldsymbol{p}_n\boldsymbol{p}_n'$ is not legitimate. By Slutsky's Theorem this limit ought to equal $\mathrm{plim}\,\boldsymbol{p}_n\,\mathrm{plim}\,\boldsymbol{p}_n'$, and $\mathrm{plim}\,\boldsymbol{p}_n$ does not exist, as the counter-example in §3.3.1 shows.

3.5.5 Asymptotic Test Criteria

The test procedures based on the assumption of Gaussian disturbances described in §2.4 can be justified in large samples on the basis of the central limit theorem. Consider the F ratio in (2.4.5). Using (3.5.2) and (3.5.6) combined with Slutsky's Theorem, and the fact that k is fixed and finite,

$$\begin{aligned}\operatorname{plim} s^2 &= \operatorname{plim}\left(\frac{n}{n-k}\right)\left(\frac{\boldsymbol{u}'\boldsymbol{u}}{n} - \frac{\boldsymbol{u}'\boldsymbol{X}}{n}\left(\frac{\boldsymbol{X}'\boldsymbol{X}}{n}\right)^{-1}\frac{\boldsymbol{X}'\boldsymbol{u}}{n}\right)\\ &= \operatorname{plim}\frac{\boldsymbol{u}'\boldsymbol{u}}{n} = \sigma^2. \end{aligned} \tag{3.5.14}$$

On the other hand, consider

$$\frac{\boldsymbol{u}'\boldsymbol{Q}\boldsymbol{u}}{\sigma^2} = \frac{1}{\sigma^2}\frac{\boldsymbol{u}'\boldsymbol{X}}{\sqrt{n}}\left(\frac{\boldsymbol{X}'\boldsymbol{X}}{n}\right)^{-1}\frac{\boldsymbol{X}'\boldsymbol{u}}{\sqrt{n}}. \tag{3.5.15}$$

In view of (3.5.10), Theorems 3.1.3, 3.3.5 and C.3.2,

$$\frac{\boldsymbol{u}'\boldsymbol{Q}\boldsymbol{u}}{\sigma^2} \xrightarrow{\text{D}} \chi^2(k) \tag{3.5.16}$$

and therefore, by Theorem 3.1.2(iii), an asymptotic version of (2.4.5) is

$$\frac{(\hat{\boldsymbol{\beta}}-\boldsymbol{\beta})'\boldsymbol{X}'\boldsymbol{X}(\hat{\boldsymbol{\beta}}-\boldsymbol{\beta})}{s^2} \xrightarrow{\text{D}} \chi^2(k). \tag{3.5.17}$$

Notice how we do not divide through by k in this instance, this factor being required in (2.4.5) solely because of the conventional definition of the F distribution. The result allows approximate confidence ellipsoids to be constructed, and can be extended in parallel with the development in §2.4 to derive tests of linear restrictions on the regression coefficients. Given r such restrictions, the large-sample counterpart of (2.4.20) is

$$n\frac{\dot{\boldsymbol{u}}'\dot{\boldsymbol{u}} - \hat{\boldsymbol{u}}'\hat{\boldsymbol{u}}}{\hat{\boldsymbol{u}}'\hat{\boldsymbol{u}}} \xrightarrow{\text{D}} \chi^2(k) \text{ on } H_0 : \boldsymbol{R\beta} = \boldsymbol{c}. \tag{3.5.18}$$

If H_0 is false, imposing the restriction must penalize the fit of the model in the limit, such that

$$\operatorname{plim}\frac{\dot{\boldsymbol{u}}'\dot{\boldsymbol{u}}}{n} - \operatorname{plim}\frac{\hat{\boldsymbol{u}}'\hat{\boldsymbol{u}}}{n} > 0. \tag{3.5.19}$$

It can be seen that in this case the test statistic is $O_p(n)$ as $n \to \infty$, and hence the test is *consistent.* A false hypothesis is rejected with probability 1 as $n \to \infty$.

The tabulation of the $\chi^2(r)$ distribution can be used to obtain critical values for a test based on (3.5.18). On the other hand, the same argument justifies using the usual F statistic from (2.4.20) and the critical values from the $F(k, n-k)$ tabulation to generate an approximate test. One cannot distinguish between these procedures on the basis of the asymptotic theory, but the regular F procedure probably provides at least as good a small sample approximation in many cases.

3.6 Linear CAN Estimators and Asymptotic Efficiency

Consider two closely related questions. First, does the asymptotic distribution of least squares have efficiency properties comparable to the best linear unbiased property established in §2.2.3? And second, can least squares be related to a more general class of feasible estimators with comparable properties? To answer these we focus on estimators formed as linear functions of the dependent variable, for no better reason than that these are amenable to our current methods of analysis, and consider the properties of consistency and asymptotic normality as defining the class of cases of interest. An efficiency result is derived for least squares as a member of the class of linear estimators for which CAN can be proved without invoking additional assumptions, apart from regularity assumptions.

3.6.1 The Linear CAN Class

In §2.2.3, a class of linear estimators of the regression model was defined having the general form

$$\boldsymbol{\beta}_L = \sum_{t=1}^{n} \boldsymbol{l}_{nt} y_t = \boldsymbol{L}\boldsymbol{y}. \tag{3.6.1}$$

where the $\boldsymbol{l}_{nt}$ form the columns of the matrix $\boldsymbol{L}$ in (2.2.10). The indexing of these by sample size is an important step in the asymptotic analysis. The collection

$$\{\boldsymbol{l}_{nt},\ t = 1, \dots, n,\ n = k, k+1, k+2, \dots\} \tag{3.6.2}$$

is formally known as a *triangular stochastic array.*[8] OLS is of course the member of the class for which

$$\boldsymbol{l}_{nt} = \left(\sum_{t=1}^{n} \boldsymbol{x}_t \boldsymbol{x}_t'\right)^{-1} \boldsymbol{x}_t. \tag{3.6.3}$$

Suppose that Assumptions 2.2.1–2.2.3 hold for each n. Substituting from $\boldsymbol{y} = \boldsymbol{X}\boldsymbol{\beta} + \boldsymbol{u}$ into (3.6.1) gives

$$\boldsymbol{\beta}_L - \boldsymbol{\beta} = (\boldsymbol{L}\boldsymbol{X} - \boldsymbol{I})\boldsymbol{\beta} + \boldsymbol{L}\boldsymbol{u} = \boldsymbol{L}\boldsymbol{u}. \tag{3.6.4}$$

The conditions for $\boldsymbol{\beta}_L$ to be CAN are therefore that $\operatorname{plim} \boldsymbol{L}\boldsymbol{u} = \boldsymbol{0}$, that

$$\operatorname{plim} n\boldsymbol{L}\boldsymbol{L}' = \boldsymbol{M}_{LL} < \infty \text{ (positive definite)} \tag{3.6.5}$$

and that

$$\sqrt{n}(\boldsymbol{\beta}_L - \boldsymbol{\beta}) = \sqrt{n}\boldsymbol{L}\boldsymbol{u} \xrightarrow{\mathrm{D}} \mathrm{N}(\boldsymbol{0}, \sigma^2 \boldsymbol{M}_{LL}). \tag{3.6.6}$$

Following the analysis of §2.2.3, let

$$\boldsymbol{D} = \boldsymbol{L} - (\boldsymbol{X}'\boldsymbol{X})^{-1}\boldsymbol{X}'. \tag{3.6.7}$$

---

[8] In this case the array is vector-valued, but this is not an essential feature of the definition.

Taking Assumption 2.2.3 to the limit then yields

$$M_{LL} = M_{XX}^{-1} + \text{plim}\, n\boldsymbol{DD}'. \tag{3.6.8}$$

This establishes the asymptotic counterpart of the Gauss–Markov theorem, which says that OLS is BAN in the class of estimators defined by (3.6.1), subject to the assumptions and regularity conditions specified.

However, just as unbiasedness does not require Assumption 2.2.3, so on considering (3.6.4) we see that consistency does not require it, and

$$\boldsymbol{LX} \xrightarrow{\text{pr}} \boldsymbol{I}_k \tag{3.6.9}$$

is sufficient. The existence of conditional bias has interesting repercussions for the asymptotic distribution. If instead of (3.6.4) it is necessary to write

$$\sqrt{n}(\boldsymbol{\beta}_L - \boldsymbol{\beta}) = \sqrt{n}(\boldsymbol{LX} - \boldsymbol{I})\boldsymbol{\beta} + \sqrt{n}\boldsymbol{Lu} \tag{3.6.10}$$

then if the first right-hand side term does not vanish identically it is not asymptotically negligible, assuming convergence to the limit in (3.6.9) at the rate $\sqrt{n}$. However, it is a sum of n terms having zero mean. Under appropriate regularity conditions it could be asymptotically normal, implying that the conditionally biased estimators are CAN, albeit with an asymptotic variance matrix different from $\sigma^2 \boldsymbol{M}_{LL}$. Hence, the claim that OLS is BAN is also dependent on Assumption 2.2.3.

It is a slightly unsatisfactory feature of the analysis that conditional unbiasedness has to be imposed for convenience in obtaining the result, and has no obvious rationale derived from the interpretation of the model. However, so long as no plausible rivals appear to be excluded by it, the proposition that OLS has asymptotic optimality properties is reasonably well-founded.

3.6.2 The Instrumental Variables Class

The analysis of the last section is problematic in another way, in that given the degree of generality permitted, it is difficult to determine how the regularity conditions can be satisfied. The convergence in (3.6.6) does not follow from results given in §3.3 because of the array structure of the sum.[9] However, there is little loss of generality in confining attention to a sub-class of linear estimators for which the CAN property can be established using the tools developed in §3.5. In this spirit, define a class of estimators $\boldsymbol{\beta}_W$ by setting $\boldsymbol{l}_{nt} = \boldsymbol{P}_n \boldsymbol{w}_t$ in (3.6.1), so that

$$\boldsymbol{\beta}_W = \boldsymbol{P}_n \boldsymbol{W}'\boldsymbol{y} \tag{3.6.11}$$

where $\boldsymbol{W}$ is a $n \times m$ matrix of variables with rows $\boldsymbol{w}_t'$, and $\boldsymbol{P}_n$ is a $k \times m$ matrix with $\text{plim}\, n\boldsymbol{P}_n = \boldsymbol{P} < \infty$, having full rank $k \leq m$. That OLS belongs to this class, with $m = k$, is evident from (3.6.3). It is called the *instrumental variables*

[9] Some results on convergence for stochastic arrays are given in §10.5 and §12.4.1. See also Davidson (1994a) for additional details.

(IV) class of linear estimators. These estimators are constructed by familiar averaging procedures analogous to OLS, and allow consideration of a feasible class of alternatives.

With this setup, Assumptions 2.2.1–2.2.3 can be restated in the following form.

Assumption 3.6.1 $E(\boldsymbol{u}|\boldsymbol{X},\boldsymbol{W}) = \mathbf{0}$ a.s. □

Assumption 3.6.2 $E(\boldsymbol{u}\boldsymbol{u}'|\boldsymbol{X},\boldsymbol{W}) = \sigma^2\boldsymbol{I}_n$ a.s. □

Assumption 3.6.3 $\boldsymbol{P}_n\boldsymbol{W}'\boldsymbol{X} = \boldsymbol{I}_k$ a.s. and uniformly in n. □

Given Assumption 2.1.1, Assumption 3.6.1 is satisfied if the $\boldsymbol{w}_t$ are valid conditioning variables, in terms of the categorization suggested in §1.4.3. Assumption 3.6.2 can be justified in the same terms, implying specifically the absence of conditional heteroscedasticity as defined in §2.3, in the context of this wider set of variables. The conditions

$$\operatorname{plim}\frac{1}{n}\sum_{t=1}^{n}\boldsymbol{w}_t\boldsymbol{w}_t' = \boldsymbol{M}_{WW} < \infty, \text{ positive definite} \tag{3.6.12}$$

$$\operatorname{plim} n^{-1}\sum_{t=1}^{n}\boldsymbol{w}_t\boldsymbol{x}_t' = \boldsymbol{M}_{WX} < \infty \tag{3.6.13}$$

can be established by the ordinary weak law of large numbers, subject to the usual regularity conditions. Condition (3.6.12) requires the instruments to vary independently in the limit and rules out 'asymptotically degenerate' choices, such as the $1/t$ case cited in §3.5.1.

Assumption 3.6.3 has a particularly interesting implication. Given (A.3.3), it requires that both $n\boldsymbol{P}_n$ and $n^{-1}\boldsymbol{W}'\boldsymbol{X}$ have full rank k almost surely, uniformly in n, which means, in effect, that $\boldsymbol{M}_{WX}$ must have full rank. This is not a trivial condition, for it implies that $\boldsymbol{X}$ and $\boldsymbol{W}$ need to be correlated. The best way to see what is involved here is to assume the variables in $\boldsymbol{w}_t$ are wholly uncorrelated with those in $\boldsymbol{x}_t$. With distributions not depending on t, the WLLN gives

$$\boldsymbol{M}_{WX} = E(\boldsymbol{w}_t\boldsymbol{x}_t') = E(\boldsymbol{w}_t)E(\boldsymbol{x}_t)' \tag{3.6.14}$$

by Theorem B.7.1, which is a matrix of rank 1, not of rank k, note. This is an extreme case, but it is clear that full rank calls for a full pattern of independent relationships.

Now, subject to the assumption

$$E|\boldsymbol{\lambda}'\boldsymbol{w}_t u_t|^{2+\delta} \le B < \infty \quad \delta > 0,\ \forall\, t,\ \forall \text{ fixed } \boldsymbol{\lambda} \text{ with } \boldsymbol{\lambda}'\boldsymbol{\lambda} = 1 \tag{3.6.15}$$

Theorem 3.3.2 yields

$$\frac{1}{\sqrt{n}}\sum_{t=1}^{n}\boldsymbol{w}_t u_t \xrightarrow{\mathrm{D}} \mathrm{N}(\mathbf{0},\sigma^2\boldsymbol{M}_{WW}) \tag{3.6.16}$$

and, hence, by Cramér's Theorem,

$$\sqrt{n}(\boldsymbol{\beta}_W - \boldsymbol{\beta}) \xrightarrow{\text{D}} \text{N}(\mathbf{0}, \sigma^2 \boldsymbol{P}\boldsymbol{M}_{WW}\boldsymbol{P}'). \tag{3.6.17}$$

We are now in a position to consider the efficiency issue. There are two distinct results involved here, which have independent interest.

Theorem 3.6.1 Given variables $\boldsymbol{w}_t$ satisfying the regularity conditions, the asymptotically efficient choice of $\boldsymbol{P}_n$ is

$$\boldsymbol{P}_n = [\boldsymbol{X}'\boldsymbol{W}(\boldsymbol{W}'\boldsymbol{W})^{-1}\boldsymbol{W}'\boldsymbol{X}]^{-1}\boldsymbol{X}'\boldsymbol{W}(\boldsymbol{W}'\boldsymbol{W})^{-1}. \tag{3.6.18}$$

Proof Given (3.6.17), this follows by Lemma A.7.5 noting that the condition $\boldsymbol{P}_n\boldsymbol{W}'\boldsymbol{X} = \boldsymbol{I}_k$ is satisfied, and

$$n\boldsymbol{P}_n \xrightarrow{\text{pr}} \boldsymbol{P} = (\boldsymbol{M}_{XW}\boldsymbol{M}_{WW}^{-1}\boldsymbol{M}_{WX})^{-1}\boldsymbol{M}_{XW}\boldsymbol{M}_{WW}^{-1} \tag{3.6.19}$$

by (3.6.13), (3.6.12) and Slutsky's Theorem. ∎

A useful spin-off from this finding is that the asymptotic properties of the $\boldsymbol{\beta}_W$ class can be established using the standard asymptotic results, without further specialized assumptions. The optimal choice of $\boldsymbol{P}_n$ is a simple function of sample moments and its convergence to $\boldsymbol{P}$ depends only on $\boldsymbol{w}_t$ and $\boldsymbol{x}_t$ satisfying the regularity conditions, plus the rank condition of Assumption 3.6.3 to ensure the existence of the inverse matrix.

The remaining issue is the choice of $\boldsymbol{w}_t$, and as expected there is the following result.

Theorem 3.6.2 OLS is asymptotically efficient (BAN) in the class $\boldsymbol{\beta}_W$.

Proof Setting $\boldsymbol{W} = \boldsymbol{X}$ yields the result $\boldsymbol{P}_n = (\boldsymbol{X}'\boldsymbol{X})^{-1}$ from (3.6.18) so OLS satisfies the condition of Theorem 3.6.1, and it remains to justify this choice. After substituting from (3.6.19) and simplifying, note that

$$\boldsymbol{P}\boldsymbol{M}_{WW}\boldsymbol{P}' = (\boldsymbol{M}_{XW}\boldsymbol{M}_{WW}^{-1}\boldsymbol{M}_{WX})^{-1} \tag{3.6.20}$$

so that the theorem holds if $(\boldsymbol{M}_{XW}\boldsymbol{M}_{WW}^{-1}\boldsymbol{M}_{WX})^{-1} - \boldsymbol{M}_{XX}^{-1}$ is positive definite for $\boldsymbol{W} \neq \boldsymbol{X}$. In view of Lemma A.7.6, this follows from the positive definiteness of $\boldsymbol{M}_{XX} - \boldsymbol{M}_{XW}\boldsymbol{M}_{WW}^{-1}\boldsymbol{M}_{WX}$. The latter result follows on considering

$$\begin{aligned} \boldsymbol{a}'(\boldsymbol{M}_{XX} - \boldsymbol{M}_{XW}\boldsymbol{M}_{WW}^{-1}\boldsymbol{M}_{WX})\boldsymbol{a} &= \begin{bmatrix} \boldsymbol{a}' & \boldsymbol{b}' \end{bmatrix} \begin{bmatrix} \boldsymbol{M}_{XX} & \boldsymbol{M}_{XW} \\ \boldsymbol{M}_{WX} & \boldsymbol{M}_{WW} \end{bmatrix} \begin{bmatrix} \boldsymbol{a} \\ \boldsymbol{b} \end{bmatrix} \\ &> 0 \end{aligned} \tag{3.6.21}$$

where $\boldsymbol{b} = -\boldsymbol{M}_{WW}^{-1}\boldsymbol{M}_{WX}\boldsymbol{a}$, since the partitioned matrix on the right is a moment matrix, and is positive definite by construction. ∎

Chapter 8 considers the IV class of estimators in much greater detail, and motivates their use. These estimators acquire importance when the assumptions of the regression model fail, such that some or all elements of $\boldsymbol{x}_t$ are not members of the set of valid conditioning variables. Then, OLS is inconsistent, but a consistent IV estimator may be available. The question of efficiency can still be answered with reference to Theorem 3.6.1, but extends to the best choice of instruments $\boldsymbol{w}_t$, drawn from the set satisfying either Assumptions 3.6.1 and 3.6.2, or the generalizations of these appropriate to sampling model C. See §8.2.5 for the details.

Further Reading: Surveys of asymptotic theory relevant to econometrics can be found in Davidson (1994a), White (1984), McCabe and Tremayne (1993), Amemiya (1985), Pötscher and Prucha (1997), Bierens (1994). For more advanced treatments from the statistical literature, see for example Serfling (1980) and Billingsley (1986).

Part II

Dynamic Regression Theory

Chapter 4

Modelling Economic Time Series

4.1 Data Generation Processes

Let $\boldsymbol{x}_t$ denote an $m \times 1$ vector of economic variables generated at time t. Such variables are typically inter-related both contemporaneously and across time. The collection $\{\boldsymbol{x}_t, -\infty < t < \infty\}$ is called a (vector-valued) random sequence. An economic data set is to be thought of as a finite segment, say $\{\boldsymbol{x}_1, \dots, \boldsymbol{x}_n\}$, of this infinite sequence. We entertain the belief that there are economic laws of motion underlying these series that will explain their interactions, and allow us to predict one from another and test theories of behaviour. There are also substantial random, inexplicable components, because of shocks to the system and mistakes by agents, as well as the noise and distortion introduced by the processes of measurement, and aggregation over agents, commodities and time.

We define the data generation process (DGP) for these variables as a statement of the joint probability law under which the sequence is generated, embodying all these influences. Thanks to the fact that time flows always in the same direction, past events can be treated as given in the explanation of current events. The idea of sequential conditioning is therefore fundamental. Assume, temporarily and purely for simplicity of exposition, that the data are continuously distributed. Then, the DGP is completely represented by the conditional density

$$D_t(\boldsymbol{x}_t | \mathcal{X}_{t-1}) \tag{4.1.1}$$

where $\mathcal{X}_{t-1} = \sigma(\boldsymbol{x}_{t-1}, \boldsymbol{x}_{t-2}, \boldsymbol{x}_{t-3}, \dots)$. This notation is a shorthand for the σ-field representing knowledge of the past history of the system. Technically, $\mathcal{X}_t$ is defined as the smallest σ-field of events with respect to which the random variables $\boldsymbol{x}_{t-j}$ are measurable for all $j \geq 0$.[1] Note how the density D_t is allowed to depend on time, because the data are not assumed to be stationary (see §4.4) and in

[1] See §B.10 for a summary of the relevant theory.

particular, allowance must be made for features such as seasonal variations, and changes in technology, regulatory regime, and so forth.

4.1.1 DGPs and Models

A dynamic econometric model is a family of functions of the data, of relatively simple form, devised by an investigator, which are intended to mimic aspects of the DGP, either D_t itself or functions derived from D_t such as moments. Formally, a model is a family of functions

$$\{M(\boldsymbol{x}_t, \boldsymbol{x}_{t-1}, \boldsymbol{x}_{t-2}, \ldots, \boldsymbol{d}_t; \boldsymbol{\psi}), \boldsymbol{\psi} \in \Psi\}, \quad \Psi \subseteq \mathbb{R}^p. \tag{4.1.2}$$

In particular, let the notation M_D denote a model of the complete DGP. Models of the conditional moments $E(\boldsymbol{x}_t|\mathcal{X}_{t-1})$ and $\mathrm{Var}(\boldsymbol{x}_t|\mathcal{X}_{t-1})$, which can be represented by M_E and M_V respectively, are the other leading cases. Models depend on a finite collection of parameters, p in number, denoted $\boldsymbol{\psi}$. These are calibrating constants that are common to every t in the sequence. Their values are not specified in the statement of a model, and Ψ denotes the set of admissible parameter values, the *parameter space.* The various members of the family are called the model elements. The vector $\boldsymbol{d}_t$ represents variables, treated as non-stochastic, which are intended to capture the changes in the DGP over time.

The relationship between the DGP and the model is a difficult issue. Since the main business of econometricians is estimating parameters, it may appear surprising that the DGP is not represented as depending on Ψ. However, parameterization is always a feature of the model, not explicitly of the DGP. A point to be emphasized in the following analysis is that many different parameterizations of the DGP are possible, and may be of interest for different purposes. The *axiom of correct specification* (compare §1.4) is the assumption that there exists a model element that is identical to the corresponding function of the DGP. Thus, M_D is correctly specified if there exists $\boldsymbol{\psi}_0 \in \Psi$ such that

$$M_D(\boldsymbol{x}_t, \boldsymbol{x}_{t-1}, \boldsymbol{x}_{t-2}, \ldots, \boldsymbol{d}_t; \boldsymbol{\psi}_0) = D_t(\boldsymbol{x}_t|\mathcal{X}_{t-1}). \tag{4.1.3}$$

Similarly, M_E and M_V are correct if the conditions

$$M_E(\boldsymbol{x}_t, \boldsymbol{x}_{t-1}, \boldsymbol{x}_{t-2}, \ldots, \boldsymbol{d}_t; \boldsymbol{\psi}_0) = \int \boldsymbol{x} D_t(\boldsymbol{x}|\mathcal{X}_{t-1}) d\boldsymbol{x} \tag{4.1.4}$$

and

$$\begin{aligned} M_V(\boldsymbol{x}_t, \boldsymbol{x}_{t-1}, \boldsymbol{x}_{t-2}, \ldots, \boldsymbol{d}_t; \boldsymbol{\psi}_0) &= \int \boldsymbol{x}\boldsymbol{x}' D_t(\boldsymbol{x}|\mathcal{X}_{t-1}) d\boldsymbol{x} \\ &\quad - \int \boldsymbol{x} D_t(\boldsymbol{x}|\mathcal{X}_{t-1}) d\boldsymbol{x} \int \boldsymbol{x}' D_t(\boldsymbol{x}|\mathcal{X}_{t-1}) d\boldsymbol{x} \end{aligned} \tag{4.1.5}$$

hold, respectively. In general, correct specification in practical modelling exercises is an implausible assumption. Models always incorporate features, linearity or Gaussianity for example, which are motivated by the need for analytical tractability rather than the quest for realism. The models studied in this chapter can be used to generate artificial series on the computer that have features in common with observed economic series but, obviously, the actual series were not generated in precisely this way. However, it is often convenient to invoke the axiom of correct specification as an aid to structuring and interpreting the statistical analysis, even though we do not believe it literally.

The hope is, of course, that (4.1.3), or (4.1.4)+(4.1.5), are true in essentials, or to an adequate approximation for a particular purpose such as testing theories, policy simulation, or forecasting. Here the term 'adequate' may be interpreted in terms of the costs of improving the model (collecting more data, say) as well as the achievement of the research goals that have been specified (e.g., useful forecasts). These adequacy conditions may well be weaker than (4.1.3) or (4.1.4)+(4.1.5). As we show in Chapters 7 and 12, there exists a battery of specification tests that allow us to check whether a model fulfils the criteria set. These tests have the important property that it is not necessary to know the form of D_t to make valid use of them, even though that knowledge could indicate which ones were the most important. Certain model features that are routinely detectable are incompatible with the status of DGP. Models that survive such trials should accordingly be more useful in practice than those that do not.

4.1.2 Nonstochastic Time Variation

Allowing $D_t(\boldsymbol{x}_t|\mathcal{X}_{t-1})$ to depend on t other than through its stochastic arguments is an essential feature of any time series model, and such effects are sometimes modelled by variations in parameters; in this spirit, the notation $\boldsymbol{\psi}_t$ might be introduced. However, parameters that vary hardly deserve the name, and the same effect is achieved by defining the vector $\boldsymbol{d}_t$ in (4.1.2), which could be used to define parametric functions $\boldsymbol{\psi}_t = \boldsymbol{f}(\boldsymbol{\psi}, \boldsymbol{d}_t)$ if desired. The $\boldsymbol{d}_t$ variables differ from elements of $\boldsymbol{x}_t$ in being determined outside the economic system. In the terminology to be introduced in §4.5, they are strongly exogenous with respect to the generation of $\boldsymbol{x}_t$. The possibility of a stochastic generation process need not be excluded, but in practical modelling exercises they are more likely to be *dummy variables*, constructed by the investigator to represent a particular source of variation, rather than measured directly. Among the possibilities are: mathematical *trend functions*, such as t^k for $k \neq 0$, which could represent demographic growth or technical progress; *seasonal dummies*, which cycle through a fixed sequence of values to capture seasonal effects; and *intervention dummies*, which are typically set equal to 1 over certain historical periods, and 0 otherwise, representing particular policy regimes, for example.

4.1.3 General Distributions

While continuous distributions have been assumed to simplify the exposition, and D_t referred to as a density, we might also wish to consider cases where the distribution of the variables is either discrete or mixed continuous/discrete. The term 'mixed' has two senses here, that the distributions of particular elements of $\boldsymbol{x}_t$ may have points of positive marginal probability as well as being continuous in other regions, and that the marginal distributions of the elements may be of different types, continuous, discrete and mixed continuous-discrete as the case may be. Discrete distributions could be used to model choices over a finite set of alternatives (e.g. policy regimes) or counts (e.g. numbers of strikes, takeovers, bankruptcies, etc. in a period). A mixed discrete-continuous distribution can arise when observations are censored over a certain range. In the well-known Tobit model for example (see §11.2.5) a zero is reported if a continuously distributed 'latent' variable is negative, and so arises with positive probability.

Such distributions can in principle be included in our framework, by defining $D_t(\cdot|\mathcal{X}_{t-1})$ to represent either a density or a probability, depending on the point of evaluation. It can also be, in effect, a density with respect to some elements of the argument, and a probability function for others. How such distributions might be represented is explained in §B.5 and §B.6. In practice, however, extensions of this sort in time series analysis are unusual. The construction of such models is difficult, and in any case the nature of aggregate economic data means that continuous distributions are appropriate in most cases. Assuming $D_t(\cdot|\mathcal{X}_{t-1})$ to be a joint density function will rarely do violence to the facts, and is often convenient from the expositional point of view.

4.2 The VAR(1) Process

The remainder of this chapter surveys important properties and concepts associated with DGPs, and at the same time develops some examples that are, explicitly, models. In other words, they are far too simple in structure to be confused with real DGPs. The concepts of DGP and model are liable to be used interchangeably in the literature, which can be confusing. The examples aim to provide insight into the way models are often constructed and used in practice, but it remains for the reader to keep clearly in his/her mind the distinctions drawn in §4.1.1.

The leading example is a simple representation of the conditional mean of $\boldsymbol{x}_t$ that gives rise to the *first-order vector autoregressive process*, otherwise VAR(1). Suppose

$$E(\boldsymbol{x}_t|\mathcal{X}_{t-1}) = \boldsymbol{\delta}_t + \boldsymbol{\Lambda}\boldsymbol{x}_{t-1} \tag{4.2.1}$$

where $\boldsymbol{\delta}_t$ is a nonstochastic m-vector, and $\boldsymbol{\Lambda}$ an $m \times m$ matrix of coefficients. Define

$$\boldsymbol{\varepsilon}_t = \boldsymbol{x}_t - \boldsymbol{\delta}_t - \boldsymbol{\Lambda}\boldsymbol{x}_{t-1} \tag{4.2.2}$$

which is the vector of *mean innovations.* Note that

$$E(\boldsymbol{\varepsilon}_t|\mathcal{X}_{t-1}) = \mathbf{0} \tag{4.2.3}$$

by construction, and hence $E(\boldsymbol{\varepsilon}_t) = \mathbf{0}$ by the LIE. A more usual representation of the VAR(1) is

$$\boldsymbol{x}_t = \boldsymbol{\delta}_t + \boldsymbol{\Lambda}\boldsymbol{x}_{t-1} + \boldsymbol{\varepsilon}_t. \tag{4.2.4}$$

By a further application of the LIE,

$$E(\boldsymbol{\varepsilon}_t \boldsymbol{x}'_{t-j}) = E(E(\boldsymbol{\varepsilon}_t|\mathcal{X}_{t-1})\boldsymbol{x}'_{t-j}) = \mathbf{0}, \text{ all } j > 0. \tag{4.2.5}$$

By construction, the innovations are uncorrelated with all lagged variables, including their own lags. Since $\boldsymbol{\varepsilon}_{t-j} = \boldsymbol{x}_{t-j} - \boldsymbol{\delta}_t - \boldsymbol{\Lambda}\boldsymbol{x}_{t-j-1}$ it is easily shown that $E(\boldsymbol{\varepsilon}_t\boldsymbol{\varepsilon}'_{t-j}) = \mathbf{0}$.

4.2.1 The Gaussian DGP

A DGP is completely specified by (4.2.4) if a conditional distribution is assigned to $\boldsymbol{\varepsilon}_t$. In most applications the simplest possible assumptions are made, in particular that

$$E(\boldsymbol{\varepsilon}_t\boldsymbol{\varepsilon}'_t|\mathcal{X}_{t-1}) = \boldsymbol{\Omega} \tag{4.2.6}$$

where $\boldsymbol{\Omega}$ is a constant matrix, hence equal to the unconditional variance matrix of $\boldsymbol{\varepsilon}_t$. There are no compelling theoretical grounds to support this assumption, but any other approach is technically difficult to implement. Moreover, if the primary goal is to predict the level of $\boldsymbol{x}_t$ and hence estimate the parameters of (4.2.1), valid (albeit less than optimal) statistical inference procedures are available for this purpose, even if the conditional variance is misspecified. See §7.3 for further details of these results, and also §5.6 to see what may be involved in relaxing assumption (4.2.6).

It is also usual to assume that the conditional distribution of $\boldsymbol{\varepsilon}_t|\mathcal{X}_{t-1}$ is Gaussian, so that from (C.1.10) the conditional density function takes the form

$$D_t(\boldsymbol{x}_t|\mathcal{X}_{t-1}) = (2\pi)^{-m/2}|\boldsymbol{\Omega}|^{-1/2} \times \exp\left\{-\tfrac{1}{2}(\boldsymbol{x}_t - \boldsymbol{\delta}_t - \boldsymbol{\Lambda}\boldsymbol{x}_{t-1})'\boldsymbol{\Omega}^{-1}(\boldsymbol{x}_t - \boldsymbol{\delta}_t - \boldsymbol{\Lambda}\boldsymbol{x}_{t-1})\right\}. \tag{4.2.7}$$

When $\boldsymbol{\varepsilon}_t$ is Gaussian with fixed mean and variance, and serially uncorrelated, it is also identically and independently distributed. The special feature of the Gaussian distribution is that equations (4.2.1) and (4.2.6) completely describe the distribution.

The VAR(1) is a convenient paradigm case to illustrate many of the key concepts in econometric modelling and estimation. The main simplification is the exclusion of higher order lags, but it is shown in §4.3.4 how extended lag structures can be cast in the VAR(1) form. Also excluded is the possibility of *moving average* errors, as described in §5.2 below. However, moving average models can be recast as AR models of infinite order, and can be approximated in turn by AR models of finite order. The framework therefore allows more generality than may be apparent. The assumption of identically distributed Gaussian innovations is more restrictive than needed for the subsequent statistical analysis of estimation, but is made for clarity and tractability. We shall be able to work through explicit examples using well-known formulae for factorizing the Gaussian density.

4.2.2 The Structural Form

Except in special cases, conditional mean equations do not *directly* represent the behavioural and technical relationships specified by economic theory. These may be both contemporaneous and dynamic in character. They might be written either in the form

$$\boldsymbol{B}E(\boldsymbol{x}_t|\mathcal{X}_{t-1}) = \boldsymbol{\Gamma}\boldsymbol{d}_t + \boldsymbol{C}\boldsymbol{x}_{t-1} \tag{4.2.8}$$

where $|\boldsymbol{B}| \neq 0$, for direct comparison with (4.2.1), or equivalently as

$$\boldsymbol{B}\boldsymbol{x}_t = \boldsymbol{\Gamma}\boldsymbol{d}_t + \boldsymbol{C}\boldsymbol{x}_{t-1} + \boldsymbol{u}_t \tag{4.2.9}$$

where $E(\boldsymbol{u}_t|\mathcal{X}_{t-1}) = \boldsymbol{0}$. This is called the *structural form* of the model, for contrast with the *reduced form*, which in this case is the conditional mean equation in (4.2.1). The vector $\boldsymbol{d}_t$ consists of dummy variables, one of which is equal to 1 in all periods, representing the intercept of the linear relations, and the others might include trends and seasonals, as detailed in §4.1.2. Defining $E(\boldsymbol{u}_t\boldsymbol{u}_t'|\mathcal{X}_{t-1}) = \boldsymbol{\Sigma}$ to complete the set of structural parameters, the relations between the structural and reduced form parameters are given by

$$\boldsymbol{\Lambda} = \boldsymbol{B}^{-1}\boldsymbol{C}, \quad \boldsymbol{\delta}_t = \boldsymbol{B}^{-1}\boldsymbol{\Gamma}\boldsymbol{d}_t, \quad \boldsymbol{\varepsilon}_t = \boldsymbol{B}^{-1}\boldsymbol{u}_t, \quad \boldsymbol{\Omega} = \boldsymbol{B}^{-1}\boldsymbol{\Sigma}(\boldsymbol{B}')^{-1} \tag{4.2.10}$$

Note how (4.2.9) defines an infinite set of alternative parameterizations for this model. Many different structures corresponding to different matrices $\boldsymbol{B}$ can correspond to the same VAR equation. However, there may be restrictions on $\boldsymbol{B}$, $\boldsymbol{C}$, $\boldsymbol{\Gamma}$, and $\boldsymbol{\Sigma}$ that allow us to distinguish one structure from another, such as the omission of certain variables from certain equations (zero restrictions). Dependence on a small number of 'deep parameters' $\boldsymbol{\psi}$ can be shown by writing $\boldsymbol{B}(\boldsymbol{\psi})$, $\boldsymbol{C}(\boldsymbol{\psi})$, $\boldsymbol{\Gamma}(\boldsymbol{\psi})$, $\boldsymbol{\Sigma}(\boldsymbol{\psi})$, and hence also $\boldsymbol{\Lambda}(\boldsymbol{\psi})$, $\boldsymbol{\delta}_t(\boldsymbol{\psi})$ and $\boldsymbol{\Omega}(\boldsymbol{\psi})$. This issue is explored further in §8.3 under the heading of *identification*.

4.2.3 Example: A Simple Keynesian Model

To illustrate these concepts consider the very well-known, very simplified, model of an economy, commonly known as the Haavelmo model (Haavelmo 1943, 1947). Let C denote aggregate real consumption, Y real national income, and I real investment. Then the equation

$$Y = C + I \tag{4.2.11}$$

corresponds to the equilibrium condition, 'savings = investment', and

$$C = f(Y) \tag{4.2.12}$$

is the Keynesian consumption function. Assume I to be generated autonomously with respect to the consumption decision. Consider the problem of constructing a statistical model of the economy, using the theoretical model (4.2.11) +(4.2.12) as a foundation. The three main components of the statistical model can be specified as follows.

1. Equation (4.2.11) holds as a measurement identity in the national accounts, and its empirical counterpart is

$$Y_t \equiv C_t + I_t. \tag{4.2.13}$$

The assumption of equilibrium is therefore crucial, since if investment and planned savings are different, the statistical assumptions are invalid.

2. Assume linearity of the consumption function and add a disturbance to get the empirical counterpart

$$C_t = \alpha + \beta Y_t + u_{1t}. \tag{4.2.14}$$

For simplicity the linear functional form is treated as correct here, not an approximation as in §1.4.1.

3. In the absence of a more complete theory, postulate an autonomous investment process exhibiting some inertia as well as a response to autonomous shocks,

$$I_t = \delta + \gamma I_{t-1} + u_{2t}. \tag{4.2.15}$$

For the moment little will be said about the properties of u_{1t} and u_{2t} except to assume they are innovations, unpredictable from information dated $t-1$ and earlier. There are some important issues here that we return to in §8.1.

Eliminating the identity by substitution of (4.2.13) into (4.2.14) yields

$$Y_t(1-\beta) = \alpha + I_t + u_{1t}. \tag{4.2.16}$$

Putting this equation together with (4.2.15), the model can be written down in the form of (4.2.9) with

$$\boldsymbol{x}_t = \begin{bmatrix} Y_t \\ I_t \end{bmatrix}, \quad \boldsymbol{u}_t = \begin{bmatrix} u_{1t} \\ u_{2t} \end{bmatrix}, \quad d_t = 1 \tag{4.2.17}$$

$$\boldsymbol{B} = \begin{bmatrix} 1-\beta & -1 \\ 0 & 1 \end{bmatrix}, \quad \boldsymbol{C} = \begin{bmatrix} 0 & 0 \\ 0 & \gamma \end{bmatrix}, \quad \boldsymbol{\Gamma} = \begin{bmatrix} \alpha \\ \delta \end{bmatrix}. \tag{4.2.18}$$

The VAR form in (4.2.4) is evidently given by

$$\boldsymbol{\delta}_t = \begin{bmatrix} (\alpha+\delta)/(1-\beta) \\ \delta \end{bmatrix}, \quad \boldsymbol{\Lambda} = \begin{bmatrix} 0 & \gamma/(1-\beta) \\ 0 & \gamma \end{bmatrix} \tag{4.2.19}$$

($\boldsymbol{\delta}_t$ not depending on t in this instance) and

$$\boldsymbol{\varepsilon}_t = \begin{bmatrix} (u_{1t}+u_{2t})/(1-\beta) \\ u_{2t} \end{bmatrix}. \tag{4.2.20}$$

4.3 Distribution of the VAR Process

The model specifies the conditional distribution of $\boldsymbol{x}_t|\mathcal{X}_{t-1}$. An important step in the analysis is to determine from this the distribution of the sequence $\{\boldsymbol{x}_t\}$ as a whole, for example, the ordinary (unconditional) moments $E(\boldsymbol{x}_t)$ and $\text{Var}(\boldsymbol{x}_t)$, assuming these exist. Be careful to understand what these things are. Suppose for the sake of argument that the process starts at time $t=0$. If $E(\boldsymbol{x}_t|\mathcal{X}_{t-1})$ is the expected value of $\boldsymbol{x}_t$ in this realization of the process, given the history from time 0 to $t-1$, then $E(\boldsymbol{x}_t)$ is the expectation across realizations. Given fixed

$t^* > 0$, imagine generating the distribution of $\boldsymbol{x}_{t*}$ experimentally, by repeatedly re-starting the process at $t = 0$ (with $\boldsymbol{x}_0$ fixed) letting it run, and building up the frequency distribution of its positions at time t^*. By a slightly greater stretch of the imagination we could let $\boldsymbol{x}_t$ be started at time $t = -\infty$ (the 'remote past') instead of $t = 0$ for each run. In this case care is needed, since $E(\boldsymbol{x}_t)$ and/or $\text{Var}(\boldsymbol{x}_t)$ might be continually increasing with t where t, although finite, is now infinitely far from the starting point.

4.3.1 Stability Conditions

One solution to the problem is to manipulate the expected value formulae by repeated substitution. Consider $E(\boldsymbol{x}_t)$ first:

$$\begin{aligned} E(\boldsymbol{x}_t) &= \boldsymbol{\delta}_t + \boldsymbol{\Lambda} E(\boldsymbol{x}_{t-1}) \\ &= \boldsymbol{\delta}_t + \boldsymbol{\Lambda}\boldsymbol{\delta}_{t-1} + \boldsymbol{\Lambda}^2 E(\boldsymbol{x}_{t-2}) \\ &= \cdots \\ &= \sum_{j=0}^{n-1} \boldsymbol{\Lambda}^j \boldsymbol{\delta}_{t-j} + \boldsymbol{\Lambda}^n E(\boldsymbol{x}_{t-n}). \end{aligned} \tag{4.3.1}$$

Clearly, the value of this sum depends on the behaviour of $\boldsymbol{\Lambda}^n$ as n increases, and to determine this calls for some standard results in matrix theory. Let $\mu_1, \ldots, \mu_m$ be the eigenvalues of $\boldsymbol{\Lambda}$, the solutions to the characteristic equation $|\boldsymbol{\Lambda} - \mu \boldsymbol{I}_m| = 0$ (see §A.5 for details). Then $\boldsymbol{\Lambda}$ can be decomposed as

$$\boldsymbol{\Lambda} = \boldsymbol{Q}\boldsymbol{M}\boldsymbol{Q}^{-1} \tag{4.3.2}$$

where $\boldsymbol{M}$ is the diagonal matrix having the eigenvalues on the diagonal, if these are all distinct. In this case it is easy to see that $\boldsymbol{\Lambda}^n = \boldsymbol{Q}\boldsymbol{M}^n\boldsymbol{Q}^{-1}$, where $\boldsymbol{M}^n = \text{diag}\{\mu_1^n, \ldots, \mu_m^n\}$. Hence if $|\mu_i| < 1$ for $i = 1, \ldots, m$, $\boldsymbol{\Lambda}^n \to 0$ as $n \to \infty$. Even if $\boldsymbol{M}$ is not diagonal but has the Jordan canonical form, it is easy to show that the same result applies. On the other hand if $|\mu_i| \geq 1$ for any i, then one or more elements of $\boldsymbol{\Lambda}^n$ are not vanishing, and may be tending to ∞. The μ_i may be complex numbers, and they must lie inside the unit circle for convergence to zero to occur. These are known as the stability conditions of the system.

4.3.2 The Mean and Variance

Subject to convergence of $\boldsymbol{\Lambda}^n$, letting $n \to \infty$ gives

$$E(\boldsymbol{x}_t) = \boldsymbol{\mu}_t = \sum_{j=0}^{\infty} \boldsymbol{\Lambda}^j \boldsymbol{\delta}_{t-j}. \tag{4.3.3}$$

If $\boldsymbol{\delta}_t = \boldsymbol{\delta}$, not dependent on t, the unconditional mean of $\boldsymbol{x}_t$ is likewise a constant, say $\boldsymbol{\mu}_x$. This has a closed form solution, for evidently $\boldsymbol{\Lambda}\boldsymbol{\mu}_x = \boldsymbol{\Lambda}\boldsymbol{\delta} + \boldsymbol{\Lambda}\boldsymbol{\delta}^2 + \cdots = \boldsymbol{\mu}_x - \boldsymbol{\delta}$ and hence

$$\boldsymbol{\mu}_x = (\boldsymbol{I} - \boldsymbol{\Lambda})^{-1}\boldsymbol{\delta}. \tag{4.3.4}$$

Consider the variance similarly. In mean deviation form the process is

$$\boldsymbol{x}_t - \boldsymbol{\mu}_t = \boldsymbol{\Lambda}(\boldsymbol{x}_{t-1} - \boldsymbol{\mu}_{t-1}) + \boldsymbol{\varepsilon}_t, \tag{4.3.5}$$

noting that $\boldsymbol{\delta}_t = \boldsymbol{\mu}_t - \boldsymbol{\Lambda}\boldsymbol{\mu}_{t-1}$. For simplicity of notation, assume that $\boldsymbol{x}_t$ is expressed in mean deviation form and hence put $\boldsymbol{\delta}_t = \mathbf{0}$ for all t. Substituting repeatedly for lagged $\boldsymbol{x}$ gives

$$\boldsymbol{x}_t = \boldsymbol{\varepsilon}_t + \boldsymbol{\Lambda}\boldsymbol{\varepsilon}_{t-1} + \boldsymbol{\Lambda}^2\boldsymbol{\varepsilon}_{t-2} + \cdots + \boldsymbol{\Lambda}^{n-1}\boldsymbol{\varepsilon}_{t-n+1} + \boldsymbol{\Lambda}^n\boldsymbol{x}_{t-n} \tag{4.3.6}$$

and assuming stability the final term can be neglected as $n \to \infty$. Since

$$E(\boldsymbol{\varepsilon}_{t-j}\boldsymbol{\varepsilon}'_{t-k}) = \begin{cases} \boldsymbol{\Omega}, & j = k \\ \mathbf{0}, & j \neq k \end{cases} \tag{4.3.7}$$

it follows that

$$\begin{aligned} E(\boldsymbol{x}_t\boldsymbol{x}'_t) &= E(\boldsymbol{\varepsilon}_t + \boldsymbol{\Lambda}\boldsymbol{\varepsilon}_{t-1} + \boldsymbol{\Lambda}^2\boldsymbol{\varepsilon}_{t-2} + \cdots)(\boldsymbol{\varepsilon}_t + \boldsymbol{\Lambda}\boldsymbol{\varepsilon}_{t-1} + \boldsymbol{\Lambda}^2\boldsymbol{\varepsilon}_{t-2} + \cdots)' \\ &= \sum_{j=0}^{\infty} \boldsymbol{\Lambda}^j\boldsymbol{\Omega}(\boldsymbol{\Lambda}')^j = \boldsymbol{\Omega}_{\boldsymbol{x}} \end{aligned} \tag{4.3.8}$$

(say). To write down the closed form of this solution requires the Vec and Kronecker product notation (see §A.10). Let

$$\boldsymbol{\Omega}_{\boldsymbol{x}} = E(\boldsymbol{\Lambda}\boldsymbol{x}_{t-1} + \boldsymbol{\varepsilon}_t)(\boldsymbol{\Lambda}\boldsymbol{x}_{t-1} + \boldsymbol{\varepsilon}_t)' = \boldsymbol{\Lambda}\boldsymbol{\Omega}_{\boldsymbol{x}}\boldsymbol{\Lambda}' + \boldsymbol{\Omega}. \tag{4.3.9}$$

The second equality used the fact that $E(\boldsymbol{x}_t\boldsymbol{x}'_t) = E(\boldsymbol{x}_{t-1}\boldsymbol{x}'_{t-1})$, noting that (4.3.8) does not depend on t, and also used $E(\boldsymbol{x}_{t-1}\boldsymbol{\varepsilon}'_t) = \mathbf{0}$. Using (A.10.6) yields the form

$$\operatorname{Vec}\boldsymbol{\Omega}_{\boldsymbol{x}} = (\boldsymbol{I}_{m^2} - \boldsymbol{\Lambda}\otimes\boldsymbol{\Lambda})^{-1}\operatorname{Vec}\boldsymbol{\Omega} \quad (m^2 \times 1) \tag{4.3.10}$$

although note that some of the elements of this vector are repeated, due to symmetry of $\boldsymbol{\Omega}_{\boldsymbol{x}}$.

Finally, consider the sequence of autocovariances. For each $j > 0$, since $E(\boldsymbol{x}_{t-j}\boldsymbol{\varepsilon}'_{t-k}) = 0$ for $k < j$,

$$\begin{aligned} E(\boldsymbol{x}_t\boldsymbol{x}'_{t-j}) &= E[(\boldsymbol{\varepsilon}_t + \boldsymbol{\Lambda}\boldsymbol{\varepsilon}_{t-1} + \boldsymbol{\Lambda}^2\boldsymbol{\varepsilon}_{t-2} + \cdots + \boldsymbol{\Lambda}^{j-1}\boldsymbol{\varepsilon}_{t-j+1} + \boldsymbol{\Lambda}^j\boldsymbol{x}_{t-j})\boldsymbol{x}'_{t-j}] \\ &= \boldsymbol{\Lambda}^j\boldsymbol{\Omega}_{\boldsymbol{x}}. \end{aligned} \tag{4.3.11}$$

4.3.3 The Sample Density

Subject to the stability restrictions, $\operatorname{Var}(\boldsymbol{x}_t)$ has been shown not to depend on t and $\operatorname{Cov}(\boldsymbol{x}_t, \boldsymbol{x}'_{t-j})$ to depend only on j, at least when t is infinitely far from the starting point of the sequence. However, more than this can be deduced. According to Theorem C.1.1, finite linear combinations of Gaussian variables are also Gaussian. Since $\boldsymbol{\Lambda}^n \to \mathbf{0}$, (4.3.6) shows that $\boldsymbol{x}_t$ is arbitrarily well approximated by a finite linear combination of the $\boldsymbol{\varepsilon}_{t-j}$, $j > 0$. When $\boldsymbol{\varepsilon}_t \sim \mathrm{N}(\mathbf{0}, \boldsymbol{\Omega})$, which follows by the assumption in (4.2.7) since the conditional distribution of $\boldsymbol{\varepsilon}_t|\mathcal{X}_{t-1}$ is independent of the conditioning variables, it follows that $\boldsymbol{x}_t \sim \mathrm{N}(\boldsymbol{\mu}_t, \boldsymbol{\Omega}_x)$, and has the *marginal* density

$$D(\boldsymbol{x}_t) = (2\pi)^{-m/2}|\boldsymbol{\Omega}_x|^{-1/2}\exp\left\{-\tfrac{1}{2}(\boldsymbol{x}_t - \boldsymbol{\mu}_t)'\boldsymbol{\Omega}_x^{-1}(\boldsymbol{x}_t - \boldsymbol{\mu}_t)\right\}. \qquad (4.3.12)$$

The joint density of a sample $\boldsymbol{x}_1, \ldots, \boldsymbol{x}_n$ can therefore be constructed by applying the rules for conditional densities sequentially:

$$\begin{aligned} D(\boldsymbol{x}_1, \ldots, \boldsymbol{x}_n) &= D(\boldsymbol{x}_1)D(\boldsymbol{x}_2, \ldots, \boldsymbol{x}_n|\boldsymbol{x}_1) \\ &= D(\boldsymbol{x}_1)D(\boldsymbol{x}_2|\boldsymbol{x}_1)D(\boldsymbol{x}_3, \ldots, \boldsymbol{x}_n|\boldsymbol{x}_1, \boldsymbol{x}_2) \\ &= \cdots \\ &= D(\boldsymbol{x}_1)\prod_{t=2}^{n} D(\boldsymbol{x}_t|\boldsymbol{x}_1, \ldots, \boldsymbol{x}_{t-1}). \end{aligned} \qquad (4.3.13)$$

For the VAR(1) the $n-1$ factors in the final member[2] of (4.3.13) are just the conditional densities already specified.

4.3.4 Higher Order Dynamics

It is not difficult, though notationally rather cumbersome, to obtain generalizations of these results for the VAR(p) process for $p > 1$. Consider (assuming mean deviation form for simplicity)

$$\boldsymbol{x}_t = \boldsymbol{\Lambda}_1\boldsymbol{x}_{t-1} + \boldsymbol{\Lambda}_2\boldsymbol{x}_{t-2} + \cdots + \boldsymbol{\Lambda}_p\boldsymbol{x}_{t-p} + \boldsymbol{\varepsilon}_t. \qquad (4.3.14)$$

For most purposes the generalization of the previous results is straightforward. Formulae for the unconditional mean and variance could be obtained after tedious derivation, but these would not be very enlightening in themselves. However, one thing we do need to know is how to generalize the condition $\boldsymbol{\Lambda}^n \to \mathbf{0}$.

A neat solution to this problem is to write the equations in *companion form.* It can be verified that

$$\begin{bmatrix} \boldsymbol{x}_t \\ \boldsymbol{x}_{t-1} \\ \boldsymbol{x}_{t-2} \\ \vdots \\ \boldsymbol{x}_{t-p} \end{bmatrix} = \begin{bmatrix} \boldsymbol{\Lambda}_1 & \boldsymbol{\Lambda}_2 & \cdots & \boldsymbol{\Lambda}_p & \mathbf{0} \\ \boldsymbol{I}_m & \mathbf{0} & \cdots & \mathbf{0} & \mathbf{0} \\ \mathbf{0} & \boldsymbol{I}_m & \cdots & \mathbf{0} & \mathbf{0} \\ \vdots & \vdots & \ddots & \vdots & \vdots \\ \mathbf{0} & \mathbf{0} & \cdots & \boldsymbol{I}_m & \mathbf{0} \end{bmatrix} \begin{bmatrix} \boldsymbol{x}_{t-l} \\ \boldsymbol{x}_{t-2} \\ \vdots \\ \boldsymbol{x}_{t-p} \\ \boldsymbol{x}_{t-p-1} \end{bmatrix} + \begin{bmatrix} \boldsymbol{\varepsilon}_t \\ \mathbf{0} \\ \mathbf{0} \\ \vdots \\ \mathbf{0} \end{bmatrix} \qquad (4.3.15)$$

which may be written more compactly as

$$\boldsymbol{x}_t^* = \boldsymbol{\Lambda}^*\boldsymbol{x}_{t-1}^* + \boldsymbol{\varepsilon}_t^*. \quad (m(p+1) \times 1) \qquad (4.3.16)$$

In other words, a pth-order process can be expressed as a first-order process of higher dimension. If $\boldsymbol{x}_t$ is a process with fixed finite variance and an autocovariance sequence that converges to zero at an exponential rate as in (4.3.11), then $\boldsymbol{x}_t^*$ must

[2] The 'members' of an equation are the links in the chain of equalities or inequalities. Don't confuse with 'terms' which is used in the sense of the components of a sum or series.

share these properties. This is ensured by having the $m(p+1)$ eigenvalues of $\mathbf{\Lambda}^*$ lie inside the unit circle. The determinant defining the characteristic equation is partitioned as

$$|\mathbf{\Lambda}^* - \mu \boldsymbol{I}_{m(p+1)}| = \begin{vmatrix} \mathbf{\Lambda}_1 - \mu \boldsymbol{I}_m & \mathbf{\Lambda}_2 & \cdots & \mathbf{\Lambda}_p & \mathbf{0} \\ \boldsymbol{I}_m & -\mu \boldsymbol{I}_m & \cdots & \mathbf{0} & \mathbf{0} \\ \mathbf{0} & \boldsymbol{I}_m & \ddots & \vdots & \vdots \\ \vdots & \vdots & \ddots & -\mu \boldsymbol{I}_m & \mathbf{0} \\ \mathbf{0} & \mathbf{0} & \cdots & \boldsymbol{I}_m & -\mu \boldsymbol{I}_m \end{vmatrix} \tag{4.3.17}$$

where the $(p+1)^2$ blocks are each of dimension $m \times m$. The right-hand side can be simplified by applying the partitioned determinant formula in (A.2.12) recursively. The partitioning adopted is by the last (right-most) column block and last row block of $|\mathbf{\Lambda}^* - \mu \boldsymbol{I}|$, yielding

$$|\mathbf{\Lambda}^* - \mu \boldsymbol{I}_{m(p+1)}| = (-\mu)^m \begin{vmatrix} \mathbf{\Lambda}_1 - \mu \boldsymbol{I}_m & \mathbf{\Lambda}_2 & \cdots & \mathbf{\Lambda}_p \\ \boldsymbol{I}_m & -\mu \boldsymbol{I} & \cdots & \mathbf{0} \\ \mathbf{0} & \boldsymbol{I}_m & \ddots & \vdots \\ \vdots & \vdots & \ddots & -\mu \boldsymbol{I}_m \end{vmatrix} \quad (p^2 \text{ blocks}). \tag{4.3.18}$$

Repeating the same substitution p times gives

$$\begin{aligned} &|\mathbf{\Lambda}^* - \mu \boldsymbol{I}_{m(p+1)}| \\ &= (-\mu)^{2m} \begin{vmatrix} \mathbf{\Lambda}_1 - \mu \boldsymbol{I}_m & \mathbf{\Lambda}_2 & \cdots & \mathbf{\Lambda}_{p-1} + \mu^{-1}\mathbf{\Lambda}_p \\ \boldsymbol{I}_m & -\mu \boldsymbol{I}_m & \cdots & \mathbf{0} \\ \mathbf{0} & \boldsymbol{I}_m & \ddots & \vdots \\ \vdots & \vdots & \ddots & -\mu \boldsymbol{I}_m \end{vmatrix} \quad ((p-1)^2 \text{blocks}) \\ &= \cdots \\ &= (-\mu)^{pm} \left| \mathbf{\Lambda}_1 - \mu \boldsymbol{I}_m + \mu^{-1}\mathbf{\Lambda}_2 + \mu^{-2}\mathbf{\Lambda}_3 + \cdots + \mu^{-(p-1)}\mathbf{\Lambda}_p \right| \\ &= -(-\mu)^m \left| \mu^p \boldsymbol{I}_m - \mu^{p-1}\mathbf{\Lambda}_1 - \cdots - \mathbf{\Lambda}_p \right|. \end{aligned} \tag{4.3.19}$$

Evidently, the characteristic equation $|\mathbf{\Lambda}^* - \mu \boldsymbol{I}_{m(p+1)}| = 0$ has $m(p+1)$ roots, of which m are clearly zero. The required condition is therefore that the roots of the equation

$$\left| \mu^p \boldsymbol{I}_m - \mu^{p-1}\mathbf{\Lambda}_1 - \cdots - \mathbf{\Lambda}_p \right| = 0 \tag{4.3.20}$$

(a polynomial of order pm) must lie inside the unit circle.

4.4 Sequence Properties

4.4.1 Stationarity

A random sequence $\{\boldsymbol{x}_t\}$ is said to be *stationary in the wide sense* (or *covariance-stationary*) if the mean, the variance and the sequence of jth-order autocovariances for $j > 0$ are all independent of t. It is also said to be *stationary in the strict sense* if for every $k > 0$, the joint distributions of all collections $(\boldsymbol{x}_t, \boldsymbol{x}_{t+1}, \boldsymbol{x}_{t+2}, \ldots, \boldsymbol{x}_{t+k})$ do not depend in any way on t. In the case of a Gaussian process, strict sense and wide sense stationarity are the same thing.

Three conditions are necessary for the stationarity of the VAR process. The first is the absence of mean shifts, with $\boldsymbol{\delta}_t = \boldsymbol{\delta}$. The second is that the vectors $\{\boldsymbol{\varepsilon}_t\}$ are identically distributed, for all t. The third is the stability condition on $\boldsymbol{\Lambda}$, such that $\boldsymbol{\Lambda}^n \to 0$. The latter condition is sometimes referred to as 'the' stationarity condition, in the context of models where the first two conditions are already imposed for simplicity. This can be rather misleading, and the term stability condition is preferable.

4.4.2 Mixing

The mean deviations of the Gaussian VAR process form a stationary process subject to the stability condition, with fixed means $\mathbf{0}$, variances $\boldsymbol{\Omega}_{\boldsymbol{x}}$ and autocovariances $\boldsymbol{\Lambda}^j\boldsymbol{\Omega}_{\boldsymbol{x}}$. In this case the jth autocovariance tends to 0 as $j \to \infty$, and hence the Gaussian pair $\boldsymbol{x}_t$ and $\boldsymbol{x}_{t-j}$ are tending to independence. This characteristic of a sequence is called restricted memory, or *mixing*. In a mixing sequence (see Definition 6.4.1) the realization of the sequence at time t contains no information about the realization at either $t-j$ or $t+j$, when j is sufficiently large. The present contains no information about either the remote past or the remote future.

The assumption of random sampling from a large population is equivalent to the assumption that the members of the sample are independently distributed. In time series this is called serial independence, and in most cases is too strong an assumption for realism. However, the mixing property ensures that points in the sequence appear randomly sampled when they are far enough apart. Be careful to note that stationarity and mixing are quite distinct properties, and it is really fortuitous that in the Gaussian VAR they both depend on the stability condition. A mixing sequence need not be stationary (the stable VAR with $\boldsymbol{\delta}_t$ depending on t is such a case) and a stationary sequence need not be mixing.

For example, consider the sequence $y_t = x_t + z$ where x_t is an i.i.d. process with $E(x_t) = 0$, and z is any random variable not depending on t, with $E(z) = 0$, and independent of x_t for all t. Then

$$\text{Cov}(y_t, y_{t-j}) \to \text{Var}(z) > 0 \tag{4.4.1}$$

and y_t is not mixing. Consider the time average of y_t, that is, $\bar{y}_n = n^{-1}\sum_{t=1}^{n} y_t$. Since $\bar{x}_n \to 0$ in probability as $n \to \infty$ by Theorem 3.2.1 it is evident that $\bar{y}_n \to z$ in probability, and although $E(z) = 0$, a continuous distribution implies that $z \neq 0$ with probability 1. Another term for $E(x_t)$ is the *ensemble mean*, the expectation of x_t for fixed t across the ensemble of all the possible realizations of the sequence. Since $E(y_t) = E(x_t) + E(z) = 0$ the ensemble mean, even if it does not depend on t, can be different from the probability limit of the time average. It is worth bearing in mind that when we observe an actual economic time series, this is just one realization out of all the possible ways the world might have turned out. We are doomed to observe just the one world we inhabit. A time average is the only sort of average we can compute, and it is therefore important to know what this can tell us about the generation process of the sequence.

4.4.3 Ergodicity

A stationary sequence having the property that a random event involving every member of the sequence always has probability either 0 or 1 is called *ergodic*. The example just given is not an ergodic sequence in general, since an event involving every member of the sequence can only be an event relating to z. For the sequence to be ergodic, z must assume the same value almost surely over the distribution of realizations of the process. In other words, $z = E(z)$ with probability 1. One of the most famous results in probability is the Ergodic Theorem, a leading case of the strong law of large numbers. This result states that in an ergodic sequence, time averages converge almost surely to the ensemble mean. Formally:

Theorem 4.4.1 If $\{x_t\}$ is a stationary ergodic sequence, and $E(x_1)$ exists, $\bar{x}_n \to E(x_1)$ with probability 1. □

For the proof see Davidson (1994a) Theorem 13.2.

A stationary mixing sequence, for example, can be shown to be ergodic. Only DGPs having the property that time averaging is a valid method of estimating parameters are amenable to statistical investigation, so ergodicity of the generated sequences is a potentially important property for DGPs to possess.

However, the concept of ergodicity is relevant only to the stationary case. Mixing sequences need not be stationary, and it is often possible to analyse statistically some time-invariant aspect of a model of nonstationary series. In fact, this is what econometricians do all the time. The VAR process does have the mixing property, although interestingly enough, this cannot be asserted solely on the strength of the stable eigenvalue condition. It is possible to exhibit stable AR processes that are not mixing – see §6.4. However, these counter-examples have discretely distributed shocks, and Gaussianity plus stability are jointly sufficient for mixing.

4.5 Marginalizing, Conditioning and Exogeneity

In this section we invoke the axiom of correct specification explicitly by discussing properties of the DGP, which is assumed to depend on a vector of parameters that we wish to estimate. However, the discussion is purely conceptual. The results demonstrate that, under the right conditions, only the part of the DGP that is of interest to the investigator actually needs to be modelled in practice.

4.5.1 Conditioning Variables

Let $\boldsymbol{x}_t$ denote the vector of all the variables in the economy. In principle, the DGP of the economic system as a whole might be written down, exploiting (4.1.3), in the form

$$D(\boldsymbol{x}_t|\mathcal{X}_{t-1};\boldsymbol{d}_t,\boldsymbol{\psi}). \tag{4.5.1}$$

Clearly, (4.5.1) is an unimaginably complex construction, and the dimension of ψ is astronomical. Its form cannot be completely specified any more than all the elements of x_t can be observed. Any feasible econometric exercise will focus on a small part of the total system.[3] Usually, this means attempting to explain the behaviour of a subset of variables y_t in terms both of the history of the system *and* of a contemporaneous subset z_t, where the latter are treated as given for the purposes of the exercise, and hence as valid conditioning variables. The question as issue is whether this partitioning of the complete model can be a valid procedure, in which no relevant information is lost.

Treating z_t as given is usually motivated by the assumption that z_t 'causes' y_t. The notion of causation in econometrics is a notoriously slippery one. It is never a directly *observable* phenomenon (as opposed to a matter of knowing the underlying mechanisms involved) unless there is a measurable time interval between the cause and the effect. Except in this case, we may choose to regard variables as 'simultaneous' or 'jointly determined', in the sense that they are related but no causal ordering can be assigned. Economic variables may be set simultaneously by agents in a joint decision, which is true simultaneity, but apparent simultaneity can also arise through the aggregation of causal relations over agents and over time. Thus, on a week-to-week basis the individual household's consumption expenditure cannot feed back to effect its income. But measured as annual flows, it is clear that aggregate consumption can interact with aggregate personal income, through the multiplier. It is reasonable to postulate either that such aggregation effects exist within the observation period, or they do not, and therefore, that the contemporaneous relations observed in aggregate data are either simultaneous or causal in nature. To take an obvious counter-example, if the average rainfall in a given year is correlated with the price of wheat in the same year, this is an unambiguously causal relation even if some of the rainfall measurements postdate the harvest. There need be no contradiction in assuming one variable to cause another, even if the observations bear the same date. In particular, this would imply the absence of significant feedback-with-a-lag from the caused to the causing variable, within the observation period.

4.5.2 Factorization of the Density

Let w_t denote those variables in x_t not belonging to either y_t or z_t, that are not considered in this exercise and in general not even observed. Inevitably, the overwhelming majority of variables must fall into w_t. Consider the factorization of the joint density in (4.5.1),

$$D = D_{w,y,z} = D_{w|y,z}D_{y|z}D_z. \qquad (4.5.2)$$

Here, the subscripts refer to the current-dated variables. The conditioning on the lagged variables, as well as the time dependence of the density, is not shown

[3] Here, 'small' means that a small number of parameters are to be specified, which could mean looking at a small sector of the economy, but more often means working at a high level of aggregation and ignoring details.

explicitly. Such factorizations exist for any partition of the variables, but this one is of particular interest when y_t and z_t are related in the postulated manner. To define these relations formally, let the symbols $\rightarrow$ or $\leftarrow$ ($\nrightarrow$ or $\nleftarrow$) connecting two vectors denote the presence (absence) of contemporaneous causation in the indicated direction, of at least one element by at least one element in the sense defined in §4.5.1, of the absence of feedback within the observation period. Let $\leftrightarrow$ ($\nleftrightarrow$) denote the presence (absence) of simultaneous relations similarly. Then, if $z_t \rightarrow\nleftrightarrow\nleftarrow y_t$ and $w_t \nrightarrow\nleftrightarrow y_t$, the factor $D_{y|z}$ completely represents the stochastic mechanism generating y_t. Note that $y_t \rightarrow w_t$ is allowed, and no restriction on the relationships between w_t and z_t is required, for this to be true.

Let us emphasize that contemporaneous correlations among variables cannot reveal a direction of causation. Except in special circumstances, to be detailed in §4.7, the factorization in (4.5.2) reflects nothing but a theoretical construction placed on the evidence. The condition $w_t \nrightarrow\nleftrightarrow y_t$ is however satisfied trivially if y_t and w_t are conditionally independent (i.e., independent in the distribution conditional on z_t). Another point to remark is that $z_t \nrightarrow y_t$ is a possible special case, in which the model of y_t can be called conditionally *closed.*[4]

To pursue this analysis, a flexible way of representing a set of conditioning variables is needed, and to this end the following notation is adopted. As already established for x_t, a calligraphic symbol will represent the σ-field generated by the history of the relevant vector up to time t, so that for example $\mathcal{Y}_{t-1} = \sigma(y_{t-1}, y_{t-2}, y_{t-3}, \ldots)$, with similar definitions for $\mathcal{W}_{t-1}$ and $\mathcal{Z}_{t-1}$. When a conditional distribution is written, the conditioning information will sometimes be represented as a set of random variables and previously defined σ-fields written after the '|'. This has the natural interpretation. For example $D(\cdot|z_t, \mathcal{Z}_{t-1})$ is shorthand for $D(\cdot|\sigma(z_t) \vee \mathcal{Z}_{t-1})$, denoting the density conditional on $\sigma(z_t, z_{t-1}, \ldots)$, while $D(\cdot|\mathcal{Z}_{t-1}, \mathcal{W}_{t-1})$ represents conditioning on $\sigma(z_{t-1}, w_{t-1}, z_{t-2}, w_{t-2}, \ldots)$, and could also be written $D(\cdot|\mathcal{Z}_{t-1} \vee \mathcal{W}_{t-1})$.[5]

Given (4.5.2), the set of assumptions on which the econometric analysis of $D_{y|z}$ implicitly relies can now be stated. Assume there exists a partition of ψ into subvectors $\psi_1 \in \Psi_1$ and $\psi_2 \in \Psi_2$, such that $\Psi = \Psi_1 \times \Psi_2$, and

$$D_{w|y,z} = D_{w|y,z}(w_t|y_t, z_t, \mathcal{W}_{t-1}, \mathcal{Y}_{t-1}, \mathcal{Z}_{t-1}; d_t, \psi_2) \tag{4.5.3a}$$

$$D_{y|z} = D_{y|z}(y_t|z_t, \mathcal{Y}_{t-1}, \mathcal{Z}_{t-1}; d_t, \psi_1) \tag{4.5.3b}$$

$$D_z = D_z(z_t|\mathcal{W}_{t-1}, \mathcal{Y}_{t-1}, \mathcal{Z}_{t-1}; d_t, \psi_2) \tag{4.5.3c}$$

The content of these conditions is three-fold. First, $D_{w|y,z}$ and D_z must not depend on ψ_1 whereas $D_{y|z}$ must not depend on ψ_2. Second, $D_{y|z}$ must also not depend on w_{t-j} for $j > 0$, in the sense that either conditioning or not conditioning on these variables has the same effect. Third, under the condition $\Psi = \Psi_1 \times \Psi_2$ the admissible values of ψ_1 may not depend on ψ_2, so that knowledge of the latter cannot improve inferences about the former. In this case ψ_1 and ψ_2 are said to be *variation free.*

---

[4]The model would be unconditionally closed if y_t depended only on its own past values.

[5]For discussion of combining σ-fields and a definition of the symbol $\vee$, see §B.10.

Under conditions (4.5.3) nothing need be known about the forms of $D_{w|y,z}$ and D_z to analyse $D_{y|z}$ since these do not depend on ψ_1, whereas we are not interested in ψ_2 since $D_{y|z}$ does not depend on it. The analysis is said to be *conditional* on z_t, whereas the model is *marginalized* with respect to w_t. The marginalization process is often taken for granted in empirical work, the set of variables actually observed tending to be regarded as the whole economic universe. However, if a variable that should be in z_t is incorrectly assigned to w_t, its omission from $D_{y|z}$ constitutes a misspecification.

4.5.3 Parameters of Interest and Weak Exogeneity

The key contribution on these questions is Engle et. al. (1983). The separation of ψ into two sets defined by the factorization of the density is called by these authors a *sequential cut* of the parameters. The sets ψ_1 and ψ_2 are respectively 'those that matter' to the investigation and 'the rest', and while the representations in (4.5.3a) and (4.5.3c) allow that $D_{w|y,z}$ and D_z may actually have parameters in common, this is merely for full generality. Most likely, these two factors define a further cut of ψ_2, but this possibility is of no particular interest to us for the present purpose. In any case, model parameterizations are never unique. Given *any* function f that is '1-to-1, onto', such that $\phi = f(\psi)$, ϕ can represent an alternative parameterization of the model, equivalent to the original apart from interpretation. Suppose that $D_{y|z}$ depends on a vector θ of parameters of interest, whose values form the focus of the investigation. To make the desired factorization of the DGP, it is only necessary that there exists *some* parameterization ψ such that (4.5.3) holds, with ψ_1 and ψ_2 variation free, and $\theta = g(\psi_1)$. Note that g need not be 1-to-1. It could be a selection function, for example, such that θ is a subvector of ψ_1.

In this analysis, the y_t are called the *endogenous* variables, and Engle et. al. (1983) call the z_t *weakly exogenous*. It is generally convenient to think of the parameters of interest θ themselves as defining the investigation. Then, y_t would be defined merely as the smallest subset of the data such that the factorization defined by (4.5.3) holds, with ψ_1 and ψ_2 variation free, and $\theta = g(\psi_1)$. In this characterization of the problem, z_t is said to be 'weakly exogenous for θ'. Since it is usually the case that the parameters of interest are linked to the conditional modelling of y_t, it is also usual for the sequential cut defined by (4.5.3) to correspond to the pattern of relationships described following (4.5.2). However, because this connection is so natural, we must be very careful not to overlook the fact that weak exogeneity is a relationship between parameters and variables, and is *not* a property of the variables, as such. Without the required cut of the parameters, the factorization in (4.5.2) is not relevant to the investigation. Thus, it is incorrect to say that z_t is weakly exogenous with respect to y_t, even though this statement might seem almost equivalent to the preceding one.[6] The weak exogeneity des-

[6] It is difficult to illustrate this assertion within the linear VAR framework of the present chapter, but a good counter-example is provided by the rational expectations model of §5.5.3. It is clear that the pair of equations represented by (5.5.13a) and equation (5.5.22), with Gaussian

ignation depends solely on the nature of the investigation and has no *necessary* connection with causality, naturally linked though the concepts may be.

4.5.4 Granger Causality and Strong Exogeneity

As noted in §4.5.1, for a causal relation to be unambiguous a measurable time interval must normally separate cause and effect. A concept of causality often cited in econometrics, embodying this idea, is *Granger causality* (Granger 1969). $\boldsymbol{y}_t$ is said to cause $\boldsymbol{z}_t$ in Granger's sense if knowledge of $\boldsymbol{y}_t$ aids the prediction of $\boldsymbol{z}_{t+j}$, for some $j > 0$. Granger causality does not actually require a direct causal mechanism linking $\boldsymbol{y}_t$ and $\boldsymbol{z}_t$ to exist. They could be connected by nothing except a common causal factor that (say) operates on $\boldsymbol{y}_t$ with a lag of one period, and on $\boldsymbol{z}_t$ with a lag of two periods. All that matters here is observable predictive power.

Since $\mathcal{X}_{t-1}$ appears as the conditioning variables in D_z, $\boldsymbol{y}_t$ may Granger-cause $\boldsymbol{z}_t$ without violating the weak exogeneity of $\boldsymbol{z}_t$. However, suppose there exists the factorization

$$D_z(\boldsymbol{z}_{1t}, \boldsymbol{z}_{2t}|\mathcal{X}_{t-1}) = D_{z_1|z_2}(\boldsymbol{z}_{1t}|\boldsymbol{z}_{2t}, \mathcal{X}_{t-1}) D_{z_2}(\boldsymbol{z}_{2t}|\mathcal{W}_{t-1}, \mathcal{Z}_{t-1}) \tag{4.5.4}$$

In this case, $\boldsymbol{y}_t$ does not Granger-cause $\boldsymbol{z}_{2t}$. Granger non-causality is a property of the DGP, under which $\boldsymbol{y}_{t-j}$ for $j > 0$ can innocuously be excluded from the conditioning variables in the right-hand factor in (4.5.4). In contrast to weak exogeneity, it is unambiguously a relationship between variables. However, if $\boldsymbol{z}_{2t}$ is both not Granger-caused by $\boldsymbol{y}_t$ and weakly exogenous for $\boldsymbol{\theta}$, these variables are said by Engle et. al. (1983) to be *strongly exogenous* for $\boldsymbol{\theta}$.

Thus, the 'weakness' of the weak exogeneity concept is that it does not rule out feedback from the endogenous variables to the exogenous variables, with a lag. Whereas the existence of lagged feedback is compatible with making efficient inferences about $\boldsymbol{\theta}$, it rules out treating $\boldsymbol{z}_t$ as given in multi-step forecasting and policy simulation exercises involving $\boldsymbol{y}_t$. For these purposes, the absence of strong exogeneity in $\boldsymbol{z}_{1t}$ requires the factor $D_{z_1|z_2}$ in (4.5.4) to be incorporated into the model. On the other hand, strongly exogenous variables can be regarded as fixed to all intents and purposes, and from a statistical viewpoint can be treated like the deterministic variables $\boldsymbol{d}_t$.

4.5.5 A Bivariate Example

The concepts of the last section can be illustrated very clearly in the bivariate Gaussian VAR(1). For simplicity assume there are no marginalized variables, so that $\boldsymbol{x}_t = (y_t, z_t)'$. Let the structural equations corresponding to (4.2.8) be

$$y_t + \alpha_{12} z_t = \gamma_1 + \beta_{11} y_{t-1} + \beta_{12} z_{t-1} + u_{1t} \tag{4.5.5a}$$

$$\alpha_{21} y_t + z_t = \gamma_2 + \beta_{21} y_{t-1} + \beta_{22} z_{t-1} + u_{2t} \tag{4.5.5b}$$

disturbances, represent $D_{y|z}$ where $\boldsymbol{y}_t = (x_t, y_t)$ and $\boldsymbol{z}_t = (w_t, z_t)$. However, the parameters of interest must include λ_1 and λ_2, since otherwise γ and δ are unidentified. There is no cut of the parameters between $D_{y|z}$ and D_z, and $\boldsymbol{z}_t$ is not weakly exogenous for $(\alpha, \beta, \gamma, \delta)$.

where

$$\begin{bmatrix} u_{1t} \\ u_{2t} \end{bmatrix} \sim \text{NI}\left(\begin{bmatrix} 0 \\ 0 \end{bmatrix}, \begin{bmatrix} \sigma_{11} & \sigma_{12} \\ \sigma_{21} & \sigma_{22} \end{bmatrix} \right) \tag{4.5.6}$$

and 'NI' denotes that the vector is normal and serially independent. Observe the normalization restrictions on $\boldsymbol{B}$, and also the fact that $\sigma_{21} = \sigma_{12}$.

Suppose the parameters of interest are $\boldsymbol{\theta} = (\alpha_{12}, \gamma_1, \beta_{11}, \beta_{12})'$. Using formula (4.2.7), the joint density of the variables is

$$D(y_t, z_t | y_{t-1}, z_{t-1})$$
$$= \frac{1}{2\pi} \begin{vmatrix} \omega_{11} & \omega_{12} \\ \omega_{21} & \omega_{22} \end{vmatrix}^{-1/2} \exp\left\{ -\tfrac{1}{2} \begin{bmatrix} \varepsilon_{1t} \ \varepsilon_{2t} \end{bmatrix} \begin{bmatrix} \omega_{11} & \omega_{21} \\ \omega_{21} & \omega_{22} \end{bmatrix}^{-1} \begin{bmatrix} \varepsilon_{1t} \\ \varepsilon_{2t} \end{bmatrix} \right\} \tag{4.5.7}$$

where $\boldsymbol{\varepsilon}_t = \boldsymbol{B}^{-1}\boldsymbol{u}_t$ and $\boldsymbol{\Omega} = \boldsymbol{B}^{-1}\boldsymbol{\Sigma}(\boldsymbol{B}')^{-1}$. To factorize this formula into conditional and marginal components note that $\omega_{21} = \omega_{12}$ by symmetry, that

$$\begin{vmatrix} \omega_{11} & \omega_{12} \\ \omega_{21} & \omega_{22} \end{vmatrix} = \left(\omega_{11} - \frac{\omega_{21}^2}{\omega_{22}} \right) \omega_{22} \tag{4.5.8}$$

and that

$$\begin{bmatrix} \varepsilon_{1t} \ \varepsilon_{2t} \end{bmatrix} \begin{bmatrix} \omega_{11} & \omega_{21} \\ \omega_{21} & \omega_{22} \end{bmatrix}^{-1} \begin{bmatrix} \varepsilon_{1t} \\ \varepsilon_{2t} \end{bmatrix} = \frac{\left(\varepsilon_{1t} - \dfrac{\omega_{21}}{\omega_{22}} \varepsilon_{2t} \right)^2}{\omega_{11} - \dfrac{\omega_{21}^2}{\omega_{22}}} + \frac{\varepsilon_{2t}^2}{\omega_{22}}. \tag{4.5.9}$$

Therefore the factors are

$$D_{y|z}(y_t | z_t, y_{t-1}, z_{t-1})$$
$$= \frac{1}{\sqrt{2\pi \left(\omega_{11} - \dfrac{\omega_{21}^2}{\omega_{22}} \right)}} \exp\left\{ -\frac{\left(\varepsilon_{1t} - \dfrac{\omega_{21}}{\omega_{22}} \varepsilon_{2t} \right)^2}{2\left(\omega_{11} - \dfrac{\omega_{21}^2}{\omega_{22}} \right)} \right\} \tag{4.5.10}$$

and

$$D_z(z_t | y_{t-1}, z_{t-1}) = \frac{1}{\sqrt{2\pi\omega_{22}}} \exp\left\{ -\frac{\varepsilon_{2t}^2}{2\omega_{22}} \right\}. \tag{4.5.11}$$

Remember that $\varepsilon_{1t} = y_t - E(y_t | y_{t-1}, z_{t-1})$ and $\varepsilon_{2t} = z_t - E(z_t | y_{t-1}, z_{t-1})$, so that ε_{2t} is treated as conditionally fixed in $D_{y|z}$.

Does the factorization divide the parameters into subsets $\boldsymbol{\psi}_1$ and $\boldsymbol{\psi}_2$, where $\boldsymbol{\theta} = \boldsymbol{g}(\boldsymbol{\psi}_1)$? Unfortunately, the answer is no, in general. Write out the structural form-reduced form relationships according to (4.2.10), as

$$\begin{bmatrix} \varepsilon_{1t} \\ \varepsilon_{2t} \end{bmatrix} = \frac{1}{1 - \alpha_{21}\alpha_{12}} \begin{bmatrix} u_{1t} - \alpha_{12}u_{2t} \\ u_{2t} - \alpha_{21}u_{1t} \end{bmatrix} \tag{4.5.12}$$

and

$$\begin{bmatrix}\omega_{11} & \omega_{12}\\ \omega_{21} & \omega_{22}\end{bmatrix} = \frac{1}{(1-\alpha_{21}\alpha_{12})^2} \times$$
$$\begin{bmatrix}\sigma_{11} - 2\alpha_{12}\sigma_{21} + \alpha_{12}^2\sigma_{22} & (1+\alpha_{12}\alpha_{21})\sigma_{21} - \alpha_{12}\sigma_{22} - \alpha_{21}\sigma_{11}\\ * & \sigma_{22} - 2\alpha_{21}\sigma_{21} + \alpha_{21}^2\sigma_{11}\end{bmatrix} \quad (4.5.13)$$

where '$*$' denotes substitution of the upper-right element, by symmetry. Inspection shows that all the parameters appear in both factors, in general.

However, in the case that $\alpha_{21} = 0$ and $\sigma_{21} = 0$, it is easy to verify that the conditional and marginal factors become, respectively,

$$D_{y|z}(y_t|z_t, y_{t-1}, z_{t-1}; \boldsymbol{\psi}_1) = \frac{1}{\sqrt{2\pi\sigma_{11}}}\exp\left\{-\frac{u_{1t}^2}{2\sigma_{11}}\right\} \quad (4.5.14)$$

$$D_z(z_t|y_{t-1}, z_{t-1}; \boldsymbol{\psi}_2) = \frac{1}{\sqrt{2\pi\sigma_{22}}}\exp\left\{-\frac{u_{2t}^2}{2\sigma_{22}}\right\} \quad (4.5.15)$$

where $\boldsymbol{\psi}_1 = (\alpha_{12}, \gamma_1, \beta_{11}, \beta_{12}, \sigma_{11})'$ (containing $\boldsymbol{\theta}$) and $\boldsymbol{\psi}_2 = (\gamma_2, \beta_{21}, \beta_{22}, \sigma_{22})'$. These conditions are both necessary and sufficient for the factorization to cut the parameters as required. The model is said to have a *statistically recursive* structure. Causality is manifestly 'one way', from z_t to y_t, for y_t depends on both u_{1t} and u_{2t} (the latter through z_t), but z_t does not depend on u_{1t}, which is independent of u_{2t}.

However, note that mere observation of the variables without knowing the structure of the DGP is not sufficient to establish this fact, given that y_t and z_t have the same date. The disturbances u_{1t} and u_{2t} are unobservables, and all that can be measured from simple observation is the contemporaneous correlation of the variables. Setting $\alpha_{21} \neq 0$ and $\alpha_{12} = 0$ would reverse the causation, but with suitable values of the parameters exactly the same data correlations as before could be obtained. On the other hand, if $\beta_{21} = 0$ it is equally clear that y_t does not Granger-cause z_t, which is predictable only from its own past values (consider the VAR form). The three conditions $\sigma_{21} = \alpha_{21} = \beta_{21} = 0$ yield strong exogeneity. In this case, z_t can be treated as if fixed in repeated samples.

4.5.6 Exogeneity and Regression

The last example illustrates the well-known result that if a variable is weakly exogenous, it is valid to treat it as a regressor in least squares estimation of the equation of interest. The equation of interest is

$$y_t = -\alpha_{12}z_t + \gamma_1 + \beta_{11}y_{t-1} + \beta_{12}z_{t-1} + u_{1t} \quad (4.5.16)$$

It is proved in §7.1 that the least squares estimator is consistent (by construction, note) for the coefficients of the conditional expectation $E(y_t|z_t, x_{t-1}, z_{t-1})$, and for present purposes let this result be taken for granted. To evaluate these coefficients, note from the conditional density formula (4.5.10) that

$$y_t - E(y_t|z_t, y_{t-1}, z_{t-1}) = \varepsilon_{1t} - \frac{\omega_{12}}{\omega_{22}}\varepsilon_{2t}. \quad (4.5.17)$$

Substitution from (4.5.12) and (4.5.5) and some simplification shows that

$$E(y_t|z_t, y_{t-1}, z_{t-1}) = \frac{\omega_{12}}{\omega_{22}} z_t + (P\gamma_1 - Q\gamma_2) + (P\beta_{11} - Q\beta_{21})y_{t-1} + (P\beta_{12} - Q\beta_{22})z_{t-1} \quad (4.5.18)$$

where

$$P = \frac{1 + \alpha_{21}\omega_{12}/\omega_{22}}{1 - \alpha_{21}\alpha_{12}}, \quad Q = \frac{\alpha_{12} + \omega_{12}/\omega_{22}}{1 - \alpha_{21}\alpha_{12}}.$$

Least squares regression of y_t on z_t, y_{t-1} and z_{t-1} will yield consistent estimates of these coefficients, and nothing else. A moment's inspection shows that when

$$\frac{\omega_{12}}{\omega_{22}} = -\alpha_{12} \quad (4.5.19)$$

$P = 1$ and $Q = 0$, and the regression coefficients coincide with the parameters of interest. Referring to (4.5.13),

$$\frac{\omega_{12}}{\omega_{22}} = \frac{(1 + \alpha_{12}\alpha_{21})\sigma_{21} - \alpha_{12}\sigma_{22} - \alpha_{21}\sigma_{11}}{\sigma_{22} - 2\alpha_{21}\sigma_{21} + \alpha_{21}^2\sigma_{11}}. \quad (4.5.20)$$

Sure enough, the weak exogeneity restrictions $\alpha_{21} = \sigma_{21} = 0$ are exactly what are needed to obtain (4.5.19) from (4.5.20). This provides another interpretation of exogeneity in the Gaussian linear model. It is the condition on the joint distribution of $(y_t, z_t)'$ under which the parameters of the conditional sub-model of $y_t|z_t$ can be estimated by least squares. In fact, this result holds true for any model in which conditional expectations are linear functions of the conditioning variables. Gaussianity is sufficient but not necessary for this property to hold.

4.5.7 Other Notions of Exogeneity

Exogeneity is sometimes defined in terms of the independence of the variables in question from the disturbances in a model. If in the regression model $y_t = \boldsymbol{x}_t'\beta + u_t$, $\boldsymbol{x}_t$ is independent of u_{t+j} for all $j \geq 0$, $\boldsymbol{x}_t$ is often said to be *predetermined* in this equation. If the independence holds for all j, $\boldsymbol{x}_t$ is said to be *strictly exogenous.*

In the model just considered, it is clear that when z_t is weakly exogenous for $\boldsymbol{\theta}$, u_{1t} is indeed independent of z_t, and also of z_{t-j} for all $j \geq 0$. Likewise, independence of u_{1t} and z_t holds only if $\alpha_{21} = 0$ and $\sigma_{21} = 0$, and hence predeterminedness and weak exogeneity are equivalent in this model. Strict and strong exogeneity are equivalent similarly. However, even if weak exogeneity does not hold, it is equally clear that if

$$e_{1t} = y_t - \frac{\omega_{12}}{\omega_{22}} z_t - (P\gamma_1 - Q\gamma_2) - (P\beta_{11} - Q\beta_{21})y_{t-1} - (P\beta_{12} - Q\beta_{22})z_{t-1} \quad (4.5.21)$$

then z_t and e_{1t} are independent by construction. Since the variables are jointly Gaussian, this follows from the condition $E(e_{1t}|z_t, y_{t-1}, z_{t-1}) = 0$. Moreover, since $e_{1t} = \varepsilon_{1t} - (\omega_{12}/\omega_{22})\varepsilon_{2t}$ from (4.5.17) it is independent of all lagged variables, again by construction. It appears equally valid to claim that z_t is a predetermined variable under these assumptions. Notice that this regression has the same variables in it as the 'structural' regression of (4.5.16), so predeterminedness, as here defined, is not a property of variables. It has no meaning until the interpretation of the parameters in the equation has been given, exactly what is done in the definition of weak exogeneity.

This discussion brings us back to the analysis of §1.4.3. The key question in any conditional analysis is what variables are allocated to the conditioning set. In a regression, all right-hand side variables are 'conditioned on' by default, since the regression always estimates the conditional mean. In the present analysis, by contrast, z_t was not initially allocated to the conditioning set. The VAR structure of the model implies that the data generation processes of the variables are inherently interdependent, so this might not be legitimate. Instead, we asked if it would make a difference to the analysis if we *did* condition on z_t. The weak exogeneity restrictions are just what are needed to make the answer to this question 'no'. This is an issue we return to in more detail in §8.1.3.

An important moral of this story is to remember that disturbances are *not data.* It is not just that they are unobserved. They are fictional constructs that have no reality outside of the particular model and parameterization we have chosen. The underlying model assumptions have implications for the properties of the disturbances, and it's often convenient to formulate the assumptions in these terms. A statement such as 'assume z_t is strictly exogenous' often appears in the preamble to a piece of analysis, and this is perfectly legitimate since it tells the reader what formal assumption is being used to get the result. However, this is merely shorthand for 'let the structure of the model be such as to make z_t independent of u_{t+j} for all j'. It is not of itself a statement about the structure.

4.6 The General Conditional Model

Let us briefly indicate how the example in §4.5.5 can be generalized to more than two variables, and embedded in the general VAR framework. Let $\boldsymbol{x}_t = (\boldsymbol{y}_t', \boldsymbol{z}_t')'$ where $\boldsymbol{y}_t$ is $m_1 \times 1$ and $\boldsymbol{z}_t$ is $m_2 \times 1$. The partitioned structural form of the VAR(1) is

$$\boldsymbol{B}_{11}\boldsymbol{y}_t + \boldsymbol{B}_{12}\boldsymbol{z}_t = \boldsymbol{\Gamma}_1\boldsymbol{d}_t + \boldsymbol{C}_{11}\boldsymbol{y}_{t-1} + \boldsymbol{C}_{12}\boldsymbol{z}_{t-1} + \boldsymbol{u}_{1t} \quad (4.6.1a)$$
$$\boldsymbol{B}_{21}\boldsymbol{y}_t + \boldsymbol{B}_{22}\boldsymbol{z}_t = \boldsymbol{\Gamma}_2\boldsymbol{d}_t + \boldsymbol{C}_{21}\boldsymbol{y}_{t-1} + \boldsymbol{C}_{22}\boldsymbol{z}_{t-1} + \boldsymbol{u}_{2t} \quad (4.6.1b)$$

where

$$\begin{bmatrix} \boldsymbol{u}_{1t} \\ \boldsymbol{u}_{2t} \end{bmatrix} \sim \mathrm{NI}\left(\begin{bmatrix} \boldsymbol{0} \\ \boldsymbol{0} \end{bmatrix}, \begin{bmatrix} \boldsymbol{\Sigma}_{11} & \boldsymbol{\Sigma}_{12} \\ \boldsymbol{\Sigma}_{21} & \boldsymbol{\Sigma}_{22} \end{bmatrix} \right). \quad (4.6.2)$$

Let the parameters of interest be the unrestricted elements of $\boldsymbol{B}_{11}, \boldsymbol{B}_{12}, \boldsymbol{\Gamma}_1$, $\boldsymbol{C}_{11}$, $\boldsymbol{C}_{12}$ and $\boldsymbol{\Sigma}_{11}$. The earlier analysis is generalized using the results in §C.2 to obtain the general case of the density factorization. The conditions $\boldsymbol{B}_{21} = \boldsymbol{0}$ and $\boldsymbol{\Sigma}_{12} = \boldsymbol{0}$ can be shown to be necessary and sufficient for the sequential cut of the parameters to be made. In this case $\boldsymbol{B}$ is said to be upper-block triangular, $\boldsymbol{\Sigma}$ to be block diagonal, and a model with this structure to be statistically block-recursive.

For brevity let $\boldsymbol{r}_t = (\boldsymbol{d}_t, \boldsymbol{y}'_{t-1}, \boldsymbol{z}'_{t-1})$, and define $\boldsymbol{\Delta}_1 = [\boldsymbol{\Gamma}_1 \ \boldsymbol{C}_{11} \ \boldsymbol{C}_{12}]$ and $\boldsymbol{\Delta}_2 = [\boldsymbol{\Gamma}_2 \ \boldsymbol{C}_{21} \ \boldsymbol{C}_{22}]$. Subject to the weak exogeneity restrictions, it can be verified that the VAR form of the model is

$$\boldsymbol{y}_t = (\boldsymbol{B}_{11}^{-1}\boldsymbol{\Delta}_1 - \boldsymbol{B}_{11}^{-1}\boldsymbol{B}_{12}\boldsymbol{B}_{22}^{-1}\boldsymbol{\Delta}_2)\boldsymbol{r}_t + \boldsymbol{\varepsilon}_{1t} \tag{4.6.3a}$$

$$\boldsymbol{z}_t = \boldsymbol{B}_{22}^{-1}\boldsymbol{\Delta}_2\boldsymbol{r}_t + \boldsymbol{\varepsilon}_{2t} \tag{4.6.3b}$$

where

$$\boldsymbol{\varepsilon}_{1t} = \boldsymbol{B}_{11}^{-1}\boldsymbol{u}_{1t} - \boldsymbol{B}_{11}^{-1}\boldsymbol{B}_{12}\boldsymbol{B}_{22}^{-1}\boldsymbol{u}_{2t} \tag{4.6.4a}$$

$$\boldsymbol{\varepsilon}_{2t} = \boldsymbol{B}_{22}^{-1}\boldsymbol{u}_{2t}. \tag{4.6.4b}$$

To construct the factorization of the joint density, it is sufficient to write down the means and variances for the conditional and marginal blocks. From (4.6.3b) the marginal model is specified by

$$E(\boldsymbol{z}_t|\mathcal{X}_{t-1}) = \boldsymbol{B}_{22}^{-1}\boldsymbol{\Delta}_2\boldsymbol{r}_t \tag{4.6.5}$$

and

$$\mathrm{Var}(\boldsymbol{z}_t|\mathcal{X}_{t-1}) = \boldsymbol{B}_{22}^{-1}\boldsymbol{\Sigma}_{22}(\boldsymbol{B}_{22}^{-1})' = \boldsymbol{\Omega}_{22} \tag{4.6.6}$$

which involve no parameters of interest. On the other hand, the conditional model is

$$\begin{aligned} E(\boldsymbol{y}_t|\boldsymbol{z}_t, \mathcal{X}_{t-1}) &= (\boldsymbol{B}_{11}^{-1}\boldsymbol{\Delta}_1 - \boldsymbol{B}_{11}^{-1}\boldsymbol{B}_{12}\boldsymbol{B}_{22}^{-1}\boldsymbol{\Delta}_2)\boldsymbol{r}_t + E(\boldsymbol{\varepsilon}_{1t}|\boldsymbol{z}_t, \mathcal{X}_{t-1}) \\ &= -\boldsymbol{B}_{11}^{-1}\boldsymbol{B}_{12}\boldsymbol{z}_t + \boldsymbol{B}_{11}^{-1}\boldsymbol{\Delta}_1\boldsymbol{r}_t \end{aligned} \tag{4.6.7}$$

where the second equality is got by substituting from (4.6.4), and

$$\mathrm{Var}(\boldsymbol{y}_t|\boldsymbol{z}_t, \mathcal{X}_{t-1}) = \boldsymbol{B}_{11}^{-1}\boldsymbol{\Sigma}_{11}(\boldsymbol{B}_{11}^{-1})' = \boldsymbol{\Omega}_{11}. \tag{4.6.8}$$

These equations depend only on parameters of interest, and the sequential cut operates. The conditional model can be expressed in structural form as

$$\boldsymbol{B}_{11}E(\boldsymbol{y}_t|\boldsymbol{z}_t, \mathcal{X}_{t-1}) = -\boldsymbol{B}_{12}\boldsymbol{z}_t + \boldsymbol{\Delta}_1\boldsymbol{r}_t. \tag{4.6.9}$$

The statistical treatment of this type of model is a specialized topic, to be examined in detail in Chapter 8.

4.7 Structural Change

4.7.1 Observational Equivalence

A qualification to the analysis in §4.5.2 concerns the role of the exogenous shift variables $\boldsymbol{d}_t$. Imagine first that there are no shift variables, so that the densities do not depend on t and the data are accordingly strictly stationary. Suppose that instead of explaining $\boldsymbol{y}_t$ by $\boldsymbol{z}_t$, you wished to explain $\boldsymbol{z}_t$ by $\boldsymbol{y}_t$. This might arise because the brief was to forecast z_{n+1} given observations of y_{n+1}, since for some reason the former variable can only be observed with a further lag. The density $D_{z|y}$ is a natural tool for this task. For illustration, consider the model in (4.5.5) which with the exogeneity restrictions imposed takes the form

$$y_t + \alpha_{12}z_t = \gamma_1 + \beta_{11}y_{t-1} + \beta_{12}z_{t-1} + u_{1t} \tag{4.7.1a}$$

$$z_t = \gamma_2 + \beta_{21}y_{t-1} + \beta_{22}z_{t-1} + u_{2t} \tag{4.7.1b}$$

where

$$\begin{bmatrix} u_{1t} \\ u_{2t} \end{bmatrix} \sim \text{NI}\left(\begin{bmatrix} 0 \\ 0 \end{bmatrix}, \begin{bmatrix} \sigma_{11} & 0 \\ 0 & \sigma_{22} \end{bmatrix}\right). \tag{4.7.2}$$

Consider the forecasting equation obtained from the regression of z_t on y_t, y_{t-1} and z_{t-1}, notwithstanding that this is a 'false' model. This is derived like (4.5.18), and if P' and Q' correspond to P and Q in (4.5.18) with the subscripts interchanged,

$$E(z_t|y_t, y_{t-1}, z_{t-1}) = \frac{\omega_{12}}{\omega_{11}}y_t + (P'\gamma_2 - Q'\gamma_1) + (P'\beta_{21} - Q'\beta_{11})y_{t-1} + (P'\beta_{22} - Q'\beta_{12})z_{t-1} \tag{4.7.3}$$

The estimated parameters do not correspond to α_{21}, β_{21}, β_{22} in (4.5.5), and in particular, the coefficient of y_t is not zero but is given, using (4.5.13), by

$$\frac{\omega_{12}}{\omega_{11}} = -\frac{\alpha_{12}\sigma_{22}}{\sigma_{11} + \alpha_{12}^2\sigma_{22}} \tag{4.7.4}$$

However, this fact is irrelevant to the task at hand, given that a stable prediction equation is still available. In fact, if anyone were to query the procedure you could even reply "Oh no, that old theory was wrong. We now think $\alpha_{12} = 0$ and $\alpha_{21} \neq 0$". In that case you would indeed have $\omega_{21}/\omega_{11} = -\alpha_{21}$, and no evidence could be cited to contradict you. As noted in §4.5.2, the two theories are observationally equivalent since all that is observed is a contemporaneous correlation.

In a stationary world one can as well predict z_t from y_t or y_t from z_t, since prediction is simply a matter of extrapolating observed correlations. The 'true' model might be more parsimonious than the other, as for example if $\beta_{11} = 0$ in (4.5.5), so that y_{t-1} was not needed to forecast y_t. Such simplifying restrictions are less likely to hold in the 'false' model since there the coefficients are composites. This issue aside, the 'false' model is perfectly sound as a forecasting device. From this point of view, weak exogeneity can be seen as just a model construct, that can be irrelevant to an atheoretical exercise such as prediction.

4.7.2 Super-exogeneity

In a heterogeneous world, however, exogeneity can have directly observable consequences. To illustrate this, partition the vector $\boldsymbol{d}_t$ into subvectors $\boldsymbol{d}_{1t}$ and $\boldsymbol{d}_{2t}$, and suppose that condition (4.5.3b) now has the form

$$D_{y|z} = D_{y|z}(\boldsymbol{y}_t|\boldsymbol{z}_t, \mathcal{Y}_{t-1}, \mathcal{Z}_{t-1}; \boldsymbol{d}_{1t}, \boldsymbol{\psi}_1) \tag{4.7.5}$$

such that $D_{y|z}$ does not depend on $\boldsymbol{d}_{2t}$. If z_t is weakly exogenous for $\boldsymbol{\theta} = \boldsymbol{g}(\boldsymbol{\psi}_1)$, and $\boldsymbol{d}_{2t}$ is both a nontrivial argument of D_z and varies over the sample period $t = 1, \ldots, n$, then following Engle et. al. (1983), (at least one element of) z_t is said to be (nontrivially) *super-exogenous* for $\boldsymbol{\theta}$. More formally, super-exogeneity is the property that the conditional distribution depending on $\boldsymbol{\theta}$ is invariant to changes in the distribution of z_t.

By assumption, the form of $D_{y|z}$ is time-invariant once the effects of $\boldsymbol{d}_{1t}$ have been taken into account. However, the form of $D_{z|y}$ is not invariant unless the effects of $\boldsymbol{d}_{2t}$ are taken into account. To illustrate, suppose $\boldsymbol{d}_t = (1, d_t)'$ where $\boldsymbol{d}_{2t} = d_t$ is a dummy variable that takes the value 0 up to a date t^*, and 1 thereafter. This might be capturing the effect of a policy-maker's intervention, for example. Let the example take the form

$$\begin{aligned} y_t + \alpha_{12} z_t &= \gamma_{11} + \beta_{11} y_{t-1} + \beta_{12} z_{t-1} + u_{1t} \\ z_t &= \gamma_{21} + \gamma_{22} d_t + \beta_{21} y_{t-1} + \beta_{22} z_{t-1} + u_{2t} \end{aligned} \tag{4.7.6}$$

The mean of z_t jumps by an amount γ_{22} at date t^*, and the mean of y_t jumps at the same moment, initially by the amount $-\alpha_{12}\gamma_{22}$, and eventually by a total of $(-\alpha_{12} + \beta_{12})\gamma_{22}/(1 - \beta_{11})$. However, note that the function $E(y_t | z_t, y_{t-1}, z_{t-1})$ is invariant to the shift and continues to predict y_t correctly both before and after it, without modification.

Now consider the function $E(z_t | y_t, y_{t-1}, z_{t-1})$ derived in (4.7.3), but which must now be modified by substituting for the intercept the term $P'(\gamma_{21} - Q'\gamma_{11}) + P'\gamma_{22} d_t$. This jumps at time t^*, so that the equation predicting z_t from y_t is not invariant. This removes the symmetry in the relationship between y_t and z_t in a vital way. Knowledge of the intervention at time t^* is not needed to predict y_t successfully from z_t, but it is needed to predict z_t from y_t It can be said unambiguously that z_t causes y_t, even though there is no observable time lag involved.

As noted, super-exogeneity can be trivial if no intervention occurs over the time period relevant to the investigation. However, interventions anywhere in the economic system that feed through to z_t, directly or indirectly, can make it super-exogenous. Take one further example to illustrate the possibilities. Let the structural model be enlarged to

$$y_t + \alpha_{12} z_t = \gamma_{11} + \beta_{11} y_{t-1} + \beta_{12} z_{t-1} + u_{1t} \tag{4.7.7a}$$

$$z_t + \alpha_{23} w_t = \gamma_{21} + \beta_{21} y_{t-1} + \beta_{22} z_{t-1} + \beta_{23} w_{t-1} + u_{2t} \tag{4.7.7b}$$

$$w_t = \gamma_{31} + \gamma_{32} d_t + \beta_{31} y_{t-1} + \beta_{32} z_{t-1} + \beta_{33} w_{t-1} + u_{3t} \tag{4.7.7c}$$

where

$$\begin{bmatrix} u_{1t} \\ u_{2t} \\ u_{3t} \end{bmatrix} \sim \mathrm{NI}\left(\begin{bmatrix} 0 \\ 0 \\ 0 \end{bmatrix} \begin{bmatrix} \sigma_{11} & 0 & 0 \\ 0 & \sigma_{22} & 0 \\ 0 & 0 & \sigma_{33} \end{bmatrix} \right). \tag{4.7.8}$$

Staying with the context of being interested in the first equation, which must not depend on w_t, this is a fairly general set-up. The third equation cannot contain y_t since this would compromise the weak exogeneity of z_t for the set

$(\alpha_{12}, \gamma_{11}, \beta_{11}, \beta_{12})$,[7] but it would make no difference (except to the complexity) if z_t and w_t were jointly determined. The marginal density D_z is found by substituting the third equation into the second to eliminate w_t, and in particular, the conditional mean has the form

$$E(z_t|y_{t-1}, z_{t-1}, w_{t-1}) = \gamma_{21} + \alpha_{23}(\gamma_{31} + \gamma_{32}d_t) + \text{terms in } w_{t-1}, y_{t-1}, z_{t-1} \tag{4.7.9}$$

It follows that z_t is super-exogenous for $(\alpha_{12}, \gamma_{11}, \beta_{11}, \beta_{12})$.

The important part of the definition of super-exogeneity is the exclusion of d_{2t} from $D_{y|z}$. Characteristically, interventions arise in policy functions, such as equations describing the setting of taxes or interest rates. They do not appear so often in equations describing the private decisions of agents in the economy. As the last illustration shows, these effects are liable to be transferred willy-nilly to derived (reduced form) relations such as (4.7.9). The stability of an equation with respect to policy interventions is important evidence in favour of it being structural rather than a reduced form, and in this sense, the super-exogeneity of z_t is a concomitant of the density $D_{y|z}$ having a structural interpretation.

Further Reading: The theory of dynamic econometric modelling has been researched very extensively by David Hendry, with co-authors Jean-François Richard, Robert Engle and others. Key readings are Hendry and Richard (1982, 1983), Engle, Hendry and Richard (1983), Hendry, Pagan and Sargan (1984). Hendry (1995) summarizes a great deal of relevant material. On the vector autoregression model (§4.2, §4.3) see Hamilton (1994), Lütkepohl (1991), Box and Tiao (1981), Giannini (1992), Sims (1980), Leamer (1985). On sequence properties (§4.4) see Davidson (1994a), and also McCabe and Tremayne (1993), Breiman (1992). On exogeneity and causality (§4.5) see Koopmans (1950b), Granger (1969), Engle, Hendry and Richard (1983), Geweke (1982, 1983), Favero and Hendry (1992), Sims (1972, 1987), Feige and Pearce (1979), Christiano and Ljungqvist (1988). On structural change (§4.7) see Hendry (1995) and Engle and Hendry (1993).

[7]In §4.5.2 it was stated that $y_t \to w_t$ was allowed. However, the presence of y_t as an explanatory variable in (4.7.7c) would entail $y_t \to w_t \to z_t \to y_t$, which is impossible, since the last relation implies feedback. Such a structure has to mean $y_t \leftrightarrow w_t$.

Chapter 5

Principles of Dynamic Modelling

5.1 The Lag Operator

5.1.1 Definition

Let x_t be a random time series observation. Define the symbol L (some authors use B) by the relation

$$Lx_t = x_{t-1}. \tag{5.1.1}$$

That is, L denotes the operation of replacing x_t by the observation preceding it in the time series. L is what in mathematics is called an operator. It does not represent a coefficient, nor even a number, but can be treated like one in many algebraic manipulations. We do not need to follow the mathematical reasoning behind this fact, just to have confidence that the device works.

Thus, $L^2x_t = L(Lx_t) = Lx_{t-1} = x_{t-2}$, and in general, $L^nx_t = x_{t-n}$. Also, $L^{-1} = x_{t+1}$, and so on. The expression

$$\alpha(L) = \alpha_0 + \alpha_1 L + \alpha_2 L^2 + \cdots + \alpha_p L^p \tag{5.1.2}$$

is called a polynomial in the lag operator of order p. If applied to a time series variable, it generates a weighted moving average of the time series, i.e.,

$$\alpha(L)x_t = \alpha_0 x_t + \alpha_1 x_{t-1} + \alpha_2 x_{t-2} + \cdots + \alpha_p x_{t-p}. \tag{5.1.3}$$

Another commonly used operator symbol is

$$\Delta = 1 - L \tag{5.1.4}$$

the difference operator. $\Delta x_t = x_t - x_{t-1}$ is the change in x at period t. Also, note:

$$\Delta_n = 1 - L^n \tag{5.1.5}$$

is the n-period difference operator, but

$$\Delta^n = (1 - L)^n \tag{5.1.6}$$

is the nth-order difference operator. For example, $\Delta_2 x_t = x_t - x_{t-2}$, but $\Delta^2 x_t = \Delta x_t - \Delta x_{t-1} = x_t - 2x_{t-1} + x_{t-2}$. Be careful not to confuse these two.

5.1.2 Inverting Lag Polynomials

The lag operator allows a great economy of notation in operations on dynamic time series models. For example, if $\alpha(L)$ and $\beta(L)$ are two lag polynomials, the effect of applying these moving average operators to a time series in succession is found by evaluating the product $\beta(L)\alpha(L)$. The interesting question of undoing the effect of a moving average operation can also be examined, by finding the polynomial $\beta(L)$, if such exists, for which $\beta(L)\alpha(L) = 1$. We could write $\beta(L) = \alpha(L)^{-1}$, and call this operator the inverse of $\alpha(L)$.

Since L is an operator and not a variable, it is mathematically tidier to consider the properties of the polynomials $\alpha(z)$ and $\beta(z)$, where z is a complex variable, having the form $z = a + ib$ where a and b are real numbers and $i = \sqrt{-1}$. It is necessary to use complex numbers in this theory because, as is well known, the solutions to equations of the form $\alpha(z) = 0$ (the roots of the polynomial) may not exist as real numbers. Recall that the *conjugate* of a complex number z is the number $\bar{z} = a - ib$, and its *modulus* (absolute value) is the real number

$$|z| = \sqrt{z\bar{z}} = \sqrt{a^2 + b^2} \tag{5.1.7}$$

to be interpreted as the radial distance of z from the origin in the complex plane, in which a and b are measured on the coordinate axes. If $|z| > (=, <)\ 1$, z is said to be 'outside (on, inside) the unit circle'. It turns out that the properties derived for polynomials in z can be used directly to interpret the effects of lag operators.

Take the very simple case of the polynomial $1 + \alpha_1 z$ where α_1 is a real number. Postulate that the inverse $\delta(z) = (1 + \alpha_1 z)^{-1}$ exists, having the property

$$\delta(z)(1 + \alpha_1 z) = 1. \tag{5.1.8}$$

Further conjecture that this is also a polynomial, of indeterminate order,

$$\delta(z) = \delta_0 + \delta_1 z + \delta_2 z^2 + \delta_3 z^3 + \cdots \tag{5.1.9}$$

where the δ_i, $i = 0, 1, 2, \ldots$ are constants to be determined. It is easily verified that

$$\delta(z)(1 + \alpha_1 z) = \delta_0 + (\delta_1 + \delta_0 \alpha_1)z + (\delta_2 + \delta_1 \alpha_1)z^2 + \cdots \tag{5.1.10}$$

To satisfy the identity (5.1.8) requires $\delta_0 = 1$ and

$$\delta_j = -\delta_{j-1}\alpha_1, \ j = 1, 2, 3, \ldots \tag{5.1.11}$$

Note that the series is non-terminating. Therefore, the existence of the inverse depends on the absolute magnitude of α_1. If $|\alpha_1| < 1$, the terms in $\delta(z)$ form a convergent, summable series,

$$\delta(z) = 1 + \alpha_1 z - \alpha_1^2 z^2 + \alpha_1^3 z^3 - \cdots . \tag{5.1.12}$$

This series is convergent (i.e. the terms have a finite sum) for any z in the unit disk (i.e. the unit circle plus its interior, such that $|z| \leq 1$). However, if $|\alpha_1| \geq 1$ the series on the right-hand side is infinite for at least some such points. The single root of this polynomial is the real number $-\alpha_1^{-1}$. The condition that the root lies outside the unit circle, equivalent to $|\alpha_1| < 1$, is called the *invertibility condition* for the polynomial. The inverse function is finite for all $|z| < |\alpha_1|^{-1}$.

5.1.3 The General Case

The secret of extending this result to higher order polynomials is to factorize them. The second order (quadratic) case will serve to illustrate the principle. The factorization is

$$\alpha(z) = 1 + \alpha_1 z + \alpha_2 z^2 = (1 - \mu_1 z)(1 - \mu_2 z) \tag{5.1.13}$$

where it is easily checked that $\alpha_1 = -(\mu_1 + \mu_2)$ and $\alpha_2 = \mu_1\mu_2$. The roots of the polynomial are μ_1^{-1} and μ_2^{-1}, which may be either real or a complex conjugate pair. If the roots are outside the unit circle, then $|\mu_1| < 1$ and $|\mu_2| < 1$ and

$$\frac{1}{1 + \alpha_1 z + \alpha_2 z^2} = \frac{1}{1 - \mu_1 z} \cdot \frac{1}{1 - \mu_2 z} = \sum_{j=0}^{\infty} \mu_1^j z^j \cdot \sum_{j=0}^{\infty} \mu_2^j z^j. \tag{5.1.14}$$

Both of the series in this product are convergent for points z in the unit disk since (applying the triangle inequality)

$$\left|\sum_{j=0}^{\infty} \mu_j^j z^j\right| \leq \sum_{j=0}^{\infty} |\mu_k|^j |z|^j < \infty \tag{5.1.15}$$

for $k = 1$ and 2. The form of the inverse is found by multiplying the two series together and collecting terms in z^j for $j = 0, 1, 2, \ldots$ Clearly, the same argument can be extended to the general pth order polynomial $\alpha(z)$, and the invertibility condition is the same. All the roots of the equation $\alpha(z) = 0$, which are either real numbers or complex conjugate pairs, must lie strictly outside the unit circle.

The actual evaluation of the convergent solution in (5.1.14) would be tedious, and the higher order cases even more so. In practice it is often more important to check the existence of the inverse than to compute it, but the following trick to handle the quadratic case can be useful. Let constants a and b be defined by the identity

$$\frac{a}{1 - \mu_1 z} + \frac{b}{1 - \mu_2 z} = \frac{1}{(1 - \mu_1 z)(1 - \mu_2 z)}. \tag{5.1.16}$$

This implies $a(1 - \mu_2 z) + b(1 - \mu_1 z) = 1$, which is satisfied if and only if $a + b = 1$ and $a\mu_2 + b\mu_1 = 0$. For the case $\mu_1 \neq \mu_2$,

$$a = \frac{\mu_1}{\mu_1 - \mu_2}, \quad b = \frac{-\mu_2}{\mu_1 - \mu_2} \tag{5.1.17}$$

have the required properties. Substituting these values yields

$$\frac{1}{(1-\mu_1 z)(1-\mu_2 z)} = \frac{1}{\mu_1-\mu_2}\left(\frac{\mu_1}{1-\mu_1 z} - \frac{\mu_2}{1-\mu_2 z}\right)$$
$$= \sum_{j=0}^{\infty}\left(\frac{\mu_1^{j+1}-\mu_2^{j+1}}{\mu_1-\mu_2}\right) z^j \tag{5.1.18}$$

For the case $\mu_1 = \mu_2$ one can show (write $\mu_2 = \mu_1 + \delta$ and let $\delta \to 0$, using l'Hôpital's rule) that the required formula is

$$\frac{1}{(1-\mu_1 z)^2} = \sum_{j=0}^{\infty}(j+1)\mu_1^j z^j. \tag{5.1.19}$$

5.2 Autoregressive and Moving Average Dynamic Structures

5.2.1 Innovation Processes

Following the approach of Chapter 4, the notion of an innovation process lies at the heart of time series modelling. The idea is to model a time series as a linear combination of random increments whose properties are simple enough to allow a tractable analysis. Let $\{\varepsilon_t, -\infty < t < \infty\}$ denote a stochastic process, and let $\mathcal{E}_{t-1}$ denote the σ-field of events that are predictable when the past history of the process ε_t is known. Assume

$$E(\varepsilon_t|\mathcal{E}_{t-1}) = 0 \tag{5.2.1}$$
$$E(\varepsilon_t^2|\mathcal{E}_{t-1}) = \sigma^2 \tag{5.2.2}$$

where σ^2 is a constant independent of t. Our shorthand for these assumptions will be, $\varepsilon_t|\mathcal{E}_{t-1} \sim (0,\sigma^2)$. The process is thereby wide sense stationary. It is serially uncorrelated (see §4.2) and if also Gaussian, is identically and independently distributed. However, Gaussianity is not a requirement. Technically, the processes ε_t and $\varepsilon_t^2 - \sigma^2$ are *martingale difference sequences.* This is a concept that is explained in detail in §6.2, but it suffices for the present to think of them as unpredictable in mean, and in particular, serially uncorrelated. A process that is wide sense stationary and serially uncorrelated is sometimes called *white noise* and while the present assumptions are a little stronger than this, they are equivalent under Gaussianity. Also, for reasons to be examined in later chapters, they may often be more natural in an economic modelling framework. Figure 5.1 shows a realization of 500 independent N(0, 1) random variables generated on the computer. The time ordering of the sequence is actually arbitrary, and the appearance of any permutation of the points should be similar to the original.

Although our main business in econometrics is the study of relationships between variables, dynamic models describing the time path of a single variable are important modelling tools. Consider first the stable AR(p) process,

$$\alpha(L)x_t = \mu + \varepsilon_t,\ \varepsilon_t|\mathcal{E}_{t-1} \sim (0,\sigma^2) \tag{5.2.3}$$

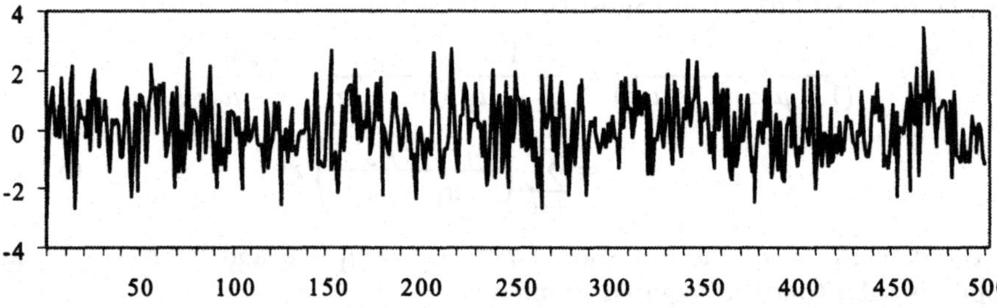

Figure 5.1: Gaussian White Noise

where the term 'stable' means that the polynomial $\alpha(z)$ is invertible in the sense of the previous section. If initialised in the remote past, at $t = -\infty$, this process is wide-sense stationary, possessing fixed, finite unconditional variance and autocovariances of all orders. It has an infinite moving average (MA) representation

$$x_t = \alpha(L)^{-1}(\mu + \varepsilon_t) = \delta(1)\mu + \delta(L)\varepsilon_t, \tag{5.2.4}$$

also called the solution of the process.

To illustrate, consider the first-order case, whose vector generalization has been analysed at length in Chapter 4. This is defined by

$$x_t = \mu + \lambda x_{t-1} + \varepsilon_t, \ |\lambda| < 1. \tag{5.2.5}$$

In operator notation this has the form $(1 - \lambda L)x_t = \varepsilon_t$, and referring to (5.1.12), the solution is clearly

$$x_t = \frac{\varepsilon_t + \mu}{1 - \lambda L} = \varepsilon_t + \mu + \lambda(\varepsilon_{t-1} + \mu) + \lambda^2(\varepsilon_{t-2} + \mu) + \cdots \tag{5.2.6}$$

where the '$\cdots$' indicates that the expansion is taken to an arbitrary number of terms, since beyond a certain finite point, the remainder is small enough to be neglected. This is exactly the solution obtained for the VAR case by iterated substitution for lagged x in the formula, compare equation (4.3.6). To formalize the notion of 'negligible' in the context of random variables, the correct step is to evaluate the moments. The geometric series $1 + \lambda + \lambda^2 + \lambda^3 + \cdots$ has the finite value of $1/(1 - \lambda)$, and hence

$$E(x_t) = \mu + \lambda\mu + \lambda^2\mu + \cdots = \frac{\mu}{1 - \lambda} \tag{5.2.7}$$

and

$$E[x_t - E(x_t)]^2 = \sigma^2 + \lambda^2\sigma^2 + \lambda^4\sigma^2 + \cdots = \frac{\sigma^2}{1 - \lambda^2} < \infty. \tag{5.2.8}$$

These formulae merely specialize (4.3.3) and (4.3.8). Note that (5.2.8) is obtained on multiplying out the square because the variables ε_{t-j} are serially uncorrelated.

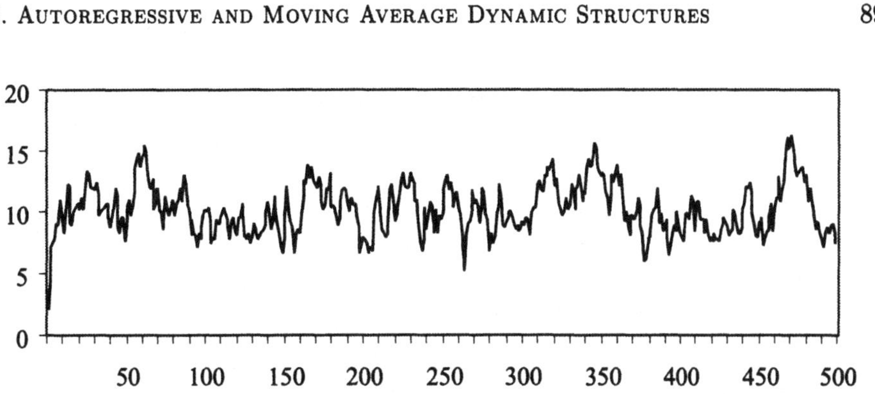

Figure 5.2: AR(1) Process

However, under the invertibility condition the double sum of the cross-product terms would be finite in expectation even if the serial covariances of the ε_t were nonzero to every order. The disappearance of this infinite sum of terms is therefore rigorously established.

Figure 5.2 shows a realization of the process $x_t = 2 + 0.8x_{t-1} + \varepsilon_t$, where $x_0 = 0$ and the ε_t sequence is that represented in Figure 5.1. The mean of the sequence is therefore 10 and the variance is 2.77. Other points to notice are the 'memory' of the process (i.e., decreased frequency of crossings of the mean) but also the mean reversion property, easiest to see by noting the initial value.

Next, consider the MA(q) process

$$x_t = \mu + \theta(L)\varepsilon_t, \ \varepsilon_t|\mathcal{E}_{t-1} \sim (0, \sigma^2) \tag{5.2.9}$$

where $\theta(z)$ is a lag polynomial of finite order q. This is wide-sense stationary for any choice of $\theta(z)$, because it is nothing but a finite sum of random variables. The invertibility condition is nonetheless of interest in this case, because when $\theta(z)$ is invertible the process can be represented as an infinite-order (but effectively truncatible) autoregression. We return to this important question in §5.2.6.

5.2.2 The ARMA Process

Putting the AR and MA structures together defines the ARMA(p, q) process

$$\alpha(L)x_t = \mu + \theta(L)\varepsilon_t, \quad \varepsilon_t|\mathcal{E}_{t-1} \sim (0, \sigma^2) \tag{5.2.10}$$

where by convention, $\alpha_0 = \theta_0 = 1$. The ARMA is said to be stationary and invertible when both polynomials are invertible. In this case it has both MA(∞) and AR(∞) representations, with MA coefficients given by $\delta(z) = \alpha(z)^{-1}\theta(z)$, and AR coefficients by $\delta(z)^{-1}$, respectively.

Generalizing the argument in §5.1.3, note that lag polynomials can always be expressed in factorised form, with

$$\alpha(z) = \prod_{j=1}^{p}(1 - \mu_j z) \tag{5.2.11}$$

where the μ_j denote the inverse roots. Applying this representation to both sides of (5.2.10) it is also evident that given any ARMA(p,q), it is possible to create a ARMA$(p+1,q+1)$ by multiplying both sides of the equation by $1-\lambda L$, for any real λ. An arbitrary complex conjugate pair of roots could be included similarly. This model must be observationally equivalent to the original, since nothing has actually changed, and it follows that the parameter λ is *underidentified*. That is to say, λ cannot be estimated from the data. In other words, any ARMA(p,q) in which one of the AR roots is equal to one of the MA roots is observationally equivalent to an ARMA$(p-1,q-1)$. This fact is of minor interest from the modelling point of view, but can gives rise to complications in the estimation and testing of ARMA models, where the properties of the model at arbitrary points in the parameter space need to be considered. See §12.3.4 for an example of the difficulties that arise.

5.2.3 The Wold Decomposition

The following famous result (Wold 1938) shows that in a stationary world, the infinite order MA representation of a time series plays a fundamental role.

Theorem 5.2.1 If the zero-mean process x_t is wide sense stationary (implying $E(x_t^2)<\infty$) it has the representation

$$x_t = \sum_{j=0}^{\infty} \theta_j \varepsilon_{t-j} + v_t \tag{5.2.12}$$

where $\theta_0 = 1$, $\sum_{j=0}^{\infty}\theta_j^2 < \infty$, $\{\varepsilon_t\}$ is a serially uncorrelated process, $E(v_t\varepsilon_{t-j}) = 0$ for all j, and there exist constants $\alpha_0, \alpha_1, \alpha_2, \ldots$ such that $\mathrm{Var}(\sum_{j=0}^{\infty}\alpha_j v_t) = 0$. □

Thus, $\{\varepsilon_t\}$ is what has been called a white noise process in §5.2.1. The distribution of $\{v_t\}$ is said to be singular, since $v_t = -\sum_{j=1}^{\infty}(\alpha_j/\alpha_0)v_{t-j}$ with probability 1 and hence is perfectly predictable one step ahead. Such a process is called deterministic. If $v_t = 0$, x_t is called a purely non-deterministic process. Another case is suggested by the example given in §4.4.2. Letting $v_t = z$ for all t, where z is a zero-mean random variable not depending on t, this is deterministic since any set of constants summing to 0 satisfy the definition.

The non-deterministic component of any wide-sense stationary process can therefore be approximated by an ARMA(p,q) model, with p and q large enough. This is a famous and important result, but it should not be overlooked that the characterization of a time series as stationary and uncorrelated does not rule out other forms of time dependence. For example, the stationary GARCH process (see §5.6) is a nonlinear process in which the *squares* of the process exhibit autocorrelation. This is not incompatible with the white noise property. However, also recall that in the jointly Gaussian process, where the autocovariances contain all the information about the dependence, white noise is the same thing as i.i.d.

5.2.4 Linear Processes

The foregoing analysis has distinguished four ways to restrict the distribution of an innovation process, and it may be helpful to contrast these formally, as follows:

$$\varepsilon_t \sim (0, \sigma^2) \text{ and } E(\varepsilon_t \varepsilon_s) = 0, t \neq s \tag{5.2.13a}$$

$$\varepsilon_t | \mathcal{E}_{t-1} \sim (0, \sigma^2) \tag{5.2.13b}$$

$$\varepsilon_t \sim \text{i.i.d.}(0, \sigma^2) \tag{5.2.13c}$$

$$\varepsilon_t \sim \text{NI}(0, \sigma^2). \tag{5.2.13d}$$

These conditions form a hierarchy, each implying the one above, but not implied by it.[1] All imply wide-sense stationarity, but only the last two imply strict stationarity. Condition (5.2.13a) is the property of the innovations in the Wold decomposition, and allows serial dependence of the GARCH type, while case (5.2.13b) does not. Both of conditions (5.2.13a) and (5.2.13c) have been referred to as 'white noise' in the literature. This term derives from spectral analysis, and refers to the property of a constant spectrum, with equal magnitude at all frequencies. As such, it depends solely on the properties of the autocorrelation function and so relates to (5.2.13a), but the i.i.d. assumption may be introduced to motivate it.[2] The two definitions are equivalent under condition (5.2.13d). The reason for focusing on (5.2.13b) is that this is the basic condition yielding a tractable asymptotic analysis, to be explored in the next chapter. Strict stationarity does not need to be imposed for this purpose, and for maximum generality we avoid doing so. The consequences of relaxing it are explored in §6.5.

A process having the form

$$x_t = \sum_{j=0}^{\infty} \theta_j \varepsilon_{t-j} \tag{5.2.14}$$

in which $\{\varepsilon_t\}$ satisfies condition (5.2.13c), of which (5.2.13d) is a special case, is called a *linear process.* The key feature is that the serial dependence of the process depends wholly on the coefficient sequence $\{\theta_j, j \geq 0\}$. Other forms of serial dependence are called nonlinear. Our characterization of an ARMA process has not imposed linearity, so that non-Gaussian cases are allowed to exhibit nonlinear dependence, although assumption (5.2.13b) rules out the GARCH case. Any possible nonlinearity is confined to the higher-order moments under this assumption, and models of such processes have yet to be considered in the literature, so the loss of generality in going from (5.2.13b) to (5.2.13c) appears small. For the sake of fixing ideas and avoiding potential complications, the processes in the analysis that follows will be generally thought of as linear if not Gaussian, the important exceptions being the subject of §5.6.

---

[1] The fact that (5.2.13b) implies (5.2.13a) is shown in §6.2.2.

[2] For background on spectral analysis see for example Fishman (1969) and Granger and Hatanaka (1964).

5.2.5 Autocovariance Analysis

Let the autocovariances of a wide-sense stationary series x_t be denoted by $\gamma_j = \text{Cov}(x_t, x_{t-j})$, constants independent of t. The sequence $\{\rho_j,\ j \geq 0\}$ where $\rho_j = \gamma_j/\gamma_0$ is called the *correlogram*, and the ρ_j are the autocorrelation coefficients. Because of stationarity, γ_0 is the variance of x_t and of x_{t-j} so this definition is consistent with the usual definition of a correlation coefficient. The correlogram is the 'fingerprint' of a stationary linear process, and the parameters of the ARMA(p, q) that generated the process can in principle be solved from it. The autocovariances are consistently estimated under the present assumptions by their sample counterparts,

$$g_j = \frac{1}{n-j}\sum_{t=j+1}^{n}(x_t - \bar{x})(x_{t-j} - \bar{x}_{-j}) \tag{5.2.15}$$

where $\bar{x}$ and $\bar{x}_{-j}$ are the means of the sub-samples from $j+1$ to n and 1 to $n-j$ respectively.[3]

We already know that if $x_t = \mu + \lambda x_{t-1} + \varepsilon_t$ where $\varepsilon_t \sim$ i.i.d.$(0, \sigma^2)$, then $\gamma_0 = \sigma^2/(1-\lambda^2)$, and $\gamma_j = \lambda^j\gamma_0$, $j = 1, 2, 3, \ldots$ and hence $\lambda = \gamma_1/\gamma_0$ and $\sigma^2 = \gamma_0 - \gamma_1^2/\gamma_0$. Replacing γ_j with g_j, it can be verified that the corresponding estimates are asymptotically equivalent to the least squares estimates of the AR(1) regression, say $\hat{\lambda}$ and s^2, although not actually identical because certain sums run from 2 to n instead of 1 to $n-1$, and the degrees of freedom adjustment is neglected.

It is not hard, in principle, to extend this analysis to higher-order cases. Consider the AR(2) model

$$x_t = \lambda_1 x_{t-1} + \lambda_2 x_{t-2} + \varepsilon_t \quad \varepsilon_t \sim \text{i.i.d.}(0, \sigma^2). \tag{5.2.16}$$

The intercept is suppressed here by assuming the process is expressed as deviations from the mean. To determine the relationship between the parameters of the model and the autocovariances, multiply equation (5.2.16) through by x_{t-j} for $j = 0, 1, 2, \ldots$ and take expectations to yield the so-called *Yule–Walker equations*,

$$\begin{aligned}
\gamma_0 - \lambda_1\gamma_1 - \lambda_2\gamma_2 &= \sigma^2 \\
\gamma_1 - \lambda_1\gamma_0 - \lambda_2\gamma_1 &= 0 \\
\gamma_2 - \lambda_1\gamma_1 - \lambda_2\gamma_0 &= 0 \\
\gamma_3 - \lambda_1\gamma_2 - \lambda_2\gamma_1 &= 0 \\
&\;\;\vdots
\end{aligned} \tag{5.2.17}$$

These equations can be used to solve λ_1, λ_2 and σ^2 from the correlogram, or to determine the correlogram from λ_1, λ_2 and σ^2. For the first of these solutions, rearrange the first three equations as

$$\begin{bmatrix} 1 & \gamma_1 & \gamma_2 \\ 0 & \gamma_0 & \gamma_1 \\ 0 & \gamma_1 & \gamma_0 \end{bmatrix} \begin{bmatrix} \sigma^2 \\ \lambda_1 \\ \lambda_2 \end{bmatrix} = \begin{bmatrix} \gamma_0 \\ \gamma_1 \\ \gamma_2 \end{bmatrix} \tag{5.2.18}$$

---

[3] This assertion is not proved as such, but the justification for it can be deduced from the material in Chapter 6.

Replacing the γ_j by g_j in the solutions yields estimates of λ_1, λ_2 and σ^2 that are asymptotically equivalent to the least squares regression of x_t on x_{t-1} and x_{t-2}. Alternatively, to derive the correlogram of the AR(2) solve

$$\begin{bmatrix} 1 & -\lambda_1 & -\lambda_2 \\ -\lambda_1 & 1-\lambda_2 & 0 \\ -\lambda_2 & -\lambda_1 & 1 \end{bmatrix} \begin{bmatrix} \gamma_0 \\ \gamma_1 \\ \gamma_2 \end{bmatrix} = \begin{bmatrix} \sigma^2 \\ 0 \\ 0 \end{bmatrix} \tag{5.2.19}$$

directly to obtain

$$\gamma_0 = \sigma^2(1-\lambda_2)/D \tag{5.2.20a}$$

$$\gamma_1 = \sigma^2\lambda_1/D \tag{5.2.20b}$$

$$\gamma_2 = \sigma^2(\lambda_2 + \lambda_1^2 - \lambda_2^2)/D \tag{5.2.20c}$$

where $D = 1 - \lambda_2 - \lambda_1^2 - \lambda_2\lambda_1^2 - \lambda_2^2 + \lambda_2^3$. The autocovariances of higher order are then obtained from the difference equation

$$\gamma_j = \lambda_1\gamma_{j-1} + \lambda_2\gamma_{j-2} \quad j = 3, 4, 5, \ldots \tag{5.2.21}$$

The AR(1) formulae can be seen to drop out on setting $\lambda_2 = 0$. .

For higher order AR processes one can generalize this scheme in the obvious manner. Given the starting conditions, solved from the Yule–Walker equations, the sequence of autocovariances is generated by the difference equation whose coefficients derive from the lag polynomial. As might be expected, the condition that this sequence converges to 0 is precisely the same invertibility condition that ensures the existence of the stable solution of the process. The result also shows that the finite order autocorrelations of the AR process are never 0, although like the lag coefficients they converge to 0 at an exponential rate as the lag increases.

5.2.6 Representing the MA(q) Process

Contrast this result with that for the moving average process of order $q < \infty$. It is easy to verify that the autocovariances have the form

$$\gamma_j = \begin{cases} \sigma^2(\theta_0\theta_j + \cdots + \theta_{q-j}\theta_q), & j = 0, \ldots, q \\ 0, \quad j > q. \end{cases} \tag{5.2.22}$$

Thus, the sequence of autocorrelations is truncated at q lags, and in principle the AR and MA structures can be distinguished by inspection of the correlograms. However, an interesting problem arises when attempting to back-solve for the lag coefficients from the autocorrelations. This is conveniently illustrated by the first-order case. If

$$x_t = \varepsilon_t + \theta_1\varepsilon_{t-1} \quad \varepsilon_t \sim \text{i.i.d.}(0, \sigma^2) \tag{5.2.23}$$

(5.2.22) yields the relation

$$\rho_1(1 + \theta_1^2) - \theta_1 = 0 \tag{5.2.24}$$

which is a quadratic in θ_1 with solutions for $\rho_1 \neq 0$ of

$$\theta_1 = \frac{1 \pm \sqrt{1-4\rho_1^2}}{2\rho_1}. \qquad (5.2.25)$$

Note that no real solutions exist for $|\rho_1| > 0.5$. At $\rho_1 = 0.5$ and $\rho_1 = -0.5$ there are unique solutions $\theta_1 = 1$ and $\theta_1 = -1$ respectively, and for other values of ρ_1 there are two solutions, say θ_1 and $1/\theta_1$ for each $\theta_1 \in (0,1)$, as is easily seen by multiplying (5.2.24) through by $1/\theta_1^2$. This is the identification problem for MA processes. Replacing θ_1 by $1/\theta_1$ and assuming that the (unobserved) shock process has a variance of $\theta_1^2\sigma^2$ instead of σ^2 yields a process with the same autocorrelation structure as the original process.

This problem exists in a more general form for any MA(q) process. Given $\theta(L)$ in (5.2.9), replacing any number of the roots of $\theta(z) = 0$ by their reciprocals yields another MA process which has the same correlogram as the original, although the implied variance σ^2, given γ_0, is different in each case. In other words there are 2^p representations of the process having the same correlogram. Given that σ^2 is not known *a priori*, and the autocorrelations represent all the available information about the dependence, these models are all observationally equivalent.[4]

However, at most one of these representations is 'invertible' such that the AR(∞) form

$$\theta(L)^{-1}x_t = \varepsilon_t \qquad (5.2.26)$$

exists with all it coefficients finite. This is the one that has all the roots of $\theta(z) = 0$ outside the unit circle. It is therefore customary to overcome the identification problem by imposing the invertibility condition. Of course, if any roots are actually on the unit circle these are also non-invertible, but they are equal to their reciprocals and therefore unique. Given a real root of unity, for example, write

$$x_t = \theta(L)\varepsilon_t = \theta^*(L)\Delta\varepsilon_t. \qquad (5.2.27)$$

and take the invertible form of $\theta^*(L)$. A process with MA roots of unity is called *over-differenced.*

The elementary mistake to avoid here is to confuse the invertibility condition for MA processes with the stability condition for AR processes. Finite order MA processes cannot be unstable. The root condition is the same in each case, but the interpretation of the condition is quite different.

5.2.7 Integrated Processes

While there are many economic time series that do not have the appearance of stationary processes, because of trend components, it is often believed that their differences of some order may do so. What became known as the Box–Jenkins forecasting methodology (Box and Jenkins 1976) relied on fitting ARMA models to time series, possibly after differencing the series to remove trends. Time series

[4] Davidson (1981) considers the implications of this fact for estimation.

whose dth differences have a stationary, invertible ARMA(p,q) representation are called integrated processes of order d, or I(d). The corresponding representation,

$$\alpha(L)\Delta^d x_t = \mu + \theta(L)\varepsilon_t \tag{5.2.28}$$

is known as the ARIMA (p,d,q) model (d is usually 0 or 1, and occasionally 2). Another variant is seasonal differencing, for example, in quarterly data one might model $\Delta_4 x_t$ and in monthly data $\Delta_{12} x_t$ as the ARMA(p,q), instead of Δx_t, aiming to account for the seasonal pattern.

As a simple example of this type of process, consider the integrated moving average or IMA(1,1),

$$\Delta x_t = (1-\theta L)\varepsilon_t. \tag{5.2.29}$$

Figure 5.3 shows a realization of this process with $\theta = 0.5$ and $x_0 = 0$, and the

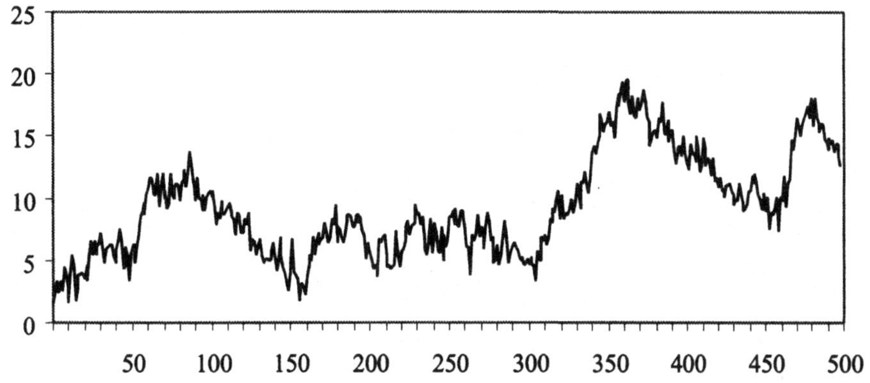

Figure 5.3: IMA(1,1) Process

driving process ε_t being again that in Figure 5.1. The special feature of integrated processes is their tendency to wander arbitrarily far from the initial point, so that the variance is diverging to infinity with t. There is no mean reversion tendency. For this reason they cannot be assumed to have started in the remote past and an initial value must be specified. Observe that there is no intercept in model (5.2.29) and the trend is an entirely stochastic feature of the realization. It could just as easily be decreasing as increasing. The properties of these processes are examined in more detail in Chapter 14.

The IMA model has two features that make it an interesting nonstationary case. One is that as θ approaches 1, the $1-\theta L$ is tending to $1 - L = \Delta$, and at this point (5.2.29) collapses to $x_t = u_t$. The model can therefore represent a 'nearly' stationary process. An interesting interpretation is found by considering a model of the form

$$x_t = z_t + u_t \quad u_t \sim \text{i.i.d.}(0, \sigma_u^2) \tag{5.2.30}$$

where

$$z_t = z_{t-1} + v_t \quad v_t \sim \text{i.i.d.}(0, \sigma_v^2). \tag{5.2.31}$$

In words, x_t is the sum of a random walk (the cumulation of an independent process) and an independent process. This process might represent an economic variable that is the sum of a 'permanent' component z_t and a 'transitory' component u_t. Consumers' income has often been cited as an example, see Hall (1978), Sargent (1979). Its properties depend on the relative magnitudes of the two variances. Note that

$$\Delta x_t = v_t + \Delta u_t \tag{5.2.32}$$

and hence, assuming the permanent and transitory components are independent of each other,

$$\text{Var}(\Delta x_t) = \sigma_v^2 + 2\sigma_u^2 \tag{5.2.33}$$

whereas

$$\text{Cov}(\Delta x_t, \Delta x_{t-j}) = \begin{cases} -\sigma_u^2, & j = 1 \\ 0, & j > 1. \end{cases} \tag{5.2.34}$$

This autocovariance pattern is the 'signature' of an MA(1) process. If the disturbances are i.i.d., Δx_t is a linear process and its serial dependence is fully described by the covariances. Therefore it *is* an MA(1), and x_t is an IMA(1,1). The coefficient θ can be calculated using (5.2.25) where

$$\rho_1 = \frac{-\sigma_u^2}{\sigma_v^2 + 2\sigma_u^2}. \tag{5.2.35}$$

Note that $|\rho_1| < .5$, and θ ranges from 0 to -1 as σ_u^2/σ_v^2 ranges from 0 to ∞.

5.2.8 Vector Autoregressions

Consider the VAR(p) model of §4.3.4. The generalization of lag operator notation to matrices provides no difficulty. With the variables expressed as deviations from the mean to avoid including intercept terms, write in place of (4.3.14)

$$\mathbf{\Lambda}(L)\boldsymbol{x}_t = (\boldsymbol{I} - \mathbf{\Lambda}_1 L - \cdots - \mathbf{\Lambda}_p L^p)\boldsymbol{x}_t = \boldsymbol{\varepsilon}_t \tag{5.2.36}$$

where $\mathbf{\Lambda}(L)$ is a $m \times m$ matrix whose elements have the form $1 - \sum_{k=1}^{p} \lambda_{kii} L^k$ on the diagonal, and $-\sum_{k=1}^{p} \lambda_{kij} L^k$ elsewhere. Indeed, there is no difficulty in principle in constructing a vector ARMA, or VARMA(p, q) model, having the form

$$\mathbf{\Lambda}(L)\boldsymbol{x}_t = \mathbf{\Theta}(L)\boldsymbol{\varepsilon}_t \tag{5.2.37}$$

where $\mathbf{\Theta}(L)$ is a $m \times m$ polynomial matrix of order q. This specification is less popular than the simple VAR, because of its complexity and practical difficulties with estimation. To fix ideas we focus on the case of (5.2.36).

The solution of the system in (5.2.36) is found by analogy with the scalar case, by inverting $\boldsymbol{\Lambda}(L)$. Consider the parallel problem of the matrix polynomial $\boldsymbol{\Lambda}(z)$. This inverse is written in the usual manner as

$$\boldsymbol{\Lambda}(z)^{-1} = \frac{1}{|\boldsymbol{\Lambda}(z)|} \operatorname{adj} \boldsymbol{\Lambda}(z) \tag{5.2.38}$$

where $|\boldsymbol{\Lambda}(z)|$ is a scalar polynomial of maximum order mp, and the elements of $\operatorname{adj} \boldsymbol{\Lambda}(z)$ are likewise polynomials of finite order. Subject to the invertibility of $|\boldsymbol{\Lambda}(z)|$, it is evident that the solution of the VAR might be written as

$$\boldsymbol{x}_t = \boldsymbol{\Lambda}(L)^{-1}\boldsymbol{\varepsilon}_t = \frac{1}{|\boldsymbol{\Lambda}(L)|} \operatorname{adj} \boldsymbol{\Lambda}(L)\boldsymbol{\varepsilon}_t. \tag{5.2.39}$$

This is the so-called *final form* of the VAR model (see Theil and Boot 1962) and if it exists the system is said to be stable. The stability condition is that the roots of the equation $|\boldsymbol{\Lambda}(z)| = 0$, up to mp in number, must all lie strictly outside the unit circle.

Applying this result to the case $p = 1$ calls for the roots of $|\boldsymbol{I} - z\boldsymbol{\Lambda}| = 0$ to be evaluated. These are, apart from a change of sign, the reciprocals of the roots of

$$|\boldsymbol{\Lambda} - z\boldsymbol{I}| = 0 \tag{5.2.40}$$

which are none other than the eigenvalues of $\boldsymbol{\Lambda}$. The analysis is therefore unified with the earlier approach of §4.3, which called for the eigenvalues of $\boldsymbol{\Lambda}$ to be inside the unit circle, with the present one calling for roots of $|\boldsymbol{\Lambda}(z)| = 0$ to be outside the unit circle. A bit more work will link up the pth order generalization of §4.3.4 with the general case in (5.2.36). Use of the lag operator generally makes the solution a great deal simpler, however.

The final form of the system may always be written as

$$|\boldsymbol{\Lambda}(L)|\boldsymbol{x}_t = \operatorname{adj} \boldsymbol{\Lambda}(L)\boldsymbol{\varepsilon}_t \tag{5.2.41}$$

which defines a vector of univariate ARMA processes. Writing $\alpha(L)$ for $|\boldsymbol{\Lambda}(L)|$ and $a_{ij}^*(L)$ for the elements of $\operatorname{adj} \boldsymbol{\Lambda}(L)$ gives (5.2.41) in the form

$$\alpha(L)x_{it} = \sum_{j=1}^{m} a_{ij}^*(L)\varepsilon_{jt}, \quad i = 1, \ldots, m. \tag{5.2.42}$$

The right-hand side of (5.2.42) is the sum of m finite-order moving average processes, driven by shock processes $\varepsilon_{1t}, \ldots, \varepsilon_{mt}$ respectively. Assuming the latter to be white noise, the linear representation of this aggregate can be deduced from the form of its correlogram. By an extension of the argument in §5.2.7, the sum of a collection of MA(q) processes can be shown to have itself an MA(q) representation. Although the AR component $\alpha(L)$ may all appear to be the same for all the equations, there is the possibility that common factors will cancel from each side of (5.2.42), and in particular, some equations might be stable even when the system as a whole is unstable. However, all the AR roots in the system are roots of $|\boldsymbol{\Lambda}(z)| = 0$, so the stability of the system ensures that each final form equation is a stable ARMA.

5.2.9 The Simple Keynesian Model Again

To illustrate the assertions of the last paragraph, consider the example in §4.2.3. In this case,

$$|I - \Lambda L| = \begin{vmatrix} 1 & -\dfrac{\gamma}{1-\beta}L \\ 0 & 1-\gamma L \end{vmatrix} = 1 - \gamma L. \tag{5.2.43}$$

This would generally be a polynomial of second order, but for the fact that here the first column of the matrix Λ is zero. The stability of the model therefore depends, as might be expected, on the condition $|\gamma| < 1$. The final form of the system is

$$(1-\gamma L)\begin{bmatrix} Y_t \\ I_t \end{bmatrix} = \begin{bmatrix} \dfrac{\alpha(1-\gamma)+\delta}{1-\beta} \\ \delta \end{bmatrix} + \begin{bmatrix} 1-\gamma L & \dfrac{\gamma}{1-\beta}L \\ 0 & 1 \end{bmatrix}\begin{bmatrix} \varepsilon_{1t} \\ \varepsilon_{2t} \end{bmatrix} \tag{5.2.44}$$

The second equation just reproduces (4.2.15). In the first equation, the disturbance term takes the form

$$\varepsilon_{1t} - \gamma\varepsilon_{1t-1} + \frac{\gamma}{1-\beta}\varepsilon_{2t-1} = \frac{u_{1t} - \gamma u_{1t-1} + u_{2t}}{1-\beta} = v_t \tag{5.2.45}$$

(say) using (4.2.20). Suppose u_{1t} and u_{2t} are white noise with variances σ_1^2 and σ_2^2 and covariance σ_{12}. Then

$$\mathrm{Var}(v_t) = \frac{(1+\gamma^2)\sigma_1^2 + \sigma_2^2 + 2\sigma_{12}}{(1-\beta)^2} \tag{5.2.46}$$

$$\mathrm{Cov}(v_t, v_{t-1}) = \frac{-\gamma\sigma_1^2}{(1-\beta)^2} \tag{5.2.47}$$

and $\mathrm{Cov}(v_t, v_{t-j}) = 0$ for $j > 1$. This is the autocorrelation structure of an MA(1) process, with

$$\rho_1 = \frac{-\gamma\sigma_1^2}{(1+\gamma^2)\sigma_1^2 + \sigma_2^2 + 2\sigma_{12}}. \tag{5.2.48}$$

There exists a white noise process η_t having variance $\mathrm{Var}(v_t)/(1+\theta^2)$, where θ is the unique solution of equation (5.2.24) subject to $|\theta| < 1$, such that the process $\eta_t + \theta\eta_{t-1}$ has the same correlogram as v_t. In this sense, the final form equation for y_t has a representation as an ARMA(1,1) process. If the structural errors are i.i.d., the same argument show that the final form is ARMA(1,1) in the stronger sense of being a linear process with this form, having innovations η_t that are also i.i.d. For the model of §4.2, this holds in the special case of Gaussianity.

5.3 Dynamic Regression Models

5.3.1 The General ARMADL Model

The remainder of this chapter considers the application of dynamic modelling concepts to regression models and some simple, and not so simple, behavioural explanations of dynamics. Let y_t be a variable to be modelled and let $\boldsymbol{z}_t$ $(k \times 1)$ be a vector of explanatory variables, assumed weakly exogenous with respect to the parameters of interest. In other words, the conditioning set for this problem is $\mathcal{I}_t = \sigma(\boldsymbol{z}_t, \boldsymbol{z}_{t-1}, \boldsymbol{z}_{t-2}, \dots, y_{t-1}, y_{t-2}, \dots, \dots ? \dots)$. As in §4.5.2, this notation is shorthand for the statement that $\mathcal{I}_t$ is the σ-field generated by the indicated variables. The question mark indicates that the list of eligible conditioning variables generally extends beyond those actually playing a role in the model.

Assuming linearity, the models of interest take the general form

$$y_t = \boldsymbol{\delta}'\boldsymbol{d}_t + \boldsymbol{\beta}_0'\boldsymbol{z}_t + \boldsymbol{\beta}_1'\boldsymbol{z}_{t-1} + \cdots + \boldsymbol{\beta}_m'\boldsymbol{z}_{t-m} + \alpha_1 y_{t-1} + \cdots + \alpha_p y_{t-p} + u_t + \theta_1 u_{t-1} + \cdots + \theta_q u_{t-q} \tag{5.3.1}$$

where $E(u_t|\mathcal{I}_t) = 0$. As before, $\boldsymbol{d}_t$ denotes dummy variables (intercept, seasonals, etc.). This is an *autoregressive moving average distributed lag* model or ARMADL (also called an ARMAX model). The lagged innovations belong to the conditioning set $\mathcal{I}_t$, but there is no need to list them explicitly. By repeated substitution of the model into itself u_t can be represented as a function of an infinite number of lags of $\boldsymbol{z}_t$ and y_t, although with coefficients converging to 0.

The lag operator provides a more compact notation for these models. Defining the k-vector of lag polynomials

$$\boldsymbol{\beta}(L) = \boldsymbol{\beta}_0 + \boldsymbol{\beta}_1 L + \boldsymbol{\beta}_2 L^2 + \cdots + \boldsymbol{\beta}_m L^m \tag{5.3.2}$$

the model can be written as

$$\alpha(L) y_t = \boldsymbol{\delta}'\boldsymbol{d}_t + \boldsymbol{\beta}(L)'\boldsymbol{z}_t + \theta(L) u_t \tag{5.3.3}$$

where $\alpha(L) = 1 - \alpha_1 L - \cdots - \alpha_p L^p$ and $\theta(L) = 1 + \theta_1 L + \cdots + \theta_q L^q$.

An alternative representation of (5.3.3) is

$$\frac{\alpha(L)}{\theta(L)} y_t = \boldsymbol{\delta}^{*\prime}\boldsymbol{d}_t^* + \frac{\boldsymbol{\beta}(L)'}{\theta(L)}\boldsymbol{z}_t + u_t. \tag{5.3.4}$$

This is a compact way of representing the operation of substituting out the lagged errors, expressing them as functions of lagged variables. The ratio of two finite-order lag polynomials (called a rational lag structure) can be expressed by consideration of the results in §5.1 as a polynomial of infinite order, although with geometrically declining weights. The transformation of the dummy variables in (5.3.3) must be treated with care, since lagging a dummy may produce a variable that is perfectly collinear with the original set. In the leading case $d_t = 1$, such that δ represents the intercept of equation (5.3.3), $\delta/\theta(L) = \delta/\theta(1)$ is the intercept in (5.3.4). If there is a trend term t in the model, its lag, $t - 1$, is a linear combination of trend and intercept. In general, applying the operator $1/\theta(L)$ to

$\boldsymbol{\delta}'\boldsymbol{d}_t$ must be represented by a recombination and reparameterization, where $\boldsymbol{d}_t^*$ represents the linearly independent components of the set $d_t, \ldots, d_{t-q}$.

Equation (5.3.3) defines a generic dynamic model, but it would be unusual for a model to be specified with all these features in practice. The following are the main specializations, and variations on the basic setup.

5.3.2 The Autoregressive Distributed Lag Model

Explicitly omitting the moving average component $\theta(L)$ yields

$$\alpha(L)y_t = \boldsymbol{\delta}'\boldsymbol{d}_t + \boldsymbol{\beta}(L)'\boldsymbol{z}_t + u_t \tag{5.3.5}$$

called an ARDL model, which can be estimated by OLS. This is probably the commonest type of model fitted in practice, just because of its simplicity. The structural equations of the VAR(p) system have this form. We can always choose to think of these as finite-order approximations to equations like (5.3.4).

5.3.3 Common Factors

Suppose there exists a lag polynomial $\rho(L)$ such that

$$\alpha(L) = \rho(L)\alpha^+(L) \tag{5.3.6}$$

$$\boldsymbol{\beta}(L) = \rho(L)\boldsymbol{\beta}^+(L) \tag{5.3.7}$$

and $\rho(L)$ is a common factor in the lag structure of each variable. The common factor model has the general form of an ARDL model with an ARMA error term,

$$\alpha^+(L)y_t = \boldsymbol{\delta}^{+\prime}\boldsymbol{d}_t^+ + \boldsymbol{\beta}^+(L)'\boldsymbol{z}_t + \frac{\theta(L)}{\rho(L)}u_t. \tag{5.3.8}$$

$\boldsymbol{d}_t^+$ represents the recombination of the dummies after transformation by $1/\rho(L)$, as before. Because of estimation difficulties, ARMA errors are not usually fitted in a regression model; but in the context of the ARDL model, (5.3.8) becomes an AR error term,

$$\alpha^+(L)y_t = \boldsymbol{\delta}^{+\prime}\boldsymbol{d}_t^+ + \boldsymbol{\beta}^+(L)'\boldsymbol{z}_t + \frac{1}{\rho(L)}u_t. \tag{5.3.9}$$

This is a very popular scheme, and routines for computing the estimates have been widely implemented (see §10.2.3). However, the major reason for this popularity in the older literature was as a 'fix' for serial correlation in the residuals of static regressions (see §7.7.3) rather than as a special form of dynamic model. Thus, in the case where $\alpha^+(z) = 1$ and $\boldsymbol{\beta}^+(z) = \boldsymbol{\beta}^+$ (constant), the model is said to exhibit no systematic dynamics, but only error dynamics. See for example Hendry and Mizon (1978), Mizon (1995) for a critique of this approach.

5.3.4 Rational Lags

If $\alpha(L) = \theta(L)$ in (5.3.3), the model can be put in the form

$$y_t = \boldsymbol{\delta}^{*\prime} \boldsymbol{d}_t^* + \frac{\boldsymbol{\beta}(L)'}{\alpha(L)} \boldsymbol{z}_t + u_t. \tag{5.3.10}$$

This is known as the rational lag model (Jorgenson 1966). It is a way of representing an infinite number of lags with a finite number of parameters, by having the coefficients decline geometrically beyond a certain point. The transformation back to

$$\alpha(L) y_t = \boldsymbol{\delta}' \boldsymbol{d}_t + \boldsymbol{\beta}(L)' \boldsymbol{z}_t + \alpha(L) u_t \tag{5.3.11}$$

is called the Koyck transformation (Koyck, 1954). The rational lag model can be implemented in practice by estimating (5.3.11), but it is important not to neglect the induced moving average disturbance. See §10.2 for further details on this estimation problem.

5.3.5 Polynomial Distributed Lags

Here is another scheme for reducing the number of parameters in a model with long lags, a variant of that due to Almon (1965). Consider for simplicity a model with just one explanatory variable,

$$y_t = \sum_{j=0}^{l} \beta_j x_{t-j} + u_t \tag{5.3.12}$$

where l is finite but large relative to the sample size. The problem is to make the β_j depend on a small number of underlying parameters in a plausible way, and a natural approach is to make the weights vary with j in a smooth manner. Let

$$\beta_j = \alpha_0 + \alpha_1 j + \alpha_2 j^2 + \cdots + \alpha_p j^p \tag{5.3.13}$$

where $p \ll l$, and the α_i, $i = 0, \ldots, p$ are the parameters. Choosing $p = 2$ or $p = 3$ in (5.3.13) makes the β_j lie along a quadratic or cubic curve. The constraints are imposed very simply by constructing new regressors

$$z_{it} = \sum_{j=0}^{l} j^i x_{t-j} \quad i = 0, \ldots, p \tag{5.3.14}$$

since then

$$\sum_{j=0}^{l} \beta_j x_{t-j} = \sum_{i=0}^{p} \alpha_i z_{it}. \tag{5.3.15}$$

Several variations on the same basic idea can be considered. For example, imposing the end-point restriction $\beta_{l+1} = 0$ is achieved by replacing (5.3.13) with

$$\beta_j = \alpha_0^* + \alpha_1^*(l - j + 1) + \cdots + \alpha_p^*(l - j + 1)^p. \tag{5.3.16}$$

The constructed regressors for this model are

$$z^*_{it} = \sum_{j=0}^{l}(l-j+1)^i x_{t-j} \quad i = 0, \dots, p. \tag{5.3.17}$$

In this case $\beta_{l+1} = \alpha^*_0$, and imposing the end-point restriction is a simple matter of omitting z_{0t} from the regression. This also means the restriction can be tested by a significance test on z_{0t}. Note that α^*_1 is the slope of the approximating polynomial at the point $j+1$, so that omitting z_{1t} also imposes a natural smoothness restriction, making the curve tangent to the horizontal axis at the terminal point.[5]

5.3.6 The Error Correction Model

The dynamics of a linear time series process can always be expressed in terms of the level and a lag polynomial in the differences. Given a polynomial $\alpha(z)$ of order p, there exists the equivalent representation

$$\alpha(z) = \alpha(1) + \alpha^*(z)(1-z) \tag{5.3.18}$$

where the coefficients of the $p-1$-order polynomial $\alpha^*(z)$ are

$$\alpha^*_j = -\sum_{k=j+1}^{p} \alpha_k,\ j = 0, \dots, p-1. \tag{5.3.19}$$

The first and second order cases are

$$\alpha_0 + \alpha_1 z = (\alpha_0 + \alpha_1) - \alpha_1(1-z) \tag{5.3.20}$$

$$\alpha_0 + \alpha_1 z + \alpha_2 z^2 = (\alpha_0 + \alpha_1 + \alpha_2) - (\alpha_1 + \alpha_2)(1-z) - \alpha_2 z(1-z). \tag{5.3.21}$$

This is known as the *Beveridge–Nelson decomposition* (see Beveridge and Nelson 1981). A further rearrangement yields

$$\alpha(z) = \alpha(1)z + \alpha^{**}(z)(1-z) \tag{5.3.22}$$

where $\alpha^{**}(z) = \alpha^*(z) + \alpha(1)$. Transforming $\beta(z)$ similarly, the ARDL model can be written in the so-called error correction model (ECM) form,

$$\alpha^{**}(L)\Delta y_t = \boldsymbol{\delta}'\boldsymbol{d}_t + \boldsymbol{\beta}^{**}(L)'\Delta \boldsymbol{z}_t - \alpha(y_{t-1} - \boldsymbol{\theta}'\boldsymbol{z}_{t-1}) + u_t \tag{5.3.23}$$

where $\alpha = \alpha(1)$ and $\boldsymbol{\theta} = \boldsymbol{\beta}(1)/\alpha$. Note how this involves no restrictions on the model, but is merely a matter of reparameterization. The parameters $\boldsymbol{\theta}$ can be thought of as representing the long-run equilibrium relations of the model, those that would prevail if $\boldsymbol{z}_t$ were constant and $u_t = 0$ for an indefinitely long period.

The ECM parameterization, first exploited by Sargan (1964) and popularised by Davidson, Hendry, Srba and Yeo (1978), has a number of attractive features. The long-run relations play an explicit role in the so-called 'error correction term'

[5] See also Sargan (1980), and Shiller (1973). The latter author suggests imposing only a *smoothness prior*, by allowing random deviations of the β_j from the curve.

whereas they are merely implicit in (5.3.5). The model gives a very natural behavioural interpretation to the lag structure, by which agents react both to change and to perceived deviations from the desired state. In many cases one can more easily accept that (5.3.23) represents the 'true' and (5.3.5) the 'derived' parameterization, than the converse. The variables enter the model either as differences, or in the lagged deviations from equilibrium, which is particularly useful when the data are nonstationary, because it is plausible to suppose that Δy_t, $\Delta \boldsymbol{z}_t$ and $y_t - \boldsymbol{\theta}'\boldsymbol{z}_t$ are stationary. This consideration touches on the very large topic of unit roots and cointegration models which are the subject of Part IV, but note that the ECM has a useful application to the stationary world to which the models of this chapter are implicitly applied. The main disadvantage of the ECM is that if $\boldsymbol{\theta}$ is unknown the model is nonlinear, although the point estimates are easily solved from the linear regression of Δy_t on $\Delta \boldsymbol{z}_t$, y_{t-1}, $\boldsymbol{z}_{t-1}$ and the lagged differences. See §10.2.7 and §15.2.5 for discussions of the statistical treatment in the stationary and integrated cases, respectively.

5.4 Models of Dynamic Behaviour

Early econometric time series research often proceeded by taking static relationships (demand and supply functions, the solutions of a comparative-static analysis, etc.) and fitting these to time series data. These endeavours were often unsuccessful; see for example Davis (1952). Econometricians came to accept, as an empirical fact, that 'lags matter', and various approaches to incorporating dynamic elements into models of economic behaviour have since been explored. There was an early vogue for error dynamics (the common factor model), since this approach represented the minimal tampering with the original behavioural model, but the restrictions involved are often found to be invalid when subjected to test (see Hendry and Mizon 1978). Another approach is to add lags of the explanatory variables on a purely ad hoc basis, taking the view that economic theory is not able to explain the timing of decisions, but can only be informative about the long-run equilibrium (conveniently solved out in the ECM form). Thirdly, attempts can be made to model systematic dynamics in terms of the costs of adjustment, the formation of subjective expectations, or some combination of these features. Here, we examine some simple examples of systematic dynamics. These approaches date mainly from an era spanning roughly 1950 to 1975, representing the first attack on the problem of dynamic econometric modelling, While this literature now needs to be read from the standpoint of today's more sophisticated views of time series analysis and model building, incorporating features such as unit roots, much of it is insightful and ingenious, and continues to repay study.

5.4.1 The Partial Adjustment Model

Suppose $y_t^* = \boldsymbol{\beta}'\boldsymbol{x}_t$ represents the desired level of an economic variable y_t. For example, the optimal level of inventories held by a firm will relate to factors such as storage costs, expected future sales, etc. The partial adjustment (PA) model of planned end-of-period inventories is

$$y_t^p = \gamma y_{t-1} + (1-\gamma)y_t^* \quad 0 \le \gamma < 1. \tag{5.4.1}$$

That is, at the start of the planning period (t) the firm aims at an inventory intermediate between the current actual and ideal levels. See Lovell (1961), and also Brown (1952) for an early application to consumption, based on the notion of 'habit persistence'. For a behavioural justification for this scheme, consider the one-period cost-minimization problem. Let y_t^p be chosen to minimize a cost function

$$C = (y_t^p - y_t^*)^2 + \alpha(y_t^p - y_{t-1})^2 \tag{5.4.2}$$

which is quadratic in both the extent of departure from the optimum and the amount of adjustment required, with cost-of-adjustment parameter $\alpha > 0$. The first-order condition

$$\frac{dC}{dy_t^p} = 2(1+\alpha)y_t^p - 2\alpha y_{t-1} - 2y_t^* = 0 \tag{5.4.3}$$

rearranges as (5.4.1) where $\gamma = \alpha/(1+\alpha)$.

The regression equation is obtained by adding a disturbance term to represent the difference between plan and outcome y_t:

$$y_t = y_t^p + u_t = \gamma y_{t-1} + (1-\gamma)\boldsymbol{\beta}'\boldsymbol{x}_t + u_t. \tag{5.4.4}$$

Since $|\gamma| < 1$ the model is stable, and if $\boldsymbol{x}_t$ is a stationary process so is y_t. If $E(\boldsymbol{x}_t) = \boldsymbol{\mu}_x$ and $E(u_t) = 0$,

$$E(y_t) = \gamma E(y_{t-1}) + (1-\gamma)\boldsymbol{\beta}'\boldsymbol{\mu}_x = \boldsymbol{\beta}'\boldsymbol{\mu}_x \tag{5.4.5}$$

since $E(y_t) = E(y_{t-1})$ by stationarity. In a stationary steady state, the desired level $y^* = \boldsymbol{\beta}'\boldsymbol{\mu}_x$ is realised.

The simple PA model is naive in several respects. It behaves unrealistically in a growing economy, since y_t^p is interpolating between the desired and the previous level, and lags behind a growing target even if the growth is smooth and predictable. The costs of anticipated change should be lower than those of unpredictable change. A modified cost function, embodying only the costs of change other than perceived trend change, is

$$C = (y_t^p - y_t^*)^2 + \alpha(y_t^p - y_{t-1} - c\Delta y_t^*)^2 \quad \alpha > 0,\ c \ge 0 \tag{5.4.6}$$

where c is a weight that represents the conservatism of the agent's growth forecast. Solving $dC/dy_t^p = 0$ as before yields

$$y_t^p = \gamma y_{t-1} + (1-\gamma)y_t^* + c\gamma\Delta y_t^*. \tag{5.4.7}$$

in place of (5.4.1). However, substituting $y_{t-1}^* + \Delta y_t^*$ for y_t^*, subtracting y_{t-1} from both sides and rearranging the equation yields

$$y_t^p - y_{t-1} = \mu\Delta y_t^* - \delta(y_{t-1} - y_{t-1}^*) \tag{5.4.8}$$

where $\mu = (1 + \alpha c)/(1 + \alpha)$ and $\delta = 1 - \gamma = 1/(1 + \alpha)$, with $0 < \delta \leq 1$. Putting $y_t = y_t^p + u_t$ gives the regression model

$$\Delta y_t = \mu \Delta y_t^* - \delta(y_{t-1} - y_{t-1}^*) + u_t. \tag{5.4.9}$$

The interest of this, still rather simple, model is that it unifies several different approaches to modelling dynamics. Substituting for y_t^* gives an ECM,

$$\Delta y_t = \mu \boldsymbol{\beta}' \Delta \boldsymbol{x}_t - \delta(y_{t-1} - \boldsymbol{\beta}' \boldsymbol{x}_{t-1}) + u_t \tag{5.4.10}$$

although this is a special case in that the coefficients of $\Delta \boldsymbol{x}_t$ differ from those of $\boldsymbol{x}_{t-1}$ only by a factor of proportionality. In other words, the rule-of-thumb adjustments to growth are in proportion to the equilibrium relations, which could be a reasonable restriction. If $c = 0$ the model reduces to the partial adjustment model. On the other hand if $c = 1$, then $\mu = 1$ and the rule is to adjust fully to shifts in the target. Rearranging (5.4.10) as

$$y_t = \boldsymbol{\beta}' \boldsymbol{x}_t + \gamma(y_{t-1} - \boldsymbol{\beta}' \boldsymbol{x}_{t-1}) + u_t \tag{5.4.11}$$

with $\gamma = 1 - \delta$ reveals a case of the common factor model,

$$y_t = \boldsymbol{\beta}' \boldsymbol{x}_t + \frac{u_t}{1 - \gamma L}. \tag{5.4.12}$$

Of the models considered, this one has the special property that if the disturbance is set to zero, the target is attained exactly, and $y_t = y_t^*$ no matter how y_t^* may be growing. Errors in attaining the target may persist, but are as likely to represent overshoots as undershoots. This is what it means to say that the model has no systematic dynamics, only error dynamics.

5.4.2 Adaptive Expectations

The adaptive expectations (AE) scheme was proposed originally by Cagan (1956) as part of a model of hyperinflation. If x_{t+1}^e denotes the subjective forecast of x_{t+1} made by agents at time t, under the adaptive scheme it is assumed to be generated according to

$$x_{t+1}^e = \lambda x_t^e + (1 - \lambda) x_t \quad 0 \leq \lambda < 1. \tag{5.4.13}$$

This model can be solved in terms of observable x by repeatedly lagging and substituting for x^e, but a neater approach is to use the lag operator. Write the model as

$$(1 - \lambda L) x_{t+1}^e = (1 - \lambda) x_t \tag{5.4.14}$$

and solve it as

$$x_{t+1}^e = \left(\frac{1 - \lambda}{1 - \lambda L} \right) x_t = (1 - \lambda) \sum_{j=0}^{\infty} \lambda^k x_{t-j}. \tag{5.4.15}$$

This is an exponentially weighted moving average (EWMA). Suppose a variable y_t depends on the expectation of a future variable, $x_{1,t+1}$, and other variables x_{2t}. Inserting this expectations model into the regression gives

$$\begin{aligned} y_t &= \beta_1 x^e_{1,t+1} + \boldsymbol{\beta}_2' \boldsymbol{x}_{2t} + u_t \\ &= \beta_1 \left(\frac{1-\lambda}{1-\lambda L} \right) x_{1t} + \boldsymbol{\beta}_2' \boldsymbol{x}_{2t} + u_t. \end{aligned} \tag{5.4.16}$$

A 'solution' that immediately suggests itself is the Koyck transformation,

$$y_t = \lambda y_{t-1} + (1-\lambda)\beta_1 x_{1t} + \boldsymbol{\beta}_2' \boldsymbol{x}_{2t} - \lambda \boldsymbol{\beta}_2' \boldsymbol{x}_{2,t-1} + v_t \tag{5.4.17}$$

where $v_t = u_t - \lambda u_{t-1}$. However, equation (5.4.17) is not the appropriate form for estimation. The moving average disturbance term has to be solved out, which in effect gets us back to (5.4.16). See §10.2.6 for the details of estimating this model.

5.4.3 Stock Adjustment

Models of stocks (fixed capital, inventories, durable household commodities etc.) suffer from the problem that the stock is not directly measured, except possibly by infrequent surveys. There are only data for the flows of expenditure on these items, the gross additions to the stocks in each period. Consider the following simple approach to the problem (see for example Stone and Rowe 1960, Jorgenson 1963). If q_t denotes expenditures in period t at constant prices, and S_t, stocks at end of period, then

$$S_t = S_{t-1} + q_t - D_t \tag{5.4.18}$$

where D_t = depreciation. This is also not observed directly, but might be modelled by

$$D_t = \delta S_{t-1} \tag{5.4.19}$$

such that depreciation in the period is a constant fraction of the opening stock. Substituting for D_t yields

$$S_t = q_t + (1-\delta) S_{t-1} \tag{5.4.20}$$

a difference equation that has the solution

$$S_t = \frac{q_t}{1-(1-\delta)L} = \sum_{j=0}^{t-1} (1-\delta)^j q_{t-j} + (1-\delta)^t S_0 \tag{5.4.21}$$

where $S_0 = \sum_{j=0}^{\infty} (1-\delta)^j q_{-j}$. One can generate a stock series recursively from the expenditures series given a benchmark S_0. It is as easy to extrapolate backwards as forwards, and given a pair of benchmarks, S_0 and S_n say, one can estimate δ by choosing the value satisfying

$$S_n = \sum_{j=0}^{n-1} (1-\delta)^j q_{n-j} + (1-\delta)^n S_0. \tag{5.4.22}$$

Like the adaptive expectations model, this is the exponentially weighted moving average of an observed series, although the weights summed to unity in the former case, which is not required here. In the absence of stock benchmarks the model can also be incorporated directly into a regression, and estimated in the same manner as AE.

5.5 Rational Expectations Models

The rational expectations hypothesis equates an agent's subjective expectation of a variable x_t with the conditional mathematical expectation given an information set $\mathcal{R}_t$, corresponding to what the agent in question is assumed to observe and act on. Technically, $\mathcal{R}_t$ represents the σ-field of events such that the agent knows at time t whether or not each has occurred. In the large literature incorporating this idea into econometric modelling that has developed since the seminal article of Muth (1961), the aim has been to model the rational expectation simultaneously with the agent's economic behaviour in response to it.

$\mathcal{R}_t$ could correspond to the maximal information set containing, in effect, everything observable at time t. This can be identified with the conditioning set for a regression model, as discussed in §1.4.3.[6] In this case the agent is said to be strongly rational. The agent might also base his forecast on a restricted information set, just the past history of the variable for example, with $\mathcal{R}_t = \sigma(x_t, x_{t-1}, x_{t-2}, \dots)$,[7] and this case is sometimes called weak rationality. Rational expectations does not imply omniscience on the part on agents, only that they make rational use of the information available to them. The essential implication is that agents learn from experience about the generation process of the variable they are trying to forecast, and hence there is a dependence between the parameters of the forecasting scheme and those of the DGP of the variable in question.

The properties of RE models are easily deduced from the properties of conditional expectations, in particular the law of iterated expectations. The prediction errors are uncorrelated with any function of the information set, so that if $f_t \in \mathcal{R}_t$ then

$$E[(x_{t+1} - E(x_{t+1}|\mathcal{R}_t)).f_t] = 0 \tag{5.5.1}$$

and in particular, have unconditional mean of zero (put $f_t = 1$).[8] However, if $\mathcal{R}_t \subset \mathcal{I}_t$ the random variable $E[x_{t+1} - E(x_{t+1}|\mathcal{R}_t)|\mathcal{I}_t]$ is nonzero in general, although it has a mean of zero.[9] Rational prediction errors are not necessarily equivalent to regression disturbances in a model.

---

[6] In the context of the dynamic regression, this information set is to be formally defined and given the symbol $\mathcal{I}_t$ in §7.1.1.

[7] See §4.1 on the $\sigma(\cdot)$ notation.

[8] See Corollary B.6.1. The notation $f_t \in \mathcal{R}_t$ is used here to indicate that f_t is an $\mathcal{R}_t$-measurable random variable, which is loosely interpreted to mean that it is 'in the information set'. See also §7.1.

[9] See Davidson (1994a), Theorem 10.26(ii).

The second important property is the multi-step prediction rule,

$$E(x_{t+2}|\mathcal{R}_t) = E[E(x_{t+2}|\mathcal{R}_{t+1})|\mathcal{R}_t] \tag{5.5.2}$$

which follows since the information sets $\mathcal{R}_t$ increase monotonically, with $\mathcal{R}_{t-1} \subseteq \mathcal{R}_t \subseteq \mathcal{R}_{t+1} \cdots$. In the interests of brevity, notations such as $E_t x_{t+j}$ will be used to denote $E(x_{t+j}|\mathcal{R}_t)$, once the information set in question is understood. The multi-step prediction rule generalizes to

$$E_t E_{t+j} x_{t+j+k} = E_t x_{t+j+k} \text{ for } k, j > 0. \tag{5.5.3}$$

Now consider some examples.

5.5.1 The ARMA(1,1) Process

To forecast x_{t+1} in

$$x_t = \alpha + \rho x_{t-1} + \varepsilon_t + \gamma\varepsilon_{t-1} \quad \varepsilon_t \sim \text{i.i.d.}(0, \sigma^2) \tag{5.5.4}$$

the model must be solved for ε_t in terms of lagged values of x. Assuming $|\gamma| < 1$, the model can be written

$$\left(\frac{1-\rho L}{1-\gamma L}\right) x_t = \frac{\alpha}{1-\gamma} + \varepsilon_t \tag{5.5.5}$$

where

$$\left(\frac{1-\rho L}{1-\gamma L}\right) = \sum_{j=0}^{\infty}(\gamma^j L^j - \rho\gamma^j L^{j+1}) = 1 + (\gamma - \rho)\sum_{j=0}^{\infty}\gamma^j L^{j+1}. \tag{5.5.6}$$

It follows that

$$x_t = \frac{\alpha}{1-\gamma} + (\rho - \gamma)(x_{t-1} + \gamma x_{t-2} + \gamma^2 x_{t-3} + \cdots) + \varepsilon_t \tag{5.5.7}$$

and hence

$$\begin{aligned} E(x_{t+1}|x_t, x_{t-1}, x_{t-2}, \ldots) &= \frac{\alpha}{1-\gamma} + (\rho - \gamma)(x_t + \gamma x_{t-1} + \gamma^2 x_{t-2} + \cdots) \\ &= \frac{\alpha}{1-\gamma} + \frac{\rho - \gamma}{1-\gamma L} x_t. \end{aligned} \tag{5.5.8}$$

The pure AR(1) and pure MA(1) cases are easily deduced from this formula by suppressing one or other parameter. The most interesting special case has $\alpha = 0$ and $\rho = 1$. This is the IMA(1,1) process and is nonstationary; see §5.2.7. In this case

$$E_t x_{t+1} = \left(\frac{1-\gamma}{1-\gamma L}\right) x_t \tag{5.5.9}$$

which is the adaptive expectations formula. This is the unique case in which AE coincides with the rational forecast.

5.5.2 A System with Lagged Expectations

Consider the linear dynamic system

$$\boldsymbol{B}\boldsymbol{y}_t = \boldsymbol{A}E_{t-1}\boldsymbol{y}_t + \boldsymbol{C}\boldsymbol{z}_t + \boldsymbol{u}_t. \tag{5.5.10}$$

This case is considered by Wallis (1977). Either strong or weak rationality implies $E_{t-1}\boldsymbol{u}_t = \boldsymbol{0}$, and hence taking conditional expectations through,

$$\boldsymbol{B}E_{t-1}\boldsymbol{y}_t = \boldsymbol{A}E_{t-1}\boldsymbol{y}_t + \boldsymbol{C}E_{t-1}\boldsymbol{z}_t \tag{5.5.11}$$

with solution $E_{t-1}\boldsymbol{y}_t = (\boldsymbol{B} - \boldsymbol{A})^{-1}\boldsymbol{C}E_{t-1}\boldsymbol{z}_t$. Making the supplementary assumption $E_{t-1}\boldsymbol{z}_t = \boldsymbol{\Lambda}\boldsymbol{z}_{t-1}$, the estimatible form of the system is

$$\boldsymbol{B}\boldsymbol{y}_t = \boldsymbol{C}\boldsymbol{z}_t + \boldsymbol{A}(\boldsymbol{B} - \boldsymbol{A})^{-1}\boldsymbol{C}\boldsymbol{\Lambda}\boldsymbol{z}_{t-1} + \boldsymbol{u}_t. \tag{5.5.12}$$

Notice the rather daunting implications of this result. There seems to be no possibility of estimating one equation in isolation here, in the way that was explored in §5.3. The solved equations are highly interdependent and nonlinear, and with rational expectations there is in general no such thing as a weakly exogenous variable. The generation process of the $\boldsymbol{z}_t$ must be specified, because it enters into the behaviour of agents through their subjective forecasts of the economy.

5.5.3 Systems with Current Expectations

These cases are more complex, and most easily developed in the context of a simple, two-equation example,

$$x_t = \alpha y_t + \beta z_t + u_t \tag{5.5.13a}$$

$$y_t = \gamma E_t x_{t+1} + \delta w_t + v_t \tag{5.5.13b}$$

where $|\alpha\gamma| < 1$. This might be a system determining prices (x_t) and wages (y_t), the latter depending on expected future prices; see for example McCallum (1976). Here, z_t and w_t are any relevant exogenous variables, which we assume to be driven by univariate AR(1) processes

$$z_t = \lambda_1 z_{t-1} + \varepsilon_{1t} \tag{5.5.14}$$

$$w_t = \lambda_2 w_{t-1} + \varepsilon_{2t} \tag{5.5.15}$$

where $E_{t-1}\varepsilon_{1t} = E_{t-1}\varepsilon_{2t} = 0$.

Eliminating y_t gives

$$x_t = \alpha\gamma E_t x_{t+1} + \beta z_t + \alpha\delta w_t + u_t + \alpha v_t \tag{5.5.16}$$

but to make further progress requires a new technique. There are various approaches to solving (5.5.16), but the nature of the solution can be most easily grasped by adding and then subtracting $\alpha\gamma x_{t+1}$ to give

$$x_t = \alpha\gamma x_{t+1} + \beta z_t + \alpha\delta w_t + u_t + \alpha v_t - \alpha\gamma\eta_{t+1} \tag{5.5.17}$$

where $\eta_{t+1} = x_{t+1} - E_t x_{t+1}$. Be careful to note that (5.5.17) does not represent the DGP of x_t. Rather, it defines the sequence η_t. It can however be solved forwards by repeated substitution for x_{t+j}, as

$$x_t = \sum_{j=0}^{n} (\alpha\gamma)^j (\beta z_{t+j} + \alpha\delta w_{t+j} + u_{t+j} + \alpha v_{t+j} - \alpha\gamma\eta_{t+j+1}) + (\alpha\gamma)^{n+1} x_{t+n+1}. \tag{5.5.18}$$

Assuming the generation processes of z_t and w_t are suitably behaved, a solution is obtained by leading (5.5.18) one period, letting n tend to infinity and taking expectations conditional on time t to give

$$E_t x_{t+1} = \sum_{j=0}^{\infty} (\alpha\gamma)^j (\beta E_t z_{t+j+1} + \alpha\delta E_t w_{t+j+1}). \tag{5.5.19}$$

We have to say 'a' solution because it is obtained by imposing the transversality condition,

$$(\alpha\gamma)^{n+1} x_{t+n+1} \to 0 \text{ as } n \to \infty. \tag{5.5.20}$$

The existence of explosive solutions cannot be ruled out, but these are uninteresting since not observed in practice. If there is a finite solution then $E_t x_{t+1}$ must have the form of (5.5.19).

Using the specialization of (5.5.8) and also the multi-step prediction rule (5.5.3) gives $E_t z_{t+j} = \lambda_1^j z_t$ and $E_t w_{t+j} = \lambda_2^j w_t$. Substitution in (5.5.19) then produces

$$\begin{aligned} E_t x_{t+1} &= \beta\lambda_1 \sum_{j=0}^{\infty} (\alpha\gamma\lambda_1)^j z_t + \alpha\delta\lambda_2 \sum_{j=0}^{\infty} (\alpha\gamma\lambda_2)^j w_t \\ &= \frac{\beta\lambda_1}{1-\alpha\gamma\lambda_1} z_t + \frac{\alpha\delta\lambda_2}{1-\alpha\gamma\lambda_2} w_t \end{aligned} \tag{5.5.21}$$

assuming $|\alpha\gamma\lambda_1| < 1$ and $|\alpha\gamma\lambda_2| < 1$. It is interesting to note that stability of the exogenous variables is not necessary for this solution, and $\lambda_1 = 1$ and $\lambda_2 = 1$ (integrated processes) are possible cases. The solved equation for y_t emerges after some simplification as

$$y_t = \frac{\gamma\beta\lambda_1}{1-\alpha\gamma\lambda_1} z_t + \frac{\delta}{1-\alpha\gamma\lambda_2} w_t + v_t. \tag{5.5.22}$$

5.5.4 Dynamic Optimization

We remarked that the PA model of §5.4.1 was naive, and now pursue this theme further. The agent's behaviour is myopic in that it fails to distinguish permanent and transitory changes in the target variable. The error correction model was introduced as a crude way of overcoming the problem, by letting a proportion of the current growth in the target proxy for its expected growth. It would be more satisfactory to model a multi-period planning rule, and allow for rational expectations. See, among many applications of this idea, Kennan (1979), Nickell (1985), Hall (1978), Hansen and Sargent (1980, 1981), Hansen and Singleton (1982).

An individual with foresight, who aims to set a variable y near to a target y^* in future periods as well as at the present, might choose a planned path $\{y^p_{t+j}, j = 0, 1, 2, \ldots, n\}$ to minimize the quadratic cost function

$$C = E_t \sum_{j=0}^{n} b^j [(y^p_{t+j} - y^*_{t+j})^2 + \alpha(y^p_{t+j} - y^p_{t+j-1})^2] \tag{5.5.23}$$

where $\alpha > 0$ is the cost-of-adjustment parameter, b is the discounting factor in weighing future against present losses, $0 \leq b \leq 1$ and $y^p_{t-1} = y_{t-1}$ (given). The random (since unobserved) component here is the sequence $y^*_{t+1}, \ldots, y^*_{t+n}$.

According to Theorem B.10.1 the derivatives of C with respect to the y^p_{t+j} can be found by differentiating inside the conditional expectation operator. C being the conditional expectation of quadratic terms, the derivatives are linear in the terms $E_t y^*_{t+j}$ and it follows that $\partial C / \partial y^p_{t+j} = \partial C^* / \partial y^p_{t+j}$ where

$$C^* = \sum_{j=0}^{n} b^j [(y^p_{t+j} - E_t y^*_{t+j})^2 + \alpha(y^p_{t+j} - y^p_{t+j-1})^2]. \tag{5.5.24}$$

From this fact there follows the certainty equivalence theorem, which states that minimizing C is equivalent to the easier problem of minimizing C^*.

It further simplifies matters to let n approach infinity. The solution to the problem is then found as follows. For convenience of notation write x_j for y^p_{t+j}, and w_j for $E_t y^*_{t+j}$. Then

$$\begin{aligned} C^* = {} & (x_0 - w_0)^2 + \alpha(x_0 - x_{-1})^2 \\ & + b[(x_1 - w_1)^2 + \alpha(x_1 - x_0)^2] \\ & + b^2[(x_2 - w_2)^2 + \alpha(x_2 - x_1)^2] \\ & + b^3[\cdots \end{aligned} \tag{5.5.25}$$

and hence for $j = 0, 1, 2, \ldots$

$$\frac{\partial C^*}{\partial x_j} = 2b^j[(x_j - w_j) + \alpha(x_j - x_{j-1})] - 2\alpha b^{j+1}(x_{j+1} - x_j). \tag{5.5.26}$$

Equating the derivatives (5.5.26) to zero yields the first-order conditions for the optimal path, or *Euler equations*. If $\alpha = 0$, the solution is to set $x_j = w_j$ in each period. Otherwise, cancel $2b^j$ and make the substitution $a = 1/\alpha$ to give these in the form

$$bx_{j+1} - (1 + a + b)x_j + x_{j-1} = -aw_j \quad j = 0, 1, 2, \ldots \tag{5.5.27}$$

This is a second-order difference equation in x_j which may be written using the lag operator as

$$[b - (1 + a + b)L + L^2]x_{j+1} = -aw_j. \tag{5.5.28}$$

To solve (5.5.28) for the sequence x_j requires the inversion of this quadratic in L. Let the roots be μ_1 and μ_2 such that

$$b - (1 + a + b)L + L^2 = (\mu_1 - L)(\mu_2 - L). \tag{5.5.29}$$

Given $0 \leq b \leq 1$ and $a > 0$, the solution to the equations

$$\mu_1 \mu_2 = b \tag{5.5.30a}$$

$$\mu_1 + \mu_2 = 1 + a + b \tag{5.5.30b}$$

must satisfy two conditions: (i) both roots positive, since both must have the same sign by (5.5.30a) and at least one positive by (5.5.30b); (ii) at least one root less than one (hence unstable) to satisfy (5.5.30a). The other root is stable however, since assuming $\mu_1 < 1$,

$$\mu_2 = 1 + a + \mu_1 \mu_2 - \mu_1 = \frac{1 + a - \mu_1}{1 - \mu_1} > 1. \tag{5.5.31}$$

Because of the unstable root, equation (5.5.28) must be solved *forward.* Let $\theta = 1/\mu_2$, such that $0 < \theta < 1$ and also $\mu_1 = b\theta$. Rewriting the Euler equations in the form

$$(1/\theta - L)(b\theta - L)L^{-1}x_j = -aw_j \tag{5.5.32}$$

and multiplying through by $-\theta$ produces

$$(1 - \theta L)(1 - b\theta L^{-1})x_j = \theta a w_j = (1 - \theta)(1 - b\theta)w_j \tag{5.5.33}$$

where the second equality comes from $1 + a + b = 1/\theta + b\theta$. The solution of (5.5.33) (restoring the definitions of x_j and w_j) is therefore

$$y^p_{t+j} = \frac{1 - \theta}{1 - \theta L}(1 - b\theta)\sum_{k=0}^{\infty}(b\theta)^k E_t y^*_{t+j+k} \quad j = 0, 1, 2, \ldots \tag{5.5.34}$$

The model requires only that we specify the plan for the current period corresponding to $j = 0$, and with $y^p_{t-1} = y_{t-1}$ given, and this is

$$y^p_t = \theta y_{t-1} + (1 - \theta)(1 - b\theta)\sum_{k=0}^{\infty}(b\theta)^k E_t y^*_{t+k}. \tag{5.5.35}$$

This completes the derivation, except for the expectations, which have to be specified with reference to the target process. It reproduces the PA model when $b = 0$ (remembering that $E_t y^*_t = y^*_t$). However, the interesting exercise is to see what other kinds of models emerge, given different processes for y^*_t.

Consider two cases. First, the AR(1) process

$$y^*_t = \lambda y^*_{t-1} + v_t \tag{5.5.36}$$

for which $E_t y^*_{t+k} = \lambda^k y^*_t$. If $|b\theta\lambda| < 1$, substituting in (5.5.35) yields

$$y^p_t = \theta y_{t-1} + \frac{(1 - \theta)(1 - b\theta)}{1 - b\theta\lambda} y^*_t \tag{5.5.37}$$

This resembles the PA solution, which is the case $b = 0$. The other case in which the weights sum to unity is if $\lambda = 1$, in which case y^*_t is a random walk and $E_t y^*_{t+k} = y^*_t$, the same as the myopic forecast.

The second example is explicitly nonstationary, with y_t^* an ARI(1,1) process, being the integral of an autoregressive process,

$$\Delta y_t^* = \beta \Delta y_{t-1}^* + v_t. \tag{5.5.38}$$

It is a little trickier to find the k-step ahead expectation in this case, but $E_t \Delta y_{t+k}^* = \beta^k \Delta y_t^*$ which suggests a recursive solution

$$\begin{aligned} E_t y_{t+k}^* &= E_t y_{t+k-1}^* + \beta^k \Delta y_t^* \\ &= E_t y_{t+k-2}^* + \beta^{k-1} \Delta y_t^* + \beta^k \Delta y_t^* \\ &= \cdots \\ &= y_t^* + (\beta + \beta^2 + \cdots + \beta^k) \Delta y_t^* \end{aligned} \tag{5.5.39}$$

since of course $E_t y_t^* = y_t^*$. Substituting (5.5.39) into (5.5.35) and simplifying on the assumption $|b\theta\beta| < 1$ produces

$$y_t^p = \theta y_{t-1} + (1-\theta) y_t^* + \frac{(1-\theta) b\theta\beta}{1 - b\theta\beta} \Delta y_t^* \tag{5.5.40}$$

or equivalently

$$y_t^p - y_{t-1} = (1-\theta)(y_{t-1}^* - y_{t-1}) + \frac{1-\theta}{1-b\theta\beta} \Delta y_t^* \tag{5.5.41}$$

Compare this with (5.4.8). We have once again arrived at an error correction model. Again, the PA model emerges if either $b = 0$ or $\beta = 0$. With $b = \beta = 1$ the model has no systematic dynamics, but AR(1) disturbances. If $\beta = 1$ the target is I(2), implying a pronounced and highly predictable trend. For more discussion of integrated processes see Chapters 15 and 16.

5.6 Conditional Heteroscedasticity

So far in this chapter, we have implicitly maintained at least assumptions (5.2.1) and (5.2.2) wherever assumptions about the error term were required. This is convenient and conventional but, as has already been remarked, the second assumption has no compelling justification. To relax it, a natural class of models to consider is one involving a clustering of (absolutely) large or small innovations, such that ε_t^2 tends to be large if this is true of ε_{t-j}^2, for small values of j. This approach, first proposed by Engle (1982a), has since given rise to a large applied literature, particularly in the field of finance where volatility modelling and prediction is a problem of special importance.

Letting h_t denote $E(\varepsilon_t^2 | \mathcal{E}_{t-1})$ one can always write

$$\varepsilon_t = \sqrt{h_t} u_t \tag{5.6.1}$$

where u_t is a process having conditional mean 0 and conditional variance 1, and hence is uncorrelated in both levels and squares. If u_t is Gaussian, these properties are equivalent to i.i.d. Then

$$E(\varepsilon_t | \mathcal{E}_{t-1}) = \sqrt{h_t} E(u_t | \mathcal{E}_{t-1}) = 0 \tag{5.6.2a}$$

$$E(\varepsilon_t^2|\mathcal{E}_{t-1}) = h_t E(u_t^2|\mathcal{E}_{t-1}) = h_t \tag{5.6.2b}$$

where both equations use the fact that h_t is conditionally fixed with respect to the information set $\mathcal{E}_{t-1}$. The first-order *autoregressive conditional heteroscedasticity* (ARCH) model has the specification

$$h_t = \alpha_0 + \alpha_1 \varepsilon_{t-1}^2. \tag{5.6.3}$$

This form of dependence does not contradict the white noise property of the process. It is stationary, subject to certain restrictions on the new parameters α_0 and α_1 to ensure finiteness and time-independence of the unconditional variance. The conditions $\alpha_0 > 0$ and $\alpha_1 \geq 0$ are necessary to ensure the conditional variance is positive with probability 1, which is an obvious requirement. Assuming that stationarity holds, so that the unconditional variance is independent of t, applying the LIE to (5.6.3) yields immediately

$$E(\varepsilon_t^2) = \alpha_0 + \alpha_1 E(\varepsilon_{t-1}^2) = \frac{\alpha_0}{1-\alpha_1}. \tag{5.6.4}$$

Hence, $\alpha_0 > 0$ and $0 \leq \alpha_1 < 1$ are required to ensure that ε_t is both stationary and nondegenerate.

Suppose that a process x_t is generated by the model represented by

$$x_t = \lambda x_{t-1} + \varepsilon_t \tag{5.6.5}$$

together with (5.6.1) and (5.6.3), where $u_t \sim$ i.i.d.(0, 1). Combining these equations gives the representation

$$x_t = \lambda x_{t-1} + u_t\sqrt{\alpha_0 + \alpha_1(x_{t-1} - \lambda x_{t-2})^2} \tag{5.6.6}$$

so x_t can be viewed as a form of nonlinear autoregressive process, although still driven by an i.i.d. innovation process. Also note that

$$h_t = \alpha_0 + \alpha_1 h_{t-1} u_{t-1}^2 \tag{5.6.7}$$

which can be solved recursively by substitution for the lagged h_t, as a complicated function of all u_{t-j} for $j > 0$. Clearly, a representation of x_t as an infinite-order 'nonlinear moving average' of the driving process is also possible.

The simple ARCH model can be generalized by adding further lags in (5.6.3) in the obvious manner. An alternative form of elaboration is the GARCH (generalized ARCH) model, due to Bollerslev (1986). The GARCH(1,1) takes the form

$$h_t = \alpha_0 + \alpha_1 \varepsilon_{t-1}^2 + \beta_1 h_{t-1} = \frac{\alpha_0}{1-\beta_1} + \alpha_1 \sum_{j=0}^{\infty} \beta_1^j \varepsilon_{t-j-1}^2 \tag{5.6.8}$$

subject to $\alpha_0 > 0$, $\alpha_1 \geq 0$ and $\beta_1 \geq 0$. The stationarity condition may be verified similarly to the ARCH case to be $\alpha_1 + \beta_1 < 1$, and subject to this condition,

$$E(\varepsilon_t^2) = \frac{\alpha_0}{1-\alpha_1-\beta_1} \tag{5.6.9}$$

by analogy with (5.6.4).

The GARCH(1,1) is found in practice to be a parsimonious representation that can represent conditional heteroscedasticity as effectively as a higher-order ARCH model, although it can itself be generalized in the obvious way by introducing further lags. A convenient way to analyse the properties of the GARCH is to represent it as an ARMA model in the squares of the disturbances. This fact can be appreciated by rewriting (5.6.8) as

$$\varepsilon_t^2 = \alpha_0 + (\alpha_1 + \beta_1)\varepsilon_{t-1}^2 - \beta_1 v_{t-1} + v_t \tag{5.6.10}$$

where

$$v_t = \varepsilon_t^2 - h_t = (u_t^2 - 1)h_t. \tag{5.6.11}$$

The stationarity condition $\alpha_1 + \beta_1 < 1$ can readily be understood in terms of the usual autoregressive root property. However, while the new 'disturbance' v_t satisfies the condition

$$E(v_t|\mathcal{E}_{t-1}) = 0 \tag{5.6.12}$$

similarly to (5.2.1), it cannot be i.i.d. and is highly conditionally heteroscedastic. Under the assumption $u_t \sim \text{NI}(0,1)$, $E(u_t^2 - 1)^2 = 2$ by (C.1.4), and

$$E(v_t^2|\mathcal{E}_{t-1}) = 2h_t^2. \tag{5.6.13}$$

The ARCH and GARCH are univariate models in the same mould as the ARMA class, but once the notion of modelling the conditional variance has been introduced, any suitably transformed lagged variable can in principle be assumed to drive h_t. Moreover, h_t can itself play a role in explaining the conditional mean, as in the so-called GARCH-M model. There is no need to assume that u_t is Gaussian. See for example Engle (1995) for a survey of the possibilities.

There is also an extension to the system case. If $\boldsymbol{\varepsilon}_t$ is $m \times 1$, and $E(\boldsymbol{\varepsilon}_t|\mathcal{E}_{t-1}) = \mathbf{0}$, a possible approach to generalizing the GARCH model (see Engle and Kroner 1995) would be to write

$$E(\boldsymbol{\varepsilon}_t\boldsymbol{\varepsilon}_t'|\mathcal{E}_{t-1}) = \boldsymbol{H}_t \quad (m \times m). \tag{5.6.14}$$

The difficulty is to choose a parameterization of $\boldsymbol{H}_t$ that is both reasonably parsimonious (economical with parameters) and preserves positive definiteness. One possibility is to postulate

$$\boldsymbol{H}_t = \boldsymbol{A}_0 + \boldsymbol{A}_1\boldsymbol{\varepsilon}_{t-1}\boldsymbol{\varepsilon}_{t-1}'\boldsymbol{A}_1' + \boldsymbol{B}_1\boldsymbol{H}_{t-1}\boldsymbol{B}_1' \tag{5.6.15}$$

where $\boldsymbol{A}_0$ is positive definite, and $\boldsymbol{A}_1$ and $\boldsymbol{B}_1$ are $m \times m$ matrices of parameters. For tractability one might need to impose severe simplifying restrictions on $\boldsymbol{A}_1$ and $\boldsymbol{B}_1$, such as having these matrices diagonal. This model can be rewritten in vector form using (A.10.6) as

$$\text{Vec}\,\boldsymbol{H}_t = \text{Vec}\,\boldsymbol{A}_0 + \boldsymbol{A}_1 \otimes \boldsymbol{A}_1'\,\text{Vec}\,\boldsymbol{\varepsilon}_{t-1}\boldsymbol{\varepsilon}_{t-1}' + \boldsymbol{B}_1 \otimes \boldsymbol{B}_1'\,\text{Vec}\,\boldsymbol{H}_{t-1} \tag{5.6.16}$$

and the dynamic properties of the model can be analysed by generalizing the foregoing arguments. Similarly to (4.3.10), the unconditional variance matrix $\boldsymbol{\Omega}$ is defined by the equation

$$\operatorname{Vec}\boldsymbol{\Omega} = (\boldsymbol{I}_{m^2} - \boldsymbol{A}_1 \otimes \boldsymbol{A}_1' - \boldsymbol{B}_1 \otimes \boldsymbol{B}_1')^{-1} \operatorname{Vec} \boldsymbol{A}_0 \tag{5.6.17}$$

subject to the implied stationarity condition, that $\boldsymbol{I}_{m^2} - \boldsymbol{A}_1 \otimes \boldsymbol{A}_1' - \boldsymbol{B}_1 \otimes \boldsymbol{B}_1'$ be nonsingular.

A second possibility is to let

$$\boldsymbol{H}_t = \boldsymbol{A}_0^* + \boldsymbol{A}_1^* \odot \boldsymbol{\varepsilon}_{t-1}\boldsymbol{\varepsilon}_{t-1}' + \boldsymbol{B}_1^* \odot \boldsymbol{H}_{t-1} \tag{5.6.18}$$

where for $m \times m$ matrices $\boldsymbol{A}$ and $\boldsymbol{B}$, $\boldsymbol{A} \odot \boldsymbol{B}$ is the *Hadamard product*, the $m \times m$ matrix whose elements are $a_{ij}b_{ij}$, for $i, j = 1, \ldots, m$. $\boldsymbol{H}_t$ is symmetric and positive definite if this is true of $\boldsymbol{A}_0^*$, $\boldsymbol{A}_1^*$, $\boldsymbol{B}_1^*$ and $\boldsymbol{H}_{t-1}$, see Attanasio (1991) for details. Extensions to higher orders of lag in both of these models can be easily made, just as in the univariate models.

An alternative approach to reducing the number of parameters is to define the elements of $\boldsymbol{H}_t$ as

$$h_{ijt} = \rho_{ij}\sqrt{h_{iit}h_{jjt}} \tag{5.6.19}$$

where $\rho_{ii} = 1$, and the h_{iit} for $i = 1, \ldots, m$ are modelled as GARCH. In other words, the variances are time varying, but the correlation matrix is fixed. See Bollerslev (1990) for an application.

Further Reading: For the basics of ARMA modelling (§5.2) there are many references to consult. Hamilton (1994), Lütkepohl (1991), Harvey (1981) are all excellent texts. Anderson (1971), and Nerlove, Grether and Carvalho (1979) offer more advanced treatments. Box and Jenkins (1976) popularised the use of these models in forecasting. Wallis (1977) and Prothero and Wallis (1976), are two important articles on econometric modelling. The literature on dynamic model building (§5.3, §5.4) links up with the subject matter of Chapter 4. In addition to Hendry (1995), some older textbooks on these topics that are still of interest include Desai (1976) and Wallis (1973). Classic survey articles include Hendry, Pagan and Sargan (1983), Nerlove (1972), Dhrymes (1971), Griliches (1967). See Pagan (1978) on polynomial lags. The literature on rational expectations (§5.5) is voluminous. Monographs which consider the econometric issues include Begg (1982), Whiteman (1983), and Pesaran (1987). Important articles on the econometric implications include Shiller (1978), Wallis (1980), Pagan (1984a). Finally. Lucas and Sargent (1981) is a collection of classic readings. On ARCH models (§5.6), Hamilton (1994) has an excellent chapter, Bollerslev, Engle and Nelson (1994) is a comprehensive survey, and Engle(1995) collects some important readings.

5.7 Appendix: Proof of Theorem 5.2.1

Let $\{x_t\}$ be a wide-sense stationary process with zero mean. Define $w_{1t} = x_{t-1}$ and for $j = 2, \ldots, k$ let $w_{jt} = x_{t-j} - \beta_{1j}x_{t-1} - \cdots - \beta_{j-1,j}x_{t-j+1}$ where the β_{mj} are the linear regression coefficients that minimize $E(x_{t-j} - \beta_{1j}x_{t-1} - \cdots - \beta_{j-1,j}x_{t-j+1})^2$. Note that for $j > 1$ the variables w_{jt} are uncorrelated with x_{t-i} for $i = 1, \ldots, j-1$, and so mutually uncorrelated, by construction. Therefore, in the least squares regression

$$x_t = \gamma_1 w_{1t} + \cdots + \gamma_k w_{kt} + \varepsilon_{kt} \tag{5.7.1}$$

$\gamma_j = E(w_{jt}x_t)/E(w_{jt}^2)$ for $j = 1, \ldots, k$, not depending on k, and

$$E(\varepsilon_{kt}^2) = E(x_t^2) - \sum_{j=1}^{k} \gamma_j^2 E(w_{jt}^2). \tag{5.7.2}$$

The sequence defined by (5.7.2) for $k = 1, 2, 3, \ldots$ is monotone non-increasing, but also bounded below, and hence converges to a limit as $k \to \infty$. The Cauchy convergence condition

$$E(\varepsilon_{k+l,t} - \varepsilon_{kt})^2 = \sum_{j=k+1}^{k+l} \gamma_j^2 E(w_{jt}^2) \to 0 \text{ as } k, l \to \infty \tag{5.7.3}$$

is sufficient for the mean-square convergence of the sequence $\{\varepsilon_{kt}, k \geq 1\}$ so there exists a random variable ε_t such that $E(\varepsilon_{kt} - \varepsilon_t)^2 \to 0$ as $k \to \infty$. Write

$$x_t = \sum_{j=1}^{\infty} \gamma_j w_{jt} + \varepsilon_t. \tag{5.7.4}$$

However, it is also possible to write this in the form

$$\begin{aligned} x_t &= \gamma_1 x_{t-1} + \gamma_2(x_{t-2} - \beta_{12}x_{t-1}) + \gamma_3(x_{t-3} - \beta_{13}x_{t-1} - \beta_{23}x_{t-2}) + \cdots + \varepsilon_t \\ &= \sum_{j=1}^{\infty} \alpha_j x_{t-j} + \varepsilon_t \end{aligned} \tag{5.7.5}$$

where $\alpha_j = \gamma_j - \sum_{m=j+1}^{\infty} \gamma_m \beta_{jm}$, so that x_t possesses an infinite order AR representation. Note that $E(\varepsilon_t w_{jt}) = 0$ for $j > 0$ by the least squares property, from which it follows by recursion that $E(\varepsilon_t x_{t-r}) = 0$ for $r > 0$ and hence $E(\varepsilon_t \varepsilon_{t-r}) = 0$ for $r > 0$.

Next consider the least squares regression of x_t on $\varepsilon_{t-1}, \ldots, \varepsilon_{t-h}$. Since these variables are uncorrelated one may write, similarly to (5.7.1),

$$x_t = \sum_{j=0}^{h} \theta_j \varepsilon_{t-j} + v_{ht} \tag{5.7.6}$$

where $\theta_j = E(x_t \varepsilon_{t-j})/E(\varepsilon_{t-j}^2)$, not depending on h. It is easily verified that $\theta_0 = 1$. In the same manner as before the existence of a random variable v_t is deduced, the mean square limit of v_{ht} as $h \to \infty$, such that

$$x_t = \sum_{j=0}^{\infty} \theta_j \varepsilon_{t-j} + v_t \tag{5.7.7}$$

where $E(v_t \varepsilon_{t-j}) = 0$ for all j, and since x_t has finite variance by hypothesis, $\sum_{j=0}^{\infty} \theta_j^2 < \infty$ must hold.

It remains to show that v_t is deterministic. Substituting for x_{t-j} in (5.7.5), using (5.7.7), we obtain

$$\varepsilon_t = x_t - \sum_{j=1}^{\infty} \alpha_j x_{t-j} = \varepsilon_t + \sum_{j=1}^{\infty} \theta_j \varepsilon_{t-j} + v_t - \sum_{j=1}^{\infty} \alpha_j \left(\varepsilon_{t-j} + \sum_{k=1}^{\infty} \theta_k \varepsilon_{t-j-k} + v_{t-j} \right)$$

$$= \varepsilon_t + \sum_{j=1}^{\infty} \delta_j \varepsilon_{t-j} + v_t - \sum_{j=1}^{\infty} \alpha_j v_{t-j}. \tag{5.7.8}$$

where $\delta_j = \theta_j - \sum_{l=1}^{j} \alpha_l \theta_{j-l}$. Squaring both sides of (5.7.8) and taking expectations yields

$$E(\varepsilon_t^2) = E(\varepsilon_t^2)(1 + \delta_1^2 + \delta_2^2 + \cdots) + E\left(v_t - \sum_{j=1}^{\infty} \alpha_j v_{t-j}\right)^2. \tag{5.7.9}$$

Hence, $\delta_1 = \delta_2 = \cdots = 0$, and

$$E\left(v_t - \sum_{j=1}^{\infty} \alpha_j v_{t-j}\right)^2 = 0. \quad \blacksquare \tag{5.7.10}$$

Chapter 6

Asymptotics for Dynamic Models

6.1 The Simple Autoregressive Model

This chapter introduces some fundamental theory for the treatment of dynamic regression models. Although some of the material is quite general, we structure the analysis around the simplest possible dynamic model, the first-order autoregression. Consider

$$x_t = \lambda x_{t-1} + u_t \tag{6.1.1}$$

where x_t is a scalar random variable. The intercept is omitted here solely for simplicity, but the omission implies that the process has a mean of zero if u_t does. Equation (6.1.1) is intended to describe how the random process x_t evolves through time, but its content obviously depends on the properties assigned to the innovation process $\{u_t\}$.

Textbook treatments often proceed by requiring u_t to be independently and identically distributed, and also Gaussian. From these powerful assumptions one can derive a correspondingly powerful set of distributional results. However, in the real world such assumptions cannot be relied on and it is helpful to know what weaker ones allow us to conclude.

An important case is where (6.1.1) represents nothing but a regression-based approximation to the true, unspecified generation process. In other words, pose the following question. Given an arbitrary, zero-mean time series $\{x_t\}$, what properties can the autoregression coefficient

$$\hat{\lambda} = \frac{\sum_{t=2}^{n} x_{t-1}x_t}{\sum_{t=2}^{n} x_{t-1}^2} \tag{6.1.2}$$

be expected to have? If we are allowed to assume nothing at all about the process there is, correspondingly, nothing to be said about the distribution of $\hat{\lambda}$. However, assumptions of quite a non-specific type can yield a useful result. If the time series is strictly stationary and ergodic (see §4.4) the following result is available.

Theorem 6.1.1 Measurable, finite-lag functions of a strictly stationary and ergodic process are also strictly stationary and ergodic. □

The proof is given in §6.6. Thus, the properties extend from $\{x_t\}$ to sequences such as $\{x_t x_{t-1}\}$ and $\{x_{t-1}^2\}$, although be careful to note that stationarity does not hold for a process such as $\{x_t + x_0\}$, which involves lags of indefinite order. Theorems 4.4.1 and 6.1.1, together with the fact that convergence almost surely is sufficient for convergence in probability, yield the results

$$\text{plim}\,\frac{1}{n}\sum_{t=2}^{n} x_{t-1}x_t = E(x_1x_2) \tag{6.1.3}$$

$$\text{plim}\,\frac{1}{n}\sum_{t=2}^{n} x_{t-1}^2 = E(x_1^2). \tag{6.1.4}$$

Applying the Slutsky Theorem (Theorem 3.1.1) it follows that

$$\text{plim}\,\hat{\lambda} = \frac{E(x_1x_2)}{E(x_1^2)}. \tag{6.1.5}$$

If this ratio is equated with λ in (6.1.1) then *by construction* the disturbance u_t is uncorrelated with x_{t-1}. Also note, in passing, that $\hat{x}_t = \hat{\lambda}x_{t-1}$ represents the minimum mean-squared error linear predictor of x_t based on x_{t-1}. All these statements are true whether or not x_t is actually generated by an autoregressive process, either of first or higher order.

By an elementary substitution, write

$$\sqrt{n}(\hat{\lambda} - \lambda) = \frac{n^{-1/2}\sum_{t=2}^{n} x_{t-1}u_t}{n^{-1}\sum_{t=2}^{n} x_{t-1}^2}. \tag{6.1.6}$$

Focusing attention on the numerator on the right-hand side, notice that $E(x_{t-1}u_t) = 0$ by construction, and this term also has a finite, albeit unknown, variance. It is therefore tempting to speculate that this scaled sum obeys a central limit theorem. However, it is clear that additional assumptions will have to be introduced in order to obtain this result. There is no reason to suppose, without imposing more structure on the problem, that the terms u_t are independent or have other properties that might allow a CLT to operate.

A general approach to this kind of problem is outlined in §6.5, but initially we consider assumptions of a specialist type. Suppose there is a sense in which (6.1.1) is a 'correct', or at least an 'adequate' representation of the true generation process. By making one rather specific (but reasonable) assumption, it turns out that a comprehensive set of asymptotic results is obtainable with very modest additional assumptions. Indeed, it is possible to discard the undesirable (because arbitrary) assumption of strict stationarity.

6.2 Martingale Difference Processes

6.2.1 Definitions

This section introduces some stochastic process theory to meet the requirements posed in the last paragraph. A revision of the material in §B.10 may be helpful at this point, although it is possible to appreciate the theory quite adequately at an intuitive level, by thinking of a σ-field $\mathcal{F}_t$ as either representing a collection of random variables to be held conditionally fixed in certain arguments, or simply as an 'information set', in the context of a subjective interpretation of probability and expectation.

Thus, let a sequence of σ-fields $\{\mathcal{F}_t,\ t = \ldots, -1, 0, 1, 2, \ldots\}$ denote 'known history to date t' in some specified observational situation. A plausible property of any time-ordered sequence of information sets is *nesting*, with $\ldots \mathcal{F}_{t-1} \subseteq \mathcal{F}_t \subseteq \mathcal{F}_{t+1} \subseteq \ldots$. In other words, knowledge accumulates with time, and is not lost. Let there also be a random sequence, $\{x_t,\ t = \ldots, -1, 0, 1, 2, \ldots\}$ in general, for which $\sigma(x_t, x_{t-1}, \ldots) \subseteq \mathcal{F}_t$; that is, the information contained in $\mathcal{F}_t$ includes the realized path of the sequence to date. In this case x_t is said to be 'measurable with respect to $\mathcal{F}_t$', or just $\mathcal{F}_t$-measurable. If x_t is $\mathcal{F}_t$-measurable for every t, the sequence $\{x_t\}$ is said to be *adapted* to $\{\mathcal{F}_t\}$ and the sequence of pairs $\{x_t,\ \mathcal{F}_t\}$ is called an adapted sequence. The sequence has been defined with an unspecified starting date, and in some cases this can be $-\infty$, while in others it must be in the finite past, say $t = 1$. In this case one could set $\mathcal{F}_0 = \emptyset$.

Measurability implies that if the conditional expectations exist (for which the condition $E|x_t| < \infty$ is sufficient, see §B.10) then $E(x_t|\mathcal{F}_t) = x_t$ a.s., because the information set includes the realization of the process up to date t. On the other hand, $E(x_t|\mathcal{F}_{t-1})$, where it exists, is a random variable that represents the best predictor of x_t given the information available at time $t-1$.

Definition 6.2.1 The adapted sequence $\{s_t,\ \mathcal{F}_t\}$ is called a martingale if for every t the following conditions hold:

(a) $E|s_t| < \infty$

(b) $E(s_t|\mathcal{F}_{t-1}) = s_{t-1}$ a.s. □

Recall that the tag 'a.s.', equivalent to 'with probability 1', is needed here as a technical caveat, since these are statements about random variables that cannot be guaranteed to be true for every possible random outcome. What can be said is that any failure to hold is guaranteed not to have any practical consequences, in particular, cannot alter the values of expectations involving these random variables. Condition (a) is included in the definition as the condition sufficient for $E(s_t|\mathcal{F}_{t-1})$ to exist, as just noted.

A companion definition, which is more important from our point of view, is as follows.

Definition 6.2.2 The adapted sequence $\{x_t, \mathcal{F}_t\}$ is called a martingale difference (m.d.) if for every t,

(a) $E|x_t| < \infty$

(b) $E(x_t|\mathcal{F}_{t-1}) = 0$ a.s. □

Thus, if s_t denotes a martingale, letting $x_t = s_1$ and $x_t = s_t - s_{t-1}$ for $t > 1$ generates a m.d. This is a sequence that is almost surely unpredictable in mean, one step ahead. Notice that the sigma fields $\mathcal{F}_{t-1}$ can be the same in these definitions, since the information sets $\sigma(x_t, x_{t-1}, \dots)$ and $\sigma(s_t, s_{t-1}, \dots)$ contain exactly the same information.

To avoid using σ-fields explicitly, which might be desirable in a less technical treatment, an m.d. can also be defined in terms of the condition

(b′) $E(x_t|x_{t-1}, x_{t-2}, \dots) = 0$ a.s.

It is quite permissible to adopt this special case, but there are several reasons why the σ-field notation is preferable. One, as noted, is the equivalence of information sets under transformations of the series such as differencing, but a more important reason is that other variables, that cannot be specified explicitly, are included in the conditioning set.

6.2.2 Properties

Here is a fundamental property of m.d. processes.

Theorem 6.2.1 Let $\{x_t\}$ be an m.d. sequence and let $g_{t-1} = g(x_{t-1}, x_{t-2}, \dots)$ be any measurable, integrable function of the lagged values of the sequence. Then $x_t g_{t-1}$ is also an m.d., and x_t and g_{t-1} are uncorrelated.

Proof $x_t g_{t-1}$ is an m.d. sequence since $E(x_t g_{t-1}|\mathcal{F}_{t-1}) = E(x_t|\mathcal{F}_{t-1})g_{t-1} = 0$ a.s. By the law of iterated expectations,

$$E(x_t) = E[E(x_t|\mathcal{F}_{t-1})] = E(0) = 0 \tag{6.2.1}$$

and

$$E(x_t g_{t-1}) = E[g_{t-1}E(x_t|\mathcal{F}_{t-1})] = E(g_{t-1} \cdot 0) = 0 \tag{6.2.2}$$

Hence,

$$\text{Cov}(g_{t-1}x_t) = E(g_{t-1}x_t) - E(x_t)E(g_{t-1}) = 0 - 0 = 0. \quad \blacksquare \tag{6.2.3}$$

Notice how this proof uses the argument that $\sigma(x_{t-1}, x_{t-2}, \dots) \subseteq \mathcal{F}_{t-1}$, and hence $E(g_{t-1}|\mathcal{F}_{t-1}) = g_{t-1}$ a.s. In other words, the information contained in $\mathcal{F}_{t-1}$ is sufficient for g_{t-1} to be known (almost) with certainty. It can be treated as if it were a constant in expectations conditional on $\mathcal{F}_{t-1}$, and taken outside the expectation.

In particular, putting $g_{t-1} = x_{t-j}$ for any $j > 0$, the theorem implies

$$\text{Cov}(x_t, x_{t-j}) = 0. \tag{6.2.4}$$

In other words, the m.d. property implies uncorrelatedness of the sequence, although it is a weaker property than independence. It can be thought of as intermediate between these two properties, although unlike either of them it is asymmetric. After placing the observations in reverse time order an independent (or uncorrelated) sequence is still independent (or uncorrelated), but the m.d. property does not generally survive such a reversal.

Given an arbitrary sequence $\{y_t\}$ satisfying $E|y_t| < \infty$ and $\sigma(y_t, y_{t-1}, \ldots) \subseteq \mathcal{F}_t$, an m.d. sequence can always be generated as the *centred* sequence (or sequence of innovations) $\{x_t\}$, where

$$x_t = y_t - E(y_t|\mathcal{F}_{t-1}). \tag{6.2.5}$$

x_t is a function of y_s for $s \leq t$ and hence $\sigma(x_{t-1}, x_{t-2}, \ldots) \subseteq \sigma(y_{t-1}, y_{t-2}, \ldots)$. In other words, knowing the history of $\{y_t\}$ we also know that of $\{x_t\}$. Also

$$\begin{aligned} E(x_t|\mathcal{F}_{t-1}) &= E[y_t - E(y_t|\mathcal{F}_{t-1})|\mathcal{F}_{t-1}] \\ &= E(y_t|\mathcal{F}_{t-1}) - E(y_t|\mathcal{F}_{t-1}) = 0 \text{ a.s.} \end{aligned} \tag{6.2.6}$$

so that condition (b) of Definition 6.2.2 is satisfied. To show that condition (a) also holds, apply the triangle inequality and Jensen's inequality for conditional expectations. Formally,

$$E|(y_t - E(y_t|\mathcal{F}_{t-1})| \leq E|y_t| + E[E(|y_t||\mathcal{F}_{t-1})] = 2E|y_t| < \infty \tag{6.2.7}$$

where the final equality is by the LIE.

6.2.3 Limit Results

The importance of m.d. sequences is due to the coincidence of two facts. First, because econometric models contain innovations (disturbances) these sequences naturally arise in our study of estimator properties. Second, subject to suitable extra conditions, m.d. sequences obey laws of large numbers and central limit theorems.

The following results parallel Theorems 3.2.1 and 3.2.2.

Theorem 6.2.2 Let the sequence $\{x_t\}$ be a m.d. sequence. Then, $\operatorname{plim} \bar{x}_n = 0$ if either of the following conditions hold.

(i) The sequence is strictly stationary and $E|x_t| < \infty$.

(ii) $E|x_t|^{1+\delta} \leq B < \infty \quad \delta > 0, \forall\, t$.

Proof For the first part, this follows from Corollary 19.8 of Davidson (1994a). The second part follows similarly using Theorem 18.13 and Theorem 12.11 of the same source. ■

The first case is virtually equivalent to Khinchine's theorem, with the m.d. property replacing independence. In the second case the sequence can be nonstationary, but the $1 + \delta$-order moments are required to be uniformly finite, which as noted in §3.1.2 is stronger than merely having them finite for every t.

Theorem 3.2.3 (Chebyshev's Theorem) does not make any stipulations about the type of dependence, but m.d. processes are uncorrelated, so that the variance of the sum of terms is the sum of the variances. The application of this result to m.d. processes is therefore transparent.

The following central limit theorems for m.d.s. parallel Theorems 3.3.1 and 3.3.2

Theorem 6.2.3 Let $\{x_t, \mathcal{F}_t\}$ be a m.d. sequence with $E(x_t^2) = \sigma_t^2$, and let $\bar{\sigma}_n^2 = n^{-1}\sum_{t=1}^n \sigma_t^2$. If

(a) $n^{-1}\sum_{t=1}^n (x_t^2 - \sigma_t^2) \xrightarrow{\text{pr}} 0$, and

(b) either

(i) the sequence is strictly stationary or

(ii) $\dfrac{\max_{1\le t\le n}\|x_t\|_{2+\delta}}{\bar{\sigma}_n} \le B < \infty \quad \delta > 0, \forall\, n \ge 1$

then $\omega_n = \sqrt{n}\bar{x}_n \,/\bar{\sigma}_n \xrightarrow{\text{D}} \omega \sim \text{N}(0,1)$.

Proof These are corollaries of Theorem 24.3 of Davidson (1994a). The sufficiency of condition (b) follows by the argument of Theorem 24.4 and Theorem 12.11 of the same source. ∎

Note the discussion of the set-up and conditions following Theorem 3.3.2, which apply just as much to this case. The main thing that makes these conditions different from the independent case is the need to establish the WLLN for the squared sequence. This is an essential step in the proof of the CLT. There is no very simple way to state conditions for this, because the fact that $\{x_t\}$ is an m.d. does *not* mean that the same is true of the squared sequence, even after centring. It will be necessary to check this condition from a WLLN for dependent processes. Theorems 4.4.1, 6.2.2, and also 6.4.4 below offer three alternative possibilities.

6.3 Properties of the Autoregression

6.3.1 Consistency

If equation (6.1.1) has status as a representation of the generation process of $\{x_t\}$, it is natural to think of it as modelling the conditional mean, as in (5.2.5). That is,

$$E(x_t|\mathcal{X}_{t-1}) = \lambda x_{t-1} \text{ a.s.} \quad |\lambda| < 1 \tag{6.3.1}$$

where $\mathcal{X}_{t-1} = \sigma(x_{t-1}, x_{t-2}, \dots)$, and $|\lambda| < 1$ is the stability condition. As detailed in Chapter 4 the extension to more general cases, either the VAR or additional lags or both, is mainly a matter of additional notational overhead. Applying the LIE in the manner of (1.3.3) yields the relation

$$E(x_t x_{t-1}) = \lambda E(x_{t-1}^2) \tag{6.3.2}$$

for any t. In this case, $\hat{\lambda}$ in (6.1.2) defines a natural estimator of λ, in the sense that it replaces population moments by sample moments. It is not essential to assume that the population moments are independent of t provided their ratio is constant as in (6.3.2), although it may be convenient to do so.

Letting $u_t = x_t - \lambda x_{t-1}$ as before, the sequence $\{u_t, \mathcal{X}_{t-1}\}$ is a martingale difference, by construction. This is not a sufficient condition of itself to obtain results, and some additional restrictions on the distribution of $\{u_t\}$ must be imposed. There is some latitude in the choice of conditions, but pursuing the theme of correct specification, a set of assumptions sufficient for consistency of $\hat{\lambda}$, while not entailing stationarity of the process, is the following.

Assumption 6.3.1

(a) $E(u_t|\mathcal{X}_{t-1}) = 0$ a.s.

(b) $E(u_t^2|\mathcal{X}_{t-1}) = \sigma^2 < \infty$ a.s.

(c) Either x_t is strictly stationary, or $E|u_t|^r \leq B < \infty \quad r > 2, \forall\, t$. □

Condition (a) simply restates the m.d. property of u_t, and in view of (c), condition (b) asserts that $u_t^2 - \sigma^2$ is also a m.d. Notice, these are just the univariate specializations of (4.2.3) and (4.2.6) respectively. They imply wide-sense (though not strict) stationarity of u_t, since the LIE gives $E(u_t^2) = \sigma^2$, not depending on t, while the m.d. property makes the autocovariances all zero. Noting the analysis of §5.2.4, this means in turn that x_t is wide sense stationary. Condition (b) also rules out ARCH effects (see §5.6). Don't overlook the fact that while imposing the existence of second moments, this is primarily a restriction on the memory of the sequence.

The following two results are together sufficient for the consistency of $\hat{\lambda}$.

Theorem 6.3.1 Under Assumption 6.3.1, $\operatorname{plim} n^{-1}\sum_{t=2}^{n} x_{t-1}u_t = 0$.[1]

Proof By the LIE,

$$E(x_{t-1}u_t) = E[x_{t-1}E(u_t|\mathcal{X}_{t-1})] = 0 \qquad (6.3.3)$$

$$E(x_{t-1}^2u_t^2) = E[x_{t-1}^2E(u_t^2|\mathcal{X}_{t-1})] = \sigma_x^2\sigma^2 = \frac{\sigma^4}{1-\lambda^2} \qquad (6.3.4)$$

and also for $s > t$

$$E(x_{t-1}u_tx_{s-1}u_s) = E[x_{t-1}u_tx_{s-1}E(u_s|\mathcal{X}_{s-1})] = 0 \qquad (6.3.5)$$

[1]One might want to take $n-1$ as the divisor here, not n, since there are only $n-1$ terms in the sum after taking the lag. Since the property in question is asymptotic, however, this detail is unimportant.

and trivially, the first member of (6.3.5) is also 0 for $t > s$. The sequence $\{x_1u_2, \dots, x_{n-1}u_n\}$ is therefore uncorrelated, and has finite variance, and so satisfies the conditions of the Chebyshev law of large numbers (Theorem 3.2.3). Hence,

$$\operatorname{plim} \frac{1}{n}\sum_{t=2}^{n} x_{t-1}u_t = E(x_{t-1}u_t) = 0. \quad \blacksquare \tag{6.3.6}$$

Theorem 6.3.2 Under Assumption 6.3.1,

$$\operatorname{plim} \frac{1}{n}\sum_{t=2}^{n} x_{t-1}^2 = \frac{\sigma^2}{1-\lambda^2}. \tag{6.3.7}$$

Proof Note that

$$\begin{aligned}\operatorname{plim} \frac{1}{n}\sum_{t=2}^{n} x_t^2 &= \operatorname{plim} \frac{1}{n}\sum_{t=2}^{n} (\lambda x_{t-1} + u_t)^2 \\ &= \frac{1}{1-\lambda^2}\left(2\operatorname{plim} \frac{1}{n}\sum_{t=2}^{n} x_{t-1}u_t + \operatorname{plim} \frac{1}{n}\sum_{t=2}^{n} u_t^2\right) \end{aligned} \tag{6.3.8}$$

where the second equality is got by multiplying out the square, and noting that the difference between $\sum_{t=2}^{n} x_t^2$ and $\sum_{t=2}^{n} x_{t-1}^2$ is $x_n^2 - x_1^2 = O_p(1)$. The first right-hand term is zero by Theorem 6.3.1. To deal with the second term, apply Theorem 6.2.2 to the process $\{u_t^2 - \sigma^2\}$. To verify the conditions in the nonstationary case, set $\delta = \frac{1}{2}r - 1$. By the Minkowski inequality,

$$\|u_t^2 - \sigma^2\|_{r/2} \le \|u_t^2\|_{r/2} + \sigma^2 = (E|u_t|^r)^{2/r} + \sigma^2. \tag{6.3.9}$$

Taking the $(r/2)$th power of both sides of (6.3.9),

$$E|u_t^2 - \sigma^2|^{r/2} \le (B^{2/r} + \sigma^2)^{r/2} < \infty. \quad \blacksquare \tag{6.3.10}$$

The consistency of $\hat{\lambda}$ follows immediately from Theorems 6.3.1 and 6.3.2 by Slutsky's theorem.

$$\operatorname{plim} \hat{\lambda} - \lambda = \frac{\operatorname{plim} n^{-1}\sum_{t=2}^{n} x_{t-1}u_t}{\operatorname{plim} n^{-1}\sum_{t=2}^{n} x_{t-1}^2} = \frac{0}{\sigma^2/(1-\lambda^2)} = 0. \tag{6.3.11}$$

However, notice the importance of both conditions, the numerator converging to zero and the denominator converging to a nonzero limit.

In the Gaussian model of §4.2, since the full distribution is specified and strict stationarity follows from wide-sense stationarity, the assumptions given in that section are sufficient for least squares to be consistent. There is, naturally, a multivariate generalization of the last argument that can operate directly on the full model. However, suppose it is necessary to admit some ignorance about the complete distribution beyond specifying the first two conditional moments. In particular, suppose it was feared this was not constant over time. What has been shown here is that such a lack of complete information is compensated by having an absolute moment a fraction higher than the second exist uniformly. This suffices to rule out pathological cases of the sort discussed in §3.2 and §3.3.

6.3.2 Finite Sample Bias

Although consistent, it is well-known that $\hat{\lambda}$ is biased towards 0 in finite samples. Evaluating a first-order approximation to the bias provides some insight into the difficulties of investigating exact distributions in dynamic models. This problem was first investigated by Hurwitz (1950). A relatively simple approach is to apply the so-called Nagar expansion (Nagar 1959). The method requires the assumption that the distribution of u_t is truncated, such that its support is a bounded interval. This is not a strictly realistic assumption since the bound is specified by the requirements of the argument, but at least if the distribution possesses all its moments (is Gaussian for example), it is innocuous in practice.

Define $s_x^2 = n^{-1}\sum_{t=2}^n x_{t-1}^2$, and let $d = 1 - s_x^2/\sigma_x^2$, where $\sigma_x^2 = \operatorname{plim} s_x^2 = \sigma^2/(1-\lambda^2)$ by Theorem 6.3.2. and moreover, by a manipulation similar to (6.3.8),

$$s_x^2 - \sigma_x^2 = \frac{2\lambda n^{-1}\sum_{t=1}^{n-1} x_{t-1}u_t + n^{-1}\sum_{t=1}^{n-1}(u_t^2 - \sigma^2) + \lambda^2(x_{n-1}^2 - x_0^2)}{1-\lambda^2}. \tag{6.3.12}$$

By the Chebyshev LLN, $n^{-1}\sum_{t=2}^n x_{t-1}u_t = O_p(n^{-1/2})$. Also, given that at least fourth moments exist, the same reasoning gives $n^{-1}\sum_{t=2}^n (u_t^2 - \sigma^2) = O_p(n^{-1/2})$. Each of these random variables has a variance of $O(n^{-1})$, and hence $d = O_p(n^{-1/2})$. The bias can be written as

$$E(\hat{\lambda} - \lambda) = \frac{1}{n\sigma_x^2} E\left(\frac{\sum_{t=2}^n x_{t-1}u_t}{1-d}\right). \tag{6.3.13}$$

We must assume that $|d| < 1$ with probability 1, which is the purpose of the boundedness assumption. Given the orders of magnitude involved, this probability can be made arbitrarily close to 1 by taking n large enough. Expanding $1/(1-d)$ in geometric series, write

$$\begin{aligned} E(\hat{\lambda} - \lambda) &= \frac{1}{n\sigma_x^2} E\left((1 + d + d^2 + \cdots)\sum_{t=2}^n x_{t-1}u_t\right) \\ &= \frac{2}{n\sigma_x^2} E\left(\sum_{t=2}^n x_{t-1}u_t\right) - \frac{1}{n^2\sigma_x^4} E\left(\sum_{t=2}^n x_{t-1}^2 \sum_{t=2}^n x_{t-1}u_t\right) \\ &\quad + O(n^{-3/2}) \end{aligned} \tag{6.3.14}$$

where the remainder contains the expectation of terms involving $d^2 n^{-1}\sum x_{t-1}u_t$ or smaller.

The first expectation on the right-hand side of (6.3.14) is zero. To work out the expectation of the second term is straightforward, but tedious. It involves substituting the representation $x_{t-1} = \sum_{j=0}^\infty \lambda^j u_{t-j-1}$, multiplying out, and collecting the terms with non-zero expectation. Observe that

$$x_t^2 = \sum_{j=0}^\infty \lambda^{2j}\left(u_{t-j}^2 + 2\sum_{k=1}^\infty \lambda^k u_{t-j}u_{t-j-k}\right) \tag{6.3.15}$$

for any $t = 1, \ldots, n-1$, and similarly

$$x_s u_{s+1} = \sum_{l=0}^\infty \lambda^l u_{s-l}u_{s+1}. \tag{6.3.16}$$

For any choice of t and s from $(1, \ldots, n-1)$ the product $x_t^2 x_s u_{s+1}$ is a weighted sum of terms of the form $u_{t-j}u_{t-j-k}u_{s-l}u_{s+1}$. Using the martingale difference property and the law of iterated expectations, the expectations of these products are either zero or σ^4, where the latter case corresponds to the subscripts being equal in pairs. For these cases, $t-j=s+1$ and $t-j-k=s-l$, which jointly imply $k=l+1>0$. Substituting from (6.3.15) and (6.3.16) and retaining only the terms satisfying these conditions yields

$$E\left(\sum_{t=2}^{n} x_{t-1}^2 \sum_{t=1}^{n} x_t u_{t+1}\right) = 2(n-1)\sum_{j=0}^{\infty}\lambda^{2j}\left(\sum_{l=0}^{\infty}\lambda^{2l+1}\right)\sigma^4$$
$$= \frac{2\lambda(n-1)\sigma^4}{\left(1-\lambda^2\right)^2}. \tag{6.3.17}$$

whence, from (6.3.14),

$$E(\hat{\lambda}-\lambda) = -2\lambda/n + O(n^{-3/2}). \tag{6.3.18}$$

The approximation could be made more precise by evaluating $E(d^j \sum x_{t-1}u_t)$ for $j>1$, though this would probably entail more labour than it was worth.

This formula is obtained under the simplest possible assumptions. If an intercept is included in the regression (equivalent to expressing x_t in sample mean deviations) the bias formula is different, although it can be obtained by elaborating the same technique, if desired.

6.3.3 Asymptotic Distribution

Consider (6.1.6) once again. Since the probability limit of $n^{-1}\sum_{t=2}^{n} x_{t-1}^2$ has been shown to be a positive constant, asymptotic normality of $\sqrt{n}(\hat{\lambda}-\lambda)$ follows from asymptotic normality of $n^{-1/2}\sum_{t=2}^{n} x_{t-1}u_t$ by Cramér's Theorem (Theorem 3.3.5)

The terms $x_{t-1}u_t$ are uncorrelated but not independent, since x_{t-1} depends on u_{t-j} for all $j>0$. Appeal must therefore be made to a central limit theorem for dependent processes. The original result was proved in a famous paper by Mann and Wald (1943b) who showed that the Liapunov central limit theorem could be applied in an adapted form, given the asymptotic independence of the terms $x_{t-1}u_t$. However, the martingale approach is neater and simpler.

By Theorem 6.2.1 the sequence $\{x_{t-1}u_t, \mathcal{X}_t\}$ is an m.d., with fixed and finite variance $\sigma^4/(1-\lambda^2)$ by (6.3.4). In the same way, given Assumption 6.3.1(b) the sequence $\{x_{t-1}^2(u_t^2-\sigma^2), \mathcal{X}_t\}$ is an m.d.

Assumption 6.3.1 is not quite sufficient for the CLT in the nonstationary case. There is a choice between enforcing stationarity, or further restricting the dependence, or the moment conditions. Any of the following extra assumptions is sufficient:

Assumption 6.3.2 x_t is strictly stationary. □

Assumption 6.3.3 $E(|u_t|^r|\mathcal{X}_{t-1}) = \mu_r < \infty$ a.s., $r>2$. □

Assumption 6.3.4 $E|u_t|^{2r} \leq B < \infty$, $r > 2$. □

Since r can be taken arbitrarily close to 2, Assumption 6.3.3 might be thought of as a very minor extension of Assumption 6.3.1. On the other hand, it is somewhat unintuitive and difficult to interpret (except perhaps in the context of complete independence of the u_t) and it may therefore be useful to know that Assumption 6.3.4 can be substituted.

Theorem 6.3.3 Under Assumption 6.3.1, and one of Assumptions 6.3.2, 6.3.3 or 6.3.4,

$$\frac{1}{\sqrt{n}}\sum_{t=2}^{n} x_{t-1}u_t \xrightarrow{\text{D}} \text{N}\left(0, \frac{\sigma^4}{1-\lambda^2}\right). \quad \square \tag{6.3.19}$$

See §6.6 for the proof. Putting together Cramér's Theorem with Theorem 6.3.3 and Theorem 6.3.2 now yields the desired result, that $\hat{\lambda}$ is consistent and asymptotically normal (CAN):

$$\sqrt{n}(\hat{\lambda} - \lambda) \xrightarrow{\text{D}} \text{N}(0, 1 - \lambda^2). \tag{6.3.20}$$

The asymptotic normality result can be used to test hypotheses of the form $H_0 : \lambda = \lambda_0$ in large samples, based on the 't-ratio'

$$\sqrt{n}\frac{\hat{\lambda} - \lambda_0}{\sqrt{1 - \hat{\lambda}^2}}. \tag{6.3.21}$$

This formula is asymptotically equivalent to a more familiar one. Write

$$\frac{1 - \hat{\lambda}^2}{n} \approx \frac{1}{\sum_{t=2}^{n} x_{t-1}^2}\frac{1}{n}\left(\sum_{t=2}^{n} x_t^2 - \hat{\lambda}\sum_{t=2}^{n} x_{t-1}x_t\right) = \frac{\hat{\sigma}^2}{\sum_{t=2}^{n} x_{t-1}^2} \tag{6.3.22}$$

where '$\approx$' indicates the asymptotic equivalence of $n^{-1}\sum_{t=2}^{n} x_t^2$ and $n^{-1}\sum_{t=2}^{n} x_{t-1}^2$, and

$$\hat{\sigma}^2 = \frac{1}{n}\left(\sum_{t=2}^{n} x_t^2 - \hat{\lambda}\sum_{t=2}^{n} x_{t-1}x_t\right) = \frac{1}{n}\sum_{t=2}^{n} \hat{u}_t x_t = \frac{1}{n}\sum_{t=2}^{n} \hat{u}_t^2. \tag{6.3.23}$$

Note that the last step is due to the orthogonality of the least squares residual $\hat{u}_t = x_t - \hat{\lambda}x_{t-1}$ with x_{t-1}. The right hand side of (6.3.22) is the usual formula for the estimated variance of the least squares coefficient. In other words, $[(1 - \hat{\lambda}^2)/n]^{1/2}$ approximates the usual standard error of $\hat{\lambda}$ that is reported by standard regression packages.

6.4 Mixing and Near-Epoch Dependence

6.4.1 Basic Concepts

There are important cases where the martingale difference property, convenient as it is, cannot be relied on to hold. Alternative approaches are generally based on the mixing condition introduced informally in §4.4. Two precise definitions are as follows.

Definition 6.4.1 Let $\{x_t, -\infty < t < +\infty\}$ be a random sequence, and for $t \geq s$ let $\mathcal{F}_s^t = \sigma(x_s, \dots, x_t)$. Then define the quantities[2]

$$\alpha_m = \sup_t \sup_{A \in \mathcal{F}_{t+m}^{+\infty}, B \in \mathcal{F}_{-\infty}^t} |P(A \cap B) - P(A)P(B)| \tag{6.4.1}$$

$$\phi_m = \sup_t \sup_{A \in \mathcal{F}_{t+m}^{+\infty}, B \in \mathcal{F}_{-\infty}^t, P(B)>0} |P(A|B) - P(A)| \tag{6.4.2}$$

The sequence is said to be α-mixing (or strong mixing) if $\alpha_m \to 0$ as $m \to \infty$, and ϕ-mixing (or uniform mixing) if $\phi_m \to 0$ as $m \to \infty$. □

These conditions represent alternative versions of the notion of asymptotic independence of a sequence. Since $P(A|B) = P(A \cap B)/P(B)$ where $P(B) \leq 1$, observe that $\alpha_m \leq \phi_m$. Thus, α-mixing is implied by ϕ-mixing and is the weaker concept, the designation 'strong' notwithstanding. It may not be obvious that they differ in a significant way, but it is possible to devise examples (involving sets with very small probability) in which α_m converges but ϕ_m does not. The notions can be refined by specifying the rate of convergence of the mixing coefficients. If $\alpha_m = O(m^{-\lambda})$ for $\lambda > \lambda_0$, the sequence is said to be α-mixing of *size* $-\lambda_0$, with analogous terminology for the ϕ-mixing case.

The following result, proved in Davidson (1994a), Theorem 14.1, may be compared with Theorem 6.1.1.

Theorem 6.4.1 Measurable, finite-lag functions of mixing processes are also mixing, of the same size. □

For example, a finite-order moving average of mixing increments is also mixing. This property yields great flexibility, and a number of powerful results exist for mixing sequences. Nonetheless, the assumption is not ideal, being really too strong for many practical purposes. If it is required that the supremum of (for example) $|P(A \cap B) - P(A)P(B)|$ over all possible sets A and B from the specified collections converge, there is the possibility that odd counter-examples will frustrate mixing on the definition, even when all the pairs of events relevant to (for example) proving the CLT are independent in the limit. The difficulty is liable to arise when processes are generated as functions of the whole history (past and/or future) of another process, such as a shock process. Such models are common in econometrics, since they arise whenever a variable depends on its own previous value. Although the infinite-order dependence may appear quite innocuous, one needs to be careful. Andrews (1984) considers an AR(1) process,

$$x_t = \rho x_{t-1} + Z_t = Z_t + \rho Z_{t-1} + \rho^2 Z_{t-2} + \cdots \tag{6.4.3}$$

[2] The supremum of a set of real numbers is the smallest real number that is at least as great as any member of the set. It need not belong to the set, and as such is different from the maximum value, which does not exist if the set is open above. The infimum is defined similarly.

with $0 < \rho < \frac{1}{2}$, in which the shock process Z_t is composed of i.i.d. Bernoulli random variables. That is, $Z_t = 1$ with fixed probability p, and 0 with probability $1 - p$. In spite of the fact that the dependence of x_t on past shocks declines exponentially, Andrews exhibits a counter-example showing that strong mixing is contradicted. To be sure that the AR(1) is strong mixing, not only must the distribution of Z_t be continuous but the density must itself exhibit certain smoothness properties. The conditions for uniform mixing of the AR(1) appear to be tougher still, requiring Z_t to be bounded with probability 1.[3]

These difficulties mean that mixing needs to be supplemented with another notion of limited dependence. This is effectively provided by the concept of *near-epoch dependence* (McLeish 1975, Andrews 1988).

Definition 6.4.2 Let $x_t = g(\dots, Z_{t-1}, Z_t, Z_{t+1}, \dots)$ represent a function of (potentially) the whole past and future history of a process $\{Z_t, -\infty < t < +\infty\}$. Let $\mathcal{F}_s^t = \sigma(Z_s, \dots, Z_t)$ for $s \leq t$. x_t is called near-epoch dependent in L_p-norm (L_p-NED) on $\{Z_t\}$, for $p > 0$, if

$$\left\| x_t - E(x_t | \mathcal{F}_{t-m}^{t+m}) \right\|_p \leq d_t \nu_m \tag{6.4.4}$$

where $\{d_t\}$ is a sequence of scaling constants, and $\nu_m \to 0$ as $m \to \infty$.[4] □

The idea in this definition may be best understood by recognizing that $E(x_t|\mathcal{F}_{-\infty}^{+\infty}) = x_t$ by definition. In other words, if we know the whole history of $\{Z_t\}$ we can predict x_t exactly. If x_t is mainly dependent on the 'near-epoch' of $\{Z_t\}$, the random variable $x_t - E(x_t|\mathcal{F}_{t-m}^{t+m})$ should be close to 0 when m gets large, in a suitable sense and relative to a suitably chosen scale variable. As with the mixing notion, the size of the sequence $\{\nu_m\}$ is defined to be $-\mu_0$ when $\nu_m = O(m^{-\mu})$ for $\mu > \mu_0$.

6.4.2 Application to the AR(1)

The simplest example to demonstrate near-epoch dependence is again the autoregressive process. Like most econometric data generation processes this is one-sided, in that there is dependence on the past, but none on the future. Let

$$x_t = \sum_{j=0}^{\infty} \rho^j Z_{t-j} = \sum_{j=0}^{m} \rho^j Z_{t-j} + \rho^{m+1} x_{t-m-1} \tag{6.4.5}$$

where $|\rho| < 1$ and Z_t is a zero-mean sequence (but otherwise arbitrary). Since Z_{t-j} for $0 \leq j \leq m$ is perfectly predictable from $\mathcal{F}_{t-m}^{t+m}$,

$$E(x_t|\mathcal{F}_{t-m}^{t+m}) = \sum_{j=0}^{m} \rho^j Z_{t-j} + \rho^{m+1} E(x_{t-m-1}|\mathcal{F}_{t-m}^{t+m}). \tag{6.4.6}$$

[3] See Davidson (1994a) §14.4 for details of these results.

[4] See (B.4.15) for the definition of $\|.\|_p$.

Hence,

$$\begin{aligned}\|x_t - E(x_t|\mathcal{F}_{t-m}^{t+m})\|_2 &= |\rho|^{m+1}\|x_{t-m-1} - E(x_{t-m-1}|\mathcal{F}_{t-m}^{t+m})\|_2 \\ &\leq 2|\rho|^{m+1}\|x_{t-m-1}\|_2. \end{aligned} \tag{6.4.7}$$

The last inequality here is got by the Minkowski inequality and the conditional Jensen inequality. Choosing $d_t = 2\max_{m\geq 0}\|x_{t-m-1}\|_2$, assuming this is finite, gives $\nu_m = |\rho|^{m+1}$. This sequence goes to zero exponentially fast, so that the size of the near-epoch dependence (absolutely) exceeds $-\mu$, for every positive μ. It is said to be L_2-NED of size $-\infty$. Note that $\{x_t\}$ does not need to be stationary, or in other words $\{Z_t\}$ does not need to be stationary, but if it is then d_t becomes a constant. Also note that the result depends on the serial dependence in the $\{Z_t\}$ only to the extent that $\|x_t\|_2$ must be finite for each t. It is a measure only of the dynamic relationship between the Z_t and the x_t, not of the serial dependence of the x_t as such, although in the case that Z_t is serially independent, it gives a direct measure of the dependence in x_t.

The linear model is relatively straightforward to analyse, but perhaps the most important feature of NED is that the condition is not related to the form of the model. In principle it can be proved for nonlinear dynamic models, subject to suitably formulated stability conditions. For example, Hansen (1991) shows that the GARCH(1,1) model in (5.6.8) is L_p-NED, subject to the condition

$$E(|\alpha_1\varepsilon_{t-1}^2 + \beta_1|^p|\mathcal{E}_{t-1}) \leq c < 1 \text{ a.s. } \forall\, t \tag{6.4.8}$$

where the sequence of NED numbers is $\{c^{m/p}\}$. If ε_t is i.i.d., (6.4.8) reduces to $\|\alpha_1\varepsilon_{t-1}^2+\beta_1\|_p < 1$. By appealing to the NED property, conditions for convergence can be cited that may be satisfied by a range of possible data generation processes.

6.4.3 Properties and Limit Results

Unlike mixing, the NED property is not invariant to arbitrary transformations of the variables. It is necessary to appeal to the properties of individual cases, of which the following are probably the most useful. For the proofs see respectively Davidson (1994a) Theorem 17.8, and Davidson (1994a) Theorems 17.9 and 17.16 and Example 17.17.

Theorem 6.4.2 Let x_t and y_t be L_p-NED of size $-\varphi$, for $p \geq 1$, on the same stochastic process $\{Z_t\}$, with respect to constants d_t^x and d_t^y. Then $x_t + y_t$ is L_p-NED on $\{Z_t\}$ of size $-\varphi$, with respect to constants $\max\{d_t^x, d_t^y\}$. □

Theorem 6.4.3 Let x_t and y_t be L_2-NED, of size $-\varphi$, for $p \geq 1$, on the same stochastic process $\{Z_t\}$, with respect to constants d_t^x and d_t^y. Then

(i) $x_t y_t$ is L_1-NED on $\{Z_t\}$ of size $-\varphi$, with respect to constants

$$\max\{\|x_t\|_2 d_t^y,\; d_t^x\|y_t\|_2,\; d_t^x d_t^y\}.$$

(ii) If $\|x_t\|_{2r} < \infty$ and $\|y_t\|_{2r} < \infty$ for $r > 2$, then $x_t y_t$ is L_2-NED on $\{Z_t\}$ of size $-\varphi(r-2)/2(r-1)$ with respect to constants

$$\max\left\{\|x_t\|_{2r}^{(3r-2)/2(r-1)},\ \|y_t\|_{2r}^{(3r-2)/2(r-1)}\right\}\max\{d_t^x,\ d_t^y\}. \quad \square$$

By making the process in question near-epoch dependent on a mixing process, with the sizes suitably constrained, serial dependence is restricted sufficiently for a CLT or WLLN to apply subject to the usual type of moment condition. Just one result is given from each of a range of results of each type that are available.[5] For the WLLN, here is the NED-mixing counterpart of Theorem 6.2.2. It follows by combining Theorems 19.11, 17.5 and 12.11 of Davidson (1994a).

Theorem 6.4.4 Let the zero-mean sequence $\{x_t\}$ be L_1-NED on an α-mixing process. If

$$E|x_t|^{1+\delta} \leq B < \infty \quad \delta > 0, \forall\, t \tag{6.4.9}$$

then $\text{plim}\,\bar{x}_n = 0$. $\square$

In other words, exactly the same moment restrictions are needed as in the m.d. or independent case. Notice that no size restrictions are required. Any rate of convergence of α_m and ν_m to 0 is sufficient.

A CLT for near-epoch dependent processes, which is a special case of Theorem 2 of de Jong (1997), is as follows.

Theorem 6.4.5 Let $\{x_t\}$ be a zero-mean sequence that is L_2-NED of size $-\frac{1}{2}$, on either a strong mixing process of size $-(1+2/\delta)$ or a uniform mixing process of size $-(2+\delta)/2(1+\delta)$ for $\delta > 0$,[6] and for the same δ,

$$\sqrt{n}\frac{\max_{1\leq t\leq n}\|x_t\|_{2+\delta}}{s_n} \leq B < \infty \quad \forall\, n \geq 1 \tag{6.4.10}$$

where $s_n^2 = E\left(\sum_{t=1}^n x_t\right)^2$. Then, $\omega_n = \sum_{t=1}^n x_t/s_n \xrightarrow{D} \omega \sim N(0,1)$. $\square$

The remarks following Theorem 3.3.2 are again of relevance, but there are some interesting differences between this theorem and Theorems 3.3.2 and 6.2.3. It can be verified that ω_n is identical with $\bar{x}_n$ divided by its standard deviation, which is s_n/n, but here the summands are not necessarily uncorrelated. The variance of the sum is not, in general, the sum of the variances, but contains up to n^2 terms, having the form

$$s_n^2 = \sum_{t=1}^n E(x_t^2) + 2\sum_{t=2}^n\sum_{j=1}^{t-1} E(x_t x_{t-j}). \tag{6.4.11}$$

---

[5] For a survey of recent strong law results of this type, see de Jong and Davidson (1997). This article illustrates the trade-offs involved between restrictions on the dependence and on the higher-order moments.

[6] Writing $r = 2+\delta$, these mixing sizes can be expressed respectively as $-r/(r-2)$ for the strong-mixing case and $-r/2(r-1)$ for the uniform mixing case. The conditions are often given in this form.

Another novel feature is the trade-off between the amount of dependence and the order of moments that are permitted to exist, noting that the constant δ appears in both conditions. If all finite-order moments exist (as in the Gaussian distribution) δ can be taken arbitrarily large, and hence the α-mixing size can be arbitrarily close to -1. However, if δ must be chosen small to satisfy the moment condition the mixing size must be correspondingly (absolutely) large. With an independent sequence δ can be put arbitrarily close to 0, which gets us back to Theorem 3.3.2. However, Theorem 6.2.3 is different in kind, for it restricts not so much the degree of dependence as the type of dependence. This is not a special case of Theorem 6.4.5, and both types of theorem may be needed for different purposes.

When definition (6.4.11) applies, there is nothing in condition (6.4.10) that rules out $s_n^2/n \to \infty$, even if the variances are uniformly bounded. However, this possibility *is* ruled out by the restrictions on the dependence. The following theorem is an implication of Lemma 3 of De Jong (1997).

Theorem 6.4.6 Let x_t be a uniformly $L_{2+\delta}$-bounded sequence, $\delta > 0$, which is L_2-NED of size $-\frac{1}{2}$ on either a strong-mixing process of size $-(1 + 2/\delta)$ or a uniform mixing process of size $-(2 + \delta)/2(1 + \delta)$. Then

$$\sum_{j=0}^{\infty} |E(x_t x_{t-j})| < \infty. \quad \square \tag{6.4.12}$$

In this case the autocovariances are said to be absolutely summable. Under the conditions of Theorem 6.4.6, $s_n^2 = O(n)$, so that the variance of the sum increases no faster than the sum of the variances. This has the implication that $\text{Var}(\bar{x}_n) = O(n^{-1})$, the same rate of convergence to zero as for an uncorrelated process.

6.5 Application: the Misspecified AR(1)

The analysis of §6.3.1 and §6.3.3 is elegant and powerful. Certain restrictions on the dependence and heterogeneity of the innovations not only allow consistency and asymptotic normality, but yield a simple test statistic formula. It is now possible to pose certain more challenging questions. In particular, suppose that while the characterization of (6.1.1) is valid, Assumption 6.3.1 is not available. How much of the analysis survives? Consider first the following assumptions.

Assumption 6.5.1

(a) $E(u_t|\mathcal{X}_{t-1}) = 0$ a.s.

(b) u_t is a mixing process.

(c) $E|u_t|^{2r} \le B < \infty \quad r > 2, \ \forall\, t.$ $\square$

In other words, the basic martingale difference assumption is retained, but Assumption 6.3.1(b) is swapped for a general restriction on the dependence, and also Assumption 6.3.4 replaces 6.3.1(c). Think of this as a model in which there could be neglected ARCH effects,[7] or other heterogeneity of the innovation variances, for example, seasonal effects, one-off changes in the economic environment, or even an upward trend in the variances. It is no longer possible to claim wide sense stationarity and therefore we should write $E(u_t^2) = \sigma_t^2$, depending on t in general, and define $\bar{\sigma}_n^2 = n^{-1}\sum_{t=2}^n \sigma_t^2$.

6.5.1 Consistency

Theorem 6.5.1 Under Assumption 6.5.1, $\text{plim}\, n^{-1}\sum_{t=2}^n x_{t-1}u_t = 0$. □

The proof is given in §6.6. Note that the role of Assumption 6.3.1(b) in Theorem 6.3.1 is revealed to be to reduce the order of moment needed to exist uniformly in t, from $2r$ to r. Also,

Theorem 6.5.2 Under Assumption 6.5.1,

$$\text{plim}\,\frac{1}{n}\sum_{t=2}^{n} x_{t-1}^2 = \sigma_x^2 = \frac{\bar{\sigma}^2}{1-\lambda^2} \tag{6.5.1}$$

where $\bar{\sigma}^2 = \lim_{n\to\infty}\bar{\sigma}_n^2 < \infty$. □

The proof is given in §6.6. Consistency now follows just as before.

Unlike Theorem 6.3.1, Theorem 6.5.1 did not provide a formula for $E(x_{t-1}^2 u_t^2)$. These variances do exist, however, since

$$E(x_{t-1}^2 u_t^2) = E\left[\left(\sum_{j=0}^{\infty}\lambda^j u_{t-j}\right)^2 u_t^2\right] = \left(\sum_{j=0}^{\infty}\sum_{k=0}^{\infty}\lambda^{j+k}E(u_{t-j}u_{t-k}u_t^2)\right). \tag{6.5.2}$$

By a double application of the Cauchy–Schwarz inequality, followed by Liapunov's inequality,

$$\begin{aligned} E|u_{t-j}u_{t-k}u_t^2| &\le \sqrt{E(u_{t-j}^2u_{t-k}^2)Eu_t^4} \\ &\le \sqrt[4]{Eu_{t-j}^4Eu_{t-k}^4}\sqrt{Eu_t^4} \le B^{2/r} < \infty. \end{aligned} \tag{6.5.3}$$

Hence,

$$E(x_{t-1}^2u_t^2) \le B^{2/r}\left(\sum_{j=0}^{\infty}\lambda^j\right)^2 = \frac{B^{2/r}}{(1-\lambda)^2} < \infty. \tag{6.5.4}$$

In contrasting (6.3.4) with (6.5.4), be careful to note how the denominators differ. This is of course a bound on the variance, not a formula for it.

---

[7]While we have remarked in §6.4.2 that ARCH processes can be NED, conditions under which they are also mixing are unknown and would have to be assumed implicitly. The present results are for illustration only, and variants appropriate to specific cases such as ARCH are interesting projects for future research.

6.5.2 Asymptotic Normality

The final task is to prove asymptotic normality, and the martingale CLT still serves under Assumption 6.5.1. The new requirement is to prove condition (a) of Theorem 6.2.3, which will need an application of Theorem 6.4.4.

Theorem 6.5.3 Under Assumption 6.5.1,

$$\frac{1}{\sqrt{n}}\sum_{t=2}^{n} x_{t-1}u_t \xrightarrow{\mathrm{D}} \mathrm{N}(0, a^2) \tag{6.5.5}$$

where

$$a^2 = \lim_{n\to\infty}\frac{1}{n}\sum_{t=2}^{n} E(x_{t-1}^2 u_t^2) < \infty. \quad \square \tag{6.5.6}$$

For the proof see §6.6.

Application of Cramér's Theorem now shows that

$$\sqrt{n}(\hat{\lambda}-\lambda) \xrightarrow{\mathrm{D}} \mathrm{N}\left(0, \frac{a^2(1-\lambda^2)^2}{\bar{\sigma}^4}\right) \tag{6.5.7}$$

Thus, the main problem with the failure of Assumption 6.3.1 is that the variance formula in (6.3.20) is no longer valid. This need not be a drawback, provided we know how to estimate the true variance consistently. Of the three unknown parameters in the variance in (6.5.7), λ can be consistently estimated by $\hat{\lambda}$ as before, and $\bar{\sigma}^2$ is the probability limit of $n^{-1}\sum_{t=2}^{n} u_t^2$ according to (6.6.7). Let

$$\hat{u}_t = x_t - \hat{\lambda}x_{t-1} = u_t - (\hat{\lambda}-\lambda)x_{t-1} \tag{6.5.8}$$

and note that

$$\frac{1}{n}\sum_{t=2}^{n}\hat{u}_t^2 = \frac{1}{n}\sum_{t=2}^{n}u_t^2 - 2(\hat{\lambda}-\lambda)\frac{1}{n}\sum_{t=2}^{n}x_{t-1}u_t + (\hat{\lambda}-\lambda)^2\frac{1}{n}\sum_{t=2}^{n}x_{t-1}^2 \tag{6.5.9}$$

Taking probability limits all the way through and applying Slutsky's Theorem, it is clear from (6.5.9) that $\operatorname{plim} n^{-1}\sum_{t=2}^{n}\hat{u}_t^2 = \bar{\sigma}^2$. In other words, the least squares residuals can successfully proxy for the innovations. The remaining problem is to estimate a^2 consistently, and for this purpose, consider the sample counterpart of (6.5.6),

$$\begin{aligned}\hat{a}^2 &= \frac{1}{n}\sum_{t=2}^{n}x_{t-1}^2\hat{u}_t^2\\ &= \frac{1}{n}\sum_{t=2}^{n}x_{t-1}^2u_t^2 - 2(\hat{\lambda}-\lambda)\frac{1}{n}\sum_{t=2}^{n}x_{t-1}^3u_t + (\hat{\lambda}-\lambda)^2\frac{1}{n}\sum_{t=2}^{n}x_{t-1}^4.\end{aligned} \tag{6.5.10}$$

Theorem 6.5.4 Under Assumptions 6.5.1 and 6.3.4, $\hat{a}^2 \xrightarrow{\mathrm{pr}} a^2$. $\square$

See §6.6 for the proof. Formula (6.5.7) can therefore be used to generate approximate confidence intervals for $\hat{\lambda}$, using consistent estimates of the asymptotic variance. Whether Assumption 6.3.1 (rather than Assumption 6.5.1) holds is therefore less important than knowing whether it holds, and hence which variance formula to use, although it should be noted that the formula in (6.5.7) is valid under either assumption. However, Assumption 6.3.3 is not likely to be available to us without Assumption 6.3.1, so perhaps the most critical issue is to know whether or not the tougher moment restriction of 6.3.4 is necessary.

Further Reading: This chapter applies to the AR(1) model some fundamental concepts from limit theory under dependence. Davidson (1994a) covers the relevant topics in detail, and is the recommended companion text for those wanting to go further. Other useful books include White (1984), McCabe and Tremayne (1993), Bierens (1994) and Pötscher and Prucha (1997). The articles by Pötscher and Prucha (1991a, 1991b) and Andrews (1987, 1988) are technical, but addressed to econometricians. For more 'deep background' on the probability fundamentals, consult Hall and Heyde (1980), Breiman (1992) or Billingsley (1986).

6.6 Appendix: Additional Proofs

Proof of Theorem 6.1.1. If the process $\{x_t\}$ is stationary then the joint distribution of the variables $(x_{t+1}, \ldots, x_{t+m+k})$, for $m > 0$ and $k > 0$, does not depend on t. It follows that the joint distributions of the vectors $\boldsymbol{x}_{t+j} = (x_{t+1+j}, \ldots, x_{t+k+j})'$, for $j = 1, \ldots, m$ do not depend on t, and hence that the joint distributions of measurable functions $g(\boldsymbol{x}_{t+1}), \ldots, g(\boldsymbol{x}_{t+m})$ do not depend on t. A sequence is ergodic if every invariant random event A has probability 0 or 1, where 'invariant' means that changing the time subscript of every element of the sequence from t to $t+k$, for any $k > 0$, leaves A unchanged. If this property holds for the distribution of $\{x_t\}$, it must also hold for the distribution of the sequence of vectors $\{\boldsymbol{x}_t\}$ just defined and, likewise, for the distribution of the sequence $\{g(\boldsymbol{x}_t)\}$. ∎

Proof of Theorem 6.3.3 The fact that the variable $n^{-1/2}\sum_{t=2}^{n} x_{t-1}u_t$ has the mean and variance indicated, for any sample size, follows from (6.3.3), (6.3.4) and (6.3.5). To show that condition (a) of Theorem 6.2.3 is met, note that $\{x_{t-1}^2(u_t^2 - \sigma^2), \mathcal{X}_t\}$ is an m.d. in view of (6.3.4) and Theorem 6.2.1. Hence by Theorem 6.2.2, any of Assumptions 6.3.2, 6.3.3 or 6.3.4 is sufficient to show that

$$\operatorname{plim} n^{-1}\sum_{t=2}^{n} x_{t-1}^2 u_t^2 = \sigma^2 \operatorname{plim} n^{-1}\sum_{t=2}^{n} x_{t-1}^2 = \frac{\sigma^4}{1-\lambda^2}. \tag{6.6.1}$$

It remains to show that condition (b) of Theorem 6.2.3 holds. Under Assumption 6.3.2 there is nothing more to show. Otherwise, given that $\bar{\sigma}_n^2 = \sigma^2$ we only need to show that $E|x_{t-1}u_t|^{2+\delta}$ has a finite bound. Since $x_{t-1} = \sum_{j=0}^{\infty}\lambda^j u_{t-1-j}$,

$$\|x_{t-1}u_t\|_{2+\delta} \le \sum_{j=0}^{\infty}|\lambda|^j\|u_{t-j-1}u_t\|_{2+\delta} \le \frac{\max_{j\ge 0}\|u_{t-j-1}u_t\|_{2+\delta}}{1-|\lambda|} \tag{6.6.2}$$

where the first inequality applies Minkowski's inequality. The problem is to show that the right-hand member of (6.6.2) is finite. Under Assumption 6.3.3 choosing $\delta \le r-2$,

$$E|u_{t-j-1}u_t|^{2+\delta} = E[|u_{t-j-1}|^{2+\delta}E(|u_t|^{2+\delta}|\mathcal{X}_{t-1})]$$

$$= E|u_{t-j-1}|^{2+\delta}\mu_r = \mu_r^2 \tag{6.6.3}$$

using the LIE to obtain the first equality. Therefore, since (6.6.3) holds for all j and t, the right-hand member of (6.6.2) is bounded as required. Alternatively, under Assumption 6.3.4, simply set $\delta = r - 2$ and apply the Cauchy–Schwarz inequality to obtain

$$E|u_{t-j-1}u_t|^{2+\delta} \le \sqrt{E|u_{t-j-1}|^{4+2\delta}E|u_t|^{4+2\delta}} \le B < \infty \tag{6.6.4}$$

yielding the same conclusion as before. ∎

Proof of Theorem 6.5.1 Much as in the proof of Theorem 6.3.3, use Minkowski's inequality to write

$$\|x_{t-1}u_t\|_{1+\delta} \le \sum_{j=0}^{\infty}|\lambda|^j\|u_{t-j-1}u_t\|_{1+\delta} \le \frac{\max_{j\ge 0}\|u_{t-j-1}u_t\|_{1+\delta}}{1-|\lambda|} \tag{6.6.5}$$

and the Cauchy–Schwarz inequality to give

$$E|u_{t-j-1}u_t|^{1+\delta} \le \sqrt{E|u_{t-j-1}|^{2+2\delta}E|u_t|^{2+2\delta}} \le B < \infty. \tag{6.6.6}$$

Since $\{x_{t-1}u_t, \mathcal{X}_t\}$ is a m.d. sequence by Theorem 6.2.1, the required conclusion follows by Theorem 6.2.2. ∎

Proof of Theorem 6.5.2 The proof of Theorem 6.3.2 goes through broadly unchanged, except that we must now show $n^{-1}\sum_{t=2}^n u_t^2 \xrightarrow{\text{pr}} \bar{\sigma}^2$, where $\bar{\sigma}^2 < \infty$ since $\sigma_t^2 \le B^{2/r} < \infty$ for every t by Assumption 6.5.1(c) and Liapunov's inequality (B.4.16). This is equivalent to

$$\text{plim}\,\frac{1}{n}\sum_{t=2}^{n}\{u_t^2 - \sigma_t^2\} = 0 \tag{6.6.7}$$

which follows by Theorem 6.4.4 with $\delta = r - 1$. Condition (6.4.9) holds since

$$E|u_t^2 - \sigma_t^2|^r \le (B^{1/r} + \sigma_t^2)^r < \infty. \tag{6.6.8}$$

A mixing process is trivially L_1-NED on itself so the conditions are satisfied, and any rate of mixing will do. ∎

Proof of Theorem 6.5.3 Since $x_{t-1}u_t$ is a m.d. under Assumption 6.5.1, condition (b) of Theorem 6.2.3 is satisfied by the argument from Assumption 6.3.4, which matches Assumption 6.5.1(c) in the proof of Theorem 6.3.3. The m.d. assumption also ensures the terms $x_{t-1}u_t$ are uncorrelated which validates the assertion in (6.5.6).

To prove that condition (a) of Theorem 6.2.3 is satisfied, note first that x_t is L_2-NED on $\{u_s\}$ of size $-\infty$ according to (6.4.7), and since

$$\|x_t\|_{2r} \le \sum_{j=0}^{\infty}|\lambda|^j\|u_{t-j}\|_{2r} \le \frac{B}{(1-|\lambda|)} < \infty \tag{6.6.9}$$

x_t^2 is also L_2-NED on $\{u_s\}$ of size $-\infty$ by Theorem 6.4.3(ii). Since, u_t^2 is L_2-NED on itself (trivially), it follows from Theorem 6.4.3(i) that $x_{t-1}^2u_t^2$ is L_1-NED on $\{u_s\}$ of size $-\infty$. Moreover, two applications of the Cauchy–Schwarz inequality give

$$E|u_{t-j}u_{t-k}u_t^2|^{r/2} \le \sqrt[4]{E|u_{t-j}|^{2r}E|u_{t-k}|^{2r}}\sqrt{E|u_t|^{2r}} \le B. \tag{6.6.10}$$

Hence by the Jensen inequality (noting $(\cdot)^{r/2}$ is a convex function) and the Minkowski inequality,

$$\|x_{t-1}^2u_t^2 - E(x_{t-1}^2u_t^2)\|_{r/2} \le 2\|x_{t-1}^2u_t^2\|_{r/2}$$

$$\leq 2\sum_{j=0}^{\infty}\sum_{k=0}^{\infty}|\lambda|^{j+k}\|u_{t-j-1}u_{t-k-1}u_t^2\|_{r/2}$$

$$\leq \frac{2B^{2/r}}{(1-|\lambda|)^2} < \infty. \tag{6.6.11}$$

Since $r/2 > 1$ the conditions of Theorem 6.4.4 therefore hold, and

$$\text{plim}\,\frac{1}{n}\sum_{t=2}^{n}[x_{t-1}^2u_t^2 - E(x_{t-1}^2u_t^2)] = 0. \tag{6.6.12}$$

This completes the proof. ∎

Proof of Theorem 6.5.4 The convergence of the first of the three terms on the right of (6.5.10) to a^2 has been established in the proof of Theorem by 6.5.3, see (6.6.12). Since $\hat{\lambda} - \lambda = O_p(n^{-1/2})$, the second and third terms vanish provided the means of x_t^4 and $x_{t-1}^3u_t$ converge in probability to finite limits. These results are argued just like the case of $x_{t-1}^2u_t^2$. x_t^4 is shown to be L_1-NED on $\{u_s\}$ by applying Theorem 6.4.3(ii) to x_t and then Theorem 6.4.3(i) to x_t^2. Then, similarly to (6.6.11).

$$\begin{aligned}\|x_t^4 - E(x_t^4)\|_{r/2} &\leq 2\|x_t^4\|_{r/2}\\ &\leq 2\sum_{j=0}^{\infty}\sum_{k=0}^{\infty}\sum_{l=0}^{\infty}\sum_{m=0}^{\infty}|\lambda|^{j+k+l+m}\|u_{t-j}u_{t-k}u_{t-l}u_{t-m}\|_{r/2}\\ &\leq \frac{B^{2/r}}{(1-|\lambda|)^4} < \infty.\end{aligned} \tag{6.6.13}$$

The argument for $x_{t-1}^3u_t$ is similar. ∎

Chapter 7

Estimation and Testing

7.1 The Dynamic Regression Model

Chapter 6 demonstrated the style of argument required to establish the asymptotic properties of regression, by working through a simple case. Now we consider the generalization of these results to practical cases. Necessarily, this will require 'higher-level' assumptions. Properties that before could be proved from primitive conditions on the DGP (like stability conditions on the autoregressive roots) must now be assumed directly. In fact, all the results can be proved at the same level as before by assuming, for example, that the equation of interest is embedded in a stationary Gaussian VAR, as in Chapter 4. Apart from the complexity of this exercise, it would not be the most helpful approach because the results actually apply much more widely. We exhibit a sufficient collection of conditions, and these can be put to practical use by showing that they hold in a given application; or more truthfully, devoutly hoping that they do. As the reader knows, economists rarely hesitate to assume things that they would like to be true, and we shall follow this honourable tradition.

7.1.1 The Setup

The model to be studied corresponds to sampling model C, in the categorization of §1.3. To cope with dynamic elements of the specification, and the fact that variables are typically related to their own lags in the sequence of observations, it is necessary to introduce conditioning assumptions less stringent that we were able to use in sampling model B. Let $\mathcal{I}_t$ represent a 'set of conditioning variables'. The mathematically correct way to express this representation is to say that $\mathcal{I}_t$ is the smallest σ-field of events containing the σ-fields generated by the conditioning variables, but this is rather a mouthful. We commit a mild abuse of notation by using the inclusion symbol $\in$ to indicate that a random vector is measurable with respect to the indicated σ-field, and so write things like $\boldsymbol{x}_t \in \mathcal{I}_t$. Although there is an important distinction between the set of random variables and the set of events with respect to which the variables are measurable, for the present purpose it is convenient to use one as shorthand for the other. See §B.10 for the relevant background.

The models studied take the basic form[1]

$$y_t = \boldsymbol{x}_t'\boldsymbol{\beta} + u_t \tag{7.1.1}$$

where $\boldsymbol{x}_t$ $(k \times 1) \in \mathcal{I}_t$. The fundamental assumption is

Assumption 7.1.1 $E(u_t|\mathcal{I}_t) = 0$ a.s. □

A subclass of models enjoying certain extra desirable properties satisfy a further condition,

Assumption 7.1.2 $E(u_t^2|\mathcal{I}_t) = \sigma^2$ a.s. □

The parameter σ^2 is defined, in either case, to equal $E(u_t^2)$. Initially we analyse the models that satisfy both assumptions, and subsequently note the consequences of dropping Assumption 7.1.2.

The most important feature of the setup is the specification of the set $\mathcal{I}_t$ of valid conditioning variables. This is the complement of the set of variables specifically excluded, by the model, from the explanation or prediction of y_t. The latter typically include any dated $t+j$ for $j > 0$, and any regarded as being determined jointly with y_t. A very large collection remains, generally including all the variables in the following categories:

- deterministic variables, such as the intercept, seasonal dummies, etc.:
- lagged variables, dated $t-j$ for $j > 0$;
- current dated variables that are weakly exogenous for $(\boldsymbol{\beta}, \sigma^2)$.

Moreover, any Borel-measurable function of variables in $\mathcal{I}_t$ is also in $\mathcal{I}_t$. Thus, $u_{t-j} \in \mathcal{I}_t$ since $u_{t-j} = y_{t-j} - \boldsymbol{\beta}'\boldsymbol{x}_{t-j}$. One implication of Assumption 7.1.1 is that the disturbances must be serially uncorrelated.

To take a specific example, suppose that $(y_t, \boldsymbol{z}_t)$ is a vector of variables generated by a dynamic data generation process, represented by the density with factorization

$$D_t(y_t, \boldsymbol{z}_t|\mathcal{Y}_{t-1}, \mathcal{Z}_{t-1}; \boldsymbol{\psi}) = D_t(y_t|\boldsymbol{z}_t, \mathcal{Y}_{t-1}, \mathcal{Z}_{t-1}; \boldsymbol{\psi}_1)D_t(\boldsymbol{z}_t|\mathcal{Y}_{t-1}, \mathcal{Z}_{t-1}; \boldsymbol{\psi}_2) \tag{7.1.2}$$

and that $\boldsymbol{x}_t'\boldsymbol{\beta}$ is the mean of y_t under the first conditional factor where $\boldsymbol{x}_t$ is composed of elements of $\boldsymbol{z}_{t-j}$ for $j \geq 0$ and y_{t-j} for $j > 0$, and $\boldsymbol{\beta}$ and σ^2 are elements of $\boldsymbol{\psi}_1$. In this case $\mathcal{I}_t = \sigma(\boldsymbol{z}_t) \vee \mathcal{Z}_{t-1} \vee \mathcal{Y}_{t-1}$ and the decomposition corresponds to (4.5.3), specialized here by taking y_t to be a scalar. If the conditional factor in (7.1.2) is Gaussian then $\boldsymbol{\psi}_1 = (\boldsymbol{\beta}, \sigma^2)$, but note that the Gaussianity assumption is not needed for the results.

---

[1] The symbol $\boldsymbol{x}_t$ is being used here to denote the vector of regressors, to match the conventional usage in Chapters 1-3. We avoid the usage $\boldsymbol{x}_t = (y_t, \boldsymbol{z}_t')'$, as employed in Chapter 4.

Additional regularity conditions are needed to validate the asymptotic analysis, of which the most important is

$$\operatorname*{plim}_{n\to\infty}\frac{1}{n}\sum_{t=1}^{n}x_t x_t' = \lim_{n\to\infty}\frac{1}{n}\sum_{t=1}^{n}E(x_t x_t') = M_{XX} < \infty \text{ (positive definite).} \tag{7.1.3}$$

This is of course identical to (3.5.2), but the underlying conditions would be quite different in the two cases. All that is needed with independent data is to verify that the moment conditions for the law of large numbers is obeyed. Here, we should need either a generalization of Theorem 6.3.2, or an invocation of mixing or NED properties. If the data are stationary then $M_{XX} = E(x_t x_t')$, but this isn't necessary.

7.1.2 Consistency

The least squares estimator, reproducing equation (3.5.4) here for the sake of emphasis, is

$$\hat{\beta} = \left(\sum_{t=1}^{n}x_t x_t'\right)^{-1}\sum_{t=1}^{n}x_t y_t = \beta + \left(\sum_{t=1}^{n}x_t x_t'\right)^{-1}\sum_{t=1}^{n}x_t u_t. \tag{7.1.4}$$

As before, the analysis of consistency begins with the vector $x_t u_t$ $(k \times 1)$. Since $x_t \in \mathcal{I}_t$, the properties of conditional expectations imply

$$E(x_t u_t|\mathcal{I}_t) = x_t E(u_t|\mathcal{I}_t) = 0 \text{ a.s.} \tag{7.1.5}$$

Define $\mathcal{I}_t^* = \sigma(y_t) \vee \mathcal{I}_t$, or in words, the σ-field with respect to which all the variables contained in the model are measurable. Since $y_{t-1} \in \mathcal{I}_t$, note that $\mathcal{I}_{t-1}^* \subseteq \mathcal{I}_t$. Hence, (7.1.5) further implies, using the LIE, that

$$E(x_t u_t|\mathcal{I}_{t-1}^*) = E[E(x_t u_t|\mathcal{I}_t)|\mathcal{I}_{t-1}^*] = 0 \text{ a.s.} \tag{7.1.6}$$

Since each element of the vector $x_t u_t$ is $\mathcal{I}_t^*$-measurable, it accordingly forms a martingale difference sequence with respect to this information set. In fact a stronger property obtains, which is that the sequence $\{x_t u_t, \mathcal{I}_t^*\}$ is a *vector martingale difference* (v.m.d.).

One way to define a v.m.d. is as a vector sequence, say $\{y_t, \mathcal{F}_t\}$, such that for any fixed, finite vector λ, $\{\lambda' y_t, \mathcal{F}_t\}$ is an m.d. sequence. This is not the same as a vector of m.d. sequences. Consider the vector $y_t = (x_t, x_{t-1})'$ where x_t is a m.d. sequence. In general $\lambda' y_t = \lambda_1 x_t + \lambda_2 x_{t-1}$ is a serially correlated sequence, and so cannot be a m.d.

Assumptions 7.1.1 and 7.1.2 also make $\{\text{Vec}\, x_t x_t'(u_t^2 - \sigma^2), \mathcal{I}_t^*\}$ a v.m.d. The properties generalize naturally from the univariate case, and in particular, the following results hold.

$$E(x_t u_t) = 0 \tag{7.1.7}$$

$$\text{Var}(x_t u_t) = E(u_t^2 x_t x_t') = E[E(u_t^2|\mathcal{I}_t)x_t x_t'] = \sigma^2 E(x_t x_t') \tag{7.1.8}$$

$$\text{Cov}(x_t u_t, x_s u_s) = E(u_t u_s x_t x_s') = E[E(u_t|\mathcal{I}_t)u_s x_t x_s'] = 0 \quad t > s. \tag{7.1.9}$$

(7.1.8) and (7.1.3) together imply

$$\frac{1}{n}\sum_{t=1}^{n}\text{Var}(\boldsymbol{x}_t u_t) = \sigma^2 \frac{1}{n}\sum_{t=1}^{n} E(\boldsymbol{x}_t \boldsymbol{x}_t') \to \sigma^2 \boldsymbol{M}_{XX} < \infty \text{ as } n \to \infty. \tag{7.1.10}$$

Together with conditions (7.1.7) and (7.1.9), (7.1.10) is sufficient for the Chebyshev WLLN to hold for each element of the vector, yielding

$$\text{plim}\,\frac{1}{n}\sum_{t=1}^{n} \boldsymbol{x}_t u_t = \boldsymbol{0}. \tag{7.1.11}$$

Applying the Slutsky Theorem and (7.1.3) now gives $\text{plim}\,\hat{\boldsymbol{\beta}} = \boldsymbol{\beta}$, by the argument paralleling (3.5.7).

7.1.3 Asymptotic Normality

For asymptotic normality, either strict stationarity or the assumption

$$E|\boldsymbol{\lambda}'\boldsymbol{x}_t u_t|^{2+\delta} \leq B < \infty \quad \delta > 0,\ \forall\, t,\ \forall \text{ fixed } \boldsymbol{\lambda} \text{ with } \boldsymbol{\lambda}'\boldsymbol{\lambda} = 1 \tag{7.1.12}$$

is all that is needed. Since $\{\text{Vec}\,\boldsymbol{x}_t\boldsymbol{x}_t'(u_t^2 - \sigma^2), \mathcal{I}_t^*\}$ is a v.m.d., this condition is sufficient by Theorem 6.2.2 for

$$\frac{1}{n}\sum_{t=1}^{n}(\boldsymbol{\lambda}'\boldsymbol{x}_t)^2(u_t^2 - \sigma^2) \xrightarrow{\text{pr}} 0. \tag{7.1.13}$$

Hence, in view of (7.1.3) and (7.1.10) and arguments similar to §3.5.3, the conditions of Theorem 6.2.3 are also satisfied, and

$$\frac{1}{\sqrt{n}}\sum_{t=1}^{n} \boldsymbol{\lambda}'\boldsymbol{x}_t u_t \xrightarrow{\text{D}} \text{N}(0, \sigma^2\boldsymbol{\lambda}'\boldsymbol{M}_{XX}\boldsymbol{\lambda}) \tag{7.1.14}$$

for each such $\boldsymbol{\lambda}$. A point to note is that (7.1.12) is not enough for (7.1.3), and (7.1.13) imposes no restrictions on the memory of the $\boldsymbol{x}_t$ process, as (7.1.3) does. Given the m.d. property, the moment conditions are enough here.

The argument leading to (3.5.11) now applies identically, leading to the conclusion

$$\sqrt{n}(\hat{\boldsymbol{\beta}} - \boldsymbol{\beta}) = \left(\frac{1}{n}\sum_{t=1}^{n}\boldsymbol{x}_t\boldsymbol{x}_t'\right)^{-1} \frac{1}{\sqrt{n}}\sum_{t=1}^{n}\boldsymbol{x}_t u_t \xrightarrow{\text{D}} \text{N}(0, \sigma^2\boldsymbol{M}_{XX}^{-1}). \tag{7.1.15}$$

This completes the proof of the following theorem.

Theorem 7.1.1 If Assumptions 7.1.1 and 7.1.2 plus conditions (7.1.3) and (7.1.12) hold, the OLS estimator of $\boldsymbol{\beta}$ is CAN, with the distribution given in (7.1.15). □

The practical application of these results is straightforward. They imply that in large samples, the interval estimates and test procedures described in §2.4 can be applied in the present context, basically without modification. A consistent estimate of $\sigma^2 M_{XX}^{-1}$ is provided by $ns^2(X'X)^{-1}$ where s^2 is the usual residual variance estimate, so that according to the Cramér Theorem, the usual t statistics for the significance of individual regressors are asymptotically $\mathrm{N}(0,1)$ on the null hypothesis. Similarly, the 'F tests' of linear restrictions in §2.4.3 can be performed in the usual manner, although the degrees of freedom corrections are optional and the tests are often interpreted as chi-squared tests; that is to say, the test statistic in (2.4.12) multiplied by r, the number of restrictions under test, is treated as asymptotically $\chi^2(r)$ under the null hypothesis. In practice, as argued in §3.5.5, the $F(n-k,r)$ distribution may provide at least as good an approximation to the true unknown distribution of the F statistic, with finite n, as does $\chi^2(r)/r$.

7.1.4 A VAR Application

As an example that extends the analysis of Chapter 6 in the crucial way, suppose the equation of interest is embedded in a structural VAR of the form (4.2.9). To fix ideas, consider the simple system

$$y_t = \beta x_t + \gamma y_{t-1} + u_t \tag{7.1.16a}$$

$$x_t = \lambda x_{t-1} + v_t \tag{7.1.16b}$$

in which u_t at least satisfies Assumptions 7.1.1 and 7.1.2, and the disturbances are contemporaneously uncorrelated, so that the first equation is a legitimate regression model with $\mathcal{I}_t = \sigma(x_{t-j}, y_{t-j-1},\ j > 0)$. The key condition to be checked, subject to these assumptions, is (7.1.3). The reduced or VAR form of the system is

$$\begin{bmatrix} y_t \\ x_t \end{bmatrix} = \begin{bmatrix} \gamma & \beta\lambda \\ 0 & \lambda \end{bmatrix} \begin{bmatrix} y_{t-1} \\ x_{t-1} \end{bmatrix} + \begin{bmatrix} u_t + \beta v_t \\ v_t \end{bmatrix} \tag{7.1.17}$$

or in vector form,

$$z_t = \Lambda z_{t-1} + \varepsilon_t. \tag{7.1.18}$$

The characteristic equation of the system is

$$|\Lambda - \mu I| = \mu^2 - (\gamma + \lambda)\mu + \lambda\gamma = 0 \tag{7.1.19}$$

which has solutions of γ and λ so the stability conditions, as is evident by inspection, are $|\gamma| < 1$ and $|\lambda| < 1$.

Subject to stability, the sample moments $n^{-1}\sum_{t-2}^{n} x_t^2$, $n^{-1}\sum_{t-2}^{n} y_{t-1}^2$ and $n^{-1}\sum_{t-2}^{n} x_t y_{t-1}$ must be shown to converge in probability and the nature of the limits determined. The first of these problems has already been dealt with in Chapter 6, and one possible approach is to undertake a vector generalization of the analysis in §6.3.1. However, this approach is based on Assumption 6.3.1, which as noted there, is quite restrictive in requiring the model to be 'correct' in essential respects. In particular, the m.d. property was required of the shocks, which in this context would have to be extended to all the equations of the system, not just the equation of interest. It is clearly better to be able to assume that the specification is incomplete, such that some elements of ε_t (v_t, in the example) are mixing processes, but not necessarily serially uncorrelated. Therefore we adopt the approach of checking the conditions of Theorem 6.4.4. This also provides a good excuse to explore the use of this theory, whose application is potentially wider than just to linear models.

The next part of the analysis applies to VARs of any dimension (assume p) and also any order, via the companion form. To check the near-epoch dependence condition expand the VAR as in (4.3.6) and use the approach of (6.4.7). Assume the eigenvalues of $\boldsymbol{\Lambda}$ are distinct, so that the decomposition $\boldsymbol{\Lambda} = \boldsymbol{QMQ}^{-1}$ holds as in (4.3.2), where $\boldsymbol{M}$ is diagonal. Defining the vectors $\boldsymbol{z}_t^* = \boldsymbol{Q}^{-1}\boldsymbol{z}_t$ and $\boldsymbol{\varepsilon}_t^* = \boldsymbol{Q}^{-1}\boldsymbol{\varepsilon}_t$, note that $\boldsymbol{z}_t^*$ has the representation as a vector of univariate AR processes with the form

$$z_{jt}^* = \mu_j z_{j,t-1}^* + \varepsilon_{jt}^* = \sum_{k=0}^{m} \mu_j^k \varepsilon_{j,t-k}^* + \mu_j^{m+1} z_{j,t-m-1}^* \tag{7.1.20}$$

for $j = 1, \dots, p$.[2] Letting $\mathcal{F}_s^t = \sigma(\boldsymbol{\varepsilon}_s, \dots, \boldsymbol{\varepsilon}_t)$ for $t \geq s$, and applying (6.4.7),

$$\|z_{jt}^* - E(z_{jt}^* | \mathcal{F}_{t-m}^{t+m})\|_2 \leq 2|\mu_j|^{m+1} \|z_{j,t-m-1}^*\|_2. \tag{7.1.21}$$

In a stable system with $|\mu_j| < 1$ for each j the elements of $\boldsymbol{z}_t^*$ are accordingly L_2-NED on $\boldsymbol{\varepsilon}_t$ of size $-\infty$. Finally consider the vector $\boldsymbol{z}_t = \boldsymbol{Q}\boldsymbol{z}_t^*$. Minkowski's inequality gives

$$\|z_{it} - E(z_{it} | \mathcal{F}_{t-m}^{t+m})\|_2 \leq \sum_{j=1}^{p} |q_{ij}| \|z_{jt}^* - E(z_{jt}^* | \mathcal{F}_{t-m}^{t+m})\|_2 \tag{7.1.22}$$

which shows that these elements share the L_2-NED property.

The weak law of large numbers is to be proved for the squares and cross products of the variables, but these are L_1-NED of the same size as the variables themselves by Theorem 6.4.3(i). It only remains to check the uniform moment condition imposed by Theorem 6.4.4, and in view of the Cauchy–Schwarz inequality it is enough to check this for the squared terms. First note that, for $1 \leq i \leq m$,

$$\|z_{it}^2\|_{1+\delta}^{1/2} = \|z_{it}\|_{2+2\delta} \leq \sum_{j=1}^{p} |q_{ij}| \|z_{jt}^*\|_{2+2\delta} \tag{7.1.23}$$

and substituting from (7.1.20) with $m = \infty$, the Minkowski inequality gives

$$\|z_{jt}^*\|_{2+2\delta} \leq \sum_{k=0}^{\infty} |\mu_j|^k \|\varepsilon_{j,t-k}^*\|_{2+2\delta} \leq \sum_{k=0}^{\infty} |\mu_j|^k \sum_{i=1}^{p} |q^{ji}| \|\varepsilon_{i,t-k}\|_{2+2\delta} \tag{7.1.24}$$

where the q^{ji} denote the elements of $\boldsymbol{Q}^{-1}$. Since the $\{|\mu_j|^k, k = 0, 1, 2, \dots\}$ form a summable sequence when $|\mu_j| < 1$, putting together (7.1.23) and (7.1.24) leads to

---

[2] Although in the example the eigenvalues are real they can be complex in general, and then the z_{jt}^* are complex-valued. The following analysis applies unchanged, noting that the L_2-norm of a complex r.v. x is $(E|x|^2)^{1/2}$ where $|x|$ is the modulus of x.

the conclusion that, if $\|\varepsilon_{j,t-k}\|_{2+2\delta} < \infty$ uniformly in t, the conditions of Theorem 6.4.4 are satisfied. Note that for this result, the only restriction needed on the distribution of the shocks is that they are mixing, and possess the moments of the required order.

Having established the existence of the limit M_{XX}, the next step (in principle at least) should be to determine its form, and check that it is positive definite. While the following analysis is perfectly general, it is easiest to revert to the simple example to see how it works since the calculations are potentially burdensome. Also for the sake of simplicity let u_t and v_t satisfy Assumptions 7.1.1 and 7.1.2, with variances σ_u^2 and σ_v^2. The idea is to form suitable equations in the second moments by operating directly on (7.1.16). Inspection easily shows that the following relations hold:

$$E(y_t^2) = \beta^2 E(x_t^2) + \gamma^2 E(y_{t-1}^2) + 2\beta\gamma E(x_t y_{t-1}) + \sigma_u^2 \tag{7.1.25a}$$

$$E(x_t^2) = \lambda^2 E(x_{t-1}^2) + \sigma_v^2 \tag{7.1.25b}$$

$$E(x_t y_t) = \beta E(x_t^2) + \gamma E(x_t y_{t-1}) \tag{7.1.25c}$$

$$E(x_t y_{t-1}) = \lambda E(x_{t-1} y_{t-1}). \tag{7.1.25d}$$

Equations (7.1.25a) and (7.1.25b) are got by squaring both sides of (7.1.16a) and (7.1.16b), and (7.1.25c) and (7.1.25d) by multiplying them through by x_t and y_{t-1} respectively. Since the system is stable and the shocks are white noise the variables are wide-sense stationary, so $E(y_t^2) = E(y_{t-1}^2)$, $E(x_t^2) = E(x_{t-1}^2)$ and $E(x_t y_t) = E(x_{t-1} y_{t-1})$. These substitutions leave four equations in four unknowns, of which three are of interest. It is easy to verify that the solutions are

$$E(x_t^2) = \frac{\sigma_v^2}{1-\lambda^2} \tag{7.1.26a}$$

$$E(x_t y_{t-1}) = \frac{\lambda\beta\sigma_v^2}{(1-\gamma\lambda)(1-\lambda^2)} \tag{7.1.26b}$$

$$E(y_{t-1}^2) = \frac{\sigma_u^2}{1-\gamma^2} + \frac{\beta^2(1+\gamma\lambda)\sigma_v^2}{(1-\gamma^2)(1-\lambda^2)(1-\gamma\lambda)}. \tag{7.1.26c}$$

Subject to the stability conditions these solutions exist and, as can be verified, form a positive definite matrix.

7.1.5 Asymptotic Efficiency

The efficiency analysis in §3.6 extends more or less unchanged to the present case, once the CAN property is established, with a few additional considerations. We considered a class of linear estimators of the form

$$\beta_L = \sum_{t=1}^{n} l_{nt} y_t \tag{7.1.27}$$

and then a subclass β_W for which

$$l_{nt} = P_n w_t. \tag{7.1.28}$$

To apply Theorems 3.6.1 and 3.6.2 to Model C, replace Assumptions 3.6.1 and 3.6.2 with $\boldsymbol{w}_t \in \mathcal{I}_t$. Subject to the usual regularity conditions, the results

$$\text{plim}\,\frac{1}{n}\sum_{t=1}^{n}\boldsymbol{w}_t u_t = \mathbf{0} \tag{7.1.29}$$

$$\frac{1}{\sqrt{n}}\sum_{t=1}^{n}\boldsymbol{w}_t u_t \xrightarrow{\text{D}} \text{N}(\mathbf{0}, \sigma^2 \boldsymbol{M}_{WW}) \tag{7.1.30}$$

follow from Assumptions 7.1.1 and 7.1.2, and the analysis can proceed as before.

There is virtually no loss of generality in confining attention to the class of instrumental variables estimators, defined by (7.1.28). Argue as follows. Any member of the class $\boldsymbol{\beta}_L$ can be represented using the form (7.1.28) if $\boldsymbol{w}_t$ is allowed to bear an array subscript, as $\boldsymbol{w}_{nt}$. One may simply write $\boldsymbol{l}_{nt} = \boldsymbol{P}_n \boldsymbol{w}_{nt}$ and if necessary choose $\boldsymbol{P}_n = n^{-1}\boldsymbol{I}_k$. Since any multiplicative scaling factors can be incorporated in $\boldsymbol{P}_n$, the main distinctive role for the array subscript would be to allow $\boldsymbol{w}_{nt}$ to depend in some way on the whole sample of data. Results (7.1.29) and (7.1.30) hold under the assumptions because $\boldsymbol{w}_t \in \mathcal{I}_t$, but do *not* hold in general if $\boldsymbol{w}_t \in \mathcal{I}_s$ for $s > t$. In particular, $\boldsymbol{w}_t$ is only allowed to depend on data up to and including date t. The only way such a vector could not be unambiguously labelled with the single subscript t would be due to some form of non-multiplicative transformation of the data depending on sample size. If such unusual possibilities are neglected, (7.1.28) represents the maximum generality compatible with consistency.

7.2 Extensions of the Basic Model

7.2.1 Dummy Regressors

We have a good idea of what is required to enforce condition (7.1.3) when the regressors are stochastic. The conditions of a weak law of large numbers must be satisfied, which, if the data are generated by a VAR, involves stable roots and suitable moment and/or dependence restrictions on the innovations. However, the case of dummy (deterministic) regressors, as discussed in §4.1.2, also needs consideration, and some care is needed in treating these when the sample size is being extended to infinity.

Write $\boldsymbol{x}_t = (\boldsymbol{s}_t', \boldsymbol{d}_t')'$, where $\boldsymbol{s}_t$ denotes stochastic variables, and $\boldsymbol{d}_t$ nonstochastic variables. A sequence of real numbers $\{a_t,\ t = 1, 2, 3, \dots\}$ is said to be *Cesàro-summable* if it has the property $|\bar{a}| < \infty$, where

$$\bar{a} = \lim_{n\to\infty}\frac{1}{n}\sum_{t=1}^{n} a_t. \tag{7.2.1}$$

The constant $\bar{a}$ is called the Cesàro sum of the sequence. Clearly, to satisfy (7.1.3) the elements of the matrix $\boldsymbol{d}_t\boldsymbol{d}_t'$ must be Cesàro-summable. If this holds, and the elements of $\boldsymbol{s}_t$ obey the WLLN, there should typically be no difficulty in showing that elements of the product matrix $\boldsymbol{d}_t\boldsymbol{s}_t'$ also obey the WLLN. The intercept (equals 1 in every period) satisfies the Cesàro-summability condition trivially, and the seasonal dummies, taking the value 1 every fourth (or twelfth) period and zero otherwise, have Cesàro sums of 1/4 or 1/12, as the case may be. Any variable that cycles through a fixed pattern of values in this way should satisfy Cesàro-summability, and the Cesàro sum is identical to the integral with respect to the probability measure that assigns the relative frequency of each value in the sequence.[3]

Intervention dummies are variables designed to isolate a particular period of the sample (a war, strike, policy reform, or similar) being set equal to 1 in the period in question, 0 otherwise. They ought probably to be regarded as stochastic since, unlike the case of seasonal patterns, it would not make sense to argue that these phenomena always fall in the same periods, when considering the ensemble distribution of the time series. The motivation for 'dummying' such effects is not that they are non-random, but that the assumptions about the disturbance distribution would otherwise be violated. Any sequence that is different from zero only for a finite set of time periods, as $n \to \infty$, has a Cesàro sum of zero. The corresponding column of $\boldsymbol{M}_{XX}$ is likewise zero. In the analyses of either §3.5 or §7.1 such cases must obviously be excluded. The only kind of intervention admissible in an asymptotic inference framework is one where a fixed fraction of the observations are dummied as n increases.

Strictly speaking, 'unique' interventions, which will not recur as the sample is extended, ought to be modelled stochastically, incorporating them into the error distribution. By definition, the influence of these observations is negligible in the limit. If in practice they are unduly influential in the sample available, they ought to be dropped or modified, and dummying can be thought of as an ad hoc device for achieving this. Note that the dummying of a single observation has exactly the same effect on the estimates as dropping this observation from the sample. The CAN property cannot be claimed for the coefficients of such dummies, and tests of significance have no validity on asymptotic criteria.[4]

The other type of dummy variable often introduced is the polynomial trend dummy, having the form $d_t = t^r$ for $r \geq 1$. Such series are not Cesàro-summable, so once again the conventional analysis breaks down. However, they can be dealt with by applying the modifications described in the next section.

7.2.2 Global Nonstationarity

The analyses of §3.5 and §7.1 built in a simplifying but unnecessary feature, that the convergence of all the estimates is at the rate $\sqrt{n}$. While it is possible to define data series that do not yield this result, the CAN property can in some cases still be obtained with a suitable normalization. Define a diagonal $k \times k$ matrix $\boldsymbol{K}_n$ whose diagonal elements are positive functions of n for $i = 1, \ldots, k$. This allows a different scaling to be applied to each regressor, although setting $\boldsymbol{K}_n = n\boldsymbol{I}_k$ in

[3] See Gallant (1977), or Burguete, Gallant and Souza (1982) for further details.

[4] See §7.2.2, and also §7.6.5 for an example.

what follows will reproduce the previous analysis. Instead of (7.1.3), assume that

$$\operatorname{plim} \boldsymbol{K}_n^{-1/2} \sum_{t=1}^{n} \boldsymbol{x}_t \boldsymbol{x}_t' \boldsymbol{K}_n^{-1/2} = \lim_{n \to \infty} \boldsymbol{K}_n^{-1/2} \sum_{t=1}^{n} E(\boldsymbol{x}_t \boldsymbol{x}_t') \boldsymbol{K}_n^{-1/2}$$
$$= \boldsymbol{M}_{XX} < \infty \tag{7.2.2}$$

(positive definite). Since $\operatorname{Var}(\boldsymbol{\lambda}'\boldsymbol{x}_t u_t) = O(\boldsymbol{\lambda}'\boldsymbol{K}_n\boldsymbol{\lambda}/n)$, (7.1.12) must be replaced by

$$\sqrt{n}\frac{\max_{1\le t\le n} \|\boldsymbol{\lambda}'\boldsymbol{x}_t u_t\|_{2+\delta}}{(\boldsymbol{\lambda}'\boldsymbol{K}_n\boldsymbol{\lambda})^{1/2}} \le B < \infty \quad \delta > 0,\ n \ge 1,\ \forall \text{ fixed } \boldsymbol{\lambda} \text{ with } \boldsymbol{\lambda}'\boldsymbol{\lambda} = 1. \tag{7.2.3}$$

Theorems 6.2.3 and 3.3.3 then allow us to say that

$$\boldsymbol{K}_n^{-1/2} \sum_{t=1}^{n} \boldsymbol{x}_t u_t \xrightarrow{\mathrm{D}} \mathrm{N}(0, \sigma^2 \boldsymbol{M}_{XX}). \tag{7.2.4}$$

Instead of (7.1.15) the conclusion becomes

$$\boldsymbol{K}_n^{1/2}(\hat{\boldsymbol{\beta}} - \boldsymbol{\beta}) \xrightarrow{\mathrm{D}} \mathrm{N}(0, \sigma^2 \boldsymbol{M}_{XX}^{-1}). \tag{7.2.5}$$

Global stationarity describes the situation in which, if the sample is split into contiguous parts of fixed relative size, for example, $t = 1, \ldots, [n/2]$ and $t = [n/2] + 1, \ldots, n$, each subsample shows the same average behaviour in the limit.[5] This is weaker than stationarity because it does not rule out local heterogeneity such as seasonal or cyclical patterns. Stationarity is not necessary for (7.1.3), but global stationarity is necessary.

A case of nonstationarity often considered is so-called *trend stationarity*,[6] meaning that the time series can be thought of as the weighted sum of a linear trend term and a stationary process. If y_t is of this form, the regression model that explains it must include another trend-stationary variable in the regressors. The simplest case is where this regressor is just the trend dummy. In other words, suppose that $x_{1t} = t$, the other regressors satisfying the usual assumptions. Cesàro-summability does not hold, as noted, and (7.1.3) fails. However, since $n^{-3}\sum_{t=1}^{n} t^2 \to 1/3$,[7] setting $(\boldsymbol{K}_n)_{11} = n^3$ will satisfy (7.2.2). With $\lambda_1 \neq 0$, $\|\boldsymbol{\lambda}'\boldsymbol{x}_t u_t\|_{2+\delta} = O(t)$, and hence its maximum is of $O(n)$ which matches the order of magnitude of $(\boldsymbol{\lambda}'\boldsymbol{K}_n\boldsymbol{\lambda}/n)^{1/2}$, and (7.2.3) is satisfied. The coefficient of a linear trend is asymptotically Gaussian, but the rate of convergence is $n^{3/2}$, not $\sqrt{n}$. This is a case of 'super-consistency'.

---

[5] This is a somewhat simplified description. See Davidson (1994a) §13.4 for further discussion of this question.

[6] This terminology is accepted but somewhat misleading. 'Trend-nonstationarity' would be a more descriptive usage here.

[7] Two useful formulae are $\sum_{t=1}^{n} t = n(n+1)/2$, and $\sum_{t=1}^{n} t^2 = n(n+1)(2n+1)/6$. Gauss is said to have derived the first as a schoolboy, perhaps the reader can! A useful hint is to consider the squares of the chessboard – how many squares fall on or below the diagonal?

This is the situation that obtains when there is just one trending variable among the regressors. However, an interesting situation arises if two or more regressors are trend-stationary. Suppose for illustration that $\boldsymbol{x}_t = \boldsymbol{v}_t + \boldsymbol{\gamma} t$ where $n^{-1}\sum_{t=1}^{n} \boldsymbol{v}_t \boldsymbol{v}_t' \xrightarrow{\text{pr}} \boldsymbol{M}_{vv}$ and $\boldsymbol{\gamma}$ is a vector of constants.[8] In this case, $\boldsymbol{K}_n = n^3 \boldsymbol{I}_k$ would appear to be the appropriate scaling matrix. However,

$$\frac{1}{n^3}\sum_{t=1}^{n} \boldsymbol{x}_t \boldsymbol{x}_t' \xrightarrow{\text{pr}} \tfrac{1}{3}\boldsymbol{\gamma}\boldsymbol{\gamma}' \tag{7.2.6}$$

which is a singular matrix, having rank 1. The least squares estimator is therefore inconsistent, being undefined in the limit. This can be interpreted as a case of extreme limiting multicollinearity where the deterministic components of $\boldsymbol{x}_t$, which cannot be distinguished, eventually dominate the stochastic components.

Strangely enough, this problem is resolved rather easily by adding the trend dummy to the regression.[9] This does not, as might be thought, make the problem worse. Writing the model as

$$y_t = \boldsymbol{\beta}'\boldsymbol{x}_t + u_t = \boldsymbol{\beta}'\boldsymbol{v}_t + \boldsymbol{\beta}'\boldsymbol{\gamma} t + u_t \tag{7.2.7}$$

it can be seen that the effects of $\boldsymbol{x}_t$ on y_t can be separated into the stationary components and a single trend component with coefficient $\boldsymbol{\beta}'\boldsymbol{\gamma}$. Switching to full-sample notation, let $\boldsymbol{d} = (1, 2, \ldots, n)'$ denote the dummy vector and consider running the regression

$$\boldsymbol{y} = \boldsymbol{X}\boldsymbol{\beta} + \theta\boldsymbol{d} + \boldsymbol{u} \tag{7.2.8}$$

where the true value of θ is actually 0. The partitioned algebra of §1.2.5 reveals the properties of this regression. Writing $\boldsymbol{X} = \boldsymbol{V} + \boldsymbol{d}\boldsymbol{\gamma}'$, observe that $\boldsymbol{M}_d\boldsymbol{X} = \boldsymbol{V}$ where $\boldsymbol{M}_d = \boldsymbol{I}_n - \boldsymbol{d}(\boldsymbol{d}'\boldsymbol{d})^{-1}\boldsymbol{d}'$. Therefore, if $\hat{\boldsymbol{\beta}} = (\boldsymbol{X}'\boldsymbol{M}_d\boldsymbol{X})^{-1}\boldsymbol{X}\boldsymbol{M}_d\boldsymbol{y}$ note that

$$\sqrt{n}(\hat{\boldsymbol{\beta}} - \boldsymbol{\beta}) = \left(\frac{\boldsymbol{V}'\boldsymbol{V}}{n}\right)^{-1}\frac{\boldsymbol{V}'\boldsymbol{u}}{\sqrt{n}} \xrightarrow{\text{D}} \mathrm{N}(\boldsymbol{0}, \sigma^2\boldsymbol{M}_{VV}^{-1}). \tag{7.2.9}$$

On the other hand, the coefficient of the dummy is

$$\hat{\theta} = (\boldsymbol{d}'\boldsymbol{d})^{-1}\boldsymbol{d}'(\boldsymbol{y} - \boldsymbol{X}\hat{\boldsymbol{\beta}}) = (\boldsymbol{d}'\boldsymbol{d})^{-1}\boldsymbol{d}'\boldsymbol{M}_V\boldsymbol{u} - \boldsymbol{\gamma}'(\hat{\boldsymbol{\beta}} - \boldsymbol{\beta}) = O_p(n^{-1/2}) \tag{7.2.10}$$

where $\boldsymbol{M}_V = \boldsymbol{I}_n - \boldsymbol{V}(\boldsymbol{V}'\boldsymbol{V})^{-1}\boldsymbol{V}'$. Therefore, the usual scale factor of $\sqrt{n}$ is appropriate to this case. The penalty of having collinear trends explaining the dependent variable, relative to a single trend, is that the 'super-consistency' represented by the $n^{3/2}$ rate of convergence is lost.

There are other varieties of global nonstationarity, that exhibit 'super-consistency' and can in principle be analysed in this way, but caution is needed since the limiting distributions are generally not Gaussian. These are the cases where

---

[8] The constant term is omitted for simplicity here.

[9] It is assumed here that the trend dummy is not one of the variables already included. If it is, the following analysis applies with minor modifications, allowing the dummy to have a nonzero true coefficient.

$\boldsymbol{x}_t$ contains integrated stochastic processes, having the form $\sum_{s=1}^{t} z_s$ where z_t is a stationary process and not the difference of a stationary process. Then there is no choice of $\boldsymbol{K}_n$ that will satisfy (7.2.2) with $\boldsymbol{M}_{XX}$ a non-stochastic matrix. Part IV of the book is devoted to the cases of this type.

Other cases where the asymptotic analysis does not apply, for wholly different reasons, are the intervention dummies discussed in §7.2.1, which are characterized as equal to zero except for a finite number of time periods. For these it is appropriate to put the corresponding elements of $\boldsymbol{K}_n$ to $n^0 = 1$. Under this normalization, $\boldsymbol{M}_{XX}$ is finite and nonsingular in the limit. The failure of asymptotic normality of the coefficients is evident on setting the other elements of $\boldsymbol{\lambda}$ (relating to the regular regressors) to 0, for then the denominator in (7.2.3) is $O(n^{-1})$, and the numerator is $O(1)$. However, as can be shown by considering the relevant partition of $\hat{\boldsymbol{\beta}}$, the CAN property continues to hold for the coefficients of the regular regressors, for which one can set $(\boldsymbol{K}_n)_{ii} = n^r$ for $r \geq 1$.

7.3 Consequences of Misspecification

Assumptions 7.1.1 and 7.1.2 define a model that is correctly specified in the strong sense, when $\mathcal{I}_t$ is the maximal set of valid conditioning variables. However, it is reasonable to ask the following question: if all the asymptotic distribution results go through when the conditioning set is defined to be smaller than $\mathcal{I}_t$, how does it matter if these conditions are violated? In other words, are some misspecifications innocuous?

7.3.1 Misspecification in Mean

Suppose first that $(y_t, \boldsymbol{x}_t')'$ is an i.i.d. vector. In this case, for reasons related to the discussion in §1.4.2, all our results hold in the case $\mathcal{I}_t = \sigma(\boldsymbol{x}_t)$. The interpretation of the estimated parameter vector will of course depend on the choice of $\boldsymbol{x}_t$, and a 'relevant' variable, in this context, might be defined as either one whose coefficient is a parameter of interest, or one to whose inclusion the values of parameters of interest are sensitive, in the sense that $\boldsymbol{\beta}$ in (1.4.9) is different from $\boldsymbol{\gamma}$ in (1.4.12). However, so long as $\boldsymbol{\beta}$ is defined in terms of the equation

$$E(y_t|\boldsymbol{x}_t) = \boldsymbol{\beta}'\boldsymbol{x}_t \tag{7.3.1}$$

the CAN property of OLS estimates will go through for *any* choice of $\boldsymbol{x}_t$. In fact, even linearity of $E(y_t|\boldsymbol{x}_t)$ can be dispensed with, as indicated in §1.4.1.

In the time series context, things are different because of serial dependence. If there is serial correlation of the disturbance terms, equation (7.1.9) no longer holds and while the CAN property may still hold,[10] the asymptotic variance formula in (7.1.14) is no longer valid, since

$$\mathrm{Var}\left(\frac{1}{\sqrt{n}}\sum_{t=1}^{n} \boldsymbol{x}_t u_t\right) \neq \frac{1}{n}\sum_{t=1}^{n} \mathrm{Var}(\boldsymbol{x}_t u_t). \tag{7.3.2}$$

[10] For a justification of this statement see §10.5.

To validate the asymptotic distribution results, the inclusion of u_{t-j} in the conditioning set for all $j > 0$ is therefore *not* optional. Given equation (7.1.1), this means conditioning on the lags of all included variables, at least. Strictly speaking there is no need to condition on any other variables, but this is the case only because the included variables can act as proxies for the excluded ones.

Consider an example. Let there exist a conditioning variable, z_t say, which explains y_t, but is independent of $\boldsymbol{x}_t$ so that $\boldsymbol{\beta}$ is invariant to its inclusion in the model. In other words,

$$E(y_t|\boldsymbol{x}_t, z_t) = \boldsymbol{\beta}'\boldsymbol{x}_t + \gamma z_t \tag{7.3.3}$$

holds, where $\gamma \neq 0$, but $E(z_t|\boldsymbol{x}_t) = 0$ and hence $\boldsymbol{\beta}$ is the same in (7.3.1) and in (7.3.3). In the case of i.i.d. data, OLS applied to the smaller model certainly yields CAN estimates of $\boldsymbol{\beta}$, although since the residual variance is reduced by including z_t, this would be desirable on the grounds of asymptotic efficiency. In the time series case, however, if the series $e_t = y_t - \boldsymbol{\beta}'\boldsymbol{x}_t - \gamma z_t$ is a martingale difference then $u_t = y_t - \boldsymbol{\beta}'\boldsymbol{x}_t$ cannot also be, in general. This would only be true if z_t itself were an m.d., which would be the exception to the rule for economic time series. If z_t is not in the data set, and the autocorrelation in u_t can be approximated by a finite-order AR form, its omission could be alleviated by including lags of u_t as explanatory variables in the model.[11] Clearly, omission of z_t is not innocuous in the same way as it would be in a random sampling framework. This is a major distinction between sampling model C and the other cases discussed in §1.3.

7.3.2 Misspecification in Variance

The assumption $E(u_t^2|\mathcal{I}_t) = \sigma^2$ is likewise not necessary for the CAN property, but its failure also results in the variance formula being incorrect, in this case because of the failure of equation (7.1.8). This failure is the condition known as conditional heteroscedasticity, although since $\mathcal{I}_t$ can be thought of as including deterministic variables the case of ordinary heteroscedasticity, where $E(u_t^2)$ is a deterministic function of t, is subsumed under the definition. In this case the condition in (7.1.10) must be replaced by the assumption

$$\frac{1}{n}\sum_{t=1}^{n} \text{Var}(\boldsymbol{x}_t u_t) \to \boldsymbol{A} \text{ as } n \to \infty \tag{7.3.4}$$

where $\boldsymbol{A}$ is some finite, positive definite matrix. Maintaining the other assumptions as before, so that the vectors $\boldsymbol{x}_t u_t$ form a v.m.d. and are serially uncorrelated,

$$\frac{1}{\sqrt{n}}\sum_{t=1}^{n} \boldsymbol{x}_t u_t \xrightarrow{\text{D}} \text{N}(\boldsymbol{0}, \boldsymbol{A}) \tag{7.3.5}$$

and hence

$$\sqrt{n}(\hat{\boldsymbol{\beta}} - \boldsymbol{\beta}) \xrightarrow{\text{D}} \text{N}(\boldsymbol{0}, \boldsymbol{M}_{XX}^{-1}\boldsymbol{A}\boldsymbol{M}_{XX}^{-1}) \tag{7.3.6}$$

---

[11] See §10.2.3 on the implementation of this technique.

which is, however, different from (7.1.15). This misspecification will therefore result in biased inferences if it is ignored.

It can be overcome by simply using a consistent estimate of the variance, which is generally available. Applying the kind of argument leading to Theorem 6.5.4, it can be assumed that $\boldsymbol{A}$ is consistently estimated by

$$\hat{\boldsymbol{A}} = \frac{1}{n}\sum_{t=1}^{n} \boldsymbol{x}_t \boldsymbol{x}_t' \hat{u}_t^2 \tag{7.3.7}$$

where $\hat{u}_t$ denotes the OLS residual. Formula (7.3.6) can therefore be used to generate asymptotically valid standard errors for $\hat{\boldsymbol{\beta}}$, defined as the square roots of the diagonal elements of the matrix $n\hat{\boldsymbol{M}}_{XX}^{-1}\hat{\boldsymbol{A}}\hat{\boldsymbol{M}}_{XX}^{-1}$, where $\hat{\boldsymbol{M}}_{XX} = n^{-1}\sum_{t=1}^{n} \boldsymbol{x}_t\boldsymbol{x}_t'$. Originally proposed by Eicker (1963) and independently by White (1980a), these are usually known as the *White standard errors.*

7.4 The Model Selection Problem

The biggest problem we face in econometrics is the uncertainty about the correct specification of our models. Because of the non-experimental nature of economics, we are never sure how the observed data were generated. The test of any hypothesis in economics always turns out to depend on additional assumptions necessary to specify a reasonably parsimonious model, which may or may not be justified. Specification testing, and diagnostic testing, are synonymous terms used to describe procedures for determining whether a model is contradicted when confronted by a data set. A model that is not rejected in this way may be said to be *data coherent.*[12]

7.4.1 Spurious Regression

Let us first of all dispose of a notorious fallacy. Many textbooks describe what is called the 'test of significance of the regression'. Assuming $x_{kt} = 1$ (the intercept term), this is the joint test of the significance of $x_{1t}, \ldots, x_{k-1,t}$ by the technique of §2.4.5. It is easy to verify that this test statistic takes the form

$$F = \frac{R^2}{1-R^2}\cdot\frac{n-k}{k-1} \tag{7.4.1}$$

where R^2 is defined in (1.2.12). The test formalizes the notion that a large R^2 implies a 'significant' explanation of y_t by $\boldsymbol{x}_t$, and under the assumptions listed in Chapter 2, the statistic is distributed as $F(k-1, n-k)$ on $H_0 : \beta_1 = \cdots = \beta_{k-1} = 0$.

However, it is clear that this test is valid only if y_t is randomly sampled. When the data in question are time series it is generally misleading, in the sense that

[12] The term data coherent was introduced by Hendry and Richard (1982) to describe a property effectively equivalent to this one. Note that Hendry (1995) has defined the term 'data congruent' to refer to a somewhat more elaborate concept of correct specification.

the probability of rejecting the null hypothesis when it is true is higher than the nominal significance level of the test. This is easy to see on considering the null hypothesis for the test which, treating (7.4.1) as an exact F statistic, is just

$$H_0 : y_t = \beta_0 + u_t \sim \mathrm{NI}(\beta_0, \sigma^2). \tag{7.4.2}$$

If y_t is a time series this null is invariably false, and there is no reason to expect rejection in 5% of cases. In practice, rejection can be much more frequent than 5%, so that completely irrelevant regressors appear to 'explain' y_t.

This fact has long been known (see Yule 1926), but was brought to the attention of econometricians in a famous paper by Granger and Newbold (1974). These authors performed a Monte Carlo experiment,[13], constructing time series using the random walk equation

$$x_{jt} = x_{j,t-1} + \varepsilon_{jt} \quad \varepsilon_{jt} \sim \mathrm{NI}(0,1) \tag{7.4.3}$$

for $t = 1, \ldots, n$ with $x_{j0} = 0$, and $j = 1, \ldots, m+1$. The ε_{jt} are generated such that $E(\varepsilon_{jt}\varepsilon_{kt}) = 0$ for all $j \neq k$, so these series are guaranteed to be totally unrelated. Letting one series be y_t and the others the m-vector $\boldsymbol{x}_t$, the exercise of regressing y_t on $\boldsymbol{x}_t$ was repeated 100 times with independently generated samples. In a typical result, with $n = 50$ and $m = 3$, the F test yielded a rejection at the 5% level in 93 out of 100 trials. That is to say, a 'relationship' was discovered 93% of the time, where no relationship actually existed.

This phenomenon is known as spurious regression. It is not just a property of the random walk model,[14] although this case illustrates it in the most dramatic form. Whenever the y_t process exhibits dependence between the observations, the hypothesis in (7.4.2) is false and the F test is invalid. Indeed, the t tests on the individual regression coefficients are not valid either, in general. The intended null hypothesis in these tests is that there is no relationship between y_t and the test regressor. The t statistic has its null distribution only if the remaining regressors fully account for the serial dependence in y_t, which is not usually equivalent to the intended null.

The bottom line is that significant correlation (or partial correlation) is not a valid criterion of correct model specification in dependent samples, and time series data in particular. To determine whether relationships are true or spurious, we must pose the stronger question 'what does the model leave unexplained about y_t?' In other words, out of all the potentially valid explanations of y_t, can we reject the hypothesis that our explanation is correct and complete?

7.4.2 Data Coherency and Theory Consistency

In the context of the regression model (7.1.1), the 'potentially valid' explanations are those based on the conditioning variables $\mathcal{I}_t$. In terms of a model of economic

---

[13] In a Monte Carlo experiment, the distribution of an estimator is investigated by performing a large number of replications of a computer simulation. A computer algorithm generates 'pseudo-random' numbers to simulate the shocks driving the DGP.

[14] See Granger, Hyung and Jeon (1998) for an analysis of the stationary case.

behaviour, the variables $\mathcal{I}_t$ are (for example) those that are potentially observable by agents when the plan of economic action the model represents is being formulated. The inclusion of lagged variables in this category is usually non-contentious, but (as noted in §4.7.1) deciding which contemporaneous variables are weakly exogenous can only be a matter of theory. Examining the data cannot in general resolve this question.

Given $\mathcal{I}_t$, the model selection problem is to decide which of its elements belong in x_t, and the decision should be based, in principle, on verification of Assumptions 7.1.1 and 7.1.2. A battery of diagnostic test procedures has been devised to check these assumptions. Defining data coherency in terms of these conditions is in one sense arbitrary, since there are other conditions that we might expect a valid model to fulfil. However, these are the assumptions is that were used to establish the asymptotic distribution theory for the least squares estimator. Inferences from the model could be unreliable unless both are valid. Misspecifications (which must exist, given that a model is always a simplification of reality) can be tolerated so long as they do not contradict the assumptions. Since $\mathcal{I}_t$ is large, it is difficult or impossible to *establish* that a model is data coherent, but coherency can be rejected by finding a single element of $\mathcal{I}_t$ that can predict u_t and/or u_t^2. According to Karl Popper's famous proposition (Popper, 1959), falsifiability is the criterion for judging a theory scientific. This points to the desirability of having a large battery of different tests, and of testing where possible against rather general alternatives.

Of course, data coherency is not the only criterion for model selection. We also usually possess a set of theoretical prejudices about the model. The content of $\mathcal{I}_t$ represents a fundamental theoretical input to the model, but typically we also have views on the expected signs and magnitudes of certain coefficients. Demand curves should slope down, for example. Variables belonging to $\mathcal{I}_t$ may nonetheless have coefficients constrained to 0 by hypothesis. A fundamental prejudice is the principle of parsimony, the belief that behaviour can be adequately described by a simple model involving no more parameters than can be effectively estimated from the available observations. Models that do not contradict our prejudices will be called theory consistent. Thus, think of the set of all possible models of y_t, relative to $\mathcal{I}_t$. The data coherent models form one subset, and the theory consistent models are another. The object of empirical research is typically to discover models lying in the intersection of these two sets.

Ideally this set of eligible models will be found to contain just a single element. If it contains more than one, this provides an opportunity to refine the theory, and select a preferred specification on the basis of conventional significance tests. On the other hand, if the set of eligible models appears to be empty, the theory might need to be reconsidered.

7.5 Model-Building Methodology

In econometrics, regression models are often constructed by a repeated process of estimation and testing, followed by re-estimation. Given the non-experimental nature of economic data, and uncertainty about the form of data generation processes, the investigator must appeal to the data set to select the various features of a model on which economic theory or prior knowledge offers no guide. If the evidence indicates that a chosen model is not data coherent, the model must be revised. A leading case of model uncertainty in time series regression is the form of dynamics and the length of lags. Economic theory may tell us whether to include a particular variable in the regression, but not whether it should be the current value, or last period's value, or both. We must rely on tests of Assumptions 7.1.1 and 7.1.2 to tell us when we have made the right choice, usually applying the parsimony principle that if a regressor can be omitted without infringing either these conditions or consistency with theory, then it should be.

7.5.1 Variable Addition/Deletion Tests

The basic tool for the selection of regressors is the F test of significance discussed in §2.4.5. Consider adding a vector of p regressors $\boldsymbol{z}_t \in \mathcal{I}_t$ to equation (7.1.1). It is convenient to use full-sample notation, letting $\boldsymbol{Z}$ $(n \times p)$ denote the matrix whose rows are the $\boldsymbol{z}_t$, and letting

$$\boldsymbol{y} = \boldsymbol{X\beta} + \boldsymbol{Z\delta} + \boldsymbol{e} \tag{7.5.1}$$

represent the regression in which is tested $H_0 : \boldsymbol{\delta} = \boldsymbol{0}$. If Assumption 7.1.1 is satisfied, these additional variables should be insignificant. These tests are often called variable addition tests, but can equally well be motivated as quantifying the penalty incurred by deleting $\boldsymbol{z}_t$ from the enlarged model.

Under the present assumptions, only a large sample version of the test is available. However, the results in §3.5.5 are appropriate since they simply apply the convergence results (law of large numbers and central limit theorem) that have been established under these assumptions. Letting $\hat{\boldsymbol{u}}$ denote the original residuals, and $\hat{\boldsymbol{e}}$ the residuals from the extended regression, the decision is based on the result

$$n\frac{\hat{\boldsymbol{u}}'\hat{\boldsymbol{u}} - \hat{\boldsymbol{e}}'\hat{\boldsymbol{e}}}{\hat{\boldsymbol{e}}'\hat{\boldsymbol{e}}} \begin{cases} \xrightarrow{\text{D}} \chi^2(p), & H_0 \text{ true} \\ = O_p(n), & H_0 \text{ false.} \end{cases} \tag{7.5.2}$$

When $p = 1$ this test can also be implemented as an asymptotic t test as in (2.4.25), and it is possible to perform a 1-tailed test if the sign of the scalar coefficient δ under the alternative is known.

Another way to view the variable addition test is as a direct test of Assumption 7.1.1. This can be seen by rewriting the test regression in the form

$$\hat{\boldsymbol{u}} = \boldsymbol{X\theta} + \boldsymbol{Z\delta} + \boldsymbol{e}. \tag{7.5.3}$$

Since $\hat{\boldsymbol{u}} = \boldsymbol{y} - \boldsymbol{X}\hat{\boldsymbol{\beta}}$, note that $\boldsymbol{\theta} = \boldsymbol{\beta} - \hat{\boldsymbol{\beta}}$. It is an easy exercise in partitioned regression algebra (see §1.2.5) to show that in the least squares estimation of (7.5.3), $\hat{\boldsymbol{\theta}} = \tilde{\boldsymbol{\beta}} - \hat{\boldsymbol{\beta}}$ where $\tilde{\boldsymbol{\beta}}$ is the least squares coefficient from (7.5.1), and also that the estimates of $\boldsymbol{\delta}$ from each regression are identical. The residuals $\hat{\boldsymbol{e}}$ are also identical in each regression. Letting $R^2 = 1 - \hat{\boldsymbol{e}}'\hat{\boldsymbol{e}}/\hat{\boldsymbol{u}}'\hat{\boldsymbol{u}}$ denote the coefficient of determination from the regression in (7.5.3) observe that

$$n\frac{\hat{\boldsymbol{u}}'\hat{\boldsymbol{u}} - \hat{\boldsymbol{e}}'\hat{\boldsymbol{e}}}{\hat{\boldsymbol{e}}'\hat{\boldsymbol{e}}} = n\frac{R^2}{1-R^2}. \tag{7.5.4}$$

In other words, this test can be thought of as a test of significance of regression (7.5.3) (compare (7.4.1)) and hence as a direct test of Assumption 7.1.1, where the least squares residual is used to estimate the unobserved disturbance term.

Some care is needed in interpreting this result. Since $\boldsymbol{X}$ and $\hat{\boldsymbol{u}}$ are orthogonal by construction (see Theorem 1.2.1) it might appear that the $\boldsymbol{X}$ variables are superfluous in (7.5.3). It is important they be included, nonetheless, because any relationships with the $\boldsymbol{Z}$ variables must be taken into account. Testing the significance of the regression of $\hat{\boldsymbol{u}}$ on $\boldsymbol{Z}$ alone will not give the correct result unless $\boldsymbol{X}$ and $\boldsymbol{Z}$ are asymptotically orthogonal. For an illustration of the problems that can arise, see §7.8.

The form in equation (7.5.4) suggests a possible alternative test statistic,

$$nR^2 = n\frac{\hat{\boldsymbol{u}}'\hat{\boldsymbol{u}} - \hat{\boldsymbol{e}}'\hat{\boldsymbol{e}}}{\hat{\boldsymbol{u}}'\hat{\boldsymbol{u}}}. \tag{7.5.5}$$

Since under the null hypothesis, $\hat{\boldsymbol{u}}'\hat{\boldsymbol{u}}/n$ and $\hat{\boldsymbol{e}}'\hat{\boldsymbol{e}}/n$ converge in probability to the same limit σ^2, these two tests are asymptotically equivalent, in the sense of having the same asymptotic distribution under H_0. This does not contradict the fact that the statistic in (7.5.4) is always larger, and so rejects more frequently. This is of course true whether H_0 is true or false, but this property may make it more attractive to practitioners who wish to err on the side of caution when using approximate criteria. We shall see in §12.3.3 that tests taking the form of (7.5.5) can be derived using the Lagrange multiplier principle.

7.5.2 Significance Tests and Diagnostic Tests

Econometric model building characteristically involves two kinds of tests.

Significance tests are done when a variable, or set of variables, is a candidate for inclusion in the model. As a rule, if the test results in a rejection the test variables are included, and otherwise they are excluded. Obviously, the choice of significance level (see §2.4.2) is critical here, because subsequent decisions based on the model (tests of economic hypotheses or forecasts) will depend for their validity on the correct decisions being made at the model construction stage. The rule of thumb of setting the significance level to 5% is often adopted routinely, as a probability small enough to ignore, appropriate when the null should be rejected only on convincing evidence. However, as a model selection criterion it could be excessively stringent, since while the retention of an irrelevant variable (a Type 1 error) may be relatively innocuous, the exclusion of an important one (a Type 2 error) could be damaging. It might be better at least to equalize the error probabilities as far as possible. Since the tests are consistent (see §3.5.5) the probability of a Type 2 error shrinks as the sample size increases and it therefore makes sense to link the significance level to sample size also.

Diagnostic tests are specialized procedures for detecting failures of the data coherency assumptions, 7.1.1 and 7.1.2, in a routine context where the investigator does not have any specific extension of the model in mind, but simply wants to be alerted to potential problems. Some leading examples of diagnostic tests are described in §7.6. The characteristic feature of a diagnostic test is the *dummy alternative hypothesis*. The dummy acts as proxy for misspecifications of unknown form. The investigator should not, in general, take the alternative to be true if the null is found to be false. Rejection in a diagnostic test should trigger a re-examination of the specification, but not, as a rule, the inclusion of the test variables themselves in the model.

The choice of significance level for diagnostic tests should therefore be guided by different considerations from that of significance tests. It is a commonly adopted rule of thumb to treat a model as adequate if non-rejection is achieved on all of a standard battery of diagnostic tests. If Type 1 errors were too frequent in this situation, the investigator would have expend an unacceptable degree of effort chasing up the 'false positives'. Diagnostic tests are appropriate to the situation where the investigator *thinks* that he/she has a well-specified model, and is seeking confirmation. It is natural to require relatively firm data evidence of a problem before acting on it, and the customary significance level of 5% is more appropriate to this case.

7.5.3 Encompassing and Non-Nested Testing

Often, researchers are faced with the problem of choosing between rival models, where neither is a special case of the other. In this case the hypotheses are said to be *non-nested*. Comparing a proposed model of a variable y_t with models put forward by other researchers is a natural approach to model selection. Consider choosing between alternatives A and B. Model A is said to *encompass* Model B if all the results obtained by confronting B with the data can be accounted for by assuming A to be the true model. Clearly, any model that can explain why its rivals fail has a relatively strong claim to be taken seriously. Many model evaluation test procedures can be placed in an encompassing framework; see Mizon (1984) and Mizon and Richard (1986) for discussion.

In the application to linear regression, there are in general three sets of explanatory variables from $\mathcal{I}_t$ to be distinguished, those that appear only in Model A ($\boldsymbol{x}_t$, $k_1 \times 1$) those that appear only in Model B ($\boldsymbol{z}_t$, $k_2 \times 1$) and any that are common to both models ($\boldsymbol{w}_t$, $k_3 \times 1$). The alternative hypotheses are therefore

$$\text{A. } E(y_t|\mathcal{I}_t) = \boldsymbol{\beta}'\boldsymbol{x}_t + \boldsymbol{\theta}'\boldsymbol{w}_t \tag{7.5.6}$$

$$\text{B. } E(y_t|\mathcal{I}_t) = \boldsymbol{\gamma}'\boldsymbol{z}_t + \boldsymbol{\eta}'\boldsymbol{w}_t. \tag{7.5.7}$$

Suppose that A is true. In this case model B is merely defined by

$$\boldsymbol{\gamma}'\boldsymbol{z}_t + \boldsymbol{\eta}'\boldsymbol{w}_t = E(y_t|\boldsymbol{z}_t, \boldsymbol{w}_t). \tag{7.5.8}$$

Consider the composite model that is correct under both hypotheses,

$$E(y_t|\mathcal{I}_t) = \boldsymbol{\beta}'\boldsymbol{x}_t + \boldsymbol{\delta}'\boldsymbol{z}_t + \boldsymbol{\theta}'\boldsymbol{w}_t \tag{7.5.9}$$

such that $\boldsymbol{\delta} = \mathbf{0}$ under model A, and $\boldsymbol{\beta} = \mathbf{0}$, $\boldsymbol{\gamma} = \boldsymbol{\delta}$ and $\boldsymbol{\eta} = \boldsymbol{\theta}$ under model B. Applying the LIE, note that

$$\begin{aligned} E(y_t|\boldsymbol{z}_t, \boldsymbol{w}_t) &= E[E(y_t|\mathcal{I}_t)|\boldsymbol{z}_t, \boldsymbol{w}_t] \\ &= \boldsymbol{\beta}' E(\boldsymbol{x}_t|\boldsymbol{z}_t, \boldsymbol{w}_t) + \boldsymbol{\delta}'\boldsymbol{z}_t + \boldsymbol{\theta}'\boldsymbol{w}_t \\ &= (\boldsymbol{\beta}'\boldsymbol{P} + \boldsymbol{\delta}')\boldsymbol{z}_t + (\boldsymbol{\beta}'\boldsymbol{Q} + \boldsymbol{\theta}')\boldsymbol{w}_t \end{aligned} \tag{7.5.10}$$

where $\boldsymbol{P}$ and $\boldsymbol{Q}$ are the respective matrices of coefficients in the regression of $\boldsymbol{x}_t$ on $\boldsymbol{z}_t$ and $\boldsymbol{w}_t$. Comparing (7.5.10) and (7.5.8) shows that a test of parametric encompassing of B by A would be a test of the k_2-dimensional equality

$$\boldsymbol{\gamma}' = \boldsymbol{\beta}'\boldsymbol{P}. \tag{7.5.11}$$

In other words, model A predicts that model B's regression coefficients are nothing but composites of the true parameters $\boldsymbol{\beta}$ and the nuisance parameters $\boldsymbol{P}$. However, it is also evident that the restriction has the equivalent form $\boldsymbol{\delta} = \mathbf{0}$. The parametric encompassing test is nothing but the familiar significance test on $\boldsymbol{z}_t$ in the composite regression (7.5.9).

In one sense, therefore, encompassing in linear models is merely a way of formalising the established notion of a test of significance. The solution to the problem of non-nested hypotheses is to create a nested hypothesis by merging the rival models. However, the encompassing approach provides a new way of thinking about the model selection problem. The tables can be turned by choosing model B as the null hypothesis, and testing it against A. The full comparison of two non-nested rival models has four possible outcomes: either one model encompasses the other but is not encompassed by it (only one of the tests rejects); or each encompasses the other (both tests reject); or neither encompasses the other (neither test rejects). In the first case, we have clearly learned something important. One model fails in both directions, and can be discounted with some confidence, though the survivor is not necessarily correct. If each encompasses the other, there is evidence that neither model is correct. Hopefully the results point the direction for further research, and a possible synthesis. However, if neither model can reject the other, all that has been learned is that the data are too weak and uninformative to allow discrimination between the alternatives.

There is also a class of tests, developed from an original suggestion of Cox (1961, 1962), with a specifically non-nested flavour. Applications to regression models have been considered by Pesaran (1974), Pesaran and Deaton (1978). These are tests with one degree of freedom, comparing the predictive power of the rival models, in contrast to the k_2-degree-of-freedom parametric encompassing test.

One of the simplest procedures in this class is the Davidson and MacKinnon (1981) J test. To test A against B requires only the *predictions* from Model B, say $\hat{y}_{Bt}$ for $t = 1, \ldots, n$. There is no need to distinguish the variables common to both models in this case so let model A, true under H_0, be represented by (7.1.1) as usual. The idea is again to formulate a pooled model that includes both models as special cases, in this case

$$y_t = (1 - \alpha)\boldsymbol{\beta}'\boldsymbol{x}_t + \alpha\hat{y}_{Bt} + e_t. \tag{7.5.12}$$

While the model is nominally nonlinear,[15] it can be estimated in practice by letting $(1-\alpha)\boldsymbol{\beta}$ be the unrestricted coefficients of $\boldsymbol{x}_t$, so this is just a variable addition test, performed by the simple t test of significance of $\hat{y}_{Bt}$. It can also be computed in the form comparable to (7.5.3),

$$\hat{u}_t = (1-\alpha)(\boldsymbol{\beta}-\hat{\boldsymbol{\beta}})'\boldsymbol{x}_t + \alpha(\hat{y}_{Bt} - \hat{\boldsymbol{\beta}}'\boldsymbol{x}_t) + e_t. \tag{7.5.13}$$

In this set-up it can be seen that, under H_0, the difference between the two predictions cannot explain the residuals from model A. While it is true that $\hat{y}_{Bt}$ depends on y_t through the estimated coefficients of model B, it can generally be assumed that these coefficients are converging in probability to constants defined as the best predictors under the 'wrong' model (compare §1.4.1). Therefore, provided the explanatory variables in model B are drawn from $\mathcal{I}_t$, it can be assumed that $\hat{y}_{Bt}$ is $\mathcal{I}_t$-measurable asymptotically, and this is a valid regression.

Note that when $k_2 = 1$, the encompassing and J tests are identical. Otherwise they provide alternative tests, although the J test and other Cox-type tests can also be applied to discriminate between nonlinear alternatives, such as linear and log-linear versions of a model (see Aneuryn-Evans and Deaton 1980). Intriguing evidence in Pesaran (1982) suggests that the one-degree-of-freedom procedures may be more powerful than the parametric encompassing test, in cases where $k_2 > 1$.

7.6 Diagnostic Tests

This section describes some diagnostic tests in common use. Most of the following tests are variable addition tests. For reasons mainly of precedent, the test statistic in (7.5.5) is generally used in this context, and the resulting tests referred to as Lagrange multiplier tests. In fact, the statistic in (7.5.4) can equally well be used, as may the regular F test for finite samples. The derivation of tests from the Lagrange multiplier principle is considered further in §12.3.3.

7.6.1 Residual Autocorrelation

A natural set of variables from $\mathcal{I}_t$ to consider for predicting u_t are its own lags. Variable addition tests of this form (motivated as Lagrange multiplier tests) were first proposed by Breusch (1978) and Godfrey (1978a,b). In the presence of any misspecification, these may have predictive power for the reasons discussed in §7.3.1. In practice, the disturbances must be estimated by the least squares residuals, so that $\boldsymbol{z}_t$ in (7.5.3) is chosen as $(\hat{u}_{t-1}, \ldots, \hat{u}_{t-p})'$, where $p \geq 1$. A natural choice of p might be 4 in quarterly data, or 12 in monthly data. Note that the residuals are consistent estimates of the disturbances when the null hypothesis is

---

[15] Davidson and MacKinnon (1981) suggest this procedure for comparing nonlinear regressions, and they propose a test based on a linearized form of model A that they call the P test. When model A is linear as assumed here, the distinction between the two tests disappears.

true, and the asymptotic distribution under H_0 is the same as if the actual disturbances were observed. The 'dummy alternative hypothesis' in this case is either an AR(p) or an MA(p) process in the error term. See §12.3.4 for additional details.

7.6.2 The Durbin–Watson Test

By far the best known test for residual autocorrelation is the Durbin–Watson (DW) test (Durbin and Watson 1950, 1951). The DW statistic takes the form

$$d = \frac{\sum_{t=2}^{n}(\Delta\hat{u}_t)^2}{\sum_{t=1}^{n}\hat{u}_t^2}. \tag{7.6.1}$$

It can be verified that $d \approx 2(1-\hat{\rho})$ where

$$\hat{\rho}_1 = \frac{\sum_{t=2}^{n}\hat{u}_t\hat{u}_{t-1}}{\sum_{t=2}^{n}\hat{u}_{t-1}^2} \tag{7.6.2}$$

is the estimate of ρ in the regression $\hat{u}_t = \rho_1\hat{u}_{t-1} + \varepsilon_t$. Hence, this is a test of first-order autocorrelation ($p = 1$). When H_0 is true, $\rho_1 = 0$ and $\delta \approx 2$. If $\rho_1 > 0$ then on average $d < 2$, and if $\rho < 0$ then $d > 2$.

Durbin and Watson's test is not asymptotic, but is based on the assumption of fixed (i.e. strongly exogenous) regressors and Gaussian disturbances. Since $\hat{u}_t$ is used to proxy for u_t, the null distribution depends on the regressors, and can only be determined within upper and lower bounds. The critical values are tabulated (for each n and k) as d_U and d_L. Relaxing the Gaussianity assumption, the DW can be treated as an asymptotic test, and by an application of the theory in Chapter 6 it can be shown that[16]

$$\sqrt{n}(1 - \tfrac{1}{2}d) \approx \sqrt{n}\hat{\rho} \xrightarrow{\text{D}} \text{N}(0,1) \text{ on } H_0 : \rho = 0. \tag{7.6.3}$$

The DW statistic has to be used with care, since it is not valid, whether as a bounds test or an asymptotic test, without the strong exogeneity assumption. This problem is analysed in §7.8. Not only is the lagged dependent variable, (y_{t-j}, $j > 0$) ruled out as a regressor, but any variable that is correlated with u_{t-1}. This includes the lag of any variable jointly determined with or explained by y_t. Since such cases are rather common in macroeconomic models, the DW statistic does not really deserve the role of primary diagnostic still accorded to it for reasons of habit and tradition. Durbin's (1970) h test provides a correction to the asymptotic test in (7.6.3) (see §7.8 for details) for the lagged dependent variable case. However, the strong recommendation is to always use the variable addition procedure described in §7.6.1. This is valid in any situation.

---

[16]It is of interest to note that Granger and Newbold (1974), in their study cited in §7.4.1, computed the DW statistic for their simulated regressions. For the case cited ($n = 50$, $m = 3$) the average value of d was 0.55, which converts into an average value of 5 for a statistic that would be approximately N(0, 1) under H_0. The hypothesis of no autocorrelation was correctly rejected in the overwhelming majority of cases. Evidently, a spurious regression may easily be detected by diagnostic checks.

7.6.3 The Q test

The Box and Pierce (1970) portmanteau test, or Q test, is an alternative test against m-order autocorrelation. This was proposed as a diagnostic for use in ARIMA time series modelling, or as a test for autocorrelation in 'raw' directly measured time series. The basic Q statistic is

$$Q = n\sum_{j=1}^{m} \hat{r}_j^2 \xrightarrow{\text{D}} \chi^2(\nu) \text{ on } H_0 : \rho_j = 0,\ j = 1, \dots, m \tag{7.6.4}$$

where ρ_j is the jth correlogram point, and $\hat{r}_j$ its sample counterpart. By stationarity, r_1 is asymptotically equivalent to $\hat{\rho}_1$ defined in (7.6.3), and the Q test applied to regression residuals reduces to the asymptotic version of the DW test in the case $m = 1$. Box and Pierce show that when the $\hat{u}_t$ is the residual from a fitted ARMA(p, q), the degrees of freedom for the asymptotic distribution of the test are $\nu = m - p - q$ to a good approximation When they are residuals from a regression in which the regressors are strongly exogenous we can set $\nu = m$, although the picture is less clear in the case of general dynamic regression models. Like the DW test the Q test should be used with caution, although there is a presumption that m would overstate the degrees of freedom in such cases. A variant of this test due to Ljung and Box (1978), having the same asymptotic distribution under the null but incorporating a small-sample correction, is based on

$$Q^* = n(n+2)\sum_{j=1}^{m} \frac{r_j^2}{n-j}. \tag{7.6.5}$$

7.6.4 Unrestricted Dynamics

As a natural generalization of tests for autocorrelated disturbances, the dynamic specification of an equation can always be checked by testing the inclusion of additional lags of the regressors. This may be called the unrestricted dynamic equation (UDE) test. Write $z_t = (y_{t-1}, x_{t-1})^*$ where the * denotes the omission of redundant lags, such that x_t and z_t have no elements in common. Thus, if x_t contains y_{t-1} then z_t should not duplicate it, but it should contain y_{t-2}. Other variables redundant when lagged are dummies such as the intercept, seasonals and trend. The UDE test generalizes in an obvious way to include higher order lags, setting $z_t = (y_{t-1}, x_{t-1}, \dots, y_{t-p}, x_{t-p})^*$. When fitting an equation with unknown dynamics, the UDE might be estimated with as many lags of all variables as is feasible given the sample size. As a rule of thumb, the number of parameters fitted in total should not exceed $n/3$ where n is the sample size. Since $\hat{u}_{t-j} = y_{t-j} - \hat{\beta}' x_{t-j}$ the UDE test should have power to detect residual autocorrelation, but since it specifies a less restrictive alternative than tests for autocorrelation, it should also detect a wider range of dynamic misspecifications.

7.6.5 Parameter Stability

Chow's (1960) tests described in §2.5 are both examples of variable addition tests that can be used as diagnostic tests. Correct specification naturally carries the implication that the model applies to the whole sample of data under consideration. The added variables in the parameter stability test are the dummies constructed to equal zero up to a chosen break point, and to duplicate the regressors thereafter, as in (2.5.4).

In the prediction test, the added variables are the set of n_p dummies, each equal to 1 in one of the prediction periods, and 0 for every other period, as in (2.5.15). There is no need for the test observations to be the last n_p periods of the sample. They can be any observations at all. The test can be calculated either by reordering the observations, or by constructing the dummy variables for the relevant periods and forming the usual F statistic (or asymptotic equivalent) of their significance. However, the prediction test is not robust to failures of conditional Gaussianity of the dependent variable. It is comparable to a test on intervention dummies, as discussed in §7.2.2. This is one of the few examples of a test in common use that is derived directly from the distribution of the data, not by appeal to the central limit theorem.

7.6.6 Nonlinear Functional Form

Ramsey's RESET test (Ramsey 1969, Ramsey and Schmidt 1976) is a test for possible nonlinearity of the functional form of the regression. The null hypothesis $y_t = \boldsymbol{\beta}'\boldsymbol{x}_t + u_t$ is tested for adequacy against a general alternative $y_t = g(\boldsymbol{x}_t) + u_t$. One approach would be to see whether $\hat{u}_t$ can be explained by nonlinear transformations (squares, cubes, etc.) of the elements of $\boldsymbol{x}_t$. All of these are in $\mathcal{I}_t$ if $\boldsymbol{x}_t$ is. The number of test variables would become unreasonably large in a model of any complexity, and a more tractable alternative hypothesis is based on the functional form $g(\boldsymbol{x}_t) = h(\boldsymbol{\beta}'\boldsymbol{x}_t)$. Assuming $h(\cdot)$ to be well approximated by a low order polynomial, write

$$h(\boldsymbol{\beta}'\boldsymbol{x}_t) = \boldsymbol{\beta}'\boldsymbol{x}_t + \delta_1(\boldsymbol{\beta}'\boldsymbol{x}_t)^2 + \delta_2(\boldsymbol{\beta}'\boldsymbol{x}_t)^3 + \ldots + \delta_p(\boldsymbol{\beta}'\boldsymbol{x}_t)^{p+1}. \qquad (7.6.6)$$

The variable addition test having p degrees of freedom is performed by constructing test regressors $(\hat{\boldsymbol{\beta}}'\boldsymbol{x}_t)^j$ for $j = 2, \ldots, p+1$, where $\hat{\boldsymbol{\beta}}$ is the OLS coefficient vector. The usual implementation of the test for routine diagnostic use is to choose $p = 1$.

7.6.7 Conditional Heteroscedasticity

The tests described so far are tests of Assumption 7.1.1. Tests of Assumption 7.1.2, or $E(u_t^2|\mathcal{I}_t) = \sigma^2$, are equally critical to valid least squares inference using the conventional criteria, but these cases are trickier to deal with. Under the alternative hypothesis the variance of u_t becomes a function of explanatory variables, and such models are not amenable to estimation by least squares. The theory of testing in this situation is treated in a later chapter, but for completeness we mention here that suitable tests can be derived. Postulate an alternative hypothesis of the form

$$E(u_t^2|\mathcal{I}_t) = h(\alpha_0 + \boldsymbol{\alpha}_1'\boldsymbol{z}_t) \quad \boldsymbol{z}_t \in \mathcal{I}_t \qquad (7.6.7)$$

where h is a differentiable function that is always positive (e.g. square or exponential), $\boldsymbol{\alpha}_1 = (\alpha_1, \ldots, \alpha_p)'$ and $\boldsymbol{z}_t$ is a p-vector of conditioning variables. The null hypothesis to be tested is $H_0 : \boldsymbol{\alpha}_1 = \mathbf{0}$. In §12.3.5 we show that this hypothesis is validly tested by running the regression of $\hat{u}_t^2$ on $\boldsymbol{z}_t$, with the statistic nR^2 being distributed asymptotically as $\chi^2(p)$ under H_0. This has the appearance of a variable addition test, but be careful to note that $\boldsymbol{x}_t$ is *not* included in this regression. The test is invariant to the functional form of $h(\cdot)$, which does not need to be specified explicitly. A common implementation for routine diagnostic use, with $p = 1$, is to let $z_t = (\hat{\boldsymbol{\beta}}'\boldsymbol{x}_t)^2$ where $\hat{\boldsymbol{\beta}}$ is the OLS coefficient vector, similarly to the RESET test.

7.6.8 ARCH Effects

An important case of conditional heteroscedasticity is ARCH (see §5.6). The simplest variant of the ARCH hypothesis takes the form $u_t|\mathcal{I}_t \sim \mathrm{N}(0, h_t)$, where

$$h_t = E(u_t^2|\mathcal{I}_t) = \alpha_1 + \alpha_2 u_{t-1}^2 \quad \alpha_1 > 0,\ 0 \leq \alpha_2 < 1. \tag{7.6.8}$$

The test against this alternative proposed by Engle (1982a) is implemented by regressing $\hat{u}_t^2$ on $\hat{u}_{t-1}^2$. It is generalized to higher-order ARCH in the obvious way, by including $\hat{u}_{t-j}^2$ for $j = 1, \ldots, p$ in the test regression.

A portmanteau test for ARCH is provided by the Box–Pierce Q test (see §7.6.3) applied to the *squared* residuals, see McCleod and Li (1983) and Bollerslev (1988). Once the squares are expressed in deviations from the mean, this works in exactly the same way as the Q test for autocorrelation, in principle. In these tests the residuals should be uncorrelated in levels, if a rejection is to be interpreted correctly for evidence of ARCH. Normally, one should always compute and interpret autocorrelation and ARCH statistics in a joint diagnostic exercise.

7.6.9 Non-normality

A failure of disturbances to be Gaussian is a common feature of regressions in economic data. A typical observed pattern is leptokurtosis, meaning that the fourth moment of the data exceeds the Gaussian specification of $\mu_4 = 3\sigma^4$. In this case 'outliers' exceeding 3 or more standard deviations in absolute magnitude have greater frequency than the Gaussian distribution predicts. Heteroscedasticity may be responsible for such a pattern in the unconditional frequencies of the data points, since either systematic or random variation in the variance of sampled normal variates will give the appearance of a so-called *mixture of normals* or mixed Gaussian distribution. However, if this appearance persists after correcting for heteroscedasticity of known origin, the conclusion must be that the disturbances are not Gaussian. Skewness (nonzero third moment) is another possibility.

Non-Gaussianity does not constitute a misspecification under the framework of §7.1.1, where only assumptions about the first two moments of the data have been introduced, and the asymptotic distributions are of course invariant to it. Its existence is nonetheless of interest, because if severe, asymptotic approximations may be correspondingly poor in a sample of given size.

A popular test is due to Jarque and Bera (1980), based on measures of the deviation of the third and fourth moments from their Gaussian specifications. Letting $\hat{u}_t$ denote the regression residuals, assumed to have mean zero, the test takes the form

$$\mathrm{JB} = n\left(\frac{\hat{\mu}_3}{6s^3}\right)^2 + n\left(\frac{\hat{\mu}_4 - 3s^4}{24s^4}\right)^2 \xrightarrow{\mathrm{D}} \chi^2(2) \text{ on } H_0 \tag{7.6.9}$$

where

$$\hat{\mu}_j = \frac{1}{n}\sum_{t=1}^{n} \hat{u}_t^j. \tag{7.6.10}$$

and s^2 is the usual residual variance estimate. The two terms in JB are asymptotically independent $\chi^2(1)$ variates when the null hypothesis is true, and the test can be decomposed, if desired, into separate 1-degree of freedom tests of zero skewness and normal kurtosis. The test extends to cases where the residuals do not sum to zero identically, such as nonlinear regressions or regressions 'through the origin', but then they must be expressed in mean deviation form before constructing the moments in (7.6.10).

7.7 Modelling Strategies

7.7.1 Testing Up vs Testing Down

Model selection typically involves doing a sequence of significance tests, where the tests performed later in the sequence depend on the outcomes in earlier tests. Although there does not seem to be any practical way to avoid it, this is a problematic procedure. A well-known pitfall is that if the maintained hypothesis H_M is not true, the nominal significance level of the test differs from the actual probability of Type 1 error. It was this problem that invalidated the naive significance test described in §7.4.1, but it can also arise in more subtle forms.

Consider an example. Suppose our initial model contains regressors $\boldsymbol{x}_t$, and we consider performing two variable addition tests, involving test variables, $\boldsymbol{z}_{At}$ and $\boldsymbol{z}_{Bt}$ respectively.[17] Further, suppose that the 'true model' that satisfies Assumption 7.1.1 contains, unknown to us, the variables $(\boldsymbol{x}_t, \boldsymbol{z}_{Bt})$. However, the first test to be done is of $H_0 : \boldsymbol{x}_t$ against $H_{1A} : (\boldsymbol{x}_t, \boldsymbol{z}_{At})$. For this test, H_M is false, because of the omission of $\boldsymbol{z}_{Bt}$, so that this test will not have its nominal significance level. As we saw in §7.4.1 the true probability of rejecting the null hypothesis could be high, because the $\boldsymbol{z}_{At}$ may tend to act as proxies for the omitted $\boldsymbol{z}_{Bt}$. If this rejection occurs, we will add $\boldsymbol{z}_{At}$ to the model, so the next test done is of $H_{1A} : (\boldsymbol{x}_t, \boldsymbol{z}_{At})$ against $H_2 : (\boldsymbol{x}_t, \boldsymbol{z}_{At}, \boldsymbol{z}_{Bt})$. This test has the correct significance level, but because of the irrelevant variables, estimation is inefficient, which may render the test low-powered. This means a relatively high probability of non-rejection, and hence of selecting the wrong model, $(\boldsymbol{x}_t, \boldsymbol{z}_{At})$, at the conclusion of the test sequence.

[17] A typical case might be where $\boldsymbol{x}_t$ contain the current values of two sets of variables, $\boldsymbol{z}_{At}$ is the lagged values of the first set, and $\boldsymbol{z}_{Bt}$ is the lagged values of the second set.

The testing strategy just described is called a *particular-to-general* (PTG) strategy, otherwise 'testing up'. That is, it start with the simplest model to be considered, and progressively enlarge it in the light of test outcomes. To reduce the probability of an undesirable outcome of the sort described, a *general-to-particular* (GTP) strategy, otherwise 'testing down', would be preferred. In this type of strategy, one would make H_2 the initial point of the test sequence. For example, first test H_{1A} against H_2. In the event of non-rejection, test H_0 against H_{1A}, otherwise test H_{1B} : $(\boldsymbol{x}_t, \boldsymbol{z}_{Bt})$ against H_2, and then H_0 against H_{1B} in the event of non-rejection.[18] Note that the hypothesis playing the role of H_M in each case is either the most general possible, or has been subjected to test and not rejected at the previous stage. Interchanging the roles of $\boldsymbol{z}_{At}$ and $\boldsymbol{z}_{Bt}$ is equally valid from this point of view, and might be the more fortunate choice in the state of the world where H_{1B} is the true hypothesis, since this one is tested first.

Even in much more complex sequences of tests, the basic virtue of a GTP strategy, of validating the maintained hypothesis at each step, continues to hold. These are widely advocated as the best approach to sequential model choice. There are difficulties in applying the strategy meticulously, not least that the most general model, containing all the candidate variables, may be too large to estimate effectively with the available sample. Some compromise between the approaches is typically necessary. However, the benefits of GTP are worth emphasizing, because PTG represents the more 'natural' approach to the modelling problem. In other words, the first model an investigator is likely to fit is the simplest one suggested by theory, in the hope it proves adequate. Otherwise, the temptation is to extend it in an ad hoc fashion in response to any deficiencies, until an apparently satisfactory version is arrived at.

As a minimal recommendation, every modelling exercise ought to begin by fitting a 'baseline' model. This model should contain all the variables the investigator regards as candidates for possible inclusion, and should pass the standard battery of diagnostic tests at reasonable significance levels. The parameters of this over-fitted model are of not interest, only the residual sum of squares, which measures the best fit to the data possible in the given sample. Any models considered subsequently, in whatever order, should be compared with the baseline model by an F test. In other words, a model should be accepted only if it does not fit significantly worse than the baseline model, after taking the differences in degrees of freedom into account.

7.7.2 Significance Levels in Multiple Tests

Even if the best modelling strategy is adopted, sequential testing presents a further difficulty. Consider three 'nested' hypotheses, $H_0 \subset H_1 \subset H_2$, where H_1 might represent either of H_{1A} and H_{1B} in the last example, and the notation indicates that each hypothesis is a restricted case of the next. Suppose that, using GTP, hypothesis H_1 is tested against H_2 at the α significance level. If it is not rejected,

[18] In this context the designation 'variable deletion tests' seems the appropriate one.

we go on to test H_0 against H_1. If the second test is also conducted with a nominal significance level of α, we shall not actually reject H_0 with probability α when it is true. The true Type 1 error probability is higher, because H_1 may be rejected at the first stage, in which case the second test is never performed, but H_0 is implicitly rejected by being contained in H_1. The overall significance level of the procedure can at best be bounded above. Letting E_i represent the event that the test of H_i leads to rejection, for $i = 0, 1$, the probability calculus (see §B.1 and §B.2) gives

$$\begin{aligned} P(\text{reject } H_0) &= P[E_1 \cup (E_0 \cap E_1^c)] \\ &\leq P(E_1) + P(E_0) = 2\alpha. \end{aligned} \tag{7.7.1}$$

This calculation suggests choosing the nominal significance level for each test conservatively, say at half the level that would be chosen for a simple test of H_0 against H_2. In extended test sequences the true significance levels may be much larger than the nominal level, and also difficult to determine.[19] Because of this difficulty, purist practitioners tend to dismiss sequential testing (where such problems are implicitly ignored) as an abuse of statistical method. In econometrics there are no easy choices, since the specification problem remains. However, for some purposes the model selection procedures described in §9.4.1 represent an increasingly favoured alternative approach. In these methods there is no attempt to assess the probability of a wrong decision, but simply to choose the best model on an arbitrary, but consistent, criterion.[20]

7.7.3 Data Mining

It is sometimes suggested that sequential testing can be misused to construct models that *appear* data coherent, but are really not. This undesirable practice is called data mining, see for example Lovell (1983). Consider a variable addition test, call it Test A, that specifies an arbitrary set of variables $\boldsymbol{z}_{At} \subset \mathcal{I}_t$, and tests the hypothesis

$$E(u_t | \boldsymbol{x}_t, \boldsymbol{z}_{At}) = 0. \tag{7.7.2}$$

If and only if the hypothesis is rejected, the data miner adds $\boldsymbol{z}_{At}$ to the explanatory variables, so that the new model is coherent according to Test A. He/she then moves on to Tests B, C, and so on, repeating the procedure. In this way, a model can easily be tailored so as not to be rejected by any specified set of tests, in the particular sample of data.

It is sometimes recommended that every model should be tested against data that were not used to construct it. For example, some observations at the end

[19] Savin (1980) gives a formal analysis of significance levels in multiple testing.

[20] The material in §9.4.1 is pitched at a greater level of generality than the present discussion, but everything in that section can be read as applying to the present case. Simply treat the 'criterion function' C_n as equal to the normalized sum of squares function $n^{-1}\boldsymbol{u}'\boldsymbol{u}$ for the regression model in question, and read $\boldsymbol{\beta}$ for $\boldsymbol{\theta}$.

of the sample should be 'held back' from the modelling exercise and then used at the final stage to validate it. Chow's (1960) prediction test might be used for this purpose, see §2.5.2, and §7.6.5. This prescription is obviously self-defeating, however, since there is no way to respond to a rejection of the model at this stage except by ignoring it – the data are always going to end up being used in constructing the model, one way or another, if they are available. We will not find salvation from this direction.

While there is no doubt that model building methods are open to bad practice, and that apparently good models may have been merely tailored to fit the available data, it needs to be emphasized that in the longer term the adverse effects of data mining ought to be self-limiting. In principle, there is always a remedy against it. There are three points to consider here. First, the chance of a 'mined' model being truly theory-consistent ought to be small, especially taking into account the principle of parsimony. Second, the use of diagnostic tests against dummy alternative hypotheses is a desirable strategy because one cannot 'fix' the model in the event of rejection by adding the test variables, instead of re-examining the specification. At least, such 'fixes' are now widely discredited. A very popular fix in the early days of dynamic modelling was the autoregressive-error model. Given rejection of the hypothesis of serially independent errors against the AR(1) alternative as in §7.6.1, the autocorrelation can be effectively removed, without tampering with the model's structure, by simply applying the AR(1) model itself to the equation residuals. Methods for implementing this fix, such as the Cochrane and Orcutt (1949) algorithm and its more recent refinements, are implemented in nearly every commercially available estimation package. Indeed, such an algorithm is described in §10.2.3. The point is that although AR(1) errors may well be the correct specification, they impose a common-factor parameter restriction on the equation (see §5.3.3) that requires to be tested.[21] It would nowadays be regarded as bad practice to impose the AR(1) model without testing the implicit restriction.

Third, if model evaluation is carried out conscientiously (a big if) the sheer number of variables typically contained in $\mathcal{I}_t$ is the ultimate insurance against misleading inferences. However many model validation tests are performed, there are always more that can, in principle, be generated, by choosing different sets of candidate variables to set up variable addition tests. Subject to allowance for possible Type 1 error, only a single rejection is sufficient to reveal a model as non-coherent. False models are unlikely to survive indefinitely in the face of systematic evaluation.

Further Reading: Hendry (1995) develops the 'theory of reduction', an approach to model selection that refines and elaborates the ideas sketched rather briefly here. See also Hendry (1980, 1983, 1993) and Hendry and Richard (1982, 1983). Spanos (1986) is another textbook that takes these issues seriously. For an alternative view of the model selection problem, often regarded as a rival 'system', see Leamer (1978, 1983a,b). Granger (1990) is a collection of essential readings on the methodology issue, including contributions from these protagonists. Two important monographs are Godfrey (1988)

---

[21] The common factor restriction can be tested by the methods described in §12.2 and §12.3.2

who surveys the theory of specification tests, and White (1994), an ambitious and technical analysis of the specification problem. Finally Pagan (1984b) surveys the variable addition principle, and Savin (1983) the multiple test problem.

Computing Resources Since this is in part a practical chapter, it is a good point to reference computer packages where the kind of modelling methods discussed in §7.5–§7.7 can be implemented. Eviews 3 (Quantitative Micro Software), PcGive for Windows (Timberlake Consultants Ltd.) and Microfit 4 (Oxford University Press) are PC packages with a Windows interface, that between them cover most options in single equation modelling. Unfortunately, none of them is best for every task, so the prospective user should evaluate these and other alternatives carefully (this list is by no means exhaustive) to decide which is best for his/her purposes. PcGive and Microfit have excellent manuals that can be purchased separately, see Doornik and Hendry (1999) and Pesaran and Pesaran (1997) respectively. These books summarize the relevant econometric theory and are useful as textbooks.

7.8 Appendix: Pitfalls With Autocorrelation Testing

The Durbin–Watson test (see §7.6.2) is derived on the assumption that the regressors are strongly exogenous. If this assumption fails the test is biased. In other words its true size is smaller than α, the nominal significance level, and there are alternatives for which the probability of rejection is less than α.[22] The problem, analysed in Durbin (1970), arises because the tests are based on the regression residuals, rather than the true disturbances. Consider the asymptotic distribution of $\sqrt{n}\hat{\rho}$ in (7.6.3) under $H_0 : \rho = 0$, further assuming that the maintained model of (7.1.1) is true. The residuals are

$$\hat{u}_t = u_t - \boldsymbol{x}_t'(\hat{\boldsymbol{\beta}} - \boldsymbol{\beta}) \tag{7.8.1}$$

although under H_0, $\hat{\boldsymbol{\beta}}$ is consistent for $\boldsymbol{\beta}$ and hence $\hat{u}_t$ is consistent for u_t. It follows that

$$\operatorname{plim} \frac{1}{n} \sum_{t=1}^{n} \hat{u}_{t-1}^2 = \operatorname{plim} \frac{1}{n} \sum_{t=1}^{n} u_{t-1}^2 = \sigma^2 \tag{7.8.2}$$

and by Cramér's Theorem it will suffice to consider the distribution of the numerator of $\sqrt{n}\hat{\rho}$. This, on substitution from (7.8.1), takes the form

$$\begin{aligned}\frac{1}{\sqrt{n}} \sum_{t=2}^{n} \hat{u}_t \hat{u}_{t-1} = \frac{1}{\sqrt{n}} \sum_{t=2}^{n} u_t u_{t-1} &- \sqrt{n}(\hat{\boldsymbol{\beta}} - \boldsymbol{\beta})' \left(\frac{1}{n} \sum_{t=2}^{n} \boldsymbol{x}_t u_{t-1} \right) \\ &- \sqrt{n}(\hat{\boldsymbol{\beta}} - \boldsymbol{\beta})' \left(\frac{1}{n} \sum_{t=2}^{n} \boldsymbol{x}_{t-1} u_t \right) \\ &+ \sqrt{n}(\hat{\boldsymbol{\beta}} - \boldsymbol{\beta})' \left(\frac{1}{n} \sum_{t=2}^{n} \boldsymbol{x}_t \boldsymbol{x}_{t-1}' \right) (\hat{\boldsymbol{\beta}} - \boldsymbol{\beta}). \end{aligned} \tag{7.8.3}$$

Consider these four terms in turn. Remembering u_t is serially uncorrelated on H_0, the first one converges in distribution to $\mathrm{N}(0, \sigma^4)$, by the arguments in §6.5. If it were

[22]See §12.1.1 for details and definitions of these testing concepts.

possible to neglect the remaining terms, then putting this result together with (7.8.2) would indeed yield (7.6.3). However, this depends critically on the assumptions about x_t. Since $\sqrt{n}(\hat{\beta}-\beta) = O_p(1)$, the fourth term in (7.8.3) is $O_p(n^{-1/2})$, and can be neglected. The third term also vanishes because according to the maintained hypothesis, $x_{t-1} \in \mathcal{I}_t$ and hence u_t and x_{t-1} are uncorrelated, and

$$\text{plim}\,\frac{1}{n}\sum_{t=2}^{n} x_{t-1}u_t = 0. \qquad (7.8.4)$$

The second term is problematic, however, since the assumptions do not require that x_t and u_{t-1} should be uncorrelated. To take a specific instance, y_{t-1} may be an element of x_t, and on H_0, $\text{Cov}(u_{t-1}, y_{t-1}) = \sigma^2$.

Substituting from (7.1.15), discarding the asymptotically vanishing terms, and substituting probability limits according to Cramér's Theorem yields the conclusion that

$$\sqrt{n}\hat{\rho} \underset{\text{asy}}{\sim} \frac{1}{\sigma^2\sqrt{n}}\sum_{t=2}^{n}(u_{t-1} - c'M_{XX}^{-1}x_t)u_t \qquad (7.8.5)$$

where

$$c = \text{plim}\,\frac{1}{n}\sum_{t=2}^{n} x_t u_{t-1} = \lim_{n\to\infty}\frac{1}{n}\sum_{t=2}^{n} E(x_t u_{t-1}) \qquad (7.8.6)$$

the second equality holding by assumption. Note that the terms of the sum in (7.8.5) are serially uncorrelated on H_0, so the variance of the sum is the sum of the variances. However,

$$E(u_t^2(u_{t-1} - c'M_{XX}^{-1}x_t)^2) = \sigma^4 - 2\sigma^2 c'M_{XX}^{-1}E(x_t u_{t-1}) + \sigma^2 c'M_{XX}^{-1}E(x_t x_t')M_{XX}^{-1}c. \qquad (7.8.7)$$

The middle terms have the same sum over n as the last one, apart from sign. Hence, appealing to the CLT as usual yields the result

$$\sqrt{n}\hat{\rho} \xrightarrow{\text{D}} N\left(0, 1 - \frac{c'M_{XX}^{-1}c}{\sigma^2}\right). \qquad (7.8.8)$$

Unless $c = 0$, the asymptotic variance is smaller than 1, and hence, the test based on $\sqrt{n}\hat{\rho}$ is too conservative.

The solution to the problem is clear enough, which is to make an adjustment to the statistic so that its variance is unity under H_0. Take the case considered by Durbin (1970), in which the first element of x_t is y_{t-1} while the rest are strongly exogenous, so that $c' = (\sigma^2, 0, \ldots, 0)$. The variance in (7.8.8) is $1 - \sigma^2(M_{XX}^{-1})_{11}$, where the second term is the asymptotic variance of the coefficient of y_{t-1} in the regression. Durbin proposed the h-test, based on the statistic

$$h = \hat{\rho}\sqrt{\frac{n}{1-n\hat{V}}} \xrightarrow{\text{D}} \text{N}(0,1) \text{ on } H_0. \qquad (7.8.9)$$

where $\hat{V}$ is the actual, estimated variance of the coefficient of y_{t-1} (the square of the usual OLS standard error) and $n\hat{V} \xrightarrow{\text{pr}} \sigma^2(M_{XX}^{-1})_{11}$.

The h test provides a solution to a particular problem, but a solution to the general problem would be more useful. The obvious fix is to estimate c by the corresponding sample average, and construct the sample counterpart of the variance formula in (7.8.8) directly. There is a very simple way to do this. which is to run the regression of $\hat{u}_t$ on

$\hat{u}_{t-1}$ *and* $\boldsymbol{x}_t$, and take the usual t statistic for the significance of $\hat{u}_{t-1}$ as the test statistic. To see why this works, consider the partitioned regression algebra of §1.2.5. Applying the partitioned inverse formula shows that the variance in (7.8.8) is the (1,1) element of the asymptotic covariance matrix for this regression, which is

$$\sigma^2\left(\operatorname{plim}\frac{1}{n}\sum_{t=1}^{n}\begin{bmatrix}\hat{u}_{t-1}^2 & \hat{u}_{t-1}\boldsymbol{x}_t' \\ \hat{u}_{t-1}\boldsymbol{x}_t & \boldsymbol{x}_t\boldsymbol{x}_t'\end{bmatrix}\right)^{-1} = \sigma^2\begin{bmatrix}\sigma^2 & \boldsymbol{c}' \\ \boldsymbol{c} & \boldsymbol{M}_{XX}\end{bmatrix}^{-1}. \qquad (7.8.10)$$

Of course, this procedure is exactly the one performed in the variable addition test.

Chapter 8

Simultaneous Equations

8.1 The Consumption Model Revisited

8.1.1 Statistical Assumptions

In §4.2.3 we considered the dynamics of the Keynesian-style model linking consumption C_t, income Y_t and investment I_t, consisting of equations (4.2.13), (4.2.14) and (4.2.15). We now analyse this model from a statistical point of view. In this very simple world the relevant conditioning set can be defined as

$$\mathcal{X}_{t-1} = \sigma(Y_{t-j}, I_{t-j}; j > 0). \tag{8.1.1}$$

It would be redundant to include all three variables in the set, because of the identity. Assume that (4.2.15) is a regression equation satisfying Assumptions 7.1.1 and 7.1.2, such that

$$u_{2t} = I_t - E(I_t|\mathcal{X}_{t-1}). \tag{8.1.2}$$

However, let the second statistical hypothesis be

$$E(C_t|\mathcal{X}_{t-1}) = \alpha + \beta E(Y_t|\mathcal{X}_{t-1}) \tag{8.1.3}$$

which corresponds to (4.2.14) when

$$u_{1t} = C_t - E(C_t|\mathcal{X}_{t-1}) - \beta(Y_t - E(Y_t|\mathcal{X}_{t-1})) \tag{8.1.4}$$

and hence $E(u_{1t}|\mathcal{X}_{t-1}) = 0$. This implies that u_{1t} is not predictable from $\mathcal{X}_{t-1}$. However, because Y_t is not in the conditioning set, (4.2.14) is *not* a regression equation.[1]

---

[1] The term 'regression' is sometimes used to refer to any equation that represents one variable as a function of others. However, in a statistical context its proper application is specifically to equations in which the right-hand side variables, except the disturbance, are conditionally fixed in the distribution of the left-hand side variable. Note that regression means literally 'backward movement', as in 'regression to the mean'. In geometrical terms, the appropriate analogy is with the projection of the regressand 'back' on to the space spanned by the regressors, to predict the former from the latter.

Let the u_{it} have fixed conditional variances $E(u_{it}^2|\mathcal{X}_{t-1}) = \sigma_{ii}$ for $i = 1, 2$, and covariance $E(u_{1t}u_{2t}|\mathcal{X}_{t-1}) = \sigma_{12}$. The assumption that investment is autonomous implies that u_{1t} and u_{2t} are independently distributed, and hence $\sigma_{12} = 0$. How believable it is to assume that the random shocks experienced by firms and households are unrelated may be a matter for debate, but this is a useful and (as we see in §8.1.3) testable restriction.

8.1.2 Estimation with Instrumental Variables

It is convenient to eliminate the intercept terms in the equations by expressing the variables as mean deviations. Letting $c_t = C_t - E(C_t)$, $y_t = Y_t - E(Y_t)$ and $i_t = I_t - E(I_t)$, the model equations become

$$y_t = c_t + i_t \tag{8.1.5}$$

$$c_t = \beta y_t + u_{1t} \tag{8.1.6}$$

$$i_t = \gamma i_{t-1} + u_{2t}. \tag{8.1.7}$$

Consider the problem of estimating β in (8.1.6). If this was a true regression equation then

$$\beta = \frac{E(c_t y_t)}{E(y_t^2)} \tag{8.1.8}$$

as in (1.3.4), or equivalently, $E(u_{1t}y_t) = 0$. To check this condition, solve out the reduced form equation

$$y_t = \frac{\gamma i_{t-1} + u_{1t} + u_{2t}}{1 - \beta} \tag{8.1.9}$$

and note that $E(u_{1t}i_{t-1}) = 0$ by definition, since $i_{t-1} \in \mathcal{X}_{t-1}$. Hence, multiplying (8.1.9) through by u_{1t} and taking expectations produces

$$E(u_{1t}y_t) = \frac{0 + \sigma_{11} + \sigma_{12}}{1 - \beta} \neq 0. \tag{8.1.10}$$

It follows from (8.1.10) that OLS cannot be a consistent estimator of β.

Consider another approach. Choose a variable from $\mathcal{X}_{t-1}$, multiply both sides of (8.1.6) by this variable (in mean deviations) and take expectations of both sides. Selecting I_{t-1} for example gives

$$E(i_{t-1}c_t) = \beta E(i_{t-1}y_t) + E(i_{t-1}u_{1t}). \tag{8.1.11}$$

Since $E(i_{t-1}u_{1t}) = 0$ as just pointed out,

$$\beta = \frac{E(i_{t-1}c_t)}{E(i_{t-1}y_t)} \tag{8.1.12}$$

so long as $E(i_{t-1}y_t) \neq 0$. To test this last condition, take equation (8.1.9), multiply by i_{t-1} and take expectations to obtain $E(i_{t-1}y_t) = \gamma E(i_{t-1}^2)/(1 - \beta)$, which is nonzero as long as $\gamma \neq 0$. (8.1.12) suggests as a consistent estimator

$$\tilde{\beta}(I_{-1}) = \frac{\sum_{t=1}^n i_{t-1}c_t}{\sum_{t=1}^n i_{t-1}y_t}. \tag{8.1.13}$$

To prove consistency of (8.1.13), divide top and bottom of the ratio by $1/n$, and take probability limits using Slutsky's Theorem to give

$$\text{plim}\,\tilde{\beta}(I_{-1}) = \frac{E(i_{t-1}c_t)}{E(i_{t-1}y_t)} \tag{8.1.14}$$

which agrees with (8.1.12).

This is called the method of instrumental variables (IV), and in this case I_{t-1} is the instrumental variable in question. The application of this idea to econometric problems originates with Sargan (1958, 1959). Be careful to note that (8.1.12) is not the unique representation of β. Any other variable in $\mathcal{X}_{t-1}$ that is also correlated with Y_t, such as Y_{t-1}, I_{t-2}, Y_{t-2}, etc., can be substituted for I_{t-1} in (8.1.12), and the equation will still hold. Any of these variables could be used as instruments to define a consistent IV estimator.

The usual criterion for the choice of best instrument is that of (asymptotic) efficiency. Letting Z_t denote the instrument, the 'generic' IV estimator is

$$\tilde{\beta}(z) = \frac{\sum_{t=1}^{n} z_t c_t}{\sum_{t=1}^{n} z_y y_t}. \tag{8.1.15}$$

It is shown in §8.2.4 that, subject to the usual assumptions on u_{1t}, the estimator is CAN with asymptotic variance formula

$$\text{AVar}\big(\tilde{\beta}(z)\big) = \frac{\sigma_{11}\,\text{Var}(Z_t)}{[\text{Cov}(Z_t, Y_t)]^2}. \tag{8.1.16}$$

According to this formula, Z_t should be chosen to be as highly correlated as possible with Y_t, subject to $\text{Cov}(Z_t u_{1t}) = 0$.

8.1.3 Testing Exogeneity

The assumption $\sigma_{12} = 0$ implies that I_t is an exogenous variable in the sub-model that jointly determines C_t and Y_t, and hence that it is a valid instrument. That is to say,

$$E(i_t u_{1t}) = \gamma E(i_{t-1}u_{1t}) + E(u_{2t}u_{1t}) = 0 + \sigma_{12} = 0. \tag{8.1.17}$$

Hence, $\beta = E(i_t c_t)/E(i_t y_t)$, and $\tilde{\beta}(I)$ is another consistent estimator. I_t is also the preferred instrument in this case. It can be verified using (8.1.16) that the corresponding estimator $\tilde{\beta}(I)$ is more efficient than $\tilde{\beta}(I_{-1})$, in effect because the disturbance u_{2t} is treated as observed instead of unobserved.

If and only if $\sigma_{12} = 0$, I_t can be treated as given when C_t and Y_t are determined, since then there is no simultaneous feedback from consumption to investment. It is valid to write

$$E(C_t|I_t, \mathcal{X}_{t-1}) = \alpha + \beta E(Y_t|I_t, \mathcal{X}_{t-1}) \tag{8.1.18}$$

However, equation (8.1.3) is also valid. This fact is important because it means that the hypothesis $\sigma_{12} = 0$ is testable. Since the estimator $\tilde{\beta}(I)$ is consistent only under H_0 and another less efficient one $\tilde{\beta}(I_{-1})$ (among others) consistent in either event, comparing these can reveal whether H_0 is true or not. The test based on this principle is known as the Hausman test (Hausman, 1978).[2] It is based on the following result.[3]

Lemma 8.1.1 Let $\hat{\beta}$ be an estimator of β that is consistent and asymptotically efficient when H_0 is true, but inconsistent when H_0 is false. Let $\tilde{\beta}$ be an estimator that is consistent under both null and alternative hypotheses. Under H_0,

$$\text{AVar}(\tilde{\beta} - \hat{\beta}) = \text{AVar}(\tilde{\beta}) - \text{AVar}(\hat{\beta}). \tag{8.1.19}$$

Proof Since both $\tilde{\beta}$ and $\hat{\beta}$ are consistent under H_0, so is $\lambda\tilde{\beta} + (1-\lambda)\hat{\beta}$, for any real λ. Efficiency of $\hat{\beta}$ means that this composite estimator has maximum efficiency when $\lambda = 0$. Its asymptotic variance is

$$\begin{aligned}\text{AVar}[\lambda\tilde{\beta} + (1-\lambda)\hat{\beta}] = \lambda^2\,\text{AVar}(\tilde{\beta}) + (1-\lambda)^2\,\text{AVar}(\hat{\beta})& \\ + 2\lambda(1-\lambda)\,\text{ACov}(\tilde{\beta}, \hat{\beta})&\end{aligned} \tag{8.1.20}$$

and hence

$$\begin{aligned}\frac{d}{d\lambda}\text{AVar}[\lambda\tilde{\beta} + (1-\lambda)\hat{\beta}] = 2\lambda\,\text{AVar}(\tilde{\beta}) - 2(1-\lambda)\,\text{AVar}(\hat{\beta})& \\ + 2(1-2\lambda)\,\text{ACov}(\tilde{\beta}, \hat{\beta})&\end{aligned} \tag{8.1.21}$$

Equating this expression to 0, evaluating at $\lambda = 0$ and rearranging gives

$$2\,\text{AVar}(\hat{\beta}) = 2\,\text{ACov}(\tilde{\beta}, \hat{\beta}) = \text{AVar}\,(\tilde{\beta}) + \text{AVar}\,(\hat{\beta}) - \text{AVar}\,(\tilde{\beta} - \hat{\beta}) \tag{8.1.22}$$

and the lemma follows. ∎

This result gives a test of the null hypothesis based on the statistic

$$t = \frac{\tilde{\beta} - \hat{\beta}}{\sqrt{\widehat{\text{AVar}}(\tilde{\beta}) - \widehat{\text{AVar}}(\hat{\beta})}} \tag{8.1.23}$$

where the hats denote the substitution of the usual variance estimates. If both estimators are CAN under H_0, this ratio is asymptotically $N(0,1)$ when H_0 is true.

This test is particularly well adapted to testing exogeneity. It can be used to test whether a particular variable such as I_t is exogenous in the consumption function by comparing the IV estimator using this variable as instrument with another that is valid under the alternative. It could also be used to test whether Y_t is exogenous in the consumption function (something that our model rules out, but another might not) by comparing the OLS estimator of β with an IV estimator.

---

[2]This test principle is also due to Durbin (1954) and Wu (1973), hence this is sometimes known as the Durbin-Wu-Hausman (DWH) test.

[3]This is a case of (12.3.9) below. It might be noted that the relationship of the lemma is also valid for the exact variances of a pair of estimators of which one is BLUE under H_0 but biased otherwise, the other unbiased in either case.

Care must be taken not to misinterpret this result. If the exogeneity of a variable is defined as the property of belonging to the conditioning set, it is not a testable hypothesis. The validity of conditioning on contemporaneous variables is always a theoretical prejudice, never a datum (compare §4.7.1). However, in the present case we maintain the hypothesis that I_t is not in the conditioning set; in other words, we have assumed that (8.1.3) (not (8.1.18)) is the correct model. Strictly, the Hausman test is a test, not of whether I_t is exogenous, but of whether it *behaves* as if it were; it might be better to call it a test of 'autonomy'.

Thus, if it was assumed at the outset that I_t was exogenous, and that equation (8.1.18) was the correct representation of the consumption function, the Hausman test could not contradict this assumption, since (8.1.3) is then irrelevant. Consider three alternative economic theories:

1. investment is determined simultaneously and jointly with income;

2. investment and income are determined simultaneously, but autonomously ($\sigma_{12} = 0$);

3. investment is determined prior to income, in the sense that households observe its realised value when they make their consumption/labour supply decision.

The Hausman test allows us to discriminate between 1 and 2, but 3 defines the consumption function in terms of a different conditioning set, and is not directly comparable with the others. However, under H_0 the last two hypotheses are observationally equivalent, and the exogeneity assumption is innocuous.

8.2 Estimating Simultaneous Equations

8.2.1 Structural and Reduced Forms

The statistical model studied in §8.1 is an example of the general simultaneous system

$$\mathbf{B}E(\boldsymbol{y}_t|\mathcal{I}_t) = \boldsymbol{\Gamma}\boldsymbol{z}_t \tag{8.2.1}$$

where $\boldsymbol{y}_t$ is $G \times 1$ (the endogenous variables) $\boldsymbol{z}_t \in \mathcal{I}_t$ is $M \times 1$. In the notation of §4.5.2, one can typically think of the conditioning set as defined by $\mathcal{I}_t = \sigma(\boldsymbol{z}_t) \vee \mathcal{Y}_{t-1} \vee \mathcal{Z}_{t-1}$ where $\mathcal{Y}_t$ and $\mathcal{Z}_t$ are the σ-fields generated by the histories of $\boldsymbol{y}_t$ and $\boldsymbol{z}_t$ respectively. $\mathbf{B}$ $(G \times G)$, invertible, and $\boldsymbol{\Gamma}$ $(G \times M)$ are matrices containing structural coefficients, although many of the elements will typically be zeros. Also, each row of $\mathbf{B}$ has one element set to one (the normalization restriction). In the example $\mathcal{I}_t$ contained only the lagged variables of the system, but more generally it can contain contemporaneous variables whose exogeneity is being asserted. Since the model is complete (G independent equations in G endogenous variables) the reduced form

$$E(\boldsymbol{y}_t|\mathcal{I}_t) = \boldsymbol{\Pi}\boldsymbol{z}_t \quad \boldsymbol{\Pi} = \mathbf{B}^{-1}\boldsymbol{\Gamma} \tag{8.2.2}$$

is defined, and can be recognised as a vector generalization of the regression model. The structural disturbance term is conventionally defined as

$$\boldsymbol{u}_t = \mathbf{B}(\boldsymbol{y}_t - E(\boldsymbol{y}_t|\mathcal{I}_t)) = \mathbf{B}\boldsymbol{y}_t - \boldsymbol{\Gamma}\boldsymbol{z}_t \tag{8.2.3}$$

and the innovations in $\boldsymbol{y}_t$, otherwise called the reduced form disturbances, are

$$\boldsymbol{v}_t = \mathbf{B}^{-1}\boldsymbol{u}_t = \boldsymbol{y}_t - \boldsymbol{\Pi}\boldsymbol{z}_t. \tag{8.2.4}$$

One way to generate the model was shown in §4.6, with (8.2.1) corresponding to equation (4.6.9) once the symbols are redefined appropriately.

By the considerations discussed in Chapter 1 and elsewhere,

$$\boldsymbol{\Pi} = \boldsymbol{M}_{YZ}\boldsymbol{M}_{ZZ}^{-1} \tag{8.2.5}$$

where if the data are stationary, $\boldsymbol{M}_{YZ} = E(\boldsymbol{y}_t\boldsymbol{z}_t')$ and $\boldsymbol{M}_{ZZ} = E(\boldsymbol{z}_t\boldsymbol{z}_t')$, but more generally it is legitimate to write

$$\boldsymbol{M}_{ZZ} = \lim_{n\to\infty}\frac{1}{n}\sum_{t=1}^{n}E(\boldsymbol{z}_t\boldsymbol{z}_t') \tag{8.2.6}$$

$$\boldsymbol{M}_{YZ} = \lim_{n\to\infty}\frac{1}{n}\sum_{t=1}^{n}E(\boldsymbol{y}_t\boldsymbol{z}_t') \tag{8.2.7}$$

whenever these limits exist. Let us assume without stating conditions formally at this point that the weak law of large numbers applies, such that

$$\boldsymbol{M}_{ZZ} = \operatorname*{plim}_{n\to\infty}\frac{1}{n}\sum_{t=1}^{n}\boldsymbol{z}_t\boldsymbol{z}_t' \tag{8.2.8}$$

$$\boldsymbol{M}_{YZ} = \operatorname*{plim}_{n\to\infty}\frac{1}{n}\sum_{t=1}^{n}\boldsymbol{y}_t\boldsymbol{z}_t'. \tag{8.2.9}$$

Sufficient conditions for (8.2.9) to hold given (8.2.8) can be expressed in the form of conditions on $\boldsymbol{v}_t$, paralleling Assumptions 7.1.1 and 7.1.2, specifically,

$$E(\boldsymbol{v}_t|\mathcal{I}_t) = \mathbf{0} \tag{8.2.10a}$$

$$E(\boldsymbol{v}_t\boldsymbol{v}_t'|\mathcal{I}_t) = \boldsymbol{\Omega}. \tag{8.2.10b}$$

Subject to these conditions, $\boldsymbol{\Pi}$ can be consistently estimated by the regression of the elements of $\boldsymbol{y}_t$ on $\boldsymbol{z}_t$, although this estimator is inefficient, since the constraints implicit in (8.2.2) are ignored. In any case, there is usually more interest in the structural coefficients themselves.

8.2.2 Setup and Notation

Consider the first equation in (8.2.1), with no loss of generality since the rows can be reordered at will. Let the normalized element of $\boldsymbol{y}_t$ in this equation be y_{1t} (a scalar); let the vector containing those other elements of $\boldsymbol{y}_t$ appearing in this equation be denoted $\boldsymbol{y}_{1At}$ $(g_1 \times 1)$, such that $\boldsymbol{y}_t$ is partitioned as $(y_{1t}, \boldsymbol{y}_{1At}', \boldsymbol{y}_{1Bt}')'$

with y_{1Bt} the excluded endogenous variables; and let the vector of elements of z_t appearing in the equation be denoted z_{1At} $(m_1 \times 1)$, such that z_t is partitioned as $(z'_{1At}, z'_{1Bt})'$, with z_{1Bt} the predetermined variables excluded from the first equation, although appearing in the model as a whole. Assume the columns of $\mathbf{B}$ and $\mathbf{\Gamma}$ have been reordered to permit these partitions, relevant to the first equation.

Letting $\beta'_1 = (1, \beta^{*\prime}_{1A}, 0')$ and $\gamma'_1 = (\gamma'_{1A}, 0')$ be the top rows of $\mathbf{B}$ and $\mathbf{\Gamma}$ respectively, the equation can be written

$$E(y_{1t}|\mathcal{I}_t) = -\beta^{*\prime}_{1A} E(y_{1At}|\mathcal{I}_t) + \gamma'_{1A} z_{1At}. \tag{8.2.11}$$

Alternatively, defining

$$u_{1t} = \beta'_1 v_t = v_{1t} + \beta^{*\prime}_{1A} v_{1At} \tag{8.2.12}$$

such that $E(u_{1t}|\mathcal{I}_t) = 0$ according to (8.2.10a), (8.2.11) is equivalent to

$$y_{1t} = -\beta^{*\prime}_{1A} y_{1At} + \gamma'_{1A} z_{1At} + u_{1t} = \delta'_1 x_{1t} + u_{1t} \tag{8.2.13}$$

where $x_{1t} = (y'_{1At}, z'_{1At})'$ and $\delta_1 = (-\beta^{*\prime}_{1A}, \gamma'_{1A})'$. In full-sample notation this becomes

$$y_1 = X_1 \delta_1 + u_1 \quad (n \times 1). \tag{8.2.14}$$

8.2.3 Two-stage Least Squares

Equation (8.2.13) is not a true regression, since $E(u_{1t}|y_{1At}, \mathcal{I}_t) \neq 0$. However, the stochastic equation corresponding to (8.2.11), which is

$$y_{1t} = -\beta^{*\prime}_{1A} E(y_{1At}|\mathcal{I}_t) + \gamma'_{1A} z_{1At} + v_{1t} \tag{8.2.15}$$

where $v_{1t} = y_{1t} - E(y_{1t}|\mathcal{I}_t)$ and hence $E(\varepsilon_{1t}|\mathcal{I}_t) = 0$, *is* a regression equation. The problem is that it contains some unobservable regressors. However, (8.2.15) can be consistently estimated by least squares given a suitable proxy for $E(y_{1At}|\mathcal{I}_t)$. Note that according to the reduced form equations (8.2.2),

$$E(y_{1At}|\mathcal{I}_t) = \mathbf{\Pi}^*_{1A} z_t \tag{8.2.16}$$

where $\mathbf{\Pi}^*_{1A}$ $(g_1 \times M)$ is the matrix consisting of the rows of $\mathbf{\Pi}$ corresponding to the elements of y_{1At}. A simple feasible procedure for generating the proxy is to estimate $\mathbf{\Pi}^*_{1A}$ unrestrictedly by least squares regression of each element of y_{1At} on z_t. The latter variables are called the instruments, or instrumental variables, for the equation.

Switching to full-sample notation, let Y_{1A} $(n \times g_1)$ and Z $(n \times M)$ be the data matrices whose rows are y_{1At} and z'_t. The OLS estimator of $\mathbf{\Pi}^*_{1A}$ is

$$\hat{\mathbf{\Pi}}^*_{1A} = Y'_{1A} Z (Z'Z)^{-1}. \tag{8.2.17}$$

Accordingly, let the least squares predictor $\hat{y}_{1At} = \hat{\mathbf{\Pi}}^*_{1A} z_t$ be the estimate of $E(y_{1At}|\mathcal{I}_t)$ and consider running, instead of (8.2.15), the regression

$$y_{1t} = -\beta^{*\prime}_{1A} \hat{y}_{1At} + \gamma'_{1A} z_{1At} + w_{1t}. \tag{8.2.18}$$

It would simplify the analysis of this estimator to avoid having to partition the vector of regressors. This can be done by noting that when $\boldsymbol{z}_{1At} \in \mathcal{I}_t$, $E(\boldsymbol{z}_{1At}|\mathcal{I}_t) = \boldsymbol{z}_{1At}$, so that it is legitimate to write

$$y_{1t} = \boldsymbol{\delta}_1' E(\boldsymbol{x}_{1t}|\mathcal{I}_t) + v_{1t}. \tag{8.2.19}$$

Likewise, the least squares predictor of $\boldsymbol{z}_{1At}$ from a set of variables including itself is itself, identically. The OLS predictor is obtained by premultiplication by the $n \times n$ projection matrix $\boldsymbol{Q_Z} = \boldsymbol{Z}(\boldsymbol{Z}'\boldsymbol{Z})^{-1}\boldsymbol{Z}'$, a familiar symmetric idempotent form. For example, the matrix whose rows are $\hat{\boldsymbol{y}}_{1At}'$ is

$$\hat{\boldsymbol{Y}}_{1A} = \boldsymbol{Z}\hat{\boldsymbol{\Pi}}_{1A}^{*\prime} = \boldsymbol{Z}(\boldsymbol{Z}'\boldsymbol{Z})^{-1}\boldsymbol{Z}'\boldsymbol{Y}_{1A} = \boldsymbol{Q_Z}\boldsymbol{Y}_{1A}. \tag{8.2.20}$$

Consider $\boldsymbol{Z}_{1A}$ similarly, with the aid of the $M \times m_1$ selection matrix

$$\boldsymbol{H}_1 = \begin{bmatrix} \boldsymbol{I}_{m_1} \\ \boldsymbol{0} \end{bmatrix} \begin{matrix} {\scriptstyle m_1} \\ {\scriptstyle M-m_1} \end{matrix}. \tag{8.2.21}$$

It is easily checked that $\boldsymbol{ZH}_1 = \boldsymbol{Z}_{1A}$, and hence that

$$\boldsymbol{Q_Z}\boldsymbol{Z}_{1A} = \boldsymbol{Q_Z}\boldsymbol{ZH}_1 = \boldsymbol{ZH}_1 = \boldsymbol{Z}_{1A}. \tag{8.2.22}$$

Now let $\boldsymbol{X}_1 = \begin{bmatrix}\boldsymbol{Y}_{1A} & \boldsymbol{Z}_{1A}\end{bmatrix}$ $(n \times k_1)$, where $k_1 = g_1 + m_1$, be the matrix of all right-hand side variables in the equation, and

$$\hat{\boldsymbol{X}}_1 = \boldsymbol{Q_Z}\boldsymbol{X}_1 = \begin{bmatrix}\boldsymbol{Q_Z}\boldsymbol{Y}_{1A} & \boldsymbol{Z}_{1A}\end{bmatrix} = \begin{bmatrix}\hat{\boldsymbol{Y}}_{1A} & \boldsymbol{Z}_{1A}\end{bmatrix}. \tag{8.2.23}$$

$\hat{\boldsymbol{X}}_1$ can also be written as $\boldsymbol{Z}\hat{\boldsymbol{P}}_{1A}^{*\prime}$ where $\hat{\boldsymbol{P}}_{1A}^{*\prime} = \begin{bmatrix}\hat{\boldsymbol{\Pi}}_{1A}^{*\prime} & \boldsymbol{H}_1\end{bmatrix}$. In words, any column of $\hat{\boldsymbol{X}}_1$ that is a predetermined variable is identical to the corresponding column of $\boldsymbol{X}_1$.

Therefore, (8.2.18) can be represented simply as

$$\boldsymbol{y}_1 = \hat{\boldsymbol{X}}_1\boldsymbol{\delta}_1 + \boldsymbol{w}_1 \tag{8.2.24}$$

and the least squares estimator is

$$\tilde{\boldsymbol{\delta}}_1 = (\hat{\boldsymbol{X}}_1'\hat{\boldsymbol{X}}_1)^{-1}\hat{\boldsymbol{X}}_1'\boldsymbol{y}_1. \tag{8.2.25}$$

This is the two stage least squares (2SLS) estimator, due to Theil (1953) and Basmann (1957). While conceptually it can be thought of as being obtained by means of two least squares regressions, (8.2.17) and then (8.2.25), in practice is simpler to compute it in a single step using the formula

$$\tilde{\boldsymbol{\delta}}_1 = [\boldsymbol{X}_1'\boldsymbol{Z}(\boldsymbol{Z}'\boldsymbol{Z})^{-1}\boldsymbol{Z}'\boldsymbol{X}_1]^{-1}\boldsymbol{X}_1'\boldsymbol{Z}(\boldsymbol{Z}'\boldsymbol{Z})^{-1}\boldsymbol{Z}'\boldsymbol{y}_1. \tag{8.2.26}$$

2SLS is also an instrumental variables estimator. Using idempotency/symmetry of $\boldsymbol{Q_Z}$ again, a formulation equivalent to (8.2.25) is

$$\tilde{\boldsymbol{\delta}}_1 = (\hat{\boldsymbol{X}}_1'\boldsymbol{X}_1)^{-1}\hat{\boldsymbol{X}}_1'\boldsymbol{y}_1. \tag{8.2.27}$$

Clearly, equations (8.1.15) and (8.2.27) have a family resemblance. 2SLS specializes the IV principle by using the OLS predictors of the right-hand side variables as instruments. Considering the case of (8.1.13), note that the predictor in that case is just $\hat{y}_t = \hat{\pi}_1 i_{t-1}$, where $\hat{\pi}_1$ is the estimate of the reduced form coefficient $\gamma/(1-\beta)$ in (8.1.9). Since $\hat{\pi}_1$ cancels in the ratio, (8.1.13) is actually identical in form to (8.2.27). This cancellation can be made whenever the number of instruments is equal to the number of right-hand side variables, in other words $k_1 = M$. In this case, $\boldsymbol{Z}'\boldsymbol{X}_1$ is square $M \times M$ and using (A.2.3), (8.2.26) becomes

$$\tilde{\boldsymbol{\delta}}_1 = (\boldsymbol{Z}'\boldsymbol{X}_1)^{-1}\boldsymbol{Z}'\boldsymbol{Z}(\boldsymbol{X}_1'\boldsymbol{Z})^{-1}\boldsymbol{X}_1'\boldsymbol{Z}(\boldsymbol{Z}'\boldsymbol{Z})^{-1}\boldsymbol{Z}'\boldsymbol{y}_1 = (\boldsymbol{Z}'\boldsymbol{X}_1)^{-1}\boldsymbol{Z}'\boldsymbol{y}_1. \tag{8.2.28}$$

Such an equation is said to be *just-identified.*

Yet another rationalization of (8.2.26) is as a back-solution from OLS estimation of the reduced form. Letting $\boldsymbol{P}' = [\boldsymbol{\Pi}' \; \boldsymbol{I}_M]$ denote the complete matrix of reduced form coefficients, where the identities $\boldsymbol{z}_t = \boldsymbol{z}_t$ are included in the system, the M-vector $\hat{\boldsymbol{p}}_{y_1} = (\boldsymbol{Z}'\boldsymbol{Z})^{-1}\boldsymbol{Z}'\boldsymbol{y}_1$ and $M \times k_1$ matrix $\hat{\boldsymbol{P}}_{X_1}' = (\boldsymbol{Z}'\boldsymbol{Z})^{-1}\boldsymbol{Z}'\boldsymbol{X}_1$ are just the least squares estimates of the relevant reduced form equations. The vector $\boldsymbol{\delta}_1$ satisfies by, construction, the equations of the structural form back-solution, or

$$\boldsymbol{P}_{X_1}'\boldsymbol{\delta}_1 = \boldsymbol{p}_{y_1}. \tag{8.2.29}$$

However, since these are M equations in $k_1 \le M$ unknowns, for *arbitrary* $\boldsymbol{P}$ there is no unique $\boldsymbol{\delta}_1$ to satisfy them, in general. The unrestricted least squares estimator $\hat{\boldsymbol{P}}$, in particular, does not satisfy the relevant restrictions except in the limit. The solution to this problem that is implemented by 2SLS is to form k_1 linear combinations of the equations, of the form

$$\hat{\boldsymbol{N}}\hat{\boldsymbol{P}}_{X_1}'\boldsymbol{\delta}_1 = \hat{\boldsymbol{N}}\hat{\boldsymbol{p}}_{y_1}. \tag{8.2.30}$$

where $\hat{\boldsymbol{N}}$ is a sample-based $k_1 \times M$ matrix of weights. These equations have a unique solution for $\boldsymbol{\delta}_1$. Any choice of $\hat{\boldsymbol{N}}$ that has full rank asymptotically will yield consistent estimates. The particular choice $\hat{\boldsymbol{N}} = n^{-1}\boldsymbol{X}_1'\boldsymbol{Z}$ which yields the 2SLS solution $\tilde{\boldsymbol{\delta}}_1$ is justified on the grounds of asymptotic efficiency, as shown in §8.2.5. In the just-identified case, where $k_1 = M$, equations (8.2.29) do have a unique solution, and in that case the solution reduces to (8.2.28). For this reason the just-identified estimator is sometimes called *indirect least squares.*

8.2.4 Asymptotic Properties of 2SLS

The exercise of deriving the asymptotic properties of the estimator is formally similar to the development in §7.1. To check on the consistency of $\tilde{\boldsymbol{\delta}}_1$, rewrite (8.2.11) (simplified and transposed) as

$$E(y_{1t}|\mathcal{I}_t) = E(\boldsymbol{x}_{1t}'|\mathcal{I}_t)\boldsymbol{\delta}_1. \tag{8.2.31}$$

Premultiply both sides of this equation by $\boldsymbol{z}_t$, and take unconditional expectations, to obtain

$$E(\boldsymbol{z}_t y_{1t}) = E(\boldsymbol{z}_t\boldsymbol{x}_{1t}')\boldsymbol{\delta}_1 \quad (M \times 1). \tag{8.2.32}$$

If the data are stationary one can write $E(\boldsymbol{z}_t y_{1t}) = \boldsymbol{m}_{ZY_1}$ and $E(\boldsymbol{z}_t \boldsymbol{x}_{1t}') = \boldsymbol{M}_{ZX_1}$ for all t. More generally, define

$$\boldsymbol{m}_{ZY_1} = \lim_{n\to\infty} \frac{1}{n} \sum_{t=1}^{n} E(\boldsymbol{z}_t y_{1t}) \tag{8.2.33}$$

$$\boldsymbol{M}_{ZX_1} = \lim_{n\to\infty} \frac{1}{n} \sum_{t=1}^{n} E(\boldsymbol{z}_t \boldsymbol{x}_{1t}') \tag{8.2.34}$$

and in either case, (8.2.32) implies

$$\boldsymbol{m}_{ZY_1} = \boldsymbol{M}_{ZX_1}\boldsymbol{\delta}_1. \tag{8.2.35}$$

The results

$$\boldsymbol{m}_{ZY_1} = \text{plim}\frac{1}{n}\boldsymbol{Z}'\boldsymbol{y}_1 \tag{8.2.36}$$

$$\boldsymbol{M}_{ZX_1} = \text{plim}\frac{1}{n}\boldsymbol{Z}'\boldsymbol{X}_1 \tag{8.2.37}$$

can be extracted from (8.2.8) and (8.2.9).[4] $\boldsymbol{M}_{ZX_1}$ is of dimension $M \times k_1$ and hence not invertible, in general, but if (this is the key condition) the $k_1 \times k_1$ matrix $\boldsymbol{P}_{1A}^*\boldsymbol{M}_{ZX_1}$ is invertible, where

$$\boldsymbol{P}_{1A}^* = \begin{bmatrix} \boldsymbol{\Pi}_{1A}^* \\ \boldsymbol{H}_1' \end{bmatrix} \quad (k_1 \times M) \tag{8.2.38}$$

then

$$\boldsymbol{\delta}_1 = (\boldsymbol{P}_{1A}^*\boldsymbol{M}_{ZX_1})^{-1}\boldsymbol{P}_{1A}^*\boldsymbol{m}_{ZY_1}. \tag{8.2.39}$$

If (8.2.39) holds consistency is immediate, since applying Slutsky's Theorem and the WLLN in the usual way,

$$\begin{aligned} \text{plim } \tilde{\boldsymbol{\delta}}_1 &= \text{plim}(\hat{\boldsymbol{X}}_1'\boldsymbol{X}_1)^{-1}\hat{\boldsymbol{X}}_1'\boldsymbol{y}_1 \\ &= \text{plim}(\hat{\boldsymbol{P}}_{1A}^*\boldsymbol{Z}'\boldsymbol{X}_1)^{-1}\hat{\boldsymbol{P}}_{1A}^*\boldsymbol{Z}'\boldsymbol{y}_1 \\ &= \left[\text{plim}\hat{\boldsymbol{P}}_{1A}^* \,\text{plim}\left(\frac{\boldsymbol{Z}'\boldsymbol{X}_1}{n}\right)\right]^{-1} \text{plim}\hat{\boldsymbol{P}}_{1A}^* \,\text{plim}\left(\frac{\boldsymbol{Z}'\boldsymbol{y}_1}{n}\right) \\ &= (\boldsymbol{P}_{1A}^*\boldsymbol{M}_{ZX_1})^{-1}\boldsymbol{P}_{1A}^*\boldsymbol{m}_{ZY_1} = \boldsymbol{\delta}_1. \end{aligned} \tag{8.2.40}$$

It can be verified that

$$\boldsymbol{P}_{1A}^* = \boldsymbol{M}_{X_1Z}\boldsymbol{M}_{ZZ}^{-1} \tag{8.2.41}$$

where $\boldsymbol{M}_{X_1Z} = \boldsymbol{M}_{ZX_1}'$. Given linear independence of the instruments, such that $\boldsymbol{M}_{ZZ}$ is nonsingular, the necessary and sufficient condition for consistency is

$$\text{rank}(\boldsymbol{M}_{X_1Z}) = k_1. \tag{8.2.42}$$

[4]In fact, (8.2.9) is only required to hold for the relevant elements of $\boldsymbol{y}_t$, y_{1t} and $\boldsymbol{y}_{1At}$ for this demonstration.

This is called the identification condition.

A necessary condition for (8.2.42) to hold is that $M \geq k_1$ so that there are at least as many linearly independent instruments as right-hand side variables. Since $k_1 - g_1 = m_1$, this condition is equivalent to $M - m_1 \geq g_1$, so that there must be at least as many excluded conditioning variables[5] as there are included right-hand side endogenous variables. The proxies for the g_1 endogenous variables must be linearly independent both of each other and of the included exogenous variables if the rank condition is to be met, and a sufficient number of excluded conditioning variables,[6] at least one for each included endogenous variables, is an obvious requirement. As noted the case of equality, in which there are just enough instruments but no surplus, is called just-identification. When there are more than enough instruments the equation is said to be overidentified.

Since

$$\sqrt{n}(\tilde{\boldsymbol{\delta}}_1 - \boldsymbol{\delta}_1) = \left(\hat{\boldsymbol{P}}^*_{1A}\frac{\boldsymbol{Z}'\boldsymbol{X}_1}{n}\right)^{-1}\hat{\boldsymbol{P}}^*_{1A}\frac{\boldsymbol{Z}'\boldsymbol{u}_1}{\sqrt{n}} \tag{8.2.43}$$

where

$$\begin{aligned}\left(\hat{\boldsymbol{P}}^*_{1A}\frac{\boldsymbol{Z}'\boldsymbol{X}_1}{n}\right)^{-1}\hat{\boldsymbol{P}}^*_{1A} &\xrightarrow{\text{pr}} (\boldsymbol{P}^*_{1A}\boldsymbol{M}_{ZX_1})^{-1}\boldsymbol{P}^*_{1A} \\ &= (\boldsymbol{M}_{X_1Z}\boldsymbol{M}_{ZZ}^{-1}\boldsymbol{M}_{ZX_1})^{-1}\boldsymbol{M}_{X_1Z}\boldsymbol{M}_{ZZ}^{-1}\end{aligned} \tag{8.2.44}$$

the asymptotic distribution of the estimator is found by a straightforward application of the methods of §7.1. Simply make the assumption

$$\frac{\boldsymbol{Z}'\boldsymbol{u}_1}{\sqrt{n}} \xrightarrow{\text{D}} \text{N}(\boldsymbol{0}, \sigma_{11}\boldsymbol{M}_{ZZ}) \tag{8.2.45}$$

where $\sigma_{11} = \text{Var}(u_{1t})$, sufficient conditions for which can be extracted straightforwardly from the earlier discussion. In particular, note that the counterparts of Assumptions 7.1.1 and 7.1.2,

$$E(u_{1t}|\mathcal{I}_t) = 0 \tag{8.2.46a}$$

$$E(u_{1t}^2|\mathcal{I}_t) = \sigma_{11} \tag{8.2.46b}$$

(where $\sigma_{11} = \boldsymbol{\beta}_1'\boldsymbol{\Omega}\boldsymbol{\beta}_1$, note) hold by (8.2.10). Cramér's Theorem gives the asymptotic variance formula

$$\begin{aligned}\text{AVar}(\tilde{\boldsymbol{\delta}}_1) &= (\boldsymbol{M}_{X_1Z}\boldsymbol{M}_{ZZ}^{-1}\boldsymbol{M}_{ZX_1})^{-1}\boldsymbol{M}_{X_1Z}\boldsymbol{M}_{ZZ}^{-1}\sigma_{11}\boldsymbol{M}_{ZZ}\boldsymbol{M}_{ZZ}^{-1}\boldsymbol{M}_{ZX_1} \\ &\qquad \times (\boldsymbol{M}_{X_1Z}\boldsymbol{M}_{ZZ}^{-1}\boldsymbol{M}_{ZX_1})^{-1} \\ &= \sigma_{11}(\boldsymbol{M}_{X_1Z}\boldsymbol{M}_{ZZ}^{-1}\boldsymbol{M}_{ZX_1})^{-1}\end{aligned} \tag{8.2.47}$$

---

[5] The z_t variables in the model are often spoken of as the 'exogenous' variables. We try to avoid this usage, since as noted in §4.5.3 and §4.5.7 the term has several conflicting meanings. Conditioning variables are variables from $\mathcal{I}_t$, and in general consist of weakly exogenous variables plus lags of any variable.

[6] 'Excluded' means excluded from this equation, but at the same time included somewhere in the model as a whole.

and the conclusion is

$$\sqrt{n}(\tilde{\boldsymbol{\delta}}_1 - \boldsymbol{\delta}_1) \xrightarrow{\text{D}} \text{N}(\mathbf{0},\ \sigma_{11}(\boldsymbol{M}_{X_1Z}\boldsymbol{M}_{ZZ}^{-1}\boldsymbol{M}_{ZX_1})^{-1}). \tag{8.2.48}$$

The variance formula is used to construct standard errors and test statistics, estimating the second-moment matrices by their sample counterparts and σ_{11} by

$$\tilde{\sigma}_{11} = \frac{(\boldsymbol{y}_1 - \boldsymbol{X}_1\tilde{\boldsymbol{\delta}}_1)'(\boldsymbol{y}_1 - \boldsymbol{X}_1\tilde{\boldsymbol{\delta}}_1)}{n}. \tag{8.2.49}$$

Be careful to note that this is *not* the residual variance from the second-stage regression. In other words the explanatory variables in (8.2.49) are $\boldsymbol{X}_1$ not $\hat{\boldsymbol{X}}_1$.

8.2.5 Asymptotic Efficiency of 2SLS

The asymptotic efficiency analysis parallels and generalizes that of §3.6 and §7.1.5. There it was shown that OLS is the asymptotically optimal CAN linear estimator for the regression model. The same method of reasoning can be applied to the present case, subject to the fact that now, $\boldsymbol{x}_{1t} \notin \mathcal{I}_t$. In parallel with the analysis of §3.6.2, there are two issues to be considered, the choice of instruments and the way they are employed. Therefore, begin by considering an arbitrary set of instruments, say $\boldsymbol{w}_t \in \mathcal{I}_t$ $(M^* \times 1)$ where $M^* \geq k_1$. If $\boldsymbol{W}$ $(n \times M^*)$ is the matrix with rows $\boldsymbol{w}_t'$, a class of linear estimators of $\boldsymbol{\delta}_1$ is defined by

$$\tilde{\boldsymbol{\delta}}_{1W} = \boldsymbol{L}_n \boldsymbol{W}'\boldsymbol{y}_1 \tag{8.2.50}$$

where $\boldsymbol{L}_n$ $(k_1 \times M^*)$ is a matrix to be chosen, such that $\text{plim}\, n\boldsymbol{L}_n = \boldsymbol{L}$ having rank k_1. Subject to the basic assumption

$$\frac{\boldsymbol{W}'\boldsymbol{u}_1}{\sqrt{n}} \xrightarrow{\text{D}} \text{N}(\mathbf{0}, \sigma_{11}\boldsymbol{M}_{WW}) \tag{8.2.51}$$

where $\boldsymbol{M}_{WW}$ is the second moment matrix of the instruments as usual, it is easy to verify (just substitute $\boldsymbol{y}_1 = \boldsymbol{X}_1\boldsymbol{\delta}_1 + \boldsymbol{u}_1$ in (8.2.50)) that a member of this class is CAN if

$$\boldsymbol{L}_n \boldsymbol{W}'\boldsymbol{X}_1 = \boldsymbol{I}_k \text{ a.s., uniformly in } n. \tag{8.2.52}$$

In this case it is straightforward to show that $\text{AVar}(\tilde{\boldsymbol{\delta}}_{1W}) = \sigma_{11}\boldsymbol{L}\boldsymbol{M}_{WW}\boldsymbol{L}'$, and applying Theorem 3.6.1 shows that an asymptotically efficient choice of $\boldsymbol{L}_n$ must have the property

$$\text{plim}\, n\boldsymbol{L}_n = (\boldsymbol{M}_{X_1W}\boldsymbol{M}_{WW}^{-1}\boldsymbol{M}_{WX_1})^{-1}\boldsymbol{M}_{X_1W}\boldsymbol{M}_{WW}^{-1}. \tag{8.2.53}$$

Since 2SLS represents the choice

$$\boldsymbol{L}_n = [\boldsymbol{X}_1'\boldsymbol{W}(\boldsymbol{W}'\boldsymbol{W})^{-1}\boldsymbol{W}'\boldsymbol{X}_1]^{-1}\boldsymbol{X}_1'\boldsymbol{W}(\boldsymbol{W}'\boldsymbol{W})^{-1}$$

it follows that 2SLS is asymptotically efficient in the class $\tilde{\boldsymbol{\delta}}_{1W}$. This result has the slightly unsatisfactory feature noted in §3.6.1, that the class considered is smaller than the CAN class, in which (8.2.52) need hold only in the limit. However, the practical conclusion remains, that 2SLS represents for most purposes the efficient use of the information contained in the instruments.

The question of the choice of instruments can be resolved, in turn, by an extension of the argument in Theorem 3.6.2. Let $\boldsymbol{e}_{1t} = E(\boldsymbol{x}_{1t}|\mathcal{I}_t) = \boldsymbol{P}_{1A}^{*}\boldsymbol{z}_t$, where $\boldsymbol{P}_{1A}^{*}$ is defined by (8.2.16) and (8.2.38), and write $\boldsymbol{E}_1 = \boldsymbol{Z}\boldsymbol{P}_{1A}^{*\prime}$ for the matrix whose rows are $\boldsymbol{e}_{1t}'$. Observe that $E(\boldsymbol{x}_{1t} - \boldsymbol{e}_{1t}|\mathcal{I}_t) = \boldsymbol{0}$ by construction and hence, by the LIE, $E(\boldsymbol{w}_t\boldsymbol{x}_{1t}') = E(\boldsymbol{w}_t\boldsymbol{e}_{1t})'$. Subject to the usual application of the WLLN, it must therefore be the case that

$$\boldsymbol{M}_{WX_1} = \text{plim}\,\frac{\boldsymbol{W}'\boldsymbol{X}_1}{n} = \text{plim}\,\frac{\boldsymbol{W}'\boldsymbol{E}_1}{n} = \boldsymbol{M}_{WE_1}. \tag{8.2.54}$$

It follows that

$$\boldsymbol{M}_{E_1E_1} - \boldsymbol{M}_{X_1W}\boldsymbol{M}_{WW}^{-1}\boldsymbol{M}_{WX_1} = \boldsymbol{M}_{E_1E_1} - \boldsymbol{M}_{E_1W}\boldsymbol{M}_{WW}^{-1}\boldsymbol{M}_{WE_1} \tag{8.2.55}$$

where the right-hand member is a positive semi-definite matrix in view of the argument in (3.6.21). However, note from (8.2.41) that

$$\boldsymbol{M}_{E_1E_1} = \boldsymbol{P}_{1A}^{*}\boldsymbol{M}_{ZZ}\boldsymbol{P}_{1A}^{*\prime} = \boldsymbol{M}_{X_1Z}\boldsymbol{M}_{ZZ}^{-1}\boldsymbol{M}_{ZX_1}. \tag{8.2.56}$$

Therefore, $\boldsymbol{M}_{X_1W}\boldsymbol{M}_{WW}^{-1}\boldsymbol{M}_{WX_1}$ does not exceed $\boldsymbol{M}_{X_1Z}\boldsymbol{M}_{ZZ}^{-1}\boldsymbol{M}_{ZX_1}$, in the matrix sense. By an argument paralleling Theorem 3.6.2, making use of Lemma A.7.6, it follows that the vector $\boldsymbol{z}_t$ specified by (8.2.1) is indeed the optimal choice of instruments. Notice that this result is true regardless of whether M^* is greater or smaller than M. Adding extra variables to the set $\boldsymbol{z}_t$ cannot reduce the asymptotic variance any more than omitting variables can do so.

However, while (8.2.1) defines the optimal instrument set, we have also demonstrated the possibility of classes of CAN estimators with different instruments, and that 2SLS is always the asymptotically efficient member of those classes. As long as at least k_1 valid, linearly independent instruments are available, the omission of others or inclusion of irrelevant ones may reduce the asymptotic efficiency of the estimator, but will not lead to failure of the CAN property. The obvious case to consider is where (8.2.1) has been misspecified. Let $\boldsymbol{z}_t^* \in \mathcal{I}_t$ and consider the equations

$$\mathbf{B}^*E(\boldsymbol{y}_t|\boldsymbol{z}_t^*) = \boldsymbol{\Gamma}^*\boldsymbol{z}_t^*. \tag{8.2.57}$$

Provided $\boldsymbol{z}_{1At} \subset \boldsymbol{z}_t^*$ the first equation of this system must be the same as the first equation of (8.2.1), even though the top row of $\boldsymbol{\Gamma}^*$ will have zero elements in different positions from $\boldsymbol{\Gamma}$, and rows 2 to G of $\mathbf{B}^*$ may be different from those of $\mathbf{B}$. The whole analysis of §8.2.3 and §8.2.4, applied to this system, goes through in just the same way whether $\boldsymbol{z}_t^* = \boldsymbol{z}_t$ or not.

A last point to note is that the 2SLS estimator makes use only of the knowledge of the list of additional variables in the system. It is not necessary to know any of the restrictions on the other equations. If this information is available it can be used to obtain an asymptotically more efficient estimator (3SLS) than $\tilde{\boldsymbol{\delta}}_1$ by estimating the system as a whole. See Chapter 13 for details of this approach.

8.3 The Rank Condition for Identification

While it is not necessary to know the specification of the complete model to estimate the first equation, it is necessary to know it in order to verify that the identification condition is satisfied. Consider how to check this condition. Let

$$\mathbf{A} = \begin{bmatrix}\mathbf{B} & -\boldsymbol{\Gamma}\end{bmatrix} \quad (G \times (G+M)) \tag{8.3.1}$$

denote the matrix of all the structural coefficients, such that if $\boldsymbol{x}_t = (\boldsymbol{y}_t', \boldsymbol{z}_t')'$ and $\boldsymbol{u}_t = \mathbf{B}(\boldsymbol{y}_t - E(\boldsymbol{y}_t|\mathcal{I}_t))$, the model takes the form

$$\mathbf{A}\boldsymbol{x}_t = \mathbf{B}\boldsymbol{y}_t - \boldsymbol{\Gamma}\boldsymbol{z}_t = \boldsymbol{u}_t. \tag{8.3.2}$$

Notice that the structural models

$$\mathbf{B}^+ E(\boldsymbol{y}_t|\mathcal{I}_t) = \boldsymbol{\Gamma}^+ \boldsymbol{z}_t \tag{8.3.3}$$

where $\mathbf{B}^+ = \boldsymbol{D}\mathbf{B}$ and $\boldsymbol{\Gamma}^+ = \boldsymbol{D}\boldsymbol{\Gamma}$ where $\boldsymbol{D}$ is any nonsingular matrix, all have the same reduced form matrix $(\boldsymbol{D}\mathbf{B})^{-1}\boldsymbol{D}\boldsymbol{\Gamma} = \mathbf{B}^{-1}\boldsymbol{D}^{-1}\boldsymbol{D}\boldsymbol{\Gamma} = \boldsymbol{\Pi}$. Knowledge of the data moments $\boldsymbol{M}_{YZ}$ and $\boldsymbol{M}_{ZZ}$ will allow us to determine $\boldsymbol{\Pi}$, but the structural model corresponding to $\boldsymbol{\Pi}$ is not unique. The alternative models with structures $\begin{bmatrix}\boldsymbol{D}\mathbf{B} & -\boldsymbol{D}\boldsymbol{\Gamma}\end{bmatrix}$ are observationally equivalent unless sufficient prior information about $\mathbf{B}$ and $\boldsymbol{\Gamma}$ is available to be able to rule out all of these except the case $\boldsymbol{D} = \boldsymbol{I}$. This means that the economic theory must fix some elements of these structural matrices in advance. When there are not sufficient prior restrictions to rule out observationally equivalent structures, the model is said to be underidentified, in whole or in part.

Consider as before the first equation of the set; partition $\mathbf{A}$ as

$$\mathbf{A} = \begin{bmatrix}\boldsymbol{\alpha}_1' \\ \mathbf{A}_2\end{bmatrix} \begin{matrix} 1 \\ G-1 \end{matrix} \tag{8.3.4}$$

so that the equation of interest has the form $\boldsymbol{\alpha}_1'\boldsymbol{x}_t = u_{1t}$. If $\boldsymbol{d}_1'\mathbf{A}$ $(1 \times (G+M))$ is an arbitrary linear combination of the rows of $\mathbf{A}$, the case of interest is $\boldsymbol{d}_1 = \boldsymbol{e}_1 = (1, 0, \ldots, 0)'$, and the problem is to find an estimator that rules out all other cases. One relatively trivial piece of information is the normalizing restriction, which says that some arbitrary element of the vector must be set to 1. In a linear modelling context, other prior information about the equation will take the form of linear restrictions. The coefficients of certain variables are either 0 (the variable does not appear in equation 1) or are linear functions of other coefficients. These restrictions, R_1 in number, can be represented in implicit form by equations $\boldsymbol{\alpha}_1'\boldsymbol{\phi}_{1i} = 0$, $i = 1, \ldots, R_1$, or simply

$$\boldsymbol{\alpha}_1'\boldsymbol{\Phi}_1 = \mathbf{0}' \quad (1 \times R_1) \tag{8.3.5}$$

where $\boldsymbol{\Phi}_1$ $((G+M) \times R_1)$ is the matrix whose columns are the $\boldsymbol{\phi}_{1i}$. Here are some examples.

1. Suppose $G+M = 5$ and $\boldsymbol{\alpha}_1' = (1,\ 0,\ \alpha_{13},\ 0,\ \alpha_{15})$. Then (8.3.5) holds where

$$\boldsymbol{\Phi}_1 = \begin{bmatrix} 0 & 0 \\ 1 & 0 \\ 0 & 0 \\ 0 & 1 \\ 0 & 0 \end{bmatrix}. \tag{8.3.6}$$

2. If $\alpha_1' = (1,\ \alpha_{12}, -\alpha_{12},\ c,\ \alpha_{15})$ where c is a known constant, then

$$\mathbf{\Phi}_1 = \begin{bmatrix} 0 & -c \\ 1 & 0 \\ 1 & 0 \\ 0 & 1 \\ 0 & 0 \end{bmatrix}. \tag{8.3.7}$$

Notice how the normalized element can be used to introduce constant terms into the restrictions, notwithstanding their homogeneous form. Since $\alpha_1' = e_1'\mathbf{A}$, the restrictions can be written in the form

$$e_1'\mathbf{A}\mathbf{\Phi}_1 = \mathbf{0}' \tag{8.3.8}$$

where the matrix $\mathbf{A}\mathbf{\Phi}_1$ is $G \times R_1$.

Now, suppose there exists $d_1 \neq \lambda e_1$ (λ a nonzero scalar) such that

$$d_1'\mathbf{A}\mathbf{\Phi}_1 = \mathbf{0}'. \tag{8.3.9}$$

This would imply that the vector $d_1'\mathbf{A}$ satisfies the same restrictions as α_1', and our prior knowledge would not allow us to distinguish these two. To avoid this possibility the system of implicit equations in (8.3.9) must have e_1 as the unique solution, up to a scale factor. Note that $\lambda \neq 1$ is ruled out by the normalization restriction. The condition for a system of homogeneous linear equations to have a unique solution (up to a scale factor) is a standard result from linear algebra and is

$$\text{rank}(\mathbf{A}\mathbf{\Phi}_1) = G - 1. \tag{8.3.10}$$

Notice that $\text{rank}(\mathbf{A}\mathbf{\Phi}_1) \leq G-1$ by construction, since equation (8.3.8) must be satisfied. However, if $\text{rank}(\mathbf{A}\mathbf{\Phi}_1) < G-1$ there are an infinity of solutions d_1, and the first structural equation is said to be underidentified. To avoid this condition calls for at least $G-1$ independent linear prior restrictions on the equation.

Another way to view the problem is as attempting to solve for the elements of α_1 given information from two sources, the structural restrictions on the one hand (theory), and the reduced form coefficients $\mathbf{\Pi}$ on the other (observation). Put $P = \begin{bmatrix} \mathbf{\Pi} \\ I_M \end{bmatrix}$ $((G+M) \times M)$, and from the set of equations $\mathbf{B\Pi} - \mathbf{\Gamma} = \mathbf{A}P = \mathbf{0}$ $(G \times M)$, extract the subset $\alpha_1 P = \mathbf{0}'$ $(1 \times M)$. The complete set of equations to be solved for α_1 $((G+M) \times 1)$ is

$$\alpha_1'\left[P \ \ \mathbf{\Phi}_1\right] = \mathbf{0}. \tag{8.3.11}$$

For these to have a unique solution up to a scale factor, the rank of the matrix $\left[P \ \ \mathbf{\Phi}_1\right]$, which is of dimension $(G+M) \times (M+R_1)$, must be $G+M-1$. This is an equivalent form of the rank condition (8.3.10). Note that $\mathbf{A}\left[P \ \ \mathbf{\Phi}_1\right] = \left[\mathbf{0} \ \ \mathbf{A}\mathbf{\Phi}_1\right]$, and (8.3.10) is necessary and sufficient for the first row of $\mathbf{A}$ to be the unique solution to (8.3.11), apart from normalization. Notice too that the rank condition can be satisfied only if $R_1 \geq G-1$, which is the order condition for identification, necessary but not sufficient.

Let us focus on the case of zero restrictions, in which certain variables are present in the model as a whole, but are excluded from equation 1. In this case $\boldsymbol{\alpha}_1' = (\boldsymbol{\beta}_{1A}', \mathbf{0}', \boldsymbol{\gamma}_{1A}', \mathbf{0}')$, and

$$\mathbf{A} = \begin{bmatrix}\mathbf{B} & \boldsymbol{\Gamma}\end{bmatrix} = \underset{g_1+1 \quad G-g_1-1 \quad m_1 \quad M-m_1}{\begin{bmatrix}\boldsymbol{\beta}_{1A}' & \mathbf{0}' & \boldsymbol{\gamma}_{1A}' & \mathbf{0}' \\ \mathbf{B}_{2A} & \mathbf{B}_{2B} & \boldsymbol{\Gamma}_{2A} & \boldsymbol{\Gamma}_{2B}\end{bmatrix}} \begin{matrix} 1 \\ G-1 \end{matrix} \tag{8.3.12}$$

Then,

$$\boldsymbol{\Phi}_1 = \begin{bmatrix}\mathbf{0} & \mathbf{0} \\ I_{G-g_1-1} & \mathbf{0} \\ \mathbf{0} & \mathbf{0} \\ \mathbf{0} & I_{M-m_1}\end{bmatrix} \tag{8.3.13}$$

and

$$\mathbf{A}\boldsymbol{\Phi}_1 = \begin{bmatrix}\mathbf{0}' & \mathbf{0}' \\ \mathbf{B}_{2B} & \boldsymbol{\Gamma}_{2B}\end{bmatrix}. \tag{8.3.14}$$

The rank condition is that the matrix $\mathbf{A}_{2B} = \begin{bmatrix}\mathbf{B}_{2B} \, \boldsymbol{\Gamma}_{2B}\end{bmatrix}$, of dimension $(G-1)\times (G-g_1-1-M-m_1)$, must have full rank. It is easy to see how violations of this condition might lead to underidentification; it will fail if, for example, all the variables omitted from equation 1 are also omitted from some other equation (so that $\mathbf{A}_{2B}$ has a zero row), which would imply that prior information does not allow us to distinguish equation 1 from a linear combination of the two.

The remaining problem is to make the connection between this rank condition and the rank condition of (8.2.42). Applying the further partition $\boldsymbol{\beta}_{1A} = (1, \boldsymbol{\beta}_{1A}^{*\prime})'$ where $\boldsymbol{\beta}_{1A}^{*}$ $(g_1 \times 1)$ was defined in (8.2.8), the equations in (8.3.11) have the fully partitioned form

$$\begin{bmatrix}1 & \boldsymbol{\beta}_{1A}^{*\prime} & \boldsymbol{\beta}_{1B}' & \boldsymbol{\gamma}_{1A}' & \boldsymbol{\gamma}_{1B}'\end{bmatrix} \begin{bmatrix}\boldsymbol{\pi}_{1AA}' & \boldsymbol{\pi}_{1AB}' & \mathbf{0}' & \mathbf{0}' \\ \boldsymbol{\Pi}_{1AA}^{*} & \boldsymbol{\Pi}_{1AB}^{*} & \mathbf{0} & \mathbf{0} \\ \boldsymbol{\Pi}_{1BA} & \boldsymbol{\Pi}_{1BB} & I_{G-g_1-1} & \mathbf{0} \\ I_{m_1} & \mathbf{0} & \mathbf{0} & \mathbf{0} \\ \mathbf{0} & I_{M-m_1} & \mathbf{0} & I_{M-m_1}\end{bmatrix}$$

$$= \begin{bmatrix}\mathbf{0}' & \mathbf{0}' & \mathbf{0}' & \mathbf{0}'\end{bmatrix} \tag{8.3.15}$$

where the matrix $\boldsymbol{\Pi}$ has been partitioned into blocks of m_1 and $M-m_1$ columns, and 1, g_1 and $G-g_1-1$ rows. These equations can be written out in partially solved form as $\boldsymbol{\beta}_{1B} = \mathbf{0}$, $\boldsymbol{\gamma}_{1B} = \mathbf{0}$, and

$$\underset{g_1 \qquad m_1}{\begin{bmatrix}\boldsymbol{\beta}_{1A}^{*\prime} & \boldsymbol{\gamma}_{1A}'\end{bmatrix}} \begin{bmatrix}\boldsymbol{\Pi}_{1AA}^{*} & \boldsymbol{\Pi}_{1AB}^{*} \\ I_{m_1} & \mathbf{0}\end{bmatrix} = -\underset{m_1 \qquad M-m_1}{\begin{bmatrix}\boldsymbol{\pi}_{1AA}' & \boldsymbol{\pi}_{1AB}'\end{bmatrix}}. \tag{8.3.16}$$

Identification requires that the $k_1 \times M$ matrix on the left-hand side have rank $k_1 = g_1 + m_1$, to permit a unique solution for the structural coefficients. This matrix is evidently identical with the matrix $\boldsymbol{P}^*_{1A}$. In particular, $\left[\boldsymbol{\Pi}^*_{1AA}\ \boldsymbol{\Pi}^*_{1AB}\right] = \boldsymbol{\Pi}^*_{1A}$, and $\left[\boldsymbol{I}_{m_1}\ \boldsymbol{0}\right] = \boldsymbol{H}'_1$. In view of (8.2.41), this condition is the same as (8.2.42).

In the case of linear homogeneous restrictions other than exclusion restrictions the story is a little more complicated, but by redefining the variables in the model as linear combinations of the original variables, all such restrictions can be set up as exclusion restrictions. For example: the condition that the coefficients of z_{1t} and z_{2t} be equal can be parameterized as the condition that in a model containing variables and $z_{2t} + z_{1t}$ and z_{2t}, the coefficient of the latter is 0. Another possibility that complicates the story is that prior restrictions on the error covariances can provide additional identifying information. These extensions will not be considered, but see for example Schmidt (1976), Hsiao (1983), Rothenberg (1971) for details.

8.4 Testing the IV Specification

8.4.1 More on Testing Exogeneity

One way to think about simultaneity is as a problem of omitted variables in regression. Were $\boldsymbol{v}_{1At}$ observable, equation (8.2.13) could be written using (8.2.12) as

$$y_{1t} = \boldsymbol{\delta}'_1 \boldsymbol{x}_{1t} + \boldsymbol{\theta}' \boldsymbol{v}_{1At} + v_{1t}. \tag{8.4.1}$$

Fitting this equation by least squares would be consistent for $\boldsymbol{\delta}_1$, albeit less efficient than imposing the restriction $\boldsymbol{\theta} = \boldsymbol{\beta}^*_{1A}$ which would be the same as running regression (8.2.15). 2SLS, which was motivated as the replacement of $\boldsymbol{y}_{1At}$ by $\hat{\boldsymbol{y}}_{1At}$, can also be computed by running the regression in (8.4.1) with $\boldsymbol{v}_{1At}$ replaced by $\hat{\boldsymbol{v}}_{1At} = \boldsymbol{y}_{1At} - \hat{\boldsymbol{y}}_{1At}$. To see that this is so, consider the partitioned regression

$$\boldsymbol{y}_1 = \boldsymbol{X}_1 \boldsymbol{\delta}_1 + \hat{\boldsymbol{V}}_{1A} \boldsymbol{\theta} + \boldsymbol{v}_1. \tag{8.4.2}$$

Note that $\hat{\boldsymbol{V}}_{1A} = \boldsymbol{M}_Z \boldsymbol{Y}_{1A}$ where $\boldsymbol{M}_Z = \boldsymbol{I}_n - \boldsymbol{Q}_Z$, and that the partitioned regression formula for the OLS estimator of $\boldsymbol{\delta}_1$ therefore gives

$$\begin{aligned}
&[\boldsymbol{X}'_1(\boldsymbol{I} - \boldsymbol{M}_Z \boldsymbol{Y}_{1A}(\boldsymbol{Y}'_{1A}\boldsymbol{M}_Z \boldsymbol{Y}_{1A})^{-1} \boldsymbol{Y}'_{1A}\boldsymbol{M}_Z)\boldsymbol{X}_1]^{-1} \\
&\qquad \times \boldsymbol{X}'_1(\boldsymbol{I}_n - \boldsymbol{M}_Z \boldsymbol{Y}_{1A}(\boldsymbol{Y}'_{1A}\boldsymbol{M}_Z \boldsymbol{Y}_{1A})^{-1} \boldsymbol{Y}'_{1A}\boldsymbol{M}_Z)\boldsymbol{y}_1 \\
&\quad = (\boldsymbol{X}'_1 \boldsymbol{Q}_Z \boldsymbol{X}_1)^{-1} \boldsymbol{X}'_1 \boldsymbol{Q}_Z \boldsymbol{y}_1 = \tilde{\boldsymbol{\delta}}_1.
\end{aligned} \tag{8.4.3}$$

The first equality in (8.4.3) can be verified by further partitioning $\boldsymbol{X}_1$ as $\left[\boldsymbol{Y}_{1A}\ \boldsymbol{Z}_{1A}\right]$ and considering each block in turn. However, be careful to note that the residuals from this regression are

$$\hat{\boldsymbol{v}}_1 = (\boldsymbol{I} - \hat{\boldsymbol{V}}_{1A}(\hat{\boldsymbol{V}}'_{1A}\hat{\boldsymbol{V}}_{1A})^{-1}\hat{\boldsymbol{V}}'_{1A})(\boldsymbol{y}_1 - \boldsymbol{X}_1\tilde{\boldsymbol{\delta}}_1) \tag{8.4.4}$$

and $\operatorname{plim} n^{-1}\hat{\boldsymbol{v}}'_1\hat{\boldsymbol{v}}_1 = \omega_{11}$ from (8.2.10b), not σ_{11} in general.

Given this interpretation, also note that when $E(v_{1t}\boldsymbol{v}_{1At}) = \boldsymbol{0}$, $\boldsymbol{\delta}_1$ is consistently and efficiently estimated by OLS with the constraint $\boldsymbol{\theta} = \boldsymbol{0}$ imposed. When this restriction holds, $\boldsymbol{Y}_{1A}$ can be treated from the viewpoint of running the regression as if it were in $\mathcal{I}_t$, and a test of this restriction is equivalent to what was described in §8.1.3 as an exogeneity test. Running the regressions

$$\boldsymbol{y}_1 = \boldsymbol{X}_1\boldsymbol{\delta}_1 + \boldsymbol{u}_1 \tag{8.4.5}$$

and (8.4.2), the usual variable-addition test statistic

$$n\frac{\hat{\boldsymbol{u}}_1'\hat{\boldsymbol{u}}_1 - \hat{\boldsymbol{v}}_1'\hat{\boldsymbol{v}}_1}{\hat{\boldsymbol{v}}_1'\hat{\boldsymbol{v}}_1} \tag{8.4.6}$$

is asymptotically $\chi^2(g_1)$ when H_0 is true. The test can be modified to apply to any subset of the endogenous regressors in the obvious manner, by deleting only the corresponding columns of $\hat{\boldsymbol{V}}_{1A}$ from the null regression.

This test can be rationalized as a generalization of the Hausman test from §8.1.3 based on the difference of the OLS and 2SLS estimators of $\boldsymbol{\delta}_1$. Formula (1.2.35) shows that

$$\begin{aligned}\hat{\boldsymbol{u}}_1'\hat{\boldsymbol{u}}_1 - \hat{\boldsymbol{v}}_1'\hat{\boldsymbol{v}}_1 &= \boldsymbol{y}_1'\boldsymbol{M}_{X_1}\boldsymbol{M}_Z\boldsymbol{Y}_{1A}(\boldsymbol{Y}_{1A}'\boldsymbol{M}_Z\boldsymbol{M}_{X_1}\boldsymbol{M}_Z\boldsymbol{Y}_{1A})^{-1}\boldsymbol{Y}_{1A}'\boldsymbol{M}_Z\boldsymbol{M}_{X_1}\boldsymbol{y}_1 \\ &= \boldsymbol{y}_1'\boldsymbol{M}_{X_1}\boldsymbol{Q}_Z\boldsymbol{Y}_{1A}(\boldsymbol{Y}_{1A}'\boldsymbol{Q}_Z\boldsymbol{M}_{X_1}\boldsymbol{Q}_Z\boldsymbol{Y}_{1A})^{-1}\boldsymbol{Y}_{1A}'\boldsymbol{Q}_Z\boldsymbol{M}_{X_1}\boldsymbol{y}_1 \end{aligned} \tag{8.4.7}$$

where $\boldsymbol{M}_{X_1} = \boldsymbol{I} - \boldsymbol{X}_1(\boldsymbol{X}_1'\boldsymbol{X}_1)^{-1}\boldsymbol{X}_1'$. Note that $\boldsymbol{Q}_Z$ can replace $\boldsymbol{M}_Z$ in the second equality because $\boldsymbol{Y}_{1A}$ is the first g_1 columns of $\boldsymbol{X}_1$ so that $\boldsymbol{M}_{X_1}\boldsymbol{Y}_{1A} = \boldsymbol{0}$. If $\tilde{\boldsymbol{\delta}}_1$ and $\hat{\boldsymbol{\delta}}_1$ are respectively the 2SLS and OLS estimators, note that

$$\begin{aligned}\tilde{\boldsymbol{\delta}}_1 - \hat{\boldsymbol{\delta}}_1 &= (\boldsymbol{X}_1'\boldsymbol{Q}_Z\boldsymbol{X}_1)^{-1}[\boldsymbol{X}_1'\boldsymbol{Q}_Z\boldsymbol{y}_1 - \boldsymbol{X}_1'\boldsymbol{Q}_Z\boldsymbol{X}_1(\boldsymbol{X}_1'\boldsymbol{X}_1)^{-1}\boldsymbol{X}_1\boldsymbol{y}_1] \\ &= (\boldsymbol{X}_1'\boldsymbol{Q}_Z\boldsymbol{X}_1)^{-1}\boldsymbol{X}_1'\boldsymbol{Q}_Z\boldsymbol{M}_{X_1}\boldsymbol{y}_1 \\ &= (\boldsymbol{X}_1'\boldsymbol{Q}_Z\boldsymbol{X}_1)^{-1}\begin{bmatrix}\boldsymbol{Y}_{1A}'\boldsymbol{Q}_Z\boldsymbol{M}_{X_1}\boldsymbol{y}_1 \\ \boldsymbol{0}\end{bmatrix}. \end{aligned} \tag{8.4.8}$$

The last m_1 elements of the right-hand vector vanish since $\boldsymbol{Z}_{1A}\boldsymbol{Q}_Z\boldsymbol{M}_{X_1} = \boldsymbol{Z}_{1A}\boldsymbol{M}_{X_1} = \boldsymbol{0}$, but the first g_1 elements are a component of the quadratic form in (8.4.7). The connection is most explicit in the case where $m_1 = 0$, so that $\boldsymbol{X}_1 = \boldsymbol{Y}_{1A}$ and $\boldsymbol{\delta}_1 = -\boldsymbol{\beta}_{1A}$. In this case, using (8.4.8) it is easy to put the variable-addition statistic into the form

$$\begin{aligned}n\frac{\hat{\boldsymbol{u}}_1'\hat{\boldsymbol{u}}_1 - \hat{\boldsymbol{v}}_1'\hat{\boldsymbol{v}}_1}{\hat{\boldsymbol{v}}_1'\hat{\boldsymbol{v}}_1} &= (\tilde{\boldsymbol{\beta}}_{1A} - \hat{\boldsymbol{\beta}}_{1A})'\big[\hat{\sigma}_{11}(\boldsymbol{Y}_{1A}'\boldsymbol{Q}_Z\boldsymbol{Y}_{1A})^{-1} \\ &\qquad - \hat{\sigma}_{11}(\boldsymbol{Y}_{1A}'\boldsymbol{Y}_{1A})^{-1]}\big]^{-1}(\tilde{\boldsymbol{\beta}}_{1A} - \hat{\boldsymbol{\beta}}_{1A})\end{aligned} \tag{8.4.9}$$

where $\hat{\sigma}_{11} = n^{-1}\hat{\boldsymbol{v}}_1'\hat{\boldsymbol{v}}_1$. Clearly, the square of the t statistic in (8.1.23) is asymptotically equivalent to the case of (8.4.9) for $g_1 = 1$. If $\hat{\sigma}_{11}$ were to be replaced by the OLS and 2SLS residual variances, respectively, the formulae would be identical. Note that all three estimators are consistent for σ_{11} under H_0.

Tests of this type were first proposed by Durbin (1954), and independently by Wu (1973) as well as Hausman (1978), and are known as Durbin–Wu–Hausman (DWH) tests; also see Nakamura and Nakamura (1981). These tests are placed in a more general theoretical context in §12.3. It is worth emphasizing once more that, although they are called tests of exogeneity, the null hypothesis is that the unpredictable parts of $\boldsymbol{y}_{1At}$ relative to $\mathcal{I}_t$ are uncorrelated with the equation disturbance, so that it is innocuous to condition on them. Membership of $\mathcal{I}_t$ is always a matter of theory, and we are entitled to treat $\boldsymbol{y}_{1At}$ as exogenous if theory so dictates, whether or not the DWH test rejects.

8.4.2 Testing Overidentifying Restrictions

If an equation is specified to be overidentified, some predetermined variables from the model are excluded from it for use as additional instruments, which could be added as explanatory variables without losing identification. The exclusion represents a restriction whose validity can be tested, providing a test of specification. This test is attributed to Sargan (1964). Considering the equation in (8.2.13), the null hypothesis is, as usual, of the form $E(u_{1t}|\mathcal{I}_t) = 0$ where in this case it is the instrumental variables $\boldsymbol{z}_t \in \mathcal{I}_t$ that are the subject of the test. If the hypothesis is false, this means that some or all of these variables should be added to the equation, given that their status as conditioning variables is accepted. This is sometimes called a 'test of validity of the instruments', but this is a correct designation only in the sense of validly excluding the additional instruments. It cannot establish whether it is valid to condition on $\boldsymbol{z}_t$, any more than the exogeneity test can.

The standard 'F-test' approach of comparing sums of squares is not obviously applicable in this case because least squares has not been used for estimation, even under the null hypothesis. There are various ways to approach the problem of formulating a test. One way is to compare the second stage regressions of two-stage least squares, for the restricted and unrestricted cases. In the restricted (overidentified) case, the sum of squares is

$$\begin{aligned}(\boldsymbol{y}_1 - \hat{\boldsymbol{X}}_1\tilde{\boldsymbol{\delta}}_1)'(\boldsymbol{y}_1 - \hat{\boldsymbol{X}}_1\tilde{\boldsymbol{\delta}}_1) &= \boldsymbol{y}_1'\boldsymbol{y}_1 - \boldsymbol{y}_1'\hat{\boldsymbol{X}}_1'(\hat{\boldsymbol{X}}_1'\hat{\boldsymbol{X}}_1)^{-1}\hat{\boldsymbol{X}}_1')\boldsymbol{y}_1 \\ &= \boldsymbol{y}_1'\boldsymbol{y}_1 - \boldsymbol{y}_1'\boldsymbol{Q}_Z\boldsymbol{X}_1(\boldsymbol{X}_1'\boldsymbol{Q}_Z\boldsymbol{X}_1)^{-1}\boldsymbol{X}_1'\boldsymbol{Q}_Z\boldsymbol{y}_1. \qquad (8.4.10)\end{aligned}$$

In the unrestricted (just identified) case, enough of the surplus instruments have been added to the equation to give exactly M explanatory variables in total. It turns out that it does not matter which variables we add back. Letting $\boldsymbol{X}_1^*$ be the augmented matrix and $\boldsymbol{\delta}_1^*$ the corresponding coefficients, it is easily verified using that fact that $\boldsymbol{Z}'\boldsymbol{X}_1^*$ is square $M \times M$ and invertible that

$$(\boldsymbol{y}_1 - \hat{\boldsymbol{X}}_1^*\tilde{\boldsymbol{\delta}}_1^*)'(\boldsymbol{y}_1 - \hat{\boldsymbol{X}}_1^*\tilde{\boldsymbol{\delta}}_1^*) = \boldsymbol{y}_1'\boldsymbol{y}_1 - \boldsymbol{y}_1'\boldsymbol{Q}_Z\boldsymbol{y}_1. \qquad (8.4.11)$$

In other words, in the just identified case the sum of squared residuals from the second stage regression is identical to that obtained from an unrestricted regression of $\boldsymbol{y}_1$ on $\boldsymbol{Z}$. Therefore, the choice of $\boldsymbol{X}_1^*$ is irrelevant. The difference of the two sums of squares is

$$\begin{aligned}&\boldsymbol{y}_1'(\boldsymbol{Q}_Z - \boldsymbol{Q}_Z\boldsymbol{X}_1(\boldsymbol{X}_1'\boldsymbol{Q}_Z\boldsymbol{X}_1)^{-1}\boldsymbol{X}_1'\boldsymbol{Q}_Z)\boldsymbol{y}_1 \\ &\qquad = \boldsymbol{u}_1'(\boldsymbol{Q}_Z - \boldsymbol{Q}_Z\boldsymbol{X}_1(\boldsymbol{X}_1'\boldsymbol{Q}_Z\boldsymbol{X}_1)^{-1}\boldsymbol{X}_1'\boldsymbol{Q}_Z)\boldsymbol{u}_1 \qquad (8.4.12)\end{aligned}$$

where the equality is obtained by substituting from (8.2.14) and noting that the matrix in the expression is orthogonal to X_1. Also note from (8.2.45) that on H_0,

$$\omega_n = M_{ZZ}^{-1/2}\frac{Z'u_1}{\sqrt{\sigma_{11}n}} \xrightarrow{\mathrm{D}} \mathrm{N}(0, I_M) \tag{8.4.13}$$

and hence,

$$\begin{aligned}
&\frac{y_1'(Q_Z - Q_Z X_1(X_1'Q_Z X_1)^{-1}X_1'Q_Z)y_1}{\tilde{\sigma}_{11}} \\
&\underset{\text{asy}}{\sim} \omega_n'(I_M - M_{ZZ}^{-1/2}M_{ZX_1}(M_{X_1Z}M_{ZZ}^{-1}M_{ZX_1})^{-1}M_{X_1Z}M_{ZZ}^{-1/2})\omega_n \\
&\xrightarrow{\mathrm{D}} \chi^2(M - k_1)
\end{aligned} \tag{8.4.14}$$

where $\tilde{\sigma}_{11}$ defined in (8.2.49) is a consistent estimate of σ_{11} on H_0. The final result follows from Theorem C.3.3, because the matrix in parentheses in the second member of (8.4.14) is idempotent of rank $M - k_1$.[7] On the other hand, when H_0 is false there is a correlation between u_{1t} and z_t, and the statistic is $O_p(n)$.

Another way to view this test is as a direct test of non-correlation between z_t and u_{1t}. Therefore, it is helpful to note that it can be derived as a kind of variable addition test. It can be verified by direct simplification that

$$\begin{aligned}
\frac{y_1'(Q_Z - Q_Z X_1(X_1'Q_Z X_1)^{-1}X_1'Q_Z)y_1}{\tilde{\sigma}_{11}} &= n\frac{(y_1 - X_1\tilde{\delta}_1)'Q_Z(y_1 - X_1\tilde{\delta}_1)}{(y_1 - X_1\tilde{\delta}_1)'(y_1 - X_1\tilde{\delta}_1)} \\
&= nR^2
\end{aligned} \tag{8.4.15}$$

where the R^2 is from the regression of the 2SLS residuals on z_t. This formulation provides an easy way to compute the test.[8].

8.5 Nonlinear Simultaneous Equations

8.5.1 Fisher's Identification Analysis

Interesting variants of the rank condition for identification arise when there are nonlinear relationships in the model. By this is meant, specifically, *nonlinear in variables.* The models to be considered in this section are linear in the parameters and can be estimated consistently by two stage least squares, but nonlinear functions of the endogenous variables are connected by equations of the model. Such cases arise when, for example, linear equations are combined with multiplicative identities having a log-linear representation, (e.g. expenditure = price × quantity) or alternatively, logarithmic equations might need to be combined with linear identities. Such a model takes the general form

$$\mathbf{A}q(y_t, z_t) = u_t \tag{8.5.1}$$

[7] Use the 'rank = trace' rule to obtain the rank.

[8] Observe that this regression omits the intercept. The 2SLS residuals do not sum to zero by construction like the OLS residuals so this omission is not trivial, although since X_1 and Z normally include the unit vector, the residual mean should be converging to 0 under H_0.

where $\mathbf{A}$ is a $G \times (G+N)$ matrix of coefficients, $\boldsymbol{q}(\boldsymbol{y}_t, \boldsymbol{z}_t)$ is a N-vector of functions of the $G+M$ arguments, not depending on any unknown parameters, $\boldsymbol{z}_t \in \mathcal{I}_t$, and

$$E(\boldsymbol{u}_t|\mathcal{I}_t) = \mathbf{0}. \tag{8.5.2}$$

Assume we are interested in estimating the first equation, written as

$$\boldsymbol{\alpha}_1' \boldsymbol{q}(\boldsymbol{y}_t, \boldsymbol{z}_t) = u_{1t} \tag{8.5.3}$$

where it is known that $\boldsymbol{\alpha}_1$ satisfies a set of R_1 linear restrictions

$$\boldsymbol{\alpha}_1' \boldsymbol{\Phi}_1 = \mathbf{0}' \tag{8.5.4}$$

where $\boldsymbol{\Phi}_1$ $(N \times R_1)$ is a matrix of known constants. The question then arises: do there exist conditions comparable to the rank and order conditions of the linear model, which are necessary and/or sufficient for identification of $\boldsymbol{\alpha}_1$? This question was first studied by Fisher (1961, 1965, 1966), whose results were extended and corrected by Brown (1983).

Assume the model possesses a unique reduced form solution, written schematically as

$$\boldsymbol{y}_t = \boldsymbol{G}(\boldsymbol{z}_t, \boldsymbol{u}_t, \mathbf{A}) \tag{8.5.5}$$

although these functions need not exist in closed form. The condition for identification can then be stated much as before: there must not exist any G-vector $\boldsymbol{d}_1 \neq \lambda \boldsymbol{\alpha}_1$ for scalar λ, such that $\boldsymbol{d}_1' \boldsymbol{\Phi}_1 = \mathbf{0}'$ and

$$E[\boldsymbol{d}_1' \boldsymbol{q}(\boldsymbol{G}(\boldsymbol{z}_t, \boldsymbol{u}_t, \mathbf{A}), \boldsymbol{z}_t)|\mathcal{I}_t] = 0. \tag{8.5.6}$$

Following Fisher's approach, assume that $\boldsymbol{u}_t$ in the true model is actually independent of $\mathcal{I}_t$, a stronger restriction than (8.5.2). This means that for any measurable and integrable function $h : \mathbb{R}^G \mapsto \mathbb{R}$, $E(h(\boldsymbol{u}_t)|\mathcal{I}_t)$ is by definition a constant, not depending on the conditioning variables. Suppose there exist equations of the form

$$h_j(\boldsymbol{u}_t) = h_j(\mathbf{A}\boldsymbol{q}(\boldsymbol{y}_t, \boldsymbol{z}_t)) = \boldsymbol{c}_j' \boldsymbol{q}(\boldsymbol{y}_t, \boldsymbol{z}_t). \tag{8.5.7}$$

Provided the equations in (8.5.1) have unrestricted intercepts, so that the last element of $\boldsymbol{q}(\boldsymbol{y}_t, \boldsymbol{z}_t)$ is equal to 1, the last element of $\boldsymbol{c}_j$ can be always chosen to make $E(h_j(\boldsymbol{u}_t)|\mathcal{I}_t) = 0$. Hence, any linear combination of this equation with the others in the model that satisfies condition (8.5.6) and also satisfies (8.5.4) is liable to be confounded with (8.5.3), meaning that the equation would be underidentified.

There can be at most $N-G$ *implied equations* of the form (8.5.7) such that the $\boldsymbol{c}_j$ are linearly independent of both each other and the rows of $\mathbf{A}$, and of course, there may be none at all. Supposing that there are H such equations, define the *augmented model*

$$\mathbf{A}^* \boldsymbol{q}(\boldsymbol{y}_t, \boldsymbol{z}_t) = \boldsymbol{u}_t^* \;\; ((G+H) \times 1) \tag{8.5.8}$$

where, if $\boldsymbol{C}$ is the matrix with rows $\boldsymbol{c}_1', \dots \boldsymbol{c}_H'$ and $\boldsymbol{w}_t$ the vector of implied disturbances,

$$\mathbf{A}^* = \begin{bmatrix} \mathbf{A} \\ \boldsymbol{C} \end{bmatrix}, \quad \boldsymbol{u}_t^* = \begin{bmatrix} \boldsymbol{u}_t \\ \boldsymbol{w}_t \end{bmatrix}. \tag{8.5.9}$$

(8.5.8) represents the full set of equations that are both linear in $\boldsymbol{q}(\boldsymbol{y}_t, \boldsymbol{z}_t)$ and independent of $\mathcal{I}_t$. Therefore, the condition

$$\text{rank}(\mathbf{A}^*\mathbf{\Phi}_1) = G + H - 1 \tag{8.5.10}$$

is necessary and sufficient for $\boldsymbol{\alpha}_1$ to be distinguishable from any linear combination of the rows of $\mathbf{A}^*$. This is Fisher's generalized form of the rank condition for identification.

8.5.2 Example

The following example is from Gallant (1977). Let u_{1t} and u_{2t} be jointly Gaussian and independent of x_t in the equations

$$y_{1t} + a_1 y_{2t} + a_2 x_t + a_3 = u_{1t} \tag{8.5.11a}$$

$$\log y_{2t} + b_2 x_t + b_3 = u_{2t}. \tag{8.5.11b}$$

Thus, $\boldsymbol{q}_t = (y_{1t}, y_{2t}, \log y_{2t}, x_t, 1)'$ and

$$\mathbf{A} = \begin{bmatrix} 1 & a_1 & 0 & a_2 & a_3 \\ 0 & 0 & 1 & b_2 & b_3 \end{bmatrix}. \tag{8.5.12}$$

The model has reduced form

$$\begin{bmatrix} y_{1t} \\ y_{2t} \end{bmatrix} = \begin{bmatrix} u_{1t} - a_1 e^{u_{2t} - b_2 x_t - b_3} - a_2 x_t - a_3 \\ e^{u_{2t} - b_2 x_t - b_3} \end{bmatrix}. \tag{8.5.13}$$

The second equation is recursive and so trivially identified, and is consistently estimated by regression of $\log y_{2t}$ on x_t. Inspection shows that there are no implied equations in this case, so the rank condition for identification of the second equation is satisfied if rank $\mathbf{A}\mathbf{\Phi}_1 = 1$, where $\mathbf{\Phi}_1 = (0, 0, 1, 0, 0)'$. To estimate it requires one or more additional instrumental variables, but nonlinear transformations of x_t can serve this purpose.

Thus, write the reduced form predictions as

$$E(y_{1t}|\mathcal{I}_t) = -a_1 c e^{-b_2 x_t} - a_2 x_t - a_3 \tag{8.5.14}$$

$$E(y_{2t}|\mathcal{I}_t) = c e^{-b_2 x_t} \tag{8.5.15}$$

where $c = \exp\{\frac{1}{2}\sigma_{22} - b_3\}$ and $\sigma_{22} = \text{Var}(u_{2t})$, and the formula in (8.5.15) is a standard result, using (C.1.4) and the power series expansion of the exponential function. For example, consider using x_t^2 as an additional instrument. In the notation of (8.2.42), letting $\boldsymbol{x}_{1t} = (y_{2t}, x_t, 1)'$ and $\boldsymbol{z}_t = (1, x_t, x_t^2)$ the moment matrix

$$\boldsymbol{M}_{X_1 Z} = \text{plim}\, \frac{1}{n} \sum_{t=1}^{n} \begin{bmatrix} c e^{-b_2 x_t} & x_t c e^{-b_2 x_t} & x_t^2 c e^{-b_2 x_t} \\ x_t & x_t^2 & x_t^3 \\ 1 & x_t & x_t^2 \end{bmatrix} \tag{8.5.16}$$

must have rank 3. Given sufficient variation in x_t over the population, this condition is satisfied provided $b_2 \neq 0$, and two stage least squares applied to this equation would be consistent.[9] However, given knowledge of b_2 a more efficient estimation procedure is provided in this case by using $e^{-b_2 x_t}$ itself as the additional instrument, and the estimate obtained from the second regression could be substituted for the true b_2 to yield an asymptotically equivalent result, that is also asymptotically efficient in the IV class.[10]

Now consider the case where $b_2 = 0$. It is immediate that consistency fails in this case, because y_{2t} is no longer correlated with the instruments. In terms of the Fisher condition, there is now an implied equation obtained by letting $h(\cdot)$ be the exponential function applied to u_{2t}. This has the form

$$y_{2t} - c = w_t \tag{8.5.17}$$

in which $E(w_t|\mathcal{I}_t) = 0$ when c has the same definition as before. Therefore, the augmented system is

$$\mathbf{A}^* = \begin{bmatrix} 1 & a_1 & 0 & a_2 & a_3 \\ 0 & 0 & 1 & 0 & b_3 \\ 0 & 1 & 0 & 0 & c \end{bmatrix}. \tag{8.5.18}$$

and it is evident that $\text{rank}(\mathbf{A}^*\mathbf{\Phi}_1) = 1$. The equation fails the extended rank condition, as expected.

8.5.3 Kelejian's Approach

A general problem with Fisher's analysis is to find the implied equations. If the model is not too complex these might be determined by inspection, as in Gallant's example. More generally, Fisher suggested that only eligible $\mathbf{c}_j$ vectors satisfy the condition

$$\boldsymbol{Q}'(\boldsymbol{y}, \boldsymbol{z})\mathbf{c}_j = \mathbf{0} \tag{8.5.19}$$

for all $\boldsymbol{y}$ and $\boldsymbol{z}$ such that $\mathbf{A}\boldsymbol{q}(\boldsymbol{y}, \boldsymbol{z}) = \mathbf{0}$, where $\boldsymbol{Q} = \partial \boldsymbol{q}/\partial(\boldsymbol{z}', \boldsymbol{y}')$. However, Brown (1983) shows that Fisher's condition is necessary but not sufficient, and the necessary and sufficient criterion is somewhat more complicated.

Moreover, the assumption of independence of $\boldsymbol{u}_t$ and $\mathcal{I}_t$ may be unnecessarily stringent. In an unpublished paper, Kelejian (1970)[11] gives an alternative derivation of the implied equations, assuming only $E(\boldsymbol{u}_t|\mathcal{I}_t) = \mathbf{0}$.

After suitable reordering, partition the system as

$$\mathbf{A}_1\boldsymbol{q}_{1t} + \mathbf{A}_2\boldsymbol{q}_{2t} = \boldsymbol{u}_t \tag{8.5.20}$$

where all the elements of $\boldsymbol{q}_{1t}$ $(G\times 1)$ must depend on $\boldsymbol{y}_t$ and $\mathbf{A}_1$ is $G\times G$ nonsingular, but $\boldsymbol{q}_{2t}$ may have elements depending only on $\boldsymbol{z}_t$.[12] This system can be 'solved' as

$$E(\boldsymbol{q}_{1t}|\mathcal{I}_t) = -\mathbf{A}_1^{-1}\mathbf{A}_2 E(\boldsymbol{q}_{2t}|\mathcal{I}_t). \tag{8.5.21}$$

---

[9] The qualification here is not trivial. In practice moment matrices with this sort of structure can be poorly conditioned even in a large sample, if the range of variation of x_t is limited.

[10] For a proof of this assertion see §10.3

[11] See Goldfeld and Quandt (1972), Chapter 8, for a summary of Kelejian's paper.

[12] The existence of the solution (8.5.5) is generally going to require this decomposition to exist.

Now, suppose that there exists a matrix $\boldsymbol{D}$ with H^* rows $(0 \leq H^* \leq N - G)$ such that

$$\boldsymbol{D}E(\boldsymbol{q}_{2t}|\mathcal{I}_t) = \boldsymbol{D}E(\boldsymbol{q}_2(\boldsymbol{G}(\boldsymbol{z}_t, \boldsymbol{u}_t), \boldsymbol{z}_t)|\mathcal{I}_t) = \mathbf{0}. \tag{8.5.22}$$

There is no need to consider equations containing $E(\boldsymbol{q}_{1t}|\mathcal{I}_t)$ because these can be substituted out using (8.5.21). Let $\boldsymbol{w}_t = \boldsymbol{D}\boldsymbol{q}_{2t}$ be the corresponding vector with zero conditional mean, and note that there exists an augmented system of the form

$$\mathbf{A}^{**}\boldsymbol{q}_t = \boldsymbol{u}_t^{**} \tag{8.5.23}$$

where $E(\boldsymbol{u}_t^{**}|\mathcal{I}_t) = \mathbf{0}$, in which

$$\mathbf{A}^{**} = \begin{bmatrix} \mathbf{A}_1 & \mathbf{A}_2 \\ \mathbf{0} & \boldsymbol{D} \end{bmatrix}. \tag{8.5.24}$$

Note that the extra row in (8.5.18) can be generated in this way.

If $\boldsymbol{D}$ has full rank then so does $\mathbf{A}^{**}$, by construction. Kelejian's approach does not assume independence, although under independence, the space spanned by the rows of $\mathbf{A}^{**}$ must clearly contain those of $\mathbf{A}^*$ in (8.5.8). Since every vector that has its error uncorrelated with the instruments lies in this space, by definition, the usual rank condition, that the matrix $\mathbf{A}^{**}\boldsymbol{\Phi}_1$ has rank equal to its row order less 1, is necessary and sufficient for consistency of 2SLS.

The problem with Kelejian's approach is that the functions $E(\boldsymbol{q}_{2t}|\mathcal{I}_t)$ do not generally exist as closed-form functions of $\boldsymbol{z}_t$. It may be impossible to verify (8.5.22) directly, but at worst the analysis provides some important information. If no more than G of the elements of $\boldsymbol{q}_t$ depend on $\boldsymbol{y}_t$, this means $\boldsymbol{q}_{2t}$ depends only on $\boldsymbol{z}_t$ and there can be no implied equations. More generally, at most $N - G$ of the elements of $\boldsymbol{q}_t$ are involved in the implied equations, including all those not depending on $\boldsymbol{y}_t$.

Further Reading: The theory of simultaneous equations estimation was largely developed at the Cowles Commission, University of Chicago, in the 1940s. Two path-breaking volumes are Koopmans (1950a) and Koopmans and Hood (1953). Many textbooks give accounts of the theory, and Malinvaud (1970), Theil (1971), Dhrymes (1970), Schmidt (1976), Madansky (1976), are all excellent. Useful survey articles include Hsiao (1983) and Hausman (1983). On the nonlinear case, see Goldfeld and Quandt (1972) and Gallant (1987).

Part III

Advanced Estimation Theory

Chapter 9

Optimization Estimators I: Theory

9.1 Preliminaries

In this chapter a set of limit results for econometric estimation and testing are developed in a very general framework, general enough to cover the great majority of situations met with in practice. The basic unifying notion is that most econometric estimators are defined as the minimizers of certain functions constructed from the sample data, called *criterion functions*, to be denoted C_n. As in §3.4, let $\Theta \subseteq \mathbb{R}^p$ denote the parameter space. For present purposes this is the set of possible values (p-vectors $\boldsymbol{\theta}$) that an investigator is willing to entertain, and within which the search for a sample-based estimate is conducted. Let $\boldsymbol{\theta}_0 \in \Theta$ $(p \times 1)$ represent the 'true' value, whose precise definition in this theory will emerge as we proceed. The symbol $\boldsymbol{\theta}$, without decorations, will be used to denote the generic point of the parameter space.

Define an estimator of $\boldsymbol{\theta}_0$ based on a data set of size n by

$$\hat{\boldsymbol{\theta}}_n = \arg\min_{\boldsymbol{\theta} \in \Theta} C_n(\boldsymbol{\theta}). \tag{9.1.1}$$

The class of estimators defined in this way goes by several different names, including M-estimators (M standing for maximization/minimization), extremum estimators, and optimization estimators (OEs). For no special reason, the last of these is adopted in this book. Ordinary least squares for the linear regression model is the OE we are most familiar with, in which C_n is the sum of squares function. There is no need to study its properties in the present framework since we already know the answers by other means, but it is always a useful example to bear in mind in studying the theory of OEs.

The analysis that follows is centred around the properties of C_n and its derivatives. The notations

$$\nabla C_n = \frac{\partial C_n}{\partial \boldsymbol{\theta}} = \begin{bmatrix} \partial C_n/\partial \theta_1 \\ \vdots \\ \partial C_n/\partial \theta_p \end{bmatrix} \quad (p \times 1) \tag{9.1.2}$$

are used for the gradient vector, and the Hessian matrix is similarly

$$\nabla^2 C_n = \frac{\partial^2 C_n}{\partial \boldsymbol{\theta} \partial \boldsymbol{\theta}'} = \begin{bmatrix} \partial^2 C_n/\partial \theta_1^2 & \cdots & \partial^2 C_n/\partial \theta_1 \partial \theta_p \\ \vdots & \ddots & \vdots \\ \partial^2 C_n/\partial \theta_p \partial \theta_1 & \cdots & \partial^2 C_n/\partial \theta_p^2 \end{bmatrix} \quad (p \times p) \tag{9.1.3}$$

Also define $\boldsymbol{q}_n(\boldsymbol{\theta}) = \nabla C_n$ and $\boldsymbol{Q}_n(\boldsymbol{\theta}) = \nabla^2 C_n$ as functional notations. It is not essential for all the results that these derivatives exist, but the assumption is very useful. Be careful to keep in mind the dual nature of all these quantities, as random variables and functions on the parameter space.

Criterion functions can be thought of as having the generic form

$$C_n(\boldsymbol{\theta}) = \phi\left(\frac{1}{n}\sum_{t=1}^{n} \boldsymbol{\psi}_t(\boldsymbol{\theta})\right) \tag{9.1.4}$$

where $\phi(\cdot)$ is a continuous function of r variables, and $\boldsymbol{\psi}_t(\boldsymbol{\theta})$ is an r-vector of continuous functions of $\boldsymbol{\theta}$, also depending on the sample observations.[1] The factor $1/n$ is optional from the point of view of computing the solution to problem (9.1.1), but ensures that C_n is bounded in the limit as $n \to \infty$. This is essential in the discussion of asymptotic properties.

A variety of specific forms for ϕ and $\boldsymbol{\psi}_t$ arise in different contexts. The most familiar is where $r = 1$ and ϕ is the identity function, so that $C_n(\boldsymbol{\theta})$ corresponds to a sum of terms, to be jointly made as small as possible by choice of $\boldsymbol{\theta}$. Ordinary least squares has

$$C_n(\boldsymbol{\theta}) = \frac{\boldsymbol{u}(\boldsymbol{\theta})'\boldsymbol{u}(\boldsymbol{\theta})}{n} \tag{9.1.5}$$

so that ψ_t is the squared residual. However, note that the characterization in (9.1.4) is usually not unique. Equation (10.1.5), for example, shows how OLS can also be thought of as a case with $r = (k+1)^2$, where k is the number of parameters. Different characterizations may be useful for different purposes.

In the *maximum likelihood* estimator (Chapter 11) ψ_t, again a scalar, corresponds to the negative of the log-probability or log-probability density associated with each observation. Such methods can often be shown by the general arguments of this chapter to have useful properties even when the distributional assumptions are incorrect. This is called quasi-maximum likelihood or pseudo-maximum likelihood, see Gourieroux, Monfort and Trognon (1984).

---

[1] This is true of all the cases considered in this book. On considering the arguments in §9.3, it is clear that other forms would not in general yield OEs with the CAN property.

Method of moments estimators are constructed as the solutions to sets of equations relating data moments and unknown parameters, the moments in question being replaced by sample averages to obtain the estimates. These can often be viewed as OEs. The natural case is where certain functions of data and true parameters are assumed to be uncorrelated. The criterion function is accordingly defined as a quadratic form in the vector of covariances. An example already encountered is the instrumental variables (IV) estimator derived in §3.6.2 and then in §8.2. The criterion function in this case can be written in vector notation as

$$C_n(\boldsymbol{\theta}) = \frac{\boldsymbol{u}(\boldsymbol{\theta})'\boldsymbol{Z}(\boldsymbol{Z}'\boldsymbol{Z})^{-1}\boldsymbol{Z}'\boldsymbol{u}(\boldsymbol{\theta})}{n} \tag{9.1.6}$$

where $\boldsymbol{u}(\boldsymbol{\theta}) = \boldsymbol{y}_1 - \boldsymbol{X}_1\boldsymbol{\theta}$ and $\boldsymbol{\theta} = \boldsymbol{\delta}_1$. It can be verified using calculus that the formula in (8.2.26) is indeed the minimizer of C_n. In this case

$$\boldsymbol{\psi}_t = (\boldsymbol{z}_t'u_t(\boldsymbol{\theta}), (\mathrm{Vec}\,\boldsymbol{z}_t\boldsymbol{z}_t')^{*\prime})' \tag{9.1.7}$$

where the '$*$' denotes that elements redundant by symmetry are omitted, and $r = M + \frac{1}{2}M(M+1)$. This example shows that the elements of $\boldsymbol{\psi}_t$ need not all depend on $\boldsymbol{\theta}$. Some can be just functions of sample data, whose averages are usually required to converge in a specified manner to establish the asymptotic properties of the OE.

This can also be rationalised as a *minimum distance estimator* (MDE). One can think of an MDE as a procedure that minimises the length of a vector $\boldsymbol{x}$ under a particular metric, such that the length is measured as $\boldsymbol{x}'\boldsymbol{Q}\boldsymbol{x}$ for some symmetric positive definite matrix $\boldsymbol{Q}$. While the method resembles another MDE, the GLS method of §2.3, be careful to note how the motivation is different in each case. In GLS, the vector whose length is to be minimised is $\boldsymbol{u}$, and $\boldsymbol{Q} = \boldsymbol{\Omega}^{-1}$ $(n \times n)$ while in IV, $\boldsymbol{x}$ corresponds to $\boldsymbol{Z}'\boldsymbol{u}$, and $\boldsymbol{Q} = (\boldsymbol{Z}'\boldsymbol{Z})^{-1}$ $(M \times M)$. There is no sense in which the length of $\boldsymbol{u}$ is minimised in this latter case, although as is apparent from inspection of (8.2.26), OLS is the case of IV where $\boldsymbol{Z} = \boldsymbol{X}_1$. OLS is of special interest, in belonging to both classes of MDE.

A fourth class of cases are the *least generalized variance* estimators, for which the criterion is either the determinant of a variance matrix, or the ratio of two such determinants; see §13.3. Here, $\boldsymbol{\psi}_t$ denotes the vectorized elements of the matrix, or matrices, of squares and products, whose means represent the sample variances and covariances. These estimators can therefore be seen as generalizing the least squares principle.

A possibility that features in certain estimation problems is where $C_n(\cdot)$ depends on previously obtained estimates of some model parameters, usually variance parameters, which are treated as given as the criterion is optimized. This is called *two-stage estimation.*[2] A well-known example (the name notwithstanding) is the three-stage least squares (3SLS) estimator for sets of simultaneous equations, which depends on preliminary estimates of the covariance matrix of the disturbances (see §13.1). There is the option of *iterating* a two-stage procedure,

[2] Don't confuse this with *two-step* estimation, to be considered in §9.4.2 below. These concepts are quite distinct.

feeding the estimates obtained at the second stage back into the procedure, and repeating this loop until the inputs and outputs agree. Indeed, it is sometimes possible to show that the resulting estimators are the optimizers of some more general criterion function, but this does not appear to be true generally; see §13.5 for further discussion. The theory of inference in two-stage estimation cannot be derived simply from OE theory, although it is possible to obtain results for specific cases by considering the properties of the model in question. The leading examples of this approach are discussed in §13.1 and §13.5.

A possible way to simplify the estimation procedure is to *concentrate* the criterion with respect to a subset of the parameters. Suppose the full set of parameters is $(\boldsymbol{\theta}, \boldsymbol{\lambda})$. Holding $\boldsymbol{\theta}$ fixed, one can optimize $C_n(\boldsymbol{\theta}, \boldsymbol{\lambda})$ with respect to $\boldsymbol{\lambda}$. Denoting the corresponding conditional estimate of $\boldsymbol{\lambda}$ by $\boldsymbol{\lambda}(\boldsymbol{\theta})$, one can then define the concentrated criterion function

$$C_n^*(\boldsymbol{\theta}) = C_n(\boldsymbol{\theta}, \boldsymbol{\lambda}(\boldsymbol{\theta})). \tag{9.1.8}$$

It is straightforward to demonstrate that optimizing $C_n^*(\boldsymbol{\theta})$ with respect to $\boldsymbol{\theta}$ leads to the same result as optimizing the original function. The concentrated optimization solves the first-order conditions

$$\frac{dC_n(\boldsymbol{\theta}, \boldsymbol{\lambda}(\boldsymbol{\theta}))}{d\boldsymbol{\theta}} = \frac{\partial C_n}{\partial \boldsymbol{\theta}} + \left.\frac{\partial C_n}{\partial \boldsymbol{\lambda}'}\right|_{\boldsymbol{\lambda}=\boldsymbol{\lambda}(\boldsymbol{\theta})} \frac{\partial \boldsymbol{\lambda}(\boldsymbol{\theta})'}{\partial \boldsymbol{\theta}} = \mathbf{0} \tag{9.1.9}$$

to obtain $\hat{\boldsymbol{\theta}}_n$. However,

$$\left.\frac{\partial C_n}{\partial \boldsymbol{\lambda}'}\right|_{\boldsymbol{\lambda}=\boldsymbol{\lambda}(\boldsymbol{\theta})} = \mathbf{0}' \tag{9.1.10}$$

for all $\boldsymbol{\theta}$ by definition of $\boldsymbol{\lambda}(\boldsymbol{\theta})$, so that (9.1.9) implies

$$\left.\frac{\partial C_n}{\partial \boldsymbol{\theta}}\right|_{\boldsymbol{\theta}=\hat{\boldsymbol{\theta}}_n} = \mathbf{0}. \tag{9.1.11}$$

It follows that $\hat{\boldsymbol{\theta}}_n$ is also the partial solution to the original problem. The estimator of $\boldsymbol{\lambda}$ is of course $\hat{\boldsymbol{\lambda}}_n = \boldsymbol{\lambda}(\hat{\boldsymbol{\theta}}_n)$.

The obvious application for this technique is where there exists a closed analytic form for $\boldsymbol{\lambda}(\boldsymbol{\theta})$, and there are some important cases where this useful situation is found, in particular, in Gaussian maximum likelihood estimation where the elements of $\boldsymbol{\lambda}$ are error variances and covariances. However, OEs are defined by a *property*, not by a formula, and often the only way to obtain them is by a systematic search for the minimum, computing C_n at a succession of trial values. These methods are the topic of the next section.

9.2 Numerical Optimization

Although we cannot always derive a formula for the minimum of C_n, we can always program a computer to evaluate the function and also, in most cases, its derivatives. It can be verified whether any particular point in the parameter space minimizes the criterion locally, by checking that first and second order conditions hold at that point, or by simply evaluating C_n at closely neighbouring points in the space.

More generally, the values of the function and derivatives at an arbitrary point can provide clues as to the direction of the minimum. A useful analogy can be drawn with the problem of descending a mountain in dense fog. This can hopefully be achieved using only local information, such as the reading of an altimeter, and knowing which direction is 'downhill'. A computer-based search algorithm is a rule for generating a sequence of trial values that, with luck and a well-chosen starting point, will approach the minimum after a finite number of steps. There are many different search methods, but most in common use are based on the idea of quadratic approximation. The quadratic is the one function for which a closed form expression for the extremum exists. Most of the methods described here have the property of *quadratic convergence*. That is to say, when they are applied to a quadratic function (such as the sum of squares for the linear regression model) the optimization problem is solved in a single iteration of the algorithm, or at worst a finite sequence of iterations.

9.2.1 Line Search

As a first, simple illustration, consider a function of one variable, $f(\theta)$. Suppose two points on the line 'bracket' the minimum; say $\theta_1 < \theta_2$, such that if $\theta_3 = (\theta_1 + \theta_2)/2$, then $f(\theta_1) > f(\theta_3) < f(\theta_2)$. It can be verified that a quadratic function passing through these three points is

$$g(\theta) = \frac{f(\theta_1) + f(\theta_2) - 2f(\theta_3)}{2h^2}(\theta - \theta_3)^2 + \frac{f(\theta_2) - f(\theta_1)}{2h}(\theta - \theta_3) + f(\theta_3) \quad (9.2.1)$$

where $h = \theta_3 - \theta_1 = \theta_2 - \theta_3$, and its minimum is

$$\theta^* = \theta_3 - \frac{h[f(\theta_2) - f(\theta_1)]}{2[f(\theta_1) + f(\theta_2) - 2f(\theta_3)]}. \quad (9.2.2)$$

θ^* should be a close approximation to the minimum of f, so long as h is small.

This basic step needs to be implemented in conjunction with some form of grid search to find the bracketing points. Here is such a procedure, based on the algorithm of Davies, Swann and Campey (1964). Start at an initial point θ^1 (say 0, if no information is available to suggest a better one), and choose an initial step length, h_1. Evaluate the function at θ^1 and $\theta^2 = \theta^1 + h_1$. If $f(\theta^1) < f(\theta^2)$, reverse the direction of search by setting $h_2 = -2h_1$. Then, for $r = 3, 4, 5, \ldots$, set $\theta^r = \theta^{r-1} + h_{r-1}$ and if $f(\theta^r) < f(\theta^{r-1})$, set $h_r = 2h_{r-1}$, and repeat so long as this inequality holds. Doubling the length of each step allows a small step to be taken initially, while ensuring rapid progress towards the minimum.

When the condition $f(\theta^r) > f(\theta^{r-1})$ is met, the minimum has been overshot; let R denote the step where this occurs. Take half a step *back*, by setting $\theta^{R+1} = \theta^R - h_R/2$, and we have four equally spaced points such that necessarily[3] either

[3] Assuming the minimum is unique, of course.

$f(\theta^{R-1}) > f(\theta^{R+1}) < f(\theta^R)$, or $f(\theta^{R-2}) > f(\theta^{R-1}) < f(\theta^{R+1})$. Discard either θ^{R-2} or θ^R, accordingly, let the remaining triplet of points stand for θ_1, θ_2 and θ_3 in (9.2.2), and compute θ^*. The entire procedure can now be repeated, starting at the smaller of θ^* and θ_3 with step set to $\theta^* - \theta_3$ or $\theta_3 - \theta^*$ as appropriate, continuing until h is smaller than the required tolerance. This might be related to the number of significant digits held by the computer, although in the case of the line searches of a multivariate minimization routine as in (9.2.9) below, for which this type of search is most commonly used, accuracy may be beneficially traded for computing time per search.

Something that must always be kept in mind about such search methods is that they converge on the first *local* minimum to be located. If there are several local minima of the function, one must detect all of these to find the global minimum or *minimum minimorum.* The only way to do this is to start the procedure at different points.

Minimizing a differentiable function can be cast into the same framework as finding the zeros of a function, where the latter function is the derivative of the former. Let $q(\theta) = df/d\theta$. The so-called *Method of False Position* assumes that the zero of a function q is bracketed by two known points, $\theta_1 < \theta_2$, such that $q(\theta_1) < 0$ and $q(\theta_2) > 0$. The point

$$\theta^* = \theta_1 - q(\theta_1)\frac{\theta_2 - \theta_1}{q(\theta_2) - q(\theta_1)} \tag{9.2.3}$$

can easily be verified to be the point of intersection of the chord joining the points $q(\theta_1)$ and $q(\theta_2)$ with the zero axis, and satisfies $\theta_1 < \theta^* < \theta_2$. Here, q is being approximated by a linear function, equivalent to approximating f by a quadratic. The method can be iterated by replacing either θ_1 or θ_2 by θ^*, according to whether $q(\theta^*) < 0$ or $q(\theta^*) > 0$. It is clear that the iterations must converge on the point $\hat{\theta}$, such that $q(\hat{\theta}) = 0$.

The updating formula in (9.2.2) applied to the minimization problem has an obvious affinity to (9.2.3) since it simply uses a difference approximation for q. The ratio in (9.2.3) itself has the interpretation of a difference approximation, in this case to the inverse of $dq/d\theta$, or equivalently, of $d^2f/d\theta^2$. This observation suggests the search procedure known as *Newton's Method,* which uses the updating step

$$\theta^{r+1} = \theta^r - \frac{q(\theta^r)}{q'(\theta^r)} \tag{9.2.4}$$

where q' represents the derivative of q (second derivative of f). If f is a quadratic in θ, the step in (9.2.4) is equivalent to the analytical solution of the minimum problem. For such cases, Newton's method converges in one step, and is said to be quadratically convergent. It has the property of very rapid convergence in most cases once the minimum is close, basically when q' is positive, but can clearly diverge from points at which $q' < 0$. Although Newton's method is conceptually very important, in most applications of line searches in econometrics one would wish to avoid computing derivatives, and simple interpolation methods using function values only are generally the most useful.

9.2.2 Gradient Methods for Multivariate Optimization

Let $C(\boldsymbol{\theta})$ be the criterion function of p variables to be minimized.[4] To implement a quadratic approximation method requires the computation of both the function C itself and the gradient vector, $\boldsymbol{q} = \boldsymbol{\nabla} C$. Hence, these methods are also called gradient methods. The estimator $\hat{\boldsymbol{\theta}}$ is defined implicitly by the first-order conditions $\boldsymbol{q}(\hat{\boldsymbol{\theta}}) = \boldsymbol{0}$, subject to the second-order conditions for a minimum.

Let $\boldsymbol{H}_r$ $(p \times p)$ denote some suitable symmetric, positive definite matrix. Alternative choices of $\boldsymbol{H}_r$ define alternative algorithms, so for the moment we leave it unspecified. A quadratic approximation to C at a point $\boldsymbol{\theta}^r \in \Theta$ is

$$C_r(\boldsymbol{\theta}) = \tfrac{1}{2}\boldsymbol{\theta}'\boldsymbol{H}_r\boldsymbol{\theta} + \boldsymbol{b}_r'\boldsymbol{\theta} + c_r. \tag{9.2.5}$$

Given $\boldsymbol{H}_r$, let $\boldsymbol{b}_r$ be chosen so that C and C_r have the same gradient at $\boldsymbol{\theta}^r$. Applying (A.9.1),

$$\boldsymbol{\nabla} C_r = \boldsymbol{b}_r + \boldsymbol{H}_r\boldsymbol{\theta} \tag{9.2.6}$$

which equated with $\boldsymbol{q}_r = \boldsymbol{q}(\boldsymbol{\theta}^r)$ gives

$$\boldsymbol{b}_r = \boldsymbol{q}_r - \boldsymbol{H}_r\boldsymbol{\theta}^r. \tag{9.2.7}$$

c_r is a scalar that does not enter the problem further and whose role is purely cosmetic. If it is chosen to make $C(\boldsymbol{\theta}^r) = C_r(\boldsymbol{\theta}^r)$, then C and C_r are tangent to one another at the point $\boldsymbol{\theta}^r$. The idea is that $\boldsymbol{\theta}^{*r}$, the minimum of C_r, should provide an approximation to the minimum of C that improves on $\boldsymbol{\theta}^r$. $\boldsymbol{\theta}^{*r}$ is calculated by equating (9.2.6) to zero, which substituting from (9.2.7) gives

$$\boldsymbol{\theta}^{*r} = -\boldsymbol{H}_r^{-1}\boldsymbol{b}_r = \boldsymbol{\theta}^r - \boldsymbol{H}_r^{-1}\boldsymbol{q}_r. \tag{9.2.8}$$

One may take $\boldsymbol{\theta}^{*r}$ as the new estimate of the minimum, set $\boldsymbol{\theta}^{r+1} = \boldsymbol{\theta}^{*r}$, and iterate the sequence of calculations for $r = 2, 3, 4$, etc.

Two other requirements to implement this search procedure are an initial point $\boldsymbol{\theta}^1$, and a criterion for stopping the search. As the sequence of steps approaches the true minimum $\hat{\boldsymbol{\theta}}$, $\boldsymbol{q}$ approaches $\boldsymbol{q}(\hat{\boldsymbol{\theta}}) = \boldsymbol{0}$, and hence the iterations should converge, such that the norm $\|\boldsymbol{\theta}^{r+1} - \boldsymbol{\theta}^r\|$ is tending to 0.[5] A stopping criterion can be based on a test of this quantity after each iteration, although one could also monitor $\|\boldsymbol{q}(\boldsymbol{\theta}^r)\|$, or even both quantities. The iterations are stopped if the test values are within the desired accuracy of estimation, or the tolerance (rounding error) of the computer, if this is greater.

If computers were infinitely fast, the procedure described, with the gradient being re-calculated at each step, could not really be improved on provided $\boldsymbol{H}_r$ is suitably chosen. However, the computer time needed to obtain $\boldsymbol{q}_r$ and $\boldsymbol{H}_r$ is often significant when p is large, and these quantities can be used more intensively before being updated. What is commonly done is to take the vector $-\boldsymbol{H}_r^{-1}\boldsymbol{q}_r$

---

[4] The n subscripts are dropped in this section for clarity of notation.

[5] See (A.1.6) for the definition of $\|\cdot\|$.

as indicating the *direction* of the minimum, and conduct a line search in this direction. In other words, writing $\boldsymbol{d}_r = -\boldsymbol{H}_r^{-1}\boldsymbol{q}_r$, minimize

$$f(\lambda) = C(\boldsymbol{\theta}^r + \lambda \boldsymbol{d}_r) \tag{9.2.9}$$

with respect to λ by a line search method, such as described in §9.2.1. The updating step is to choose

$$\boldsymbol{\theta}^{r+1} = \boldsymbol{\theta}^r - \lambda^r \boldsymbol{H}_r^{-1}\boldsymbol{q}_r \tag{9.2.10}$$

where λ^r is the best point found on the line. Note that if $\boldsymbol{H}_r$ is positive definite then using Lemma A.7.2,

$$\left.\frac{df}{d\lambda}\right|_{\lambda=0} = \boldsymbol{q}_r'\boldsymbol{d}_r = -\boldsymbol{q}_r'\boldsymbol{H}_r^{-1}\boldsymbol{q}_r < 0 \tag{9.2.11}$$

which shows that, subject to the positive definiteness, a line search (over positive values of λ, note) can always reduce the function, assuming the minimum is not already attained with $\boldsymbol{q}_r = \boldsymbol{0}$.

What distinguishes different gradient methods is the choice of the matrices $\boldsymbol{H}_r$. Choosing $\boldsymbol{H}_r = \boldsymbol{I}$ for every r is called the method of *steepest descent.* It is simple to implement and robust (should always find the minimum eventually) but very slow to converge, since the approximation of C_r to C is very poor. Another obvious choice for $\boldsymbol{H}_r$ is $\boldsymbol{Q}_r$, the true Hessian matrix of the criterion function at the current point. This method, the multivariate generalization of Newton's method in (9.2.4), is called the *Newton–Raphson* algorithm. If the derivatives are exact the Newton–Raphson method is quadratically convergent, meaning that when applied to a quadratic function of p variables,

$$C(\boldsymbol{\theta}) = \tfrac{1}{2}\boldsymbol{\theta}'\boldsymbol{A}\boldsymbol{\theta} + \boldsymbol{b}'\boldsymbol{\theta} + c \tag{9.2.12}$$

it converges in just 1 step, putting $C_1 = C$. While apparently irrelevant since we know already that $\hat{\boldsymbol{\theta}} = -\boldsymbol{A}^{-1}\boldsymbol{b}$ in this case, quadratic convergence is an important property since it indicates that the algorithm will also converge rapidly in more general cases, particularly from points in the neighbourhood of the minimum.

A problem with Newton–Raphson is that the Hessian matrix is not guaranteed to be either nonsingular or positive definite except at the minimum. If these conditions are not observed at every step, the search routine could either diverge or break down altogether. To avoid this type of behaviour, one expedient is to augment the diagonal elements of the matrix, for example, setting

$$\boldsymbol{H}_r = \boldsymbol{Q}_r + \mu_r \boldsymbol{I}. \tag{9.2.13}$$

Here, μ_r is a scalar that is decreased at each step, say by a factor of 10, so long as $\boldsymbol{Q}_r$ is well-conditioned, but is increased if, for example, the ratio of the largest to the smallest eigenvalue of $\boldsymbol{Q}_r$ is excessive; the Goldfeld–Quandt–Trotter (1966) algorithm is an example. This type of method interpolates the search direction between Newton–Raphson and steepest descent, tending to the latter method when the function contours are awkwardly shaped, but switching to the former as the

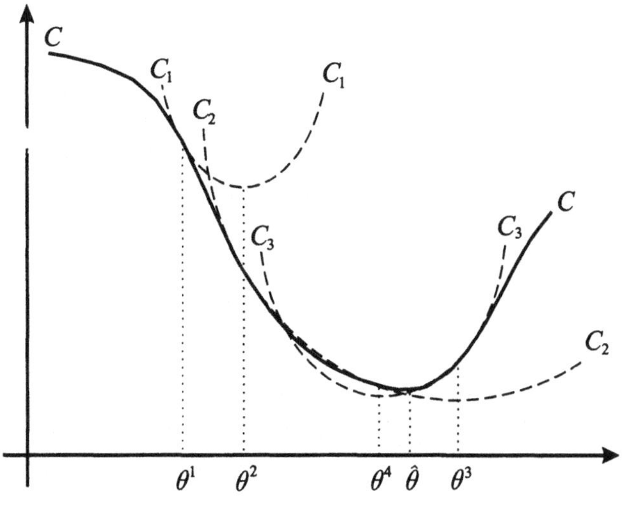

Figure 9.1: Quadratic Approximation

minimum is approached. The methods discussed in the next section develop this idea further.

Figure 9.1 illustrates the implementation of such an algorithm, drawn in one dimension. At the starting point θ^1, the approximating quadratic is the curve C_1, chosen to have the same gradient as the criterion C at θ^1. Since the second derivative of C is actually negative at that point, an adjustment such as (9.2.13) has to be made to ensure reduction of the function, so this curve does not fit C closely. The first step takes us to point θ^2, the minimum of C_1. Here, the approximating quadratic can be chosen by the Newton–Raphson rule,[6] so that C_2 matches both first and second derivatives of C at θ^2. Minimizing this function takes us to θ^3, and repeating the same rule takes us to θ^4. From here, further iterations of the same sort will rapidly approach the minimum $\hat{\theta}$. To appreciate the advantage conveyed by Newton–Raphson, the reader might like to imagine applying the steepest descent method to this case. This would be similar to duplicating C_1 to form the approximating function, for every iteration. This method is sure to converge, but will take considerably more steps to do so.

There are several gradient methods that exploit the particular form of the optimand, notably the *Gauss–Newton* algorithm for least squares-type problems (Hartley 1961, Marquardt 1963) and the algorithm of Berndt, Hall, Hall and Haus-

[6] In one dimension this is just the Newton step. 'Newton–Raphson' is the multivariate generalization, which the reader must imagine.

man (1974) (BHHH) for maximum likelihood-type problems. These methods are discussed in context, in §10.2.1 and §11.3.5.

9.2.3 Quasi-Newton Methods

The most popular methods suitable for general optimands are the *quasi-Newton* (QN) algorithms, also called variable-metric methods. These use simple formulae for updating $\boldsymbol{H}_r^{-1}$ from one iteration to the next, so that no explicit inversions have to be carried out. Let the search direction at step r be denoted $-\boldsymbol{B}_r\boldsymbol{q}_r$, defining $\boldsymbol{H}_r$ implicitly by $\boldsymbol{B}_r = \boldsymbol{H}_r^{-1}$. The initial step is usually a steepest descent, such that $\boldsymbol{B}_1 = \boldsymbol{I}$. Now define $\boldsymbol{\gamma}_r = \boldsymbol{q}_{r+1} - \boldsymbol{q}_r$ and $\boldsymbol{\delta}_r = \boldsymbol{\theta}^{r+1} - \boldsymbol{\theta}^r = -\lambda_r\boldsymbol{B}_r\boldsymbol{q}_r$. Note that $\boldsymbol{\delta}_r$ represents the direction of search at step r. The key property of the QN approach is to choose $\boldsymbol{B}_{r+1}$ to be positive definite and to satisfy the relation

$$\boldsymbol{B}_{r+1}\boldsymbol{\gamma}_r = \boldsymbol{\delta}_r \tag{9.2.14}$$

which is called the quasi-Newton equation. The significance of this condition can be appreciated by considering the mean value expansion of the gradient vector,

$$\boldsymbol{q}_{r+1} - \boldsymbol{q}_r = \boldsymbol{Q}^*(\boldsymbol{\theta}^{r+1} - \boldsymbol{\theta}^r) \tag{9.2.15}$$

where $\boldsymbol{Q}^*$ denotes the matrix whose rows are the rows of the Hessian $\boldsymbol{Q}$, evaluated at different points on the line segment connecting $\boldsymbol{\theta}^r$ and $\boldsymbol{\theta}^{r+1}$. Clearly, when the updates at step r are small, as when the neighbourhood of the minimum is approached with $\boldsymbol{q}_r \approx \boldsymbol{q}(\hat{\boldsymbol{\theta}}) = \boldsymbol{0}$, $\boldsymbol{B}_{r+1}$ should approximate $\boldsymbol{Q}(\hat{\boldsymbol{\theta}})$, provided it is positive definite. Thus, QN methods have the desirable property of approximating the Newton–Raphson algorithm in the neighbourhood of the minimum.

To operationalize the method, an updating formula is required to obtain $\boldsymbol{B}_{r+1}$ given $\boldsymbol{B}_r$. Many different schemes exist. The leading cases are members of the *Broyden family* of algorithms (Broyden, 1967). In these formulae a matrix of rank 2 is added to $\boldsymbol{B}_r$, with the form

$$\boldsymbol{B}_{r+1} = \boldsymbol{B}_r + \boldsymbol{u}_r(\boldsymbol{E}_r + \phi_r\boldsymbol{F}_r)\boldsymbol{u}_r' \tag{9.2.16}$$

where

$$\boldsymbol{u}_r = \begin{bmatrix}\boldsymbol{\delta}_r & \boldsymbol{B}_r\boldsymbol{\gamma}_r\end{bmatrix} \quad (p \times 2)$$

$$\boldsymbol{E}_r = \begin{bmatrix} \dfrac{1}{\boldsymbol{\delta}_r'\boldsymbol{\gamma}_r} & 0 \\ 0 & -\dfrac{1}{\boldsymbol{\gamma}_r'\boldsymbol{B}_r\boldsymbol{\gamma}_r} \end{bmatrix}, \qquad \boldsymbol{F}_r = \begin{bmatrix} \dfrac{\boldsymbol{\gamma}_r'\boldsymbol{B}_r\boldsymbol{\gamma}_r}{(\boldsymbol{\delta}_r'\boldsymbol{\gamma}_r)^2} & -\dfrac{1}{\boldsymbol{\delta}_r'\boldsymbol{\gamma}_r} \\ -\dfrac{1}{\boldsymbol{\delta}_r'\boldsymbol{\gamma}_r} & \dfrac{1}{\boldsymbol{\gamma}_r'\boldsymbol{B}_r\boldsymbol{\gamma}_r} \end{bmatrix}$$

are 2×2 matrices, and $\phi_r \geq 0$ is a scalar that defines the family member. Note that $\boldsymbol{F}_r$ has rank 1 and that $\boldsymbol{u}_r\boldsymbol{F}_r\boldsymbol{u}_r' = \boldsymbol{v}_r\boldsymbol{v}_r'$ where

$$\boldsymbol{v}_r = \sqrt{\boldsymbol{\gamma}_r'\boldsymbol{B}_r\boldsymbol{\gamma}_r}\left(\frac{\boldsymbol{\delta}_r}{\boldsymbol{\delta}_r'\boldsymbol{\gamma}_r} - \frac{\boldsymbol{B}_r\boldsymbol{\gamma}_r}{\boldsymbol{\gamma}_r'\boldsymbol{B}_r\boldsymbol{\gamma}_r}\right). \tag{9.2.17}$$

Since $\boldsymbol{v}_r'\boldsymbol{\gamma}_r = 0$ and

$$\boldsymbol{u}_r'\boldsymbol{\gamma}_r = \begin{bmatrix} \boldsymbol{\delta}_r'\boldsymbol{\gamma}_r \\ \boldsymbol{\gamma}_r'\boldsymbol{B}_r\boldsymbol{\gamma}_r \end{bmatrix} \tag{9.2.18}$$

it is easily verified that the quasi-Newton equation is satisfied by (9.2.16) for any choice of ϕ_r. Similar updating formulae for the matrices $\boldsymbol{H}_r = \boldsymbol{B}_r^{-1}$ can be derived from these, using the Sherman–Morrison formula (A.2.14).

The Broyden family has two important properties. The first is:

Theorem 9.2.1 Let $\boldsymbol{B}_r$ be symmetric and positive definite, and let rth step be computed by an exact line search in the direction $-\boldsymbol{B}_r\boldsymbol{q}_r$. Then $\boldsymbol{B}_{r+1}$ computed by (9.2.16) is also symmetric and positive definite. □

See §9.5 for the proof. The second property is quadratic convergence. With exact line searches, a quadratic function is optimized in just $p+1$ steps. Observe that if C is given by (9.2.12) then

$$\boldsymbol{\gamma}_r = \boldsymbol{A}\boldsymbol{\delta}_r \tag{9.2.19}$$

and in view of the quasi-Newton equation the algorithms therefore satisfy

$$\boldsymbol{B}_{r+1}\boldsymbol{A}\boldsymbol{\delta}_r = \boldsymbol{\delta}_r. \tag{9.2.20}$$

Theorem 9.2.2 If a Broyden algorithm is applied to (9.2.12) with exact line searches then $\boldsymbol{B}_p = \boldsymbol{A}^{-1}$. □

See §9.5 for the proof. Quadratic convergence follows immediately, since

$$\boldsymbol{\theta}^{p+1} = \boldsymbol{\theta}_p - \boldsymbol{A}^{-1}\boldsymbol{q}_p = -\boldsymbol{A}^{-1}\boldsymbol{b} = \hat{\boldsymbol{\theta}}. \tag{9.2.21}$$

These facts are remarkable in that the initial values, $\boldsymbol{\theta}^1$ and $\boldsymbol{B}_1$ are unspecified The latter can be any symmetric positive definite matrix, such as $\boldsymbol{I}_p$.

The most important members of the Broyden family are the *Davidon–Fletcher–Powell* (DFP) algorithm[7], which sets $\phi_r = 0$ for all r, and the *Broyden-Fletcher-Goldfarb-Shanno* (BFGS) algorithm,[8] for which $\phi_r = 1$. Of these, the BFGS is often said to perform best, and is widely implemented. Notwithstanding that the important properties just derived assume exact line searches, the methods work very successfully with approximate (and hence rapid) line searches. A balance always has to be struck between the advantages of thorough search in an existing direction, and the updating of the direction in the light of new information.

---

[7]See Davidon (1959), Fletcher and Powell (1963).

[8]See Broyden (1970), Fletcher (1970), Goldfarb (1970), Shanno (1970).

9.2.4 Direct Search Methods

A class of methods exist for multivariate problems that make no use of derivatives. They may be appropriate in cases where the existence of continuous derivatives is not guaranteed, or for large dimensioned problems where the computation of derivatives is very laborious, although they are generally less efficient than gradient methods when derivatives do exist.

A very simple example is *axial search*, in which a line search is conducted with respect to each argument in turn, holding the others constant. In other words, the search directions are the vectors $\boldsymbol{e}_i = (0, \ldots, 0, 1, 0, \ldots)'$ (the ith column of the identity matrix), running from $i = 1$ up to $i = p$, and then back to 1 again. While very easy to implement, axial searches can be very inefficient, since like steepest descent methods, they fail to make use of the information acquired during the search about the local contours of the criterion function.

A much more efficient direct search method is the *conjugate directions* method due to Powell (1964). This method is actually quadratically convergent. An iteration of the Powell method is performed by conducting a sequence of line searches, after which (unlike the axial search method) the direction set is updated for the next iteration. The initial set of directions can be any collection of p linearly independent vectors, but the axial directions are a natural choice. Let $(\boldsymbol{\xi}_1^r, \ldots, \boldsymbol{\xi}_p^r)$ denote the current collection of directions at the rth iteration, and let the current point be $\boldsymbol{\theta}^r$. The iteration consists of three steps.

1. Conduct line searches in each of the p current directions in turn, to reach successive points $\boldsymbol{\theta}_1^r, \ldots, \boldsymbol{\theta}_p^r$.

2. Make one further search from $\boldsymbol{\theta}_p^r$ in the *direction of total progress* $\boldsymbol{\theta}_p^r - \boldsymbol{\theta}^r$, to obtain $\boldsymbol{\theta}^{r+1}$.

3. Update the direction set with the direction of total progress, setting
$$(\boldsymbol{\xi}_1^{r+1}, \ldots, \boldsymbol{\xi}_p^{r+1}) = (\boldsymbol{\xi}_2^r, \ldots, \boldsymbol{\xi}_p^r, \boldsymbol{\theta}_p^r - \boldsymbol{\theta}^r). \tag{9.2.22}$$

To demonstrate the quadratic convergence of this method, consider the application to (9.2.12). Write

$$\boldsymbol{\theta} = \boldsymbol{\theta}^r + \sum_{j=1}^{p} \lambda_j \boldsymbol{\xi}_j^r \tag{9.2.23}$$

and suppose that the directions $\boldsymbol{\xi}_j^r$ are all $\boldsymbol{A}$-*conjugate*, meaning that $\boldsymbol{\xi}_j^{r\prime} \boldsymbol{A} \boldsymbol{\xi}_k^r = 0$ for $j \neq k$. Subject to this condition, (9.2.12) becomes

$$C(\boldsymbol{\theta}) = C(\boldsymbol{\theta}^r) + \sum_{j=1}^{p} \left[\lambda_j \boldsymbol{\xi}_j^{r\prime}(\boldsymbol{b} + \boldsymbol{A}\boldsymbol{\theta}^r) + \tfrac{1}{2}\lambda_j^2 \boldsymbol{\xi}_j^{r\prime} \boldsymbol{A} \boldsymbol{\xi}_j^r\right]. \tag{9.2.24}$$

C has been expressed as the sum of p scalar quadratic functions, and minimizing it with respect to $\boldsymbol{\theta}$ is achieved by minimizing each of these functions with respect

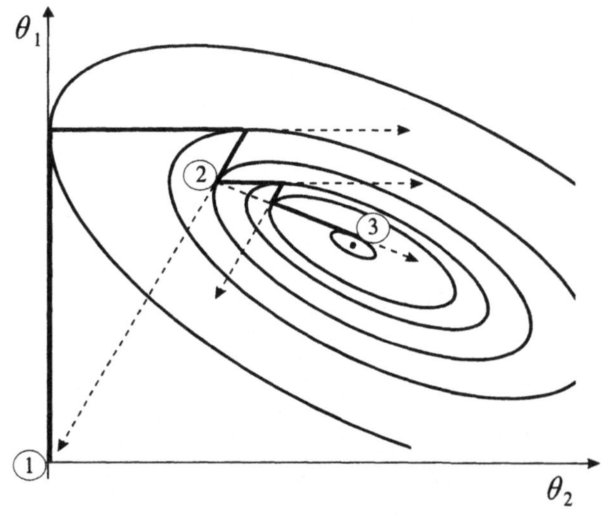

Figure 9.2: Conjugate Directions

to the λ_j. The line search in the jth conjugate direction depends only on $\boldsymbol{\theta}^r$ and $\boldsymbol{\xi}_j^r$, and the solutions

$$\lambda_j^r = -\frac{\boldsymbol{\xi}_j^{r\prime}(\boldsymbol{b} + \boldsymbol{A}\boldsymbol{\theta}^r)}{\boldsymbol{\xi}_j^{r\prime}\boldsymbol{A}\boldsymbol{\xi}_j^r} \tag{9.2.25}$$

are independent of the order in which the searches are conducted. Substituting these solutions back into (9.2.24) and simplifying shows that $\boldsymbol{\theta} = -\boldsymbol{A}^{-1}\boldsymbol{b}$ is indeed the solution to this minimization problem.

It remains to show that the directions of total progress generated by the algorithm are $\boldsymbol{A}$-conjugate.

Theorem 9.2.3 $(\boldsymbol{\theta}_p^r - \boldsymbol{\theta}^r)'\boldsymbol{A}(\boldsymbol{\theta}_p^j - \boldsymbol{\theta}^j) = 0$ for $j = 1, \ldots, r-1$ and $r = 2, \ldots, p$. □

See §9.5 for the proof. Note that after p iterations, all of the initially specified directions have been replaced by directions of total progress, and the direction set is $\boldsymbol{A}$-conjugate. Thus, at step $p+1$ the algorithm simply solves the problem of minimizing (9.2.24), and returns the minimum exactly.

Figure 9.2 shows the contour map of a function in $\mathbb{R}^2$. The function contours are roughly elliptical, so that the function is well approximated by a quadratic. The path traced out by Powell's algorithm is shown as the heavy line, with the direction vectors broken lines. The line searches locate the points of tangency of the search vectors with the contours of the criterion function. The initial point is the origin (point 1 on the diagram) and the initial directions are the axial directions, first the θ_1 direction, then the θ_2 direction. The first iteration takes us to point

2, the second to point 3. Note how the search virtually locates the minimum in two iterations, and had the function been exactly quadratic, the final direction would have passed exactly through the minimum. It can be also be appreciated, by tracing out a couple of steps with ruler and pencil, how much less efficient the axial search would be. With a quadratic function whose contours are not parallel to the axes (corresponding to $\boldsymbol{A}$ being non-diagonal) convergence could be extremely slow. The $\boldsymbol{A}$-conjugacy property means merely that the directions are aligned with the contours, and it is this feature that the directions of total progress exhibit.

9.2.5 Practical Implementation

Methods such as these are widely implemented in computer software for econometric research. The user may encounter them both built into purpose-built estimation packages such as TSP, RATS, Eviews, PC-Give, Microfit and others, and also as components of specialized programming languages such as GAUSS and Ox. In the former case their operation is often transparent to the user, at least on a fast computer where the time taken for the search is not appreciable. In the latter case, the user will have to supply the program with a procedure to evaluate the criterion function at any given point of the parameter space, and optionally, its first and even second partial derivatives as well. In all but very simple problems the effort required to evaluate the derivatives analytically and code the formulae would be disproportionate, and it is usually quite satisfactory to have the computer approximate these by finite differences.

Consider the partial derivative of $C(\boldsymbol{\theta})$ with respect to θ_i, where $\boldsymbol{\theta}$ is $p \times 1$. Letting $\boldsymbol{e}_i$ be the p-vector that has a 1 in the ith position and zeros elsewhere, and choosing a suitably small scalar h, the forward difference approximation at the point $\boldsymbol{\theta}$ is obtained as

$$\frac{\partial C(\boldsymbol{\theta})}{\partial \theta_i} \approx \frac{C(\boldsymbol{\theta} + \boldsymbol{e}_i h) - C(\boldsymbol{\theta})}{h} \qquad i = 1, \dots, p \tag{9.2.26}$$

requiring $p+1$ evaluations of the function C in total. For greater accuracy, though at greater computational cost requiring $2p$ function evaluations, one may also use the central difference approximation,

$$\frac{\partial C(\boldsymbol{\theta})}{\partial \theta_i} \approx \frac{C(\boldsymbol{\theta} + \boldsymbol{e}_i h/2) - C(\boldsymbol{\theta} - \boldsymbol{e}_i h/2)}{h} \qquad i = 1, \dots, p. \tag{9.2.27}$$

Second derivatives can be obtained similarly, and generalizing the forward difference method gives

$$\frac{\partial^2 C(\boldsymbol{\theta})}{\partial \theta_i \partial \theta_j} \approx \frac{C(\boldsymbol{\theta} + \boldsymbol{e}_i h + \boldsymbol{e}_j h) - C(\boldsymbol{\theta} + \boldsymbol{e}_i h) - C(\boldsymbol{\theta} + \boldsymbol{e}_j h) + C(\boldsymbol{\theta})}{h^2} \tag{9.2.28}$$

for $i, j = 1, \dots, p$. Even without central differencing, computing the Hessian matrix of the criterion function calls for $p(p+1)/2$ additional function evaluations (not counting the ones needed to compute the gradient) and optimization methods such as Newton Raphson, are therefore computationally rather expensive.

Even with the benefit of state-of-the-art methods, numerical optimization has not yet been relegated to a purely automated procedure. Human intervention is sometimes required, if the search fails to converge or converges to the wrong place. Here are some of the things that can go wrong.

The matrices defining the search metric, either $\boldsymbol{Q}_r$ in Newton–Raphson, $\boldsymbol{B}_r$ in the QN procedures, or the matrix Ξ^r of conjugate directions in Powell's method, can tend to indefiniteness or singularity as the iterations proceed. Matrix inversions may fail, and even when the method does not explicitly perform inversions, a singular metric means that the search becomes trapped in a lower-dimensioned subspace of the parameter space, from which it cannot escape unaided. It is therefore necessary to monitor the condition of these matrices at each step. As noted, a good measure of condition is the ratio of the largest to the smallest eigenvalues, which should not be too large. (The eigenvalues must be positive to have the matrix positive definite.) If necessary, corrections can be made, such as adding a diagonal matrix similarly to (9.2.13), or diagonalizing the matrix and directly augmenting eigenvalues that are becoming too small. In variable metric methods one can always reset to the initial matrix $\boldsymbol{I}_p$, and so re-start the search with a steepest-descent step. All implementations employ some method such as these for recovering from a breakdown of the algorithm, but experience suggests that they cannot always prevent convergence failure. This is especially true when the function is very flat in certain directions, or otherwise not well conditioned.

The choice of starting point can be critical, not only to avoid the sort of problems just described but to avoid false minima. All search algorithms converge at best to the nearest local minimum, which is not always the global minimum of the function. Ideally (though this rule is probably observed most often in the breach) one should repeat every search from a number of different starting points. This can reveal that the global minimum has not been attained, but unfortunately, nothing but an exhaustive mapping of the parameter space can confirm the global minimum.

Rounding and approximation error can also degrade the performance of an algorithm, and here differences of scale can be critical. The determinant of a poorly conditioned matrix is the small difference of two large numbers, and rounding can make such calculations inaccurate. The accuracy of finite-difference approximations to derivatives is also sensitive to large differences in scale. The elements of $\boldsymbol{\theta}$ should ideally be of similar orders of magnitude, and in most cases this is easy to ensure by choosing units of measurement appropriately. Re-scaling the data should always be considered if failure of convergence is experienced.

9.3 Asymptotic Properties

9.3.1 Existence of OEs

A fundamental collection of results show that, subject to various regularity conditions that it is our task to establish in particular cases, OEs satisfy the usual properties demanded of econometric estimators. The first and most fundamental relates to existence. That there could be a problem with this may sound surprising, but the issue is, simply, does the estimator exist *as a random variable* (a measurable function of the data)? This is just a matter of validating the application of probabilistic methods to the estimation problem. This question usually has a straightforward answer when the estimator is obtained from the data by an explicit formula (like OLS) but OEs are defined implicitly, by a property, and a problem cannot be ruled out without specifying something about the model.

Probably the seminal paper on the asymptotic analysis of OEs is Jennrich (1969). Jennrich's paper gives a simple sufficient existence condition, of which the following slightly more general formulation is due to Gallant and White (1988):

Lemma 9.3.1 Let $(\Omega, \mathcal{F})$ be a measurable space, and Θ a compact (closed and bounded) subset of $\mathbb{R}^p$. Let C: $\Omega \times \Theta \mapsto \mathbb{R}$ be a function, such that $C(\cdot, \boldsymbol{\theta})$ is $\mathcal{F}/\mathcal{B}$ measurable for every $\boldsymbol{\theta} \in \Theta$ and $C(\omega, \cdot)$ is continuous on Θ for every $\omega \in F$, for some $F \in \mathcal{F}$. Then there exists a $\mathcal{F}/\mathcal{B}^p$ measurable function $\hat{\boldsymbol{\theta}} : \Omega \mapsto \Theta$ such that for all $\omega \in F$,

$$C(\omega, \hat{\boldsymbol{\theta}}(\omega)) = \inf_{\boldsymbol{\theta} \in \Theta} C(\omega, \boldsymbol{\theta}). \quad \square \tag{9.3.1}$$

The concepts relating to measurability that appear in this lemma are explained in Appendix B, but in any case will not be required explicitly in what follows. The proof is a simple exercise in measure theory, and can be found in the cited references. The basic ideas are straightforward. Think of ω as an idealised representation of the data set. Measurability of $C(\cdot, \boldsymbol{\theta})$ means that this can be treated as a random variable when the data are random variables, having a well-defined distribution. Since C is an explicit function this condition ought to be directly checkable, and is in any case mild. The set F can be chosen freely, but would in most cases be Ω itself. The important conditions here are continuity of $C(\omega, \cdot)$ as a function of $\boldsymbol{\theta}$ for given data and compactness of the parameter space.

Continuity is a mild restriction, implied by the differentiability generally needed to derive a distribution for $\hat{\boldsymbol{\theta}}$ (see §9.3.4). However, compactness of Θ is a trickier matter. Boundedness is intuitively an innocuous requirement, since arbitrarily large parameter values are unreasonable, but there are often particular finite parameter values that are also regarded as unacceptable. For example, they might give a rise to a singular matrix when that matrix has to be inverted to solve the model, or imply nonstationary behaviour when stationarity has been assumed to construct the estimator. Usually, the implication is that C could not be evaluated – and hence would not be continuous – at these points, and they must be ruled out *a priori*. However, it is not enough to merely exclude them from Θ, if as a result this set does not contain all its closure points. For example: Θ cannot be specified to be an open interval (a, b), on the grounds that points $\theta \leq a$ and $\theta \geq b$ are to be excluded *a priori*. The problem is that the minimum of a function on a set may not exist *as a member of the set*, unless the set is closed. For full rigour, to exclude a and b from Θ requires specifying a closed interval $[a + \varepsilon, b - \varepsilon]$, for some suitably small $\varepsilon > 0$.

Fortunately, this slightly artificial aspect of the theory rarely intrudes. The lemma says that results not predicted by the theory can arise if its conditions are not met, but it does not say that they *will* arise. In practice, estimation is almost always successfully performed by unconstrained optimization of the criterion. Furthermore, the asymptotic analysis is only concerned with the behaviour of the estimator on a small open neighbourhood of the true point $\boldsymbol{\theta}_0$. If it is possible to construct a closed set Θ within such a neighbourhood, of which $\boldsymbol{\theta}_0$ is itself an interior point, all the asymptotic arguments go through if we are willing to maintain the fiction that $\hat{\boldsymbol{\theta}}$ is defined as the minimum of C on Θ so defined. Viewing the matter from this angle also tells us that the asymptotic distribution theory will fail only when $\boldsymbol{\theta}_0$ lies arbitrarily close to a problematic parameter point.

9.3.2 Consistency

To analyse the consistency question, some new convergence concepts need to be defined. Let $\{X_n(\boldsymbol{\theta}), n = 1, 2, \dots\}$ be a random sequence whose members are functions of parameters $\boldsymbol{\theta}$, on a domain Θ.

Definition 9.3.1 If $X_n(\boldsymbol{\theta}) \xrightarrow{\text{pr}} X(\boldsymbol{\theta})$ for every $\boldsymbol{\theta} \in \Theta$, X_n is said to converge in probability to X *pointwise* on Θ. □

Definition 9.3.2 If $\sup_{\boldsymbol{\theta}\in\Theta} |X_n(\boldsymbol{\theta}) - X(\boldsymbol{\theta})| \xrightarrow{\text{pr}} 0$, X_n is said to converge in probability to X *uniformly* on Θ. □

This distinction between modes of convergence is technical, and it is only in a class of pathological cases that uniform convergence is not implied by pointwise convergence. See Amemiya (1985) and Davidson (1994a) for details and examples.

Theorem 9.3.1 If

(a) Θ is compact

(b) $C_n(\boldsymbol{\theta}) \xrightarrow{\text{pr}} \bar{C}(\boldsymbol{\theta})$ (a non-stochastic function of $\boldsymbol{\theta}$) uniformly in Θ

(c) $\boldsymbol{\theta}_0 \in \text{int}(\Theta)$ is the unique minimum of $\bar{C}(\boldsymbol{\theta})$[9]

then $\text{plim}\, \hat{\boldsymbol{\theta}}_n = \boldsymbol{\theta}_0$. □

See §9.5 for the proof, which is adapted from Amemiya (1985). Condition (a) has already been discussed. Condition (c) is called the identification condition, ensuring that the estimation problem is properly specified, and is discussed in §9.3.3. If (c) is satisfied for a given vector $\boldsymbol{\theta}_0$, this defines the probability limit of the estimator by construction. This could be a 'true value' in the sense of representing some interpretable parameters of an economic model, but could also merely represent the best parametric approximation to some unspecified model. See for example §1.4.1 for an application of this sort, and also §10.5 for a fuller analysis.

[9] See §3.4 for the definition of int(·) and discussion of this restriction.

The role of condition (b), as noted, is to rule out certain pathological conditions that frustrate the proof. Meeting it does not normally present a problem in practice, once Θ is defined appropriately. It can also be stated in the form

$$\sup_{\theta\in\Theta}\left|C_n(\boldsymbol{\theta}) - \bar{C}(\boldsymbol{\theta})\right| \xrightarrow{\text{pr}} 0. \tag{9.3.2}$$

The problem of verifying this condition has been investigated by a number of authors, see Pötscher and Prucha (1989), Andrews (1987, 1992), Newey (1991) and also Davidson (1994a) Chapter 21, for a survey. It depends essentially on the vectors $\boldsymbol{\psi}_t(\boldsymbol{\theta})$ in (9.1.4), for if their average converges uniformly, this property will carry over to C_n by Slutsky's Theorem, given that $\phi(\cdot)$ is continuous. A sufficient condition on the sequences $\{\psi_{it}(\boldsymbol{\theta}),\ t = 1, 2, 3, \ldots\}$ for $i = 1, \ldots, r$ is *stochastic uniform equicontinuity*. Think of this as requiring each $\psi_{it}(\boldsymbol{\theta})$ to be uniformly continuous, not merely for every finite t, but also in the limit.

A little care is needed here with the term 'uniform'. In previous applications it has referred to uniformity over all t in a time series (as in uniform boundedness of moments) and uniformity over all $\boldsymbol{\theta} \in \Theta$ (as in uniform convergence of C_n) In the present context, *both* notions of uniformity are being invoked. This makes for terminological trouble, and the prefix 'equi-' is therefore used to indicate the uniformity over t. We forego the technical definition, but the following result employs a neat sufficient condition due to Andrews (1987):

Theorem 9.3.2 Let C_n have the form in (9.1.4) with $\phi(\cdot)$ continuous. Condition (9.3.2) holds if

(a) $n^{-1}\sum_{t=1}^{n} \boldsymbol{\psi}_t(\boldsymbol{\theta}) \xrightarrow{\text{pr}} \bar{\boldsymbol{\psi}}(\boldsymbol{\theta})$, pointwise on Θ, where $\bar{C}(\boldsymbol{\theta}) = \phi(\bar{\boldsymbol{\psi}}(\boldsymbol{\theta}))$, and

(b) for $i = 1, \ldots, r$, and every $\boldsymbol{\theta}_1, \boldsymbol{\theta}_2 \in \Theta$ with $\|\boldsymbol{\theta}_1 - \boldsymbol{\theta}_2\| < \varepsilon$,

$$|\psi_{it}(\boldsymbol{\theta}_1) - \psi_{it}(\boldsymbol{\theta}_2)| < B_{it}h(\varepsilon) \tag{9.3.3}$$

for all t with probability 1, where $B_{it} = O_p(1)$ and $h(\cdot)$ is a nonnegative function with $h(\varepsilon) \to h(0) = 0$ as $\varepsilon \to 0$. □

See §9.5 for the proof. It is the presence of the factor B_{it} that changes the condition from equicontinuity to stochastic equicontinuity. If B_{it} were replaced by 1 the condition in (9.3.3) is sure to be violated for some t unless the ψ_{it} are bounded almost surely, and the condition would become impossibly strong. A suitable choice of B_{it} picks up the random variations in scale, for example $B_{it} = |\psi_{it}(\boldsymbol{\theta}_c)|$ where $\boldsymbol{\theta}_c$ is some fixed value from the parameter space, but any random variable satisfying the conditions would serve.

Theorem 9.3.1 makes no mention of the derivatives $\boldsymbol{q}_n$ and $\boldsymbol{Q}_n$, and differentiability of C_n is not necessary for consistency. If the derivatives do exist however, necessary conditions for condition (c) of the theorem to hold can be stated.

Assumption 9.3.1 C_n is twice continuously differentiable with respect to $\boldsymbol{\theta}$, at all interior points of Θ, with probability 1. The expectations $E(C_n)$, $E(\boldsymbol{q}_n)$, and $E(\boldsymbol{Q}_n)$ exist, with $E(C_n) \to \bar{C}$, $E(\boldsymbol{q}_n) \to \bar{\boldsymbol{q}}$ and $E(\boldsymbol{Q}_n) \to \bar{\boldsymbol{Q}}$, uniformly in Θ. □

Theorem 9.3.3 Let Assumption 9.3.1 hold, and let $\boldsymbol{\theta}_0 \in \text{int}(\Theta)$. If $\boldsymbol{\theta}_0$ is the unique minimum of $\bar{C}$ then $\bar{\boldsymbol{q}}(\boldsymbol{\theta}_0) = \mathbf{0}$ and $\bar{\boldsymbol{Q}}(\boldsymbol{\theta}_0)$ is positive definite.

Proof If $\boldsymbol{\theta}$ is an interior point of Θ,

$$\nabla E[C_n(\boldsymbol{\theta})] = E[\boldsymbol{q}_n(\boldsymbol{\theta})] \tag{9.3.4}$$

$$\nabla^2 E[C_n(\boldsymbol{\theta})] = E[\boldsymbol{Q}_n(\boldsymbol{\theta})] \tag{9.3.5}$$

by an application of Theorem B.4.1. Therefore, by the standard result of multivariate calculus (see e.g. Intriligator 1971 Chapter 3.1), $E(\boldsymbol{q}_n) = \mathbf{0}$ and $E(\boldsymbol{Q}_n)$ positive definite are necessary and sufficient conditions for a unique local minimum of $E(C_n)$. The result follows on letting n tend to ∞. ∎

If the existence of multiple local minima could be ruled out, the conditions of Theorem 9.3.3 would be both necessary and sufficient for condition (c) of Theorem 9.3.1, since the positive definiteness ensures local uniqueness of the minimum. However, this is possible only in special cases, as when C_n is quadratic.

9.3.3 Identification

It is condition (c) of Theorem 9.3.1 that ensures the estimation problem is properly formulated. In other words, the question being posed in this estimation exercise is capable of being answered with reference to the data, and the chosen criterion function is suited to its purpose. Whether these conditions hold is what is broadly referred to as the identification problem, although be careful to note that this term has a particular meaning when the criterion in question is the likelihood function. This aspect is taken up in §11.3.2.

The basic requirement for a consistent estimator is that the 'true structure' can be distinguished from alternative possibilities, given sufficient data. The concept of *observational equivalence* defines the circumstances in which this requirement fails.

Definition 9.3.3 Structures $\boldsymbol{\theta}_1$ and $\boldsymbol{\theta}_2$ are said to be observationally equivalent with respect to C_n if for every $\varepsilon > 0$ there exists $n_\varepsilon \geq 1$ such that for all $n \geq n_\varepsilon$,

$$P(|C_n(\boldsymbol{\theta}_1) - C_n(\boldsymbol{\theta}_2)| < \varepsilon) > 1 - \varepsilon. \quad \square \tag{9.3.6}$$

Thus, the criterion changes by only an arbitrarily small amount between points $\boldsymbol{\theta}_1$ and $\boldsymbol{\theta}_2$ of the parameter space, with probability arbitrarily close to 1. In almost every sample of size exceeding n_ε, it is not possible to distinguish between the two structures using C_n. Observational equivalence needs to be defined in this asymptotic sense because it is possible to construct examples in which (9.3.6) is not true for some finite n while holding in the limit. Consider as a slightly trivial example the sum of squares criterion $C_n(\boldsymbol{\theta}) = n^{-1}\sum_{t=1}^{n} a_t u_t^2$ where $a_1, \dots, a_n$ are nonnegative constant weights. If all but a finite number of the weights are set to 0 as $n \to \infty$, $C_n(\boldsymbol{\theta}) \to 0$ at all points of the parameter space.

Definition 9.3.4 The true structure $\boldsymbol{\theta}_0$ is said to be globally (locally) identified by C_n if no other point in Θ (in an open neighbourhood of $\boldsymbol{\theta}_0$) is observationally equivalent to $\boldsymbol{\theta}_0$ with respect to C_n. □

Identification by C_n is equivalent to condition (c) of Theorem 9.3.1, in the following sense:

Theorem 9.3.4 Let $C_n(\boldsymbol{\theta}) \stackrel{\text{pr}}{\to} \bar{C}(\boldsymbol{\theta})$ uniformly in Θ and let $\boldsymbol{\theta}_0$ be a global (local) minimum of $\bar{C}(\boldsymbol{\theta})$. The minimum is unique (unique in an open neighbourhood of $\boldsymbol{\theta}_0$) if and only if $\boldsymbol{\theta}_0$ is asymptotically globally (locally) identified by C_n. □

See §9.5 for the proof.

The distinction between local and global identification is best explained by means of examples. The following are again rather trivial, but it is easy to see what is going on. First consider the regression model

$$y_t = \alpha + (\beta_1 + \beta_2)x_t + u_t \tag{9.3.7}$$

and let the criterion function be

$$C_n(\alpha, \beta_1, \beta_2) = \frac{1}{n}\sum_{t=1}^{n}(y_t - \alpha - \beta_1 x_t - \beta_2 x_t)^2. \tag{9.3.8}$$

Think of this as an extreme case of multicollinearity, in which the same regressor enters twice. It is obvious that β_1 and β_2 are not locally identified. The failure of the positive definiteness condition of Theorem 9.3.3 is something the reader can easily verify.

Second, consider

$$y_t = \alpha + \beta^2 x_t + u_t \tag{9.3.9}$$

The criterion function $C_n(\alpha, \beta) = n^{-1}\sum_{t=1}^{n}(y_t - \alpha - \beta^2 x_t)^2$ has two well-defined minima corresponding to β and $-\beta$, and the positive definiteness condition is satisfied at both points. This is a case of local identification, but global underidentification.

While there is no virtue in the local identification condition for its own sake, this is the condition that can be verified relatively easily, while checking global identification is usually more difficult. The two concepts coincide only where C_n is quadratic in $\boldsymbol{\theta}$, so that any minimum is known to be unique. OLS is the familiar case.

A fundamental theorem on local identification was given by Rothenberg (1971). A *regular point* of a matrix function $\boldsymbol{A}(\boldsymbol{\theta})$ is a point $\boldsymbol{\theta}_0$ (say) such that $\boldsymbol{A}(\boldsymbol{\theta})$ has constant rank in an open neighbourhood of $\boldsymbol{\theta}_0$. In particular, if $|\boldsymbol{A}(\boldsymbol{\theta}_0)| = 0$ there exists $\delta > 0$ such that $|\boldsymbol{A}(\boldsymbol{\theta}_0 + \delta \boldsymbol{z})| = 0$ for any $\boldsymbol{z} \neq \boldsymbol{0}$.

Theorem 9.3.5 Let Assumption 9.3.1 hold, and let $\boldsymbol{\theta}_0$ be a continuity point and a regular point of $\boldsymbol{A}_n(\boldsymbol{\theta}) = nE[\boldsymbol{q}_n(\boldsymbol{\theta})\boldsymbol{q}_n(\boldsymbol{\theta})']$. $\boldsymbol{A}_n(\boldsymbol{\theta}_0)$ is singular if and only if there exists in every open neighbourhood $\mathcal{N}(\boldsymbol{\theta}_0)$ a point $\boldsymbol{\theta} \in \mathcal{N}(\boldsymbol{\theta}_0) - \{\boldsymbol{\theta}_0\}$ such that

$$P\{C_n(\boldsymbol{\theta}) = C_n(\boldsymbol{\theta}_0)\} = 1. \quad \square \tag{9.3.10}$$

See §9.5 for the proof. The result is given by Rothenberg specifically for the log-likelihood function (Chapter 11) but it holds generally for optimization criteria. Its significance is to focus attention on the matrix $\boldsymbol{A}_n(\boldsymbol{\theta}_0)$, and in particular its limit as $n \to \infty$, to be denoted $\boldsymbol{A}_0$ in what follows. While $\boldsymbol{q}_n(\boldsymbol{\theta}_0) \xrightarrow{\text{pr}} \boldsymbol{0}$ under the assumption of consistency, $\sqrt{n}\boldsymbol{q}_n(\boldsymbol{\theta}_0)$ will (under further suitable assumptions) converge to a limit in distribution, having a mean of zero by (9.3.4), and $\boldsymbol{A}_0$ is its covariance matrix. In an identified model both this matrix and (in view of Theorem 9.3.3) the matrix $\bar{\boldsymbol{Q}}_0 = \bar{\boldsymbol{Q}}(\boldsymbol{\theta}_0)$ must have full rank.

9.3.4 Asymptotic Normality

Approximate confidence intervals and test statistics based on OEs depend on the assumption that a central limit theorem can be invoked. In particular, the form of the criterion function, juxtaposed with assumptions on the data series, must be such as to lead to the result

$$\sqrt{n}\boldsymbol{q}_{n0} \underset{\text{asy}}{\sim} \mathrm{N}(\boldsymbol{0}, \boldsymbol{A}_0) \tag{9.3.11}$$

where $\boldsymbol{q}_{n0} = \boldsymbol{q}_n(\boldsymbol{\theta}_0)$. To obtain this central limit theorem the vector in question must have the generic form

$$\sqrt{n}\boldsymbol{q}_{n0} = \boldsymbol{J}_n \frac{1}{\sqrt{n}} \sum_{t=1}^{n} \boldsymbol{v}_t \tag{9.3.12}$$

where $\boldsymbol{J}_n$ $(p \times q)$ is a random matrix converging in probability to a finite limit $\bar{\boldsymbol{J}}$ (say), with $q \geq p$, and $\boldsymbol{v}_t$ $(q \times 1)$ is a zero-mean vector. Invoking the Cramér–Wold device, the conditions specified in Theorem 6.2.3 or Theorem 6.4.5 would be required to hold for the sequences $x_t = \boldsymbol{\lambda}'\boldsymbol{v}_t$, for arbitrary vectors $\boldsymbol{\lambda}$.

Invoking the generic formula for the criterion function in (9.1.4), one possibility giving rise to (9.3.12) is that $\boldsymbol{v}_t = \boldsymbol{\nabla}\psi_t$, with $r = 1$, $q = p$, and $\boldsymbol{J}_n = \phi'\boldsymbol{I}_p$. The case of least squares, where $\psi_t = u_t^2$, is examined in detail in §10.2.2. Care is needed in generalizing this example, however, since $\boldsymbol{v}_t$ need not represent the derivatives of $\boldsymbol{\psi}_t$ but (with $r > 1$) could just as well be $\boldsymbol{\psi}_t$ itself. An example of this type is the method of moments (9.1.6) where $q = r = M$, $\boldsymbol{J}_n = (\boldsymbol{X}'\boldsymbol{Z}/n)(\boldsymbol{Z}'\boldsymbol{Z}/n)^{-1}$, and $\boldsymbol{v}_t = \boldsymbol{z}_t u_t$. Thus, the condition in (9.3.11) can be fulfilled in a variety of ways, depending on the structure of the problem. At this level of generality, it is merely asserted as a requirement. The main task of this section is to make the link between (9.3.11) and the asymptotic distribution of the estimator itself.

The essential step is a quadratic approximation argument based on an application of the mean value theorem, that is, a Taylor's expansion to first order. Writing $\bar{\boldsymbol{Q}}_0 = \bar{\boldsymbol{Q}}(\boldsymbol{\theta}_0)$, the result is as follows:

Theorem 9.3.6 If (9.3.11) holds, and

$$\boldsymbol{Q}_n(\boldsymbol{\theta}) \xrightarrow{\text{pr}} \bar{\boldsymbol{Q}}(\boldsymbol{\theta}) \tag{9.3.13}$$

uniformly in a neighbourhood of $\boldsymbol{\theta}_0$, then

$$\sqrt{n}(\hat{\boldsymbol{\theta}}_n - \boldsymbol{\theta}_0) \underset{\text{asy}}{\sim} -\bar{\boldsymbol{Q}}_0^{-1}\sqrt{n}\boldsymbol{q}_{n0} \xrightarrow{\text{D}} N(\boldsymbol{0}, \boldsymbol{V}_0) \tag{9.3.14}$$

where $\boldsymbol{V}_0 = \bar{\boldsymbol{Q}}_0^{-1}\boldsymbol{A}_0\bar{\boldsymbol{Q}}_0^{-1}$. □

Note how Theorem 9.3.3 ensures the existence of $\boldsymbol{V}_0$ under consistency. An important technical lemma (for example, see Davidson 1994a, Theorem 21.6) needed to prove Theorem 9.3.6 is worth noting here, since it has many applications.

Lemma 9.3.2 If $Y_n(\boldsymbol{\theta})$ is a stochastic function of $\boldsymbol{\theta}$, $Y_n(\boldsymbol{\theta}) \xrightarrow{\text{pr}} Y(\boldsymbol{\theta})$ uniformly in an open neighbourhood of $\boldsymbol{\theta}_0$, and $\operatorname{plim}\hat{\boldsymbol{\theta}}_n = \boldsymbol{\theta}_0$, then $\operatorname{plim} Y_n(\hat{\boldsymbol{\theta}}_n) = Y(\boldsymbol{\theta}_0)$. □

This can be thought of as an extension of Slutsky's Theorem (Theorem 3.1.1). In this case there is a sequence of stochastic functions (i.e., functions depending on random variables other than $\hat{\boldsymbol{\theta}}_n$) converging to a limit, whereas in Theorem 3.1.1 there is a single nonstochastic function.

Proof of Theorem 9.3.6 Letting $q_{ni}(\boldsymbol{\theta})$ denote the ith element of $\boldsymbol{q}_n(\boldsymbol{\theta})$, and noting that $q_{ni}(\hat{\boldsymbol{\theta}}_n) = 0$ identically by definition of $\hat{\boldsymbol{\theta}}_n$, the mean value theorem yields

$$q_{ni}(\boldsymbol{\theta}_0) + \left(\boldsymbol{\nabla} q_{ni}|_{\boldsymbol{\theta}=\boldsymbol{\theta}^*_{ni}}\right)'(\hat{\boldsymbol{\theta}}_n - \boldsymbol{\theta}_0) = 0 \quad i = 1, \ldots, p \tag{9.3.15}$$

where $\boldsymbol{\theta}^*_{ni} = \boldsymbol{\theta}_0 + \lambda_i(\hat{\boldsymbol{\theta}}_n - \boldsymbol{\theta}_0)$ for $0 \le \lambda_i \le 1$. Stacking these equations up to form a column vector, write them as

$$\boldsymbol{q}_n(\boldsymbol{\theta}_0) + \boldsymbol{Q}^*_n(\hat{\boldsymbol{\theta}}_n - \boldsymbol{\theta}_0) = \boldsymbol{0} \ (p \times 1) \tag{9.3.16}$$

where $\boldsymbol{Q}^*_n$ denotes $\boldsymbol{Q}_n$ with row i evaluated at the point $\boldsymbol{\theta}^*_{ni}$ for each i.[10]

After multiplying by $\sqrt{n}$, equation (9.3.16) can be rearranged as

$$\sqrt{n}(\hat{\boldsymbol{\theta}}_n - \boldsymbol{\theta}_0) = -(\boldsymbol{Q}^*_n)^{-1}\sqrt{n}\boldsymbol{q}_{n0}. \tag{9.3.17}$$

Since $\hat{\boldsymbol{\theta}}_n \xrightarrow{\text{pr}} \boldsymbol{\theta}_0$, $\boldsymbol{\theta}^*_{ni} \xrightarrow{\text{pr}} \boldsymbol{\theta}_0$ for each i. It follows from (9.3.13) and Lemma 9.3.2 that

$$\boldsymbol{Q}^*_n \xrightarrow{\text{pr}} \bar{\boldsymbol{Q}}(\boldsymbol{\theta}_0). \tag{9.3.18}$$

The theorem then follows from Cramér's Theorem, noting that $\bar{\boldsymbol{Q}}$ is symmetric. ■

Assuming the convergence in (9.3.13) begs a very important question, which can only be answered in the context of the particular model, and particular criterion function, to which the result is being applied. Typically it is justified by the application of a uniform law of large numbers, since $\boldsymbol{Q}_n$ turns out to consist of a sum of n functions of $\boldsymbol{\theta}$. This is true of all the cases to be considered in the sequel.

---

[10] Be careful to note that these points are not generally the same, so it would be incorrect to write, say, $\boldsymbol{Q}_n(\boldsymbol{\theta}^*)$ for this matrix.

However, it is not usually possible to appeal to the martingale difference property, or uncorrelatedness, in considering these terms. Either they are independent (in the random sampling framework) or some limited-dependence assumption such as NED-on-mixing is needed, as discussed in §6.4. The dependence restrictions must apply to the suprema of $|q_{ijn}(\boldsymbol{\theta}) - \bar{q}_{ij}(\boldsymbol{\theta})|$ on a subset of the parameter space, as specified in Lemma 9.3.2, for each element q_{ijn} of $\boldsymbol{Q}_n$. There is no problem about this if the variables on which $\boldsymbol{Q}_n$ depends are mixing, since functions of mixing processes are mixing (Theorem 6.4.1) but reliance on the NED property could pose problems, since inheritance of the property by functions has to be shown for each case.

An interesting and useful fact is that, in the leading cases of OEs to be considered, the relation

$$\boldsymbol{A}_0 = c^2 \bar{\boldsymbol{Q}}_0 \tag{9.3.19}$$

holds for a scalar constant $c > 0$. For example, in least squares and the method of moments (see §10.3) $c = \sigma$, and in maximum likelihood (see §11.3) $c = 1$, assuming in both cases that the models are correctly specified. In this case,

$$\boldsymbol{V}_0 = c^2 \bar{\boldsymbol{Q}}_0^{-1}. \tag{9.3.20}$$

This equality is rather mysterious, being a mathematical property of the criterion functions whose justification in the two cases appears quite different. In the least squares and method of moments cases it holds because the criterion is a quadratic function of white noise disturbances. In the maximum likelihood case, it is true because the criterion function is a sum of correctly specified log-densities, independent of the functional form of the densities. With Gaussian disturbances it happens that the two conditions are met simultaneously, because the likelihood and sum of squares functions are closely related (see Chapter 11 for details). No such equivalence holds for the method of moments criterion, which cannot be a log-likelihood function under any distribution.

In likelihood theory, equation (9.3.19) is called the information matrix equality, and following convention we use this term even when the criterion in question is not a log-likelihood. Where it holds, the equality substantially simplifies the computation of variance formulae. One should be cautious about relying on it uncritically, because equation (9.3.19) generally does not hold in cases where the model is misspecified, see §7.3.2 for example. However, this fact also means that it can form the basis for a test of correct specification, see §12.5.4.

9.4 Other Issues

9.4.1 Model Selection

All the usual OEs share the feature that the value of the expected criterion function at the minimum is an indicator of goodness of fit, and smaller therefore means better. This is a property whose validity is almost self-evident in those cases where C_n is a quadratic form in the model residuals. The case of the log-likelihood function is considered in §11.1, and a similar presumption holds. If we were uncertain about the true model specification, but were able to compute $\bar{C}$ itself for any candidate model, we should always want to include any additional parameters that yielded a smaller value of this function at the minimum. On the other hand, the natural criterion of a correct model is that adding parameters does not reduce $\bar{C}$ further, since the true value of these parameters is 0. To find the best model specification, one should therefore include any parameter that reduces $\min \bar{C}$, but delete any parameter when this can be done without increasing $\min \bar{C}$.

In practice $\bar{C}$ is not observed, only the sample criterion C_n, and adding new parameters will invariably reduce C_n whether or not they belong in the model. Thus, in OLS regression it is well known that an extra regressor will always raise R^2, which is merely a monotonic transformation of the sum of squares function, and indeed, the sum of squares can be reduced to 0 by merely including n regressors. In other words, there is a degrees of freedom problem. The same phenomenon will arise in one form or another whichever criterion is adopted. The problem disappears as $n \to \infty$ and C_n converges to $\bar{C}$, but in finite samples the strategy of choosing the model giving the 'smallest minimum' of C_n has to be modified.

A natural approach is to attach a penalty term that increases with the number of fitted parameters, but is of smaller order of magnitude in n than C_n so that its effect disappears in the limit. Consider the problem of choosing amongst a set of M models, indexed by $j = 1, \ldots, M$, where p_j denotes the number of fitted parameters in model j. Let C_{jn} denote the criterion function for model j, and define

$$C^*_{jn} = \min C_{jn} \tag{9.4.1}$$

that is, the minimized criterion (with respect to the p_j included parameters) for model j. Then, consider the model choice strategy of choosing j to minimize the criterion

$$A_{jn} = C^*_{jn} + \frac{p_j r_n}{n} \tag{9.4.2}$$

where r_n is an increasing function of n with the property $r_n \to \infty$ as $n \to \infty$, but $r_n/n \to 0$. The question is, whether this model selection strategy is *consistent*, meaning that when n is large enough, it will always give the same result as choosing j to minimize p_j subject to $\bar{C}^*_j \leq \bar{C}^*_k$ for $k \neq j$.

Let $j = m$ denote the solution to the latter problem, and consider first a case where the jth model is incorrect in the sense that $\bar{C}^*_j > \bar{C}^*_m$. In this case, by assumption,

$$\frac{C^*_{jn} + p_j r_n/n}{C^*_{mn} + p_m r_n/n} \xrightarrow{pr} \frac{\bar{C}^*_j}{\bar{C}^*_m} > 1. \tag{9.4.3}$$

The false model is therefore rejected with probability approaching 1 as $n \to \infty$. On the other hand, suppose $\bar{C}^*_j = \bar{C}^*_m$ but $p_j > p_m$. Note that

$$\frac{C^*_{jn} + p_j r_n/n}{C^*_{mn} + p_m r_n/n} = 1 + \frac{(C^*_{jn} - C^*_{mn}) + (p_j - p_m) r_n/n}{C^*_{mn} + p_m r_n/n}. \tag{9.4.4}$$

While the second term on the right of (9.4.4) is converging in probability to 0, the question of interest is the direction of approach. Suppose that

$$\frac{n}{r_n}(C^*_{jn} - C^*_{mn}) \xrightarrow{\text{pr}} 0 \tag{9.4.5}$$

which is equivalent to

$$\frac{C^*_{jn} + p_j r_n/n}{C^*_{mn} + p_m r_n/n} - 1 = \frac{r_n}{n}\Big(\frac{p_j - p_m}{C^*_{mn} + p_m r_n/n} + o_p(1)\Big). \tag{9.4.6}$$

The probability that the right hand side term in parentheses is positive, so that model m is selected, can be made as large as desired by taking n large enough. It does not matter how small r_n/n has to be to attain this probability, since this ratio is positive for any finite n. In this sense, the selection procedure is consistent.

In practice, the sequence r_n has to be chosen to make sure that the condition in (9.4.5) holds. For illustration consider the regression model

$$\boldsymbol{y} = \boldsymbol{X\beta} + \boldsymbol{Z\gamma} + \boldsymbol{u} \tag{9.4.7}$$

where in model m, $\boldsymbol{\gamma} = \boldsymbol{0}$ and in model j, $\boldsymbol{\gamma} \neq \boldsymbol{0}$. The difference of the two normalized sums of squared residuals, using a 'dot' to denote the restricted case and a 'hat' the unrestricted, is

$$\frac{\dot{\boldsymbol{u}}'\dot{\boldsymbol{u}}}{n} - \frac{\hat{\boldsymbol{u}}'\hat{\boldsymbol{u}}}{n} = \hat{\boldsymbol{\gamma}}'\Big(\frac{\boldsymbol{Z}'\boldsymbol{M}_X\boldsymbol{Z}}{n}\Big)\hat{\boldsymbol{\gamma}} = O_p(n^{-1}) \tag{9.4.8}$$

(compare (2.4.20) and (2.4.23)) where the stochastic order of magnitude follows since $\hat{\boldsymbol{\gamma}} = O_p(n^{-1/2})$ under model m. The same conclusion can be verified in other leading cases, under the usual regularity conditions. In this case, any increasing sequence will satisfy the consistency condition.

Two well-known consistent selection criteria are the Schwarz (1978) Bayesian criterion,[11] and the Hannan–Quinn (1979) criterion. When applied to sum of squares criteria, these have the respective forms

$$\text{SBC} = \ln\Big(\frac{\hat{\boldsymbol{u}}'\hat{\boldsymbol{u}}}{n}\Big) + \frac{p \ln n}{n} \tag{9.4.9}$$

$$\text{HQC} = \ln\Big(\frac{\hat{\boldsymbol{u}}'\hat{\boldsymbol{u}}}{n}\Big) + \frac{2p \ln\ln n}{n} \tag{9.4.10}$$

where in each case $\hat{\boldsymbol{u}}'\hat{\boldsymbol{u}}$ is the minimised sum of squares and p the number of parameters fitted. The criterion functions appear in log form in these formulae since the criteria are derived assuming the disturbances are Gaussian, and these are therefore log-likelihood functions, with signs reversed. The consistency property of the criteria holds since, for any variables x_1 and x_2,

$$\ln(x_1) - \ln(x_2) = \ln(x_1/x_2) \approx \frac{x_1 - x_2}{x_2} \tag{9.4.11}$$

[11] The designation 'Bayesian' is conventional, but the only property of Schwarz's criterion we appeal to here is consistency.

where the approximation is better as x_1 and x_2 are closer together. If the denominator on the right-hand side in (9.4.11) is $O_p(1)$ and not $o_p(1)$, which is the case with the normalized sum of squares criteria, then the difference of the logs is also $O_p(n^{-1})$.

The SBC and HQC illustrate two choices for r_n, the log and the log-log, which are both consistent although the former will tend to favour more parsimoniously specified models than the latter in a finite sample. Not all selection criteria are consistent, and a well-known alternative is the Akaike information criterion (Akaike 1973, 1974) that for sums of squares criteria takes the form

$$\mathrm{AIC} = \ln\left(\frac{\hat{\boldsymbol{u}}'\hat{\boldsymbol{u}}}{n}\right) + \frac{2p}{n}. \tag{9.4.12}$$

Another statistic directly comparable with these is 'R-bar-squared', or

$$\bar{R}^2 = 1 - \frac{\hat{\boldsymbol{u}}'\hat{\boldsymbol{u}}/(n-k)}{(\boldsymbol{y}'\boldsymbol{y} - n\bar{y}^2)/(n-1)}, \tag{9.4.13}$$

which is a natural modification of (1.2.12). A little manipulation can put $1 - \bar{R}^2$ into the form of (9.4.2), where r_n is now a complicated stochastic sequence that, however, does not tend to ∞, so this is also not a consistent criterion. In practice, however, the log and more especially the log-log functions increase very slowly, and all these criteria will often agree with each other in small samples.

These selection criteria are increasingly favoured for decisions such as the choice of lag length, orders of ARMA models, and others on which there is little theoretical basis for a choice. An important feature of the procedures is that there is no need to assume that a special 'true' model was represented in the set of alternatives. However the alternative C_{jn}s are constructed, there must always be one in the set such that $\bar{C}_j$ achieves its minimum with the smallest number of parameters, and this must be the most interesting of the set. This case can be given a special interpretation when the criterion is a log-likelihood function, and this issue is discussed further in §11.3.4, but the consistency criterion applies quite generally.

Perhaps the chief issue to consider here is the respective merits of selection criteria and significance tests on the doubtful parameters, as methods of model choice. With the selection criteria no attempt is made to quantify error probabilities, but against this must be weighed the fact that when a sequence of significance tests is performed, as in the process of choosing between M alternative models, the true significance levels are in any case unknown. See §7.7.2 for further discussion.

9.4.2 Two-step Estimation

In the age of cheap, fast computers, computing the exact optimum of C_n by numerical methods is rarely an insuperable problem, but in earlier days such methods could be difficult and expensive to implement. Even today, there are times when to have an estimation method that does not require iteration could be useful. Numerical optimization requires specialist software that is not installed on every system, whereas most computers have a spreadsheet program installed on them that allows quite sophisticated 'hand calculations', such as linear regressions.

In many cases, *consistent* estimates can be calculated by straightforward methods. The obvious example would be a regression that is subject to nonlinear restrictions on the parameters, of which several examples are studied in Chapter 10. If the restrictions are relaxed the coefficients can be calculated by OLS, but the resulting estimates won't be unique, or as efficient as if the restrictions were imposed.

However, if one step of an appropriate search algorithm to minimize C_n is performed, starting at the consistent point (call this $\boldsymbol{\theta}^1$) then the resulting value, $\boldsymbol{\theta}^2$, is an estimate that is asymptotically equivalent to $\hat{\boldsymbol{\theta}} = \arg\min_{\boldsymbol{\theta}} C_n$. Asymptotically equivalent means that the limiting distribution of $\sqrt{n}(\boldsymbol{\theta}^2 - \boldsymbol{\theta}_0)$ is the same as that of $\sqrt{n}(\hat{\boldsymbol{\theta}} - \boldsymbol{\theta}_0)$. An 'appropriate' search algorithm is one for which the matrix $\boldsymbol{H}_n(\boldsymbol{\theta}^1)$, that which corresponds to $\boldsymbol{H}_r$ in (9.2.8) for $r = 1$, converges in probability to $\bar{\boldsymbol{Q}}_0$. One way this could be achieved is of course to choose $\boldsymbol{H}_n = \boldsymbol{Q}_n$, but simpler formulae may suffice, for example by omitting any terms in $\boldsymbol{Q}_n$ that have zero expectation or otherwise disappear asymptotically. The result, due to Rothenberg and Leenders (1964), is as follows.

Theorem 9.4.1 Let $\boldsymbol{\theta}^1$ be a consistent estimator of $\boldsymbol{\theta}_0$ such that $\sqrt{n}(\boldsymbol{\theta}^1 - \boldsymbol{\theta}_0) = O_p(1)$. If

$$\boldsymbol{\theta}^2 = \boldsymbol{\theta}^1 - \boldsymbol{H}_n(\boldsymbol{\theta}^1)^{-1}\boldsymbol{q}_n(\boldsymbol{\theta}^1) \tag{9.4.14}$$

where $\boldsymbol{H}_n - \boldsymbol{Q}_n \xrightarrow{\text{pr}} 0$ uniformly in an open neighbourhood of $\boldsymbol{\theta}_0$, and both matrices have full rank on the same neighbourhood, then $\sqrt{n}(\boldsymbol{\theta}^2 - \hat{\boldsymbol{\theta}}) = o_p(1)$.

Proof Consider the first iterative step defined by (9.2.8). Apply the mean value theorem to the elements of $\boldsymbol{q}_n$ between $\boldsymbol{\theta}^1$ and $\boldsymbol{\theta}_0$ to obtain

$$\begin{aligned}\boldsymbol{\theta}^2 &= \boldsymbol{\theta}^1 - \boldsymbol{H}_n^{-1}(\boldsymbol{\theta}^1)\boldsymbol{q}_n(\boldsymbol{\theta}^1)\\ &= \boldsymbol{\theta}^1 - \boldsymbol{H}_n^{-1}(\boldsymbol{\theta}^1)[\boldsymbol{q}_{n0} + \boldsymbol{Q}_n^{**}(\boldsymbol{\theta}^1 - \boldsymbol{\theta}_0)].\end{aligned} \tag{9.4.15}$$

where '$**$' denotes that the rows of $\boldsymbol{Q}_n$ are evaluated at points intermediate between $\boldsymbol{\theta}^1$ and $\boldsymbol{\theta}_0$. Subtracting $\hat{\boldsymbol{\theta}}$ from both sides of (9.4.15), weighting by $\sqrt{n}$, and substituting from (9.3.17), yields

$$\begin{aligned}\sqrt{n}(\boldsymbol{\theta}^2 - \hat{\boldsymbol{\theta}}) &= \sqrt{n}(\boldsymbol{\theta}^1 - \boldsymbol{\theta}_0) + (\boldsymbol{Q}_n^*)^{-1}\sqrt{n}\boldsymbol{q}_{n0}\\ &\quad - \boldsymbol{H}_n(\boldsymbol{\theta}^1)^{-1}\sqrt{n}[\boldsymbol{q}_{n0} + \boldsymbol{Q}_n^{**}(\boldsymbol{\theta}^1 - \boldsymbol{\theta}_0)]\\ &= \big(\boldsymbol{H}_n(\boldsymbol{\theta}^1)^{-1} - (\boldsymbol{Q}_n^*)^{-1}\big)\sqrt{n}\boldsymbol{q}_{n0}\\ &\quad + \boldsymbol{H}_n(\boldsymbol{\theta}^1)^{-1}\big(\boldsymbol{H}_n(\boldsymbol{\theta}^1) - \boldsymbol{Q}_n^{**}\big)\sqrt{n}(\boldsymbol{\theta}^1 - \boldsymbol{\theta}_0).\end{aligned} \tag{9.4.16}$$

Consider the two right-hand side terms. Since both $\boldsymbol{\theta}^1$ and $\hat{\boldsymbol{\theta}}$ are consistent, the matrices in parentheses are each tending to 0 in probability, by the assumptions and Lemma 9.3.2. The random variables multiplying them are $O_p(1)$, and it follows that $\sqrt{n}(\boldsymbol{\theta}^2 - \hat{\boldsymbol{\theta}}) \xrightarrow{\text{pr}} 0$. This implies that $\sqrt{n}(\boldsymbol{\theta}^2 - \boldsymbol{\theta}_0)$ and $\sqrt{n}(\hat{\boldsymbol{\theta}} - \boldsymbol{\theta}_0)$ have the same limiting distribution. ∎

Applications of this result are considered in §10.2. Implementation can require just two applications of least squares regression.

9.4.3 Estimation of Covariance Matrices

To implement the theory of §9.3.4, to construct confidence intervals and test hypotheses, requires replacing $\boldsymbol{A}_0$ and $\bar{\boldsymbol{Q}}_0$ with consistent estimates of these matrices. Assumption (9.3.13) in combination with Lemma 9.3.2 ensures that the required estimator of $\bar{\boldsymbol{Q}}_0$ is provided by $\boldsymbol{Q}_n(\hat{\boldsymbol{\theta}})$. This, in turn, can usually be computed to a good approximation using a finite difference formula such as (9.2.28). Indeed, if the Newton–Raphson method is being used to optimize the criterion then this matrix is just a by-product of the iterative process on convergence.

However, estimating $\boldsymbol{A}_0$ represents a new problem to be solved, whether this corresponds to estimating the scalar c in cases where (9.3.19) holds, or to estimating the entire matrix in other cases. By definition,

$$\boldsymbol{A}_0 = \lim_{n\to\infty} nE[\boldsymbol{q}_n(\boldsymbol{\theta}_0)\boldsymbol{q}_n(\boldsymbol{\theta}_0)']. \tag{9.4.17}$$

Since $\boldsymbol{q}_n(\boldsymbol{\theta}_0)$ must have the generic form in (9.3.12), let the assumption in (9.3.11) be replaced by

$$\frac{1}{\sqrt{n}}\sum_{t=1}^{n} \boldsymbol{v}_{t0} \underset{\text{asy}}{\sim} N(\boldsymbol{0}, \boldsymbol{B}_0) \tag{9.4.18}$$

say, where $\boldsymbol{v}_{t0} = \boldsymbol{v}_t(\boldsymbol{\theta}_0)$, and $\boldsymbol{B}_0 = \boldsymbol{B}(\boldsymbol{\theta}_0)$ is a covariance matrix of dimension $q \times q$ such that, applying the Cramér Theorem, $\boldsymbol{A}_0 = \bar{\boldsymbol{J}}\boldsymbol{B}_0\bar{\boldsymbol{J}}'$. In practice $\boldsymbol{v}_{t0}$ must be replaced by $\hat{\boldsymbol{v}}_t = \boldsymbol{v}_t(\hat{\boldsymbol{\theta}})$, and also, in most cases, the derivatives by difference approximations. The matrix $\boldsymbol{B}$ may be written out as a sum of n^2 terms,

$$\begin{aligned}\boldsymbol{B} &= \frac{1}{n}\sum_{t=1}^{n}\sum_{s=1}^{n} E(\boldsymbol{v}_t\boldsymbol{v}_s') \\ &= \frac{1}{n}\sum_{t=1}^{n} E(\boldsymbol{v}_t\boldsymbol{v}_t') + \frac{1}{n}\sum_{t=2}^{n} E(\boldsymbol{v}_t\boldsymbol{v}_{t-1}' + \boldsymbol{v}_{t-1}\boldsymbol{v}_t') \\ &\quad + \frac{1}{n}\sum_{t=3}^{n} E(\boldsymbol{v}_t\boldsymbol{v}_{t-2}' + \boldsymbol{v}_{t-2}\boldsymbol{v}_t') + \cdots + \frac{1}{n}(\boldsymbol{v}_n\boldsymbol{v}_1' + \boldsymbol{v}_1\boldsymbol{v}_n').\end{aligned} \tag{9.4.19}$$

If $\boldsymbol{v}_{t0}$ is a serially uncorrelated sequence (which includes the vector martingale difference and serially independent cases) all except the n terms of this sum in which $t = s$ are zero. In this case $\boldsymbol{B}_0$ may be estimated by its direct sample counterpart

$$\hat{\boldsymbol{B}}_n = \frac{1}{n}\sum_{t=1}^{n} \hat{\boldsymbol{v}}_t\hat{\boldsymbol{v}}_t'. \tag{9.4.20}$$

This orthogonality property holds under model B of §1.3, assuming $\boldsymbol{v}_t$ depends only on the tth observation. It also holds for the correctly specified dynamic linear regression model of §7.1, in which case $\boldsymbol{v}_t = \boldsymbol{x}_t u_t$, and in the correctly specified structural equation estimated by IV (see §8.2) in which case $\boldsymbol{v}_t = \boldsymbol{z}_t u_t$, as shown. It holds too for the case of correctly specified maximum likelihood, see §11.3.2.

More generally, however, particularly in incompletely specified dynamic models, the orthogonality of the terms cannot be assumed. To estimate $\boldsymbol{B}$ in (9.4.19) by its direct sample counterpart obviously won't work. Removing the expectation signs just gives the outer product of the vector in (9.4.18) with itself, which is a random matrix of rank 1 for any sample size, and does not converge in probability.[12] However, note how the assumption $\boldsymbol{B} < \infty$ implies that each of the sequences of covariances $\{E(\boldsymbol{v}_t\boldsymbol{v}_{t-m}'),\ m = 1,2,3,\dots\}$ is summable. In other words, so many of the expectations in (9.4.19) are either zero or arbitrarily close to zero, that the sum of the n^2 terms only grows at the rate n. This suggests $\boldsymbol{B}$ might be estimated by, in effect, deleting all the terms from the sum except when the lag j is suitably small, relative to the sample size. Following Newey and West (1987), consider the general class of estimators

$$\hat{\boldsymbol{B}}_n = \frac{1}{n}\left(\sum_{t=1}^{n}\hat{\boldsymbol{v}}_t\hat{\boldsymbol{v}}_t' + \sum_{j=1}^{n-1} w_{nj}\sum_{t=j+1}^{n}(\hat{\boldsymbol{v}}_t\hat{\boldsymbol{v}}_{t-j}' + \hat{\boldsymbol{v}}_{t-j}\hat{\boldsymbol{v}}_t')\right) \tag{9.4.21}$$

where $w_{nj} = k(j/m_n)$ for some function $k(x)$ that is suitably close to 0 for large values of $|x|$, and m_n, called the *bandwidth*, is a function increasing to infinity with n, although more slowly. Thus, setting $k(x) = 1$ for $|x| \le 1$, and 0 otherwise, has exactly the effect of omitting terms involving lags greater than m_n.

More generally, (9.4.21) defines a *kernel estimator* of $\boldsymbol{B}$, and k is known as a *kernel function.* The particular case described is called the truncated kernel. Here are some of the more popular choices:

1. Bartlett: $k(x) = \begin{cases} 1 - |x|, & |x| \le 1 \\ 0, & \text{otherwise} \end{cases}$

2. Parzen: $k(x) = \begin{cases} 1 - 6x^2 + 6|x|^3, & |x| \le \frac{1}{2} \\ 2(1 - |x|)^3, & \frac{1}{2} \le |x| \le 1 \\ 0, & \text{otherwise} \end{cases}$

3. Tukey-Hanning: $k(x) = \begin{cases} \frac{1}{2}(1 + \cos(\pi x)|), & |x| \le 1 \\ 0, & \text{otherwise} \end{cases}$

4. Quadratic spectral: $k(x) = \dfrac{25}{12\pi^2x^2}\left(\dfrac{\sin(6\pi x/5)}{6\pi x/5} - \cos(6\pi x/5)\right)$

In all these cases, the role of the kernel function is to taper the contribution of the longer lags smoothly to zero, rather than cutting it off abruptly. A difficulty with kernel estimators of $\boldsymbol{B}$ is that, even if consistent, the estimate may not be

[12] Compare §3.5.4.

guaranteed positive semi-definite in finite samples. The four kernels listed all have this property, but the truncated kernel does not, implying that the latter is not a good practical choice.

More formally, consider a class of kernel functions $\mathcal{K}$ as follows:

Assumption 9.4.1 $k \in \mathcal{K}$ if $k(x) = k(-x)$ for $x > 0$, $|k(x)| < 1$, $k(0) = 1$, k is continuous at 0 and all but at most a finite number of other points,

$$\int_{-\infty}^{\infty} |k(x)|dx < \infty \tag{9.4.22}$$

and

$$\int_{-\infty}^{\infty} |\psi(\xi)|\, d\xi < \infty \tag{9.4.23}$$

where ψ is the Fourier transform of k, that is,

$$\psi(\xi) = \int_{-\infty}^{\infty} k(x)e^{i\xi x}dx. \quad \square \tag{9.4.24}$$

The properties specified in Assumption 9.4.1 are mainly self-explanatory, with (9.4.22) ensuring that k gets suitably small as $x \to \infty$. Condition (9.4.23) is a technical condition whose role is not so easy to explain in simple terms. However, these conditions are not severe in practice. All of the four examples belong to $\mathcal{K}$. Any kernel that ensures positive semi-definiteness must (it can be shown) satisfy (9.4.23). Regarding consistency, the following result from De Jong and Davidson (2000a) can be stated.

Theorem 9.4.2 Let $\boldsymbol{\lambda}'\boldsymbol{v}_t(\boldsymbol{\theta}_0)$ satisfy the conditions of Theorem 6.4.5 for each fixed vector $\boldsymbol{\lambda}$ of unit length. Then (9.4.18) holds, and $\hat{\boldsymbol{B}}_n \xrightarrow{\text{pr}} \boldsymbol{B}_0$ for any $k \in \mathcal{K}$ and $\gamma_n = o(n)$. $\square$

This result is unusual in the literature because it allows nonstationarity, and does not impose the existence of fourth moments of the data. The conditions are matched closely to the best-known sufficient conditions for the central limit theorem, which suits the present application. However, the result does not offer guidance on the best choice of kernel, nor on the crucial choice of the bandwidth function. Such guidance is available only when at least fourth moments of the data exist. Then a choice can be based on the consideration of minimizing the asymptotic mean squared error of estimate (MSE). Let $q \geq 0$ be defined as the largest number such that

$$\lim_{x \to 0} \frac{1 - k(x)}{|x|^q} < \infty. \tag{9.4.25}$$

This is an index of the smoothness of the kernel function close to 0. The asymptotic MSE criterion indicates the rule $\gamma_n = O(n^{1/(2q+1)})$ as optimal (see Andrews 1991). This rule leads to the choices of $\gamma_n = O(n^{1/3})$ for the Bartlett kernel, and $\gamma_n = O(n^{1/5})$ for the other three cases. While these recommendations are based on the existence of fourth moments of the data there is, at least, no known reason to think they are not suitable generally. However, fixing the rate of growth of the bandwidth still leaves considerable latitude in the choice. Under mild extra conditions on k that are satisfied by cases 1–4, De Jong and Davidson (2000a) show that the consistency result still holds when γ_n is replaced by a stochastic sequence, say $\hat{\alpha}_n n^{1/(2q+1)}$ where $\hat{\alpha}_n$ can depend on the sample data, provided it is bounded away from both ∞ and 0 in the limit. Various 'plug-in' methods have been proposed for constructing $\hat{\alpha}_n$ on the basis of a prior examination of the data. See Andrews and Monahan (1992), Newey and West (1994), for details.

Further Reading: Books on numerical optimization include Fletcher (1980), Gill, Murray and Wright (1981), Wolfe (1978), Box, Davies and Swann (1969). Also see Quandt's (1983) survey article, as well as Goldfeld and Quandt (1972). On the theory of optimization estimators, useful textbooks include Amemiya (1985), Gallant (1987), Gourieroux and Monfort (1995). Gallant and White (1988) and White (1994) are two important monographs, and Pötscher and Prucha (1997) survey the asymptotic theory. Also see the articles by Burguete, Gallant and Souza (1982) and Bates and White (1985), and the Handbook of Econometrics surveys by Newey and McFadden (1994), Wooldridge (1994) and Andrews (1994).

Computing Resources A feature of the methods described in this chapter is that they can be adapted by the advanced user to a large range of problems, both established and new. To implement them as computer algorithms may require programming. A number of purpose-designed computer languages, including GAUSS (Aptech Systems, Inc.) and Jurgen Doornik's Ox (Timberlake Consultants Ltd.) have been created to make this kind of thing as easy as possible. These are matrix languages, in which matrix expressions can be written directly into lines of code, and they come equipped with good optimization algorithms as reviewed in §9.2. Ox is available free on the Internet to academic users, at http://www.nuff.ox.ac.uk/Users/Doornik/

9.5 Appendix: Additional Proofs

Proof of Theorem 9.2.1 The symmetry is immediate. From (9.2.16) note that for arbitrary $\boldsymbol{z} \neq \boldsymbol{0}$,

$$\boldsymbol{z}'\boldsymbol{B}_{r+1}\boldsymbol{z} = \boldsymbol{z}'\boldsymbol{B}_r\boldsymbol{z} - \frac{\boldsymbol{z}'\boldsymbol{B}_r\boldsymbol{\gamma}_r\boldsymbol{\gamma}_r'\boldsymbol{B}_r\boldsymbol{z}}{\boldsymbol{\gamma}_r'\boldsymbol{B}_r\boldsymbol{\gamma}_r} + \frac{(\boldsymbol{z}'\boldsymbol{\delta}_r)^2}{\boldsymbol{\delta}_r'\boldsymbol{\gamma}_r} + \phi_r(\boldsymbol{v}_r'\boldsymbol{z})^2. \tag{9.5.1}$$

If $\boldsymbol{B}_r$ is positive definite, the sum of the first two terms of (9.5.1) is nonnegative by the Cauchy–Schwarz inequality. It therefore suffices to show that $\boldsymbol{\delta}_r'\boldsymbol{\gamma}_r > 0$. Note that

$$\boldsymbol{\delta}_r'\boldsymbol{\gamma}_r = -\lambda_r\boldsymbol{q}_r'\boldsymbol{B}_r(\boldsymbol{q}_{r+1} - \boldsymbol{q}_r) \tag{9.5.2}$$

where λ_r solves the line search problem, and $\lambda_r > 0$ by (9.2.11). However,

$$\begin{aligned} -\boldsymbol{q}_r'\boldsymbol{B}_r\boldsymbol{q}_{r+1} &= -\boldsymbol{q}_r'\boldsymbol{B}_r\ \nabla C|_{\boldsymbol{\theta}=\boldsymbol{\theta}_r-\lambda_r\boldsymbol{B}_r\boldsymbol{q}_r} \\ &= \left.\frac{df}{d\lambda}\right|_{\lambda=\lambda_r} = 0 \end{aligned} \tag{9.5.3}$$

and hence

$$\boldsymbol{\delta}_r'\boldsymbol{\gamma}_r = \lambda_r\boldsymbol{q}_r'\boldsymbol{B}_r\boldsymbol{q}_r > 0. \quad \blacksquare \tag{9.5.4}$$

Proof of Theorem 9.2.2 In view of (9.2.20),

$$\boldsymbol{\delta}_r'\boldsymbol{A}\boldsymbol{\delta}_{r-1} = -\lambda_r \boldsymbol{q}_r'\boldsymbol{B}_r\boldsymbol{A}\boldsymbol{\delta}_{r-1} = -\lambda_r\lambda_{r-1}\boldsymbol{q}_r'\boldsymbol{B}_{r-1}\boldsymbol{q}_{r-1} = 0 \tag{9.5.5}$$

for $1 < r \leq p$, by (9.5.3). So consider step r for $r > 2$. (If $p \leq 2$ there is nothing more to show.) We argue by induction to show that if, for any r and $j < r$,

$$\boldsymbol{\delta}_r'\boldsymbol{A}\boldsymbol{\delta}_j = 0 \tag{9.5.6}$$

$$\boldsymbol{B}_r\boldsymbol{A}\boldsymbol{\delta}_j = \boldsymbol{\delta}_j \tag{9.5.7}$$

then the same equalities hold for $j-1$. Since we already know by (9.2.20) and (9.5.5) that they hold for $j = r-1$, it follows that they hold for $1 \leq j < r$. From (9.2.16),

$$\boldsymbol{B}_r\boldsymbol{A}\boldsymbol{\delta}_{j-1} = \boldsymbol{B}_j\boldsymbol{A}\boldsymbol{\delta}_{j-1} + \sum_{i=j}^{r-1}\boldsymbol{u}_i(\boldsymbol{E}_i + \phi_i\boldsymbol{F}_i)\boldsymbol{u}_i'\boldsymbol{A}\boldsymbol{\delta}_{j-1}. \tag{9.5.8}$$

However,

$$\boldsymbol{u}_i'\boldsymbol{A}\boldsymbol{\delta}_{j-1} = \begin{bmatrix}\boldsymbol{\delta}_i'\boldsymbol{A}\boldsymbol{\delta}_{j-1}\\ \boldsymbol{\gamma}_i'\boldsymbol{B}_i\boldsymbol{A}\boldsymbol{\delta}_{j-1}\end{bmatrix} = \boldsymbol{0} \quad j \leq i < r \tag{9.5.9}$$

applying (9.5.6) and (9.5.7) which hold by the inductive hypothesis with i substituted for r, and also (9.2.19). Hence,

$$\boldsymbol{B}_r\boldsymbol{A}\boldsymbol{\delta}_{j-1} = \boldsymbol{B}_j\boldsymbol{A}\boldsymbol{\delta}_{j-1} = \boldsymbol{\delta}_{j-1} \tag{9.5.10}$$

as required, where the second equality applies (9.2.20). Also note that

$$\boldsymbol{q}_r'\boldsymbol{\delta}_{j-1} = \boldsymbol{q}_j'\boldsymbol{\delta}_{j-1} + \sum_{i=j}^{r-1}\boldsymbol{\gamma}_i'\boldsymbol{\delta}_{j-1} = \boldsymbol{q}_j'\boldsymbol{\delta}_{j-1} + \sum_{i=j}^{r-1}\boldsymbol{\delta}_i'\boldsymbol{A}\boldsymbol{\delta}_{j-1} = 0 \tag{9.5.11}$$

where the second equality uses (9.2.19), and the last one (9.5.6) and (9.5.3). Hence, (9.5.10) implies that

$$\boldsymbol{\delta}_r'\boldsymbol{A}\boldsymbol{\delta}_{j-1} = -\lambda_r\boldsymbol{q}_r'\boldsymbol{B}_r\boldsymbol{A}\boldsymbol{\delta}_{j-1} = -\lambda_r\boldsymbol{q}_r'\boldsymbol{\delta}_{j-1} = 0 \tag{9.5.12}$$

as required.

Finally, consider the case $r = p$. Let $\boldsymbol{\Delta}$ represent the $p \times p$ matrix whose columns are the search directions $\boldsymbol{\delta}_1, \dots, \boldsymbol{\delta}_p$. Since $\boldsymbol{A}$ has full rank, the matrix $\boldsymbol{\Delta}'\boldsymbol{A}\boldsymbol{\Delta}$ is diagonal and has full rank by (9.5.6), so that $\boldsymbol{\Delta}$ is nonsingular. Since (9.5.7) implies

$$\boldsymbol{B}_p\boldsymbol{A}\boldsymbol{\Delta} = \boldsymbol{\Delta} \tag{9.5.13}$$

and $\boldsymbol{A}$ and $\boldsymbol{B}_p$ are symmetric,

$$\boldsymbol{B}_p = \boldsymbol{A}^{-1} \tag{9.5.14}$$

and the proof is complete. ■

Proof of Theorem 9.2.3 The proof is by induction. Note that according to the algorithm,

$$\boldsymbol{\xi}_{p-j}^r = \boldsymbol{\theta}_p^{r-j-1} - \boldsymbol{\theta}^{r-j-1} \tag{9.5.15}$$

for $j = 0, \dots, r-2$ and $r = 2, \dots, p+1$. Assume that at the rth iteration these generated directions are $\boldsymbol{A}$-conjugate, in other words that

$$\boldsymbol{\xi}_j^{r\prime}\boldsymbol{A}\boldsymbol{\xi}_k^r = 0 \text{ for } j = p-r+2, \dots, p-1,\ j < k \leq p. \tag{9.5.16}$$

It suffices to show that (9.5.16) implies

$$\boldsymbol{\xi}_j^{r\prime} \boldsymbol{A}(\boldsymbol{\theta}_p^r - \boldsymbol{\theta}^r) = 0 \text{ for } j = p - r + 2, \ldots, p. \tag{9.5.17}$$

First note that, similarly to (9.2.24),

$$C(\boldsymbol{\theta}_p^r) = C(\boldsymbol{\theta}_{p-r+1}^r) + \sum_{j=p-r+2}^{p} [\lambda_j^r \boldsymbol{\xi}_j^{r\prime}(\boldsymbol{b} + \boldsymbol{A}\boldsymbol{\theta}_{p-r+1}^r) + \tfrac{1}{2}(\lambda_j^r)^2 \boldsymbol{\xi}_j^{r\prime} \boldsymbol{A} \boldsymbol{\xi}_j^r]. \tag{9.5.18}$$

By the first-order conditions for minimization of (9.5.18) with respect to the λ_j,

$$\begin{aligned} 0 &= \boldsymbol{\xi}_j^{r\prime}(\boldsymbol{b} + \boldsymbol{A}(\boldsymbol{\theta}_{p-r+1}^r + \lambda_j^r \boldsymbol{\xi}_j^r)) \\ &= \boldsymbol{\xi}_j^{r\prime}\left(\boldsymbol{b} + \boldsymbol{A}\left(\boldsymbol{\theta}_{p-r+1}^r + \sum_{i=p-r+2}^{p} \lambda_i^r \boldsymbol{\xi}_i^r\right)\right) = \boldsymbol{\xi}_j^{r\prime}(\boldsymbol{b} + \boldsymbol{A}\boldsymbol{\theta}_p^r) \end{aligned} \tag{9.5.19}$$

for $j = p - r + 2, \ldots, p$, where the second equation uses (9.5.16).

Applying the same arguments to the case $r - 1$, note first that

$$\boldsymbol{\theta}^r = \boldsymbol{\theta}_{p-r+2}^{r-1} + \sum_{j=p-r+3}^{p} \lambda_j^{r-1} \boldsymbol{\xi}_j^{r-1} + \lambda_{p+1}^{r-1}(\boldsymbol{\theta}_p^{r-1} - \boldsymbol{\theta}^{r-1}). \tag{9.5.20}$$

Similarly to (9.5.19) write

$$\boldsymbol{\xi}_j^{r-1\prime}(\boldsymbol{b} + \boldsymbol{A}\boldsymbol{\theta}^r) = 0 \tag{9.5.21}$$

for $j = p - r + 3, \ldots, p$, and

$$(\boldsymbol{\theta}_p^{r-1} - \boldsymbol{\theta}^{r-1})'(\boldsymbol{b} + \boldsymbol{A}\boldsymbol{\theta}^r) = 0. \tag{9.5.22}$$

However, the algorithm sets $\boldsymbol{\xi}_{j-1}^r = \boldsymbol{\xi}_j^{r-1}$ for $j = 2, \ldots, p$ and $\boldsymbol{\xi}_p^r = \boldsymbol{\theta}_p^{r-1} - \boldsymbol{\theta}^{r-1}$. Hence we can write (9.5.21) and (9.5.22) in the equivalent form

$$\boldsymbol{\xi}_j^{r\prime}(\boldsymbol{b} + \boldsymbol{A}\boldsymbol{\theta}^r) = 0 \quad j = p - r + 2, \ldots, p \tag{9.5.23}$$

Subtracting (9.5.23) from (9.5.19) yields (9.5.17). ■

Proof of Theorem 9.3.1 We have to show that $\lim_{n\to\infty} P(\hat{\boldsymbol{\theta}}_n \in N(\delta)) = 1$ for every $\delta > 0$ where

$$N(\delta) = \{\boldsymbol{\theta} : \|\boldsymbol{\theta} - \boldsymbol{\theta}_0\| < \delta\}. \tag{9.5.24}$$

$N^c(\delta)$, the complement of $N(\delta)$ in $\mathbb{R}^p$, is closed and $N^c(\delta) \cap \Theta$ is compact by condition (a). Since every function on a compact set has a minimum on the set, the vector $\boldsymbol{\theta}^\delta = \arg\min_{N^c(\delta)\cap\Theta} \bar{C}(\boldsymbol{\theta})$ exists. For some $\varepsilon > 0$ define the event

$$A_n = \left\{\sup_{\boldsymbol{\theta}\in\Theta} \left|C_n(\boldsymbol{\theta}) - \bar{C}(\boldsymbol{\theta})\right| < \tfrac{1}{2}\varepsilon\right\} \tag{9.5.25}$$

so that $\lim_{n\to\infty} P(A_n) = 1$ by condition (b). Note that $\left|C_n(\boldsymbol{\theta}) - \bar{C}(\boldsymbol{\theta})\right| < \frac{1}{2}\varepsilon$ implies that both $C_n(\boldsymbol{\theta}) - \frac{1}{2}\varepsilon < \bar{C}(\boldsymbol{\theta})$ and $\bar{C}(\boldsymbol{\theta}) - \frac{1}{2}\varepsilon < C_n(\boldsymbol{\theta})$. Since $\hat{\boldsymbol{\theta}}_n \in \Theta$ and $\boldsymbol{\theta}_0 \in \Theta$, if A_n occurs then both of the following events occur:

$$\bar{C}(\hat{\boldsymbol{\theta}}_n) - \tfrac{1}{2}\varepsilon < C_n(\hat{\boldsymbol{\theta}}_n) \tag{9.5.26}$$

and

$$C_n(\boldsymbol{\theta}_0) - \tfrac{1}{2}\varepsilon < \bar{C}(\boldsymbol{\theta}_0). \tag{9.5.27}$$

Since $C_n(\hat{\boldsymbol{\theta}}_n) \le C_n(\boldsymbol{\theta}_0)$ by definition of $\hat{\boldsymbol{\theta}}_n$, A_n therefore implies

$$\bar{C}(\hat{\boldsymbol{\theta}}_n) - \varepsilon < \bar{C}(\boldsymbol{\theta}_0). \tag{9.5.28}$$

In particular, the preceding remarks hold for the case

$$\varepsilon = \bar{C}(\boldsymbol{\theta}^{\delta}) - \bar{C}(\boldsymbol{\theta}_0) \tag{9.5.29}$$

where the positivity of ε is assured by uniqueness of the minimum, condition (c). Hence (9.5.28) implies

$$\bar{C}(\hat{\boldsymbol{\theta}}_n) < \bar{C}(\boldsymbol{\theta}^{\delta}). \tag{9.5.30}$$

Given the definition of $\boldsymbol{\theta}^{\delta}$, it follows that $\hat{\boldsymbol{\theta}}_n \in N(\delta)$. We have shown that the occurrence of A_n implies the latter event, so

$$P(A_n) \le P(\hat{\boldsymbol{\theta}}_n \in N(\delta)). \tag{9.5.31}$$

Since δ is arbitrary, the theorem follows. ∎

Proof of Theorem 9.3.2 The main step is a case of Theorem 21.11 of Davidson (1994a), which establishes that the elements of the vector

$$\boldsymbol{f}_n(\boldsymbol{\theta}) = n^{-1} \sum_{t=1}^{n} \boldsymbol{\psi}_t(\boldsymbol{\theta}) \tag{9.5.32}$$

are stochastically equicontinuous (s.e.) as $n \to \infty$. The conditions of Theorem 21.11 of Davidson (1994a) are satisfied under the present conditions, letting q_{nt} in the former theorem correspond to $n^{-1}\psi_{it}$ where $\boldsymbol{\psi}_t = (\psi_{1t}, \dots, \psi_{rt})'$. Also, if

$$\sup_{\boldsymbol{\theta}} \sup_{\boldsymbol{\theta}' \in S(\boldsymbol{\theta},\delta)} \left| f_i(\boldsymbol{\theta}) - f_i(\boldsymbol{\theta}') \right| \to 0 \tag{9.5.33}$$

as $\delta \downarrow 0$ for $i = 1, \dots, r$, and $\phi(\cdot)$ is a continuous function of r variables, it follows that

$$\sup_{\boldsymbol{\theta}} \sup_{\boldsymbol{\theta}' \in S(\boldsymbol{\theta},\delta)} \left| \phi(\boldsymbol{f}(\boldsymbol{\theta})) - \phi(\boldsymbol{f}(\boldsymbol{\theta}')) \right| \to 0 \tag{9.5.34}$$

as $\delta \downarrow 0$ where $\boldsymbol{f} = (f_1, \dots, f_r)'$. In other words, considering the definitions in Section 21.3 of Davidson (1994a), if a vector function $\boldsymbol{f}_n(\boldsymbol{\theta})$ is s.e. so is $\phi(\boldsymbol{f}_n(\boldsymbol{\theta}))$. The result now follows by Theorem 21.9 of Davidson (1994a). ∎

Proof of Theorem 9.3.4 Consider the identity

$$\bar{C}(\boldsymbol{\theta}_0) - \bar{C}(\boldsymbol{\theta}_1) = [C_n(\boldsymbol{\theta}_0) - C_n(\boldsymbol{\theta}_1)] + [C_n(\boldsymbol{\theta}_1) - \bar{C}(\boldsymbol{\theta}_1)] - [C_n(\boldsymbol{\theta}_0) - \bar{C}(\boldsymbol{\theta}_0)] \tag{9.5.35}$$

Suppose $\boldsymbol{\theta}_0$ is asymptotically globally (locally) underidentified according to Definition 9.3.3. Then for some $\boldsymbol{\theta}_1$ in Θ (in an open neighbourhood of $\boldsymbol{\theta}_0$),

$$C_n(\boldsymbol{\theta}_0) - C_n(\boldsymbol{\theta}_1) \xrightarrow{\text{pr}} 0. \tag{9.5.36}$$

The plims of the second and third terms of (9.5.35) also vanish by the assumed uniform WLLN. Since the left hand side of (9.5.35) is a constant not depending on n, it follows that $\bar{C}(\boldsymbol{\theta}_0) = \bar{C}(\boldsymbol{\theta}_1)$.

On the other hand suppose $\bar{C}(\boldsymbol{\theta}_0) = \bar{C}(\boldsymbol{\theta}_1)$. Using the triangle inequality in (9.5.35),

$$|C_n(\boldsymbol{\theta}_0) - C_n(\boldsymbol{\theta}_1)| \le \left|C_n(\boldsymbol{\theta}_0) - \bar{C}(\boldsymbol{\theta}_0)\right| + \left|C_n(\boldsymbol{\theta}_1) - \bar{C}(\boldsymbol{\theta}_1)\right|. \tag{9.5.37}$$

Uniform convergence in probability implies that for any $\varepsilon > 0$, $\exists\, n_\varepsilon \ge 1$ such that

$$P[\left|C_n(\boldsymbol{\theta}) - \bar{C}(\boldsymbol{\theta})\right| < \tfrac{1}{2}\varepsilon] > 1 - \varepsilon \quad n \ge n_\varepsilon \tag{9.5.38}$$

for all $\boldsymbol{\theta} \in \boldsymbol{\Theta}$. This implies by (9.5.37)

$$P[|C_n(\boldsymbol{\theta}_0) - C_n(\boldsymbol{\theta}_1)| < \varepsilon] > 1 - \varepsilon \quad n \geq n_\varepsilon \tag{9.5.39}$$

which contradicts identification, and so completes the proof. ■

Proof of Theorem 9.3.5 We first prove necessity. Let $C_n(\boldsymbol{\theta}, \omega)$, $\omega \in \Omega$, where Ω is the sample space, represent a particular outcome from the distribution of $C_n(\boldsymbol{\theta})$, and note that by the mean value theorem,

$$C_n(\boldsymbol{\theta}, \omega) - C_n(\boldsymbol{\theta}_0, \omega) = \boldsymbol{q}_n(\boldsymbol{\theta}^*(\omega), \omega)'(\boldsymbol{\theta} - \boldsymbol{\theta}_0) \tag{9.5.40}$$

where $\boldsymbol{\theta}^*(\omega)$ is a point on the line segment joining $\boldsymbol{\theta}$ and $\boldsymbol{\theta}_0$. Let $A \subseteq \Omega$ denote the set of outcomes ω for which there exists a Cauchy sequence $\{\boldsymbol{\theta}_m\}$ converging to $\boldsymbol{\theta}_0$ such that $C_n(\boldsymbol{\theta}_m, \omega) = C_n(\boldsymbol{\theta}_0, \omega)$ for all m. Construct a sequence $\{\boldsymbol{d}_m\}$ of points on the unit sphere, where

$$\boldsymbol{d}_m = \frac{\boldsymbol{\theta}_m - \boldsymbol{\theta}_0}{\|\boldsymbol{\theta}_m - \boldsymbol{\theta}_0\|}. \tag{9.5.41}$$

Denoting the limit of this sequence as $\boldsymbol{\theta}_m \longrightarrow \boldsymbol{\theta}_0$ by $\boldsymbol{d}$, it follows from (9.5.40) that

$$\boldsymbol{q}_n(\boldsymbol{\theta}_m, \omega)'\boldsymbol{d} = 0 \quad \forall\, \omega \in A. \tag{9.5.42}$$

An expected value is invariant to values assumed by an r.v. on sets of measure 0, and hence if $P(A) = 1$,

$$0 = nE(\boldsymbol{q}_n(\boldsymbol{\theta}_0)'\boldsymbol{d})^2 = \boldsymbol{d}'\boldsymbol{A}_n(\boldsymbol{\theta}_0)\boldsymbol{d}. \tag{9.5.43}$$

Since $\boldsymbol{A}_n(\boldsymbol{\theta}_0)$ is symmetric and positive semidefinite by construction, (9.5.43) implies it is singular.

To prove sufficiency, let $\boldsymbol{A}_n(\boldsymbol{\theta})$ be singular at $\boldsymbol{\theta}_0$ and hence, by regularity, everywhere in an open neighbourhood $\mathcal{N}(\boldsymbol{\theta}_0)$, and let $\boldsymbol{c}(\boldsymbol{\theta})$ ($p \times 1$) be an eigenvector of $\boldsymbol{A}_n(\boldsymbol{\theta})$ corresponding to a zero root in $\mathcal{N}(\boldsymbol{\theta}_0)$, so that

$$0 = \boldsymbol{c}(\boldsymbol{\theta})'\boldsymbol{A}_n(\boldsymbol{\theta})\boldsymbol{c}(\boldsymbol{\theta}) = nE[\boldsymbol{c}(\boldsymbol{\theta})'\boldsymbol{q}_n(\boldsymbol{\theta})]^2. \tag{9.5.44}$$

This implies that

$$P[\boldsymbol{q}_n(\boldsymbol{\theta})'\boldsymbol{c}(\boldsymbol{\theta}) = 0] = 1 \tag{9.5.45}$$

for all $\boldsymbol{\theta} \in \mathcal{N}(\boldsymbol{\theta}_0)$. Define a sequence of points in $\mathcal{N}(\boldsymbol{\theta}_0)$ by a vector function $\boldsymbol{\theta}(\lambda)$, λ a scalar, defined as the solution to the vector of differential equations

$$\frac{d\boldsymbol{\theta}}{d\lambda} = \boldsymbol{c}(\boldsymbol{\theta}(\lambda)). \tag{9.5.46}$$

Then note that

$$\frac{dC_n}{d\lambda} = \boldsymbol{q}_n(\boldsymbol{\theta}(\lambda))'\boldsymbol{c}(\boldsymbol{\theta}(\lambda)) \tag{9.5.47}$$

so that in view of (9.5.45), C_n is constant on the path $\boldsymbol{\theta}(\lambda)$ with probability 1. Since $\boldsymbol{A}_n$ is continuous at $\boldsymbol{\theta}_0$, so is $\boldsymbol{c}(\boldsymbol{\theta})$ and also hence $\boldsymbol{\theta}(\lambda)$. Every open neighbourhood of $\boldsymbol{\theta}_0$ therefore contains points of the path. This completes the proof. ■

Chapter 10

Optimization Estimators II: Examples

In this chapter we look at a number of cases where the regression theory of Chapter 7 cannot help us to determine the asymptotic properties of estimators. The theory of OEs is very useful in understanding these cases. It is worth remarking that treatments of some these topics, those in §10.4.1 and §10.4.2 for example, are more often to be found in textbooks under the heading of 'maximum likelihood', since this is what they correspond to under the assumption of Gaussianity. However, as we show, the results are available under a broader set of assumptions.

Before embarking on the more exotic cases, a good place to start is to reprise the theory of ordinary least squares from Chapter 3, in the light of the OE approach.

10.1 Linear Least Squares

As before, let the model be $\boldsymbol{y} = \boldsymbol{X\beta} + \boldsymbol{u}$, with $E(\boldsymbol{u}|\boldsymbol{X}) = \boldsymbol{0}$, $E(\boldsymbol{uu}'|\boldsymbol{X}) = \sigma^2\boldsymbol{I}$, and

$$\operatorname{plim} \frac{1}{n}\boldsymbol{X}'\boldsymbol{X} = \boldsymbol{M}_{XX} < \infty \text{ (positive definite).} \tag{10.1.1}$$

Define the least squares estimator of $\boldsymbol{\beta}$ as

$$\hat{\boldsymbol{\beta}}_n = \arg\min_{\boldsymbol{b}} S_n(\boldsymbol{b}) \tag{10.1.2}$$

where

$$\begin{aligned} S_n(\boldsymbol{b}) &= (\boldsymbol{y} - \boldsymbol{Xb})'(\boldsymbol{y} - \boldsymbol{Xb}) \\ &= [\boldsymbol{u} - \boldsymbol{X}(\boldsymbol{b} - \boldsymbol{\beta})]'[\boldsymbol{u} - \boldsymbol{X}(\boldsymbol{b} - \boldsymbol{\beta})] \\ &= \boldsymbol{u}'\boldsymbol{u} - 2\boldsymbol{u}'\boldsymbol{X}(\boldsymbol{b} - \boldsymbol{\beta}) + (\boldsymbol{b} - \boldsymbol{\beta})'\boldsymbol{X}'\boldsymbol{X}(\boldsymbol{b} - \boldsymbol{\beta}). \end{aligned} \tag{10.1.3}$$

In conformity with the notation of Chapters 1 and 2, $\boldsymbol{\beta}$ is used for the true value and $\boldsymbol{b}$ as the argument of $C_n = S_n/n$.

The standard consistency proof for OLS operates on the formula for the estimator, but OEs are defined implicitly, and no formula need exist. The asymptotic properties of $\hat{\boldsymbol{\beta}}$ can be derived without explicitly using the fact that $\hat{\boldsymbol{\beta}} = (\boldsymbol{X}'\boldsymbol{X})^{-1}\boldsymbol{X}'\boldsymbol{y}$ at any point.

To show consistency, assume the WLLN holds, such that $\operatorname{plim} n^{-1}\boldsymbol{X}'\boldsymbol{u} = \boldsymbol{0}$ and $\operatorname{plim} n^{-1}\boldsymbol{u}'\boldsymbol{u} = \sigma^2$ together with (10.1.1). Then, pointwise on $\mathbb{R}^k$,

$$\operatorname{plim} \frac{S_n(\boldsymbol{b})}{n} = \bar{S}(\boldsymbol{b}) = \sigma^2 + (\boldsymbol{b} - \boldsymbol{\beta})'\boldsymbol{M}_{XX}(\boldsymbol{b} - \boldsymbol{\beta}) \tag{10.1.4}$$

which takes a unique minimum at the point $\boldsymbol{b} = \boldsymbol{\beta}$ when $\boldsymbol{M}_{XX}$ is positive definite. This establishes condition (c) of Theorem 9.3.1, and the demonstration is completed in view of (10.1.4) by checking the stochastic equicontinuity condition in (9.3.3). The sum of squares criterion can be cast in the form

$$\frac{S_n(\boldsymbol{b})}{n} = \frac{1}{n}\sum_{t=1}^{n} y_t^2 - 2\sum_{j=1}^{k} b_j\left(\frac{1}{n}\sum_{t=1}^{n} x_{jt}y_t\right) + \sum_{j=1}^{k}\sum_{m=1}^{k} b_j b_m\left(\frac{1}{n}\sum_{t=1}^{n} x_{jt}x_{mt}\right) \tag{10.1.5}$$

so that in (9.1.4) the vector $\boldsymbol{\psi}_t$ can be thought of as having elements of the form $b_j x_{jt} y_t$ and $b_j b_m x_{jt} x_{mt}$, with $r = (k+1)^2$. Choosing B_{it} to be $x_{jt}y_t$ or $x_{jt}x_{mt}$ as the case may be, it is clear that in this case the conditions of Theorem 9.3.2 are satisfied, completing the proof of consistency.

Next, it is easily verified that $\boldsymbol{q}_n(\boldsymbol{b}) = \boldsymbol{X}'\boldsymbol{X}(\boldsymbol{b}-\boldsymbol{\beta}) - \boldsymbol{X}'\boldsymbol{u}$, and $\boldsymbol{Q}_n(\boldsymbol{b}) = \boldsymbol{X}'\boldsymbol{X}$. Thus, $\boldsymbol{q}_n(\boldsymbol{\beta}) = \boldsymbol{X}'\boldsymbol{u}$,

$$E(\boldsymbol{q}_n(\boldsymbol{\beta})\boldsymbol{q}_n(\boldsymbol{\beta})') = E(\boldsymbol{X}'\boldsymbol{u}\boldsymbol{u}'\boldsymbol{X}) = \sigma^2 E(\boldsymbol{X}'\boldsymbol{X}) \tag{10.1.6}$$

and condition (9.3.19) is satisfied with $c = \sigma$. If $\boldsymbol{X}$ and $\boldsymbol{u}$ satisfy the requisite conditions for

$$\frac{\boldsymbol{X}'\boldsymbol{u}}{\sqrt{n}} \underset{\text{asy}}{\sim} \mathrm{N}(\boldsymbol{0}, \sigma^2\boldsymbol{M}_{XX}) \tag{10.1.7}$$

as in (7.1.14), it follows directly that

$$\sqrt{n}(\hat{\boldsymbol{\beta}}_n - \boldsymbol{\beta}) \underset{\text{asy}}{\sim} \mathrm{N}(\boldsymbol{0}, \sigma^2\boldsymbol{M}_{XX}^{-1}). \tag{10.1.8}$$

10.2 Nonlinear Least Squares

The dynamic equations of Chapter 5 are often of a nonlinear-in-parameters form. Consider the general nonlinear regression model,

$$\boldsymbol{y} = \boldsymbol{g}(\boldsymbol{\theta}) + \boldsymbol{u} \tag{10.2.1}$$

where $\boldsymbol{g}$ $(n \times 1)$ is a continuous function of parameters $\boldsymbol{\theta}$ $(p \times 1)$. The least squares (NLLS) estimator $\hat{\boldsymbol{\theta}}$ is the minimizer of

$$S_n(\boldsymbol{\theta}) = [\boldsymbol{y} - \boldsymbol{g}(\boldsymbol{\theta})]'[\boldsymbol{y} - \boldsymbol{g}(\boldsymbol{\theta})]. \tag{10.2.2}$$

While it is not essential for $\boldsymbol{g}$ to be differentiable for NLLS to exist and be consistent, this property usually obtains in practice and is assumed below where required. Among other studies of this model see White (1980c), White and Domowitz (1984) and Amemiya (1983).

10.2.1 Computation

The principle of estimation by minimizing the sum of the squared residuals still applies, but the sum of squares is no longer a quadratic function of the parameters. A numerical method on the lines of §9.2 is necessary to solve the least squares problem.

A convenient search algorithm for the least squares problem is Gauss–Newton (GN) see Hartley (1961), Marquardt (1963), Hartley and Booker (1965). This is based on the principle of approximating the nonlinear equation by a linear equation and estimating this by ordinary least squares.

Let the $n \times p$ gradient matrix with elements $\partial g_t / \partial \theta_j$ be denoted $\nabla \boldsymbol{g}$. If $\boldsymbol{\theta}^r$ denotes the current guess at the minimum, the Taylor's expansion of $\boldsymbol{g}$ around $\boldsymbol{\theta}^r$ yields

$$\boldsymbol{g}(\boldsymbol{\theta}) = \boldsymbol{g}(\boldsymbol{\theta}^r) + \boldsymbol{D}_r(\boldsymbol{\theta} - \boldsymbol{\theta}^r) + \boldsymbol{r}_r. \qquad (10.2.3)$$

where

$$\boldsymbol{D}_r = \nabla \boldsymbol{g}(\boldsymbol{\theta}^r) \qquad (10.2.4)$$

and $\boldsymbol{r}_r$ is the remainder term. The linearized equation is therefore

$$\boldsymbol{y}_r^* = \boldsymbol{D}_r \boldsymbol{\theta} + \boldsymbol{u}_r^* \qquad (10.2.5)$$

where $\boldsymbol{u}_r^* = \boldsymbol{u} + \boldsymbol{r}_r$ and

$$\boldsymbol{y}_r^* = \boldsymbol{y} - \boldsymbol{g}(\boldsymbol{\theta}^r) + \boldsymbol{D}_r \boldsymbol{\theta}^r. \qquad (10.2.6)$$

Note that $\boldsymbol{y}_r^*$ and $\boldsymbol{D}_r$ are both computable, given $\boldsymbol{\theta}^r$. The GN algorithm at the rth step can be computed as the regression of these variables yielding

$$\boldsymbol{\theta}^{r+1} = (\boldsymbol{D}_r' \boldsymbol{D}_r)^{-1} \boldsymbol{D}_r' \boldsymbol{y}_r^* \qquad (10.2.7)$$

although substituting (10.2.6) into (10.2.7) and cancelling shows that this is equivalent to an updating rule for $\boldsymbol{\theta}^r$,

$$\boldsymbol{\theta}^{r+1} = \boldsymbol{\theta}^r + (\boldsymbol{D}_r' \boldsymbol{D}_r)^{-1} \boldsymbol{D}_r' [\boldsymbol{y} - \boldsymbol{g}(\boldsymbol{\theta}^r)]. \qquad (10.2.8)$$

This can be recognised as an iterative step with the form of (9.2.8), with $\boldsymbol{H}_r = \boldsymbol{D}_r' \boldsymbol{D}_r$. The step is easily computed by the regression of the residuals $\boldsymbol{u}_r = \boldsymbol{y} - \boldsymbol{g}(\boldsymbol{\theta}^r)$ on $\boldsymbol{D}_r$.

10.2.2 Asymptotic Properties

The CAN property of NLLS is derived by application of the results in §9.3, although some of the arguments bear a close resemblance to those invoked for the linear regression in §7.1. Let $\{\mathcal{I}_t\}$ be an increasing sequence of σ-fields such that the random variable $g_t(\boldsymbol{\theta})$, the tth element of $\boldsymbol{g}$, is $\mathcal{I}_t$-measurable for any fixed $\boldsymbol{\theta} \in \Theta$. Also, let $\boldsymbol{\theta}_0$ denote the true value of $\boldsymbol{\theta}$, such that if

$$\boldsymbol{u} = \boldsymbol{y} - \boldsymbol{g}(\boldsymbol{\theta}_0) \qquad (10.2.9)$$

then under the axiom of correct specification, the elements of $\boldsymbol{u}$ satisfy

$$E(u_t|\mathcal{I}_t) = 0 \text{ a.s.} \tag{10.2.10a}$$

$$E(u_t^2|\mathcal{I}_t) = \sigma^2 \text{ a.s.} \tag{10.2.10b}$$

for $t = 1, \dots, n$. Then, $\{u_t, \mathcal{I}_t^*\}$ and $\{u_t^2 - \sigma^2, \mathcal{I}_t^*\}$ are m.d. sequences, where $\mathcal{I}_t^*$ is defined after (7.1.5). Since g_t is $\mathcal{I}_t$-measurable it follows, subject to integrability, that $\{g_t(\boldsymbol{\theta})u_t, \mathcal{I}_t^*\}$ is a m.d. sequence, at any point $\boldsymbol{\theta} \in \Theta$.

To show consistency, rewrite (10.2.9) as

$$\boldsymbol{y} - \boldsymbol{g}(\boldsymbol{\theta}) = \boldsymbol{u} + \boldsymbol{g}(\boldsymbol{\theta}_0) - \boldsymbol{g}(\boldsymbol{\theta}) \tag{10.2.11}$$

so that

$$\begin{aligned} C_n(\boldsymbol{\theta}) &= \frac{[\boldsymbol{y} - \boldsymbol{g}(\boldsymbol{\theta})]'[\boldsymbol{y} - \boldsymbol{g}(\boldsymbol{\theta})]}{2n} \\ &= \frac{\boldsymbol{u}'\boldsymbol{u}}{2n} + \frac{[\boldsymbol{g}(\boldsymbol{\theta}_0) - \boldsymbol{g}(\boldsymbol{\theta})]'\boldsymbol{u}}{n} + \frac{[\boldsymbol{g}(\boldsymbol{\theta}_0) - \boldsymbol{g}(\boldsymbol{\theta})]'[\boldsymbol{g}(\boldsymbol{\theta}_0) - \boldsymbol{g}(\boldsymbol{\theta})]}{2n}. \end{aligned} \tag{10.2.12}$$

The first term on the right-hand side in (10.2.12) does not depend on $\boldsymbol{\theta}$ and, after centring by subtracting $\frac{1}{2}\sigma^2$, is a mean of martingale differences. The middle term is a mean of martingale differences for any value of $\boldsymbol{\theta}$. Under appropriate regularity conditions it should therefore be possible to show that

$$2\bar{C}(\boldsymbol{\theta}) = \sigma^2 + \operatorname{plim} \frac{1}{n}[\boldsymbol{g}(\boldsymbol{\theta}_0) - \boldsymbol{g}(\boldsymbol{\theta})]'[\boldsymbol{g}(\boldsymbol{\theta}_0) - \boldsymbol{g}(\boldsymbol{\theta})]. \tag{10.2.13}$$

However, note that the last term is not a mean of m.d.s, and a mixing or near-epoch dependence condition will have to be established. To satisfy the conditions of Theorem 9.3.1, this convergence must be uniform in Θ and the last term must be minimized uniquely by $\boldsymbol{\theta} = \boldsymbol{\theta}_0$ This, hopefully, imposes straightforwardly verifiable conditions on $\boldsymbol{g}$. Note that derivatives are not needed at this point.

For asymptotic normality, derivatives are needed, and differentiability of the criterion function follows from differentiability of $\boldsymbol{g}$ to the required order. Writing $\boldsymbol{D}(\boldsymbol{\theta}) = \boldsymbol{\nabla g}$ $(n \times p)$, the gradient of C_n is $\boldsymbol{q}_n = -n^{-1}\boldsymbol{D}(\boldsymbol{\theta})'[\boldsymbol{y} - \boldsymbol{g}(\boldsymbol{\theta})]$. It will be necessary to show that

$$\frac{\boldsymbol{D}(\boldsymbol{\theta})'\boldsymbol{D}(\boldsymbol{\theta})}{n} \xrightarrow{\text{pr}} \boldsymbol{M}_{dd}(\boldsymbol{\theta}) \tag{10.2.14}$$

uniformly in an open neighbourhood of $\boldsymbol{\theta}_0$, where $\boldsymbol{M}_{dd}(\boldsymbol{\theta}_0)$ is finite and positive definite. Letting $\boldsymbol{d}_t$ denote the transposed tth row of $\boldsymbol{D}$, the sequences $\{\boldsymbol{d}_t(\boldsymbol{\theta}_0)u_t, \mathcal{I}_t^*\}$ and $\{\text{Vec}\, \boldsymbol{d}_t(\boldsymbol{\theta}_0)\boldsymbol{d}_t(\boldsymbol{\theta}_0)'(u_t^2 - \sigma^2), \mathcal{I}_t^*\}$ are both vector m.d.s. The argument leading to (7.1.14) can now be applied more or less unchanged, with $\boldsymbol{d}_t(\boldsymbol{\theta}_0)$ replacing $\boldsymbol{x}_t$ and required to have similar sequence properties, and the condition

$$E\left|\boldsymbol{\lambda}'\boldsymbol{d}_t(\boldsymbol{\theta}_0)u_t\right|^{2+\delta} \le B < \infty \quad \delta > 0,\ \forall t,\ \text{all fixed } \boldsymbol{\lambda} \text{ with } \boldsymbol{\lambda}'\boldsymbol{\lambda} = 1 \tag{10.2.15}$$

is sufficient for

$$\frac{1}{\sqrt{n}}\boldsymbol{D}(\boldsymbol{\theta}_0)'\boldsymbol{u} \xrightarrow{\text{D}} \text{N}(\boldsymbol{0}, \sigma^2\boldsymbol{M}_{dd}(\boldsymbol{\theta}_0)). \tag{10.2.16}$$

Next, apply Theorem 9.3.6. Let

$$\boldsymbol{\nabla} \boldsymbol{D} = \boldsymbol{\nabla}^2 \boldsymbol{g} \quad (pn \times p) \tag{10.2.17}$$

represent the matrix of second derivatives of $\boldsymbol{g}$, such that the tth block of dimension $p \times p$ is the Hessian matrix of the element $g_t(\boldsymbol{\theta})$, and note that

$$\boldsymbol{\nabla}^2 C_n = \frac{\boldsymbol{D}'\boldsymbol{D}}{n} - \frac{\boldsymbol{\nabla} \boldsymbol{D}'(\boldsymbol{y} - \boldsymbol{g}(\boldsymbol{\theta}) \otimes \boldsymbol{I}_p)}{n} \quad (p \times p). \tag{10.2.18}$$

However, if this matrix is evaluated at the point $\boldsymbol{\theta}_0$, the terms of the second sum on the right-hand side are $p \times p$ matrices of the form $\boldsymbol{\nabla} \boldsymbol{d}_t(\theta_0)u_t$, where $\{\text{Vec}\, \boldsymbol{\nabla} \boldsymbol{d}_t(\theta_0)u_t, \mathcal{I}_t^*\}$ is also a v.m.d. Therefore, subject to the usual regularity conditions, this term converges in probability to $\mathbf{0}$ and

$$\text{plim}\, \boldsymbol{\nabla}^2 C_n(\boldsymbol{\theta}_0) = \boldsymbol{M}_{dd}(\boldsymbol{\theta}_0). \tag{10.2.19}$$

The conclusion is

$$\sqrt{n}(\hat{\boldsymbol{\theta}} - \boldsymbol{\theta}_0) \underset{\text{asy}}{\sim} \text{N}(\mathbf{0}, \boldsymbol{V}_0) \tag{10.2.20}$$

where $\boldsymbol{V}_0 = \sigma^2 \boldsymbol{M}_{dd}(\boldsymbol{\theta}_0)^{-1}$. In view of (10.2.16) and (10.2.19), equality (9.3.19) can be seen to apply in this case. The matrix is consistently estimated by

$$\hat{\boldsymbol{V}} = ns^2(\hat{\boldsymbol{D}}'\hat{\boldsymbol{D}})^{-1} \tag{10.2.21}$$

where $\hat{\boldsymbol{D}}$ is the matrix of derivatives evaluated at $\hat{\boldsymbol{\theta}}$, and $s^2 = S(\hat{\boldsymbol{\theta}})/n$.

Two important conclusions follow from these results. The first is that approximate standard errors are obtained as an instant by-product of the GN algorithm, since the components of (10.2.21) are computed at the final iteration where convergence is achieved. Equation (10.2.21) is just the OLS variance formula, calculated with $\boldsymbol{d}_t$ instead of $\boldsymbol{x}_t$. The second conclusion, in view of (10.2.19) is that the conditions of Theorem 9.4.1 are satisfied. Given a consistent estimator of $\boldsymbol{\theta}$, a two step estimator can be implemented using the GN algorithm, to yield estimates asymptotically equivalent to NLLS.

The problem is, of course, to verify the regularity conditions that have been invoked in this analysis for particular cases. In the following subsections, the theory is illustrated by some nonlinear dynamic equations drawn from Chapter 5. In each case, only first-order lags are considered for simplicity, but the generalizations to higher order cases are easily made.

10.2.3 The AR(1) Error Model: Computation

Consider the case

$$g_t = \boldsymbol{\beta}'\boldsymbol{x}_t + \rho y_{t-1} - \rho\boldsymbol{\beta}'\boldsymbol{x}_{t-1} \tag{10.2.22}$$

which is obtained by transforming the k-variable linear model with autoregressive errors,

$$y_t = \boldsymbol{\beta}'\boldsymbol{x}_t + \nu_t \quad \nu_t = \rho\nu_{t-1} + u_t = \frac{u_t}{1 - \rho L}. \tag{10.2.23}$$

Given (10.2.22), the unconstrained regression of y_t on $\boldsymbol{x}_t$, y_{t-1} and $\boldsymbol{x}_{t-1}$ yields consistent estimates of $\boldsymbol{\beta}$ and ρ, and these can provide a starting point for the GN iterations. The coefficients of $\boldsymbol{x}_{t-1}$ in this regression are simply discarded. Letting $\boldsymbol{\theta} = (\boldsymbol{\beta}', \rho)'$ the derivatives are

$$\left.\frac{\partial g_t}{\partial \boldsymbol{\beta}}\right|_{\boldsymbol{\theta}=\boldsymbol{\theta}^r} = \boldsymbol{x}_t - \rho^r \boldsymbol{x}_{t-1} \ (k \times 1) \tag{10.2.24a}$$

$$\left.\frac{\partial g_t}{\partial \rho}\right|_{\boldsymbol{\theta}=\boldsymbol{\theta}^r} = y_{t-1} - \boldsymbol{\beta}^{r\prime}\boldsymbol{x}_{t-1}. \tag{10.2.24b}$$

In principle, there are now two different ways to implement the GN algorithm. The usual procedure would be to obtain the updates $\boldsymbol{\beta}^{r+1} - \boldsymbol{\beta}^r$ and $\rho^{r+1} - \rho^r$ by regressing the residuals $u_t^r = y_t - g_t(\boldsymbol{\theta}^r)$ on the derivatives in (10.2.24). However, according to (10.2.6),

$$\begin{aligned} y_t^{*r} &= y_t - (\boldsymbol{\beta}^{r\prime}\boldsymbol{x}_t + \rho^r y_{t-1} - \rho^r \boldsymbol{\beta}^{r\prime}\boldsymbol{x}_{t-1}) \\ &\qquad + \boldsymbol{\beta}^{r\prime}(\boldsymbol{x}_t - \rho^r \boldsymbol{x}_{t-1}) + (y_{t-1} - \boldsymbol{\beta}^{r\prime}\boldsymbol{x}_{t-1})\rho^r \\ &= y_t - \rho^r \boldsymbol{\beta}^{r\prime}\boldsymbol{x}_{t-1}. \end{aligned} \tag{10.2.25}$$

The algorithm could also be implemented by constructing the right hand member of (10.2.25) and performing the least squares regression of y_t^{*r} on the derivatives, to obtain $\boldsymbol{\beta}^{r+1}$ and ρ^{r+1} directly, rather than the vectors of updates. This model is well adapted to the application of the two-step method discussed in §9.4.2, since the initial point is consistent, and the GN step is performed in either case by an application of least squares. In §10.2.2 it is shown that the conditions of Theorem 9.4.1 are satisfied by the GN algorithm. This is known as Hatanaka's two-step estimator (Hatanaka 1974).

A third method of computing the GN update is obtained by adding and then subtracting $\rho^r y_{t-1}$ in (10.2.25), to give

$$y_t^{*r} = (y_t - \rho^r y_{t-1}) + \rho^r(y_{t-1} - \boldsymbol{\beta}^{r\prime}\boldsymbol{x}_{t-1}). \tag{10.2.26}$$

$\boldsymbol{\beta}^{r+1}$ and ρ^{r+1} are therefore obtained by applying least squares to the equation

$$(y_t - \rho^r y_{t-1}) = \boldsymbol{\beta}'(\boldsymbol{x}_t - \rho^r \boldsymbol{x}_{t-1}) + (\rho - \rho^r)(y_{t-1} - \boldsymbol{\beta}^{r\prime}\boldsymbol{x}_{t-1}) + u_t^{*r}. \tag{10.2.27}$$

This regression yields the new value of $\boldsymbol{\beta}$ and the update in ρ. The interest in this method lies in the comparison with the well-known Cochrane and Orcutt (1949) (CO) procedure. The latter is a stepwise (or 'flip-flop') algorithm, in which each iteration consists of a regression in the 'quasi-differenced' variables,

$$(y_t - \rho^r y_{t-1}) = \boldsymbol{\beta}'(\boldsymbol{x}_t - \rho^r \boldsymbol{x}_{t-1}) + u_t^{+r} \tag{10.2.28}$$

followed by estimation of ρ in a separate autoregression on the residuals from (10.2.28). The two methods have an obvious family resemblance, in that (10.2.28) matches (10.2.27) except for the second right-hand side term.

It can be shown that the CO algorithm will locate the minimum of the sum of squares function if iterated until convergence, and hence iterated GN and iterated CO define the same estimator. As two-step methods they have quite different properties, however. In earlier times, the two-step CO estimator was often implemented by taking the initial $\boldsymbol{\beta}$ from the OLS regression of y_t on $\boldsymbol{x}_t$, so that ρ was implicitly initialized at 0. In this case, the second step is not even guaranteed to be consistent, if the equation contains lagged endogenous variables. Durbin (1960) proposed estimating the unrestricted form of (10.2.22) by OLS to obtain consistent initial estimates, but even then, the CO method is not asymptotically equivalent to NLLS unless iterated to convergence.

Another point of interest is that these methods can be interpreted as feasible implementations of the GLS formula in (2.3.8), at least in large samples. The AR disturbances imply that the matrix $\boldsymbol{\Omega}$ in (2.3.1) depends on ρ. Its form can easily be reconstructed using the formulae in §5.2.5. After factorizing $\boldsymbol{\Omega}^{-1}$ into $\boldsymbol{KK}'$, rows 2 to n of $\boldsymbol{KX}$ and $\boldsymbol{Ky}$ in (2.3.5) are just the 'quasi-differences' shown in (10.2.28). If the true ρ were known and used to implement the step, (10.2.27) and (10.2.28) would be identical. True GLS would be implemented in exactly this manner, except that $\boldsymbol{x}_1$ and y_1 multiplied by $\sqrt{1-\rho^2}$ should added as the first observation in the transformed data set. This is called the Prais–Winsten (1954) correction. Provided $|\rho| < 1$ the correction is asymptotically negligible.

10.2.4 The AR(1) Error Model: Asymptotics

The next job is to check out each of the assumptions needed for consistency and asymptotic normality. Write (10.2.22) in the form

$$g_t = \boldsymbol{\beta}'\boldsymbol{x}_t - \rho\boldsymbol{\beta}'\boldsymbol{x}_{t-1} + \rho u_{t-1} + \rho g_{t-1}. \tag{10.2.29}$$

This representation emphasizes the fact that y_{t-1} cannot be treated as a datum in this analysis, since the model has to be solved for different values of $\boldsymbol{\theta}$ given $\boldsymbol{x}_t$ and u_t, whose properties are given by assumption.

For condition (b) of Theorem 9.3.1 to hold, it must be shown in view of (10.2.12) that the sequences $g_t(\boldsymbol{\theta})u_t$ and $[g_t(\boldsymbol{\theta}_0) - g_t(\boldsymbol{\theta})]^2$ satisfy the WLLN pointwise on Θ, and are stochastically equicontinuous. Theorem 6.4.4 can establish the pointwise convergence, subject to the required dependence and moment conditions being established. Assuming the stability condition $|\rho| < 1$, g_t can be expanded as

$$g_t = \boldsymbol{\beta}'\boldsymbol{x}_t + \sum_{j=0}^{\infty}\rho^j u_{t-j-1}. \tag{10.2.30}$$

Also assume that $\boldsymbol{x}_t$ has a stable VAR representation, $\boldsymbol{x}_t = \boldsymbol{\Lambda}\boldsymbol{x}_{t-1} + \boldsymbol{v}_t$. Then, similarly to the argument in §7.1.4,

$$g_t = \boldsymbol{\beta}'\boldsymbol{Q}\sum_{k=0}^{\infty}\boldsymbol{M}^k\boldsymbol{v}_{t-k}^* + \sum_{j=0}^{\infty}\rho^j u_{t-j-1} \tag{10.2.31}$$

where $\boldsymbol{v}_t^* = \boldsymbol{Q}^{-1}\boldsymbol{v}_t$ and $\boldsymbol{M}$ is the diagonal matrix of eigenvalues of $\boldsymbol{\Lambda}$ (assumed distinct). Applying the result in (6.4.7) as before, the argument shows that g_t is a linear combination of processes that are L_2-NED on $(\boldsymbol{v}_t, u_t)$ of size $-\infty$. Hence, it is itself such a process, by Theorem 6.4.2.

More generally, one might want to think of $\boldsymbol{x}_t$ as embedded in a larger VAR system. This is easily accommodated by inserting the relevant VAR into (10.2.31), replacing $\boldsymbol{\beta}$ by a selection vector, containing the elements of $\boldsymbol{\beta}$ in the positions corresponding to the included regressors, and zeros in the other positions. Higher order lag models can be incorporated similarly using the companion form of the system.

Given the assumptions about u_t, the moment conditions imposed by Theorem 6.4.4 are satisfied if $E|g_t(\boldsymbol{\theta})|^r < \infty$ uniformly in t and for $r > 2$. Once again, it is not difficult to adapt the arguments from §7.1.4 to the present case. According to those arguments, the L_r-norm of g_t in (10.2.31) is finite when $|\rho| < 1$, subject to the same condition being observed by u_t and $\boldsymbol{v}_t$. However, there is the problem that the finiteness is required at every point of Θ, which must be a compact set. Ideally, Θ should include all values $|\rho| < 1$. Since the moment condition fails at the point $\rho = 1$ this must be excluded from the sample space, but the need for Θ to be closed requires a bound to be imposed, of the form $|\rho| \leq 1 - a$. for $a > 0$.[1]

Having established pointwise convergence on Θ, the next job is to convert this to uniform convergence. To check stochastic equicontinuity the conditions of Theorem 9.3.2 must be verified for the terms $\psi_{1t} = g_t^2$, $\psi_{2t} = g_t(\boldsymbol{\theta}_0)g_t$, and $\psi_{3t} = g_t u_t$. It will suffice to examine the first case, since the others follow similar lines. The trick is to use the mean value theorem. Using the Cauchy–Schwarz inequality in the form (B.5.14) with $p = q = 2$,

$$\begin{aligned}\left|g_t(\boldsymbol{\theta}_1)^2 - g_t(\boldsymbol{\theta}_2)^2\right| &= 2|g_t(\boldsymbol{\theta}^*)\nabla g_t(\boldsymbol{\theta}^*)'(\boldsymbol{\theta}_1 - \boldsymbol{\theta}_2)| \\ &\leq 2|g_t(\boldsymbol{\theta}^*)|\|\nabla g_t(\boldsymbol{\theta}^*)\|\,\|\boldsymbol{\theta}_1 - \boldsymbol{\theta}_2\| \qquad (10.2.32)\end{aligned}$$

where the '$*$' denotes evaluation at a point on the line segment joining $\boldsymbol{\theta}_1$ and $\boldsymbol{\theta}_2$. The inequality shows it is sufficient if

$$B_{1t} = 2|g_t(\boldsymbol{\theta})|\|\nabla g_t(\boldsymbol{\theta})\| = O_p(1) \quad \forall \boldsymbol{\theta} \in \Theta. \qquad (10.2.33)$$

The fact that $|g_t(\boldsymbol{\theta})| = O_p(1)$ has already been established. The derivative vector ∇g_t is partitioned into components[2]

$$\nabla_\beta g_t = \boldsymbol{x}_t - \rho \boldsymbol{x}_{t-1} + \rho \nabla_\beta g_{t-1} \qquad (10.2.34a)$$

$$\nabla_\rho g_t = -\boldsymbol{\beta}'\boldsymbol{x}_{t-1} + u_{t-1} + g_{t-1} + \rho \nabla_\rho g_{t-1} \qquad (10.2.34b)$$

Stacking these two equations together with (10.2.29) yields a recursive (lower triangular) system of stochastic difference equations, whose driving variables $\boldsymbol{x}_t$ and u_t are $O_p(1)$. The methods of §4.3 or §5.2.8 easily establish the stability of this system, whose eigenvalues are all equal to ρ. This holds for any point in the parameter space. Extending this argument to the other cases shows there is no problem about uniform convergence.

---

[1]With ρ close to 1, the adequacy of the asymptotic approximation to the finite sample distribution is in any case poor (i.e. a very large sample is needed to be close to the limit) so such a restriction is reasonable in practice.

[2]It may seem odd that these formulae are different from (10.2.24). As noted, the difference is that in the computational framework y_t is treated as given, so that changing parameter values changes u_t. Here u_t is given, and changing parameter values changes y_t.

The last step in proving consistency is to establish condition (c) of Theorem 9.3.1. This requires a little ingenuity. Let $g_{0t} - g_t$ denote $g_t(\boldsymbol{\theta}_0) - g_t(\boldsymbol{\theta})$. Using (10.2.29) and some rearrangement produces

$$\begin{aligned} g_{0t} - g_t &= (\boldsymbol{\beta}_0 - \boldsymbol{\beta})'\boldsymbol{x}_t - (\rho_0\boldsymbol{\beta}_0 - \rho\boldsymbol{\beta})'\boldsymbol{x}_{t-1} + (\rho_0 - \rho)u_{t-1} + \rho_0 g_{0,t-1} - \rho g_{t-1} \\ &= (\boldsymbol{\beta}_0 - \boldsymbol{\beta})'(\boldsymbol{x}_t - \rho\boldsymbol{x}_{t-1}) + (\rho_0 - \rho)v_{t-1} + \rho(g_{0,t-1} - g_{t-1}) \qquad (10.2.35) \end{aligned}$$

where $v_t = u_t + g_{0t} - \boldsymbol{\beta}_0'\boldsymbol{x}_t$. Define the $k+1$-vector $\boldsymbol{z}_t = (\boldsymbol{x}_t' - \rho\boldsymbol{x}_{t-1}', v_{t-1})'$, which depends on ρ, although note that v_t depends only on ρ_0 and $\boldsymbol{\beta}_0$ and is nothing but the 'true' unadjusted residual. Squaring, summing and taking plims yields

$$\begin{aligned} (1-\rho^2)\,\text{plim}\,\frac{1}{n}\sum_{t=1}^{n}(g_{0t} - g_t)^2 &= 2\rho(\boldsymbol{\theta}_0 - \boldsymbol{\theta})'\,\text{plim}\,\frac{1}{n}\sum_{t=1}^{n}\boldsymbol{z}_t(g_{0t} - g_t) \\ &\quad + (\boldsymbol{\theta}_0 - \boldsymbol{\theta})'\,\text{plim}\,\frac{1}{n}\sum_{t=1}^{n}\boldsymbol{z}_t\boldsymbol{z}_t'(\boldsymbol{\theta}_0 - \boldsymbol{\theta}). \qquad (10.2.36) \end{aligned}$$

To verify that the left-hand side is equal to 0 uniquely at the point $\boldsymbol{\theta} = \boldsymbol{\theta}_0$, note first that the first right-hand side term must be 0 identically whenever the left-hand side is 0, since the latter is a sum of nonnegative terms that must all vanish. Hence, all depends on the second right-hand side term. A sufficient condition for identification now emerges, which is that the second moment matrix of $\boldsymbol{z}_t$ has full rank of $k+1$ for all ρ such that $|\rho| < 1 - a$. So long as the matrix of regressors has full rank asymptotically, essentially condition (7.1.3), there should not be any problem about meeting this condition.

This completes the check on consistency conditions, and most of the work is also done for establishing the asymptotic distribution. This requires simply that $\nabla g_t(\boldsymbol{\theta}_0)u_t$ is a m.d. process satisfying (10.2.15), which certainly follows given (10.2.34). There is one more result to be verified, and this is the convergence in (10.2.19). This requires the second moments of the derivatives to converge, which can be shown using the previous approach, checking the dependence and moment conditions for Theorem 6.4.4. Using (10.2.34) these follow straightforwardly. However, (10.2.19) also specifies that the average product of u_t and the matrix of second derivatives converges to zero, which is an application of the weak law for martingale differences, but requires verification that the second derivatives also satisfy the requisite moment conditions. These are

$$\nabla^2_{\beta\beta}g_t = \rho\nabla^2_{\beta\beta}g_{t-1} \qquad (10.2.37a)$$

$$\nabla^2_{\rho\rho}g_t = 2\nabla_{\rho}g_{t-1} + \rho\nabla^2_{\rho\rho}g_{t-1} \qquad (10.2.37b)$$

$$\nabla^2_{\beta\rho}g_t = -\boldsymbol{x}_{t-1} + \nabla_{\beta}g_{t-1} + \rho\nabla^2_{\beta\rho}g_t \qquad (10.2.37c)$$

Stacking these three equations together with (10.2.34) and (10.2.29) yields a recursive system of 6 difference equations, which are once again stable with common eigenvalues of ρ. This completes, in outline, the full asymptotic analysis of the model.

10.2.5 The MA(1) Error Model

Now let

$$g_t = \boldsymbol{\beta}'\boldsymbol{x}_t + \theta u_{t-1} = \boldsymbol{\beta}'\boldsymbol{x}_t + \theta(y_{t-1} - g_{t-1}) \tag{10.2.38}$$

where repeated substitution would show g_t to be a function of x_{t-j} and y_{t-j-1} for all $j > 0$. The derivatives required for estimation by Gauss–Newton are

$$\frac{\partial g_t}{\partial \boldsymbol{\beta}} = \boldsymbol{x}_t - \theta \frac{\partial g_{t-1}}{\partial \boldsymbol{\beta}} \tag{10.2.39a}$$

$$\frac{\partial g_t}{\partial \theta} = y_{t-1} - g_{t-1} - \theta \frac{\partial g_{t-1}}{\partial \theta}. \tag{10.2.39b}$$

These formulae can be solved recursively for $t = 1, \ldots, n$ given initial values g_0, $\partial g_0/\partial \boldsymbol{\beta}$ and $\partial g_0/\partial \theta$. The initial values might be set at zero, which represents an error of small order asymptotically and is influential in practice only when θ is close to 1.

By choosing $x_t = y_{t-1}$, this provides a simple method of estimating the ARMA(1,1) model. The generalization to ARMA$(p, 1)$ should be obvious, but one can also generalize to ARMA(p, q) for $q > 1$ without too much difficulty. This method, like the AR procedures, can be shown to be as asymptotically equivalent to feasible GLS, under the MA(1) error assumption.

The asymptotic analysis of the MA model is more straightforward than the AR model, because the relevant representation of g_t is given by the first equality in (10.2.38). The duality between the two models is emphasized by the fact that a recursive solution is needed for computational purposes in the MA case, and for the asymptotic analysis in the AR case. On the other hand, closed form equations appear in the computation of the AR, and in the asymptotics of the MA. The demonstration of consistency and asymptotic normality of the estimates is comparatively straightforward, adapting the techniques of the previous section.

10.2.6 The Adaptive Expectations/Stock Adjustment Model

This model is described in §5.4.2. Consider specifically equation (5.4.17), which gives after rearrangement,

$$g_t = (1 - \lambda)\beta_1 x_{1t} + \boldsymbol{\beta}_2'\boldsymbol{x}_{2t} - \lambda\boldsymbol{\beta}_2'\boldsymbol{x}_{2,t-1} + \lambda g_{t-1}. \tag{10.2.40}$$

The derivatives required to perform the Gauss–Newton iterations are

$$\frac{\partial g_t}{\partial \beta_1} = (1 - \lambda)x_{1t} + \lambda \frac{\partial g_{t-1}}{\partial \beta_1} \tag{10.2.41a}$$

$$\frac{\partial g_t}{\partial \boldsymbol{\beta}_2} = \boldsymbol{x}_{2t} - \lambda \boldsymbol{x}_{2,t-1} + \lambda \frac{\partial g_{t-1}}{\partial \boldsymbol{\beta}_2} \tag{10.2.41b}$$

$$\frac{\partial g_t}{\partial \lambda} = -\beta_1 x_{1t} - \boldsymbol{\beta}_2'\boldsymbol{x}_{2,t-1} + g_{t-1} + \lambda \frac{\partial g_{t-1}}{\partial \lambda} \tag{10.2.41c}$$

to be evaluated recursively, where the recursions can be initialized at 0, as before.

The asymptotic analysis provides another variant on the approach in §10.2.4, for this time note that g_t has the expanded form

$$g_t = (1-\lambda)\beta_1 \sum_{j=0}^{\infty} \lambda^j x_{1,t-j} + \boldsymbol{\beta}_2' \boldsymbol{x}_{2t}. \tag{10.2.42}$$

This resembles the expansion in (10.2.30), except that the variable that now appears in an infinite distributed lag is not a disturbance term but the observed variable x_{1t}, which may be expected to have a serial dependence structure of its own. For simplicity assume that this is a stable AR(1), say

$$x_{1t} = \sum_{k=0}^{\infty} \alpha^k v_{t-k}. \tag{10.2.43}$$

Substituting into (10.2.42) produces

$$\begin{aligned} g_t &= (1-\lambda)\beta_1 \sum_{j=0}^{\infty} \lambda^j \sum_{k=0}^{\infty} \alpha^k v_{t-k-j} + \boldsymbol{\beta}_2' \boldsymbol{x}_{2t} \\ &= (1-\lambda)\beta_1 \sum_{k=0}^{\infty} \left(\sum_{j=0}^{k} \lambda^j \alpha^{k-j} \right) v_{t-k} + \boldsymbol{\beta}_2' \boldsymbol{x}_{2t}. \end{aligned} \tag{10.2.44}$$

Now note that

$$\sum_{j=0}^{k} \lambda^j \alpha^{k-j} = O((k+1)\max\{\lambda, \alpha\}^k). \tag{10.2.45}$$

These terms converge exponentially to 0 just as like λ^k or α^k. The only difference is that their sum is a bit bigger than either of these, and the conclusion that g_t is L_2-NED on v_t still holds good. However, there is a twist to this result, since as pointed out in §5.5.1, adaptive expectations only coincide with the *rational* expectation when x_{1t} is an IMA process, corresponding here to $\alpha = 1$. In this case the assumptions fail and the least squares estimates, while consistent, are not asymptotically normal. See Chapter 15 for the analysis of regressions of this sort.

10.2.7 The Error Correction Model

One last example illustrates the usefulness of the asymptotic theory in situations even where the estimation problem has a trivial solution. Consider equation (5.3.23). This is nothing but a linear regression of the form

$$\alpha^{**}(L)\Delta y_t = \boldsymbol{\delta}' \boldsymbol{d}_t + \boldsymbol{\beta}^{**}(L)' \Delta \boldsymbol{z}_t - \alpha y_{t-1} + \boldsymbol{\gamma}' \boldsymbol{z}_{t-1} + u_t. \tag{10.2.46}$$

where the parameters of interest include $\boldsymbol{\theta} = -\boldsymbol{\gamma}/\alpha$. There is no difficulty here in computing the point estimates since the nonlinearity does not impose any restrictions. Simply obtain $\hat{\alpha}$ and $\hat{\boldsymbol{\gamma}}$ by least squares and compute $\hat{\boldsymbol{\theta}} = -\hat{\boldsymbol{\gamma}}/\hat{\alpha}$. While the theory of linear regression does not show how to construct standard errors for the derived estimates $\hat{\boldsymbol{\theta}}$ and test hypotheses, it is evident that the solution is to use formula (10.2.21) for this purpose. Nonlinearity in the parameters is not always a matter of imposing restrictions, but may also be implied by a derived parameterization.

There is, again, a caveat to be observed. While the application of the ECM to stationary data is perfectly valid, the commonest application of this type of model is to integrated time series, in which the regularity conditions for the CLT are violated. The statistical treatment of the nonstationary case is considered in §15.2.5.

10.3 Generalized Method of Moments

Let the results of the last section now be adapted to the general case where conditions (10.2.10) hold for the elements of the vector

$$\boldsymbol{f}(\boldsymbol{\theta}_0) = \boldsymbol{u} \tag{10.3.1}$$

but the vector $\boldsymbol{f}$ $(n \times 1)$ does not have the form previously assumed. Specifically, it does not have the form $\boldsymbol{y} - \boldsymbol{g}(\boldsymbol{\theta})$ where $\boldsymbol{y}$ does not depend on unknown parameters, and the elements g_t are $\mathcal{I}_t$-measurable. The class of estimators suited to this kind of problem are known as 'generalized method of moments' (GMM) and also as nonlinear instrumental variables (NLIV). They are defined as minimizing the function

$$C_n(\boldsymbol{\theta}) = \frac{1}{2n}\boldsymbol{f}(\boldsymbol{\theta})'\boldsymbol{Z}(\boldsymbol{Z}'\boldsymbol{Z})^{-1}\boldsymbol{Z}'\boldsymbol{f}(\boldsymbol{\theta}) \tag{10.3.2}$$

where $\boldsymbol{Z}$ $(n \times M)$ is a matrix whose rows $\boldsymbol{z}_t'$ are $\mathcal{I}_t$-measurable random variables; see Amemiya (1974, 1975), Hansen (1982). In the case where g_t is linear (but not $\mathcal{I}_t$-measurable) they correspond to the 2SLS method of §8.2. These methods have been exploited especially in the estimation of rational expectations models, since the Euler equations implied by optimum choices under rational expectations characteristically define a function of data and parameters such as (10.3.1) with conditional mean zero; see for example Hansen and Singleton (1982), Epstein and Zin (1991).

10.3.1 Asymptotic Theory

Letting

$$\boldsymbol{D}(\boldsymbol{\theta}) = \boldsymbol{\nabla}\boldsymbol{f}(\boldsymbol{\theta}) \quad (n \times p) \tag{10.3.3}$$

the minimizer $\hat{\boldsymbol{\theta}}$ solves the p equations

$$\boldsymbol{\nabla}C_n(\boldsymbol{\theta}) = \frac{\boldsymbol{D}(\boldsymbol{\theta})'\boldsymbol{Z}(\boldsymbol{Z}'\boldsymbol{Z})^{-1}\boldsymbol{Z}'\boldsymbol{f}(\boldsymbol{\theta})}{n} = \boldsymbol{0}. \tag{10.3.4}$$

In the usual way, the assumptions must be such as to lead to the result

$$\frac{1}{\sqrt{n}}\boldsymbol{Z}'\boldsymbol{f}(\boldsymbol{\theta}_0) \xrightarrow{\text{D}} \text{N}(\boldsymbol{0}, \sigma^2\boldsymbol{M}_{ZZ}). \tag{10.3.5}$$

The arguments in §7.1 and §10.2.2 apply here with little amendment. The combination of assumption (10.2.10) and suitable regularity conditions holding for $\boldsymbol{z}_t$ are sufficient to obtain (10.3.5), similarly to (7.1.14). The $p \times p$ matrix of second derivatives of the criterion function, by analogy with (10.2.18), is

$$\nabla^2 C_n = \frac{\boldsymbol{D}'\boldsymbol{Z}(\boldsymbol{Z}'\boldsymbol{Z})^{-1}\boldsymbol{Z}'\boldsymbol{D}}{n} - \frac{\nabla \boldsymbol{D}'\boldsymbol{Z}(\boldsymbol{Z}'\boldsymbol{Z})^{-1}\boldsymbol{Z}'[\boldsymbol{f}(\boldsymbol{\theta}) \otimes \boldsymbol{I}_p]}{n}. \qquad (10.3.6)$$

In view of (10.3.1) and the same argument as before, the second term is $O_p(n^{-1/2})$ at the point $\boldsymbol{\theta}_0$, and under suitable assumptions,

$$\begin{aligned}\operatorname{plim} \nabla^2 C_n(\boldsymbol{\theta}_0) &= \operatorname{plim} \frac{\boldsymbol{D}(\boldsymbol{\theta}_0)'\boldsymbol{Z}(\boldsymbol{Z}'\boldsymbol{Z})^{-1}\boldsymbol{Z}'\boldsymbol{D}(\boldsymbol{\theta}_0)}{n} \\ &= \boldsymbol{M}_{DZ}(\boldsymbol{\theta}_0)\boldsymbol{M}_{ZZ}^{-1}\boldsymbol{M}_{ZD}(\boldsymbol{\theta}_0) \qquad (10.3.7)\end{aligned}$$

where the limit matrix must be finite and positive definite, with rank p (so that in particular, $M \geq p$ is necessary). The required conclusion is

$$\sqrt{n}(\hat{\boldsymbol{\theta}} - \boldsymbol{\theta}_0) \xrightarrow{\text{D}} \text{N}(\boldsymbol{0}, \sigma^2[\boldsymbol{M}_{DZ}(\boldsymbol{\theta}_0)\boldsymbol{M}_{ZZ}^{-1}\boldsymbol{M}_{ZD}(\boldsymbol{\theta}_0)]^{-1}). \qquad (10.3.8)$$

In view of (10.3.4) and (10.3.7), it can be seen that equality (9.3.19) holds in this case, as for the least squares estimators.

The question of interest is the choice of the variables $\boldsymbol{z}_t$ that make this estimator asymptotically efficient in the class. This analysis is a straightforward generalization of §8.2.5. Let $\boldsymbol{E}(\boldsymbol{\theta}_0)$ denote the matrix whose transposed rows are the $\mathcal{I}_t$-measurable random vectors $E(\boldsymbol{d}_t(\boldsymbol{\theta}_0)|\mathcal{I}_t)$, and note that

$$\operatorname{plim} \frac{\boldsymbol{Z}'\boldsymbol{E}(\boldsymbol{\theta}_0)}{n} = \boldsymbol{M}_{ZD}(\boldsymbol{\theta}_0) \qquad (10.3.9)$$

in view of the fact that the vectors $\boldsymbol{d}_t(\boldsymbol{\theta}_0) - E(\boldsymbol{d}_t(\boldsymbol{\theta}_0)|\mathcal{I}_t)$ are uncorrelated with $\mathcal{I}_t$-measurable $\boldsymbol{z}_t$. Arguing analogously to (8.2.54) and (8.2.55) with $\boldsymbol{D}$ replacing $\boldsymbol{X}$, and also using Lemma A.7.6, the matrix

$$[\boldsymbol{M}_{DZ}(\boldsymbol{\theta}_0)\boldsymbol{M}_{ZZ}^{-1}\boldsymbol{M}_{ZD}(\boldsymbol{\theta}_0)]^{-1} - \boldsymbol{M}_{EE}(\boldsymbol{\theta}_0)^{-1} \qquad (10.3.10)$$

may be shown to be positive semi-definite, where

$$\boldsymbol{M}_{EE}(\boldsymbol{\theta}_0) = \operatorname{plim} \frac{\boldsymbol{E}(\boldsymbol{\theta}_0)'\boldsymbol{E}(\boldsymbol{\theta}_0)}{n}. \qquad (10.3.11)$$

Choosing $\boldsymbol{z}_t = E(\boldsymbol{d}_t(\boldsymbol{\theta}_0)|\mathcal{I}_t)$ is therefore the asymptotically efficient case. This is not generally a feasible estimator since these functions typically have unknown form, although if they were known, substituting a preliminary consistent estimate of $\boldsymbol{\theta}$ for $\boldsymbol{\theta}_0$ in the formulae should yield an asymptotically efficient two-stage estimator.[3] A feasible alternative is to attempt to estimate $E(\boldsymbol{d}_t(\boldsymbol{\theta}_0)|\mathcal{I}_t)$ by projecting

---

[3]This claim needs to be established, and such an argument must usually proceed by applying a Taylor's expansion to the random functions $E(\boldsymbol{d}_t(\boldsymbol{\theta})|\mathcal{I}_t)$, to determine the order of magnitude of the error due to estimation. This is not attempted here, but see §13.5.3 for the analysis of a closely related problem, where the derivatives depend on estimated variance parameters.

$\boldsymbol{d}_t(\boldsymbol{\theta}_0)$ (or a consistent equivalent) linearly on to a collection of $\mathcal{I}_t$-measurable variables, a vector $\boldsymbol{w}_t$ (say). Defining $\check{\boldsymbol{D}} = \boldsymbol{W}(\boldsymbol{W}'\boldsymbol{W})^{-1}\boldsymbol{W}'\boldsymbol{D}$ to be this projection, and setting $\boldsymbol{Z} = \check{\boldsymbol{D}}$, observe that

$$\boldsymbol{D}'\check{\boldsymbol{D}}(\check{\boldsymbol{D}}'\check{\boldsymbol{D}})^{-1}\check{\boldsymbol{D}}'\boldsymbol{D} = \boldsymbol{D}'\boldsymbol{W}(\boldsymbol{W}'\boldsymbol{W})^{-1}\boldsymbol{W}'\boldsymbol{D}. \tag{10.3.12}$$

In other words, this approach is equivalent to choosing $\boldsymbol{Z} = \boldsymbol{W}$. Kelejian (1971) suggests using powers of the conditioning variables as additional instruments. A more elaborate solution to the problem would be to estimate $\boldsymbol{E}$ nonparametrically, see Newey (1990) and Robinson (1991).

10.3.2 A Nonlinear Example

A model with a single dependent variable that is unsuited to least squares estimation, but can be estimated by GMM, takes the form

$$y_t^\gamma - \alpha - \beta x_t = u_t \tag{10.3.13}$$

where $y_t > 0$, and $x_t > 0$ is $\mathcal{I}_t$-measurable. The problem with least squares is that the derivatives

$$\boldsymbol{d}_t' = (y_t^\gamma \log y_t,\ 1,\ x_t) \tag{10.3.14}$$

are not $\mathcal{I}_t$-measurable, in respect of the first element.

There is no way to evaluate $E(y_t^\gamma \log y_t|\mathcal{I}_t)$, where $y_t = (\alpha + \beta x_t + u_t)^{1/\gamma}$, in closed form. GMM might be implemented with a set of instruments $\boldsymbol{z}_t = (1,\ x_t,\ f(x_t))'$, where $f(\cdot)$ is a function chosen to mimic the unobserved expectation as far as possible. For example, $x_t \log(x_t)$ might be considered. In principle the matrix $\boldsymbol{M}_{ZD}$ constructed from these components should have full rank, and feasible GMM with these instruments is consistent. However, monotone transformations of a variable tend to be quite highly collinear unless the range of variation is wide. The condition of this matrix and hence the efficiency of the procedure depends on x_t exhibiting sufficient variation in the sample.

10.3.3 Application to Rational Expectations

Next, consider the model in §5.5.3. Without attempting to solve the model, simply consider directly the structural equation (5.5.13b). Define a conditioning set $\mathcal{R}_t$ containing only the variables used by agents for forming expectations of x_{t+1}. The variable $E_t x_{t+1} = E(x_{t+1}|\mathcal{R}_t)$ is unobservable, but defining

$$f_t(\gamma, \delta) = y_t - \gamma x_{t+1} - \delta w_t = v_t - \gamma\eta_{t+1} \tag{10.3.15}$$

it is immediate that $E(f_t(\gamma,\delta)|\mathcal{R}_t) = 0$. In this example the equation is actually linear in the variables. Given a suitable instrument vector $\boldsymbol{z}_t \in \mathcal{R}_t$, it can be estimated by two-stage least squares as in (8.2.26) with the single novelty of an endogenous explanatory variable dated $t+1$, which is acting as a proxy for the unobservable. In the model of §5.5.3 suitable instruments would be $\boldsymbol{z}_t = (z_t, w_t)'$, although the assumptions such as (5.5.14) and (5.5.15), that were introduced to ensure a tractable solution the model, are inessential for the present approach.

The use of instrumental variables in such a case is proposed by McCallum (1976). He points out that to avoid inconsistent estimates, it is essential to select instruments satisfying the theoretical orthogonality condition. If agents are not strongly rational then $\mathcal{R}_t \subset \mathcal{I}_t$ where $\mathcal{I}_t$ is the information set containing the candidate instruments. There is a risk that $E(\eta_t|\mathcal{I}_t) \neq 0$ so that assumption (10.2.10a) fails. In other words, any variable not used by agents for prediction can be correlated with the prediction error. For a variable to be a valid instrument, it is not enough to be a valid conditioning variable in the usual sense.

10.3.4 Nonlinear 2SLS

The last example is the case of nonlinearity in parameters with endogenous explanatory variables. Write the model in vector form as

$$\boldsymbol{y}_1 - \boldsymbol{Y}_2\boldsymbol{\beta}(\boldsymbol{\theta}) - \boldsymbol{Z}_1\boldsymbol{\gamma}(\boldsymbol{\theta}) = \boldsymbol{u}_1 \tag{10.3.16}$$

where $\boldsymbol{Y}_2$ and $\boldsymbol{X}_1$ are matrices of variables, and the problem is that $\boldsymbol{y}'_{2t}$ (row t of $\boldsymbol{Y}_2$) is not $\mathcal{I}_t$-measurable and is correlated with u_{1t}. The derivatives may in this case be written in the form

$$\boldsymbol{D} = \begin{bmatrix}\boldsymbol{Y}_2 & \boldsymbol{Z}_1\end{bmatrix}\begin{bmatrix}\boldsymbol{\nabla\beta} \\ \boldsymbol{\nabla\gamma}\end{bmatrix} \tag{10.3.17}$$

where the right-hand matrix is composed of the Jacobian matrices of the coefficient vectors with respect to $\boldsymbol{\theta}$. Suppose that the model can be completed by linear reduced form equations

$$\boldsymbol{Y}_2 = \boldsymbol{Z}\boldsymbol{\Pi}'_2 + \boldsymbol{U}_2 \tag{10.3.18}$$

where $\boldsymbol{Z} = \begin{bmatrix}\boldsymbol{Z}_1 & \boldsymbol{Z}_2\end{bmatrix}$, the tth row of this matrix is $\mathcal{I}_t$-measurable, and $E(\boldsymbol{u}_{2t}|\mathcal{I}_t) = \boldsymbol{0}$. The optimal instrument matrix is $\boldsymbol{Z\Psi}$ where

$$\boldsymbol{\Psi} = \boldsymbol{\Pi}'_2\boldsymbol{\nabla\beta} + \begin{bmatrix}\boldsymbol{\nabla\gamma} \\ \boldsymbol{0}\end{bmatrix}. \tag{10.3.19}$$

If the instrument matrix is to have rank p, there must be at least p linearly independent columns in $\boldsymbol{Z}$. This condition generalizes the order condition for identification given in §8.3. However, in this case the matrix $\begin{bmatrix}\boldsymbol{\nabla\beta}' & \boldsymbol{\nabla\gamma}'\end{bmatrix}$ must also have rank p everywhere in Θ, which is a supplementary identification condition. If these conditions are satisfied, the optimal GMM estimator can be evidently be computed using the matrix $\boldsymbol{Z}$ as instruments, by the argument of (10.3.12). An identical form of the estimator is obtained by replacing $\boldsymbol{Y}_2$ by $\hat{\boldsymbol{Y}}_2 = \boldsymbol{Z}(\boldsymbol{Z}'\boldsymbol{Z})^{-1}\boldsymbol{Z}'\boldsymbol{Y}_2$, and then applying nonlinear least squares. This procedure might be called nonlinear 2SLS.

However, this is a specific exception to the rule that nonlinear 2SLS and GMM are *not* equivalent. Consider a nonlinear simultaneous equations model of the form

$$y_{1t} = g(\boldsymbol{y}_{2t}, \boldsymbol{z}_{1t}, \boldsymbol{\theta}) + u_{1t} \tag{10.3.20}$$

$$\boldsymbol{y}_{2t} = \boldsymbol{\Pi}_2\boldsymbol{z}_t + \boldsymbol{u}_{2t} \tag{10.3.21}$$

where u_{1t} and u_{2t} are correlated. The nonlinear regression of y_{1t} on $g(\hat{y}_{2t}, z_{1t}, \theta)$, where $\hat{y}_{2t} = \hat{\Pi}_2 z_t$, is generally inconsistent. The term 'nonlinear two-stage least squares' has sometimes been used as a synonym for GMM (e.g. Amemiya 1974), so care should be taken to note that, except for the linear-in-variables case of (10.3.16), this particular two-stage procedure is improper.

10.4 Modelling Second Moments

10.4.1 Residual Variance Estimation

Chapter 7 reviewed least squares estimation at length, but the problem of estimating the residual variance was treated as a side issue. Estimating the variance σ^2 of a zero-mean data series u_t by the sample average $\hat{\sigma}^2 = n^{-1}\sum_{t=1}^n u_t^2$ (i.e., the method of moments) was shown to be consistent by direct methods.

Suppose momentarily that u_t is an observed process with mean 0. The method of moments can be rationalised as an optimization estimator by noting that $\hat{\sigma}^2$ minimises the criterion

$$C_n(v) = \frac{\sum_{t=1}^n u_t^2}{2nv} + \frac{\ln v}{2}. \tag{10.4.1}$$

Note that C_n has the form of (9.1.4) where $\psi_t(v) = (v,\, u_t^2)'$.[4] If $E(u_t^2) = \sigma^2$ for any t, the expected value of C_n is

$$\bar{C}(v) = \frac{\sigma^2}{2v} + \frac{\ln v}{2} \tag{10.4.2}$$

for any n, and hence also in the limit as $n \to \infty$. The first-order conditions

$$\frac{d\bar{C}(v)}{dv} = -\frac{\sigma^2}{2v^2} + \frac{1}{2v} = 0 \tag{10.4.3}$$

have solution $v = \sigma^2$, and checking the second-order conditions (or inspection) shows that σ^2 is the minimum of $\bar{C}$, and is clearly unique. The conditions of Theorem 9.3.1 are evidently satisfied under suitable assumptions on u_t, and minimizing $C_n(v)$ should yield a consistent estimator of σ^2, although to satisfy condition (a) of the theorem requires specifying a parameter space that is bounded below by some small positive value. Since the function is tending to $+\infty$ as v approaches 0, there is no difficulty about ensuring an interior minimum in practice.

Now extend the analysis, replacing u_t by the regression disturbance having properties specified in §7.1. The criterion function for this case is

$$C_n(b, v) = \frac{\sum_{t=1}^n (y_t - x_t'b)^2}{2nv} + \frac{\ln v}{2}. \tag{10.4.4}$$

Note that its asymptotic expectation is

$$\bar{C}(b, v) = \frac{\sigma^2 + (b - \beta)' M_{XX} (b - \beta)}{2v} + \frac{\ln v}{2}$$

---

[4]The divisor 2 has been inserted to avoid carrying a 2 through the gradient formulae when u_t depends on parameters.

which is minimised uniquely by $\boldsymbol{b} = \boldsymbol{\beta}$ and $v = \sigma^2$, and hence Theorem 9.3.1 may be applied as before. As we see in Chapter 11, C_n corresponds to the negative of the log-likelihood function for the Gaussian case, and hence might be called a quasi-likelihood function. However, to demonstrate the CAN property there is no need for any more distributional assumptions than are given in §7.1.

The derivatives are as follows:

$$q_{bn} = \frac{\partial C_n}{\partial \boldsymbol{b}} = \frac{\sum_{t=1}^n \boldsymbol{x}_t(y_t - \boldsymbol{b}'\boldsymbol{x}_t)}{nv} \tag{10.4.5a}$$

$$q_{vn} = \frac{\partial C_n}{\partial v} = -\frac{\sum_{t=1}^n (y_t - \boldsymbol{x}_t'\boldsymbol{b})^2}{2nv^2} + \frac{1}{2v} \tag{10.4.5b}$$

$$\boldsymbol{Q}_{bbn} = \frac{\partial^2 C_n}{\partial \boldsymbol{b}\partial \boldsymbol{b}'} = \frac{\sum_{t=1}^n \boldsymbol{x}_t\boldsymbol{x}_t'}{nv} \tag{10.4.5c}$$

$$Q_{vvn} = \frac{\partial^2 C_n}{\partial v^2} = \frac{\sum_{t=1}^n (y_t - \boldsymbol{x}_t'\boldsymbol{b})^2}{nv^3} - \frac{1}{2v^2} \tag{10.4.5d}$$

$$\boldsymbol{Q}_{bvn} = \frac{\partial^2 C_n}{\partial \boldsymbol{b}\partial v} = -\frac{\sum_{t=1}^n \boldsymbol{x}_t(y_t - \boldsymbol{b}'\boldsymbol{x}_t)}{nv^2} \tag{10.4.5e}$$

Equating (10.4.5a) to zero yields the least squares normal equations with the usual solution $\hat{\boldsymbol{\beta}}$, independently of the value of v, so that also equating (10.4.5b) to 0 and solving the pair of first-order conditions yields $\hat{\boldsymbol{\beta}}$ and $\hat{\sigma}^2$. Second-order conditions for a minimum can be easily verified. The divisor in $\hat{\sigma}^2$ is n, not $n-k$ as required for an unbiased estimator, but the bias is of small order in n and $\hat{\sigma}^2$ is consistent.

The variance matrix of the gradient involves the third and fourth moments of the disturbances, and Assumptions 7.1.1 and 7.1.2 need to be augmented by assuming these moments to exist and to be identical for all t under the conditional distributions. Let these be denoted respectively by

$$\mu_3 = E(u_t^3|\mathcal{I}_t) \tag{10.4.6}$$

$$\mu_4 = E(u_t^4|\mathcal{I}_t). \tag{10.4.7}$$

The components of $\mathrm{Var}[\sqrt{n}\boldsymbol{q}_n(\boldsymbol{\beta}, \sigma^2)]$, and their asymptotic limits, are

$$nE(\boldsymbol{q}_{bn}\boldsymbol{q}_{bn}') = \frac{E(\sum_{t=1}^n \boldsymbol{x}_t\boldsymbol{x}_t')}{n\sigma^2} \to \frac{\boldsymbol{M}_{XX}}{\sigma^2} \tag{10.4.8}$$

$$\begin{aligned} nE(q_{vn}^2) &= \frac{n}{4\sigma^8}E\left(\frac{\sum_{t=1}^n u_t^2}{n} - \sigma^2\right)^2 \\ &= \frac{n}{4\sigma^8}\left(\frac{\mu^4}{n} + \frac{n(n-1)}{n^2}\sigma^4 - \sigma^4\right) \\ &\to \frac{\mu_4 - \sigma^4}{4\sigma^8} \end{aligned} \tag{10.4.9}$$

$$nE(\boldsymbol{q}_{bn}q_{vn}) = -\frac{E(\sum_{t=1}^n \boldsymbol{x}_t u_t \sum_{t=1}^n u_t^2)}{2n\sigma^6} + \frac{E(\sum_{t=1}^n \boldsymbol{x}_t u_t)}{2\sigma^4}$$

$$\to -\frac{\mu_3}{2\sigma^6}\bar{\boldsymbol{\mu}}_x \tag{10.4.10}$$

where $\bar{\boldsymbol{\mu}}_x = \lim_{n\to\infty} n^{-1}\sum_{t=1}^{n} E(\boldsymbol{x}_t)$, in view of the fact that

$$E(\boldsymbol{x}_s u_s u_t^2) = \begin{cases} E(\boldsymbol{x}_t)\mu_3, & s = t \\ \mathbf{0}, & s \neq t \end{cases} \tag{10.4.11}$$

an easily verified consequence of the assumptions. Also,

$$E(\boldsymbol{Q}_{bbn}) = \frac{\boldsymbol{M}_{XX}}{\sigma^2} \tag{10.4.12a}$$

$$E(Q_{vvn}) = \frac{1}{2\sigma^4} \tag{10.4.12b}$$

$$E(\boldsymbol{Q}_{bvn}) = \mathbf{0}. \tag{10.4.12c}$$

The application of Theorem 6.2.3 to establish the central limit theorem calls for either stationarity/ergodicity or

$$E|\boldsymbol{\lambda}_1'\boldsymbol{x}_t u_t + \lambda_2(u_t^2 - \sigma^2)|^{2+\delta} \leq B < \infty \quad \delta > 0,\ \forall\, t \tag{10.4.13}$$

for every vector $\boldsymbol{\lambda} = (\boldsymbol{\lambda}_1', \lambda_2)'$ of unit length. In particular, note that (10.4.13) specifies the existence of moments of u_t of order strictly exceeding 4. Applying Theorem 9.3.6 gives

$$\sqrt{n}\begin{bmatrix} \hat{\boldsymbol{\beta}} - \boldsymbol{\beta} \\ \hat{\sigma}^2 - \sigma^2 \end{bmatrix} \xrightarrow{\text{D}} \text{N}\left(\begin{bmatrix} \mathbf{0} \\ 0 \end{bmatrix}, \begin{bmatrix} \sigma^2\boldsymbol{M}_{XX}^{-1} & -\mu_3\boldsymbol{M}_{XX}^{-1}\bar{\boldsymbol{\mu}}_x \\ -\mu_3\bar{\boldsymbol{\mu}}_x'\boldsymbol{M}_{XX}^{-1} & \mu_4 - \sigma^4 \end{bmatrix}\right). \tag{10.4.14}$$

Notice that the information matrix equality (9.3.20) does *not* apply here in general, because the criterion function is neither a quadratic form nor, in general, a density. The exception is the special case where both $\mu_3 = 0$ (symmetry around 0) and $\mu_4 = 3\sigma^4$ (mesokurtosis). Gaussian disturbances possess these properties and in this case the method corresponds to maximum likelihood, as noted. Also, $\hat{\boldsymbol{\beta}}$ and $\hat{\sigma}^2$ are asymptotically independent subject to the symmetry restriction, but not more generally. In most applications σ^2 is thought of as a nuisance parameter, not subject to interesting restrictions, so fortunately the distribution of the disturbances is not a crucial issue. However, since non-Gaussianity is not typically regarded as a misspecification in econometric modelling it is desirable to bear the distinction between the two cases in mind.

In any event, the assumptions are sufficient for Theorem 6.2.2 to apply to u_t^3 and u_t^4. Hence, μ_3 and μ_4 are consistently estimated by

$$\hat{\mu}_3 = \frac{1}{n}\sum_{t=1}^{n}\hat{u}_t^3 \tag{10.4.15}$$

$$\hat{\mu}_4 = \frac{1}{n}\sum_{t=1}^{n}\hat{u}_t^4. \tag{10.4.16}$$

The substitution of $\hat{u}_t$ for u_t in these formulae does not pose a difficulty, noting that

$$\hat{\mu}_3 = \frac{1}{n}\sum_{t=1}^{n}[u_t + O_p(n^{-1/2})]^3 = \frac{1}{n}\sum_{t=1}^{n}u_t^3 + O_p(n^{-1/2}) \tag{10.4.17}$$

and similarly,

$$\hat{\mu}_4 = \frac{1}{n}\sum_{t=1}^{n}[u_t + O_p(n^{-1/2})]^4 = \frac{1}{n}\sum_{t=1}^{n}u_t^2 + O_p(n^{-1/2}). \tag{10.4.18}$$

Approximate confidence regions for the parameters can therefore be constructed.

To conclude this section, note an important extension that is left for the interested reader to explore. The covariance matrix $\mathbf{\Sigma} = E(\boldsymbol{u}_t\boldsymbol{u}_t')$ of a zero-mean vector $\boldsymbol{u}_t$ can be shown to be consistently estimated by

$$\hat{\mathbf{\Sigma}} = n^{-1}\sum_{t=1}^{n}\boldsymbol{u}_t\boldsymbol{u}_t'. \tag{10.4.19}$$

This turns out to be the minimizer of the function

$$C_n(\boldsymbol{S}) = \frac{|\sum_{t=1}^{n}\boldsymbol{u}_t\boldsymbol{u}_t'|}{2n|\boldsymbol{S}|} + \frac{\ln|\boldsymbol{S}|}{2} \tag{10.4.20}$$

where $|.|$ denotes the determinant, and the asymptotic distribution of $\hat{\mathbf{\Sigma}}$ can therefore be derived by arguments similar to the foregoing. This approach assumes importance in the estimation of systems of related equations, to be pursued in Chapter 13. There are clearly interesting restrictions to test on $\mathbf{\Sigma}$, such as diagonality, and for this kind of application the validity of the information matrix equality is critical. The issue of valid testing is pursued further, in a general framework, in Chapter 12.

10.4.2 Conditional Heteroscedasticity and ARCH Models

The last analysis can be extended to consider a regression model that cannot be treated by the methods of Chapter 7. This is the case $y_t = \boldsymbol{x}_t'\boldsymbol{\beta} + u_t$ where

$$E(u_t|\mathcal{I}_t) = 0 \tag{10.4.21a}$$

$$E(u_t^2|\mathcal{I}_t) = h(\alpha_0 + \boldsymbol{\alpha}_1'\boldsymbol{z}_t) \tag{10.4.21b}$$

where $\boldsymbol{x}_t \in \mathcal{I}_t$, $\boldsymbol{z}_t \in \mathcal{I}_t$, and $h(\cdot)$ is a monotone, positive, twice-differentiable positive function of its argument. Harvey (1976), for example, considers a model of this type. The vectors $\boldsymbol{x}_t$ $(k \times 1)$ and $\boldsymbol{z}_t$ $(p \times 1)$ could have elements in common, possibly after a nonlinear transformation. Thus, $\boldsymbol{z}_t$ could contain the squares of conditioning variables, and then h could be the identity function subject to the constraints $\alpha_0 >$ and $\boldsymbol{\alpha}_1 \geq 0$. The framework and assumptions match those of Chapter 7, except for the possibility of conditional heteroscedasticity. The model contains the homoscedastic model as the case $\boldsymbol{\alpha}_1 = \mathbf{0}$, with $\sigma^2 = h(\alpha_0)$.

For compactness write $\boldsymbol{w}_t = (1,\ \boldsymbol{z}_t')'$, and $\boldsymbol{\alpha} = (\alpha_0,\ \boldsymbol{\alpha}_1')'$. A suitable criterion function, following the pattern of (10.4.4), is

$$C_n(\boldsymbol{b}, \boldsymbol{a}) = \frac{1}{2n}\sum_{t=1}^{n}\left(\frac{(y_t - \boldsymbol{b}'\boldsymbol{x}_t)^2}{h(\boldsymbol{a}'\boldsymbol{w}_t)} + \ln h(\boldsymbol{a}'\boldsymbol{w}_t)\right). \tag{10.4.22}$$

There is no alternative to optimizing this function numerically with respect to the unknowns. Writing h_t as shorthand for $h(\boldsymbol{a}'\boldsymbol{w}_t)$, the derivatives are

$$\boldsymbol{q}_{bn} = -\frac{1}{n}\sum_{t=1}^{n}\frac{u_t}{h_t}\boldsymbol{x}_t \tag{10.4.23}$$

$$\boldsymbol{q}_{an} = -\frac{1}{2n}\sum_{t=1}^{n}\frac{h_t'}{h_t}\left(\frac{u_t^2}{h_t} - 1\right)\boldsymbol{w}_t \tag{10.4.24}$$

$$\boldsymbol{Q}_{bbn} = \frac{1}{n}\sum_{t=1}^{n}\frac{1}{h_t}\boldsymbol{x}_t\boldsymbol{x}_t' \tag{10.4.25}$$

$$\boldsymbol{Q}_{aan} = \frac{1}{2n}\sum_{t=1}^{n}\left[\left(\frac{(h_t')^2}{h_t^2}\right)\frac{u_t^2}{h_t} - \left(\frac{h_t''}{h_t} - \frac{(h_t')^2}{h_t^2}\right)\left(\frac{u_t^2}{h_t} - 1\right)\right]\boldsymbol{w}_t\boldsymbol{w}_t' \tag{10.4.26}$$

$$\boldsymbol{Q}_{ban} = \frac{1}{n}\sum_{t=1}^{n}\left(\frac{h_t'}{h_t^2}\right)u_t\boldsymbol{x}_t\boldsymbol{w}_t' \tag{10.4.27}$$

where h_t' and h_t'' are respectively the first and second derivatives of $h(\cdot)$ with respect to its argument, evaluated at $\boldsymbol{w}_t$. It is convenient to choose $h(\cdot) = \exp\{\cdot\}$, because then the ratios h_t'/h_t and h_t''/h_t reduce to 1, or to choose h as the identity function, so that the terms in h'' disappear.

To verify consistency calls for checking the uniform convergence of $C_n(\boldsymbol{b}, \boldsymbol{a})$, which will depend on the choice of h. In the representation of (9.1.4), $r = 1$ and the functions ψ_t are the terms of the sum in (10.4.22). The stochastic equicontinuity condition of Theorem 9.3.2 presents no problem if $h(\boldsymbol{a}'\boldsymbol{w}_t) > 0$ with probability 1. To verify condition (c) of Theorem 9.3.1, apply the LIE to give

$$\begin{aligned} E[C_n(\boldsymbol{b}, \boldsymbol{a})] &= \frac{1}{2n}E\left[\sum_{t=1}^{n}E\left(\frac{u_t^2 - 2(\boldsymbol{b}-\boldsymbol{\beta})'\boldsymbol{x}_t u_t + (\boldsymbol{b}-\boldsymbol{\beta})'\boldsymbol{x}_t\boldsymbol{x}_t'(\boldsymbol{b}-\boldsymbol{\beta})}{h(\boldsymbol{a}'\boldsymbol{w}_t)}\right.\right. \\ &\qquad\qquad \left.\left. + \ln h(\boldsymbol{a}'\boldsymbol{w}_t)\,\middle|\,\mathcal{I}_t\right)\right] \\ &= \frac{1}{2n}\sum_{t=1}^{n}E\left(\frac{h(\boldsymbol{\alpha}'\boldsymbol{w}_t)}{h(\boldsymbol{a}'\boldsymbol{w}_t)} + \ln h(\boldsymbol{a}'\boldsymbol{w}_t)\right) \\ &\quad + \frac{1}{2n}\sum_{t=1}^{n}(\boldsymbol{b}-\boldsymbol{\beta})'E\left(\frac{\boldsymbol{x}_t\boldsymbol{x}_t'}{h(\boldsymbol{a}'\boldsymbol{w}_t)}\right)(\boldsymbol{b}-\boldsymbol{\beta}). \end{aligned} \tag{10.4.28}$$

The last member of (10.4.28) must be minimized uniquely by $\boldsymbol{b} = \boldsymbol{\beta}$ and $\boldsymbol{a} = \boldsymbol{\alpha}$. Consider the first term, which involves only $\boldsymbol{a}$. The random functions whose expectations enter the sum are minimised at $\boldsymbol{\alpha}$ by the usual argument, for any choice of $\boldsymbol{w}_t$. These minima need not be unique (as when some element of $\boldsymbol{w}_t$ is equal to 0, for example) but provided the identification condition cited following (10.4.30) below is met, $\boldsymbol{\alpha}$ is the unique value that minimises these functions for any $\boldsymbol{w}_t$, with probability 1. From this it follows by differentiating under the integral sign (see Theorem B.4.1) that the expected function is minimised uniquely at $\boldsymbol{\alpha}$. Next consider the second term. This is minimised uniquely at the point $\boldsymbol{b} = \boldsymbol{\beta}$, for any $\boldsymbol{a}$, subject to the quadratic forms being positive definite. Therefore, $E[C_n(\boldsymbol{b}, \boldsymbol{a})]$ is minimized uniquely at $(\boldsymbol{\beta}, \boldsymbol{\alpha})$ if the positive definiteness condition is satisfied at $\boldsymbol{\alpha}$, which constitutes another identification condition.

Theorem 9.3.5 provides another approach to checking the identification conditions. Let

$$\boldsymbol{A}_0 = \lim_{n\to\infty} E\begin{bmatrix} \boldsymbol{q}_{bn}\boldsymbol{q}_{bn}' & \boldsymbol{q}_{bn}\boldsymbol{q}_{an}' \\ \boldsymbol{q}_{an}\boldsymbol{q}_{bn}' & \boldsymbol{q}_{an}\boldsymbol{q}_{an}' \end{bmatrix} = \lim_{n\to\infty}\frac{1}{n}\sum_{t=1}^{n}\begin{bmatrix} \boldsymbol{A}_{bbt} & \boldsymbol{A}_{bat} \\ \boldsymbol{A}_{abt} & \boldsymbol{A}_{aat} \end{bmatrix} \tag{10.4.29}$$

where

$$\boldsymbol{A}_{bbt} = E(\boldsymbol{x}_t\boldsymbol{x}_t'/h_t) \tag{10.4.30a}$$

$$\boldsymbol{A}_{aat} = \tfrac{1}{4}E[(h_t'/h_t)^2(u_t^4/h_t^2 - 1)\boldsymbol{w}_t\boldsymbol{w}_t'] \tag{10.4.30b}$$

$$\boldsymbol{A}_{abt} = \tfrac{1}{2}E[(u_t^3h_t'/h_t^3)\boldsymbol{w}_t\boldsymbol{x}_t'] \tag{10.4.30c}$$

and the "0" subscript on $\boldsymbol{A}_0$ denotes evaluation at the point $\boldsymbol{b} = \boldsymbol{\beta}$, $\boldsymbol{a} = \boldsymbol{\alpha}$. It is clear that the uniqueness conditions specified in the preceding paragraph are met when $\boldsymbol{A}_0$ has full rank, with $(\boldsymbol{\alpha}, \boldsymbol{\beta})$ a regular point of the matrix. This imposes the usual type of restrictions on the generation processes of $\boldsymbol{x}_t$ and $\boldsymbol{w}_t$, to ensure that these vary independently in the limit.

To verify asymptotic normality, consider (10.4.21), (10.4.23) and (10.4.24), and observe that the $(k+p)$-vector sequence

$$\left\{\left[\frac{u_t}{h_t}\boldsymbol{x}_t' \quad \frac{h_t'}{h_t}\left(\frac{u_t^2}{h_t} - 1\right)\boldsymbol{w}_t'\right]', \mathcal{I}_t^*\right\} \tag{10.4.31}$$

is a vector martingale difference – compare (7.1.5). Subject to the requisite moment conditions analogous to (7.1.12), which will require as a minimum the existence of $E|u_t|^{4+\delta}$ for $\delta > 0$, asymptotic normality will follow. By Theorem 9.3.6, the limiting distribution is given (subject to the existence of the specified limits) by

$$\sqrt{n}\begin{bmatrix} \hat{\boldsymbol{\beta}} - \boldsymbol{\beta} \\ \hat{\boldsymbol{\alpha}} - \boldsymbol{\alpha} \end{bmatrix} \xrightarrow{\text{D}} \text{N}(\boldsymbol{0}, \bar{\boldsymbol{Q}}_0^{-1}\boldsymbol{A}_0\bar{\boldsymbol{Q}}_0^{-1}), \tag{10.4.32}$$

where

$$\bar{\boldsymbol{Q}}_0 = \lim_{n\to\infty}\frac{1}{n}\sum_{t=1}^{n}\begin{bmatrix} E(\boldsymbol{Q}_{bbt}) & E(\boldsymbol{Q}_{bat}) \\ E(\boldsymbol{Q}_{abt}) & E(\boldsymbol{Q}_{aat}) \end{bmatrix} \tag{10.4.33}$$

and $E(\boldsymbol{Q}_{bbt}) = \boldsymbol{A}_{bbt}$, $E(\boldsymbol{Q}_{aat}) = \frac{1}{2}E[(h_t'/h_t)^2\boldsymbol{w}_t\boldsymbol{w}_t']$, and $E(\boldsymbol{Q}_{abt}) = \boldsymbol{0}$. As in the fixed-variance case of (10.4.14), these formulae simplify in the conditionally Gaussian case, since then assumptions (10.4.21) can be augmented with $E(u_t^3|\mathcal{I}_t) = 0$ and $E(u_t^4|\mathcal{I}_t) = 3h_t^2$, and the information matrix equality $\bar{\boldsymbol{Q}}_0 = \boldsymbol{A}_0$ holds. However, with or without this restriction the asymptotic variance matrix of $\sqrt{n}(\hat{\boldsymbol{\beta}}-\boldsymbol{\beta})$ is equal to

$$(\bar{\boldsymbol{Q}}_0^{-1})_{bb} = \left(\lim_{n\to\infty}\frac{1}{n}\sum_{t=1}^{n}E\left(\frac{\boldsymbol{x}_t\boldsymbol{x}_t'}{h_t}\right)\right)^{-1}. \tag{10.4.34}$$

These variance matrices can be consistently estimated under the standard assumptions by replacing the expectations by the corresponding functions of the data, also replacing $\boldsymbol{\beta}$ and $\boldsymbol{\alpha}$ by $\hat{\boldsymbol{\beta}}$ and $\hat{\boldsymbol{\alpha}}$, by appeal to Lemma 9.3.2.

The ARCH and GARCH models are similar to this case, except in one important respect. The vector $\boldsymbol{w}_t$ contains latent variables, u_{t-j}^2 and h_{t-j} for $j > 0$, which in practice are represented as functions of lagged ($\mathcal{I}_t$-measurable) variables and unknown parameters, elements of both $\boldsymbol{\alpha}$ and $\boldsymbol{\beta}$. The presence of the latter complicates the derivative formulae. Consider the GARCH(1,1) in which

$$h_t = \alpha_0 + \alpha_1 u_{t-1}^2 + \alpha_2 h_{t-1}. \tag{10.4.35}$$

Note that

$$q_{bn} = -\frac{1}{n}\sum_{t=1}^{n}\left(\frac{u_t}{h_t}\boldsymbol{x}_t + \frac{1}{2h_t}\left(\frac{u_t^2}{h_t} - 1\right)\frac{\partial h_t}{\partial \boldsymbol{\beta}}\right) \tag{10.4.36}$$

where

$$\frac{\partial h_t}{\partial \boldsymbol{\beta}} = -2\alpha_1 u_{t-1}\boldsymbol{x}_{t-1} + \alpha_2\frac{\partial h_{t-1}}{\partial \boldsymbol{\beta}} \tag{10.4.37}$$

a formula that must be evaluated recursively from suitable initial values. Similarly

$$q_{an} = -\frac{1}{2n}\sum_{t=1}^{n}\frac{1}{h_t}\left(\frac{u_t^2}{h_t} - 1\right)\frac{\partial h_t}{\partial \boldsymbol{\alpha}} \tag{10.4.38}$$

where

$$\frac{\partial h_t}{\partial \boldsymbol{\alpha}} = \begin{bmatrix}\partial h_t/\partial \alpha_0\\ \partial h_t/\partial \alpha_1\\ \partial h_t/\partial \alpha_2\end{bmatrix} = \begin{bmatrix}1\\ u_{t-1}^2 + \alpha_2\partial h_{t-1}/\partial \alpha_1\\ h_{t-1} + \alpha_2\partial h_{t-1}/\partial \alpha_2\end{bmatrix}. \tag{10.4.39}$$

The remaining details of this model are left as an exercise for the interested reader.

It is especially useful that Gaussianity is not a required assumption for the CAN property in these models, because it is often found to be inappropriate. Excess kurtosis is commonly found, especially in high-frequency financial data sets, even after correcting for GARCH. There is just one caveat, to be taken up in §12.3.5. The information matrix equality is a required assumption in certain common tests for conditional heteroscedasticity.

10.5 Misspecified Regression Models

Our final application is of particular importance in applied research, since the question of whether the standard linear parameterization of an economic relationship is justified is always in the background. It also raises special problems, and the analysis will call for some new concepts in the asymptotic theory. Important work in this area has been done by White (1980b, 1981, 1982) and Domowitz and White (1982).

In this analysis, no model will be written down beyond the trivial statement

$$E(y_t|\boldsymbol{x}_t) = f_t(\boldsymbol{x}_t) \tag{10.5.1}$$

where the $f_t(\cdot)$ are arbitrary unknown functions. We simply want to know the consequences of approximating $f_t(\boldsymbol{x}_t)$ by the linear function $\boldsymbol{\beta}'\boldsymbol{x}_t$, where the criterion to be optimized is the average predictive accuracy of the regression. Theorems 1.4.1 and 1.4.2 show that $E(y_t - \boldsymbol{b}'\boldsymbol{x}_t)^2$ is minimized by choosing $\boldsymbol{b} = \boldsymbol{\beta}_t = E(\boldsymbol{x}_t\boldsymbol{x}_t')^{-1}E(\boldsymbol{x}_t y_t)$. However, it is not possible to estimate $\boldsymbol{\beta}_t$ for a single observation, and one must consider the average squared error over the sample size n. As in (1.4.7) write

$$\boldsymbol{\beta}_n = \left(\sum_{t=1}^{n} E(\boldsymbol{x}_t\boldsymbol{x}_t')\right)^{-1} \sum_{t=1}^{n} E(\boldsymbol{x}_t y_t) \tag{10.5.2}$$

and note that

$$\begin{aligned}
E[S_n(\boldsymbol{b})] &= \sum_{t=1}^{n} E(y_t - \boldsymbol{b}'\boldsymbol{x}_t)^2 \\
&= \sum_{t=1}^{n} E[y_t - \boldsymbol{\beta}_n'\boldsymbol{x}_t + (\boldsymbol{\beta}_n - \boldsymbol{b})'\boldsymbol{x}_t]^2 \\
&= \sum_{t=1}^{n} E(y_t - \boldsymbol{\beta}_n'\boldsymbol{x}_t)^2 + (\boldsymbol{\beta}_n - \boldsymbol{b})'\left(\sum_{t=1}^{n} E(\boldsymbol{x}_t\boldsymbol{x}_t')\right)(\boldsymbol{\beta}_n - \boldsymbol{b}) \\
&\quad + 2(\boldsymbol{\beta}_n - \boldsymbol{b})'\left(\sum_{t=1}^{n} E(\boldsymbol{x}_t y_t) - \sum_{t=1}^{n} E(\boldsymbol{x}_t\boldsymbol{x}_t')\boldsymbol{\beta}_n\right).
\end{aligned} \tag{10.5.3}$$

It is not difficult to see that the cross-product term vanishes, and hence that

$$\boldsymbol{\beta}_n = \arg\min_{\boldsymbol{b}} E[S_n(\boldsymbol{b})]. \tag{10.5.4}$$

We may therefore pose the following questions: does $\boldsymbol{\beta}_n$ converge to a unique limit, $\boldsymbol{\beta}_0$ say, as $n \to \infty$; and is $\hat{\boldsymbol{\beta}}_n$, the minimizer of the sample sum of squares S_n, a CAN estimator of $\boldsymbol{\beta}_0$? Of course, if the data have a stationary distribution then $\boldsymbol{\beta}_n = \boldsymbol{\beta}_0$ for all n. Otherwise, the uniqueness question is resolved by looking at (10.5.3) and noting that $\boldsymbol{\beta}_n$ is unique if $\sum_{t=1}^{n} E(\boldsymbol{x}_t\boldsymbol{x}_t')$ is positive definite. To ensure this property holds in the limit, such that

$$\boldsymbol{\beta}_0 = \arg\min_{\boldsymbol{b}} \lim_{n\to\infty} \frac{1}{n} E[S_n(\boldsymbol{b})] \tag{10.5.5}$$

is unique, requires that the matrix

$$\lim_{n\to\infty}\frac{1}{n}\sum_{t=1}^{n}E(\boldsymbol{x}_t\boldsymbol{x}_t') = \boldsymbol{M}_{XX} \tag{10.5.6}$$

exists, and is finite and positive definite. Given this, to show consistency it suffices in view of Theorem 9.3.1 to verify that

$$\sup_{\boldsymbol{b}}\left|\frac{1}{n}S_n(\boldsymbol{b}) - \frac{1}{n}E[S_n(\boldsymbol{b})]\right| \xrightarrow{\text{pr}} 0. \tag{10.5.7}$$

Note that

$$\begin{aligned}\frac{1}{n}S_n(\boldsymbol{b}) - \frac{1}{n}E[S(\boldsymbol{b})] &= \frac{1}{n}\sum_{t=1}^{n}[(y_t - \boldsymbol{b}'\boldsymbol{x}_t)^2 - E(y_t - \boldsymbol{b}'\boldsymbol{x}_t)^2]\\ &= \frac{1}{n}\sum_{t=1}^{n}[y_t^2 - E(y_t^2)] - 2\boldsymbol{b}'\frac{1}{n}\sum_{t=1}^{n}[\boldsymbol{x}_t y_t - E(\boldsymbol{x}_t y_t)]\\ &\quad + \boldsymbol{b}'\frac{1}{n}\sum_{t=1}^{n}[\boldsymbol{x}_t\boldsymbol{x}_t' - E(\boldsymbol{x}_t\boldsymbol{x}_t')]\boldsymbol{b}.\end{aligned} \tag{10.5.8}$$

The question therefore reduces to that of whether the weak law of large numbers applies to the variables y_t^2, $\boldsymbol{x}_t y_t$, and $\boldsymbol{x}_t\boldsymbol{x}_t'$. If so, the uniform convergence follows by the same arguments as used in §10.1.

Interestingly, the answer to this latter question is much the same, whether the data are independently sampled (sampling model B of §1.3) or are time series (sampling model C). In either case, the absolute moments of order $2+\delta$ of the variables $(y_t, \boldsymbol{x}_t)$ must exist for $\delta > 0$ to permit an appeal to Theorem 6.4.4. Under independence the mixing assumption is trivially satisfied. Likewise, there is no problem if it is possible to assume that y_t and $\boldsymbol{x}_t$ are mixing, since this property extends directly to the products. Under the near-epoch dependence assumption (for example, if the variables are generated by stochastic difference equations with mixing innovations) it will also be necessary to appeal to Theorem 6.4.3(ii), putting $x_t = y_t$ in the statement of that theorem to obtain the result for the squares. In any case, the following statement covers all eventualities:

Theorem 10.5.1 If the variables $(y_t, \boldsymbol{x}_t)$ are L_2-NED on a mixing process, and have uniformly bounded absolute moments of order $2+\delta$ for $\delta > 0$, then $\hat{\boldsymbol{\beta}}_n \xrightarrow{\text{pr}} \boldsymbol{\beta}_0$. □

The question of asymptotic normality is a bit trickier. Taking the criterion function to be $C_n = S_n/2n$, the derivatives are

$$\boldsymbol{q}_n(\boldsymbol{b}) = -\frac{1}{n}\sum_{t=1}^{n}\boldsymbol{x}_t(y_t - \boldsymbol{x}_t'\boldsymbol{b}) \tag{10.5.9}$$

and also

$$\boldsymbol{Q}_n = \frac{1}{n}\sum_{t=1}^{n}\boldsymbol{x}_t\boldsymbol{x}_t'. \tag{10.5.10}$$

Unless the model really is linear, the terms of the sum in (10.5.9) do not have a mean of $\mathbf{0}$ at the point $\boldsymbol{\beta}_0$, and Theorem 6.4.5 cannot be applied directly. However, note that

$$E[\boldsymbol{q}_n(\boldsymbol{\beta}_n)] = \mathbf{0} \tag{10.5.11}$$

by definition of $\boldsymbol{\beta}_n$. Hence, if $\boldsymbol{\mu}_{nt} = E(\boldsymbol{x}_t\boldsymbol{x}_t'\boldsymbol{\beta}_n - \boldsymbol{x}_t y_t)$ then $\sum_{t=1}^n \boldsymbol{\mu}_{nt} = \mathbf{0}$ by definition. Therefore, the terms

$$\boldsymbol{v}_{nt} = \boldsymbol{x}_t\boldsymbol{x}_t'\boldsymbol{\beta}_n - \boldsymbol{x}_t y_t - \boldsymbol{\mu}_{nt} \tag{10.5.12}$$

have zero mean by construction and

$$\boldsymbol{q}_n(\boldsymbol{\beta}_n) = \frac{1}{n}\sum_{t=1}^n \boldsymbol{v}_{nt}. \tag{10.5.13}$$

However, there is a problem, because the terms of this sum depend on both t and n. The collection $\{\boldsymbol{v}_{nt},\ t = 1,\dots,n,\ n = k+1, k+2,\dots\}$ form a triangular stochastic array (see §3.6.1). Happily, the concept of near-epoch dependence extends straightforwardly to the array case. The following formal definition (contrast with Definition 6.4.2) will serve the present purpose, although a definition that extends the array notation to the underlying process $\{Z_t\}$ may also be given:

Definition 10.5.1 Let $\{x_{nt},\ t = 1,\dots,n,\ n \geq 1\}$ denote a triangular array of functions of a stochastic process $\{Z_t\}$ of the form $x_{nt} = g_n(\dots, Z_{t-1}, Z_t, Z_{t+1}, \dots)$. Let $\mathcal{F}_s^t = \sigma(Z_s, \dots, Z_t)$ for $s \leq t$. x_{nt} is called L_p-NED on $\{Z_t\}$ if

$$\left\| x_{nt} - E(x_{nt}|\mathcal{F}_{t-m}^{t+m})\right\|_p \leq d_{nt}\nu_m \tag{10.5.14}$$

where $\{d_{nt}, t = 1,\dots,n, n \geq 1\}$ is a triangular array of scaling constants, and $\nu_m \to 0$. □

The usual size terminology applies here, see §6.4.1. The central limit theorems of Chapter 6 are not valid for arrays as given, but the required generalization of Theorem 6.4.5 is easily stated. This follows by Theorem 2 of De Jong (1997).

Theorem 10.5.2 Let $\{x_{nt}\}$ be a triangular array of zero-mean r.v.s, which are L_2-NED of size $-\frac{1}{2}$, on either a strong mixing process of size $-(1+2/\delta)$ or a uniform mixing process of size $-(2+\delta)/2(1+\delta)$ for some $\delta > 0$. If for the same δ

$$\sqrt{n}\frac{\max_{1\leq t\leq n}\|x_{nt}\|_{2+\delta}}{s_n} \leq B < \infty \quad \forall\, n \geq 1 \tag{10.5.15}$$

where $s_n^2 = E(\sum_{t=1}^n x_{nt})^2$, then $\sum_{t=1}^n x_{nt}/s_n \xrightarrow{\text{D}} \mathrm{N}(0,1)$. □

This is a somewhat more general statement of the CLT than Theorem 6.4.5, and it is easy to see that it contains the earlier result. By taking the case

$$x_{nt} = \frac{x_t}{\sqrt{E(\sum_{t=1}^n x_t)^2}} \tag{10.5.16}$$

note that $s_n^2 = 1$ by construction. In this case conditions (10.5.15) and (6.4.10) are equivalent, under the appropriate definitions of s_n^2.

To apply this theorem in conjunction with Theorem 3.3.3 to obtain a central limit result for $\sqrt{n}\boldsymbol{q}_n$, assume that for all conformable fixed vectors $\boldsymbol{\lambda}$ of unit length, the scalar array

$$\boldsymbol{\lambda}'\boldsymbol{v}_{nt} = \boldsymbol{\lambda}'\boldsymbol{x}_t\boldsymbol{x}_t'\boldsymbol{\beta}_n - \boldsymbol{\lambda}'\boldsymbol{x}_t y_t - \boldsymbol{\lambda}'\boldsymbol{\mu}_{nt} \tag{10.5.17}$$

is L_2-NED on a mixing process. Given that this is true for y_t and $x_{1t}, \dots, x_{kt}$, the required result for $\boldsymbol{\lambda}'\boldsymbol{v}_{nt}$ can be obtained by applying Theorems 6.4.2 and 6.4.3(ii).

Theorem 10.5.3 If $\boldsymbol{\beta}_n \to \boldsymbol{\beta}_0$, and the random variables y_t and $x_{1t}, \dots, x_{kt}$ in (10.5.1) are L_{2r}-bounded and L_2-NED of size $-(r-1)/(r-2)$ for $r > 2$, on mixing processes of size $-r/(r-2)$ for $\delta > 0$, then

(i) $\displaystyle \frac{1}{n}\sum_{t=1}^{n}\sum_{s=1}^{n} E(\boldsymbol{v}_{nt}\boldsymbol{v}_{ns}') \to \boldsymbol{A} < \infty$

(ii) $\sqrt{n}\boldsymbol{q}_n(\boldsymbol{\beta}_n) \xrightarrow{\text{D}} \text{N}(\boldsymbol{0}, \boldsymbol{A})$. □

See §10.6 for the proof. The final step in the argument parallels Theorem 9.3.6, and in this case is straightforward because the second derivative of S_n does not depend on $\boldsymbol{\beta}_n$.

Theorem 10.5.4 $\sqrt{n}(\hat{\boldsymbol{\beta}}_n - \boldsymbol{\beta}_n) \xrightarrow{\text{D}} \text{N}(\boldsymbol{0}, \boldsymbol{M}_{XX}^{-1}\boldsymbol{A}\boldsymbol{M}_{XX}^{-1})$, where $\boldsymbol{M}_{XX}$ is defined in (10.5.6).

Proof From (10.5.9) and (10.5.10),

$$\hat{\boldsymbol{\beta}}_n - \boldsymbol{\beta}_n = \boldsymbol{Q}_n^{-1}\boldsymbol{q}_n(\boldsymbol{\beta}_n) \tag{10.5.18}$$

and $\boldsymbol{Q}_n \xrightarrow{\text{pr}} \boldsymbol{M}_{XX}$ by an element-by-element application of Theorem 6.4.4, whose conditions are clearly satisfied in the present case. The result therefore follows by applications of the Slutsky and Cramér Theorems. ■

All of this analysis is of course a good deal simplified if $\boldsymbol{\beta}_n = \boldsymbol{\beta}_0$ for every n, but except in this case, care is necessary in the application of the last result. In particular, it need not imply that

$$\sqrt{n}(\hat{\boldsymbol{\beta}} - \boldsymbol{\beta}_0) \xrightarrow{\text{D}} \text{N}(\boldsymbol{0}, \boldsymbol{M}_{XX}^{-1}\boldsymbol{A}\boldsymbol{M}_{XX}^{-1}). \tag{10.5.19}$$

This would only be true if $\boldsymbol{\beta}_n - \boldsymbol{\beta}_0 = o(n^{-1/2})$, for except in this case,

$$\sqrt{n}(\hat{\boldsymbol{\beta}} - \boldsymbol{\beta}_0) = \sqrt{n}(\hat{\boldsymbol{\beta}}_n - \boldsymbol{\beta}_n) + \sqrt{n}(\boldsymbol{\beta}_n - \boldsymbol{\beta}_0), \tag{10.5.20}$$

where the second term is not converging to $\boldsymbol{0}$, and is possibly diverging. However, it is likely that any restrictions needing to be tested apply to $\boldsymbol{\beta}_n$ for all n, not just to $\boldsymbol{\beta}_0$, and hence this feature of the asymptotic distribution is not a drawback in practice.

This point aside, it has been shown that least squares analysis of a misspecified model can yield useful results, in the sense that a sensible 'pseudo-parameterization' can be defined, for which least squares can yield consistent and asymptotically normal estimates. There are just two difficulties that need to be borne in mind. First, since the regression errors lack the martingale difference property, restrictions on the general dependence must be imposed, together with moment conditions that are tougher than before by a factor of two, to obtain the asymptotic distribution. Second, for the same reason, the usual least squares formula for the standard errors is incorrect, and to estimate the asymptotic variance a kernel-based estimator for $\boldsymbol{A}$ must be used, of the type discussed in §9.4.3. However, such estimators are consistent under the present assumptions and the conditions on the kernel function specified in Theorem 9.4.2. The array generalization of the latter result is given in De Jong and Davidson (2000a).

Further Reading: Davidson and MacKinnon (1993) is an excellent source for many of these topics. On nonlinear regression see also Amemiya (1983), White (1987), Harvey (1990). On the generalized method of moments see Hamilton (1994), Manski (1994). On ARCH models see Engle (1995), Bollerslev, Engle and Nelson (1994). On misspecified models, see Gallant (1987), Gallant and White (1988), White (1994). The other readings cited in Chapter 9 may also be helpful.

10.6 Appendix: Proof of Theorem 10.5.3

Since $\boldsymbol{\beta}_n \to \boldsymbol{\beta}_0$ by assumption, there exists $n_1 \geq 1$ such that $\boldsymbol{\beta}_n$ is bounded uniformly in $n \geq n_1$. Define the $K+1$-vector $\boldsymbol{z}_t = (\boldsymbol{x}_t', y_t)'$, and note that the elements of the vector $\boldsymbol{v}_{nt}$ are linear combinations of elements of the form $z_{it}z_{jt}$ weighted by elements from $\boldsymbol{\beta}_n$, and elements of $\boldsymbol{\mu}_{nt}$. The latter are uniformly bounded in t, and $n \geq n_1$, by assumption. Also the terms $z_{it}z_{jt}$ are L_2-NED of size $-\frac{1}{2}$ on strong-mixing processes by Theorem 6.4.3(ii) and hence, by Theorem 6.4.6 the terms of the form $E(z_{it}z_{jt}z_{k,t-m}z_{l,t-m})$ for $m \geq 0$ are summable over m, for i, j, k, and l drawn from $1, \dots, K+1$. Part (i) of the theorem follows directly, on considering the elements of the matrices $E(\boldsymbol{v}_{nt}\boldsymbol{v}_{ns}')$ one by one.

Part (ii) of the theorem is an application of Theorem 10.5.2 to the triangular arrays of the form $\boldsymbol{\lambda}'\boldsymbol{v}_{nt}$ for $\boldsymbol{\lambda}'\boldsymbol{\lambda} = 1$. Note that

$$\boldsymbol{\lambda}'\boldsymbol{v}_{nt} = \sum_{i=1}^{k}\sum_{j=1}^{k} \lambda_i \beta_{nj} x_{it}x_{jt} - \sum_{i=1}^{k} \lambda_i x_{it} y_t - \boldsymbol{\lambda}'\boldsymbol{\mu}_{nt} \tag{10.6.1}$$

and applying the Minkowski inequality,

$$\begin{aligned}\left\|\boldsymbol{\lambda}'\boldsymbol{v}_{nt} - E(\boldsymbol{\lambda}'\boldsymbol{v}_{nt}|\mathcal{F}_{t-m}^{t+m})\right\|_2 &\leq \sum_{i=1}^{k}\sum_{j=1}^{k} \lambda_i\beta_{nj} \left\|x_{it}x_{jt} - E(x_{it}x_{jt}|\mathcal{F}_{t-m}^{t+m})\right\|_2 \\ &\quad + \sum_{i=1}^{k} \lambda_i \left\|x_{it}y_t - E(x_{it}y_t|\mathcal{F}_{t-m}^{t+m})\right\|_2 \end{aligned} \tag{10.6.2}$$

Applying Theorem 6.4.3(ii) to the terms in the sums on the right-hand side of (10.6.2), and then applying Definition 10.5.1 and Theorem 6.4.2, the triangular array $\boldsymbol{\lambda}'\boldsymbol{v}_{nt}$ is

L_2-NED of size $-\frac{1}{2}$ on the specified mixing processes, with respect to the constant array

$$d_{nt} = \max\left\{\max_{i,j}\left\{\lambda_i\beta_{nj}\max\left\{\|x_{it}\|_{2r}\|x_{jt}\|_{2r}\right\}^{(3r-2)/2(r-1)}\max\left\{d_{kit}, d_{kjt}\right\}\right\},\right.$$
$$\left.\max_i\left\{\lambda_i\max\left\{\|x_{it}\|_{2r}, \|y_t\|_{2r}\right\}^{(3r-2)/2(r-1)}\max\left\{d_{xit}, d_{yt}\right\}\right\}\right\} \qquad (10.6.3)$$

which is uniformly bounded over t and $n \geq n_1$, by assumption. The conditions of Theorem 10.5.2 hold, for any choice of $\boldsymbol{\lambda}$, for the case $\delta = r-2$. Putting $s_n^2 = E(\sum_{t=1}^n \boldsymbol{\lambda}'\boldsymbol{v}_{nt})^2$, note that $s_n^2/n \to \boldsymbol{\lambda}'\boldsymbol{A}\boldsymbol{\lambda}$ as $n \to \infty$, and hence

$$\sqrt{n}\boldsymbol{\lambda}'\boldsymbol{q}_n(\boldsymbol{\beta}_n) = \frac{1}{\sqrt{n}}\sum_{t=1}^n \boldsymbol{\lambda}'\boldsymbol{v}_{nt} \xrightarrow{\mathrm{D}} \mathrm{N}(0, \boldsymbol{\lambda}'\boldsymbol{A}\boldsymbol{\lambda}). \qquad (10.6.4)$$

The theorem now follows from the usual application of the Cramér–Wold device. ∎

Chapter 11

The Method of Maximum Likelihood

11.1 Introduction

Let $\boldsymbol{X}_n^1 = \left[\boldsymbol{x}_1 \cdots \boldsymbol{x}_n\right]'$ $(n \times m)$ denote a matrix of random variables, formed from n observations of an m-vector $\boldsymbol{x}_t \in \mathbb{S} \subseteq \mathbb{R}^m$. When the context is clear this matrix will just be called $\boldsymbol{X}$, for simplicity. Think of each such matrix as a point in the sample space $\mathbb{S}^n \subseteq \mathbb{R}^{nm}$, written as $\boldsymbol{X} \in \mathbb{S}^n$. Supposing the data are continuously distributed, let the joint probability density function (p.d.f.) of these data be denoted $D(\boldsymbol{X}; \boldsymbol{\theta}_0)$, a member of a family of functions $D(.; \boldsymbol{\theta})$, $\boldsymbol{\theta} \in \Theta$, where Θ is the parameter space. $D(\cdot; \boldsymbol{\theta})$ is a function from $\mathbb{S}^n$ to $\mathbb{R}$ (the real line), representing the density associated with each point in $\mathbb{S}^n$, for a given $\boldsymbol{\theta}$. However, thinking of D as a function from Θ to $\mathbb{R}$ for a given $\boldsymbol{X} \in \mathbb{S}^n$ it is called the *likelihood function*, and is denoted by a different symbol, usually $\mathcal{L}(\cdot; \boldsymbol{X})$. Here $\boldsymbol{X}$ is to be thought of as a sample that has been observed, and $\mathcal{L}(\boldsymbol{\theta}; \boldsymbol{X})$ represents the p.d.f. that would be associated with the sample $\boldsymbol{X}$ had it been generated by the data generation process (DGP) with parameters $\boldsymbol{\theta}$.

If the data have a discrete distribution, $D(\cdot, \boldsymbol{\theta})$ can represent the probability associated with each of the discrete points of $\mathbb{S}$, and apart from this modification the likelihood function is defined in the same way as before. Mixed continuous-discrete cases are also possible, in which the p.d.f. is defined except at a countable number of points of S^n. At these points the cumulative distribution function (c.d.f.) has discontinuities (points of positive probability mass). In this case, define the likelihood function to be the counterpart, in the sense described, to either the density function or the probability, according to the point of $\mathbb{S}^n$ at which it is evaluated. Examples of all these cases are discussed in §11.2.

The likelihood function can provide the basis for inferences from a sample $\boldsymbol{X}$ about the unknown vector $\boldsymbol{\theta}$. The maximum likelihood estimator (MLE) is

$$\hat{\boldsymbol{\theta}}(\boldsymbol{X}) = \arg\min_{\boldsymbol{\theta} \in \Theta} \mathcal{L}(\boldsymbol{\theta}; \boldsymbol{X}). \tag{11.1.1}$$

The intuition underlying this approach to point estimation is that the sample $\boldsymbol{X}$ is representative of the distribution from which it was drawn – an assumption that becomes more plausible as the sample size increases – so that the value of $\boldsymbol{\theta}$ for which $\mathcal{L}$ is largest is 'most likely' in the sense of attributing the highest probability or probability density to $\boldsymbol{X}$. The sketches in Figure 11.1 illustrate this point, showing respectively (a) the sample space $\mathbb{S}$ and (b) the parameter space Θ, in one dimension. The likelihood function is drawn as bimodal only to

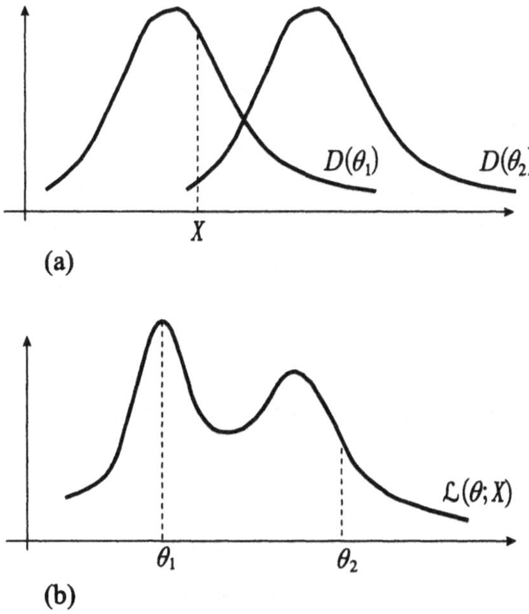

Figure 11.1: Densities and Likelihood Function

emphasize that such shapes are possible. To determine its form at a given point of the sample space, one must consider the entire family of density functions, of which two members only are shown in part (a) of the figure.

From the computational point of view, $\mathcal{L}$ does not need to be identical with an actual p.d.f. or probability function. Any factors that do not depend on the parameters $\boldsymbol{\theta}$ can be omitted. An obvious case is the constants, such as the powers of $(2\pi)^{-1/2}$ in the Gaussian density, whose role is to make the density integrate to 1 over $\mathbb{S}^n$. This property has no relevance to the likelihood. More important, if the density can be factorized into conditional and marginal factors, only one of which depends on $\boldsymbol{\theta}$, the irrelevant factor can be omitted – see the examples in §11.2.1 and §11.2.3. It is also customary to work with the natural logarithm of $\mathcal{L}$, denoted L. This is a monotone transformation that does not change the value of the maximum so that replacing $\mathcal{L}$ by L in (11.1.1) yields the same solution, but the log-likelihood is both computationally more convenient, and has special statistical properties too.

The MLE has a special place among estimators, since by definition it uses all the information in the sample. It is shown in §11.3.6 that the MLE is asymptotically efficient in the class of CAN estimators. However, it is worth being reminded that there is rarely enough genuine information to construct the true MLE. At best, economic theory will provide a specification for the first one or two moments of the distribution, and the rest is often dealt with by assuming, with no special justification, that the distribution is Gaussian. In this case, the estimator is properly called quasi-maximum likelihood (QML), or less kindly, pseudo-ML.

It is often the case that QML is consistent even when the distributional assumptions are wrong, because the estimator can also be motivated as an OE, and the arguments from Chapter 9 apply. Some of the optimization estimators reviewed in Chapter 10 are cases in point, especially those in §10.4.1 where the criterion function is in fact the negative of the log-likelihood for the Gaussian regression model, apart from constants. We were careful to emphasize merely the fact that these estimators had the CAN property for all the parameters, under mild assumptions. Many estimators commonly known to practitioners as 'maximum likelihood' are better thought of as OEs which possess the MLE property when certain more stringent assumptions are also observed. There are, however, other estimators that possess no independent justification. Either they are MLEs, or they run the risk of being inconsistent. After deriving the classic equivalence between least squares and ML, the next section focuses on cases of this type as leading examples.

11.2 Examples

11.2.1 The Classical Gaussian Regression Model

Consider the Gaussian version of the regression model explored in Chapters 2 and 3, under the assumptions of sampling model B. When the data are independently sampled from a large population, the joint density of the sample is merely the product of the marginal densities of the observations. Considering the partition $\boldsymbol{X}_n^1 = [\boldsymbol{y}_n^1 \; \boldsymbol{Z}_n^1]$ (respectively, the first column and last $m-1$ columns) suppose the joint sample density can be factored so that the parameters of interest are all in the conditional factor, say

$$\begin{aligned} D(\boldsymbol{y}_n^1, \boldsymbol{Z}_n^1; \boldsymbol{\theta}, \boldsymbol{\psi}) &= D_{y|Z}(\boldsymbol{y}_n^1 | \boldsymbol{Z}_n^1; \boldsymbol{\theta}) \cdot D_Z(\boldsymbol{Z}_n^1; \boldsymbol{\psi}) \\ &= \prod_{t=1}^{n} D(y_t | \boldsymbol{z}_t; \boldsymbol{\theta}) D_Z(\boldsymbol{Z}_n^1; \boldsymbol{\psi}) \end{aligned} \tag{11.2.1}$$

where under the Gaussianity assumption

$$D(y_t | \boldsymbol{z}_t; \boldsymbol{\theta}) = \frac{1}{\sqrt{2\pi}\sigma} \exp\left\{ -\frac{(y_t - \boldsymbol{\beta}' \boldsymbol{z}_t)^2}{2\sigma^2} \right\} \tag{11.2.2}$$

and $\boldsymbol{\theta} = (\boldsymbol{\beta}, \sigma^2)$. The factor D_Z does not depend on $\boldsymbol{\theta}$ and so can be ignored. It is not necessary to know what form it takes, nor even whether the $\boldsymbol{z}_t$ are randomly sampled. Any variables that do not appear in the conditional factor can be ignored altogether. The set-up is comparable to the factorization in (4.5.2) and (4.5.3) except that there is no sequential conditioning on past variables here, and the joint distribution of the whole sample may be factorised according to the first equality of (11.2.1), not merely that of individual observations. In the terminology of §4.5 $\boldsymbol{z}_t$ is strongly exogenous for $\boldsymbol{\theta}$, since there is no feedback from lagged y_t to $\boldsymbol{z}_t$ to consider.

The likelihood function in this case is

$$\mathcal{L}(\boldsymbol{\beta}, \sigma^2; \boldsymbol{X}) = \left(\frac{1}{\sqrt{2\pi}\sigma}\right)^n \exp\left\{-\frac{S(\boldsymbol{\beta})}{2\sigma^2}\right\} \tag{11.2.3}$$

where $S(\boldsymbol{\beta}) = \sum_{t=1}^n (y_t - \boldsymbol{\beta}'\boldsymbol{z}_t)^2$. Hence the log-likelihood function is

$$L(\boldsymbol{\beta}, \sigma^2) = -\frac{n}{2}\ln(\sigma^2) - \frac{S(\boldsymbol{\beta})}{2\sigma^2}. \tag{11.2.4}$$

This is the same criterion that was discussed in §10.4.1, and the same remarks apply. The MLE of $\boldsymbol{\beta}$ is just the minimizer of S, in other words, identical with the OLS estimator. The MLE of σ^2 is

$$\hat{\sigma}^2 = \frac{S(\hat{\boldsymbol{\beta}})}{n} \tag{11.2.5}$$

where $\hat{\boldsymbol{\beta}}$ is the MLE of $\boldsymbol{\beta}$, different from the unbiased estimator $s^2 = S(\hat{\boldsymbol{\beta}})/(n-k)$ where $k = m - 1$. ML estimators are not infrequently biased in finite samples.

11.2.2 The Stationary Gaussian AR Model

Consider the model $\boldsymbol{x}_t|\mathcal{X}_{t-1} \sim \mathrm{N}(\boldsymbol{\delta} + \boldsymbol{\Lambda}\boldsymbol{x}_{t-1}, \boldsymbol{\Omega})$ where $\mathcal{X}_{t-1} = \sigma(\boldsymbol{x}_{t-1}, \boldsymbol{x}_{t-2}, \ldots)$, as studied in §4.2. The exact likelihood function for a sample $\boldsymbol{x}_1, \ldots, \boldsymbol{x}_n$ is

$$\mathcal{L}(\boldsymbol{\delta}, \boldsymbol{\Lambda}, \boldsymbol{\Omega}; \boldsymbol{x}_1, \ldots, \boldsymbol{x}_n) = D(\boldsymbol{x}_1)\prod_{t=2}^n D(\boldsymbol{x}_t|\mathcal{X}_{t-1}) \tag{11.2.6}$$

where the formulae for $D(\boldsymbol{x}_1)$ and $D(\boldsymbol{x}_t|\mathcal{X}_{t-1})$ are given in (4.3.12) and (4.2.7) respectively. The matrix formulation of the model introduces special problems of notation, and discussion of these is postponed until system estimation is discussed generally in Chapter 13. To appreciate the main issues arising in the ML estimation of dynamic models, it suffices to consider the scalar version of the model, $x_t|\mathcal{X}_{t-1} \sim \mathrm{N}(\lambda x_{t-1}, \sigma^2)$. In this case the likelihood formula reduces to

$$\begin{aligned}\mathcal{L}(\lambda, \sigma^2) &= D(x_1)\prod_{t=2}^n D(x_t|\mathcal{X}_{t-1}) \\ &= \left(\frac{1}{\sqrt{2\pi}\sigma}\right)^n \sqrt{1-\lambda^2} \\ &\quad \times \exp\left\{-\frac{1}{2\sigma^2}(1-\lambda^2)x_1^2 - \frac{1}{2\sigma^2}\sum_{t=2}^n (x_t - \lambda x_{t-1})^2\right\}\end{aligned} \tag{11.2.7}$$

The maximand, after taking logarithms and dropping constants, becomes

$$L(\lambda,\sigma^2) = -\frac{n}{2}\ln\sigma^2 + \tfrac{1}{2}\ln(1-\lambda^2) - \frac{1}{2\sigma^2}[(1-\lambda^2)x_1^2 + S(\lambda)] \qquad (11.2.8)$$

where $S(\lambda) = \sum_{t=2}^{n}(x_t - \lambda x_{t-1})^2$. There is no closed expression for the MLE $\hat{\lambda}$ which maximizes (11.2.8), although given $\hat{\lambda}$, the solution

$$\hat{\sigma}^2 = \frac{(1-\hat{\lambda}^2)x_1^2 + S(\hat{\lambda})}{n} \qquad (11.2.9)$$

is obtained by analogy with the previous cases.

There are two possible approaches to the estimation problem. Either find the true maximum of L directly, by numerical methods, or compute an approximation to the MLE by discarding the terms derived from $D(x_1)$, and simply minimize $S(\lambda)$. That is, apply OLS to observations x_2 to x_n. Provided λ is not too large and n not too small, the exact and approximate MLEs should be similar, noting that $S(\lambda) = O_p(n)$ while the other terms are $O_p(1)$ as $n \to \infty$.

If the exact likelihood is to be maximized, a convenient technique is to concentrate the function (see §9.1) with respect to any parameters for which an analytic partial solution exists, in this case, the parameter σ^2. . Substituting the maximizing value of σ^2 as a function of λ, noting the cancellation in the exponent term and dropping constants as usual, the concentrated log-likelihood is

$$\begin{aligned} L^*(\lambda) &= L(\lambda, \sigma^2(\lambda)) + \frac{n}{2} \\ &= -\frac{n}{2}\ln\left(\frac{(1-\lambda^2)x_1^2 + S(\lambda)}{n}\right) + \frac{\ln(1-\lambda^2)}{2}. \end{aligned} \qquad (11.2.10)$$

Equation (9.1.9) shows that the value of λ that maximizes L^* is also the MLE.

Since $L^*(\lambda)$ is a function of a single variable defined in the interval $(-1,+1)$, the maximum can be found by a line search technique as in §9.2.1. Even a simple grid search will serve. The maximum can be located to the desired accuracy by evaluating the function at regularly spaced points over the interval to 'bracket' it, and then repeating the procedure over successively finer grids. Note that at points close to ± 1 the negative term $\ln(1-\lambda^2)$ is tending to $-\infty$, and hence the maximum is driven away from these points. By contrast, the OLS approximation to ML is not prevented from occurring in the unstable region, outside $(-1,+1)$.

The OLS estimator can be justified formally by assuming that the stochastic process did not exist prior to time $t=1$. Either x_1 is a fixed, unique value (which is to be thought of as the same for all possible random realizations of the process) or x_1 is a drawing from some distribution whose parameters are irrelevant to the problem at hand. Then the likelihood function is just

$$\mathcal{L}(\lambda,\sigma^2) = D(x_2,\ldots,x_n|\mathcal{X}_1) = \prod_{t=2}^{n} D(x_t|\mathcal{X}_{t-1}) \qquad (11.2.11)$$

where now $\mathcal{X}_1 = \sigma(x_1)$ and $\mathcal{X}_t = \sigma(x_1,\ldots,x_t)$ for $t > 1$. Maximizing L now gives the same result as minimizing S. However, the assumption needed to yield this result is patently fictitious in the majority of cases, where the date of the initial observation has no significance for the data generation process. Except in this case, information is clearly lost by ignoring $D(x_1)$, and the only valid justification is in terms of an approximation that is negligible in large samples.

11.2.3 The Dynamic Regression Model

As a natural synthesis of the classical regression model and the closed VAR process, there is a temptation to cast the dynamic model of Chapter 7 into the same framework. Suppose the model of (7.1.1) is augmented by the specific conditional Gaussian assumption

$$D(y_t|\mathcal{I}_t;\boldsymbol{\beta},\sigma^2) = \frac{1}{\sqrt{2\pi}\sigma}\exp\left\{-\frac{(y_t - \boldsymbol{x}_t'\boldsymbol{\beta})^2}{2\sigma^2}\right\} \tag{11.2.12}$$

corresponding to the conditional factor in (7.1.2), where $\mathcal{I}_t = \sigma(\boldsymbol{z}_t) \vee \mathcal{Y}_{t-1} \vee \mathcal{Z}_{t-1}$. If p represents the maximum lag on any variables contained in $\boldsymbol{x}_t$,

$$\mathcal{L}(\boldsymbol{\beta},\sigma^2) = \prod_{t=p+1}^{n} D(y_t|\mathcal{I}_t;\boldsymbol{\beta},\sigma^2) \tag{11.2.13}$$

can be regarded as the approximate likelihood function of the sample. It is interesting to note that, unlike the first factor in (11.2.1), the expression in (11.2.13) is *not* a joint density function in general, even as an approximation. Since $\boldsymbol{z}_t$ may depend on lagged values of y_t, (i.e. be weakly but not strongly exogenous) the marginal factors $D(\boldsymbol{z}_t|\mathcal{Y}_{t-1},\mathcal{Z}_{t-1})$ are needed to describe the joint distribution of $(y_{p+1},\dots,y_n)$. The justification for regarding the maximizers of $\mathcal{L}(\boldsymbol{\beta},\sigma^2)$ as the MLEs rests on the fact that the joint density is the product of terms of which only those in (11.2.13) depend on $\boldsymbol{\beta}$ and σ^2.

However, while the approximate likelihood can be constructed in this manner, there is no hope of constructing the exact likelihood corresponding to (11.2.6), because the term representing the initial conditions cannot be factorised in the same way. As a simple illustration, consider the model of (4.5.5). Under the exogeneity conditions $\alpha_{21} = \sigma_{21} = 0$, the conditional densities can be factorized as in (4.5.14) and (4.5.15). The product of these terms is analogous to the terms $D(\boldsymbol{x}_t|\mathcal{X}_{t-1})$ in (11.2.6), where $\boldsymbol{x}_t = (y_t, \boldsymbol{z}_t')'$, but factorizing the term $D(\boldsymbol{x}_1)$ in (11.2.6) is impossible, as can be seen by considering the formulae for $\boldsymbol{\mu}_x$ in (4.3.4) and $\boldsymbol{\Omega}_x$ in (4.3.10). Ignoring the initial conditions is not merely a computational short-cut in this case but the only way, given that in practice $\boldsymbol{z}_t$ represents a large set of weakly exogenous variables, to make the problem tractable. The best that can be done is to say that least squares is asymptotically equivalent to the MLE when the disturbances are Gaussian.

11.2.4 Conditional Heteroscedasticity

The models analysed in §10.4.2 can be written down in a conditional Gaussian framework, and form a natural extension of (11.2.12). The conditional Gaussian density satisfying the assumptions of (10.4.21) is

$$D(y_t|\mathcal{I}_t;\boldsymbol{\beta},\boldsymbol{\alpha}) = \frac{1}{\sqrt{2\pi h(\boldsymbol{\alpha}'\boldsymbol{w}_t)}}\exp\left\{-\frac{(y_t-\boldsymbol{\beta}'\boldsymbol{x}_t)^2}{2h(\boldsymbol{\alpha}'\boldsymbol{w}_t)}\right\}. \tag{11.2.14}$$

where $(\boldsymbol{x}_t, \boldsymbol{w}_t) \in \mathcal{I}_t$. In this case the estimation methods discussed in §10.4.2 have the interpretation of maximum likelihood. There are however important differences between the properties of the estimator motivated by (10.4.21) alone, and that motivated by (11.2.14). In the latter case, as noted, the conditions

$$E(u_t^3|\mathcal{I}_t) = 0 \tag{11.2.15a}$$

$$E(u_t^4|\mathcal{I}_t) = 3h(\boldsymbol{\alpha}'\boldsymbol{w}_t)^2 \tag{11.2.15b}$$

apply and hence the information matrix equality holds. It is going to be important for an investigator to decide whether to impose these assumptions. The discussions in §12.3.5 and in §12.5.4 are highly relevant to this issue.

11.2.5 Discrete and Censored Data Models

It is of greatest interest to focus on cases where the MLE does not have a least squares *alter ego*. The models of this section are typically associated with sampling model B of §1.3, surveys of households or firms. The peculiarity of these models is that the conditional distributions are either discrete or mixed continuous-discrete. In the first example the distribution is binary, with the variable to be explained consisting of Yes/No responses to questions such as 'Does the family own a car?', 'Is the respondent employed?' and the like.

The sample consists of n responses, coded as

$$y_t = \begin{cases} 1, & \text{if answer is Yes} \\ 0, & \text{if answer is No} \end{cases} \tag{11.2.16}$$

together with vectors of explanatory variables $\boldsymbol{z}_t$, for $t = 1, \ldots, n$. The y_t can be thought of as conditional Bernoulli random variables, where $P(y_t = 1|\boldsymbol{z}_t)$ is a function of $\boldsymbol{z}_t$. The problem is to specify the functional form of these probabilities. In the *probit* model, a latent variable y_t^* is postulated, with the property

$$y_t^*|\boldsymbol{z}_t \sim \mathrm{N}(\boldsymbol{\alpha}'\boldsymbol{z}_t, \sigma^2) \tag{11.2.17}$$

where $\boldsymbol{\alpha}$ is a vector of constant parameters. In the case of car ownership, y_t^* might be thought to represent a latent demand for the services of a car. Because of the indivisibility involved, these are only translated into an effective demand above the break-even point $y_t^* = 0$. The only information available to an observer is

$$y_t = \begin{cases} 1, & \text{if } y_t^* > 0 \\ 0, & \text{if } y_t^* \le 0. \end{cases} \tag{11.2.18}$$

If Z is used to denote a standard Gaussian r.v.,

$$P(y_t^* > 0) = P\Big(\frac{y_t^* - \boldsymbol{\alpha}'\boldsymbol{z}_t}{\sigma} > -\frac{\boldsymbol{\alpha}'\boldsymbol{z}_t}{\sigma}\Big|\boldsymbol{z}_t\Big)$$

$$= P\left(Z > -\frac{\alpha' z_t}{\sigma}\Big| z_t\right) = P\left(Z \leq \frac{\alpha' z_t}{\sigma}\Big| z_t\right). \tag{11.2.19}$$

where the last equality is by symmetry of the distribution. Hence,

$$p_t = P(y_t = 1|z_t) = \Phi\left(\frac{\alpha' z_t}{\sigma}\right). \tag{11.2.20}$$

where $\Phi(z) = (2\pi)^{-1/2} \int_{-\infty}^{z} e^{-\zeta^2/2} d\zeta$ is the standard Gaussian c.d.f.

If z_t is continuously distributed, note that the joint distribution of the observations (y_t, z_t) has a mixed continuous-discrete form (see §B.5). However, assuming the parameters of interest α/σ are confined to the conditional (discrete) factor, only this component needs to be analysed. Under independent sampling the joint probability of the sample, conditional on $z_1, \ldots, z_n$, is the product of the probabilities of the observations:

$$D(W_n^1|Z_t^1) = \prod_{t \in I_1} p_t \prod_{t \in I_0} (1 - p_t) \tag{11.2.21}$$

where I_1 is the set of observations for which $y_t = 1$, and I_0 the remainder. The log-likelihood is

$$\ln L(\alpha/\sigma) = \sum_{t \in I_0} \ln \left(1 - \Phi\left(\frac{\alpha' z_t}{\sigma}\right)\right) + \sum_{t \in I_1} \ln \Phi\left(\frac{\alpha' z_t}{\sigma}\right). \tag{11.2.22}$$

Note that α and σ are not separately identified, and only the ratio α/σ can be estimated. Note too that the estimator obtained by maximizing (11.2.22) has no obvious justification, even in large samples, if (11.2.17) is not true. In other words, without fully specifying the distribution of y_t^*, it is not possible to claim in general that α is consistent for the parameters of the mean equation.

The *logit* model is similar to the probit, except that a different distribution for the y_t variables is postulated. It is assumed that

$$p_t = P(y_t = 1|z_t) = \frac{\exp\{\alpha' z_t\}}{1 + \exp\{\alpha' z_t\}}. \tag{11.2.23}$$

In this model the log-odds in favour of the answer Yes are linear in the explanatory variables, so that

$$\ln\left(\frac{p_t}{1 - p_t}\right) = \alpha' z_t. \tag{11.2.24}$$

The logistic transformation can be thought of as a convenient way to map a variable $\alpha' z_t$, defined on the real line $(-\infty, +\infty)$, into the unit interval as required to model a probability. In practice, the logistic curve has a shape quite similar to the normal c.d.f.

A variable y_t may be observed that is continuously distributed in some regions of the sample space, and discrete in other regions. Consider purchases of tobacco. Those who smoke purchase positive amounts, while non-smokers purchase none, regardless of price or income. There is a positive probability associated with zero purchases. To treat the zero observations in the same way as the positive ones and include them in a regression of y_t on z_t, would clearly violate Assumptions 2.1.1 and 2.1.2. However, consider the effect of an alternative ploy, of deleting the zero observations from the sample. To do this it is necessary to postulate a model of the data generation process, and such a model is the *Tobit*.[1] Assume

$$y_t^* = \alpha' z_t + \varepsilon_t, \ \varepsilon_t | z_t \sim \mathrm{N}(0, \sigma^2) \tag{11.2.25}$$

represents the distribution of a latent variable that can take negative values. On the other hand, the observed variable is

$$y_t = \max\{y_t^*, 0\}. \tag{11.2.26}$$

The resulting distribution of y_t is mixed discrete-continuous:

$$\begin{aligned} \text{p.d.f.}(y_t | y_t > 0, z_t) &= \frac{1}{\sqrt{2\pi}\sigma} \exp\left\{-\tfrac{1}{2}\left(\frac{y_t - \alpha' z_t}{\sigma}\right)^2\right\} \\ &= \frac{1}{\sigma}\phi\left(\frac{y_t - \alpha' z_t}{\sigma}\right) \end{aligned} \tag{11.2.27}$$

where $\phi(z) = (2\pi)^{-1/2} e^{-z^2/2}$, while

$$\begin{aligned} P(y_t = 0 | z_t) &= P(y_t^* \leq 0 | z_t) \\ &= P\left(\frac{y_t^* - \alpha' z_t}{\sigma} \leq \frac{-\alpha' z_t}{\sigma} \middle| z_t\right) \\ &= \Phi\left(\frac{-\alpha' z_t}{\sigma}\right) = 1 - \Phi\left(\frac{\alpha' z_t}{\sigma}\right). \end{aligned} \tag{11.2.28}$$

If this is in fact how the data are generated, it is possible to see the effect of censoring the observations. Consider the log-likelihood function, which in this case is a mixture of probabilities and densities, depending on whether y_t is observed to be zero or not:

$$L(\alpha, \sigma) = \sum_{t \in I_0} \ln\left(1 - \Phi\left(\frac{\alpha' z_t}{\sigma}\right)\right) + \sum_{t \in I_+} \ln\left(\sigma^{-1}\phi\left(\frac{y_t - \alpha' z_t}{\sigma}\right)\right) \tag{11.2.29}$$

where I_0 is the set of zero observations and I_+ the set of positive observations. Omitting the first term, and maximizing the second term alone is equivalent to fitting the least squares line to the positive observations only. If there is a positive probability of zero observations, the two estimates of α must have different probability limits.

A comparable result would be obtained whatever the true distribution of the latent variables, and it can be concluded that censoring the observations leads to inconsistent estimates. If the Gaussian assumption is true then maximizing the Tobit likelihood is consistent and has the optimal properties associated with the MLE, to be explored in the next section. If the Gaussian assumption is false, however, one cannot draw firm conclusions about this method.

[1] So called since it was proposed by Tobin (1958) as a variation on the probit model.

11.3 Properties of the MLE

11.3.1 Preliminaries

As the foregoing examples make clear, to consider the case of dependent sampling (model C of §1.3) the likelihood function has to be constructed as the product of sequentially conditional densities or probabilities. Given an adapted stochastic sequence $\{\boldsymbol{x}_t, \mathcal{X}_t\}$, let

$$l_t(\boldsymbol{\theta}) = \ln D_t(\boldsymbol{x}_t|\mathcal{X}_{t-1};\boldsymbol{\theta}) \quad \boldsymbol{\theta} \in \Theta. \tag{11.3.1}$$

It is assumed that, for some $\boldsymbol{\theta}_0 \in \text{int}(\Theta)$, $D_t(\cdot|\mathcal{X}_{t-1};\boldsymbol{\theta}_0)$ represents, with probability 1, the true conditional probability function of $\boldsymbol{x}_t$. As such, the axiom of correct specification is adopted throughout this section. According to (11.3.1), the likelihood represents a closed dynamic model of the complete vector $\boldsymbol{x}_t$, conditioned only on the past, without the factoring-out of weakly exogenous components, in the manner exemplified by (11.2.1), and discussed in the dynamic context in §11.2.3. However, this is purely to facilitate the analysis, since the parameters of interest $\boldsymbol{\theta}$ are confined to the conditional factor of D_t. The marginal factor can be carried along in the derivations, but drops out at the end since it does not depend on $\boldsymbol{\theta}$. It does not need to be specified at any point. Also, in the case of independent observations, sequentially conditioned probability functions reduce to marginal probability functions, and one could write simply $D_t(\cdot)$. This case is subsumed in what follows.

If $\boldsymbol{x}_t|\mathcal{X}_{t-1}$ is continuously distributed, D_t is the density function at the point $\boldsymbol{x}_t$, whereas if the distribution is discrete, D_t is the probability of $\boldsymbol{x}_t$ and equal to zero except at a countable number of points of $\mathbb{R}^m$. A mixed continuous-discrete distribution is also possible within this general framework. However, for the sake of clarity the results of this section will be given for continuous distributions. The general case involves some extra technical complications, and is examined in §11.4.

Under dependent sampling the log-likelihood is, as noted, the sum of the l_ts over the sample plus a term representing initial conditions, as in (11.2.6). For the asymptotic analysis it is legitimate to ignore the latter term, which should be of small order as $n \to \infty$ under the assumptions to be introduced. The MLE will be treated as the OE minimizing the criterion

$$-\frac{1}{n}L_n(\boldsymbol{\theta}) = -\frac{1}{n}\sum_{t=1}^{n} l_t(\boldsymbol{\theta}). \tag{11.3.2}$$

In reviewing the properties of $\hat{\boldsymbol{\theta}}$ along the lines followed in §9.3.2 and §9.3.4 keep in mind the rather complex nature of the terms $l_t(\boldsymbol{\theta})$ defined in (11.3.1). One can view these in two distinct ways. When the probability function is evaluated at the point $\boldsymbol{x}_t$ (the observed data) they can be thought of as mappings from $\Theta \times \Omega$ to $\mathbb{R}$, where Ω denotes the underlying sample space. For each fixed $\omega \in \Omega$ they are mappings from Θ to $\mathbb{R}$, and for each fixed $\boldsymbol{\theta}$ they are $\mathcal{X}_t$-measurable random variables. However, their special form is particularly useful when it comes to considering the distribution conditional on $\mathcal{X}_{t-1}$. Replacing the stochastic data point $\boldsymbol{x}_t$ by a fixed argument $\boldsymbol{x}$, writing say $l_t(\boldsymbol{\theta}, \boldsymbol{x})$, they may be thought of as mappings from $\Theta \times \mathbb{S} \times \Omega$ to $\mathbb{R}$, which at each fixed point $(\boldsymbol{\theta}, \boldsymbol{x})$ are $\mathcal{X}_{t-1}$-measurable random variables. The same dual characterization applies to the various partial derivatives with respect to the elements of $\boldsymbol{\theta}$, both the first derivatives and the second cross-partials.

The fundamental results on asymptotic properties are due to Cramér (1946) and Wald (1949). As a preliminary, consider a fundamental inequality, which will be stated in general terms for a data set $\boldsymbol{x}$, assumed continuously distributed with joint density D. Let $G(\boldsymbol{x})$ be a nonnegative, measurable function of the data satisfying $\int G(\boldsymbol{\xi})d\boldsymbol{\xi} = 1$, thereby having the mathematical form of a p.d.f. Letting S denote the support of the distribution, the set of sample points $\boldsymbol{x}$ on which $D(\boldsymbol{x}) > 0$, suppose that D and G have the same support with $G(\boldsymbol{x}) = 0$ if and only if $D(\boldsymbol{x}) = 0$. A pair of probability measures with this property are said to be *equivalent*. G is therefore an equivalent p.d.f. to be thought of as a candidate for the role of approximating D. In view of Jensen's inequality (B.4.23),

$$E\left[\ln\left(\frac{G}{D}\right)\right] = \int_S \ln\left(\frac{G(\boldsymbol{\xi})}{D(\boldsymbol{\xi})}\right) D(\boldsymbol{\xi})d\boldsymbol{\xi} \le \ln\left(\int_S G(\boldsymbol{\xi})d\boldsymbol{\xi}\right) = 0. \tag{11.3.3}$$

Since the logarithm is strictly concave, the inequality holds as an equality only in the case where $G(\boldsymbol{X}) = D(\boldsymbol{X})$ for almost every $\boldsymbol{X} \in S$, such that the exceptions form a set of measure 0 in S. This is the so-called *information inequality*, and the quantity $E[\ln(G/D)]$, which measures the closeness of G to D over the sample space, is called the *Kullback–Leibler information criterion* or KLIC (Kullback and Leibler 1951). Obvious choices of G include the other members, with $\boldsymbol{\theta} \neq \boldsymbol{\theta}_0$, of the family of densities representing the model, under the axiom of correct specification. However, note that this is not a stipulation, and G can be entirely arbitrary.

The important feature of this analysis is that the information inequality holds, almost surely, for the case of conditional expectations; see (B.10.3). Assume, uncontroversially, that the conditional distribution is regular, such that for any $\omega \in C$ with $P(C) = 1$, and fixed $\boldsymbol{\theta} \in \Theta$, $D_t(\cdot|\mathcal{X}_{t-1}; \boldsymbol{\theta})(\omega)$ is a p.d.f.[2] Writing $E(\cdot|\mathcal{X}_{t-1})$ to denote $\int(\cdot)D_t(\boldsymbol{\xi}|\mathcal{X}_{t-1}; \boldsymbol{\theta}_0)d\boldsymbol{\xi}$ and applying this result yields

$$\begin{aligned} E\left(\ln\frac{D_t(\boldsymbol{x}_t|\mathcal{X}_{t-1};\boldsymbol{\theta})}{D_t(\boldsymbol{x}_t|\mathcal{X}_{t-1};\boldsymbol{\theta}_0)}\,\middle|\,\mathcal{X}_{t-1}\right) &\le \ln E\left(\frac{D_t(\boldsymbol{x}_t|\mathcal{X}_{t-1};\boldsymbol{\theta})}{D_t(\boldsymbol{x}_t|\mathcal{X}_{t-1};\boldsymbol{\theta}_0)}\,\middle|\,\mathcal{X}_{t-1}\right) \\ &= 0 \text{ a.s.} \end{aligned} \tag{11.3.4}$$

where the last equality follows exactly as in (11.3.3).

11.3.2 Consistency and Identification

The main result is that under the axiom of correct specification, condition (c) of Theorem 9.3.1 holds for the MLE.

Theorem 11.3.1 $E[L_n(\boldsymbol{\theta})]$ is maximized at $\boldsymbol{\theta}_0$.

[2] See §B.10 on regular conditional distributions.

Proof Applying (11.3.4) with (11.3.1) gives

$$E[l_t(\boldsymbol{\theta})|\mathcal{X}_{t-1}] - E[l_t(\boldsymbol{\theta}_0)|\mathcal{X}_{t-1}] \leq 0 \text{ a.s.} \tag{11.3.5}$$

This is true for any value of $\boldsymbol{\theta}$ because D_t is a p.d.f. in every case. Using the LIE,

$$E[L_n(\boldsymbol{\theta})] = E\left(\sum_{t=1}^{n} E[l_t(\boldsymbol{\theta})|\mathcal{X}_{t-1}]\right) \tag{11.3.6}$$

for any $\boldsymbol{\theta}$. The sum of random functions appearing under the expectation on the right is maximized by $\boldsymbol{\theta}_0$ with probability 1, since according to (11.3.5) this is true for each term in the sum. Hence $E[L_n(\boldsymbol{\theta})]$ has the same maximum. ■

Given this result, consistency of the MLE by Theorem 9.3.1 follows, subject to restrictions of two sorts. First, conditions (a) and (b) of the theorem must be met. These are regularity conditions – limited dependence, stochastic equicontinuity, uniformly bounded moments, etc. – whose analysis follows the same lines as the examples considered in Chapter 10. Second, there is the uniqueness specified in condition (c). The following definitions may be compared with Definitions 9.3.3 and 9.3.4:

Definition 11.3.1 Structures $\boldsymbol{\theta}_1$ and $\boldsymbol{\theta}_2$ are said to be observationally equivalent if $L_n(\boldsymbol{\theta}_1, \boldsymbol{X}) = L_n(\boldsymbol{\theta}_2, \boldsymbol{X})$ for almost all $\boldsymbol{X} \in \mathbb{S}^n$, and all $n \geq 1$. □

Definition 11.3.2 A model is said to be globally (locally) identified if the true structure $\boldsymbol{\theta}_0$ is not observationally equivalent to any other point of Θ (of an open neighbourhood of $\boldsymbol{\theta}_0$). □

Since the likelihood, by assumption, embodies all the information in the sample about the structure that generated it, Definition 11.3.1 represents a strong notion of observational equivalence. Letting E_0 denote the expectation under the true distribution, the KLIC for the complete sample takes the form

$$E_0[L_n(\boldsymbol{\theta})] \leq E_0[L_n(\boldsymbol{\theta}_0)] \tag{11.3.7}$$

where the right-hand side does not depend on $\boldsymbol{\theta}$, and underidentification in the sense of Definition 11.3.2 can be interpreted as the failure of the KLIC to have a unique zero at $\boldsymbol{\theta}_0$. It also implies that the criterion $-L_n/n$ fails the uniqueness requirement of condition (c) of Theorem 9.3.1

In the general context of OEs, identification has been defined as a property of the estimator in relation to the distribution of the data. It is possible that two structures could be observationally equivalent in the sense of Definition 9.3.3 with respect to some criterion C_n that ignores certain features of the data, and yet not with respect to the likelihood function. The fact that a given estimator fails to identify certain parameters does not mean that another estimator might not put the data to better use and succeed. The MLE is the exception to this rule. Underidentification means that no consistent estimator exists, and the parameters are simply inaccessible to empirical investigation.

11.3.3 Asymptotic Normality

As with other OEs, these results hinge on the properties of the gradient of L_n at $\boldsymbol{\theta}_0$, popularly known as the 'score vector'. For the results of this section some mild regularity conditions on the model are needed.

Assumption 11.3.1 $l_t(\boldsymbol{\theta}, \boldsymbol{x})$ is twice continuously differentiable with respect to $\boldsymbol{\theta}$ everywhere on int(Θ) $\times \mathbb{S}$ with probability 1, and the derivatives are $L_{2+\delta}$-bounded uniformly in t. □

Be careful to note that the qualification 'with probability 1' here refers to the fact that $l_t(\boldsymbol{\theta}, \boldsymbol{x})$ is a $\mathcal{X}_{t-1}$-measurable random variable at each point of $\Theta \times \mathbb{S}$. A particular role of the assumption is to validate differentiation inside the conditional expectation operator, according to Theorem B.10.1. In view of the definition of l_t there is a useful equivalence,

$$\frac{\partial D_t}{\partial \boldsymbol{\theta}} = D_t \frac{\partial l_t}{\partial \boldsymbol{\theta}} \text{ a.s.} \tag{11.3.8}$$

It is convenient to define the operator

$$E_{\boldsymbol{\theta}}(\cdot|\mathcal{X}_{t-1}) = \int (\cdot) D_t(\boldsymbol{\xi}|\mathcal{X}_{t-1}; \boldsymbol{\theta}) d\boldsymbol{\xi} \tag{11.3.9}$$

representing the conditional expectation of any function of $\boldsymbol{x}_t$ when $\boldsymbol{\theta}$ is the 'true parameter'.

Lemma 11.3.1 $E\left(\left.\frac{\partial l_t}{\partial \boldsymbol{\theta}}\right|_{\boldsymbol{\theta}=\boldsymbol{\theta}_0} \middle| \mathcal{X}_{t-1} \right) = \mathbf{0}$ a.s.

Proof In view of (11.3.8),

$$\begin{aligned} E_{\boldsymbol{\theta}}\left(\frac{\partial l_t}{\partial \boldsymbol{\theta}} \middle| \mathcal{X}_{t-1} \right) &= \int \frac{\partial l_t}{\partial \boldsymbol{\theta}} D_t(\boldsymbol{\xi}|\mathcal{X}_{t-1}; \boldsymbol{\theta}) d\boldsymbol{\xi} \\ &= \int \frac{\partial D_t(\boldsymbol{\xi}|\mathcal{X}_{t-1}; \boldsymbol{\theta})}{\partial \boldsymbol{\theta}} d\boldsymbol{\xi} \\ &= \frac{\partial}{\partial \boldsymbol{\theta}} \int D_t(\boldsymbol{\xi}|\mathcal{X}_{t-1}; \boldsymbol{\theta}) d\boldsymbol{\xi} = \mathbf{0} \text{ a.s.} \end{aligned} \tag{11.3.10}$$

since the final integral is identically equal to 1. Interchanging the order of differentiation and integration in the third equality of (11.3.10) is permitted by Theorem B.4.1 under Assumption 11.3.1. In particular, this equality holds for the case $\boldsymbol{\theta} = \boldsymbol{\theta}_0$. ■

Subject to Assumption 11.3.1, the adapted sequence $\{(\partial/\partial\boldsymbol{\theta}) l_t(\boldsymbol{\theta}_0), \mathcal{X}_t\}$ is therefore a vector m.d. Applying the martingale CLT (Theorem 6.2.3 plus the Cramér–Wold device, Theorem 3.3.3) and arguments basically similar to those of §7.1.3 and §10.2.2 yields

$$\frac{1}{\sqrt{n}} \left.\frac{\partial L_n}{\partial \boldsymbol{\theta}}\right|_{\boldsymbol{\theta}_0} \xrightarrow{\text{D}} \text{N}(\mathbf{0}, \mathfrak{I}_0) \tag{11.3.11}$$

where $\mathfrak{I}_0 = \lim_{n\to\infty} n^{-1}\mathfrak{I}_{n0}$, and

$$\mathfrak{I}_{n0} = E\left(\frac{\partial L_n}{\partial \boldsymbol{\theta}}\frac{\partial L_n}{\partial \boldsymbol{\theta}'}\bigg|_{\boldsymbol{\theta}_0}\right) = \sum_{t=1}^{n} E\left(\frac{\partial l_t}{\partial \boldsymbol{\theta}}\frac{\partial l_t}{\partial \boldsymbol{\theta}'}\bigg|_{\boldsymbol{\theta}_0}\right). \tag{11.3.12}$$

The matrix $\mathfrak{I}_{n0}$ is called the *information matrix*, being thought of as measuring the amount of information about $\boldsymbol{\theta}_0$ in the sample. $\mathfrak{I}_0$ may similarly be called the limiting information matrix, or limiting average information. In view of the next result, the information matrix plays a key role in the distribution theory.

Theorem 11.3.2

$$\mathfrak{I}_{n0} = -E\left(\frac{\partial L_n^2}{\partial \boldsymbol{\theta}\partial \boldsymbol{\theta}'}\bigg|_{\boldsymbol{\theta}_0}\right). \tag{11.3.13}$$

Proof Differentiating (11.3.10) with respect to $\boldsymbol{\theta}'$ yields a $p \times p$ matrix of zeros by construction. It follows that

$$\begin{aligned}
\mathbf{0} &= \frac{\partial}{\partial \boldsymbol{\theta}'}\int \frac{\partial l_t}{\partial \boldsymbol{\theta}} D_t(\boldsymbol{\xi}|\mathcal{X}_{t-1};\boldsymbol{\theta})d\boldsymbol{\xi} \\
&= \int \left(\frac{\partial^2 l_t}{\partial \boldsymbol{\theta}\partial \boldsymbol{\theta}'} + \frac{\partial l_t}{\partial \boldsymbol{\theta}}\cdot\frac{\partial l_t}{\partial \boldsymbol{\theta}'}\right) D_t(\boldsymbol{\xi}|\mathcal{X}_{t-1};\boldsymbol{\theta})d\boldsymbol{\xi} \\
&= E_{\boldsymbol{\theta}}\left(\frac{\partial^2 l_t}{\partial \boldsymbol{\theta}\partial \boldsymbol{\theta}'}\bigg|\mathcal{X}_{t-1}\right) + E_{\boldsymbol{\theta}}\left(\frac{\partial l_t}{\partial \boldsymbol{\theta}}\frac{\partial l_t}{\partial \boldsymbol{\theta}'}\bigg|\mathcal{X}_{t-1}\right).
\end{aligned} \tag{11.3.14}$$

The theorem follows on considering the case $\boldsymbol{\theta} = \boldsymbol{\theta}_0$, summing over n, and taking unconditional expectations using the LIE. ∎

This is the information matrix equality of (9.3.19), in which $c = 1$. Note that the minus sign on the right-hand side of (11.3.13) is appropriate since $-L/n$ is the criterion function relevant to the theory of Chapter 9. Theorem 9.3.6 therefore provides the neat result

$$\sqrt{n}(\hat{\boldsymbol{\theta}}_n - \boldsymbol{\theta}_0) \xrightarrow{\mathrm{D}} \mathrm{N}(\mathbf{0}, \mathfrak{I}_0^{-1}). \tag{11.3.15}$$

For an intuitive appreciation of the asymptotic distributions (11.3.11) and (11.3.15), consider the case of scalar θ. Repeated sampling generates a distribution of sample log-likelihood functions whose expectation takes its maximum at θ_0 (Theorem 11.3.1). The sketches in Figure 11.2 show two expected log-likelihoods relating to samples of fixed size n, where in case (a) the data contain more information about θ_0 than in case (b). These curves represent the average values of the sample criterion functions at each θ, and by imagining the sampling distributions that gave rise to them, it is easy to appreciate that in case (a) the proportion of sample functions taking their modes close to θ_0 must be higher than in case (b). The sampling distribution of $\hat{\theta}_n$ must therefore have more probability mass concentrated near θ_0 in the former case.

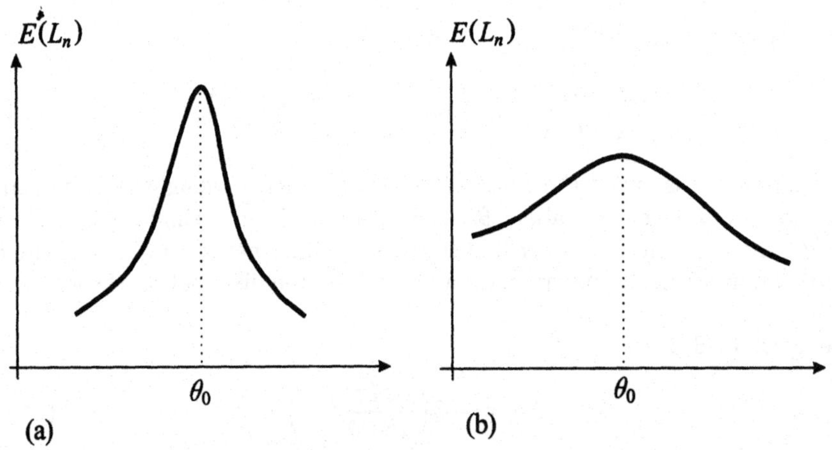

Figure 11.2: Expected Log-likelihoods

The difference between the cases is characterized by the sharpness (second order curvature) of the peaks, measured by

$$-\left.\frac{\partial^2 E(L_n)}{\partial\theta^2}\right|_{\theta=\theta_0}. \tag{11.3.16}$$

Since the differentiation and integration operators can be interchanged under the regularity conditions in Assumption 11.3.1, this is the same as

$$\mathfrak{I}_{n0} = -E\left(\left.\frac{\partial^2 L_n}{\partial\theta^2}\right|_{\theta=\theta_0}\right). \tag{11.3.17}$$

Under the regularity conditions a function is arbitrarily well approximated by a quadratic within a sufficiently small neighbourhood of a point, a fact exploited in deriving the asymptotic distribution of $\hat{\theta}_n$. In the limit $\mathfrak{I}_0$ becomes the sole relevant measure of the curvature, so it is easy to see that the limiting variance of $\sqrt{n}(\hat{\theta}_n - \theta_0)$ must be inversely related to this quantity.

11.3.4 Model Selection

Return now to consider the methods discussed in §9.4.1, as they apply to the log likelihood function. Since the likelihood purports to represent the full distribution of the data set, the question of when the model is 'true' assumes a special significance, and is also precisely answered in this case, through the information inequality. The function G in (11.3.3) does not need to be a member of the family $D(\boldsymbol{\theta})$, $\boldsymbol{\theta} \in \Theta$, but can be any equivalent p.d.f. at all, and can therefore represent an alternative model of the data. Consider alternatives G_1 and G_2. If these are equivalent p.d.f.s having support S in common with the true density D, observe that

$$E(\ln G_1) - E(\ln G_2) = \int_S \ln(G_1/D)Dd\boldsymbol{\xi} - \int_S \ln(G_2/D)Dd\boldsymbol{\xi}. \tag{11.3.18}$$

If the difference is positive, this favours G_1 over G_2. If $\ln G_1$ and $\ln G_2$ are the maximised log-likelihoods for two competing models, comparing them directly is equivalent to comparing them on the basis of the KLIC. As in §9.4.1, it is desirable to correct for different numbers of parameters when comparing sample average likelihoods in finite samples. The Schwarz (1978), Hannan–Quinn (1979) and Akaike (1973) criteria are usually given in the form

$$SBC = L_n(\hat{\boldsymbol{\theta}}) - \tfrac{1}{2}p\ln n \qquad (11.3.19)$$

$$HQC = L_n(\hat{\boldsymbol{\theta}}) - p\ln\ln n \qquad (11.3.20)$$

$$AIC = L_n(\hat{\boldsymbol{\theta}}) - p. \qquad (11.3.21)$$

Since the maximised value of the Gaussian log-likelihood in the regression model has the form

$$L_n(\hat{\boldsymbol{\beta}}, \hat{\sigma}^2) = \text{constant} - \frac{n\ln\hat{\sigma}^2}{2} \qquad (11.3.22)$$

from (11.2.4) and (11.2.5), the relationship between these formulae and those in §9.4.1 should be evident. The decision whether or not to scale by sample size is of little consequence, but note that these criteria are in the form 'bigger = better' in contrast to the sum of squares form in §9.4.1 where 'smaller = better'. There does not seem to be any consensus about the way to report these, so care is necessary when interpreting output from unfamiliar computer packages or research reports.

11.3.5 Computational Issues

The special structure of the log-likelihood function can be exploited to define efficient methods of computing the ML estimates and associated test statistics. The function $-L_n/n$ that is to be minimized takes the generic form of C_n in (9.1.4) where ϕ is the identity function, $r = 1$, and $\psi_t = -l_t$. The gradient is the score vector, the sum of terms of the form $-\partial l_t/\partial\boldsymbol{\theta}$.

Moreover, according to Theorem 11.3.2 the matrix of second derivatives, when evaluated at $\boldsymbol{\theta}_0$, has the same expectation as the matrix

$$\sum_{t=1}^{n}\frac{\partial l_t}{\partial\boldsymbol{\theta}}\frac{\partial l_t}{\partial\boldsymbol{\theta}'}. \qquad (11.3.23)$$

This is called the *outer product of the gradient* or OPG matrix. These results suggests a computationally economical way to define a search algorithm of the form (9.2.8), in which the search direction is computed as a regression. Thus, the search direction has the form

$$\boldsymbol{d}_r = \left(\sum_{t=1}^{n}\frac{\partial l_t}{\partial\boldsymbol{\theta}}\frac{\partial l_t}{\partial\boldsymbol{\theta}'}\right)^{-1}\sum_{t=1}^{n}\frac{\partial l_t}{\partial\boldsymbol{\theta}}\bigg|_{\boldsymbol{\theta}=\boldsymbol{\theta}^r}. \qquad (11.3.24)$$

Letting $\boldsymbol{L}$ $(n\times p)$ denote the matrix whose rows are $\partial l_t/\partial\boldsymbol{\theta}'$, and $\boldsymbol{\iota}$ the n-dimensional unit vector $(1, 1, \ldots, 1)'$, the direction is calculated by the 'OPG regression' formula,

$$\boldsymbol{d}_r = (\boldsymbol{L}'\boldsymbol{L})^{-1}\boldsymbol{L}'\boldsymbol{\iota}. \qquad (11.3.25)$$

This is the BHHH algorithm (Berndt et. al. 1974). It has apparent affinities with the Gauss–Newton algorithm of (10.2.8), but be careful to note that BHHH applied to the sum of squares function is different from GN. For the case

$$l_t = [y_t - g_t(\boldsymbol{\theta})]^2 \tag{11.3.26}$$

the BHHH direction is

$$\boldsymbol{d}_r = \left(\sum_{t=1}^{n}(y_t - g_t)^2\frac{\partial g_t}{\partial \boldsymbol{\theta}}\frac{\partial g_t}{\partial \boldsymbol{\theta}'}\right)^{-1}\sum_{t=1}^{n}\frac{\partial g_t}{\partial \boldsymbol{\theta}}(y_t - g_t)\Bigg|_{\boldsymbol{\theta}=\boldsymbol{\theta}^r} \tag{11.3.27}$$

which differs from GN by the inclusion of the squared residuals, weighting the terms of the outer product matrix.

11.3.6 Asymptotic Efficiency

The result in (11.3.15) is interesting, not only for its simplicity, but for the efficiency theorem to which it leads, the Cramér–Rao Theorem.

Theorem 11.3.3 (Cramér–Rao) If $\boldsymbol{t}_n$ is any unbiased estimator of $\boldsymbol{\theta}_0$, the matrix $\text{Var}(\boldsymbol{t}_n) - \mathfrak{I}_{n0}^{-1}$ is positive semi-definite.

Proof Consider the unconditional expectation of $\boldsymbol{t}_n$. Using the LIE, this can be constructed from the conditional densities using the recursion

$$E(\boldsymbol{t}_n) = E[E(E(\dots E(\boldsymbol{t}_n|\mathcal{X}_{n-1})\dots|\mathcal{X}_2)|\mathcal{X}_1)]. \tag{11.3.28}$$

If $\boldsymbol{\theta}$ represents the true model, this has the representation

$$E_{\boldsymbol{\theta}}(\boldsymbol{t}_n) = \int_1 \dots \int_n \boldsymbol{t}(\boldsymbol{\xi}_1,\dots,\boldsymbol{\xi}_n)D_1(\boldsymbol{\xi}_1;\boldsymbol{\theta})d\boldsymbol{\xi}_1\prod_{t=2}^{n}D_t(\boldsymbol{\xi}_t|\mathcal{X}_{t-1};\boldsymbol{\theta})d\boldsymbol{\xi}_t \tag{11.3.29}$$

where it is understood that the multiple integrations are performed sequentially from n back to 1,[3] where at stage t the integration is with respect to the density D_t conditional on $\mathcal{X}_{t-1}$, and for $t < n$ the integrands are

$$\int_{t+1}\dots\int_n \boldsymbol{t}(\boldsymbol{x}_1,\dots,\boldsymbol{x}_{t-1},\boldsymbol{\xi}_t,\dots,\boldsymbol{\xi}_n)\prod_{s=t+1}^{n}D_s(\boldsymbol{\xi}_s|\mathcal{X}_{s-1};\boldsymbol{\theta})d\boldsymbol{\xi}_s. \tag{11.3.30}$$

The final expectation with respect to density D_1 is unconditional.

Differentiating under the integral sign, using the product rule for differentiation, and substituting from (11.3.8) yields

$$\frac{\partial E_{\boldsymbol{\theta}}(\boldsymbol{t}_n)}{\partial \boldsymbol{\theta}'}$$

[3] This stepwise integration is permissible by Fubini's Theorem because the integrals are with respect to Lebesgue measure. Note the assumption of continuous distributions here. The generalization to non-continuous cases is discussed in §11.4.

$$= \int \cdots \int t_n(\xi_1, \ldots, \xi_n)\frac{\partial}{\partial \theta'}\left(D_1(\xi_1;\theta)d\xi_1 \prod_{t=2}^{n} D_t(\xi_t|\mathcal{X}_{t-1};\theta)d\xi_t\right)$$
$$= \int \cdots \int t_n(\xi_1, \ldots, \xi_n)\frac{\partial L_n}{\partial \theta'}D_1(\xi_1;\theta)d\xi_1 \prod_{t=2}^{n} D_t(\xi_t|\mathcal{X}_{t-1};\theta)d\xi_t$$
$$= E_\theta\left(t_n\frac{\partial L_n}{\partial \theta'}\right) \tag{11.3.31}$$

where $L_n = \sum_{t=1}^{n} l_t$. Taking the case $\theta = \theta_0$, since $E_\theta(\partial/\partial\theta)L_n(\theta) = \mathbf{0}$ the right-hand member is the covariance matrix of the vectors t_n and $(\partial/\partial\theta)L_n(\theta_0)$. If t_n is unbiased, then by definition $E_\theta(t_n) = \theta$, and $\partial\theta/\partial\theta' = I_p$ for any value of θ. It follows that

$$\text{Cov}\left(t_n\frac{\partial L_n}{\partial \theta'}\right) = I_p \tag{11.3.32}$$

and hence, using (11.3.12)

$$\text{Var}\begin{bmatrix} t_n \\ (\partial/\partial\theta)L_n(\theta_0)\end{bmatrix} = \begin{bmatrix}\text{Var}(t_n) & I_p \\ I_p & \mathfrak{I}_{n0}\end{bmatrix} \quad (2p \times 2p). \tag{11.3.33}$$

As a covariance matrix, this must be positive semi-definite. For any fixed p-vector a, form the $2p \times 1$ vector

$$b = \begin{bmatrix} a \\ -\mathfrak{I}_{n0}^{-1}a\end{bmatrix} \tag{11.3.34}$$

such that

$$a'(\text{Var}(t_n) - \mathfrak{I}_{n0}^{-1})a = b'\begin{bmatrix}\text{Var}(t_n) & I_p \\ I_p & \mathfrak{I}_{n0}\end{bmatrix}b \geq 0 \tag{11.3.35}$$

which is the required inequality. ■

This is an exact result for unbiased estimators, although there is no suggestion that an estimator attaining the bound always exists. However, under the limiting distribution of $\sqrt{n}(t_n - \theta_0)$, where t_n is asymptotically unbiased, the inequality implies that for all a,

$$a'(\text{AVar}(t_n) - \mathfrak{I}_0^{-1})a \geq 0 \tag{11.3.36}$$

where $\text{AVar}(t_n) = \lim_{n\to\infty} n\,\text{Var}(t_n)$, the variance of $\sqrt{n}(t_n - \theta_0)$ under the limiting distribution. Since $\text{AVar}(\hat{\theta}_{ML}) = \mathfrak{I}_0^{-1}$, the MLE attains the CR variance bound asymptotically. It is therefore BAN, or in other words, asymptotically efficient in the class of CAN estimators.[4] This is an intuitively plausible conclusion,

[4]Amemiya (1985) points out that 'superefficient' CAN estimators can be constructed that improve on the CR bound for certain values of θ_0. Since these counter-examples occupy no more than a set of Lebesgue measure 0 in Θ, they do not have much practical significance.

given that the MLE is based on a complete specification of the probability law of the observations, and so puts all the sample information to use.

These results relate back to the discussions of identification in §11.3.2 and §9.3.3. Theorems 9.3.4 and 9.3.5 jointly show that $\mathfrak{I}_0$ is singular in the unidentified case. The MLE is inconsistent, and its asymptotic variance is accordingly undefined. Inequality (11.3.36) rules out the possibility of any alternative consistent estimator.

11.4 General Distributions

The foregoing arguments were cast explicitly in the context of continuous distributions, so it is important to appreciate that they hold for general distributions, including the discrete and mixed discrete-continuous cases. Some examples of how the likelihood function can be constructed in such cases were provided in §11.2.5. It would, however, be reassuring to see how the arguments of §11.3 might be followed through. To give a flavour of these extensions, which necessarily are complex in the full generality of m dimensions (see §B.5 on the bivariate case), consider a univariate dynamic model where the scalar variable x_t is mixed discrete-continuous.

Let Δ denote the set of points (finite or at most countably infinite) at which x_t assumes positive probability, under the distribution conditional on $\mathcal{X}_{t-1}$. If x_t is purely discrete, Δ is simply the set of all possible values the variables may assume under the distribution, and in the mixed case it is the set of jump points of the conditional c.d.f. Define the log-likelihood as $L_n = \sum_{t=1}^n l_t$ where $l_t = \ln D(x_t|\mathcal{X}_{t-1};\boldsymbol{\theta})$ and

$$D(x_t|\mathcal{X}_{t-1};\boldsymbol{\theta}) = \begin{cases} p(x_t|\mathcal{X}_{t-1};\boldsymbol{\theta}), & x_t \in \Delta \\ f(x_t|\mathcal{X}_{t-1};\boldsymbol{\theta}), & \text{otherwise} \end{cases} \tag{11.4.1}$$

where $p(\cdot|\mathcal{X}_{t-1};\boldsymbol{\theta})$ is a probability, and $f(\cdot|\mathcal{X}_{t-1};\boldsymbol{\theta})$ is the density function for the continuous part of the distribution.

$D(\cdot|\mathcal{X}_{t-1})$ defines, with probability 1, a mixed continuous-discrete probability measure. For any integrable, $\mathcal{X}_{t-1}$-measurable function $g(\cdot)$, the expectation with respect to this conditional distribution is

$$E(g(x_t)|\mathcal{X}_{t-1}) = \int g(\xi)f(\xi|\mathcal{X}_{t-1})d\xi + \sum_{\xi_i\in\Delta} g(\xi_i)p(\xi_i|\mathcal{X}_{t-1}). \tag{11.4.2}$$

Conditional expectations as in (11.4.2) can be substituted into the various arguments of this chapter involving conditional densities. Consider (11.3.4), for example, which contains the case

$$g(x_t) = \frac{D(x_t|\mathcal{X}_{t-1};\boldsymbol{\theta})}{D(x_t|\mathcal{X}_{t-1};\boldsymbol{\theta}_0)} = \begin{cases} \dfrac{p(x_t|\mathcal{X}_{t-1};\boldsymbol{\theta})}{p(x_t|\mathcal{X}_{t-1};\boldsymbol{\theta}_0)}, & x_t \in \Delta \\[2ex] \dfrac{f(x_t|\mathcal{X}_{t-1};\boldsymbol{\theta})}{f(x_t|\mathcal{X}_{t-1};\boldsymbol{\theta}_0)}, & \text{otherwise.} \end{cases} \tag{11.4.3}$$

The Jensen inequality applies generally, and the equality with the third member also holds as before, making use of (B.3.9), in the form

$$E\Big(\frac{D(x_t|\mathcal{X}_{t-1};\boldsymbol{\theta})}{D(x_t|\mathcal{X}_{t-1};\boldsymbol{\theta}_0)}\Big|\mathcal{X}_{t-1}\Big) = \int \frac{f(\xi|\mathcal{X}_{t-1};\boldsymbol{\theta})}{f(\xi|\mathcal{X}_{t-1};\boldsymbol{\theta}_0)}f(\xi|\mathcal{X}_{t-1};\boldsymbol{\theta}_0)d\xi + \sum_{\xi_i\in\Delta}\frac{p(\xi_i|\mathcal{X}_{t-1};\boldsymbol{\theta})}{p(\xi_i|\mathcal{X}_{t-1};\boldsymbol{\theta}_0)}p(\xi_i|\mathcal{X}_{t-1};\boldsymbol{\theta}_0) = 1. \tag{11.4.4}$$

The extensions for Lemma 11.3.1 and Theorem 11.3.2 are precisely similar, except that the cases $g = \partial l_t/\partial\boldsymbol{\theta}_j$, $j = 1,\dots,p$, appear in the equalities that replace (11.3.10) and (11.3.14).

Theorem 11.3.3 extends in a similar manner, although here the key relation (11.3.31) involves the whole sample rather than individual observations. Letting $\boldsymbol{g}_n = \boldsymbol{t}_n$ and also letting $\boldsymbol{g}_{t-1} = E(\boldsymbol{g}_t|\mathcal{X}_{t-1})$ for $t = n,\ n-1,\dots,1$, these are defined by the recursion

$$\boldsymbol{g}_{t-1} = \int \boldsymbol{g}_t f(\xi|\mathcal{X}_{t-1})d\xi + \sum_{\xi_i\in\Delta}\boldsymbol{g}_t p(\xi_i|\mathcal{X}_{t-1}). \tag{11.4.5}$$

The number of terms doubles at each substitution, so that $E(\boldsymbol{t}_n)$ consists of a sum of 2^n such terms. The structure is best illustrated by the case $n = 2$. For this there are the four groups of terms

$$\begin{aligned} E[\boldsymbol{t}(x_1,x_2)] = &\int\int \boldsymbol{t}(\xi_1,\xi_2)f(\xi_2|\mathcal{X}_1)f(\xi_1)d\xi_1 d\xi_2 \\ &+ \sum_{\xi_1\in\Delta}\int \boldsymbol{t}(\xi_{1i},\xi_2)f(\xi_2|\mathcal{X}_1)d\xi_2 p(\xi_{1i}) \\ &+ \int\sum_{\xi_{2i}\in\Delta}\boldsymbol{t}(\xi_1,\xi_{2i})p(\xi_{2i}|\mathcal{X}_1)f(\xi_1)d\xi_1 \\ &+ \sum_{\xi_{1i}\in\Delta}\sum_{\xi_{2i}\in\Delta}\boldsymbol{t}(\xi_{1i},\xi_{2i})p(\xi_{2i}|\mathcal{X}_1)p(\xi_{1i}). \end{aligned} \tag{11.4.6}$$

Each of these terms corresponds to the Lebesgue–Stieltjes integral of $\boldsymbol{t}_n$ over a particular region of the sample space, and each contains the n-fold product of factors, either f or p, that corresponds to the likelihood function as it is defined for that region of the space. The same decomposition applies to $E_{\theta}(\cdot)$, for any choice of $\boldsymbol{\theta}$. Thus, differentiating these terms with respect to $\boldsymbol{\theta}$, using (11.3.8) where D denotes either $f(\cdot|\mathcal{X}_{t-1};\boldsymbol{\theta})$ or $p(\cdot|\mathcal{X}_{t-1};\boldsymbol{\theta})$ as appropriate, yields the same conclusion as in (11.3.31). By considering the analysis in §B.5, and especially equation (B.5.8), the reader may visualize how this analysis could be extended to the multivariate case.

Further Reading: The literature on maximum likelihood estimation in econometrics is of course voluminous, although very often the material is relevant to general optimization estimators, and is equally useful in connection with Chapters 9 and 10. Recommended textbook treatments are Gourieroux and Monfort (1995), Davidson and MacKinnon (1993) and for a concise and elegant introduction, Silvey (1975). Rothenberg (1973) explores the issues of identification and efficient estimation. On the dynamic Gaussian linear model see Hamilton (1994), Harvey (1990). On limited dependent variable models, see Maddala's (1983) monograph, the survey article by McFadden (1983), and also Amemiya (1981, 1984, 1985).

Chapter 12

Testing Hypotheses

12.1 Basic Ideas

12.1.1 Concepts and Definitions

A good place to begin this chapter is by reviewing the contents of §4.1. Once the modelling apparatus of density functions and the like outlined there is taken as given, a parametric model is defined by the parameter space $\Theta \subseteq \mathbb{R}^p$, to be thought of as the set of all admissible parameter values. Invoking the axiom of correct specification, as will be done throughout this chapter, the DGP is represented by the point $\boldsymbol{\theta}_0$ of the set. In the language of hypothesis testing, Θ represents the *maintained hypothesis*, written as H_M.

A hypothesis partitions Θ into two subsets by stating that $\boldsymbol{\theta}_0$ falls in one of these. Let ω and $\Theta - \omega$ denote the sets in question, and then, in the conventional terminology, the null hypothesis is

$$H_0 : \boldsymbol{\theta}_0 \in \omega \tag{12.1.1}$$

and the alternative hypothesis, that which is true when H_0 is false, is

$$H_A : \boldsymbol{\theta}_0 \in \Theta - \omega. \tag{12.1.2}$$

A null hypothesis that imposes a restriction and so is a special case relative to H_A is said to be *nested* in the alternative. The non-nested tests considered in §7.5.3, by contrast, compare two special cases of H_M, neither one contained in the other, but that approach will not be specifically considered in this chapter. In the present framework ω is defined by an equality restriction,

$$\boldsymbol{g}(\boldsymbol{\theta}_0) = \boldsymbol{0} \tag{12.1.3}$$

where $\boldsymbol{g}$ is a $r \times 1$ vector of functions and $1 \le r \le p$. The alternative is

$$H_A : \boldsymbol{g}(\boldsymbol{\theta}_0) \neq \boldsymbol{0} \tag{12.1.4}$$

such that at least one element of the equality does not hold. Accordingly, ω is a set of dimension less than p and nearly all the points of Θ fall into the alternative hypothesis. $\boldsymbol{g}$ is assumed to be differentiable at all interior points of Θ, and the Jacobian matrix

$$\boldsymbol{G}(\boldsymbol{\theta}) = \frac{\partial \boldsymbol{g}}{\partial \boldsymbol{\theta}'} \; (r \times p) \tag{12.1.5}$$

is assumed to have full rank r, at least in an open neighbourhood of $\boldsymbol{\theta}_0$. To visualize the kind of restrictions implied by $\boldsymbol{g}$, consider the case where Θ is a region of the plane $\mathbb{R}^2$. An implicit function of the form $g(\theta_1, \theta_2) = 0$ defines a line or curve (one-dimensional set) in the plane. A pair of such functions define a pair of curves whose intersection defines at most a finite collection of points. The curve ($r = 1$) or points ($r = 2$) represent the θ-values permitted under H_0.

The test is a decision to reject or not reject H_0 on the basis of the sample evidence. For example, one approach to testing to be considered in this chapter, the Wald principle, is to evaluate the restrictions at the estimated parameters $\hat{\boldsymbol{\theta}}_n$. When n is finite the equality $\boldsymbol{g}(\hat{\boldsymbol{\theta}}_n) = \mathbf{0}$ will hold exactly only with probability 0, but the question to be decided is whether the deviation is small enough to be attributed merely to sampling error, or is large enough to suggest that $\boldsymbol{g}(\boldsymbol{\theta}_0) \neq \mathbf{0}$. Two distinct types of error can be committed in making this decision. A Type 1 error is to reject when H_0 is in fact true, whereas a Type 2 error is not to reject when H_0 is in fact false.

The most widely accepted approach to testing hypotheses is that due to Neyman and Pearson (1928, 1933). The Neyman–Pearson approach is to fix the probability of a Type 1 error at or below a certain known level α, called the ***significance level*** of the test. A test procedure having significance level α is chosen, such that the probability of making a Type 2 error (denoted β) is as small as possible.

If $\boldsymbol{X}$ is the $n \times m$ matrix representing the data set (n observations on m variables), let $\mathfrak{X} \subseteq \mathbb{R}^{mn}$ denote the space of all possible samples. The test procedure is, in effect, to partition $\mathfrak{X}$ into two sets. The *critical region*, $\mathfrak{X}_c$, is the set such that if $\boldsymbol{X} \in \mathfrak{X}_c$, we shall reject H_0 and accept H_A. The complementary set, $\mathfrak{X} - \mathfrak{X}_c$, is called the *acceptance region*. The way these regions are usually defined is to construct a *test statistic* $\tau(\boldsymbol{X}) \in \mathbb{R}$ and adopt a decision rule of the form 'reject H_0 if $\tau(\boldsymbol{X}) > k$', for some real value k, called the *critical value*. The terminology of critical and acceptance regions is usually extended to this partition of the line into values exceeding and not exceeding the critical value.[1] Letting

$$\alpha(\boldsymbol{\theta}) = P_{\boldsymbol{\theta}}(\boldsymbol{X} \in \mathfrak{X}_c) \tag{12.1.6}$$

where $P_{\boldsymbol{\theta}}(\cdot)$ denotes the probability in the state of the world in which $D_n(\boldsymbol{X}, \boldsymbol{\theta})$ is the joint distribution of the sample, $\mathfrak{X}_c$ must be chosen such that

$$\alpha(\boldsymbol{\theta}) \leq \alpha \;\forall\; \boldsymbol{\theta} \in \omega. \tag{12.1.7}$$

The quantity $\sup_{\boldsymbol{\theta} \in \omega} \alpha(\boldsymbol{\theta})$ is called the *size* of the test based on $\mathfrak{X}_c$. The Neyman–Pearson procedure is to choose $\mathfrak{X}_c$ (which means in practice, to find a method of

---

[1] In some cases the critical region lies in the negative half-line so that this definition is reversed, but it nearly every case rejection is triggered when the statistic is absolutely large.

computing $\tau(\boldsymbol{X})$ and choosing the critical value k) such that the size of the test does not exceed α.

If it has the property that $\alpha(\boldsymbol{\theta}) = \alpha$ for all $\boldsymbol{\theta} \in \omega$, the test is called *similar*. This property is desirable, if not essential, because without it the performance of the test depends on the values of the parameters not constrained by H_0, and in general unknown.

Assuming there are several ways to construct a test of significance level α, the choice must be based on making the probability of Type 2 error as small as possible. The *power* of the test is defined as $1 - \beta(\boldsymbol{\theta})$ where

$$\beta(\boldsymbol{\theta}) = P_{\boldsymbol{\theta}}(\boldsymbol{X} \in \mathfrak{X} - \mathfrak{X}_c). \tag{12.1.8}$$

The problem is that the power depends on $\boldsymbol{\theta}$. Clearly, a useful test needs to have the property that

$$1 - \beta(\boldsymbol{\theta}) \geq \alpha \text{ for all } \boldsymbol{\theta} \in \Theta - \omega \tag{12.1.9}$$

so that the probability of rejecting H_0 when it is false is never less than when it is true, and such tests are said to be *unbiased*. However, the choice among unbiased α-level tests is not always clear cut. A *uniformly most powerful* α-level test, one that has the greatest power against all alternatives $\boldsymbol{\theta} \in \Theta - \omega$, does not exist except in certain special cases, so the choice of test generally involves a compromise. A test should as far as possible have power against alternatives of interest, or alternatives that are believed to be the plausible cases in the event that H_0 is false.

To apply this theory, the problem to be solved is to construct test statistics $\tau(\boldsymbol{X})$ that have a known distribution under H_0, not depending on nuisance parameters. All the statistics discussed in this book are of this type. Since the distribution theory to be employed is mainly asymptotic, the tests likewise have an asymptotic justification, and test sizes can only be fixed approximately in finite samples. A test that rejects all alternatives $\boldsymbol{\theta} \in \Theta - \omega$ with probability 1 as $n \to \infty$ is called a *consistent* test. While consistency is obviously a desirable property, there will usually be a choice of consistent tests. One solution to the problem of choosing between them is to consider a sequence of local alternatives approaching ω at a suitable rate as n increases, so that comparisons can be made under the respective asymptotic distributions of the statistics. This approach is discussed in §12.4.

12.1.2 Test Principles

A number of different testing principles based on OE estimators can be identified. One of these already mentioned, the *Wald* (W) principle (Wald 1943), is to construct a statistic based on the restriction vector $\boldsymbol{g}$, evaluated at unrestricted estimates of the model. The idea of the *Lagrange multiplier* (LM) principle due to Silvey (1959) and Aitchison and Silvey (1958, 1960) is, as the name implies, to consider the penalty implied by estimation of the model subject to the restrictions. This turns out to be effectively identical to the *score test* proposed by Rao (1948), based on the gradient of the unrestricted criterion function evaluated at the restricted estimates. The *Durbin–Wu–Hausman* (DWH) principle (Durbin 1954, Hausman 1978, Wu 1973) compares the restricted and unrestricted estimates while the *likelihood ratio* (LR) or (referring to the general case) the *analogue likelihood ratio* (ALR) principle compares the values of the criterion function itself at the restricted and unrestricted optima. A fifth testing principle, the M or moment principle, does not fit so neatly into a schema as the other four, but is related to the LM principle.

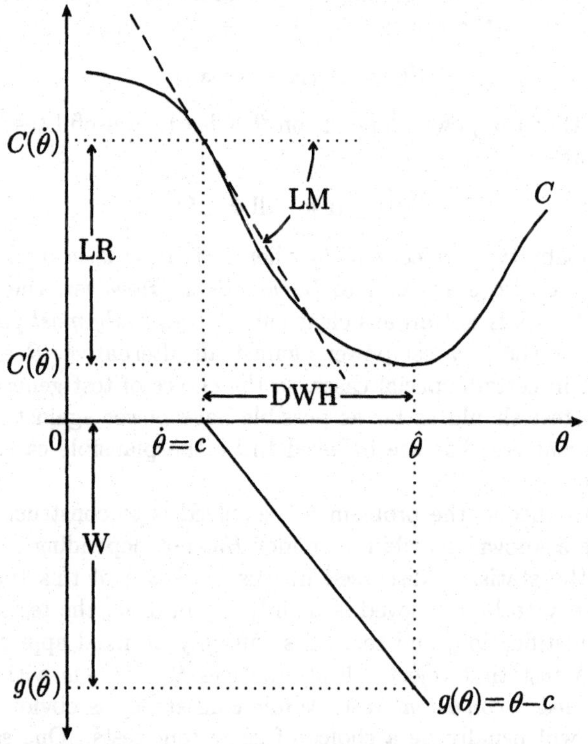

Figure 12.1: Test Principles Compared

The differences between the four can be illustrated by a diagram, as in Figure 12.1. The model has one parameter θ, and the restriction in question is just $\theta = c$, where c is a given constant. The diagram plots both the criterion function C and the constraint function g (vertical axes) against the parameter value (horizontal axis). The distances marked W, DWH, and LR, and the angle marked LM, are the quantities examined under each test principle. After scaling these quantities by their standard deviations, the tests represent decisions whether they differ enough from 0 to warrant rejection of the null hypothesis. One or two points can be appreciated from the diagram alone. First, if the criterion function was a quadratic function (that it has deliberately been drawn not to resemble) then simple geometry implies that the three distances and the angle bear a fixed relationship to one another. Knowing one, and the formula for the curve, we could calculate all the others. The implication is that the tests are all asymptotically equivalent. When the sample is large, consistency means that only a strictly local deviation of the restricted from the unrestricted minimum could leave the outcome of a test in doubt (otherwise the test has unit power, trivially). Only a small neighbourhood of the minimum matters to the outcome, but any twice-differentiable function is arbitrarily well approximated by a quadratic over such a neighbourhood, once it is small enough that the remainder in the Taylor's expansion can be neglected.

The asymptotic theory of testing exploits the idea of quadratic approximation (and hence, linear approximation to the gradient) to approximate the distributions of nonlinear functions and apply the central limit theorem. This gives the approach wide application, but also liable to give misleading answers if the assumptions are unwarranted. In finite samples, the different test principles can contradict each other, yielding different decisions. In general, the further the alternative is taken from the unconditional minimum the larger the different test statistics become, suggesting that test power should be increasing for alternatives further from the null. The notable exception to this rule is LM, for the gradient of C has been drawn to become flatter as we move to the left of point c, suggesting that power of the test could actually be lower for more remote points. In the case of a quadratic criterion this cannot happen of course, since the gradient rises monotonically as we move away.

What the diagram is not able to show is the case of restrictions in a p-dimensional space for $p > 1$. Then, it is not only the distances but the *direction* in p-space that can determine the power of the test. If the criterion function is very flat in certain directions, tests will have little power to distinguish alternative points in those directions. While it might seem that the W and DWH distances in the diagram do not depend on the local gradient, their variances of course do, and in this respect the diagram cannot give the whole picture.

12.2 The Wald Test

Tests of the Wald class (there may be several variants) are based on approximating the distribution under H_0 of $\boldsymbol{g}$ evaluated at $\hat{\boldsymbol{\theta}}_n$, the unrestricted OE estimator of $\boldsymbol{\theta}_0$. The basic mathematical tool for deriving the test is the mean value expansion

$$\boldsymbol{g}(\hat{\boldsymbol{\theta}}_n) = \boldsymbol{g}(\boldsymbol{\theta}_0) + \boldsymbol{G}^*(\hat{\boldsymbol{\theta}}_n - \boldsymbol{\theta}_0) \tag{12.2.1}$$

where $\boldsymbol{G}^*$ is the Jacobian matrix in (12.1.5) with its rows evaluated at different points lying between $\hat{\boldsymbol{\theta}}_n$ and $\boldsymbol{\theta}_0$; compare (9.3.16). Hence, by Theorems 3.1.1 (Slutsky) and 3.3.5 (Cramér)

$$\sqrt{n}\boldsymbol{g}(\hat{\boldsymbol{\theta}}_n) = \sqrt{n}\boldsymbol{G}^*(\hat{\boldsymbol{\theta}}_n - \boldsymbol{\theta}_0) \xrightarrow{\text{D}} \text{N}(\boldsymbol{0}, \boldsymbol{G}_0\boldsymbol{V}_0\boldsymbol{G}_0') \text{ on } H_0 \tag{12.2.2}$$

where $\boldsymbol{V}_0$ is the asymptotic covariance matrix of $\sqrt{n}(\hat{\boldsymbol{\theta}}_n - \boldsymbol{\theta}_0)$, and $\boldsymbol{G}_0 = \boldsymbol{G}(\boldsymbol{\theta}_0)$. Using Theorems C.3.2 and 3.1.3 (continuous mapping theorem) a test of the joint null hypothesis is usually obtained from the result

$$n\boldsymbol{g}(\hat{\boldsymbol{\theta}}_n)'(\boldsymbol{G}_0\boldsymbol{V}_0\boldsymbol{G}_0')^{-1}\boldsymbol{g}(\hat{\boldsymbol{\theta}}_n) \xrightarrow{\text{D}} \chi^2(r) \text{ on } H_0 \tag{12.2.3}$$

where $\chi^2(r)$ denotes the central chi-squared distribution with r degrees of freedom. For an operational test, $\boldsymbol{V}_0$ and $\boldsymbol{G}_0$ in this formula are replaced by consistent estimates obtained from $\boldsymbol{X}$, and in particular, from substituting $\hat{\boldsymbol{\theta}}_n$ for $\boldsymbol{\theta}_0$. According to Theorem 3.3.5, this substitution does not affect the asymptotic distribution. If (9.3.20) holds, the Wald test is based on

$$\mathrm{W} = \frac{\boldsymbol{g}(\hat{\boldsymbol{\theta}}_n)'(\hat{\boldsymbol{G}}_n\hat{\boldsymbol{Q}}_n^{-1}\hat{\boldsymbol{G}}_n')^{-1}\boldsymbol{g}(\hat{\boldsymbol{\theta}}_n)}{\hat{c}^2} \xrightarrow{\mathrm{D}} \chi^2(r) \text{ on } H_0. \tag{12.2.4}$$

The symbol $\hat{c}$ here stands for either c in (9.3.20) if this number is known (the maximum likelihood case) or a consistent estimate of c if it is unknown. To compute the expression in (12.2.4), the various derivatives can be approximated by the finite difference methods exemplified by (9.2.26) or (9.2.27). The test may be performed by comparing W with the critical value obtained from the tabulation of the $\chi^2(r)$ distribution. The statistic should be compared with the formula in (2.4.12), which gives the F test for the case $\boldsymbol{g}(\boldsymbol{\beta}) = \boldsymbol{R}\boldsymbol{\beta} - \boldsymbol{c}$ in the Gaussian linear model. The latter test is asymptotically equivalent to W, noting that $rF(r, n-k)$ converges to $\chi^2(r)$ in distribution. The present result gives an asymptotic justification to the F test in the case when the disturbances are not Gaussian.

In spite of often being onerous to calculate, since estimation under the alternative involves more parameters and sometimes nonlinearity as well, the W test was formerly thought of as one of the best tests for general use in econometrics. It was believed to have generally more power than the LM, for example. However, a major disadvantage with W tests, pointed out by Gregory and Veall (1985), is that they are liable to give a poor approximation to the asymptotic distribution if the constraint function is nonlinear, and not constructed in the best manner.[2] Quite simply, the linear approximation in (12.2.1) may be poor, and very different values of W can be obtained for the *same* restriction on the same model.

To take a rather dramatic example, consider the restriction

$$g(\theta_1, \theta_2) = \theta_2 - a/\theta_1 = 0 \tag{12.2.5}$$

where $a \neq 0$ is a known constant, which has Jacobian matrix

$$\boldsymbol{G} = \begin{bmatrix} a\theta_1^{-2} & 1 \end{bmatrix}. \tag{12.2.6}$$

In a state of the world in which $\theta_1 = 0$ the hypothesis in (12.2.5) is certainly false, yet applying the statistic in (12.2.4), it can easily be verified that $\mathrm{W} = O_p(n\hat{\theta}_1^2) = O_p(1)$. Hence, the test is inconsistent. On the other hand, the apparently equivalent restriction

$$h(\theta_1, \theta_2) = \theta_1\theta_2 - a \tag{12.2.7}$$

has Jacobian matrix

$$\boldsymbol{H} = \begin{bmatrix} \theta_2 & \theta_1 \end{bmatrix}. \tag{12.2.8}$$

[2] Also see Lafontaine and White (1986), Gregory and Veall (1987), and Park and Phillips (1988).

The W test applied to (12.2.7) in the same case behaves normally, and $W = O_p(n)$. This is an extreme case in which the test fails even asymptotically, but it is clear that the Wald test can have low power and also be incorrectly sized in finite samples, if there are regions of the parameter space where the restrictions approach non-differentiability and the asymptotic approximation fails. The moral of the example is to use the W test with care for nonlinear problems, and always to consider the consequences of alternative forms of the restriction.

12.3 Tests Based on Constrained Estimation

12.3.1 Distribution of the Constrained OE

The criterion $C_n(\boldsymbol{\theta})$ is minimized subject to the restriction $\boldsymbol{g}(\boldsymbol{\theta}) = \mathbf{0}$ at a stationary point with respect to $\boldsymbol{\theta}$ and $\boldsymbol{\lambda}$ of the Lagrangian function

$$L(\boldsymbol{\theta}) = C_n(\boldsymbol{\theta}) + \boldsymbol{g}(\boldsymbol{\theta})'\boldsymbol{\lambda}. \tag{12.3.1}$$

The first-order conditions for the problem are

$$\dot{\boldsymbol{q}}_n + \dot{\boldsymbol{G}}_n'\dot{\boldsymbol{\lambda}}_n = \mathbf{0} \tag{12.3.2a}$$

$$\dot{\boldsymbol{g}}_n = \mathbf{0}. \tag{12.3.2b}$$

The solutions of these $p + r$ equations will be denoted $\dot{\boldsymbol{\theta}}_n$ and $\dot{\boldsymbol{\lambda}}_n$, and dots above functions of $\boldsymbol{\theta}$ such as $\boldsymbol{q}$, $\boldsymbol{g}$ and $\boldsymbol{G}$ denote evaluation at these restricted estimates.

Taking a Taylor's expansion of the first-order conditions about $\boldsymbol{\theta}_0$ and solving yields two fundamental results for the cases where the information matrix equality (9.3.19) holds. After scaling by the square root of n, the equations become

$$\sqrt{n}\boldsymbol{q}_{n0} + \boldsymbol{Q}_n^*\sqrt{n}(\dot{\boldsymbol{\theta}}_n - \boldsymbol{\theta}_0) + \sqrt{n}\dot{\boldsymbol{G}}_n'\dot{\boldsymbol{\lambda}}_n = \mathbf{0} \tag{12.3.3a}$$

$$\boldsymbol{G}_n^*\sqrt{n}(\dot{\boldsymbol{\theta}}_n - \boldsymbol{\theta}_0) = \mathbf{0} \tag{12.3.3b}$$

where as before, $\boldsymbol{Q}_n^*$ and $\boldsymbol{G}_n^*$ denote the matrices $\boldsymbol{Q}$ and $\boldsymbol{G}$ with rows evaluated at points between $\dot{\boldsymbol{\theta}}_n$ and $\boldsymbol{\theta}_0$, remembering that $\dot{\boldsymbol{\theta}}_n$ is consistent under H_0. Rearrangement yields

$$\begin{bmatrix} \boldsymbol{Q}_n^* & \dot{\boldsymbol{G}}_n' \\ \boldsymbol{G}_n^* & \mathbf{0} \end{bmatrix} \begin{bmatrix} \sqrt{n}(\dot{\boldsymbol{\theta}}_n - \boldsymbol{\theta}_0) \\ \sqrt{n}\dot{\boldsymbol{\lambda}}_n \end{bmatrix} = \begin{bmatrix} -\sqrt{n}\boldsymbol{q}_{n0} \\ \mathbf{0} \end{bmatrix}. \tag{12.3.4}$$

From (12.3.4) and (9.3.11), which is also the distribution of $-\sqrt{n}\boldsymbol{q}_0$, by the symmetry of the normal distribution, and Theorem 3.3.5 and Lemma 9.3.2, the asymptotic distribution of $\sqrt{n}(\dot{\boldsymbol{\theta}}_n - \boldsymbol{\theta}_0)$ and $\sqrt{n}\dot{\boldsymbol{\lambda}}_n$ can be solved from these equations, after substituting plim $\dot{\boldsymbol{G}}_n$ = plim $\boldsymbol{G}_n^* = \boldsymbol{G}_0$, and plim $\boldsymbol{Q}_n^* = \bar{\boldsymbol{Q}}_0$. The partitioned inverse formula gives

$$\begin{bmatrix} \bar{\boldsymbol{Q}}_0 & \boldsymbol{G}_0' \\ \boldsymbol{G}_0 & \mathbf{0} \end{bmatrix}^{-1} = \begin{bmatrix} \boldsymbol{E}_0 & \bar{\boldsymbol{Q}}^{-1}\boldsymbol{G}_0'(\boldsymbol{G}_0\bar{\boldsymbol{Q}}_0^{-1}\boldsymbol{G}_0')^{-1} \\ (\boldsymbol{G}_0\bar{\boldsymbol{Q}}_0^{-1}\boldsymbol{G}_0')^{-1}\boldsymbol{G}_0\bar{\boldsymbol{Q}}_0^{-1} & -(\boldsymbol{G}_0\bar{\boldsymbol{Q}}_0^{-1}\boldsymbol{G}_0')^{-1} \end{bmatrix} \tag{12.3.5}$$

where $\boldsymbol{E}_0 = \bar{\boldsymbol{Q}}_0^{-1} - \boldsymbol{K}_0$ and $\boldsymbol{K}_0 = \bar{\boldsymbol{Q}}_0^{-1}\boldsymbol{G}_0'(\boldsymbol{G}_0\bar{\boldsymbol{Q}}_0^{-1}\boldsymbol{G}_0')^{-1}\boldsymbol{G}_0\bar{\boldsymbol{Q}}_0^{-1}$. $\boldsymbol{E}_0$ is symmetric and has rank $p - r$, as can be seen from the fact that $\boldsymbol{E}_0\boldsymbol{G}_0' = \boldsymbol{0}$, the matrix $\boldsymbol{G}_0'$ having r linearly independent columns. Accordingly, from (12.3.4) and Theorem 3.3.5,

$$\sqrt{n}(\dot{\boldsymbol{\theta}}_n - \boldsymbol{\theta}_0) \underset{\text{asy}}{\sim} -\sqrt{n}\boldsymbol{E}_0\boldsymbol{q}_{n0} \xrightarrow{\text{D}} \text{N}(\boldsymbol{0}, \boldsymbol{E}_0\boldsymbol{A}_0\boldsymbol{E}_0) \tag{12.3.6}$$

where the covariance matrix has rank $p - r$, and the notation (given that $\boldsymbol{E}_0$ is singular) means that any $p - r$ independent linear combinations of the vector $\sqrt{n}(\dot{\boldsymbol{\theta}} - \boldsymbol{\theta}_0)$ have a multivariate Gaussian distribution asymptotically. If the information matrix equality (9.3.19) holds, the covariance matrix in (12.3.6) takes the form

$$c^2\boldsymbol{E}_0\bar{\boldsymbol{Q}}_0\boldsymbol{E}_0 = c^2\boldsymbol{E}_0 \tag{12.3.7}$$

using the fact that $\boldsymbol{K}_0\bar{\boldsymbol{Q}}_0\boldsymbol{K}_0 = \boldsymbol{K}_0$.

If both the constrained and the unconstrained estimates are computed, comparing the two provides one test of the constraints. By (9.3.14) and (9.3.11) respectively, when H_0 is true,

$$\begin{aligned}\sqrt{n}(\hat{\boldsymbol{\theta}}_n - \dot{\boldsymbol{\theta}}_n) &\underset{asy}{\sim} \sqrt{n}(\bar{\boldsymbol{Q}}_0^{-1} - \boldsymbol{E}_0)\boldsymbol{q}_{n0} \\ &= \sqrt{n}\boldsymbol{K}_0\boldsymbol{q}_{n0} \xrightarrow{\text{D}} \text{N}(\boldsymbol{0}, \boldsymbol{K}_0\boldsymbol{A}_0\boldsymbol{K}_0).\end{aligned} \tag{12.3.8}$$

Again, suppose that (9.3.19) holds. Then

$$\boldsymbol{K}_0\boldsymbol{A}_0\boldsymbol{K}_0 = c^2\boldsymbol{K}_0 = c^2\bar{\boldsymbol{Q}}_0^{-1} - c^2\boldsymbol{E}_0. \tag{12.3.9}$$

In other words, the asymptotic covariance matrix of the difference between the unrestricted and restricted estimates is equal to the difference of the respective asymptotic covariance matrices. This distribution is also singular in general, with rank r, but it could in principle be used to generate tests based on suitable functions of $\hat{\boldsymbol{\theta}}_n - \dot{\boldsymbol{\theta}}_n$, including particular elements of the vector. The Hausman test derived in Lemma 8.1.1 is just such a case,[3] and see also §8.4.1. As well as the references given in §8.4.1, see also Holly (1982), Holly and Monfort (1986) and for another application, White (1981).

12.3.2 The Likelihood Ratio Test

While an asymptotic χ^2 test of the restrictions might be based on the distribution specified in (12.3.8), using the generalized inverse of the covariance matrix (see (A.8.7)), this is rarely done in practice. A more popular technique is to compare the criterion functions themselves. A Taylor's expansion of C_n to second order around the unconstrained estimator $\hat{\boldsymbol{\theta}}_n$ gives

$$C_n(\dot{\boldsymbol{\theta}}_n) = C_n(\hat{\boldsymbol{\theta}}_n) + \hat{\boldsymbol{q}}_n'(\dot{\boldsymbol{\theta}}_n - \hat{\boldsymbol{\theta}}_n) + \tfrac{1}{2}(\dot{\boldsymbol{\theta}}_n - \hat{\boldsymbol{\theta}}_n)'\boldsymbol{Q}_n(\boldsymbol{\theta}_n^*)(\dot{\boldsymbol{\theta}}_n - \hat{\boldsymbol{\theta}}_n) \tag{12.3.10}$$

[3]In the proof of Lemma 8.1.1 it was assumed that one of the estimators was efficient. In this generalized version of the result (9.3.19) has to hold, which is the property of the efficient estimator in the CAN class (the MLE), although $\dot{\boldsymbol{\theta}}$ is not required to be the MLE. The result also allows comparisons between GMM estimators, for example.

where $\boldsymbol{\theta}^*$ is a point on the line segment joining $\dot{\boldsymbol{\theta}}_n$ and $\hat{\boldsymbol{\theta}}_n$. Since $\hat{\boldsymbol{q}}_n = \mathbf{0}$ by definition of $\hat{\boldsymbol{\theta}}_n$, and plim $\boldsymbol{Q}_n(\boldsymbol{\theta}_n^*) = \bar{\boldsymbol{Q}}_0$ under H_0,

$$\begin{aligned} 2n[C(\dot{\boldsymbol{\theta}}) - C(\hat{\boldsymbol{\theta}})] &\underset{\text{asy}}{\sim} n(\dot{\boldsymbol{\theta}} - \hat{\boldsymbol{\theta}})'\bar{\boldsymbol{Q}}_0(\dot{\boldsymbol{\theta}} - \hat{\boldsymbol{\theta}}) \\ &\underset{\text{asy}}{\sim} n\boldsymbol{q}_{n0}'\boldsymbol{K}_0'\bar{\boldsymbol{Q}}_0\boldsymbol{K}_0\boldsymbol{q}_{n0} \\ &= n\boldsymbol{q}_{n0}'\bar{\boldsymbol{Q}}_0^{-1}\boldsymbol{G}_0'(\boldsymbol{G}_0\bar{\boldsymbol{Q}}_0^{-1}\boldsymbol{G}_0')^{-1}\boldsymbol{G}_0\bar{\boldsymbol{Q}}_0^{-1}\boldsymbol{q}_{n0} \end{aligned} \tag{12.3.11}$$

where the notation implies that if one side of the equivalence has a well-defined asymptotic distribution, it is shared by the other side. If H_0 is false, both sides are expected to be $O_p(n)$ as $n \to \infty$.

The formula in (12.3.11) may not look very promising, but if the information matrix equality $\boldsymbol{A}_0 = c^2\bar{\boldsymbol{Q}}_0$ holds it yields a useful result. Let $\boldsymbol{A}_0^{1/2}$ denote the square root matrix such that $\boldsymbol{A}_0^{-1/2}\boldsymbol{A}_0(\boldsymbol{A}_0^{-1/2})' = \boldsymbol{I}$ by Lemma A.7.4, and so

$$\sqrt{n}\boldsymbol{A}_0^{-1/2}\boldsymbol{q}_0 \xrightarrow{\text{D}} \boldsymbol{Z} \sim \text{N}(\mathbf{0}, \boldsymbol{I}). \tag{12.3.12}$$

Then,

$$\begin{aligned} &n\boldsymbol{q}_{n0}'\bar{\boldsymbol{Q}}_0^{-1}\boldsymbol{G}_0'(\boldsymbol{G}_0\bar{\boldsymbol{Q}}_0^{-1}\boldsymbol{G}_0')^{-1}\boldsymbol{G}_0\bar{\boldsymbol{Q}}_0^{-1}\boldsymbol{q}_{n0} \\ &\qquad \underset{\text{asy}}{\sim} c^2\boldsymbol{Z}'\boldsymbol{A}_0^{-1/2}\boldsymbol{G}_0'(\boldsymbol{G}_0'\boldsymbol{A}_0^{-1}\boldsymbol{G}_0')^{-1}\boldsymbol{G}_0(\boldsymbol{A}_0^{-1/2})'\boldsymbol{Z} \\ &\qquad = c^2\boldsymbol{Z}'\boldsymbol{B}\boldsymbol{Z} \end{aligned} \tag{12.3.13}$$

where the second line of (12.3.13) substitutes the information matrix equality and the last line defines the matrix $\boldsymbol{B}$. It is easily verified that $\boldsymbol{B}$ is symmetric and idempotent of rank r, and it follows by Theorem C.3.3 that $\boldsymbol{Z}'\boldsymbol{B}\boldsymbol{Z} \sim \chi^2(r)$. Using (12.3.11), this leads directly to the test statistic

$$\text{ALR} = 2n\frac{C(\dot{\boldsymbol{\theta}}) - C(\hat{\boldsymbol{\theta}})}{\hat{c}^2} \xrightarrow{\text{D}} \chi^2(r) \text{ on } H_0 \tag{12.3.14}$$

where $\hat{c}$ denotes a consistent estimate of c, as before. In the context of maximum likelihood estimation where $C = -L/n$ and $c^2 = 1$, the test based on (12.3.14) takes the form

$$\text{LR} = 2[L(\hat{\boldsymbol{\theta}}) - L(\dot{\boldsymbol{\theta}})] = 2\ln\frac{\mathcal{L}(\hat{\boldsymbol{\theta}})}{\mathcal{L}(\dot{\boldsymbol{\theta}})}. \tag{12.3.15}$$

This is the likelihood ratio test, hence the designation LR. In the general context of optimization estimators, we refer to it here as the analogue likelihood ratio or ALR test.

It's important to be aware, however, that the ALR principle depends specifically on the validity of the information matrix equality. Without it the asymptotic equivalence in (12.3.13) does not hold. It is therefore valid for least squares and GMM estimators, with or without Gaussianity, provided both the fundamental assumptions (10.2.10) hold under H_0. It is not valid without (10.2.10b), however. Nor is it available for models such as those in §10.4.2 except with Gaussian shocks. These facts do not always seem to be widely appreciated, and should not be overlooked because, whereas the evaluation of an estimator covariance matrix at least gives the opportunity to question whether the formula being used is correct, simply comparing criterion functions gives the (deceptive) impression of being a straightforward and robust procedure.

In the case of the linear regression model of §2.1 or §7.1, in which $C(\hat{\theta}) = \hat{u}'\hat{u}/n$ is consistent for $\frac{1}{2}c^2$, the test has the familiar form

$$\text{ALR} = n\frac{\dot{u}'\dot{u} - \hat{u}'\hat{u}}{\hat{u}'\hat{u}} \tag{12.3.16}$$

and is just the asymptotic form of the F test from (2.4.20) or (7.5.2). It is also equivalent to the W test, given (2.4.12) and the equivalence in (2.4.19). An asymptotically equivalent test is obtained by estimating $\frac{1}{2}c^2$ by $C(\dot{\theta}) = \dot{u}'\dot{u}/n$. Also, taking the Gaussian regression model from §11.2.1 and substituting (11.2.5) into (11.2.4) shows that the true LR statistic (12.3.15) for this case takes the form

$$\text{LR} = n\ln\left(\frac{\dot{u}'\dot{u}}{\hat{u}'\hat{u}}\right). \tag{12.3.17}$$

However, the inequalities implied by the series expansions of $\ln(1+x)$ for $0 \le x < 1$ and $-1 < x \le 0$ respectively imply

$$n\frac{\dot{u}'\dot{u} - \hat{u}'\hat{u}}{\dot{u}'\dot{u}} \le n\ln\left(\frac{\dot{u}'\dot{u}}{\hat{u}'\hat{u}}\right) \le n\frac{\dot{u}'\dot{u} - \hat{u}'\hat{u}}{\hat{u}'\hat{u}} \tag{12.3.18}$$

the equalities being strict unless the two sums of squares are equal. All these forms of the ALR/LR test are asymptotically equivalent, in the sense of having the same limiting distribution under H_0. It is true that being the largest, the 'W' form will always reject the most frequently, but this is the case whether the null hypothesis is true or false, so this fact it has no implications for the respective powers of the tests. It does however allow us to decide in which direction we prefer to err, when using an asymptotic approximation to a finite sample distribution.

12.3.3 The Lagrange Multiplier Test

Equation (12.3.4) also yields the limiting distribution of the Lagrange multipliers under H_0,

$$\begin{aligned} \sqrt{n}\dot{\lambda} &\underset{\text{asy}}{\sim} \sqrt{n}(G_0\bar{Q}_0^{-1}G_0')^{-1}G_0\bar{Q}_0^{-1}q_0 \\ &\xrightarrow{\text{D}} \text{N}(0,\ (G_0\bar{Q}_0^{-1}G_0')^{-1}G_0\bar{Q}_0^{-1}A_0\bar{Q}_0^{-1}G_0'(G_0\bar{Q}_0^{-1}G_0')^{-1}). \end{aligned} \tag{12.3.19}$$

Assuming the information matrix equality (9.3.19), this simplifies to

$$\sqrt{n}\dot{\lambda} \xrightarrow{\text{D}} \text{N}(0, c^2(G_0\bar{Q}_0^{-1}G_0')^{-1}) \tag{12.3.20}$$

leading to the result

$$n\frac{\dot{\lambda}'G_0\bar{Q}_0^{-1}G_0'\dot{\lambda}}{c^2} \xrightarrow{\text{D}} \chi^2(r) \text{ on } H_0. \tag{12.3.21}$$

To obtain an operational form of this test, one can use the facts that $\dot{\boldsymbol{q}}_n = -\dot{\boldsymbol{G}}_n'\dot{\boldsymbol{\lambda}}_n$ from (12.3.2), that plim $\dot{\boldsymbol{G}}_n = \boldsymbol{G}_0$, and that plim $\dot{\boldsymbol{Q}}_n = \bar{\boldsymbol{Q}}_0$. Applying Theorem 3.3.5 yields the third operational test principle, based on

$$\mathrm{LM} = n\frac{\dot{\boldsymbol{q}}_n'\dot{\boldsymbol{Q}}_n^{-1}\dot{\boldsymbol{q}}_n}{\dot{c}^2} \xrightarrow{\mathrm{D}} \chi^2(r) \text{ on } H_0. \tag{12.3.22}$$

Tests based on (12.3.22) are known as Lagrange multiplier tests and also as score tests, where the score is the gradient of the log-likelihood, corresponding here to the vector $\boldsymbol{q}_n$. If c^2 is different from 1 in these formulae it will have to be replaced by a consistent estimate, and this is indicated by $\dot{c}^2$ in (12.3.22) because it is customary to think of the Lagrange multiplier statistic as being computed exclusively using $\dot{\boldsymbol{\theta}}$, so that estimation under the alternative hypothesis is avoided. However, replacing $\dot{c}^2$ by $\hat{c}^2$ (estimation under the alternative) leads to the same asymptotic distribution under H_0.

Similar caveats to those noted in §12.3.2 apply in this case with regard to failure of the information matrix inequality. There is however a remedy in this case, which is to go back to (12.3.19) and work directly with the statistic

$$\begin{aligned}\mathrm{LM} &= n\dot{\boldsymbol{\lambda}}'\dot{\boldsymbol{G}}_n\dot{\boldsymbol{Q}}_n^{-1}\dot{\boldsymbol{G}}_n'(\dot{\boldsymbol{G}}_n\dot{\boldsymbol{Q}}_n^{-1}\dot{\boldsymbol{A}}_n\dot{\boldsymbol{Q}}_n^{-1}\dot{\boldsymbol{G}}_n')^{-1}\dot{\boldsymbol{G}}_n\dot{\boldsymbol{Q}}_n^{-1}\dot{\boldsymbol{G}}_n'\dot{\boldsymbol{\lambda}}_n \\ &= \dot{\boldsymbol{q}}_n'\dot{\boldsymbol{Q}}_n^{-1}\dot{\boldsymbol{G}}_n'(\dot{\boldsymbol{G}}_n\dot{\boldsymbol{Q}}_n^{-1}\dot{\boldsymbol{A}}_n\dot{\boldsymbol{Q}}_n^{-1}\dot{\boldsymbol{G}}_n')^{-1}\dot{\boldsymbol{G}}_n\dot{\boldsymbol{Q}}_n^{-1}\dot{\boldsymbol{q}}_n.\end{aligned} \tag{12.3.23}$$

Either of formulae (12.3.22) and (12.3.23) may be referred to Lagrange multiplier statistics, and the latter should always be used when the validity of the information matrix equality is in doubt.

To illustrate the use of the LM principle, consider the nonlinear least squares model of §10.2. This is a useful case because even models that are linear under the null hypothesis are often nonlinear under the postulated alternative. There is no need to actually estimate the nonlinear model to construct the LM statistic, merely to extract some formulae from it. If the criterion is the sum of squares function, then direct from (10.2.19) and (12.3.22),

$$\mathrm{LM} = \frac{\dot{\boldsymbol{u}}'\dot{\boldsymbol{D}}(\dot{\boldsymbol{D}}'\dot{\boldsymbol{D}})^{-1}\dot{\boldsymbol{D}}'\dot{\boldsymbol{u}}}{\dot{\sigma}^2} = n\frac{\dot{\boldsymbol{u}}'\dot{\boldsymbol{D}}(\dot{\boldsymbol{D}}'\dot{\boldsymbol{D}})^{-1}\dot{\boldsymbol{D}}'\dot{\boldsymbol{u}}}{\dot{\boldsymbol{u}}'\dot{\boldsymbol{u}}} \tag{12.3.24}$$

where the dots denote evaluation of the equation and its derivatives subject to the restriction. Thus, the LM statistic can be constructed as nR^2 from the regression of the residuals on the model derivatives, all computed at the constrained estimates. Another way to think about this regression is as the first Gauss Newton step in the computation of the unrestricted model, taking the restricted model as the starting point, as in (10.2.8).

The formula in (2.4.15) shows that the F test in the linear model can also be constructed like (12.3.21) and so is like an LM test. Strictly speaking it is not an LM test, however, because c^2 is estimated under the alternative, being equal in this case to $s^2 = \hat{\boldsymbol{u}}'\hat{\boldsymbol{u}}/(n-k)$. The substitution s^2 for $\dot{\sigma}^2$ turns nR^2 into $(n-k)R^2/(1-R^2)$, and it is clear that this substitution always yields an asymptotically equivalent test,[4] the two statistics having the same asymptotic distribution under H_0, since $R^2 \xrightarrow{\text{pr}} 0$ in that case.

Further, comparison with (12.3.18) shows that the LM in this case is the same as the smallest variant of the ALR test. The relations between the tests for the Gaussian linear model are expressed by the well-known inequalities

$$\text{LM} < \text{LR} < \text{W} \tag{12.3.25}$$

(see Berndt and Savin 1977, Evans and Savin 1982). However, note that these relations do not necessarily generalize to arbitrary models and estimation criteria.

12.3.4 Testing for Autocorrelation

In §7.6.1, variable addition tests for autocorrelation were described that we can now rationalize as LM tests, and in so doing learn a bit more about their properties; see Breusch (1978) and Godfrey (1978a,b). Suppose the model under the alternative has AR(p) disturbances. Then

$$y_t = f_t + u_t \tag{12.3.26}$$

where

$$f_t = \boldsymbol{\beta}'\boldsymbol{x}_t + \sum_{j=1}^{p} \rho_j (y_{t-j} - \boldsymbol{\beta}'\boldsymbol{x}_{t-j}). \tag{12.3.27}$$

Generalizing the formulae in §10.2.3 from the first-order case to the p-order case, the derivatives are

$$\frac{\partial f_t}{\partial \boldsymbol{\beta}} = \boldsymbol{x}_t - \rho_1 \boldsymbol{x}_{t-1} - \cdots - \rho_p \boldsymbol{x}_{t-p} \tag{12.3.28}$$

$$\frac{\partial f_t}{\partial \rho_j} = y_{t-j} - \boldsymbol{\beta}'\boldsymbol{x}_{t-j} = u_{t-j} \quad j = 1, \ldots, p \tag{12.3.29}$$

These terms are computed at the constrained estimates and therefore, as indicated in §7.6.1, the additional variables to be tested in the regression are the lagged OLS residuals up to order p. Now consider the MA(p) alternative. The model in this case has the form of (12.3.26) where

$$f_t = \boldsymbol{\beta}'\boldsymbol{x}_t + \sum_{j=1}^{p} \theta_j (y_{t-j} - f_{t-j}). \tag{12.3.30}$$

The derivatives are

$$\frac{\partial f_t}{\partial \boldsymbol{\beta}} = \boldsymbol{x}_t - \sum_{j=1}^{p} \theta_j \frac{\partial f_{t-j}}{\partial \boldsymbol{\beta}} \tag{12.3.31}$$

[4] The choice between multipliers n and $n-k$ is of course asymptotically irrelevant under both null and alternative.

$$\frac{\partial f_t}{\partial \theta_j} = y_{t-j} - f_{t-j} - \sum_{i=1}^{p} \theta_i \frac{\partial f_{t-i}}{\partial \theta_j} \quad j = 1, \ldots, p. \tag{12.3.32}$$

Under the null hypothesis with $\theta_j = 0$ for each j, note that $f_{t-j} = \boldsymbol{\beta}'\boldsymbol{x}_{t-j}$, so that the LM test against the MA(p) alternative is actually identical to the test against AR(p).

This finding raises the interesting question of a test against an ARMA(p, q) alternative. As the reader can easily verify by combining these formulae, the derivatives with respect to the AR and MA parameters, constrained under the null hypothesis, are the same. They are the lagged OLS residuals in both cases. As noted in §5.2.2, the ARMA model is underidentified at the point of zero roots since these are equal, and cancel from each side of the equation. In practice, this problem is overcome by simply discarding the redundant derivatives. The LM test against the ARMA(p, q) alternative is the usual variable addition test with $\max\{p, q\}$ lagged residuals added to the equation.

This test has another interesting feature, which can be exhibited by writing out the numerator of the statistic in partitioned form. Since $\dot{\boldsymbol{D}} = [\boldsymbol{X}\ \dot{\boldsymbol{U}}_-]$ where $\dot{\boldsymbol{U}}_-$ denotes the matrix of lagged OLS residuals, and $\boldsymbol{X}'\dot{\boldsymbol{u}} = \boldsymbol{0}$ by construction since $\dot{\boldsymbol{u}}$ is the current OLS residual, applying the partitioned inverse formula yields

$$\dot{\boldsymbol{u}}'\dot{\boldsymbol{D}}(\dot{\boldsymbol{D}}'\dot{\boldsymbol{D}})^{-1}\dot{\boldsymbol{D}}'\dot{\boldsymbol{u}} = \frac{1}{n}\dot{\boldsymbol{u}}'\dot{\boldsymbol{U}}_-\left(\frac{\dot{\boldsymbol{U}}_-'\dot{\boldsymbol{U}}_-}{n} - \frac{\dot{\boldsymbol{U}}_-'\boldsymbol{X}}{n}\left(\frac{\boldsymbol{X}'\boldsymbol{X}}{n}\right)^{-1}\frac{\boldsymbol{X}'\dot{\boldsymbol{U}}_-}{n}\right)^{-1}\dot{\boldsymbol{U}}_-'\dot{\boldsymbol{u}}. \tag{12.3.33}$$

Now, suppose that the columns of $\boldsymbol{X}$ consist of variables that are asymptotically uncorrelated with the columns of $\dot{\boldsymbol{U}}_-$ under the null hypothesis. This would be the case provided the regressors are strongly exogenous, and do not include the lagged dependent variable. Then $n^{-1}\dot{\boldsymbol{U}}_-'\boldsymbol{X} \xrightarrow{\text{pr}} \boldsymbol{0}$, and it follows that

$$\text{LM} \underset{\text{asy}}{\sim} n\frac{\dot{\boldsymbol{u}}'\dot{\boldsymbol{U}}_-(\dot{\boldsymbol{U}}_-'\dot{\boldsymbol{U}}_-)^{-1}\dot{\boldsymbol{U}}_-'\dot{\boldsymbol{u}}}{\dot{\boldsymbol{u}}'\dot{\boldsymbol{u}}}. \tag{12.3.34}$$

However, observe that under the null hypothesis

$$\frac{\dot{\boldsymbol{U}}_-'\dot{\boldsymbol{U}}_-}{n} \xrightarrow{\text{pr}} \sigma^2\boldsymbol{I}_p \tag{12.3.35}$$

where $n^{-1}\dot{\boldsymbol{u}}'\dot{\boldsymbol{u}} \xrightarrow{\text{pr}} \sigma^2$ also. Therefore,

$$\text{LM} \underset{\text{asy}}{\sim} n\sum_{j=1}^{p} r_j^2 \tag{12.3.36}$$

where

$$r_j^2 = \frac{(\dot{\boldsymbol{u}}'\dot{\boldsymbol{u}}_{-j})^2}{(\dot{\boldsymbol{u}}'\dot{\boldsymbol{u}})(\dot{\boldsymbol{u}}_{-j}'\dot{\boldsymbol{u}}_{-j})} \tag{12.3.37}$$

is the squared jth-order autocorrelation coefficient. With strongly exogenous regressors, the LM test is asymptotically equivalent to the Box–Pierce Q test (see §7.6.3). In the case $p = 1$, it is accordingly equivalent to the Durbin Watson test.

Finally, suppose that $p = 1$, that

$$\boldsymbol{X} = \left[\boldsymbol{y}_{-1}\ \boldsymbol{X}_2\right] \tag{12.3.38}$$

where $\boldsymbol{y}_{-1}$ is the lagged dependent variable, and that $\boldsymbol{X}_2$ contains only strongly exogenous variables, so that $n^{-1}\boldsymbol{X}_2'\dot{\boldsymbol{u}}_{-1} \xrightarrow{\text{pr}} \boldsymbol{0}$. Noting that $n^{-1}\boldsymbol{y}_{-1}'\dot{\boldsymbol{u}}_{-1} \xrightarrow{\text{pr}} \sigma^2$, and considering the special case of (12.3.33) it is easily shown that

$$\text{LM} \underset{\text{asy}}{\sim} \frac{nr_1^2}{1 - s^2(\boldsymbol{y}_{-1}'(\boldsymbol{I}_n - \boldsymbol{X}_2(\boldsymbol{X}_2'\boldsymbol{X}_2)^{-1}\boldsymbol{X}_2')\boldsymbol{y}_{-1})^{-1}} = h^2 \tag{12.3.39}$$

where h is the Durbin (1970) test statistic. See also §7.8 for discussion of the case where strong exogeneity is violated.

12.3.5 Testing for Heteroscedasticity

We review one other example of the LM procedure in detail, as exemplifying the special features of the method as well as linking interestingly to other approaches. This is the linear regression model with heteroscedastic disturbances analysed in §10.4.2. The model has a number of interesting features, especially related to the fact that the information matrix equality does not hold except with Gaussian restrictions on third and fourth moments. This is an opportunity to see what difference the equality can make in practice. The model is given by (10.4.21) and under the null hypothesis to be tested, $\boldsymbol{\alpha}_1 = \boldsymbol{0}$ and

$$h(\boldsymbol{\alpha}'\boldsymbol{w}_t) = h(\alpha_0) = \sigma^2. \tag{12.3.40}$$

From (10.4.23) and (10.4.24), the gradient vector evaluated under H_0 has components

$$\dot{\boldsymbol{q}}_{bn} = -\frac{1}{n\dot{\sigma}^2}\sum_{t=1}^{n}\boldsymbol{x}_t\dot{u}_t = \boldsymbol{0} \tag{12.3.41}$$

$$\dot{\boldsymbol{q}}_{an} = -\frac{1}{2n}\sum_{t=1}^{n}\dot{\kappa}\left(\frac{\dot{u}_t^2}{\dot{\sigma}^2} - 1\right)\boldsymbol{w}_t \tag{12.3.42}$$

where $\kappa = h'/h$. Note that $\boldsymbol{G}$ $(p\times(k+p+1))$ is just the selection matrix that picks $\alpha_1, \ldots, \alpha_p$ from $\boldsymbol{\theta} = (\boldsymbol{\beta}', \alpha')'$. As in §10.4.2, partition $\boldsymbol{w}_t$ as $(1,\ \boldsymbol{z}_t')'$. Calculations using the partitioned inverse formula then show that

$$(\boldsymbol{G}_0\bar{\boldsymbol{Q}}_0^{-1}\boldsymbol{G}_0')^{-1} = \tfrac{1}{2}\kappa^2(\boldsymbol{M}_{ZZ} - \bar{\boldsymbol{\mu}}_Z\bar{\boldsymbol{\mu}}_Z') \tag{12.3.43}$$

and

$$\boldsymbol{G}_0\bar{\boldsymbol{Q}}_0^{-1}\boldsymbol{A}_0\bar{\boldsymbol{Q}}_0^{-1}\boldsymbol{G}_0' = \kappa^{-2}\left(\frac{\mu_4}{\sigma^4} - 1\right)(\boldsymbol{M}_{ZZ} - \bar{\boldsymbol{\mu}}_Z\bar{\boldsymbol{\mu}}_Z')^{-1} \tag{12.3.44}$$

where $\bar{\boldsymbol{\mu}}_Z = \operatorname{plim}\bar{\boldsymbol{z}}$ where $\bar{\boldsymbol{z}} = n^{-1}\sum_{t=1}^{n}\boldsymbol{z}_t$, and $\boldsymbol{M}_{ZZ}$ is the usual asymptotic moment matrix. Therefore, the asymptotic chi-squared statistic derived from (12.3.23) takes the form

$$\text{LM} = \frac{\displaystyle\sum_{t=1}^{n}\left(\frac{\dot{u}_t^2}{\dot{\sigma}^2} - 1\right)\boldsymbol{z}_t'\left(\sum_{t=1}^{n}\boldsymbol{z}_t\boldsymbol{z}_t' - n\bar{\boldsymbol{z}}\bar{\boldsymbol{z}}'\right)^{-1}\sum_{t=1}^{n}\left(\frac{\dot{u}_t^2}{\dot{\sigma}^2} - 1\right)\boldsymbol{z}_t}{\dfrac{\dot{\mu}_4}{\dot{\sigma}^4} - 1} \tag{12.3.45}$$

where

$$\dot{\mu}_4 = \frac{1}{n}\sum_{t=1}^{n} \dot{u}_t^4 \tag{12.3.46}$$

and $\dot{\sigma}^4$ is the square of the usual variance estimator (see Koenker 1981).

This formula has a number of interesting features. First note that the constant κ cancels in the ratio, so the test does not depend on the functional form of $h(\cdot)$. Second, observe that

$$\sum_{t=1}^{n}\left(\frac{\dot{u}_t^2}{\dot{\sigma}^2} - 1\right)z_t = \sum_{t=1}^{n}(z_t - \bar{z})\frac{\dot{u}_t^2}{\dot{\sigma}^2} \tag{12.3.47}$$

in view of the fact that the terms $\dot{u}_t^2/\dot{\sigma}^2 - 1$ sum to zero identically. Therefore it can be rewritten in the form

$$\mathrm{LM} = n\frac{\sum_{t=1}^{n}(z_t - \bar{z})\dot{u}_t^2\left(\sum_{t=1}^{n} z_t z_t' - n\bar{z}\bar{z}'\right)^{-1}\sum_{t=1}^{n}(z_t - \bar{z})\dot{u}_t^2}{\sum_{t=1}^{n}\dot{u}_t^4 - n\dot{\sigma}^4} \tag{12.3.48}$$

which is none other than the nR^2 from the regression of $\dot{u}_t^2$ on z_t, including an intercept. The test is therefore very easily computed. For an alternative derivation of the test, see §12.5.2.

If the disturbances are Gaussian, the denominator of (12.3.45) is simply an estimator of 2. Actually replacing it by 2 gives the statistic proposed by Breusch and Pagan (1979) and Godfrey (1978c), who follow the derivation of this section while assuming Gaussian disturbances. Observe that, with this restriction, $\bar{\boldsymbol{Q}}_0 = \boldsymbol{A}_0$ in the formulae. Given that the information matrix equality holds, these authors' derivations are simplified by being based on (12.3.22). However, if the disturbances are really leptokurtic, having $\mu_4 > 3\sigma^4$, the denominator is too small and the test is incorrectly sized, rejecting more frequently under H_0 than the nominal significance level indicates even asymptotically.

12.4 Power Calculations

12.4.1 Pitman Drift

If H_0 is false, we would like to know the probability that it will be rejected. Since we are working with asymptotic distribution criteria the answer to this question is '1' for any fixed element of $\Theta - \omega$, assuming the test to be consistent, which is rather unsatisfactory. We do not want to know the situation in an infinite sample, but to find an approximation for the case of a finite but reasonably large sample. Since a larger sample will always provide a more discriminating test, other things being equal, it is natural to tailor the question to be posed about test power to the relevant sample size. This idea leads naturally to the device known as *Pitman drift*, (Pitman 1949) by which elements of H_A specific to n are considered.

For the sake of argument, suppose that $\boldsymbol{g}(\boldsymbol{\theta}_0) = \boldsymbol{0}$ but that the data in a sample of size n are generated by the model element

$$\boldsymbol{\theta}_{0n} = \boldsymbol{\theta}_0 + \frac{\boldsymbol{\delta}}{\sqrt{n}} \tag{12.4.1}$$

with $\boldsymbol{\delta}$ a fixed p-vector. The power of a consistent test against the sequence of alternatives in which $\boldsymbol{\theta} = \boldsymbol{\theta}_{0n}$ is a value independent of n, providing a basis for comparing alternative asymptotic tests.

Using the Pitman drift technique requires certain modifications to the convergence theorems of 6.2 and §6.4. To appreciate the problem, consider the argument in §9.3.4 where it was assumed a CLT held for $\sqrt{n}\boldsymbol{q}_n(\boldsymbol{\theta}_0)$. Since $\boldsymbol{\theta}_0$ is a fixed vector there was no need to indicate how the matrix $\boldsymbol{J}_n$ and vectors $\boldsymbol{v}_t$ depended on it. However, writing (9.3.12) as

$$\sqrt{n}\boldsymbol{q}_n(\boldsymbol{\theta}_{0n}) = \boldsymbol{J}_n \frac{1}{\sqrt{n}} \sum_{t=1}^{n} \boldsymbol{v}_{nt} \tag{12.4.2}$$

where $\boldsymbol{v}_{nt} = \boldsymbol{v}_t(\boldsymbol{\theta}_{0n})$, note that the latter random variable is an element of a triangular array. Some theory was developed for arrays in §10.5, including a law of large numbers and CLT for near-epoch dependent arrays. An array can also be a martingale difference, according to the following definition.

Definition 12.4.1 The adapted triangular array $\{(x_{nt}, \mathcal{F}_{nt})\ t = 1, \dots, n,\ n \geq 1\}$ is called a martingale difference if

(a) $E|x_{nt}| < \infty$, all t and n

(b) $E(x_{nt}|\mathcal{F}_{n,t-1}) = 0$ a.s., all t and all $n > 1$. □

The n subscript from $\mathcal{F}_{nt}$ might be omitted here, since in our applications the σ-fields do not in fact depend on n, but it is conventional to allow this.

A stationary array (strict or wide sense) is one for which the distributions are stationary with respect to t for each fixed $n > 1$. Given these definitions, it is possible to state a CLT for m.d. arrays, as follows. The proof is as for Theorem 6.2.3, which is just the special case where $x_{nt} = x_t$ for all n. Theorem 24.3 of Davidson (1994a) is actually given for the array case.

Theorem 12.4.1 Let $\{x_{nt}, \mathcal{F}_{nt}\}$ be a m.d. array with $E(x_{nt}^2) = \sigma_{nt}^2$, and let $s_n^2 = \sum_{t=1}^n \sigma_{nt}^2$. If

(a) $s_n^{-1} \sum_{t=1}^n (x_{nt}^2 - \sigma_{nt}^2) \xrightarrow{\text{pr}} 0$, and

(b) either

  (i) the array is strictly stationary or

  (ii) $\sqrt{n} \dfrac{\max_{1 \leq t \leq n} \|x_{nt}\|_{2+\delta}}{s_n} \leq B < \infty \quad \delta > 0, \forall\, n \geq 1$

then $\sum_{t=1}^{n} x_{nt}/s_n \xrightarrow{D} N(0,1)$. □

This result may be useful in proving results about Pitman drift, and is certainly appropriate under independence in sampling model B of §1.3, for example, but there is an important caveat. If the sequence $\{\boldsymbol{v}_t(\boldsymbol{\theta}_0),\ t = 1,\dots,n\}$ is a martingale difference, then this will not necessarily be true of the array $\{\boldsymbol{v}_t(\boldsymbol{\theta}_{0n}),\ t = 1,\dots,n\}$. Think of a regression model for example. If $u_t = y_t - \boldsymbol{x}_t'\boldsymbol{\beta}_0$ is a m.d. process, then in general this will not be true for

$$y_t - \boldsymbol{x}_t'\boldsymbol{\beta}_{0n} = u_t + \boldsymbol{x}_t'(\boldsymbol{\beta}_0 - \boldsymbol{\beta}_{0n}). \tag{12.4.3}$$

Therefore, appeal to a CLT allowing general dependence such as Theorem 10.5.2 may be essential. However, armed with both Theorems 12.4.1 and 10.5.2, all the results on asymptotic distributions previously derived can be extended to the case of Pitman drift, provided the relevant regularity conditions hold.

12.4.2 Asymptotic Distributions under H_A

For each n, $\boldsymbol{\theta}_{0n}$ is the true model. For any fixed $n^* \geq 1$, imagine drawing the element $\sqrt{n^*}(\hat{\boldsymbol{\theta}}_{n^*} - \boldsymbol{\theta}_{0n^*})$ from a sequence $\sqrt{n}(\hat{\boldsymbol{\theta}}_n - \boldsymbol{\theta}_{0n^*})$ converging in the usual manner. By considering the sequence generated by such drawings for $n^* = 1, 2, 3, \dots$ and letting $n^* \to \infty$, it is clear since $\boldsymbol{\theta}_{0n} \to \boldsymbol{\theta}_0$ that

$$\sqrt{n}(\hat{\boldsymbol{\theta}}_n - \boldsymbol{\theta}_{0n}) \xrightarrow{D} N(\boldsymbol{0},\ \bar{\boldsymbol{Q}}_0^{-1}\boldsymbol{A}_0\bar{\boldsymbol{Q}}_0^{-1}). \tag{12.4.4}$$

Note that this implies

$$\sqrt{n}(\hat{\boldsymbol{\theta}}_n - \boldsymbol{\theta}_0) = \sqrt{n}(\hat{\boldsymbol{\theta}}_n - \boldsymbol{\theta}_{0n}) + \boldsymbol{\delta} \xrightarrow{D} N(\boldsymbol{\delta},\ \bar{\boldsymbol{Q}}_0^{-1}\boldsymbol{A}_0\bar{\boldsymbol{Q}}_0^{-1}) \tag{12.4.5}$$

so that in this sense the null hypothesis, represented by $\boldsymbol{\theta} = \boldsymbol{\theta}_0$ where $\boldsymbol{g}(\boldsymbol{\theta}_0) = \boldsymbol{0}$, is asymptotically false.

Applying the mean value expansion to the vector of restrictions under the alternatives gives

$$\boldsymbol{g}(\boldsymbol{\theta}_{0n}) = \frac{\boldsymbol{G}_n^*\boldsymbol{\delta}}{\sqrt{n}} \tag{12.4.6}$$

where $\boldsymbol{G}_n^*$ denotes $\boldsymbol{G}$ with rows evaluated at points on the line segment joining $\boldsymbol{\theta}_0$ and $\boldsymbol{\theta}_{0n}$. Consider the Wald statistic. Using (12.4.6) in (12.2.1) yields

$$\boldsymbol{g}(\hat{\boldsymbol{\theta}}_n) = \frac{\boldsymbol{G}_n^*\boldsymbol{\delta}}{\sqrt{n}} + \boldsymbol{G}_n^{**}(\hat{\boldsymbol{\theta}}_n - \boldsymbol{\theta}_{0n}) \tag{12.4.7}$$

where $\boldsymbol{G}_n^{**}$ has its rows evaluated at points between $\hat{\boldsymbol{\theta}}_n$ and $\boldsymbol{\theta}_{0n}$. Hence, applying Theorems 3.1.1 (Slutsky) and 3.3.5 (Cramér) in the usual way to (12.4.5) combined with (12.4.7) yields the result

$$\sqrt{n}\boldsymbol{g}(\hat{\boldsymbol{\theta}}_n) \xrightarrow{D} N(\boldsymbol{G}_0\boldsymbol{\delta},\ \boldsymbol{G}_0\bar{\boldsymbol{Q}}_0^{-1}\boldsymbol{A}_0\bar{\boldsymbol{Q}}_0^{-1}\boldsymbol{G}_0') \tag{12.4.8}$$

where $\boldsymbol{G}_0 = \boldsymbol{G}(\boldsymbol{\theta}_0)$, which is both the limit of $\boldsymbol{G}_n^*$ and the probability limit of $\boldsymbol{G}_n^{**}$. It follows immediately from the facts given in §C.3 that the limiting distribution of W is the non-central chi-squared distribution with r degrees of freedom and noncentrality parameter $\lambda = \boldsymbol{\delta}'\boldsymbol{G}_0'(\boldsymbol{G}_0\bar{\boldsymbol{Q}}_0^{-1}\boldsymbol{A}_0\bar{\boldsymbol{Q}}_0^{-1}\boldsymbol{G}_0')^{-1}\boldsymbol{G}_0\boldsymbol{\delta}$. Assuming the information matrix equality (9.3.19) this becomes

$$\lambda = \frac{\boldsymbol{\delta}'\boldsymbol{G}_0'(\boldsymbol{G}_0\bar{\boldsymbol{Q}}_0^{-1}\boldsymbol{G}_0')^{-1}\boldsymbol{G}_0\boldsymbol{\delta}}{c^2}. \tag{12.4.9}$$

This distribution (whose tabulation can be approximated from the central χ^2 tables, as discussed in §C.3) can be used to approximate the power of the test against alternatives that lie in particular directions away from $\boldsymbol{\theta}_0$, corresponding to the value of $\boldsymbol{\delta}$. Directions lying in the kernel of $\boldsymbol{G}_0$, such that $\boldsymbol{G}_0\boldsymbol{\delta} = \boldsymbol{0}$ and hence $\lambda = 0$, span a space of dimension $p - r$ and represent, at least locally, elements of the null hypothesis. The test inevitably has low local power against alternatives that lie close to the null, in the sense of yielding a small λ.

To obtain the corresponding result for the tests based on the constrained estimates, note letting $\boldsymbol{q}_{n0} = \boldsymbol{q}_n(\boldsymbol{\theta}_{0n})$ that equations (12.3.3) become

$$\frac{\boldsymbol{q}_{n0}}{\sqrt{n}} + \frac{\boldsymbol{Q}_n^{**}}{n}\sqrt{n}(\dot{\boldsymbol{\theta}}_n - \boldsymbol{\theta}_{0n}) + \frac{\dot{\boldsymbol{G}}_n'\dot{\boldsymbol{\lambda}}_n}{\sqrt{n}} = \boldsymbol{0} \tag{12.4.10a}$$

$$\boldsymbol{G}_n^{**}\sqrt{n}(\dot{\boldsymbol{\theta}}_n - \boldsymbol{\theta}_{0n}) + \boldsymbol{G}_n^*\boldsymbol{\delta} = \boldsymbol{0} \tag{12.4.10b}$$

where (12.4.6) has been substituted. Under the sequence of local alternatives, $\boldsymbol{G}_n^*$, $\boldsymbol{G}_n^{**}$ and $\dot{\boldsymbol{G}}_n$ all converge to $\boldsymbol{G}_0$, and plim $n^{-1}\boldsymbol{Q}_n^{**} = \bar{\boldsymbol{Q}}_0$ by the same arguments as before, so solving these equations in the limit yields

$$\begin{aligned}\sqrt{n}(\dot{\boldsymbol{\theta}}_n - \boldsymbol{\theta}_{0n}) &\underset{\text{asy}}{\sim} -\frac{\boldsymbol{E}_0\boldsymbol{q}_{n0}}{\sqrt{n}} - \bar{\boldsymbol{Q}}_0^{-1}\boldsymbol{G}_0'(\boldsymbol{G}_0\bar{\boldsymbol{Q}}_0^{-1}\boldsymbol{G}_0')^{-1}\boldsymbol{G}_0\boldsymbol{\delta} \\ &\xrightarrow{\text{D}} \text{N}(-\bar{\boldsymbol{Q}}_0^{-1}\boldsymbol{G}_0'(\boldsymbol{G}_0\bar{\boldsymbol{Q}}_0^{-1}\boldsymbol{G}_0')^{-1}\boldsymbol{G}_0\boldsymbol{\delta},\ \boldsymbol{E}_0\boldsymbol{A}_0\boldsymbol{E}_0).\end{aligned} \tag{12.4.11}$$

Also, using (12.4.4) to adapt (12.3.8),

$$\begin{aligned}\sqrt{n}(\dot{\boldsymbol{\theta}}_n - \hat{\boldsymbol{\theta}}_n) &\underset{asy}{\sim} -\frac{\boldsymbol{K}_0\boldsymbol{q}_{n0}}{\sqrt{n}} - \bar{\boldsymbol{Q}}_0^{-1}\boldsymbol{G}_0'(\boldsymbol{G}_0\bar{\boldsymbol{Q}}_0^{-1}\boldsymbol{G}_0')^{-1}\boldsymbol{G}_0\boldsymbol{\delta} \\ &\xrightarrow{\text{D}} \text{N}(-\bar{\boldsymbol{Q}}_0^{-1}\boldsymbol{G}_0'(\boldsymbol{G}_0\bar{\boldsymbol{Q}}_0^{-1}\boldsymbol{G}_0')^{-1}\boldsymbol{G}_0\boldsymbol{\delta},\ \boldsymbol{K}_0\boldsymbol{A}_0\boldsymbol{K}_0).\end{aligned} \tag{12.4.12}$$

Substituting these formulae into the second member of (12.3.11) and following through the same argument as previously with the obvious variations, the asymptotic distribution of the ALR statistic is obtained as $\chi^2(r,\lambda)$ where λ is given by (12.4.9). Thus, the Wald and ALR tests are asymptotically equivalent with respect to a sequence of local alternatives. Solving for $\dot{\boldsymbol{\lambda}}_n$ from (12.4.10a), the same result is found to hold for the LM test. It is also clear that the robust versions of the tests, avoiding the information matrix equality, behave similarly. These steps are left as an exercise for the reader.

12.5 M Tests

12.5.1 Theory

Although we can conceive of constrained estimation being performed by solving the equations in (12.3.2), this is not how it is done in practice. More usually, the constraints are used to substitute out a subset of the parameters. Forming the partition $\boldsymbol{\theta} = (\boldsymbol{\alpha}, \boldsymbol{\gamma})$, where $\boldsymbol{\alpha}$ is $q \times 1$ and $\boldsymbol{\gamma}$ is $r \times 1$, where $p = r + q$, define a vector of solutions to (12.1.3) as $\boldsymbol{\gamma} = \boldsymbol{h}(\boldsymbol{\alpha})$ $(r \times 1)$, such that

$$\boldsymbol{g}(\boldsymbol{\alpha}, \boldsymbol{h}(\boldsymbol{\alpha})) = \mathbf{0}. \tag{12.5.1}$$

See (2.4.28) for the linear case. The vector $\boldsymbol{\alpha}$ defines the parameterization of the constrained model. Define the criterion function subject to these constraints as having the implicit form

$$C_n^*(\boldsymbol{\alpha}) = C_n(\boldsymbol{\alpha}, \boldsymbol{h}(\boldsymbol{\alpha})) \tag{12.5.2}$$

with the corresponding gradient and Hessian matrix,

$$\boldsymbol{s}_n(\boldsymbol{\alpha}) = \frac{\partial C_n^*}{\partial \boldsymbol{\alpha}} \qquad \boldsymbol{S}_n(\boldsymbol{\alpha}) = \frac{\partial^2 C_n^*}{\partial \boldsymbol{\alpha} \partial \boldsymbol{\alpha}'}. \tag{12.5.3}$$

By construction, $\boldsymbol{s}_n$ has the property $\boldsymbol{s}_n(\dot{\boldsymbol{\alpha}}) = \mathbf{0}$ where $\dot{\boldsymbol{\alpha}}$ denotes the first q elements of $\dot{\boldsymbol{\theta}}$, and $\dot{\boldsymbol{\gamma}} = \boldsymbol{h}(\dot{\boldsymbol{\alpha}})$. When H_0 is true, applying the analysis of §9.3.4 as usual yields

$$\sqrt{n}(\dot{\boldsymbol{\alpha}} - \boldsymbol{\alpha}_0) \underset{\text{asy}}{\sim} \bar{\boldsymbol{S}}_0^{-1}\sqrt{n}\boldsymbol{s}_{n0} \xrightarrow{\text{D}} \text{N}(\mathbf{0}, \bar{\boldsymbol{S}}_0^{-1}\boldsymbol{D}_0\bar{\boldsymbol{S}}_0^{-1}) \tag{12.5.4}$$

where $\boldsymbol{D}_0$ denotes the asymptotic covariance matrix of $\sqrt{n}\boldsymbol{s}_{n0}$. Since $\dot{\boldsymbol{\alpha}}$ is necessarily the same solution to the constrained optimization problem as that defined by (12.3.2), the variance matrix in (12.5.4) is identical to the upper-left $q \times q$ submatrix of $\boldsymbol{E}_0\boldsymbol{A}_0\boldsymbol{E}_0$ in (12.3.6).

The situation in which $\boldsymbol{\alpha}$ is estimated by optimizing C_n^* arises when this setup, embodying the restrictions $\boldsymbol{g}$, is initially hypothesised to be the correct specification for the model. The Lagrange multiplier technique provides a method of testing such a restricted specification without actually estimating the unrestricted model, but nevertheless requires this model to be known. The unrestricted score vector $\boldsymbol{q}_n$ must be evaluated at the point $\dot{\boldsymbol{\theta}}$, even though there is no need to compute the unrestricted vector $\hat{\boldsymbol{\theta}}$. By contrast, we now consider how to construct tests of the null hypothesis without specifying the alternative explicitly, aiming simply to check the adequacy of $C_n^*(\boldsymbol{\alpha})$ as the correct model.[5]

This is possible, because there often exist functions of the data and parameters, to be denoted $\boldsymbol{w}_t(\boldsymbol{\alpha}, \boldsymbol{\gamma})$ $(s \times 1)$, having the property

$$E[\boldsymbol{w}_t(\boldsymbol{\alpha}_0, \boldsymbol{h}(\boldsymbol{\alpha}_0))] = \mathbf{0} \quad t = 1, \dots, n \tag{12.5.5}$$

[5] In effect, C_n^* is 'the' criterion, and $\boldsymbol{s}_n$, $\boldsymbol{D}_0$, $\boldsymbol{S}_n$ and $\bar{\boldsymbol{S}}_0$, from the point of view of calculating test statistics, are equivalent to $\boldsymbol{q}_n$, $\boldsymbol{A}_0$, $\boldsymbol{Q}_n$ and $\bar{\boldsymbol{Q}}_0$ defined in §9.3.4.

but

$$E[\boldsymbol{w}_t(\boldsymbol{\alpha}_0, \boldsymbol{\gamma}_0)] \neq \mathbf{0} \quad \text{when } \boldsymbol{\gamma}_0 \neq \boldsymbol{h}(\boldsymbol{\alpha}_0). \tag{12.5.6}$$

Such functions are called *indicators* of correct specification. Note that $\boldsymbol{h}$ need not depend on $\boldsymbol{\alpha}$ and could be just an r-vector of zeros, corresponding to the suppression of these extra parameters. Define the vector of sample moments

$$\boldsymbol{m}_n = \frac{1}{n}\sum_{t=1}^{n} \boldsymbol{w}_t \quad (s \times 1). \tag{12.5.7}$$

Condition (12.5.5) implies that $\boldsymbol{m}_n(\boldsymbol{\alpha}_0, \boldsymbol{h}(\boldsymbol{\alpha}_0))$ has a mean of zero, and under H_0 the same ought to be approximately true of $\boldsymbol{m}_n(\dot{\boldsymbol{\alpha}}, \boldsymbol{h}(\dot{\boldsymbol{\alpha}}))$, to be denoted by $\dot{\boldsymbol{m}}_n$. Tests of correct specification based on (12.5.5), first suggested by Newey (1985) and Tauchen (1985), are called M tests, or moment tests.

A statistic is derived by constructing the usual type of mean value expansion. If

$$\boldsymbol{\Delta}_n = \frac{\partial \boldsymbol{m}_n}{\partial \boldsymbol{\alpha}'} = \frac{1}{n}\sum_{t=1}^{n} \frac{\partial \boldsymbol{w}_t}{\partial \boldsymbol{\alpha}'} \quad (s \times q) \tag{12.5.8}$$

defines the Jacobian matrix of the moments,

$$\begin{aligned} \sqrt{n}\dot{\boldsymbol{m}}_n &= \sqrt{n}\boldsymbol{m}_{n0} + \boldsymbol{\Delta}_n^*\sqrt{n}(\dot{\boldsymbol{\alpha}}_n - \boldsymbol{\alpha}_0) \\ &\underset{\text{asy}}{\sim} \sqrt{n}\boldsymbol{m}_{n0} - \boldsymbol{\Delta}_0\bar{\boldsymbol{S}}_0^{-1}\sqrt{n}\boldsymbol{s}_{n0} \\ &\xrightarrow{\text{D}} \text{N}(\mathbf{0}, \boldsymbol{V}_{m0}) \end{aligned} \tag{12.5.9}$$

where, letting $\boldsymbol{C}_0$ denote the asymptotic variance matrix of $\sqrt{n}\boldsymbol{m}_{n0}$, and $\boldsymbol{F}_0$ the matrix of asymptotic covariances with $\sqrt{n}\boldsymbol{s}_{n0}$,

$$\boldsymbol{V}_{m0} = \begin{bmatrix} \boldsymbol{I}_s & -\bar{\boldsymbol{\Delta}}_0\bar{\boldsymbol{S}}_0^{-1} \end{bmatrix} \begin{bmatrix} \boldsymbol{C}_0 & \boldsymbol{F}_0 \\ \boldsymbol{F}_0' & \boldsymbol{D}_0 \end{bmatrix} \begin{bmatrix} \boldsymbol{I}_s \\ -\bar{\boldsymbol{S}}_0^{-1}\bar{\boldsymbol{\Delta}}_0' \end{bmatrix}. \tag{12.5.10}$$

This leads to the result

$$M = n\dot{\boldsymbol{m}}_n'\dot{\boldsymbol{V}}_m^{-1}\dot{\boldsymbol{m}}_n \xrightarrow{\text{D}} \chi^2(s) \text{ on } H_0 \tag{12.5.11}$$

where $\dot{\boldsymbol{V}}_m$ is a consistent estimate of the covariance matrix. To compute this matrix it is necessary to estimate $\bar{\boldsymbol{\Delta}}_0$ by $\dot{\boldsymbol{\Delta}}_n$ and $\bar{\boldsymbol{S}}_0$ by $\dot{\boldsymbol{S}}_n$, corresponding to the sample matrices in (12.5.8) and (12.5.3) respectively, evaluated at the point $\dot{\boldsymbol{\alpha}}$, and also to estimate $\boldsymbol{C}_0, \boldsymbol{D}_0$ and $\boldsymbol{F}_0$. If there is no simple analytic formula available for the evaluation of $\boldsymbol{\Delta}_n$, a difference approximation around the point $\dot{\boldsymbol{\alpha}}$ might be computed as in (9.2.26). Under the null hypothesis, and assuming that $\sqrt{n}\boldsymbol{s}_n$ has the representation in (9.3.12), these matrices have the form

$$\begin{bmatrix} \boldsymbol{C}_0 & \boldsymbol{F}_0 \\ \boldsymbol{F}_0' & \boldsymbol{D}_0 \end{bmatrix} = \lim_{n\to\infty}\frac{1}{n}E\left(\sum_{t=1}^{n}\begin{bmatrix} \boldsymbol{w}_{t0} \\ \bar{\boldsymbol{J}}\boldsymbol{v}_{t0} \end{bmatrix}\sum_{t=1}^{n}\begin{bmatrix} \boldsymbol{w}_{t0}' & \boldsymbol{v}_{t0}'\bar{\boldsymbol{J}}' \end{bmatrix}\right). \tag{12.5.12}$$

If the sample is independent, this matrix can be computed by the obvious generalization of (9.4.20). For dependent data problems on the other hand, there is *in general* no reason for the sequence $\{\boldsymbol{w}_{t0}\}$ to be a martingale difference, even if the null hypothesis is true, when this takes the form of (12.5.5). For such cases, (12.5.12) can be estimated by the methods discussed in §9.4.3. The important exception to this statement is when the null hypothesis can actually be given in the form

$$E[\boldsymbol{w}_t(\boldsymbol{\alpha}_0, \boldsymbol{h}(\boldsymbol{\alpha}_0))|\mathcal{I}_t] = \mathbf{0} \text{ a.s.} \quad t = 1, \dots, n. \tag{12.5.13}$$

Note that (12.5.13) implies (12.5.5) but is not implied by it. When the null hypothesis takes this form, these are called conditional moment (CM) tests. All CM tests are also M tests, in the sense that if (12.5.13) holds, so does (12.5.5). In an independent sample the distinction disappears. Under sample dependence, however, there is the possibility of rejecting in the CM test because the $\boldsymbol{C}$ matrix assumed under H_0 is the wrong variance matrix, and yet not rejecting in the M test in which $\boldsymbol{C}$ is estimated in an autocorrelation-consistent fashion.

A natural context for M tests is the regression model of Chapter 7. Consider the correct specification criteria, Assumptions 7.1.1 and 7.1.2, and the tests of these conditions that were discussed in §7.5.1 and §7.6. In the model $y_t = \boldsymbol{\beta}'\boldsymbol{x}_t + u_t$, consider a test of the restriction

$$H_0 : E(u_t|\mathcal{I}_t) = 0 \tag{12.5.14}$$

where as usual, $\mathcal{I}_t$ is the σ-field generated by a set of variables that contains, but is larger than, $\boldsymbol{x}_t$. Moments known to be constrained to zero under the null hypothesis, but possibly not under the alternative, are the covariances between u_t and additional variables from $\mathcal{I}_t$. Thus, letting $\boldsymbol{z}_t$ $(s \times 1)$ be $\mathcal{I}_t$-measurable,

$$E(u_t\boldsymbol{z}_t) = E(E(u_t|\mathcal{I}_t)\boldsymbol{z}_t) = \mathbf{0} \tag{12.5.15}$$

under H_0. Defining $\boldsymbol{Z}$ $(n \times s)$ as the matrix having rows $\boldsymbol{z}_t'$ and $\dot{\boldsymbol{u}}$ $(n \times 1)$ as the vector of least squares residuals, the candidate vector of estimated moments is

$$\dot{\boldsymbol{m}}_n = \frac{\boldsymbol{Z}'\dot{\boldsymbol{u}}}{n}. \tag{12.5.16}$$

Assuming that $E(u_t^2|\mathcal{I}_t) = \sigma^2$, and that u_s is $\mathcal{I}_t$-measurable for $s < t$, then defining $\boldsymbol{X}$ $(n \times k)$ to be the matrix with rows $\boldsymbol{x}_t'$, estimates of the various matrices required are $\dot{\boldsymbol{\Delta}}_n = -n^{-1}\boldsymbol{Z}'\boldsymbol{X}$, $\dot{\boldsymbol{S}}_n = n^{-1}\boldsymbol{X}'\boldsymbol{X}$, $\dot{\boldsymbol{C}}_n = \dot{\sigma}^2 n^{-1}\boldsymbol{Z}'\boldsymbol{Z}$, $\dot{\boldsymbol{D}}_n = \dot{\sigma}^2\boldsymbol{S}_n$, and $\dot{\boldsymbol{F}}_n = -\dot{\sigma}^2\dot{\boldsymbol{\Delta}}_n$ where $\dot{\sigma}^2 = n^{-1}\dot{\boldsymbol{u}}'\dot{\boldsymbol{u}}$. Substituting into (12.5.11) gives

$$M = \frac{\dot{\boldsymbol{u}}'\boldsymbol{Z}\left(\boldsymbol{Z}'\boldsymbol{Z} - \boldsymbol{Z}'\boldsymbol{X}(\boldsymbol{X}'\boldsymbol{X})^{-1}\boldsymbol{X}'\boldsymbol{Z}\right)^{-1}\boldsymbol{Z}'\dot{\boldsymbol{u}}}{\dot{\sigma}^2} = nR^2 \tag{12.5.17}$$

where the R^2 is that from the regression of $\dot{\boldsymbol{u}}$ on $\boldsymbol{Z}$ and $\boldsymbol{X}$. This is, of course, identical with the variable addition test of §7.5.1, and has the interpretation of an LM test, as remarked in §12.3.4, for example. Once again a new testing 'principle', applied to a standard problem, yields the usual solution.

12.5.2 M Tests for Heteroscedasticity

Consider a test of the null hypothesis of conditional homoscedasticity in the linear model. This is the same problem for which the LM test was derived in §12.3.5, and the comparison is instructive. The test can be based on the criterion function in (10.4.4), although there is no need to specify the parameterized form of the alternative, as in (10.4.22). Just let $\boldsymbol{z}_t$ $(s \times 1)$ be a vector of $\mathcal{I}_t$-measurable candidate variables believed to explain, in some manner, the deviations of u_t^2 from its unconditional mean σ^2. Since correlation is the obvious property to seek, the logical moment vector to consider is

$$\dot{\boldsymbol{m}}_n = \frac{1}{n}\sum_{t=1}^{n} \boldsymbol{z}_t\left(\frac{\dot{u}_t^2}{\dot{\sigma}^2} - 1\right) \tag{12.5.18}$$

where $\dot{u}_t$ and $\dot{\sigma}^2$ are defined as before. In this case $\boldsymbol{\alpha} = (\boldsymbol{\beta}, \sigma^2)$, and

$$\boldsymbol{\Delta}_n = \frac{1}{n}\sum_{t=1}^{n}\left[\frac{2u_t}{\sigma^2}\boldsymbol{z}_t\boldsymbol{x}_t' \quad -\frac{u_t^2}{\sigma^4}\boldsymbol{z}_t\right] \quad (s \times (k+1)). \tag{12.5.19}$$

Assuming H_0 is true, and making additional assumptions (10.4.6) and (10.4.7), assemble the following asymptotic formulae. Letting $\boldsymbol{M}_{ZZ}$ and $\boldsymbol{M}_{ZX}$ denote the relevant moment matrices of the $\boldsymbol{z}_t$ and $\boldsymbol{x}_t$ variables, and $\bar{\boldsymbol{\mu}}_Z$ the limiting mean vector of the $\boldsymbol{z}_t$,

$$\boldsymbol{C}_0 = \left(\frac{\mu_4}{\sigma^4} - 1\right)\boldsymbol{M}_{ZZ} \quad (s \times s) \tag{12.5.20}$$

$$\boldsymbol{F}_0 = \left[\mu_3\sigma^{-4}\boldsymbol{M}_{ZX} \quad -\frac{1}{2\sigma^2}\left(\frac{\mu_4}{\sigma^4} - 1\right)\bar{\boldsymbol{\mu}}_Z'\right] \quad (s \times (k+1)) \tag{12.5.21}$$

using (10.4.5a) and (10.4.5b), and

$$\bar{\boldsymbol{\Delta}}_0 = \left[\boldsymbol{0} \quad -\frac{1}{\sigma^2}\bar{\boldsymbol{\mu}}_Z\right]. \tag{12.5.22}$$

The formulae for $\bar{\boldsymbol{S}}_0$ and $\bar{\boldsymbol{D}}_0$ are available from (10.4.12a)–(10.4.12c) and (10.4.8)–(10.4.10) respectively, from which we may readily compute

$$\boldsymbol{V}_{m0} = \left(\frac{\mu_4}{\sigma^4} - 1\right)(\boldsymbol{M}_{ZZ} - \bar{\boldsymbol{\mu}}_Z\bar{\boldsymbol{\mu}}_Z'). \tag{12.5.23}$$

This test turns out to be effectively identical to the LM test derived in §12.3.5. However, the result was arrived at without having to write down a specific model of heteroscedasticity such as (10.4.21b), from which the LM test was derived.

12.5.3 Tests of Functional Form

There are other applications of the M test for which a test would be difficult to derive in any other manner. Consider the analysis of the misspecified regression model in §10.5. There, we just assumed

$$E(y_t|\boldsymbol{x}_t) = f_t(\boldsymbol{x}_t) \tag{12.5.24}$$

where the f_t are arbitrary functions. How should the hypothesis that f_t has a particular form be tested? Linearity of the regression is tested by the RESET test (§7.6.6) which being a variable addition test, clearly has the interpretation of an M test where $\boldsymbol{z}_t$ is a vector of powers of the elements of $\boldsymbol{x}_t$. The M principle offers a different approach that easily generalizes to a non-linear null hypothesis.

Nonetheless, take the linear null for the sake of illustration and consider the case $f(\boldsymbol{x}_t) = \boldsymbol{\beta}'\boldsymbol{x}_t$. Clearly, there is no scope for testing the hypothesis

$$H_0 : E(y_t|\boldsymbol{x}_t) = \boldsymbol{\beta}'\boldsymbol{x}_t \tag{12.5.25}$$

by examining the sample covariance between $\dot{u}_t$ and $\boldsymbol{x}_t$, which is zero in the sample by construction. However, this property is achieved in the least squares estimates by trading off one part of the sample against another, and has nothing to do with the expectations of the individual terms $\boldsymbol{x}_t(y_t - \boldsymbol{\beta}'\boldsymbol{x}_t)$. These can all differ from zero, and in general will do so, unless H_0 is true. In particular, given a set of positive scalar weights $w(\boldsymbol{x}_1), \dots, w(\boldsymbol{x}_n)$, these is no reason to expect that

$$\dot{m}_n = \frac{1}{n}\sum_{t=1}^{n}(y_t - \dot{\boldsymbol{\beta}}'\boldsymbol{x}_t)w(\boldsymbol{x}_t) \tag{12.5.26}$$

should be close to 0 in general, *except* when H_0 is true. There are many ways a one-degree-of freedom M test of this type might be implemented. For example, if the observations fell naturally into groups across which the conditional expectation function might differ, $w(\boldsymbol{x}_t)$ could be chosen as the indicator of such a group. However, the goal should be to find a general misspecification test that can be used for routine diagnosis.

Bierens (1991) suggests constructing functions of the form

$$w(\boldsymbol{x}_t) = e^{\boldsymbol{\xi}'\boldsymbol{\psi}(\boldsymbol{x}_t)} \tag{12.5.27}$$

where $\boldsymbol{\xi}$ is any k-vector, and $\boldsymbol{\psi}(\cdot)$ is a *bounded* measurable mapping from $\mathbb{R}^p$ into $\mathbb{R}^p$. The motivation for this proposal is the fact that if $P[E(u|\boldsymbol{x}) = 0] < 1$, and $\boldsymbol{x}$ is bounded, then the set of vectors $\boldsymbol{\xi}$ such that

$$E(ue^{\boldsymbol{\xi}'\boldsymbol{x}}) = 0 \tag{12.5.28}$$

has Lebesgue measure zero. Being a measurable function of $\boldsymbol{x}$, $\boldsymbol{\psi}(\boldsymbol{x})$ is equivalent to it from the point of view of the latter property. Bierens suggests letting $\psi_i(\boldsymbol{x}_t) = \arctan x_{it}$ for $i = 1, \dots, k$, and further suggests putting the variables into standardised form, with zero means and unit variances, to avoid the problem of $w(\boldsymbol{x}_t)$ being effectively invariant to changes in some arguments due to scale factors. Almost any choice of $\boldsymbol{\xi}$ will give the test some power to detect misspecifications, and one obtains a consistent test with probability 1 by choosing $\boldsymbol{\xi}$ at random from some bounded set T (a k-dimensional cube, say).

Maximizing the test statistic M by choice of $\boldsymbol{\xi}$ would seem to ensure the most powerful test, but this will not yield a $\chi^2(1)$ statistic under H_0. Instead, Bierens suggests computing the statistic at a fixed value $\boldsymbol{\xi}_0$ from T, and *also* locating $\hat{\boldsymbol{\xi}}$ such that $M(\hat{\boldsymbol{\xi}}) \geq M(\boldsymbol{\xi})$ for all $\boldsymbol{\xi} \in T$. Then, one bases the test on $M(\boldsymbol{\xi}_0)$ if $M(\hat{\boldsymbol{\xi}}) - M(\boldsymbol{\xi}_0) \leq \gamma n^\rho$ for some $\gamma > 0$ and $\rho \in (0,1)$, but on $M(\hat{\boldsymbol{\xi}})$ otherwise. The point of this strategy is that asymptotically one must choose $M(\boldsymbol{\xi}_0)$ with probability 1 under H_0, so that the asymptotic $\chi^2(1)$ distribution applies.

12.5.4 The Information Matrix Test

One of the best-known tests that has an M-test interpretation is White's (1980a) information matrix test. This test of the information matrix equality (11.3.13) is a potentially powerful test of model specification. The setting for the test we develop is the case $C^* = L$, the log-likelihood function under H_0 depending on parameters $\boldsymbol{\alpha}$, although it might be adapted to more the general cases represented by (9.3.19) for criteria different from the log-likelihood. There are $p(p+1)/2$ equalities to be tested, although in the face of a dimensionality problem one might confine attention to a subset, say the diagonal elements.

This is a conditional moment test, and the restrictions to be tested are given in (11.3.14). The moment vector can be written in the form

$$\boldsymbol{m}_n = \operatorname{Vec}\left(n^{-1}\sum_{t=1}^{n}(\boldsymbol{q}_t\boldsymbol{q}_t' - \boldsymbol{Q}_t)\right)^* = n^{-1}\sum_{t=1}^{n}\boldsymbol{w}_t \tag{12.5.29}$$

where $\boldsymbol{q}_t = \partial l_t/\partial\boldsymbol{\alpha}$ and $\boldsymbol{Q}_t = \partial^2 l_t/\partial\boldsymbol{\alpha}\partial\boldsymbol{\alpha}'$, and the $*$ denotes omission of the elements of the vector that are redundant through symmetry.

The major problem in this case would appear to be the evaluation of $\boldsymbol{\Delta}_n$ the derivatives of $\boldsymbol{m}_n$ with respect to $\boldsymbol{\alpha}$. Fortunately this can be solved, or rather evaded, by a neat trick using the OPG regression of §11.3.5.

The argument is closely related to the one used to derive the information matrix equality itself. For simplicity assume the distribution is continuous, although the argument might be generalized similarly to §11.4. Under the null hypothesis,

$$E_\alpha[\boldsymbol{w}_t(\boldsymbol{\alpha})|\mathcal{X}_{t-1}] = \int \boldsymbol{w}_t(\boldsymbol{\alpha})D_t(\boldsymbol{x}_t|\mathcal{X}_{t-1};\boldsymbol{\alpha})d\boldsymbol{x}_t = \boldsymbol{0} \text{ a.s.} \tag{12.5.30}$$

where the operator $E_\alpha(\cdot|\mathcal{X}_{t-1})$ is defined as in (11.3.9). Differentiating this equality with respect to $\boldsymbol{\alpha}$ yields, similarly to (11.3.14),

$$\begin{aligned}\boldsymbol{0} &= \frac{\partial}{\partial\boldsymbol{\alpha}'}\int \boldsymbol{w}_t(\boldsymbol{\alpha})D_t(\boldsymbol{x}_t|\mathcal{X}_{t-1};\boldsymbol{\alpha})d\boldsymbol{x}_t \\ &= \int\left(\frac{\partial\boldsymbol{w}_t(\boldsymbol{\alpha})}{\partial\boldsymbol{\alpha}'} + \boldsymbol{w}_t(\boldsymbol{\alpha})\frac{\partial l_t}{\partial\boldsymbol{\alpha}'}\right)D_t(\boldsymbol{x}_t|\mathcal{X}_{t-1};\boldsymbol{\alpha})d\boldsymbol{x}_t \\ &= E_\alpha\left(\frac{\partial\boldsymbol{w}_t(\boldsymbol{\alpha})}{\partial\boldsymbol{\alpha}'}\Big|\mathcal{X}_{t-1}\right) + E_\alpha\left(\boldsymbol{w}_t(\boldsymbol{\alpha})\frac{\partial l_t}{\partial\boldsymbol{\alpha}'}\Big|\mathcal{X}_{t-1}\right).\end{aligned} \tag{12.5.31}$$

It follows by the application of the LIE to the last member of (12.5.31) that

$$E_\alpha(\boldsymbol{\Delta}_n) = -E_\alpha\left(\frac{1}{n}\sum_{t=1}^{n}\boldsymbol{w}_t\frac{\partial l_t}{\partial\boldsymbol{\alpha}'}\right). \tag{12.5.32}$$

Define $\boldsymbol{W}$ as the matrix whose rows are $\boldsymbol{w}_t'$, $\boldsymbol{L}$ as the matrix whose rows are $\partial l_t/\partial\boldsymbol{\alpha}_t'$, and $\boldsymbol{\iota}$ as the summation vector, the n-vector of 1s. Assuming the limits of expectations can be equated with probability limits, and using the information matrix equality, validly under H_0, a version of (12.5.9) is

$$\sqrt{n}\dot{\boldsymbol{m}}_n = \frac{\dot{\boldsymbol{W}}'\boldsymbol{\iota}}{\sqrt{n}}$$

$$\underset{\text{asy}}{\sim} \frac{\boldsymbol{W}_0'\boldsymbol{\iota} - \boldsymbol{W}_0'\boldsymbol{L}_0(\boldsymbol{L}_0'\boldsymbol{L}_0)^{-1}\boldsymbol{L}_0'\boldsymbol{\iota}}{\sqrt{n}}$$
$$\xrightarrow{\text{D}} \text{N}(\boldsymbol{0}, \boldsymbol{V}_{m0}). \tag{12.5.33}$$

Since this is a conditional moment test where the essential equality being tested is (11.3.14), the rows of $\boldsymbol{W}$ are serially uncorrelated in exactly the same way that the rows of $\boldsymbol{L}$ are uncorrelated because of (11.3.10). Under H_0,

$$E(\boldsymbol{W}_0'\boldsymbol{\iota}\boldsymbol{\iota}'\boldsymbol{W}_0) = E(\boldsymbol{W}_0'\boldsymbol{W}_0) \tag{12.5.34}$$

and

$$E(\boldsymbol{L}_0'\boldsymbol{\iota}\boldsymbol{\iota}'\boldsymbol{L}_0) = E(\boldsymbol{L}_0'\boldsymbol{L}_0). \tag{12.5.35}$$

It follows that

$$\boldsymbol{V}_{m0} = \text{plim}\, n^{-1}\boldsymbol{W}_0'(\boldsymbol{I}_n - \boldsymbol{L}_0(\boldsymbol{L}_0'\boldsymbol{L}_0)^{-1}\boldsymbol{L}_0')\boldsymbol{W}_0. \tag{12.5.36}$$

The M statistic can therefore be computed by running the modified OPG regression

$$\boldsymbol{\iota} = \dot{\boldsymbol{L}}\boldsymbol{b} + \dot{\boldsymbol{W}}\boldsymbol{c} + \boldsymbol{e} \tag{12.5.37}$$

where as usual, the dots over the matrices denote estimation under H_0. Since $\dot{\boldsymbol{L}}'\boldsymbol{\iota} = \boldsymbol{0}$ by definition, this is not unlike the variable addition test regression in (7.5.1). As in that case, the test statistic may be calculated from the regression as the nR^2 from the regression in (12.5.37). This statistic has the asymptotic chi-squared distribution with $p(p+1)/2$ degrees of freedom under H_0. Note that computing $\boldsymbol{L}$ and $\boldsymbol{W}$ is generally a straightforward problem since the relevant derivatives of the log-likelihood are already computed as a by-product of the estimation algorithm, and in any case, the rows of $\boldsymbol{L}$ are just a component of the rows of $\boldsymbol{W}$.

Further Reading: On the general theory of statistical inference Silvey (1975) provides a nice introduction. Many econometrics textbooks give good surveys, but for a very comprehensive treatment see Gourieroux and Monfort (1995). Other important references, though not econometrically oriented, are Lehmann (1986), Kendall and Stuart (1979), and Cox and Hinkley (1974). On LM tests see Engle (1982b, 1983) and Godfrey (1988). On M testing see Davidson and MacKinnon (1993) and Bierens (1994).

Chapter 13

System Estimation

The estimation of linear equation systems is one of earliest problems to have been researched in econometrics, with important work being done at the Cowles Commission, University of Chicago, in the 1940s. The problem of stacking several equations together for estimation provides an important role for the generalized least squares principle, met with briefly in §2.3, but otherwise there is rather less here in the way of new concepts than of new notation. The estimators are based either on the instrumental variables principle, or (quasi-) maximum likelihood. However, nonlinear system estimation (see §13.4 and §13.5) does introduce some interesting new problems and insights into the theory of optimization estimators.

13.1 Three-stage Least Squares

Recalling the set-up and notation of §8.2.1, assume a set of equations of the form

$$\mathbf{B}\boldsymbol{y}_t = \boldsymbol{\Gamma}\boldsymbol{z}_t + \boldsymbol{u}_t \ (H \times 1) \tag{13.1.1}$$

where, if $\mathcal{I}_t = \sigma(\boldsymbol{z}_t) \vee \mathcal{Y}_{t-1} \vee \mathcal{Z}_{t-1}$ as before, then

$$E(\boldsymbol{u}_t|\mathcal{I}_t) = \mathbf{0} \tag{13.1.2a}$$

$$E(\boldsymbol{u}_t\boldsymbol{u}_t'|\mathcal{I}_t) = \boldsymbol{\Sigma}. \tag{13.1.2b}$$

This need not be a *complete* system, having as many equations as endogenous variables; $\boldsymbol{y}_t$ is of dimension $G \times 1$ and $\mathbf{B}$ of dimension $H \times G$ with $1 < H \leq G$. All the equations must satisfy the rank condition for identification (see §8.3) which might need to be verified with reference to the complete system, but any subset of the equations can be estimated jointly by the three stage least squares (3SLS) method proposed by Zellner and Theil (1962).

13.1.1 Construction of 3SLS

As in §8.2.2 let the individual equations of the system be written

$$y_{it} = \boldsymbol{\delta}_i'\boldsymbol{x}_{it} + u_{it} \quad i = 1, \ldots, H \tag{13.1.3}$$

where $\boldsymbol{\delta}_i = (\boldsymbol{\beta}^{*\prime}_{iA}, \boldsymbol{\gamma}'_{iA})'$ ($k_i \times 1$, where $k_i = g_i + m_i$) and $\boldsymbol{x}_{it} = (\boldsymbol{y}'_{iAt}, \boldsymbol{z}'_{iAt})'$. Write these in full-sample notation as

$$\boldsymbol{y}_i = \boldsymbol{X}_i\boldsymbol{\delta}_i + \boldsymbol{u}_i \;(n \times 1) \quad i = 1, \dots, H \tag{13.1.4}$$

where $\boldsymbol{X}_i$ ($n \times k_i$) is the matrix whose tth row is $\boldsymbol{x}'_{it}$ and $\boldsymbol{y}_i$ and $\boldsymbol{u}_i$ are the n-vectors with elements y_{it} and u_{it}. These equations are stacked up into a single super-equation,

$$\boldsymbol{y}^* = \boldsymbol{X}^*\boldsymbol{\delta} + \boldsymbol{u}^* \quad (Hn \times 1) \tag{13.1.5}$$

where

$$\boldsymbol{y}^* = \begin{bmatrix} \boldsymbol{y}_1 \\ \vdots \\ \boldsymbol{y}_H \end{bmatrix} \quad \underset{(Hn\times k)}{\boldsymbol{X}^*} = \begin{bmatrix} \boldsymbol{X}_1 & \boldsymbol{0} & \cdots & \boldsymbol{0} \\ \boldsymbol{0} & \boldsymbol{X}_2 & & \\ \vdots & & \ddots & \vdots \\ \boldsymbol{0} & \cdots & & \boldsymbol{X}_H \end{bmatrix} \quad \boldsymbol{u}^* = \begin{bmatrix} \boldsymbol{u}_1 \\ \vdots \\ \boldsymbol{u}_H \end{bmatrix} \quad \underset{(k\times 1)}{\boldsymbol{\delta}} = \begin{bmatrix} \boldsymbol{\delta}_1 \\ \vdots \\ \boldsymbol{\delta}_H \end{bmatrix}$$

and $k = \sum_{i=1}^{H} k_i$.

There are two difficulties to be dealt with in estimating equation (13.1.5). First there is simultaneity, which will require the use of an IV method. The matrix $\boldsymbol{Z}^* = (\boldsymbol{I}_H \otimes \boldsymbol{Z})$ ($Hn \times HM$) will make a suitable matrix of instruments for this purpose.[1] Then there is the fact that the elements of the vector $\boldsymbol{u}^*$ are correlated. Assumption (13.1.2) says there is no serial correlation but that contemporaneous disturbances from different equations have correlations σ_{ij}, such that

$$E(\boldsymbol{u}^*\boldsymbol{u}^{*\prime}) = E\begin{bmatrix} \boldsymbol{u}_1\boldsymbol{u}'_1 & \cdots & \boldsymbol{u}_1\boldsymbol{u}'_H \\ \vdots & \ddots & \vdots \\ \boldsymbol{u}_H\boldsymbol{u}'_1 & \cdots & \boldsymbol{u}_H\boldsymbol{u}'_H \end{bmatrix} = \begin{bmatrix} \sigma_{11}\boldsymbol{I}_n & \cdots & \sigma_{1H}\boldsymbol{I}_n \\ \vdots & \ddots & \vdots \\ \sigma_{H1}\boldsymbol{I}_n & \cdots & \sigma_{HH}\boldsymbol{I}_n \end{bmatrix}$$
$$= \boldsymbol{\Sigma} \otimes \boldsymbol{I}_n. \tag{13.1.6}$$

Applying the GLS principle of §2.3, let $\boldsymbol{K}$ be the matrix such that $\boldsymbol{K}'\boldsymbol{K} = \boldsymbol{\Sigma}^{-1}$, and $\boldsymbol{K\Sigma K}' = \boldsymbol{I}_H$.[2] Let $\boldsymbol{K}^* = (\boldsymbol{K} \otimes \boldsymbol{I}_n)$, and then let $\boldsymbol{v}^* = \boldsymbol{K}^*\boldsymbol{u}^*$ such that

$$E(\boldsymbol{v}^*\boldsymbol{v}^{*\prime}) = (\boldsymbol{K} \otimes \boldsymbol{I}_n)(\boldsymbol{\Sigma} \otimes \boldsymbol{I}_n)(\boldsymbol{K}' \otimes \boldsymbol{I}_n) = (\boldsymbol{K\Sigma K}' \otimes \boldsymbol{I}_n) = \boldsymbol{I}_{Hn}. \tag{13.1.7}$$

Premultiplying (13.1.5) by $\boldsymbol{K}^*$, the equation

$$\boldsymbol{K}^*\boldsymbol{y}^* = \boldsymbol{K}^*\boldsymbol{X}^*\boldsymbol{\delta} + \boldsymbol{v}^* \;(Hn \times 1) \tag{13.1.8}$$

is seen to have uncorrelated disturbances. $\boldsymbol{\Sigma}$ is unknown, but it can be estimated consistently by

$$\tilde{\boldsymbol{\Sigma}} = \frac{1}{n}\sum_{t=1}^{n} \begin{bmatrix} \tilde{u}_{1t}^2 & \cdots & \tilde{u}_{1t}\tilde{u}_{Ht} \\ \vdots & \ddots & \vdots \\ \tilde{u}_{Ht}\tilde{u}_{1t} & \cdots & \tilde{u}_{Ht}^2 \end{bmatrix} \tag{13.1.9}$$

---

[1] For explanation of the Kronecker product operator see §A.10

[2] See Lemma A.7.4 for details of this factorization.

where $\tilde{u}_{it}$ is the residual from 2SLS estimation of equation i. Accordingly, let $\tilde{\boldsymbol{K}}$ and $\tilde{\boldsymbol{K}}^*$ be the estimated counterparts of $\boldsymbol{K}$ and $\boldsymbol{K}^*$. By analogy with single equation 2SLS, the 3SLS estimator is

$$\tilde{\boldsymbol{\delta}}^* = [\boldsymbol{X}^{*\prime}\tilde{\boldsymbol{K}}^{*\prime}\boldsymbol{Z}^*(\boldsymbol{Z}^{*\prime}\boldsymbol{Z}^*)^{-1}\boldsymbol{Z}^{*\prime}\tilde{\boldsymbol{K}}^*\boldsymbol{X}^*]^{-1} \\ \times \boldsymbol{X}^{*\prime}\tilde{\boldsymbol{K}}^{*\prime}\boldsymbol{Z}^*(\boldsymbol{Z}^{*\prime}\boldsymbol{Z}^*)^{-1}\boldsymbol{Z}^{*\prime}\tilde{\boldsymbol{K}}^*\boldsymbol{y}^*. \qquad (13.1.10)$$

A partitioned version of this formula can be constructed using the Kronecker product algebra. Using (A.10.3)–(A.10.5),

$$\begin{aligned}\boldsymbol{Z}^*(\boldsymbol{Z}^{*\prime}\boldsymbol{Z}^*)^{-1}\boldsymbol{Z}^{*\prime} &= (\boldsymbol{I}\otimes\boldsymbol{Z})[(\boldsymbol{I}\otimes\boldsymbol{Z})'(\boldsymbol{I}\otimes\boldsymbol{Z})]^{-1}(\boldsymbol{I}\otimes\boldsymbol{Z})' \\ &= \boldsymbol{I}\otimes\boldsymbol{Z}(\boldsymbol{Z}'\boldsymbol{Z})^{-1}\boldsymbol{Z}' \\ &= \boldsymbol{I}\otimes\boldsymbol{Q}_Z \end{aligned} \qquad (13.1.11)$$

and hence

$$\begin{aligned}\tilde{\boldsymbol{K}}^{*\prime}\boldsymbol{Z}^*(\boldsymbol{Z}^{*\prime}\boldsymbol{Z}^*)^{-1}\boldsymbol{Z}^{*\prime}\tilde{\boldsymbol{K}}^* &= (\tilde{\boldsymbol{K}}\otimes\boldsymbol{I}_n)'(\boldsymbol{I}\otimes\boldsymbol{Q}_Z)(\tilde{\boldsymbol{K}}\otimes\boldsymbol{I}_n) \\ &= \tilde{\boldsymbol{K}}'\tilde{\boldsymbol{K}}\otimes\boldsymbol{Q}_Z \\ &= \begin{bmatrix}\tilde{\sigma}^{11}\boldsymbol{Q}_Z & \cdots & \tilde{\sigma}^{1H}\boldsymbol{Q}_Z \\ \vdots & \ddots & \vdots \\ \tilde{\sigma}^{H1}\boldsymbol{Q}_Z & \cdots & \tilde{\sigma}^{HH}\boldsymbol{Q}_Z\end{bmatrix}\end{aligned} \qquad (13.1.12)$$

where $\tilde{\sigma}^{ij}$ is the (i,j)th element of $\tilde{\boldsymbol{\Sigma}}^{-1}$. The partitioned form is therefore

$$\begin{bmatrix}\tilde{\boldsymbol{\delta}}_1^* \\ \vdots \\ \tilde{\boldsymbol{\delta}}_H^*\end{bmatrix} = \begin{bmatrix}\tilde{\sigma}^{11}\boldsymbol{X}_1'\boldsymbol{Q}_Z\boldsymbol{X}_1 & \cdots & \tilde{\sigma}^{1H}\boldsymbol{X}_1'\boldsymbol{Q}_Z\boldsymbol{X}_H \\ \vdots & \ddots & \vdots \\ \tilde{\sigma}^{H1}\boldsymbol{X}_H'\boldsymbol{Q}_Z\boldsymbol{X}_1 & \cdots & \tilde{\sigma}^{HH}\boldsymbol{X}_H'\boldsymbol{Q}_Z\boldsymbol{X}_H\end{bmatrix}^{-1}\begin{bmatrix}\sum_{j=1}^H\tilde{\sigma}^{1j}\boldsymbol{X}_1'\boldsymbol{Q}_Z\boldsymbol{y}_j \\ \vdots \\ \sum_{j=1}^H\tilde{\sigma}^{Hj}\boldsymbol{X}_H'\boldsymbol{Q}_Z\boldsymbol{y}_j\end{bmatrix} \qquad (13.1.13)$$

Yet another way to write the estimator is

$$\begin{bmatrix}\tilde{\boldsymbol{\delta}}_1^* \\ \vdots \\ \tilde{\boldsymbol{\delta}}_H^*\end{bmatrix} = \left(\begin{bmatrix}\boldsymbol{X}_1'\boldsymbol{Z} & & 0 \\ & \ddots & \\ 0 & & \boldsymbol{X}_H'\boldsymbol{Z}\end{bmatrix}(\tilde{\boldsymbol{\Sigma}}^{-1}\otimes(\boldsymbol{Z}'\boldsymbol{Z})^{-1})\begin{bmatrix}\boldsymbol{Z}'\boldsymbol{X}_1 & & 0 \\ & \ddots & \\ 0 & & \boldsymbol{Z}'\boldsymbol{X}_H\end{bmatrix}\right)^{-1} \\ \times\begin{bmatrix}\boldsymbol{X}_1'\boldsymbol{Z} & & 0 \\ & \ddots & \\ 0 & & \boldsymbol{X}_H'\boldsymbol{Z}\end{bmatrix}(\tilde{\boldsymbol{\Sigma}}^{-1}\otimes(\boldsymbol{Z}'\boldsymbol{Z})^{-1})\begin{bmatrix}\boldsymbol{Z}'\boldsymbol{y}_1 \\ \vdots \\ \boldsymbol{Z}'\boldsymbol{y}_H\end{bmatrix}. \qquad (13.1.14)$$

13.1.2 Distribution of 3SLS

Substituting for $\boldsymbol{y}_1, \ldots, \boldsymbol{y}_H$ from (13.1.4), the familiar relationship between the estimator and the error-of-estimate applies in this case, i.e.,[3]

$$\begin{bmatrix} \tilde{\boldsymbol{\delta}}_1^* \\ \vdots \\ \tilde{\boldsymbol{\delta}}_H^* \end{bmatrix} = \begin{bmatrix} \boldsymbol{\delta}_1 \\ \vdots \\ \boldsymbol{\delta}_H \end{bmatrix} + \begin{bmatrix} \tilde{\sigma}^{11}\boldsymbol{X}_1'\boldsymbol{Q}_Z\boldsymbol{X}_1 & \cdots & \tilde{\sigma}^{1H}\boldsymbol{X}_1'\boldsymbol{Q}_Z\boldsymbol{X}_H \\ \vdots & \ddots & \vdots \\ \tilde{\sigma}^{H1}\boldsymbol{X}_H'\boldsymbol{Q}_Z\boldsymbol{X}_1 & \cdots & \tilde{\sigma}^{HH}\boldsymbol{X}_H'\boldsymbol{Q}_Z\boldsymbol{X}_H \end{bmatrix}^{-1} \times \begin{bmatrix} \sum_{j=1}^{H}\tilde{\sigma}^{1j}\boldsymbol{X}_1'\boldsymbol{Q}_Z\boldsymbol{u}_j \\ \vdots \\ \sum_{j=1}^{H}\tilde{\sigma}^{Hj}\boldsymbol{X}_H'\boldsymbol{Q}_Z\boldsymbol{u}_j \end{bmatrix}. \quad (13.1.15)$$

The analysis of this section operates directly on formula (13.1.15), generalizing the approach in §8.2.4, and avoids using OE theory. This is fortunate, because the dependence of $\tilde{\boldsymbol{\delta}}^*$ on $\tilde{\boldsymbol{\Sigma}}$ would otherwise represent a major complication. This complication does need to be confronted when we come to consider the nonlinear case, however, and this case is dealt with in §13.5.

Assume, in line with the 2SLS theory of §8.2.4, that the variables have the various desirable asymptotic properties. In particular, assume

$$\operatorname{plim}\frac{\boldsymbol{Z}'\boldsymbol{Z}}{n} = \boldsymbol{M}_{ZZ} \text{ (positive definite)} \quad (13.1.16)$$

$$\operatorname{plim}\frac{\boldsymbol{X}_i'\boldsymbol{Z}}{n} = \boldsymbol{M}_{X_iZ} \quad i = 1, \ldots, H \quad (13.1.17)$$

where the latter matrices all have full rank k_i, and

$$\frac{1}{\sqrt{n}}\begin{bmatrix} \boldsymbol{Z}'\boldsymbol{u}_1 \\ \vdots \\ \boldsymbol{Z}'\boldsymbol{u}_H \end{bmatrix} = \frac{1}{\sqrt{n}}\sum_{t=1}^{n}\begin{bmatrix} \boldsymbol{z}_t u_{1t} \\ \vdots \\ \boldsymbol{z}_t u_{Ht} \end{bmatrix} \xrightarrow{\text{D}} \text{N}(\boldsymbol{0}, \boldsymbol{\Sigma}\otimes\boldsymbol{M}_{ZZ}) \quad (HM \times 1) \quad (13.1.18)$$

The matrix $\boldsymbol{\Sigma}\otimes\boldsymbol{M}_{ZZ}$ has diagonal $M \times M$ blocks of the form $\sigma_{ii}\boldsymbol{M}_{ZZ}$ that match those appearing in (8.2.45) for the individual equations. The off-diagonal blocks are of the form $\sigma_{ij}\boldsymbol{M}_{ZZ}$ for $i \neq j$, and the fact of all these convergences was really implicit in the earlier treatment. What is new here is the assumption of *joint* convergence of the whole vector.

Also assume $\operatorname{plim}\tilde{\boldsymbol{\Sigma}} = \boldsymbol{\Sigma}$. Then, application of Cramér's Theorem and some rather cumbersome manipulations (which nonetheless closely parallel the 2SLS case) yield

$$\frac{1}{\sqrt{n}}\begin{bmatrix} \sum_{j=1}^{H}\tilde{\sigma}^{1j}\boldsymbol{X}_1'\boldsymbol{Q}_Z\boldsymbol{u}_j \\ \vdots \\ \sum_{j=1}^{H}\tilde{\sigma}^{Hj}\boldsymbol{X}_H'\boldsymbol{Q}_Z\boldsymbol{u}_j \end{bmatrix} \xrightarrow{\text{D}} \text{N}(\boldsymbol{0}, \boldsymbol{M}_{XZ}^*(\boldsymbol{\Sigma}^{-1}\otimes\boldsymbol{M}_{ZZ}^{-1})\boldsymbol{M}_{ZX}^*) \quad (13.1.19)$$

[3]Formula (13.1.14) may be the most intuitive form for this demonstration. It's always a useful exercise to work through the two-equation cases of formulae of this sort.

where

$$\boldsymbol{M}_{XZ}^{*} = \begin{bmatrix} \boldsymbol{M}_{X_1Z} & & 0 \\ & \ddots & \\ 0 & & \boldsymbol{M}_{X_HZ} \end{bmatrix} \tag{13.1.20}$$

is a matrix of rank k, and $\boldsymbol{M}_{ZX}^{*} = \boldsymbol{M}_{XZ}^{*\prime}$. Also,

$$\begin{aligned} \operatorname{plim} \frac{1}{n} & \begin{bmatrix} \tilde{\sigma}^{11}\boldsymbol{X}_1'\boldsymbol{Q}_Z\boldsymbol{X}_1 & \cdots & \tilde{\sigma}^{1H}\boldsymbol{X}_1'\boldsymbol{Q}_Z\boldsymbol{X}_H \\ \vdots & \ddots & \vdots \\ \tilde{\sigma}^{H1}\boldsymbol{X}_H'\boldsymbol{Q}_Z\boldsymbol{X}_1 & \cdots & \tilde{\sigma}^{HH}\boldsymbol{X}_H'\boldsymbol{Q}_Z\boldsymbol{X}_H \end{bmatrix} \\ &= \begin{bmatrix} \sigma^{11}\boldsymbol{M}_{X_1Z}\boldsymbol{M}_{ZZ}^{-1}\boldsymbol{M}_{ZX_1} & \cdots & \sigma^{1H}\boldsymbol{M}_{X_1Z}\boldsymbol{M}_{ZZ}^{-1}\boldsymbol{M}_{ZX_H} \\ \vdots & \ddots & \vdots \\ \sigma^{H1}\boldsymbol{M}_{X_HZ}\boldsymbol{M}_{ZZ}^{-1}\boldsymbol{M}_{ZX_1} & \cdots & \sigma^{HH}\boldsymbol{M}_{X_HZ}\boldsymbol{M}_{ZZ}^{-1}\boldsymbol{M}_{ZX_H} \end{bmatrix} \\ &= \boldsymbol{M}_{XZ}^{*}(\boldsymbol{\Sigma}^{-1} \otimes \boldsymbol{M}_{ZZ}^{-1})\boldsymbol{M}_{ZX}^{*}. \end{aligned} \tag{13.1.21}$$

It follows that

$$\sqrt{n}(\tilde{\boldsymbol{\delta}}^{*} - \boldsymbol{\delta}^{*}) \xrightarrow{D} \mathrm{N}\big(\mathbf{0},\ [\boldsymbol{M}_{XZ}^{*}(\boldsymbol{\Sigma}^{-1} \otimes \boldsymbol{M}_{ZZ}^{-1})\boldsymbol{M}_{ZX}^{*}]^{-1}\big). \tag{13.1.22}$$

To judge the advantages of doing the third stage of 3SLS, as opposed to stopping at 2SLS, the asymptotic distribution in (13.1.22) should be compared with (8.2.48). There is an efficiency gain in estimating the system, as against one equation at a time. Consider the two-equation case. Applying the partitioned inverse formula and the formula for $\boldsymbol{\Sigma}^{-1}$ and doing some manipulations yields

$$\begin{aligned} \mathrm{AVar}(\tilde{\boldsymbol{\delta}}_1^{*}) = \sigma_{11}\bigg(& \boldsymbol{M}_{X_1Z}\boldsymbol{M}_{ZZ}^{-1}\boldsymbol{M}_{ZX_1} + \frac{\sigma_{12}^2}{\sigma_{11}\sigma_{22} - \sigma_{12}^2}\big[\boldsymbol{M}_{X_1Z}\boldsymbol{M}_{ZZ}^{-1}\boldsymbol{M}_{ZX_1} \\ & - \boldsymbol{M}_{X_1Z}\boldsymbol{M}_{ZZ}^{-1}\boldsymbol{M}_{ZX_2}\left(\boldsymbol{M}_{X_2Z}\boldsymbol{M}_{ZZ}^{-1}\boldsymbol{M}_{ZX_2}\right)^{-1}\boldsymbol{M}_{X_2Z}\boldsymbol{M}_{ZZ}^{-1}\boldsymbol{M}_{ZX_1}\big]\bigg)^{-1} \end{aligned} \tag{13.1.23}$$

In general, the term in square brackets is positive semi-definite so that 3SLS has smaller asymptotic variance than 2SLS, and this is true for any equation.

There is a down-side to this efficiency gain, apart from the extra computational labour. If *any* of the equations is misspecified such that assumption (13.1.18) fails in respect of one or more of the blocks, then $\tilde{\boldsymbol{\delta}}_1^{*}$ is generally inconsistent, regardless of whether equation 1 is correctly specified. A trade-off of efficiency for robustness is a phenomenon often encountered in estimation theory, compare §8.1.3 for example. To make the best of the trade-off in this case, the best strategy may be to estimate jointly any subset of equations whose specification is known with confidence, but to omit the doubtful cases.

13.1.3 Special Cases

There are a number of models for which the 3SLS estimator assumes a simpler form.

1. $\boldsymbol{\Sigma}$ is diagonal.

If diagonality of $\tilde{\boldsymbol{\Sigma}}$ is imposed, (13.1.13) reduces to 2SLS on each equation;

$$\begin{bmatrix} \tilde{\boldsymbol{\delta}}_1^* \\ \vdots \\ \tilde{\boldsymbol{\delta}}_H^* \end{bmatrix} = \begin{bmatrix} \tilde{\sigma}_{11}^{-1}\boldsymbol{X}_1'\boldsymbol{Q}_Z\boldsymbol{X}_1 & & 0 \\ & \ddots & \\ 0 & & \tilde{\sigma}_{HH}^{-1}\boldsymbol{X}_H'\boldsymbol{Q}_Z\boldsymbol{X}_H \end{bmatrix}^{-1} \begin{bmatrix} \tilde{\sigma}_{11}^{-1}\boldsymbol{X}_1'\boldsymbol{Q}_Z\boldsymbol{y}_1 \\ \vdots \\ \tilde{\sigma}_{HH}^{-1}\boldsymbol{X}_H'\boldsymbol{Q}_Z\boldsymbol{y}_H \end{bmatrix}$$
$$= \begin{bmatrix} \tilde{\sigma}_{11}(\boldsymbol{X}_1'\boldsymbol{Q}_Z\boldsymbol{X}_1)^{-1}\tilde{\sigma}_{11}^{-1}\boldsymbol{X}_1'\boldsymbol{Q}_Z\boldsymbol{y}_1 \\ \vdots \\ \tilde{\sigma}_{HH}(\boldsymbol{X}_H'\boldsymbol{Q}_Z\boldsymbol{X}_H)^{-1}\tilde{\sigma}_{HH}^{-1}\boldsymbol{X}_H'\boldsymbol{Q}_Z\boldsymbol{y}_H \end{bmatrix} = \begin{bmatrix} \tilde{\boldsymbol{\delta}}_1 \\ \vdots \\ \tilde{\boldsymbol{\delta}}_H \end{bmatrix}. \quad (13.1.24)$$

If this restriction holds for the true $\boldsymbol{\Sigma}$, the asymptotic distribution of 3SLS is the same as that of 2SLS on each equation.

2. $\boldsymbol{X}_i = \boldsymbol{X}$, all i.

When every equation has the same set of right-hand side variables, 3SLS is identical to 2SLS. In this case $\boldsymbol{X}^* = \boldsymbol{I}_H \otimes \boldsymbol{X}$, and formula (13.1.10) reduces to

$$\begin{aligned} \tilde{\boldsymbol{\delta}}^* &= [(\boldsymbol{I}_H \otimes \boldsymbol{X}')(\boldsymbol{K}' \otimes \boldsymbol{I}_n)(\boldsymbol{I}_H \otimes \boldsymbol{Q}_Z)(\boldsymbol{K} \otimes \boldsymbol{I}_n)(\boldsymbol{I}_H \otimes \boldsymbol{X})]^{-1} \\ &\qquad \times (\boldsymbol{I}_H \otimes \boldsymbol{X}')(\boldsymbol{K}' \otimes \boldsymbol{I}_n)(\boldsymbol{I}_H \otimes \boldsymbol{Q}_Z)(\boldsymbol{K} \otimes \boldsymbol{I}_n)\boldsymbol{y}^* \\ &= (\boldsymbol{\Sigma}^{-1} \otimes \boldsymbol{X}'\boldsymbol{Q}_Z\boldsymbol{X})^{-1}(\boldsymbol{\Sigma}^{-1} \otimes \boldsymbol{X}'\boldsymbol{Q}_Z)\boldsymbol{y}^* \\ &= \begin{bmatrix} (\boldsymbol{X}'\boldsymbol{Q}_Z\boldsymbol{X})^{-1}\boldsymbol{X}'\boldsymbol{Q}_Z\boldsymbol{y}_1 \\ \vdots \\ (\boldsymbol{X}'\boldsymbol{Q}_Z\boldsymbol{X})^{-1}\boldsymbol{X}'\boldsymbol{Q}_Z\boldsymbol{y}_H \end{bmatrix} = \begin{bmatrix} \tilde{\boldsymbol{\delta}}_1 \\ \vdots \\ \tilde{\boldsymbol{\delta}}_H \end{bmatrix}. \end{aligned} \quad (13.1.25)$$

3. All of the equations are just identified.

In this case the identification conditions $k_i \leq M$ are all satisfied as equalities, and the matrices $\boldsymbol{Z}'\boldsymbol{X}_i$ are square $M \times M$. Then,

$$\begin{bmatrix} \tilde{\boldsymbol{\delta}}_1 \\ \vdots \\ \tilde{\boldsymbol{\delta}}_H^* \end{bmatrix} = \left(\begin{bmatrix} \boldsymbol{X}_1'\boldsymbol{Z} & & 0 \\ & \ddots & \\ 0 & & \boldsymbol{X}_H'\boldsymbol{Z} \end{bmatrix} (\tilde{\boldsymbol{\Sigma}}^{-1} \otimes (\boldsymbol{Z}'\boldsymbol{Z})^{-1}) \begin{bmatrix} \boldsymbol{Z}'\boldsymbol{X}_1 & & 0 \\ & \ddots & \\ 0 & & \boldsymbol{Z}\boldsymbol{X}_H \end{bmatrix} \right)^{-1}$$
$$\times \begin{bmatrix} \boldsymbol{X}_1'\boldsymbol{Z} & & 0 \\ & \ddots & \\ 0 & & \boldsymbol{X}_H'\boldsymbol{Z} \end{bmatrix} (\tilde{\boldsymbol{\Sigma}}^{-1} \otimes (\boldsymbol{Z}'\boldsymbol{Z})^{-1}) \begin{bmatrix} \boldsymbol{Z}'\boldsymbol{y}_1 \\ \vdots \\ \boldsymbol{Z}'\boldsymbol{y}_H \end{bmatrix}$$
$$= \begin{bmatrix} (\boldsymbol{Z}'\boldsymbol{X}_1)^{-1}\boldsymbol{Z}'\boldsymbol{y}_1 \\ \vdots \\ (\boldsymbol{Z}'\boldsymbol{X}_H)^{-1}\boldsymbol{Z}'\boldsymbol{y}_H \end{bmatrix} = \begin{bmatrix} \tilde{\boldsymbol{\delta}}_1 \\ \vdots \\ \tilde{\boldsymbol{\delta}}_H \end{bmatrix}. \quad (13.1.26)$$

Compare this formula with (8.2.28).

4. $\mathbf{B} = I_H$.

Every equation in the system is a proper regression, such that all the columns of X_i are also columns of Z. Then $Q_Z X_i = X_i$ and the estimator reduces to

$$\begin{bmatrix} \tilde{\delta}_1^* \\ \vdots \\ \tilde{\delta}_H^* \end{bmatrix} = \begin{bmatrix} \tilde{\sigma}^{11} X_1' X_1 & \cdots & \tilde{\sigma}^{1H} X_1' X_H \\ \vdots & \ddots & \vdots \\ \tilde{\sigma}^{H1} X_H' X_1 & \cdots & \tilde{\sigma}^{HH} X_H' X_H \end{bmatrix}^{-1} \begin{bmatrix} \sum_{j=1}^H \tilde{\sigma}^{1j} X_1' y_j \\ \vdots \\ \sum_{j=1}^H \tilde{\sigma}^{Hj} X_H' y_j \end{bmatrix}. \tag{13.1.27}$$

This is the *seemingly unrelated regressions* (SUR) estimator due to Zellner (1962). The feasible form of the estimator will be computed in this instance by estimating $\tilde{\Sigma}$ from the residuals from OLS estimation of each equation.

13.2 Full Information Maximum Likelihood

13.2.1 Set-up and Computation

Suppose the model (13.1.1) + (13.1.2) is complete, so that $H = G$ and $\mathbf{B}$ is $G \times G$ invertible. Also assume that

$$u_t | \mathcal{I}_t \sim \mathrm{N}(\mathbf{0}, \boldsymbol{\Sigma}). \tag{13.2.1}$$

Full specification of the conditional distribution of y_t permits construction of the approximate maximum likelihood estimator for the system, although when the equations are dynamic some small-order terms must be neglected; compare §11.2.3, noting the remarks therein about the start-up conditions. Subject to such omissions, the joint density of the sample is

$$D(y_1, z_1, \ldots, y_n, z_n) = \prod_{t=1}^{n} D(y_t|\mathcal{I}_t) D(z_t|\mathcal{Y}_{t-1}, \mathcal{Z}_{t-1}) \tag{13.2.2}$$

where, applying the formula in (B.9.1),[4]

$$\begin{aligned} D(y_t|\mathcal{I}_t) &= |\det \mathbf{B}| D(u_t) \\ &= (2\pi)^{-G/2} |\det \mathbf{B}| (\det \boldsymbol{\Sigma})^{-1/2} \exp\left\{-\tfrac{1}{2} u_t' \boldsymbol{\Sigma}^{-1} u_t\right\}. \end{aligned} \tag{13.2.3}$$

Assuming weak exogeneity of z_t, the product of these factors alone is taken as the likelihood function. In full-sample notation the $n \times G$ matrix whose transposed rows are $u_t = \mathbf{B} y_t - \boldsymbol{\Gamma} z_t$ may be written

$$U = Y\mathbf{B}' - Z\boldsymbol{\Gamma}'. \tag{13.2.4}$$

Omitting the constants, the log-likelihood function is written

$$L(\mathbf{B}, \boldsymbol{\Gamma}, \boldsymbol{\Sigma}) = n \ln |\det \mathbf{B}| - \frac{n}{2} \ln \det \boldsymbol{\Sigma}$$

---

[4] $|\det \mathbf{B}|$ denotes the absolute value of the determinant of $\mathbf{B}$. The notational conventions are somewhat confusing here, since $|\mathbf{B}|$ is also used for the determinant of $\mathbf{B}$. The rule is: if what is inside $|\cdot|$ is a matrix, the resulting expression is a determinant.

$$-\tfrac{1}{2}\operatorname{tr}\mathbf{\Sigma}^{-1}(\mathbf{B}\boldsymbol{Y}'-\mathbf{\Gamma}\boldsymbol{Z}')(\boldsymbol{Y}\mathbf{B}'-\boldsymbol{Z}\mathbf{\Gamma}') \tag{13.2.5}$$

where the last term is just another way of writing

$$-\tfrac{1}{2}\sum_{t=1}^{n}(\boldsymbol{y}_t-\mathbf{\Gamma}\boldsymbol{z}_t)'\mathbf{\Sigma}^{-1}(\mathbf{B}\boldsymbol{y}_t-\mathbf{\Gamma}\boldsymbol{z}_t). \tag{13.2.6}$$

The first step is to concentrate the likelihood with respect to $\mathbf{\Sigma}$, holding $\mathbf{B}$ and $\mathbf{\Gamma}$ fixed. Applying formulae (A.9.5) and (A.9.7) to (13.2.5), not forgetting that $\ln\det\mathbf{\Sigma}^{-1} = -\ln\det\mathbf{\Sigma}$, yields the first-order conditions

$$\frac{\partial L}{\partial\mathbf{\Sigma}^{-1}} = \frac{n}{2}\mathbf{\Sigma} - \tfrac{1}{2}(\mathbf{B}\boldsymbol{Y}'-\mathbf{\Gamma}\boldsymbol{Z}')(\boldsymbol{Y}\mathbf{B}'-\boldsymbol{Z}\mathbf{\Gamma}') = \mathbf{0} \tag{13.2.7}$$

which solve to give

$$\hat{\mathbf{\Sigma}}(\mathbf{B},\mathbf{\Gamma}) = \frac{(\mathbf{B}\boldsymbol{Y}'-\mathbf{\Gamma}\boldsymbol{Z}')(\boldsymbol{Y}\mathbf{B}'-\boldsymbol{Z}\mathbf{\Gamma}')}{n}. \tag{13.2.8}$$

Substituting the latter formula for $\mathbf{\Sigma}$ in (13.2.5), notice that there is a cancellation in the final term which reduces to $Gn/2$. The concentrated log-likelihood function is (again omitting constants)

$$L^*(\mathbf{B},\mathbf{\Gamma}) = n\ln|\det\mathbf{B}| - \frac{n}{2}\ln\det\hat{\mathbf{\Sigma}}(\mathbf{B},\mathbf{\Gamma}). \tag{13.2.9}$$

Maximizing this function with respect to the unrestricted elements of $\mathbf{B}$ and $\mathbf{\Gamma}$, which must be done numerically, defines the full information maximum likelihood (FIML) estimator. [5] This estimator was proposed by Koopmans, Rubin and Leipnik (1950) at a remarkably early date in the development of econometrics, when few computers that could make it an operational procedure were in existence.

13.2.2 Properties

Maximum likelihood theory (see §11.3) tells us that subject to correct specification these estimates are CAN, and efficient in the CAN class. However, OE theory can also be used to show that the CAN property of FIML holds without the Gaussianity assumption, although not the asymptotic efficiency, which is an application of the Cramér–Rao Theorem. A direct approach to the proof of this proposition by establishing the conditions of Theorem 9.3.1 is outlined in §13.4.4. A straightforward alternative, although one still needing some fairly heroic manipulations to switch notation from $\mathbf{B},\mathbf{\Gamma}$ to $\tilde{\boldsymbol{\delta}}^*$ and construct the derivatives, is to show that FIML has the same asymptotic distribution as 3SLS applied to the full system. We will not pursue this course rigorously,[6] but an informal comparison of the two procedures is instructive.

Recall from (8.2.23) the relation

$$\boldsymbol{Q}_Z\boldsymbol{X}_1 = \boldsymbol{Z}\hat{\boldsymbol{P}}^{*\prime}_{1A} \quad (M\times k_1) \tag{13.2.10}$$

[5] See §9.2 and §11.3.5 on methods for optimizing the likelihood function.

[6] See for example Schmidt (1976) or Theil (1971) for a formal proof.

where $\hat{\boldsymbol{P}}^{*\prime}_{1A} = \left[\hat{\boldsymbol{\Pi}}^{*\prime}_{1A}\ \boldsymbol{H}_1\right]$. The first g_1 columns of this matrix, after transposition, are consistent but generally inefficient estimates of certain rows of the matrix $\boldsymbol{\Pi} = \mathbf{B}^{-1}\boldsymbol{\Gamma}$. The full collection of these estimates is $\hat{\boldsymbol{\Pi}} = \boldsymbol{Y}'\boldsymbol{Z}(\boldsymbol{Z}'\boldsymbol{Z})^{-1}$. If $\tilde{\mathbf{B}}$ and $\tilde{\boldsymbol{\Gamma}}$ are the 3SLS estimates of the structural matrices, with the unknown elements replaced by the relevant elements of $\tilde{\boldsymbol{\delta}}^*$ in (13.1.10), it is clear that $\hat{\boldsymbol{\Pi}} \neq \tilde{\mathbf{B}}^{-1}\tilde{\boldsymbol{\Gamma}}$. In other words, 3SLS fails to reconcile all the information in the data, such that all the estimates are internally consistent with each other. In the same way, if $\boldsymbol{\Sigma}$ is estimated from the 3SLS residuals, this will not agree with the 2SLS-based estimator $\hat{\boldsymbol{\Sigma}}$ used to obtain it.

In FIML, by contrast, all the parameter estimates are consistent with one another. Let

$$\hat{\boldsymbol{P}}'_{iA} = \left[[\hat{\mathbf{B}}^{-1}\hat{\boldsymbol{\Gamma}}]^*_{iA}\ \boldsymbol{H}_i\right] \quad i = 1, \dots, G \tag{13.2.11}$$

where $\hat{\mathbf{B}}$ and $\hat{\boldsymbol{\Gamma}}$ are understood to contain the elements of the vector $\hat{\boldsymbol{\delta}}$, the FIML estimator, and similarly let $\hat{\sigma}^{ij}$ denote the elements of $\hat{\boldsymbol{\Sigma}}^{-1}$, where $\hat{\boldsymbol{\Sigma}} = n^{-1}\hat{\boldsymbol{U}}'\hat{\boldsymbol{U}}$ computed from (13.2.4), also evaluated at $\hat{\boldsymbol{\delta}}$. The estimator can be characterized as the solution to the equations

$$\begin{bmatrix} \hat{\boldsymbol{\delta}}_1 \\ \vdots \\ \hat{\boldsymbol{\delta}}_G \end{bmatrix} = \begin{bmatrix} \hat{\sigma}^{11}\hat{\boldsymbol{P}}_{1A}\boldsymbol{Z}'\boldsymbol{X}_1 & \cdots & \hat{\sigma}^{1G}\hat{\boldsymbol{P}}_{1A}\boldsymbol{Z}'\boldsymbol{X}_G \\ \vdots & \ddots & \vdots \\ \hat{\sigma}^{G1}\hat{\boldsymbol{P}}_{GA}\boldsymbol{Z}'\boldsymbol{X}_1 & \cdots & \hat{\sigma}^{GG}\hat{\boldsymbol{P}}_{GA}\boldsymbol{Z}'\boldsymbol{X}_G \end{bmatrix}^{-1} \begin{bmatrix} \sum_{j=1}^G \hat{\sigma}^{1j}\hat{\boldsymbol{P}}_{1A}\boldsymbol{Z}'\boldsymbol{y}_j \\ \vdots \\ \sum_{j=1}^G \hat{\sigma}^{Gj}\hat{\boldsymbol{P}}_{GA}\boldsymbol{Z}'\boldsymbol{y}_j \end{bmatrix} \tag{13.2.12}$$

There is no closed form solution to these equations, but one might attempt to solve them by the Jacobi iteration method.[7] Starting with the 2SLS estimator, say $\hat{\boldsymbol{\delta}}^{(0)}$, compute the sequence

$$\begin{bmatrix} \hat{\boldsymbol{\delta}}_1^{(r+1)} \\ \vdots \\ \hat{\boldsymbol{\delta}}_G^{(r+1)} \end{bmatrix} = \begin{bmatrix} \hat{\sigma}^{(r)11}\hat{\boldsymbol{P}}^{(r)}_{1A}\boldsymbol{Z}'\boldsymbol{X}_1 & \cdots & \hat{\sigma}^{(r)1G}\hat{\boldsymbol{P}}^{(r)}_{1A}\boldsymbol{Z}'\boldsymbol{X}_G \\ \vdots & \ddots & \vdots \\ \hat{\sigma}^{(r)G1}\hat{\boldsymbol{P}}^{(r)}_{GA}\boldsymbol{Z}'\boldsymbol{X}_1 & \cdots & \hat{\sigma}^{(r)GG}\hat{\boldsymbol{P}}^{(r)}_{GA}\boldsymbol{Z}'\boldsymbol{X}_G \end{bmatrix}^{-1} \times \begin{bmatrix} \sum_{j=1}^G \hat{\sigma}^{(r)1j}\hat{\boldsymbol{P}}^{(r)}_{1A}\boldsymbol{Z}'\boldsymbol{y}_j \\ \vdots \\ \sum_{j=1}^G \hat{\sigma}^{(r)Gj}\hat{\boldsymbol{P}}^{(r)}_{GA}\boldsymbol{Z}'\boldsymbol{y}_j \end{bmatrix} \tag{13.2.13}$$

iteratively, for $r = 0, 1, 2, 3, \dots$, where the (r) superscripts on the right-hand side denote evaluation at the point $\hat{\boldsymbol{\delta}}^{(r)}$. It can be shown that the FIML estimator is a fixed point of these iterations.

The application of Theorem 9.4.1 now yields the asymptotic equivalence of FIML and 3SLS, as shown by Rothenberg and Leenders (1964). $\hat{\boldsymbol{\Pi}}^*$ and $\tilde{\boldsymbol{\Sigma}}$ are consistent estimators of $\boldsymbol{\Pi}$ and $\boldsymbol{\Sigma}$, as is $\hat{\boldsymbol{\delta}}^{(0)}$ of $\boldsymbol{\delta}$, and in a large enough sample, the iterations in (13.2.13) converge in a single step.

[7] See for example Quandt (1983).

13.2.3 Least Generalized Variance

A special case of interest is $\mathbf{B} = \boldsymbol{I}_G$, which corresponds to the SUR model. For this case the FIML estimator reduces to the minimizer of

$$|\hat{\boldsymbol{\Sigma}}(\boldsymbol{\Gamma})| = \left|\frac{(\boldsymbol{Y} - \boldsymbol{Z}\boldsymbol{\Gamma})'(\boldsymbol{Y} - \boldsymbol{Z}\boldsymbol{\Gamma})}{n}\right|. \tag{13.2.14}$$

This is called the *least generalized variance* estimator, and it corresponds to the case of (13.1.27) (with the $\boldsymbol{\delta}_j$ representing the unrestricted elements of the jth row of $\boldsymbol{\Gamma}$) where the FIML property, that the estimate of the covariance matrix is consistent with the structural parameter estimates, is satisfied. In the case where $\boldsymbol{\Gamma}$ is unrestricted, so that every variable in $\boldsymbol{z}_t$ appears in every equation, minimizing (13.2.14) turns out to yield OLS estimation of each equation. This may be shown by differentiating the criterion function. Using (A.9.4) and exploiting the symmetry of $\hat{\boldsymbol{\Sigma}}$ and the chain rule yields the derivative formula

$$\frac{\partial|\hat{\boldsymbol{\Sigma}}|}{\partial\gamma_{jk}} = \sum_p\sum_q \frac{\partial|\hat{\boldsymbol{\Sigma}}|}{\partial\hat{\sigma}_{pq}}\frac{\partial\hat{\sigma}_{pq}}{\partial\gamma_{jk}} = 2\sum_q \mathrm{adj}(\hat{\boldsymbol{\Sigma}})_{jq}(\boldsymbol{y}_q - \boldsymbol{Z}\boldsymbol{\gamma}_q)'\boldsymbol{z}_k \tag{13.2.15}$$

where γ_{jk} is the coefficient of z_{kt} in equation j, and $\boldsymbol{z}_k$ is the kth column of $\boldsymbol{Z}$. Stacking these expressions into a matrix produces

$$\frac{\partial|\hat{\boldsymbol{\Sigma}}|}{\partial\boldsymbol{\Gamma}} = 2\,\mathrm{adj}(\hat{\boldsymbol{\Sigma}})(\boldsymbol{Y}' - \boldsymbol{\Gamma}\boldsymbol{Z}')\boldsymbol{Z} \tag{13.2.16}$$

and equating to zero and solving for $\boldsymbol{\Gamma}$ yields the unrestricted OLS formula

$$\hat{\boldsymbol{\Gamma}} = \boldsymbol{Y}'\boldsymbol{Z}(\boldsymbol{Z}'\boldsymbol{Z})^{-1}. \tag{13.2.17}$$

13.3 Least Generalized Variance Ratio

13.3.1 Subsystem Estimation

FIML is an estimator for a complete system, with the number of equations equal to the number of endogenous variables. In other words, $\mathbf{B}$ must be square. However, there is a related OE estimator that applies to incomplete systems, and reduces to FIML in the complete system case. Let the set-up be given as before by model (13.1.1), with $H < G$ possible. The proposed criterion function is the generalized variance ratio, or ratio of determinants, taking the form

$$\Lambda(\mathbf{B},\boldsymbol{\Gamma}) = \frac{|\hat{\boldsymbol{\Sigma}}(\mathbf{B},\boldsymbol{\Gamma})|}{|\mathbf{B}\boldsymbol{W}\mathbf{B}'|} \tag{13.3.1}$$

where $\boldsymbol{W} = n^{-1}(\boldsymbol{Y}'\boldsymbol{Y} - \boldsymbol{Y}'\boldsymbol{Z}(\boldsymbol{Z}'\boldsymbol{Z})^{-1}\boldsymbol{Z}'\boldsymbol{Y})$, $\boldsymbol{Y}$ $(n \times H)$ and $\boldsymbol{Z}$ $(n \times M)$ are the matrices of the variables, and $\hat{\boldsymbol{\Sigma}}$ is as in (13.2.8).

Notice first that (13.2.8) has an alternative form,

$$\hat{\boldsymbol{\Sigma}} = \mathbf{B}\frac{(\boldsymbol{Y}' - \boldsymbol{\Pi}\boldsymbol{Z}')(\boldsymbol{Y} - \boldsymbol{Z}\boldsymbol{\Pi}')}{n}\mathbf{B}' \tag{13.3.2}$$

where $\mathbf{\Pi} = \mathbf{B}^{-1}\mathbf{\Gamma}$ (for any choice of $\mathbf{B}$ and $\mathbf{\Gamma}$) whereas

$$\mathbf{B}W\mathbf{B}' = \mathbf{B}\frac{(Y' - \hat{\mathbf{\Pi}}Z')(Y - Z\hat{\mathbf{\Pi}}')}{n}\mathbf{B}' \tag{13.3.3}$$

where $\hat{\mathbf{\Pi}} = Y'Z(Z'Z)^{-1}$ is the unrestricted OLS estimator of the reduced form coefficients. As shown in §13.2.3, the latter matrix is the solution to the problem of minimizing $|\hat{\mathbf{\Sigma}}(\mathbf{\Pi})|$ unrestrictedly; read $\mathbf{\Pi}$ for $\mathbf{\Gamma}$ in (13.2.17) for this particular case. It follows that $\Lambda(\mathbf{B},\mathbf{\Gamma}) \geq 1$ for all choices of $\mathbf{B}$ and $\mathbf{\Gamma}$. Moreover, notice that $\mathbf{B}W\mathbf{B}'$ and $\hat{\mathbf{\Sigma}}(\mathbf{B},\mathbf{\Gamma})$ provide two alternative estimators of $\mathbf{\Sigma}$, since $W \xrightarrow{\text{pr}} \mathbf{\Omega} = E[(y_t - \mathbf{\Pi}z_t)(y_t - \mathbf{\Pi}z_t)']$ and $\mathbf{\Sigma} = \mathbf{B}\mathbf{\Omega}\mathbf{B}'$. If $\hat{\mathbf{B}}$ and $\hat{\mathbf{\Gamma}}$ are consistent for $\mathbf{B}$ and $\mathbf{\Gamma}$, it must therefore be the case that

$$\Lambda(\hat{\mathbf{B}},\hat{\mathbf{\Gamma}}) \xrightarrow{\text{pr}} 1. \tag{13.3.4}$$

Applying Theorem 9.3.1 shows that under suitable conditions the minimizer of Λ (the LGVR estimator) is a consistent estimator of $(\mathbf{B},\mathbf{\Gamma})$, and OE theory can likewise show that the estimator is CAN.

The second point to note about (13.3.1) is that if $\mathbf{B}$ is actually $G \times G$, then

$$\ln \Lambda(\mathbf{B},\mathbf{\Gamma}) = \ln \det \hat{\mathbf{\Sigma}}(\mathbf{B},\mathbf{\Gamma}) - 2\ln|\det \mathbf{B}| - \ln \det W \tag{13.3.5}$$

and since W depends only on data and not on unknown parameters, this minimand is equivalent apart from sign and irrelevant constants to the maximand in (13.2.9). It is also possible to show (we will not do this) that if the likelihood function is set up for a complete Gaussian system in which a subset of the equations are unrestricted reduced forms, the parameters of these equations can be concentrated out analytically and the resulting estimator of the remaining parameters is identical to LGVR. Hence, this estimator has a ML interpretation, and is often called the (subsystem) *limited information maximum likelihood* (LIML)estimator.

13.3.2 LIML

The original proposal for LIML due to Anderson and Rubin (1949, 1950) relates to the case $H = 1$, in which the two determinants reduce to scalar variance estimates. In this case it is referred to as least variance ratio (LVR), and as ordinary LIML for Gaussian models. Assume that the equation in question is the first in the system. As in §8.2.2 put $\beta_1 = (\beta_{1A}', 0')'$ and $\gamma_1 = (\gamma_{1A}', 0')'$ for the top rows of $\mathbf{B}$ and $\mathbf{\Gamma}$ respectively. Then the minimand is

$$\Lambda(\beta_{1A}, \gamma_{1A}) = \frac{\hat{\sigma}_{11}(\beta_{1A}, \gamma_{1A})}{\beta_1' W \beta_1} = \frac{\hat{\sigma}_{11}(\beta_{1A}, \gamma_{1A})}{\beta_{1A}' W^* \beta_{1A}} \tag{13.3.6}$$

where

$$\hat{\sigma}_{11}(\beta_{1A}, \gamma_{1A}) = \frac{(Y_{1A}^+\beta_{1A} - Z_{1A}\gamma_{1A})'(Y_{1A}^+\beta_{1A} - Z_{1A}\gamma_{1A})}{n} \tag{13.3.7}$$

where $Y_{1A}^+ = [y_1 \; Y_{1A}]$, and also

$$W^* = \frac{Y_{1A}^{+\prime} Y_{1A} - Y_{1A}^{+\prime} Z(Z'Z)^{-1}Z'Y_{1A}^+}{n}. \tag{13.3.8}$$

Since γ_{1A} appears only in the numerator of (13.3.6) it can be concentrated out by least squares. Regressing $\boldsymbol{Y}_{1A}^{+}\boldsymbol{\beta}_{1A}$ on $\boldsymbol{Z}_{1A}$, yields

$$\hat{\gamma}_{1A}(\boldsymbol{\beta}_{1A}) = (\boldsymbol{Z}_{1A}'\boldsymbol{Z}_{1A})^{-1}\boldsymbol{Z}_{1A}'\boldsymbol{Y}_{1A}^{+}\boldsymbol{\beta}_{1A}. \tag{13.3.9}$$

and substituting this formula in (13.3.7) and simplifying gives

$$\hat{\sigma}_{11}(\boldsymbol{\beta}_{1A}, \hat{\gamma}_{1A}) = \boldsymbol{\beta}_{1A}'\boldsymbol{W}^{**}\boldsymbol{\beta}_{1A} \tag{13.3.10}$$

where

$$\boldsymbol{W}^{**} = \frac{\boldsymbol{Y}_{1A}^{+\prime}\boldsymbol{Y}_{1A}^{+} - \boldsymbol{Y}_{1A}^{+\prime}\boldsymbol{Z}_{1A}(\boldsymbol{Z}_{1A}'\boldsymbol{Z}_{1A})^{-1}\boldsymbol{Z}_{1A}'\boldsymbol{Y}_{1A}^{+}}{n}. \tag{13.3.11}$$

The concentrated minimand is therefore

$$\Lambda^*(\boldsymbol{\beta}_{1A}) = \frac{\boldsymbol{\beta}_{1A}'\boldsymbol{W}^{**}\boldsymbol{\beta}_{1A}}{\boldsymbol{\beta}_{1A}'\boldsymbol{W}^{*}\boldsymbol{\beta}_{1A}} \tag{13.3.12}$$

and the first-order conditions for a minimum with respect to $\boldsymbol{\beta}_{1A}$ are

$$\frac{\partial\Lambda^*}{\partial\boldsymbol{\beta}_{1A}} = \frac{\boldsymbol{W}^{**}\boldsymbol{\beta}_{1A}}{\boldsymbol{\beta}_{1A}'\boldsymbol{W}^{*}\boldsymbol{\beta}_{1A}} - \Lambda^*\frac{\boldsymbol{W}^{*}\boldsymbol{\beta}_{1A}}{\boldsymbol{\beta}_{1A}'\boldsymbol{W}^{*}\boldsymbol{\beta}_{1A}} = \mathbf{0}. \tag{13.3.13}$$

Evidently the solution, $\hat{\boldsymbol{\beta}}_{1A}$ say, is an eigenvector of the generalized eigenvalue problem

$$|\boldsymbol{W}^{**} - \lambda\boldsymbol{W}^{*}| = 0 \tag{13.3.14}$$

where $\lambda = \Lambda^*(\hat{\boldsymbol{\beta}}_{1A})$ is the corresponding eigenvalue – necessarily, this has to be the *smallest* eigenvalue of (13.3.14). The solution is unique in view of the normalization restriction, such that $\hat{\boldsymbol{\beta}}_{1A} = (1, \hat{\boldsymbol{\beta}}_{1A}^{*\prime})'$. The estimator of γ_{1A} is given by

$$\hat{\gamma}_{1A} = (\boldsymbol{Z}_{1A}'\boldsymbol{Z}_{1A})^{-1}\boldsymbol{Z}_{1A}'\boldsymbol{Y}_{1A}^{+}\hat{\boldsymbol{\beta}}_{1A}. \tag{13.3.15}$$

13.3.3 Asymptotic Equivalence of LIML and 2SLS

Just as FIML and 3SLS are asymptotically equivalent estimators, so are LIML and 2SLS. The implementation of 2SLS being so much simpler in practice, the LIML procedure has been little used in applied work. To demonstrate this equivalence, write $\boldsymbol{Q}_{Z1A} = \boldsymbol{Z}_{1A}(\boldsymbol{Z}_{1A}'\boldsymbol{Z}_{1A})^{-1}\boldsymbol{Z}_{1A}'$, such that $\boldsymbol{W}^{*} = \boldsymbol{Y}_{1A}^{+\prime}\boldsymbol{Q}_Z\boldsymbol{Y}_{1A}^{+}$ and $\boldsymbol{W}^{**} = \boldsymbol{Y}_{1A}^{+\prime}\boldsymbol{Q}_{Z1A}\boldsymbol{Y}_{1A}^{+}$. Then the equations to be solved for $\hat{\boldsymbol{\beta}}_{1A}$ take the form

$$(\boldsymbol{W}^{**} - \lambda\boldsymbol{W}^{*})\hat{\boldsymbol{\beta}}_{1A} = \left[\boldsymbol{Y}_{1A}^{+\prime}\{\boldsymbol{I} - \boldsymbol{Q}_{Z1A} - \lambda(\boldsymbol{I} - \boldsymbol{Q}_Z)\}\boldsymbol{Y}_{1A}^{+}\right]\hat{\boldsymbol{\beta}}_{1A} = \mathbf{0}. \tag{13.3.16}$$

Let $\boldsymbol{P} = \boldsymbol{I} - \boldsymbol{Q}_{Z1A} - \lambda(\boldsymbol{I} - \boldsymbol{Q}_Z)$ and partition these $g_1 + 1$ equations as

$$\begin{bmatrix} \boldsymbol{y}_1' \\ \boldsymbol{Y}_{1A}' \end{bmatrix} \boldsymbol{P} \begin{bmatrix} \boldsymbol{y}_1 & \boldsymbol{Y}_{1A} \end{bmatrix} \begin{bmatrix} 1 \\ \hat{\boldsymbol{\beta}}_{1A}^* \end{bmatrix} = \begin{bmatrix} \boldsymbol{y}_1'\boldsymbol{P}\boldsymbol{y}_1 - \boldsymbol{y}_1'\boldsymbol{P}\boldsymbol{Y}_{1A}\hat{\boldsymbol{\beta}}_{1A}^* \\ \boldsymbol{Y}_{1A}'\boldsymbol{P}\boldsymbol{y}_1 - \boldsymbol{Y}_{1A}'\boldsymbol{P}\boldsymbol{Y}_{1A}\hat{\boldsymbol{\beta}}_{1A}^* \end{bmatrix} = \begin{bmatrix} 0 \\ \mathbf{0} \end{bmatrix} \tag{13.3.17}$$

The last g_1 equations yield the solution

$$-\hat{\boldsymbol{\beta}}_{1A}^* = (\boldsymbol{Y}_{1A}'\boldsymbol{P}\boldsymbol{Y}_{1A})^{-1}\boldsymbol{Y}_{1A}'\boldsymbol{P}\boldsymbol{y}_1$$

$$= \left[\{\lambda Y_{1A}'Q_Z Y_{1A} + (1-\lambda) Y_{1A}' Y_{1A}\} - Y_{1A}' Q_{Z1A} Y_{1A}\right]^{-1}$$
$$\times \left[\{\lambda Y_{1A}'Q_Z Y_{1A} + (1-\lambda) Y_{1A}' y_1\} - Y_{1A}' Q_{Z1A} y_1\right]. \quad (13.3.18)$$

The partitioned inverse formula shows that equations (13.3.18) and (13.3.15) can be written together as

$$\hat{\delta}_1(\lambda) = \begin{bmatrix} -\hat{\beta}_{1A}^* \\ \hat{\gamma}_{1A} \end{bmatrix} = \begin{bmatrix} \lambda Y_{1A}'Q_Z Y_{1A} + (1-\lambda) Y_{1A}' Y_{1A} & Y_{1A}' Z_{1A} \\ Z_{1A}' Y_{1A} & Z_{1A}' Z_{1A} \end{bmatrix}^{-1} \times \begin{bmatrix} \lambda Y_{1A}' Q_Z y_1 + (1-\lambda) Y_{1A}' y_1 \\ Z_{1A}' y_1 \end{bmatrix}. \quad (13.3.19)$$

Since $\lambda \xrightarrow{\text{pr}} 1$ it is evident that (13.3.19) is converging to the same probability limit as the 2SLS estimator, and given that 2SLS is consistent, so is LIML. What has yet to be established is the *rate* of convergence. While $\hat{\delta}_1(\lambda) - \delta_1 = O_p(n^{-\alpha})$ where $\alpha > 0$, we do not yet know what α is.[8] In fact, $\alpha = \frac{1}{2}$, and it follows that LIML and 2SLS have the same asymptotic distribution. To show this, first write

$$\lambda - 1 = \frac{\hat{\beta}_{1A}' W^{**} \hat{\beta}_{1A}}{\hat{\beta}_{1A}' W^{*} \hat{\beta}_{1A}} - 1 = \frac{\hat{\beta}_{1A}' (W^{**} - W^{*}) \hat{\beta}_{1A}}{\hat{\beta}_{1A}' W^{*} \hat{\beta}_{1A}}. \quad (13.3.20)$$

Using (13.3.15), the numerator is

$$\begin{aligned} \hat{\beta}_{1A}'(W^{**} - W^{*})\hat{\beta}_{1A} &= \frac{\hat{\beta}_{1A}' Y_{1A}^{+\prime} Q_Z Y_{1A}^{+} \hat{\beta}_{1A}}{n} - \frac{\hat{\beta}_{1A}' Y_{1A}^{+\prime} Q_{Z1A} Y_{1A}^{+} \hat{\beta}_{1A}}{n} \\ &= \hat{\beta}_1' \hat{\Pi} \left(\frac{Z'Z}{n}\right) \hat{\Pi}' \hat{\beta}_1 - \hat{\gamma}_{1A}' \left(\frac{Z_{1A}' Z_{1A}}{n}\right) \hat{\gamma}_{1A} \\ &= (\hat{\beta}_1' \hat{\Pi} - \hat{\gamma}_1') \left(\frac{Z'Z}{n}\right) (\hat{\Pi}' \hat{\beta}_1 - \hat{\gamma}_1) \end{aligned} \quad (13.3.21)$$

where $\hat{\beta}_1 = (\hat{\beta}_{1A}', 0')'$, $\hat{\gamma}_1 = (\hat{\gamma}_{1A}', 0')'$, and $\hat{\Pi} = Y'Z(Z'Z)^{-1}$. Since $\hat{\Pi} - \Pi = O(n^{-1/2})$ and $\Pi'\beta_1 = \gamma_1$ by definition of Π, it follows that

$$\begin{aligned} \hat{\Pi}' \hat{\beta}_1 - \hat{\gamma}_1 &= (\hat{\Pi} - \Pi)' \hat{\beta}_1 + \Pi' (\hat{\beta}_1 - \beta_1) - (\hat{\gamma}_1 - \gamma_1) \\ &= O_p(\max\{n^{-\alpha}, n^{-1/2}\}) \end{aligned} \quad (13.3.22)$$

and hence $\lambda - 1 = O_p(\max\{n^{-2\alpha}, n^{-1}\})$.

Now,

$$\hat{\delta}_1(\lambda) - \delta_1 = \begin{bmatrix} \lambda \frac{Y_{1A}' Q_Z Y_{1A}}{n} + (1-\lambda) \frac{Y_{1A}' Y_{1A}}{n} & \frac{Z_{1A}' Y_{1A}}{n} \\ \frac{Y_{1A}' Z_{1A}}{n} & \frac{Z_{1A} Z_{1A}}{n} \end{bmatrix}^{-1}$$

[8] This is a slight simplification. It is possible to have a random sequence converge in probability to 0 slower that $n^{-\alpha}$ for any $\alpha > 0$. For example, this is true of $(\ln n)^{-1}$. Taking this possibility into account would complicate the argument without adding anything material.

$$\times \begin{bmatrix} \lambda \dfrac{Y_{1A}' Q_Z u_1}{n} + (1-\lambda)\dfrac{Y_{1A} u_1}{n} \\ \dfrac{Z_{1A}' u_1}{n} \end{bmatrix} \tag{13.3.23}$$

where the inverse matrix is $O_p(1)$ and in the vector on the right, the terms $n^{-1} Y_{1A}' Q_Z u_1$ and $n^{-1} Z_{1A}' u_1$ are $O_p(n^{-1/2})$. However, $n^{-1} Y_{1A}' u_1 = O_p(1)$ since the Y_{1A} are endogenous and correlated with the u_1. It follows that

$$\hat{\delta}_1(\lambda) - \delta_1 = O_p(\max\{n^{-2\alpha}, n^{-1/2}\}) \tag{13.3.24}$$

and hence that $\alpha = \min\{2\alpha, \frac{1}{2}\}$. Since $\alpha > 0$, this implies $\alpha = \frac{1}{2}$. Hence $\hat{\delta}_1(\lambda) - \delta_1 = O_p(n^{-1/2})$.

By the same token $\lambda - 1 = O_p(n^{-1})$, and hence

$$\begin{aligned} \frac{1}{\sqrt{n}} \left(\lambda \frac{Y_{1A}' Q_Z u_1}{n} + (1-\lambda) \frac{Y_{1A} u_1}{n} \right) &= \frac{1}{\sqrt{n}} \lambda Y_{1A}' Q_Z u_1 + O_p(n^{-1/2}) \\ &\underset{\text{asy}}{\sim} \frac{1}{\sqrt{n}} Y_{1A}' Q_Z u_1. \end{aligned} \tag{13.3.25}$$

Therefore by the usual argument from the Cramér Theorem,

$$\sqrt{n}(\hat{\delta}_1(\lambda) - \delta_1) \underset{\text{asy}}{\sim} \left(\operatorname{plim} \begin{bmatrix} \dfrac{Y_{1A}' Q_Z Y_{1A}}{n} & \dfrac{Z_{1A}' Y_{1A}}{n} \\ \dfrac{Y_{1A}' Z_{1A}}{n} & \dfrac{Z_{1A}' Z_{1A}}{n} \end{bmatrix} \right)^{-1} \begin{bmatrix} \dfrac{Y_{1A}' Q_Z u_1}{\sqrt{n}} \\ \dfrac{Y_{1A}' u_1}{\sqrt{n}} \end{bmatrix} \tag{13.3.26}$$

The partitioning aside, it should be evident that the distribution of the vector on the right is that shown in (8.2.48).

13.4 Nonlinear FIML

13.4.1 Preliminaries

The model to be considered next has the form

$$f(y_t, z_t; \alpha) = u_t \quad \mathbb{Y} \times \mathbb{Z} \times \Theta_\alpha \mapsto \mathbb{R}^G \tag{13.4.1}$$

for $t = 1, \ldots, n$ where y_t and u_t are $G \times 1$, z_t is $M \times 1$ and as usual $\mathcal{I}_t$-measurable, $\mathbb{Y}$ and $\mathbb{Z}$ are subsets of $\mathbb{R}^G$ and $\mathbb{R}^M$ respectively, Θ_α is a compact subset of $\mathbb{R}^p$, and it is assumed that (13.1.2) and possibly also (13.2.1) hold at the 'true' point $\alpha = \alpha_0$, an interior point of Θ_α. f is assumed to be differentiable with respect to its first argument everywhere on $\mathbb{Y}$. It is convenient to reparameterize the model in terms of the inverse of Σ, and letting σ^{ij} represent the indicated element of Σ^{-1}, the distinct variance parameters (allowing for symmetry) are

$$\sigma = (\sigma^{11}, \sigma^{12}, \sigma^{22}, \sigma^{13}, \ldots, \sigma^{GG})' \quad (G(G+1)/2 \times 1). \tag{13.4.2}$$

The complete set of parameters is therefore $\boldsymbol{\theta} = (\boldsymbol{\alpha}', \boldsymbol{\sigma}')' \in \Theta = \Theta_\alpha \times \Theta_\sigma$, where Θ_σ is a compact subset of $\mathbb{R}^{G(G+1)/2}$.

This set-up, of course, contains those that have been considered already, and the opportunity has been taken to set out in a rigorous fashion some assumptions that were previously implicit. Among the special cases are the linear simultaneous equations model, and the system that is linear in variables but nonlinear in the parameters. By considering the reduced form, either of these cases can be set up as a nonlinear SUR system with nonlinear cross-equation restrictions on the coefficients. However, the cases to be examined in this section are special, being characterised by the non-existence of closed-form expressions for the reduced form equations

$$\boldsymbol{y}_t = \boldsymbol{\pi}(\boldsymbol{u}_t, \boldsymbol{z}_t; \boldsymbol{\alpha}) \quad \mathbb{R}^G \times \mathbb{Z} \times \Theta_\alpha \mapsto \mathbb{Y}. \tag{13.4.3}$$

These solutions may be obtainable numerically at given values of the argument, but are not guaranteed to exist everywhere without further restrictions on the system. The condition that the structural form-reduced form mapping exists and is 1-1 invertible at all points of $\mathbb{Y} \times \mathbb{Z} \times \Theta$ is called *coherency*.[9] For each t let

$$\boldsymbol{J}_t = \frac{\partial \boldsymbol{f}_t}{\partial \boldsymbol{y}_t'} \quad (G \times G). \tag{13.4.4}$$

These are called the Jacobian matrices of the system. In the linear model (13.1.1) for example, $\boldsymbol{J}_t = \mathbf{B}$ for every t. A necessary condition for coherency is that $|\det \boldsymbol{J}_t| > 0$ at every point of $\mathbb{Y} \times \mathbb{Z} \times \Theta$. See §9.3.1 for the implications of this requirement for defining Θ. In the linear case it means that points on which $|\mathbf{B}| = 0$ have to be excluded from Θ, a restriction that was implicit in the earlier discussion. There are parametric implications in the nonlinear case too, though these can be more subtle.

Consider maximizing the Gaussian log-likelihood function, which (omitting constants as before) takes the form

$$L(\boldsymbol{\alpha}, \boldsymbol{\Sigma}) = \sum_{t=1}^{n} \ln|\det \boldsymbol{J}_t| - \frac{n}{2} \ln\det \boldsymbol{\Sigma} - \tfrac{1}{2} \operatorname{tr} \boldsymbol{\Sigma}^{-1} \boldsymbol{U}'\boldsymbol{U} \tag{13.4.5}$$

where $\boldsymbol{U}$ $(n \times G)$ is the matrix whose rows are $\boldsymbol{u}_t'$; compare (13.2.5).

13.4.2 Computation

After concentrating out $\boldsymbol{\Sigma}$ as for the linear case, the function to be maximised is

$$L^*(\boldsymbol{\alpha}) = \sum_{t=1}^{n} \ln|\det \boldsymbol{J}_t| - \frac{n}{2} \ln\det \hat{\boldsymbol{\Sigma}} \tag{13.4.6}$$

where

$$\hat{\boldsymbol{\Sigma}} = \frac{1}{n} \boldsymbol{U}'\boldsymbol{U}. \tag{13.4.7}$$

---

[9] See Gourieroux, Laffont and Monfort (1980). Note that this usage of the term *coherent* is different from the one in §7.4.

The gradient of the maximand has elements $\partial L^*/\partial\alpha_m$, $m = 1, \dots, p$ equal to the difference of the terms

$$\frac{\partial}{\partial\alpha_m}\sum_t \ln|\det \boldsymbol{J}_t| = \sum_{t=1}^{n}\left(\sum_{i=1}^{G}\sum_{j=1}^{G}(\boldsymbol{J}_t'^{-1})_{ij}\frac{\partial(\boldsymbol{J}_t)_{ij}}{\partial\alpha_m}\right)$$

$$= \sum_{t=1}^{n}\left(\sum_{i=1}^{G}\sum_{j=1}^{G}(\boldsymbol{J}_t'^{-1})_{ij}\frac{\partial^2 u_{it}}{\partial y_{jt}\partial\alpha_m}\right) \tag{13.4.8}$$

and

$$\frac{n}{2}\frac{\partial \ln\det\hat{\boldsymbol{\Sigma}}}{\partial\alpha_m} = \frac{n}{2}\sum_{i=1}^{G}\sum_{j=1}^{G}\frac{\partial\ln\det\hat{\boldsymbol{\Sigma}}}{\partial\hat{\sigma}_{ij}}\frac{\partial\hat{\sigma}_{ij}}{\partial\alpha_m}$$

$$= \sum_{t=1}^{n}\left(\sum_{i=1}^{G}\sum_{j=1}^{G}\hat{\sigma}^{ij}\frac{\partial u_{it}}{\partial\alpha_m}u_{jt}\right). \tag{13.4.9}$$

These formulae, together with L^* itself, are all that are needed to construct an optimization algorithm; see Eisenpress and Greenstadt (1966), Fair and Parke (1980) for details. Equating the difference of the tth terms in parentheses in (13.4.9) and (13.4.8) with the gradient contribution $\partial l_t/\partial\alpha_m$, the BHHH algorithm (see §11.3.5) can be implemented straightforwardly, in principle. However, the heavy computational burden involved in inverting the n matrices $\boldsymbol{J}_t$ at each iteration should be remarked.

13.4.3 Consistency of the MLE

The asymptotic properties of this estimator have been studied by Jorgenson and Laffont (1974), Amemiya (1977, 1982), Gallant and Holly (1980), and Phillips (1982). Let $(\boldsymbol{\sigma}_0, \boldsymbol{\alpha}_0)$ denote the true values of the parameters. On the usual assumption that limiting expectations can be equated with probability limits, it needs to be shown according to Theorem 9.3.3 that

$$\operatorname{plim}\frac{1}{n}\left.\frac{\partial L}{\partial\boldsymbol{\sigma}}\right|_{\boldsymbol{\alpha}_0,\boldsymbol{\sigma}_0} = \mathbf{0} \tag{13.4.10a}$$

$$\operatorname{plim}\frac{1}{n}\left.\frac{\partial L}{\partial\boldsymbol{\alpha}}\right|_{\boldsymbol{\alpha}_0,\boldsymbol{\sigma}_0} = \mathbf{0}. \tag{13.4.10b}$$

Since $\partial L/\partial\boldsymbol{\sigma}$ is a selection of elements from $\partial L/\partial\boldsymbol{\Sigma}^{-1}$, (13.4.10a) follows immediately given the fact that

$$\left.\frac{\partial L}{\partial\boldsymbol{\Sigma}^{-1}}\right|_{\boldsymbol{\alpha}_0,\boldsymbol{\sigma}_0} = \frac{n}{2}\boldsymbol{\Sigma}_0 - \tfrac{1}{2}\boldsymbol{F}(\boldsymbol{\alpha}_0)'\boldsymbol{F}(\boldsymbol{\alpha}_0). \tag{13.4.11}$$

where $\boldsymbol{F}(\cdot)$ is the matrix whose rows are $\boldsymbol{f}(\boldsymbol{y}_t, \boldsymbol{z}_t, \cdot)'$. Next, in view of (13.4.5) we have to evaluate the elements

$$\frac{\partial L}{\partial\alpha_m} = \frac{\partial}{\partial\alpha_m}\left(\sum_{t=1}^{n}\ln|\det\boldsymbol{J}_t| - \tfrac{1}{2}\operatorname{tr}\boldsymbol{\Sigma}^{-1}\boldsymbol{F}'\boldsymbol{F}\right) \tag{13.4.12}$$

for $m = 1, \ldots, p$. It is convenient to define

$$g_{itm} = \frac{\partial f_i(\boldsymbol{y}_t, \boldsymbol{z}_t, \boldsymbol{\alpha})}{\partial \alpha_m} \tag{13.4.13}$$

for $i = 1, \ldots, G$ so that

$$\tfrac{1}{2}\frac{\partial}{\partial \alpha_m} \operatorname{tr} \boldsymbol{\Sigma}^{-1}\boldsymbol{F}'\boldsymbol{F} = \sum_{i=1}^{G}\sum_{j=1}^{G}\sigma^{ij}\sum_{t=1}^{n} g_{itm}u_{jt} \tag{13.4.14}$$

and

$$\frac{\partial}{\partial \alpha_m} \ln|\det \boldsymbol{J}_t| = \sum_{i=1}^{G}\sum_{j=1}^{G}(\boldsymbol{J}_t'^{-1})_{ij}\frac{\partial g_{itm}}{\partial y_{jt}}. \tag{13.4.15}$$

By the chain rule of differentiation,

$$\frac{\partial g_{itm}}{\partial y_{jt}} = \sum_{k=1}^{G}\frac{\partial g_{itm}}{\partial u_{kt}}\frac{\partial u_{kt}}{\partial y_{jt}} \tag{13.4.16}$$

for $j = 1, \ldots, G$, which, in matrix notation is equivalent to

$$\frac{\partial g_{itm}}{\partial \boldsymbol{y}_t} = \boldsymbol{J}_t'\frac{\partial g_{itm}}{\partial \boldsymbol{u}_t}. \tag{13.4.17}$$

Combining (13.4.12), (13.4.14), (13.4.15) and (13.4.17) yields

$$\frac{\partial L}{\partial \alpha_m} = \sum_{t=1}^{n}\sum_{i=1}^{G}\left(\frac{\partial g_{itm}}{\partial u_{it}} - g_{itm}\sum_{j=1}^{G}\sigma^{ij}u_{jt}\right) \quad m = 1, \ldots, p. \tag{13.4.18}$$

Letting $\boldsymbol{g}_{it}$ denote the p vector whose elements are g_{itm} evaluated at the point $(\boldsymbol{\alpha}_0, \boldsymbol{\sigma}_0)$, and $\boldsymbol{\sigma}^i$ the ith column of $\boldsymbol{\Sigma}^{-1}$ and assuming plims and asymptotic expectations may be equated as usual, (13.4.10b) holds if[10]

$$\sum_{i=1}^{G} E\left(\frac{\partial \boldsymbol{g}_{it}}{\partial u_{it}} - \boldsymbol{g}_{it}\boldsymbol{u}_t'\boldsymbol{\sigma}^i \middle| \mathcal{I}_t\right) = \boldsymbol{0} \text{ a.s.} \quad t = 1, \ldots, n. \tag{13.4.19}$$

A useful special case is where there are no cross-equation restrictions so that it is possible to partition $\boldsymbol{\alpha}$ into G vectors $\boldsymbol{\alpha}_i$ ($p_i \times 1$) such that the ith element of $\boldsymbol{f}$ is $f_i(\boldsymbol{y}_t, \boldsymbol{z}_t, \boldsymbol{\alpha}_i)$. Then $g_{itm} = 0$ unless the mth parameter is in $\boldsymbol{\alpha}_i$, and the elements of the vector in (13.4.19) contain most one nonzero term in the sum.

The following lemma establishes a set of sufficient conditions for (13.4.19).

Lemma 13.4.1 Let $\boldsymbol{u}_t \sim \mathrm{N}(\boldsymbol{0}, \boldsymbol{\Sigma})$. If $h(\boldsymbol{u})$ is an absolutely continuous[11] function on $\mathbb{R}^G$, and $E|\partial h/\partial u_i| < \infty$, then

$$E\left(\frac{\partial h}{\partial u_i} - h\sum_j \sigma^{ij}u_j\right) = 0. \quad \square \tag{13.4.20}$$

---

[10] In fact, (13.4.10b) holds if the random variables in (13.4.19) are distributed with a mean of **0** in the limit, but for simplicity we don't consider any case more general than the one stated.

[11] Absolute continuity is a technical property that imposes differentiability of the function at almost all points.

For the formal proof, see the discussions in Phillips (1982), Stein (1981) and Amemiya (1982). A heuristic argument can be sketched as follows. Let

$$\phi = (2\pi)^{-G/2}|\boldsymbol{\Sigma}|^{-1/2}\exp\left\{-\tfrac{1}{2}\boldsymbol{u}'\boldsymbol{\Sigma}^{-1}\boldsymbol{u}\right\}. \tag{13.4.21}$$

Setting $i = 1$, integration by parts with respect to u_1 holding $u_2, \ldots, u_G$ fixed yields

$$\int_{-a}^{a}\left(\frac{\partial h}{\partial u_1} - h\sum_j \sigma^{1j}u_j\right)\phi du_1 = \int_{-a}^{a}\left(\frac{\partial(h\phi)}{\partial u_1}\right)du_1 = [h\phi]_{u_1=-a}^{u_1=a}. \tag{13.4.22}$$

Under the assumptions, the right hand side of (13.4.22) can be shown to converge to 0 as $a \to \infty$, since ϕ does so, whereas integrating the left hand side with respect to $u_2, \ldots, u_G$ yields the expectation in (13.4.20) in the limit.

Letting h correspond to g_{itm}, the lemma clearly contributes to the proof of consistency when the distribution is conditionally Gaussian. However, to prove the required uniform law of large numbers as in (9.3.2), it is clear that $\boldsymbol{J}_t$ must be a nonsingular matrix, with probability 1, at every point of Θ; compare Theorem 9.3.2. This is the coherency requirement noted previously. In view of (13.4.17), the distribution of $\partial g_{itm}/\partial u_{it}$ is also going to depend on this vital condition, and the integrability condition of the lemma will fail without it.

To illustrate, take a nonlinear version of the Keynesian model in §4.2.3 with a log-linear consumption function:

$$\ln C_t = \alpha + \beta \ln Y_t + u_t \tag{13.4.23a}$$

$$Y_t = C_t + I_t \tag{13.4.23b}$$

where $u_t \sim \mathrm{N}(0, \sigma^2)$ and I_t is a nonnegative-valued exogenous variable. Substituting out C_t gives

$$\ln(Y_t - I_t) = \alpha + \beta \ln Y_t + u_t. \tag{13.4.24}$$

Therefore, the Jacobian of the system is

$$J_t = \frac{du_t}{dY_t} = \frac{1}{Y_t - I_t} - \frac{\beta}{Y_t} \tag{13.4.25}$$

and it is clear that if $0 \le \beta < 1$, the coherency condition is satisfied since $J_t > 0$ at every point of the sample space. However, suppose $\beta = 1$, which is not implausible since this is the unit elasticity case. Then, as u_t approaches $-\alpha$ from above, it can be seen that $Y_t \to \infty$, and $J_t \to 0$. The model in incoherent if Θ includes points where $\beta \ge 1$.

13.4.4 Quasi-FIML

Condition (13.4.19) leads to a generic condition for consistency of the quasi-ML procedure, in which the only thing assumed about the disturbances is that (13.1.2) holds. The following result is then available.

Theorem 13.4.1 Suppose

$$f(y_t, z_t, \alpha) = B(z_t, \alpha) y_t + c(z_t, \alpha) \tag{13.4.26}$$

where $B(z_t, \alpha)$ is a matrix of functions that is nonsingular with probability 1 on $\mathbb{Z} \times \Theta$. Then condition (13.4.19) holds.

Proof Recalling (13.4.13), note that

$$g_{it} = L_{it} u_t + k_{it} \tag{13.4.27}$$

where

$$L_{it} = \frac{\partial b_i(z_t, \alpha)'}{\partial \alpha} B(z_t, \alpha_0)^{-1} \quad (p \times G) \tag{13.4.28}$$

where b_i' is the ith row of B and similarly

$$k_{it} = \frac{\partial c_i(z_t, \alpha)}{\partial \alpha} - \frac{\partial b_i(z_t, \alpha)'}{\partial \alpha} B(z_t, \alpha_0)^{-1} c(z_t, \alpha_0) \quad (p \times 1). \tag{13.4.29}$$

Therefore

$$\frac{\partial g_{it}}{\partial u_{it}} - g_{it} u_t' \sigma^i = (L_{it})_i - L_{it} u_t u_t' \sigma^i - k_{it} u_t' \sigma^i. \tag{13.4.30}$$

where $(L_{it})_i$ denotes the ith column of the matrix. The conditional expectation of the second term on the right-hand side of (13.4.30), holding L_{it} and k_{it} fixed and evaluated at α_0, is

$$L_{it} \Sigma \sigma^i = (L_{it})_i \tag{13.4.31}$$

by definition of σ^i, while the third term has conditional expectation zero. Therefore the terms of (13.4.19) are equal to zero a.s. for each i. ∎

The class of models represented by (13.4.26) includes nonlinear SUR models, where $B(z_t, \alpha) = I$, as well as the linear simultaneous setup where B is a constant matrix. This provides the proof of the consistent-OE status of linear FIML that was promised earlier. Clearly, quasi-ML does have a potentially wide range of applications. However, this result also serves as a warning that under general nonlinearities in the endogenous variables, correctness of the Gaussian specification is required. From consideration of counterexamples such as (13.4.23), it appears that (13.4.26) is a necessary condition for consistency. Caution in the use of procedures of this type must be advised.

The example provides an interesting twist to the story, because it might be supposed that the coherency difficulty associated with $\beta = 1$ could be overcome by assuming that the distribution of u_t is truncated below at $-\alpha$. The data must conform to this restriction given $C_t < Y_t$, but it contradicts Gaussianity, so QML must be inconsistent, in one way or the other, if $\beta = 1$ is admitted to the parameter space. This is of course a highly simplified model, and would probably not be entertained if the data actually varied in such a way that these restrictions made a difference to the estimates. The conclusion is nonetheless unexpected, given the popularity of the log-linear specification in applied work and the plausibility of a unit elasticity.

13.5 System GMM

13.5.1 The One-stage Estimator

If both the Gaussianity and the linearity assumptions of the model in (13.4.1) are unavailable, or if only $H < G$ equations of the model are specified, FIML is not an option. An alternative estimator may be sought in a generalization of the GMM procedure of §10.3. Studies of this method include Jorgenson and Laffont (1974), Amemiya (1977), Gallant (1977), and Gallant and Jorgenson (1979). It is commonly known as 'nonlinear three stage least squares' in this literature, but this is clearly a misnomer, and in particular, we want to keep in mind the distinction between regular OEs and those based on preliminary estimates. The question of two-stage estimation was touched on in §9.1.

The model is defined by

$$\boldsymbol{f}(\boldsymbol{y}_t, \boldsymbol{z}_t; \boldsymbol{\alpha}) = \boldsymbol{u}_t \quad \mathbb{Y} \times \mathbb{Z} \times \Theta_\alpha \mapsto \mathbb{R}^H,\ H \leq G \tag{13.5.1}$$

or in other words, a subset of the equations in (13.4.1) where $\boldsymbol{u}_t$ satisfies (13.1.2) when evaluated at $\boldsymbol{\alpha} = \boldsymbol{\alpha}_0$. A convenient notation is found, as before, by stacking the equations. Let $\boldsymbol{U}$ $(n \times H)$ be the matrix whose rows are $\boldsymbol{u}_t'$, and $\boldsymbol{u}^* = \mathrm{Vec}\,\boldsymbol{U}$ $(nH \times 1)$, with covariance matrix given by $\boldsymbol{\Sigma} \otimes \boldsymbol{I}_n$ from (13.1.6). Let a stacked matrix of N 'instruments' be

$$\boldsymbol{W} = \begin{bmatrix} \boldsymbol{W}_1 \\ \vdots \\ \boldsymbol{W}_H \end{bmatrix} \quad (nH \times N) \tag{13.5.2}$$

for $N \geq p$. The tth row of $\boldsymbol{W}_i$ must be $\mathcal{I}_t$-measurable for each i. The final ingredient of the estimators of this section is a $H \times H$ symmetric positive definite matrix $\boldsymbol{S}$. This must not be an estimate of $\boldsymbol{\Sigma}$ depending on the sample, simply a given matrix. If $\boldsymbol{\Sigma}$ were known one should set $\boldsymbol{S} = \boldsymbol{\Sigma}$, but otherwise let $\boldsymbol{S}$ be any fixed matrix of suitable type, such as $\boldsymbol{I}_H$. The optimand to be considered is the quadratic form

$$C_S(\boldsymbol{\alpha}) = \frac{\boldsymbol{u}^{*\prime}\boldsymbol{\Lambda}^{-1}\boldsymbol{W}(\boldsymbol{W}'\boldsymbol{\Lambda}^{-1}\boldsymbol{W})^{-1}\boldsymbol{W}'\boldsymbol{\Lambda}^{-1}\boldsymbol{u}^*}{2n}. \tag{13.5.3}$$

where $\boldsymbol{\Lambda} = \boldsymbol{S} \otimes \boldsymbol{I}_n$.

Letting

$$\boldsymbol{D} = \begin{bmatrix} \boldsymbol{D}_1 \\ \vdots \\ \boldsymbol{D}_H \end{bmatrix} = \frac{\partial \boldsymbol{u}^*}{\partial \boldsymbol{\alpha}'} \quad (nH \times p) \tag{13.5.4}$$

the first-order conditions for a minimum are

$$\boldsymbol{\nabla} C_S(\boldsymbol{\alpha}) = \frac{1}{n}\boldsymbol{D}(\boldsymbol{\alpha})'\boldsymbol{\Lambda}^{-1}\boldsymbol{W}(\boldsymbol{W}'\boldsymbol{\Lambda}^{-1}\boldsymbol{W})^{-1}\boldsymbol{W}'\boldsymbol{\Lambda}^{-1}\boldsymbol{u}^*(\boldsymbol{\alpha}) = \boldsymbol{0} \quad (p \times 1). \tag{13.5.5}$$

The GMM estimator depending on $\boldsymbol{S}$, $\hat{\boldsymbol{\alpha}}^S$, is the solution to these equations. When $p = N$, the solution is the same as that of the equations

$$\frac{1}{n}\boldsymbol{W}'\boldsymbol{\Lambda}^{-1}\boldsymbol{u}^*(\boldsymbol{\alpha}) = \mathbf{0} \tag{13.5.6}$$

and $C_S(\hat{\boldsymbol{\alpha}}^S) = 0$ identically. The system is said to be just-identified in this case.

Under assumptions (13.1.2), and the usual regularity conditions applied to $\boldsymbol{W}$, it can be verified that

$$\frac{1}{\sqrt{n}}\boldsymbol{W}'\boldsymbol{\Lambda}^{-1}\boldsymbol{u} \xrightarrow{\mathrm{D}} \mathrm{N}(\mathbf{0},\ \boldsymbol{B}_0) \tag{13.5.7}$$

where

$$\boldsymbol{B}_0 = \operatorname{plim}\frac{\boldsymbol{W}'(\boldsymbol{S}^{-1}\boldsymbol{\Sigma}\boldsymbol{S}^{-1}\otimes \boldsymbol{I}_n)\boldsymbol{W}}{n} = \sum_{i=1}^{H}\sum_{j=1}^{H}\boldsymbol{s}^{i\prime}\boldsymbol{\Sigma}\boldsymbol{s}^j\boldsymbol{M}_{ij} \quad (N\times N) \tag{13.5.8}$$

where $\boldsymbol{s}^i$ is the ith column of $\boldsymbol{S}^{-1}$ and $\boldsymbol{M}_{ij} = \operatorname{plim} n^{-1}\boldsymbol{W}_i'\boldsymbol{W}_j$. Let

$$\boldsymbol{C} = \operatorname{plim}\frac{\boldsymbol{W}'\boldsymbol{\Lambda}^{-1}\boldsymbol{W}}{n} = \sum_{i=1}^{H}\sum_{j=1}^{H}s^{ij}\boldsymbol{M}_{ij} \quad (N\times N) \tag{13.5.9}$$

where s^{ij} is the $(i,j)$the element of $\boldsymbol{S}^{-1}$, and also, if $\boldsymbol{D}_0$ denotes $\boldsymbol{D}$ evaluated at $\boldsymbol{\alpha}_0$, let

$$\boldsymbol{N}_0 = \operatorname{plim}\frac{\boldsymbol{D}_0'\boldsymbol{\Lambda}^{-1}\boldsymbol{W}}{n} = \sum_{i=1}^{H}\sum_{j=1}^{H}s^{ij}\operatorname{plim}\frac{\boldsymbol{D}_{0i}'\boldsymbol{W}_j}{n} \quad (p\times N). \tag{13.5.10}$$

The usual application of OE theory shows the estimator to be CAN with

$$\sqrt{n}(\hat{\boldsymbol{\alpha}}^S - \boldsymbol{\alpha}_0) \xrightarrow{\mathrm{D}} \mathrm{N}(\mathbf{0},\ \bar{\boldsymbol{Q}}_0^{-1}\boldsymbol{A}_0\bar{\boldsymbol{Q}}_0^{-1}) \tag{13.5.11}$$

where $\bar{\boldsymbol{Q}}_0 = \boldsymbol{N}_0\boldsymbol{C}^{-1}\boldsymbol{N}_0'$ and $\boldsymbol{A}_0 = \boldsymbol{N}_0\boldsymbol{C}^{-1}\boldsymbol{B}_0\boldsymbol{C}^{-1}\boldsymbol{N}_0'$. Note that if $\boldsymbol{S} = \boldsymbol{\Sigma}$ then $\boldsymbol{B}_0 = \boldsymbol{C}$ and $\bar{\boldsymbol{Q}}_0 = \boldsymbol{A}_0$, so that

$$\sqrt{n}(\hat{\boldsymbol{\alpha}}^{\Sigma} - \boldsymbol{\alpha}_0) \xrightarrow{\mathrm{D}} \mathrm{N}(\mathbf{0},\ \bar{\boldsymbol{Q}}_0^{-1}). \tag{13.5.12}$$

In this case the information matrix equality (9.3.19) holds with $c = 1$.

13.5.2 The Efficient Case

To approach the question of the optimal choices of $\boldsymbol{W}$ and $\boldsymbol{S}$ formally, reconsider the result in §10.3.1, treating the stacked system as, in effect, a single equation. Assuming $\boldsymbol{\Sigma}$ is known, let the disturbances be transformed as

$$\boldsymbol{u}^+ = (\boldsymbol{\Sigma}^{-1/2}\otimes \boldsymbol{I}_n)\boldsymbol{u}^* \tag{13.5.13}$$

such that $E(\boldsymbol{u}^+\boldsymbol{u}^{+\prime}) = \boldsymbol{I}_{nH}$. Write the candidate instrument matrix for this model as $\boldsymbol{W}^+$, but since the disturbances are now uncorrelated set $\boldsymbol{S} = \boldsymbol{I}_H$. $\boldsymbol{\Lambda}$ can be suppressed in the formulae, and the criterion function is just

$$\frac{\boldsymbol{u}^{+\prime}\boldsymbol{W}^+(\boldsymbol{W}^{+\prime}\boldsymbol{W}^+)^{-1}\boldsymbol{W}^{+\prime}\boldsymbol{u}^+}{2n} \tag{13.5.14}$$

which is formally equivalent to (10.3.2). Following the argument leading to (10.3.8), this OE, say $\hat{\boldsymbol{\alpha}}^+$, satisfies

$$\sqrt{n}(\hat{\boldsymbol{\alpha}}^+ - \boldsymbol{\alpha}_0) \xrightarrow{\text{D}} \text{N}(\mathbf{0},\ [\boldsymbol{M}_{DW}^+(\boldsymbol{M}_{WW}^+)^{-1}\boldsymbol{M}_{WD}^+]^{-1}) \tag{13.5.15}$$

in which $\boldsymbol{M}_{DW}^+ = \text{plim}\, n^{-1}\boldsymbol{D}_0^{+\prime}\boldsymbol{W}^+$ where

$$\boldsymbol{D}_0^+ = \left.\frac{\partial \boldsymbol{u}^+}{\partial \boldsymbol{\alpha}'}\right|_{\alpha=\alpha_0} \tag{13.5.16}$$

and $\boldsymbol{M}_{WW}^+$ has the obvious definition. By the argument that follows (10.3.8), the optimal choice of $\boldsymbol{W}^+$ is $\boldsymbol{E}_0^+$, the matrix whose rows are $E(\boldsymbol{d}_{it}^{+\prime}|\mathcal{I}_t)$ where $\boldsymbol{d}_{it}^{+\prime}$ is tth row of block i of $\boldsymbol{D}_0^+$, in the partition analogous to (13.5.4). However, since

$$\boldsymbol{E}_0^+ = (\boldsymbol{\Sigma}^{-1/2} \otimes \boldsymbol{I}_n)\boldsymbol{E}_0 \tag{13.5.17}$$

where $\boldsymbol{E}_0$ is the counterpart of $\boldsymbol{E}_0^+$ for the original equations $\boldsymbol{u}^*$, it easily follows that the asymptotically efficient GMM estimator is obtained by minimizing the criterion

$$\frac{\boldsymbol{u}^{*\prime}\boldsymbol{\Lambda}_0^{-1}\boldsymbol{E}_0(\boldsymbol{E}_0'\boldsymbol{\Lambda}_0^{-1}\boldsymbol{E}_0)^{-1}\boldsymbol{E}_0'\boldsymbol{\Lambda}_0^{-1}\boldsymbol{u}^*}{2n}. \tag{13.5.18}$$

where $\boldsymbol{\Lambda}_0 = \boldsymbol{\Sigma} \otimes \boldsymbol{I}_n$. In particular note that, as expected, $\boldsymbol{\Sigma}$ is the optimal choice for $\boldsymbol{S}$.

This formula is infeasible on two counts,[12] the fact that $\boldsymbol{\Sigma}$ is unknown, and the fact that the conditional expectations do not generally exist in closed form, as discussed in §10.3.1. $\boldsymbol{\Sigma}$ can be estimated, and this issue is addressed in the next section. The possibilities for constructing a proxy for $\boldsymbol{E}_0$ reviewed in the earlier discussion apply equally here, and in particular note from (10.3.12) that letting a matrix $\boldsymbol{W}^+$ replace $\boldsymbol{E}_0^+$ in the formula is equivalent to estimating the latter by least squares projection of $\boldsymbol{D}^+$ onto $\boldsymbol{W}^+$. Replacing $\boldsymbol{E}_0$ by $\boldsymbol{W}$ in (13.5.18) can be motivated in the corresponding way.

To allow full generality, the analysis above has assumed the availability of at least pH instruments, with $N \geq p$ employed for each equation. Fortunately, these do not all have to be distinct and linearly independent. It is permissible, for example, to have $\boldsymbol{W}_1 = \boldsymbol{W}_2 = \cdots = \boldsymbol{W}_H$ in (13.5.2) (the same set of instruments for each equation) and then one can write $\boldsymbol{M}_{ij} = \boldsymbol{M}$ for all i and j.in (13.5.8).

Moreover, the set-up has allowed the possibility of every parameter arising in every equation, whereas this is obviously an exceptional case. More often cross-equation restrictions are absent, so that $\boldsymbol{\alpha} = (\boldsymbol{\alpha}_1', \dots, \boldsymbol{\alpha}_H')'$ where $\boldsymbol{\alpha}_i$ $(p_i \times 1)$ appears only in equation i, and $\sum_{i=1}^H p_i = p$. Then (13.5.4) becomes block-diagonal, so that

$$\boldsymbol{D} = \begin{bmatrix} \boldsymbol{D}_{11} & & 0 \\ & \ddots & \\ 0 & & \boldsymbol{D}_{HH} \end{bmatrix} \tag{13.5.19}$$

[12] 'Feasibility' here refers to the asymptotic formula, in which the replacement of $\boldsymbol{\alpha}_0$ by the consistent estimate $\hat{\boldsymbol{\alpha}}$ for practical purposes is taken as given.

where D_{ii} is $n \times p_i$, and E is structured similarly. Nothing is then lost by choosing

$$W = \begin{bmatrix} W_{11} & & 0 \\ & \ddots & \\ 0 & & W_{HH} \end{bmatrix} \tag{13.5.20}$$

where W_{ii} is a $n \times N_i$ matrix of instruments with $\sum_{i=1}^{H} N_i = N$. In this case, (13.5.9) becomes

$$C = \begin{bmatrix} s^{11}M_{11} & \cdots & s^{1H}M_{1M} \\ \vdots & \ddots & \vdots \\ s^{H1}M_{H1} & \cdots & s^{HH}M_{HH} \end{bmatrix} \tag{13.5.21}$$

where $M_{ij} = n^{-1}W_{ii}'W_{jj}$, and (13.5.10) becomes

$$N_0 = \begin{bmatrix} s^{11}\operatorname{plim} n^{-1}D_{11}'W_{11} & \cdots & s^{1H}\operatorname{plim} n^{-1}D_{1H}'W_{1H} \\ \vdots & \ddots & \vdots \\ s^{H1}\operatorname{plim} n^{-1}D_{H1}'W_{H1} & \cdots & s^{HH}\operatorname{plim} n^{-1}D_{HH}'W_{HH} \end{bmatrix}. \tag{13.5.22}$$

Having $W_{11} = W_{22} = \cdots = W_{HH}$ is a permitted option, and then $C = S^{-1} \otimes M$ where M is the common moment matrix. These restrictions, together with linearity of the equations so that D reduces to the block-diagonal matrix of explanatory variables, equates this set-up with the ordinary three-stage least squares estimator. Since in that case the optimal instruments are the reduced form predictions of the latter variables, the asymptotic efficiency of 3SLS in the GMM class is an implication of the present analysis (subject to the material in §13.5.3) that may be contrasted with the discussion in §13.2.2.

13.5.3 The Two-stage Estimator

The problem now is to extend this analysis to the case where $S = \hat{\Sigma}$, a consistent estimate of Σ. The obvious way to implement the estimator is to initially run the one-stage GMM algorithm setting (say) $S = I_H$, giving $\sqrt{n}$-consistent estimates $\hat{\alpha}^0$ according to (13.5.11). Then compute

$$\hat{\Sigma} = \frac{\hat{U}'\hat{U}}{n} \tag{13.5.23}$$

where $\hat{u}_t = f(y_t, z_t, \hat{\alpha}^0)$. Since $\hat{\alpha}^0$ is $\sqrt{n}$-consistent, $\hat{U} = U + O_p(n^{-1/2})$ by a first-order Taylor's expansion, and so

$$\begin{aligned} \Delta_n &= \hat{\Sigma} - \Sigma \\ &= \left(\frac{\hat{U}'\hat{U}}{n} - \frac{U'U}{n}\right) + \left(\frac{U'U}{n} - \Sigma\right) = O_p(n^{-1/2}). \end{aligned} \tag{13.5.24}$$

It must be determined how this substitution affects the asymptotic distribution of the estimator. The following argument summarizes the proof of Jorgenson and

Laffont (1974), with some details left for the reader to supply. For arbitrary square matrices $\boldsymbol{A}$ and $\boldsymbol{\Delta}$ of the same order such that both $\boldsymbol{A}$ and $\boldsymbol{A}+\boldsymbol{\Delta}$ are nonsingular, define $\boldsymbol{\Upsilon} = (\boldsymbol{A}+\boldsymbol{\Delta})^{-1} - \boldsymbol{A}^{-1}$ and note the identity

$$\boldsymbol{A\Upsilon}+\boldsymbol{\Delta A}^{-1}+\boldsymbol{\Delta\Upsilon}=\boldsymbol{0}. \tag{13.5.25}$$

Since the inverse is (elementwise) continuously differentiable to all orders, $\boldsymbol{\Upsilon} = O(\boldsymbol{\Delta})$ as $\boldsymbol{\Delta} \to \boldsymbol{0}$ and hence

$$\boldsymbol{\Upsilon}= -\boldsymbol{A}^{-1}\boldsymbol{\Delta A}^{-1}+O(\boldsymbol{\Delta}^2). \tag{13.5.26}$$

Applying (13.5.26) to the case of (13.5.24) gives

$$\hat{\boldsymbol{\Sigma}}^{-1}-\boldsymbol{\Sigma}^{-1}=-\boldsymbol{\Sigma}^{-1}\boldsymbol{\Delta}_n\boldsymbol{\Sigma}^{-1}+O_p(n^{-1})=O_p(n^{-1/2}). \tag{13.5.27}$$

Now define

$$\boldsymbol{Q}_n(\boldsymbol{S})=\frac{1}{n}\boldsymbol{N}'(\boldsymbol{S}^{-1}\otimes\boldsymbol{I}_n)\boldsymbol{W}[\boldsymbol{W}'(\boldsymbol{S}^{-1}\otimes\boldsymbol{I}_n)\boldsymbol{W}]^{-1}\boldsymbol{W}'(\boldsymbol{S}^{-1}\otimes\boldsymbol{I}_n)\boldsymbol{N} \tag{13.5.28}$$

Note that

$$\frac{1}{n}\boldsymbol{N}'[(\hat{\boldsymbol{\Sigma}}^{-1}-\boldsymbol{\Sigma}^{-1})\otimes\boldsymbol{I}_n]\boldsymbol{W}=O_p(n^{-1/2}) \tag{13.5.29}$$

under the assumptions on the matrices $\boldsymbol{N}$ and $\boldsymbol{W}$, and similarly with $\boldsymbol{W}'$ replacing $\boldsymbol{N}'$. Applying the arguments in (13.5.26) and (13.5.29) repeatedly shows that

$$\boldsymbol{Q}_n(\hat{\boldsymbol{\Sigma}})^{-1}=\boldsymbol{Q}_n(\boldsymbol{\Sigma})^{-1}+O_p(n^{-1/2}). \tag{13.5.30}$$

Similarly, if

$$\boldsymbol{q}(\boldsymbol{S})=\frac{1}{n}\boldsymbol{N}'(\boldsymbol{S}^{-1}\otimes\boldsymbol{I}_n)\boldsymbol{W}(\boldsymbol{W}'(\boldsymbol{S}^{-1}\otimes\boldsymbol{I}_n)\boldsymbol{W})^{-1}\boldsymbol{W}'(\boldsymbol{S}^{-1}\otimes\boldsymbol{I}_n)\boldsymbol{u}^* \tag{13.5.31}$$

note in particular that

$$\frac{1}{\sqrt{n}}\boldsymbol{W}'[(\hat{\boldsymbol{\Sigma}}^{-1}-\boldsymbol{\Sigma}^{-1})\otimes\boldsymbol{I}_n]\boldsymbol{u}^*=O_p(n^{-1/2}). \tag{13.5.32}$$

Let $\hat{\boldsymbol{\alpha}}^{\Sigma}$ denote the infeasible estimator using the true $\boldsymbol{\Sigma}$, and $\hat{\boldsymbol{\alpha}}^1$ the feasible estimator using $\hat{\boldsymbol{\Sigma}}$. Plugging the above expressions into equation (9.3.17) yields

$$\begin{aligned}\sqrt{n}(\hat{\boldsymbol{\alpha}}^1-\boldsymbol{\alpha}_0)&=-\boldsymbol{Q}_n^*(\hat{\boldsymbol{\Sigma}})^{-1}\sqrt{n}\boldsymbol{q}_0(\hat{\boldsymbol{\Sigma}})\\&=[\boldsymbol{Q}_n^*(\boldsymbol{\Sigma})^{-1}+O_p(n^{-1/2})][\sqrt{n}\boldsymbol{q}_0(\boldsymbol{\Sigma})+O_p(n^{-1/2})]\\&=\sqrt{n}(\hat{\boldsymbol{\alpha}}^{\Sigma}-\boldsymbol{\alpha}_0)+O_p(n^{-1/2}).\end{aligned} \tag{13.5.33}$$

The asymptotic distributions of $\hat{\boldsymbol{\alpha}}^1$ and $\hat{\boldsymbol{\alpha}}^{\Sigma}$ are therefore the same. This means that OE theory can be used to analyse the properties of $\hat{\boldsymbol{\alpha}}^1$, and issues such as identification, for example, can be considered, by simply working with the OE $\hat{\boldsymbol{\alpha}}^{\Sigma}$, having confidence that the same conclusions apply asymptotically to $\hat{\boldsymbol{\alpha}}^1$.

Given this result, there is a natural temptation to iterate the procedure. The residuals computed from $\hat{\boldsymbol{\alpha}}^1$ can be used to compute $\hat{\boldsymbol{\Sigma}}^1$ (say) to obtain $\hat{\boldsymbol{\alpha}}^2$, and thence $\hat{\boldsymbol{\alpha}}^3$, $\hat{\boldsymbol{\alpha}}^4$, and so on until the sequence converges. This possibility raises a number of interesting questions: whether the sequence will converge, and if it does, whether the limit can be thought of as an OE. Is it, for example, equivalent to minimizing

$$C^*(\boldsymbol{\alpha}, \boldsymbol{S}) = C(\boldsymbol{\alpha}, \boldsymbol{S}) + \text{Vec}(\boldsymbol{S} - n^{-1}\boldsymbol{U}'\boldsymbol{U})' \,\text{Vec}(\boldsymbol{S} - n^{-1}\boldsymbol{U}'\boldsymbol{U}) \qquad (13.5.34)$$

where $C(\boldsymbol{\alpha}, \boldsymbol{S})$ is the quadratic form in (13.5.3) considered as a function of all the unknowns, and the second term is a function of $\boldsymbol{\alpha}$ as well as $\boldsymbol{S}$, through the $\boldsymbol{u}_t$s? The answer to this latter question is in general *no*, because there is no reason for the criterion in (13.5.34) to take its minimum at a point where the second term is equal to 0. We do not even know, without checking the conditions, if this particular OE is consistent.

Nor can the iterated procedure be justified as an OE, although it has the same asymptotic distribution as the two-stage GMM estimator, and hence as that of $\hat{\boldsymbol{\alpha}}^{\Sigma}$, since this is true of every step in the sequence. Iteration is at worst innocuous, since asymptotically the sequence converges in one step. However, it is worth noting that the derivation of the properties of the two-stage estimator required us to move outside OE theory, and operate on the formula for the criterion function and its derivatives. There exists no general result to validate two-stage estimators, and each case has to be considered on its merits, as was done in this case. Fortunately, system GMM is the only major case of a two-stage OE estimator that we meet, in this book at least.

13.5.4 Nonlinear SUR

A related case of interest is the nonlinear SUR model in which the equations take the form of (13.4.26) with $\boldsymbol{B} = \boldsymbol{I}_H$. The minimand in this case, given fixed $\boldsymbol{S}$, takes the form

$$C(\boldsymbol{\alpha}) = \tfrac{1}{2}\boldsymbol{u}^{*\prime}\boldsymbol{\Lambda}^{-1}\boldsymbol{u}^* = \tfrac{1}{2}\,\text{tr}\,\boldsymbol{S}^{-1}\boldsymbol{U}'\boldsymbol{U} \qquad (13.5.35)$$

where the second equality is easily verified from the definitions of $\boldsymbol{u}^*$ and $\boldsymbol{\Lambda}$. Note that this is a MDE of the GLS type, rather than the GMM type (see §9.1). Moreover, the Gaussian log-likelihood for this case can be written, apart from constants, as

$$L(\boldsymbol{\alpha}, \boldsymbol{\Sigma}) = -\frac{n}{2}\ln\det\boldsymbol{\Sigma} - \tfrac{1}{2}\,\text{tr}\,\boldsymbol{\Sigma}^{-1}\boldsymbol{U}'\boldsymbol{U}. \qquad (13.5.36)$$

Concentrating out $\boldsymbol{\Sigma}$ in the usual manner gives the maximand

$$L^*(\boldsymbol{\alpha}) = -\frac{n}{2}\ln\det\boldsymbol{U}'\boldsymbol{U}. \qquad (13.5.37)$$

The obvious question now arises, whether iterating the minimization of (13.5.35) with respect to $\boldsymbol{S}$ is equivalent to maximizing (13.5.37), so that the matrix obtained on convergence maximizes L. The answer to this question is *yes*. Since the first term in (13.5.36) does not depend on $\boldsymbol{\alpha}$, maximizing $L(\boldsymbol{\alpha}, \boldsymbol{S})$ with respect to $\boldsymbol{\alpha}$ holding $\boldsymbol{S}$ fixed is the same as minimizing $C(\boldsymbol{\alpha})$ in (13.5.35) with fixed $\boldsymbol{S}$. And, if

$\boldsymbol{S}$ is chosen to maximize $L(\boldsymbol{\alpha}, \boldsymbol{S})$ given $\boldsymbol{\alpha}$, (13.5.23) must be obtained, by the usual derivation. Joint maximization of (13.5.36) by the stepwise method, alternating between $\boldsymbol{\alpha}$ and $\boldsymbol{S}$ (a valid technique) is equivalent to iterating the minimization of $C(\boldsymbol{\alpha})$, with respect to $\boldsymbol{S}$, to convergence. See Phillips (1976) for further details.

Further Reading: Koopmans (1950a) and Koopmans and Hood (1953) are the seminal references. Many textbooks cover the linear simultaneous model, notably Schmidt (1976), Theil (1971), Christ (1966), and Dhrymes (1970). On the nonlinear model see Gallant (1987).

Part IV

Cointegration Theory

Chapter 14

Unit Roots

14.1 The Random Walk Model

Chapter 6 gave a detailed analysis of the OLS estimator of the AR(1) model

$$x_t = \lambda x_{t-1} + u_t \qquad (14.1.1)$$

subject to the stability condition $|\lambda| < 1$, under a range of assumptions about u_t. For the case $\lambda = 1$, the asymptotic theory is quite different from the stable case. This is a member of the class of integrated or I(1) processes, defined in §5.2.7. Borrowing the terminology from §5.1.2, they are also called unit root processes. In this case $u_t = \Delta x_t$, and the designation I(d) generally refers to the number of differencing operations needed to produce a process having the 'usual' stability properties, which is the I(0) case. To give a rigorous definition of I(0) is quite tricky. In §5.2.7 an I(0) process was characterized, in effect, as one having a stationary invertible ARMA representation, and this is the most usual definition, but is rather restrictive. It rules out stationary but nonlinear cases, such as GARCH processes, that could well arise in practice. Perhaps the best working definition to keep in mind, to avoid being too specific, is that an I(0) process should be amenable to the methods of statistical analysis applied up to this point in the book. In other words, it should obey the law of large numbers and central limit theorem, when suitably centred and normalized. As we now show, I(1) processes fail this test and have distinctive non-standard asymptotic properties.

If u_t is i.i.d. (14.1.1) is known as a *random walk*, and this simple case is a good one to start with. With $x_0 = 0$ the model $x_t = x_{t-1} + u_t$ solves as

$$x_t = \sum_{s=1}^{t} u_s. \qquad (14.1.2)$$

Since the u_t are uncorrelated,

$$E(x_t x_{t+s}) = t\sigma^2 \text{ for } s = 0, 1, 2, 3, \ldots, \; t \geq 1. \qquad (14.1.3)$$

The variance of the process (the case $s = 0$) is therefore tending to infinity as $t \to \infty$, and the autocovariances do not tend to 0 as the time separation increases.

Next consider the sample mean $\bar{x}_n = n^{-1}\sum_{t=1}^{n} x_t$. Substitution yields

$$\bar{x}_n = \frac{1}{n}\sum_{t=1}^{n}\Bigl(\sum_{s=1}^{t} u_s\Bigr) = \sum_{t=1}^{n}\Bigl(\frac{n-t+1}{n}\Bigr)u_t. \tag{14.1.4}$$

All the weights in this sum of random terms lie between 0 and 1. These terms are martingale differences that satisfy the conditions of Theorem 6.2.3 if this is true of the u_t themselves, so consider the behaviour of the random variable $n^{-1/2}\bar{x}_n$ in the limit. Its mean is 0, and its variance is[1]

$$E\Bigl(\frac{\bar{x}_n}{\sqrt{n}}\Bigr)^2 = \frac{\sigma^2}{n}\sum_{t=1}^{n}\Bigl(\frac{n-t+1}{n}\Bigr)^2 \to \frac{\sigma^2}{3}. \tag{14.1.5}$$

Applying an appropriate CLT shows that

$$\frac{\bar{x}_n}{\sqrt{n}} \xrightarrow{D} \mathrm{N}\Bigl(0, \frac{\sigma^2}{3}\Bigr). \tag{14.1.6}$$

The sample mean itself is therefore diverging.

Although this particular result yields an asymptotic normal distribution, this is the attribute of the partial sums of x_t scaled by $n^{-3/2}$, *not* $n^{-1/2}$. To extend the analysis further calls for a new kind of limit theory.

14.2 The Probability Background

14.2.1 Function Spaces

The most important departure is to transform the probability model from an infinite sequence of random variables to a random function on the closed interval $[0, 1]$. Let an I(1) time series, more formally called a partial-sum process, be $S_t = x_t - x_0 = \sum_{s=1}^{t} u_s$ for $t = 1, \dots, n$. Define a function from $[0, 1]$ to $\mathbb{R}$ by

$$Y_n(r) = \begin{cases} \dfrac{S_{j-1} + (nr - j - 1)u_j}{\sqrt{n}\sigma}, & (j-1)/n \le r < j/n, \\ & j = 1, \dots, n \\ \dfrac{S_n}{\sqrt{n}\sigma} & r = 1. \end{cases} \tag{14.2.1}$$

This may be written more compactly as

$$Y_n(r) = \frac{S_{[nr]} + (nr - [nr])u_{[nr]+1}}{\sqrt{n}\sigma} \quad 0 \le r < 1 \tag{14.2.2}$$

where $[nr]$ is the largest integer not exceeding nr. In graphical terms, this transformation just represents the joining up of dots with line segments. Figure 14.1

---

[1] See the second of the useful formulae in the footnote on page 149.

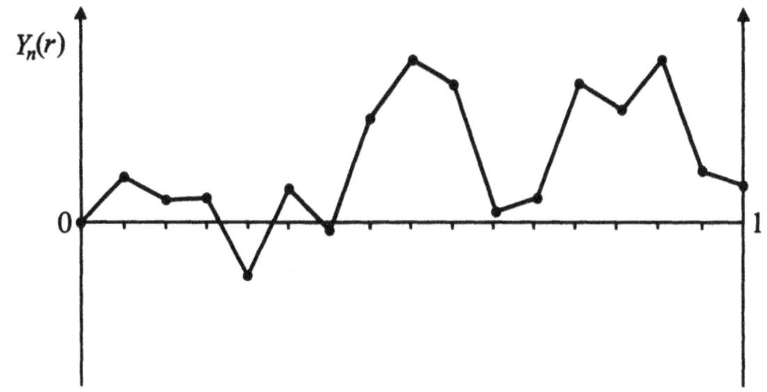

Figure 14.1: An Element of $C[0,1]$

provides a simple illustration, the vertices at points j/n on the horizontal axis representing the points $S_j/\sqrt{n}\sigma$. This resembles the usual sort of time series plot of points $S_1, \ldots, S_n$, and while the difference is crucial, it lies only in the axes. The horizontal axis is a continuum instead of representing n discrete points, and the vertical axis is re-scaled by the $1/\sqrt{n}\sigma$. Because the set $(u_1, \ldots, u_n)$ are random variables, Y_n can be thought of as a random drawing from the sample space $C[0,1]$ of *all possible* continuous functions on $[0,1]$. The interesting departure is to consider the distribution of these functions, and in particular, the limit of this distribution, if such can be shown to exist, as $n \to \infty$. Since the width of the interval is fixed, increasing n crams more and more points into the same space until, ultimately, their horizontal separation vanishes to give a curve that is 'all corners'. At the same time the variation of the partial sums is normalized so that the vertical scale can remain unchanged. This promises to be a limit of a rather interesting sort.

To handle this problem mathematically some structure must be imposed on the space $C[0,1]$, to be known simply as C when there is no risk of ambiguity. Let an element of C (that is, any continuous curve traversing the unit interval) be denoted x. The real numbers $x(r)$ representing the unique values of x at points $r \in [0,1]$ are called the *coordinates* of x. Given any two elements of the space, say $x \in C$ and $y \in C$, we need to be able to say how close together they are. Technically, C must be assigned a *metric*. For example, for any pair of real numbers x and y a distance between them is defined, the nonnegative number $d_E(x,y) = |x-y|$. d_E is known as the *Euclidean* metric, and the pair $(\mathbb{R}, d_E)$ (the set of points paired with the distance measure) defines a *metric space*, in this case Euclidean space. To be a metric, the function d must satisfy the properties

$$d(x,y) \geq 0, \text{and } d(x,y) = 0 \text{ if and only if } x = y \tag{14.2.3a}$$
$$d(y,x) = d(x,y) \tag{14.2.3b}$$
$$d(x,y) \leq d(x,z) + d(y,z). \tag{14.2.3c}$$

It can be verified that the Euclidean metric on $\mathbb{R}$ does so. In fact this is not the only way to define a metric on $\mathbb{R}$. The *discrete* metric, taking the value 0 if $x = y$ and 1 otherwise, also satisfies conditions (14.2.3).

For elements of C there are also several ways to define a metric. A convenient choice is the *uniform* metric,

$$d_U(x, y) = \sup_{0 \leq r \leq 1} |x(r) - y(r)| \tag{14.2.4}$$

This is just the largest vertical separation between the pair of functions over the interval, and can be verified to satisfy the definition. (C, d_U) is a metric space. Intuitively, is helpful to think of metric spaces as sharing certain essential properties with the real numbers. In particular, there is the generalization of the notion of an open interval. Sets of the form $\{x : d_u(x, y) < r\}$ can be defined, called the *open spheres* with centre y and radius r. The σ-field generated from the open spheres of a metric space is called the Borel field of the space, the generalization of the concept defined in §B.3 for the real line. The Borel field of (C, d_U) is denoted $\mathcal{B}_C$, and probabilities can be assigned to the elements of $\mathcal{B}_C$ to define a probability space $(C, \mathcal{B}_C, \mu)$. In many ways this is analogous to the familiar distribution on the line, although unlike $\mathbb{R}$ there is no ordering of elements defined on C, and hence no natural counterpart of the c.d.f. to represent μ.

Now let us focus attention on elements of C such as the one illustrated in Figure 14.1. The key idea is that these have a distribution derived from the joint distribution of the elements $u_1, \ldots, u_n$. For example, this might be designated as i.i.d. with mean 0 and variance σ^2. Let μ_n denote the distribution in question, such that $\mu_n(A)$ represents the probability of the curve lying in the set A, for each $A \in \mathcal{B}_C$.

Now consider the sequence $\{\mu_n, n = 1, 2, 3, \ldots\}$, to correspond with increasing sample sizes, and a tighter packing of sample points into the unit interval. If there exists a limiting distribution μ such that $\mu_n(A) \to \mu(A)$ for every $A \in \mathcal{B}_C$, possibly excepting cases where $\mu(\partial A) > 0$ where ∂A denotes the boundary points of A, μ_n is said to *converge weakly* to μ, denoted $\mu_n \Longrightarrow \mu$. This is the natural generalization of Definition 3.1.1 for distributions on $\mathbb{R}$. The earlier stipulation of convergence only at 'continuity points of F' specializes the condition just given, allowing the convergence to fail for sets whose boundaries have positive measure.

14.2.2 Brownian Motion

If $u_t \sim \text{i.i.d.}(0, \sigma^2)$, something is already known about the postulated convergence. Since the increments u_t are small relative to their sums from 0 to t according to (14.1.5), the limit curves should retain their continuity. The interesting thing is that, as a consequence of the central limit phenomenon, their evolution follows a normal law. Start with the case $Y_n(1)$. Looking at (14.2.1), the Lindeberg–Lévy CLT implies that $Y_n(1) = S_n/\sqrt{n}\sigma \xrightarrow{D} N(0, 1)$ on the stated assumptions. However if $n \to \infty$, so does nr for any $r > 0$. It is therefore also the case that

$$\frac{S_{[nr]}}{\sqrt{nr}\sigma} \xrightarrow{D} N(0, 1) \tag{14.2.5}$$

and hence

$$Y_n(r) = \sqrt{r}\frac{S_{[nr]}}{\sqrt{nr}\sigma} + \frac{(nr - [nr])u_{[nr]+1}}{\sqrt{n}\sigma} \xrightarrow{\text{D}} \text{N}(0, r) \tag{14.2.6}$$

noting that the second of the two terms is $O_p(n^{-1/2})$. Pursuing the same logic further still, one can say using the independence of the increments that

$$Y_n(r_2) - Y_n(r_1) \xrightarrow{\text{D}} \text{N}(0,\ r_2 - r_1) \tag{14.2.7}$$

for all $0 \le r_1 < r_2 \le 1$. To see this, let Y represent the limit of Y_n and note that, for example, $Y(\frac{1}{2})$ and $Y(1) - Y(\frac{1}{2})$ are a pair of independent normals each with variance of $\frac{1}{2}$, given that $Y(0) = 0$ with probability 1. Their sum $Y(1)$ clearly has a variance of 1, as required.

A random function that possesses these properties of Y is known as a *Wiener process* or *Brownian motion process.* Formally:

Definition 14.2.1 A Brownian motion B is a real random function on the unit interval,[2] with the following properties:

(a) $B \in C$ with probability 1.

(b) $B(0) = 0$ with probability 1.

(c) for any set of subintervals defined by arbitrary $0 \le r_1 < r_2 < \ldots < r_k \le 1$, the increments $B(r_1)$, $B(r_2) - B(r_1)$, ... , $B(r_k) - B(r_{k-1})$ are totally independent.

(d) $B(t) - B(s) \sim \text{N}(0, t - s)$ for $0 \le s < t \le 1$. □

Given property (a), B can be thought of as a random drawing from the probability space $(C, \mathcal{B}_C, W)$, where W is the probability measure that assigns probabilities to B in accordance with the definition, called *Wiener measure.*

Although continuous, the sample paths of the Wiener process are extremely tortuous. They are curves of the class named *fractals* by Mandelbrot (1983). Even when traversing a finite interval they are curves of infinite length, for note that

$$\frac{1}{\sqrt{n}}\sum_{j=1}^{n}|u_j| = O_p(\sqrt{n}). \tag{14.2.8}$$

Almost every point is a corner, and they are nondifferentiable at every point of $[0, 1]$ with probability 1. To see this, note that

$$\frac{B(r+h) - B(r)}{h} \sim \text{N}(0, h^{-1}) \quad \text{all } h > 0. \tag{14.2.9}$$

Letting h tend to 0 does not yield a well-defined limit in distribution.

---

[2]Brownian motion can be defined on any interval of the line, including $[0, \infty)$. The present definition is the relevant one for our purposes.

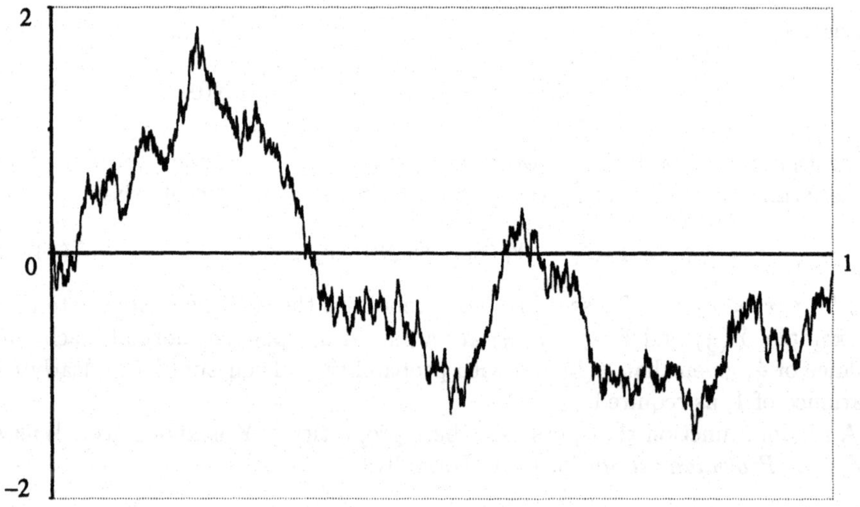

Figure 14.2: A Realization of B

Figure 14.2 gives an idea of the appearance of these sample paths,[3] and may be compared with the finite realization of an integrated process shown in Figure 5.3. Realizations of B have the interesting property of exhibiting purposeful-seeming local trends. At any point the curve rises or falls with the same probability, and S_n has zero mean for every n, but it can keep the same sign for very long periods.

14.2.3 The Functional CLT

The basic weak convergence result, to be thought of as the generalization to a function space of the Lindeberg–Lévy CLT, is *Donsker's Theorem* (Donsker, 1951).

Theorem 14.2.1 If $\{u_j\ ,\ j = 1, 2, 3, \dots\}$ is i.i.d.$(0, \sigma^2)$, then $Y_n \xrightarrow{\text{D}} B$. □

This is a case of the *functional central limit theorem* (FCLT). The term *invariance principle* is also used to refer to a result in which the weak limit of a stochastic process is invariant to the distribution of the underlying components.

The proof of the FCLT involves two fundamental steps, one of which is obvious in view of the earlier discussion. This is to show that the finite-dimensional distributions of the process (joint distributions of finite collections of coordinates) converge to those of the limit process. As remarked, the Lindeberg–Lévy theorem achieves this in the present case. However, the convergence of the finite dimensional distributions does *not* suffice by itself. These do not define all the

[3] The figure was constructed by plotting 3600 points of a partial sum of independent N(0, 1) increments. Since this number approaches the maximum resolution of the graphics software, adding more points would not change the overall appearance of the curve.

characteristics of a continuous stochastic process. To cite just one example, they do not reveal what the distribution of $\max_{0 \leq r \leq 1} |Y(r)|$ is.

However, if the sequence of distributions $\{\mu_n,\ n = 1, 2, 3, \dots\}$ does possess a well defined limit, this can only be W. The problem is to demonstrate that the limit exists, and it will do so only if the sequence of distributions is *uniformly tight.* Tightness of a distribution is the condition that prohibits the escape of probability mass to infinity. For example, consider the sequence of distributions on $\mathbb{R}$ defined by (14.2.9) with $h = 1/n$. The distributions $\{N(0, n),\ n = 1, 2, 3, \dots\}$ are tight for each n, but the limit of the sequence would appear to assign positive probability to infinitely large values. In fact, it is not a well-defined distribution, and this sequence is not uniformly tight. In the context of a sequence of probability measures on C, a tight distribution, roughly speaking, is one which is both bounded at the origin and assigns arbitrarily small probability to functions with discontinuities. Fortunately, uniform tightness of the distributions of the Y_n is readily shown by a technical argument under the condition of i.i.d. increments, completing the proof of the Donsker FCLT.

The foregoing approach to the problem is neat in principle, but algebraically rather untidy. In (14.2.6), it might seem desirable to omit the asymptotically negligible term at the outset, and working directly with the simple partial-sum function X_n where

$$X_n(r) = \frac{S_{[nr]}}{\sqrt{n}\sigma} \quad 0 \leq r \leq 1 \tag{14.2.10}$$

in place of Y_n. This function is drawn in Figure 14.3 for comparison with the continuous version in Figure 14.1. The substitution looks trivial but, unfortunately,

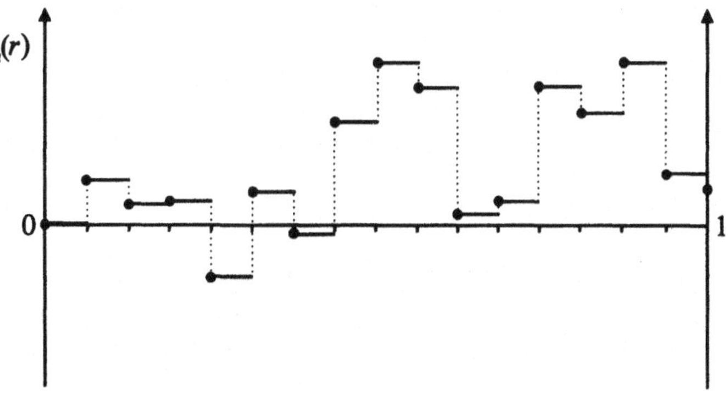

Figure 14.3: An Element of $D[0, 1]$

is not as straightforward as it might appear. The problem is that X_n is not an element of $C\,[0, 1]$. Technically, it belongs to the space $D\,[0, 1]$ of *cadlag* functions, to be written simply as D when there is no risk of ambiguity.[4] Such functions may

[4]This is a French acronym, standing for 'continue à droite, limites à gauche'.

have discontinuities, although every *decreasing* sequence of points on a function segment has a limit point, and a small enough *increase* in r never need result in a jump in $X_n(r)$; whereas neither of these statements is true if the directions are interchanged. The space C forms a subset of D, and hence in particular a Brownian motion is an element of D. In this case condition (a) is an important component of Definition 14.2.1.

It is possible to make D a metric space by associating the uniform metric with it, but here is where the problems arise. The space (D, d_U) is *nonseparable.* A separable metric space is one that contains a countable,[5] dense subset, a subset being *dense* if every point of the space is arbitrarily close to one of its elements. For example, $\mathbb{R}$ is separable because the rational numbers are both countable and dense in $\mathbb{R}$. It is possible to show that (C, d_U) is also separable. However, if

$$x_\theta(r) = \begin{cases} 0, & 0 \leq r < \theta \\ 1, & \theta \leq r \leq 1 \end{cases} \tag{14.2.11}$$

the functions x_θ are elements of D for each $\theta \in [0,1]$. There are an uncountable number of these, but $d_U(x_\theta, x_{\theta+\delta}) = 1$ for *every* $0 < \delta \leq 1 - \theta$. So no countable subset of (D, d_U) can exist that is arbitrarily close to all of these functions. The problem with nonseparability is that the Borel field of (D, d_U) contains 'too many sets'. It is not possible to associate probabilities with all these sets without running into contradictions.

The favoured solution to the nonseparability problem is to adopt a different metric for D. Common sense suggests that x_θ and $x_{\theta+\delta}$ should be thought of as close when δ is small. A suitable metric with this property has been constructed by Billingsley (1968).[6] Letting d_B denote Billingsley's metric, and $\mathcal{B}_D$ the associated Borel field, probability spaces of the form $((D, d_B), \mathcal{B}_D, \mu)$ are well-defined. With this set-up, the asymptotic analysis of the processes X_n can proceed just as for the continuous Y_n, with a worthwhile gain in simplicity.

For econometric problems we would also like to extend the FCLT beyond the case of i.i.d. increments. A route can be followed similar to the one pursued in Chapter 6. The following result has conditions nearly the same as those for the CLT, but with a crucial extra condition:

Theorem 14.2.2 Let $S_n = \sum_{t=1}^{n} u_t$, where the sequence $\{u_t,\ t = 1, \ldots, n\}$ has mean of zero, variances $\sigma_t^2 < \infty$, and meets the conditions specified for $\{X_t\}$ in at least one of Theorems 3.3.1, 3.3.2, 6.2.3 and 6.4.5. In addition, assume

$$\frac{E(S_n^2)}{n} \to \sigma^2 < \infty. \tag{14.2.12}$$

If $X_n(r) = S_{[nr]}/\sqrt{n}\sigma$, then $X_n \xrightarrow{\text{D}} B$. □

---

[5] An infinite set is countable if its elements can be labelled by the natural numbers $n = 1, 2, 3, \ldots$ The points of the line $0 \leq r \leq 1$ are uncountable, representing a higher order of infinity.

[6] Billingsley's metric has the technical property of inducing the so-called *Skorokhod topology* on the space.

A proof is given in Davidson (1994a), Theorems 27.14 and 29.6.[7] Condition (14.2.12) is *global* wide-sense stationarity. Notice that σ^2 is not the same thing as $\sigma_u^2 = \lim_{n\to\infty} n^{-1}\sum \sigma_t^2$ unless the increments are uncorrelated. Otherwise, all the terms $E(u_t u_{t-j})$ for $j > 0$ and $1 \le t \le n$ are included in the sum. This extra condition is sufficient for uniform tightness of the distributions, and ensures that

$$\frac{S_{[nr]}}{\sqrt{n}\sigma} \xrightarrow{\text{D}} \text{N}(0, r) \tag{14.2.13}$$

for each r in $(0, 1]$. For the ordinary CLT this need hold only for the case $r = 1$, and technically (14.2.12) need not hold, though it is a fairly innocuous condition and would be expected to hold in most applications of the CLT in any case.

Always paired with the FCLT is the function-space version of the continuous mapping theorem (Theorem 3.1.3). The following is a special case of Davidson (1994a) Theorem 26.13.

Theorem 14.2.3 Let $h : D \mapsto \mathbb{R}$ be a measurable functional[8] that is continuous except on a set $D_h \subset D$ with $P(B \in D_h) = 0$. If $X_n \xrightarrow{\text{D}} B$ then $h(X_n) \xrightarrow{\text{D}} h(B)$. □

Examples of continuous functionals of X_n include the coordinate functions $X_n(r)$ for any fixed r, and also integrals over $[0, 1]$, of X_n and of transformations such as X_n^2.

14.3 The Unit Root Autoregression

14.3.1 Basic Convergence Results

Consider the asymptotic properties of the autoregression in the model

$$x_t = \lambda x_{t-1} + u_t \quad \lambda = 1. \tag{14.3.1}$$

For the main development, it is not necessary to make any assumptions about u_t beyond what is specified in Theorem 14.2.2. The initial value x_0 is assumed to be observed, so that the error-of-estimate takes the form

$$\hat{\lambda} - 1 = \frac{\sum_{t=1}^n u_t x_{t-1}}{\sum_{t=1}^n x_{t-1}^2} = \frac{\sum_{t=1}^n (x_t - x_{t-1})x_{t-1}}{\sum_{t=1}^n x_{t-1}^2}. \tag{14.3.2}$$

If in fact $x_0 = 0$, this is equivalent to summing from 2 to n. Recall that $S_t = x_t - x_0$ and $X_n(r) = n^{-1/2}S_{[nr]}/\sigma$. Note that $\int_{(t-1)/n}^{t/n} dr = n^{-1}$, and therefore

$$S_{t-1} = nS_{t-1}\int_{(t-1)/n}^{t/n} dr = n\int_{(t-1)/n}^{t/n} S_{[nr]}dr = n^{3/2}\sigma\int_{(t-1)/n}^{t/n} X_n(r)dr \tag{14.3.3}$$

---

[7] De Jong and Davidson (2000b) prove the FCLT under even weaker conditions than these.

[8] A functional is function that takes another function as its argument. The integral of a function is a familiar example.

and

$$S_{t-1}^2 = nS_{t-1}^2 \int_{(t-1)/n}^{t/n} dr = n \int_{(t-1)/n}^{t/n} S_{[nr]}^2 dr = n^2\sigma \int_{(t-1)/n}^{t/n} X_n(r)^2 dr. \quad (14.3.4)$$

Put $S_0 = 0$, and then

$$\frac{1}{n^{3/2}}\sum_{t=1}^{n} S_{t-1} = \sigma \sum_{t=1}^{n} \int_{(t-1)/n}^{t/n} X_n(r)dr = \sigma \int_0^1 X_n(r)dr$$

$$\xrightarrow{\text{D}} \sigma \int_0^1 B(r)dr \quad (14.3.5)$$

and

$$\frac{1}{n^2}\sum_{t=1}^{n} S_{t-1}^2 = \sigma \sum_{t=1}^{n} \int_{(t-1)/n}^{t/n} X_n(r)^2 dr = \sigma \int_0^1 X_n(r)^2 dr$$

$$\xrightarrow{\text{D}} \sigma^2 \int_0^1 B(r)^2 dr \quad (14.3.6)$$

where σ^2 is defined in (14.2.12). The indicated convergence follows from Theorems 14.2.2 and 14.2.3, noting that the expressions are both continuous functionals of X_n.

The random variables $\int_0^1 Bdr$ and $\int_0^1 B^2 dr$ are called *functionals of Brownian motion.* The convergence in (14.3.5) has already been encountered in a different form as (14.1.6); in other words, it has been shown that $\int_0^1 Bdr \sim \mathrm{N}(0, \frac{1}{3})$.[9] However, no such simple closed form exists for the density function of $\int_0^1 B^2 dr$. Although analytical formulae for the distributions of these statistics can be obtained,[10] these methods are difficult and inflexible. The preferred method of actually tabulating such distributions is by Monte Carlo simulation. To obtain a good approximation to the limiting distribution of $\int_0^1 B^2 dr$, for example, the integral might be approximated by the formula on the left-hand side of (14.3.6), with the S_t obtained as the partial sums of N(0, 1) random numbers, and n chosen suitably large (say 1000). The distribution is built up experimentally from a still larger number of replications of the variable. Percentiles can be estimated quite accurately with 10,000 or more replications. This kind of computation can be done routinely on a fast PC.

14.3.2 Tests of the I(1) Hypothesis

Now consider the limiting distribution of the ratio in (14.3.2) multiplied by a suitable scale factor. First, the denominator. Since $x_t = S_t + x_0$,

$$\frac{1}{n^2}\sum_{t=1}^{n} x_{t-1}^2 = \frac{1}{n^2}\sum_{t=1}^{n} S_{t-1}^2 + \frac{2x_0}{n^2}\sum_{t=1}^{n} S_{t-1} + \frac{x_0^2}{n}. \quad (14.3.7)$$

---

[9] (14.1.6) was shown for the uncorrelated case, but since (14.3.5) holds generally, the two limits must coincide.

[10] See Evans and Savin (1981), also Tanaka (1996).

The fact that $x_0 n^{-2}\sum_{t=1}^{n} S_{t-1} = O_p(n^{-1/2})$ follows from (14.3.5), and hence the last two terms converge in probability to zero. Invoking Theorem 3.1.2(i) gives the result

$$\frac{1}{n^2}\sum_{t=1}^{n} x_{t-1}^2 \xrightarrow{\mathrm{D}} \sigma^2 \int_0^1 B^2 dr. \tag{14.3.8}$$

Thus, the distribution does not depend on x_0, which may be either a constant or a random variable.

The next task is to consider the numerator in (14.3.2). Since $S_t = S_{t-1} + u_t$,

$$\begin{aligned}\frac{1}{n}\sum_{t=1}^{n} S_{t-1}u_t &= \frac{1}{2n}\sum_{t=1}^{n}(S_t^2 - S_{t-1}^2 - u_t^2)\\ &= \frac{1}{2n}\left(S_n^2 - \sum_{t=1}^{n} u_t^2\right)\\ &= \frac{\sigma^2}{2}\left(X_n(1)^2 - \frac{1}{n\sigma^2}\sum_{t=1}^{n} u_t^2\right)\\ &\xrightarrow{\mathrm{D}} \frac{\sigma^2}{2}\left(B(1)^2 - \frac{\sigma_u^2}{\sigma^2}\right)\end{aligned} \tag{14.3.9}$$

where Theorem 6.4.4, for example, is used to show that $\operatorname{plim} n^{-1}\sum_{t=1}^{n} u_t^2 = \sigma_u^2$, and Theorem 3.1.2(i) is applied in the final step. It follows from the same sort of reasoning that $\operatorname{plim} n^{-1}\sum_{t=1}^{n} u_t = 0$, and hence that

$$\frac{1}{n}\sum_{t=1}^{n} x_{t-1}u_t = \frac{1}{n}\sum_{t=1}^{n} S_{t-1}u_t + x_0\frac{1}{n}\sum_{t=1}^{n} u_t \xrightarrow{\mathrm{D}} \frac{\sigma^2}{2}\left(B(1)^2 - \frac{\sigma_u^2}{\sigma^2}\right). \tag{14.3.10}$$

Note that $B(1) \sim \mathrm{N}(0,1)$ by the definition, and hence $B(1)^2 \sim \chi^2(1)$. Also, if u_t is serially uncorrelated then $\sigma^2 = \sigma_u^2$, as noted following Theorem 14.2.2.

It is worth digressing to note that this result provides, in effect, a proof of a famous result in stochastic calculus known as the Itô integral formula. This supplies the generalization to stochastic integrals of the formula for integration by parts. If B is standard Brownian motion, the Itô rule says that

$$\int_0^1 B(r)dB(r) = \tfrac{1}{2}[B(1)^2 - 1] \text{ a.s.} \tag{14.3.11}$$

where the left-hand side of (14.3.11) can be viewed (assuming $\sigma^2 = 1$) as the limit in distribution as $n \to \infty$ of the left hand side of (14.3.10), assuming $\sigma^2 = 1$. In contrast to (14.3.11), the formula for integration by parts applied to the ordinary Stieltjes integral with respect to a function of bounded variation $h(r) : [0,1] \mapsto \mathbb{R}$ (say) would yield

$$\int_0^1 h(r)dh(r) = \tfrac{1}{2}h(1)^2. \tag{14.3.12}$$

The appearance of the extra term of $-\frac{1}{2}$ in the Itô formula is linked to the fact, noted in §14.2.2, that almost all realizations of B are functions of unbounded variation.

Now, returning to equation (14.3.2), a further application of the continuous mapping theorem delivers the required limit result. From (14.3.8) and (14.3.10),

$$n(\hat{\lambda}-1) \xrightarrow{\text{D}} \frac{B(1)^2 - \dfrac{\sigma_u^2}{\sigma^2}}{2\int_0^1 B^2 dr}. \tag{14.3.13}$$

Contrast (14.3.13) with (6.3.20). In particular, observe the scaling factor of n in the former case, instead of $\sqrt{n}$. $\hat{\lambda}$ is not merely consistent but 'super-consistent'. If the data are serially uncorrelated the limit in (14.3.13) reduces to

$$\frac{B(1)^2 - 1}{2\int_0^1 B^2 dr}. \tag{14.3.14}$$

This is a random variable whose distribution, although nonstandard, does not depend on nuisance parameters and can be tabulated by Monte Carlo simulation. This was done originally by Dickey and Fuller, see Fuller (1976). The statistic $n(\hat{\lambda}-1)$ accordingly provides the basis for a test of $\lambda = 1$. Under the alternative hypothesis of $|\lambda| < 1$, the standard asymptotics for stationary processes apply, $\hat{\lambda}$ is $\sqrt{n}$-consistent for λ, and hence

$$n|\hat{\lambda}-1| = O_p(n). \tag{14.3.15}$$

The test is accordingly consistent.

The distribution of the conventional t statistic for the test of $\lambda = 1$ is found similarly. Writing

$$t_\lambda = \frac{\hat{\lambda}-1}{s_u}\sqrt{\sum_{t=1}^{n} x_{t-1}^2} \tag{14.3.16}$$

where s_u^2 is the least squares residual variance, note that

$$\begin{aligned} s_u^2 &= \frac{1}{n}\sum_{t=1}^{n}(u_t - (\hat{\lambda}-1)x_{t-1})^2 \\ &= \frac{1}{n}\sum_{t=1}^{n} u_t^2 - 2(1-\hat{\lambda})\frac{1}{n}\sum_{t=1}^{n} x_{t-1}u_t + (1-\hat{\lambda})^2\frac{1}{n}\sum_{t=1}^{n} x_{t-1}^2 \\ &\xrightarrow{\text{pr}} \sigma_u^2 \end{aligned} \tag{14.3.17}$$

since the last two terms in the third member of (14.3.17) are $O_p(n^{-1})$ by (14.3.10) and (14.3.8), respectively. It follows that, under the null hypothesis $\lambda = 1$,

$$t_\lambda \xrightarrow{\text{D}} \frac{\dfrac{\sigma}{2\sigma_u}\left(B(1)^2 - \dfrac{\sigma_u^2}{\sigma^2}\right)}{\sqrt{\int_0^1 B(r)^2 dr}}. \tag{14.3.18}$$

Again, if the time series is uncorrelated then the limiting distribution reduces to

$$\frac{B(1)^2 - 1}{2\sqrt{\int_0^1 B^2 dr}}. \tag{14.3.19}$$

This is free of nuisance parameters, but as with (14.3.14) is not a standard distribution. As in the case of $n(\hat{\lambda} - 1)$, it must be tabulated by Monte Carlo, and this was also done by Dickey and Fuller.

Thus, one of the basic intuitions of standard regression theory, that the t ratio has a variance standardised to 1 and a normal distribution in the limit, proves inappropriate to this case. The sample standard error that converges to a constant limit in the stable case here converges to a random variable, a functional of Brownian motion. However, it can be verified that under the alternative hypothesis $|\lambda| < 1$,

$$|t_\lambda| = O_p(\sqrt{n}) \tag{14.3.20}$$

and hence this test is also consistent.

Since the explosive case $\lambda > 1$ is ruled out (in large samples such data must approach infinity at an exponential rate), the $n(\hat{\lambda}-1)$ and t tests of a unit root are always performed as one-tail tests, with the rejection region lying under the left-hand tail. In other words, the null is rejected when the statistics take absolutely large negative values. In practice, the test is often performed by reparameterizing (14.1.1) as

$$\Delta x_t = (\lambda - 1)x_{t-1} + u_t \tag{14.3.21}$$

where $\Delta x_t = u_t$ by hypothesis. The OLS estimate and t ratio of the regression coefficient in (14.3.21) are identical to $\hat{\lambda} - 1$ and t_λ respectively. The tests based on these two statistics are the alternative versions of the so-called Dickey–Fuller test for a unit root (Dickey and Fuller 1979, 1981).

14.3.3 Serial Correlation

For the more usual case when u_t is serially correlated, two approaches have been developed. The most popular procedure is to try to model the correlation in u_t by fitting an autoregression. Instead of (14.3.21), run the regression

$$\Delta x_t = (\lambda - 1)x_{t-1} + \sum_{j=1}^{k} \beta_j \Delta x_{t-j} + u_t \tag{14.3.22}$$

assuming that for a suitable value of k, u_t so defined is an uncorrelated sequence. This is the augmented Dickey–Fuller (ADF) test. The following is the basic result needed to justify it.

Theorem 14.3.1 If (14.3.22) holds where u_t meets the conditions specified in Theorem 14.2.2, and is also serially uncorrelated, (14.3.14) and (14.3.19) are the limiting distributions of the ADF statistics $n(\hat{\lambda} - 1)$ and t_λ respectively. □

See §14.6 for the proof. The problem with this approach is to choose k appropriately. If the process generating Δx_t has moving average as well as autoregressive components, the true k is actually infinite and Theorem 14.3.1 does not apply. However, if k is made a suitable increasing function of n, it can be shown that t_λ does converge to the DF distribution under H_0. Said and Dickey (1984) show that if Δx_t is ARMA(1,1), $k = o(n^{1/3})$ is appropriate. In practice, *ad hoc* methods such as choosing k on the basis of model selection criteria (see §9.4.1) are often adopted. It should be borne in mind that over-parameterization as well as neglect of autocorrelation can affect the performance of the test in finite samples.

An alternative approach due to Phillips and Perron (see Phillips 1987, Phillips and Perron 1988) is to treat the autocorrelation nonparametrically. The nuisance parameters in (14.3.13) and (14.3.18) are estimated consistently using the methods of §9.4.3. Applying the Newey and West (1987) suggestion to use the Bartlett kernel leads to the estimator

$$s_{nl}^2 = \frac{1}{n}\left(\sum_{t=1}^{n} \hat{u}_t^2 + 2\sum_{\tau=1}^{l(n)} w_{\tau l} \sum_{t=\tau+1}^{n} \hat{u}_t\hat{u}_{t-\tau}\right) \tag{14.3.23}$$

where $\hat{u}_t = x_t - \hat{\lambda}x_{t-1}$, $w_{\tau l} = 1-\tau/(l(n)+1)$ and $l(n) = O(n^{1/3})$ is recommended, see §9.4.3 for details.

This estimator is always positive, and $s_{nl}^2 \xrightarrow{\text{pr}} \sigma^2$ under H_0. Thus, consider the Dickey–Fuller t statistic. It can be verified that inverting the formula in (14.3.18) gives

$$\frac{\sigma_u}{\sigma}t_\lambda + \frac{\sigma_u^2 - \sigma^2}{2\sigma^2\sqrt{\int_0^1 B^2 dr}} \xrightarrow{\text{D}} \frac{B(1)^2 - 1}{2\sqrt{\int_0^1 B^2 dr}} \tag{14.3.24}$$

The sample counterpart is the statistic

$$\hat{Z}_t = \frac{s_u}{s_{nl}}t_\lambda + \frac{s_u^2 - s_{nl}^2}{2s_{nl}\sqrt{n^{-2}\sum_{t=1}^n x_{t-1}^2}} \tag{14.3.25}$$

which has the same asymptotic distribution as (14.3.24).

While the formula in (14.3.25) shows how to modify the t statistic, it might be simpler to see how it is constructed directly from its constituent elements. Since

$$t_\lambda = \frac{\sum_{t=1}^n x_{t-1}\hat{u}_t}{s_u\sqrt{\sum_{t=1}^n x_{t-1}^2}}, \tag{14.3.26}$$

the modified statistic is

$$\hat{Z}_t = \frac{\sum_{t=1}^n (x_{t-1}\hat{u}_t - \hat{c})}{s_{nl}\sqrt{\sum_{t=1}^n x_{t-1}^2}} \tag{14.3.27}$$

where $\hat{c} = n^{-1}\sum_{\tau=1}^{l(n)} w_{\tau l}\sum_{t=\tau+1}^{n} \hat{u}_t\hat{u}_{t-\tau}$ from (14.3.23). Notice that $\hat{c}$ is actually the estimate of $E(x_{t-1}u_t)$, and so can be seen as a centring correction. The modifications to t_λ represented by $\hat{Z}_t$ are therefore two, the mean correction and the replacement of s_u by the consistent estimator s_{nl}. Similar corrections can be applied to the $n(\hat{\lambda}-1)$ statistic, and it is left to the interested reader to construct the modifications for this case.

14.3.4 Including an Intercept

It is usual to run a regression such as (14.3.21) including an intercept. This was not assumed in §14.3.2 and including an intercept changes the asymptotic distributions, although both estimators are consistent. The OLS estimator of $\lambda - 1$ becomes

$$\hat{\lambda} - 1 = \frac{\sum_{t=1}^{n}(x_{t-1} - \bar{x}_{-1})u_t}{\sum_{t=1}^{n} x_{t-1}^2 - n\bar{x}_{-1}^2} \tag{14.3.28}$$

where $\bar{x}_{-1} = n^{-1}\sum_{t=1}^{n} x_{t-1}$. Note that the mean deviations do not depend on x_0.

Starting with the denominator, expanding x_{t-1} yields

$$\begin{aligned}\frac{1}{n^2}\left(\sum_{t=1}^{n} x_{t-1}^2 - n\bar{x}_{-1}^2\right) &= \frac{1}{n^2}\sum_{t=1}^{n} S_{t-1}^2 - \left(\frac{1}{n^{3/2}}\sum_{t=1}^{n} S_{t-1}\right)^2 \\ &\xrightarrow{\mathrm{D}} \sigma^2\int_0^1 B^2 dr - \left(\sigma\int_0^1 B dr\right)^2. \end{aligned} \tag{14.3.29}$$

Also, extending (14.3.10),

$$\begin{aligned}\frac{1}{n}\sum_{t=1}^{n}(x_{t-1} - \bar{x}_{-1})u_t &= \frac{1}{n}\sum_{t=1}^{n} S_{t-1}u_t - \frac{1}{n^{3/2}}\sum_{t=1}^{n} S_{t-1}\frac{1}{\sqrt{n}}\sum_{t=1}^{n} u_t \\ &\xrightarrow{\mathrm{D}} \frac{\sigma^2}{2}\left(B(1)^2 - \frac{\sigma_u^2}{\sigma^2} - 2\int_0^1 B dr\cdot B(1)\right). \end{aligned} \tag{14.3.30}$$

Thus, with the data expressed in sample mean deviations the null distribution of $n(\hat{\lambda}-1)$ is given by the ratio of (14.3.30) to (14.3.29), which differs from (14.3.13). Similarly,

$$t_\lambda = \frac{\hat{\lambda} - 1}{s}\sqrt{\sum_{t=1}^{n} x_{t-1}^2 - n\bar{x}_{-1}^2} \xrightarrow{\mathrm{D}} \frac{B(1)^2 - \frac{\sigma_u^2}{\sigma^2} - 2B(1)\int_0^1 B dr}{2\frac{\sigma_u}{\sigma}\sqrt{\int_0^1 B^2 dr - \left(\int_0^1 B dr\right)^2}} \tag{14.3.31}$$

which is different from (14.3.18). Some simplification of these expressions is possible by noting that

$$\int_0^1 B^2 dr - \left(\int_0^1 B dr\right)^2 = \int_0^1 B^{*2} dr \tag{14.3.32}$$

where

$$B^* = B - \int_0^1 B dr \tag{14.3.33}$$

which is known as a *de-meaned* Brownian motion.

These distributions have also been tabulated by Dickey and Fuller, so that one has the choice of estimating either with or without an intercept provided the correct tabulation is used in each case. The corrections for serial correlation, either parametric or nonparametric, can be carried out as usual, and the data in mean deviation form can be substituted for the raw data to compute the variance in the latter case. The limiting distributions apply as before.

14.4 Allowing Deterministic Trends

14.4.1 Distribution of the AR Coefficient

So far, the assumption has been that x_t is a pure unit root process under the null hypothesis, having increments with a mean of zero. While the effect of *fitting* an intercept was considered in the last section, the assumption nonetheless remained as before, that the *true* intercept was 0.

In practice, this assumption is rather restrictive. Consider extending model (14.3.1) by assuming that the autoregressive process drives not x_t but $x_t - \alpha - \gamma t$ where either α or γ may differ from zero. Substitution into (14.3.1) yields

$$\begin{aligned} x_t &= \alpha + \gamma t + \lambda[x_{t-1} - \alpha - \gamma(t-1)] + u_t \\ &= \lambda x_{t-1} + [\alpha(1-\lambda) + \gamma] + (1-\lambda)\gamma t + u_t. \end{aligned} \tag{14.4.1}$$

When $\lambda = 1$, the trend term disappears from this equation, as does the parameter α, and the parameter γ appears to acquire the role of an intercept term. This appearance is deceptive, as is revealed by solving the difference equation to obtain

$$x_t = x_0 + S_t + \gamma t. \tag{14.4.2}$$

When $|\lambda| < 1$ and $\gamma \neq 0$, (14.4.1) describes a trend stationary process. What this means is that the process is stationary after subtracting a deterministic function of time. On the other hand, the case $\lambda = 1$ defines a difference stationary process, and in this case γ is called the drift parameter, since it represents the mean of the differences (increments). Given a series observed to possess a trend, unit root tests are a natural method for distinguishing difference stationarity from trend stationarity. The question to be decided is whether the trend has a stochastic component or is purely deterministic, the cases $\lambda = 1$ and $|\lambda| < 1$ respectively.

The first result to be established is that, although the tests derived in §14.3.4 might appear appropriate since the model under the null hypothesis contains the 'intercept' γ, this is not the case. Substituting from (14.4.2), assuming $x_0 = 0$ without loss of generality, produces

$$\begin{aligned} \sum_{t=1}^{n} x_{t-1}^2 - n\bar{x}_{-1}^2 &= \sum_{t=1}^{n} S_{t-1}^2 + 2\gamma \sum_{t=1}^{n}(t-1)S_{t-1} + \gamma^2 \sum_{t=1}^{n}(t-1)^2 \\ &\quad - \frac{1}{n}\left(\sum_{t=1}^{n}[S_{t-1} + \gamma(t-1)]\right)^2. \end{aligned} \tag{14.4.3}$$

The first three of these terms are respectively $O_p(n^2)$, $O_p(n^{5/2})$ and $O(n^3)$. The limit in distribution of the first term multiplied by n^{-2} is given by (14.3.8). For the second term the relevant limit is

$$\frac{1}{n^{5/2}} \sum_{t=1}^{n}(t-1)S_{t-1} = \sigma \sum_{t=1}^{n} \int_{t-1/n}^{t/n} \frac{t-1}{n} X_n(r)dr \xrightarrow{\mathrm{D}} \sigma \int_0^1 rB(r)dr \tag{14.4.4}$$

by the same sort of argument as in (14.3.5) and (14.3.6), and for the third,[11]

$$\frac{\gamma^2}{n^3}\sum_{t=1}^{n}(t-1)^2 \rightarrow \frac{\gamma^2}{3}. \tag{14.4.5}$$

Finally, the fourth term is

$$\frac{1}{n}\left(\sum_{t=1}^{n}[S_{t-1}+\gamma(t-1)]\right)^2 = \left(\frac{1}{\sqrt{n}}\sum_{t=1}^{n}S_{t-1}+\frac{\gamma}{2}\sqrt{n}(n-1)\right)^2. \tag{14.4.6}$$

The two terms under the square are $O_p(n)$ (by (14.3.5)) and $O(n^{3/2})$ respectively. Thus, the appropriate normalization here is n^{-3}, all the stochastic terms in (14.4.3) are of small order, and

$$\frac{1}{n^2}\left(\sum_{t=1}^{n}x_{t-1}^2 - n\bar{x}_{-1}^2\right) \xrightarrow{\text{pr}} \frac{\gamma^2}{3}-\frac{\gamma^2}{4}=\frac{\gamma^2}{12}. \tag{14.4.7}$$

Next, consider

$$\sum_{t=1}^{n}(x_{t-1}-\bar{x}_{-1})u_t = \sum_{t=1}^{n}S_{t-1}u_t+\gamma\sum_{t=1}^{n}(t-1)u_t$$
$$-\frac{1}{n}\left(\sum_{t=1}^{n}S_{t-1}+\gamma\sum_{t=1}^{n}(t-1)\right)\sum_{t=1}^{n}u_t. \tag{14.4.8}$$

which must be normalized by $n^{-3/2}$. The leading terms in the resulting expression can be written as

$$\frac{\gamma}{n^{3/2}}\sum_{t=1}^{n}\left(t-1-\frac{n-1}{2}\right)u_t = \frac{\gamma}{\sqrt{n}}\sum_{t=1}^{n}\left(\frac{t}{n}-\frac{1}{2}\right)u_t + O_p(n^{-1/2}). \tag{14.4.9}$$

By the same kind of argument that gave (14.1.5), it can be shown that

$$\frac{\gamma}{\sqrt{n}}\sum_{t=1}^{n}\left(\frac{t}{n}-\frac{1}{2}\right)u_t \xrightarrow{\text{D}} \text{N}\left(0,\ \frac{\gamma^2\sigma^2}{12}\right). \tag{14.4.10}$$

Putting (14.4.10) together with (14.4.7) yields by Theorem 3.1.2 the results

$$n^{3/2}(\hat{\lambda}-1) \xrightarrow{\text{D}} \text{N}\left(0,\ \frac{12\sigma^2}{\gamma^2}\right) \tag{14.4.11}$$

and

$$t_\lambda \xrightarrow{\text{D}} \text{N}(0,1). \tag{14.4.12}$$

Here, we find *super*-super consistency, with a rate of convergence of $n^{3/2}$. The obvious curiosity about these results is that the unit root process with drift yields a standard limit result, admittedly at different orders of magnitude in n from the stationary case, while the process without drift does not. This is deceptive, however. This is just a special case of the nonstandard asymptotics. It does not mean that the standard asymptotics apply to this model.

---

[11] See the footnote on page 149.

14.4.2 Tests of I(1)

The problem with constructing tests is that the limiting distribution for t_λ is given by (14.3.31) or (14.4.12), depending on whether $\gamma = 0$ or $\gamma \neq 0$. In the terminology of §12.1.1, tests based on an intercept correction are not similar. The solution to this difficulty is to include the trend variable in the autoregression, notwithstanding its apparent absence under the null hypothesis. Thus, consider the model

$$x_t = \mu + \tau t + \lambda x_{t-1} + u_t \tag{14.4.13}$$

where $\tau = \gamma(1-\lambda)$ and $\mu = \alpha(1-\lambda)+\gamma$. Let (14.4.13) be estimated by multiple regression on the assumption implied by the null hypothesis, $\lambda = 1$, $\tau = 0$, and $\mu = \gamma \neq 0$, in general. Let '$*$' denote deviations from the sample mean, so that for example $t^* = t - (n+1)/2$. Note from (14.4.2) that $x^*_{t-1} = S^*_{t-1} + \gamma(t-1)^*$, where $(t-1)^* = t^*$, and the OLS estimate of λ in (14.4.13) can be expressed in error-of-estimate form as

$$\begin{aligned}\hat{\lambda} - 1 &= \frac{\sum t^{*2} \sum (S^*_{t-1} + \gamma t^*)u_t - \sum t^*(S^*_{t-1} + \gamma t^*) \sum t^* u_t}{\sum t^{*2} \sum (S^*_{t-1} + \gamma t^*)^2 - [\sum t^*(S^*_{t-1} + \gamma t^*)]^2} \\ &= \frac{\sum t^{*2} \sum S^*_{t-1} u_t - \sum t^* S^*_{t-1} \sum t^* u_t}{\sum t^{*2} \sum S^{*2}_{t-1} - (\sum t^* S^*_{t-1})^2}\end{aligned} \tag{14.4.14}$$

where all sums are from 2 to n. The second equality follows by cancellation of matching terms. Similarly for the trend coefficient,

$$\begin{aligned}\hat{\tau} &= \frac{\sum (S^*_{t-1} + \gamma t^*)^2 \sum t^* u_t - \sum t(S^*_{t-1} + \gamma t^*) \sum (S^*_{t-1} + \gamma t^*) u_t}{\sum t^{*2} \sum (S^*_{t-1} + \gamma t^*)^2 - [\sum t(S^*_{t-1} + \gamma t^*)]^2} \\ &= \frac{\sum S^{*2}_{t-1} \sum t^* u_t - \sum t S^*_{t-1} \sum S^*_{t-1} u_t}{\sum t^{*2} \sum S^{*2}_{t-1} - (\sum t S^*_{t-1})^2}\end{aligned} \tag{14.4.15}$$

All the relevant limits for these expressions have already been obtained. In particular,

$$\frac{1}{n^3} \sum t^{*2} \to \int_0^1 (r - \tfrac{1}{2})^2 dr = \frac{1}{12} \tag{14.4.16}$$

$$\frac{1}{n} \sum S^*_{t-1} u_t \xrightarrow{\text{D}} \frac{\sigma^2}{2} \left(B(1)^2 - \frac{\sigma_u^2}{\sigma^2} - 2 \int_0^1 B dr \cdot B(1) \right) \tag{14.4.17}$$

from (14.3.30),

$$\frac{1}{n^{5/2}} \sum t^* S^*_{t-1} \xrightarrow{\text{D}} \sigma \int_0^1 (r - \tfrac{1}{2}) B dr \tag{14.4.18}$$

using (14.4.4) and (14.3.5),

$$\frac{1}{n^{3/2}} \sum t^* u_t \xrightarrow{\text{D}} \sigma \int_0^1 (r - \tfrac{1}{2}) dB \tag{14.4.19}$$

and finally,

$$\frac{1}{n^2}\sum S_{t-1}^{*2} \xrightarrow{D} \sigma^2 \int_0^1 B^2 dr - \left(\sigma \int_0^1 B dr\right)^2. \tag{14.4.20}$$

None of these terms depends on γ. $\hat{\lambda} - 1$ is n-consistent, the limiting distributions of $n(\hat{\lambda} - 1)$ and $n^{3/2}\hat{\tau}$ under the null hypothesis are invariant to the drift, and

$$t_\lambda \xrightarrow{D} \frac{B(1)^2 - \frac{\sigma_u^2}{\sigma^2} - 2B(1)\int_0^1 B dr - 12\int_0^1 (r - \frac{1}{2})B dr \int_0^1 (r - \frac{1}{2}) dB}{\frac{2\sigma_u}{\sigma}\sqrt{\int_0^1 B^2 dr - \left(\int_0^1 B dr\right)^2 - 12\left(\int_0^1 (r - \frac{1}{2}) B dr\right)^2}} \tag{14.4.21}$$

As with (14.3.18) and (14.3.31), this limiting distribution is independent of nuisance parameters when the increments are not serially correlated, such that $\sigma^2 = \sigma_u^2$. The augmented Dickey–Fuller and Phillips–Perron modifications are available in the same way as before, where in the former case the lags of Δx_t are now added to the regression in (14.4.13). For the latter case, s_u^2 and s_{nl}^2 are consistent for σ_u^2 and σ^2 as before.

Dickey and Fuller also tabulated critical values for these versions of the t and $n(\hat{\lambda} - 1)$ tests, so all the variants of the unit root test are feasible in practice. The most popular procedures are the t_λ test from (14.4.1), when it is given as prior knowledge that $\gamma = 0$, and the test from (14.4.13), if the case $\gamma \neq 0$ is admitted. MacKinnon (1991) provides a much more extensive set of simulations using different sample sizes. These are used to construct 'response surface'[12] formulae, allowing the distributions to be approximated for small samples.

14.5 Testing the Null of I(0)

A feature of the Dickey–Fuller and Phillips–Perron tests is that they make the unit root the null hypothesis. This is a natural choice when we think of nesting the unit root model in the family of autoregressive forms, but has the drawback that a lack of test power may encourage practitioners to 'find' unit roots when none exist. Therefore, the devising of a test that sets 'I(0)' as the null hypothesis is an important extension. Such a test is proposed by Kwiatkowski, Phillips, Schmidt and Shin (1992). The KPSS test can be motivated in a number of ways, but perhaps the simplest way to approach it is to ask 'What is the particular characteristic of a I(0) process?'. A natural answer might be: 'A process that, when integrated, yields a process with exactly one unit root.' This is something distinct from a process that has no unit roots, because it must not be over-differenced, which is the I(−1) case. It is also different from a process that integrates to I(d)

[12] In a response surface estimation, the test critical values estimated by Monte Carlo simulation for a range of different values of n form an experimental sample. These data are regressed on n^{-1} and n^{-2}. The intercept in these regressions estimates the asymptote, and the regression predictions can be used to formulate small sample corrections.

for $d \geq 2$, and the proposed test is consistent against all alternatives of the latter type.

Suppose the series under test is $x_1, \ldots, x_n$, and is assumed under H_0 to satisfy one of the conditions specified in Theorem 14.2.2. Take these to define what can legitimately be called an I(0) process (compare the remarks in the first paragraph of this chapter) noting in particular that the I(−1) process does not satisfy them. The latter process has no trend, but its scaled partial sums do not satisfy the conditions for a FCLT. Expressing the sample in mean deviations, consider the partial sum series

$$S_t = \sum_{s=1}^{t}(x_t - \bar{x}) = \sum_{s=1}^{t} x_s - \frac{t}{n}\sum_{st=1}^{n} x_s \tag{14.5.1}$$

for $t = 1, \ldots, n$. This series has the property $S_n = 0$. Define, similarly to (14.2.10),

$$V_n(r) = \frac{1}{\sqrt{n}\sigma} S_{[nr]} \quad 0 \leq r \leq 1 \tag{14.5.2}$$

where $\sigma^2 = \lim_{n\to\infty} n^{-1}E(S_n^2)$, which exists and is finite and nonzero by assumption. Theorems 14.2.2 and 14.2.3 applied to the terms in (14.5.1) yield $V_n \xrightarrow{\mathrm{D}} V$ where

$$V(r) = B(r) - rB(1). \tag{14.5.3}$$

This limit process, which can be seen to have the property $V(0) = V(1) = 0$ a.s., is called a *Brownian bridge*, and also a 'tied-down Brownian motion'.

The statistic to be considered has the form

$$\hat{\eta}_\mu = \frac{1}{n^2 s_{nl}^2}\sum_{t=1}^{n} S_t^2 \tag{14.5.4}$$

where s_{nl}^2 is a consistent kernel estimator of σ^2 of the form (14.3.23). In this case, it is necessary to specify that $l(n) = o(n^{-1/2})$. Applying the continuous mapping theorem in the usual manner leads to the conclusion that, under the null hypothesis,

$$\hat{\eta}_\mu \xrightarrow{\mathrm{D}} \int_0^1 V(r)^2 dr. \tag{14.5.5}$$

This distribution can be tabulated by simulation, as for the Dickey–Fuller statistics.

To show that the test is consistent against the I(1) alternative, consider the distribution of $\hat{\eta}_\mu$ when x_t contains a unit root. The alternative hypothesis can be posed in a general form, as

$$x_t = x_0 + \sum_{i=1}^{t} u_i + \varepsilon_t$$

where both u_t and ε_t are processes satisfying the assumptions of Theorem 14.2.2. In fact, the contribution of ε_t to the asymptotic distribution is of small order and can be ignored. The partial sums of x_t must be normalized by $n^{-3/2}$, and then by application of previous arguments

$$\frac{1}{n^{3/2}\sigma}S_{[nr]} \xrightarrow{D} \int_0^r B(u)du - r\int_0^1 B(u)du = \int_0^r B^*(u)du \tag{14.5.6}$$

where B^* is the de-meaned Brownian motion defined in (14.3.33). This in fact is the limit in distribution of an I(2) process, in deviations from the mean. Hence,

$$\frac{1}{n^4}\sum_{t=1}^{n} S_t^2 \xrightarrow{D} \sigma^2 \int_0^1 \left(\int_0^r B^*(u)du\right)^2 dr \tag{14.5.7}$$

under the alternative hypothesis.

On the other hand, the denominator of $\hat{\eta}_\mu$ can be written, using (14.3.23) as

$$s_{nl}^2 = \frac{1}{n}\left(\sum_{t=1}^{n}(x_t - \bar{x})^2 + 2\sum_{\tau=1}^{l(n)} w_{\tau l} \sum_{t=\tau+1}^{n} (x_t - \bar{x})(x_{t-\tau} - \bar{x})\right) \tag{14.5.8}$$

where

$$\sum_{t=\tau+1}^{n} (x_t - \bar{x})(x_{t-\tau} - \bar{x}) = \sum_{t=\tau+1}^{n} (x_{t-\tau} - \bar{x})^2 + \sum_{t=\tau+1}^{n} (x_{t-\tau} - \bar{x})\Delta x_{t-\tau+1} + \cdots + \sum_{t=\tau+1}^{n} (x_{t-\tau} - \bar{x})\Delta x_t. \tag{14.5.9}$$

Using (14.3.30), note that all the terms in (14.5.9) except the first, τ in number, are of $O_p(n)$. Therefore, defining $w_{0l} = \frac{1}{2}$ and applying the assumption that $l(n) = o(n^{-1/2})$,

$$\begin{aligned}\frac{s_{nl}^2}{nl(n)} &= \frac{2}{n^2 l(n)}\left(\sum_{\tau=0}^{l(n)} w_{\tau l} \sum_{t=\tau+1}^{n} (x_{t-\tau} - \bar{x})^2\right) + O_p(l(n)^2/n) \\ &\xrightarrow{D} \sigma^2 \int_{-1}^{1} k(\xi)d\xi \int_0^1 B^*(r)dr.\end{aligned} \tag{14.5.10}$$

where $k(\cdot)$ is the kernel function specified for the variance estimator (see §9.4.3). Combining (14.5.10) and (14.5.7) shows that $\hat{\eta}_\mu = O_p(n/l(n))$, which proves consistency. Also note how the distribution is free of nuisance parameters under the alternative, apart from the (known) integral of $k(\cdot)$.

The extension of the KPSS statistic to allow for deterministic trends is straightforward. In this case the test is of the null of trend stationarity, with difference stationarity as the alternative. In (14.5.1), the mean deviations must be replaced by residuals from the regression of x_t on the intercept and trend terms. Following a development closely similar to §14.4, define a process V_{2n} by

$$V_{2n}(r) = \frac{1}{\sqrt{n}\sigma}S_{[nr]} \quad 0 \le r \le 1 \tag{14.5.11}$$

where now

$$S_t = \sum_{s=1}^{t}\left((x_t - \bar{x}) - \frac{\sum_s (s-\bar{s})x_s}{\sum_s (s-\bar{s})^2}(t-\bar{t})\right). \tag{14.5.12}$$

Let the statistic corresponding to (14.5.4) with this definition of S_t be denoted $\hat{\eta}_\tau$. It can be shown straightforwardly, adapting previous arguments, that

$$\hat{\eta}_\tau \xrightarrow{\text{D}} \int_0^1 V_2(r)^2 dr \tag{14.5.13}$$

where V_2 is the limit in distribution of V_{2n} and is defined by

$$V_2(r) = B(r) - rB(1) - 6(r^2 - r)\int_0^1 (s - \tfrac{1}{2})dB(s). \tag{14.5.14}$$

V_2 is called a second level Brownian bridge. The distribution of $\hat{\eta}_\tau$ can be tabulated by simulation just like the other cases.

An interesting feature of the test, as has been developed here, is that it tests a nonparametric hypothesis to the effect that the series in question satisfies the conditions of Theorem 14.2.2, without specifying a parametric model of the process. It is nonetheless possible to construct parametric models in which the relevant null is a special case. It can be rationalised as an LM test of $\sigma_v^2 = 0$ in the model represented by (5.2.30) and (5.2.31). Equivalently, consider the IMA(1,1) model of §5.2.7, which (after including a drift term) has the form

$$x_t = \gamma + x_{t-1} + \varepsilon_t - \theta\varepsilon_{t-1}. \tag{14.5.15}$$

The test can now be seen as a test of $\theta = 1$, against the alternative $\theta < 1$. However, these are special cases, and the null distribution will be obtained simply under the stated assumptions on the process in question.

Further Reading: On the probability background, the books by Davidson (1994a) and McCabe and Tremayne (1993) provide an introduction. The renowned monograph by Billingsley (1968) has been hugely influential in this field, and is still widely quoted as a source of useful results. Pollard (1984) provides some additional background, and explores some alternative methods of setting up the required probability measures. On the asymptotics of the unit root AR(1), the article by Phillips (1987) is a sound introduction. Thorough treatments are found in Hamilton (1994), and the survey by Stock (1994), which also looks at the problem of structural breaks in detail. The monographs by Banerjee et. al. (1993), Hatanaka (1996) and Tanaka (1996) also give in-depth coverage. Fuller's (1976) textbook is often cited as the source of the original Dickey–Fuller tabulations.

14.6 Appendix: Proof of Theorem 14.3.1

Let $\mathbf{z}_t$ denote the vector whose elements are $\Delta x_{t-1}, \ldots, \Delta x_{t-k}$, with $E(\mathbf{z}_t) = \mathbf{0}$ and $E(\mathbf{z}_t\mathbf{z}_t') = \mathbf{\Sigma}_{zz}$. Use the Frisch-Waugh theorem to construct the ADF regression in two stages. When H_0 is true, regressing Δx_t on $\boldsymbol{z}_t$ yields consistent estimates of the coefficients $\beta_1, \ldots, \beta_k$, and the residuals

$$\hat{u}_t = \Delta x_t - \boldsymbol{z}_t \left(\sum_{t=1}^{n} \boldsymbol{z}_t \boldsymbol{z}_t' \right)^{-1} \sum_{t=1}^{n} \boldsymbol{z}_t \Delta x_t \tag{14.6.1}$$

converge in probability to the u_t in (14.3.22).

On the other hand, note that the elements of $\boldsymbol{z}_t x_{t-1}$ are $\Delta x_{t-i} x_{t-1} = \Delta x_{t-i} x_{t-i-1} + \sum_{j=1}^{i} \Delta x_{t-i} \Delta x_{t-j}$ for $i = 1, \ldots, k$. Therefore, under H_0 the coefficient in the regression of x_{t-1} on $\boldsymbol{z}_t$, using Theorem 15.2.3, is

$$\hat{\boldsymbol{d}} = \left(\sum_{t=1}^{n} \boldsymbol{z}_t \boldsymbol{z}_t' \right)^{-1} \sum_{t=1}^{n} \boldsymbol{z}_t x_{t-1} \xrightarrow{\text{D}} \boldsymbol{\Sigma}_{zz}^{-1} \boldsymbol{\iota} \sigma^2 \int_0^1 B dB + \boldsymbol{\psi} \tag{14.6.2}$$

where $\boldsymbol{\iota}$ is the k-vector of ones and $\boldsymbol{\psi}$ is the constant vector with elements

$$\psi_i = \sum_{j=1-i}^{\infty} \text{Cov}(\Delta x_{t-1}, \Delta x_{t-j}), \; i = 1, \ldots, k. \tag{14.6.3}$$

Note that $\hat{\boldsymbol{d}}$ is a random vector asymptotically. However, the residuals from this regression are $\hat{v}_t = x_{t-1} - \hat{\boldsymbol{d}}' \boldsymbol{z}_t$ where the first term is a unit root process under H_0, but the second term is $O_p(1)$. Applying Theorem 3.1.2(i), it follows that

$$\frac{\hat{v}_{[nr]}}{\sqrt{n}} \xrightarrow{\text{D}} \sigma B(r) \tag{14.6.4}$$

which is the same limit in distribution as $n^{-1/2} x_{[nr]}$. In other words, the correction of x_{t-1} for the lagged differences is asymptotically negligible.

Putting these two results together, it follows that the ADF regression

$$n(\hat{\lambda} - 1) = \frac{n \sum_{t=1}^{n} \hat{v}_t \hat{u}_t}{n^2 \sum_{t=1}^{n} \hat{v}_t^2} \tag{14.6.5}$$

is equivalent under H_0 to the simple regression of u_t in (14.3.22) on x_{t-1}. The tabulated Dickey–Fuller distributions therefore apply. ∎

Chapter 15

Cointegrating Regression

15.1 Cointegrated Time Series

15.1.1 Basic Concepts

Application of the unit root tests of the last chapter has lead to the observation that many economic time series are I(1). The well-known study of Nelson and Plosser (1982) was the first to document this phenomenon. Such variables do not exhibit a long-run mean reversion tendency. They appear to vary around a local point of central tendency that shifts permanently with the passage of time; see Figure 5.3 for an (artificial) example of the type of pattern often observed.

Such phenomena were traditionally modelled by making the mean a deterministic function of time, but unless the rate of trend is able to change, such models will break down eventually. An I(1) process contains a stochastic trend that can change its direction as a result of random events, which is how economic variables like real GDP or employment appear to behave. Typically, there may be a combination of deterministic and stochastic trend elements (for example, GDP has always tended to increase in the very long run) but stochastic trends are found to be generally important.

The recognition of stochastic trends in individual time series leads to the idea that relationships between such variables over time may be manifested by common trends.

Definition 15.1.1 If $\boldsymbol{x}_t$ is an m-vector of I(1) time series processes, and there exists an m-vector $\boldsymbol{\beta}$ such that $\boldsymbol{\beta}'\boldsymbol{x}_t \sim \mathrm{I}(0)$, the variables are said to be *cointegrated.* $\boldsymbol{\beta}$ is called a *cointegrating vector.* □

Recall the discussion of spurious regression in §7.4. The question of whether a genuine (as opposed to spurious) relationship exists between a set of I(1) time series can be posed as the question: are the variables cointegrated? This is a question that can be answered in principle without any reference to the short-run dynamics of the relationship. It is sufficient that the residual obtained after taking an appropriate linear combination of the variables is an I(0) component that can be modelled by ordinary time series techniques. It is possible that $\boldsymbol{\beta}$ is not unique, and there are several linearly independent vectors, say $\boldsymbol{\beta}_1, \ldots, \boldsymbol{\beta}_s$, each of which is a cointegrating vector for $\boldsymbol{x}_t$. The space spanned by these vectors is called the *cointegrating space* for $\boldsymbol{x}_t$ and s is the *cointegrating rank* of the variables.

The following section introduces the algebra of vector ARMA systems with unit roots. Thereafter, this chapter will focus on the case $s = 1$, in which the cointegrating vector is unique.[1] In this case the analysis can in principle be pursued as a single-equation problem. Chapter 16 will look at the general case, where there may be multiple cointegrating vectors.

15.1.2 Cointegrated Equation Systems

Consider the n-vector of variables $\boldsymbol{x}_t$ having the representation

$$\Delta \boldsymbol{x}_t = \boldsymbol{C}(L)\boldsymbol{\varepsilon}_t \tag{15.1.1}$$

where $\boldsymbol{C}(\cdot)$ represents a matrix-valued polynomial, possibly of infinite order, and $\boldsymbol{\varepsilon}_t$ is a random sequence having at least zero mean and finite variance matrix $\boldsymbol{\Sigma}$, plus additional properties to be specified, to ensure that $\Delta \boldsymbol{x}_t \sim \mathrm{I}(0)$. It is conventional in this kind of analysis to assume something on the lines of $\boldsymbol{\varepsilon}_t \sim \mathrm{i.i.d.}(\boldsymbol{0}, \boldsymbol{\Sigma})$. This is harmless for the sake of exposition although more restrictive than is needed for the results of this chapter. For a statement of sufficient conditions with discussion, see §15.2.1.

Equation (15.1.1) may be thought of as the Wold representation (see §5.2.3) of $\Delta \boldsymbol{x}_t$. If

$$\boldsymbol{C}(z) = \boldsymbol{A}^{+}(L)^{-1}\boldsymbol{D}(L) \tag{15.1.2}$$

where both $\boldsymbol{A}^{+}(L)$ and $\boldsymbol{D}(L)$ are finite order polynomials, (15.1.1) could also be thought of as the final form of the vector ARMA (VARMA) system

$$\boldsymbol{A}(L)(\boldsymbol{x}_t - \boldsymbol{x}_0) = \boldsymbol{D}(L)\boldsymbol{\varepsilon}_t \tag{15.1.3}$$

where

$$\boldsymbol{A}(L) = \boldsymbol{A}^{+}(L)(1 - L). \tag{15.1.4}$$

As in §5.1, the properties of $\boldsymbol{C}(\cdot)$ and similar constructions are conveniently discussed by treating them as functions of a complex variable z. The following properties are assumed. First, $\boldsymbol{C}(z)$ must be summable, such that $|[\boldsymbol{C}(1)]_{ij}| < \infty$ for each i and j. An example of a polynomial that is not summable is one that contains a factor $(1 - z)^{-1} = 1 + z^2 + z^3 + \ldots$, which is undefined at the point $z = 1$. Second, it is assumed is that

$$\boldsymbol{C}(1) \neq \boldsymbol{0} \tag{15.1.5}$$

[1]That is, unique apart from the choice of normalization, which is always arbitrary. If $\boldsymbol{\beta}$ is cointegrating, so is $\lambda\boldsymbol{\beta}$ for any scalar $\lambda \neq 0$.

which rules out the case

$$C(z) = (1 - z)C^*(z) \tag{15.1.6}$$

where $C^*(z)$ is summable. This would imply that (15.1.1) is *over*-differenced, with a factor $1 - L$ that can be cancelled from each side.

Under these assumptions, $\boldsymbol{x}_t \sim \mathrm{I}(1)$. In particular, the factor Δ cannot be cancelled, and a solution to (15.1.3) of the form

$$\boldsymbol{x}_t - \boldsymbol{x}_0 = C^*(L)\boldsymbol{\varepsilon}_t \tag{15.1.7}$$

with $C^*(z)$ summable is ruled out by (15.1.5). The solution is obtained by treating $(1 - L)^{-1}$ applied to a time series starting at time $t = 0$ as a summation (integration) operator, so that if $\boldsymbol{\eta}_t = C(L)\boldsymbol{\varepsilon}_t$ for $t = 1, 2, 3, \ldots$ then

$$\boldsymbol{x}_t - \boldsymbol{x}_0 = \sum_{s=1}^{t} \boldsymbol{\eta}_s. \tag{15.1.8}$$

Thus, to avoid infinities it is necessary to specify a finite starting date for an I(1) process. Since the increments have zero mean, it is sometimes assumed that $\boldsymbol{x}_t$ has a mean of zero for each $t \geq 0$, but by subtracting out the initial value $\boldsymbol{x}_0$ a fixed, nonzero mean that disappears in this transformation can also be assumed.

A simple example illustrates these points. Let $m = 2$ and suppose

$$x_{1t} - \lambda x_{2t} = \varepsilon_{1t} \tag{15.1.9a}$$

$$\Delta x_{2t} = \varepsilon_{2t} \tag{15.1.9b}$$

where $x_{10} = x_{20} = 0$. The model has the form of (15.1.3) where $D(z) = I$ and

$$A(z) = \begin{bmatrix} 1 & -\lambda \\ 0 & 1 - z \end{bmatrix}. \tag{15.1.10}$$

Note that $|A(z)| = 1 - z$ and

$$C(z) = (1 - z)A(z)^{-1} = \begin{bmatrix} 1 - z & \lambda \\ 0 & 1 \end{bmatrix}. \tag{15.1.11}$$

The Wold representation in differences is therefore

$$\Delta x_{1t} = \Delta\varepsilon_{1t} + \lambda\varepsilon_{2t} \tag{15.1.12a}$$

$$\Delta x_{2t} = \varepsilon_{2t}. \tag{15.1.12b}$$

15.1.3 The VECM Representation

The roots of the characteristic equation $|A(z)| = 0$, as defined in §5.2.8, are also the reciprocals of the eigenvalues of the companion form of the model as in §4.3.4. As pointed out in those discussions, stability of the dynamic system requires all the roots to lie outside the unit circle. By contrast, in an integrated system $|A(z)|$ has one or more roots of unity, as evidenced by the example.[2] By a

[2] See Engle and Granger (1987) Lemma 1, and Davidson (1991) Theorem 2.1(ii).

straightforward generalization of (5.3.18), the Beveridge–Nelson decomposition of a pth-order matrix polynomial $\boldsymbol{A}(z)$ is

$$\boldsymbol{A}(z) = \boldsymbol{A}(1) + (1-z)\boldsymbol{A}^*(z) \tag{15.1.13}$$

where $\boldsymbol{A}^*(z)$ is of order $p-1$. By consideration of the formula for a determinant,

$$|\boldsymbol{A}(z)| = |\boldsymbol{A}(1) + (1-z)\boldsymbol{A}^*(z)| = |\boldsymbol{A}(1)| + (1-z)f(z) \tag{15.1.14}$$

where $f(z)$ is some scalar polynomial of finite order. For $|\boldsymbol{A}(z)| = 0$ to have one or more roots of unity, it is necessary and sufficient that $\boldsymbol{A}(1)$ be singular.

Suppose that $\boldsymbol{A}(1)$ has rank $s < m$. For such a matrix there always exists a decomposition,

$$\boldsymbol{A}(1) = \boldsymbol{\rho}\boldsymbol{\beta}' \tag{15.1.15}$$

where $\boldsymbol{\rho}$ and $\boldsymbol{\beta}$ are $m \times s$ matrices with rank s, whose columns span the column space and row space of $\boldsymbol{A}(1)$, respectively. The decomposition is not unique, but the VARMA model always has a representation

$$\boldsymbol{A}(L)(\boldsymbol{x}_t - \boldsymbol{x}_0) = \boldsymbol{\rho}(\boldsymbol{\beta}'\boldsymbol{x}_t - \boldsymbol{\mu}) + \boldsymbol{A}^*(L)\Delta\boldsymbol{x}_t = \boldsymbol{D}(L)\boldsymbol{\varepsilon}_t \tag{15.1.16}$$

where $\boldsymbol{\mu} = \boldsymbol{\beta}'\boldsymbol{x}_0$. In the example of (15.1.9), a valid decomposition is

$$\boldsymbol{\beta}' = \begin{pmatrix} 1 & -\lambda \end{pmatrix} \quad \boldsymbol{\rho} = \begin{bmatrix} 1 \\ 0 \end{bmatrix} \quad \boldsymbol{A}^*(z) = \begin{bmatrix} 0 & 0 \\ 0 & 1 \end{bmatrix}. \tag{15.1.17}$$

Suppose that $\boldsymbol{x}_t \sim \mathrm{I}(1)$, and accordingly that $\boldsymbol{A}^*(L)\Delta\boldsymbol{x}_t \sim \mathrm{I}(0)$. Since $\boldsymbol{D}(L)\boldsymbol{\varepsilon}_t \sim \mathrm{I}(0)$, it follows that $\boldsymbol{\beta}'\boldsymbol{x}_t - \boldsymbol{\mu} \sim \mathrm{I}(0)$ since otherwise equation (15.1.16) does not balance. There must therefore exist s independent linear combinations of an I(1) vector process that are I(0). The vector process $\boldsymbol{x}_t$ is said to be cointegrated with cointegrating rank s. Note that if the rows of $\boldsymbol{\beta}'$ are cointegrating, so are those of $\boldsymbol{d\beta}'$ for any nonsingular $s \times s$ matrix $\boldsymbol{d}$.

Alternatively, one can say that the integrated processes share a set of common trends. An integrated system, while not stable, generates only a restricted set of independent stochastic trends, equal in number to the nullity of $\boldsymbol{A}(1)$, or $m-s$. Only in the case $\boldsymbol{A}(1) = \boldsymbol{0}$ does an I(1) VAR process fail to be cointegrated, and then it generates m independent stochastic trends.[3]

The need to specify $\boldsymbol{x}_t \sim \mathrm{I}(1)$ is a hint that the class of unit root models to be considered here is not exhaustive. Note that the matrix $\boldsymbol{A}^*(L)$ defines a difference equation in $\Delta\boldsymbol{x}_t$ that must be stable, containing no integrating factors, or else the assumption $\boldsymbol{x}_t \sim \mathrm{I}(1)$ is unwarranted. For example, if (15.1.9b) were to be changed to $\Delta^2 x_{2t} = u_{2t}$ then $\boldsymbol{A}^*(z)$ acquires a factor $1-z$ and $\boldsymbol{A}(z)^{-1}$ would contain factors of $(1-z)^{-2}$. The model then generates I(2) processes. These are a legitimate case, but are outside the scope of these chapters.[4]

---

[3] See for example Stock and Watson (1988a,b).

[4] See Johansen (1988a) and Davidson (1991) for a discussion of these conditions, and also Johansen (1995b,c) on the statistical treatment of I(2) systems.

A small rearrangement of (15.1.16) gives

$$\boldsymbol{A}^{**}(L)\Delta\boldsymbol{x}_t + \boldsymbol{\rho}(\boldsymbol{\beta}'\boldsymbol{x}_{t-1} - \boldsymbol{\mu}) = \boldsymbol{D}(L)\boldsymbol{\varepsilon}_t \tag{15.1.18}$$

where $\boldsymbol{A}^{**}(z) = \boldsymbol{A}^*(z) + \boldsymbol{A}(1)$. This is a more convenient form of the system, since current $\boldsymbol{x}_t$ appears in only one term and $\boldsymbol{A}_0^{**} = \boldsymbol{A}_0$. This is the error correction (EC) form of the VAR system, also known as the VECM system. The result that the cointegrated VAR system has an error correction representation is known as the Granger representation theorem, see Engle and Granger (1987) and also Granger (1981, 1983), Granger and Weiss (1983). Engle and Yoo (1991) give an alternative derivation using the Smith–Macmillan decomposition of a rational polynomial matrix.

15.2 Limit Theory for Cointegrating Regressions

A fundamental result in cointegration theory pointed out by Engle and Granger (1987) is that a unique cointegrating vector is consistently estimated by least squares regression. This holds true regardless of the simultaneity structure of the model generating $\boldsymbol{x}_t$ and of the short-run dynamics, although these factors do influence the asymptotic distribution. Assuming $s = 1$, let $\boldsymbol{\beta}$ $(m \times 1)$ denote the cointegrating vector, unique apart from normalization. Fixing the first element at 1 by appropriate definition of $\boldsymbol{\rho}$ in (15.1.15), write

$$\boldsymbol{\beta}'\boldsymbol{x}_t = x_{1t} - \boldsymbol{\gamma}'\boldsymbol{x}_{2t} \tag{15.2.1}$$

so that $\boldsymbol{\beta}' = (1, -\gamma_1, \dots, -\gamma_{m-1})$. Accordingly, consider the regression

$$x_{1t} = \mu + \boldsymbol{\gamma}'\boldsymbol{x}_{2t} + u_t. \tag{15.2.2}$$

The asymptotic analysis of this model was first undertaken by Phillips and Durlauf (1986).

15.2.1 Limit Theory Preliminaries

Consider a vector of random variables $\boldsymbol{\eta}_t = (\eta_{1t}, \dots, \eta_{mt})'$. Let $\boldsymbol{S}_t = \sum_{j=1}^t \boldsymbol{\eta}_j$ $(m \times 1)$ with $\boldsymbol{S}_0 = \boldsymbol{0}$, and define

$$\boldsymbol{\Sigma} = \lim_{n\to\infty} \frac{1}{n} \sum_{t=1}^n E(\boldsymbol{\eta}_t\boldsymbol{\eta}_t') \tag{15.2.3}$$

$$\boldsymbol{\Lambda} = \lim_{n\to\infty} \frac{1}{n} \sum_{t=1}^n E(\boldsymbol{S}_{t-1}\boldsymbol{\eta}_t') = \lim_{n\to\infty} \frac{1}{n} \sum_{t=2}^n \sum_{j=1}^{t-1} E(\boldsymbol{\eta}_j\boldsymbol{\eta}_t'). \tag{15.2.4}$$

Note that $\boldsymbol{\Lambda} = \boldsymbol{0}$ in the case where $\boldsymbol{\eta}_t$ is serially uncorrelated.

Also, let $D^m[0,1]$ denote the Cartesian product of m copies of the space $D[0,1]$, that is, the space of m-vectors of cadlag functions. Then, if

$$\boldsymbol{x}_n(r) = \frac{1}{\sqrt{n}}\boldsymbol{S}_{[nr]} = \frac{1}{\sqrt{n}}\boldsymbol{S}_{j-1} \quad (j-1)/n \le r < j/n \tag{15.2.5}$$

$\boldsymbol{x}_n(r)$ is a random element of $D^m[0,1]$. The following generalization of Theorem 14.2.2 is a special case of Theorem 3.1 of De Jong and Davidson (2000b).

Theorem 15.2.1 Let each element of $\boldsymbol{\eta}_t$ satisfy the conditions of at least one of Theorems 3.3.1, 3.3.2, 6.2.3, and 6.4.5, and also assume

$$\lim_{n\to\infty} n^{-1}E(\boldsymbol{S}_n\boldsymbol{S}_n') = \boldsymbol{\Omega} = \boldsymbol{\Sigma} + \boldsymbol{\Lambda} + \boldsymbol{\Lambda}' < \infty \tag{15.2.6}$$

where $\boldsymbol{\Omega}$ is positive definite. Then

$$\boldsymbol{x}_n \xrightarrow{\mathrm{D}} \boldsymbol{B} \tag{15.2.7}$$

where $\boldsymbol{B}$ is a m-dimensional vector Brownian motion with covariance matrix $\boldsymbol{\Omega}$, such that for $0 \le s < t \le 1$,

$$E[\boldsymbol{B}(t) - \boldsymbol{B}(s)][\boldsymbol{B}(t) - \boldsymbol{B}(s)]' = (t-s)\boldsymbol{\Omega}. \quad \square \tag{15.2.8}$$

Equivalently, we may say that $\boldsymbol{B} = \boldsymbol{\Omega}^{1/2}\boldsymbol{W}$, where $\boldsymbol{W}$ is an m-vector of independent standard Wiener processes. This theorem implies that each element of $\boldsymbol{S}_n$ behaves asymptotically like the scalar I(1) process analysed in Chapter 14. In considering the assumptions of this theorem, it should be noted that these will have to be satisfied by $\Delta\boldsymbol{x}_t$ in the analysis. If the data are generated by a model like (15.1.3), this imposes conditions jointly on the polynomials $\boldsymbol{A}(z)$ and $\boldsymbol{D}(z)$ and the driving process $\boldsymbol{\varepsilon}_t$. If the processes are in fact VARMA, in which $\boldsymbol{A}^+(z)$ in (15.1.4) and $\boldsymbol{D}(z)$ are of finite order with all roots outside the unit circle, it is actually sufficient for $\boldsymbol{\varepsilon}_t$ itself to satisfy the stated conditions, since by NED theory, sufficient properties carry straight over to $\Delta\boldsymbol{x}_t$. The kind of arguments that can be adopted here are discussed in several earlier sections of the book including §6.3.3, §6.5 and §7.1.4.

There is also the vector generalization of the continuous mapping theorem, as in Davidson (1994a), Theorem 26.13.

Theorem 15.2.2 Let $h : D^m[0,1] \to \mathbb{R}$ be a measurable functional that is continuous except on a set of Wiener measure zero. Then $h(\boldsymbol{x}_n) \xrightarrow{\mathrm{D}} h(\boldsymbol{B})$. $\square$

By straightforward generalization of equations (14.3.5) and (14.3.6), the last two results give

$$\frac{1}{n^{3/2}}\sum_{t=1}^{n}\boldsymbol{S}_t \xrightarrow{\mathrm{D}} \int_0^1 \boldsymbol{B}dr \ (m\times 1) \tag{15.2.9}$$

$$\frac{1}{n^2}\sum_{t=1}^{n}\boldsymbol{S}_t\boldsymbol{S}_t' \xrightarrow{\mathrm{D}} \int_0^1 \boldsymbol{B}\boldsymbol{B}'dr \ (m\times m). \tag{15.2.10}$$

In the scalar case, the counterparts of Theorems 15.2.1 and 15.2.2 were sufficient to prove all the results needed to study the autoregression. However, this is not the case when two or more variables are involved. One further result called for is the following, which is by Theorem 4.1 of Davidson and De Jong (2000b).

Theorem 15.2.3 Under the assumptions of Theorem 15.2.1,

$$\frac{1}{n}\sum_{t=1}^{n}\boldsymbol{S}_{t-1}\boldsymbol{\eta}_t' \xrightarrow{\mathrm{D}} \int_0^1 \boldsymbol{B}d\boldsymbol{B}' + \boldsymbol{\Lambda}. \quad \square \tag{15.2.11}$$

The first right-hand side term is a random matrix whose elements have zero mean, called the stochastic integral of $\boldsymbol{B}$ with respect to itself. The scalar counterpart of this result is (14.3.9), which is evidently not comparable. The multivariate version of the Itô rule in (14.3.11) is

$$\int_0^1 \boldsymbol{W}d\boldsymbol{W}' + \int_0^1 d\boldsymbol{W}\boldsymbol{W}' = \boldsymbol{W}(1)\boldsymbol{W}(1)' - \boldsymbol{I}_m \tag{15.2.12}$$

and after transforming to $\boldsymbol{B} = \boldsymbol{\Omega}^{1/2}\boldsymbol{W}$, it can be seen that the argument in (14.3.9) generalizes directly to

$$\frac{1}{n}\sum_{t=1}^{n}(\boldsymbol{S}_{t-1}\boldsymbol{\eta}_t' + \boldsymbol{\eta}_t\boldsymbol{S}_{t-1}') \xrightarrow{\text{D}} \boldsymbol{B}(1)\boldsymbol{B}(1)' - \boldsymbol{\Sigma}. \tag{15.2.13}$$

However, to derive the limiting distribution of the left-hand side of (15.2.11) needs arguments additional to those of Theorems 15.2.1 and 15.2.2, and cannot be deduced from (15.2.13).

15.2.2 Static Least Squares

'Static' least squares means the estimation of the cointegrating relationship by OLS without any attempt to correct for dynamic effects, or simultaneity between the elements $\boldsymbol{x}_t$. In other words, the problems and solutions discussed in Part II for the case of the I(0) regression are ignored.

The OLS estimators of $\boldsymbol{\gamma}$ and μ are

$$\hat{\boldsymbol{\gamma}} = \left(\sum_{t=1}^{n}\boldsymbol{x}_{2t}\boldsymbol{x}_{2t}' - n\bar{\boldsymbol{x}}_2\bar{\boldsymbol{x}}_2'\right)^{-1}\sum_{t=1}^{n}\boldsymbol{x}_{2t}x_{1t} - n\bar{\boldsymbol{x}}_2\bar{x}_1 \tag{15.2.14a}$$

$$\hat{\mu} = \bar{x}_1 - \hat{\boldsymbol{\gamma}}'\bar{\boldsymbol{x}}_2 \tag{15.2.14b}$$

where $\bar{x}_1 = n^{-1}\sum_{t=1}^{n}x_{1t}$ and $\bar{\boldsymbol{x}}_2 = n^{-1}\sum_{t=1}^{n}\boldsymbol{x}_{2t}$. The limiting distributions of $n(\hat{\boldsymbol{\gamma}} - \boldsymbol{\gamma})$ and $\sqrt{n}(\hat{\mu} - \mu)$ can be derived making use of the foregoing results. Choose $\boldsymbol{\eta}_t = (u_t, \boldsymbol{\theta}_t')'$, with components of dimension 1 and $m-1$ respectively, where u_t is defined in (15.2.2), and $\boldsymbol{\theta}_t$ denotes the last $m-1$ elements of $\boldsymbol{C}(L)\boldsymbol{\varepsilon}_t$ in (15.1.1). Each of these elements is I(0) by assumption. Define in accordance with (15.1.8)

$$\boldsymbol{x}_{2t} = \boldsymbol{x}_{20} + \boldsymbol{S}_{2t} = \boldsymbol{x}_{20} + \sum_{j=1}^{t}\boldsymbol{\theta}_j. \tag{15.2.15}$$

However, be *very* careful to note that $x_{1t} \neq x_{10} + \sum_{j=1}^{t}u_j$. The partial sums of the u_j do not enter the model explicitly, and x_{1t} is defined by (15.2.2). Defining the variable $v_t = \boldsymbol{\gamma}'\boldsymbol{\theta}_t + \Delta u_t$, we could write $x_{1t} = x_{10} + \sum_{j=1}^{t}v_j$, but $v_t \neq u_t$. Because of the cointegrating relationship there are only $m-1$ distinct I(1) processes driving the m variables in $\boldsymbol{x}_t$. In fact, any element of $\boldsymbol{x}_t$ can be defined as a linear combination of the others, plus an I(0) term. The construction of $\boldsymbol{\eta}_t$ and its integral S_t is to be seen simply as a device to allow the exploitation of Theorem 15.2.3.

Define the partition $\boldsymbol{B} = (B_1, \boldsymbol{B}_2')'$, into the first and remaining $m-1$ elements, and let the covariance matrix of $\boldsymbol{B}$ be partitioned conformably as

$$\begin{bmatrix} \omega_{11} & \boldsymbol{\Omega}_{12} \\ \boldsymbol{\Omega}_{21} & \boldsymbol{\Omega}_{22} \end{bmatrix} = \begin{bmatrix} \sigma_{11} & \boldsymbol{\Sigma}_{12} \\ \boldsymbol{\Sigma}_{21} & \boldsymbol{\Sigma}_{22} \end{bmatrix} + \begin{bmatrix} \lambda_{11} & \boldsymbol{\Lambda}_{12} \\ \boldsymbol{\Lambda}_{21} & \boldsymbol{\Lambda}_{22} \end{bmatrix} + \begin{bmatrix} \lambda_{11} & \boldsymbol{\Lambda}_{21}' \\ \boldsymbol{\Lambda}_{12}' & \boldsymbol{\Lambda}_{22}' \end{bmatrix} \tag{15.2.16}$$

In particular, note

$$\boldsymbol{\Lambda}_{21} = \lim_{n\to\infty} \frac{1}{n} \sum_{t=1}^{n} E(\boldsymbol{S}_{2t-1}\eta_{1t}) = \lim_{n\to\infty} \frac{1}{n} \sum_{t=2}^{n} \sum_{j=1}^{t-1} E(\boldsymbol{\theta}_{t-j} u_t) \tag{15.2.17}$$

whereas

$$\boldsymbol{\Lambda}_{12} = \lim_{n\to\infty} \frac{1}{n} \sum_{t=2}^{n} \sum_{j=1}^{t-1} E(u_{t-j}\boldsymbol{\theta}_t'). \tag{15.2.18}$$

Now, by straightforward analogy with the univariate case,

$$\sqrt{n}\bar{\boldsymbol{x}}_2 = n^{-3/2} \sum_{t=1}^{n} \boldsymbol{S}_{2t} + \frac{1}{\sqrt{n}} \boldsymbol{x}_{20} \xrightarrow{\text{D}} \int_0^1 \boldsymbol{B}_2 dr \tag{15.2.19}$$

and

$$\frac{1}{n^2} \sum_{t=1}^{n} \boldsymbol{x}_{2t}\boldsymbol{x}_{2t}' = \frac{1}{n^2} \left(\sum_{t=1}^{n} \boldsymbol{S}_{2t}\boldsymbol{S}_{2t}' + \sum_{t=1}^{n} \boldsymbol{S}_{2t}\boldsymbol{x}_{20}' + \boldsymbol{x}_{20} \sum_{t=1}^{n} \boldsymbol{S}_{2t}' + \boldsymbol{x}_{20}\boldsymbol{x}_{20}' \right)$$

$$\xrightarrow{\text{D}} \int_0^1 \boldsymbol{B}_2 \boldsymbol{B}_2' dr \tag{15.2.20}$$

noting in both cases how the terms in the second members, other than the first, are $O_p(n^{-1/2})$ or smaller as $n \to \infty$. Also,

$$\frac{1}{n} \sum_{t=1}^{n} \boldsymbol{x}_{2t} u_t = \frac{1}{n} \sum_{t=1}^{n} (\boldsymbol{S}_{2t-1} u_t + \boldsymbol{\theta}_t u_t + \boldsymbol{x}_{20} u_t)$$

$$\xrightarrow{\text{D}} \int_0^1 \boldsymbol{B}_2 dB_1 + \boldsymbol{\Lambda}_{21} + \boldsymbol{\Sigma}_{21} \tag{15.2.21}$$

using the relevant partition of (15.2.11) and the fact that $n^{-1} \sum_{t=1}^{n} \boldsymbol{\theta}_t u_t \xrightarrow{\text{pr}} \boldsymbol{\Sigma}_{21}$. Lastly

$$\sqrt{n}\bar{u} = \frac{1}{\sqrt{n}} \sum_{t=1}^{n} u_t \xrightarrow{\text{D}} B_1(1) \tag{15.2.22}$$

which is the ordinary CLT, remembering $B_1(1) \sim \text{N}(0, \omega_{11})$. Putting the results together using the continuous mapping theorem, the conclusions are

$$n(\hat{\boldsymbol{\gamma}} - \boldsymbol{\gamma}) = \left(\frac{1}{n^2} \sum_{t=1}^{n} \boldsymbol{x}_{2t}\boldsymbol{x}_{2t}' - \frac{1}{n} \bar{\boldsymbol{x}}_2 \bar{\boldsymbol{x}}_2' \right)^{-1} \left(\frac{1}{n} \sum_{t=1}^{n} \boldsymbol{x}_{2t} u_t - \left(\frac{1}{\sqrt{n}} \bar{\boldsymbol{x}}_2 \right) \sqrt{n}\bar{u} \right)$$

$$\xrightarrow{\text{D}} \left(\int_0^1 \boldsymbol{B}_2\boldsymbol{B}_2' dr - \int_0^1 \boldsymbol{B}_2 dr \int_0^1 \boldsymbol{B}_2' dr\right)^{-1}$$
$$\times \left(\int_0^1 \boldsymbol{B}_2 dB_1 + \boldsymbol{\Lambda}_{21} + \boldsymbol{\Sigma}_{21} - \int_0^1 \boldsymbol{B}_2 dr \cdot B_1(1)\right) = \boldsymbol{\xi} \qquad (15.2.23)$$

(defining the vector $\boldsymbol{\xi}$) and

$$\sqrt{n}(\hat{\mu} - \mu) = \sqrt{n}\bar{u} - n(\hat{\boldsymbol{\gamma}} - \boldsymbol{\gamma})' \frac{\bar{\boldsymbol{x}}_2}{\sqrt{n}} \xrightarrow{\text{D}} B_1(1) - \boldsymbol{\xi}' \int_0^1 \boldsymbol{B}_2 dr. \qquad (15.2.24)$$

For ease of notation, define the de-meaned Brownian motion $\boldsymbol{B}_2^* = \boldsymbol{B}_2 - \int_0^1 \boldsymbol{B}_2 dr$, being the limit in distribution of the process $n^{-1/2}\boldsymbol{x}_{2t}^*$ where $\boldsymbol{x}_t^* = \boldsymbol{x}_t - \bar{\boldsymbol{x}}$. Then the limit in (15.2.23) is more compactly written as

$$\boldsymbol{\xi} = \left(\int_0^1 \boldsymbol{B}_2^* \boldsymbol{B}_2^{*\prime} dr\right)^{-1} \left(\int_0^1 \boldsymbol{B}_2^* dB_1 + \boldsymbol{\Sigma}_{21} + \boldsymbol{\Lambda}_{21}\right). \qquad (15.2.25)$$

This result shows that $\hat{\boldsymbol{\gamma}}$ is super-consistent, and some other interesting features of the regression are easily deduced. First, omitting the intercept from the regression still yields a n-consistent estimator of $\boldsymbol{\gamma}$, although the limiting distribution is different. It is found by omitting the 'stars' in (15.2.25). Second, in either case R^2 tends in probability to unity. The term $\boldsymbol{\gamma}'\boldsymbol{x}_{2t}$ dominates the right-hand side of (15.2.2) asymptotically, in the sense that

$$\frac{1}{n^2}\sum_{t=1}^n x_{1t}^{*2} \xrightarrow{\text{D}} \boldsymbol{\gamma}' \left(\int_0^1 \boldsymbol{B}_2^* \boldsymbol{B}_2^{*\prime} dr\right) \boldsymbol{\gamma} \qquad (15.2.26)$$

whereas $n^{-1}\sum_{t=1}^n u_t^2 \xrightarrow{\text{pr}} \sigma_{11}$. Hence

$$R^2 = 1 - \left(\sum_{t=1}^n u_t^2\right) \div \left(\sum_{t=1}^n x_{1t}^{*2}\right) \xrightarrow{\text{pr}} 1. \qquad (15.2.27)$$

As a consequence, consistency is invariant to the choice of normalization. If instead of imposing (15.2.1) we choose (say) the second element of $\boldsymbol{x}_t$ as regressand, then so long as $\gamma_1 \neq 0$ the regression consistently estimates the vector

$$-\boldsymbol{\beta}/\gamma_1 = (-1/\gamma_1, 1, -\gamma_2/\gamma_1, \dots, -\gamma_{m-1}/\gamma_1)' \qquad (15.2.28)$$

after suitable reordering. However, note that the definition of cointegration does not rule out $\boldsymbol{\beta}$ having zero elements in cases with $m > 2$, so caution is needed in choosing the normalization. We will have more to say about this point in §15.3.4.

This set of results makes an interesting contrast with standard regression theory for I(0) variables. In the latter theory, consistency of OLS for $\boldsymbol{\gamma}$ in (15.2.2) requires the condition

$$\text{Cov}(\boldsymbol{x}_{2t}, u_t) = \mathbf{0}. \qquad (15.2.29)$$

This condition may fail from one of two causes. The first is endogeneity, with x_{1t} and $\boldsymbol{x}_{2t}$ jointly determined, so that $\boldsymbol{x}_{2t}$ not weakly exogenous with respect to γ. The second is the omission of dynamic components of the DGP, terms in $\Delta\boldsymbol{x}_{2,t-j}$ and/or $\Delta x_{1,t-j}$ for $j > 0$, that are implicit in the VAR representation (15.1.18). These biases are still present in the I(1) regression, but they involve I(0) variables and so are of small order in n. It will be noted from (15.2.25) that $\boldsymbol{\Sigma}_{21}$ and $\boldsymbol{\Lambda}_{21}$, representing respectively simultaneity and autocorrelation effects, influence the central tendency in the limiting distribution of $n(\hat{\boldsymbol{\gamma}} - \boldsymbol{\gamma})$. In general this is different from zero, and there exists an asymptotic median bias,[5] and a corresponding finite sample bias of $O(n^{-1})$. Simulation studies (e.g. Banerjee et al. 1986) suggest that this bias can be severe in practice, even in quite large samples. There is also a third source of bias in the regression which has no simple parallel with the I(0) case, due to the dependence between $\boldsymbol{B}_2$ and B_1. More is said on this question in §15.2.4. The magnitude of all these biases depends on the choice of normalization, since different partitions of $\boldsymbol{B}$, $\boldsymbol{\Sigma}$ and $\boldsymbol{\Lambda}$ are involved, and to this extent the choice of normalization is not arbitrary.

Thus, as with the unit root AR(1) model, conventional asymptotic inference is not generally valid. Non-standard limiting distributions of the usual t and F statistics can be deduced easily enough by applying the same rather simple arguments that were used to obtain the parameter distributions, and these will not be derived explicitly here though it would be a good exercise for the reader to attempt. The problem is not so much that the asymptotic distributions of these statistics are not normal, or chi-squared, as that the actual distributions depend on the nuisance parameters $\boldsymbol{\Sigma}$ and $\boldsymbol{\Lambda}$, and hence they cannot be tabulated for general use. Phillips and Park (1988) propose transformations of the F statistics that they call H statistics. These transformations involve consistent estimates of the nuisance parameters employing the same general principle as in the $\hat{Z}_t$ test of the unit root hypothesis (equation (14.3.25)) whose distributions, albeit non-standard, can be tabulated. A variant of this idea that has found wider application is discussed in §15.2.6.

15.2.3 When Static Least Squares is Optimal

There is one important case where the results of §15.2.2 simplify dramatically. In particular, there is zero asymptotic median-bias *and* standard asymptotic inference is valid, even though the estimators themselves are not asymptotically Gaussian. This is the case where $\boldsymbol{\Sigma}_{21} = \boldsymbol{\Lambda}_{21} = \boldsymbol{\Lambda}'_{12} = \boldsymbol{0}$ so that $\boldsymbol{\Omega}_{21} = \boldsymbol{0}$, and hence $\boldsymbol{\Omega}$ is block-diagonal. In this case the Brownian motions B_1 and $\boldsymbol{B}_2$ are uncorrelated and hence (thanks to the Gaussianity of the increments) *independently* distributed, which means it is legitimate to hold $\boldsymbol{B}_2$ conditionally fixed. In this case, $\int_0^1 \boldsymbol{B}_2^* dB_1 | \boldsymbol{B}_2$ can be thought of as the limit in distribution of the sum $n^{-1}\sum_{t=1}^n \boldsymbol{S}_{2t}u_t$, where under the conditional distribution, $\boldsymbol{S}_{2t}$ is just a vector of constant weights. Not merely do the bias terms in (15.2.25) disappear, it is possible to show by application of a regular CLT for heterogeneous processes, such as

[5] The existence of moments for the distribution of $n(\hat{\boldsymbol{\beta}} - \boldsymbol{\beta})$ cannot be assumed, but the median will generally differ from $\boldsymbol{0}$. Cases arise below where the distribution is symmetric about $\boldsymbol{0}$, in which case the designation 'median-unbiased' is natural.

Theorem 6.4.5, that

$$\int_0^1 \boldsymbol{B}_2^* dB_1 | \boldsymbol{B}_2 \sim \mathrm{N}(\mathbf{0}, \omega_{11}\boldsymbol{G}) \tag{15.2.30}$$

where $\boldsymbol{G} = \int_0^1 \boldsymbol{B}_2^* \boldsymbol{B}_2^{*\prime} dr$. The assumptions sufficient for Theorem 15.1.1 to hold for u_t are certainly sufficient here.

The unconditional distribution is a mixture of normals, or mixed Gaussian distribution. This is to be understood as a multivariate normal distribution with variance matrix $\boldsymbol{G}$ which is itself a random drawing from the space of positive definite matrices, in this case quadratic functionals of Brownian motion.[6] The probability of a measurable set $A \subseteq \mathbb{R}^{m-1}$ under this distribution is

$$\int \left(\int_A \phi(\zeta; \mathbf{0}, \omega_{11}\boldsymbol{G}) d\zeta \right) dP(\boldsymbol{G}), \tag{15.2.31}$$

where $\phi(\cdot; \boldsymbol{\mu}, \boldsymbol{\Sigma})$ is the p.d.f. of $\mathrm{N}(\boldsymbol{\mu}, \boldsymbol{\Sigma})$. Hence the Gaussian mixture can be represented schematically as

$$\int_0^1 \boldsymbol{B}_2^* dB_1 \sim \int \mathrm{N}(\mathbf{0}, \omega_{11}\boldsymbol{G}) dP(\boldsymbol{G}). \tag{15.2.32}$$

It follows directly from (15.2.25) that

$$n(\hat{\boldsymbol{\gamma}} - \boldsymbol{\gamma}) \xrightarrow{\mathrm{D}} \int \mathrm{N}(\mathbf{0}, \omega_{11}\boldsymbol{G}^{-1}) dP(\boldsymbol{G}) \tag{15.2.33}$$

which is also a Gaussian mixture. This distribution is symmetric around zero, and hence $\hat{\boldsymbol{\gamma}}$ is said to be median-unbiased to $O(n^{-1})$. Further,

$$\begin{aligned} \sqrt{n}(\hat{\mu} - \mu) &= \sqrt{n}\bar{u} - \frac{1}{\sqrt{n}} \bar{\boldsymbol{x}}_2' n(\hat{\boldsymbol{\gamma}} - \boldsymbol{\gamma}) \\ &\xrightarrow{\mathrm{D}} \int_0^1 \left[1 - \int_0^1 \boldsymbol{B}_2' dr \left(\int_0^1 \boldsymbol{B}_2^* \boldsymbol{B}_2^{*\prime} dr \right)^{-1} \boldsymbol{B}_2^* \right] dB_1 \\ &\sim \int \mathrm{N}(0, \omega_{11} h) dP(h) \end{aligned} \tag{15.2.34}$$

where $h = 1 + \int_0^1 \boldsymbol{B}_2' dr \, \boldsymbol{G}^{-1} \int_0^1 \boldsymbol{B}_2 dr$.

The result in (15.2.33) implies that for any fixed vector $\boldsymbol{a} \neq \mathbf{0}$,

$$n \frac{\boldsymbol{a}'(\hat{\boldsymbol{\gamma}} - \boldsymbol{\gamma})}{\sqrt{\omega_{11} \boldsymbol{a}' \boldsymbol{G}^{-1} \boldsymbol{a}}} \xrightarrow{\mathrm{D}} \int \mathrm{N}(0, 1) dP(\boldsymbol{G}) = \mathrm{N}(0, 1). \tag{15.2.35}$$

If u_t is serially uncorrelated, meaning that $\lambda_{11} = 0$, then $\omega_{11} = \sigma_{11}$ and this can be consistently estimated in the usual way by $s^2 = n^{-1} \sum_{t=1}^n \hat{u}_t^2$, where $\hat{u}_t = x_{1t} - \hat{\mu} - \hat{\boldsymbol{\gamma}}' \boldsymbol{x}_{2t}$. Since

$$\hat{\boldsymbol{G}} = n^{-2} \sum_{t=1}^n \boldsymbol{x}_{2t}^* \boldsymbol{x}_{2t}^{*\prime} \xrightarrow{\mathrm{D}} \boldsymbol{G} \tag{15.2.36}$$

---

[6] Visualize the distribution as obtained from a two-stage random experiment. As a simpler example, imagine generating a scalar r.v. X by first drawing V from a distribution with support on the positive real numbers, and then letting X be an independent drawing from $\mathrm{N}(0, V)$.

the continuous mapping and Cramér theorems imply that

$$n\frac{\boldsymbol{a}'(\hat{\boldsymbol{\gamma}}-\boldsymbol{\gamma})}{\sqrt{s^2\boldsymbol{a}'\hat{\boldsymbol{G}}^{-1}\boldsymbol{a}}} \xrightarrow{\mathrm{D}} \mathrm{N}(0,1). \tag{15.2.37}$$

Thus, standard inference procedures can be applied to this model. Choosing $\boldsymbol{a} = \boldsymbol{e}_i$, ($i$th column of the identity matrix) for example would yield the standard asymptotic t-ratio for $\hat{\beta}_i$. Similar arguments show that asymptotic χ^2 statistics for tests of general restrictions on $\boldsymbol{\gamma}$ are also generated in the standard way.

However, the condition $\lambda_{11} = 0$ is not necessary for the mixed-normal limit distribution to hold. The only correction needed when $\lambda_{11} \neq 0$ is to estimate ω_{11} consistently, and this can be done using the Newey-West (1987) type of estimator. Thus, replace s^2 by

$$\hat{\omega}_{11} = \frac{1}{n}\left(\sum_{t=1}^{n}\hat{u}_t^2 + 2\sum_{t=1}^{l(n)} w_{\tau l}\sum_{t=\tau+1}^{n}\hat{u}_t\hat{u}_{t-\tau}\right) \tag{15.2.38}$$

with $l(n)$ and the $w_{\tau l}$ chosen to ensure consistency and nonnegativity, as in (14.3.23).

These are attractive results, but it is important to determine what the conditions needed to obtain them imply about the model. $\boldsymbol{\Sigma}_{21}$ and $\boldsymbol{\Lambda}_{21}$ are the covariances between the disturbances and the current and lagged increments of the regressors, respectively, and for these to disappear is a condition comparable to the weak exogeneity conditions for CAN regression in I(0) data – compare the discussion in §7.1. However, according to (15.2.18) the condition $\boldsymbol{\Lambda}_{12} = \boldsymbol{0}$ requires $E(u_t\boldsymbol{\theta}_{t+j}) = \boldsymbol{0}$ for $j > 0$. This requires $\boldsymbol{x}_{2t}$ to be *strongly* exogenous with respect to the DGP of x_{1t}, ruling out lagged feedback from u_t to $\boldsymbol{x}_{2t}$ (see §4.5). These conditions are collectively very strong and are unlikely to be satisfied in many dynamic modelling situations. The remainder of this section considers some possible ways of overcoming the failure of the conditions, and achieving the mixed Gaussian result in a modified model.

15.2.4 Including I(0) Regressors

First, consider a refinement of the simple static regression in which I(0) regressors are added to allow for 'short run' effects. The equation to be considered is

$$x_{1t} = \mu + \boldsymbol{\gamma}'\boldsymbol{x}_{2t} + \boldsymbol{\delta}'\boldsymbol{\kappa}_t + \varepsilon_t \tag{15.2.39}$$

where $\boldsymbol{\kappa}_t$ is a vector of I(0) variables, and $\varepsilon_t = u_t - \boldsymbol{\delta}'\boldsymbol{\kappa}_t$. The designation I(0) means specifically that

$$\frac{1}{\sqrt{n}}\sum_{t=1}^{[nr]}\boldsymbol{\kappa}_t = \boldsymbol{x}_3(r) \xrightarrow{\mathrm{D}} \boldsymbol{B}_3(r) \tag{15.2.40}$$

where $\boldsymbol{B}_3$ is another vector Brownian motion, so that

$$\frac{1}{\sqrt{n}}\sum_{t=1}^{[nr]}\varepsilon_t \xrightarrow{\mathrm{D}} B_1(r) - \boldsymbol{\delta}'\boldsymbol{B}_3(r). \tag{15.2.41}$$

Thus, $\boldsymbol{\kappa}_t$ could contain the differences of I(1) series in the model, current and lagged, as well as other I(0) series.

Define $\boldsymbol{\eta}_t = (u_t, \boldsymbol{\theta}_t', \boldsymbol{\kappa}_t')'$, and then define $\boldsymbol{S}_t$ and $\boldsymbol{\Omega}$ as before, but now with the three-way partition

$$\boldsymbol{\Omega} = \begin{bmatrix} \omega_{11} & \boldsymbol{\Omega}_{12} & \boldsymbol{\Omega}_{13} \\ \boldsymbol{\Omega}_{21} & \boldsymbol{\Omega}_{22} & \boldsymbol{\Omega}_{23} \\ \boldsymbol{\Omega}_{31} & \boldsymbol{\Omega}_{32} & \boldsymbol{\Omega}_{33} \end{bmatrix} = \begin{bmatrix} \sigma_{11} & \boldsymbol{\Sigma}_{12} & \boldsymbol{\Sigma}_{13} \\ \boldsymbol{\Sigma}_{21} & \boldsymbol{\Sigma}_{22} & \boldsymbol{\Sigma}_{23} \\ \boldsymbol{\Sigma}_{31} & \boldsymbol{\Sigma}_{32} & \boldsymbol{\Sigma}_{33} \end{bmatrix} + \begin{bmatrix} \lambda_{11} & \boldsymbol{\Lambda}_{12} & \boldsymbol{\Lambda}_{13} \\ \boldsymbol{\Lambda}_{21} & \boldsymbol{\Lambda}_{22} & \boldsymbol{\Lambda}_{23} \\ \boldsymbol{\Lambda}_{31} & \boldsymbol{\Lambda}_{32} & \boldsymbol{\Lambda}_{33} \end{bmatrix} + \begin{bmatrix} \lambda_{11} & \boldsymbol{\Lambda}_{21}' & \boldsymbol{\Lambda}_{31}' \\ \boldsymbol{\Lambda}_{12}' & \boldsymbol{\Lambda}_{22}' & \boldsymbol{\Lambda}_{32}' \\ \boldsymbol{\Lambda}_{13}' & \boldsymbol{\Lambda}_{23}' & \boldsymbol{\Lambda}_{33}' \end{bmatrix}. \tag{15.2.42}$$

Since $E(\boldsymbol{\kappa}_t\varepsilon_t) = \boldsymbol{0}$ is required, it must be the case that $\boldsymbol{\delta} = \boldsymbol{\Sigma}_{33}^{-1}\boldsymbol{\Sigma}_{31}$. Rewrite the regression as

$$x_{1t}^* = \boldsymbol{\gamma}'\boldsymbol{x}_{2t}^* + \boldsymbol{\delta}'\boldsymbol{\kappa}_t^* + \varepsilon_t^* \tag{15.2.43}$$

where as before, the '$*$' denotes that the variables are expressed in deviations from the sample mean. Applying the partitioned regression algebra, write (15.2.43) as

$$\breve{x}_{1t} = \boldsymbol{\delta}'\breve{\boldsymbol{\kappa}}_t + \breve{\varepsilon}_t \tag{15.2.44}$$

where the variables are the residuals from regressing x_{1t}^* and $\boldsymbol{\kappa}_t^*$ on $\boldsymbol{x}_{2t}^*$. Note that

$$\frac{1}{n}\sum_{t=1}^{n}\breve{\boldsymbol{\kappa}}_t\breve{\boldsymbol{\kappa}}_t' = \frac{1}{n}\sum_{t=1}^{n}\boldsymbol{\kappa}_t^*\boldsymbol{\kappa}_t^{*\prime} - \frac{1}{n}\left(\frac{1}{n}\sum_{t=1}^{n}\boldsymbol{\kappa}_t^*\boldsymbol{x}_{2t}^{*\prime}\right)\left(\frac{1}{n^2}\sum_{t=1t}^{n}\boldsymbol{x}_{2t}^*\boldsymbol{x}_{2t}^{*\prime}\right)^{-1}\left(\frac{1}{n}\sum_{t=1}^{n}\boldsymbol{x}_{2t}^*\boldsymbol{\kappa}_t^{*\prime}\right) \xrightarrow{\text{pr}} \boldsymbol{\Sigma}_{33} \tag{15.2.45}$$

in view of (15.2.19) and (15.2.20) and the fact that

$$\frac{1}{n}\sum_{t=1}^{n}\boldsymbol{x}_{2t}^*\boldsymbol{\kappa}_t^{*\prime} \xrightarrow{\text{D}} \int_0^1 \boldsymbol{B}_2 d\boldsymbol{B}_3' + \boldsymbol{\Lambda}_{23} + \boldsymbol{\Sigma}_{23} \tag{15.2.46}$$

by Theorem 15.2.3 applied to the extended vector $\boldsymbol{x}_t = (x_{1t}, \boldsymbol{x}_{2t}', \boldsymbol{x}_{3t}')'$. Furthermore,

$$\frac{1}{\sqrt{n}}\sum_{t=1}^{n}\breve{\boldsymbol{\kappa}}_t\breve{\varepsilon}_t = \frac{1}{\sqrt{n}}\sum_{t=1}^{n}\boldsymbol{\kappa}_t^*\varepsilon_t - \frac{1}{\sqrt{n}}\left(\frac{1}{n}\sum_{t=1}^{n}\boldsymbol{\kappa}_t^*\boldsymbol{x}_{2t}^{*\prime}\right)\left(\frac{1}{n^2}\sum_{t=1}^{n}\boldsymbol{x}_{2t}^*\boldsymbol{x}_{2t}^{*\prime}\right)^{-1}\left(\frac{1}{n}\sum_{t=1}^{n}\boldsymbol{x}_{2t}^*\varepsilon_t\right) \tag{15.2.47}$$

where it is easily verified that the second right-hand side term is $O_p(n^{-1/2})$. Therefore, if

$$\hat{\boldsymbol{\delta}} = \left(\sum_{t=1}^{n}\breve{\boldsymbol{\kappa}}_t\breve{\boldsymbol{\kappa}}_t'\right)^{-1}\sum_{t=1}^{n}\breve{\boldsymbol{\kappa}}_t\breve{x}_{1t} \tag{15.2.48}$$

the limiting distribution of $\sqrt{n}(\hat{\boldsymbol{\delta}} - \boldsymbol{\delta})$ is the same as if the regression were of u_t on $\boldsymbol{\kappa}_t$. Applying the results from §10.5,

$$\sqrt{n}(\hat{\boldsymbol{\delta}} - \boldsymbol{\Sigma}_{33}^{-1}\boldsymbol{\Sigma}_{31}) \xrightarrow{\text{D}} \text{N}(\mathbf{0},\ \boldsymbol{\Sigma}_{33}^{-1}\boldsymbol{A}\boldsymbol{\Sigma}_{33}^{-1}) \tag{15.2.49}$$

where

$$\boldsymbol{A} = \lim_{n\to\infty}\frac{1}{n}\sum_{t=1}^{n}\sum_{s=1}^{n}E(\varepsilon_t\varepsilon_s\boldsymbol{\kappa}_t^*\boldsymbol{\kappa}_s^{*\prime}). \tag{15.2.50}$$

Now reverse the roles $\boldsymbol{x}_{2t}$ and $\boldsymbol{\kappa}_t$ and apply the partitioned regression algebra again. The regression to be considered

$$\tilde{x}_{1t} = \boldsymbol{\gamma}'\tilde{\boldsymbol{x}}_{2t} + \tilde{\varepsilon}_t \tag{15.2.51}$$

where the variables are the residuals from regressing x_{1t}^* and $\boldsymbol{x}_{2t}^*$ on $\boldsymbol{\kappa}_t^*$. Analysing this regression as before yields the following results. First,

$$\begin{aligned}\frac{1}{n^2}\sum_{t=1}^{n}\tilde{\boldsymbol{x}}_{2t}\tilde{\boldsymbol{x}}_{2t}'\\ &= \frac{1}{n^2}\sum_{t=1}^{n}\boldsymbol{x}_{2t}^*\boldsymbol{x}_{2t}^{*\prime} - \frac{1}{n}\left(\frac{1}{n}\sum_{t=1}^{n}\boldsymbol{x}_{2t}^*\boldsymbol{\kappa}_t^{*\prime}\right)\left(\frac{1}{n}\sum_{t=1}^{n}\boldsymbol{\kappa}_t^*\boldsymbol{\kappa}_t^{*\prime}\right)^{-1}\left(\frac{1}{n}\sum_{t=1}^{n}\boldsymbol{\kappa}_t^*\boldsymbol{x}_{2t}^{*\prime}\right)\\ &\xrightarrow{\text{D}} \int_0^1 \boldsymbol{B}_2^*\boldsymbol{B}_2^{*\prime}dr,\end{aligned} \tag{15.2.52}$$

since the factors in parentheses in the second right-hand side term are all $O_p(1)$. Next, the fact that

$$\frac{1}{n}\sum_{t=1}^{n}\boldsymbol{\kappa}_t^*\varepsilon_t \xrightarrow{\text{pr}} \mathbf{0} \tag{15.2.53}$$

implies by (15.2.41) that

$$\begin{aligned}\frac{1}{n}\sum_{t=1}^{n}\tilde{\boldsymbol{x}}_{2t}\tilde{\varepsilon}_t &= \frac{1}{n}\sum_{t=1}^{n}\boldsymbol{x}_{2t}^*\varepsilon_t - \left(\frac{1}{n}\sum_{t=1}^{n}\boldsymbol{x}_{2t}^*\boldsymbol{\kappa}_t^{*\prime}\right)\left(\frac{1}{n}\sum_{t=1}^{n}\boldsymbol{\kappa}_t^*\boldsymbol{\kappa}_t^{*\prime}\right)^{-1}\left(\frac{1}{n}\sum_{t=1}^{n}\boldsymbol{\kappa}_t^*\varepsilon_t\right)\\ &\xrightarrow{\text{D}} \int_0^1 \boldsymbol{B}_2^*(dB_1 - d\boldsymbol{B}_3'\boldsymbol{\Sigma}_{33}^{-1}\boldsymbol{\Sigma}_{31}) + (\boldsymbol{\Sigma}_{21} + \boldsymbol{\Lambda}_{21}) - (\boldsymbol{\Sigma}_{23} + \boldsymbol{\Lambda}_{23})\boldsymbol{\Sigma}_{33}^{-1}\boldsymbol{\Sigma}_{31}.\end{aligned} \tag{15.2.54}$$

Hence, if

$$\tilde{\boldsymbol{\gamma}} = \left(\sum_{t=1}^{n}\tilde{\boldsymbol{x}}_{2t}\tilde{\boldsymbol{x}}_{2t}'\right)^{-1}\sum_{t=1}^{n}\tilde{\boldsymbol{x}}_{2t}\tilde{x}_{1t} \tag{15.2.55}$$

then in the usual way,

$$n(\tilde{\boldsymbol{\gamma}} - \boldsymbol{\gamma}) \xrightarrow{\text{D}} \left(\int_0^1 \boldsymbol{B}_2^*\boldsymbol{B}_2^{*\prime}dr\right)^{-1}\left(\int_0^1 \boldsymbol{B}_2^*(dB_1 - d\boldsymbol{B}_3'\boldsymbol{\Sigma}_{33}^{-1}\boldsymbol{\Sigma}_{31})\right.$$

$$+ (\mathbf{\Sigma}_{21} + \mathbf{\Lambda}_{21}) - (\mathbf{\Sigma}_{23} + \mathbf{\Lambda}_{23})\mathbf{\Sigma}_{33}^{-1}\mathbf{\Sigma}_{31} \Bigg). \tag{15.2.56}$$

This result says that the inclusion of I(0) regressors changes the asymptotic distribution of the cointegrating coefficients, and also suggests how this might be done to make the distribution more tractable. First, consider the bias terms. Assuming covariance stationarity, note that

$$(\mathbf{\Sigma}_{21} + \mathbf{\Lambda}_{21}) - (\mathbf{\Sigma}_{23} + \mathbf{\Lambda}_{23})\mathbf{\Sigma}_{33}^{-1}\mathbf{\Sigma}_{31} = \sum_{j=0}^{\infty} E(\boldsymbol{\theta}_{t-j}\varepsilon_t). \tag{15.2.57}$$

These terms vanish if the regression is correctly specified in the usual sense of §7.1, that $E(\varepsilon_t|\mathcal{I}_t) = 0$ where $\boldsymbol{\theta}_{t-j} \in \mathcal{I}_t$ for $j \geq 0$. For the purpose of estimating the cointegrating vector it is legitimate to condition on variables that are jointly determined in the short run, and simultaneity can be corrected in a manner analogous to (8.4.1). In fact, if $\boldsymbol{\eta}_t$ were serially uncorrelated so that $\mathbf{\Lambda} = \mathbf{0}$, one could simply choose $\boldsymbol{\kappa}_t = \boldsymbol{\theta}_t = \Delta\boldsymbol{x}_{2t}$, so that $\mathbf{\Sigma}_{21} = \mathbf{\Sigma}_{31}$ and $\mathbf{\Sigma}_{23} = \mathbf{\Sigma}_{33}$. In other words, include the current changes in the I(1) regressors as additional regressors. This condition is unlikely to arise in practice since the I(0) components (increments of the I(1) processes) are usually autocorrelated to some degree. However, by including lagged variables in $\boldsymbol{\kappa}_t$ of the form $\Delta\boldsymbol{x}_{2t-j}$ for some $j > 0$, there is the hope of making (15.2.57) suitably small. A procedure akin to the model selection methods discussed in §7.4 can be envisaged.

However, before proceeding down this path there are further problems to reckon with. Consider the process

$$B_{1.3} = B_1 - \boldsymbol{B}_3'\mathbf{\Sigma}_{33}^{-1}\mathbf{\Sigma}_{31} \tag{15.2.58}$$

which is the Brownian motion generated from the partial sums of the ε_t. Note that

$$\begin{aligned} E(\boldsymbol{B}_2 B_{1.3}) &= \mathbf{\Omega}_{21} - \mathbf{\Omega}_{23}\mathbf{\Sigma}_{33}^{-1}\mathbf{\Sigma}_{31} \\ &= \mathbf{\Sigma}_{21} + \mathbf{\Lambda}_{21} + \mathbf{\Lambda}_{12}' - (\mathbf{\Sigma}_{23} + \mathbf{\Lambda}_{23} + \mathbf{\Lambda}_{32}')\mathbf{\Sigma}_{33}^{-1}\mathbf{\Sigma}_{31}. \end{aligned} \tag{15.2.59}$$

If the adding of regressors is going to permit the condition in (15.2.30) to hold, with $B_{1.3}$ independent of $\boldsymbol{B}_2$, then this matrix must vanish. Assume that by choice of regressors one can make (15.2.57) equal to 0. Then

$$E(\boldsymbol{B}_2 B_{1.3}) = \mathbf{\Lambda}_{12}' - \mathbf{\Lambda}_{32}'\mathbf{\Sigma}_{33}^{-1}\mathbf{\Sigma}_{31} = \sum_{j=0}^{\infty} E(\boldsymbol{\theta}_{t+j}\varepsilon_t). \tag{15.2.60}$$

Unless this term also vanishes, the estimator will not be asymptotically mixed Gaussian and median-unbiased.

The problem that arises here is quite different from any encountered under the assumptions of Chapters 7 and 8. In general (15.2.60) will vanish only if $\boldsymbol{x}_{2t}$ is strongly exogenous, as pointed out in §15.2.3. There is no way that it can be removed by adding variables from the conditioning set $\mathcal{I}_t$, where this set includes only current and lagged variables. It would be necessary to add *future*-dated increments, $\Delta \boldsymbol{x}_{2,t+j}$ for $j > 0$, to the equation to purge ε_t of this correlation. This would obviously contradict the ground rules for constructing a regression model developed in Chapter 7.

See Phillips and Loretan (1991) and also Phillips (1988, 1991) for a careful analysis of the issue of dynamic specification in models like this. The problem can be understood as a form of simultaneity, in the sense of joint determination of the regressors and the error term. However, it is not a simultaneity issue in the sense of Chapter 8, since $\boldsymbol{x}_{2t}$ can be in $\mathcal{I}_t$. The essential difficulty is that the asymptotic distribution results of Chapter 6 work by a trick that does not generalize from short memory processes to I(1) processes. It follows that with I(1) variables, building single equations to satisfy the criteria of §7.1.1 is no longer an appropriate research strategy. Different approaches to dynamic modelling are needed.

15.2.5 The Error Correction Model Approach

An alternative to the augmented least squares approach of the last section is to, in effect, re-normalize the equation. If $s = 1$ then in the ECM in (15.1.18), $\boldsymbol{\rho}$ is a column m-vector. Assuming that the first element ρ_1 is nonzero, and that $\boldsymbol{D}(L) = \boldsymbol{I}$ for simplicity, write the first equation as

$$\Delta x_{1t} = \boldsymbol{\phi}_1' \Delta \boldsymbol{x}_{2t} + \boldsymbol{F}_1(L)' \Delta \boldsymbol{x}_{t-1} - \rho_1 (x_{1t-1} - \mu - \boldsymbol{\gamma}' \boldsymbol{x}_{2,t-1}) + \varepsilon_{1t}. \qquad (15.2.61)$$

where $(1, \boldsymbol{\phi}_1')$ is the top row of $\boldsymbol{A}_0^{**}$ and $\boldsymbol{F}_1(L)'$ is the top row of $\boldsymbol{A}_0^{**} - \boldsymbol{A}^{**}(L)$. Modelling restrictions may be imposed on the various dynamic terms, as appropriate. The equation is nominally nonlinear, but no restrictions are imposed, and writing it as

$$\Delta x_{1t} = \boldsymbol{\phi}_1' \Delta \boldsymbol{x}_{2t} + \boldsymbol{F}_1(L)' \Delta \boldsymbol{x}_{t-1} - \rho_1 x_{1t-1} + \nu + \boldsymbol{\psi}' \boldsymbol{x}_{2,t-1} + \varepsilon_{1t}. \qquad (15.2.62)$$

the solutions $\hat{\boldsymbol{\gamma}} = \hat{\boldsymbol{\psi}}/\hat{\rho}_1$ and $\hat{\mu} = \hat{\nu}/\hat{\rho}_1$ may be solved from the OLS estimates. In any case, this is only a matter of normalization, and the vector $(\hat{\rho}_1, \hat{\boldsymbol{\psi}}')'$ consistently estimates the cointegrating space, in the sense that this linear combination of the variables is asymptotically I(0).

This method is analysed by Stock (1987). While consistency can be proved straightforwardly, the question of interest is whether the distribution is mixed Gaussian, and can be used to generate hypothesis tests using standard asymptotics. The answer to this turns out to be 'yes' under the assumption that $\boldsymbol{x}_{2t}$ is weakly exogenous for the parameters in (15.2.61). This implies in particular that all the elements of $\boldsymbol{\rho}$ *except* ρ_1 must be zero. In other words, out of all the variables it is Δx_{1t} alone that is driven by deviations from the long-run equilibrium. It is easy to see that if the cointegrating relationship also appears in the equations for one or more elements of $\Delta \boldsymbol{x}_{2t}$, then these equations ought to be estimated jointly with the first for efficient estimation. The interesting fact is that this is also a condition for valid inference, not merely a matter of efficiency alone. As with the augmented OLS approach, the essence of the problem is that ε_{1t} has to be uncorrelated with all the increments of $\boldsymbol{x}_{2t}$, both past and future. The condition fails in the presence of feedback from current shocks to Δx_{1t} to the future evolution of $\boldsymbol{x}_{2t}$, which would be the result of having error correction terms in the latter equations.

The natural way to overcome these problems is to estimate the relevant error correction equations jointly. To be fully appreciated, these results have to be discussed in the context of system analysis and, accordingly, the proof of these assertions is deferred until §16.5.3.

15.2.6 Fully Modified Least Squares

Phillips and Hansen (1990) have another suggestion for optimal estimation of the cointegrating vector, which is to make nonparametric corrections. Going back to (15.2.2), write the system in the form

$$x_{1t} = \mu + \boldsymbol{\gamma}'\boldsymbol{x}_{2t} + u_t \tag{15.2.63a}$$

$$\Delta\boldsymbol{x}_{2t} = \boldsymbol{\theta}_t. \tag{15.2.63b}$$

Given arbitrary Brownian motions B_1 and $\boldsymbol{B}_2$, the Brownian motion

$$B_{1.2} = B_1 - \boldsymbol{\Omega}_{12}\boldsymbol{\Omega}_{22}^{-1}\boldsymbol{B}_2 \tag{15.2.64}$$

is orthogonal to $\boldsymbol{B}_2$, with

$$\boldsymbol{\Omega}^* = \mathrm{Cov}\begin{bmatrix} B_{1.2} \\ \boldsymbol{B}_2 \end{bmatrix} = \begin{bmatrix} \omega_{11.2} & \boldsymbol{0}' \\ \boldsymbol{0} & \boldsymbol{\Omega}_{22} \end{bmatrix} \tag{15.2.65}$$

where

$$\omega_{11.2} = \omega_{11} - \boldsymbol{\Omega}_{12}\boldsymbol{\Omega}_{22}^{-1}\boldsymbol{\Omega}_{21}. \tag{15.2.66}$$

As noted, $B_{1.2}$ is not merely orthogonal to $\boldsymbol{B}_2$ but is distributed independently of it, thanks to the Gaussianity of the increments. Using (15.2.25) and the relation $dB_1 = dB_{1.2} + d\boldsymbol{B}_2'\boldsymbol{\Omega}_{22}^{-1}\boldsymbol{\Omega}_{21}$, the weak limit of $n(\hat{\boldsymbol{\gamma}} - \boldsymbol{\gamma})$ can be decomposed as

$$\boldsymbol{\xi} = \left(\int_0^1 \boldsymbol{B}_2^*\boldsymbol{B}_2^{*\prime}dr\right)^{-1}\left(\int_0^1 \boldsymbol{B}_2^*dB_{1.2} + \int_0^1 \boldsymbol{B}_2^*d\boldsymbol{B}_2'\boldsymbol{\Omega}_{22}^{-1}\boldsymbol{\Omega}_{21} + \boldsymbol{\Sigma}_{21} + \boldsymbol{\Lambda}_{21}\right). \tag{15.2.67}$$

(Note, $d\boldsymbol{B}_2 = d\boldsymbol{B}_2^*$).

From the discussion in §15.2.3 the first of the four terms in (15.2.67) has a mixed Gaussian distribution, with

$$\int_0^1 \boldsymbol{B}_2^*dB_{1.2} \sim \int \mathrm{N}(\boldsymbol{0}, \omega_{11.2}\boldsymbol{G})dP(\boldsymbol{G}) \tag{15.2.68}$$

where $\boldsymbol{G} = \int_0^1 \boldsymbol{B}_2^*\boldsymbol{B}_2^{*\prime}dr$. The idea is to introduce a two-part correction that eliminates the extra terms directly. First, letting

$$v_t = u_t - \boldsymbol{\theta}_t'\boldsymbol{\Omega}_{22}^{-1}\boldsymbol{\Omega}_{21} \tag{15.2.69}$$

note that $\lim_{n\to\infty} n^{-1}\sum_{t=1}^n E(v_t^2) = \omega_{11.2}$. According to Theorem 15.2.3,

$$\frac{1}{n}\sum_{t=1}^n \boldsymbol{x}_{2t}^*\boldsymbol{\theta}_t' \xrightarrow{\mathrm{D}} \int_0^1 \boldsymbol{B}_2^*d\boldsymbol{B}_2' + \boldsymbol{\Sigma}_{22} + \boldsymbol{\Lambda}_{22} \tag{15.2.70}$$

and hence

$$\frac{1}{n}\sum_{t=1}^{n} x_{2t}^{*} v_t \xrightarrow{D} \int_0^1 B_2^* dB_{1.2} + \delta^+ \tag{15.2.71}$$

where $\delta^+ = \Sigma_{21} + \Lambda_{21} - (\Sigma_{22} + \Lambda_{22})\Omega_{22}^{-1}\Omega_{21}$.

The parameters Ω, Σ and Λ are unknown, but can be estimated consistently from Δx_{2t} and $\hat{u}_t$ (the OLS residuals), using a kernel estimator as in (14.3.23), applied element by element. Call these estimates $\hat{\Omega}$, $\hat{\Sigma}$ and $\hat{\Lambda}$. Substituting them for the true parameters will not change the asymptotic distribution of the estimators based on them. Let

$$\hat{x}_{1t}^{+} = x_{1t} + (\hat{v}_t - u_t) = x_{1t} - \Delta x_{2t}'\hat{\Omega}_{22}^{-1}\hat{\Omega}_{21} \tag{15.2.72}$$

and so define the *fully modified least squares* (FMLS) estimator as

$$\gamma^+ = \left(\sum_{t=1}^{n} x_{2t}^{*} x_{2t}^{*\prime}\right)^{-1}\left(\sum_{t=1}^{n} x_{2t}^{*}\hat{x}_{1t}^{+} - n\hat{\delta}^{+}\right) \tag{15.2.73}$$

where the 'hats' denote the substitution of estimated covariance parameters in the formulae. It is straightforward after substituting for x_{1t} from (15.2.63a) to verify that

$$\begin{aligned} n(\gamma^+ - \gamma) &= \left(\frac{1}{n^2}\sum_{t=1}^{n} x_{2t}^{*} x_{2t}^{*\prime}\right)^{-1}\left(\frac{1}{n}\sum_{t=1}^{n} x_{2t}^{*}\hat{v}_t - \hat{\delta}^{+}\right) \\ &\xrightarrow{D} \left(\int_0^1 B_2^* B_2^{*\prime} dr\right)^{-1}\int_0^1 B_2^* B_{1.2} \\ &\sim \int \mathrm{N}(0, \omega_{11.2} G^{-1}) dP(G). \end{aligned} \tag{15.2.74}$$

Thus, γ^+ is median-unbiased to $O(n^{-1})$ and standard asymptotic inference procedures apply, just as for OLS in the strongly exogenous case. The intercept is estimated as $\hat{\mu} = \hat{x}_1^+ - \beta^{+\prime}\bar{x}_2$, and it can similarly be shown in parallel with (15.2.34) that

$$\begin{aligned} \sqrt{n}(\hat{\mu} - \mu) &= \sqrt{n}\bar{v} - \frac{1}{\sqrt{n}}\bar{x}_2' n(\gamma^+ - \gamma) \\ &\xrightarrow{D} \int \mathrm{N}(0, \omega_{11.2} h) dP(h). \end{aligned} \tag{15.2.75}$$

Apart from needing to estimate $\omega_{11.2}$ consistently by $\hat{\omega}_{11} - \hat{\Omega}_{12}\hat{\Omega}_{22}^{-1}\hat{\Omega}_{21}$, standard inference procedures can be applied to γ^+, exactly as for the OLS estimator in (15.2.33). In particular, the modified standard error formulae yield true asymptotic t ratios for the coefficients. This methodology therefore generalizes the application of near-conventional regression analysis from the strongly exogenous case in §15.2.3 to the general case. The various caveats given with respect to the methods in §15.2.4 and §15.2.5 do not have to be made here, and this is therefore, potentially the most powerful of the options for single equation analysis.

Phillips (1995) has shown that, suitably implemented, FMLS remains valid even when the equation contains I(0) regressors. It is not even necessary to know whether elements of $\boldsymbol{x}_{2t}$ are I(1) or I(0), so the analysis can proceed without previously determining the orders of integration. This is not an obvious conclusion, since if an element of $\boldsymbol{x}_{2t}$ is I(0) then the long-run variance of its *difference*, as defined in (15.2.6), is zero. Thus, the matrix $\boldsymbol{\Omega}_{22}$ is singular, and the construction in (15.2.72) looks questionable. However, provided the bandwidth in the kernel estimator is chosen appropriately, the FMLS estimator nonetheless yields n-consistent mixed-Gaussian estimates for the coefficients for the I(1) regressors and $\sqrt{n}$-consistent Gaussian estimates for the I(0) regressors, and there is no practical need to distinguish between them. See Phillips (1995) for the details.

The one thing that must not be overlooked, in either OLS or FMLS estimation, is the assumption that the cointegrating vector is unique for the particular set of variables $\boldsymbol{x}_t$. We shall need to consider other approaches in the general case where several linearly independent cointegrating vectors exist for $\boldsymbol{x}_t$ and this issue is taken up in Chapter 16.

15.3 Testing for Cointegration

15.3.1 Regression Without Cointegration

The analysis of the last section *assumes* the existence of cointegration. None of the results hold if the assumption is false. To set the scene for a discussion of cointegration tests, we examine the properties of OLS when the regressors are I(1) but not cointegrated. This case was studied by simulation in the well-known paper by Granger and Newbold (1974) (see §7.4.1). The limit theory for the Granger-Newbold model is treated in Phillips (1986).

Suppose that $\boldsymbol{x}_t$ is a vector of I(1) processes with the property

$$\frac{\boldsymbol{x}_{[nr]}}{\sqrt{n}} \xrightarrow{\mathrm{D}} \boldsymbol{B} \tag{15.3.1}$$

where $\boldsymbol{B}$ is a vector Brownian motion with *full-rank* covariance matrix $\boldsymbol{\Omega}$. These variables are accordingly not cointegrated.

As before, consider the result of regressing the first column of this vector on the remainder. Equations (15.2.9) and (15.2.10) and the continuous mapping theorem yield the results

$$\hat{\boldsymbol{\gamma}} \xrightarrow{\mathrm{D}} \boldsymbol{\zeta}_B = \left(\int_0^1 \boldsymbol{B}_2^* \boldsymbol{B}_2^{*\prime} dr\right)^{-1} \int_0^1 \boldsymbol{B}_2^* B_1^* dr \tag{15.3.2}$$

and

$$\frac{\hat{\mu}}{\sqrt{n}} = \frac{1}{\sqrt{n}}(\bar{x}_1 - \hat{\boldsymbol{\gamma}}'\bar{\boldsymbol{x}}_2) \xrightarrow{\mathrm{D}} \int_0^1 B_1 dr - \boldsymbol{\zeta}_B' \int_0^1 \boldsymbol{B}_2 dr. \tag{15.3.3}$$

Thus, the slope coefficients are converging to random variables, while the intercept is tending to infinity at the rate $\sqrt{n}$. Also, R^2 is converging to a random variable,

$$R^2 \xrightarrow{\mathrm{D}} \frac{\boldsymbol{\zeta}_B' \int_0^1 \boldsymbol{B}_2^* \boldsymbol{B}_2^{*\prime} dr \boldsymbol{\zeta}_B}{\int_0^1 B_1^{*2} dr}. \tag{15.3.4}$$

Hence,

$$F = \frac{R^2}{1-R^2}\frac{n-m+1}{m-2} = O_p(n) \tag{15.3.5}$$

and the hypothesis that x_{1t} and $\boldsymbol{x}_{2t}$ are uncorrelated is rejected on the F test with probability approaching 1 as $n \to \infty$. It is for this reason we speak of a spurious regression.

However, the DW statistic is tending to zero. The residuals are

$$\hat{u}_t = x_{1t} - \hat{\mu} - \hat{\boldsymbol{\gamma}}'\boldsymbol{x}_{2t} = x^*_{1t} - \hat{\boldsymbol{\gamma}}'\boldsymbol{x}^*_{2t} \sim \mathrm{I}(1). \tag{15.3.6}$$

Hence,

$$\mathrm{DW} = \frac{\sum_t \Delta\hat{u}_t^2}{\sum_t \hat{u}_t^2} = \frac{O_p(n)}{O_p(n^2)} = O_p(n^{-1}). \tag{15.3.7}$$

The fact the regression residuals are I(1), whereas in the case of a cointegrating regression they are I(0), provides the clue for detecting a spurious regression.

15.3.2 Residual-based Tests

An early suggestion for a cointegration test was provided by Sargan and Bhargava (1983) who tabulated the distribution of the Durbin–Watson statistic for the case where the variables in the regression are independent random walks. This is known as the cointegrating regression Durbin–Watson (CRDW) test, and is like the original DW an exact bounds test. Unfortunately, there is no generalization of this test to cases where $\Delta\hat{u}_t$ is I(0) but not serially uncorrelated, which limits its usefulness. Nonetheless, a glance at the DW statistic provides a routine check on the possibility of non-cointegration in I(1) regressions, just as it can point to misspecification in I(0) regressions.

A better established procedure is to perform an analogue of the Dickey–Fuller or Phillips–Perron unit root tests on the regression residuals. Temporarily ignoring the autocorrelation problem, consider the following procedure. Retrieve the residuals $\hat{u}_t$, run the regression

$$\Delta\hat{u}_t = \phi\hat{u}_{t-1} + e_t \tag{15.3.8}$$

and examine the 't-ratio',

$$t_\phi = \frac{\sum_t \hat{u}_{t-1}\Delta\hat{u}_t}{s_e\sqrt{\sum_t \hat{u}_{t-1}^2}}. \tag{15.3.9}$$

Here H_0 is $\phi = 0$ and H_1 is $\phi < 0$, so that the null hypothesis is the hypothesis of *non*-cointegration. However, even without autocorrelation the usual Dickey–Fuller tables are not appropriate to this test.

The asymptotic distribution of t_ϕ can be analysed using (15.2.9), (15.2.10) and (15.2.13). To simplify notation, stack the regressand and regressors into a single vector $\boldsymbol{x}_t$ with increments $\boldsymbol{\eta}_t$. Let

$$\boldsymbol{\xi}'_B = \begin{bmatrix} 1 & -\boldsymbol{\zeta}'_B \end{bmatrix} \tag{15.3.10}$$

where ζ_B is defined in (15.3.2). Then,

$$\frac{1}{n}\sum_{t=1}^{n}\hat{u}_{t-1}\Delta\hat{u}_t = [1 \ -\hat{\gamma}']\left(\frac{1}{n}\sum_{t=2}^{n}\boldsymbol{x}_{t-1}^{*}\boldsymbol{\eta}_t'\right)\begin{bmatrix}1\\-\hat{\gamma}\end{bmatrix}$$

$$\xrightarrow{\text{D}} \boldsymbol{\xi}_B'\left(\int_0^1 \boldsymbol{B}^*d\boldsymbol{B}' + \boldsymbol{\Lambda}\right)\boldsymbol{\xi}_B. \tag{15.3.11}$$

Define the 'square root' matrix of $\boldsymbol{\Omega}$,

$$\boldsymbol{L} = \begin{bmatrix}\sqrt{\omega_{11.2}} & \boldsymbol{0}'\\ \boldsymbol{L}_{22}^{-1}\boldsymbol{\Omega}_{21} & \boldsymbol{L}_{22}\end{bmatrix} \tag{15.3.12}$$

where $\boldsymbol{L}_{22}'\boldsymbol{L}_{22} = \boldsymbol{\Omega}_{22}$ so that $\boldsymbol{\Omega} = \boldsymbol{L}'\boldsymbol{L}$. Let $\boldsymbol{W}$ denote a standard m-vector Brownian motion having variance matrix $\boldsymbol{I}_m$, and let $\boldsymbol{W}^* = \boldsymbol{W} - \int_0^1 \boldsymbol{W}dr$ be the de-meaned form. The representation $\boldsymbol{B}^* = \boldsymbol{L}'\boldsymbol{W}^*$ can be written in partitioned form as

$$\begin{bmatrix}B_1^*\\ \boldsymbol{B}_2^*\end{bmatrix} = \begin{bmatrix}\sqrt{\omega_{11.2}}W_1^* + \boldsymbol{\Omega}_{12}(\boldsymbol{L}_{22}^{-1})'\boldsymbol{W}_2^*\\ \boldsymbol{L}_{22}'\boldsymbol{W}_2^*\end{bmatrix}. \tag{15.3.13}$$

It follows on substituting for $\boldsymbol{B}_2^*$ and B_1^* in (15.3.2) that

$$\zeta_B = \sqrt{\omega_{11.2}}(\boldsymbol{L}_{22}^{-1})'\left(\int_0^1 \boldsymbol{W}_2^*\boldsymbol{W}_2^{*\prime}dr\right)^{-1}\int_0^1 \boldsymbol{W}_2^*W_1^*dr + \boldsymbol{\Omega}_{22}^{-1}\boldsymbol{\Omega}_{21} \tag{15.3.14}$$

and so

$$\boldsymbol{L}\boldsymbol{\xi}_B = \sqrt{\omega_{11.2}}\begin{bmatrix}1\\ -\left(\int_0^1 \boldsymbol{W}_2^*\boldsymbol{W}_2^{*\prime}dr\right)^{-1}\int_0^1 \boldsymbol{W}_2^*W_1^*dr\end{bmatrix} = \sqrt{\omega_{11.2}}\boldsymbol{\xi} \tag{15.3.15}$$

where the last equation defines $\boldsymbol{\xi}$, which is independent of nuisance parameters. Hence,

$$\boldsymbol{\xi}_B'\left(\int_0^1 \boldsymbol{B}^*d\boldsymbol{B}' + \boldsymbol{\Lambda}\right)\boldsymbol{\xi}_B = \omega_{11.2}\left(\boldsymbol{\xi}'\int_0^1 \boldsymbol{W}^*d\boldsymbol{W}'\boldsymbol{\xi} + \boldsymbol{\xi}'(\boldsymbol{L}')^{-1}\boldsymbol{\Lambda}\boldsymbol{L}^{-1}\boldsymbol{\xi}\right). \tag{15.3.16}$$

In an exactly similar way,

$$n^{-2}\sum_{t=1}^{n}\hat{u}_{t-1}^2 = [1 \ -\hat{\gamma}']\left(\frac{1}{n^2}\sum_{t=2}^{n}\boldsymbol{x}_{t-1}^{*}\boldsymbol{x}_{t-1}^{*\prime}\right)\begin{bmatrix}1\\-\hat{\gamma}\end{bmatrix}$$

$$\xrightarrow{\text{D}} \omega_{11.2}\boldsymbol{\xi}'\int_0^1 \boldsymbol{W}^*\boldsymbol{W}^{*\prime}dr\boldsymbol{\xi}. \tag{15.3.17}$$

Finally

$$s_e^2 = \frac{1}{n}\sum_{t=2}^{n}\Delta\hat{u}_t^2 - \hat{\phi}^2\frac{1}{n}\sum_{t=2}^{n}\hat{u}_{t-1}^2$$

$$= \frac{1}{n}\sum_{t=2}^{n}\left(\begin{bmatrix}1 & -\hat{\boldsymbol{\gamma}}'\end{bmatrix}\boldsymbol{\eta}_t\right)^2 - \frac{1}{n}(n\hat{\phi})^2\left(n^{-2}\sum_{t=2}^{n}\hat{u}_{t-1}^2\right). \tag{15.3.18}$$

The second term on the right-hand side of (15.3.18) is $O(n^{-1})$, and so is easily seen using (15.3.15) again that

$$s_e^2 \xrightarrow{\text{D}} \boldsymbol{\xi}_B'\boldsymbol{\Sigma}\boldsymbol{\xi}_B = \omega_{11.2}\boldsymbol{\xi}'(\boldsymbol{L}')^{-1}\boldsymbol{\Sigma}\boldsymbol{L}^{-1}\boldsymbol{\xi}. \tag{15.3.19}$$

Suppose $\boldsymbol{\eta}_t$ is not autocorrelated. Then $\boldsymbol{\Lambda} = \mathbf{0}$, $\boldsymbol{\Omega} = \boldsymbol{\Sigma}$, and $(\boldsymbol{L}')^{-1}\boldsymbol{\Sigma}\boldsymbol{L}^{-1} = \boldsymbol{I}_m$. Substitution of (15.3.16) into (15.3.11) and applying the continuous mapping theorem gives

$$t_\phi \xrightarrow{\text{D}} \frac{\boldsymbol{\xi}'\int_0^1 \boldsymbol{W}^* d\boldsymbol{W}'\boldsymbol{\xi}}{\sqrt{\boldsymbol{\xi}'\boldsymbol{\xi}}\sqrt{\boldsymbol{\xi}'\int_0^1 \boldsymbol{W}^*\boldsymbol{W}^{*\prime}dr\boldsymbol{\xi}}}. \tag{15.3.20}$$

This may be compared with (14.3.19), which is obtained for the case $m = 1$, putting $\boldsymbol{\xi} = 1$. This distribution depends only on m, the number of variables in the regression. The critical values for significance levels 1%, 5% and 10% have been computed by MacKinnon (1991) for between 1 and 5 regressors in addition to the usual Dickey–Fuller tables, or in other words for $1 \le m \le 6$.

15.3.3 Correcting for Autocorrelation

Just as for unit root testing, the issue is complicated by the presence of autocorrelation in the increments, such that $\boldsymbol{\Lambda} \neq \mathbf{0}$. We then have the problem that

$$t_\phi \xrightarrow{\text{D}} \frac{\boldsymbol{\xi}'\int_0^1 \boldsymbol{W}^* d\boldsymbol{W}'\boldsymbol{\xi} + \boldsymbol{\xi}'(\boldsymbol{L}')^{-1}\boldsymbol{\Lambda}\boldsymbol{L}^{-1}\boldsymbol{\xi}}{\sqrt{\boldsymbol{\xi}'(\boldsymbol{L}')^{-1}\boldsymbol{\Sigma}\boldsymbol{L}^{-1}\boldsymbol{\xi}}\sqrt{\boldsymbol{\xi}'\int_0^1 \boldsymbol{W}^*\boldsymbol{W}^{*\prime}dr\boldsymbol{\xi}}}, \tag{15.3.21}$$

a distribution that depends on nuisance parameters and cannot be tabulated. The easiest way to modify the approach is to consider the $\hat{Z}_t$ statistic as in (14.3.25). The kernel variance estimator as in (14.3.23) can be applied to the residuals from the test regression. While these have the form $\hat{e}_t = \Delta\hat{u}_t - \hat{\phi}\hat{u}_{t-1}$, $\hat{\phi} = O_p(n^{-1})$ under H_0 and similarly to (15.3.18),

$$\frac{1}{n}\sum_{t=\tau+2}^{n}\hat{e}_t\hat{e}_{t-\tau} = \begin{bmatrix}1 & -\hat{\boldsymbol{\gamma}}'\end{bmatrix}\frac{1}{n}\sum_{t=\tau+2}^{n}\boldsymbol{\eta}_t\boldsymbol{\eta}_{t-\tau}'\begin{bmatrix}1\\ -\hat{\boldsymbol{\gamma}}\end{bmatrix} + O_p(n^{-1}) \tag{15.3.22}$$

for any $\tau \ge 0$. Therefore,

$$s_{nl}^2 = \frac{1}{n}\left(\sum_{t=2}^{n}\hat{e}_t^2 + 2\sum_{\tau=1}^{l(n)}w_{\tau l}\sum_{t=\tau+2}^{n}\hat{e}_t\hat{e}_{t-\tau}\right) \xrightarrow{\text{D}} \boldsymbol{\xi}_B'\boldsymbol{\Omega}\boldsymbol{\xi}_B = \omega_{11.2}\boldsymbol{\xi}'\boldsymbol{\xi} \tag{15.3.23}$$

where the second equality is by (15.3.15). On the other hand,

$$s_e^2 = \frac{1}{n}\sum_{t=2}^{n}\hat{e}_t^2 \xrightarrow{\text{D}} \omega_{11.2}\boldsymbol{\xi}'(\boldsymbol{L}')^{-1}\boldsymbol{\Sigma}\boldsymbol{L}^{-1}\boldsymbol{\xi}. \tag{15.3.24}$$

Finally, note using (A.2.4) that

$$(L')^{-1}\Lambda L^{-1} = \frac{I_m - (L')^{-1}\Sigma L^{-1}}{2}. \tag{15.3.25}$$

Putting all the components together yields the result

$$\hat{Z}_t = \frac{s_e}{s_{nl}} t_\phi + \frac{s_e^2 - s_{nl}^2}{2s_{nl}\sqrt{n^{-2}\sum_{t=2}^{n} \hat{u}_{t-1}^2}} \xrightarrow{\mathrm{D}} \frac{\xi' \int_0^1 W^* dW' \xi}{\sqrt{\xi'\xi}\sqrt{\xi' \int_0^1 W^* W^{*\prime} dr \xi}} \tag{15.3.26}$$

as in (15.3.20). In other words the $\hat{Z}_t$ statistic has the same limiting distribution as that of t_ϕ in the absence of autocorrelation in the increments.

It is also possible to show that, when the lags are correctly specified, the augmented Dickey–Fuller statistic from the residual autoregression has the same distribution. The proof calls for some advanced results not covered by the material in §15.2.1. This result as well as the ones surveyed here is to be found in Phillips and Ouliaris (1990).

15.3.4 Drawbacks with Residual-based Tests

The use of these cointegration tests is widespread since they are convenient to perform, requiring only the putative 'cointegrating regression' to be fitted, and then a further regression run on the residuals, to obtain the Phillips–Perron or ADF statistic. However, they cannot be generally recommended as the best procedures. For one thing they tend to lack power, since they fail to exploit all the available information about the joint dynamic interactions of the variables. See Kremers, Ericsson and Dolado (1992) for an analysis of this issue.

Another pitfall is that the choice of normalization (which variable to make the regressand) is arbitrary. In practice the hypothesis might be rejected for one normalization and accepted for another, at the chosen level of significance. Then a decision has to be made, which outcome to accept. With three or more variables, there is the added problem that some of them could be superfluous to the cointegrating relationship. Suppose that among three variables, x_1 and x_2 (say) form a cointegrating pair, but do not cointegrate with x_3. The set nonetheless cointegrate, with $\beta_3 = 0$. Doing the tests with either x_1 or x_2 as regressand ought to lead to rejection of H_0, with the coefficient of x_3 converging to 0 in probability, but if x_3 is chosen as the regressand the tests are obviously inconsistent. It is important to repeat them under several different normalizations in cases of doubt.

The system methods to be discussed in §16.3.1 overcome both of these difficulties, and should be regarded as the best practice to follow where possible.

15.4 Trended Variables

15.4.1 Simple Regression

Suppose that

$$x_t = S_t + \tau t \tag{15.4.1}$$

where $\boldsymbol{\tau}$ is the vector of drift parameters, and consider what happens if x_{1t} is regressed on $\boldsymbol{x}_{2t}$. If the variables are cointegrated, in the sense that there exists $\boldsymbol{\beta} = (1 \quad -\boldsymbol{\gamma}')'$ with

$$\boldsymbol{\beta}'\boldsymbol{x}_t - \mu = \boldsymbol{\beta}'\boldsymbol{S}_t + \boldsymbol{\beta}'\boldsymbol{\tau}t - \mu = u_t \sim I(0) \tag{15.4.2}$$

then it must be the case that $\boldsymbol{\beta}'\boldsymbol{\tau} = \tau_1 - \boldsymbol{\gamma}'\boldsymbol{\tau}_2 = 0$. However, vectors $\boldsymbol{\beta}$ having the latter property are not unique but span a space of dimension $m-1$. Because of the greater order of magnitude of the deterministic trends,

$$\frac{1}{n^3}\sum_{t=1}^{n}\boldsymbol{x}_{2t}^{*}\boldsymbol{x}_{2t}^{*\prime} \xrightarrow{\text{pr}} \frac{\boldsymbol{\tau}_2\boldsymbol{\tau}_2'}{12} \quad ((m-1)\times(m-1)) \tag{15.4.3}$$

similarly to (14.4.5), which is a matrix of rank 1, whereas

$$\frac{1}{n^{3/2}}\sum_{t=1}^{n}\boldsymbol{x}_{2t}^{*}u_t \xrightarrow{\text{D}} \int_0^1 (r-\tfrac{1}{2})dB_1 \sim \boldsymbol{\tau}_2\text{N}\Big(0, \frac{\omega_{11}}{12}\Big). \tag{15.4.4}$$

It therefore might appear that the relevant distributions are singular, in general.[7]

Consider first the case $m = 2$ where τ_2 is a nonzero scalar, so there is no singularity. In this case $\gamma = \tau_1/\tau_2$ must hold to achieve cointegration. If $\hat{\gamma}$ is the coefficient in the regression of x_{1t} on x_{2t}, it is evident on applying (15.4.3) and (15.4.4) that

$$n^{3/2}\Big(\hat{\gamma} - \frac{\tau_1}{\tau_2}\Big) \xrightarrow{\text{D}} \text{N}\Big(0, \frac{12\omega_{11}}{\tau_2^2}\Big) \tag{15.4.5}$$

similarly to (14.4.11). Even if there is no cointegration between the variables the regression, is still $\sqrt{n}$-consistent for τ_1/τ_2, although the asymptotic distribution is no longer Gaussian. Thus,

$$\frac{1}{n^{5/2}}\sum_{t=1}^{n}x_{2t}(x_{1t} - \tau_1 t) \xrightarrow{\text{D}} \tau_2\int_0^1 (r-\tfrac{1}{2})B_1 dr \tag{15.4.6}$$

and hence

$$\sqrt{n}(\hat{\gamma} - \tau_1/\tau_2) \xrightarrow{\text{D}} \frac{12}{\tau_2}\int_0^1 (r-\tfrac{1}{2})B_1 dr. \tag{15.4.7}$$

Now consider the case $m \geq 3$. Notwithstanding the limiting singularity in (15.4.3) OLS is still consistent, but it converges at the rate n^{-1}, not $n^{-3/2}$. To show this, take the first element of $\boldsymbol{x}_{2t}$, which is x_{2t}, and let the remaining elements of $\boldsymbol{x}_{2t}$ be denoted $\boldsymbol{x}_{3t}$. Assume with no loss of generality that $\tau_2 \neq 0$, and partial out x_{2t} from the other variables. Using the pairwise result in (15.4.5), consider the residuals from the regressions of x_{jt} on x_{2t} for $j = 3, \ldots, m$, including an intercept so mean deviations are taken as usual. Letting $\hat{\pi}_j$ denote the coefficients in these

[7] Note the affinities of this analysis with the trend-stationary regression discussed in §7.2.2, where in both cases the trends dominate.

regressions, these are $\sqrt{n}$ consistent for τ_j/τ_2 according to the result in (15.4.7), so

$$\frac{1}{\sqrt{n}}(x_{jt}^* - \hat{\pi}_j x_{2t}^*) = \frac{1}{\sqrt{n}}\left(s_{jt}^* - \frac{\tau_j}{\tau_2}s_{2t}^*\right) + O_p(n^{-1/2}) \qquad (15.4.8)$$

for $j = 3, \ldots, m$ and hence, if $\hat{\boldsymbol{\pi}}$ $((m-2)\times 1)$ is the vector of the $\hat{\pi}_j$,

$$\frac{1}{\sqrt{n}}(\boldsymbol{x}_{3[nr]}^* - \hat{\boldsymbol{\pi}} x_{2[nr]}^*) \xrightarrow{\text{D}} \boldsymbol{B}_3^*(r) - \frac{\boldsymbol{\tau}_3}{\tau_2}B_2^*(r) = \boldsymbol{F}_3^*(r) \qquad (15.4.9)$$

(say). Now consider the multiple cointegrating regression in partitioned form. For the coefficients of the $\boldsymbol{x}_{3t}$ variables

$$\begin{aligned} n(\hat{\boldsymbol{\gamma}}_3 - \boldsymbol{\gamma}_3) &= \left(\frac{1}{n^2}\sum_{t=1}^{n}(\boldsymbol{x}_{3t}^* - \hat{\boldsymbol{\pi}}x_{2t}^*)(\boldsymbol{x}_{3t}^* - \hat{\boldsymbol{\pi}}x_{2t}^*)'\right)^{-1}\frac{1}{n}\sum_{t=1}^{n}(\boldsymbol{x}_{3t}^* - \hat{\boldsymbol{\pi}}x_{2t}^*)u_t \\ &\xrightarrow{\text{D}} \left(\int_0^1 \boldsymbol{F}_3^*\boldsymbol{F}_3^{*\prime}dr\right)^{-1}\left(\int_0^1 \boldsymbol{F}_3^* dB_1 + \boldsymbol{\Sigma}_{31} + \boldsymbol{\Lambda}_{31} - \frac{\boldsymbol{\tau}_3}{\tau_2}(\sigma_{21} + \lambda_{21})\right) \end{aligned} \qquad (15.4.10)$$

where the obvious partitions,

$$\boldsymbol{\Sigma}_{21} = \begin{bmatrix}\sigma_{21}\\ \boldsymbol{\Sigma}_{31}\end{bmatrix}\begin{matrix}1\\ m-2\end{matrix} \qquad \boldsymbol{\Lambda}_{21} = \begin{bmatrix}\lambda_{21}\\ \boldsymbol{\Lambda}_{31}\end{bmatrix}\begin{matrix}1\\ m-2\end{matrix}$$

have been made. The partitioned regression formula (1.2.28) now gives the coefficient of x_{2t}^* itself as

$$\hat{\gamma}_2 = \left(\sum_{t=1}^{n} x_{2t}^{*2}\right)^{-1}\sum_{t=1}^{n} x_{2t}^*(x_{1t}^* - \boldsymbol{x}_{3t}^{*\prime}\hat{\boldsymbol{\gamma}}_3) \qquad (15.4.11)$$

so that

$$\begin{aligned} n(\hat{\gamma}_2 - \gamma_2) &= -\left(n^{-3}\sum_{t=1}^{n} x_{2t}^{*2}\right)^{-1}\left(n^{-3}\sum_{t=1}^{n} x_{2t}^*\boldsymbol{x}_{3t}^{*\prime}n(\hat{\boldsymbol{\gamma}}_3 - \boldsymbol{\gamma}_3) + n^{-2}\sum_{t=1}^{n} x_{2t}^* u_t\right) \\ &\underset{\text{asy}}{\sim} -\frac{\boldsymbol{\tau}_3'}{\tau_2}n(\hat{\boldsymbol{\gamma}}_3 - \boldsymbol{\gamma}_3). \end{aligned} \qquad (15.4.12)$$

Thus, the distribution of the regression coefficients has reduced rank, to ensure that the restriction $\tau_1 = \boldsymbol{\gamma}'\boldsymbol{\tau}_2$ is satisfied by the estimates. Be sure to appreciate that the selection of x_{2t} for partialing out was completely arbitrary in this analysis, and any of the regressors could play the same role as long as its trend coefficient is nonzero.

15.4.2 Detrending the Data

Another approach to estimation is to include the trend variable as an additional regressor. Notwithstanding that the true model does not contain a trend term as such, run the regression

$$x_{1t} = \mu + \theta t + \boldsymbol{\gamma}'\boldsymbol{x}_{2t} + u_t. \qquad (15.4.13)$$

Projecting all the variables on to t has the effect of eliminating the drift components. Define $\boldsymbol{X}$ $(n \times m)$ as the sample data matrix, and let $\boldsymbol{D}$ $(n \times 2)$ denote the matrix whose columns are the intercept and trend dummies. The orthogonal projection matrix $\boldsymbol{M_D} = \boldsymbol{I} - \boldsymbol{D}(\boldsymbol{D}'\boldsymbol{D})^{-1}\boldsymbol{D}'$ annihilates the trend variable. In other words, if $\boldsymbol{X} = \boldsymbol{S} + \boldsymbol{Da}$ where $\boldsymbol{a}$ is some constant $2 \times m$ matrix, then $\boldsymbol{M_D X} = \boldsymbol{M_D S}$, not depending on $\boldsymbol{a}$. The rows of $\boldsymbol{M_D X}$ have the form

$$\boldsymbol{x}_t^{**} = \boldsymbol{x}_t^* - t^* \frac{\sum_{s=1}^n s^* \boldsymbol{x}_s^*}{\sum_{s=1}^n s^{*2}} \tag{15.4.14}$$

where $t^* = t - \frac{1}{2}(n+1)$, and

$$\sqrt{n}\boldsymbol{x}_{[nr]}^{**} \xrightarrow{\mathrm{D}} \boldsymbol{B}^{**}(r) = \boldsymbol{B}(r) - \int_0^1 \boldsymbol{B} du - 12(r - \tfrac{1}{2}) \int_0^1 (u - \tfrac{1}{2}) \boldsymbol{B} du. \tag{15.4.15}$$

The limit is a vector of de-meaned and de-trended Brownian motions, and does not depend on $\boldsymbol{\tau}$. According to the usual partitioned regression algebra, the estimator $\tilde{\gamma} = (\boldsymbol{X}_2'\boldsymbol{M_D X}_2)^{-1}\boldsymbol{X}_2'\boldsymbol{M_D x}_1$ converges on the hypothesis $S_{1t} - \gamma'\boldsymbol{S}_{2t} \sim \mathrm{I}(0)$ as

$$n(\tilde{\gamma} - \gamma) \xrightarrow{\mathrm{D}} \left(\int_0^1 \boldsymbol{B}_2^{**}\boldsymbol{B}_2^{**\prime} dr\right)^{-1} \left(\int_0^1 \boldsymbol{B}_2^{**} dB_1 + \boldsymbol{\Sigma}_{21} + \boldsymbol{\Lambda}_{21}\right). \tag{15.4.16}$$

Note that this estimator is not constrained to fit the trends together, since the trends have been accounted for by the additional parameter θ. One can extend the partitioned analysis to show that the regression coefficient $\hat{\theta}$ converges to $\tau_1 - \gamma'\boldsymbol{\tau}_2 = 0$ at the rate $n^{3/2}$. As pointed out by Hansen (1992), the restricted estimator $\hat{\gamma}$ should therefore be more asymptotically efficient than $\tilde{\gamma}$. Both of (15.4.12) and (15.4.16) are distributions depending on nuisance parameters, and are not mixed Gaussian, but both estimators can be 'fully modified' in the Phillips-Hansen (1990) manner (see §15.2.6) to yield mixed Gaussian estimators, so that asymptotic efficiency comparisons can made directly on the conditional covariance matrix. This extension is developed in Hansen (1992), and is left for the reader to explore.

15.4.3 Testing for Cointegration

Both the restricted and the unrestricted estimators can be used as the basis for tests of cointegration. Consider first the detrended regression when there is no cointegration. Following the reasoning of the previous section, (15.3.2) is replaced by

$$\tilde{\gamma} \xrightarrow{\mathrm{D}} \left(\int_0^1 \boldsymbol{B}_2^{**}\boldsymbol{B}_2^{**\prime} dr\right)^{-1} \int_0^1 \boldsymbol{B}_2^{**} B_1 dr. \tag{15.4.17}$$

This limit is independent of $\boldsymbol{\tau}$, and hence the residuals

$$\hat{u}_t = x_{1t} - \hat{\mu} - \hat{\theta}t - \tilde{\gamma}'x_{2t} = x_{1t}^{**} - \tilde{\gamma}'\boldsymbol{x}_{2t}^{**} \tag{15.4.18}$$

can form the basis for a test. The tests of §15.3.2 and §15.3.3 can be applied to these residuals in exactly the same manner as before. The only thing that changes is the critical values for the tests, because the Brownian motions in the limit distributions are detrended. These have however been tabulated as for the non-trending case by MacKinnon (1991). One point to note carefully is that in the unit root tests of §14.4 the dummy variables, either intercept or intercept plus trend, are added to the test regression itself. In this test of noncointegration, on the other hand, the dummies are added to the candidate cointegrating regression, but the test autoregression on the residuals is performed with no dummies included.

A test can also be generated from the restricted regression, and here an interesting trick can be exploited to indicate the nature of the distribution. Note that the regression can be transformed (compare §1.2.4) as

$$\begin{aligned} x_{1t} &= \mu + \gamma_2 x_{2t} + \boldsymbol{\gamma}_3' \boldsymbol{x}_{3t} + u_t \\ &= \mu + (\gamma_2 + \tau_2^{-1} \boldsymbol{\gamma}_3' \boldsymbol{\tau}_3) x_{2t} + \boldsymbol{\gamma}_3' (\boldsymbol{x}_{3t} - \tau_2^{-1} \boldsymbol{\tau}_3 x_{2t}) + u_t \\ &= \mu + \gamma_2^+ x_{2t} + \boldsymbol{\gamma}_3' \boldsymbol{x}_{3t}^+ + u_t \end{aligned} \tag{15.4.19}$$

The residuals from the regression of x_{1t} on x_{2t} and $\boldsymbol{x}_{3t}^+$ are identical to those from the regression on x_{2t} and $\boldsymbol{x}_{3t}$. However, in the former case, the $\boldsymbol{x}_{3t}^+$ variables are de-trended. They are pure stochastic trend processes, although the trends have the form $\boldsymbol{S}_{3t} - \tau_2^{-1} \boldsymbol{\tau}_3 S_{2t}$, and hence do not match those of the $\boldsymbol{x}_{3t}$ variables. On the other hand x_{2t} is dominated asymptotically by the trend component.

In fact, as pointed out by Hansen (1992), the regression is equivalent in the limit to one including a deterministic trend term and $m - 2$ drift-free regressors. Therefore, a test for cointegration based on the ADF or $\hat{Z}_t$ statistics is distributed like the detrended case in (15.4.16), provided the number of regressors is counted as one less than the actual number when consulting the tabulations. If there is only one regressor to start with, then the effective number becomes zero, which means that the relevant critical value is taken from the Dickey–Fuller tabulation for the unit root autoregression with drift, see §14.4.2. There is one potential problem with this approach to unit root testing, even though greater test power is claimed for the procedure. If there is in fact no drift in the data, then the correct tabulation to use is the one referred to in §15.3.2. It is therefore necessary to know in advance whether trends are present. The advantage of the test based on the detrended regression is that it is equally valid whether trends are present or not.

15.5 A Postscript on OE Analysis

The analysis of this chapter in some ways parallels the linear model theory of Chapter 7 for the I(0) data case, and so provokes an obvious question. How might the theory of optimization estimators be incorporated into cointegration analysis? The answer is, only with some difficulty.

In the theory of Chapter 9, the cornerstone of the analysis is the fact that with the appropriate normalization of n^{-1}, the criterion function $C_n(\boldsymbol{\theta})$ converges to a nonstochastic function of $\boldsymbol{\theta}$. The gradient of C_n evaluated at $\boldsymbol{\theta}_0$, after normalizing by $\sqrt{n}$, converges to a Gaussian limit, but all the other relevant sequences, and especially the second derivatives, converge in probability to constants. Everything else in the theory follows from these essential facts.

In the present analysis, the criterion function (the sum of squares) after normalizing by n^{-2} converges to a random function in the limit. After partialing out the intercept for simplicity, the result that parallels (10.1.4) for the cointegrating regression of (15.2.2) is

$$n^{-2}S_n(\boldsymbol{g}) \xrightarrow{\text{D}} (\boldsymbol{g}-\boldsymbol{\gamma})' \int_0^1 \boldsymbol{B}_2^* \boldsymbol{B}_2^{*\prime} dr (\boldsymbol{g}-\boldsymbol{\gamma}). \tag{15.5.20}$$

This function does take its minimum value of zero, identically, at the cointegrating point $\boldsymbol{g} = \boldsymbol{\gamma}$, but it is clear why the standard asymptotics as in §9.3.4 fail. In particular, there is no normalization that yields a nonzero fixed limit for the Hessian matrix. The arguments may sometimes apply in a modified form by conditioning with respect to the regressors, but in general, the asymptotic distributions derived in this chapter involve ratios of correlated random variables. Even when the distributions are free of nuisance parameters they generally do not follow standard distributions, and need be tabulated for each special case. This problem is circumvented in methods such as fully modified least squares by applying tailor-made fixes to the regression formulae. However, the project of deriving a general asymptotic theory like that of Chapter 9 for integrated processes, embracing all kinds of nonlinear models, is not a straightforward one.

There is the additional fact that cointegration is an inherently linear modelling framework, because integration is itself a linear operator. Nonlinear transformations of I(1) processes are not in general I(1), in the sense of converging under suitable normalization to Brownian motion. While models that combine nonstationarity and nonlinearity will continue to be the subject of intensive research, it is likely that the cases where 'one tabulation fits all' will remain unusual.

Further Reading: The number of textbooks treating this theory in depth is still quite small, but Hamilton (1994) has a good chapter. See also Banerjee et. al. (1993), Hatanaka (1996), Hargreaves (1994), and the Handbook of Econometrics survey by Watson (1994).

Chapter 16

Cointegrated Systems

16.1 The VECM Framework

16.1.1 Modelling Issues

In Chapter 15 matters were simplified by assuming the existence of a single cointegrating vector, such that in the VAR representation of the system, $\boldsymbol{A}(1)$ has rank 1. The case $s > 1$ is more complicated because clearly, the cointegrating regression cannot be expected to estimate any particular column of $\boldsymbol{\beta}$. In general, what will be estimated is an arbitrary linear combination of the columns.

Consider the structural VAR of (15.1.18),

$$\boldsymbol{A}(L)(\boldsymbol{x}_t - \boldsymbol{x}_0) = \boldsymbol{A}^{**}(L)\Delta\boldsymbol{x}_t + \boldsymbol{\rho}(\boldsymbol{\beta}'\boldsymbol{x}_{t-1} - \boldsymbol{\mu}) = \boldsymbol{u}_t \quad (m \times 1) \tag{16.1.1}$$

for the general case where $\operatorname{rank}\boldsymbol{\beta} = s$, $0 \le s < m$. For simplicity, the present analysis will neglect the possibility of MA components and just assume that $\boldsymbol{u}_t = \boldsymbol{A}_0\boldsymbol{\varepsilon}_t$ where $\boldsymbol{A}_0$, recall, is the zero-order term of $\boldsymbol{A}^{**}(z)$. To clarify the initial results let it be assumed that $\boldsymbol{\varepsilon}_t \sim \text{i.i.d.}(\boldsymbol{0}, \boldsymbol{\Sigma})$. As usual, weaker conditions than this allowing some heterogeneity and limited dependence may be sufficient for the results, but are less easy to state compactly. The process must at least be serially uncorrelated, however.

Premultiply (16.1.1) by $\boldsymbol{A}_0^{-1}$ to obtain the reduced form (or VAR form) of the system. Assuming $\boldsymbol{A}(z)$ is of order p, let $\boldsymbol{\Pi}_j = -\boldsymbol{A}_0^{-1}\boldsymbol{A}_j^{**}$ for $j = 1, \dots, p-1$ and let $\boldsymbol{\alpha} = -\boldsymbol{A}_0^{-1}\boldsymbol{\rho}$, so that

$$\Delta\boldsymbol{x}_t = \boldsymbol{\Pi}(L)\Delta\boldsymbol{x}_{t-1} + \boldsymbol{\alpha}\boldsymbol{\beta}'\boldsymbol{x}_{t-1} + \boldsymbol{\nu} + \boldsymbol{\varepsilon}_t \tag{16.1.2}$$

where $\boldsymbol{\Pi}(z) = \boldsymbol{\Pi}_1 + \boldsymbol{\Pi}_2 z + \cdots + \boldsymbol{\Pi}_k z^{k-1}$, $\boldsymbol{\nu} = -\boldsymbol{\alpha}\boldsymbol{\mu}$ and $\boldsymbol{\varepsilon}_t = \boldsymbol{A}_0^{-1}\boldsymbol{u}_t$. It is apparent that (16.1.2) corresponds to the Wold representation of the system as in (15.1.1). Rewriting (16.1.2) in the form

$$[(\boldsymbol{I} - L\boldsymbol{\Pi}(L))(1 - L) - \boldsymbol{\alpha}\boldsymbol{\beta}'L](\boldsymbol{x}_t - \boldsymbol{x}_0) = \boldsymbol{\varepsilon}_t \tag{16.1.3}$$

and premultiplying through by $\boldsymbol{C}(L)$, (15.1.1) evidently implies that

$$\boldsymbol{C}(z)[(\boldsymbol{I} - z\boldsymbol{\Pi}(z))(1 - z) - \boldsymbol{\alpha}\boldsymbol{\beta}'z] = (1 - z)\boldsymbol{I}. \tag{16.1.4}$$

Evaluating this relation at $z = 1$ gives $\boldsymbol{C\alpha\beta}' = \mathbf{0}$, and since $\boldsymbol{\beta}'$ has full rank this implies

$$\boldsymbol{C\alpha} = \mathbf{0}. \tag{16.1.5}$$

Apply the Beveridge–Nelson decomposition $\boldsymbol{C}(z) = \boldsymbol{C} + (1 - z)\boldsymbol{C}^*(z)$ where $\boldsymbol{C} = \boldsymbol{C}(1)$ similarly to (15.1.13). Assuming $\boldsymbol{\varepsilon}_t = \mathbf{0}$ for $t \leq 0$,[1] (15.1.1) can be solved as

$$\boldsymbol{x}_t - \boldsymbol{x}_0 = \boldsymbol{C}\boldsymbol{w}_t + \boldsymbol{C}^*(L)\boldsymbol{\varepsilon}_t \quad t \geq 1 \tag{16.1.6}$$

where $\boldsymbol{w}_t = \sum_{j=1}^{t} \boldsymbol{\varepsilon}_j$. $\boldsymbol{C}\boldsymbol{w}_t \sim \mathrm{I}(1)$, whereas the second term on the right is I(0). Premultiplying by $\boldsymbol{\beta}'$ yields

$$\boldsymbol{\beta}'\boldsymbol{x}_t - \boldsymbol{\mu} = \boldsymbol{\beta}'\boldsymbol{C}\boldsymbol{w}_t + \boldsymbol{\beta}'\boldsymbol{C}^*(L)\boldsymbol{\varepsilon}_t. \tag{16.1.7}$$

For $\boldsymbol{\beta}$ to span the space of cointegrating vectors it is necessary that $\boldsymbol{\beta}'\boldsymbol{x}_t - \boldsymbol{\mu} \sim \mathrm{I}(0)$ and hence that

$$\boldsymbol{\beta}'\boldsymbol{C} = \mathbf{0}. \tag{16.1.8}$$

Conditions (16.1.8) and (16.1.5) will be important in subsequent developments.

The treatment of the intercept term in this model requires care, since formulation (16.1.2) allows for two quite different interpretations. Suppose instead of (16.1.1) the model had the form

$$\boldsymbol{A}^{**}(L)\Delta\boldsymbol{x}_t + \boldsymbol{\rho}(\boldsymbol{\beta}'\boldsymbol{x}_{t-1} - \boldsymbol{\mu}) + \boldsymbol{\xi}^* = \boldsymbol{u}_t \; (m \times 1) \tag{16.1.9}$$

where $\boldsymbol{\xi}^*$ is a constant vector of drift parameters. The reduced form becomes

$$\Delta\boldsymbol{x}_t = \boldsymbol{\Pi}(L)\Delta\boldsymbol{x}_{t-1} + \boldsymbol{\alpha}(\boldsymbol{\beta}'\boldsymbol{x}_{t-1} - \boldsymbol{\mu}) + \boldsymbol{\xi} + \boldsymbol{\varepsilon}_t \tag{16.1.10}$$

where $\boldsymbol{\xi} = -\boldsymbol{A}_0^{-1}\boldsymbol{\xi}^*$, which is identical to (16.1.2) except that $\boldsymbol{\nu} = \boldsymbol{\xi} - \boldsymbol{\alpha\mu}$. By repeating the previous analysis with $\boldsymbol{\xi}$ treated as a component of the disturbance process, one can easily see that the Wold representation is

$$\Delta\boldsymbol{x}_t = \boldsymbol{C}(L)(\boldsymbol{\xi} + \boldsymbol{\varepsilon}_t) = \boldsymbol{C\xi} + \boldsymbol{C}(L)\boldsymbol{\varepsilon}_t. \tag{16.1.11}$$

The apparent equivalence between (16.1.2) and (16.1.10) is deceptive, because $\boldsymbol{C\nu} = \boldsymbol{C\xi}$ by (16.1.5), and $\boldsymbol{\mu}$ does not act as a drift parameter. The two constant terms play distinct roles, centring the error correction term on the one hand, and inducing a drift on the other. In the case of drift the solution of the system becomes

$$\boldsymbol{x}_t - \boldsymbol{x}_0 = \boldsymbol{C\xi}t + \boldsymbol{C}\boldsymbol{w}_t + \boldsymbol{C}^*(L)\boldsymbol{\varepsilon}_t \quad t \geq 1. \tag{16.1.12}$$

Both of the first two terms on the right of (16.1.12) are annihilated by $\boldsymbol{\beta}'$ so that cointegration still occurs, but otherwise the properties of the variables are very different. For the sale of clarity the assumption $\boldsymbol{\xi} = \mathbf{0}$ is maintained in the initial exposition. The case of drifts is considered in §16.4.

---

[1] Otherwise the solution must contain the additional term $-\boldsymbol{C}^*(L)\boldsymbol{\varepsilon}_0$.

16.1.2 Least Squares Analysis

With $\boldsymbol{w}_t = \sum_{j=1}^{t} \boldsymbol{\varepsilon}_j$, define a vector Brownian motion (BM) process $\boldsymbol{B}_w$ $(m \times 1)$ by

$$\frac{\boldsymbol{w}_{[nr]}}{\sqrt{n}} \xrightarrow{\mathrm{D}} \boldsymbol{B}_w(r) \quad 0 \leq r \leq 1. \tag{16.1.13}$$

Since $\boldsymbol{\varepsilon}_t \sim \text{i.i.d.}(\mathbf{0}, \boldsymbol{\Sigma})$, $\text{Var}(\boldsymbol{B}_w) = \boldsymbol{\Sigma}$. From (16.1.6) and Theorem 15.2.1,

$$\frac{\boldsymbol{x}_{[nr]}}{\sqrt{n}} = \frac{\boldsymbol{w}_{[nr]}}{\sqrt{n}} + O_p(n^{-1/2}) \xrightarrow{\mathrm{D}} \boldsymbol{C}\boldsymbol{B}_w(r). \tag{16.1.14}$$

In mean-deviation form, with $\boldsymbol{x}_t^* = \boldsymbol{x}_t - \bar{\boldsymbol{x}}$ where $\bar{\boldsymbol{x}} = n^{-1}\sum_{t=1}^{n} \boldsymbol{x}_t$ and $\boldsymbol{w}_t^*$ and $\boldsymbol{\varepsilon}_t^*$ defined similarly,

$$\boldsymbol{x}_t^* = \boldsymbol{C}(L)\boldsymbol{w}_t^* = \boldsymbol{C}\boldsymbol{w}_t^* + \boldsymbol{C}^*(L)\boldsymbol{\varepsilon}_t^* \tag{16.1.15}$$

and

$$\frac{\boldsymbol{x}_{[nr]}^*}{\sqrt{n}} \xrightarrow{\mathrm{D}} \boldsymbol{C}\boldsymbol{B}_w^*(r) \tag{16.1.16}$$

where $\boldsymbol{B}_w^* = \boldsymbol{B}_w - \int_0^1 \boldsymbol{B}_w dr$ is the de-meaned BM. Then, by Theorem 15.2.2,

$$\frac{1}{n^2}\sum_{t=1}^{n} \boldsymbol{w}_t^* \boldsymbol{w}_t^{*\prime} \xrightarrow{\mathrm{D}} \int_0^1 \boldsymbol{B}_w^* \boldsymbol{B}_w^{*\prime} dr \tag{16.1.17}$$

and substituting from (16.1.15), it follows that

$$\boldsymbol{M}_n = \frac{1}{n^2}\sum_{t=1}^{n} \boldsymbol{x}_t^* \boldsymbol{x}_t^{*\prime} \xrightarrow{\mathrm{D}} \boldsymbol{C}\int_0^1 \boldsymbol{B}_w^* \boldsymbol{B}_w^{*\prime} dr\, \boldsymbol{C}'. \tag{16.1.18}$$

Also, by Theorem 15.2.3,

$$\frac{1}{n}\sum_{t=1}^{n} \boldsymbol{w}_t^* \boldsymbol{\varepsilon}_t^{*\prime} = \frac{1}{n}\sum_{t=1}^{n} \boldsymbol{w}_{t-1}^* \boldsymbol{\varepsilon}_t^{*\prime} + \frac{1}{n}\sum_{t=1}^{n} \boldsymbol{\varepsilon}_t^* \boldsymbol{\varepsilon}_t^{*\prime} \xrightarrow{\mathrm{D}} \int_0^1 \boldsymbol{B}_w^* d\boldsymbol{B}_w' + \boldsymbol{\Sigma} \tag{16.1.19}$$

noting $d\boldsymbol{B}_w^* = d\boldsymbol{B}_w$. For any finite j this result extends to

$$\frac{1}{n}\sum_{t=j+1}^{n} \boldsymbol{w}_t^* \boldsymbol{\varepsilon}_{t-j}^{*\prime} = \frac{1}{n}\sum_{t=j+1}^{n} \boldsymbol{w}_{t-j}^* \boldsymbol{\varepsilon}_{t-j}^{*\prime} + \sum_{k=1}^{j}\left(\frac{1}{n}\sum_{t=j+1}^{n} \boldsymbol{\varepsilon}_{t-j+k}^* \boldsymbol{\varepsilon}_{t-j}^{*\prime}\right)$$

$$\xrightarrow{\mathrm{D}} \int_0^1 \boldsymbol{B}_w^* d\boldsymbol{B}_w' + \boldsymbol{\Sigma} \tag{16.1.20}$$

because the autocovariance matrices in the second member are converging to $\mathbf{0}$, by assumption. Therefore, using (16.1.7) and (16.1.8),

$$n\boldsymbol{M}_n\boldsymbol{\beta} = \frac{1}{n}\sum_{t=1}^{n} \boldsymbol{C}\boldsymbol{w}_t^* \boldsymbol{\varepsilon}_t^{*\prime} \boldsymbol{C}^*(L)'\boldsymbol{\beta} + \frac{1}{n}\sum_{t=1}^{n} \boldsymbol{C}^*(L)\boldsymbol{\varepsilon}_t^* \boldsymbol{\varepsilon}_t^{*\prime} \boldsymbol{C}^*(L)'\boldsymbol{\beta}$$

$$\xrightarrow{\mathrm{D}} C\int_0^1 B_w^* dB_w' C^{*\prime}\beta + (C + C^*)\Sigma C^{*\prime}\beta \tag{16.1.21}$$

where $C^* = C^*(1)$.

Thus,

$$M_n\beta = O_p(n^{-1}). \tag{16.1.22}$$

The limiting matrix on the right side of (16.1.18) has a singular distribution, for CB_w has covariance matrix $C\Sigma C'$ with rank $m - s$, such that $\beta' CB_w = 0$. This is the asymptotic counterpart of the condition $\beta' x_t - \mu \sim \mathrm{I}(0)$. The fact that the columns of β span the null space of M_n asymptotically points directly to a consistent estimation procedure.

However, β is not unique and our problem is properly thought of as estimating, not a set of parameters, but rather the *space* spanned by the cointegrating vectors. As remarked in §15.1.3, if the rows of β' are cointegrating so are those of $d\beta'$ for nonsingular d, and choosing $d = (\beta'\beta)^{-1/2}$, for example, is equivalent to imposing orthonormality restrictions $\beta'\beta = I_s$.

As a simple first approach to this problem, one could consider applying the least squares principle, by solving the problem.

$$\min_b \operatorname{tr}(b' M_n b) \text{ subject to } b'b = I_s. \tag{16.1.23}$$

In other words, minimize $n^{-2}\sum_{i=1}^s \sum_{t=1}^n (b_i' x_t^*)^2$ subject to the stated normalization, generalizing the OLS procedure of §15.2.2. This is a standard problem in multivariate analysis whose solution, $\check{\beta}$ say, is the matrix whose columns are the eigenvectors corresponding to the s smallest eigenvalues of M_n. These eigenvalues take the form $\check{\beta}_i' M_n \check{\beta}_i$ for $i = 1, \ldots, s$, and it is clear from (16.1.18) and (16.1.21) that they are converging to 0 as $n \to \infty$, reflecting the asymptotic rank of the matrix. The intercepts μ may be estimated by $\hat{\mu} = \check{\beta}'\bar{x}$.

These estimators can be shown to be consistent, but since the short-run dynamics of the model are ignored, they clearly suffer from the same drawbacks as the single equation OLS procedure. Refining the approach to correct for the short run dynamics leads to the well-known methods due to Johansen.

16.2 Johansen's Analysis

16.2.1 The General Dynamic Model

The general framework for these results is the system[2]

$$\Delta x_t = \alpha\beta' x_{t-1} + \nu + \Pi_1 \Delta x_{t-1} + \cdots + \Pi_k \Delta x_{t-k} + \Theta d_t + \varepsilon_t \tag{16.2.1}$$

[2] Johansen (1988b, 1991) considers the case $\Delta x_t = \nu + \Pi_1 \Delta x_{t-1} + \ldots + \Pi_{k-1}\Delta x_{t-k+1} + \alpha\beta' x_{t-k} + \varepsilon_t$. The choice of lag for the levels term affects nothing but the interpretation of the Π_j parameters, and if these are unrestricted it is irrelevant. Our k is equivalent to his $k - 1$.

where $\boldsymbol{d}_t$ represents a vector of Cesàro-summable nonstochastic variables (see §7.2.1).[3] These may include dummies such as seasonals, but not the intercept, which is included separately, nor trend dummies which require a modified analysis, to be discussed in §16.4. They can be assumed to have Cesàro sums of 0 with no loss of generality. The joint role of the I(0) regressors is to ensure that $\boldsymbol{\varepsilon}_t$ is, at worst, uncorrelated with lagged variables. This is important, since the results make a key use of the latter assumption.[4]

Johansen's (1988b, 1991) approach to the estimation problem is to apply a pseudo-maximum likelihood procedure to (16.2.1). The least generalized variance (LGV) estimator (see §13.3) minimizes the determinant

$$\Lambda_s(\boldsymbol{\beta}, \boldsymbol{\alpha}, \boldsymbol{\nu}, \boldsymbol{\Pi}_1, \ldots, \boldsymbol{\Pi}_k, \boldsymbol{\Theta}) = \left| \frac{1}{n} \sum_{t=1}^{n} \boldsymbol{\varepsilon}_t \boldsymbol{\varepsilon}_t' \right|. \tag{16.2.2}$$

For a reduced form system this method corresponds to (13.2.14), and also to maximum likelihood when $\boldsymbol{\varepsilon}_t$ is Gaussian. The method is also called reduced rank regression, since the restriction 'rank $= s < m$' is imposed on the $m \times m$ matrix of coefficients of $\boldsymbol{x}_{t-1}$. Since the system is linear in all the parameters except $\boldsymbol{\alpha}$ and $\boldsymbol{\beta}$ it is straightforward to concentrate Λ with respect to these. Let $\boldsymbol{R}_{0t}$ and $\boldsymbol{R}_{1t}$ represent the residuals obtained from regressing $\Delta \boldsymbol{x}_t$ and $\boldsymbol{x}_{t-1}$, respectively, on $(1, \Delta \boldsymbol{x}_{t-1}, \ldots, \Delta \boldsymbol{x}_{t-k}, \boldsymbol{d}_t)$. The minimum of Λ_s with respect to $\boldsymbol{\nu}, \boldsymbol{\Pi}_1, \ldots, \boldsymbol{\Pi}_k, \boldsymbol{\Theta}$, as a function of $\boldsymbol{\alpha}$ and $\boldsymbol{\beta}$, is then

$$\Lambda_s^*(\boldsymbol{\alpha}, \boldsymbol{\beta}) = \left| \frac{1}{n} \sum_{t=1}^{n} (\boldsymbol{R}_{0t} - \boldsymbol{\alpha\beta}' \boldsymbol{R}_{1t})(\boldsymbol{R}_{0t} - \boldsymbol{\alpha\beta}' \boldsymbol{R}_{1t})' \right|. \tag{16.2.3}$$

To simplify what is already a very complex analysis, we proceed on the tacit assumption that $\boldsymbol{R}_{0t}$ and $\boldsymbol{R}_{1t}$ in the reduced rank regression

$$\boldsymbol{R}_{0t} = \boldsymbol{\alpha\beta}' \boldsymbol{R}_{1t} + \boldsymbol{\varepsilon}_t \tag{16.2.4}$$

are just data expressed in deviations from the mean, with $\boldsymbol{\varepsilon}_t$ uncorrelated with $\boldsymbol{R}_{1t}$. By a generalization of the argument in Theorem 14.3.1 it can be shown that this assumption is justified in the sense that the asymptotic analysis is equivalent. In the sequel, frequent use is made of the $m \times m$ sample moment matrices

$$\boldsymbol{S}_{00} = \frac{1}{n} \sum\nolimits_t \boldsymbol{R}_{0t} \boldsymbol{R}_{0t}' \tag{16.2.5a}$$

$$\boldsymbol{S}_{10} = \frac{1}{n} \sum\nolimits_t \boldsymbol{R}_{1t} \boldsymbol{R}_{0t}' \tag{16.2.5b}$$

---

[3] It is in fact permissible for $\boldsymbol{d}_t$ to contain I(0) exogenous stochastic variables. Exogeneity in the relevant sense need not exclude being Granger-caused by $\Delta \boldsymbol{x}_{t-j}$, $j > 0$. However, these extensions will not be pursued here.

[4] In practice k is unknown and has to be estimated. Model selection criteria (§9.4.1) might be used for this purpose. A possibility usually neglected in the system analysis is that the VAR is approximating a VARMA dynamic structure, so that $k = \infty$. It is possible to choose k finite but increasing with n at a suitable rate in these cases, so as to obtain the correct asymptotic distributions. Refinements of this sort are not considered.

$$S_{11} = \frac{1}{n}\sum\nolimits_t R_{1t}R_{1t}' \tag{16.2.5c}$$

$$S_{1\varepsilon} = S_{10} - S_{11}\beta\alpha'. \tag{16.2.5d}$$

Letting $\bar{\alpha} = \alpha(\alpha'\alpha)^{-1}$, the process

$$z_t = \beta' R_{1t} = \bar{\alpha}'(R_{0t} - \varepsilon_t) \ (s \times 1) \tag{16.2.6}$$

is I(0), although autocorrelated in general. If $n^{-1/2}\sum_{t=1}^{[nr]} z_t \xrightarrow{\mathrm{D}} y(r)$ then

$$S_{11}\beta \xrightarrow{\mathrm{D}} \int_0^1 B_w^* dy' + \Sigma_{xy} + \Lambda_{xy} = \Psi \ (m \times s) \tag{16.2.7}$$

(say) as the limit analogous to (16.1.21) for this somewhat more general model. There will be no need to work with this formula beyond assuming the existence of the limit. Following (16.1.16), (16.1.19) and (16.1.18), it is assumed without further justification that

$$\frac{1}{\sqrt{n}} R_{1[nr]} \xrightarrow{\mathrm{D}} CB_w^*(r) \tag{16.2.8}$$

$$\frac{1}{n} S_{11} \xrightarrow{\mathrm{D}} C \int_0^1 B_w^* B_w^{*\prime} dr \, C' \tag{16.2.9}$$

$$S_{10} = S_{11}\beta\alpha' + S_{1\varepsilon} \xrightarrow{\mathrm{D}} \Psi\alpha' + C \int_0^1 B_w^* dB_w' \tag{16.2.10}$$

where Ψ is defined in (16.2.7).

16.2.2 Reduced Rank Regression

Given (16.2.3), the next computational step is to concentrate the criterion with respect to α, while holding β fixed. This is achieved by the unrestricted regression of R_{0t} on $\beta' R_{1t}$. The conditional estimator of α is

$$\alpha(\beta) = S_{01}\beta(\beta' S_{11}\beta)^{-1} \tag{16.2.11}$$

and the concentrated criterion function (the generalized variance of the residuals from this regression) is

$$\Lambda_s^{**}(\beta) = |S_{00} - S_{01}\beta(\beta' S_{11}\beta)^{-1}\beta' S_{10}|. \tag{16.2.12}$$

Minimizing this function with respect to β yields the same result as direct minimization of Λ_s in (16.2.2).

Using (A.2.12),

$$\begin{aligned} \begin{vmatrix} S_{00} & S_{01}\beta \\ \beta' S_{10} & \beta' S_{11}\beta \end{vmatrix} &= |\beta' S_{11}\beta||S_{00} - S_{01}\beta(\beta' S_{11}\beta)^{-1}\beta' S_{10}| \\ &= |S_{00}||\beta' S_{11}\beta - \beta' S_{10} S_{00}^{-1} S_{01}\beta|. \end{aligned} \tag{16.2.13}$$

The term to be minimized is the second factor in the second member of (16.2.13). Since S_{00} does not depend on β, this is equivalent to minimizing

$$\frac{|\beta' S_{11}\beta - \beta' S_{10} S_{00}^{-1} S_{01}\beta|}{|\beta' S_{11}\beta|}. \tag{16.2.14}$$

This problem has a standard solution from multivariate analysis (Anderson 1951) similar to the LIML estimation problem of §13.3.2. The columns of β are estimated by the eigenvectors corresponding to the s *largest* solutions of the generalized eigenvalue problem[5]

$$|\lambda S_{11} - S_{10} S_{00}^{-1} S_{01}| = 0. \tag{16.2.15}$$

Assuming the eigenvalues are ranked with $\lambda_1 > \ldots > \lambda_m$, these are solutions to

$$(\lambda_j S_{11} - S_{10} S_{00}^{-1} S_{01})\beta_j = \mathbf{0} \tag{16.2.16}$$

for $j = 1, \ldots, s$.

Defining L by $LL' = S_{11}^{-1}$, such that $L' S_{11} L = I_m$, note that

$$|\lambda S_{11} - S_{10} S_{00}^{-1} S_{01}| = |\lambda I_m - L' S_{10} S_{00}^{-1} S_{01} L||S_{11}|. \tag{16.2.17}$$

There is an equivalent simple eigenvalue problem whose solutions are the first s columns of the orthonormal matrix Q^* satisfying

$$Q^* D = L' S_{10} S_{00}^{-1} S_{01} L Q^* \tag{16.2.18}$$

where $D = \text{diag}(\lambda_1, \ldots, \lambda_m)$. The eigenvalues in the original problem are the same as these, but the original eigenvectors are the columns of the matrix $Q = LQ^*$ which have the normalization

$$Q' S_{11} Q = I_m. \tag{16.2.19}$$

Premultiplying (16.2.18) by L, note first that the eigenvectors are also solutions to the equations

$$(\lambda_j I_m - S_{11}^{-1} S_{10} S_{00}^{-1} S_{01}) q_j = \mathbf{0}. \tag{16.2.20}$$

The λ_j are the squared *canonical correlations* between R_{0t} and R_{1t}. In other words, the vector q_1 is the set of weights that gives the variables $q_1' R_{1t}$ the maximum multiple correlation with R_{0t} (i.e., maximum regression R^2) subject to $n^{-1}\sum_t (q_1' R_{1t})^2 = q_1' S_{11} q_1 = 1$. The corresponding coefficient is λ_1. Then the vector q_2 maximizes the multiple correlation (which is λ_2) subject to the constraints $q_2' S_{11} q_2 = 1$ and $q_2' S_{11} q_1 = 0$. And so on. The λ_j therefore lie in the interval $[0, 1]$. For further details see Anderson (1984).

The canonical correlations should be maximized when the q_j estimate cointegrating vectors. Premultiplying (16.2.20) by $q_j' S_{11}$ shows that

$$\lambda_j = q_j' S_{10} S_{00}^{-1} S_{01} q_j \quad j = 1, \ldots, m. \tag{16.2.21}$$

[5] Compare (13.3.12) and its solution from (13.3.14). In the present case the solutions correspond to choosing the smallest values of $1 - \lambda$.

However, because $S_{11} = O_p(n)$, the normalization of the q_j does not make the nature of the solutions explicit. Instead let $r_j = (q_j'q_j)^{-1/2}q_j$ having length 1. Then the last equation can be written as

$$\lambda_j = \frac{r_j' S_{10} S_{00}^{-1} S_{01} r_j}{r_j' S_{11} r_j} \tag{16.2.22}$$

where $r_j'S_{11}r_j = (q_j'q_j)^{-1}$. For any unit-length vector r_j we can show that $r_j'S_{10}S_{00}^{-1}S_{01}r_j = O_p(1)$. This follows by considering the convergence in (15.2.11). On the other hand, $r_j'S_{11}r_j = O_p(1)$ *only* if $r_j'R_{1t} \sim \mathrm{I}(0)$ in the limit, such that r_j (and hence q_j) is converging to a point in the space spanned by the cointegrating vectors. Otherwise, on comparing (16.1.18) and (16.1.21), it is evident that this term must be $O_p(n)$. Either $\lambda_j = O_p(1)$, and q_j lies in the cointegrating space asymptotically in this sense, or $\lambda_j = O_p(n^{-1})$. Since S_{11} is nonsingular, the vectors

$$\hat{\beta} = (q_1, \dots, q_s) \tag{16.2.23}$$

corresponding to the s largest eigenvalues span the space containing β asymptotically, and in this special sense, are consistent estimates of β. In view of (16.2.19), note that

$$\hat{\beta}' S_{11} \hat{\beta} = I_s \tag{16.2.24}$$

by construction. In other words, under this normalization the cointegrating residuals $\hat{z}_t = \hat{\beta}' R_{1t}$ are normalized to be orthogonal with unit variance. Given (16.2.23), α can be estimated by substituting $\hat{\beta}$ into (16.2.11), which in view of (16.2.24) yields simply

$$\hat{\alpha} = S_{01}\hat{\beta}. \tag{16.2.25}$$

The required property of the eigenvalues is established in the following section. While one can speak of $\hat{\beta}$ as consistent for β, note that the normalization is arbitrary, and any matrix spanning the same space is equivalent to it from this point of view. Comparing $\hat{\beta}$ with $\check{\beta}$ that solves (16.1.23), note that since $M_n = n^{-1}S_{11}$, in the present notation this is

$$\check{\beta} = \arg\min_{b} \operatorname{tr}(b' S_{11} b) \text{ subject to } b'b = I_s. \tag{16.2.26}$$

Since the terms in this criterion function are the denominators of (16.2.22), the consistency of the two estimators follows by very similar reasoning.

16.3 Inference in the Cointegrating VAR

16.3.1 Tests for Cointegrating Rank

All the foregoing discussion has assumed that the true cointegrating rank of the system is s. However, this assumption has only been imposed on the estimation by electing to treat the first s eigenvectors as estimates of cointegrating vectors. A test of the hypothesis is suggested by the fact that $\lambda_j = O_p(1)$ if $\boldsymbol{q}_j$ is in the cointegrating space, but otherwise $\lambda_j = O_p(n^{-1})$. To be precise, we can test the hypothesis that the rank of the cointegrating space is at most s, against the alternative that it exceeds s.

Consider a matrix $\boldsymbol{\gamma}$ $(m \times (m-s))$ such that $\boldsymbol{A} = [\boldsymbol{\beta} \;\; \boldsymbol{\gamma}]$ $(m \times m)$ has rank m, $\boldsymbol{\gamma}'\boldsymbol{\beta} = \boldsymbol{0}$, and

$$\boldsymbol{\gamma}'\boldsymbol{C\Sigma C}'\boldsymbol{\gamma} = \boldsymbol{I}_{m-s}. \tag{16.3.1}$$

Note that the columns of $\boldsymbol{\beta}$ are eigenvectors of $\boldsymbol{C\Sigma C}'$ corresponding to zero eigenvalues, by (16.1.8). The columns of $\boldsymbol{\gamma}$ can be constructed as eigenvectors corresponding to the positive eigenvalues, divided by the square roots of the latter.[6] Maintaining the hypothesis that the cointegrating rank is s, define

$$\boldsymbol{S}_j = \lambda_j \boldsymbol{S}_{11} - \boldsymbol{S}_{10}\boldsymbol{S}_{00}^{-1}\boldsymbol{S}_{01} \tag{16.3.2}$$

where λ_j is one of the solutions of (16.2.15), such that $|\boldsymbol{S}_j| = 0$. Note that

$$\begin{aligned} |\boldsymbol{\beta}'\boldsymbol{S}_j\boldsymbol{\beta}||\boldsymbol{\gamma}'(\boldsymbol{S}_j - \boldsymbol{S}_j\boldsymbol{\beta}(\boldsymbol{\beta}'\boldsymbol{S}_j\boldsymbol{\beta})^{-1}\boldsymbol{\beta}'\boldsymbol{S}_j)\boldsymbol{\gamma}| &= \begin{vmatrix} \boldsymbol{\beta}'\boldsymbol{S}_j\boldsymbol{\beta} & \boldsymbol{\beta}'\boldsymbol{S}_j\boldsymbol{\gamma} \\ \boldsymbol{\gamma}'\boldsymbol{S}_j\boldsymbol{\beta} & \boldsymbol{\gamma}'\boldsymbol{S}_j\boldsymbol{\gamma} \end{vmatrix} \\ &= |\boldsymbol{A}'\boldsymbol{S}_j\boldsymbol{A}| = |\boldsymbol{A}|^2|\boldsymbol{S}_j| = 0 \end{aligned} \tag{16.3.3}$$

where the first equality is similar to (16.2.13). Consider one of the $m - s$ smallest eigenvalues. Write

$$n\lambda_j \xrightarrow{\text{D}} \bar{\lambda}_j \tag{16.3.4}$$

for $s+1 \le j \le m$, where the limiting distribution on the right-hand side is assumed to exist and is now to be determined, and consider the limiting distributions of the terms in (16.3.3).

Given the normalization of $\boldsymbol{\beta}$ (compare (16.2.24))

$$\boldsymbol{\beta}'\boldsymbol{S}_{11}\boldsymbol{\beta} \xrightarrow{\text{pr}} \boldsymbol{I}_s \tag{16.3.5}$$

$$\boldsymbol{S}_{01}\boldsymbol{\beta} \xrightarrow{\text{pr}} \boldsymbol{\alpha} \tag{16.3.6}$$

$$\boldsymbol{S}_{00} \xrightarrow{\text{pr}} \boldsymbol{\Sigma}_{00} = \boldsymbol{\Sigma} + \boldsymbol{\alpha\alpha}' \tag{16.3.7}$$

where all the limits are finite constant matrices. The limits in (16.3.6) and (16.3.7) result from substituting from (16.2.4) and assuming $E(\boldsymbol{\varepsilon}_t\boldsymbol{\varepsilon}_t') = \boldsymbol{\Sigma}$ and $E(\boldsymbol{\varepsilon}_t\boldsymbol{R}_{1t}'\boldsymbol{\beta}) = \boldsymbol{0}$. The latter condition depends on correct modelling of dynamic effects, and is crucial to what follows. Since $\lambda_j = O_p(n^{-1})$,

$$\boldsymbol{\beta}'\boldsymbol{S}_j\boldsymbol{\beta} = \lambda_j\boldsymbol{\beta}'\boldsymbol{S}_{11}\boldsymbol{\beta} - \boldsymbol{\beta}'\boldsymbol{S}_{10}\boldsymbol{S}_{00}^{-1}\boldsymbol{S}_{01}\boldsymbol{\beta} \xrightarrow{pr} -\boldsymbol{\alpha}'\boldsymbol{\Sigma}_{00}^{-1}\boldsymbol{\alpha}. \tag{16.3.8}$$

Since $\boldsymbol{\alpha}$ has rank s by assumption, it follows that $\boldsymbol{\beta}'\boldsymbol{S}_j\boldsymbol{\beta}$ has full rank asymptotically, which in view of (16.3.3) means that the equality

$$|\boldsymbol{\gamma}'\boldsymbol{S}_j\boldsymbol{\gamma} - \boldsymbol{\gamma}'\boldsymbol{S}_j\boldsymbol{\beta}(\boldsymbol{\beta}'\boldsymbol{S}_j\boldsymbol{\beta})^{-1}\boldsymbol{\beta}'\boldsymbol{S}_j\boldsymbol{\gamma}| = 0 \tag{16.3.9}$$

[6] If $\boldsymbol{\gamma}$ satisfies these conditions so does $\boldsymbol{\gamma d}$ where $\boldsymbol{d}$ $((m-s) \times (m-s))$ is any orthonormal matrix, satisfying $\boldsymbol{d}'\boldsymbol{d} = \boldsymbol{I}_{m-s}$.

must hold in the limit.

Consider the various terms in (16.3.9). Applying (16.2.9)-(16.2.10) gives

$$\begin{aligned}\gamma' S_j \gamma \xrightarrow{\mathrm{D}} \bar{\lambda}_j \gamma' C \int_0^1 B_w^* B_w^{*\prime} dr\, C' \gamma \\ - \left(\gamma' \Psi \alpha' + \gamma' C \int_0^1 B_w^* dB_w'\right) \Sigma_{00}^{-1} \left(\alpha \Psi' \gamma + \int_0^1 dB_w B_w^{*\prime} C' \gamma\right) \end{aligned} \tag{16.3.10}$$

and similarly, since $\lambda_j = O_p(n^{-1})$ and applying (16.3.6),

$$\begin{aligned}\gamma' S_j \beta &= \lambda_j \gamma' S_{11} \beta - \gamma' S_{10} S_{00}^{-1} S_{01} \beta \\ &\xrightarrow{\mathrm{D}} - \left(\gamma' \Psi \alpha' + \gamma' C \int_0^1 B_w^* dB_w'\right) \Sigma_{00}^{-1} \alpha. \end{aligned} \tag{16.3.11}$$

Define

$$N = \Sigma_{00}^{-1} - \Sigma_{00}^{-1} \alpha (\alpha' \Sigma_{00}^{-1} \alpha)^{-1} \alpha' \Sigma_{00}^{-1} \quad (m \times m) \tag{16.3.12}$$

a symmetric, positive semi-definite matrix having rank $m-s$ in view of the evident fact that $N\alpha = 0$. Also, by (16.3.7),

$$N = N \Sigma_{00} N = N(\Sigma + \alpha\alpha')N = N \Sigma N. \tag{16.3.13}$$

Factorize this matrix as

$$N = PP' \tag{16.3.14}$$

where P $(m \times (m-s))$ is of rank $m - s$, $P'\alpha = 0$, and in view of (16.3.13), $P'\Sigma P = I_{m-s}$. In view of (16.3.1) γ can be chosen to satisfy

$$P = C'\gamma. \tag{16.3.15}$$

Also write $\gamma' C B_w^* = W^*$ where $W^* = W - \int_0^1 W dr$ and W is a $(m-s)$-dimensional standard BM, having covariance matrix $\gamma' C \Sigma C' \gamma = I_{m-s}$. Putting together the foregoing limit expressions, doing some rearrangement, and using the properties of N yields

$$\begin{aligned}&\gamma'(S_j - S_j\beta(\beta' S_j \beta)^{-1} \beta' S_j)\gamma \\ &\xrightarrow{\mathrm{D}} \bar{\lambda}_j \int_0^1 W^* W^{*\prime} dr \\ &\quad - \left(\gamma' \Psi \alpha' + \int_0^1 W^* dB_w'\right) N \left(\alpha \Psi' \gamma + \int_0^1 dB_w W^{*\prime}\right) \\ &= \bar{\lambda}_j \int_0^1 W^* W^{*\prime} dr - \left(\int_0^1 W^* dB_w'\right) PP' \left(\int_0^1 dB_w W^{*\prime}\right) \\ &= \bar{\lambda}_j \int_0^1 W^* W^{*\prime} dr - \left(\int_0^1 W^* dW\right)\left(\int_0^1 dW W^{*\prime}\right) \end{aligned} \tag{16.3.16}$$

This matrix is singular asymptotically from (16.3.9). The eigenvalue problem

$$|\rho B - AA'| = 0 \tag{16.3.17}$$

where A and B are nonsingular has the same solutions as the problem[7]

$$|\rho I - A'B^{-1}A| = 0 \qquad (16.3.18)$$

so the $\bar{\lambda}_j$ can be viewed as the eigenvalues of the stochastic $(m - s) \times (m - s)$ matrix

$$\bar{Q}_W = \int_0^1 dWW^{*\prime}\left(\int_0^1 W^* W^{*\prime} dr\right)^{-1}\int_0^1 W^* dW'. \qquad (16.3.19)$$

Since W is a standard BM, $\bar{Q}_W$ does not depend on nuisance parameters and, in particular, the distribution of its eigenvalues may be tabulated.

All the foregoing argument has been based on the assumption that the cointegrating rank is s. Consider a test of $H_0 : s = s_0$ where s_0 is the hypothesised cointegrating rank of the system, with alternative hypothesis $H_A : s > s_0$. If H_0 is true, the random variables $n\lambda_{s_0+1}, \dots, n\lambda_m$ are $O_p(1)$, and are converging to eigenvalues of $\bar{Q}_W$. On the other hand, if H_A is true the maximal eigenvalue of the set, which is λ_{s_0+1} since they are in rank order, is not vanishing and $n\lambda_{s_0+1} = O_p(n)$. Hence, a consistent test of H_0 can be based on $n\lambda_{s_0+1}$, whose limiting null distribution is found as the distribution of the maximal eigenvalue of $\bar{Q}_W$. This is called the *maximal eigenvalue* test.

However, consider the alternative statistic

$$\mathrm{J} = n \sum_{j=s_0+1}^{m} \lambda_j. \qquad (16.3.20)$$

When H_0 is true, J is converging to the sum of the eigenvalues of $\bar{Q}_W$, which is just the trace of the matrix. The distribution of this random variable can again be tabulated, and the test based on J is called the *trace test.* Both of these distributions have been tabulated by simulation, see for example Osterwald-Lenum (1992).

An interesting special case is where $s_0 = m - 1$, because then under the alternative hypothesis the data must be stationary, being generated by a full-rank VAR. The test becomes in effect a test of I(1), with a single common trend existing under H_0. In this case, the maximal eigenvalue and trace statistics coincide and the test statistic is converging to a random variable equal to $\bar{Q}_W$, in this case a scalar. The asymptotic null distribution is that of the square of the Dickey–Fuller t statistic, as in (14.3.19).

16.3.2 Likelihood Ratio Tests

Johansen (1988b, 1991) derives the tests for cointegrating rank by assuming the shock processes are Gaussian. In this case, the maximal eigenvalue and trace tests just described are asymptotically equivalent to likelihood ratio tests. The function $-\frac{1}{2}n \ln \Lambda_s^{**}(\beta)$ obtained from (16.2.12) is the Gaussian concentrated log

[7] This follows by applications of (A.2.11).

likelihood function apart from additive constants, derived on the assumption that the cointegrating rank is s. Since $\boldsymbol{Q}'\boldsymbol{S}_{11}\boldsymbol{Q} = \boldsymbol{I}_m$, premultiplying (16.2.18) through by $\boldsymbol{Q}'\boldsymbol{S}_{11}\boldsymbol{L}$ yields the diagonal matrix having the eigenvalues on the diagonal,

$$\boldsymbol{Q}'\boldsymbol{S}_{10}\boldsymbol{S}_{00}^{-1}\boldsymbol{S}_{01}\boldsymbol{Q} = \boldsymbol{D}. \tag{16.3.21}$$

Since $\hat{\boldsymbol{\beta}}$ is the first s columns of $\boldsymbol{Q}$, it follows that the maximized value of the log-likelihood is

$$\begin{aligned} -\frac{n}{2}\ln \hat{\Lambda}_s^{**} &= -\frac{n}{2}\ln \frac{|\hat{\boldsymbol{\beta}}'\boldsymbol{S}_{11}\hat{\boldsymbol{\beta}} - \hat{\boldsymbol{\beta}}'\boldsymbol{S}_{10}\boldsymbol{S}_{00}^{-1}\boldsymbol{S}_{01}\hat{\boldsymbol{\beta}}|}{|\hat{\boldsymbol{\beta}}'\boldsymbol{S}_{11}\hat{\boldsymbol{\beta}}|} \\ &= -\frac{n}{2}\ln|\boldsymbol{I}_s - \boldsymbol{D}| = -\frac{n}{2}\ln\prod_{j=1}^{s}(1-\lambda_j). \end{aligned} \tag{16.3.22}$$

The maximized log-likelihood function under the assumption that the cointegrating rank is $s+u$ is identical to this expression except with s replaced by $s+u$. The values of the first s eigenvalues are the same in the solutions to either problem, as are the corresponding eigenvectors. Hence the usual likelihood ratio statistic as defined in (12.3.15), of the test of H_0 against the alternative that the cointegrating rank is s_0+u, takes the form

$$n(\ln \hat{\Lambda}_{s_0+u}^{**} - \ln \hat{\Lambda}_{s_0}^{**}) = -n\sum_{j=s+1}^{s+u}\ln(1-\lambda_j). \tag{16.3.23}$$

Note that when λ_j is close to 0, it is correspondingly close to $-\ln(1-\lambda_j)$, according to the series expansion of the logarithmic function. On this basis it can be shown that this test is asymptotically equivalent to the test based on $n\sum_{j=s+1}^{s+u}\lambda_j$.

The maximal eigenvalue test is therefore asymptotically equivalent to the LR test of H_0 against the alternative of $s = s_0+1$, while the trace test is the LR test against the alternative $s = m$. Of course, both tests will have power against alternatives intermediate between these cases. In practice, it is the LR forms of the test that are usually conducted. These will reject slightly more frequently under both null and alternative than those based directly on the maximal eigenvalue and the trace statistic, because of the convexity of the transformation.

16.3.3 Inference on $\boldsymbol{\beta}$

The purpose of this section is to show that the estimated cointegrating vectors have a mixed Gaussian distribution when appropriately normalized, and to derive the conditional covariance matrix. These results need careful interpretation in view of the fact that the columns of $\boldsymbol{\beta}$ have been arbitrarily constructed to span the cointegrating space. Their elements have no obvious status as parameters of interest, and it is not immediately clear how confidence intervals and test statistics relating to these parameters could be applied. In fact, there is a way to test hypotheses relating to the cointegrating relations, making use of the present results, and this issue is dealt with in detail in §16.6.3.

It is, however, not possible to derive the asymptotic distribution of $\hat{\boldsymbol{\beta}}$ as defined by (16.2.23). We must consider a derived estimator $\tilde{\boldsymbol{\beta}}$, which is actually infeasible because it depends on the true $\boldsymbol{\beta}$. However, this is not a problem in practice because the difference between the two is only in the choice of normalization. $\hat{\boldsymbol{\beta}}$ and $\tilde{\boldsymbol{\beta}}$ span the same space, and yield the same value for the estimation criterion, provided $\boldsymbol{\alpha}$ is renormalized to match. As will be shown in §16.6.3, the change of normalization is actually immaterial to the type of restrictions that it is useful to test.

The purpose of the renormalization is to project the error-of-estimate into the space orthogonal to $\boldsymbol{\beta}$. Since $\boldsymbol{A} = [\boldsymbol{\beta} \;\; \boldsymbol{\gamma}]$ has full rank, every m-vector $\boldsymbol{a}$ has the decomposition

$$\boldsymbol{a} = \boldsymbol{\beta}\bar{\boldsymbol{\beta}}'\boldsymbol{a} + \boldsymbol{\gamma}\bar{\boldsymbol{\gamma}}'\boldsymbol{a} \tag{16.3.24}$$

where $\bar{\boldsymbol{\beta}} = \boldsymbol{\beta}(\boldsymbol{\beta}'\boldsymbol{\beta})^{-1}$ and $\bar{\boldsymbol{\gamma}} = \boldsymbol{\gamma}(\boldsymbol{\gamma}'\boldsymbol{\gamma})^{-1}$. The two components lie in orthogonal subspaces spanned by $\boldsymbol{\beta}$ and $\boldsymbol{\gamma}$ respectively. Defining

$$\tilde{\boldsymbol{\beta}} = \hat{\boldsymbol{\beta}}(\bar{\boldsymbol{\beta}}'\hat{\boldsymbol{\beta}})^{-1} \tag{16.3.25}$$

note that since $\boldsymbol{\gamma}'\boldsymbol{\beta} = \mathbf{0}$,

$$\tilde{\boldsymbol{\beta}} - \boldsymbol{\beta} = \boldsymbol{\gamma}\bar{\boldsymbol{\gamma}}'\tilde{\boldsymbol{\beta}} = \boldsymbol{\gamma}\bar{\boldsymbol{\gamma}}'(\tilde{\boldsymbol{\beta}} - \boldsymbol{\beta}). \tag{16.3.26}$$

The corresponding renormalization of $\boldsymbol{\alpha}$, such that $\tilde{\boldsymbol{\alpha}}\tilde{\boldsymbol{\beta}}' = \hat{\boldsymbol{\alpha}}\hat{\boldsymbol{\beta}}'$, is

$$\tilde{\boldsymbol{\alpha}} = \boldsymbol{S}_{01}\tilde{\boldsymbol{\beta}}(\tilde{\boldsymbol{\beta}}'\boldsymbol{S}_{11}\tilde{\boldsymbol{\beta}})^{-1} = \hat{\boldsymbol{\alpha}}\hat{\boldsymbol{\beta}}'\bar{\boldsymbol{\beta}}. \tag{16.3.27}$$

Consider the joint optimization with respect to $\boldsymbol{\alpha}$ and $\boldsymbol{\beta}$ of the criterion function $\Lambda_s^*(\boldsymbol{\alpha}, \boldsymbol{\beta}) = |\boldsymbol{\Sigma}(\boldsymbol{\alpha}, \boldsymbol{\beta})|$ where

$$\boldsymbol{\Sigma}(\boldsymbol{\alpha}, \boldsymbol{\beta}) = \frac{1}{n}\sum_{t=1}^{n} \boldsymbol{\varepsilon}_t\boldsymbol{\varepsilon}_t' = \boldsymbol{S}_{00} - \boldsymbol{S}_{01}\boldsymbol{\beta}\boldsymbol{\alpha}' - \boldsymbol{\alpha}\boldsymbol{\beta}'\boldsymbol{S}_{10} + \boldsymbol{\alpha}\boldsymbol{\beta}'\boldsymbol{S}_{11}\boldsymbol{\beta}\boldsymbol{\alpha}'. \tag{16.3.28}$$

The problem is analogous to minimizing (13.2.14), except for the nonlinearity in parameters. Letting $\boldsymbol{\Gamma} = \boldsymbol{\alpha}\boldsymbol{\beta}'$ with typical element

$$\gamma_{jk} = \sum_{i=1}^{s} \alpha_{ji}\beta_{ki} \tag{16.3.29}$$

it can be verified that

$$\begin{aligned}\frac{\partial \Lambda_s^*}{\partial \beta_{uv}} &= \sum_p \sum_q \sum_j \sum_k \frac{\partial |\Sigma|}{\partial \sigma_{pq}} \frac{\partial \sigma_{pq}}{\partial \gamma_{jk}} \frac{\partial \gamma_{jk}}{\partial \beta_{uv}} \\ &= 2\sum_q \sum_j \operatorname{adj}(\boldsymbol{\Sigma})_{jq} \sum_{t=1}^{n} \varepsilon_{qt}(\boldsymbol{R}_{1t})_u \alpha_{jv}.\end{aligned} \tag{16.3.30}$$

Equating to 0 for each u and v and writing this expression out in matrix form yields first-order conditions equivalent to

$$(\boldsymbol{S}_{10} - \boldsymbol{S}_{11}\tilde{\boldsymbol{\beta}}\tilde{\boldsymbol{\alpha}}')\hat{\boldsymbol{\Sigma}}^{-1}\tilde{\boldsymbol{\alpha}} = \mathbf{0} \tag{16.3.31}$$

where the tildes denote the solution values and $\hat{\Sigma} = \Sigma(\tilde{\alpha}, \tilde{\beta})$.[8] Premultiply this expression by γ'. In view of the consistency of the estimators $\tilde{\alpha}$, $\tilde{\beta}$ and $\hat{\Sigma}$ (see Johansen 1995b Section 13.3 for details) the expression becomes

$$\begin{aligned} 0 &= \gamma'[S_{1\varepsilon} - S_{11}(\tilde{\beta}\tilde{\alpha}' - \beta\alpha')]\hat{\Sigma}^{-1}\tilde{\alpha} \\ &= \gamma' S_{1\varepsilon}\hat{\Sigma}^{-1}\tilde{\alpha} - \gamma' S_{11}(\tilde{\beta} - \beta)\tilde{\alpha}'\hat{\Sigma}^{-1}\tilde{\alpha} - \gamma' S_{11}\beta(\tilde{\alpha} - \alpha)'\hat{\Sigma}^{-1}\tilde{\alpha} \\ &= \gamma' S_{1\varepsilon}\Sigma^{-1}\alpha - \gamma' S_{11}\gamma\bar{\gamma}'(\tilde{\beta} - \beta)\alpha'\Sigma^{-1}\alpha + o_p(1) \end{aligned} \tag{16.3.32}$$

which solves as

$$n\bar{\gamma}'(\tilde{\beta} - \beta) = \left(\frac{\gamma' S_{11}\gamma}{n}\right)^{-1}\gamma' S_{1\varepsilon}\Sigma^{-1}\alpha(\alpha'\Sigma^{-1}\alpha)^{-1} + o_p(1). \tag{16.3.33}$$

The final step is to apply (16.3.26) to obtain

$$\begin{aligned} n(\tilde{\beta} - \beta) &= \gamma\left(\frac{\gamma' S_{11}\gamma}{n}\right)^{-1}\gamma' S_{1\varepsilon}\Sigma^{-1}\alpha(\alpha'\Sigma^{-1}\alpha)^{-1} + o_p(1) \\ &\xrightarrow{\mathrm{D}} \gamma\left(\int_0^1 W^* W^{*\prime} ds\right)^{-1}\int_0^1 W^* dB_w'\Sigma^{-1}\alpha(\alpha'\Sigma^{-1}\alpha)^{-1} \end{aligned} \tag{16.3.34}$$

where, as previously, $W = \gamma' C B_w$ is a standard BM of dimension $m - s$ and W^* denotes the de-meaned process. Now observe that

$$E(\gamma' C B_w B_w' \Sigma^{-1}\alpha) = \gamma' C\Sigma\Sigma^{-1}\alpha = 0 \tag{16.3.35}$$

so that the BM $\alpha'\Sigma^{-1}B_w$ is distributed independently of W with covariance matrix $\alpha'\Sigma^{-1}\alpha$. This implies that the distribution in (16.3.34) is mixed Gaussian (see §15.2.3).

This result shows that conventional asymptotic inference can be performed on $\tilde{\beta}$, and it remains to derive the conditional covariance matrix. It is convenient to vectorize the limiting matrix in (16.3.34) using (A.10.6), and so obtain the mixed Gaussian distribution in the form

$$\begin{aligned} n\,\mathrm{Vec}(\tilde{\beta} - \beta) &\xrightarrow{\mathrm{D}} (\alpha'\Sigma^{-1}\alpha)^{-1} \otimes \gamma G_W^{-1}\,\mathrm{Vec}\int_0^1 W^* dB_w'\Sigma^{-1}\alpha \\ &\sim \int \mathrm{N}(0,\ (\alpha'\Sigma^{-1}\alpha)^{-1} \otimes \gamma G_W^{-1}\gamma')\,dG_W \end{aligned} \tag{16.3.36}$$

where

$$G_W = \int_0^1 W^* W^{*\prime} ds. \tag{16.3.37}$$

This covariance matrix is singular of rank $m(m-s)$ reflecting the fact that some linear combinations of the errors of estimate are known with certainty, specifically, $\bar{\beta}'(\tilde{\beta} - \beta) = 0$. This is simply an alternative to the convention of normalizing certain coefficients to 1 or 0.

---

[8] Don't forget that $(\tilde{\alpha}, \tilde{\beta})$ and $(\hat{\alpha}, \hat{\beta})$ are equivalent solutions to the optimization.

To construct a sample counterpart of the asymptotic conditional covariance matrix it is required to estimate $\gamma G_W^{-1}\gamma$. Let $\hat{v} = (q_{s+1}, \ldots, q_m)$ $(m \times (m-s))$ denote the non-cointegrating eigenvectors, and following (16.3.24) write

$$\hat{v} = \beta\bar{\beta}'\hat{v} + \gamma\bar{\gamma}'\hat{v}. \tag{16.3.38}$$

By (16.2.19), $\hat{v}'S_{11}\hat{v} = I_{m-s}$, but since $S_{11} = O_p(n)$ from (16.2.9), whereas $S_{11}\beta = O_p(1)$ from (16.2.7), the projection of $\hat{v}$ into the space spanned by γ must dominate this expression in the limit. In other words,

$$\hat{e}'\gamma' S_{11}\gamma\hat{e} \xrightarrow{\text{pr}} I_{m-s}. \tag{16.3.39}$$

where $\hat{e} = \bar{\gamma}'\hat{v}$ is $(m-s)\times(m-s)$. Rearranging (16.3.38) in the form $\gamma\hat{e} = M_\beta\hat{v}$ where $M_\beta = I_m - \beta\bar{\beta}'$ and using (16.3.39) yields

$$\begin{aligned} nM_\beta\hat{v}\hat{v}'M_\beta &\underset{\text{asy}}{\sim} \gamma\hat{e}\Big(\frac{\hat{e}'\gamma'S_{11}\gamma\hat{e}}{n}\Big)^{-1}\hat{e}'\gamma' \\ &= \gamma\Big(\frac{\gamma'S_{11}\gamma}{n}\Big)^{-1}\gamma' \xrightarrow{\text{D}} \gamma G_W^{-1}\gamma'. \end{aligned} \tag{16.3.40}$$

Replacing M_β by $\hat{M}_\beta$, in which β is replaced by $\hat{\beta}$, gives a matrix with the same limit in distribution. Also note from (16.2.19) that $S_{11}^{-1} = QQ' = \hat{\beta}\hat{\beta}' + \hat{v}\hat{v}'$. Therefore, an alternative method of computing the variance matrix is indicated by the relation

$$\hat{M}_\beta\hat{v}\hat{v}'\hat{M}_\beta = \hat{M}_\beta S_{11}^{-1}\hat{M}_\beta. \tag{16.3.41}$$

It remains to find an estimator of $(\alpha'\Sigma^{-1}\alpha)^{-1}$. This can of course be computed directly from the solution values of these parameters, but a neat result, proved in §16.7, is the following.

Lemma 16.3.1

$$(\hat{\alpha}'\hat{\Sigma}^{-1}\hat{\alpha})^{-1} = D_1^{-1} - I_s \tag{16.3.42}$$

where $D_1 = \text{diag}\{\lambda_1, \ldots, \lambda_s\}$. □

16.3.4 The Other Parameters

Estimates of the other parameters in the model are recovered straightforwardly by running the regression in (16.2.1) with $\beta' x_t$ replaced by new regressors $\hat{\beta}' x_t$. These converge at the conventional rate of $\sqrt{n}$, so that $\hat{\beta}$ can be regarded as equivalent to β in the limiting distribution. Standard errors can also be computed conventionally, as required.

Considering the case of the adjustment parameters α, the first-order conditions analogous to (16.3.31) take the form

$$\begin{aligned} 0 &= \hat{\Sigma}^{-1}(S_{01} - \tilde{\alpha}\tilde{\beta}'S_{11})\tilde{\beta} \\ &= \hat{\Sigma}^{-1}[S_{\varepsilon 1}\tilde{\beta} - (\tilde{\alpha} - \alpha)\tilde{\beta}'S_{11}\tilde{\beta} + \alpha(\tilde{\beta} - \beta)'S_{11}\tilde{\beta}] \end{aligned} \tag{16.3.43}$$

which rearranges as

$$\sqrt{n}(\tilde{\alpha} - \alpha) = \frac{1}{\sqrt{n}} S_{\varepsilon 1}\beta(\beta' S_{11}\beta)^{-1} + o_p(1) \tag{16.3.44}$$

in view of the fact that $(\tilde{\beta} - \beta) = O_p(n^{-1})$. Thus, the standard asymptotic analysis leads to

$$\begin{aligned}\sqrt{n}\,\mathrm{Vec}(\tilde{\alpha} - \alpha) &= (I_m \otimes (\beta' S_{11}\beta)^{-1})\frac{1}{\sqrt{n}} \mathrm{Vec}\, S_{\varepsilon 1}\beta \\ &\underset{\text{asy}}{\sim} \frac{1}{\sqrt{n}} \mathrm{Vec}\, S_{\varepsilon 1}\beta \xrightarrow{\mathrm{D}} \mathrm{N}(0, \Sigma \otimes I_s).\end{aligned} \tag{16.3.45}$$

The fact that the 'regressors' $\beta' R_{1t}$ have covariance matrix converging to I_s is of course a feature of the chosen normalization of the model.

Given the intercept term $\hat{\nu}$ one can estimate the intercepts in the cointegrating relations as

$$\hat{\mu} = -(\hat{\alpha}'\hat{\alpha})^{-1}\hat{\alpha}'\hat{\nu} \tag{16,3.46}$$

recalling that $\xi = 0$ by assumption. However, the latter assumption has not been imposed. To estimate μ directly and obtain its asymptotic distribution it is necessary to impose the zero-drift restriction on the model. This is done in §16.4.3.

16.4 Allowing Deterministic Trends

16.4.1 Modifications to the Analysis

Consider the VECM with drift,

$$\Delta x_t = \alpha(\beta' x_{t-1} - \mu) + \xi + \Pi(L)\Delta x_{t-1} + \Theta d_t + \varepsilon_t. \tag{16.4.1}$$

Putting $\tau = C\xi$ in (16.1.12),

$$\frac{x_{[nr]} - \bar{x}}{n} \xrightarrow{\mathrm{pr}} \tau(r - \tfrac{1}{2}) \tag{16.4.2}$$

replaces (16.1.16). Much as in §15.4,

$$\frac{S_{11}}{n^2} \xrightarrow{\mathrm{pr}} \tau\tau' \int_0^1 (r - \tfrac{1}{2})^2 dr = \frac{\tau\tau'}{12} \tag{16.4.3}$$

which is a matrix of rank 1. Although $\beta'\tau = \beta' C\xi = 0$, the space of vectors orthogonal to τ actually has dimension $m - 1$. There exists a full-rank matrix φ $(m \times (m - s - 1))$ orthogonal to β and τ, such that $\varphi' x_t$ is a drift-free I(1) process. In (16.2.22), $r_j' S_{11} r_j = O_p(1)$ when r_j lies in the space spanned by φ, and $O_p(n^2)$ otherwise. In this theory the properties of matrix rank and stochastic order of magnitude are subtly intertwined.

To derive the tests for cointegrating rank we retrace the arguments of §16.3.1 with one important variation. Previously the matrix γ was chosen to satisfy $\gamma' C\Sigma C'\gamma = I_{m-s}$. Now φ is chosen to satisfy the conditions

$$\varphi' C\Sigma C'\varphi = I_{m-s-1} \tag{16.4.4a}$$

$$\boldsymbol{\varphi}'\boldsymbol{\tau} = \mathbf{0}. \tag{16.4.4b}$$

Such a matrix can be constructed as $\boldsymbol{\varphi} = \boldsymbol{\gamma} \boldsymbol{c}$, where each column of the full-rank matrix $\boldsymbol{c}$ $((m-s) \times (m-s-1))$ is orthogonal to the $(m-s)$-vector $\boldsymbol{\gamma}'\boldsymbol{\tau}$, and is orthonormalized such that $\boldsymbol{c}'\boldsymbol{c} = \boldsymbol{I}_{m-s-1}$.[9] The matrix $[\boldsymbol{\beta}\ \ \boldsymbol{\varphi}\ \ \boldsymbol{\tau}]$ is $m \times m$ of full rank. However, the matrix that will play the role of $\boldsymbol{A}$ in (16.3.3) is $\boldsymbol{A}_n = [\boldsymbol{\beta}\ \ \boldsymbol{\varphi}\ \ n^{-1/2}\bar{\boldsymbol{\tau}}]$ where $\bar{\boldsymbol{\tau}} = \boldsymbol{\tau}(\boldsymbol{\tau}'\boldsymbol{\tau})^{-1}$, which also has full rank. Note that $\bar{\boldsymbol{\tau}}'\boldsymbol{\tau} = 1$.

According to (16.1.12),

$$\boldsymbol{\varphi}'(\boldsymbol{x}_t - \boldsymbol{x}_0) = \boldsymbol{\varphi}'\boldsymbol{C}\boldsymbol{w}_t + \boldsymbol{\varphi}'\boldsymbol{C}^*(L)\boldsymbol{\varepsilon}_t \quad t \geq 1 \tag{16.4.5}$$

so that $\boldsymbol{\varphi}'\boldsymbol{x}_t$ is a $(m-s-1)$-dimensional drift-free I(1). Now apply to $\boldsymbol{\varphi}'\boldsymbol{x}_t$ the analysis that was applied previously to $\boldsymbol{\gamma}'\boldsymbol{x}_t$, leading to

$$\begin{aligned} &\boldsymbol{\varphi}'(\boldsymbol{S}_j - \boldsymbol{S}_j\boldsymbol{\beta}(\boldsymbol{\beta}'\boldsymbol{S}_j\boldsymbol{\beta})^{-1}\boldsymbol{\beta}'\boldsymbol{S}_j)\boldsymbol{\varphi} \\ &\xrightarrow{\text{D}} \boldsymbol{c}'\left(\bar{\lambda}_j \int_0^1 \boldsymbol{W}^*\boldsymbol{W}^{*\prime}dr - \int_0^1 \boldsymbol{W}^* d\boldsymbol{W}' \int_0^1 d\boldsymbol{W}\boldsymbol{W}^{*\prime}\right)\boldsymbol{c} \end{aligned} \tag{16.4.6}$$

in place of (16.3.16). On the other hand, from (16.4.2),

$$\frac{\bar{\boldsymbol{\tau}}'(\boldsymbol{x}_{[nr]} - \bar{\boldsymbol{x}})}{n} \xrightarrow{\text{pr}} r - \tfrac{1}{2}. \tag{16.4.7}$$

Hence, similarly to (15.4.3) and (15.4.4) the following hold:

$$\frac{\lambda_j}{\sqrt{n}}\bar{\boldsymbol{\tau}}'\boldsymbol{S}_{11}\boldsymbol{\varphi} \xrightarrow{\text{D}} \bar{\lambda}_j\left(\int_0^1 (r - \tfrac{1}{2})\,\boldsymbol{W}'dr\right)\boldsymbol{c} \tag{16.4.8}$$

$$\frac{\lambda_j}{n}\bar{\boldsymbol{\tau}}'\boldsymbol{S}_{11}\bar{\boldsymbol{\tau}} \xrightarrow{\text{D}} \bar{\lambda}_j \int_0^1 (r - \tfrac{1}{2})^2 dr = \frac{1}{12}\bar{\lambda}_j \tag{16.4.9}$$

$$\frac{1}{\sqrt{n}}\bar{\boldsymbol{\tau}}'\boldsymbol{S}_{11}\boldsymbol{\beta} \xrightarrow{\text{D}} \int_0^1 (r - \tfrac{1}{2})d\boldsymbol{y}' = \boldsymbol{\Psi}^* \tag{16.4.10}$$

$$\frac{1}{\sqrt{n}}\bar{\boldsymbol{\tau}}'\boldsymbol{S}_{10} \xrightarrow{\text{D}} \boldsymbol{\Psi}^*\boldsymbol{\alpha}' + \int_0^1 (r - \tfrac{1}{2})d\boldsymbol{B}_w' \tag{16.4.11}$$

where $\boldsymbol{\Psi}^*$ is defined here by analogy with (16.2.7).[10] With these results, the arguments leading to (16.3.16) can be extended to show

$$\begin{aligned} &\frac{1}{\sqrt{n}}\bar{\boldsymbol{\tau}}'(\boldsymbol{S}_j - \boldsymbol{S}_j\boldsymbol{\beta}(\boldsymbol{\beta}'\boldsymbol{S}_j\boldsymbol{\beta})^{-1}\boldsymbol{\beta}'\boldsymbol{S}_j)\boldsymbol{\varphi} \\ &\xrightarrow{\text{D}} \left(\bar{\lambda}_j \int_0^1 (r - \tfrac{1}{2})\,\boldsymbol{W}^{*\prime}dr - \int_0^1 (r - \tfrac{1}{2})d\boldsymbol{W}' \int_0^1 d\boldsymbol{W}\boldsymbol{W}^{*\prime}\right)\boldsymbol{c} \end{aligned} \tag{16.4.12}$$

and

$$\frac{1}{n}\bar{\boldsymbol{\tau}}'(\boldsymbol{S}_j - \boldsymbol{S}_j\boldsymbol{\beta}(\boldsymbol{\beta}'\boldsymbol{S}_j\boldsymbol{\beta})^{-1}\boldsymbol{\beta}'\boldsymbol{S}_j)\bar{\boldsymbol{\tau}}$$

---

[9] Note that if $\boldsymbol{A}$ is any matrix of full column rank, $\boldsymbol{A}(\boldsymbol{A}'\boldsymbol{A})^{-1/2}$ is orthonormal.

[10] $\boldsymbol{\Psi}^*$ and $\int_0^1 (r - \frac{1}{2})d\boldsymbol{B}_w'$ are in fact Gaussian variables, according to the regular CLT.

$$\xrightarrow{\text{D}} \left(\frac{1}{12}\bar{\lambda}_j - \int_0^1 (r-\tfrac{1}{2})d\boldsymbol{W}' \int_0^1 (r-\tfrac{1}{2})d\boldsymbol{W}\right). \qquad (16.4.13)$$

The result replacing (16.3.16) is

$$\begin{bmatrix} \boldsymbol{\varphi}' \\ n^{-1/2}\bar{\boldsymbol{\tau}}' \end{bmatrix} (\boldsymbol{S}_j - \boldsymbol{S}_j\boldsymbol{\beta}(\boldsymbol{\beta}'\boldsymbol{S}_j\boldsymbol{\beta})^{-1}\boldsymbol{\beta}'\boldsymbol{S}_j) \begin{bmatrix} \boldsymbol{\varphi} & n^{-1/2}\bar{\boldsymbol{\tau}} \end{bmatrix}$$

$$\xrightarrow{\text{D}} \left(\bar{\lambda}_j \int_0^1 \boldsymbol{V}\boldsymbol{V}'dr - \int_0^1 \boldsymbol{V}d\boldsymbol{W}' \int_0^1 d\boldsymbol{W}\boldsymbol{V}'\right) \qquad (16.4.14)$$

where

$$\boldsymbol{V}(r) = \begin{bmatrix} \boldsymbol{c}'\boldsymbol{W}^*(r) \\ r - \frac{1}{2} \end{bmatrix} \begin{matrix} m-s-1 \\ 1 \end{matrix}. \qquad (16.4.15)$$

The final step is to choose a $(m-s)$ vector $\boldsymbol{d}$, of unit length and orthogonal to $\boldsymbol{c}$, such that $\boldsymbol{O} = [\boldsymbol{c}\ \boldsymbol{d}]$ is a $(m-s)\times(m-s)$ orthonormal matrix with $\boldsymbol{O}'\boldsymbol{O} = \boldsymbol{O}\boldsymbol{O}' = \boldsymbol{I}_{m-s}$. Then, $\boldsymbol{U} = \boldsymbol{O}'\boldsymbol{W} = \begin{bmatrix} \boldsymbol{c}'\boldsymbol{W} \\ \boldsymbol{d}'\boldsymbol{W} \end{bmatrix}$ is a standard BM of dimension $m-s$. The first $m-s-1$ elements of $\boldsymbol{V}(r)$ are also the first $m-s-1$ elements of $\boldsymbol{U}(r) - \int_0^1 \boldsymbol{U}(s)ds$, and

$$\int_0^1 \boldsymbol{V}d\boldsymbol{W}' \int_0^1 d\boldsymbol{W}\boldsymbol{V}' = \int_0^1 \boldsymbol{V}d\boldsymbol{W}'\boldsymbol{O}\boldsymbol{O}' \int_0^1 d\boldsymbol{W}\boldsymbol{V}'$$
$$= \int_0^1 \boldsymbol{V}d\boldsymbol{U}' \int_0^1 d\boldsymbol{U}\boldsymbol{V}'. \qquad (16.4.16)$$

The matrix

$$\bar{\boldsymbol{Q}}_V = \int_0^1 d\boldsymbol{U}\boldsymbol{V}'\left(\int_0^1 \boldsymbol{V}\boldsymbol{V}'dr\right)^{-1} \int_0^1 \boldsymbol{V}d\boldsymbol{U}' \qquad (16.4.17)$$

is entirely a function of standard BMs and known constants, and the distribution of its eigenvalues can be tabulated. The tests for cointegrating rank can now be performed just as before.

In the case with $m-s=1$, $\int_0^1 \boldsymbol{V}\boldsymbol{V}'dr$ reduces to the scalar $\int_0^1 (r-\frac{1}{2})^2 dr = \frac{1}{12}$, and $\int_0^1 \boldsymbol{V}d\boldsymbol{u}' \sim \text{N}(0, \frac{1}{12})$. In this case $\bar{\boldsymbol{Q}}_V$ is just a $\chi^2(1)$ random variable. This may be compared with the integration test for drift models of (14.4.12) and confirms a previous remark, that while models with drift can yield standard asymptotics, these are only special cases of a generally non-standard distribution theory.

16.4.2 The Cointegrating Vectors

The modifications to the analysis of §16.3.3 follows similar lines to that already seen, and it suffices to summarize the main results. The decomposition in (16.3.24) is replaced by[11]

$$\boldsymbol{a} = \boldsymbol{\beta}\bar{\boldsymbol{\beta}}'\boldsymbol{a} + \boldsymbol{\varphi}\bar{\boldsymbol{\varphi}}'\boldsymbol{a} + \bar{\boldsymbol{\tau}}\boldsymbol{\tau}'\boldsymbol{a}. \qquad (16.4.18)$$

[11]Note that $\bar{\boldsymbol{\tau}}\boldsymbol{\tau}' = \boldsymbol{\tau}\bar{\boldsymbol{\tau}}'$, and $\bar{\boldsymbol{\tau}}(\bar{\boldsymbol{\tau}}'\bar{\boldsymbol{\tau}})^{-1} = \boldsymbol{\tau}$. This is the appropriate representation given the definition of $\boldsymbol{\tau}$.

so that (16.3.26) becomes

$$\tilde{\boldsymbol{\beta}} - \boldsymbol{\beta} = \boldsymbol{\varphi}\bar{\boldsymbol{\varphi}}'(\tilde{\boldsymbol{\beta}} - \boldsymbol{\beta}) + \bar{\boldsymbol{\tau}}\boldsymbol{\tau}'(\tilde{\boldsymbol{\beta}} - \boldsymbol{\beta}). \tag{16.4.19}$$

The key feature of the analysis is that the vectors $\boldsymbol{\varphi}\bar{\boldsymbol{\varphi}}'(\tilde{\boldsymbol{\beta}} - \boldsymbol{\beta})$ and $\bar{\boldsymbol{\tau}}\boldsymbol{\tau}'(\tilde{\boldsymbol{\beta}} - \boldsymbol{\beta})$ converge at different rates, n and $n^{3/2}$ respectively. Arguments closely paralleling those in §16.3.3 yield

$$\begin{bmatrix} n\bar{\boldsymbol{\varphi}}'(\tilde{\boldsymbol{\beta}} - \boldsymbol{\beta}) \\ n^{3/2}\boldsymbol{\tau}(\tilde{\boldsymbol{\beta}} - \boldsymbol{\beta}) \end{bmatrix} = \left(\begin{bmatrix} \boldsymbol{\varphi}' \\ n^{-1/2}\bar{\boldsymbol{\tau}}' \end{bmatrix} \frac{\boldsymbol{S}_{11}}{n} \begin{bmatrix} \boldsymbol{\varphi} & n^{-1/2}\bar{\boldsymbol{\tau}} \end{bmatrix} \right)^{-1}$$
$$\times \begin{bmatrix} \boldsymbol{\varphi}' \\ n^{-1/2}\bar{\boldsymbol{\tau}}' \end{bmatrix} \boldsymbol{S}_{1\varepsilon}\boldsymbol{\Sigma}^{-1}\boldsymbol{\alpha}(\boldsymbol{\alpha}'\boldsymbol{\Sigma}^{-1}\boldsymbol{\alpha})^{-1} + o_p(1). \tag{16.4.20}$$

Hence,

$$n(\tilde{\boldsymbol{\beta}} - \boldsymbol{\beta}) = \begin{bmatrix} \boldsymbol{\varphi} & n^{-1/2}\bar{\boldsymbol{\tau}} \end{bmatrix} \left(\begin{bmatrix} \boldsymbol{\varphi}' \\ n^{-1/2}\bar{\boldsymbol{\tau}}' \end{bmatrix} \frac{\boldsymbol{S}_{11}}{n} \begin{bmatrix} \boldsymbol{\varphi} & n^{-1/2}\bar{\boldsymbol{\tau}} \end{bmatrix} \right)^{-1}$$
$$\times \begin{bmatrix} \boldsymbol{\varphi}' \\ n^{-1/2}\bar{\boldsymbol{\tau}}' \end{bmatrix} \boldsymbol{S}_{1\varepsilon}\boldsymbol{\Sigma}^{-1}\boldsymbol{\alpha}(\boldsymbol{\alpha}'\boldsymbol{\Sigma}^{-1}\boldsymbol{\alpha})^{-1} + o_p(1)$$
$$\xrightarrow{\mathrm{D}} \begin{bmatrix} \boldsymbol{\varphi} & \mathbf{0} \end{bmatrix} \left(\int_0^1 \boldsymbol{V}\boldsymbol{V}' ds \right)^{-1} \int_0^1 \boldsymbol{V} d\boldsymbol{B}_w' \boldsymbol{\Sigma}^{-1}\boldsymbol{\alpha}(\boldsymbol{\alpha}'\boldsymbol{\Sigma}^{-1}\boldsymbol{\alpha})^{-1}$$
$$= \boldsymbol{\varphi} \left(\int_0^1 \boldsymbol{V}^* \boldsymbol{V}^{*\prime} ds \right)^{-1} \int_0^1 \boldsymbol{V}^* d\boldsymbol{B}_w' \boldsymbol{\Sigma}^{-1}\boldsymbol{\alpha}(\boldsymbol{\alpha}'\boldsymbol{\Sigma}^{-1}\boldsymbol{\alpha})^{-1} \tag{16.4.21}$$

where the last equality in (16.4.21) is got using the partitioned inverse formula. $\boldsymbol{V}$ is defined in (16.4.15) and

$$\boldsymbol{V}^*(r) = \boldsymbol{c}'\boldsymbol{W}^*(r) - \frac{1}{12}(r - \tfrac{1}{2}) \int_0^1 (u - \tfrac{1}{2})\boldsymbol{c}'\boldsymbol{W}^*(u) du. \tag{16.4.22}$$

$\boldsymbol{V}^*$ can be thought of as the $m - s - 1$-dimensional Brownian motion corrected for both mean and trend. The limiting distribution can be represented as

$$n\,\mathrm{Vec}(\tilde{\boldsymbol{\beta}} - \boldsymbol{\beta}) \xrightarrow{\mathrm{D}} \int \mathrm{N}(\mathbf{0},\ (\boldsymbol{\alpha}'\boldsymbol{\Sigma}^{-1}\boldsymbol{\alpha})^{-1} \otimes \boldsymbol{\varphi}\boldsymbol{G}_V^{-1}\boldsymbol{\varphi}') d\boldsymbol{G}_V \tag{16.4.23}$$

where

$$\boldsymbol{G}_V = \int_0^1 \boldsymbol{V}^* \boldsymbol{V}^{*\prime} ds. \tag{16.4.24}$$

Note that this distribution has rank $m(m - s - 1)$.

To estimate $\boldsymbol{\varphi}\boldsymbol{G}_V^{-1}\boldsymbol{\varphi}'$, exactly the same procedure as for the drift-free case applies. Now,

$$\hat{\boldsymbol{v}} = \boldsymbol{\beta}\bar{\boldsymbol{\beta}}'\hat{\boldsymbol{v}} + \boldsymbol{\varphi}\bar{\boldsymbol{\varphi}}'\hat{\boldsymbol{v}} + \bar{\boldsymbol{\tau}}\boldsymbol{\tau}'\hat{\boldsymbol{v}} \tag{16.4.25}$$

and similarly to (16.3.39),

$$\hat{\boldsymbol{v}}' \begin{bmatrix} \bar{\boldsymbol{\varphi}} & \boldsymbol{\tau} \end{bmatrix} \begin{bmatrix} \boldsymbol{\varphi}' \\ n^{-1/2}\bar{\boldsymbol{\tau}}' \end{bmatrix} \boldsymbol{S}_{11} \begin{bmatrix} \boldsymbol{\varphi} & n^{-1/2}\bar{\boldsymbol{\tau}} \end{bmatrix} \begin{bmatrix} \bar{\boldsymbol{\varphi}}' \\ \boldsymbol{\tau}' \end{bmatrix} \hat{\boldsymbol{v}} \xrightarrow{\text{pr}} \boldsymbol{I}_{m-s}. \tag{16.4.26}$$

Therefore, similarly to (16.3.40)

$$\begin{aligned} n\boldsymbol{M}_\beta \hat{\boldsymbol{v}}\hat{\boldsymbol{v}}'\boldsymbol{M}_\beta \underset{\text{asy}}{\sim} &\begin{bmatrix} \boldsymbol{\varphi} & n^{-1/2}\bar{\boldsymbol{\tau}} \end{bmatrix} \left(\begin{bmatrix} \boldsymbol{\varphi}' \\ n^{-1/2}\bar{\boldsymbol{\tau}}' \end{bmatrix} \boldsymbol{S}_{11} \begin{bmatrix} \boldsymbol{\varphi} & n^{-1/2}\bar{\boldsymbol{\tau}} \end{bmatrix} \right)^{-1} \begin{bmatrix} \boldsymbol{\varphi}' \\ n^{-1/2}\bar{\boldsymbol{\tau}}' \end{bmatrix} \\ &\xrightarrow{\text{D}} \boldsymbol{\varphi} \boldsymbol{G}_V^{-1} \boldsymbol{\varphi}'. \end{aligned} \tag{16.4.27}$$

noting that the terms in $\bar{\boldsymbol{\tau}}$ are of smaller order of magnitude and disappear in the limit.

16.4.3 Restricting and Testing Trends

$\bar{\boldsymbol{Q}}_V$ and $\bar{\boldsymbol{Q}}_W$ are the matrices whose eigenvalues are the limits of the $m-s$ smallest solutions to same sample eigenvalue problem, (16.2.15), in the cases $\boldsymbol{\xi} \neq \boldsymbol{0}$ and $\boldsymbol{\xi} = \boldsymbol{0}$, respectively. However, what we would clearly like to do is to estimate the model *subject to* the restriction $\boldsymbol{\xi} = \boldsymbol{0}$. This restriction is imposed in the following way. Write (16.4.1) with trend suppressed as

$$\Delta \boldsymbol{x}_t = \boldsymbol{\alpha}\boldsymbol{\beta}^{*\prime}\boldsymbol{x}^*_{t-1} + \boldsymbol{\Pi}(L)\Delta\boldsymbol{x}_{t-1} + \boldsymbol{\Theta}\boldsymbol{d}_t + \boldsymbol{\varepsilon}_t. \tag{16.4.28}$$

where $\boldsymbol{\beta}^{*\prime} = \begin{bmatrix} \boldsymbol{\beta}' & \boldsymbol{\mu} \end{bmatrix}$ $(s \times (m+1))$ and $\boldsymbol{x}^*_t = (\boldsymbol{x}_t',\ 1)'$. This regression should be estimated 'through the origin', without taking mean deviations. Defining $\boldsymbol{R}^*_{0t}$ and $\boldsymbol{R}^*_{1t}$ as the residuals from the regressions of $\Delta\boldsymbol{x}_t$ and $\boldsymbol{x}^*_{t-1}$ respectively on $(\Delta\boldsymbol{x}_{t-1}, \dots, \Delta\boldsymbol{x}_{t-k}, \boldsymbol{d}_t)$, excluding the intercept, define

$$\boldsymbol{S}^*_{00} = \frac{1}{n}\sum\nolimits_t \boldsymbol{R}^*_{0t}\boldsymbol{R}^{*\prime}_{0t} \quad (m \times m) \tag{16.4.29a}$$

$$\boldsymbol{S}^*_{01} = \frac{1}{n}\sum\nolimits_t \boldsymbol{R}^*_{1t}\boldsymbol{R}^{*\prime}_{0t} \quad (m \times (m+1)) \tag{16.4.29b}$$

$$\boldsymbol{S}^*_{11} = \frac{1}{n}\sum\nolimits_t \boldsymbol{R}^*_{1t}\boldsymbol{R}^{*\prime}_{1t} \quad ((m+1) \times (m+1)) \tag{16.4.29c}$$

$$\boldsymbol{S}^*_{1\varepsilon} = \boldsymbol{S}^*_{10} - \boldsymbol{S}^*_{11}\boldsymbol{\beta}^*\boldsymbol{\alpha}' \quad ((m+1) \times m). \tag{16.4.29d}$$

Notice that the elements of the $(m+1)$th row and column of $\boldsymbol{S}^*_{11}$ are identically equal to 1, whereas the $(m+1)$th column of $\boldsymbol{S}^*_{01}$ is converging in probability to $\boldsymbol{0}$ when the restriction holds. In this case reduced rank regression yields an estimate of $\boldsymbol{\mu}$, which more generally is underidentified.

In place of (16.3.2), define

$$\boldsymbol{S}^*_j = \lambda_j\boldsymbol{S}^*_{11} - \boldsymbol{S}^*_{10}\boldsymbol{S}^{*-1}_{00}\boldsymbol{S}^*_{01} \quad j = 1, \dots, m+1 \tag{16.4.30}$$

and in place of $\boldsymbol{A}$ or $\boldsymbol{A}_n$ let

$$\boldsymbol{A}^*_n = \begin{bmatrix} \boldsymbol{\beta} & \boldsymbol{\gamma} & \boldsymbol{0} \\ \boldsymbol{\mu}' & \boldsymbol{0}' & \sqrt{n} \end{bmatrix} \quad (m+1) \times (m+1). \tag{16.4.31}$$

Then,

$$|S_j^* - S_j^*\beta^*(\beta^{*\prime}S_j^*\beta^*)^{-1}\beta^{*\prime}S_j^*| = |A_n^{*\prime}(S_j^* - S_j^*\beta^*(\beta^{*\prime}S_j^*\beta^*)^{-1}\beta^{*\prime}S_j^*)A_n^*| \tag{16.4.32}$$

where the last $m-s+1$ roots are $O_p(n^{-1})$. An easy extension of previous results leads to

$$\begin{bmatrix}\gamma' & 0\\ 0' & \sqrt{n}\end{bmatrix}(S_j^* - S_j^*\beta^*(\beta^{*\prime}S_j^*\beta^*)^{-1}\beta^{*\prime}S_j^*)\begin{bmatrix}\gamma & 0\\ 0' & \sqrt{n}\end{bmatrix}$$
$$\xrightarrow{\text{D}} \left(\bar{\lambda}_j\int_0^1 HH'dr - \int_0^1 H\,dW'\int_0^1 dWH'\right) \tag{16.4.33}$$

where $H(r) = \begin{bmatrix} W(r)\\ 1\end{bmatrix}$.

The generalized eigenvalue problem

$$|\rho B - AA'| = 0 \tag{16.4.34}$$

where B is $(m-s+1)\times(m-s+1)$ nonsingular and A is $(m-s+1)\times(m-s)$ with rank $m-s$, has one solution at 0, since AA' is singular, with the corresponding eigenvector in the null space of A'. The other eigenvalues are the same as those of

$$|\rho I_{m-s} - A'B^{-1}A| = 0 \tag{16.4.35}$$

although the corresponding eigenvectors take the form $A'q$ ($(m-s)\times 1$) if q is an eigenvector of the original problem. The stochastic matrix relevant to the testing problem is nonetheless

$$\bar{Q}_H = \int_0^1 dWH'\left(\int_0^1 HH'dr\right)^{-1}\int_0^1 H\,dW. \tag{16.4.36}$$

The trace and maximal eigenvalue of this matrix provide the distributions for the two tests of cointegrating rank, subject to the constraint that the model is free of drift.

The matrix β is estimated in this case as the eigenvectors corresponding to $\lambda_1,\dots,\lambda_s$ from (16.4.30). Suppose first that there is no drift, with $\xi = 0$. Then, although these estimates are numerically different from (16.2.23) because the zero-drift restriction is imposed, the asymptotic distribution of the normalized estimates turns out to be the same as in (16.3.36); in other words, the same as the unrestricted estimates when there is in fact no drift. This fact can be verified by adapting previous arguments in the obvious manner, noting by the partitioned inverse formula that the top-left $m\times m$ submatrix of the inverse in (16.4.36) is equal to G_W in (16.3.37). When there is a drift, on the other hand, the distributions differ since the unrestricted estimator follows (16.4.23).

If model (16.4.28) is mistakenly applied when in fact $\xi \neq 0$, a 'spurious' cointegrating vector may be discovered. That is to say, when there are s cointegrating vectors, the largest of the $m-s$ smallest eigenvalues is actually $O_p(1)$ not $O_p(n^{-1})$, leading to rejection of the null hypothesis of at most s cointegrating vectors, with probability 1 in the limit. To see that this is so one can verify the limit results

$$\frac{\boldsymbol{S}_{11}^{*}}{n^2} \xrightarrow{\text{pr}} \begin{bmatrix} \frac{1}{3}\boldsymbol{\tau}\boldsymbol{\tau}' & \mathbf{0} \\ \mathbf{0}' & 0 \end{bmatrix} \tag{16.4.37}$$

$$\frac{\boldsymbol{S}_{01}^{*}}{n} \xrightarrow{\text{pr}} \begin{bmatrix} \frac{1}{2}\boldsymbol{\tau}\boldsymbol{\tau}' & \mathbf{0} \end{bmatrix}. \tag{16.4.38}$$

For any vector $\boldsymbol{r}$ of unit length, as in (16.2.22), if $\boldsymbol{r}'\boldsymbol{\tau} \neq \mathbf{0}$ then $\boldsymbol{r}'\boldsymbol{S}_{11}^{*}\boldsymbol{r} = O(n^2)$ and $\boldsymbol{r}'\boldsymbol{S}_{10}^{*}\boldsymbol{S}_{00}^{*-1}\boldsymbol{S}_{01}^{*}\boldsymbol{r} = O(n^2)$. At least one of the normalized eigenvectors must have this property, not lying in $\boldsymbol{\beta}$-space since $\boldsymbol{\beta}'\boldsymbol{\tau} = \mathbf{0}$, and the corresponding eigenvalue is evidently $O_p(1)$.

However, this fact provides a simple test of the hypothesis $\boldsymbol{\xi} = \mathbf{0}$. Formula (A.2.13) supplies the result

$$\begin{bmatrix} \boldsymbol{E}' & \boldsymbol{F}' \end{bmatrix} \begin{bmatrix} \boldsymbol{A} & \boldsymbol{B}' \\ \boldsymbol{B} & \boldsymbol{D} \end{bmatrix}^{-1} \begin{bmatrix} \boldsymbol{E} \\ \boldsymbol{F} \end{bmatrix}$$
$$= (\boldsymbol{E} - \boldsymbol{B}'\boldsymbol{D}^{-1}\boldsymbol{F})'(\boldsymbol{A} - \boldsymbol{B}'\boldsymbol{D}^{-1}\boldsymbol{B})^{-1}(\boldsymbol{E} - \boldsymbol{B}'\boldsymbol{D}^{-1}\boldsymbol{F}) + \boldsymbol{F}'\boldsymbol{D}^{-1}\boldsymbol{F}. \tag{16.4.39}$$

Applying this to (16.4.36) with the substitutions $\boldsymbol{A} = \int_0^1 \boldsymbol{W}\boldsymbol{W}'dr$, $\boldsymbol{B} = \int_0^1 \boldsymbol{W}dr$, $\boldsymbol{D} = 1$, $\boldsymbol{E} = \int_0^1 \boldsymbol{W}d\boldsymbol{W}'$ and $\boldsymbol{F} = \int_0^1 d\boldsymbol{W}' = \boldsymbol{W}(1)'$, observe that

$$\bar{\boldsymbol{Q}}_H = \bar{\boldsymbol{Q}}_W + \boldsymbol{W}(1)\boldsymbol{W}(1)'. \tag{16.4.40}$$

Thus, if $\bar{\boldsymbol{Q}}_W$ is the true limiting matrix for model (16.4.1) on $H_0 : \boldsymbol{\xi} = \mathbf{0}$, and $\bar{\boldsymbol{Q}}_H$ is the limiting matrix for model (16.4.28) under the same hypothesis, then

$$\operatorname{tr} \bar{\boldsymbol{Q}}_H - \operatorname{tr} \bar{\boldsymbol{Q}}_W = \operatorname{tr} \boldsymbol{W}(1)\boldsymbol{W}(1)' \sim \chi^2(m-s). \tag{16.4.41}$$

Under H_0, the difference between the trace statistics in (16.3.20) computed for models (16.4.28) and (16.4.1), is asymptotically $\chi^2(m-s)$, whereas under H_A : $\boldsymbol{\xi} \neq \mathbf{0}$ the first of these statistics does not converge to tr $\bar{\boldsymbol{Q}}_H$ but is $O_p(n)$.

To sum up: there are two models, but three different limiting distributions, the cases $\bar{\boldsymbol{Q}}_W$, $\bar{\boldsymbol{Q}}_V$ and $\bar{\boldsymbol{Q}}_H$ respectively. The maximal eigenvalue and trace statistics have been tabulated for each case; see Johansen and Juselius (1990) as well as Osterwald-Lenum (1992). If model (16.4.1) is estimated allowing the presence of a drift, the tabulation of $\bar{\boldsymbol{Q}}_W$ is appropriate if in fact $\boldsymbol{\xi} = \mathbf{0}$ and that of $\bar{\boldsymbol{Q}}_V$ if $\boldsymbol{\xi} \neq \mathbf{0}$. To test the hypothesis of drift, estimate both models and perform the χ^2 test. If the null is not rejected, or if a drift is ruled out *a priori*, one has the option of using the restricted estimates from (16.4.28) and the $\bar{\boldsymbol{Q}}_H$ tabulation to test cointegrating rank.

16.4.4 Trends in the Cointegration Space

The models of this section have a natural generalization, that may be written in the form[12]

$$\Delta \boldsymbol{x}_t = \boldsymbol{\alpha}(\boldsymbol{\beta}'\boldsymbol{x}_{t-1} - \boldsymbol{\mu} - \boldsymbol{\psi}t) + \boldsymbol{\xi} + \boldsymbol{\zeta}t + \boldsymbol{\Pi}(L)\Delta\boldsymbol{x}_{t-1} + \boldsymbol{\varepsilon}_t. \tag{16.4.42}$$

[12]The deterministic variables are omitted here for clarity.

This is equivalent to inserting a trend term into the VECM with coefficient $\boldsymbol{\nu}_1 = \boldsymbol{\zeta} - \boldsymbol{\alpha\psi}$. It can be verified that the solution of this model is

$$\boldsymbol{x}_t - \boldsymbol{x}_0 = (\boldsymbol{C\xi} + \boldsymbol{C}^*\boldsymbol{\alpha\psi})t + \tfrac{1}{2}\boldsymbol{C\zeta}t(t+1) + \boldsymbol{Cw}_t + \boldsymbol{C}^*(L)\boldsymbol{\varepsilon}_t \quad t \geq 1 \qquad (16.4.43)$$

where $\boldsymbol{C}^* = \boldsymbol{C}^*(1)$. Quadratic trends do not seem to arise very often in economic data so as a rule the case $\boldsymbol{\zeta} \neq \boldsymbol{0}$ can be overlooked, but the case $\boldsymbol{\psi} \neq \boldsymbol{0}$, in which there is a drift in the cointegrating relationship, appears quite plausible. Note that this induces a linear trend in the time series additional to that due to $\boldsymbol{\xi}$. To estimate this model the trend term should be partialed out along with the other regressors to define $\boldsymbol{R}_{1t}$ and $\boldsymbol{R}_{0t}$. The asymptotic analysis of this case, with $\boldsymbol{\xi}$ constrained to $\boldsymbol{0}$ or otherwise, follows a natural generalization of the foregoing results. The distributions are again different from the previous cases, but can be derived by the same approach as before.

16.5 Partial Models and Exogeneity

16.5.1 The Conditional Model

A feature of the analysis in this chapter so far has been the closed VECM framework. The more common framework in econometrics, as discussed in §4.5, is to estimate conditional partial models, and the next task is to consider whether this can be done here. For compactness let $\boldsymbol{r}_t = (1, \Delta\boldsymbol{x}'_{t-1}, \ldots, \Delta\boldsymbol{x}'_{t-k}, \boldsymbol{d}'_t)'$ and $\boldsymbol{\Upsilon} = [\boldsymbol{\nu}\ \boldsymbol{\Pi}_1 \cdots \boldsymbol{\Pi}_k\ \boldsymbol{\Theta}]$, and hence write model (16.2.1) in partitioned form as

$$\begin{bmatrix}\Delta\boldsymbol{x}_{at}\\ \Delta\boldsymbol{x}_{bt}\end{bmatrix} = \begin{bmatrix}\boldsymbol{\alpha}_a\\ \boldsymbol{\alpha}_b\end{bmatrix}\boldsymbol{\beta}'\boldsymbol{x}_{t-1} + \begin{bmatrix}\boldsymbol{\Upsilon}_a\\ \boldsymbol{\Upsilon}_b\end{bmatrix}\boldsymbol{r}_t + \begin{bmatrix}\boldsymbol{\varepsilon}_{at}\\ \boldsymbol{\varepsilon}_{bt}\end{bmatrix} \qquad (16.5.1)$$

where $\boldsymbol{x}_t = (\boldsymbol{x}'_{at}, \boldsymbol{x}'_{bt})'$, the subvectors are of dimension m_a and $m_b = m - m_a$, and

$$E\begin{bmatrix}\boldsymbol{\varepsilon}_{at}\\ \boldsymbol{\varepsilon}_{bt}\end{bmatrix}\begin{bmatrix}\boldsymbol{\varepsilon}'_{at}\ \boldsymbol{\varepsilon}'_{bt}\end{bmatrix} = \begin{bmatrix}\boldsymbol{\Sigma}_{aa} & \boldsymbol{\Sigma}_{ab}\\ \boldsymbol{\Sigma}_{ba} & \boldsymbol{\Sigma}_{bb}\end{bmatrix}. \qquad (16.5.2)$$

The question to be considered is the effect of estimating just the first m_a equations, while treating the variables $\boldsymbol{x}_{bt}$ as valid conditioning variables in the model of $\boldsymbol{x}_{at}$. In particular we want to know whether the cointegrating space can be validly estimated in this way. The restriction

$$\boldsymbol{\alpha}_b = \boldsymbol{0} \qquad (16.5.3)$$

turns out to be of central importance in this discussion, since in this case the second block of equations do not depend on $\boldsymbol{\beta}$. One can therefore say in the terminology of §4.5.3 that the variables $\boldsymbol{x}_{bt}$ are weakly exogenous for $\boldsymbol{\beta}$. A conditional analysis should be equivalent from this point of view to analysing the complete model. While it is not imposed in the derivations, this restriction makes a crucial difference to the asymptotic distributions arising in the conditional analysis. Notice the implication of (16.5.3), that the set $\boldsymbol{x}_{bt}$ are not independently cointegrated in the marginal model. In other words, $\boldsymbol{\beta}$ represents all the cointegrating relations for $\boldsymbol{x}_t$.

Letting $\mathcal{X}_t = \sigma(\boldsymbol{x}_t, \boldsymbol{x}_{t-1}, \dots)$ as usual, the relevant conditional relations take the form[13]

$$E(\Delta \boldsymbol{x}_{at}|\Delta \boldsymbol{x}_{bt}, \mathcal{X}_{t-1}) = \boldsymbol{\alpha}_a \boldsymbol{\beta}' \boldsymbol{x}_{t-1} + \boldsymbol{\Upsilon}_a \boldsymbol{r}_t + E(\boldsymbol{\varepsilon}_{at}|\Delta \boldsymbol{x}_{bt}, \mathcal{X}_{t-1}). \tag{16.5.4}$$

Assuming the disturbances are not contemporaneously independent, it is necessary to augment the system with a model of this dependence. In the spirit of linearity it is natural to assume

$$E(\boldsymbol{\varepsilon}_{at}|\boldsymbol{\varepsilon}_{bt}) = \boldsymbol{\phi} \boldsymbol{\varepsilon}_{bt} \tag{16.5.5}$$

where $\boldsymbol{\phi} = \boldsymbol{\Sigma}_{ab}\boldsymbol{\Sigma}_{bb}^{-1}$ $(m_a \times m_b)$. Of course, this relation holds automatically when the disturbances are jointly Gaussian, but it is this assumption rather than Gaussianity itself than is needed to validate the analysis. Letting $\boldsymbol{\kappa} = [\boldsymbol{I}_{m_a} \quad -\boldsymbol{\phi}]$, (16.5.4) rearranges under (16.5.5) as

$$\Delta \boldsymbol{x}_{at} = \boldsymbol{\phi} \Delta \boldsymbol{x}_{bt} + \boldsymbol{\kappa} \boldsymbol{\alpha} \boldsymbol{\beta}' \boldsymbol{x}_{t-1} + \boldsymbol{\kappa} \boldsymbol{\Upsilon} \boldsymbol{r}_t + \boldsymbol{\eta}_t \tag{16.5.6}$$

where $\boldsymbol{\eta}_t = \boldsymbol{\kappa} \boldsymbol{\varepsilon}_t$.

The role of exogeneity is clarified by considering the structural form of the system as in (16.1.1), in the light of the exogeneity analysis of §4.6. If the structural model takes the form

$$\begin{bmatrix} \boldsymbol{B}_{aa} & \boldsymbol{B}_{ab} \\ \boldsymbol{B}_{ba} & \boldsymbol{B}_{bb} \end{bmatrix} \begin{bmatrix} \Delta \boldsymbol{x}_{at} \\ \Delta \boldsymbol{x}_{bt} \end{bmatrix} = \begin{bmatrix} \boldsymbol{\rho}_a \\ \boldsymbol{\rho}_b \end{bmatrix} \boldsymbol{\beta}' \boldsymbol{x}_{t-1} + \begin{bmatrix} \boldsymbol{\Delta}_a \\ \boldsymbol{\Delta}_b \end{bmatrix} \boldsymbol{r}_t + \begin{bmatrix} \boldsymbol{u}_{at} \\ \boldsymbol{u}_{bt} \end{bmatrix} \tag{16.5.7}$$

the weak exogeneity restrictions are $\boldsymbol{B}_{ba} = \boldsymbol{0}$, $E(\boldsymbol{u}_{at}|\boldsymbol{u}_{bt}) = \boldsymbol{0}$ and $\boldsymbol{\rho}_b = \boldsymbol{0}$. The last of these is additional to the restrictions on the stationary VAR, and is necessary because of the cross-equation restriction implicit in the VECM framework. The essential features of the relationship between (16.5.7) and the reduced form in (16.5.1), subject to weak exogeneity, are given by

$$\begin{bmatrix} \boldsymbol{\alpha}_a \\ \boldsymbol{\alpha}_b \end{bmatrix} = \begin{bmatrix} \boldsymbol{B}_{aa}^{-1} \boldsymbol{\rho}_a - \boldsymbol{B}_{aa}^{-1} \boldsymbol{B}_{ab} \boldsymbol{B}_{bb}^{-1} \boldsymbol{\rho}_b \\ \boldsymbol{B}_{bb}^{-1} \boldsymbol{\rho}_b \end{bmatrix} \tag{16.5.8}$$

and

$$\begin{bmatrix} \boldsymbol{\varepsilon}_{at} \\ \boldsymbol{\varepsilon}_{bt} \end{bmatrix} = \begin{bmatrix} \boldsymbol{B}_{aa}^{-1} \boldsymbol{u}_{at} - \boldsymbol{B}_{aa}^{-1} \boldsymbol{B}_{ab} \boldsymbol{B}_{bb}^{-1} \boldsymbol{u}_{bt} \\ \boldsymbol{B}_{bb}^{-1} \boldsymbol{u}_{bt} \end{bmatrix}. \tag{16.5.9}$$

The conditional mean equations for this model under weak exogeneity therefore take the form of (16.5.4)+(16.5.5) where $\boldsymbol{\phi} = -\boldsymbol{B}_{aa}^{-1}\boldsymbol{B}_{ab}$.[14] The most important thing is to note that $\boldsymbol{\alpha}_b = \boldsymbol{0}$ if and only if $\boldsymbol{\rho}_b = \boldsymbol{0}$, so that the former becomes the relevant restriction in the Johansen framework. Note that the restrictions do not entail strong exogeneity, because no restriction on $\boldsymbol{\Delta}_b$ in (16.5.7) is required.

---

[13] See §4.5.2 for the conventions on writing conditioning sets.

[14] In §4.6 the symbol $\boldsymbol{\Omega}$ is used for the reduced form covariance matrix corresponding to the present $\boldsymbol{\Sigma}$. Taking care not to confuse the notations, it may be verified that the two definitions of $\boldsymbol{\phi}$ derived here are equivalent.

16.5.2 Testing Cointegrating Rank

Three distinct cases are evident. If $m_a > s$, or $m_a = s$, then $\boldsymbol{\beta\alpha'\kappa'}$ has at least s columns and spans the same space as $\boldsymbol{\beta}$, although in the second case it also has full rank and so is unrestricted. In the third case $m_a < s$, and the space spanned by $\boldsymbol{\beta\alpha'\kappa'}$ has dimension lower than s. In this case it is clear that there is some loss of information about the cointegration space from dropping the equations. It is possible to estimate consistently a m_a-dimensional subspace of the cointegrating space (see Johansen 1992 for details) but optimal estimation is not possible and this case will not be considered further.

Consider the hypothesis that $s = s_0 < m_a$, with the implication that the conditional model contains unit roots. To derive a test of this hypothesis, the arguments of §16.3.1 can be adapted to the conditional model without too much difficulty. If it is false for all $s_0 < m_a$ this does not imply the series are I(0), but it does imply that all the unit roots are in the marginal equations. The stochastic trends in $\boldsymbol{x}_{at}$ are 'driven' by those in $\boldsymbol{x}_{bt}$ in that case, and the model accordingly has causal implications relevant to the long run.

Except for the fact that the generalized eigenvalue problem in (16.2.15) now has $m - m_a$ solutions that are identically zero, much the same reasoning holds as regards the estimation of $\boldsymbol{\beta}$. The limiting distributions of the test statistics are different, however, the distribution being based just on the eigenvalues numbered $j = s+1, \ldots, m_a$. To run the reduced rank regression in (16.5.6) the first step is to partial out both $\boldsymbol{r}_t$ *and* $\Delta\boldsymbol{x}_{bt}$ from $\Delta\boldsymbol{x}_{at}$ and $\boldsymbol{x}_{t-1}$, to arrive at

$$\boldsymbol{R}_{a0t} = \boldsymbol{\kappa\alpha\beta}'\boldsymbol{R}_{a1t} + \boldsymbol{\eta}_t \tag{16.5.10}$$

where $\boldsymbol{R}_{a0t}$ $(m_a \times 1)$ and $\boldsymbol{R}_{a1t}$ is $(m \times 1)$ are the residuals from the preliminary regressions. Proceeding very much as before, equation (16.3.6) is replaced by

$$\boldsymbol{S}_{a01}\boldsymbol{\beta} = \frac{1}{n}\sum\nolimits_t \boldsymbol{R}_{a0t}\boldsymbol{R}'_{a1t}\boldsymbol{\beta} \xrightarrow{\text{pr}} \boldsymbol{\kappa\alpha}\ (m_a \times s) \tag{16.5.11}$$

and (16.3.7) by

$$\boldsymbol{S}_{a00} = \frac{1}{n}\sum\nolimits_t \boldsymbol{R}_{a0t}\boldsymbol{R}'_{a0t} \xrightarrow{\text{pr}} \boldsymbol{\kappa\Sigma}_{00}\boldsymbol{\kappa}' = \boldsymbol{\kappa\Sigma\kappa}' + \boldsymbol{\kappa\alpha\alpha}'\boldsymbol{\kappa}'\ (m_a \times m_a) \tag{16.5.12}$$

where $\boldsymbol{\kappa\Sigma\kappa}' = \boldsymbol{\Sigma}_{aa} - \boldsymbol{\Sigma}_{ab}\boldsymbol{\Sigma}_{bb}^{-1}\boldsymbol{\Sigma}_{ba}$. Also define the $m_a \times m_a$ matrix

$$\boldsymbol{N}_{(a)} = (\boldsymbol{\kappa\Sigma}_{00}\boldsymbol{\kappa}')^{-1} - (\boldsymbol{\kappa\Sigma}_{00}\boldsymbol{\kappa}')^{-1}\boldsymbol{\kappa\alpha}(\boldsymbol{\alpha}'\boldsymbol{\kappa}'(\boldsymbol{\kappa\Sigma}_{00}\boldsymbol{\kappa}')^{-1}\boldsymbol{\kappa\alpha})^{-1}\boldsymbol{\alpha}'\boldsymbol{\kappa}'(\boldsymbol{\kappa\Sigma}_{00}\boldsymbol{\kappa}')^{-1} \tag{16.5.13}$$

such that $\boldsymbol{N}_{(a)}\boldsymbol{\kappa\alpha} = \boldsymbol{0}$, $\boldsymbol{\alpha}'\boldsymbol{\kappa}'\boldsymbol{N}_{(a)} = \boldsymbol{0}$ and $\boldsymbol{N}_{(a)} = \boldsymbol{N}_{(a)}\boldsymbol{\kappa\Sigma\kappa}'\boldsymbol{N}_{(a)}$. Thus, if $\boldsymbol{P}_{(a)}\boldsymbol{P}'_{(a)} = \boldsymbol{N}_{(a)}$ then $\boldsymbol{P}'_{(a)}\boldsymbol{\kappa\Sigma\kappa}'\boldsymbol{P}_{(a)} = \boldsymbol{I}_{m_a - s}$. Finally note that

$$\boldsymbol{S}_{a1\eta} = \frac{1}{n}\sum\nolimits_t \boldsymbol{R}_{a1t}\boldsymbol{\eta}'_t \xrightarrow{\text{D}} \int_0^1 \boldsymbol{B}^*_w d\boldsymbol{B}'_w\boldsymbol{\kappa}'\ (m \times m_a). \tag{16.5.14}$$

Now, letting $\boldsymbol{S}_{a11} = n^{-1}\sum_t \boldsymbol{R}_{a1t}\boldsymbol{R}'_{a1t}$ consider the matrices

$$\boldsymbol{S}_{aj} = \lambda_j\boldsymbol{S}_{a11} - \boldsymbol{S}_{a10}(\boldsymbol{S}_{a00})^{-1}\boldsymbol{S}_{a01}. \tag{16.5.15}$$

Proceeding with the analysis as before by analogy with (16.3.2) yields

$$\gamma'(S_{aj} - S_{aj}\beta(\beta' S_{aj}\beta)^{-1}\beta' S_{aj})\gamma \xrightarrow{D} \bar{\lambda}_j \gamma' C\left(\int_0^1 B_w^* B_w^{*\prime} dr\right) C'\gamma$$
$$- \gamma' C\left(\int_0^1 B_w^* dB_w'\right)\kappa' N_{(a)}\kappa\left(\int_0^1 dB_w B_w^{*\prime}\right) C'\gamma \qquad (16.5.16)$$

for $j = s+1, \ldots, m_a$. Thus $n\lambda_j \xrightarrow{D} \bar{\lambda}_j$, and these limits are the eigenvalues of the limit matrix

$$\bar{Q}_{Wa} = \int_0^1 dW_a W^{*\prime}\left(\int_0^1 W^* W^{*\prime} dr\right)^{-1} \int_0^1 W^* dW_a' \qquad (16.5.17)$$

where $W_a = P_{(a)}' \kappa B_w$ is a $(m_a - s)$-dimensional standard BM.

The question of interest is whether this distribution is free of nuisance parameters, and weak exogeneity is the key restriction here. Construct as before the matrix $N = PP'$ defined in (16.3.12), where $P = C'\gamma$ by choice of γ, as before. If (16.5.3) holds and $\kappa\alpha = \alpha_a$, applying the partitioned inverse formula shows that

$$N = \begin{bmatrix} N_{(a)} & -N_{(a)}\phi \\ -\phi' N_{(a)} & \phi' N_{(a)}\phi + \Sigma_{bb}^{-1} \end{bmatrix} \qquad (16.5.18)$$

and hence, under this restriction,

$$P = \begin{bmatrix} P_{(a)} & 0 \\ -\phi' P_{(a)} & \Sigma_{bb}^{-1/2} \end{bmatrix}. \qquad (16.5.19)$$

Therefore,

$$PE(WW_a')P_{(a)}' = N\Sigma\kappa' N_{(a)} = N \begin{bmatrix} \kappa\Sigma\kappa' \\ 0 \end{bmatrix} N_{(a)} = \begin{bmatrix} P_{(a)} \\ -\phi P_{(a)} \end{bmatrix} P_{(a)}' \qquad (16.5.20)$$

which shows that

$$E(WW_a') = \begin{bmatrix} I_{m_a - s} \\ 0 \end{bmatrix}. \qquad (16.5.21)$$

Therefore, the maximum eigenvalue and trace statistics have limiting distributions free of nuisance parameters. However, these are different from those of the statistics for the full system, and they depend on both $m - s$ and $m_a - s$. Essentially similar arguments can be applied for the case with deterministic trends.

16.5.3 Estimating β

Next consider the estimation of β. Maintaining for the moment the assumption $m_a > s$, the analysis closely follows §16.3.3, or §16.4.2 in the case of deterministic trends. For simplicity, consider the former case. The first-order conditions to be solved, paralleling (16.3.31), are now

$$(\boldsymbol{S}_{a10}\boldsymbol{\kappa}' - \boldsymbol{S}_{a11}\tilde{\boldsymbol{\beta}}\tilde{\boldsymbol{\alpha}}'\boldsymbol{\kappa}')(\boldsymbol{\kappa}\hat{\boldsymbol{\Sigma}}\boldsymbol{\kappa}')^{-1}\boldsymbol{\kappa}\tilde{\boldsymbol{\alpha}} = \boldsymbol{0}. \tag{16.5.22}$$

Similar manipulations to before yield

$$\begin{aligned} n(\tilde{\boldsymbol{\beta}} - \boldsymbol{\beta}) &= \boldsymbol{\gamma}\Big(\frac{\boldsymbol{\gamma}'\boldsymbol{S}_{11}\boldsymbol{\gamma}}{n}\Big)^{-1}\boldsymbol{\gamma}'\boldsymbol{S}_{1\epsilon}\boldsymbol{\kappa}'(\boldsymbol{\kappa}\boldsymbol{\Sigma}\boldsymbol{\kappa}')^{-1}\boldsymbol{\kappa}\boldsymbol{\alpha}[\boldsymbol{\alpha}'\boldsymbol{\kappa}'(\boldsymbol{\kappa}\boldsymbol{\Sigma}\boldsymbol{\kappa}')^{-1}\boldsymbol{\kappa}\boldsymbol{\alpha}]^{-1} + o_p(1) \\ &\xrightarrow{\mathrm{D}} \boldsymbol{\gamma}\Big(\int_0^1 \boldsymbol{W}^*\boldsymbol{W}^{*\prime}ds\Big)^{-1}\int_0^1 \boldsymbol{W}^* d\boldsymbol{B}_w' \\ &\qquad \times \boldsymbol{\kappa}'(\boldsymbol{\kappa}\boldsymbol{\Sigma}\boldsymbol{\kappa}')^{-1}\boldsymbol{\kappa}\boldsymbol{\alpha}[\boldsymbol{\alpha}'\boldsymbol{\kappa}'(\boldsymbol{\kappa}\boldsymbol{\Sigma}\boldsymbol{\kappa}')^{-1}\boldsymbol{\kappa}\boldsymbol{\alpha}]^{-1} \end{aligned} \tag{16.5.23}$$

and as before the key question is whether a mixed Gaussian distribution is obtained. Recalling that $\boldsymbol{W} = \boldsymbol{\gamma}'\boldsymbol{C}\boldsymbol{B}_w$ where $\boldsymbol{\gamma}'\boldsymbol{C} = \boldsymbol{P}'$, consider the covariance matrix

$$E(\boldsymbol{W}\boldsymbol{B}_w')\boldsymbol{\kappa}'(\boldsymbol{\kappa}\boldsymbol{\Sigma}\boldsymbol{\kappa}')^{-1}\boldsymbol{\kappa}\boldsymbol{\alpha} = \boldsymbol{P}'\boldsymbol{\Sigma}\boldsymbol{\kappa}'(\boldsymbol{\kappa}\boldsymbol{\Sigma}\boldsymbol{\kappa}')^{-1}\boldsymbol{\kappa}\boldsymbol{\alpha}. \tag{16.5.24}$$

Under the weak exogeneity assumption, using (16.5.19) yields

$$\boldsymbol{P}'\boldsymbol{\Sigma}\boldsymbol{\kappa}'(\boldsymbol{\kappa}\boldsymbol{\Sigma}\boldsymbol{\kappa}')^{-1}\boldsymbol{\alpha}_a = \begin{bmatrix} \boldsymbol{P}_{(a)}\boldsymbol{\alpha}_a \\ -\boldsymbol{\phi}'\boldsymbol{P}_{(a)}\boldsymbol{\alpha}_a \end{bmatrix} = \boldsymbol{0}. \tag{16.5.25}$$

In this case, the limit result is therefore

$$n\,\mathrm{Vec}(\tilde{\boldsymbol{\beta}} - \boldsymbol{\beta}) \xrightarrow{\mathrm{D}} \int \mathrm{N}(\boldsymbol{0},\ [\boldsymbol{\alpha}_a'(\boldsymbol{\kappa}\boldsymbol{\Sigma}\boldsymbol{\kappa}')^{-1}\boldsymbol{\alpha}_a]^{-1} \otimes \boldsymbol{\gamma}\boldsymbol{G}^{-1}\boldsymbol{\gamma}')d\boldsymbol{G}. \tag{16.5.26}$$

Thus, even if $\boldsymbol{x}_{2t}$ is not weakly exogenous a n-consistent estimator of $\boldsymbol{\beta}$ is obtainable, with limiting distribution as specified in (16.5.23). The problem is that this distribution depends on nuisance parameters, and is no use for hypothesis testing. Weak exogeneity ensures the mixed Gaussian limit in (16.5.26). Once again, comparable results to these are found in the model with deterministic trends.

An admissible case of the model is where $s = m_a$, so that $\boldsymbol{\kappa\alpha}$ is a square matrix. In this case, reduced rank regression becomes, in effect, full rank regression. One can obtain $\hat{\boldsymbol{\beta}}$ as the complete set of eigenvectors in the usual problem, but OLS can yield the same result. Writing $\boldsymbol{\Pi} = \boldsymbol{\kappa}\boldsymbol{\alpha}\boldsymbol{\beta}'$, the first-order conditions in (16.5.22) have the solution

$$\hat{\boldsymbol{\Pi}} = \boldsymbol{S}_{a01}\boldsymbol{S}_{a11}^{-1}. \tag{16.5.27}$$

In practice, the $\hat{\boldsymbol{\Pi}}$ are calculated simply as the coefficients of $\boldsymbol{x}_{t-1}$ in the regressions of the $\Delta\boldsymbol{x}_{at}$ on all the variables in equations (16.5.6). In the usual normalization one can if desired calculate

$$\hat{\boldsymbol{\beta}} = \hat{\boldsymbol{\Pi}}'(\hat{\boldsymbol{\Pi}}\boldsymbol{S}_{a11}\hat{\boldsymbol{\Pi}}')^{-1/2} \tag{16.5.28}$$

although this is not an essential step since $\hat{\boldsymbol{\Pi}}$ also estimates the cointegrating space in this case. The asymptotic distribution in (16.5.26) applies as usual, under weak exogeneity. An interesting case is where $s = m_a = 1$, so that the partial system reduces to a single equation. See §15.2.5 for additional discussion of this case.

16.6 Structural Cointegrating Relations

16.6.1 Identification

In an economic model containing cointegrating relations, it is normally assumed that the cointegration comes about because a set of long-run linear economic relationships act as 'attractors', drawing the time series together as they evolve through time. The consumption function, investment function, money demand function and other fundamental macroeconomic relationships are often thought of in this way. These will be called the *structural* cointegrating relationships. Johansen's methodology is designed to estimate the space spanned by these relationships, but it does not allow us to observe them individually. An error frequently committed by students and practitioners is to attempt to give the 'Johansen vectors' a structural interpretation.

Let $\boldsymbol{\delta}$ be used to denote the $m \times s$ 'structural' matrix. One usually normalizes such relationships by setting one of the coefficients to 1, although this is arbitrary in the present context since there is no causal priority being assumed. These are not regressions in which one variable is 'explained by' the others. On the other hand, the relations are restricted, typically by certain elements being equal to 0, and these restrictions are not arbitrary, but are a feature of the economic laws of motion that they represent. For example, in the model of King et. al. (1991) real national income is in linear cointegrating relationships with real consumption, real investment and real money holdings respectively (all variables in logarithms) where the last relationship also depends on interest rates and inflation. Each of these relationships describes a different facet of economic equilibrium, and is distinct from the others.[15]

The structural coefficient matrix is related to the Johansen matrix by a renormalizing transformation of the form

$$\boldsymbol{\beta} = \boldsymbol{\delta a} \tag{16.6.1}$$

where $\boldsymbol{a}$ is an unknown $s \times s$ nonsingular matrix, such that both matrices span the cointegrating space. The key question is: having estimated $\boldsymbol{\beta}$, can estimates of $\boldsymbol{\delta}$ be recovered? This problem parallels very closely the simultaneous equations analysis of §8.3, where the issue is to recover the structural form from the reduced form equations. In the present case the object is to recover structural relationships from the Johansen matrix. A difference between the two cases is that there is no distinction here between exogenous and endogenous variables, as in (8.2.1) and (8.2.2). However, solving back to the structural form from the reduced form is formally an identical problem to recovering structural vectors from $\boldsymbol{\beta}$, and the sufficient conditions are effectively the same. Each column of $\boldsymbol{\delta}$ must satisfy the rank condition for identification.

Suppose we are interested in recovering the first column of $\boldsymbol{\delta}$, say $\boldsymbol{\delta}_1$, normalized by putting the first element (assumed non-zero) to unity. We possess the

[15] See also Davidson (1998b) for a version of this model.

prior information that, after reordering the variables as necessary, the last $m - g_1$ elements are zero, in other words,

$$\boldsymbol{\delta}_1 = \begin{bmatrix} \boldsymbol{\delta}_{1a} \\ \mathbf{0} \end{bmatrix}. \tag{16.6.2}$$

Following the discussion of §8.3, the rank condition for identification may be summarized as follows. Let $\boldsymbol{\delta}$ be partitioned conformably with $\boldsymbol{\delta}_1$ as $\begin{bmatrix} \boldsymbol{\delta}_a \\ \boldsymbol{\delta}_b \end{bmatrix}$ where $\boldsymbol{\delta}_b$ has dimension $(m - g_1) \times s$ with its first column zero, by construction. If and only if rank $\boldsymbol{\delta}_b = s - 1$, the only choice of $\boldsymbol{r}$ $(s \times 1)$ such that the vector $\boldsymbol{\delta r}$ satisfies the known prior restrictions on $\boldsymbol{\delta}_1$ is $\boldsymbol{r} = \boldsymbol{e}_1 = (1, 0, \dots, 0)'$.

In the simultaneous equations model, identification allows the equation to be consistently estimated by solving back from the consistently estimated reduced form equations, which is accomplished, essentially, by the 2SLS estimator as shown in (8.2.30). The same principle applies in the present case,[16] but given the nature of the I(1) data, and especially the fact that there is a difference of orders of magnitude between relationships that cointegrate and those that do not, its implementation is quite different.

The following simple result is taken from Davidson (1994b).

Theorem 16.6.1 If $\boldsymbol{\delta}_1$ is identified by the rank condition, the OLS regression of the normalized variable on *only* the variables having unrestricted coefficients in $\boldsymbol{\delta}_1$ consistently estimates those coefficients.

Proof Let $\boldsymbol{d}_1$ denote the vector that has the same restricted elements as $\boldsymbol{\delta}_1$, and whose other elements are the probability limits of the regression coefficients specified in the theorem. Since the variables included in equation 1 are cointegrated (by $\boldsymbol{\delta}_1$) by hypothesis, $\boldsymbol{d}_1$ must also be cointegrating for $\boldsymbol{x}_t$. This follows from the arguments of §15.2.2, where no property is assumed other than cointegration. Hence, $\boldsymbol{d}_1$ lies in the cointegrating space, or equivalently, $\boldsymbol{d}_1 = \boldsymbol{\delta r}$ for some $\boldsymbol{r}$. Since $\boldsymbol{\delta}_1$ is identified and $\boldsymbol{d}_1$ has the same restrictions, it follows that $\boldsymbol{d}_1 = \boldsymbol{\delta}_1$. ■

It will be noted that the theorem also holds in respect of any estimator that is consistent for $\boldsymbol{\delta}_1$ when OLS is. Such cases include two-stage least squares,[17] the Phillips-Hansen fully modified estimator detailed in §15.2.6, and the error correction model approach (nonlinear least squares) of §15.2.5.

Recall that in the latter cases, the existence of a unique cointegrating vector was assumed. In other words, the cointegrating rank s of the system linking the variables was assumed to be 1. However, there is a second result, also from Davidson (1994b).

---

[16] See Johansen (1995a) for an analysis.

[17] Phillips and Hansen (1990) show that two-stage least squares is a consistent estimator of the cointegrating vector, where the intruments can be arbitrarily chosen I(1) processes or deterministic trend terms.

Theorem 16.6.2 If and only if a structural cointegrating relation is identified by the rank condition, it is *irreducible*. That is, dropping any of the variables leaves a set that is not cointegrated. □

The proof is given in §16.7. It is clear that an irreducible cointegrating vector must be unique. In other words, there cannot be two linearly independent cointegrating vectors for a set of irreducibly cointegrated variables. This follows by contradiction, for were it the case, one could form a linear combination of the two vectors one of whose elements, but choice of weights, is equal to 0. Since this combination also lies in the cointegrating space, yet omits a variable, irreducibility is contradicted.

To illustrate these concepts consider a simple example as in Davidson (1994b, 1998b), the standard market model often called the 'Marshallian cross'. Omitting the dynamic components for clarity, write this simply as

$$q_t - \alpha p_t - \lambda w_t - \theta r_t \sim \mathrm{I}(0) \qquad \text{(demand, } \alpha < 0) \tag{16.6.3a}$$

$$q_t - \beta p_t - \mu w_t - \delta r_t \sim \mathrm{I}(0) \qquad \text{(supply, } \beta > 0) \tag{16.6.3b}$$

$$w_t \sim \mathrm{I}(1) \tag{16.6.3c}$$

$$r_t \sim \mathrm{I}(1) \tag{16.6.3d}$$

where w_t and r_t are autonomous variables. Let both relations be cointegrating, but w_t and r_t not cointegrated independently, since otherwise the system should be augmented with this extra relation. The relations are therefore embedded in a cointegrating VAR system with $m = 4$ and $s = 2$.

Consider the identifiability of these six parameters, α, β, λ, μ, θ and δ. The matrix

$$\boldsymbol{\delta} = \begin{bmatrix} 1 & 1 \\ -\alpha & -\beta \\ -\lambda & -\mu \\ -\theta & -\delta \end{bmatrix} \tag{16.6.4}$$

must have rank 2, given the sign restrictions on the price parameters, so that the system has solutions for q_t and p_t, given the autonomous variables. However, if all parameters are otherwise unrestricted and different from 0, the rank condition is not satisfied in either equation. The cointegrating space can be estimated by reduced-rank regression, but there is no way to distinguish the supply and demand schedules. Note that there are four ways to construct a linear combination of the vectors that has one element equal to 0, so that any three of the four variables form a cointegrating set. In other words, neither cointegrating relation is irreducible.

Next, suppose $\theta = \mu = 0$, so that both schedules satisfy the rank condition for identification. Then both schedules are irreducible. The demand schedule is consistently estimated by regressing q_t on p_t and w_t, and the supply schedule is consistently estimated by regressing q_t on p_t and r_t. However, note that there are other irreducible cointegrating relations that are not structural. These are what are usually called the reduced form equations, estimated by regression of q_t and p_t, respectively, on the two autonomous variables. Irreducibility is not a sufficient condition for a cointegrating relation to be an identified structural equation, although it is necessary.

Consider this analysis from the point of view of the economist who wishes to estimate demand and supply elasticities consistently. If she is willing to assume that the relations are subject to identifying restrictions, running some OLS regressions is in principle all that is needed to do this. What structural relation is obtained is decided by the choice of included variables. Economic theory informs her that only relations that contain both p_t and q_t are of interest, so there is no problem in distinguishing the structural equations from the reduced forms. Moreover, given the prior restrictions on the signs of the price coefficients, she can even decide which is supply and which demand without knowing which autonomous variable drove which relationship. Even though it is not very plausible that the absence of such information could coexist with knowledge of identification, this is still a striking difference between the I(1) and I(0) analyses. In the latter case one must know which autonomous variable drives which schedule for consistent estimation, since it is necessary to use instrumental variables and correctly choose the variable to be excluded and used as the 'additional instrument'.

Next, consider the case with $\theta = \mu = \lambda = 0$, which implies that the pair (p_t, q_t) is cointegrated. When the economist discovers this fact she knows, without using *any* prior information, that this is the demand equation. The equation cannot be a reduced form, since any linear combination of supply and demand must contain at least three variables. Remember that the cointegrating rank is known to be 2, from tests on the data alone. Moreover, the sign of the price coefficient establishes the identity of the estimated equation. Obviously, a symmetric situation arises with $\theta = \mu = \delta = 0$.

These examples give an idea of what can and cannot be learned by the inspection of cointegrating regressions.[18] The main lesson is that if a set of variables is found to be cointegrated, this fact implies that their relation is structural only if all the members of the set are needed for cointegration. If the set is reducible, there are only two possibilities. Either it is an arbitrary collection that is cointegrated by virtue of appearing in a linear combination of structural equations, or it represents a structural relation which is underidentified. In both cases the estimated coefficients are just an arbitrary vector from the cointegrating space. In neither case can the coefficients have any status as economically interpretable parameters. It is therefore desirable to check the irreducibility condition before doing any further investigation of a cointegrating equation. Remember though that irreducibility is necessary but not sufficient for a relationship to be structural, so it does not guarantee anything by itself.

---

[18] See Davidson (1998b) for some additional results that can be used to help identify structural relations in certain cases. It is shown that an irreducible cointegrating relation that is 'smaller' (has fewer variables in it) than all the others in the system must be structural. Also, if a cointegrating equation is irreducible and is the *only* such vector to contain a particular variable, it too must be structural. These results do however require that the set of variables in the system as a whole is correctly specified, such that none are omitted.

16.6.2 Single Equation Analysis

The problem with the type of investigation just described is that least squares analysis has well-known drawbacks, as detailed in §15.2.2. There are really three routes that we might consider to the estimation of structural cointegrating relationships. There are single-equation methods, with a choice between the fully-modified least squares method of §15.2.6 and the error correction model approach of §15.2.5. And there is also the system approach.

The single equation methods are simple and convenient, but each depends for its validity on certain assumptions being satisfied. The most important of these is that the cointegrating relation in question is unique for the given set of variables. If the variables have cointegrating rank two or greater, then any cointegrating relation estimated by single equation methods can only be a hybrid, an arbitrary point of the cointegrating space. However, there are two very important facts in the form of Theorems 16.6.1 and 16.6.2. These say, respectively, that any structural equation whose coefficients are identified can be consistently estimated in a single equation analysis, and that there is the verifiable necessary condition of irreducibility for such an analysis to be valid.

The uniqueness of the vector has a particularly useful implication. The closed dynamic system describing the evolution of this particular set of variables, from which other variables have been eliminated by substitution, is amenable to single equation analysis. To state the result formally, consider model (16.1.1) (put $\boldsymbol{x}_0 = \boldsymbol{0}$ for simplicity) and consider the partition of $\boldsymbol{x}_t$ into subvectors $\boldsymbol{x}_{at}$ $(g_1 \times 1)$ and $\boldsymbol{x}_{bt}$ $((m - g_1) \times 1)$, such that $\boldsymbol{x}_{at}$ appears in the first structural equation according to the partition defined by (16.6.2).

Theorem 16.6.3 If $\boldsymbol{\delta}_1$ in (16.6.2) is identified, the subsystem

$$\boldsymbol{B}(L)\boldsymbol{x}_{at} = \boldsymbol{\nu}_t \tag{16.6.5}$$

solved from (16.1.1), such that $\boldsymbol{\nu}_t \sim \mathrm{I}(0)$, has cointegrating rank 1, with $\boldsymbol{B}(1) = \boldsymbol{c}(1)\boldsymbol{\rho}_{1a}\boldsymbol{\delta}'_{1a}$ where $\boldsymbol{\rho}_{1a}$ $(g_1 \times 1)$ is a vector of the error correction coefficients associated with $\boldsymbol{\delta}_1$ in g_1 of the equations of the full model, and $\boldsymbol{c}(1)$ is a diagonal matrix with the diagonal having first element 1 and the other elements either 1 or 0. □

See §16.7 for the proof. The implication of the result is that the assumptions of Chapter 15 are satisfied for the subsystem. To show this, let $\boldsymbol{\zeta} = \boldsymbol{c}(1)\boldsymbol{\rho}_{1a}$ and define a full rank matrix $\boldsymbol{G} = [\bar{\boldsymbol{\zeta}}\ \boldsymbol{G}_2]$ $(g_1 \times g_1)$ whose first column is $\bar{\boldsymbol{\zeta}} = \boldsymbol{\zeta}(\boldsymbol{\zeta}'\boldsymbol{\zeta})^{-1}$, and whose last $g_1 - 1$ columns are any matrix $\boldsymbol{G}_2$ that is orthogonal to $\boldsymbol{\zeta}$. Taking the Beveridge–Nelson decomposition $\boldsymbol{B}(z) = \boldsymbol{B}(1) + (1 - z)\boldsymbol{B}^*(z)$, write

$$\boldsymbol{G}'\boldsymbol{B}(z) = \begin{bmatrix} \boldsymbol{\delta}'_{1a} \\ \boldsymbol{0} \end{bmatrix} + (1 - z)\begin{bmatrix} \bar{\boldsymbol{\zeta}}'\boldsymbol{B}^*(z) \\ \boldsymbol{C}(z) \end{bmatrix} \tag{16.6.6}$$

where $\boldsymbol{C}(z)$ represents the last $g_1 - 1$ rows of $\boldsymbol{G}'\boldsymbol{B}^*(z)$. Premultiplying (16.6.5) by $\boldsymbol{G}'$ therefore converts the model into the form

$$\begin{bmatrix} \boldsymbol{\delta}_{1a}'\boldsymbol{x}_{at} \\ \boldsymbol{0} \end{bmatrix} + \begin{bmatrix} \bar{\boldsymbol{\zeta}}'\boldsymbol{B}^*(L)\Delta\boldsymbol{x}_{at} \\ \boldsymbol{C}(L)\Delta\boldsymbol{x}_{at} \end{bmatrix} = \begin{bmatrix} \bar{\boldsymbol{\zeta}}'\boldsymbol{\nu}_t \\ \boldsymbol{G}_2'\boldsymbol{\nu}_t \end{bmatrix}. \tag{16.6.7}$$

If $\boldsymbol{C}(z)$ is now partitioned as $[\mathbf{c}_1(z)\ \boldsymbol{C}_2(z)]$ where $\mathbf{c}_1(z)$ is the first column and $\boldsymbol{C}_2(z)$ is $(g_1 - 1) \times (g_1 - 1)$, the model can be further rearranged as

$$x_{a1,t} = \boldsymbol{\gamma}'\boldsymbol{x}_{a2,t} + u_t \tag{16.6.8a}$$

$$\Delta\boldsymbol{x}_{a2,t} = \boldsymbol{\theta}_t \tag{16.6.8b}$$

where $\boldsymbol{\delta}_{1a}' = (1,\ \boldsymbol{\gamma}')$,

$$u_t = \bar{\boldsymbol{\zeta}}'(\boldsymbol{\nu}_t - \boldsymbol{B}^*(L)\Delta\boldsymbol{x}_{at}) \tag{16.6.9}$$

and

$$\boldsymbol{\theta}_t = \boldsymbol{C}_2(L)^{-1}(\boldsymbol{G}_2'\boldsymbol{\nu}_t - \mathbf{c}_1(z)\Delta x_{a1,t}). \tag{16.6.10}$$

By construction $\boldsymbol{C}_2(z)$ has all its roots outside the unit circle, so both u_t and $\boldsymbol{\theta}_t$ are I(0) processes.

In other words, the system is in exactly the form analysed in §15.2. The model is not a finite order VAR, but the previous analyses go through since they depend on no assumptions about the form of the dynamics apart from the conditions of Theorems 15.2.1 and 15.2.3 being satisfied, and this certainly is the case if (say) $\boldsymbol{u}_t$ in (16.1.1) is i.i.d. Therefore, the results of that section go through. In particular, the Phillips-Hansen fully-modified least squares method provides a consistent, mixed-Gaussian estimator yielding standard asymptotic inference. Any irreducible cointegrating vector can be thought of as a valid parameterization in this particular sense, whether or not the coefficients have an interpretation as structural (economically interpretable) parameters.

The error correction model approach might also be considered. Care is necessary here because (16.6.5) is a solved model. The disturbances are I(0) but not i.i.d. in general, and with the exception of $\boldsymbol{\gamma}$ the parameters are solved forms not subject to zero restrictions. However, if all the variables in $\boldsymbol{x}_{a2,t}$ are weakly exogenous for $\boldsymbol{\gamma}$ in the sense of §16.5.1, this weak exogeneity holds in the solved model too. In particular, the restriction means that $\boldsymbol{\rho}_{1a}$ has all elements except the first one zero, and this is true of the corresponding reduced form adjustment vector $\boldsymbol{\alpha}_{1a}$ according to (16.5.8). To summarize: if in the complete system of equations, the variable $x_{a1,t}$ appears in an identified structural cointegrating vector with weakly exogenous $\boldsymbol{x}_{a2,t}$, estimating the error correction equation in (15.2.61) containing just these included variables by least squares can yield n-consistent mixed Gaussian estimates. Standard asymptotic inference is available. The one condition to be satisfied, which is not necessarily trivial, is that a finite order lag structure can provide an adequate approximation to the solved first equation of (16.6.5). By comparison, the great advantage of the fully-modified least squares approach is that it does not demand weakly exogenous regressors for its validity.

16.6.3 System Analysis

The alternative approach to structural modelling is full system estimation. Since any set of vectors spanning the cointegrating space is equivalent to $\boldsymbol{\beta}$ according to (16.6.1) the matrix $\boldsymbol{\delta}$ can be estimated, in principle, by simply imposing the restrictions in the construction of the criterion function. Overidentifying restrictions (such that $\boldsymbol{\delta}$ is subject to more restrictions than $\boldsymbol{\beta}$) can then be tested using the likelihood ratio principle.

Johansen (1988b, 1991) and Johansen and Juselius (1992) show how to impose certain restrictions on $\boldsymbol{\beta}$, while still using the reduced rank regression to estimate the model. For example, consider

$$\boldsymbol{\Phi}\boldsymbol{\beta} = \mathbf{0} \tag{16.6.11}$$

where $\boldsymbol{\Phi}$ is a $r \times m$ matrix of known constants imposing r independent restrictions on the columns of $\boldsymbol{\beta}$. These restrictions can also be written in the form

$$\boldsymbol{\beta} = \boldsymbol{H}\boldsymbol{\phi} \tag{16.6.12}$$

where $\boldsymbol{H}$ is a $m \times (m - r)$ constant matrix and $\boldsymbol{\phi}$ is a $(m - r) \times s$ matrix containing the unrestricted parameters. The relation $\boldsymbol{\Phi H} = \mathbf{0}$ show how the two representations are related. By substituting (16.6.12) into the model, Johansen shows how to treat $\boldsymbol{\phi}$ as arguments of the criterion function, and formulate a modified reduced rank regression problem. Simply write the reduced rank regression equation (16.2.4) in the form

$$\boldsymbol{R}_{0t} = \boldsymbol{\alpha}\boldsymbol{\phi}'\boldsymbol{H}\boldsymbol{R}_{1t} + \boldsymbol{\varepsilon}_t. \tag{16.6.13}$$

where $\boldsymbol{HR}_{1t}$ is a $m-r$-dimensional vector of generated variables, and the matrix $\hat{\boldsymbol{\phi}}$ can be obtained as the solution to an eigenvalue problem. An example of this case might be where it is known that two variables only enter the cointegrating relations in the form of a differential, $x_{1t} - x_{2t}$, despite Δx_{1t} and Δx_{2t} appearing independently in the dynamic parts of the model, so that two rows of $\boldsymbol{\beta}$ are equal and opposite in sign. To impose this particular restriction, let $\boldsymbol{\Phi} = (1, -1, 0, \dots, 0)'$.

Another example of a restriction that can be imposed through a modified reduced rank regression is where one column of $\boldsymbol{\delta}$ is actually known up to a scale factor, say $\boldsymbol{\delta}_1 = \boldsymbol{h}_1$, a vector of known constants. To estimate this model, partition $\boldsymbol{\alpha}$ in (16.2.4) by columns as

$$\boldsymbol{R}_{0t} = \boldsymbol{\alpha}_1\boldsymbol{h}_1'\boldsymbol{R}_{1t} + \boldsymbol{\alpha}_2\boldsymbol{\beta}_2'\boldsymbol{R}_{1t} + \boldsymbol{\varepsilon}_t. \tag{16.6.14}$$

The scalar $\boldsymbol{h}_1'\boldsymbol{R}_{1t}$, I(0) by assumption, can then be partialed out of the model like the other I(0) components. These restrictions can be tested by likelihood ratio tests and it can be shown that the statistics are chi-squared distributed under H_0. It is a general feature of these models that tests which do not involve unit root restrictions feature standard asymptotics. It is the tests of cointegrating rank, which do test unit root restrictions, that unavoidably entail non-standard distributions. In the non-Gaussian case these are analogue LR tests, and the lack of robustness of the likelihood ratio test to misspecification pointed out in §12.3.2 is of relevance here, and should not be overlooked.

However, it needs to be emphasized that the matrix $\boldsymbol{H\phi}$ is not in general the same as $\boldsymbol{\delta}$, the hypothesised structural cointegration matrix. It does no more than share some assumed restrictions with $\boldsymbol{\delta}$. To estimate $\boldsymbol{\delta}$ (or one or more columns thereof) directly, the system has to be estimated using numerical methods and, in effect, the problem becomes a variant of the nonlinear system estimation discussed in Chapter 13.

Before undertaking such an effort, it would be useful to test the overidentifying structural restrictions using the easily computed reduced rank regression estimate $\hat{\boldsymbol{\beta}}$. In §16.3.3 a mixed Gaussian distribution was derived for $\tilde{\boldsymbol{\beta}}$, a renormalized form of $\hat{\boldsymbol{\beta}}$ such that both span the same space. However, this derivation was not convincingly motivated at the time. It is obvious that there are no interesting restrictions to test on $\tilde{\boldsymbol{\beta}}$ directly apart from those that survive renormalization, in particular those of the form (16.6.11), and we already know how to tackle these.

What we wish to test, and all that can be tested in fact, is whether a vector satisfying particular restrictions *lies in* the cointegrating space. Suppose it is desired to test p structural restrictions of the form $\boldsymbol{H\delta}_1 = \boldsymbol{0}$ where $\boldsymbol{\delta}_1$ is the first column of $\boldsymbol{\delta}$ and $\boldsymbol{H}$ is a $p \times m$ matrix of constants. This null hypothesis can be expressed in the form:

$$\text{there exists a vector } \boldsymbol{a} \ (s \times 1) \text{ such that } \boldsymbol{H\beta a} = \boldsymbol{0}. \tag{16.6.15}$$

Consider constructing a Wald test of this hypothesis based on the matrix $\hat{\boldsymbol{\beta}}$.[19] Assume $p \geq s$, since otherwise H_0 is trivially true. This simply means that with fewer than s restrictions the order condition for identification is not satisfied, and only overidentifying restrictions can be tested. Suppose H_0 is true. Then the matrix $\boldsymbol{\beta' H' H \beta}$ $(s \times s)$ has rank of $s-1$, its smallest eigenvalue is 0, and $\boldsymbol{a}$ is the corresponding eigenvector.[20] The vector $\boldsymbol{a}$ is a continuous function of $\boldsymbol{\beta}$, differentiable to all orders, and letting $\hat{\boldsymbol{a}}$ denotes the eigenvector corresponding to the smallest eigenvalue of $\hat{\boldsymbol{\beta}}' \boldsymbol{H' H} \hat{\boldsymbol{\beta}}$, $\hat{\boldsymbol{a}}$ is consistent for $\boldsymbol{a}$. Noting that $n(\hat{\boldsymbol{\beta}} - \boldsymbol{\beta}) = O_p(1)$, write the expansion

$$n\boldsymbol{H}\hat{\boldsymbol{\beta}}\hat{\boldsymbol{a}} = n\boldsymbol{H}(\hat{\boldsymbol{\beta}} - \boldsymbol{\beta})\boldsymbol{a} + n\boldsymbol{H\beta}(\hat{\boldsymbol{a}} - \boldsymbol{a}) + o_p(1). \tag{16.6.16}$$

Using a formula from Magnus and Neudecker (1991, Ch. 8, Th. 7) the differential of an eigenvector of $\boldsymbol{\beta' H' H \beta}$ with respect to $\boldsymbol{\beta}$ corresponding to a simple eigenvalue λ has the form

$$d\boldsymbol{a} = \boldsymbol{P}(d\boldsymbol{\beta}' \boldsymbol{H' H \beta} + \boldsymbol{\beta' H' H} d\boldsymbol{\beta})\boldsymbol{a} \tag{16.6.17}$$

where $\boldsymbol{P}$ denotes the Moore–Penrose inverse of the singular matrix $\lambda \boldsymbol{I}_s - \boldsymbol{\beta' H' H \beta}$. Letting $\boldsymbol{h}_i'$ denote the ith row of $\boldsymbol{H}$,

$$\boldsymbol{h}_i' \boldsymbol{\beta} d\boldsymbol{a} = \boldsymbol{a}' \boldsymbol{\beta}' \boldsymbol{H' H} d\boldsymbol{\beta P \beta}' \boldsymbol{h}_i + \boldsymbol{h}_i' \boldsymbol{\beta P \beta}' \boldsymbol{H' H} d\boldsymbol{\beta a}$$

[19] This analysis is based on Davidson (1998a).

[20] If the rank is less than $s-1$, with two or more zero eigenvalues, the rank of the space in which the test restrictions are satisfied must be *two* or more. Therefore, there must be $p+1$ valid restrictions, including those under test. We neglect this possibility, but in such circumstances the test of p restrictions ought not to be oversized.

$$= (\boldsymbol{h}_i'\boldsymbol{\beta}\boldsymbol{P} \otimes \boldsymbol{a}'\boldsymbol{\beta}'\boldsymbol{H}'\boldsymbol{H} + \boldsymbol{a}' \otimes \boldsymbol{h}_i'\boldsymbol{\beta}\boldsymbol{P}\boldsymbol{\beta}'\boldsymbol{H}'\boldsymbol{H})\,\mathrm{Vec}\,d\boldsymbol{\beta} \tag{16.6.18}$$

and hence

$$\begin{aligned} \boldsymbol{h}_i'd(\boldsymbol{\beta}\boldsymbol{a}) &= \boldsymbol{h}_i'd\boldsymbol{\beta}\boldsymbol{a} + \boldsymbol{h}_i'\boldsymbol{\beta}d\boldsymbol{a} \\ &= (\boldsymbol{a} \otimes \boldsymbol{h}_i + \boldsymbol{P}\boldsymbol{\beta}'\boldsymbol{h}_i \otimes \boldsymbol{H}'\boldsymbol{H}\boldsymbol{\beta}\boldsymbol{a} + \boldsymbol{a} \otimes \boldsymbol{H}'\boldsymbol{H}\boldsymbol{\beta}\boldsymbol{P}\boldsymbol{\beta}'\boldsymbol{h}_i)'\,\mathrm{Vec}\,d\boldsymbol{\beta} \\ &= \boldsymbol{k}_i'\,\mathrm{Vec}\,d\boldsymbol{\beta} \end{aligned} \tag{16.6.19}$$

where the last equality defines $\boldsymbol{k}_i$ $(ms \times 1)$. The ith element of (16.6.16) is therefore approximated by

$$n\boldsymbol{h}_i'\hat{\boldsymbol{\beta}}\hat{\boldsymbol{a}} = n\boldsymbol{k}_i'\,\mathrm{Vec}(\hat{\boldsymbol{\beta}} - \boldsymbol{\beta}) + o_p(1). \tag{16.6.20}$$

Although this formula has been derived for $\hat{\boldsymbol{\beta}}$, whose asymptotic distribution is unknown, the same argument can be made in respect of $\tilde{\boldsymbol{\beta}} = \hat{\boldsymbol{\beta}}(\bar{\boldsymbol{\beta}}'\hat{\boldsymbol{\beta}})^{-1}$. Let $\tilde{\boldsymbol{a}}$ denote the solution to the problem of minimizing $\boldsymbol{a}'\tilde{\boldsymbol{\beta}}'\boldsymbol{H}'\boldsymbol{H}\tilde{\boldsymbol{\beta}}\boldsymbol{a}$ subject to $\boldsymbol{a}'\boldsymbol{a} = 1$, and note that $(\bar{\boldsymbol{\beta}}'\hat{\boldsymbol{\beta}})^{-1}\tilde{\boldsymbol{a}}$ is therefore the solution to the generalized eigenvalue problem of minimizing $\boldsymbol{a}'\hat{\boldsymbol{\beta}}'\boldsymbol{H}'\boldsymbol{H}\hat{\boldsymbol{\beta}}\boldsymbol{a}$ subject to $\boldsymbol{a}'\bar{\boldsymbol{\beta}}'\hat{\boldsymbol{\beta}}\hat{\boldsymbol{\beta}}'\bar{\boldsymbol{\beta}}\boldsymbol{a} = 1$. Therefore,

$$\begin{aligned} \mathbf{0} &= (\hat{\boldsymbol{\beta}}'\boldsymbol{H}'\boldsymbol{H}\hat{\boldsymbol{\beta}} - \lambda\bar{\boldsymbol{\beta}}'\hat{\boldsymbol{\beta}}\hat{\boldsymbol{\beta}}'\bar{\boldsymbol{\beta}})(\bar{\boldsymbol{\beta}}'\hat{\boldsymbol{\beta}})^{-1}\tilde{\boldsymbol{a}} \\ &= (\hat{\boldsymbol{\beta}}'\boldsymbol{H}'\boldsymbol{H}\hat{\boldsymbol{\beta}} - \lambda\boldsymbol{I}_s)[(\bar{\boldsymbol{\beta}}'\hat{\boldsymbol{\beta}})^{-1}\tilde{\boldsymbol{a}} - \hat{\boldsymbol{a}}] + O_p(n^{-2}) \end{aligned} \tag{16.6.21}$$

where the second equality uses the facts that $\hat{\boldsymbol{\beta}}'\bar{\boldsymbol{\beta}} - \boldsymbol{I}_s = O_p(n^{-1})$, and that $(\hat{\boldsymbol{\beta}}'\boldsymbol{H}'\boldsymbol{H}\hat{\boldsymbol{\beta}} - \lambda\boldsymbol{I}_s)\hat{\boldsymbol{a}} = \mathbf{0}$ by definition of $\hat{\boldsymbol{a}}$. Given that $\hat{\boldsymbol{\beta}}'\boldsymbol{H}'\boldsymbol{H}\hat{\boldsymbol{\beta}} - \lambda\boldsymbol{I}_s = O_p(1)$ and $\hat{\boldsymbol{a}}$ and $\tilde{\boldsymbol{a}}$ are both normalized to unit length, it follows that

$$n(\boldsymbol{h}_i'\tilde{\boldsymbol{\beta}}\tilde{\boldsymbol{a}} - \boldsymbol{h}_i'\hat{\boldsymbol{\beta}}\hat{\boldsymbol{a}}) = O_p(n^{-1}) \tag{16.6.22}$$

so that the two vectors have the same asymptotic distribution. From (16.3.36), this is

$$n\boldsymbol{h}_i'\hat{\boldsymbol{\beta}}\hat{\boldsymbol{a}} \underset{\text{asy}}{\sim} \int N\big(\mathbf{0},\ \boldsymbol{K}[(\boldsymbol{\alpha}'\boldsymbol{\Sigma}^{-1}\boldsymbol{\alpha})^{-1} \otimes \boldsymbol{\gamma}\boldsymbol{G}_W^{-1}\boldsymbol{\gamma}']\boldsymbol{K}'\big)d\boldsymbol{G}_W \tag{16.6.23}$$

where $\boldsymbol{K}$ is the matrix with rows $\boldsymbol{k}_1, \dots, \boldsymbol{k}_p$. Define

$$\hat{\boldsymbol{V}} = n\hat{\boldsymbol{K}}\big((\hat{\boldsymbol{\alpha}}'\hat{\boldsymbol{\Lambda}}^{-1}\hat{\boldsymbol{\alpha}})^{-1} \otimes \hat{\boldsymbol{M}}_\beta\hat{\boldsymbol{v}}\hat{\boldsymbol{v}}'\hat{\boldsymbol{M}}_\beta\big)\hat{\boldsymbol{K}}' \tag{16.6.24}$$

where hats denote evaluation at $\hat{\boldsymbol{\beta}}$ throughout, and provided $\hat{\boldsymbol{V}}$ is of rank p there is the unconditional result

$$n^2\hat{\boldsymbol{a}}'\hat{\boldsymbol{\beta}}\boldsymbol{H}'\hat{\boldsymbol{V}}^{-1}\boldsymbol{H}\hat{\boldsymbol{\beta}}\hat{\boldsymbol{a}} \underset{\text{asy}}{\sim} \chi^2(p) \text{ on } H_0. \tag{16.6.25}$$

Since the matrix $n\hat{\boldsymbol{M}}_\beta\hat{\boldsymbol{v}}\hat{\boldsymbol{v}}'\hat{\boldsymbol{M}}_\beta$ in (16.3.40) is of rank $m - s$, the latter requirement presents a difficulty when $p > m-s$. As noted the distribution of $n\,\mathrm{Vec}(\hat{\boldsymbol{\beta}}-\boldsymbol{\beta})$ is singular of rank $s(m-s)$, and it is not possible to test more than $m-s$ restrictions on any one column of $\boldsymbol{\delta}$, even though these can arise in practice, because of the way $\boldsymbol{\beta}$ is normalized. However, a solution is to use the Moore–Penrose inverse of the variance matrix. Diagonalizing $\hat{\boldsymbol{V}}$ as $\boldsymbol{Q}_1'\boldsymbol{\Lambda}\boldsymbol{Q}_1$ where $\boldsymbol{\Lambda}$ $(r \times r)$ is the diagonal matrix of the positive eigenvalues, with $r = \min\{p, m-s\}$, yields

$$n^2 \hat{\boldsymbol{a}}'\hat{\boldsymbol{\beta}}'\boldsymbol{H}'\boldsymbol{Q}_1'\boldsymbol{\Lambda}^{-1}\boldsymbol{Q}_1\boldsymbol{H}\hat{\boldsymbol{\beta}}\hat{\boldsymbol{a}} \underset{\text{asy}}{\sim} \chi^2(r) \text{ on } H_0. \tag{16.6.26}$$

The $m-s$ independent restrictions represented by $\boldsymbol{Q}_1\boldsymbol{H}$ will in general (though not invariably) hold only if H_0 is true.

The typical application of such tests would be to exclusion restrictions. After suitable reordering if the variables let $\boldsymbol{H} = [\boldsymbol{0} \;\; \boldsymbol{I}_p]$ for $s \le p \le m-2$. This corresponds to the hypothesis that the cointegrating space contains a vector with only $m-p$ nonzero elements, and equivalently that the first $m-p$ elements of $\boldsymbol{x}_t$ form a cointegrated subset. The cointegrating vector for this subset is directly estimated by

$$\hat{\boldsymbol{b}} = \boldsymbol{G}\hat{\boldsymbol{\beta}}\hat{\boldsymbol{a}} \quad ((m-p) \times 1) \tag{16.6.27}$$

where $\boldsymbol{G} = [\boldsymbol{I}_{m-p} \;\; \boldsymbol{0}]$, and the asymptotic distribution of $\hat{\boldsymbol{b}}$ is mixed Gaussian, being found very simply by letting $\boldsymbol{G}$ replace $\boldsymbol{H}$ in the conditional variance formula (16.6.24). If the restrictions satisfied by $\boldsymbol{H}$ represent an identified vector of $\boldsymbol{\delta}$ then $\hat{\boldsymbol{b}}$ is an asymptotically mixed Gaussian estimator of this vector, obtained without the use of iterative methods.

Recall from Theorem 16.6.2 that any identified structural cointegrating relationship is necessarily irreducible. This test can be used to check, first whether hypothetical structural restrictions are satisfied by a column of $\boldsymbol{\delta}$, but then whether any additional exclusion restrictions are also satisfied by this same vector. If so, the vector is not irreducible, and therefore its status as an identified structural form is in doubt. These methods may be useful at a preliminary stage of an investigation, before attempting to estimate a restricted model directly by numerical methods. See Davidson (1998b) for an analysis on these lines.

Further Reading: Johansen (1995b) gives an account of the reduced rank regression theory and its ramifications. Also see Hatanaka (1996) as well as Hamilton (1994) and Hendry (1995). A number of commercial estimation packages are currently available for the estimation and testing of cointegrated systems, and two deserve mention because the manuals that accompany them, respectively Doornik and Hendry (1997) and Pesaran and Pesaran (1997), are expertly written and helpful just as textbooks. These are PcFiml 9.0 (Timberlake Consultants Ltd.) and Microfit 4 (Oxford University Press).

16.7 Appendix: Additional Proofs

Proof of Lemma 16.3.1 Define $\boldsymbol{\alpha}_\perp$ $(m \times (m-s))$ to be a matrix of rank $m-s$ such that $\boldsymbol{\alpha}'\boldsymbol{\alpha}_\perp = \boldsymbol{0}$, and so construct the $m \times m$ full-rank matrix $\boldsymbol{M} = \begin{bmatrix}\boldsymbol{\alpha} & \boldsymbol{\Sigma}\boldsymbol{\alpha}_\perp\end{bmatrix}$. Note that

$$(\boldsymbol{\alpha}'\boldsymbol{\Sigma}_{00}^{-1}\boldsymbol{\alpha})^{-1}\boldsymbol{\alpha}'\boldsymbol{\Sigma}_{00}^{-1}\boldsymbol{M} = [\boldsymbol{I}_s \;\; \boldsymbol{0}] = (\boldsymbol{\alpha}'\boldsymbol{\Sigma}^{-1}\boldsymbol{\alpha})^{-1}\boldsymbol{\alpha}'\boldsymbol{\Sigma}^{-1}\boldsymbol{M} \tag{16.7.1}$$

where the first equality holds since $\boldsymbol{\Sigma}_{00}\boldsymbol{\alpha}_\perp = \boldsymbol{\Sigma}\boldsymbol{\alpha}_\perp$ by (16.3.7). Since $\boldsymbol{M}$ is invertible, this implies

$$(\boldsymbol{\alpha}'\boldsymbol{\Sigma}_{00}^{-1}\boldsymbol{\alpha})^{-1}\boldsymbol{\alpha}'\boldsymbol{\Sigma}_{00}^{-1} = (\boldsymbol{\alpha}'\boldsymbol{\Sigma}^{-1}\boldsymbol{\alpha})^{-1}\boldsymbol{\alpha}'\boldsymbol{\Sigma}^{-1}. \tag{16.7.2}$$

Now postmultiply by $\boldsymbol{\Sigma}_{00}\boldsymbol{\alpha}(\boldsymbol{\alpha}'\boldsymbol{\alpha})^{-1}$ to obtain

$$\begin{aligned}(\boldsymbol{\alpha}'\boldsymbol{\Sigma}_{00}^{-1}\boldsymbol{\alpha})^{-1} &= (\boldsymbol{\alpha}'\boldsymbol{\Sigma}^{-1}\boldsymbol{\alpha})^{-1}\boldsymbol{\alpha}'\boldsymbol{\Sigma}^{-1}(\boldsymbol{\Sigma}+\boldsymbol{\alpha}\boldsymbol{\alpha}')\boldsymbol{\alpha}(\boldsymbol{\alpha}'\boldsymbol{\alpha})^{-1} \\ &= (\boldsymbol{\alpha}'\boldsymbol{\Sigma}^{-1}\boldsymbol{\alpha})^{-1} + \boldsymbol{I}_s. \qquad (16.7.3)\end{aligned}$$

Note that since $\hat{\boldsymbol{S}}_{00} = \hat{\boldsymbol{\Sigma}} + \hat{\boldsymbol{\alpha}}\hat{\boldsymbol{\alpha}}'$, these relations are satisfied identically at the estimated values.

By (16.2.18) the diagonal matrix $\hat{\boldsymbol{D}}_1$ having the first s solution eigenvalues on its diagonal satisfies the equation

$$\hat{\boldsymbol{D}}_1 = \hat{\boldsymbol{\beta}}'\boldsymbol{S}_{10}\boldsymbol{S}_{00}^{-1}\boldsymbol{S}_{01}\hat{\boldsymbol{\beta}} = \hat{\boldsymbol{\alpha}}\boldsymbol{S}_{00}^{-1}\hat{\boldsymbol{\alpha}}. \qquad (16.7.4)$$

Therefore,

$$(\hat{\boldsymbol{\alpha}}'\hat{\boldsymbol{\Sigma}}^{-1}\hat{\boldsymbol{\alpha}})^{-1} = \hat{\boldsymbol{D}}_1^{-1} - \boldsymbol{I}_s. \quad \blacksquare \qquad (16.7.5)$$

Proof of Theorem 16.6.2 Suppose that $\boldsymbol{\delta}_1$, the first column of $\boldsymbol{\delta}$, is identified by the rank condition. This means that for no choice of $\boldsymbol{r}$ can the vector $\boldsymbol{\delta r}$ reproduce the restrictions on $\boldsymbol{\delta}_1$ except $\boldsymbol{r} = \lambda\boldsymbol{e}_1$ for any $\lambda \neq 0$. On the other hand, since $\boldsymbol{\delta}$ spans the cointegrating space, every cointegrating vector must have the form $\boldsymbol{\delta r}$. Thus, consider a candidate vector $\boldsymbol{\psi}$ which reproduces the restrictions on $\boldsymbol{\delta}_1$ and has one more restriction in addition. This cannot have the form $\lambda\boldsymbol{\delta e}_1$ (which is equal to $\boldsymbol{\delta}_1$ up to a scale constant) nor can it have the form $\boldsymbol{\delta r}$ for $\boldsymbol{r} \neq \lambda\boldsymbol{e}_1$, because the rank condition implies that no such vector can have the assumed restrictions. It follows that $\boldsymbol{\psi}$ does not lie in the cointegrating space, proving sufficiency.

Next, suppose equation 1 is underidentified by the rank condition. This means there exists a matrix $\boldsymbol{R}$ $(s \times s^*)$, with first column $\boldsymbol{e}_1$ but having rank $s^* > 1$, such that each column of $\boldsymbol{\Psi} = \boldsymbol{\delta R}$ $(m \times s^*)$ satisfies the prior restrictions on $\boldsymbol{\delta}_1$, and therefore has the partition $\begin{bmatrix}\boldsymbol{\Psi}_a \\ \boldsymbol{0}\end{bmatrix}$ where $\boldsymbol{\Psi}_a$ is $g_1 \times s^*$. Partitioning $\boldsymbol{x}_t$ conformably as $(\boldsymbol{x}_{at}', \boldsymbol{x}_{bt}')'$ note that

$$\boldsymbol{\Psi}_a'\boldsymbol{x}_{at} = \boldsymbol{R}'\boldsymbol{\delta}'\boldsymbol{x}_t \sim \mathrm{I}(0). \qquad (16.7.6)$$

Partition $\boldsymbol{\Psi}_a$ into its first $g_1 - 1$ rows and last row, as $\boldsymbol{\Psi}_a = \begin{bmatrix}\boldsymbol{C} \\ \boldsymbol{d}'\end{bmatrix}$ where $\boldsymbol{C}$ is $(g_1-1)\times s^*$. Partition $\boldsymbol{x}_{at}$ conformably as $(\boldsymbol{x}_{ct}', x_{dt})'$ where x_{dt} is a scalar. By reordering, any variable from $\boldsymbol{x}_{at}$ can be chosen to be x_{dt}.

With this setup, we show that the vector $\boldsymbol{x}_{ct}$ is cointegrated by exhibiting a $(g_1 - 1)$-vector $\boldsymbol{\gamma}$ such that $\boldsymbol{\gamma}'\boldsymbol{x}_{ct} \sim \mathrm{I}(0)$. If any element of $\boldsymbol{d}$ is zero there is no problem, since $\boldsymbol{\gamma}$ is chosen to be the corresponding column of $\boldsymbol{C}$. Otherwise, for any column $\boldsymbol{c}_j$ of $\boldsymbol{C}$, note that $(\boldsymbol{c}_j'/d_j)\boldsymbol{x}_{ct} + x_{dt} \sim \mathrm{I}(0)$. Choose $\boldsymbol{\gamma} = \boldsymbol{c}_k - d_k\boldsymbol{c}_j/d_j$, for $k \neq j$, and

$$\boldsymbol{\gamma}'\boldsymbol{x}_{ct} = \boldsymbol{c}_k'\boldsymbol{x}_{ct} + d_k x_{dt} + \mathrm{I}(0) \qquad (16.7.7)$$

as required. Note that $\boldsymbol{\gamma} \neq \boldsymbol{0}$ unless columns j and k of $\boldsymbol{\Psi}_a$ are identical, which is ruled out since $\boldsymbol{R}$ has full rank. This means that x_{dt} can be dropped from the set $\boldsymbol{x}_{at}$ without destroying cointegration, proving necessity. ■

Proof of Theorem 16.6.3 Partition the system as

$$\boldsymbol{A}_{aa}(L)\boldsymbol{x}_{at} + \boldsymbol{A}_{ab}(L)\boldsymbol{x}_{bt} = \boldsymbol{u}_{at} \ (g_1 \times 1) \qquad (16.7.8a)$$

$$\boldsymbol{A}_{ba}(L)\boldsymbol{x}_{at} + \boldsymbol{A}_{bb}(L)\boldsymbol{x}_{bt} = \boldsymbol{u}_{bt} \ (m - g_1 \times 1) \qquad (16.7.8b)$$

after ordering the equations to ensure that $A_{bb}(z)$ has full rank.[21] Next, noting $A(1) = \rho\delta'$, transform the system so that the top row of $A_{aa}(1)$ is $\rho_{11}\delta'_{1a}$ where ρ_{11} is the top-left element of ρ, and the top row of $A_{ab}(1)$ is zero. This is accomplished by letting $F = [\rho\ \varphi]^{-1}$ where φ is any full-rank matrix of dimension $m \times (m - s)$ whose columns are linearly independent of ρ, and then replacing the first row of $A(z)$ by $\rho_{11}f'_1A(z)$ where f'_1 is the first row of F, leaving rows 2 to m unchanged. In the transformed model the top row of ρ is $(\rho_{11}, 0, \dots, 0)$ by construction so that only δ_1 appears in the first equation, although note that the cointegration properties of the model as a whole are unaffected. For the rest of the proof let this transformation be implicit, though the same notation is used.

Define the $g_1 \times g_1$ polynomial matrix

$$B(z) = c(z)A_{aa}(z) - c(z)A_{ab}(z)A_{bb}(z)^{-1}A_{ba}(z) \tag{16.7.9}$$

where $c(z)$ is a diagonal matrix having diagonal elements equal either to 1 or to $1 - z$. Solving the partitioned model (16.7.8) for x_{at} yields

$$B(L)x_{at} = c(L)u_{at} - c(L)A_{ab}(L)A_{bb}(L)^{-1}u_{bt} = v_t. \tag{16.7.10}$$

Let $c(z)$ be chosen to cancel any factors of $(1 - z)^{-1}$ from the rows of $A_{ab}(z)A_{bb}(z)^{-1}$.[22] The terms in the lag polynomial in (16.7.10) are accordingly summable, and $v_t \sim \mathrm{I}(0)$.

It remains to show that $B(1)$ has the form stated. Consider the partial solution from (16.7.8b),

$$x_{bt} = -A_{bb}(L)^{-1}A_{ba}(L)x_{at} + A_{bb}(L)^{-1}u_{bt}. \tag{16.7.11}$$

Under the hypothesis $x_t \sim \mathrm{I}(1)$, this equation is balanced (having both sides I(1)) if and only if the elements of $A_{bb}(z)^{-1}A_{ba}(z)$ contain no factors of $(1 - z)^{-1}$, by cancellation or otherwise. Therefore, letting

$$E(z) = A_{bb}(z)^{-1}A_{ba}(z) \tag{16.7.12}$$

the matrix $E(1)$ is finite. Note that $A_{aa}(1) = \rho_a\delta'_a$ and $A_{ab}(1) = \rho_a\delta'_b$, and hence

$$B(1) = c(1)\rho_a[\delta'_a - \delta'_bE(1)] \tag{16.7.13}$$

and the cointegrating vectors for the solved system lie in the space spanned by $\delta_a - E(1)'\delta_b$. The first column of δ_b, and hence the first column of $E(1)'\delta_b$, is equal to $\mathbf{0}$. Hence δ'_{1a} is the first row of $\delta'_a - \delta'_bE(1)$. This cointegrating vector is irreducible, and hence unique for x_{at}, by the hypothesis of identifiability and Theorem 16.6.2. Therefore, the only solution compatible with $v_t \sim \mathrm{I}(0)$ is that the remaining columns of $\delta_a - E(1)'\delta_b$ are equal to $\mathbf{0}$, and

$$B(1) = c(1)\rho_{1a}\delta'_{1a} \tag{16.7.14}$$

where ρ_{1a} $(g_1 \times 1)$ is the first column of ρ_a.

The last point to verify is that $c(1) \neq \mathbf{0}$. Since the top row of $A_{ab}(1)$ is zero, the top row of $A_{ab}(z)A_{bb}(z)^{-1}$ contains no factors of $(1 - z)^{-1}$, and the first diagonal element of $c(z)$ is therefore equal to 1. ∎

---

[21] That is to say, $A_{bb}(z)$ must be nonsingular at all points $z \in C$ other than the finite set of solutions of $|A_{bb}(z)| = 0$.

[22] As pointed out in §15.1.2, factors of $(1 - z)^{-k}$ for $k > 1$ are ruled out by assumption. Note that Davidson (1998b) gives a version of this result that omits $c(z)$, and so implicitly deals with the case where $A_{bb}(z)^{-1}$ contains no factors $(1 - z)^{-1}$.

Part V

Technical Appendices

Appendix A

Matrix Algebra Basics

A.1 Vectors and Matrices

A *matrix* is a rectangular array of numbers,

$$A = \begin{bmatrix} a_{11} & a_{12} & \cdots & a_{1n} \\ a_{21} & a_{22} & \cdots & a_{2n} \\ \vdots & \vdots & \ddots & \vdots \\ a_{m1} & a_{m2} & \cdots & a_{mn} \end{bmatrix} \quad (m \text{ rows } \times \ n \text{ columns}) \tag{A.1.1}$$

often denoted by an upper case (Roman or Greek) letter. A matrix is called *square* if $m = n$. The generic element of a matrix is denoted a_{ij}, where usually, i is the row index and j the column index, the convention maintained in this appendix. However, in econometrics the column index sometimes appears first. For example, if a data matrix $\boldsymbol{X}$ $(n \times k)$ is arranged with variables in columns and observations in rows, x_{it} is typically in the ith column and tth row.

A *column vector* is a $m \times 1$ matrix in which the column index is suppressed, often denoted by a lower case letter:

$$\boldsymbol{a} = \begin{bmatrix} a_1 \\ a_2 \\ \vdots \\ a_m \end{bmatrix} \tag{A.1.2}$$

The name vector comes from coordinate geometry, where $\boldsymbol{a}$ may represent a point in m-dimensional space (measuring the distance from the origin in each of the m directions) and hence also a direction in space, represented by the ray through the origin passing through $\boldsymbol{a}$. In matrix algebra an ordinary real number is called a *scalar*.

The *transpose* of a matrix $\boldsymbol{A}$ $(m \times n)$, written $\boldsymbol{A}'$ (some authors use $\boldsymbol{A}^\top$) is the $n \times m$ matrix whose rows contain the elements of the columns of $\boldsymbol{A}$, so that if $\boldsymbol{B} = \boldsymbol{A}'$, $b_{ij} = a_{ji}$. In particular, the *row vector*

$$\boldsymbol{a}' = \begin{bmatrix} a_1 \, a_2 \, \cdots \, a_m \end{bmatrix} \tag{A.1.3}$$

is the transpose of column vector $\boldsymbol{a}$. If $\boldsymbol{A} = \boldsymbol{A}'$, the matrix $\boldsymbol{A}$ (necessarily square) is said to be *symmetric*.

Matrices and vectors are frequently *partitioned*, that is, expressed as matrices whose elements are submatrices. Partitioning may be by rows, by columns or both, for example,

$$\boldsymbol{A} = \begin{bmatrix} \boldsymbol{A}_1 \\ \boldsymbol{A}_2 \end{bmatrix} = \begin{bmatrix} \boldsymbol{A}_{11} & \boldsymbol{A}_{12} \\ \boldsymbol{A}_{21} & \boldsymbol{A}_{22} \end{bmatrix} \tag{A.1.4}$$

where $\boldsymbol{A}_1 = [\boldsymbol{A}_{11}\ \boldsymbol{A}_{12}]$, $\boldsymbol{A}_2 = [\boldsymbol{A}_{21}\ \boldsymbol{A}_{22}]$, and the matrices $\boldsymbol{A}_{ij}$ are of dimension $m_i \times n_j$ for $i, j = 1, 2$ where $m_1 + m_2 = m$ and $n_1 + n_2 = n$. A matrix can be thought of as a row of column vectors, or alternatively as a column of row vectors.

The sum of two matrices of the same dimensions, $\boldsymbol{C} = \boldsymbol{A} + \boldsymbol{B}$, is the matrix with elements $c_{ij} = a_{ij} + b_{ij}$. The product of a scalar a with a matrix $\boldsymbol{B}$, written $a\boldsymbol{B}$, is defined as the matrix with elements ab_{ij}. Combining these definitions lets us define the difference of two matrices as $\boldsymbol{A} - \boldsymbol{B} = \boldsymbol{A} + (-1)\boldsymbol{B}$.

The product of two matrices, $\boldsymbol{C} = \boldsymbol{AB}$, is defined when the row order of $\boldsymbol{B}$ matches the column order of $\boldsymbol{A}$, in which case $\boldsymbol{A}$ and $\boldsymbol{B}$ are said to be *conformable* for multiplication. If $\boldsymbol{A}$ is $m \times n$ and $\boldsymbol{B}$ is $n \times p$, then $\boldsymbol{C}$ is the $m \times p$ matrix with elements

$$c_{ij} = \sum_{k=1}^{n} a_{ik} b_{kj}. \tag{A.1.5}$$

Notice that $\boldsymbol{BA}$ is different from $\boldsymbol{AB}$ and does not exist unless $m = p$. In other words, matrix multiplication, unlike scalar multiplication, is not commutative. For an m-vector $\boldsymbol{a}$ and n-vector $\boldsymbol{b}$, the product $\boldsymbol{a}'\boldsymbol{b}$ exists only if $m = n$ and is a scalar called the *inner product* of the vectors, whereas $\boldsymbol{ab}'$ is an $m \times n$ matrix, the *outer product*. The nonnegative scalar

$$\|\boldsymbol{a}\| = \sqrt{\boldsymbol{a}'\boldsymbol{a}} \tag{A.1.6}$$

is called the *length* and also the *norm* of the vector $\boldsymbol{a}$. If $\boldsymbol{A}'\boldsymbol{B} = \boldsymbol{0}$ the matrices $\boldsymbol{A}$ and $\boldsymbol{B}$ are said to be *orthogonal*.

Transposition of sums and products is governed by the rules

$$(\boldsymbol{A} + \boldsymbol{B})' = \boldsymbol{A}' + \boldsymbol{B}' \tag{A.1.7}$$

$$(\boldsymbol{AB})' = \boldsymbol{B}'\boldsymbol{A}'. \tag{A.1.8}$$

Multiplication of conformably partitioned matrices is a matter of applying the usual formula for multiplication to the blocks. For example,

$$[\boldsymbol{A}_1\ \boldsymbol{A}_2] \begin{bmatrix} \boldsymbol{B}_1 \\ \boldsymbol{B}_2 \end{bmatrix} = \boldsymbol{A}_1\boldsymbol{B}_1 + \boldsymbol{A}_2\boldsymbol{B}_2 \tag{A.1.9}$$

whereas

$$\begin{bmatrix} \boldsymbol{A}_1 \\ \boldsymbol{A}_2 \end{bmatrix} [\boldsymbol{B}_1\ \boldsymbol{B}_2] = \begin{bmatrix} \boldsymbol{A}_1\boldsymbol{B}_1 & \boldsymbol{A}_1\boldsymbol{B}_2 \\ \boldsymbol{A}_2\boldsymbol{B}_1 & \boldsymbol{A}_2\boldsymbol{B}_2 \end{bmatrix}. \tag{A.1.10}$$

The sum of the diagonal elements of a square matrix $\boldsymbol{A}$ is called the *trace* of $\boldsymbol{A}$, written $\operatorname{tr}(\boldsymbol{A})$. For square matrices $\boldsymbol{A}$ and $\boldsymbol{B}$,

$$\operatorname{tr}(\boldsymbol{A}+\boldsymbol{B}) = \operatorname{tr}(\boldsymbol{A}) + \operatorname{tr}(\boldsymbol{B}) \tag{A.1.11}$$

whereas if $\boldsymbol{A}$ is $m \times n$ and $\boldsymbol{B}$ is $n \times m$, then

$$\operatorname{tr}(\boldsymbol{AB}) = \sum_{i=1}^{m}\sum_{j=1}^{n} a_{ij}b_{ji} = \operatorname{tr}(\boldsymbol{BA}) \tag{A.1.12}$$

where $\boldsymbol{AB}$ and $\boldsymbol{BA}$ are $m \times m$ and $n \times n$ respectively.

A.2 Matrix Inversion

The *inverse* of a square matrix $\boldsymbol{A}$ ($n \times n$), when it exists, is the $n \times n$ matrix denoted $\boldsymbol{A}^{-1}$ such that

$$\boldsymbol{AA}^{-1} = \boldsymbol{A}^{-1}\boldsymbol{A} = \boldsymbol{I}_n \tag{A.2.1}$$

where $\boldsymbol{I}_n$ denotes the *identity matrix* of order n,

$$\boldsymbol{I}_n = \begin{bmatrix} 1 & 0 & \cdots & 0 \\ 0 & 1 & \cdots & 0 \\ \vdots & \vdots & \ddots & \vdots \\ 0 & 0 & \dots & 1 \end{bmatrix} \quad (n \times n) \tag{A.2.2}$$

(ones on the diagonal, zeros elsewhere). This generalizes to matrices the concept of the reciprocal of a real number. A matrix whose inverse exists (the generalization of a nonzero number) is called *nonsingular*. The rules for inverting products and transposes are

$$(\boldsymbol{AB})^{-1} = \boldsymbol{B}^{-1}\boldsymbol{A}^{-1} \tag{A.2.3}$$

and

$$(\boldsymbol{A}')^{-1} = (\boldsymbol{A}^{-1})'. \tag{A.2.4}$$

To give a rule for computing the inverse of a matrix requires the definition of the *determinant* of a square matrix $\boldsymbol{A}$, usually denoted $|\boldsymbol{A}|$ and also sometimes $\det \boldsymbol{A}$. This is a scalar quantity that is calculated from the elements of $\boldsymbol{A}$. In the case of a 2×2 matrix

$$\boldsymbol{A} = \begin{bmatrix} a_{11} & a_{12} \\ a_{21} & a_{22} \end{bmatrix} \tag{A.2.5}$$

the determinant is

$$|\boldsymbol{A}| = a_{11}a_{22} - a_{12}a_{21}. \tag{A.2.6}$$

For higher order matrices, an inductive rule is used. For each i and j the (i, j)th *cofactor* of $\boldsymbol{A}$, denoted c_{ij}, is the determinant of the $(n-1) \times (n-1)$ matrix obtained by deleting the ith row and jth column from $\boldsymbol{A}$, multiplied by $(-1)^{i+j}$. That is, the sign is changed if and only if $i+j$ is odd, called for obvious reasons the *checkerboard rule*. The determinant of $\boldsymbol{A}$ $(n \times n)$ is given by the formula

$$|\boldsymbol{A}| = \sum_{j=1}^{n} a_{ij} c_{ij} \tag{A.2.7}$$

where i denotes any row of the matrix, for the formula has the same value for every i. This is called expanding the determinant on row i. For a 3×3 matrix, for example, the formula yields the result

$$\begin{aligned} |\boldsymbol{A}| = a_{11}a_{22}a_{33} - a_{11}a_{23}a_{32} + a_{12}a_{23}a_{31} - a_{12}a_{21}a_{33} \\ + a_{13}a_{21}a_{32} - a_{13}a_{22}a_{31} \end{aligned} \tag{A.2.8}$$

This latter formula is easily remembered by noting that the terms with positive signs are constructed from the left-to-right diagonals, and those with negative signs from the right-to-left diagonals. For $n > 3$, the cofactors must be obtained by applying the same rule to the various sub-matrices obtained by deleting rows and columns.

A nonsingular matrix is one for which $|\boldsymbol{A}| \neq 0$. A well-known result, given without proof, is that the inverse is

$$\boldsymbol{A}^{-1} = \frac{1}{|\boldsymbol{A}|} \operatorname{adj} \boldsymbol{A} \tag{A.2.9}$$

where adj $\boldsymbol{A}$ denotes the *adjoint matrix* of $\boldsymbol{A}$, that is, the transpose of the matrix of cofactors, having c_{ji} for its (i,j)th element.

Determinants obey the following rules:

$$\text{If } \boldsymbol{B} \text{ is } n \times n \text{ and } a \text{ is a scalar, } |a\boldsymbol{B}| = a^n|\boldsymbol{B}| \tag{A.2.10}$$

$$|\boldsymbol{AB}| = |\boldsymbol{A}||\boldsymbol{B}| \tag{A.2.11}$$

$$\begin{vmatrix} \boldsymbol{A} & \boldsymbol{B} \\ \boldsymbol{C} & \boldsymbol{D} \end{vmatrix} = \begin{cases} |\boldsymbol{A} - \boldsymbol{BD}^{-1}\boldsymbol{C}||\boldsymbol{D}| & (\boldsymbol{D} \text{ nonsingular}) \\ |\boldsymbol{D} - \boldsymbol{CA}^{-1}\boldsymbol{B}||\boldsymbol{A}| & (\boldsymbol{A} \text{ nonsingular}). \end{cases} \tag{A.2.12}$$

Note in particular that $|\boldsymbol{A}^{-1}| = 1/|\boldsymbol{A}|$ is an important case (A.2.11), since $|\boldsymbol{I}| = 1$ is easily verified. The inverse of a partitioned matrix is given by

$$\begin{bmatrix} \boldsymbol{A} & \boldsymbol{B} \\ \boldsymbol{C} & \boldsymbol{D} \end{bmatrix}^{-1} = \begin{bmatrix} \boldsymbol{E} & -\boldsymbol{EBD}^{-1} \\ -\boldsymbol{D}^{-1}\boldsymbol{CE} & \boldsymbol{D}^{-1} + \boldsymbol{D}^{-1}\boldsymbol{CEBD}^{-1} \end{bmatrix} \tag{A.2.13}$$

where $\boldsymbol{E} = (\boldsymbol{A} - \boldsymbol{BD}^{-1}\boldsymbol{C})^{-1}$. This formula should be checked by multiplying out in both directions. Note too the alternative version of the formula based on $\boldsymbol{F} = (\boldsymbol{D} - \boldsymbol{CA}^{-1}\boldsymbol{B})^{-1}$, which must be equal to the lower right submatrix of (A.2.13).

Inversion of matrices of any size is a computationally intensive task. As a general rule, the number of floating point operations (multiplications) that the computer must perform, and hence the time taken, rises with the cube of the dimension of the matrix, although there are a few cases where the task can be simplified. When the matrix is sparse, for example with either $\boldsymbol{B} = \mathbf{0}$ or $\boldsymbol{C} = \mathbf{0}$ in (A.2.13), the potential simplification is obvious. A case frequently arising in econometrics is where a matrix is constructed as a sum of outer products. It is nearly as easy to augment the inverse of such a matrix by adding a new term as it is to augment the original matrix, using the *Sherman–Morrison* formula. If $\boldsymbol{A}$ is $n \times n$ nonsingular and $\boldsymbol{u}$ and $\boldsymbol{v}$ are n-vectors it can be verified by direct multiplication that

$$(\boldsymbol{A} + \boldsymbol{u}\boldsymbol{v}')^{-1} = \boldsymbol{A}^{-1} - \frac{\boldsymbol{A}^{-1}\boldsymbol{u}\boldsymbol{v}'\boldsymbol{A}^{-1}}{1 + \boldsymbol{v}'\boldsymbol{A}^{-1}\boldsymbol{u}}. \tag{A.2.14}$$

A.3 Linear Dependence and Rank

Let $\boldsymbol{A}$ be $m \times n$. In the geometrical interpretation of matrix algebra, $\boldsymbol{A}$ represents a linear transformation, taking points $\boldsymbol{b}$ in n-dimensional space to points $\boldsymbol{c}$ in m-dimensional space, by the formula

$$\boldsymbol{c} = \boldsymbol{A}\boldsymbol{b}. \tag{A.3.1}$$

The collection of all m-vectors $\boldsymbol{c}$ having the representation (A.3.1) for some n-vector $\boldsymbol{b} \neq \mathbf{0}$ is called the *column space* of $\boldsymbol{A}$, or the *space spanned by the columns of* $\boldsymbol{A}$. Think of this as the range of the transformation $\boldsymbol{A}$.

If $\mathbf{0}$ (the vector of zeros) is not an element of the column space of $\boldsymbol{A}$, so that there exists no $\boldsymbol{b} \neq \mathbf{0}$ such that $\boldsymbol{A}\boldsymbol{b} = \mathbf{0}$, the columns of $\boldsymbol{A}$ are said to be *linearly independent.* If such a $\boldsymbol{b}$ exists, on the other hand, they are called *linearly dependent*, and the collection of all the vectors $\boldsymbol{b}$ satisfying this condition is called the *kernel* or *null space* of $\boldsymbol{A}$. The *nullity* of $\boldsymbol{A}$ is the dimension of the null space, the maximum number of linearly independent vectors contained in it. If $\boldsymbol{A}$ $(m \times n)$ has nullity p, where $0 < p \leq n$, then there exists a matrix $\boldsymbol{B}$ $(n \times p)$, whose columns are linearly independent, such that $\boldsymbol{A}\boldsymbol{B} = \mathbf{0}$ $(m \times p)$. The *rank* of $\boldsymbol{A}$ is the difference between its dimension and its nullity. This is equal to the number of linearly independent columns it contains.

Some rules for determining rank under transformations are as follows.

$$\operatorname{rank} \boldsymbol{A}' = \operatorname{rank} \boldsymbol{A}. \tag{A.3.2}$$

If $\boldsymbol{A}$ is $m \times n$ and $\boldsymbol{B}$ is $n \times p$, then

$$\operatorname{rank} \boldsymbol{A}\boldsymbol{B} \leq \min\{\operatorname{rank} \boldsymbol{A}, \operatorname{rank} \boldsymbol{B}\}. \tag{A.3.3}$$

However, if $\boldsymbol{B}$ is $n \times n$ and nonsingular, then

$$\operatorname{rank} \boldsymbol{A}\boldsymbol{B} = \operatorname{rank} \boldsymbol{A}. \tag{A.3.4}$$

A.4 Equation Systems

Let $\boldsymbol{A}$ be square $n \times n$. If $\boldsymbol{A}$ is nonsingular, then given a vector $\boldsymbol{c}$, there is a unique vector $\boldsymbol{x}$ satisfying the equations

$$\boldsymbol{A}\boldsymbol{x} = \boldsymbol{c} \tag{A.4.1}$$

given by $\boldsymbol{x} = \boldsymbol{A}^{-1}\boldsymbol{c}$. Think of $\boldsymbol{A}^{-1}\boldsymbol{c}$ as the solution to this system of linear equations. The nonsingular transformation $\boldsymbol{A}$ is accordingly one-to-one and invertible, since $\boldsymbol{x}$ can be recovered uniquely from $\boldsymbol{c}$, and $\boldsymbol{c}$ from $\boldsymbol{x}$ similarly.

An equation system of the form $\boldsymbol{Ax} = \boldsymbol{0}$ is called *homogeneous*. Since $\boldsymbol{A}^{-1}\boldsymbol{0} = \boldsymbol{0}$ it is clear that such a system has a nonzero solution only if $\boldsymbol{A}$ is singular. Since this is also the case when $\boldsymbol{A}$ has positive nullity, it follows that a square matrix has full rank if and only if it is nonsingular. If the nullity is 1 the solution is unique, but only up to a scale factor, since if $\boldsymbol{x} \neq \boldsymbol{0}$ is a solution then so is $\lambda\boldsymbol{x}$ for any scalar $\lambda \neq 0$. More generally, the set of solutions of a homogeneous system spans the null space of the matrix.

If $\boldsymbol{A}$ is $m \times n$ then (A.4.1) is a system of m equations in n unknowns, and if $m > n$ there is in general no solution, for arbitrary $\boldsymbol{c}$. If $m < n$ on the other hand, there is a multiplicity of solutions. The system imposes restrictions on $\boldsymbol{x}$ but does not determine it uniquely.

A.5 Eigenvalues and Eigenvectors

Let $\boldsymbol{A}$ be square $n \times n$. It is easy to verify that the scalar equation $|\boldsymbol{A} - \lambda\boldsymbol{I}| = 0$ is a polynomial of degree n in λ. This is called the *characteristic equation* of the matrix $\boldsymbol{A}$. The set of n roots (solutions) $\lambda_1, \dots, \lambda_n$ are called the *eigenvalues* of the matrix, and in general can be real or complex numbers. The set of n nonzero solutions $\boldsymbol{c}_1, \dots, \boldsymbol{c}_n$ to the homogeneous equations

$$(\boldsymbol{A} - \lambda_i\boldsymbol{I})\boldsymbol{c}_i = \boldsymbol{0} \quad i = 1, \dots, n \tag{A.5.1}$$

subject to normalizing constraints $\|\boldsymbol{c}_i\| = 1$ are the corresponding *eigenvectors*. Let $\boldsymbol{\Lambda}$ denote the $n \times n$ *diagonal* matrix whose diagonal elements are $\lambda_1, \dots, \lambda_n$ (conventionally arranged in descending order of magnitude) and all the off-diagonal elements are zero. If $\boldsymbol{C}$ is the matrix whose columns are $\boldsymbol{c}_1, \dots, \boldsymbol{c}_n$, one can stack up these equations in the form

$$\boldsymbol{AC} = \boldsymbol{C\Lambda}. \tag{A.5.2}$$

Given any $n \times n$ nonsingular matrix $\boldsymbol{P}$, if $\boldsymbol{B} = \boldsymbol{PAP}^{-1}$ then

$$\boldsymbol{PAC} = \boldsymbol{BPC} = \boldsymbol{PC\Lambda} \tag{A.5.3}$$

and hence the matrix $\boldsymbol{B}$ has the same eigenvalues as $\boldsymbol{A}$, and its eigenvectors are given by the columns of $\boldsymbol{PC}$. $\boldsymbol{A}$ and $\boldsymbol{B}$ are called *similar* matrices.

If the eigenvalues are all different it can be shown that the eigenvectors form a linearly independent set. In this case set $\boldsymbol{P} = \boldsymbol{C}^{-1}$, showing that $\boldsymbol{A}$ and $\boldsymbol{\Lambda}$ are similar. $\boldsymbol{A}$ has the representation

$$\boldsymbol{A} = \boldsymbol{C\Lambda C}^{-1}. \tag{A.5.4}$$

This is called the *diagonalization* of $\boldsymbol{A}$. If the eigenvalues are not all different, $\boldsymbol{C}$ may not have full rank, and then no diagonalization exists. However, there always exists a similarity transformation $\boldsymbol{B} = \boldsymbol{PAP}^{-1}$ such that $\boldsymbol{B}$ is an upper triangular matrix in which the eigenvalues lie on the diagonal, and if $\lambda_i = \lambda_{i+1}$ then the element in position $(i, i+1)$ could be 1, but otherwise all elements are zero. This is called the *Jordan canonical form* of $\boldsymbol{A}$.

A.6 Diagonalization of Symmetric Matrices

Let $\boldsymbol{A}$ be symmetric. The eigenvalues of a symmetric matrix are always real numbers. The eigenvectors corresponding to distinct eigenvalues are linearly independent and also *orthogonal*, satisfying $\boldsymbol{c}_i'\boldsymbol{c}_j = 0$ for all $i \neq j$. The latter property must hold in view of the identities

$$\boldsymbol{c}_i'\boldsymbol{A}\boldsymbol{c}_j - \lambda_j \boldsymbol{c}_i'\boldsymbol{c}_j = 0 = \boldsymbol{c}_j'\boldsymbol{A}\boldsymbol{c}_i - \lambda_i \boldsymbol{c}_j'\boldsymbol{c}_i \tag{A.6.1}$$

in which the $\lambda_j \neq \lambda_i$ but $\boldsymbol{c}_i'\boldsymbol{A}\boldsymbol{c}_j = \boldsymbol{c}_j'\boldsymbol{A}\boldsymbol{c}_i$ by symmetry.

Symmetric matrices always have a diagonalization. If k of the eigenvalues are equal, say to λ_j, then $\boldsymbol{A} - \lambda_j \boldsymbol{I}$ has rank $n - k$ and the corresponding k eigenvectors can be any set spanning the null space of $\boldsymbol{A} - \lambda_j \boldsymbol{I}$. However, k linearly independent and orthogonal vectors can be selected from these. Letting $\boldsymbol{C}$ be the $n \times n$ nonsingular matrix with columns $\boldsymbol{c}_i$, this has the property $\boldsymbol{C}'\boldsymbol{C} = \boldsymbol{C}\boldsymbol{C}' = \boldsymbol{I}$, and hence $\boldsymbol{C}' = \boldsymbol{C}^{-1}$ (an *orthonormal* matrix). It follows that $\boldsymbol{A}$ has the diagonalization (not unique unless the eigenvalues are distinct)

$$\boldsymbol{A} = \boldsymbol{C}\boldsymbol{\Lambda}\boldsymbol{C}'. \tag{A.6.2}$$

The determinant of $\boldsymbol{A}$, using (A.2.11), is

$$|\boldsymbol{A}| = |\boldsymbol{C}||\boldsymbol{C}^{-1}||\boldsymbol{\Lambda}| = |\boldsymbol{\Lambda}| = \prod_{j=1}^{n} \lambda_j. \tag{A.6.3}$$

The rank of $\boldsymbol{A}$ is similarly equal to the rank of $\boldsymbol{\Lambda}$, and hence, to the number of nonzero eigenvalues. The trace of $\boldsymbol{A}$ is equal to the trace of $\boldsymbol{\Lambda}$ by (A.1.12), and hence equal to the sum of the eigenvalues.

$\boldsymbol{A}$ is said to be *idempotent* if $\boldsymbol{A}\boldsymbol{A} = \boldsymbol{A}$. Using the diagonalization, note that

$$\boldsymbol{A}\boldsymbol{A} = \boldsymbol{C}\boldsymbol{\Lambda}\boldsymbol{C}'\boldsymbol{C}\boldsymbol{\Lambda}\boldsymbol{C}' = \boldsymbol{C}\boldsymbol{\Lambda}^2\boldsymbol{C}' \tag{A.6.4}$$

which requires $\boldsymbol{\Lambda}^2 = \boldsymbol{\Lambda}$. Hence, the eigenvalues must equal to either 0 or 1. The rank of an idempotent matrix is therefore equal to its trace.

A.7 Definite Matrices

A symmetric matrix $\boldsymbol{A}$ $(n \times n)$ is said to be *positive (semi-) definite* if $\boldsymbol{x}'\boldsymbol{A}\boldsymbol{x} > 0$ (≥ 0) for all n-vectors $\boldsymbol{x} \neq \boldsymbol{0}$. In this case, $-\boldsymbol{A}$ is called negative (semi-) definite, and a positive semi-definite matrix is also called nonnegative definite. The eigenvalues of a positive (semi-)definite matrix are always positive (nonnegative) real numbers. A positive definite matrix is nonsingular, noting that were $\boldsymbol{A}$ singular the equations $\boldsymbol{A}\boldsymbol{x} = \boldsymbol{0}$ would have a solution $\boldsymbol{x} \neq \boldsymbol{0}$, implying that $\boldsymbol{x}'\boldsymbol{A}\boldsymbol{x} = 0$.

The following are a collection of useful lemmas concerning definite matrices.

Lemma A.7.1 Given a $m \times n$ matrix $\boldsymbol{B}$, the symmetric $n \times n$ matrix $\boldsymbol{B}'\boldsymbol{B}$ is

(i) positive semi-definite

(ii) positive definite if and only if rank $(\boldsymbol{B}) = n$.

Proof For any $n \times 1$ vector $\boldsymbol{z} \neq \boldsymbol{0}$,

$$\boldsymbol{z}'\boldsymbol{B}'\boldsymbol{B}\boldsymbol{z} = \boldsymbol{w}'\boldsymbol{w} = \sum_{i=1}^{n} w_i^2 \geq 0 \tag{A.7.1}$$

where $\boldsymbol{w} = \boldsymbol{B}\boldsymbol{z}$. This proves (i). If and only if rank$(\boldsymbol{B}) = n$, $\boldsymbol{B}\boldsymbol{z} \neq \boldsymbol{0}$ for all $\boldsymbol{z} \neq \boldsymbol{0}$ by definition of linear independence, and hence $\boldsymbol{z}'\boldsymbol{B}'\boldsymbol{B}\boldsymbol{z} > 0$, proving (ii). ∎

Lemma A.7.2 If a square matrix $\boldsymbol{A}$ is symmetric and positive definite, $\boldsymbol{A}^{-1}$ is symmetric and positive definite.

Proof Symmetry is immediate from the definition of the inverse. Consider

$$\boldsymbol{z}'\boldsymbol{A}^{-1}\boldsymbol{z} = \boldsymbol{z}'\boldsymbol{A}^{-1}\boldsymbol{A}\boldsymbol{A}^{-1}\boldsymbol{z} = \boldsymbol{y}'\boldsymbol{A}\boldsymbol{y} > 0 \tag{A.7.2}$$

where $\boldsymbol{y} = \boldsymbol{A}^{-1}\boldsymbol{z}$. ∎

Lemma A.7.3 Let a quadratic function of n variables be

$$f(\boldsymbol{x}) = a + \boldsymbol{b}'\boldsymbol{x} + \boldsymbol{x}'\boldsymbol{H}\boldsymbol{x} \tag{A.7.3}$$

where $\boldsymbol{H}$ is symmetric $n \times n$, and $\boldsymbol{b}$ is $n \times 1$. f is minimized uniquely at the point $\boldsymbol{x} = \boldsymbol{0}$ if and only if $\boldsymbol{b} = \boldsymbol{0}$ and $\boldsymbol{H}$ is positive definite.

Proof Sufficiency is obvious, since $f(\boldsymbol{0}) = a$, and $f(\boldsymbol{x}) > a$ when $\boldsymbol{x} \neq \boldsymbol{0}$, by definition of positive definiteness. To show necessity, assume first that $\boldsymbol{H}$ is not positive definite, and choose $\boldsymbol{x} \neq \boldsymbol{0}$ such that $\boldsymbol{x}'\boldsymbol{H}\boldsymbol{x} \leq 0$ and $\boldsymbol{b}'\boldsymbol{x} \leq 0$. (Note that $(-\boldsymbol{x})'\boldsymbol{H}(-\boldsymbol{x}) = \boldsymbol{x}'\boldsymbol{H}\boldsymbol{x}$ and either $\boldsymbol{b}'\boldsymbol{x} \leq 0$ or $\boldsymbol{b}'(-\boldsymbol{x}) \leq 0$, for any $\boldsymbol{x}$.) On the other hand, if $\boldsymbol{H}$ is positive definite but $\boldsymbol{b} \neq \boldsymbol{0}$ put $\boldsymbol{y} = -\frac{1}{2}\boldsymbol{H}^{-1}\boldsymbol{b}$ and note that

$$f(\boldsymbol{y}) = a - \tfrac{1}{4}\boldsymbol{b}'\boldsymbol{H}^{-1}\boldsymbol{b} \leq a \tag{A.7.4}$$

by Lemma A.7.2. ∎

Lemma A.7.4 If $\boldsymbol{A}$ $(n \times n)$ is symmetric and positive definite, there exists a nonsingular matrix $\boldsymbol{K}$ $(n \times n)$ such that $\boldsymbol{K}\boldsymbol{A}\boldsymbol{K}' = \boldsymbol{I}_n$ and $\boldsymbol{K}'\boldsymbol{K} = \boldsymbol{A}^{-1}$.

Proof The diagonalization of symmetric, positive definite $\boldsymbol{A}$ has the form

$$\boldsymbol{A} = \boldsymbol{C}\boldsymbol{\Lambda}\boldsymbol{C}^{-1} = \boldsymbol{C}\boldsymbol{\Lambda}^{1/2}\boldsymbol{\Lambda}^{1/2}\boldsymbol{C}' \tag{A.7.5}$$

where $\boldsymbol{\Lambda}$ denotes the diagonal matrix of positive eigenvalues, and $\boldsymbol{\Lambda}^{1/2}$ is the corresponding matrix having the positive square roots of the eigenvalues on its diagonal. It follows by a double application of (A.2.3) that $\boldsymbol{A}^{-1} = \boldsymbol{K}'\boldsymbol{K}$ where $\boldsymbol{K} = \boldsymbol{\Lambda}^{-1/2}\boldsymbol{C}'$. Also,

$$\boldsymbol{K}\boldsymbol{A}\boldsymbol{K}' = \boldsymbol{\Lambda}^{-1/2}\boldsymbol{C}'\boldsymbol{C}\boldsymbol{\Lambda}^{1/2}\boldsymbol{\Lambda}^{1/2}\boldsymbol{C}'\boldsymbol{C}\boldsymbol{\Lambda}^{-1/2} \tag{A.7.6}$$

and the lemma follows since $\boldsymbol{C}'\boldsymbol{C} = \boldsymbol{I}_n$. ∎

The matrix $\boldsymbol{K}^{-1} = \boldsymbol{C}\boldsymbol{\Lambda}^{1/2}$ is often called the 'square root matrix' of $\boldsymbol{A}$, written $\boldsymbol{A}^{1/2}$, having the properties $\boldsymbol{A}^{1/2}(\boldsymbol{A}^{1/2})' = \boldsymbol{A}$, as well as $(\boldsymbol{A}^{-1/2})'\boldsymbol{A}^{-1/2} = \boldsymbol{A}^{-1}$.

A symmetric matrix $\boldsymbol{A}$ is said to be greater than (not less than) another such matrix $\boldsymbol{B}$, sometimes written $\boldsymbol{A} > \boldsymbol{B}$ ($\boldsymbol{A} \geq \boldsymbol{B}$), if $\boldsymbol{A} - \boldsymbol{B}$ is positive (semi)definite.[1] In this sense one can say that a symmetric matrix is the (unique) minimum of a class of such matrices if it is not greater than (strictly less than) all those in the class.

Lemma A.7.5 Let $\boldsymbol{M}$ $(l \times l)$ be positive definite. For $k \leq l$, the solution to the problem: choose $\boldsymbol{P}$ $(k \times l)$ to minimize the matrix $\boldsymbol{PMP}'$, subject to the constraint $\boldsymbol{PL} = \boldsymbol{I}_k$ for $\boldsymbol{L}$ $(l \times k)$ is

$$\boldsymbol{P}^* = (\boldsymbol{L}'\boldsymbol{M}^{-1}\boldsymbol{L})^{-1}\boldsymbol{L}'\boldsymbol{M}^{-1}. \tag{A.7.7}$$

Proof Put $\boldsymbol{P} = \boldsymbol{P}^* + \boldsymbol{D}$, so that $\boldsymbol{DL} = \boldsymbol{0}$. Note that

$$\begin{aligned}\boldsymbol{P}^*\boldsymbol{MD}' &= (\boldsymbol{L}'\boldsymbol{M}^{-1}\boldsymbol{L})^{-1}\boldsymbol{L}'\boldsymbol{M}^{-1}\boldsymbol{MD}' \\ &= (\boldsymbol{L}'\boldsymbol{M}^{-1}\boldsymbol{L})^{-1}\boldsymbol{L}'\boldsymbol{D}' = \boldsymbol{0}.\end{aligned} \tag{A.7.8}$$

It follows that

$$\begin{aligned}\boldsymbol{PMP}' &= \boldsymbol{P}^*\boldsymbol{MP}^{*\prime} + \boldsymbol{DMP}^{*\prime} + \boldsymbol{P}^*\boldsymbol{MD}' + \boldsymbol{DMD}' \\ &= \boldsymbol{P}^*\boldsymbol{MP}^{*\prime} + \boldsymbol{DMD}'\end{aligned} \tag{A.7.9}$$

where $\boldsymbol{DMD}'$ is positive semi-definite if $\boldsymbol{M}$ is. ∎

Lemma A.7.6 If $\boldsymbol{A}$, $\boldsymbol{B}$ and $\boldsymbol{A} - \boldsymbol{B}$ are positive definite, then $\boldsymbol{B}^{-1} - \boldsymbol{A}^{-1}$ is positive definite. □

For the proof see for example Magnus and Neudecker (1988), page 22.

A.8 Generalized Inverses

The concept of an inverse has been defined for a square nonsingular matrix. Given a matrix $\boldsymbol{A}$ $(n \times m)$ that is either not square, or singular if square, matrices derived from $\boldsymbol{A}$ with certain properties of an inverse can be defined. The *Moore–Penrose* (MP) inverse is the unique matrix $\boldsymbol{B}$ such that

$$\boldsymbol{ABA} = \boldsymbol{A} \tag{A.8.1}$$

$$\boldsymbol{BAB} = \boldsymbol{B} \tag{A.8.2}$$

and both $\boldsymbol{AB}$ and $\boldsymbol{BA}$ are symmetric. The usual notation for the MP inverse of $\boldsymbol{A}$ is $\boldsymbol{A}^+$.

[1] This notation should be used with caution since it may be confused with the property that $A - B$ is a positive (non-negative) matrix, having all its elements > 0 (≥ 0).

Here are two useful cases. First, consider a non-square matrix with $n > m$, where $\boldsymbol{A}$ has rank m. Then the MP inverse is

$$\boldsymbol{A}^+ = (\boldsymbol{A}'\boldsymbol{A})^{-1}\boldsymbol{A}'. \tag{A.8.3}$$

This has a role in the solution of an over-determined system of n equations in m unknowns,

$$\boldsymbol{A}\boldsymbol{x} = \boldsymbol{b}. \tag{A.8.4}$$

Premultiplying by $\boldsymbol{A}^+$ yields the solution

$$\boldsymbol{x} = (\boldsymbol{A}'\boldsymbol{A})^{-1}\boldsymbol{A}'\boldsymbol{b}. \tag{A.8.5}$$

This formula is familiar from least squares theory as the best approximate solution, in the sense that it minimizes $\|\boldsymbol{A}\boldsymbol{x} - \boldsymbol{b}\|$.

The second example of interest is a matrix that is symmetric $n \times n$ and positive semi-definite, but has rank $r < n$. Diagonalizing $\boldsymbol{A}$ as in §A.6, note that

$$\boldsymbol{A} = \boldsymbol{S}\boldsymbol{\Lambda}\boldsymbol{S}' \tag{A.8.6}$$

where $\boldsymbol{\Lambda}$ is the $r \times r$ diagonal matrix having the positive eigenvalues of $\boldsymbol{A}$ on the diagonal, and $\boldsymbol{S}$ $(n \times r)$ is the corresponding matrix of orthonormal eigenvectors satisfying $\boldsymbol{S}'\boldsymbol{S} = \boldsymbol{I}_r$. It is easily verified that in this case

$$\boldsymbol{A}^+ = \boldsymbol{S}\boldsymbol{\Lambda}^{-1}\boldsymbol{S}'. \tag{A.8.7}$$

A.9 Matrix Calculus

Let $\boldsymbol{x}$ be a n-vector, and write $f(\boldsymbol{x}) = f(x_1, \dots, x_p)$ to represent a real-valued function of p variables. The column n-vector consisting of the partial derivatives $(\partial/\partial x_i)f$ is called the *gradient* vector of f, written $(\partial/\partial \boldsymbol{x})f$ or more compactly as $\nabla_{\boldsymbol{x}} f$, or just ∇f when the argument of the function is understood. The $p \times p$ matrix of the second-partial and cross-partial derivatives $(\partial^2/\partial x_i \partial x_j)f$ is called the *Hessian* of f, written $(\partial^2/\partial \boldsymbol{x}\partial \boldsymbol{x}')f$ or $\nabla^2 f$. Both forms of notation are used in the text, with the classic partial derivative form for preference and the nabla (∇) form when compactness of notation is at a premium, or simply as a distinguishing feature (e.g. see the footnote on page 241).

Derivatives are also defined for vector-valued functions $\boldsymbol{f}(\boldsymbol{x})$ $(n \times 1)$. The $(n \times p)$ matrix $(\partial/\partial \boldsymbol{x}')\boldsymbol{f}$, also written $\nabla \boldsymbol{f}$ when the argument is understood, is called the *Jacobian matrix* of $\boldsymbol{f}$. The convention that the gradient of a column vector is taken with respect to the arguments expressed as the row vector $\boldsymbol{x}'$ is adopted implicitly in the text. If $n = p$ the real number $|\nabla \boldsymbol{f}|$ is called the Jacobian determinant, and sometimes just 'the Jacobian of $\boldsymbol{f}$'.

It is also possible to define the second derivative $\nabla^2 \boldsymbol{f}$, which is normally interpreted as the $(np \times p)$ matrix consisting of the Hessian matrices of the $f_1, \dots, f_n$ stacked one above the other. However, there are no hard and fast conventions about writing such objects.

A commonly arising case is the quadratic form $\boldsymbol{x}'\boldsymbol{A}\boldsymbol{x}$, where $\boldsymbol{A}$ is a $p\times p$ matrix. The gradient is

$$\frac{\partial(\boldsymbol{x}'\boldsymbol{A}\boldsymbol{x})}{\partial\boldsymbol{x}} = 2\boldsymbol{A}\boldsymbol{x}\ (p\times 1) \tag{A.9.1}$$

and the Hessian is

$$\frac{\partial^2(\boldsymbol{x}'\boldsymbol{A}\boldsymbol{x})}{\partial\boldsymbol{x}\partial\boldsymbol{x}'} = 2\boldsymbol{A}. \tag{A.9.2}$$

By the usual considerations of multivariate calculus, the quadratic form is minimized uniquely at the point $\boldsymbol{x} = \boldsymbol{0}$ if and only if $\boldsymbol{A}$ is positive definite, see Lemma A.7.3.

There are some useful formulae for derivatives of functions with matrix-valued arguments. If $\boldsymbol{A}$ is $n\times n$, then using (A.2.7),

$$\frac{\partial|\boldsymbol{A}|}{\partial a_{ij}} = c_{ij}. \tag{A.9.3}$$

Writing out the matrix of derivatives gives

$$\frac{\partial|\boldsymbol{A}|}{\partial\boldsymbol{A}} = \operatorname{adj}\boldsymbol{A}' \tag{A.9.4}$$

and it is clear similarly that

$$\frac{\partial\ln|\boldsymbol{A}|}{\partial\boldsymbol{A}} = (\boldsymbol{A}')^{-1}. \tag{A.9.5}$$

If $\boldsymbol{A}\boldsymbol{B}$ is square, it can be verified that

$$\frac{\partial(\operatorname{tr}\boldsymbol{A}\boldsymbol{B})}{\partial a_{ij}} = b_{ji} \tag{A.9.6}$$

and hence

$$\frac{\partial(\operatorname{tr}\boldsymbol{A}\boldsymbol{B})}{\partial\boldsymbol{A}} = \boldsymbol{B}'. \tag{A.9.7}$$

A.10 Vecs and Kronecker Products

Econometric formulae often involve stacking up matrix equations, and the following pieces of notation are very useful. If $\boldsymbol{A} = [\boldsymbol{a}_1,\dots,\boldsymbol{a}_n]$ is an $m\times n$ matrix with columns $\boldsymbol{a}_j$ $(m\times 1)$, define the *vectorization* of $\boldsymbol{A}$ as

$$\operatorname{Vec}\boldsymbol{A} = \begin{bmatrix}\boldsymbol{a}_1\\ \vdots\\ \boldsymbol{a}_n\end{bmatrix}\ (mn\times 1) \tag{A.10.1}$$

the vector formed by stacking the columns one above the other. If $\boldsymbol{A}$ $(m\times n)$ and $\boldsymbol{B}$ $(p\times q)$ are matrices, the *Kronecker product* of $\boldsymbol{A}$ and $\boldsymbol{B}$ is

$$\boldsymbol{A}\otimes\boldsymbol{B} = \begin{bmatrix}a_{11}\boldsymbol{B} & \dots & a_{1n}\boldsymbol{B}\\ \vdots & \ddots & \vdots\\ a_{m1}\boldsymbol{B} & \dots & a_{mn}\boldsymbol{B}\end{bmatrix}\ (mp\times nq). \tag{A.10.2}$$

The basic rules for manipulation of Vecs and Kronecker products are as follows:

$$(\boldsymbol{A} \otimes \boldsymbol{B})(\boldsymbol{C} \otimes \boldsymbol{D}) = \boldsymbol{AC} \otimes \boldsymbol{BD} \tag{A.10.3}$$

whenever the products exist;

$$(\boldsymbol{A} \otimes \boldsymbol{B})' = \boldsymbol{A}' \otimes \boldsymbol{B}' \tag{A.10.4}$$

$$(\boldsymbol{A} \otimes \boldsymbol{B})^{-1} = \boldsymbol{A}^{-1} \otimes \boldsymbol{B}^{-1} \tag{A.10.5}$$

whenever the inverses exist; and

$$\text{Vec}\, \boldsymbol{ABC} = (\boldsymbol{C}' \otimes \boldsymbol{A})\, \text{Vec}\, \boldsymbol{B}. \tag{A.10.6}$$

Further Reading: Many textbooks on econometrics and statistics provide summaries of the required matrix theory, in greater or lesser detail. There is no need to list them all, but distinguished examples are Rao (1973) and Theil (1971). For more specialized treatments see Rao and Rao (1998) and Magnus and Neudecker (1988).

Appendix B

Probability and Distribution Theory

B.1 Set Theory Basics

A set is any collection of objects. $x \in A$ denotes that object x is an element of set A. $A \subseteq B$ denotes the fact that set A is a subset of set B, with all elements of A also elements of B. In any analysis, the set X of all elements under consideration, the *universal set*, is defined. For example, in real analysis this might be the set $\mathbb{R}$ of the real numbers (points of the line). The *empty set*, the one having no elements, is denoted $\emptyset$.

The membership of a set may be indicated by indexing the elements, as in $A = \{x_i, i \in I\}$ where I is the *index set*. I can be finite or infinite. If $I = \mathbb{N}$ (the natural numbers 1,2,3, ...) the number of elements is said to be *countably infinite*. Some sets, such as $\mathbb{R}$, are well known to be uncountably infinite, in that their elements cannot be exhaustively labelled by elements of $\mathbb{N}$.

The *union* of A and B, written $A \cup B$, is the set of elements in either A or B, and the *intersection* of A and B, written $A \cap B$, is the set of elements in both A and B. The set of elements in A but not in B, written $A - B$ or $A \backslash B$, is the *difference* of A and B. The set $X - A$ is the *complement* of A, also written A^c.

Let $\mathcal{C} = \{A_i, i \in I\}$ be a set whose elements are sets (also called a collection). The union and intersection of these sets are written $\bigcup_{i \in I} A_i$ and $\bigcap_{i \in I} A_i$ respectively. The rules of set algebra include the associative laws,

$$\left(\bigcup\nolimits_{i \in I} A_i\right) \cap B = \bigcup\nolimits_{i \in I} (A_i \cap B) \tag{B.1.1}$$

$$\left(\bigcap\nolimits_{i \in I} A_i\right) \cup B = \bigcap\nolimits_{i \in I} (A_i \cup B) \tag{B.1.2}$$

and De Morgan's laws for complements,

$$\left(\bigcup\nolimits_{i \in I} A_i\right)^c = \bigcap\nolimits_{i \in I} A_i^c \tag{B.1.3}$$

$$\left(\bigcap_{i\in I} A_i\right)^c = \bigcup_{i\in I} A_i^c. \tag{B.1.4}$$

Given a universal set X, there are various ways to define collections of subsets of X that have useful properties in probability.

Definition B.1.1 A *field* $\mathcal{F}$ of X is a collection containing X that is closed under complementation and union, that is, it has the properties:

(a) $X \in \mathcal{F}$

(b) if $A \in \mathcal{F}$ then $A^c \in \mathcal{F}$

(c) if $A_1 \in \mathcal{F}$ and $A_2 \in \mathcal{F}$ then $A_1 \cup A_2 \in \mathcal{F}$. □

In a σ-field (say 'sigma-field') the last condition extends to countable unions.

Definition B.1.2 A σ-field is a field $\mathcal{F}$ of subsets of X that obeys the additional rule

(d) if $A_1, A_2, A_3, \ldots$ is a countably infinite collection of sets in $\mathcal{F}$, then

$$\bigcup_i A_i \in \mathcal{F}. \quad \square$$

A particular field or σ-field $\mathcal{F}$ is defined by specifying that it contains a certain collection of sets, say $\mathcal{C}$. The other elements of $\mathcal{F}$ are then defined by the rules of membership. $\mathcal{F}$ is said to be generated by $\mathcal{C}$, and may be written as $\mathcal{F}(\mathcal{C})$.

B.2 Probability

Probability is the standard mathematical framework for analysing sample data in situations where outcomes cannot be predicted with certainty. When a coin is tossed we cannot predict whether heads or tails will come up, but we believe that approximately half of a large number of tosses will be heads. Formally, we believe that (if the coin is fair) the ratio of the number of heads to the number of tosses will approach $\frac{1}{2}$ as the number of tosses tends to infinity. The *probability of heads* is a constant parameter associated with the coin-tossing experiment, and is assigned the value of $\frac{1}{2}$. However, since only a finite number of tosses can be made in finite time, the probability cannot be determined experimentally and has no objective reality. It is merely an idealised mathematical description of 'typical' behaviour in actual coin-tossing experiments. We use this mathematical model because it works well in practice, and we do not have to worry about deeper meanings unless we choose to. An alternative to this *frequentist* notion of probability is to regard it as a psychological construct, as describing an observer's *degree of belief* in the outcome.

Formally, the probabilistic model of a random experiment has three ingredients: the sample space Ω, the set of all the possible outcomes of the experiment (the universal set for this analysis); a σ-field of events $\mathcal{F}$ (subsets of Ω); and a probability measure P, that is, a function attaching a real number from the interval $[0,1]$ to each element of $\mathcal{F}$. $\mathcal{F}$ must be a σ-field to be sure that $P(A)$ is well-defined for each member of such a set. There are technical difficulties with showing this for more general collections. To be a probability measure, P must satisfy the *probability axioms:*

Definition B.2.1 The set function $P : \mathcal{F} \longmapsto [0,1]$ is a probability measure on the space $(\Omega, \mathcal{F})$ if

(a) $P(A) \geq 0$ for all $A \in \mathcal{F}$

(b) $P(\Omega) = 1$

(c) If $A_1, A_2, A_3, \ldots$ is a countably infinite collection of *disjoint* sets of $\mathcal{F}$, such that $A_1 \cap A_j = \emptyset$ whenever $i \neq j$, then $P(\bigcup_i A_i) = \sum_i P(A_i)$. □

The triple of objects $(\Omega, \mathcal{F}, P)$ defines a probability space. For example, in the case of the coin tossing experiment the probabilistic setup is fully described by the following designations:

$$\Omega = (H, T)$$
$$\mathcal{F} = \{\Omega, \{H\}, \{T\}, \emptyset\}$$
$$P(H) = \tfrac{1}{2}.$$

We can deduce from the probability axioms that $P(T) = 1 - P(H) = \frac{1}{2}$.

Taking just the pair of objects $(\Omega, \mathcal{F})$ defines a measurable space, one on which a probability measure can be defined. In the example, having $P(H) = \frac{5}{8}$ (a biased coin) would define a different probability model, but on the same measurable space as before.

B.3 Random Variables

The elements of Ω can be anything whatever; faces of a coin, poker hands, the points on the target at a rifle range, or whatever form a random experiment may take. In practice, observed outcomes are often quantified, which means that a mapping $X : \Omega \mapsto \mathbb{R}$ is defined.

For example, if 'the economy' is a point in a probability space, a particular outcome $\omega \in \Omega$ may specify that John Smith and Jane Jones (among others) have jobs, but Albert Brown and Alice White (among others) do not. This information is held on the computer at the Department of Social Security, but it is not typically in an economic researcher's database. This is more likely to contain a summary statistic, the unemployment rate for the economy as a whole. The set of manipulations and rules used by the statistical agency to reduce the employment status of every economic agent down to a single number is a mapping having Ω as domain, and the real numbers as the codomain. Here, $X(\omega) \in \mathbb{R}$ denotes the unemployment rate corresponding to a particular economic outcome ω.

The key question is whether this mapping generates a *derived* probability space on the real numbers, taking the form $(\mathbb{R}, \mathcal{B}, \mu)$, where $\mathcal{B}$ denotes the *Borel field* of $\mathbb{R}$, and μ is a probability measure on $\mathcal{B}$. $\mathcal{B}$ is defined as the smallest σ-field of $\mathbb{R}$ that contains all the *half-lines*, the sets of the form $(-\infty, x]$ for $x \in \mathbb{R}$. If for every $B \in \mathcal{B}$ there exists a set of $A \in \mathcal{F}$ such that $X(A) = B$, the function X is said to be *measurable* (or more precisely, $\mathcal{F}/\mathcal{B}$-measurable). A *random variable* (r.v.) is a measurable mapping from a probability space to the real line. It defines a derived probability space, since for every $B \in \mathcal{B}$ one can assign $\mu(B) = P(X^{-1}(B))$, knowing by measurability that $X^{-1}(B) \in \mathcal{F}$.

Applying the definition of a σ-field and the rules of set algebra, consider what sorts of sets $\mathcal{B}$ contains. By de Morgan's laws it must contain the half-open intervals $(x_1, x_2]$ for $x_1 < x_2$ (intersections of half lines). It also contains the open half lines, sets of the form $(-\infty, x)$ for $x \in \mathbb{R}$, because

$$(-\infty,\ x) = \bigcup_{n=1}^{\infty} (-\infty,\ x - 1/n] \tag{B.3.1}$$

where all the sets of the countable union are in $\mathcal{B}$. It therefore contains all open intervals, and also the singleton sets

$$(-\infty,\ x] \cap (-\infty,\ x)^c = \{x\} \tag{B.3.2}$$

for any $x \in \mathbb{R}$. Also, any sets that can be formed from finite or countably infinite unions, intersections and complements of these sets. This is quite a rich enough collection for our needs.

In the employment example, the unemployment rate is a percentage so that $0 \le X(\omega) \le 100$ for every $\omega \in \Omega$. It is sufficient just to say that $\mu([0, 100]) = 1$, and when this condition holds the set $[0, 100]$ is called the *support* of X. However, an alternative is to define the derived probability space as $([0, 100], \mathcal{B}_{[0,100]}, \mu)$, where $\mathcal{B}_{[0,100]}$ is the collection whose elements are $B \cap [0, 100]$ for each $B \in \mathcal{B}$. These two formulations are effectively equivalent.

Although conceptually random variables are derived from some underlying probability space that need not have a numerical character, in practical applications this aspect tends to be neglected. One proceeds by formulating some analytically tractable hypothesis about the form of μ, which it is hoped will reflect the nature of the underlying P. Distribution theory deals with the problems of assigning and then manipulating probability measures on the line.

Most distributions are either continuous or discrete. A discrete r.v. takes at most a countably infinite number of possible values $x_1, x_2, x_3, \ldots$ and the distribution is specified by assigning probabilities to each one, i.e.,

$$p(x_i) = P(X = x_i) > 0 \quad i = 1, 2, 3, \ldots \tag{B.3.3}$$

$$\textstyle\sum_i p(x_i) = 1. \tag{B.3.4}$$

A continuous r.v. X, by contrast, can take any real value. Its distribution is defined by a ***probability density function*** (p.d.f.), a function $f(x) \ge 0$ normalized so that

$$\int_{-\infty}^{+\infty} f(x)dx = 1 \tag{B.3.5}$$

with the property

$$\int_a^b f(x)dx = P(a \le X \le b). \tag{B.3.6}$$

When the distribution is continuous, $P(X = x) = 0$ for any specific x. Thus, $P(a \le X \le b) = P(a < X < b)$, and either of these expressions would be valid in (B.3.6). A third class of distribution in the mixed continuous-discrete case in which the variable is continuously distributed *except* at a finite or countable set of points, where it has positive probability. Such points are called *atoms* of the distribution. As an example of this type, consider the Tobit distribution of commodity demands where the probability of zero demands is positive, but the distribution of positive demands is treated as continuous (see §11.2.5).

The *cumulative distribution function* (c.d.f.) of a r.v. is the non-decreasing function of a real variable defined as

$$F(a) = P(X \le a). \tag{B.3.7}$$

Thus, $P(a < X \le b) = F(b) - F(a)$ and in particular $F(-\infty) = 0$ and $F(\infty) = 1$. The three important special cases are

$$F(a) = \int_{-\infty}^{a} f(x)dx \qquad \text{(continuous case)} \tag{B.3.8a}$$

$$F(a) = \sum_{-\infty < x_i \le a} p(x_i) \qquad \text{(discrete case)} \tag{B.3.8b}$$

$$F(a) = \int_{-\infty}^{a} f(x)dx + \sum_{-\infty < x_i \le a} p(x_i) \qquad \text{(mixed case).} \tag{B.3.8c}$$

F and μ are equivalent representations of the distribution. F assigns a probability to every half-line, $(-\infty, x]$, and the probability axioms allow probabilities derived from F to be consistently assigned to every set of $\mathcal{B}$. These assignments must agree with $\mu(B)$ for every $B \in \mathcal{B}$.

In (B.3.8c), the set $\{x_i,\ i = 1, 2, 3 \ldots\}$ are the atoms of the distribution and by implication, f is a nonnegative function with the property

$$\int_{-\infty}^{+\infty} f(x)dx = 1 - \sum_i p(x_i). \tag{B.3.9}$$

Since the atoms make a contribution of zero to the integral with respect to f, there is no need to delete these points from the domain of integration. In fact, since the value of f is arbitrary at these points, the mixed distribution can be defined by a single function, say

$$p(x) = \begin{cases} p(x_i), & x = x_i \\ f(x), & \text{otherwise.} \end{cases} \tag{B.3.10}$$

This is done implicitly when the likelihood function for a mixed distribution is constructed, see (11.2.29) for example.

B.4 Expectations

The expectation (or expected value) of an r.v. X, denoted $E(X)$, represents mathematically the central tendency of the distribution of X, giving a precise meaning to intuitive notions such as the 'average', or 'typical value'. It is not the only such representation. The *median*, defined as M such that

$$P(-\infty < x \le M) = \tfrac{1}{2} \tag{B.4.1}$$

and the *mode*, defined in the continuous case as the maximum of f, are well-known alternatives. However, for one reason or another $E(\cdot)$ is the measure of location used most often in probability.

Begin with an easy case. A *simple random variable* is a random variable assuming at most a finite number of different values, $x_1, \dots, x_n$, with probabilities p_i such that $\sum_{i=1}^n p_i = 1$.[1] In terms of the parent probability space $(\Omega, \mathcal{F}, P)$, this implies a partition of Ω into sets $A_1, \dots A_n$, with $A_i \in \mathcal{F}$ for each i, $A_i \cap A_j = \emptyset$ when $i \neq j$, and $\bigcup_{i=1}^n A_i = \Omega$, such that $X(\omega) = x_i$ when $\omega \in A_i$, and $p_i = P(A_i)$. In this case the expectation is

$$E(X) = \sum_{i=1}^n x_i p_i. \tag{B.4.2}$$

The extension to general *nonnegative* X depends on the fundamental result that such an X can be approximated arbitrarily well by a simple r.v., with n taken large enough. Approximating X 'from below' leads to the formal definition:

$$E(X) = \sup_{\phi < X}\left\{\sum_i \phi_i P(A_i)\right\} \tag{B.4.3}$$

where ϕ denotes any simple r.v. assuming values $\phi(\omega) = \phi_i$ for $\omega \in A_i$ for $i = 1, \dots, n$ for finite n, and $\phi(\omega) < X(\omega)$ for all $\omega \in \Omega$. By implication, the supremum over all these alternatives may have $n = \infty$. Mathematically, the expression in (B.4.3) defines the integral of the function $X(\omega)$ with respect to the measure P. $E(X) = \infty$ is a possible value according to (B.4.3), if the probabilities assigned to large values of X are sufficiently large.

The extension to general X (taking either sign) is done by treating the nonnegative and negative parts of X separately. Write $X^+ = \max(X, 0)$, and $X^- = X^+ - X$ (both nonnegative functions) and define $E(X) = E(X^+) - E(X^-)$. In this case $E(X)$ can fail to exist, since it is possible that the $E(X^+) = \infty$ and $E(X^-) = -\infty$ and the difference is undefined. This possibility is ruled out if both positive and negative parts are finite, or equivalently, since $|X| = X^+ + X^-$, if

$$E|X| < \infty. \tag{B.4.4}$$

This is the *integrability* condition.

---

[1] This is not the same thing as a discrete r.v., since the latter may take a (countably) infinite number of values.

An interesting feature of the definition of $E(\cdot)$ is that it does not depend on values of the random variable that occur with probability zero. This is closely connected to the important notion of an 'almost sure' event. We say that $C \in \mathcal{F}$ occurs almost surely (abbreviated as a.s.) if $P(C) = 1$, and accordingly, $P(C^c) = 0$. For example, in a continuous distribution, any individual point of the line has probability 0, and two continuous random variables that are equal except at a countably infinite number of points are equal almost surely, and have the same expectation.

$E(X)$ is sometimes written in the form

$$E(X) = \int_{\Omega} X dP \tag{B.4.5}$$

where the integral sign conveys the notion of the limiting sum in (B.4.3). However, in view of the mapping of probabilities from sets of $\mathcal{F}$ to sets of $\mathcal{B}$ through the relations $B = X(A)$, with $\mu(B) = P(A)$, the expectation can also be constructed as an integral on the line. An alternative to (B.4.5) is the *Lebesgue–Stieltjes integral* of x on $\mathbb{R}$, with respect to the c.d.f. of X, or[2]

$$E(X) = \int_{-\infty}^{+\infty} x dF(x). \tag{B.4.6}$$

Expressions (B.4.5) and (B.4.6) are merely alternative representations of the same thing, but formula (B.4.6) is useful in practice when the distribution of X is defined in terms of F. Only by formulae such as these could one actually *compute* $E(X)$. The special forms corresponding to (B.3.8) are

$$\int_{-\infty}^{+\infty} x dF = \begin{cases} \int_{-\infty}^{+\infty} x f(x) dx & \text{(continuous case)} \\ \sum_i x_i p(x_i) & \text{(discrete case)} \\ \int_{-\infty}^{+\infty} x f(x) dx + \sum_i x_i p(x_i) & \text{(mixed case).} \end{cases} \tag{B.4.7}$$

In the mixed case the integral is taken over the whole line so that the points $\{x_1, x_2, \dots\}$ are apparently double counted, but this fact can be neglected because, as noted, these points have total probability 0 under f.

X is just a particular measurable function $\Omega \mapsto \mathbb{R}$, and the expectations of other such functions are formed in the same manner. The simple r.v.

$$1_A(\omega) = \begin{cases} 1, & \omega \in A \\ 0, & \omega \notin A \end{cases} \qquad A \in \mathcal{F} \tag{B.4.8}$$

is called the *indicator function* of the set A, and this device unifies the notions of probability and expectation. If $B = X(A) \in \mathcal{B}$ (the set of points x such that $x = X(\omega)$ for some $\omega \in A$) then

$$P(A) = \int_A dP = \int 1_A dP = E(1_A) = \int_B dF = \mu(B) \tag{B.4.9}$$

[2] The regular Lebesgue integral is the case where $dF(x) = dx$.

six equivalent ways of writing down the probability of A. For the three special cases, the Lebesgue–Stieltjes integral takes the forms

$$\int_B dF = \begin{cases} \int_B f(x)dx & \text{(continuous case)} \\ \sum_{x_i \in B} p(x_i) & \text{(discrete case)} \\ \int_B f(x)dx + \sum_{x_i \in B} p(x_i) & \text{(mixed case)} \end{cases} \tag{B.4.10}$$

By letting $B = \{x : x \leq a\}$ these formulae yield the c.d.f. in (B.3.8). While the first of the formulae in (B.4.10) superficially resembles the integrals studied in elementary calculus, the rationale and method of construction is entirely different. The latter are defined only for intervals of $\mathbb{R}$, whereas the sets B may be much more general than intervals. To take an extreme example, let B represent the set $\mathbb{Q}$ of rational numbers, the numbers of the form a/b for a and b integers, $b \neq 0$. $\mathbb{Q}$ is a countable set of points of $\mathbb{R}$, and hence is in $\mathcal{B}$. For the continuous (atomless) case the Lebesgue integral in (B.4.10) evaluates to 0, since the probability of a countable union of points is the sum of the probabilities of each point, all zero in this case.

A function $g : \mathbb{R} \mapsto \mathbb{R}$ is said to be *Borel measurable* if $g(X)$ is a random variable whenever X is. This requires that $g^{-1}(B) \in \mathcal{B}$ whenever $B \in \mathcal{B}$. For Borel measurable g (subject to integrability)

$$E[g(X)] = \int g dF. \tag{B.4.11}$$

Consider for example the variance of X,

$$\text{Var}(X) = E[X - E(X)]^2 = E(X^2) - E(X)^2 \tag{B.4.12}$$

(verify the second equality). More generally, the rth *moments* of the distribution about the mean $\mu = E(X)$ (where they exist) are

$$E(X - \mu)^r \quad r = 2, 3, \ldots \tag{B.4.13}$$

The moments are a useful device for summarizing the characteristics of a distribution. For example, if this is *symmetric*, such that $P(X \geq \mu + \varepsilon) = P(X \leq \mu - \varepsilon)$ for every $\varepsilon \geq 0$, all odd-order moments about μ are zero.

If a r.v. is nonnegative it can be raised to the power of a real variable. The expectations of $|X|$ raised to positive powers are another useful device for summarizing the characteristics of a distribution, by placing a bound on the tail probabilities. For any $\varepsilon > 0$ and $p > 0$,

$$\begin{aligned} P(|X - \mu| > \varepsilon) &= \int_{\{|x-\mu|>\varepsilon\}} dF(x) \\ &\leq \int_{\{|x-\mu|>\varepsilon\}} \frac{|x - \mu|^p}{\varepsilon^p} dF(x) \leq \frac{E|X - \mu|^p}{\varepsilon^p}. \end{aligned} \tag{B.4.14}$$

The higher the order of absolute moments that are finite, the smaller the probability that the distribution will throw up 'outliers'. Inequality (B.4.14) is known as the *Markov inequality* and also for the case $r = 2$ as the *Chebyshev inequality.*

The quantities

$$\|X\|_p = (E|X|^p)^{1/p} \quad p \geq 1 \tag{B.4.15}$$

are called the L_p-norms of X (L stands for Lebesgue). The motivation for taking the pth root of the pth absolute moment in this definition is provided by the following useful inequalities. The *Liapunov inequality* states that if $0 < p \leq q$, then

$$\|X\|_p \leq \|X\|_q. \tag{B.4.16}$$

Also, if X and Y are two random variables, *Minkowski's inequality* is

$$\|X+Y\|_p \leq \|X\|_p + \|Y\|_p \tag{B.4.17}$$

for all $p \geq 1$. For the case $p = 1$ the Minkowski inequality is better known as the *triangle inequality*,

$$E|X+Y| \leq E|X| + E|Y|. \tag{B.4.18}$$

The latter inequality in particular is easily proved, because the triangle inequality $|x+y| < |x| + |y|$ is a basic property of real numbers x and y. The Minkowski inequality can be iterated to permit statements of the form

$$\left\|\sum_i X_i\right\|_p \leq \sum_i \|X_i\|_p \tag{B.4.19}$$

where the number of terms in the sum may be finite or infinite.

Jensen's inequality is a fundamental result on the transformation of expected values. If $\phi(\cdot)$ is a convex function over the support of a random variable X, then

$$E[\phi(X)] \geq \phi(E[X]) \tag{B.4.20}$$

assuming the expectations in question are well-defined. Two useful cases are

$$E|X| \geq |E(X)| \tag{B.4.21}$$

which is the *modulus inequality*, and

$$E(X^2) \geq E(X)^2 \tag{B.4.22}$$

which says that variances cannot be negative. The inequality is reversed for concave functions. For example, a positive r.v. X satisfies

$$E\log(X) \leq \log E(X). \tag{B.4.23}$$

When the convexity/concavity is strict the inequalities are strict, unless X is a constant with probability 1.

One other useful trick with expectations should be mentioned here.

Theorem B.4.1 If:

(a) for fixed real θ, $g(\theta)$ is an integrable random variable;

(b) for almost all ω in the sample space,[3] $g(\theta,\omega)$ is a function of θ, differentiable at the point θ_0, with

$$\frac{|g(\theta_0+h,\omega)-g(\theta_0,\omega)|}{h}\leq d(\omega) \tag{B.4.24}$$

for all h in an open neighbourhood of 0 not depending on ω, where d is an integrable random variable;

then

$$E\left(\left.\frac{dg}{d\theta}\right|_{\theta=\theta_0}\right)=\left.\frac{dE(g)}{d\theta}\right|_{\theta=\theta_0}. \quad \square \tag{B.4.25}$$

For the proof, see Davidson (1994a) Theorem 9.31, and also see, for example, Apostol (1974) Section 7.24 for the case of general Riemann-Stieltjes integrals. This is called differentiation under the integral sign, an essential step in various derivations in estimation theory. It extends to partial derivatives of functions of several variables in the obvious way.

B.5 Joint Distributions

A random pair X,Y is a measurable mapping from Ω to a point in the plane $\mathbb{R}^2$. To define a suitable framework for distributions on the plane, consider any pair of sets $A\in\mathcal{B}$ and $B\in\mathcal{B}$. The subset of $\mathbb{R}^2$ containing the pairs (x,y) such that $x\in A$ and $y\in B$ is called the *Cartesian product* of the sets, written $A\times B$. These product sets are called the *measurable rectangles.* For example, they include the ordinary rectangles $(a,b]\times(c,d]$ where $(a,b]$ and $(c,d]$ are intervals of the line. Let $\mathcal{B}^2$ denote the smallest σ-field that contains all the measurable rectangles. This is the Borel field of $\mathbb{R}^2$, and the triple $(\mathbb{R}^2,\mathcal{B}^2,\mu)$, where μ is a suitable probability measure, defines a probability space, the generalization to two dimensions of $(\mathbb{R},\mathcal{B},\mu)$.

The c.d.f.

$$F(x,y)=P(X\leq x,Y\leq y) \tag{B.5.1}$$

again provides an alternative representation of μ, and can be used to generate probabilities of sets in $\mathcal{B}^2$. Given a Borel-measurable integrable function $g:\mathbb{R}^2\mapsto\mathbb{R}$, the expected value is

$$E[g(X,Y)]=\int_{\mathbb{R}^2}g(x,y)dF(x,y). \tag{B.5.2}$$

In particular, for $a\in\mathbb{R}$ define the set

$$B_a=\{(x,y),-\infty<x<+\infty,-\infty<y\leq a\}\in\mathcal{B}^2. \tag{B.5.3}$$

[3] That is, for all ω in a set $C\subseteq\Omega$ where $P(C)=1$.

The *marginal distribution* of X, corresponding to the usual univariate c.d.f., is defined by the function

$$F_X(a) = \int_{\mathbb{R}^2} 1_{B_a}(x,y)dF(x,y). \tag{B.5.4}$$

Ordinary (Riemann) multiple integrals with respect to two or more variables are usually thought of as being formed iteratively. In other words, one integrates first in the y direction (say), then in the x direction. However, multiple Lebesgue-Stieltjes integrals are defined on the underlying probability space, as in (B.4.5), and should formally be treated as cases of formula (B.4.3) where the sets $A_i \in \Omega$ are mapped into sets from $\mathcal{B}^2$ by the distribution. Iterated integration is justified in certain cases by the fundamental result known as *Fubini's theorem*, which states that a double integral with respect to a *product measure* may be evaluated iteratively. This is the case where $dF(x,y)$ can be factorized as (say) $dF_X(x)dF_Y(y)$. Integrating an arbitrary $\mathcal{B}^2/\mathcal{B}$-measurable integrable function $g(X,Y)$ with respect to dF_Y yields a $\mathcal{B}/\mathcal{B}$-measurable integrable function, $\int gdF_Y$, whose integral with respect to F_X equals $E[g(X,Y)]$. One important case where iterative evaluation is legitimate is the continuous distribution, because in that case one can write

$$E[g(X,Y)] = \int_{-\infty}^{+\infty}\Big(\int_{-\infty}^{+\infty} g(x,y)f(x,y)dy\Big)dx. \tag{B.5.5}$$

Here the product measure is the Lebesgue measure $dxdy$, and Fubini's theorem applies since integrating $g(x,y)$ with respect to $f(x,y)dxdy$ is equivalent to integrating $g(x,y)f(x,y)$ with respect to Lebesgue product measure.[4]

Consider the mixed continuous-discrete class of distributions, which contains the pure discrete and pure continuous as special cases. These distributions may feature countable sets of points, $\Delta_x = \{x_i,\ i = 1,2,\dots\}$ and $\Delta_y = \{y_j,\ j = 1,2,\dots\}$, occurring with positive probability, while being continuously distributed at other points. One of the sets may be empty, as in the case of a discrete Y paired with a continuous X, say, but if both are nonempty, there is also a set of points of $\mathbb{R}^2$ having positive probability. Define this as

$$\Delta_{xy} = \{(x_k, y_k),\ k = 1,2,\dots\} \subseteq \Delta_x \times \Delta_y \tag{B.5.6}$$

though be careful to note that Δ_{xy} is not *equal* to $\Delta_x \times \Delta_y$ in general.

One can represent these distributions by defining a function $p(x,y)$ that represents either a probability or density, depending on the point of evaluation.[5] In particular, the marginal distributions have the form

$$p_X(x) = \int_{-\infty}^{+\infty} p(x,y)dy + \sum_j p(x,y_j) \tag{B.5.7}$$

[4]The other main case of valid iteration is where the variables are independent, see §B.7.

[5]The conditioning concept discussed in §B.6 is needed to describe the construction of p explicitly.

(say), where the summation is over points $y_j \in \Delta_y$. At points $x = x_i \in \Delta_x$, p_X represents the marginal probability of x_i, but for points $x \notin \Delta_x$ it is the marginal density. If Y is purely discrete the first term in (B.5.7) is zero, and if Y is purely continuous the second term is zero. With this set-up, the generalization of (B.5.5) (omitting the limits of the integrals for brevity) is

$$\begin{aligned} E[g(X,Y)] &= \int g(x,y)dF(x,y) \\ &= \int\int g(x,y)p(x,y)dxdy + \sum_j \int g(x,y_j)p(x,y_j)dx \\ &\quad + \sum_i \int g(x_i,y)p(x_i,y)dy + \sum_k g(x_k,y_k)p(x_k,y_k) \end{aligned} \tag{B.5.8}$$

where the summations over i, j and k correspond to the elements of Δ_y, Δ_x and Δ_{xy} respectively. The expression in the right-hand member of (B.5.8) is a complete representation of the distribution, because any probability can be represented by making g the indicator function of the relevant set in $\mathcal{B}^2$. For example, by setting $g = 1_A$ for $A = \{x, y : x \leq a,\ y \leq b\}$, the expectation yields $F(a, b)$ itself. In the continuous case it reduces to (B.5.5), and in the purely discrete case, only the last of the four terms appears. As in (B.4.7), there is no problem of double counting in the integrals because the points at which $p(x, y)$ does not represent a density have zero Lebesgue measure in $\mathbb{R}^2$.

Leading examples of the function $g(x, y)$ in (B.5.2) are x, x^2, y and y^2, leading to definitions of the means and variances of X and Y. In addition, put $g(x, y) = xy$ to define the *covariance*,

$$\mathrm{Cov}(X,Y) = E[X - E(X)][Y - E(Y)] = E(XY) - E(X)E(Y). \tag{B.5.9}$$

Again, the reader should verify the equivalence of these two forms.

The *Cauchy–Schwarz inequality* is

$$E(XY)^2 \leq E(X^2)E(Y^2). \tag{B.5.10}$$

This follows because for any constant a,

$$a^2E(X^2) + 2aE(XY) + E(Y^2) = E[(aX + Y)^2] \geq 0 \tag{B.5.11}$$

and (B.5.10) follows directly on setting $a = -E(XY)/E(X^2)$. Applying the inequality to the centred r.v.s. $X - E(X)$ and $Y - E(Y)$, the *correlation coefficient*

$$\rho_{XY} = \frac{\mathrm{Cov}(X,Y)}{\sqrt{\mathrm{Var}(X)\,\mathrm{Var}(Y)}} \tag{B.5.12}$$

is seen always to lie between +1 and −1.

The Cauchy–Schwarz inequality is a special case (for $p = q = 2$) of the *Hölder inequality*, which is as follows. Let X and Y be two random variables, and let $p > 1$ and $q > 1$ be two numbers such that $1/p + 1/q = 1$. (In other words, $q = p/(p-1)$.) Then

$$E|XY| \leq \|X\|_p \|Y\|_q \tag{B.5.13}$$

where $\|\cdot\|_p$ is defined in (B.4.15). This is an adaptation to the probabilistic setting of an inequality that holds for arbitrary integrals including finite sums. Thus, arbitrary pairs of real numbers (a_j, b_j), $j = 1, \ldots, n$, obey the inequality

$$\left|\sum_{j=1}^{n} a_j b_j\right| \leq \left(\sum_{j=1}^{n} |a_j|^p\right)^{1/p} \left(\sum_{j=1}^{n} |b_j|^q\right)^{1/q}. \tag{B.5.14}$$

B.6 Conditional Expectations

From the viewpoint of subjective probability, consider the problem of modelling a bivariate random experiment in which the random variables (X, Y) are revealed to an observer sequentially, first X and later Y. If $E(Y)$ represents the observer's forecast of Y before the experiment begins, then $E(Y|x)$ might be defined to represent her forecast of Y after the occurrence of the event $\{X = x\}$ is revealed. It appears reasonable to construct conditional distributions $Y|x$, which reflect the dependence between the random variables.

Consider initially the continuous case. Given the joint distribution of the pair (X, Y), the conditional p.d.f. of $Y|x$ may be defined by

$$f(y|x) = \frac{f(y, x)}{f_X(x)}. \tag{B.6.1}$$

Note that with x fixed, this function integrates to unity with respect to the argument y and is therefore a p.d.f. The expectation is accordingly

$$E(Y|x) = \int_{-\infty}^{+\infty} y f(y|x) dy. \tag{B.6.2}$$

To see how these functions are constructed for the Gaussian case, see §C.2.

To generalize this concept to the discrete and mixed continuous-discrete cases, factor the function in (B.5.8) as $p(x, y) = p(y|x)p_X(x)$, where p_X is defined in (B.5.7), and write

$$E(Y|x) = \int_{-\infty}^{+\infty} y p(y|x) dy + \sum_j y_j p(y_j|x). \tag{B.6.3}$$

This formula can be constructed whenever $p_X(x) > 0$, whether this represents a density or the probability of $x \in \Delta_x$. In the latter case, note that for $y_j \in \Delta_y$, $p(y_j|x_i) > 0$ if and only if $(x_i, y_j) \in \Delta_{xy}$. The formation of $p(x, y)$ becomes transparent under this decomposition. It is constructed as the product of two factors representing discrete, continuous or mixed univariate distributions, where the conditional factor depends in general on x.

Prior to observing X, the observer can be imagined to assign a distribution to the conditional predictions of Y that will be made after observing it. This means treating $E(Y|x)$ as a drawing from a distribution derived from that of X, and so defining a random variable, denoted $E(Y|X)$. When it exists this is a measurable function of X, although note that $E(Y|X)$ is well-defined only when Y is integrable, as in (B.4.4).

A fundamental property is the *law of iterated expectations* (LIE), which is as follows.

Theorem B.6.1 Letting $E_X(\cdot)$ denote the expectation under $F_X(\cdot)$,

$$E_X[E(Y|X)] = E(Y). \quad \square \tag{B.6.4}$$

Consider the mixed continuous-discrete class. Integrating (B.6.3) with respect to p_X yields

$$\begin{aligned} E_X[E(Y|X)] &= \int\left(\int yp(y|x)dy + \sum_j y_j p(y_j|x)\right)p_X(x)dx \\ &\quad + \sum_i\left(\int yp(y|x_i)dy + \sum_j y_j p(y_j|x_i)\right)p_X(x_i) \\ &= \int\int yp(x,y)dxdy + \int\sum_j y_j p(x,y_j)dx \\ &\quad + \sum_i \int yp(x_i,y)dy + \sum_k y_k p(x_k,y_k) = E(Y) \end{aligned} \tag{B.6.5}$$

from (B.5.8). The key step here is to apply the fact noted above, that $p(y_j|x_i) > 0$ in the final term only in the cases where (x_i, y_j) is an atom of the joint distribution. In this case the pair may be labelled by k, corresponding to a member of the set Δ_{xy} defined in (B.5.6).

The LIE has numerous applications in econometrics, and a number of useful corollaries. For example,

Corollary B.6.1 If $E(Y|X) = E(Y)$ (a constant not depending on X) then

$$\text{Cov}[Y, h(X)] = 0 \tag{B.6.6}$$

for all Borel-measurable, integrable functions $h(\cdot)$.

Proof $\text{Cov}[Y, h(X)] = E[Yh(X)] - E(Y)E[h(X)]$. However,

$$E[Yh(X)] = E_X[E(Yh(X)|X)] = E_X[E(Y|X)h(X)] = E(Y)E[h(X)] \tag{B.6.7}$$

by the LIE. ■

Notice how, in this argument, the random variable X is treated as if it were fixed for manipulations involving the conditional distribution; the conditional expectation has the usual linear property, $E[Yh(x)|x] = E(Y|x)h(x)$ for each x.

Another useful corollary of the LIE is that $E(Y|X)$ is the best predictor of Y when X is observed, in the mean squared error sense.

Corollary B.6.2 For every Borel-measurable, integrable function ϕ,

$$E[Y - E(Y|X)]^2 \leq E[Y - \phi(X)]^2. \tag{B.6.8}$$

Proof Substitute and multiply out:

$$\begin{aligned}E[Y-\phi(X)]^2 &= E[(Y-E(Y|X))+(E(Y|X)-\phi(X))]^2\\ &= E[Y-E(Y|X)]^2+2E[(Y-E(Y|X))(E(Y|X)-\phi(X)]\\ &\quad + E[E(Y|X)-\phi(X)]^2 \qquad \text{(B.6.9)}\end{aligned}$$

Put $h(X)=E(Y|X)-\phi(X)$ (a function of X alone) and then the LIE gives

$$E[(Y-E(Y|X))h(X)] = E[(E(Y|X)-E(Y|X))h(X)] = E(0) = 0 \qquad \text{(B.6.10)}$$

since $h(X)$ can be held conditionally fixed. The result now follows in view of the fact that $E[E(Y|X)-\phi(X)]^2$ is minimized when $\phi(X)=E(Y|X)$. ∎

Although straightforward from an intuitive point of view, the constructive approach to conditioning given here presents some theoretical difficulties. The conditional expectation has been constructed, in effect, by the first step of the iterated integration of the random variable Y. In the jointly continuous case, Fubini's theorem assures us that, when x is sampled from the distribution f_X, (B.6.2) yields a well defined integrable random variable, obeying the LIE. However, outside the case of product measures there is no *general* result to this effect. It is therefore difficult to develop a general theory of conditioning from the present approach. In §B.10 an alternative, abstract approach is introduced, that defines conditioning information at the level of the underlying probability space, and resolves the measurability difficulties inherent in the constructive approach. It allows problems involving three or more variables to be easily considered, as well as extensions that cannot even be envisaged in the present framework.

B.7 Independence

If the joint distribution of X and Y is a product probability measure, such that the c.d.f. factorizes as

$$F(x,y) = F_X(x)F_Y(y) \qquad \text{(B.7.1)}$$

the variables are said to be independent. If $B_1 \in \mathcal{B}$ and $B_2 \in \mathcal{B}$, then $B_1 \times B_2 \in \mathcal{B}^2$ and (B.7.1) is equivalent to the condition that $\mu(B_1 \times B_2) = \mu_X(B_1)\mu_Y(B_2)$ where μ_x and μ_Y are the marginal measures corresponding to F_x and F_Y. For the continuous and discrete cases, respectively, this implies that

$$f(x,y) = f_X(x)f_Y(y) \qquad \text{(B.7.2)}$$

$$p(x,y) = p_X(x)p_Y(y) \qquad \text{(B.7.3)}$$

for any pair $(x,y) \in \mathbb{R}^2$. In view of (B.7.3), if $p_X(x_i) > 0$ and $p_Y(y_j) > 0$ the pair (x_i, y_j) must be an atom of the joint distribution, and therefore $\Delta_{xy} = \Delta_x \times \Delta_y$ in (B.5.6). Iterated integration is generally permissible by Fubini's theorem, and equation (B.5.8) can be written as.

$$E[g(X,Y)] = \int\left(\int g(x,y)p_Y(y)dy + \sum_j g(x,y_j)p_Y(y_j)\right)p_X(x)dx$$

$$+\sum_i\Big(\int g(x_i,y)p_Y(y)dy+\sum_j g(x_i,y_j)p_Y(y_j)\Big)p_X(x_i)$$

$$=\int\Big(\int g(x,y)dF_Y(y)\Big)\,dF_X(x). \tag{B.7.4}$$

One way to appreciate the implications of independence is to note that conditional distributions are independent of the conditioning variables, and hence equal to the marginal distributions. Since $p(y|x)=p_Y(y)$ in (B.6.3) this implies

$$E(Y|x)=E(Y) \tag{B.7.5}$$

which formalizes the notion that one variable of an independent pair cannot help to predict the other. A further useful implication in the same vein is the following.

Theorem B.7.1 If X and Y are independent, $\text{Cov}(g(X),h(Y))=0$ for all Borel-measurable integrable functions g and h.

Proof Applying Fubini's Theorem,

$$\begin{aligned}E[g(X)h(Y)] &= \int\int g(x)h(y)dF_X(x)dF_Y(y)\\ &= \int g(x)dF_X(x)\int h(y)dF_Y(y).\\ &= E[g(X)]E[h(Y)] \quad \blacksquare\end{aligned} \tag{B.7.6}$$

In particular, $\text{Cov}(X,Y)=0$, so that independence implies uncorrelatedness; but uncorrelatedness does not imply independence. Comparing Theorem B.7.1 with Corollary B.6.1 shows rather clearly the relationship between independence and unpredictability, in the sense of (B.7.5). Independence is a sufficient condition for the latter property, but not a necessary one.

B.8 Random Vectors

Most of the foregoing formulae for the bivariate distribution generalize to n-variate distributions. $(\mathbb{R}^n,\mathcal{B}^n,\mu)$ is probability space with typical element $\boldsymbol{x}=(X_1,\ldots,X_n)'$,[6] where $\mathbb{R}^n$ is Euclidean n-space and $\mathcal{B}^n$ the smallest σ-field of $\mathbb{R}^n$ containing the measurable rectangles $B_1\times\ldots\times B_n$, where $B_i\in\mathcal{B}$ for each i. The joint distribution is again represented by a c.d.f., a function F of n variables defined by

$$F(\boldsymbol{a})=P(\boldsymbol{x}\le\boldsymbol{a})\quad \boldsymbol{a}\in\mathbb{R}^n. \tag{B.8.1}$$

The formulae relating to continuous distributions generalize straightforwardly, allowing the definition of the joint p.d.f. as $f(\boldsymbol{x})$, and so forth, but otherwise the

[6] Here, we let the convention of denoting a vector by a lower case bold symbol and a matrix by an upper case bold symbol take precedence over the convention in probabilty of representing a random variable by an upper case letter, with values it assumes in lower case.

constructive approach, of extending (B.5.8), is clearly intractable in general. The c.d.f. can always be defined to represent the distribution, although the usual caveat about iterated integration applies.

The condition of *total independence* of the elements of x can be defined by the factoring condition

$$F(a_1, \ldots, a_n) = F_{X_1}(a_1) \cdots F_{X_n}(a_n). \qquad \text{(B.8.2)}$$

Pairwise independence of the elements of a random vector does not imply total independence. That is, the fact that

$$F_{X_i,X_j}(a_i, a_j) = F_{X_i}(a_i)F_{X_i}(a_j) \quad \forall\, i \neq j \qquad \text{(B.8.3)}$$

does not imply (B.8.2).

The expected value of $\boldsymbol{x}$ is the vector $E(\boldsymbol{x}) = (E(X_1), \ldots, E(X_n))'$, while the mean outer product matrix is

$$E(\boldsymbol{x}\boldsymbol{x}') = \begin{bmatrix} E(X_1^2) & E(X_1X_2) & \cdots & E(X_1X_n) \\ E(X_2X_1) & E(X_2^2) & & \vdots \\ \vdots & & \ddots & \\ E(X_nX_1) & \cdots & & E(X_n^2) \end{bmatrix} \qquad \text{(B.8.4)}$$

Thus, the *covariance matrix* of $\boldsymbol{x}$ is the symmetric, positive semi-definite matrix

$$\text{Var}(\boldsymbol{x}) = E[\boldsymbol{x} - E(\boldsymbol{x})][\boldsymbol{x} - E(\boldsymbol{x})]' = E(\boldsymbol{x}\boldsymbol{x}') - E(\boldsymbol{x})E(\boldsymbol{x})'. \qquad \text{(B.8.5)}$$

A useful formula is for the variance of a linear combination of elements. For any fixed n-vector $\boldsymbol{a}$,

$$\begin{aligned} \text{Var}(\boldsymbol{a}'\boldsymbol{x}) &= E(\boldsymbol{a}'\boldsymbol{x} - \boldsymbol{a}'E(\boldsymbol{x}))^2 \\ &= E[\boldsymbol{a}'(\boldsymbol{x} - E(\boldsymbol{x}))(\boldsymbol{x} - E(\boldsymbol{x}))'\boldsymbol{a}] \\ &= \boldsymbol{a}'\,\text{Var}(\boldsymbol{x})\boldsymbol{a}. \end{aligned} \qquad \text{(B.8.6)}$$

The conditioning concepts of §B.6 generalize straightforwardly to random vectors $\boldsymbol{y}$ and $\boldsymbol{x}$ when the distributions are jointly continuous. The conditional density $f(\boldsymbol{y}|\boldsymbol{x})$, the conditional expectation $E(\boldsymbol{y}|\boldsymbol{x})$, etc., can be defined in the obvious manner. However, the constructive approach of (B.6.3) for the case of general mixed distributions becomes excessively complex. For this reason, the abstract approach to be explored in §B.10 is generally more useful.

B.9 Change of Variable

Let $Y = g(X)$ be a scalar r.v. derived from a continuously distributed X where g is a one-to-one function, and let $h = g^{-1}$, such that $X = h(Y)$. In the discrete case where $P(X = x_i) = p(x_i)$ for $i = 1, 2, 3, \ldots$,

$$P(Y = y_i) = p^*(y_i) = p(h(y_i)). \qquad \text{(B.9.1)}$$

These probabilities assume the value 0 except at the points $y_i = g(x_i)$. In the continuous case, allowance must be made for effect of the transformation of the widths of intervals. Assume additionally that both g and h are differentiable. Being one-to-one, g is either monotonically increasing or monotonically decreasing everywhere, so its derivative is either positive everywhere or negative everywhere, and never zero.

Theorem B.9.1 If X is continuously distributed with p.d.f. $f(x)$, the p.d.f. of Y is given by

$$f^*(y) = f(h(y))\left|\frac{dh}{dy}\right|. \quad \square \tag{B.9.2}$$

Extending to multivariate distributions, consider a random n-vector $\boldsymbol{x}$, and let $\boldsymbol{g}$ represent an n-vector of differentiable one-to-one functions with differentiable inverse $\boldsymbol{h} = \boldsymbol{g}^{-1}$.

Theorem B.9.2 If $\boldsymbol{x}$ is continuously distributed with p.d.f. f, the p.d.f. of $\boldsymbol{y}$ is given by

$$f^*(\boldsymbol{y}) = f(\boldsymbol{h}(\boldsymbol{y}))|J| \tag{B.9.3}$$

where J is the Jacobian determinant,

$$J = \begin{vmatrix} \frac{\partial h_1}{\partial y_1} & \cdots & \frac{\partial h_1}{\partial y_n} \\ \vdots & \ddots & \vdots \\ \frac{\partial h_n}{\partial y_1} & \cdots & \frac{\partial h_n}{\partial y_n} \end{vmatrix} = \left|\frac{\partial \boldsymbol{h}}{\partial \boldsymbol{y}'}\right|. \quad \square \tag{B.9.4}$$

B.10 Conditioning on a Sigma-field

Except in the jointly continuous case, the constructive approach to conditioning of §B.6 rapidly becomes intractable when generalized to multivariate distributions, and has been shown to present theoretical difficulties. A more abstract line of attack, embodying some measure-theoretic ideas, allows a theory that applies to any distribution, and also extends the concept of partial knowledge in a flexible way, from simply knowing the value of one member of a random pair to a general notion of information, defined at the level of the underlying probability space $(\Omega, \mathcal{F}, P)$.

Thus, consider a subset of the random events, $\mathcal{G} \subseteq \mathcal{F}$. Partial information available to an observer of a random experiment can be represented by specifying that, for each $A \in \mathcal{G}$, she knows whether or not A has occurred (i.e. whether the outcome is in A). Since if we know whether A has occurred we also know whether A^c has occurred, and if we know whether each of $A_1, A_2, A_3, \ldots$ has occurred we also know whether $\bigcup_i A_i$ has occurred, it is clear that $\mathcal{G}$ is a σ-field. The possibilities for partial knowledge range all the way from $\mathcal{G} = \mathcal{F}$, where the observer actually knows the outcome, to $\mathcal{G} = \mathcal{T}$ where $\mathcal{T} = \{\emptyset, \Omega\}$, the 'trivial σ-field', and she has no information at all.

The conditional expectation $E(Y|\mathcal{G})$, representing the best predictor of Y when observers possess partial information $\mathcal{G}$, is defined formally as a random variable on the restricted probability space $(\Omega, \mathcal{G}, P)$ that satisfies the equation

$$E[1_G E(Y|\mathcal{G})] = E(1_G Y), \ \forall \ G \in \mathcal{G} \tag{B.10.1}$$

where 1_G is the indicator of the event G. Since $\Omega \in \mathcal{G}$, a case of (B.10.1) is

$$E[E(Y|\mathcal{G})] = E(Y) \tag{B.10.2}$$

so that the definition embodies the LIE. If Y is not integrable, $E(Y|\mathcal{G})$ is not well defined. Take care to appreciate the fundamental difference between $E(Y)$ and $E(Y|\mathcal{G})$. The former represents an averaging over the points of the sample space, whereas the latter is simply a new mapping from Ω to $\mathbb{R}$, derived from that represented by Y. This fact can be emphasized by writing $E(Y|\mathcal{G})(\omega)$ as well as $Y(\omega)$. These both represent numerical values associated with the outcome ω of the random experiment, or in other words, random variables.

Special cases are $E(Y|\mathcal{F}) = Y$, a.s. and $E(Y|\mathcal{T}) = E(Y)$ a.s., the unconditional expectation. Notice how (B.10.1) holds in both these cases. The tag 'a.s.' here stands for 'almost surely', which means the same thing as 'with probability 1'. The reason for it is that the conditional expectation is defined merely by the property in (B.10.1), and is not guaranteed to be unique. Recall from §B.4 that if $W(\omega)$ and $Z(\omega)$ are two different random variables, but $W(\omega) = Z(\omega)$ except for $\omega \in M$, where $P(M) = 0$, then $E(W) = E(Z)$. There may be more than one random variable that satisfies (B.10.1), although all such r.v.s are equal except on a set of probability 0. Every statement about $E(Y|\mathcal{G})$ should be qualified with 'a.s.' as a reminder that it may not hold on such a set. This is essentially a technical detail since 'exceptional' sets rarely arise in practical problems, and often the tag is omitted once the context is clear.

To unify this approach with that of §B.6, consider the case $\mathcal{G} = \sigma(X)$, the 'σ-field generated by X'. Technically, $\sigma(X)$ is defined as the smallest σ-field with respect to which X is measurable. More familiarly, it is the collection of events defined by: '$A \in \sigma(X)$ if and only if by observing X you know whether or not A has occurred'. Knowledge of $\sigma(X)$ is therefore the same thing as knowing $X = x$ for some unspecified x. The variable $E(Y|X)$, defined previously, means exactly the same thing as $E[Y|\sigma(X)]$, which is fully general, and the former notation can be used as shorthand for the latter. It can be verified, treating the G as sets of X values, that the formulae in (B.6.2) and (B.6.3) satisfy (B.10.1).

The definition generalizes naturally to random vectors of any order, noting that, in a multivariate framework, the expression $\sigma(X, Z)$, for example, can represent the σ-field generated by the joint distribution of X and Z. A little care is needed here, because $\sigma(X, Z)$ is not just the union of the collections $\sigma(X)$ and $\sigma(Z)$. This set is not necessarily a σ-field according to the definition. Therefore, $\sigma(X, Z)$ must be defined as the smallest σ-field containing $\sigma(X)$ and $\sigma(Z)$. This is can be written, to distinguish it from the ordinary union, as $\sigma(X) \vee \sigma(Z)$.

Unlike the previous analysis, this one does not tell us how to construct the conditional expectation, but this is no drawback in the many applications where the issues arising are conceptual rather than computational. Most of the properties of ordinary expectations extend to conditional expectations, including a conditional form of Jensen's inequality,

$$E[\phi(X)|\mathcal{G}] \geq (\leq)\phi(E[X|\mathcal{G}]), \text{ a.s.} \tag{B.10.3}$$

when $\phi(\cdot)$ is a convex (concave) function. Another important case is the generalization of Theorem B.4.1.

Theorem B.10.1 Under the same assumptions on g as in Theorem B.4.1,

$$\frac{dE(g(\theta)|\mathcal{G})}{d\theta} = E\left(\frac{dg(\theta)}{d\theta}\middle|\mathcal{G}\right) \text{ a.s. } \square \tag{B.10.4}$$

(For the proof see Davidson (1994a) Theorem 10.20.) Finally, if $\mathcal{G}_1 \subseteq \mathcal{G}_2 \subseteq \mathcal{F}$, in which case the σ-fields $\mathcal{G}_1$ and $\mathcal{G}_2$ are said to be *nested*, we can also show that $E[E(Y|\mathcal{G}_2)|\mathcal{G}_1] = E(Y|\mathcal{G}_1)$ a.s. This is the conditional form of the LIE. See Davidson (1994a) Chapter 10, for additional details.

Although conditional expectations are the fundamental concept in this theory, probabilities have a representation as the expectations of indicator functions, and so conditional distributions are a natural extension. For example, one can write

$$P(B|\mathcal{G}) = E(1_B|\mathcal{G}), \; B \in \mathcal{F} \tag{B.10.5}$$

and this definition can be used to construct conditional c.d.f.s and p.d.f.s for random variables. However, a technical issue arises here. In most cases it is possible to define a random probability measure as

$$\mu_\omega(B) = P(B|\mathcal{G})(\omega). \tag{B.10.6}$$

If this probability measure is well defined for every $\omega \in C$, where $P(C) = 1$, the conditional distribution is said to be *regular*. Regular conditional distributions have all the usual properties of ordinary distributions. While it is possible to construct examples of non-regular distributions, distributions in n-dimensional Euclidean space can be shown to be regular. See Theorem 10.30 of Davidson (1994a) and also Breiman (1992) §4.3.

Further Reading: Davidson (1994a) summarizes all the concepts and results needed, and a good deal more. A good beginners' text on measure theory and probability, with econometric applications, is Gallant (1997). Other books in this field are often technically advanced, but for readers willing to be a bit more adventurous, Cramér (1946) and Breiman (1968) are two classic texts, both of which have been recently re-issued. Breiman especially gives a good flavour of the measure-theoretic ideas. There are many texts on distribution theory, among which Hogg and Craig (1995), and Freund (1992) are well established examples. Mood and Graybill (1972) and Wilks (1962) are two older texts that also highly recommended.

Appendix C

The Gaussian Distribution and its Relatives

C.1 The Univariate and Multivariate Cases

The standard Gaussian (or normal) distribution is continuous with p.d.f.

$$\phi(z) = \frac{e^{-\frac{1}{2}z^2}}{\sqrt{2\pi}}. \tag{C.1.1}$$

To indicate that Z is an r.v. with this density write $Z \sim \mathrm{N}(0, 1)$. This function has the well-known bell-shaped profile shown in Figure C.1. The main properties

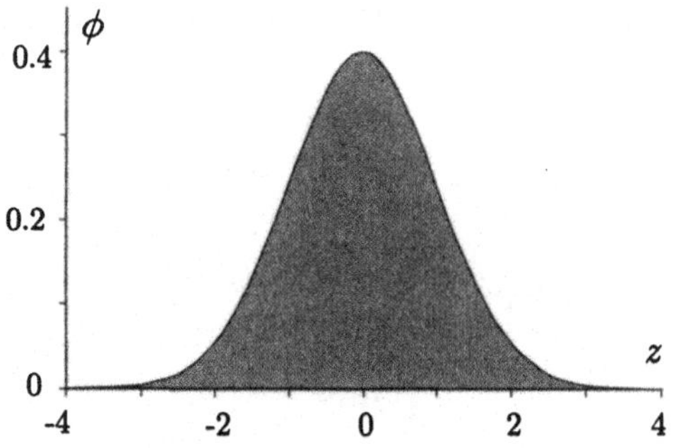

Figure C.1: The Standard Gaussian Density

of $\phi(z)$ are:

$$\phi(z) > 0, \; -\infty < z < +\infty. \tag{C.1.2}$$

$$\int_{-\infty}^{+\infty} \phi(\zeta) d\zeta = 1 \tag{C.1.3}$$

$$E(Z^r) = \int_{-\infty}^{+\infty} \zeta^r \phi(\zeta) d\zeta = \begin{cases} 0 & \text{odd integers } r \\ \dfrac{r!}{2^{r/2}(r/2)!} & \text{even integers } r. \end{cases} \tag{C.1.4}$$

Property (C.1.3) is required of a p.d.f. by definition and is ensured by the choice of constant factor $(2\pi)^{-1/2}$. Note that the support is infinite in spite of the fact, evident from the figure, that the probability mass is negligible beyond about ± 3. The geometric convergence of the tails ensures that all finite-order moments exist, as shown in (C.1.4), and for the cases $r = 1$ and $r = 2$, this implies $E(Z) = 0$ and $\mathrm{Var}(Z) = 1$.

Consider $X = \sigma Z + \mu$. Using the results on change of variable in §B.9 and the fact $|dz/dx| = 1/\sigma$

$$f(x) = \frac{1}{\sqrt{2\pi}\sigma} \exp\left\{-\tfrac{1}{2}\left(\frac{x-\mu}{\sigma}\right)^2\right\} \tag{C.1.5}$$

with $E(X) = \mu$ and $\mathrm{Var}(X) = \sigma^2$. To indicate that X has this distribution, write $X \sim \mathrm{N}(\mu, \sigma^2)$. The formulae in (C.1.4) are easily generalized to the case of $E(X - \mu)^r$ by multiplication by σ^r.

Now consider the vector $\boldsymbol{z} = (z_1, \ldots, z_n)'$ with density

$$\phi(\boldsymbol{z}) = \prod_{i=1}^{n} f(z_i) = (2\pi)^{-n/2} \exp\left\{-\frac{\boldsymbol{z}'\boldsymbol{z}}{2}\right\} \tag{C.1.6}$$

A plot of this function for $n = 2$ is shown in Figure C.2. By construction $\boldsymbol{z}$ is the

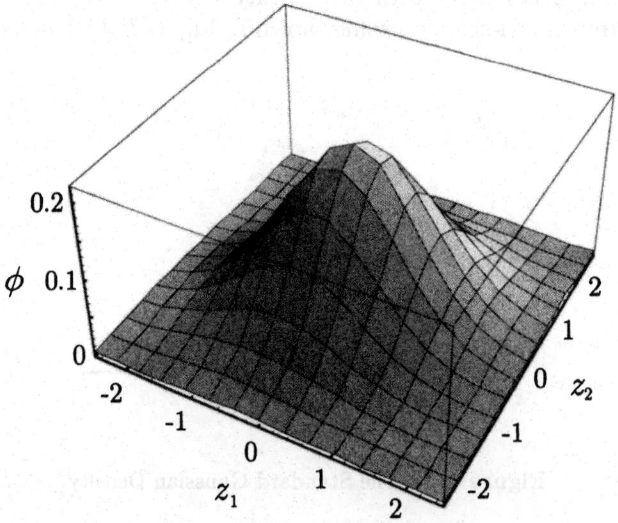

Figure C.2: The Bivariate Gaussian Density

independent standard Gaussian vector, with properties $E(\boldsymbol{z}) = \boldsymbol{0}$, $E(\boldsymbol{z}\boldsymbol{z}') = \boldsymbol{I}_n$.

The conventional way to denote this is

$$\boldsymbol{z} \sim \mathrm{N}(\boldsymbol{0}, \boldsymbol{I}_n). \tag{C.1.7}$$

Consider the affine transformation

$$\boldsymbol{x} = \boldsymbol{A}\boldsymbol{z} + \boldsymbol{\mu} \tag{C.1.8}$$

where $\boldsymbol{A}$ ($n \times n$ nonsingular) and $\boldsymbol{\mu}$ ($n \times 1$) are constants. This is a continuous one-to-one vector-valued function with inverse $\boldsymbol{z} = \boldsymbol{A}^{-1}(\boldsymbol{x} - \boldsymbol{\mu})$, having Jacobian $J = |\boldsymbol{A}^{-1}| = 1/|\boldsymbol{A}|$. Formula (B.9.3) for change of variable gives

$$\begin{aligned} f(\boldsymbol{x}) &= \phi(\boldsymbol{A}^{-1}(\boldsymbol{x} - \boldsymbol{\mu}))\,|1/|\boldsymbol{A}|| \\ &= (2\pi)^{-n/2}\,\big||\boldsymbol{A}|^{-1}\big| \exp\left\{-\tfrac{1}{2}(\boldsymbol{x} - \boldsymbol{\mu})'(\boldsymbol{A}^{-1})'\boldsymbol{A}^{-1}(\boldsymbol{x} - \boldsymbol{\mu})\right\}. \end{aligned} \tag{C.1.9}$$

Defining the positive definite matrix $\boldsymbol{\Sigma} = \boldsymbol{A}\boldsymbol{A}'$, such that $(\boldsymbol{A}^{-1})'\boldsymbol{A}^{-1} = (\boldsymbol{A}\boldsymbol{A}')^{-1} = \boldsymbol{\Sigma}^{-1}$ and $\big||\boldsymbol{A}|^{-1}\big| = |\boldsymbol{\Sigma}|^{-1/2}$, the positive square root being understood, the density may be written

$$f(\boldsymbol{x}) = (2\pi)^{-n/2}|\boldsymbol{\Sigma}|^{-1/2} \exp\left\{-\tfrac{1}{2}(\boldsymbol{x} - \boldsymbol{\mu})'\boldsymbol{\Sigma}^{-1}(\boldsymbol{x} - \boldsymbol{\mu})\right\}. \tag{C.1.10}$$

This is the general formula for the multivariate Gaussian density. Since $E(\boldsymbol{z}) = \boldsymbol{0}$, $E(\boldsymbol{x}) = \boldsymbol{\mu}$ and

$$\mathrm{Var}(\boldsymbol{x}) = E(\boldsymbol{x} - \boldsymbol{\mu})(\boldsymbol{x} - \boldsymbol{\mu})' = \boldsymbol{A}E(\boldsymbol{z}\boldsymbol{z}')\boldsymbol{A}' = \boldsymbol{A}\boldsymbol{A}' = \boldsymbol{\Sigma}. \tag{C.1.11}$$

The usual way of denoting that $\boldsymbol{x}$ is multivariate Gaussian is by $\boldsymbol{x} \sim \mathrm{N}(\boldsymbol{\mu}, \boldsymbol{\Sigma})$. According this derivation, any multivariate Gaussian vector can be expressed as a linear function of the independent standard Gaussian vector by factorizing the covariance matrix.

This is a case of the following fundamental result, that a linear transformation of Gaussian variables is also Gaussian.

Theorem C.1.1 Let $\boldsymbol{x} \sim \mathrm{N}(\boldsymbol{\mu}, \boldsymbol{\Sigma})$ ($n \times 1$), and let $\boldsymbol{B}$ ($m \times n$), $\boldsymbol{d}$ ($m \times 1$) be constants; then defining $\boldsymbol{y} = \boldsymbol{B}\boldsymbol{x} + \boldsymbol{d}$,

$$\boldsymbol{y} \sim \mathrm{N}(\boldsymbol{B}\boldsymbol{\mu} + \boldsymbol{d}, \boldsymbol{B}\boldsymbol{\Sigma}\boldsymbol{B}'). \quad \square \tag{C.1.12}$$

If $\boldsymbol{B}$ has rank m it follows that $\boldsymbol{B}\boldsymbol{\Sigma}\boldsymbol{B}'$ ($m \times m$) has rank m, and then the p.d.f. of $\boldsymbol{y}$ can be written directly as

$$f(\boldsymbol{y}) = (2\pi)^{-n/2}|\boldsymbol{B}\boldsymbol{\Sigma}\boldsymbol{B}'|^{-1/2} \exp\left\{-\tfrac{1}{2}(\boldsymbol{y} - \boldsymbol{B}\boldsymbol{\mu} - \boldsymbol{d})'(\boldsymbol{B}\boldsymbol{\Sigma}\boldsymbol{B}')^{-1}(\boldsymbol{y} - \boldsymbol{B}\boldsymbol{\mu} - \boldsymbol{d})\right\} \tag{C.1.13}$$

If $\mathrm{rank}(\boldsymbol{B}) = r < m$, $\boldsymbol{y}$ is said to have a singular distribution, and since its covariance matrix is singular certain linear combinations of the elements of $\boldsymbol{y}$ are known exactly. Nonetheless it is said to be Gaussian in the sense that for any $r \times m$ matrix $\boldsymbol{P}$ such that rank $(\boldsymbol{P}\boldsymbol{B}) = r$, the r-vector $\boldsymbol{P}\boldsymbol{y}$ has the multivariate normal p.d.f. with full-rank covariance matrix $\boldsymbol{P}\boldsymbol{B}\boldsymbol{\Sigma}\boldsymbol{B}'\boldsymbol{P}'$.

C.2 The Conditional and Marginal Distributions

Partition $\boldsymbol{x}$ into sub-vectors of dimension n_1 and n_2 respectively with corresponding partitions for $\boldsymbol{\mu}$ and $\boldsymbol{\Sigma}$,

$$\boldsymbol{x} = \begin{bmatrix} \boldsymbol{x}_1 \\ \boldsymbol{x}_2 \end{bmatrix} \quad \boldsymbol{\mu} = \begin{bmatrix} \boldsymbol{\mu}_1 \\ \boldsymbol{\mu}_2 \end{bmatrix} \quad \boldsymbol{\Sigma} = \begin{bmatrix} \boldsymbol{\Sigma}_{11} & \boldsymbol{\Sigma}_{12} \\ \boldsymbol{\Sigma}_{21} & \boldsymbol{\Sigma}_{22} \end{bmatrix}$$

where $\boldsymbol{\Sigma}_{21} = \boldsymbol{\Sigma}_{12}'$ by symmetry.

Using the partitioned determinant and inverse formulae (A.2.12) and (A.2.13), the p.d.f. becomes

$$\begin{aligned} f(\boldsymbol{x}_1, \boldsymbol{x}_2) = {} & (2\pi)^{-n/2} |\boldsymbol{\Sigma}_{11} - \boldsymbol{\Sigma}_{12}\boldsymbol{\Sigma}_{22}^{-1}\boldsymbol{\Sigma}_{21}|^{-1/2} |\boldsymbol{\Sigma}_{22}|^{-1/2} \\ & \times \exp\Big\{-\tfrac{1}{2}\big[(\boldsymbol{x}_1 - \boldsymbol{\mu}_1)'\boldsymbol{E}(\boldsymbol{x}_1 - \boldsymbol{\mu}_1) - (\boldsymbol{x}_1 - \boldsymbol{\mu}_1)'\boldsymbol{E}\boldsymbol{\Sigma}_{12}\boldsymbol{\Sigma}_{22}^{-1}(\boldsymbol{x}_2 - \boldsymbol{\mu}_2) \\ & - (\boldsymbol{x}_2 - \boldsymbol{\mu}_2)'\boldsymbol{\Sigma}_{22}^{-1}\boldsymbol{\Sigma}_{21}\boldsymbol{E}(\boldsymbol{x}_1 - \boldsymbol{\mu}_1) \\ & + (\boldsymbol{x}_2 - \boldsymbol{\mu}_2)'(\boldsymbol{\Sigma}_{22}^{-1} + \boldsymbol{\Sigma}_{22}^{-1}\boldsymbol{\Sigma}_{21}\boldsymbol{E}\boldsymbol{\Sigma}_{12}\boldsymbol{\Sigma}_{22}^{-1})(\boldsymbol{x}_2 - \boldsymbol{\mu}_2)\big]\Big\} \end{aligned} \tag{C.2.14}$$

where $\boldsymbol{E} = (\boldsymbol{\Sigma}_{11} - \boldsymbol{\Sigma}_{12}\boldsymbol{\Sigma}_{22}^{-1}\boldsymbol{\Sigma}_{21})^{-1}$. Note that the terms in the exponent may be rearranged as

$$\begin{aligned} & \big[\boldsymbol{x}_1 - \boldsymbol{\mu}_1 - \boldsymbol{\Sigma}_{12}\boldsymbol{\Sigma}_{22}^{-1}(\boldsymbol{x}_2 - \boldsymbol{\mu}_2)\big]'\boldsymbol{E}\big[\boldsymbol{x}_1 - \boldsymbol{\mu}_1 - \boldsymbol{\Sigma}_{12}\boldsymbol{\Sigma}_{22}^{-1}(\boldsymbol{x}_2 - \boldsymbol{\mu}_2)\big] \\ & \quad + (\boldsymbol{x}_2 - \boldsymbol{\mu}_2)'\boldsymbol{\Sigma}_{22}^{-1}(\boldsymbol{x}_2 - \boldsymbol{\mu}_2), \end{aligned} \tag{C.2.15}$$

so revealing the factorization $f(\boldsymbol{x}_1, \boldsymbol{x}_2) = f(\boldsymbol{x}_1|\boldsymbol{x}_2)f(\boldsymbol{x}_2)$ where

$$\begin{aligned} f(\boldsymbol{x}_1|\boldsymbol{x}_2) = {} & (2\pi)^{-n_1/2} |\boldsymbol{\Sigma}_{11} - \boldsymbol{\Sigma}_{12}\boldsymbol{\Sigma}_{22}^{-1}\boldsymbol{\Sigma}_{21}|^{-1/2} \\ & \times \exp\Big\{-\tfrac{1}{2}\big[\boldsymbol{x}_1 - \boldsymbol{\mu}_1 - \boldsymbol{\Sigma}_{12}\boldsymbol{\Sigma}_{22}^{-1}(\boldsymbol{x}_2 - \boldsymbol{\mu}_2)\big]'(\boldsymbol{\Sigma}_{11} - \boldsymbol{\Sigma}_{12}\boldsymbol{\Sigma}_{22}^{-1}\boldsymbol{\Sigma}_{21})^{-1} \\ & \big[\boldsymbol{x}_1 - \boldsymbol{\mu}_1 - \boldsymbol{\Sigma}_{12}\boldsymbol{\Sigma}_{22}^{-1}(\boldsymbol{x}_2 - \boldsymbol{\mu}_2)\big]\Big\} \end{aligned} \tag{C.2.16}$$

and

$$f(\boldsymbol{x}_2) = (2\pi)^{-n_2/2} |\boldsymbol{\Sigma}_{22}|^{-1/2} \exp\left\{-\tfrac{1}{2}(\boldsymbol{x}_2 - \boldsymbol{\mu}_2)'\boldsymbol{\Sigma}_{22}^{-1}(\boldsymbol{x}_2 - \boldsymbol{\mu}_2)\right\}. \tag{C.2.17}$$

These are respectively the conditional density of $\boldsymbol{x}_1$, given $\boldsymbol{x}_2$, and the marginal density of $\boldsymbol{x}_2$. Notice that

$$E(\boldsymbol{x}_1|\boldsymbol{x}_2) = \boldsymbol{\mu}_1 + \boldsymbol{\Sigma}_{12}\boldsymbol{\Sigma}_{22}^{-1}(\boldsymbol{x}_2 - \boldsymbol{\mu}_2) \tag{C.2.18}$$

which is a function of $\boldsymbol{x}_2$, whereas

$$\mathrm{Var}(\boldsymbol{x}_1|\boldsymbol{x}_2) = \boldsymbol{\Sigma}_{11} - \boldsymbol{\Sigma}_{12}\boldsymbol{\Sigma}_{22}^{-1}\boldsymbol{\Sigma}_{21} \tag{C.2.19}$$

which is not a function of $\boldsymbol{x}_2$, but is smaller than the marginal variance $\boldsymbol{\Sigma}_{11}$ in the matrix sense that their difference is positive definite.

C.3 The Chi-squared, F and t Distributions

Consider $\boldsymbol{z} \sim \mathrm{N}(\mathbf{0}, \boldsymbol{I})$, $(n \times 1)$. The distribution of $\omega = \boldsymbol{z}'\boldsymbol{z}$ is called the *central chi-squared with n degrees of freedom*, denoted $\chi^2(n)$. The first two moments are $E(\omega) = n$, and $\mathrm{Var}(\omega) = 2n$. Let $\boldsymbol{z}_1$ be $n_1 \times 1$ and $\boldsymbol{z}_2$ be $n_2 \times 1$, with the property

$$\begin{bmatrix} \boldsymbol{z}_1 \\ \boldsymbol{z}_2 \end{bmatrix} \sim \mathrm{N}(\mathbf{0}, \boldsymbol{I}_{n_1+n_2}) \tag{C.3.20}$$

and note that $\boldsymbol{z}_1'\boldsymbol{z}_1 = \omega_1 \sim \chi^2(n_1)$, $\boldsymbol{z}_2'\boldsymbol{z}_2 = \omega_2 \sim \chi^2(n_2)$, and

$$\omega_1 + \omega_2 = \boldsymbol{z}_1'\boldsymbol{z}_1 + \boldsymbol{z}_2'\boldsymbol{z}_2 \sim \chi^2(n_1 + n_2). \tag{C.3.21}$$

The r.v.s ω_1 and ω_2 are independent if and only if the elements of $\boldsymbol{z}_1$ and $\boldsymbol{z}_2$ are independent, and being Gaussian, uncorrelatedness is sufficient for independence. Hence the distribution has the following general property:

Theorem C.3.1 Sums of independent χ^2*s* are also χ^2, with degrees of freedom (d.f.) equal to the sum of the d.f.s of each term in the sum. □

A direct implication of Theorem C.1.1 is

Theorem C.3.2 If $\boldsymbol{x} \sim \mathrm{N}(\boldsymbol{\mu}, \boldsymbol{\Sigma})$ $(n \times 1)$, then $(\boldsymbol{x} - \boldsymbol{\mu})'\boldsymbol{\Sigma}^{-1}(\boldsymbol{x} - \boldsymbol{\mu}) \sim \chi^2(n)$. □

A closely related and fundamental result is the following.

Theorem C.3.3 Let $\boldsymbol{z} \sim \mathrm{N}(\mathbf{0}, \boldsymbol{I})$ $(n \times 1)$ and let $\boldsymbol{M}$ be a $n \times n$ symmetric idempotent matrix with rank r. Then $\boldsymbol{z}'\boldsymbol{M}\boldsymbol{z} \sim \chi^2(r)$

Proof Consider the diagonalization of $\boldsymbol{M}$. Since $\boldsymbol{M}$ is symmetric and idempotent, r of the eigenvalues are ones and the rest zeros, and after reordering,

$$\boldsymbol{\Lambda} = \begin{bmatrix} \boldsymbol{I}_r & \mathbf{0} \\ \mathbf{0} & \mathbf{0} \end{bmatrix} \begin{matrix} r \\ n-r \end{matrix} \tag{C.3.22}$$

Consider $\boldsymbol{y} = \boldsymbol{C}'\boldsymbol{z}$. By Theorem C.1.1, $\boldsymbol{y} \sim \mathrm{N}(\mathbf{0}, \boldsymbol{C}'\boldsymbol{C})$, and $\boldsymbol{C}'\boldsymbol{C} = \boldsymbol{I}$, hence, $\boldsymbol{y} = (y_1, \dots, y_n)'$ is an independent standard Gaussian vector. It follows that $\boldsymbol{z}'\boldsymbol{M}\boldsymbol{z} = \boldsymbol{z}'\boldsymbol{C}\boldsymbol{\Lambda}\boldsymbol{C}'\boldsymbol{z} = \boldsymbol{y}'\boldsymbol{\Lambda}\boldsymbol{y} = \sum_{i=1}^r y_i^2 \sim \chi^2(r)$. ■

The family of *non-central chi-squared distributions* $\chi^2(n, \lambda)$, with degrees of freedom n and noncentrality parameter λ, are the distributions of $\omega = \boldsymbol{x}'\boldsymbol{x}$ when $\boldsymbol{x} \sim \mathrm{N}(\boldsymbol{\mu}, \boldsymbol{I})$ $(n \times 1)$, with $\lambda = \boldsymbol{\mu}'\boldsymbol{\mu}$. It is easy to establish that $E(\omega) = n + \lambda$, $\mathrm{Var}(\omega) = 2n + 4\lambda$ and also the generalization of the additive property, that if $\omega_1 \sim \chi^2(n_1, \lambda_1)$ and $\omega_2 \sim \chi^2(n_2, \lambda_2)$, and these random variables are independent, then

$$\omega_1 + \omega_2 \sim \chi^2(n_1 + n_2, \lambda_1 + \lambda_2). \tag{C.3.23}$$

In applications the noncentral chi-squared can be approximated by a central chi-squared, scaled to have matching mean and variance. Defining $\rho = 1 + \lambda/(n + \lambda)$ and $n' = n + \lambda^2/(n + 2\lambda)$, these being the solutions to the equations

$$n + \lambda = \rho n' \tag{C.3.24a}$$

$$2n + 4\lambda = 2\rho^2 n' \qquad \text{(C.3.24b)}$$

the tabulation of ρ times the $\chi^2(n')$ distribution is found to give a good approximation to that of $\chi^2(n, \lambda)$.

The family of F distributions is obtained as the ratio of two independent central chi-squareds, each divided by its degrees of freedom. If $\omega_1 \sim \chi^2(n_1)$ and $\omega_2 \sim \chi^2(n_2)$, independent of one another, then

$$\frac{\omega_1/n_1}{\omega_2/n_2} \sim F(n_1, n_2). \qquad \text{(C.3.25)}$$

A related case is Student's t distribution with n degrees of freedom. This is defined as the ratio of a standard Gaussian to the square root of an independent $\chi^2(n)$ divided by n:

$$\frac{z}{\sqrt{\omega_n/n}} \sim t_n. \qquad \text{(C.3.26)}$$

Note that $t_n^2 \sim F(1, n)$.

C.4 Quadratic Forms in Normal Variables

The many applications of the F distribution depend on the following result:

Theorem C.4.1 Let $\boldsymbol{Z}'\boldsymbol{M}\boldsymbol{Z}$ and $\boldsymbol{Z}'\boldsymbol{Q}\boldsymbol{Z}$ be a pair of idempotent quadratic forms in the standard Gaussian vector $\boldsymbol{Z}$ $(n \times 1)$. If $\boldsymbol{M}\boldsymbol{Q} = \boldsymbol{0}$, these random variables are independent of one another.

Proof Let $\text{rank}(\boldsymbol{M}) = r$ and $\text{rank}(\boldsymbol{Q}) = s$. The diagonalizations of the symmetric idempotent matrices $\boldsymbol{M}$ and $\boldsymbol{Q}$ have the form

$$\boldsymbol{M} = \boldsymbol{C}\boldsymbol{\Lambda}_r\boldsymbol{C}' \qquad \text{(C.4.27)}$$

$$\boldsymbol{Q} = \boldsymbol{D}\boldsymbol{\Lambda}_s\boldsymbol{D}' \qquad \text{(C.4.28)}$$

where

$$\boldsymbol{C}\boldsymbol{C}' = \boldsymbol{C}'\boldsymbol{C} = \boldsymbol{D}\boldsymbol{D}' = \boldsymbol{D}'\boldsymbol{D} = \boldsymbol{I} \qquad \text{(C.4.29)}$$

and

$$\boldsymbol{\Lambda}_r = \begin{bmatrix} \boldsymbol{I}_r & \boldsymbol{0} \\ \boldsymbol{0} & \boldsymbol{0} \end{bmatrix} \quad \boldsymbol{\Lambda}_s = \begin{bmatrix} \boldsymbol{I}_s & \boldsymbol{0} \\ \boldsymbol{0} & \boldsymbol{0} \end{bmatrix}. \qquad \text{(C.4.30)}$$

It follows that

$$\boldsymbol{C}'\boldsymbol{M} = \boldsymbol{C}'\boldsymbol{C}\boldsymbol{\Lambda}_r\boldsymbol{C}' = \begin{bmatrix} \boldsymbol{C}_1' \\ \boldsymbol{0} \end{bmatrix} \begin{matrix} r \\ n-r \end{matrix} \qquad \text{(C.4.31)}$$

and similarly

$$\boldsymbol{D}'\boldsymbol{Q} = \begin{bmatrix} \boldsymbol{D}_1' \\ \boldsymbol{0} \end{bmatrix} \begin{matrix} s \\ n-s \end{matrix} \qquad \text{(C.4.32)}$$

where $\boldsymbol{C}_1'$ and $\boldsymbol{D}_1'$ are respectively the first r rows of $\boldsymbol{C}'$ and the first s rows of $\boldsymbol{D}'$. It follows that

$$\boldsymbol{C}'\boldsymbol{M}\boldsymbol{Q}\boldsymbol{D} = \begin{bmatrix} \boldsymbol{C}_1'\boldsymbol{D}_1 & \boldsymbol{0} \\ \boldsymbol{0} & \boldsymbol{0} \end{bmatrix}. \tag{C.4.33}$$

Define $\boldsymbol{Y}_1^M = \boldsymbol{C}_1'\boldsymbol{Z}$ and $\boldsymbol{Y}_1^Q = \boldsymbol{D}_1'\boldsymbol{Z}$ which, given the properties of $\boldsymbol{C}$ and $\boldsymbol{D}$, are independent standard Gaussian vectors of dimension r and s respectively. Note that

$$\boldsymbol{Z}'\boldsymbol{M}\boldsymbol{Z} = \boldsymbol{Z}'\boldsymbol{M}'\boldsymbol{C}\boldsymbol{C}'\boldsymbol{M}\boldsymbol{Z} = \boldsymbol{Z}'\boldsymbol{C}_1\boldsymbol{C}_1'\boldsymbol{Z} = \boldsymbol{Y}_1^{M\prime}\boldsymbol{Y}_1^M \tag{C.4.34}$$

and similarly

$$\boldsymbol{Z}'\boldsymbol{Q}\boldsymbol{Z} = \boldsymbol{Y}_1^{Q\prime}\boldsymbol{Y}_1^Q. \tag{C.4.35}$$

It remains to show that the elements of these vectors are independent of one another. Since they are Gaussian, uncorrelatedness is sufficient for independence and the $r \times s$ matrix of covariances is

$$E(\boldsymbol{Y}_1^M\boldsymbol{Y}_1^{Q\prime}) = E(\boldsymbol{C}_1'\boldsymbol{Z}\boldsymbol{Z}'\boldsymbol{D}_1) = \boldsymbol{C}_1'\boldsymbol{D}_1. \tag{C.4.36}$$

The theorem follows in view of the premise, and (C.4.33). ∎

It may seem counterintuitive that two quadratic forms in the *same* Gaussian vector $\boldsymbol{Z}$ could be independent. In fact, $\boldsymbol{M}\boldsymbol{Q} = \boldsymbol{0}$ implies that the nullity of $\boldsymbol{M}$ (say) equals or exceeds s, and hence necessarily $r + s \leq n$. The two quadratic forms actually depend on different, orthogonal components of the $\boldsymbol{Z}$ vector.

Putting the results of Theorems C.3.3 and C.4.1 together yields the fundamental theorem of Gaussian least squares inference, as follows.

Theorem C.4.2 If $\boldsymbol{X} \sim \mathrm{N}(\boldsymbol{0}, \sigma^2\boldsymbol{I})$ and $\boldsymbol{M}$ and $\boldsymbol{Q}$ are symmetric idempotent matrices of ranks r and s respectively and $\boldsymbol{M}\boldsymbol{Q} = \boldsymbol{0}$, then

$$\frac{\boldsymbol{X}'\boldsymbol{Q}\boldsymbol{X}}{\boldsymbol{X}'\boldsymbol{M}\boldsymbol{X}}\frac{r}{s} \sim F(s, r). \tag{C.4.37}$$

Proof This follows from Theorems C.3.3 and C.4.1, noting that $\boldsymbol{X}'\boldsymbol{Q}\boldsymbol{X} \sim \sigma^2\chi^2(s)$ and $\boldsymbol{X}'\boldsymbol{M}\boldsymbol{X} \sim \sigma^2\chi^2(r)$. The scale factor σ^2 cancels in the ratio. ∎

Closely related to this result is the case of the standardized mean of a Gaussian sample.

Theorem C.4.3 If $\boldsymbol{X} \sim \mathrm{N}(\mu\boldsymbol{\iota}, \sigma^2\boldsymbol{I})$ $(n \times 1)$ where μ is a scalar and $\boldsymbol{\iota}$ the unit vector (n-vector of ones), $\bar{X} = n^{-1}\sum_{i=1}^n X_i$, and $s^2 = (n-1)^{-1}\sum_{i=1}^n (X_i - \bar{X})^2$, then

$$\sqrt{n}\frac{\bar{X} - \mu}{s} \sim t_{n-1}. \tag{C.4.38}$$

Proof Let $\boldsymbol{Z} = (\boldsymbol{X} - \mu\boldsymbol{\iota})/\sigma \sim \mathrm{N}(\boldsymbol{0}, \boldsymbol{I})$. Then $\bar{Z} = (\bar{X} - \mu)/\sigma = n^{-1}\boldsymbol{\iota}'\boldsymbol{Z}$, and applying Theorem C.1.1 shows that $\sqrt{n}(\bar{X} - \mu)/\sigma = \sqrt{n}\bar{Z} \sim \mathrm{N}(0, 1)$. Also, if $\boldsymbol{M} = \boldsymbol{I} - \boldsymbol{\iota}(\boldsymbol{\iota}'\boldsymbol{\iota})^{-1}\boldsymbol{\iota}'$, it can be verified that

$$\begin{aligned}\frac{(n-1)s^2}{\sigma^2} &= \frac{1}{\sigma^2}\left[\sum_{i=1}^{n}(X_i - \mu)^2 - \frac{1}{n}\left(\sum_{i=1}^{n}(X_i - \mu)\right)^2\right] \\ &= \boldsymbol{Z}'\boldsymbol{M}\boldsymbol{Z} \\ &= \boldsymbol{Y}_1^{M\prime}\boldsymbol{Y}_1^{M} \sim \chi^2(n-1) \qquad \text{(C.4.39)}\end{aligned}$$

where $\boldsymbol{Y}_1^M$ ($(n-1) \times 1$) is defined by the decomposition in the proof of Theorem C.4.1. Lastly

$$E(\bar{Z}\boldsymbol{Y}_1^M) = n^{-1}E(\boldsymbol{\iota}'\boldsymbol{Z}\boldsymbol{Z}'\boldsymbol{C}_1) = n^{-1}\boldsymbol{\iota}'\boldsymbol{C}_1 = n^{-1}\boldsymbol{\iota}'\boldsymbol{M}\boldsymbol{C} = \boldsymbol{0} \qquad \text{(C.4.40)}$$

and $\bar{Z}$ and $\boldsymbol{Y}_1^M$ are both Gaussian, and hence independent. The result now follows by definition of the t distribution. ∎

References

Aitchison, J., and S. D. Silvey 1958: Maximum-likelihood estimation of parameters subject to restraints. *Annals of Mathematical Statistics* 29, 813–28.

Aitchison, J., and S. D. Silvey 1960: Maximum-likelihood estimation procedures and associated tests of significance. *Journal of Royal Statistical Society* Series B 22, 154–71.

Aitken, A. C. 1935: On least squares and linear combinations of observations. *Proceedings of the Royal Society of Edinburgh* 55, 42–48.

Akaike H. 1973: Information theory and the extension of the maximum likelihood principle, in B. N. Petrov and F. Csaki (eds.) *2nd International Symposium on Information Theory*, Akailseoniai-Kiudo, Budapest, 267–81.

Akaike H. 1974: A new look at the statistical identification model. *IEEE: Trans. Auto Control* 19, 716–23.

Almon, S. 1965: The distributed lag between capital appropriations and expenditures. *Econometrica* 33, 178–96.

Amemiya, T. 1974: The nonlinear two-stage least-squares estimator. *Journal of Econometrics* 2,105–10.

Amemiya, T. 1975: The nonlinear limited-information maximum-likelihood estimator and the modified nonlinear two-stage least-squares estimator. *Journal of Econometrics* 3, 375–86.

Amemiya, T. 1977: The maximum likelihood and nonlinear three stage least squares estimator in the general nonlinear simultaneous equations model. *Econometrica* 45, 955–68.

Amemiya, T. 1982: Correction to a lemma. *Econometrica* 50, 1325–8.

Amemiya, T. 1981: Qualitative response models: a survey. *Journal of Economic Literature* 19, 1483–536.

Amemiya, T. 1983: Non-linear regression models. Chapter 6 of Griliches and Intriligator (1983).

Amemiya, T. 1984: Tobit models: a survey. *Journal of Econometrics* 24, 3–61.

Amemiya, T. 1985: *Advanced Econometrics.* Oxford, Basil Blackwell

Anderson, T. W. 1951: Estimating linear restrictions on regression coefficients for multivariate normal distributions. *Annals of Mathematical Statistics* 22, 327–51.

Anderson, T. W. 1971: *The Statistical Analysis of Time Series.* New York: John Wiley & Sons.

Anderson, T. W. 1984: *An Introduction to Multivariate Statistical Analysis.* New York: John Wiley & Sons.

Anderson, T. W. and H. Rubin 1949: Estimation of the parameters of a single equation in a complete system of stochastic equations. *Annals of Mathematical Statistics* 20, 46–63.

Anderson, T. W. and H. Rubin 1950: The asymptotic properties of estimates of the parameters of a single equation in a complete system of stochastic equations. *Annals of Mathematical Statistics* 21, 570–582.

Andrews, D. W. K. 1984: Non-strong mixing autoregressive processes. *Journal of Applied Probability* 21, 930–4.

Andrews, D. W. K. 1987: Consistency in nonlinear econometric models: a generic uniform law of large numbers. *Econometrica* 55, 1465–72.

Andrews, D. W. K. 1988: Laws of large numbers for dependent non-identically distributed random variables. *Econometric Theory* 4, 458–67.

Andrews, D. W. K. 1991: Heteroscedasticity and autocorrelation consistent covariance matrix estimation. *Econometrica* 59, 817–58.

Andrews, D. W. K. 1992: Generic uniform convergence. *Econometric Theory* 8, 241–57.

Andrews, D. W. K. 1994: Empirical Process Methods in Econometrics. Chapter 37 of *Handbook of Econometrics, Volume IV* eds. R. F. Engle and D. L. McFadden, Amsterdam: Elsevier.

Andrews, D. W. K. and J. C. Monahan 1992: An improved heteroscedasticity and autocorrelation consistent covariance matrix estimator. *Econometrica* 60, 953–66.

Aneuryn-Evans, G. and A. S. Deaton 1980: Testing linear versus logarithmic regression models, *Review of Economic Studies* 47, 275–91.

Apostol, Tom M. 1974: *Mathematical Analysis*, 2nd Edition. Reading, Mass.: Addison-Wesley.

Attanasio, O. 1991: Risk, time-varying second moments and market efficiency.*Review of Economic Studies* 58, 479–94.

Banerjee, A., J. J. Dolado, D. F. Hendry and D. W. Smith 1986: Exploring equilibrium relationships in econometrics through static models: some Monte Carlo evidence. *Oxford Bulletin of Economics and Statistics* 48, 253–77.

Banerjee, A., J. J. Dolado, J. W. Galbraith and D. F. Hendry 1993: *Cointegration, Error Correction and the Econometric Analysis of Nonstationary Data.* Oxford: Oxford University Press.

Basmann, R. L. 1957: A generalized classical method of linear estimation of coefficients in a structural equation. *Econometrica* 25, 77–83.

Bates, C. and H. White 1985: A unified theory of consistent estimation for parametric models. *Econometric Theory* 1, 151–78.

Begg, D. K. H. 1982: *The Rational Expectations Revolution in Macroeconomics: Theories and Evidence.* Oxford: Philip Allan.

Berndt, E. R., and N. E. Savin 1977: Conflict among criteria for testing hypotheses in the multivariate linear regression model. *Econometrica* 45, 1263–78.

Berndt, E. R., B. H. Hall, R. E. Hall, and J. A. Hausman 1974: Estimation and inference in nonlinear structural models. *Annals of Economic and Social Measurement* 3, 653–65.

Beveridge, S. and C. R. Nelson 1981: A new approach to decomposition of economic time series into permanent and transitory components with particular attention to the measurement of the business cycle. *Journal of Monetary Economics* 7, 151–74.

Bierens, H. J. 1982: Consistent model specification tests. *Journal of Econometrics* 20, 105–34.

Bierens, H. J. 1991: Consistent conditional moment tests of functional form. *Econometrica* 58, 1443–58.

Bierens, H. J. 1994: *Topics in advanced econometrics.* Cambridge: Cambridge University Press.

Billingsley, P. 1968: *Convergence of Probability Measures.* New York: John Wiley & Sons.

Billingsley, P. 1986: *Probability and Measure*, 2nd edition. New York: John Wiley & Sons.

Bollerslev, T. 1986: Generalized autoregressive conditional heteroscedasticity. *Journal of Econometrics* 31, 307–27.

Bollerslev, T. 1988: On the correlation structure of the generalized autoregressive conditional heteroscedastic process. *Journal of Time Series Analysis* 9, 121–31.

Bollerslev, T. 1990: Modelling the coherence in short-run nominal exchange rates: a multivariate generalized ARCH model. *Review of Economics and Statistics* 72, 498–505.

Bollerslev, T., R. F. Engle and D. B. Nelson 1994: ARCH models. Chapter 49 of Engle and McFadden (1994).

Box, G. E. P. and G. M. Jenkins 1976: *Time Series Analysis: Forecasting and Control*, revised edition. San Francisco: Holden-Day.

Box, G. E. P. and D. A. Pierce 1970: The distribution of residual autocorrelations in autoregressive-integrated moving average time series models. *Journal of the American Statistical Association* 5, 1509–26.

Box, G. E. P. and G. Tiao 1981: Modelling multiple time series, with applications. *Journal of the American Statistical Association* 76, 802–16.

Box, M. J., D. Davies and W. H. Swann 1969: *Nonlinear Optimization Techniques* Edinburgh: Oliver and Boyd.

Breiman, L. 1992: *Probability.* Philadelphia: Society for Industrial and Applied Mathematics.

Breusch, T. S. 1978: Testing for autocorrelation in dynamic linear models. *Australian Economic Papers* 17, 334–55.

Breusch, T. S. and A. R. Pagan 1979: A simple test for heteroscedasticity and random coefficient variation. *Econometrica* 47, 1287–94.

Brown, B. W. 1983: The identification problem in systems nonlinear in the variables. *Econometrica* 51, 175–196.

Brown, T. M. 1952: Habit persistence and lags in consumer behaviour. *Econometrica 20*, 355–71.

Broyden, C. G. 1967: Quasi-Newton methods and their application to function minimisation. *Mathematics of Computation* 21, 368–81.

Broyden, C. G. 1970: The convergence of a class of double rank minimization algorithms, parts I and II. *Journal of the Institute of Mathematics and its Applications* 6, 76–90.

Burguete, J. F., A. R. Gallant and G. Souza 1982: On unification of the asymptotic theory of nonlinear econometric models. *Econometric Reviews* 1, 151–90.

Cagan, P. 1956: The monetary dynamics of hyperinflation, in *Studies in the Quantity Theory of Money*, ed. Milton Friedman. Chicago: University of Chicago Press.

Chow, G. C. 1960: Tests of equality between sets of coefficients in two linear regressions. *Econometrica* 28, 591–605.

Christ, C. F. 1966: *Econometric Models and Methods.* New York: John Wiley & Sons.

Christiano, L. J. and L. Ljungqvist 1988: Money does Granger-cause output in the bivariate money-output relation. *Journal of Monetary Economics*, 22, 217–35.

Cochrane, D., and G. H. Orcutt 1949: Application of least squares regression to relationships containing autocorrelated error terms. *Journal of the American Statistical Association* 44, 32–61.

Cox, D. R. 1961: Tests of separate families of hypotheses. *Proceedings of the Fourth Berkeley Symposium on Mathematical Statistics and Probability* 1, 105–23.

Cox, D. R. 1962: Further results on tests of separate families of hypotheses. *Journal of the Royal Statistical Society* Series B, 24, 406–24.

Cox, D. R. and D. V. Hinkley 1974: *Theoretical Statistics.* London: Chapman and Hall.

Cramér, H. 1946: *Mathematical Methods of Statistics.* Princeton: Princeton University Press.

Davidon, W. C. 1959: Variable metric method for minimization. AEC Research and Development Report ANL–5990.

Davidson, J. E. H. 1981: Problems with the estimation of moving average processes. *Journal of Econometrics.* 19, 295–310.

Davidson, J. E. H. 1991: The cointegration properties of vector autoregression models. *Journal of Time Series Analysis* 12, 43–62.

Davidson, J. E. H. 1994a: *Stochastic Limit Theory.* Oxford: Oxford University Press.

Davidson, J. E. H. 1994b: Identifying cointegrating regressions by the rank condition. *Oxford Bulletin of Economics and Statistics*, 56, 103–8.

Davidson, J. E. H. 1998a: A Wald test of restrictions on the cointegrating space based on Johansen's estimator. *Economics Letters* 59, 183–7.

Davidson, J. E. H. 1998b: Structural relations, cointegration and identification: some simple results and their application. *Journal of Econometrics* 87, 87–113.

Davidson, J. E. H. and R. M. De Jong 1997: Strong laws of large numbers for dependent heterogeneous processes: a synthesis of new and recent results. *Econometric Reviews* 16, 251–79.

Davidson, J. E. H., D. F. Hendry, F. Srba, and S. Yeo 1978: Econometric modelling of the aggregate time-series relationship between consumers expenditure and income in the United Kingdom. *Economic Journal* 88, 661–92.

Davidson, R., and J. G. MacKinnon 1981: Several tests for model specification in the presence of alternative hypotheses. *Econometrica* 49, 781–93.

Davidson, R., and J. G. MacKinnon 1993: *Estimation and Inference in Econometrics.* New York: Oxford University Press.

Davies, D., W. H. Swann and I. G. Campey 1964: Report on the development of a new direct search method of optimization. Central Instrument Research Laboratory Research Note 64/3, ICI Ltd.

Davis, T. E. 1952: The consumption function as a tool of prediction. *Review of Economics and Statistics* 34, 270–7.

De Jong, R. M. 1997: Central limit theorems for dependent heterogeneous random variables. *Econometric Theory* 13, 353–67.

De Jong, R. M. and J. Davidson 2000a: Consistency of kernel estimators of heteroscedastic and autocorrelated covariance matrices. *Econometrica*, forthcoming.

De Jong, R. M. and J. Davidson 2000b: The functional central limit theorem and convergence to stochastic integrals I: weakly dependent processes. *Econometric Theory*, forthcoming.

Desai, Meghnad 1976: *Applied Econometrics*. Oxford: Philip Allan.

Dhrymes, P. J. 1970: *Econometrics: Statistical Foundations and Applications*. New York: Harper and Row.

Dhrymes, P. J. 1971: *Distributed Lags: Problems of Estimation and Formulation*. San Francisco, Holden-Day.

Dickey, D. A. and W. A. Fuller 1979: Distribution of the estimators for autoregressive time series with a unit root. *Journal of the American Statistical Association* 74, 427–31.

Dickey, D. A. and W. A. Fuller 1981: Likelihood ratio statistics for autoregressive time series with a unit root. *Econometrica* 49, 1057–72.

Domowitz, I. and H. White 1982: Misspecified models with dependent observations. *Journal of Econometrics* 20, 35–58.

Donsker, M. D. 1951: An invariance principle for certain probability limit theorems. *Memoirs of the American Mathematical Society* 6, 1–12.

Doornik, J. A. and D. F. Hendry 1997: *Modelling Dynamic Systems Using PcFiml 9.0 for Windows*. London: International Thompson Business Press.

Doornik, J. A. and D. F. Hendry 1999: *Empirical Econometric Modelling Using PcGive*, Vol. 1. West Wickham: Timberlake Consultants Ltd.

Durbin, J. 1954: Errors in variables. *Review of the International Statistical Institute* 22, 23–32.

Durbin, J. 1960: Estimation of parameters in time-series regression models. *Journal of the Royal Statistical Society, Series B* 22,139–53.

Durbin, J. 1970: Testing for serial correlation in least squares regression when some of the regressors are lagged dependent variables. *Econometrica* 38, 410–21.

Durbin, J. and G. S. Watson 1950: Testing for serial correlation in least squares regression I. *Biometrika* 37, 409–28.

Durbin, J. and G. S. Watson 1951: Testing for serial correlation in least squares regression II, *Biometrika* 38, 159–78.

Eatwell, J., M. Milgate and P. Newman (eds.) 1987: *The New Palgrave: A Dictionary of Economics*. London: Macmillan.

Eicker, F 1963: Asymptotic normality and consistency of the least squares estimators for families of linear regressions, *Annals of Mathematical Statistics* 34, 447–56.

Eisenpress, H., and J. Greenstadt 1966: The estimation of nonlinear econometric systems. *Econometrica* 34, 851–61.

Engle, R. F. 1982a: Autoregressive conditional heteroscedasticity with estimates of the variance of United Kingdom inflation. *Econometrica* 50, 987–1007.

Engle, R. F. 1982b: A general approach to Lagrange Multiplier model diagnostics. *Journal of Econometrics* 20, 83–104.

Engle, R. F. 1983: Wald, likelihood ratio and Lagrange multiplier methods in econometrics. Chapter 13 of Griliches and Intriligator (1983).

Engle, R. F. 1995: *ARCH: Selected Readings*. Oxford: Oxford University Press

Engle, R. F. and C. W. J. Granger 1987: Cointegration and error correction: representation, estimation and testing, *Econometrica* 55, 251–76.

Engle, R. F. and C. W. J. Granger 1991: *Long Run Economic Relationships: Readings in Cointegration*. Oxford: Oxford University Press.

Engle, R. F. and D. F. Hendry, 1993: Testing super exogeneity and invariance in regression models. *Journal of Econometrics* 56, 119–39.

Engle, R. F. and K. Kroner 1995: Multivariate simultaneous generalized ARCH. *Econometric Theory* 11, 122–50.

Engle, R. F. and D. L. McFadden (eds.) 1994: *Handbook of Econometrics Volume 4*. Amsterdam: North-Holland.

Engle, R. F. and B. S. Yoo 1987: Forecasting and testing in cointegrated systems *Journal of Econometrics* 35, 143–59.

Engle, R. F. and B. S. Yoo 1991: Cointegrated economic time series: an overview with new results. Chapter 12 of Engle and Granger (1991).

Engle, R. F., D. F. Hendry and J.-F. Richard 1983: Exogeneity. *Econometrica* 51, 277–304.

Epstein, L. G., and S. E. Zin 1991: Substitution, risk aversion, and the temporal behavior of consumption and asset returns: an empirical analysis. *Journal of Political Economy* 99, 263–86.

Evans, G. B. A., and N. E. Savin 1981: Testing for unit roots: 1 *Econometrica* 49, 753–80.

Evans, G. B. A., and N. E. Savin 1982: Conflict among the criteria revisited: the W, LR and LM tests. *Econometrica* 50, 737–48.

Fair, R. C., and W. R. Parke 1980: Full-information estimates of a nonlinear macroeconometric model. *Journal of Econometrics* 13, 269–91.

Favero, C. and D. F. Hendry 1992: Testing the Lucas critique: a review. *Econometric Reviews* 11, 265–306.

Feige, E. L. and D. K. Pearce 1979: The casual causal relationship between money and income: some caveats for time series analysis. *Review of Economics and Statistics* 61, 521–33.

Fisher, F. M. 1961: Identifiability criteria in nonlinear systems. *Econometrica* 29, 574–90.

Fisher, F. M. 1965: Identifiability criteria in nonlinear systems: a further note. *Econometrica* 33, 197–205.

Fisher, F. M. 1966: *The Identification Problem in Econometrics.* New York: McGraw Hill.

Fishman, G. S. 1969: *Spectral Methods in Econometrics.* Cambridge, Massachusetts: Harvard University Press.

Fletcher, R. 1970: A new approach to variable metric algorithms. *Computer Journal* 13, 317–22.

Fletcher, R. 1980: *Practical Methods of Optimization, Volume 1.* Chichester: John Wiley & Sons.

Fletcher, R. and M. J. D. Powell 1963: A rapidly convergent descent method for minimization. *Computer Journal* 6, 163–8.

Freund, J. E. 1992: *Mathematical Statistics*, 5th Edition. New Jersey: Prentice Hall.

Frisch, R., and F. V. Waugh 1933: Partial time regressions as compared with individual trends, *Econometrica* 1, 387–401.

Fuller, W. A. 1976: *Introduction to Statistical Time Series.* New York: John Wiley & Sons.

Gallant, A. R. 1977: Three-stage least-squares estimation for a system of simultaneous, nonlinear, implicit equations. *Journal of Econometrics* 5, 71–88.

Gallant, A. R. 1987: *Nonlinear Statistical Models.* New York: John Wiley & Sons.

Gallant, A. R. 1997: *An Introduction to Econometric Theory.* Princeton: Princeton University Press.

Gallant, A. R. and A. Holly 1980: Statistical inference in an implicit, nonlinear, simultaneous equation model in the context of maximum likelihood estimation. *Econometrica* 48, 697–720.

Gallant, A. R. and D. W. Jorgenson 1979: Statistical inference for a system of simultaneous, non-linear, implicit equations in the context of instrumental variable estimation. *Journal of Econometrics* 11, 275–302.

Gallant, A. R. and H. White 1988: *A Unified Theory of Inference for Nonlinear Dynamic Models.* Oxford: Basil Blackwell.

Geweke, J. 1982: Causality, exogeneity and inference. Chapter 7 of W. Hildenbrand (ed.) *Advances in Econometrics.* Cambridge, Cambridge University Press.

Geweke, J. 1983: Inference and causality in economic time series models. Chapter 19 of Griliches and Intriligator (1983).

Giannini, Carlo 1992: *Topics in Structural VAR Econometrics.* New York: Springer-Verlag.

Gill, P. E., W. Murray and M. H. Wright 1981: *Practical Optimization.* New York: Academic Press.

Godfrey, L. G. 1978a: Testing against general autoregressive and moving average error models when the regressors include lagged dependent variables. *Econometrica* 46, 1293–302.

Godfrey, L. G. 1978b: Testing for higher order serial correlation in regression equations when the regressors include lagged dependent variables. *Econometrica* 46, 1303–10.

Godfrey, L. G. 1978c: Testing for multiplicative heteroscedasticity. *Journal of Econometrics* 8, 227–36.

Godfrey, L. G. 1988: *Misspecification Tests in Econometrics,* Econometric Society Monographs No. 16. Cambridge: Cambridge University Press.

Goldberger, Arthur S. 1991: *A Course in Econometrics.* Cambridge, Mass.: Harvard University Press.

Goldfarb, D. 1970: A family of variable metric methods derived by variational means. *Mathematics of Computation* 24, 23–6.

Goldfeld, S. M. and R. E. Quandt 1972: *Nonlinear Methods in Econometrics.* Amsterdam: North-Holland.

Goldfeld, S. M. and R. E. Quandt and H. F. Trotter 1966: Maximization by quadratic hill climbing. *Econometrica* 34, 541–51.

Gourieroux, C., and A. Monfort 1995: *Statistics and Econometric Models,* Volumes I and II. Cambridge: Cambridge University Press.

Gourieroux, C., J. J. Laffont and A. Monfort 1980: Coherency conditions in simultaneous linear equation models with endogenous switching regimes. *Econometrica* 48, 675–96.

Gourieroux, C., A. Monfort and A. Trognon 1984: Pseudo-maximum likelihood methods: theory. *Econometrica* 52, 681–700.

Granger, C. W. J. 1969: Investigating causal relations by econometric models and cross-spectral methods. *Econometrica* 37, 424–38.

Granger, C. W. J. 1981: Some properties of time series data and their use in econometric model specification. *Journal of Econometrics* 16, 121–30.

Granger, C. W. J. 1983: Cointegrated variables and error correction models. Discussion paper 83–13a, University of California, San Diego

Granger, C. W. J. 1990: *Modelling Economic Series Oxford:* Oxford University Press

Granger, C. W. J. and M. Hatanaka 1964: *Spectral Analysis of Economic Time Series* Princeton: Princeton University Press.

Granger, C. W. J. and P. Newbold 1974: Spurious regressions in econometrics, *Journal of Econometrics* 2, 111–20.

Granger, C. W. J. and A. A. Weiss 1983: Time series analysis of error correction models, in *Studies in Econometrics, Time Series and Multivariate Statistics* eds. S. Karlin, T. Amemiya and L. A. Goodman. New York, Academic Press.

Granger, C. W. J., N. Hyung and Y. Jeon 1998: Spurious regressions with stationary series. Discussion Paper 98–25, University of California San Diego, Department of Economics.

Gregory, A. W., and M. R. Veall 1985:. On formulating Wald tests for nonlinear restrictions. *Econometrica* 53, 1465–8.

Gregory, A. W., and M. R. Veall 1987: Formulating Wald tests of the restrictions implied by the rational expectations hypothesis. *Journal of Applied Econometrics* 2, 61–8.

Griliches, Z. 1967. Distributed Lags: A Survey. *Econometrica* 35, 16–49.

Griliches, Z. and M. D. Intriligator (eds.) 1983: *Handbook of Econometrics Volumes I-III.* Amsterdam: North-Holland.

Haavelmo, T. 1943: The statistical implications of a system of simultaneous equations. *Econometrica* 11, 1–12.

Haavelmo, T. 1947: Methods of measuring the marginal propensity to consume. *Journal of the American Statistical Association* 42, 105–22, reprinted in Koopmans and Hood (1953).

Hall, P. and C. C. Heyde 1980: *Martingale Limit Theory and its Applications*, New York, Academic Press.

Hall, R. E. 1978: Stochastic implications of the life cycle-permanent income hypothesis: theory and evidence, *Journal of Political Economy* 86, 971–87.

Hamilton, James D. 1994: *Time Series Analysis.* Princeton: Princeton University Press.

Hannan, E. J. and B. G. Quinn 1979: The determination of the order of an autoregression. *Journal of the Royal Statistical Society Series B* 41, 190–5.

Hansen, B. E. 1991: GARCH(1,1) processes are near-epoch dependent. *Economics Letters* 36, 181–6.

item Hansen, B. E. 1992: Efficient estimation and testing of cointegrating vectors in the presence of deterministic trends. *Journal of Econometrics* 53, 87–121.

Hansen, L. P. 1982: Large sample properties of generalized method of moments estimators. *Econometrica* 50, 1029–54.

Hansen, L. P. and T. Sargent 1980: Formulating and estimating dynamic linear rational expectations models. *Journal of Economic Dynamics and Control* 2, 7–46, reprinted in Lucas and Sargent (1981).

Hansen, L. P. and T. Sargent 1981: Linear rational expectations models for dynamically interrelated variables, in Lucas and Sargent (1981).

Hansen, L. P. and K. J. Singleton 1982: Generalized instrumental variables estimators of nonlinear rational expectations models. *Econometrica* 50, 1269–86.

Hargreaves, C. P. (ed.) 1994: *Nonstationary Time Series Analysis and Cointegration* Oxford: Oxford University Press.

Hartley, H. O. 1961: The modified Gauss–Newton method for the fitting of nonlinear regression functions by least squares. *Technometrics* 3, 269–80.

Hartley, H. O. and A. Booker 1965: Nonlinear least squares estimation. *Annals of Mathematical Statistics* 36, 638–50.

Harvey, A. C. 1976: Estimating regression models with multiplicative heteroscedasticity. *Econometrica* 44, 461–66.

Harvey, A. C. 1981: *Time Series Models.* Oxford: Philip Allan.

Harvey, A. C. 1990: *The Econometric Analysis of Time Series*, 2nd Edition. New York: Philip Allan.

Hatanaka, M. 1974: An efficient two-step estimator for the dynamic adjustment model with autoregressive errors. *Journal of Econometrics* 2, 199–220.

Hatanaka, M. 1996: *Time-Series-Based Econometrics.* Oxford: Oxford University Press.

Hausman, J. A. 1978: Specification tests in econometrics. *Econometrica* 46, 1251–72.

Hausman, J. A. 1983: Specification and estimation of simultaneous equation models. Chapter 7 of Griliches and Intriligator (1983).

Hendry, D. F. 1980: Econometrics: Alchemy or Science? *Economica* 47, 387–406.

Hendry, D. F. 1983: Econometric modelling: the consumption function in retrospect. *Scottish Journal of Political Economy* 30, 193–220.

Hendry, D. F. 1986: Econometric modelling with cointegrated variables: an overview. *Oxford Bulletin of Economics and Statistics* 48, 201–12.

Hendry, D. F. 1993: *Econometrics: Alchemy or Science?* Oxford: Blackwell Publishers.

Hendry, D. F. 1995: *Dynamic Econometrics.* Oxford: Oxford University Press.

Hendry, D. F. and G. E. Mizon 1978: Serial correlation as a convenient simplification not a nuisance: a comment on a study of the demand for money by the Bank of England. *Economic Journal* 88, 549–63.

Hendry, D. F. and J.-F. Richard 1982: On the Formulation of Empirical Models in Dynamic Econometrics, *Journal of Econometrics* 20, 3–34.

Hendry, D. F. and J.-F. Richard 1983: The econometric analysis of economic time series. *International Statistical Review* 51, 111–64.

Hendry, D. F. and K. F. Wallis 1984: *Econometrics and Quantitative Economics.* Oxford: Basil Blackwell.

Hendry, D. F., A. R. Pagan, and J. D. Sargan 1983: Dynamic specification, Ch. 18 of Griliches and Intriligator (1983).

Hogg, C. and A. T. Craig 1995: *Introduction to Mathematical Statistics, 5th Ed.* New Jersey: Prentice Hall.

Holly, A. 1982: A remark on Hausman's specification test. *Econometrica* 50, 749–59.

Holly, A. and A. Monfort 1986: Some useful equivalence properties of Hausman's test. *Economics Letters* 20, 39–43.

Hsiao, C. 1983: Identification. Chapter 4 of Griliches and Intriligator (1983).

Hsiao, C. 1986: *Analysis of panel data*, Econometric Society Monographs No. 11. Cambridge: Cambridge University Press.

Hurwitz, L. 1950: Least squares bias in time series. Chapter XV of Koopmans (1950).

Intriligator, M. D. 1971: *Mathematical Optimization and Economic Theory* . Englewood Cliffs: Prentice Hall.

Jarque, C. M., and A. K. Bera 1980: Efficient tests for normality, heteroscedasticity and serial independence of regression residuals. *Economics Letters* 6, 255–9.

Jennrich, R. I. 1969: Asymptotic properties of non-linear least squares estimators. *Annals of Mathematical Statistics* 40, 633–43.

Johansen, S. 1988a: The mathematical structure of error correction models. *Contemporary Mathematics* 80, 359–86.

Johansen, S. 1988b: Statistical analysis of cointegration vectors. *Journal of Economic Dynamics and Control* 12, 231–54.

Johansen, S. 1991: Estimation and hypothesis testing of cointegration vectors in Gaussian vector autoregressive models. *Econometrica* 59, 1551–80.

Johansen, S. 1992: Cointegration in partial systems and the efficiency of single equation analysis. *Journal of Econometrics* 52, 389–402.

Johansen, S. 1995a: Identifying restrictions of linear equations with applications to simultaneous equations and cointegration. *Journal of Econometrics* 69,111–32.

Johansen, S. 1995b: *Likelihood-Based Inference in Cointegrated Vector Autoregressive Models.* Oxford: Oxford University Press.

Johansen, S. 1995c: A statistical analysis of cointegration for I(2) variables. *Econometric Theory* 11, 25–59.

Johansen, S. and K. Juselius 1990: Maximum likelihood estimation and inference on cointegration, with applications to the demand for money. *Oxford Bulletin of Economics and Statistics* 52, 169–210.

Johansen, S. and K. Juselius 1992: Testing structural hypotheses in a multivariate cointegration analysis of the PPP and the UIP for UK. *Journal of Econometrics* 53, 211–44.

Johnston, J. 1972: *Econometric Methods*, 2nd Edition. Tokyo: McGraw-Hill Kogakusha.

Johnston, J. and J. DiNardo 1997: *Econometric Methods*, 4th Edition. New York: McGraw-Hill.

Jorgenson, D. W. 1963: Capital theory and investment behaviour. *American Economic Review* 53, 247–59.

Jorgenson, D. W. 1966: Rational distributed lag functions, *Econometrica* 34, 135–49.

Jorgenson, D. W. and J.-J. Laffont 1974: Efficient estimation of nonlinear simultaneous equations with additive disturbances. *Annals of Economic and Social Measurement* 3, 615–40.

Kelejian, H. H. 1970: Identification of nonlinear systems: an interpretation of Fisher. Research Paper 22, Econometric Research Program, Princeton University.

Kelejian, H. H. 1971: Two-stage least squares and econometric systems linear in parameters and nonlinear in endogenous variables. *Journal of the Americal Statistical Association* 66, 373–374

Kendall, M. G. and A. Stuart 1979: *The Advanced Theory of Statistics Volume 2: Inference and Relationship* (4th Edition). London: Charles Griffin & Co.

Kennan, J. 1979: The estimation of partial adjustment models with rational expectations. *Econometrica* 47, 1441–6.

King, R. G., C. I. Plosser, J. H. Stock, and M. W. Watson 1991: Stochastic trends and economic fluctuations. *American Economic Review* 81, 819–40.

Koenker, R. 1981: A note on studentizing a test for heteroscedasticity. *Journal of Econometrics* 17, 107–12.

Koopmans, T. C. (ed.) 1950a: *Statistical Inference in Dynamic Economic Models.* Cowles Commission Monograph 10. New York, John Wiley & Sons

Koopmans, T. C. 1950b: When is an equation system complete for statistical purposes? Chapter XVII of Koopmans (1950a).

Koopmans, T. C. and W. C. Hood 1953: *Studies in Econometric Method.* New Haven: Yale University Press.

Koopmans, T. C., H. Rubin and R. B. Leipnik, 1950: Measuring the equation systems of dynamic economics. Chapter II of Koopmans (1950).

Koyck, L. M. 1954: *Lags and Economic Behaviour.* Amsterdam: North-Holland.

Kremers, J. J. M., N. R. Ericsson, and J. J. Dolado 1992: The power of cointegration tests. *Oxford Bulletin of Economics and Statistics* 54, 325–48.

Kullback, L. and R. A. Leibler 1951: On Information and Sufficiency. *Annals of Mathematical Statistics* 22, 79–86.

Kwiatkowski, D., Phillips, P. C. B., Schmidt, P., and Shin, Y 1992: Testing the null hypothesis of stationarity against the alternative of a unit root. *Journal of Econometrics* 54, 159–78.

Lafontaine, F., and K. J. White 1986: Obtaining any Wald statistic you want. *Economics Letters* 21, 35–40.

Leamer, E. 1978: *Specification Searches: Ad Hoc Inference with Nonexperimental Data.* New York: John Wiley & Sons.

Leamer, E. 1983a: Let's take the con out of econometrics. *American Economic Review* 73, 31–43.

Leamer, E. 1983b: Model choice and specification analysis. Chapter 5 of Griliches and Intriligator (1983)

Leamer, E. 1985: Vector autoregressions for causal inference? *Carnegie-Rochester Conference Series on Public Policy* 22, 255–303.

Lehmann, E. L. 1986: *Testing Statistical Hypotheses*, 2nd Edition. New York: John Wiley & Sons.

Ljung, G. M. and G. E. P. Box 1978: On a measure of lack of fit in time-series models. *Biometrika* 65, 297–303.

Lovell, M. C. 1961: Manufacturers' inventories, sales expectations and the acceleration principle. *Econometrica* 29, 293–314.

Lovell, M. C. 1963: Seasonal adjustment of economic time series. *Journal of the American Statistical Association* 58, 993–1010.

Lovell, M. C. 1983: Data mining. *The Review of Economics and Statistics* 65, 1–12.

Lucas, R. E. and T. J. Sargent 1981: *Rational Expectations and Econometric Practice.* London: George Allen and Unwin.

Lütkepohl, H. 1991: *Introduction to Multiple Time Series Analysis.* New York: Springer-Verlag

McCabe, B. and A. Tremayne 1993: *Elements of modern asymptotic theory with statistical applications.* Manchester: Manchester University Press.

McCallum, B. T. 1976: Rational expectations and the natural rate hypothesis: some consistent estimates. *Econometrica*, 44, 43–52.

McLeod, A. I. and Li, W. K. 1983: Diagnostic checking ARMA time series models using squared-residual autocorrelations. *Journal of Time Series Analysis* 4, 269–273.

McFadden, D. L. 1983: Econometric analysis of qualitative response models. Chapter 24 of Griliches and Intriligator (1983).

MacKinnon, J. G. 1991: Critical values for cointegration tests. Chapter 13 of Engle and Granger (1991).

McLeish, D. L. 1975: A maximal inequality and dependent strong laws. *Annals of Probability* 3, 329–39.

Madansky, A. 1976: *Foundations of Econometrics.* Amsterdam: North-Holland

Maddala, G. S. 1977: *Econometrics.* Tokyo: McGraw-Hill Kogakusha.

Maddala, G. S. 1983: *Limited Dependent and Qualitative Variables in Econometrics.* Cambridge: Cambridge University Press.

Magnus, Jan R., and Heinz Neudecker 1988: *Matrix Differential Calculus with Applications in Statistics and Econometrics.* Chichester: John Wiley & Sons.

Malinvaud, E. 1970: *Statistical Methods of Econometrics*, 2nd Edition. Amsterdam: North-Holland.

Mandelbrot, B. B. 1983: *The Fractal Geometry of Nature.* New York: W. H. Freeman & Co.

Mann, H. and A. Wald 1943a: On stochastic limit and order relationships. *Annals of Mathematical Statistics* 14, 217–26.

Mann, H. and A. Wald 1943b: On the statistical treatment of linear stochastic difference equations. *Econometrica* 11, 173–220.

Manski, C. F. 1994: Analog estimation of econometric models. Chapter 43 of *Handbook of Econometrics, Volume IV* eds. R. F. Engle and D. L. McFadden, Amsterdam: Elsevier.

Marquardt, D. W. 1963: An algorithm for least squares estimation of nonlinear parameters. *Journal of the Society for Industrial and Applied Mathematics* 11, 431–41.

Mizon, G. 1984: The encompassing approach in econometrics. Chapter 6 of Hendry and Wallis (1984).

Mizon, G. 1995: A simple message to autocorrelation correctors: don't. *Journal of Econometrics* 69, 267–88.

Mizon, G. and J.-F. Richard 1986: The encompassing principle and its application to testing non-nested hypotheses. *Econometrica* 54, 657–78.

Mood, A. M. and F. A. Graybill 1972: *Introduction to the Theory of Statistics.* New York: McGraw-Hill Kogakusha

Muth, J. F. 1961: Rational expectations and the theory of price movements. *Econometrica* 19, 315–35.

Nagar, A. L. 1959: The bias and moment matrix of the general k-class estimators of the parameters in simultaneous equations, *Econometrica* 27, 575–95.

Nakamura, A., and M. Nakamura 1981: On the relationships among several specification error tests presented by Durbin, Wu and Hausman. *Econometrica* 49,1583–88.

Nelson, C. R. and C I. Plosser 1982: Trends and random walks in macroeconomic time series. *Journal of Monetary Economics* 10, 139–62.

Nerlove, M. 1963: Returns to scale in Electricity supply. Chapter 7 of *Measurement in Economics: Studies in Mathematical Economics and Econometrics in Memory of Yehuda Grunfeld.* Stanford: Stanford University Press.

Nerlove, M. 1972: Lags in economics behaviour. *Econometrica* 40, 221–51.

Nerlove, M., D. M. Grether and J. L. Carvalho 1979: *Analysis of Economic Time Series.* New York: Academic Press.

Newey, W. K. 1985: Maximum likelihood specification testing and conditional moment tests. *Econometrica* 53, 1047–70.

Newey, W. K. 1990: Efficient instrumental variables estimation of nonlinear models. *Econometrica* 58, 809–837.

Newey, W. K. 1991: Uniform convergence in probability ans stochastic equicontinuity. *Econometrica* 59, 1161–8

Newey, W. K. and D. L. McFadden 1994: Large sample estimation and hypothesis testing. Chapter 36 of *Handbook of Econometrics, Volume IV* eds. R. F. Engle and D. L. McFadden, Amsterdam: Elsevier.

Newey, W. K. and K. D. West 1987: A simple, positive semi-definite, heteroscedasticity and autocorrelation consistent covariance matrix. *Econometrica* 55, 703–8.

Newey, W. K. and K. D. West 1994: Automatic lag selection in covariance matrix estimation. *Review of Economic Studies* 61, 631–54.

Neyman, J. and E. S. Pearson 1928: On the use and interpretation of certain test criteria for purposes of statistical inference. *Biometrika* 20A 175–240, 263–94.

Neyman, J. and E. S. Pearson 1933: On the problem of the most efficient tests of statistical hypotheses. *Phil. Trans. Roy. Soc., Ser. A.* 231, 289–337.

Nickell, S. J. 1985: Error correction, partial adjustment and all that: An expository note. *Oxford Bulletin of Economics and Statistics* 47, 119–30.

Osterwald-Lenum, M. 1992: A note with quantiles of the asymptotic distribution of the maximum likelihood cointegration rank test statistics. *Oxford Bulletin of Economics and Statistics* 54, 461–72.

Pagan, A. 1978: Rational and polynomial lags. *Journal of Econometrics* 8, 242–54.

Pagan, A. 1984a: Econometric issues in the analysis of regressions with generated regressors. *International Economic Review* 25, 221–47.

Pagan, A. 1984b: Model evaluation by variable addition. Chapter 5 of Hendry and Wallis (1984)

Park, J. Y. and P. C. B. Phillips 1988: Statistical inference in regressions with integrated processes: Part 1. *Econometric Theory* 4, 468-97.

Park, J. Y. and P. C. B. Phillips 1989: Statistical inference in regressions with integrated processes: Part 2, *Econometric Theory* 5, 95–131.

Pesaran, M. H. 1974: On the general problem of model selection. *Review of Economic Studies* 41,153–71.

Pesaran, M. H. 1982: Comparison of local power of alternative tests of non-nested regression models. *Econometrica* 50, 1287–1305.

Pesaran, M. H. 1987: *The Limits to Rational Expectations.* Oxford: Basil Blackwell.

Pesaran, M. H. and A. S. Deaton, 1978: Testing non-nested nonlinear regression models. *Econometrica* 46, 677–94.

Pesaran, M. H. and B. Pesaran 1997: *Working with Microfit 4.0: Interactive Econometric Analysis* Oxford: Oxford University Press.

Phillips, P. C. B. 1976: The iterated minimum distance estimator and the quasi-maximum likelihood estimator. *Econometrica* 44, 449–60.

Phillips, P. C. B. 1982: On the consistency of nonlinear FIML. *Econometrica* 50, 1307–24.

Phillips, P. C. B. 1986: Understanding spurious regressions in econometrics, *Journal of Econometrics* 33, 311–40.

Phillips, P. C. B. 1987: Time series regression with a unit root. *Econometrica* 55, 277–301.

Phillips, P. C. B. 1988: Reflections on econometric methodology. *Economic Record* 64, 544–59.

Phillips, P. C. B. 1991: Optimal inference in cointegrated systems. *Econometrica* 59 283–306.

Phillips, P. C. B. 1995: Fully modified least squares and vector autoregression. *Econometrica* 63, 1023–79.

Phillips, P. C. B. and S. N. Durlauf 1986: Multiple time series regression with integrated processes. *Review of Economic Studies* 53, 473–96.

Phillips, P. C. B. and B. E. Hansen 1990: Statistical inference in instrumental variables regression with I(1) processes, *Review of Economic Studies* 57, 99–125.

Phillips, P. C. B. and M. Loretan 1991: Estimating long-run economic equilibria. *Review of Economic Studies* 58, 407–37.

Phillips, P. C. B. and S. Ouliaris 1990: Asymptotic properties of residual based tests for cointegration *Econometrica* 58, 165–93.

Phillips, P. C. B. and J. Y. Park 1988: On the formulation of Wald tests of nonlinear restrictions. *Econometrica* 56, 1065–83.

Phillips, P. C. B. and P. Perron 1988: Testing for unit roots in time series regression. *Biometrika* 75, 335–46.

Pitman, E, J. G. 1949: Notes on non-parametric statistical inference. Columbia University, New York, mimeo.

Pollard, D. 1984: *Convergence of Stochastic Processes.*New York: Springer-Verlag.

Popper, Karl R. 1959: *The Logic of Scientific Discovery.* London: Hutchison.

Pötscher, B. M. and I. R. Prucha 1989: A uniform law of large numbers for dependent and heterogeneous data processes. *Econometrica* 57, 675–684.

Pötscher, B. M. and I. R. Prucha 1991a: Basic structure of the asymptotic theory in dynamic nonlinear econometric models, part 1: consistency and approximation concepts. *Econometric Reviews* 10, 125–216.

Pötscher, B. M. and I. R. Prucha 1991b: Basic structure of the asymptotic theory in dynamic nonlinear econometric models, part 2: asymptotic normality. *Econometric Reviews* 10, 253–325.

Pötscher, B. M. and I. R. Prucha 1997: *Dynamic Nonlinear Econometric Models, Asymptotic Theory.* New York: Springer Verlag.

Powell, M. J. D. 1964: An efficient method of finding the minimum of a function without calculating derivatives. *Computer Journal,* 11, 302–4.

Prais, S. J. and C. B. Winsten 1954: Trend estimators and serial correlation. Cowles Commission Discussion Paper No. 383, University of Chicago.

Prothero, D. L. and Wallis, K. F. 1976: Modelling macro-economic time series (with discussion). *Journal of the Royal Statistical Society, Series A* 139, 468–500.

Quandt, R. E. 1983: Computational problems and methods. Chapter 12 of Griliches and Intriligator (1983).

Ramsey, J. B. 1969: Tests for specification errors in classical linear least-squares regression analysis. *Journal of the Royal Statistical Society, Series B* 31, 350–71.

Ramsey, J. B. and Schmidt, P. 1976: Some further results on the use of OLS and BLUS residuals in specification error tests. *Journal of the American Statistical Association* 71, 389–90.

Rao, C. R. (1948): Large sample tests of statistical hypotheses concerning several parameters with applications to problems of estimation. *Proceedings of the Cambridge Philosophical Society* 44, 50–57.

Rao, C. R. 1973: *Linear Statistical Inference and its Applications,* 2nd Edition. New York: John Wiley & Sons.

Rao, C. R. and M. B. Rao 1998: *Matrix Algebra and its Applications to Statistics and Econometrics* World Scientific Publishing.

Robinson, P. M. 1991: Best nonlinear three-stage least squares estimation of certain econometric models. *Econometrica* 59, 755–86.

Rothenberg, T. J. 1971: Identification in parametric models. *Econometrica* 39, 577–92.

Rothenberg, T. J. 1973: *Efficient Estimation with A Priori Information.* New Haven: Yale University Press.

Rothenberg, T. J. and Leenders, C. T. 1964: Efficient estimation of simultaneous equations systems. *Econometrica* 32, 57–76.

Said, S. E. and D. A. Dickey 1984: Testing for unit roots in autoregressive moving average models of unknown order. *Biometrika* 71, 599–607.

Sargan, J. D. 1958: The estimation of economic relationships using instrumental variables. *Econometrica* 26, 393–415.

Sargan, J. D. 1959: The estimation of relationships with auto-correlated residuals by the use of instrumental variables, *Journal of the Royal Statistical Society, Series B* 21, 91–105.

Sargan, J. D. 1964: Wages and prices in the United Kingdom: a study in econometric methodology, in P. E. Hart, G. Mills and J. K. Whitaker (eds.), *Econometric Analysis for National Economic Planning*, Butterworth, pp.25-54, reprinted in Hendry and Wallis (1984).

Sargan, J. D. 1980: The consumer price equation in the post war British economy: an exercise in equation specification testing. *Review of Economic Studies* 47,113–35.

Sargan, J. D. and A. Bhargava 1983: Testing residuals from least squares regression for being generated by the Gaussian random walk *Econometrica* 51, 153–75.

Sargent, Thomas J. 1979: *Macroeconomic Theory.* New York: Academic Press.

Savin, N. E. 1980: The Bonferroni and Scheffé multiple comparison procedures. *Review of Economics Studies* 67, 255–273.

Savin, N. E. 1983: Multiple hypothesis testing. Chapter 14 of Griliches and Intriligator (1983).

Schmidt, P. 1976: *Econometrics.* New York: Marcel Dekker.

Schwarz, G. 1978. Estimating the dimension of a model. *Annals of Statistics* 6, 461–4.

Seber, G. A. F. 1980: *The Linear Hypothesis: A General Theory.* London: Charles Griffin & Co.

Serfling, Robert J. 1980: *Approximation Theorems of Mathematical Statistics.* New York: John Wiley & Sons.

Shanno, D. F. 1970: Conditioning of quasi-Newton methods for function minimization. *Mathematics of Computation* 24, 647–56.

Shiller, R. J. 1973:. A distributed lag estimator derived from smoothness priors. *Econometrica* 41, 775–8.

Shiller, R. J. 1978: Rational expectations and the dynamic structure of macroeconomic models. *Journal of Monetary Economics* 4, 1–44.

Silvey, S. D. 1959: The Lagrangian multiplier test. *Annals of Mathematical Statistics* 30, 389–407.

Silvey, S. D. 1970: *Statistical Inference.* London: Chapman and Hall.

Sims, C. A. 1972: Money, Income and Causality. *American Economic Review* 62, 540–52.

Sims, C. A. 1980: Macroeconomics and reality. *Econometrica* 48, 1–48.

Sims, C. A. 1987: Multivariate time series models, in Eatwell, Milgate and Newman (1987).

Sims, C. A., J. H. Stock and M. W. Watson 1990: Inference in linear time series models with some unit roots. *Econometrica* 58, 113–44.

Spanos, A. 1986: *Statistical foundations of econometric modelling.* Cambridge: Cambridge University Press.

Stein, C. M. 1981: Estimation of the mean of a multivariate normal distribution. *Annals of Statistics* 9, 1135–51.

Stock, J. 1987: Asymptotic Properties of least squares estimators of cointegrating vectors, *Econometrica* 55 1035–56.

Stock, J. 1994: Unit roots, structural breaks and trends. Chapter 43 of *Handbook of Econometrics, Volume IV* eds. R. F. Engle and D. L. McFadden, Amsterdam: Elsevier.

Stock, J. and M. W. Watson 1988a: Testing for common trends. *Journal of the American Statistical Association* 83, 1097–107.

Stock, J. and M. W. Watson 1988b: Variable trends in economic time series. *Journal of Economic Perspectives* 2, 147–74.

Stone, R. and D. A. Rowe 1960: The durability of consumers' durable goods. *Econometrica* 28, 407–16.

Tanaka, K. 1996: *Time Series Analysis: Nonstationary and Noninvertible Distribution Theory.* New York: John Wiley & Sons.

Tauchen, G. E. 1985: Diagnostic testing and evaluation of maximum likelihood models. *Journal of Econometrics* 30, 415–43.

Theil, H. 1953: Repeated least squares applied to complete equation systems. The Hague, Central Planning Bureau, mimeo.

Theil, H. 1971: *Principles of Econometrics.* New York: John Wiley & Sons

Theil, H. and J. C. G. Boot 1962: The final form of econometric equation systems. *Review of the International Statistical Institute* 30, 136–52.

Tobin, J. 1958: Estimation of Relationships for Limited Dependent Variables. *Econometrica* 26, 24–36.

Wald, A. 1943: Tests of statistical hypotheses concerning several parameters when the number of observations is large. *Transactions of the American Mathematical Society* 54, 426–82.

Wald, A. 1949: Note on the consistency of the maximum likelihood estimate. *Annals of Mathematical Statistics* 20, 595–601.

Wallis, K. F. 1973: *Topics in Applied Econometrics.* London: Gray-Mills Publishing.

Wallis, K. F. 1977: Multiple time series analysis and the final form of econometric models. *Econometrica* 45, 1481–97.

Wallis, K. F. 1980: Econometric implications of the rational expectations hypothesis, *Econometrica* 48, 49–73.

Watson, M. W. 1994: Vector autoregressions and cointegration. Chapter 47 of *Handbook of Econometrics, Volume IV* eds. R. F. Engle and D. L. McFadden, Amsterdam: Elsevier.

White, H. 1980a: A heteroscedasticity-consistent covariance matrix estimator and a direct test for heteroscedasticity. *Econometrica*, 48, 817–38.

White, H. 1980b: Using least squares to approximate unknown regression functions. *International Economic Review* 21, 149–70.

White, H. 1980c: Nonlinear regression in cross-section data. *Econometrica* 48, 721–46.

White, H. 1981: Consequences and detection of misspecified nonlinear regression models. *Journal of the American Statistical Association* 76, 419–33.

White, H. 1982: Maximum likelihood estimation of misspecified models. *Econometrica* 50,1–26.

White, H. 1984: *Asymptotic Theory for Econometricians.* Orlando: Academic Press.

White, H. 1987: Least Squares. In Eatwell, Milgate and Newman (1987).

White, H. 1990: A consistent model selection procedure based on m-testing. Chapter 16 of Granger (1990).

White, H. 1994: *Estimation, Inference and Specification Analysis*, Econometric Society Monographs No. 22. Cambridge: Cambridge University Press.

White, H. and I. Domowitz 1984: Nonlinear regression with dependent observations. *Econometrica* 52, 143–62.

Whiteman, C. H. 1983: *Linear Rational Expectations Models.* Minneapolis: University of Minnesota Press.

Wilks, S. S. 1962: *Mathematical Statistics* New York: John Wiley & Sons.

Wold, H. 1938: *A Study in the Analysis of Stationary Time Series.* Uppsala: Almqvist and Wiksell.

Wolfe, M. A. 1978: *Numerical Methods for Unconstrained Optimization.* New York, Van Nostrand–Reinhold.

Wooldridge, J. M. 1994: Estimation and inference for dependent processes. Chapter 45 of *Handbook of Econometrics, Volume IV* eds. R. F. Engle and D. L. McFadden, Amsterdam: Elsevier.

Wu, D.-M. 1973: Alternative tests of independence between stochastic regressors and disturbances. *Econometrica* 41, 733–50.

Yule, G. U. 1926: Why do we sometimes get nonsense correlations between time series? *Journal of the Royal Statistical Society* 89, 1–64.

Zellner, A. 1962: An efficient method of estimating seemingly unrelated regressions, and tests for aggregation bias. *Journal of the American Statistical Association* 57, 348–68.

Zellner, A. and F. Palm 1974: Time series analysis and simultaneous equation econometric models. *Journal of Econometrics* 2, 17–54.

Zellner, A. and H. Theil 1962: Three-stage least squares: simultaneous estimation of simultaneous equations. *Econometrica* 30, 54–78.

Author Index

Subject Index

9 780631 215844